THE MICROPAL GUIDE TO OFFSHORE INVESTMENT FUNDS

plus Survey of the Top 350 Funds

Edited by ROBERT B. MILROY

1997/98 Edition

INTERNATIONAL OFFSHORE PUBLICATIONS

The Micropal Guide To Offshore Investment Funds – 1997/98 Edition

Internet http://www/micropal.com

Press and Media: 181-741-4100 London, 1-617-451-1585 Boston

ISBN 0 952 8558 0 1 – X

Published by:

International Offshore Publications Limited

Box 549 Les Sablons, St. Peters,

Guernsey, Channel Islands, GY1 6HS

Tel: 44-1481-66759

Fax: 44-1481-66758

E-mail: info@intl-offshore.com

Internet http://www.intl-offshore.com

US and Canada sales: 1-888-848-8844 (Toll free)

Designed and produced by Chapman Bounford and Associates, London, UK

Acknowledgements

This year's edition again has been a pleasure to create especially because the subject of offshore investments is one I enjoy and find exciting. As an author and Investment Manager, I have tried to pass on to the reader not only knowledge but also the excitement of the rapidly developing and changing world of global investing. The purpose of this book is to help you create and be better able to protect your wealth.

So many people have helped me in so many ways in this publication that I hesitate to list them, fearing that I may miss someone. Accepting this risk, I will begin with thanks to the Directors of Micropal because of their direct support through Philip Flint Wood (Chief Operating Officer), Justine Kashmiri-Goddard (Project Manager), Kerri Taylor (Static Data Supervisor), Vipul Nakum, Richard Daden, Paul Barnes, William White and the many other members of staff with whom I am constantly discussing or working out clarifications.

In creating, brainstorming, modifying and editing text I wish to thank Bruce, Andrea, Lee, Cecilia and especially Carol Railton, the publisher, for her total commitment, inspiration and support to me in seeing that the Top 350 Performers and the rest of the book could be finished on time.

This edition has come together more quickly than the first edition. Not only do I thank all the many fund managers and /or their assistants that promptly completed the surveys but also the staff at Chapman Bounford & Associates, the design and print set-up team.

International Offshore Publications Ltd. would like to thank FT Magazines, Global Asset Management and the various advertisers for their support to this edition.

Robert B. Milroy, Editor

Important Warning To Investors

The information in this Publication:

- is supplied for information & research purposes only and does not constitute a prospectus or offer to sell or solicitation to buy any of the securities featured herein;
- information concerning a security, investment vehicle, investment manager or contact mentioned in this Publication does not imply any endorsement or recommendation by Micropal, the Editor or Publisher;
- cannot and does not take into account the circumstances of any particular investor or the suitability or legality of an investor buying, selling or holding a particular security. Consequently, Micropal, the Editor and the Publisher recommend that investors seek independent expert financial advice from persons qualified to provide investment advice in the relevant territory before making any investment decision.

The value of investments and the income from them may fall as well as rise and you may not recover all of your initial investment. Past performance is not necessarily a guide to the future performance of a security or investment.

The Micropal® Star Rating™ (MSR) is a complex analytical tool devised to compare risk in relation to certain benchmarks as against the reward demonstrated by funds within the same investment sector. It is not an absolute measure of risk against reward, nor does it show the comparative performance between sectors in any event. MSR must not be taken as a simplistic guide to the best fund for a given investor looking at a given sector. More detailed explanation is available from Micropal.

Important Liability Notice

All reasonable care has been taken by the Editor, the Publisher and Micropal, including their agents and servants to ensure that the information in this Publication is correct and not misleading at the time of publication. However, neither the Editor, the Publisher nor Micropal warrant, represent or guarantee the contents of this Publication nor do they accept any responsibility for errors, inaccuracies, omissions or any inconsistency herein. Any ideas, suggestions or conclusions stated in this Publication are subject in each case to all applicable local, state, federal and national statutes, regulations and case law at the date hereof and as amended from time to time. Any slights of people or organisations contained in this Publication are unintentional.

Important Intellectual Property Notice

For assistance contact: International Offshore Publications Ltd. Telephone: 44-1481-66759.

Contents

FOREWORD

Welcome to the second edition of *The Micropal Guide to Offshore Investment Funds*. Until the first edition was published in 1996, investors were obliged to obtain information on offshore funds from a variety of diverse sources, including specialist magazines and the financial sections of newspapers. Now investors can find performance statistics and practical information on 5,500 offshore funds in just one publication. The guide which is intended for anyone intending to put their money offshore also contains pertinent information on offshore investment in collective investment vehicles such as unit trusts, mutual funds, SICAVs and closed-ended funds.

The publication aims to take the mystery out of offshore investing and to be the ultimate information source on the subject for investors and advisers who would generally be regarded as "retail" within the investment trade, in preference to private banks and public institutions that use offshore facilities for asset management.

The guide has been divided into six parts:

Part One covers the basics of offshore fund investment and answers questions such as: What is an offshore fund? Why should I use one? What funds should I use? How do I go about choosing and investing in a particular fund?

Part Two reviews the investment year of 1996. It discusses the key events that affected the financial markets during this period with an update of the first quarter of 1997. As the most recent complete year, 1996 had the greatest impact on the performance of offshore funds and is therefore a useful starting point for looking at future trends.

Part Three is a detailed survey of the 350 top performing offshore funds of 1996, including information on their investment strategies, details of past performance, charts, names of portfolio managers or advisers, portfolio holdings and charges.

Part Four looks at the performance returns on over 5,500 offshore funds within their sectors (and includes information about those sectors): fund size, launch date, currency, domicile, volatility, risk return ratio and the popular Micropal Star Rating.

Part Five is a management/marketing fund directory with addresses and telephone numbers.

The sixth and final part is an extensive appendix including the Most Frequently Asked Questions about Offshore Funds in addition to an extensive glossary and other further information.

PART 1

About Offshore Investment Funds

Those artificial barriers we call nation states are constantly being broken down by technology and the commerce that springs from it. Increasing numbers of people no longer consider themselves to be attached to any particular country. Indeed, it is not a ridiculous idea for someone to be born in one country, educated in another, work in a third, have clients mainly in a fourth, suppliers mainly from a fifth, live part-time in a sixth, plan to retire in a seventh and – significantly for this book – keep their money in an eighth. Nation states – and more particularly, the revenue-seeking governments of nation states – have not caught up with this increasingly international world of individuals.

Social and demographic changes have led to upward pressure on government expenditure, while at the same time the need for governments in democratic countries to be re-elected has put downward pressure on taxation. This squeeze has led many governments to give up on providing adequate retirement pensions and encourage their citizens to provide for themselves.

Faced with the prospect of having to finance their own retirement, many people are grasping the nettle. Those with an international outlook are beginning to wonder why they should be limited by a particular government's controls on how and where they may save and invest – and be taxed heavily for this dubious privilege. Indeed, internationally minded individuals are questioning why a particular nation state should be able to demand an interest in how they organise their personal financial security when the very same government admits that it will be able to do little to support them in the future.

It is for this reason that many investors are turning to offshore funds, which provide freedom and control for individuals to plan for their financial security without being regulated by tax-hungry governments.

Such increasing internationalisation of outlook is being spurred on by the exponential growth in world communications, in particular, the Internet. With no real national barriers to overcome, many people are surfing the net looking for global investment opportunities that do not tie them to one country's investment regime. And investors are finding such information, not the least on Micropal's own website (micropal.com), which includes much data on the performance of offshore funds.

1. WHAT IS AN OFFSHORE FUND?

The term "offshore fund" is a rather loose one. Offshore funds come in many designs and are structured to do many different things. Basically, an offshore fund is a common fund managed by a professional investment manager on behalf of investors and is based in one of the world's tax havens or low-tax areas.

In many ways most offshore funds have much in common with the mutual funds familiar to those from the US and Canada and with the unit trusts of the UK. People invest in such collective investment funds because they are a useful alternative to investing in stocks and shares directly. Useful, firstly because they have financial professionals to do the investment research and make the day-to-day investment decisions; secondly, because collective investment is a more cost-effective way of building up a diversified investment portfolio than buying individual small holdings of direct investments.

Once, investment funds were used mainly for rounding off a portfolio of investments. An individual might buy a few units in, say, a Japan fund, to obtain a little exposure to foreign markets. Today many investors use investment funds far more readily and will use them as their primary way of investing. According to recent research by the Washington D.C. based Investment Company Institute, 38 percent of US households own mutual funds. On average they own three funds with a total value of some $25,000. Just five years previously, only 20 percent of US households owned mutual funds.

Historically, during the 1970s the offshore industry began to grow when UK fund management companies set up non-domestic fund management subsidiaries, primarily in the old UK "schedule territories" of Guernsey, Jersey, the Isle of Man, Hong Kong and Bermuda. These offshore funds were designed initially for expatriate non-tax paying investors and foreign subsidiaries of UK firms. Later on in the 1970s and 1980s the offshore centres became a safe refuge for individuals and corporations with assets in the Middle East and Latin America who were primarily concerned with safeguarding their assets due to political events and/or their lack of faith in their home currency. In the 1980s Luxembourg began to develop its low-tax status from within the European Union. This tax-efficient money management trend gathered momentum with the introduction of the UCITS (Undertaking for Collective Investment in Transferable Securities) legislation in 1989. This legislation was intended to create common basic rules for collective investment schemes in the European Union. The UCITS domiciled in low-tax areas such as Luxembourg and Dublin are usually sold across one border to the promoter's home state. Luxembourg has developed more along the tax efficient lines for money market and fixed income funds, whereas Dublin has developed as a base for equity funds, due to its having more withholding tax treaties with other countries. Lately the development and expansion in offshore assets has come from US-based corporations expanding globally and striving for a lower cost of asset management.

Why go offshore?

The benefits of collective investment funds are obvious enough and will be covered in section 4. Going offshore provides wealth protection whether from punitive taxes or – if the funds are wrapped up in an offshore trust – from creditors and excessive charges due to legal damages (something which professionals in the US will understand well). Preservation of assets becomes more important when there may be a change in government and resulting inflationary effects.

As well as protection, offshore investors gain the freedom to invest in pretty well whatever they want. Onshore collective investment funds tend to have many government designed restrictions (mostly in the name of consumer protection). Offshore funds have fewer restrictions. Consequently, there are numerous weird and wonderful investment funds available offshore which the Securities Exchange Commission (SEC) in the US and the UK's Securities and Investment Board (SIB) may not have approved. This is not to say there is no consumer protection with offshore funds. Indeed, most offshore financial centres are very keen to uphold a good reputation and therefore only allow in reputable investment managers and keep a close eye on their activities. On the whole, offshore funds do have greater freedoms, not the least being the freedom from the costly process of reporting to such regulatory bodies as the SEC and SIB.

Where are they?

Offshore funds are based all over the world, and where they are located can be a puzzling question to answer. Very often the investment management, the administration, and the location where the fund is registered are in different places. However, a fund's home, or domicile, is usually considered to be where it is registered.

The definition of an offshore fund is also varied because people have different ideas as to what a tax haven is. For example, to the highly taxed Scandinavians, the UK is an excellent and convenient tax haven even though investment funds based in the UK would not ordinarily be considered to be offshore funds. However, there are offshore centres where taxes on funds for non-residents are either low or non-existent and where there is a high level of expertise available to manage the funds for overseas investors. This guide concentrates on these funds. Micropal lists over 5,500 offshore funds which are based primarily in 10 key offshore jurisdictions. The term "offshore" can be a little misleading, as some offshore centres are not islands. Indeed, the offshore centre with the most funds, Luxembourg, does not even have a coastline. The chart below shows the proportion of funds in each of the key jurisdictions. The number of offshore funds has been growing quite strongly in recent years: Micropal listed 2,000 funds five years ago, so its current figure of over 5,500 represents a 175 percent increase. The current general asset sector classification is shown in the chart below.

The size of the offshore funds ranges from less than US$1m to nearly $7bn for some European money market or short-term bond funds. In the derivative area the Quantum Fund managed by George Soros out of New York has over $4.6bn in assets, while the oldest offshore equity fund, Robeco, has assets exceeding $6bn.

Offshore Funds by Domicile

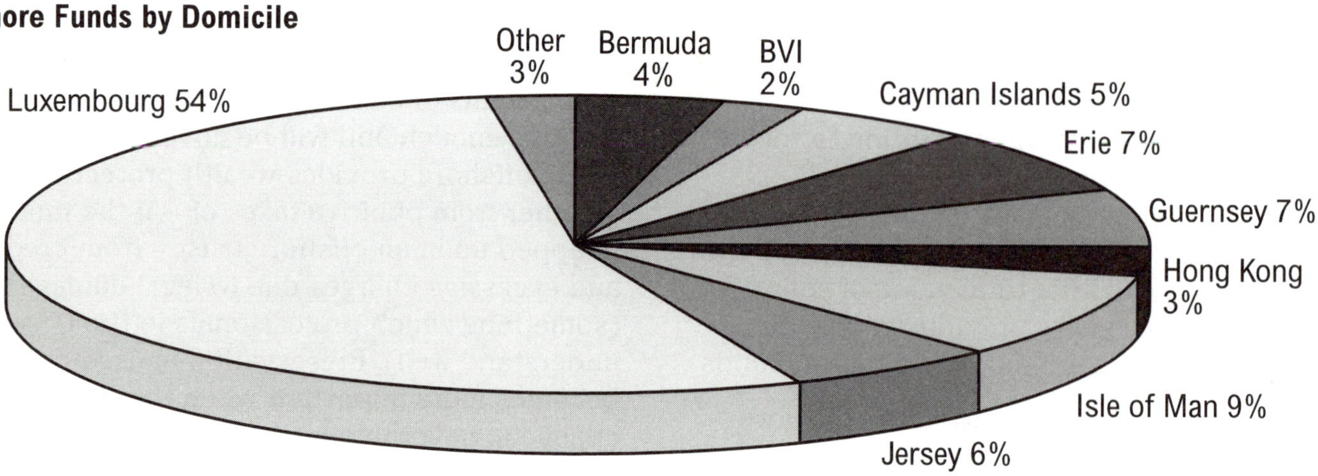

2. ABOUT THE FUNDS

With well over 5,500 offshore funds in existence, there is no shortage of choice for investors. While the funds may all be termed "offshore" funds, the similarities largely end there. The general aim of all funds is to maximise investment returns while limiting the amount of risk.

Perhaps the best way to look at the different types of offshore fund is to examine the different kinds of assets in which they invest. Micropal segregates all offshore funds into 193 sectors and nine broad categories: equity funds, money market funds, fixed interest stock (or bond) funds, laufzeitfonds, short-term bond funds, convertible bond funds, warrant funds, specialist funds and mixed (or balanced) funds. The funds in the first eight categories specialise in one type of investment, while funds in the mixed sector invest in various types of investments.

Offshore Funds by Asset Type

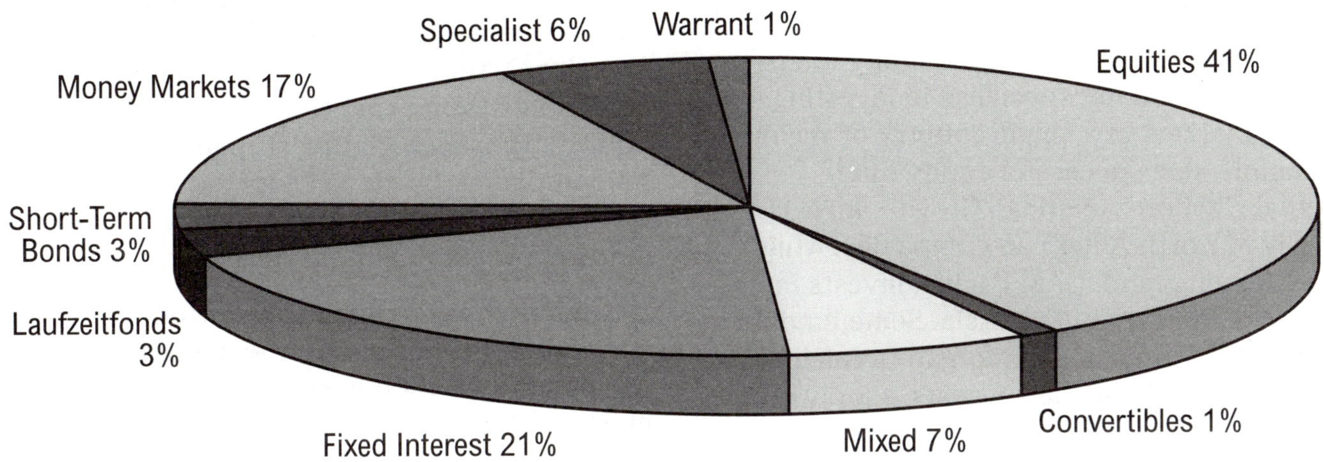

Micropal Category Breakdown

Category	Micropal sectors
Equities	61
Fixed Interest	33
Money Markets	27
Laufzeitfonds	27
Convertible Bonds	5
Short-Term Bonds	18
Specialist	4
Warrants	7
Mixed	11
TOTAL	193

Equity funds

The equity fund category is the biggest of them all. Over half of all offshore funds specialise in this particular type of investment. Equity funds invest primarily in the shares of public listed companies. The term "equities" is simply an alternative word for shares. Sometimes these are also known as company stocks or common stocks. Whatever the preferred name, in essence, the managers of equity funds will build up a portfolio of shares in various companies. The value of the fund will rise and fall as do the fortunes of those companies on the stock market.

Like offshore funds in general, equity funds are a diverse group. Many specialise in investing on the stock markets of a single country or region. For example, one successful equity fund, Perpetual Offshore American Growth, invests primarily in North American companies, while another leading fund, GAM Pacific, invests mainly in the stock markets of East Asia. Some funds are very specific. For example, Morgan Grenfell Brazil concentrates, as its name suggests, simply on the shares of Brazilian companies.

But some equity funds take a broader approach geographically. We list some 300 funds that take a largely global approach to their investment and do not specialise in any particular region. Typically, the manager of such a fund will take a view on how the world's various stock markets are likely to perform comparatively and will adjust his portfolio based upon this assessment. Once he has decided how much to invest in each region (for example, 30 percent in North America, 20 percent in Europe, etc.) he will then pick the actual shares in each market. This is known as "top down" investment management. The opposite method – "bottom up" – is employed by some managers of globally invested offshore equity funds. Here, the manager picks out the shares he thinks will perform well, irrespective of where the companies are based. Bottom-up investment management tends to be a more detailed approach. There are other approaches to globally managed funds. Some specialise in the stock markets of emerging economies. Others will invest mainly in smaller companies or the shares of companies in a particular line of business, such as health care (for example, Orbitex Health & Environment), information technology (GT Telecommunications), finance (ItalFortune International Banks & Insurance) or utility companies (Templeton Global Utilities).

This type of sector specialisation also occurs with single-country and regionally specialist funds. Take North American equity funds, for example. There are broadly based investment funds (for example, Swiss Life Proteus American), those which specialise in smaller companies (Von Ernst GP US Smaller Companies Equity), those which invest mainly in the largest US companies (such as Guinness Flight American Blue Chip), and industry specialist funds (Putnam Emerging Health Science).

Besides the top-down and bottom-up approach, there is another way of managing equity funds, which is simply to follow the market. This is what index or tracker funds do. Stock markets are covered by indices that reflect what a market is doing. Examples are the Dow Jones Industrial Average and the FT-SE 100 Index. By buying in the correct proportions, or weighting, the shares of those companies that make up such indices, a fund will simply rise and fall as the market index rises and falls. In effect, investors are taking away the fund manager's job of trying to produce high returns and trusting solely in the stock market for gains. This has two advantages. Firstly, it is often a cheaper way to run a fund, and these cost savings are passed down to the investor in lower fees. Secondly, it avoids the risk of the fund manager making bad decisions. Buying, say, CMI Passport UK Index, means that your fortunes will simply be tied to the performance of the UK stock market – and not necessarily to the skills of Clerical Medical International's fund management team.

So, there is certainly no such thing as a simple equity fund. The best way to look at equity funds is on a scale of diversity. As a rule of thumb, the more diverse the investments of a fund are, the less risky it generally will be. This is because if, say, a certain stock market goes into free fall, the diverse fund may lose out on only part of its portfolio. A specialist fund that happens to concentrate in that particular area would suffer far more.

On the whole, equity funds with their expected gains are for the long-term investor. Even diversely invested risk-averse funds will regularly make losses, and so investors must be willing to stick with their fund selections for long enough to ride through any rough patches. In the long term – at least three years but preferably five or more – equity funds will usually outperform most other types of fund, especially those funds based on bonds and government debt issues.

Money market funds

Money market funds fulfil a rather different purpose to that of equity funds. These are far lower risk than equity funds, and over the long term their returns will almost certainly be lower too.

Offshore money market funds invest in debt securities with very short maturity dates – up to 90 days. Because of their short-term nature and high level of safety, many investors consider money market funds a good alternative to lower interest bank savings accounts.

The debt securities held by money market funds come in various forms. The most common are government debt issues. Some also invest in other forms of short-term debt such as bank certificates of deposit, bankers' acceptances (debt arising from international trade transactions) and commercial paper (unsecured IOUs from corporations). Money market funds are the least risky of all offshore funds. Those which invest in the securities of stable governments – such as US Treasury Bills – are virtually free of any risk. However, those money market funds which stray away from "safe country" government debt do run some risk to the investor's capital, albeit a relatively small one.

Like equity funds, some money market funds are globally invested, while others invest in a specific region or country. Of key importance is the currency in which the investments are based. Most investors will invest in those money market funds that are denominated in the currency they use themselves. Otherwise, the small returns available on such funds could be eliminated by exchange rate movements. The flip side of this, however, is that investors find some money market funds such as the Guinness Flight Managed Currency Fund a useful way to speculate on exchange rate movements.

These managed currency funds are suitable for investors, both individuals or institutions, who want to protect the purchasing power of their liquid assets through a managed diversification of currency and interest rate exposure. Typically the fund invests in a spread of currencies, held largely in the form of bank deposits, CDs, floating rate notes, and other instruments such as short-term tail-end bonds. The currencies are monitored on a medium to long-term view, and the manager seeks undervalued currencies or situations in the currency markets that are within the risk parameters of the fund. These funds play a very important part in the global market, as they can be major buyers of Treasury Bills.

Fixed interest stock funds

Offshore funds in the fixed interest stock sector are those which invest in fixed interest securities – alternatively known as bonds – with a maturity of three years or more. This is an important sector among offshore funds. After equity funds, fixed interest funds are more numerous than any other type of offshore fund (over 1,000 of them are listed in Part 4).

The term fixed interest security covers a wide range of investment instruments, including government treasury bonds, corporate and municipal bonds. Such investments are relatively risk-free, the main risk being that the bond issuers (effectively the government or organisation which has borrowed the money) will be unable to repay it. With stable governments this risk is usually acceptable. Bonds issued by Third World governments and corporations naturally have more risk. But the riskier the bond issuer, the better the yield on the bond.

Offshore investors are attracted to fixed interest funds due to the good levels of income such funds can achieve – better than short-term bonds and money market funds – and these funds are safer than equity investments. Although they are less risky than equities, the value of bonds can fluctuate. Their value tends to run in the opposite direction to interest rates in the economies in which they are based.

Most fixed interest funds are based on instruments in a single currency. The majority of funds are based in major currencies such as the German mark, UK sterling, the US dollar and the Japanese yen, but there are some minor currency fixed interest funds, such as Kleinwort Benson (Lux) Bond Canadian Dollars (in Canadian dollars), CS Portfolio Income Lira (in Italian lira) and Multi Link Finnish Bonds (in Finnish markka). There are also over 300 globally invested fixed interest funds. Most are generally invested, although some specialise only in fixed interest stocks based on the world's key currencies (for example, Credis Bond Prime Currencies). Other funds may concentrate on bonds from emerging markets (Morgan Grenfell Emerging Markets Fixed Interest).

Laufzeitfonds

These are fixed interest bond funds sold primarily in Germany, Switzerland, Luxembourg and Belgium, and may be in differing base currencies. These funds are established with a defined maturity, or collapse date, usually within 10 years. When the funds are launched, they usually sell their units for a short period (30 to 90 days) and are then closed. Consequently, only a bid price (redemption price) or net asset value (NAV) price is published until maturity. All interest or capital gains is retained within the fund until the end of the period. The manager of the fund will buy a selection of bonds, usually in the base currency of the specific laufzeitfond, that usually mature during the time period of the laufzeitfond; but the manager is not restricted to set maturities other than that the bond portfolio will be liquidated at the term date of the fund itself. At maturity the investor will receive the NAV price of the unit. These funds have been very popular in the Luxembourg offshore market, as they are relatively risk free and attract people who wish to have funds invested in fixed securities for a set time and have the income that is generated by the fund reinvested.

Short-term bond funds

Short-term bond offshore funds can be seen as a half-way house between money market funds and fixed interest stock funds. In terms of time scale, they most certainly are. While money market funds hold investment instruments with maturities of less than twelve months and fixed interest stock (bond) funds hold mostly investment instruments which mature in more than three years' time, short-term bond offshore funds, on the other hand, cover the less than three-year time spectrum.

While money market funds are often seen as an alternative to bank deposits and fixed interest stocks are seen as rather more long-term investments, short-term bond funds fulfil a need somewhere in between. These are essentially very safe investments, but ones which should produce marginally better returns than money market funds.

There are not huge numbers of offshore funds investing primarily in short-term bonds. Most funds are invested in European fixed interest stocks – German bonds are the most popular – although there are some Canadian and US funds.

Short-term bond funds are usually dominated by the currency in which the investments are held.

Convertible bond funds

Generally a convertible bond or debenture is an unsecured loan to a corporation which may be exchanged for ordinary shares in the company, in most cases at the discretion of the holder of the bond. As an investment they tend to work in part like an equity and in part like a bond. When the share price of the company in question rises above the conversion price of the bond, the price of the bond tends to move in line with the price of the underlying shares. But should the share price be below that of the conversion price, then, as the bonds pay interest and have a limited life, they act more like bonds in their market pricing. All this tends to make their performance over time lie somewhere between that of equities and fixed interest stocks.

This has great appeal for investors looking for investment growth but who are unwilling to take on too much risk. A portfolio of convertible bonds gives an investor a stake in a rising stock market – as convertible bond prices go in tandem with share prices – while allowing some protection from the bad times, when the bonds continue to pay out interest.

Convertible bonds are not a big area for offshore investment, indeed – we list 34 such funds. The majority of convertible bond funds are invested globally, although there are area-specific funds such as those investing mainly in the convertible bond markets of Japan, the Far East, the UK and Switzerland.

Warrant funds

Warrants are a type of investment instrument which give the holder the right to subscribe for shares at some time in the future and at prices fixed when the warrants are issued. For a relatively small initial investment, warrants offer the buyer the option of a future stake in a company's equity. Some warrants expire in one or two years' time, while many are for five to ten years and others are perpetual.

Warrants are basically very speculative. Huge sums can be made by investing in warrants, and conversely huge sums can be lost. Movements in the value of a warrant tend to be exaggerated versions of the movements in the value of the underlying share on which it is based. The majority of offshore warrant funds specialise in the markets of Asia Pacific. They can be extremely volatile creatures. While some have made their investors small fortunes, others have lost their investors nearly all their stake. Consequently, warrant funds are usually not advisable for most investors. Even for investors happy to take on a bit of speculation, warrant funds should never make up a large portion of a portfolio.

Specialist funds

Specialist funds can be risky as well, being invested in a narrow range of assets such as precious metals or property. Micropal splits specialist funds into four further categories: commodity and natural resources funds, real estate funds, derivative investment funds and actively hedged funds.

The commodity and natural resources sector includes funds invested in the shares of companies operating in commodity related industries – most commonly mining – and/or which hold physical assets such as gold bullion and other precious metals. Real estate funds invest in the shares of companies in property related industries and/or hold physical real estate, quite often development sites.

Derivative investment funds concentrate on investments such as futures and options with the aim of achieving high returns. Futures are contract shares or commodities bought or sold for future delivery. These investment contracts have a price today but they also have a price for delivery on a future date. The two prices are likely to be different depending on market expectations of what the price will be in, say, three months' time. A fund may buy a future without the intention of taking up the related asset but instead will rely on price changes in order to sell at a profit ahead of delivery. A profit – or loss – can be made without ever holding the underlying share. Options are rather similar. An option is the right, but not the obligation, to buy or sell an asset at a fixed strike price within a specified period.

Actively hedged funds tend to behave rather like those in the derivative investment sector but have a somewhat broader remit. Such funds will invest in many areas such as equities, fixed interest stock or money market instruments, but specialist funds will also actively speculate in the derivatives market and/or use hedging techniques involving future and option contracts. Although hedge funds can be highly volatile, some are, in fact, less volatile than many equity funds. The use of hedging techniques can actually take much of the downside risk out of a portfolio, so making it less volatile than one which does not use hedging.

Mixed funds

Some funds do not really specialise at all and invest in a variety of asset types – be that equities, fixed interest bonds or any of the other types of investment instrument mentioned above. Being non-specialist, these funds are useful to investors who wish to leave most of the basic "asset allocation" decisions up to a fund manager who will attempt to balance the riskier equity holdings with lower returning fixed interest investments to produce a portfolio which should produce a reasonable return at a relatively low level of risk.

Most such funds are globally invested but often have very different styles of management. Some will have a mix which is geared more towards the riskier end of the asset spectrum and will have a higher than average proportion of equity holdings. Others will play it safer and will carry a high level of bonds and money market instruments. What a fund is trying to achieve is often obvious from its name. For example, Sun Life International has mixed funds with titles such as "managed growth", "balanced", and "defensive".

Portfolio management

Investors in offshore funds should not simply pick one fund and put all their money into it. One reason why there are so many different types of offshore investment funds is so that investors can, by buying into a range of funds with different investment managers, build up a diversified portfolio of investments compatible with their expectations of safety and performance. But before we look at the best ways to structure a portfolio of offshore funds, it is important to look at some basic strategies of international investment.

3. BASIC INVESTMENT STRATEGIES

As an individual, your financial circumstances are going to be very different from those of the people around you. Similarly, just as financial circumstances vary, so will the requirements you have for your investment portfolio.

It is a widely recognised fact that younger investors are more likely to be comfortable with a high-risk, high-return portfolio, while older investors with more financial responsibilities – or those concerned with retirement planning – tend to look for more conservative investments. Similarly, investors from continental Europe are more at home with bonds than shares, in direct contrast to their British and American counterparts. Investors in Asia tend to hold large amounts on deposit with banks, and if they do dabble in financial markets, they like to buy securities directly from a broker rather than putting money into a mutual fund.

Thus, we can see that even the culture you grow up in is likely to affect the sorts of investments you are prepared to make. The newspapers or magazines you read will, if locally published, reflect the preferred investment portfolio of a typical inhabitant of that country. Only the truly cerebral investor is prepared to consider all possibilities, all asset types, in his quest to build the portfolio that suits his requirements exactly.

Your goals

When sitting down to decide on what type of portfolio to build, it is important to think carefully about what you require of that portfolio, what you want it to do for you. The asset managers who advise multi-millionaires and lottery winners design portfolios for their clients only after they are fully acquainted with a client's financial position and requirements. You should do the same.

The buzz phrase here is risk tolerance. Essentially, this boils down to a balance between fantastic returns (and the potential for fantastic losses) and the safety of your assets. But there are other factors too, such as time scale. For instance, are you prepared to invest money for the long term, at least five years, or can you only spare it for a short period of time? Some portfolios are very actively traded because the investor is trying to make large gains with short-term investments: buying an investment one day in order to sell it the next. This is an effective strategy when you are trading with considerable amounts of money, where a 1 percent gain in price is going to make a big difference in the size of the return. For example, $100,000 in an investment which rises by 1 percent overnight is going to make $1,000. However, there would be no point in putting $1,000 in such an investment: $10 is hardly worth the trouble.

Diversification

Whether a long-term or a short-term investor, you should always guard against risk. This is done through a process called diversification – spreading your money in more than one investment, and preferably in more than one market. Remember the old saying: "Don't put all your eggs in one basket".

Markets can be notoriously cyclical, and you will find that when prices are plunging in one market, they can be rising in another. This is frequently because large institutional investors like to move their money around the world from one stock market to another.

During the years up to the end of 1996 when the Tokyo Stock Exchange was plunging, the New York market was climbing to record levels. Many large US investors had demonstrated their lack of confidence in Japan by selling out of Japanese stock and buying back into US shares. American institutional investors control vast sums of money. If they do not like a market and sell out, there is little a private investor can do apart from follow them as quickly as possible. A long-term investor can stay in the market, riding the rough times, waiting until the market rises again, as the Tokyo market inevitably did (although continues to falter); but those following a short-term strategy can quickly see the value of their portfolio devalued as the big pension funds flee the markets in which they are invested.

The US market makes up almost 40 percent of the total world market capitalisation, and US investors are similarly important when it comes to international flows of money. When the Mexican debt crisis hit Latin American stock markets in 1995, US investors fled en masse, and many also sold out of other emerging markets. The ripple effect hit the Philippine market, some say because its currency, the peso, has the same name as that of Mexico's. The Mexican crisis undermined heavyweight US investors' credibility in emerging markets, and consequently many of these markets suffered downturns in 1995.

This is why diversification is so important. An investor with all his savings invested in Latin American shares in early 1995 would have seen them much reduced in a matter of weeks. To put all your money in one investment, one market, or one region can leave you open to the risk of losing much of your investment's value if that market runs into difficulties. The Mexican crisis was a good example of how an entire region can be hit, and how follow-on effects can damage the price of investments in other regions. Investors who thought they were sitting safely in south-east Asian stocks would have suffered as a result of the crisis, while those with investments in Europe would have been safe, and those holding North American stocks would have profited.

If a portfolio relies solely on the progress of a single market or region, or an asset class such as international bonds, then it is vulnerable to damage if these markets fall. It is like having a chair with only one leg. The prudent investor will try to put as many legs on this chair as he can, so that if one or more break, the chair is still likely to stay upright. Generally speaking the more markets and asset classes an investment can be spread through, for the average investor the better. Diversification reduces market risk and volatility as the investment is spread over a variety of collective funds with diverse portfolios in preference to holding, say, three or four stocks. The prudent investor depending on capital availability, age, investment objective and desired market sector exposure should acquire a diversified asset mix of at least three investment funds preferably managed by different investment managers.

Assessing risk

Diversification also involves assessing risk as some markets are riskier than others. For instance, government bonds are considered much more secure than corporate bonds, because a government is less likely to default on its debts than a company is, no matter how big the company. Obviously, some governments have defaulted on debts before, and there was even a threat that the US government might be forced to do so during the federal budget crisis in early 1996; but generally speaking, major economies will not do so. Thus, we can see that US government bonds are treated by investors and risk-rating agencies as being far less of a gamble than bonds issued by a company or an African government.

The same goes for stock markets. The stock markets of Southeast Asia, for example, have proven themselves capable of giving investors some of the best returns available from equities, but they are perceived as being higher risk or more volatile than European or North American markets. This perception is generally caused by unknown determinants such as politics, a weaker currency, high national debt, social tension, and so forth. When diversifying a portfolio in order to spread your risk, it pays to keep a substantial proportion of assets in low risk markets, such as UK shares, government bonds issued by economically stable countries like Germany or the US, and in cash.

Once this safety net has been established, money can then be set aside for high-earning, high-risk markets. This is why safe but relatively low performing investments are so popular and form the foundation of any portfolio. This explains the historical popularity of UK government bonds (or gilts) which are internationally regarded as something of a safe haven by investors due to the country's relative political security and stable currency.

Currency

This is another factor which must be considered when diversifying a portfolio. Currencies can rise and fall just as quickly as stock markets, especially those of high debtor nations. The base currency of a portfolio is the one in which the original investment is made and into which profits are realised. However, if you are investing internationally, you will be exposing yourself to other currencies. Buying assets in other countries means using the currency of that country. At some stage, your base currency must be converted into the currency in which the foreign share can be bought. Once you hold that share, its value will be altered not only by being traded on the market, but also by the strength of the currency in which it is denominated relative to the base currency of the investor.

Ironically, when the Tokyo stock market was plunging in 1994-95, the yen was soaring, sometimes cancelling out some of the losses international investors were making on share prices. (The yen has since weakened considerably so making many of those losses real.)

For the purposes of diversification, however, it is best to spread yourself through as many "hard" currencies as possible. The hardest of all have been the deutschmark, the Swiss franc and, despite recent problems, the yen. This avoids the possibility of making a big loss should a single currency take a downturn. It even applies to your base currency. Dollar investors buying foreign assets are insuring their portfolios against the possibility that the dollar will weaken against other currencies. The money invested in non-dollar assets will thus not be affected by the weakening in the relative value of the investor's dollar assets (which would include any US bonds or shares held). Historically, because of its overseas debt position, the dollar has declined relative to less indebted nations.

Investors tend to make the bulk of their portfolio purchases in assets listed in their home country, using their home currency. If all you do is buy domestic investments, a currency downturn is not going to be a problem. Major world currencies are unlikely to suffer serious problems, but weaker ones, like the South African rand or the Russian rouble, cannot always be relied on. If your base currency is one you do not have confidence in, it pays to keep much of your portfolio in assets that are not denominated in this currency. The table below illustrates the returns in currency alone relative to US dollars over the previous one, three and five years to the end of 1996. Understandably, this type of return performance may not be the case in the future; but it is interesting for comparison, especially if you held assets denominated in the currencies of countries such as Canada, Italy, Spain, and the UK.

Currency Returns Relative to US Dollars to 1/1/1997

Currency	% Return 1 Year	% Return 3 years	% Return 5 Years
U S Dollar	1.00	1.00	1.00
Australian Dollar	6.77	17.02	4.53
Belgian Franc	-7.35	13.81	-1.42
Canadian Dollar	-0.50	-3.41	-15.64
Danish Krone	-6.05	15.20	0.32
Deutschmark	-7.13	12.68	-1.47
ECU	-2.30	12.22	-6.44
French Franc	-5.93	13.58	-0.07
Hong Kong Dollar	-0.04	-0.10	0.55
Irish Punt	5.60	20.11	-3.73
Italian Lire	4.33	12.60	-24.30
Japanese Yen	-11.13	-3.85	7.57
Luxembourg Franc	-7.35	13.81	-1.42
Netherlands Guilder	-7.33	12.29	-0.91
Singapore Dollar	1.12	15.02	15.87
Spanish Peseta	-6.73	9.88	-25.55
Swiss Franc	-14.30	10.60	0.92
UK Sterling	10.22	15.67	-8.34

Source: Micropal, US dollars 4/97

Geographical spread

When looking at the world's stock markets, you realise that some are more important than others. The three largest are New York, Tokyo and London – in that order. Other important markets include Hong Kong, Paris, the other major US exchanges such as Nasdaq (National Association of Securities Dealers Automated Quotation), the American Stock Exchange and the Toronto Stock Exchange.

When determining geographical spread, portfolios will tend to reflect the regional prejudices of the investor. Asian investors tend to have most of their money in Asian shares. US private investors have so much to choose from in their home markets that they rarely venture abroad. Most investors will keep the bulk of their portfolios close to home, invested in securities denominated in their base currency. However, in the interests of diversification and the pursuit of higher returns, it also pays to keep money in foreign markets too. Indeed, despite the traditional reluctance of Americans to invest outside the US, the argument for greater diversification into foreign fields seems to be winning. Recent research by the Investment Company Institute shows that the proportion of the flow of new money into mutual investing in non-US markets was nearly twice as much in 1996 than it was in 1992.

The other major markets in a portfolio will tend to be the heavyweight stock markets: the US, the UK, Europe, and Japan. This is because they are the most liquid (you can get in and out of them most easily), they have the most shares to choose from, and are situated in countries with secure governments that have good regulators and stable currencies.

Emerging markets are becoming more popular, however. These are basically the stock markets of countries in the developing world or those which have until recently been dominated by communist regimes. Eastern Europe, Russia, India, South Africa, and most Asian countries outside Japan can be classed as emerging markets.

Although very high returns have been realised in these markets in the past, they are still considered very risky compared with developed markets. It would be foolish for any portfolio to have a large exposure to emerging markets, despite the large amount of publicity they get. You need to be in the "right" emerging market. Usually at least one area of emerging markets is doing well at anyone time (last year mostly Eastern European markets) but often the rest will be heading in the opposite direction (such as Thailand in 1996).

But most asset managers argue that, with the rise of the economies of the Pacific Rim, it would be foolish for investors not to have at least some exposure to emerging Asian stocks. Investing in Pacific stock markets, they say, is betting on the future of east Asia as the fulcrum of world affairs in the 21st century. Not everyone would agree with this view, but an issue like this is a good example of the sort of factor considered when someone is trying to determine their emerging markets exposure. The world twenty years from now is going to be a very different place, and emerging markets are one way of capitalising on an historical shift in emphasis.

Liquidity

One of the pitfalls experienced in emerging markets, however, is a lack of liquidity. This is basically a measure of how easy it is to buy or sell something. It is not always possible to buy the shares you want, when you want, or to sell them for that matter. If only a small number of shares are available on a market and they are in great demand, that issue is deemed to be less liquid. This situation can sometimes be created when a single investor is trying to maintain a controlling interest in a company, and other major interested parties have also built up large blocks of stock with the aim of exercising shareholders' rights on the board of directors. A relatively tiny number of shares will thus be actively traded on the market, especially if the company is doing well, and its price is going up. Few people will be prepared to sell out. Conversely, if a company is doing badly, and it is a large company with lots of equity on the market, and everyone is selling, it may prove difficult to get a buyer.

This situation can also apply to countries, especially where governments, such as those in India and China, restrict the companies foreigners are allowed to invest in or specify that foreign ownership of a company is not allowed to exceed a certain level. A lack of activity in a market, for whatever reason, will make it illiquid. For the investor, this makes it harder to get into or out of the market. There is nothing worse than being stuck in an illiquid market, watching the price of your assets decline without being able to sell them. For the private investor, however, this is hardly a consideration, since individuals rarely trade sums large enough for the lack of liquidity to affect them. It is usually something large banks and fund managers with millions of dollars in assets have to worry about, not someone with a $200,000 portfolio. Mice can get in and out through holes which elephants cannot fit through.

Appraising portfolios

Professional investors tend to appraise their portfolios in various ways. One is the top-down strategy. Here, percentage allocations are made to specific asset types or markets. So, an investor might decide he wants 20 percent of his portfolio in financial stocks, 10 percent in industrials, 15 in consumer goods producers, and so forth. Similarly, he could make geographical allocations on the same basis.

This is a useful way of judging your exposure to various markets. You could decide in advance that you will never expose more than 10 percent of your portfolio to emerging markets, thereby limiting your risk. Decisions are made at the macro-economic level. The top-down – or asset allocation – approach involves a lot of looking at averages, assessing countries, markets, and sectors on the basis of average returns, percentage increases, inflation rates, stock market indices, risk and so forth. An index that shows the movements of the whole or part of a stock market enables the investor to have a clear picture of the overall trend in that market. It is an ideal tool in this respect for the top-down investor.

The bottom-up strategy, on the other hand, involves a more micro-economic approach. A portfolio based on a bottom-up strategy looks at the smallest denominator, often an individual share issue, or bond, or whatever. Bottom-up managers are detail oriented, reviewing the fundamentals of the companies they invest in or are considering through analysis of balance sheets and inventories. So, for instance, whereas the top-down investor will decide, for example, to make his exposure to US property 10 percent of his portfolio, the bottom-up investor will buy into a specific development or company because he likes the potential returns it is likely to offer. The bottom-up investor, or stock picker, looks to the detail. He invests in shares he knows about rather than sticking to the top 100 companies in a market or famous blue-chip shares. Bottom-up investment can be highly lucrative if you know what you're doing, because you avoid following the crowd and can get in early on an investment prospect while it is still relatively cheap. There are always stories about canny, individualistic investors who bought into a company when it was still operating out of a garden shed and sold it once it reached blue-chip status.

Few investors are either bottom-up or top-down in their approach. Most investors, including offshore fund managers, put together a portfolio of investments based upon both strategies. Indeed, it would be difficult to do otherwise. It is important to note, however, that some investment management houses put more emphasis on one approach than the other.

Timing

One of the most essential rules when it comes to managing your money in cyclical markets is to avoid the crowd. Private investors too often buy into markets once they are at their highest point and when assets are at their most expensive, while the canny institutional investors are ready to start selling their securities for a profit. Private investors like good news and buy in a bull market in the hope of realising returns that are no longer possible. Indeed, they usually lose money as the market turns from a bull into a bear.

It is important never to adopt any given type of selection method on a permanent basis. If everyone else is using your method of selecting investments, you will never stay ahead of the crowd. If you always buy the same types of securities as everyone else does, you will get the same results. Superior performance can only be achieved by doing something very different: buying when others are selling and selling when others are buying. It can seem imprudent and risky at the time, but this is frequently how top money managers make their millions. You end up acquiring investments when they are very cheap or out of favour and selling them again when they are expensive.

Such a process goes against the grain. There is always the fear that a bear market is going to go on forever, and that you will simply end up throwing your money away. But bear markets never last forever. Share prices usually turn upward from between one to twelve months before the bottom of the business cycle, and vice versa. According to Sir John Templeton, founder of the successful Templeton Fund: "Bull markets are born on pessimism, grow on scepticism, mature on optimism and die on euphoria. The time of maximum pessimism is the best time to buy, and the time of maximum optimism is the best time to sell."

Consequently, the successful investor tends to be one who does not focus on outlooks or trends, but on the relative value of the investments he makes. Thus, the best time to acquire assets is when they are undervalued and when everybody else is selling them or simply not interested in them. But you have got to be quick on your toes – the majority of major market moves are all over in the space of a few days or weeks. If you are not invested at the correct time, then by the time you are, it may be too late to gain much of the benefit.

There is a strong argument to take little notice of the market. Investors who try to second-guess where a market is going well often increase their exposure to risk without necessarily achieving any positive affect on performance. Markets run on fear (the fear of losses) and greed (the taking of risky postures). Investors should avoid being swayed by either of these emotions. Decide on a long-term course and stay with it. The key is to be consistent in your investment fund purchases if they are being bought over a period of time; for not only do you benefit from the lower price cost of dollar cost averaging, but you will also participate in the markets on an averaging basis. Markets spend almost as much time in retreat as they do in rising, so even having made the right decisions for a lot of the time, you may see the value of your investments declining. But stick with it: if you have set up your portfolio with the correct level of risk you are willing to take, do not let the fear of falling markets knock you off course. Likewise in a rising market, do not be tempted to increase your exposure to risk simply because things are going well; a sharp market correction could leave you feeling very sorry for yourself.

Business cycles

Economies tend to move through periods of upturn or recovery, followed by periods of slow growth or recession. These are called business cycles, and it is these which investors must take advantage of if they are to maximise their profits. The first phase of a cycle is usually a recovery when the economy is coming out of a recession. It is characterised by low short-term interest rates, stepped-up production by businesses and strong export growth. Interest rates will usually still be travelling downward, allowing investors to make capital gains in fixed-interest markets.

The second phase is one of expansion, the healthiest phase in a business cycle, and one which sees the economy, having recovered from its previous losses as a result of the last recession, surging ahead to new heights. Thus, unemployment falls, borrowing and spending rise, along with business and consumer confidence. It is at this stage that the stock market really appreciates and short-term interest rates bottom out, as evidenced by the US and UK stock markets in 1996. Toward the end of this phase consumer demand will outstrip production and unemployment will reach a stage where the economy will suffer from labour shortages. It is at this point that inflation will start to pick up, and the authorities will tighten up monetary policy by raising interest rates. Once this happens, the bond market goes into decline due to rising interest rates, followed shortly, usually within six months, by a jittery stock market, with investors sensing that the boom times are drawing to a close. A declining stock market presages the end of the expansion.

Now the economy starts to slow down, with continuing inflation and labour shortages. Investors lose confidence as a result of high interest rates, and financial markets deflate. Business and consumer borrowing and spending drops, with companies trimming expansion or capital spending plans.

Finally, in a recession, investors find themselves with assets worth much less than they were acquired for and with debts that are more difficult to pay off. Unemployment starts to rise, companies make losses or go bankrupt, and most people stop borrowing altogether in order to pay off existing debts. Interest rates come down as the government tries to jump-start the economy and lenders try to encourage consumers to borrow again. This is prime time for the bond market, as bond prices are peaking and interest rates are bottoming out.

Economic factors

It is important to pay close attention to economic factors when planning your entrance into a market. Prevailing interest rates are a good indication of opportunities. If they are starting to pick up, it is a bad time to commit yourself, since money supply is already beginning to tighten and the economy is overheating. Investments made at this stage are likely to lose you money, unless perhaps you keep them as long-term holdings. If interest rates have peaked, then it is time to buy stocks and long-dated bonds or short-term money market funds. When interest rates start declining, stocks and bonds will start to rise. Similarly, inflation, which rises in tandem with interest rates, is bad for investments, since as an economic phenomenon it will encourage monetary authorities to hike up interest rates. This environment is good for cash investments and gold, but not for securities.

Other trend figures to watch include measures of gross domestic product (GDP) and money supply. GDP tracks the growth of a country's economy by measuring the increase in the value of goods and services produced. Growth economies are better prospects for long-term investment exposure. Many emerging markets (like the nations of Southeast Asia, for instance) regularly record annual GDP growth rates well ahead of those of the developed world. Agencies such as the International Monetary Fund (IMF) measure money supply, which is an indication of the likely tack a government is going to take on interest rates and whether or not higher inflation is to be expected. Money supply tends to reveal which way a national economy is going. Confidence is shown by accelerating borrowing by individuals and companies. Lack of confidence is indicated by reduced (or slower accelerating) borrowing and by increased saving.

Contraction in the money supply – especially if a lot of money is going into bank accounts, money market savings accounts and certificates of deposit – is an indication that the economy is about to enter a deflationary spiral. Conversely, more money circulating in the economy is a warning of approaching inflation and rising interest rates.

Investing in those economies which look set for growth (and getting out of those ready for a downturn) is obviously a key to investment success. However, during the 1990s there has been increasing evidence that the major economies business cycles are converging. If this trend continues, it will become increasingly difficult to avoid the ups and downs of the business cycle.

Income or growth?

When building a portfolio, it is important that you decide what you want to do with the money your investments earn. Currency exposure and the types of assets you buy will depend somewhat on your requirements. The main decision to make has to be whether you wish to invest for income, growth or a bit of both.

The income investor is simply looking to earn a specific amount of income on a monthly or annual basis. If this is what you want, you must be aware of the rate of inflation in the country where you live, because high inflation may make it impossible for you to maintain purchasing power parity.

Both the value of the portfolio and the value of the income it generates will shrink in relation to the rising costs of living. In a high inflation scenario, income investors have to be prepared to assume a higher level of risk (income portfolios tend to be comprised of low-risk investments such as government bonds) in order to allow the value of the base assets to increase, thereby boosting the level of income generated. In order to maintain purchasing power parity, it is therefore important to ensure that your portfolio grows in value faster than the rate of inflation.

The other type of investor is the growth investor. When investing offshore, this strategy is frequently preferable, since most tax-friendly jurisdictions have no capital gains taxes; but the country you are living in will probably tax income you repatriate from your offshore portfolio. Therefore, it is frequently preferable for the offshore investor to allow earnings to accumulate by reinvesting them or to invest in funds that have accumulating units or to allow the income roll-up feature. In this case investors frequently have to accept an above-average level of risk and a high rate of fluctuation in asset value. In addition, they should pay close attention to other currencies, which may also provide opportunities for gain.

Model offshore portfolios

We have already discussed why a portfolio must be diversified. Ideally, it should include investments in different markets and asset types. However, just like a shopper in a supermarket, it is impossible to buy something from everything. Nobody has that kind of money.

Therefore, investors must concentrate on ensuring that they do not rely too heavily on one market. North Americans, for instance, can find themselves severely tempted to go "overweight" in US stocks simply because there is so much choice and a great deal written about them. This is particularly true when the US stock market is performing well. But by doing so, investors leave themselves open to a downturn in the US equity market. It has happened before and will no doubt happen again. By investing abroad, it is possible to offset downturns in the domestic market with gains overseas.

It is much harder to know exactly when to sell out of one market and buy into another, so most portfolio managers try to keep their fingers in as many pies as they can, and simply adjust their weightings in the various markets according to local conditions. While there are some professional investment managers who routinely commit some 40 or 50 percent of their portfolios into a single market, this is not a course of action recommended to the private investor.

The other advantage of investing internationally is that you can avoid foreign exchange risk. Although some of your assets will always be affected by downturns in the denominated currency, there are bound to be other foreign currencies you hold that will appreciate, thus off-setting your losses. Currencies tend not to fluctuate as violently as stock and bond markets and thereby bring an element of stability to a portfolio.

Generally speaking, a globally oriented portfolio will constitute the following asset categories: US large and small company stocks, international stocks, US bonds, international bonds, precious metals and money market assets. Exposure to the real estate market has not been included here, primarily because few private investors have the money to speculate in the real estate market and most investors already have exposure to this market via the homes they have purchased in addition to land or buildings they might own (a holiday condominium, for instance). There is also the fact that by investing in the shares of a company, you are frequently buying a share of an organisation that has its own real estate portfolio. Look at the large amounts of property owned by railway or oil companies. Buying their shares can be seen as an indirect play on the property market. Exactly how much of a portfolio should be weighted towards each of these asset categories depends on what individuals are hoping to achieve and their aversion to risk.

In the three tables set out below, we have put together three types of portfolios: an aggressive growth portfolio for those willing to take reasonable risks for long-term growth, a conservative growth portfolio for those looking for capital gains but less willing to run the risk of short-term losses, and an income portfolio for those looking for high income at a low level of risk.

Model Portfolio Weights

Component	Aggressive Growth Portfolio % Weighting	Conservative Growth Portfolio % Weighting	Income Portfolio % Weighting
US Large Cap Equity	10%	15%	20%
US Small Cap Equity	30%	15%	0%
International Equity	40%	15%	10%
US Bonds	0%	20%	25%
International Bonds	10%	15%	25%
Gold	10%	5%	0%
Money Markets	0%	15%	20%

Source: Micropal 4/97

Such portfolios can be maintained at the above weightings, or they can be altered according to market performance. When adjusting the balance of a portfolio, it is best to make smaller allocation adjustments and reduce exposure to a market where assets are obviously overvalued.

The three model portfolios should have all made money over recent years and are designed to reflect the duration of two bull/bear stock-market cycles (1992-1996). Using key indices, we calculate that the aggressive growth portfolio would have achieved a total return of 74.95 percent during the five years from 1992 to 1996; the conservative growth portfolio would have achieved 65.60 percent; and the income portfolio would have made 59.42 percent. For comparison, the FT-SE All-Share Index (UK equities only) increased by 84.31 percent, the S&P 500 Index (US equities only) increased by 103.00 percent, and Salomon Brothers World Government Bond Index (international bonds) increased by 50.91 percent over the same period. The table below illustrates the model portfolio components and their relative indices.

Model Offshore Portfolio Indices

Component	Index
Large Cap Equity	Wilshire Large Cap 750
US Small Cap Equity	Wilshire Small Cap 1750
International Equity	MSCI World x US
US Bonds	Salomon Brothers USA Govt Bond Index
International Bonds	Salomon Brothers World Govt Bond Index x USA & Italy
Gold	James Capel Global Gold Index
Money Markets	Salomon Brothers FNMA 30-Year

Source: Micropal 4/97

The table below shows the return over each of the years from 1992 to 1996 based on the three model portfolios and with some key indices for comparison. It can be seen that although the riskier aggressive growth portfolio produced the best return, its performance was the most erratic: a small loss in 1992, a nearly 30 percent gain in 1993, a tiny gain in 1994, just under 20 percent in 1995 and just over 10 percent in 1996. Although the conservative growth portfolio showed the same pattern of good performances in 1993, 1995 and 1996 and weak ones in 1992 and 1994, its performances were less extreme. Less extreme still were those of the income portfolio.

Model Offshore Portfolio Tables of Performance

Portfolio / Index	1992 Return (%)	1993 Return (%)	1994 Return (%)	1995 Return (%)	1996 Return (%)	Total Return (%) for 5 Years	Volatility (Standard Deviation)
Aggressive Growth Portfolio	-1.31	31.89	2.02	19.01	10.70	74.95	9.51
Conservative Growth Portfolio	3.96	20.18	0.17	21.27	9.12	65.60	5.66
Income Portfolio	5.12	14.15	0.55	22.19	8.12	59.42	4.81
S&P 500 Composite Index	7.69	9.99	1.29	37.48	23.08	103.00	8.67
FTSE A All Share Index	-3.51	24.39	-1.23	21.85	27.58	84.31	13.80
Salomon Brothers World Govt Bond Index	5.53	13.28	2.33	19.04	3.63	50.91	5.41

Source: Micropal 4/97

The greater volatility of the aggressive growth portfolio is a function of the greater risks it has taken. Indeed, measuring volatility (or standard deviation of monthly performances about their average) is a common method of measuring how risky a fund or portfolio is. We look at volatility ratings in more detail in Appendix 3.

One of the three model portfolios should suit most investors, but none is likely to be absolutely perfect. They are best seen as a base from which an investor can plan his own risk-reward profile. Age is an important factor here. Older investors tend to be more risk averse than younger investors – they are keener to preserve their capital, while the younger investor is keenest to grow his money. Consequently, older investors should hold lower levels of equities. It is useful to know the Hundred Minus Age Rule: the investor should take his current age and subtract it from 100. This figure is the percentage of equities the investor should consider holding in his portfolio. This simple "rule of thumb" works amazingly well.

Using offshore funds

A lot of the hassle of investing in international shares, bonds and other investments can be taken away with the use of offshore investment funds. While the general rules of investing remain crucial to any successful investor – such as building a diversified portfolio, deciding on the right markets to invest in – much of the foot-slogging can be taken away by utilising professional offshore fund managers. It is they, after all, who have to research the markets and find the best investments to put your money into. All you have to do is find the fund or funds which will do this most successfully.

4. RELATING INVESTMENT STRATEGIES TO OFFSHORE FUNDS

A well-balanced portfolio will contain a spread of investments such as real estate, a pension or some other provision for retirement, appropriate insurance and a deposit of cash or near cash securities to guard against the unforeseen. Those are the basics; beyond them, investors have a bewildering array of products to choose from.

It is in the stock markets that the most attractive returns have been made this century, well outperforming fixed interest vehicles such as bonds. But the difficulty for many smaller investors is that stockbrokers are not interested in the kind of money they have available; the costs of share dealing make it unrealistic to invest less than about $5,000 directly in one company, and a portfolio with any sort of balance would need to include an absolute minimum of ten stocks. Therefore, investors with less than $100,000 or so, are better off channelling capital down the collective investment route.

Those with more than $100,000 may be better off with collective investments too. Here your money is pooled with that of other investors to allow purchases to be made at large enough levels to put together a suitably broad and diversified portfolio incorporating, say, 40 or 50 stocks, and thereby increasing your chances of making some profitable selections and minimising the impact of the odd poor performance. Moreover, by pooling investment resources, dealing and administrative costs can be minimized.

Most funds contain a broad spread of asset types. Even those that, say, channel the majority of their holdings into a particular category of equities will retain an element of diversity, keeping a certain percentage in more conservative investments such as government bonds and as cash. As explained earlier, the pooled investment principle has been extended across the spectrum of investment vehicles, from gilts and bonds to money market instruments, warrants and derivatives, with widely differing risk profiles entailed. But they all operate by maintaining, to a greater or lesser extent, an array of investment types.

Many investors' portfolios will probably include onshore schemes – open-ended investment schemes such as mutual funds and unit trusts, and closed-ended schemes such as investment trusts – as well as offshore funds. Once again the principle of diversity is worth underlining: when you come to make choices about the offshore element of your investments, take into account the balance and spread of onshore funds you hold. If, onshore, you have a preponderance of North American equity funds, for example, you might choose to focus more on emerging markets and European growth prospects in your offshore holdings.

Not surprisingly, the collective investment industry has thrived globally, and new funds are continually being launched both onshore and offshore. Micropal currently lists more than 5,500 offshore funds. That is a daunting number, and the prospect of analysing and digesting the necessary detail to make informed judgements about them all is beyond the stamina of most investors. But the job is made much easier by the fact that the funds are broken down by Micropal into categories according to the principal investment vehicle, and subdivided by region or country, and in some cases by industrial sector.

Picking the right sectors

Picking the right niches is fundamental to successful investment. This may sound trite, but it is true to a remarkable extent. Although many investors focus on identifying top-performing funds, only a part of the return on a fund portfolio is determined by individual fund selection. In the long term, it is asset allocation that most shapes investment performance. In other words, your key decision might be whether to hold aggressive growth funds or emerging market funds rather than "majoring" on money market or conservatively run mixed funds. Compared with picking the right sector, picking the right fund or funds is of secondary importance.

Here we return to first principles. Investors need to decide on basic investment philosophy in terms of risk and return – the level of growth they want to see balanced against the level of loss they can stomach – and that applies when selecting individual funds as much as when making more general decisions about the overall allocation of wealth to deposit accounts/real estate/collective investments/shares.

Beating the market and earning above-average returns is all very well, but it generally entails taking greater-than-average risks with your money. So if your primary objective is simply to counteract the effects of inflation eating into your capital and achieve a modest but reliable level of growth in your fund investments, there is no point looking at the emerging market single country equity sectors, for instance.

You will be less likely to find yourself in financial hot water, and will therefore probably be more comfortable, with your money in a fund concentrating on North American or UK blue chip companies. If your circumstances prompt you to take a more cautious attitude still, you may look to a money market fund investing exclusively in treasury bills in a particular currency or to a fixed interest fund focusing on, say, US Treasury Bonds. The rewards may be nothing to write home about but the risks to your capital are minimal.

In other words, it is important to establish, firstly, what you want out of the fund or funds you are choosing (which need to be considered in the context of the rest of your portfolio of assets), and secondly, the sectors and sub-sectors in which you are likely to find funds with such a risk/return profile. In the first instance it is a question of looking carefully at the potential risk and reward entailed in the range of fund sectors.

The table below shows the average rate of return of the various categories of fund (by type of investment); and their performance can be compared not only against each other but also against those of benchmark indices such as the FT-SE 100 and the S&P 500.

Average Offshore Returns to 1/1/1997 by Sector

Sector	% Return for 1996	% Return 3 years	% Return 5 Years
Equities	13.80	20.53	71.92
Fixed Interest	6.32	25.83	42.04
Mixed	10.53	23.59	50.46
Money Market	1.84	23.49	24.70
Short Term Bonds	0.71	26.08	28.13
Others *	6.90	24.01	55.53

* others include derivatives, warrants, converibles, real estate, managed currency, physical commodity.
Source: Micropal, US dollars 4/97

Once you have established where on the spectrum of risk and volatility you are prepared to sit, it is time to take a look at the (mainly geographical) sub-sectors. In large part this is a question of personal inclination and homework. The sheer range of offshore funds means that you need to form an opinion of some kind on the attractions of particular regions or countries, whether on the grounds of personal preference or of political and economic indicators, in order to make choices between them.

In general, regional funds, spreading their investment across a number of countries, offer less risk than single-country funds. So a Latin American equities fund, holding interests in several stock markets would feel less impact in the event of political upheaval or a currency crisis in, say, Chile than would a fund investing specifically in Chile. Conversely, of course, the dramatic gains that might be made in a country like Chile during a prosperous period would have effect on only a small part of the regional fund.

A similarly neutralising effect is provided in global sectors – for example, global emerging markets equities – where the broad spread helps counterbalance what could otherwise be a relatively risky selection of stocks. The table below illustrates the principle.

World Market Indices Returns to 1/1/1997

Market Indicator	% Return 1 Year	% Return 3 years	% Return 5 Years
Australia All Ordinaries*	17.51	30.53	53.27
Canada TSE 100 TR**	27.98	44.15	59.47
Dow Jones Industrials	28.91	85.39	132.91
FTSE 100*	23.04	39.36	51.42
Germany Dax (30 stocks)**	19.03	43.60	80.38
Hong Kong Hang Seng*	33.48	13.04	214.74
Nikkei 225 Stock Average*	-13.40	6.88	-9.39
S&P 500 (Composite) – TR**	22.95	71.32	102.89
Singapore SES All Share*	-2.39	-3.34	54.60

* Price Return (no income) ** Total Return (with income)

Source: Micropal, US dollars 4/97

Picking the right fund

After narrowing your choice by selecting a category of funds and geographical or other sub-sector, it is a matter of weighing up the relative merits of the various funds. A few basic tenets are worth emphasising at this stage.

First, it is important to read the prospectus and annual report of any potentially attractive fund and to be clear about its investment goals, philosophy, its asset selection and portfolio management strategies. If that information is not forthcoming, move on to another fund. You should also establish the charging structure of the fund, start-up and management costs, as these fees eat into profitability. All other things being equal, the less you pay in charges, the better off you are.

When you have established that a fund's broad objectives and means of achieving them are in line with your own, it is time to look more closely at its track record. Whatever the risk/return profile of a fund, as spelled out in its prospectus, a good fund is one that manages to achieve its objectives, whether conservatively or aggressively.

The big problem for investors, of course, is how to measure prospective fund performance. As everyone knows (but it is all too easy to forget), a spectacular past performance, while indicating how well fund managers did under particular market conditions, is absolutely no guarantee of similar results in the future. Despite this, past performance is the mainstay of any fund choice. Last year's top performers will always attract a lot of new money, and to illustrate this fact a special section of this guide covers the Top 350 Performers for 1996.

There is little agreement as to what time period should be used when making judge ments about a fund's relative performance. Some investors take a view over the past five or ten years, others have a short-term approach. To get some idea of consistent performance within an equity sector, however, it is necessary to review results over at least three years and preferably five in addition to the Micropal Star Rating™.

A fund's stellar performance over one year may well be the consequence of lucky choices on the part of the fund manager rather than superior judgement. The influence of luck is much less likely to carry that fund through a second or third year of impressive results, let alone a fifth. A fund that appears in the top 25 percent of its group over each of the last five years represents a very strong bet, much safer for the coming years than its competitor which stormed in at the top of the table three years ago and has subsequently slumped to the bottom 25 percent.

When examining performance over a number of years, bear in mind that many funds will have grown enormously in size over their lifetimes. Such growth tends to affect both management strategy and performance. The way a fund was run and the trading decisions made when it was young and small may not work so successfully when it is much bigger, so a well-run fund will tend to evolve in management style as it grows.

The capabilities of individual fund portfolio managers has quite a lot to do with consistent performance. When sizing up past performance, it is good to check whether the portfolio manager who produced those impressive results is still running the fund. But it would be a mistake in most cases to base investment decisions purely on such a consideration (unless a fund's reputation hangs particularly heavily on the genius of one individual, in which case its outlook for the long-term future is open to question anyway).

In a choosing a fund, you should also examine its attributes – yield, cash component, the size of the companies in which it holds stocks, etc. – and try to find one that seems well placed, given your views on what the relevant market is likely to do. For instance, if you believe that a particular country or region is in for a period of economic growth, you would select a fund favouring, say, smaller or rapidly expanding companies rather than mature or blue chip firms. Familiarity with each fund's attributes also makes it easier for an investor to maintain a well-diversified portfolio.

Volatile funds

Investors should not necessarily avoid a fund that shows relatively big swings from high to low performance between years, but they should be clear that such a fund is an inherently high-risk one. Because high risk goes hand in hand with potential high returns, such funds tend to produce the largest rewards for their backers in prosperous years; and over the long term they are likely to yield better results overall than their more conservative competitors.

Shrewd market-watchers looking to buy low and sell high in the relatively short term will probably base their decisions on how a volatile fund has performed recently rather than over the past five or even three years. Volatile specialist funds in particular – for instance, gold or certain emerging markets funds – may be bought for the short term. But more generally, the less time you are prepared to leave your money in a relatively volatile fund, the more dependent on luck you become. If the market bombs out, you could lose heavily, unless you can afford to wait until it strengthens again, as it will usually do in time.

Keep in mind, too, the place of such funds in your overall portfolio. Greed – or at least over-optimism – is a dangerous and insidious emotion. When markets are rising, there is a tendency for investors to increase the risk profile of their portfolio in the pursuit of the returns they see materialising. When those markets suddenly slump, they are often caught off-guard. The sort of "real-rate of return" (investment return minus inflation) most investors look for is 3 to 4 percent a year. This is a good return and those expecting to earn more than this will only do so by increasing their risk profile.

It is also worth remembering that your attitude to volatility may change. For example, as you become older and wealthier, you may find you have more "risk capital" to allocate to such relatively speculative investments. On the other hand, you may be keen to consolidate your assets and keep your level of risk fairly low. Either way, it is important to be clear about your changing objectives and how these are reflected in the contents of your portfolio. If you find you cannot, after all, stand the heat, beat a brisk retreat from the kitchen. Peace of mind is a very valuable commodity, especially in comfortable retirement.

Old and new

Although it is only in the last decade or so that the number of collective investments, including offshore funds, has grown explosively, the concept is not a new one. In the US, more than 60 mutual funds have been around for longer than 50 years; and a dozen predate the 1929 Wall Street Crash with the oldest, the Colonial Fund, having begun in 1904. Many of these "grandfather" funds are balanced funds, investing in a ratio of stocks to bonds. The rest are either bond funds, equity income funds or mainstream growth funds. The table below lists the 20 oldest offshore funds.

The Oldest Funds in the Offshore Market

	Fund Name	Launch Year
1	Robeco	1933
2	Baring IUF North America	1957
3	Baring IUF Octopus	1957
4	Mercury ST Global Equity	1962
5	Barclays Australian Equity	1965
6	M&G Island UK	1965
7	EBC IIF Eurobond LT USD	1965
8	Rolinco	1965
9	BBL Renta Fund Intl C	1966
10	BBL Renta Fund Hard Curr D	1966
11	BBL Renta Fund Intl D	1966
12	Anchor International	1966
13	KB Bonds Income Fund	1966
14	Barclays Global Resources	1967
15	Barclays (Lux) Intl Bond	1967
16	Nippon Fund	1968
17	F&C PF Amer Sm Cos Eq	1968
18	M&G Island Global	1969
19	Mercury Energy International	1969
20	JF Japan	1969

Source: Micropal

Thus, the majority of offshore funds have a shorter pedigree. Robeco goes back to the 1930s, but the rest are far younger; in fact, only 24 funds now in existence go back to the end of the 1960s. On the back of new varieties of funds and fashionable new strategies, a plethora of collective investments has come to the market. With every new market "discovery" comes a clutch of new releases, even though quite satisfactory existing funds are already, in many cases, operating in the market. New fund launches can be attractive, but when buying into a new fund, investors should not lose sight of the shape of their overall portfolio. And of course, there is no performance record on which to assess the quality of a new launch.

As a general principle, you should wait until a fund's units or shares have been on offer to the general public for at least a year before buying. Note that some funds start as limited partnerships, and if they perform well, they are made public. Be wary of such "embryo" funds boasting impressive past returns: those returns were enjoyed by only a few investors. Another reason to be careful of new funds is that their start-up costs will be reflected in the earlier performance figures. It is fair to say that the start-up costs of Robeco have long been recovered.

The start date of each offshore fund is shown in the performance section of this guide, Part 4.

Does size matter?

Information about the size of a fund is useful as an indicator of the nature of a fund. Not surprisingly large funds have good performance track records which have attracted investment in the first place. Also the size of the fund has an effect on how it will be managed in the future. For instance, small funds are likely to be more nimble and can usually buy and sell stocks without having any effect on the markets invested in (which may be particularly helpful for those funds specialising in illiquid markets, such as emerging markets). On the other hand, small funds are likely to hold similar stocks and therefore be more volatile – if one stock holding does particularly well or badly, it may have a dramatic influence on the performance of the whole fund. Equally, larger funds are likely to be less volatile and less able to get in and out of illiquid stock markets easily. But the size of a fund is merely an indicator of its management style; there are large volatile funds and small slow-moving ones too. The table below illustrates the largest offshore funds in 1996 by asset size along with performance returns both in terms of US dollars and Swiss francs. Due to the strength of the US dollar vs the Swiss franc or deutschmark in the later part of 1996, the performance on US dollar denominated funds shows better returns when those returns are shown in Swiss francs.

The Top 100 Offshore Funds by Asset Size with Performance Returns

Offshore Fund	Currency	Fund Size in (US$) (millions)	1996 return % Chg (US$)*	1996 return % Chg (CHF)*
Credis Money Market Fund SFR	CHF	6,949.82	-12.68	1.90
UBS (Lux) Money Mkt Invst USD	USD	6,710.09	4.94	22.46
Credis Money Market Fund USD	USD	6,558.43	4.96	22.48
Robeco N.V	NLG	6,085.96	19.16	39.06
UBS (Lux) Money Mkt Invst CHF	CHF	5,805.39	-13.13	1.37
SBC Money Market Fund CHF	CHF	5,491.49	-13.06	1.45
Rodamco N.V	NLG	4,974.42	11.12	29.67
Quantum	USD	4,611.00	-1.64	14.78
CB Geldmarkt Deutschland I	DEM	4,439.79	-4.43	11.53
DBIM Rendite 2000	DEM	4,255.81	5.15	22.70
Credis Money Market Fund DEM	DEM	4,092.85	-4.09	11.92
SBC Money Market Fund USD II	USD	3,887.64	5.06	22.59
Rorento N.V	NLG	3,878.92	4.02	21.39
Mercury IIT Continental Eur	GBP	3,673.82	26.60	47.73
IBJ Asian Equity	USD	3,553.00	17.93	37.61

Offshore Fund	Currency	Fund Size in (US$) (millions)	1996 return % Chg (US$)*	1996 return % Chg (CHF)*
DekaLux S Rendite 1/98	DEM	3,542.47	-3.11	13.06
Rolinco N.V	NLG	3,303.10	16.02	35.39
SBC Money Market Fund DEM	DEM	3,213.38	-4.42	11.54
UBS (Lux) Short Term Invt DEM	DEM	3,161.67	-4.53	11.41
DBIM Eurorenta	DEM	2,701.11	10.02	28.38
Haussmann Holdings	USD	2,700.00	16.89	36.41
SBC Money Market Fund USD I	USD	2,586.00	5.07	22.61
BBL (L) Invest E-Fix Euro Core	USD	2,551.00	N.A.	N.A.
Quantum Industrial Holdings	USD	2,489.30	19.11	38.99
RG Divirente Fund	NLG	2,311.88	-5.18	10.65
Quota	USD	2,250.80	78.80	108.65
KB Bonds Income Fund	BEF	2,212.85	4.51	21.95
RG Florente Fund	NLG	2,169.79	-5.76	9.97
SBC Bond Portfolio Sfr /B	CHF	2,086.91	-10.43	4.52
Mercury IIT Pacific	GBP	2,058.34	9.90	28.25
Dit Lux DM Laufzeitfonds 99	DEM	1,987.19	-0.67	15.91
DekaLux Bond	DEM	1,920.51	3.47	20.74
Schroder Emerging Markets	USD	1,911.21	7.06	24.93
Quantum Emerging Gth	USD	1,876.00	38.02	61.06
UI Money Market DEM	DEM	1,871.77	-4.32	11.65
DBIM Rendite Garant	DEM	1,859.74	-4.62	11.30
DBIM US Dollar Reserve	USD	1,818.60	4.53	21.98
G-Treasury Intl Belgo-Lux B	LUF	1,782.92	-4.51	11.43
Dit Lux Bondspezial A	DEM	1,762.91	12.69	31.50
Quasar International	USD	1,757.80	9.31	27.55
Swissca MM Fund SFR	CHF	1,695.56	-13.00	1.52
UBS (Lux) Money Mkt Invst XEU	ECU	1,669.57	1.66	18.63
Citi Institutional Liquid Res	USD	1,651.75	5.49	23.10
UniplusKapital	DEM	1,566.34	-2.91	13.30
EMIF UK Index Plus A	GBP	1,448.23	23.63	44.27
DekaLux 10/95 (A) (3Y R-O)	DEM	1,418.20	-2.85	13.37
BBL Renta Fund Intl D	LUF	1,412.05	4.60	22.06
CB MMF D-MARK	DEM	1,393.46	-4.20	11.79
DekaLux Treasury: DM	DEM	1,384.70	-4.57	11.36

Offshore Fund	Currency	Fund Size in (US$) (millions)	1996 return % Chg (US$)*	1996 return % Chg (CHF)*
SBC Bond Portfolio DM /B	DEM	1,384.60	-0.77	15.80
UniLux	DEM	1,316.22	5.42	23.02
Capital Intl Emerging Markets	USD	1,311.25	14.44	33.55
Uni 92/99	DEM	1,285.35	-1.40	15.06
DekaLux S Rendite 4/98	DEM	1,273.46	-2.90	13.31
BBL Capital Cash C	BEF	1,244.26	-4.81	11.08
Adilux	DEM	1,232.01	4.68	22.15
UBS (Lux) Med Term Inv USD	USD	1,207.55	4.24	21.64
Short Fund LUF-BEF Cap	LUF	1,190.14	-4.92	10.90
G-Treasury Belgo-Lux B	LUF	1,161.66	-4.42	11.53
DekaLux S Rendite 10/97	DEM	1,107.05	-3.24	12.92
DBIM DM Reserve	DEM	1,076.83	-3.33	12.81
UBS (Lux) Med Term Inv SFR T	CHF	1,066.51	-11.34	3.46
M.Lynch Dollar Asset Portf	USD	1,063.27	5.08	22.63
EMIF Germany Index Plus A	DEM	1,033.97	15.00	34.00
Orbis Optimal Equity	USD	1,011.23	3.98	21.34
Schroder Japan	USD	962.17	-8.05	7.30
IHS Fonds 3	DEM	953.57	-3.23	12.93
BBL Renta Cash Sht-Med BEF C	BEF	950.28	-4.75	11.15
EMIF Netherlands Index Plus A	NLG	945.45	26.49	47.61
A.L.S.A. DM Rentplus	DEM	942.75	-3.72	12.35
Dit Lux Deutsche Renten SK	DEM	919.36	-3.00	13.19
SBC Global SFr Income /B	CHF	913.41	-8.58	6.68
A.L.S.A. Laufzeitfds 31.03.98	DEM	909.66	-2.97	13.23
Lloydstrust Gilt	GBP	893.67	17.59	37.22
Orbis Global Equity	USD	885.37	13.78	32.77
Morgan Grenfell Pacific	GBP	880.51	25.66	46.64
UBS (Lux) Money Mkt Invst ITL	ITL	879.44	13.35	32.27
SBC Bond Portfolio Sfr /A	CHF	871.65	-10.45	4.50
SBC Global SFr Yield /B	CHF	868.46	-4.18	11.82
GAM Japan	USD	868.00	0.20	16.92
DekaLux Flex	DEM	860.97	-4.10	11.91
SBC Bond Portfolio USD /B	USD	858.47	3.89	21.23
A.L.S.A. Rent	DEM	857.85	-1.85	14.53

Offshore Fund	Currency	Fund Size in (US$) (millions)	1996 return % Chg (US$)*	1996 return % Chg (CHF)*
Schroder Latin American	USD	854.04	24.91	45.77
Barclays Sterling Bond	GBP	851.30	18.28	38.02
DekaLux 1/96 (A) (3Y R-O)	DEM	848.50	-3.43	12.69
UBS (Lux) Med Term Inv DM T	DEM	845.97	-2.10	14.24
SBC Government Bond 1-3 B	USD	830.55	4.85	22.35
Uni 92/98	DEM	828.18	1.92	18.93
DBIM Delta Fonds	DEM	803.10	0.64	17.44
Cregem Bonds International Cap	BEF	800.96	4.99	22.52
Inter Cash France Securite C	FRF	789.23	-2.49	13.79
Capital International	USD	783.96	11.75	30.41
Green Way	USD	775.83	N.A.	N.A.
SBC Money Market Fund ITL	ITL	771.54	13.59	32.55
Credis Money Market Fund ECU	ECU	760.33	1.91	18.92
SBC Bond Portfolio Ecu /B	ECU	742.66	8.45	26.55
DBIM DM Renta	DEM	738.10	-0.18	16.48
A.L.S.A. Laufzeitfds 30.06.97	DEM	733.20	-3.55	12.55
SBC Money Market Fund XEU	ECU	725.91	1.81	18.80

* offer-offer,gross income reinvested

Source: Micropal 4/97

Another useful indicator of a fund's management style is information on its individual holdings, even though this information can be hard to come by. Part 3 of the guide shows each fund with a list of its top holdings along with the percentage comprised by these holdings, as supplied at year end. While the actual holdings may change regularly, this information indicates the type of holdings considered by the management. Moreover, the weightings indicate whether the manager concentrates much of the fund in a few stocks or distributes the money more widely. A fund which invests heavily in a few stocks is likely to be more volatile than an evenly-spread one.

A matter of time

Fund investment decisions, particularly those involving equities, should generally be taken for the long term, which, of course, is a notoriously vague phrase. As far as most collective investments are concerned, it generally means at least five years; and during that length of time, a consistent performer should produce the kind of return that was anticipated at the outset.

During that period, nonetheless, it is likely that different geographical and industrial sectors will have their ups and downs, as will individual funds within them – which may or may not be due to fund managers moving on. An element of volatility, no matter how small, is unavoidable; you need to understand the potential for movement both within a particular sector and within the objectives of your chosen fund.

In essence, funds should be bought and held and not sold quickly. There may be a good reason for selling a particular investment but it should not be that the stock market is sliding or looks as though it might do. The decision to sell should be related to the fund's function in your portfolio. Stock prices are always in a state of flux, and the best strategy for anyone disconcerted by market volatility is to reduce the percentage of equity funds in the portfolio and focus on more stable sectors such as money market, fixed interest or mixed funds.

When to sell

That is not to say, of course, that you should never sell a fund holding – indeed, there are many good reasons to sell. The importance of each depends on individual circumstances, and one reason alone may not be enough to trigger the selling decision. Here are the six key reasons about when to sell:

1. Your objectives may have changed. For example, retiring from work may make you more risk adverse and therefore wish to restructure your portfolio.
2. A good investment manager leaves and/or the investment strategy of the fund changes. Is this still a fund you want to hold?
3. A weak performance relative to its peers over at least twelve months.
4. The fund gets too big. The management style has to change if an actively managed fund grows fast. These factors could effect performance – and assuming you bought the fund for its good track record – performance is likely to get worse.
5. You need to re-balance your portfolio after some rather large rises or falls in various asset classes.
6. You require funds for another expenditure.

How many funds?

We have already extolled the virtues of diversification. Because of the broader spread of assets, the lower the impact of disaster in any one area on the overall portfolio. Diversification reduces risk, which is one of the benefits of investing in collective funds in the first place. But how diversified should an investor in collective investments aim to be?

It does not necessarily follow that if some diversification is a good thing, a lot more is better: the benefits decline as the numbers increase. The average equity fund will hold around 100 stocks, so an investor with ten funds in a single investment category has exposure to up to 1,000 different stocks. But an investor with only 200 stocks (or two such funds) would actually be exposed to roughly the same degree of risk. In other words, investing in ten similarly invested funds is no less risky than investing in two. In addition certain stocks will often be represented across the range of funds anyway, which tends to result in redundant transaction costs and reduce overall investment return.

It makes sense to hold more than one offshore fund, particularly if you have a fund which is a relatively specialist investment such as a single-country fund. But you can minimise portfolio duplication and the related excess costs by spreading your interests across several categories. You might choose an aggressive UK recovery fund, for example, focusing on shares that have had a hard time but seem set to make a profitable recovery, alongside a European fund investing in large, blue chip companies. The two will have few common investments. Similarly, a spread of emerging market funds is unlikely to show overlaps; regions suffering setbacks are likely to be balanced by others showing strong performances, so that your overall portfolio shows strength and consistency.

As an alternative, if you have a particular penchant for a specific fund category, you could choose several funds that employ different management styles. Because they employ different criteria in picking stock, they are likely to favour companies with markedly differing circumstances.

Be selective and resist the temptation to succumb to funds just for the sake of it. Any fund you own should conform to a clear and reasonably long-term investment plan. Do not hold more than you need and try not to duplicate. It is useful to classify them in terms of investment objective and management style, so that if you do select a new one that happens to overlap in either respect with an existing investment, you can consider weeding out the old one.

The average US household owns three mutual funds – and that is not a bad number for those uncertain about how many funds to hold. Holding three offshore funds is likely to provide diversification without duplication.

Index funds

One increasingly popular alternative to an actively managed fund is the index fund. Rather than holding specifically selected stocks, an index fund simply mirrors a particular stock market index – the FT-SE 100, the Hong Kong Hang Seng or the S&P 500 Composite, for example. This is done by buying in the correct weighted quantities every stock represented in the index (full replication) or by investing in a statistically selected set of shares which tend to reflect the larger index's movements (called optimisation).

Index funds originated in the US with the introduction of the Vanguard Index Trust in 1976 and have caught on internationally in recent years. Their popularity reflects the fact that over the long term the broad stock market averages have outperformed most actively managed portfolios. The premise is that a typical manager's ability to pick stocks or bonds is less reliable than the workings of the market. In other words, the index fund philosophy maintains that if you cannot beat it, then you are better off tracking it.

The table below illustrates several funds and how successfully they have tracked their respective indices.

Index Funds vs Indices*

	1996 % Chg	1995 % Chg	1994 % Chg	1993 % Chg	1992 % Chg	1991 % Chg
F&C RAF UK Equities	27.37	22.14	-3.35	19.96	-3.03	11.04
FTSE 100**	28.81	25.01	-1.14	22.35	-2.85	18.14
Tracking Error (- under, + over)	-1.44	-2.87	-2.21	-2.39	-0.18	-7.10
CMI GNF US Eqty Index Tracker	24.23	33.88	-0.41	9.80	6.51	27.69
S&P 500 (Composite)	22.95	37.53	1.32	10.06	7.61	30.40
Tracking Error (- under, + over)	1.28	-3.65	-0.91	-0.26	-1.10	-2.71

* US Dollars, Offer-Offer, Gross Income **Gross income, total return.

Source: Micropal 4/97

Although somewhat boring, index funds have many advantages – for instance, a fund can never seriously underperform its benchmark, though it is equally unlikely to outperform, nor will it be blighted by the mistakes or misfortunes of an individual fund manager. And because there is little stock research or trading involved, costs can be much lower than for conventional equity funds. The flip side is, of course, that when a market is in the doldrums, so are the index funds that parallel it. Essentially, buying an index fund means your fortunes are dictated by the market and not by the investment skills (or otherwise) of a fund manager.

When choosing an index fund, remember that there is little scope for differences in performance between competitors tracking a particular index and that low operating costs are one of the key attractions. All other considerations being equal, investors should make their selection from those funds with the lowest expenses and sales charges and best tracking records.

There are some 50 index funds available to offshore investors ranging in size from $.2m to $128m. The most popular indices used as the benchmark are the S&P 500 Composite (US equities), the FT-SE 100 (UK equities), the Hang Seng (Hong Kong equities) and the Nikkei Dow Jones 225 (Japan equities). As the table below shows, there are fund groups which specialise in index funds, including CCF Structured Asset Management, Clerical Medical International, Foreign & Colonial, Global Manager and Lazard.

Offshore Index Funds

Fund	Benchmark Index	Start Date	Currency
America Index Plus Fund B	S&P 500 Composite	1994	USD
American Sentinel	S&P 500 Composite	1995	GBP
Bachmann GIF Intl Eq Index	FT/S&P World Index	1995	USD
CCF Sam EMF American Index plus	S&P 500 Composite	1995	USD
CCF Sam EMF Asia Indx Track C	MSCI Far East ex Japan	1995	USD
CCF Sam EMF Lat Am Indx Tr C	IFC-Global Latin America TR	1995	USD
CMI GNF Japan Eqty Index Tr	Nikkei Dow Jones 300	1990	JPY
CMI GNF UK Eqty Index Tr	FT-All Share	1990	GBP
CMI GNF US Eqty Index Tr	S&P 500 Composite	1990	USD
CMI Passport Japanese Index	Nikkei Dow Jones 300	1995	JPY
CMI Passport UK Index	FT-All Share	1995	GBP
CMI Passport US Index	S&P 500 Composite	1995	USD
Continental Euro Sentinel	FT Actuary Europe ex UK	1995	GBP
EMIF Belgium Index Plus B	BEL 20	1990	BEF
EMIF France Index Plus B	CAC 40	1990	FRF
EMIF Germany Index plus B	FAZ Aktien	1990	DEM

Fund	Benchmark Index	Start Date	Currency
EMIF Italy Index Plus B	FT Actuary Italy	1990	ITL
EMIF Netherlands Index Plus B	AEX	1990	NLG
EMIF Spain Index Plus B	IBEX 35	1990	ESP
EMIF Switzerland Index Plus B	SBC 100	1990	CHF
EMIF UK Index Plus B	FT All share	1990	GBP
F&C RAF Contl Euro Eqtys	FT Actuary Europe ex UK	1992	DEM
F&C RAF Japanese Eq	Nikkei Dow Jones 225	1987	JPY
F&C RAF UK Equities	FT SE 100	1986	GBP
F&C RAF US Equities	S&P 500 Composite	1986	USD
Glbl Mgr German Bond Index	LIFFE long German Bund 7-10yr	1994	USD
Glbl Mgr German Index	DAX	1994	USD
Glbl Mgr HK Index	Hong Kong Hang Seng	1994	USD
Glbl Mgr Japan Index	Nikkei Dow Jones 225	1994	USD
Glbl Mgr UK Gilt Index	LIFFE long gilt 8-15yr	1994	USD
Glbl Mgr UK Index	FT SE 100	1994	USD
Glbl Mgr US Bond Index	CBOT US long bond 15-20yr	1994	USD
Glbl Mgr US Index	S&P 500 Composite	1994	USD
Hang Seng Index Fund	Hong Kong Hang Seng	1995	HKD
HSBC Guaranteed	Hong Kong Hang Seng	1996	HKD
Japanese Sentinel	Nikkei Dow Jones 225	1995	GBP
JRIA UK Tracker	FT SE 100	1993	GBP
Lazard SIT Europe Index	FT Actuary Europe ex UK	1989	GBP
Lazard SIT Japan Index	Nikkei Dow Jones 225	1989	GBP
Lazard SIT UK Index	FT All share	1989	GBP
Lazard SIT US Index	S&P 500 Composite	1989	GBP
Lion Belgium Index	Bel 20	1993	BEL
Nikko GIUF Japan Rtn Reversal	1st Section Tokyo Stock Exchange	1994	JPY
RLI/UK Index Tracker	FT SE 100	1990	GBP
Scot Amicable Euro Tracker	FT Eurotop	1994	DEM
Scot Amicable UK Index Track	FT SE 100	1994	GBP
Scot Amicable US Index Track	S&P 500 Composite	1994	USD
UK Sentinel	FT SE 100	1995	GBP
WFNIA Japan Index	1st Section Tokyo Stock Exchange	1986	JPY
Yamaichi ISS	1st Section Tokyo Stock Exchange	1990	USD

Source: Micropal4/97

Taking a back seat

Some fund investors like to run their own show. They select a range of complementary funds to give balance and diversity, and they keep an eye on the performance of their holdings and on interesting newcomers to the market. From time to time (though bearing in mind that, on the whole, collective investments are bought for the long term), these investors review their portfolios in the light of changing circumstances, and may trade part of it.

Other people, however, prefer to take a less active role. They require a diversified investment portfolio, but do not want to have to monitor and manage it. They too are catered for by the offshore funds industry.

For investors who want to spread their interests across a number of sectors and regions but who prefer to leave the choice of which ones to the professionals (or who may not have the resources to invest in as many diverse funds as they would like), the managed or mixed fund provides one solution.

By working as a sort of all-in-one personal portfolio and diversifying not only between equity groups but right across the range of assets, mixed funds aim to reduce risk while producing a satisfactory yield. For investors with limited capital, and/or limited knowledge of the relative attractions of the various categories of investment, mixed funds offer the benefit of a broad spread with minimal effort. The balance of investment between equities, fixed interest and money market securities is determined by the fund manager according to the objectives of the fund in question; some funds have distinctly less risk-averse objectives than others.

There is also a type of managed fund known as a "fund of funds" which is run by a investment management company and comprises a number of its collective investment funds. The manager makes the selection and switches between funds, or investors can make switches, at low cost or even free of charge.

A fund of funds can work well within an impressive fund management group, where there are a number high-performing sectors. But it is a mistake to extrapolate from the success of, say, the American smaller companies fund which first attracted you to the investment company and assume that its Korean equities fund will yield equally good results. Low-cost switching facilities may also tempt investors to forget the basic tenet that funds are for the long term.

Umbrella funds

At first glance there is much to recommend umbrella funds, particularly for those who prefer to take an active role in the management of their investments but want to keep the whole thing simple. An umbrella fund is composed of sub-funds or compartments so that investors can select their preferences, and switch between sub-funds without incurring initial charges or fees each time they do so.

However, there are pitfalls to balance against the advantages: it is rare for an umbrella fund to combine high-performing managers across the entire range of equities, bonds and money markets. One way around this could be to allocate an amount for each category and choose the best performing umbrella fund. But assessing the aggregate performance of all the sub-funds in an umbrella investment is not easy.

Make sure also that your preferred funds contain a sufficiently wide selection of sub-funds. If you do not have much choice, it is hardly worth restricting yourself to the umbrella format. Another consideration is cost: there is no uniformity of charging pattern, and fees can vary not only between different fund managers but even under the same roof for different sub-funds.

5. THE STRUCTURE OF OFFSHORE FUNDS

There are two basic types of offshore funds: "closed-ended" meaning the fund is a company with a fixed number of shares; and "open-ended" meaning that the manager can create new shares or units and buy them back to match investor demand. In addition there are offshore funds called SICAVs, open-ended investment companies (OEICs), mutual funds, FCPs, variable capital investment companies, unit-linked life bonds, umbrellas, unit trusts and UCITSs. The chart below shows the relationship between the different types of offshore fund.

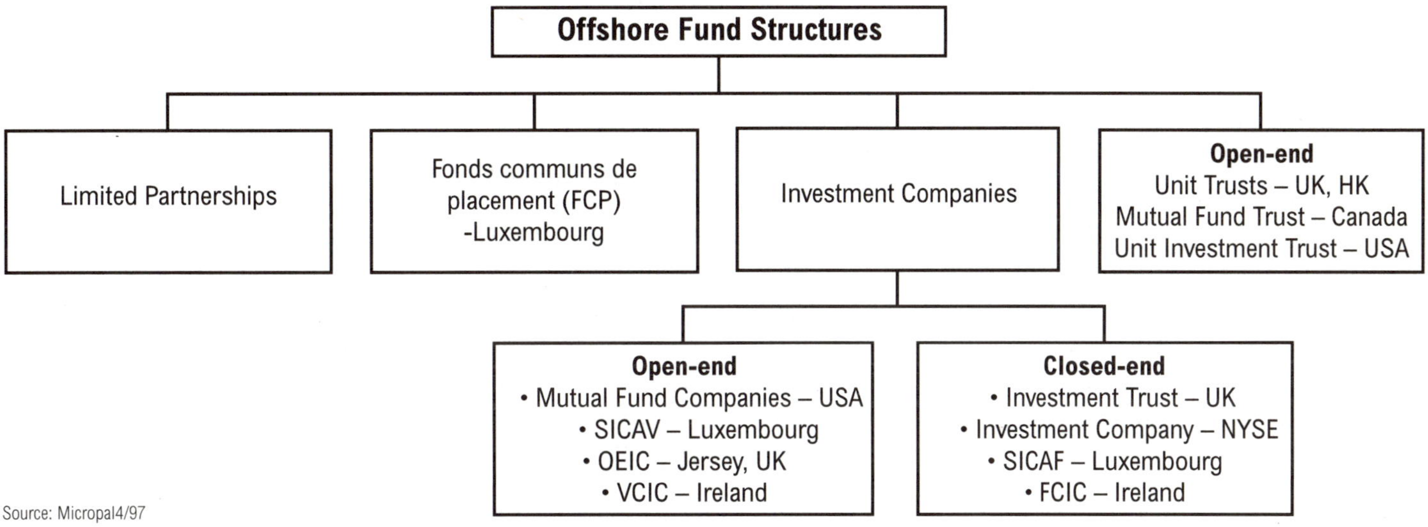

Source: Micropal4/97

Open-ended funds

Examples of open-ended funds are mutual funds in the US and unit trusts in the UK. With open-ended funds the unit price reflects the value of the investments in the fund or the "net asset value". Most of the offshore funds that individual investors are likely to encounter will be open-ended.

Such a fund might be a unit trust, a non-corporate entity with a trustee who guards the interests of investors who hold units in the fund. Or it might be an open-ended investment company, called an OEIC in the UK or a variable capital investment corporation (VCIC) in Ireland. This is a bit of a hybrid, being structured as a company with a board of directors managing and being responsible for the fund. But it is still open-ended because it has a variable number of shares and has the authority to sell and buy back its own shares.

Why is this important? The answer is in the pricing. With an offshore unit trust, typically you buy at one price (the offer price) and sell at a lower bid price. The difference between them is usually around 4 to 6 percent, but it can be more or less.

This is pretty confusing to most investors except the British, who originated the concept of unit trusts. On the other hand, OEICs typically work with a single dealing price, which international investors – such as those in US mutual funds – are already comfortable with.

In Luxembourg's giant fund market, one of the most popular forms of open structures is called the SICAV, or Société d'investissement à capital variable. It is a French concept which is very popular among fund managers looking to crack the European market. Offshore unit trusts, however, tend to be more widespread in the offshore UK centres such as the Channel Islands and the Isle of Man.

Open-ended funds can stand on their own, or they can be umbrella funds. Umbrella funds are very popular. Instead of setting up separate and stand-alone funds, a fund manager sets up one inclusive fund split into "sub-funds". Because all the rules and regulations are the same for each sub-fund, or compartment, it is easier and cheaper to add sub-funds to the umbrella should a new market look attractive. Hence, the Fleming Flagship Fund, a Luxembourg umbrella, is actually a group of 29 equity and bond funds.

In practice there is no difference between a sub-fund and an ordinary stand-alone fund, except that if you should change your mind and want to switch funds, it is usually easier and cheaper to do so within an umbrella fund. Fund managers quickly realised that umbrella funds could be used to build a cost-effective portfolio of funds for people without sufficient cash to buy a good international spread of stocks and shares.

Another bit of open-ended fund jargon is the Undertaking for Collective Investment in Transferable Securities (UCITS). This concept is based on a European Union directive designed to establish common rules for the authorisation, supervision, structure and activities of collective investment schemes among the member states. Consequently, in theory if a fund is recognised in its own country, it could be marketed within another member state. UCITS have no legal personality as the assets are owned either by the management company or by the unit-holders as co-owners depending on the agreement between the UCITS and the unit holders. UCITS tend to be invested in equities and bonds rather than other types of investment instruments, such as money markets, derivatives and physical commodities. The development of UCITS as a "single passport" within Europe has been limited due to the various differing domestic marketing rules and tax laws. The table below identifies the sector funds that can have UCITS approval.

Main Investment Objectives

UCITS	Non-UCITS
Equity Growth	Cash & Deposits
Equity Income	Flexible Portfolio
Equity Growth & Income	Futures, Options & Warrants
Fixed Interest Bonds	Managed Currency
Mixed Growth	Physical Commodity
Mixed Income	Physical Property

Source: Micropal

Closed-ended funds

Closed-ended funds are companies with a fixed number of shares, which for investors is important because the share price reflects the twin gods of supply and demand rather than the fund's value. They are known as Investment companies in the USA and Investment Trusts in the UK.

Shares can trade at a discount to the fund's value if there is negative feeling about their particular market, and at a premium if demand and hopes are high. As most closed-end funds trade at a discount, the investor must be adept at deciding at what point the discount stops looking disastrous and seems to be a good value. Open the stock market pages of any major newspaper and you will see numerous offshore closed-end funds listed, in the same way as British Telecom or IBM are. As for any public company, investors in publicly listed closed-ended funds can buy and sell shares through a stockbroker.

For a variety of reasons, these funds often have more investment "freedom" than open-ended funds have. Many closed-end funds invest solely in volatile stock markets such as that of Turkey (such as the Turkish Growth Fund), and the fund managers may also borrow or leverage against the fund's assets to enhance their returns, a process called "gearing". This can exaggerate returns drastically, so it is important to know whether the fund has this option.

Insurance bond (fund) unit-linked policies

Unit-linked policies were developed in the UK in the 1950s to cater to the demand for policyholders who wished to accept a higher investment risk and in turn expected to receive greater returns. Unlike "with profits" policies, there are no guarantees built into the returns. Instead the policy returns are linked by the life company to the performance of the selected fund or funds managed. In some cases such as Hansard/GT Healthcare, the life fund is unit-linked to another management unit fund: GT Healthcare is a sub-fund of GT Global Theme Funds, which in turn is part of the Prince of Liechtenstein Foundation. Policyholders receive ownership units in the fund based on its net asset value (NAV) which reflects the investment performance. Depending on the risk profile of the individual, the insurance provider can usually offer many different unit-linked policies, such as cash or building society funds, fixed interest funds, UK equity funds, international funds or managed (balanced) funds.

Such insurance-linked funds tend to be more expensive than "mutual fund" type offshore investments because other costs and benefits, such as life assurance cover are built in over and above the pure investment return. There is more on charges in Section 7.

Paying income – the essential factor

On a more mundane point, be clear about whether the fund pays out the income earned from investments (a "distributor" fund), or whether it reinvests the income (a "roll-up" or "accumulator" or "capitalisation" fund). If you want the income produced, make sure that you are in a distributor fund. Some funds will only accumulate or distribute, while with others there is a choice usually between two types of shares or units – income and accumulator units. These are often known as A or B shares, although this is not standard practice across the offshore fund industry; and some investment houses use "A" and "B" suffixes to mean quite different things, such as the currency denomination, front-end load versus a back-end load (redemption sales charge), or the minimum investment requirements, as one unit may have a larger management fee than another. The minimum investment is often lower on distributor funds, and this is certainly an area to be clear about before investing in any particular fund.

6. WHO'S LOOKING AFTER YOUR MONEY?

There is more to an offshore fund than an investment manager and your money. Other companies, quite often completely separate from the investment manager, may well be involved. This is for two reasons: first, as a safeguard to investors (can you really trust much of your life's savings to a company based on the other side of the world?); second, because economies of scale allow some companies to specialise in certain aspects of offshore fund work and accordingly offer their services to offshore investment houses at cheaper rates. The functional work areas of an offshore fund break down into four main categories, although some companies will undertake more than one of the functions.

The manager

The manager's main duties are setting the investment criteria restrictions and preparing the prospectus. Often the manager will also run the actual portfolio, although in many cases the investment advice part of management is separated off (see investment adviser below). Usually the manager will be involved in marketing the fund, although the actual selling is often via third parties, such as financial advisers.

The investment adviser

The investment adviser's main duties are investment strategy and the actual investment decisions. Often the adviser is also the manager, but many offshore funds have a manager in an offshore centre and investment advice originating out of the relevant market. For example, for an Asia Pacific fund, Hong Kong would be the location of the investment adviser. Many Jersey-based fund management companies take their investment advice from parent companies in London.

The administrator

The administrator carries out the day-to-day running of the fund, such as issuing contract notes, valuing the fund and responding to questions from the public. The investment manager may also carry out administration of the fund, but a lot of companies offshore have a specialised business performing administrative tasks for fund managers.

The custodian

The third function is that of the custodian (for open-ended investment companies). This is one job which should be separate from the other functions. The independent custodian's role is safeguarding investors' interests. Typically a custodian will be the guardian of the fund's assets, will police the manager to ensure that the investment parameters are maintained and that valuations are carried out properly. The custodian actually holds the assets, handles all payments, distributions and dividends or interest payments. The nature of this work means that global banks and major insurance companies often take on the custodian's role. The Bank of Bermuda, Citco, Credit Suisse and State Street Bank, for example, are leading global custodians which can offer fund managers their service from a number of offshore centres. Offshore unit trusts have trustees who are responsible for making sure their money is safe and properly invested. For funds based on a legal trust, such as a mutual trust fund or unit trust type offshore funds, the trustees take on a similar role as company directors and ensure that the fund is run as specified under the trust documentation or deed.

Regulations

Depending on the jurisdiction of the country where a fund is domiciled, the above four functions may or may not be carried out by the investment manager. Different jurisdictions apply different rules. A fund can be incorporated in the British Virgin Islands and have its manager and custodian elsewhere. A Jersey-domiciled fund must have a Jersey-based manager and a separate custodian. Similarly, Luxembourg insists that the custodian of a domiciled fund must be in the Grand Duchy. This is seen as a safety measure to protect investors' money. Some investment managers even insist on the use of sub-custodians in case the chief custodian is ever unable to perform its services.

As is always the case, there are never gold-plated guarantees for fund investors. But if the three functions are regulated, wherever they are carried out, that is a positive sign. The fund prospectus will outline who does what and where they are. For example, Jersey's Financial Services Department (FSD) licences and regulates all companies involved in any of these functions. The FSD only allows Jersey managers, custodians or administrators to service funds domiciled elsewhere if it is the sort of fund Jersey itself would accept for registration. Where a Jersey-domiciled fund has any functions carried out elsewhere, the manager must keep records sufficient for it to know at any time what the fund's investments are and their value.

7. OFFSHORE FUND CHARGES

It is very easy to get hot under the collar about the costs of investing. But an offshore fund's charges should only ever be viewed as one factor, alongside others such as the performance history and risk profile. Only where you are faced with the choice of funds with similar strategies and track records, can cost tip the scales.

Charges vary, but there are often good reasons for the differences. For example, a fund investing aggressively in Far Eastern equities is going to cost more to buy into than one investing in US dollar deposits because it is more complicated and expensive to manage. A fund investing mostly in US Treasury Bonds can be run relatively cheaply. But you can also find noticeable differences even between offshore funds which are similar. There is no single international system of charges, and offshore financial centres are different from the US and UK's domestic fund markets. Typically they do not make fund managers reveal every last charge in the brochure, nor do they impose maximums on the charges to investors.

Initial charges

North American investors who are used to "no load" funds might be surprised at the number of open-ended funds offshore which require an up-front or initial charge. This is usually around 5 percent, although it can be lower for money market funds. The sales literature may say that the initial investment is US$10,000, but once the up-front charge is taken, less will actually be invested.

Sometimes it is cheaper to buy through a bank which is selling its own offshore funds. Or you might be able to reduce the initial fee if you have a substantial amount to invest. "Substantial" certainly is not going to be around US$5,000 – more like ten times that amount as a starting point; but it is always worth enquiring.

When the fund is recommended, the intermediary, such as a financial adviser, may agree to rebate some or all of the commission paid out by the fund manager. For example, in the case of a 5 percent initial fee, rather than 95 percent of the US$10,000 going to buy units in the fund, 98 percent may be invested.

There are offshore funds which charge no initial fee, but they are still the exception in fund centres such as Guernsey, Luxembourg and the Isle of Man. Well-known names which do not charge a front-end load include the Royal Bank of Canada out of Guernsey and Regent Fund Management in Hong Kong.

North Americans may be surprised to discover that some funds, especially those offered by investment groups hailing from the other side of the Atlantic, which call themselves no-load funds, do in fact have an up-front charge. This is because many open-ended funds use a "dual pricing" system: the price at which investors buy units – the offer price – and another at which investors can sell units back to the fund – the bid price. The gap between these two prices is called the bid-offer spread.

The bid-offer spread usually includes the initial fee and commissions, and extra costs such as the dealing charges paid on all the securities in the fund. As an example, Joe Brown invests US$10,000 in the Offshore World Fund on May 1 and sells on the same day, receiving back US$9,490. The US$510 he loses represents the bid-offer spread, in this case 5.1 percent. A typical bid-offer spread is 6 percent, but fund managers do have the flexibility to change it. If this happens and you buy and sell at the wrong time, the spread can be as much as 9 percent.

Dual pricing is a throwback to the UK's unit trust industry, which still use two prices; and dual pricing is still most common in the offshore UK centres of Jersey, Guernsey and the Isle of Man. Open-ended funds which deal purely on a single price – just taking an initial fee – are the norm in most other offshore centres, and indeed around the world. However, the same fund manager may use both systems, as in the case of Guinness

Flight, a major British name, which employs dual pricing for its long established Guernsey-based funds and single pricing for its newer range in Dublin. A representative of another large British fund management house explains that it is too hard to sell non-British investors on the concept that even if the fund immediately jumps 2 percent in value, they will still lose out by selling. Further to confuse this issue, you will read elsewhere in the guide how you can buy previously issued open-ended mutual or unit trust units through a recognised stock exchange.

While single pricing is easier to understand, it is worth remembering that the fund manager still has to pay transaction charges on the bonds or equities in the fund. In most cases those costs will still filter down to the investor.

With closed-ended funds, which are structured as companies, the up-front fee is not such an issue. Investors buy shares which carry no initial charge. However, there is an up-front cost in the form of commission to the stockbroker who purchases the shares.

Annual charges

Apart from the cost of buying into the fund, other charges arise once you hold units (in open-ended funds) and shares (in closed ended funds). Depending on the type of fund, the annual management fee ranges from 0.5 percent to 2.5 percent. For a typical global equity fund this is usually about 1.5 percent; for a bond fund, 0.5 percent to 1 percent and for an emerging markets equity fund it is likely to be 2 to 2.5 percent, reflecting the higher cost of investment and research.

Sales literature tends to highlight the annual management fee, but there are other charges such as those for printing reports, marketing, transactions fees and providing safe custody for the fund's assets. You should also be aware that offshore fund management groups may not be as clear in reporting the charges on their funds as, say, US mutual fund managers are required to be.

The US has rules limiting additional charges and ensuring that investors are made aware of the total annual expenses. Offshore, few fund managers make these "total expense ratios" crystal clear in their sales and marketing literature. Intrepid investors may want to search through annual reports and accounts to find out what the expense ratio has been in the past, but this is a big job if you are interested in a broad range of funds. It makes most sense simply to narrow down the field and ask the fund managers directly about the total annual expenses and what is included in these fees.

Switching charges

Another point to remember is the charge for switching between open-ended funds run by the same manager or as part of an umbrella fund that may have a certain switch fee. In many cases a fund manager will not require the full initial fee every time you change funds and you may be charged a lower percentage or maybe just a flat fee. For example, investors in the Guinness Flight Global Strategy group of funds pay $25 per switch.

Back-end sales charges

Depending upon the type of fund, more unusual costs are back-end loads or redemption fees, often charged by funds which have no initial fee. Typically the redemption fee works on a sliding scale: for example, from 6 percent to zero, dependent on how long the investor has been with the fund (1 year – 6 percent, 7 years or more – 0 percent). Sometimes the redemption fee is at a fixed percentage, especially in the case of emerging markets funds where the redemption fee is in place due to the costs of investing in illiquid markets. This is also why emerging markets funds often only have bi-monthly or monthly dealing dates – it reflects the problem the manager has in making liquidity in an illiquid market.

Performance fees

Investors in certain funds may also pay a performance fee, whereby the manager receives 10 to 20 percent of the increase in the net asset value above a certain profit benchmark. This might be the case if the fund aims for high capital growth or if it is particularly speculative which can be in the investor's favour in that the charges will be comparatively low in poor performing years.

Unit-linked life insurance bond (fund) charges

Unit-linked charges are visible as well. The investment charges consist of the initial charge, which is the bid-offer spread usually taken each time units are allocated either monthly or annually, and this charge is expressed as a percentage of the NAV, typically 1/12 of 1 percent per month. The life assurance charges usually consist of the benefit charge, the policy fee and the front-end loading. The benefit charge for typical life coverage and optional benefits is usually taken by the cashing in of units monthly. A small policy fee is handled in a similar fashion. The front-end charge for setting up the policy and the selling costs are handled in a variety of ways.

One method is to have a nil or low income allocation to units in the initial period, which is usually two years but varies with age and other factors. Another way is to allocate initial units for the first year or two of the policy's existence. These units bear a higher monthly management charge, for example, 1/3 of 1 percent, and will have a lower bid price. After the early period, accumulation units with the normal annual charge are allocated. Irrespective of the method used by the life office, significant actual investment does not start until the initial costs have been covered.

Quoted prices

Investors who want to keep up with their fund's performance can subscribe to one of the newspapers and magazines that regularly publish offshore fund statistics. Another good source is the Internet, particularly Micropal's offshore fund site which may be found at micropal.com. Quoted prices appear in many different ways. If the performance figure is quoted "bid to bid", it is based on the rise or fall of the bid (or selling) price. If the statistics are "offer to bid", the price shown is net of any bid-offer spread. Fund managers also have to indicate whether their funds are priced on a "forward" or "historic" basis. Some funds deal once a day and others deal more or less often. If you buy a forward priced fund, it means your money will be invested at the price of the next dealing time. The historic price is where investors buy and sell units at the most recent quoted price. Forward pricing is used by most offshore open-ended funds.

8. WHERE ARE OFFSHORE FUNDS BASED, AND WHY?

Call them offshore centres, tax efficient centres or even tax havens – there are any number of jurisdictions around the world with friendly tax regimes and high levels of confidentiality. The good news for investors is that these centres do not tax the profits or income of funds that are incorporated or domiciled there.

Some, like Dublin, have passed laws especially to set up offshore or international financial centres. Others, like Luxembourg, have not done this and reject the "offshore" tag. The Cayman Islands and Bermuda levy no direct taxation, while the Isle of Man and Jersey impose relatively low income tax, but only on residents.

Luxembourg is an interesting case. It is certainly not offshore, being landlocked in the heart of Europe, and it does impose a small tax (0.06 percent per annum) on the investment funds' assets. Yet Luxembourg is the giant among "offshore" jurisdictions when it comes to investment funds, especially fixed interest funds and money market funds.

As seen in the table US$363bn has been invested in Luxembourg domiciled funds, US$81bn in Cayman, US$53bn in Jersey, US$32bn in Dublin, US$23bn in Guernsey, US$18bn in Bermuda and US$8bn in the Isle of Man.

Growth of Offshore Funds and Assets

	No of Funds			Assets ($ Billions)		
Domicile	**1995**	**1996**	**% Increase**	**1995**	**1996**	**% Increase**
Dublin	759	985	29.80%	23.39	32.34	38.30%
Jersey	845	992	17.40%	37.89	52.53	38.70%
Guernsey	674	703	4.30%	19.93	22.91	14.95%
Isle of Man	**176	**168	-4.50%	6.81	7.85	15.30%
Luxembourg	3597	3939	8.40%	308.30	363.37	17.86%
Cayman	1059	1335	26.10%	*70.23	** 80.80	15.10%
Bermuda	676	859	27.10%	13.39	18.23	36.10%
Mean/Avg			15.51%			25.19%

includes compartments or sub funds * as of October 1995 **year end estimates

Source:Micropal/97

Not all of this offshore money is held by individual investors. Typically each centre has a mixture of funds, some aimed at average investors and others at wealthy, highly sophisticated individuals and institutions. The Bermuda Monetary Authority says the vast majority of funds registered in Bermuda are for sophisticated and wealthy investors with higher risk profiles and more specific investment objectives than those of ordinary private investors. The same could be said of the Caribbean offshore centres such as the British Virgin Islands and the Cayman Islands.

Cayman is widely seen as less restrictive when it comes to dictating what fund managers can and cannot do. There are fewer restrictions on investment objectives, risks, rate of return, gearing, or other commercial issues. Relative to other offshore centres, it is not too difficult for fund promoters to get approval to set up their funds in Cayman. Because of this flexible approach, Cayman as well as the Netherlands Antilles have attracted numerous hedge-type funds that employ complex trading strategies and hold potentially high geared or leveraged investments. These tend to be for investors with large sums to invest and who appreciate the risks involved.

In contrast, Europe's offshore centres have colder climates but warmer welcomes for more risk-averse investors. They may not be as familiar to North American investors as the Caribbean names, but Jersey, Guernsey, Ireland, the Isle of Man and Luxembourg offer an enormous choice of funds to investors with more modest means: US$5,000 per fund is often sufficient, and some funds require less.

To give a flavour of the diversity, Luxembourg's big advantage is its position at the cross-roads of Europe. Geographically, culturally and linguistically, investors across the continent are familiar and comfortable with the Grand Duchy. Luxembourg is very European, reflecting the continental liking for rather conservative bond and cash investments, as well as the tendency to buy investments through a bank. Swiss, Belgian and German institutions, particularly banks, are still the source of the vast majority of Luxembourg funds. And over twice the assets held in Luxembourg funds are in bond funds rather than equity funds.

Even so, there is a growing number of fund managers with global equity expertise, particularly British and American names like Equifund Wright, Fidelity, Fleming, and Mercury. The Fleming Flagship Fund, for instance, is an umbrella with funds covering regional stock markets all over the world as well as single countries such as China and India. Its US exposure is split into funds buying big and fledgling companies.

The same is true of Jersey, Guernsey and the smaller funds market in the Isle of Man, all of which lie off the United Kingdom coast. In contrast to Luxembourg, Jersey and Guernsey funds reflect the Anglo-Saxon fondness for stock market investments. A large proportion of Jersey funds are also sterling denominated by the big fund names such as Barclays, Lloyds Bank and Midland Fund Managers. Smaller British managers such as TSB Fund Managers and Perpetual have also built up a sound reputation and track record for their funds. Perpetual has 11 funds which are mostly regional and global (European Growth and Global Bond).

However, you can also find a multitude of international names. Swiss banks account for a large slice of Jersey's fund pie, while international names running Guernsey funds include CIBC – The Canadian Imperial Bank of Canada and the Royal Bank of Canada.

Hong Kong is very different and remains a route for fund managers exploring the awakening dragon of China. Many funds invested from Hong Kong are Luxembourg registered, with a heavy bias towards the dollar-thinking investor and a particularly good selection of funds investing around the Far Eastern stock markets. Major names include Barclays, BZW, Fidelity, GAM, HSBC, Schroder and Thornton. Flexibility is the key – funds are allowed to invest in warrants, options and futures, given certain limitations. As one of the world's top five financial centres, there are many globally recognisable names.

To summarise, the environment of offshore financial centres is changing to one of more regulations and restrictions, from being tax avoidance to tax efficient centres, which are also becoming the platforms for funds to launch into more regulated areas.

Regulators

The quality of investor protection does vary around the world's offshore financial centres. Many well-established ones, including Jersey, Guernsey, Luxembourg, Bermuda, Dublin and the Isle of Man have regulatory bodies and strict procedures for vetting and monitoring any fund that is to be sold to the general public. In Luxembourg, for example, assets must be kept with a custodian, usually a bank, which cannot be the same company as the fund manager. The custodian checks the contents of the fund portfolio daily and each month reports to the regulatory body, the Institute Monetaire Luxembourgeois. In Guernsey, the Financial Services Commission must be satisfied with all the parties involved in the fund's running. Each regulator has rules and procedures which standardise financial reporting, handling of investors' money and complaints.

Compensation schemes

People usually feel more comfortable if there is a financial safety net, and certain offshore centres do have the backup of compensation. This is not enormous – Guernsey's scheme promises to pay a maximum of £60,000 compensation per investor should a fund collapse or a fund manager go under, and the figure in Jersey and the Isle of Man is £48,000. Bermuda has put no ceiling on its compensation scheme, which also applies to fund collapses as well as to negligence and wrongdoing by the managers. Cayman and Luxembourg have no compensation arrangements.

For Bermuda, Guernsey, the Isle of Man, and Jersey, compensation only applies to funds which are recognised by the UK's Securities and Investments Board (SIB), the equivalent of the SEC in the US. Compensation only applies to a very limited number of funds: 210 out of 703 approved schemes (subfunds included) in Guernsey. These funds have different names such as "Class A" in Guernsey and "UK designated status" in Bermuda. A glance at the *Financial Times* will tell you which funds are recognised by SIB, and this information will also be stated in a fund's brochure. These funds are more restricted than their offshore brethren in terms of where they can invest. At present there is much discussion going on between the UK and these centres to give recognised funds a freer hand. Jersey, for instance, recently decided to let recognised funds go into previously banned areas such as Taiwan and Eastern Europe.

Why are recognised investment funds important? Again it comes down to safety. Recognised funds can be sold into the UK, but in order to do this, the offshore centres have had to set up investor protection and regulations which are at least equivalent to the UK's. Of course there are never any fool-proof guarantees, but this is an added badge of respectability. After all, Bermuda's focus might not be on the private investor, as its Monetary Authority says this stresses its financial supervisory quality and reflects more upon competing with much bigger offshore centres.

Confidentiality

Hand in hand with low– or no– tax, the investor's confidentiality is crucial to the offshore centres' credibility. Some jurisdictions have made it a criminal offence to reveal information about investors, while in others it is a practice which carries very heavy weight. Non-resident investors' money would pour out of any offshore centre which opened up its books to the inspection of outsiders.

In general, outside bodies such as criminal investigators will only be allowed to access information where a criminal offence, typically drug dealing and money laundering, is involved. Cayman, for example, has a particularly strong tradition of secrecy, yet it signed a Mutual Legal Assistance Treaty in 1993 with the US and the UK. This states that where there is evidence of criminal activity, there can be an exchange of information between authorities.

Whatever the offshore centre, questions from tax authorities who suspect tax evasion would be rebuffed, although there are rumours of tax authorities threatening banks and other offshore players with dire consequences if they do not divulge information. When asked about such sensitive issues, bankers and fund managers in the offshore centres are, not surprisingly, tight-lipped.

9. ANALYSING OFFSHORE FUND PERFORMANCE

The first thing to understand about investment performance is that a fund with a good track record is in no way certain to continue to perform well. This year's top performer could easily be next year's laggard.

So why spend time looking at the past performance of offshore funds? Simply because it is one of the best indicators we have of how a fund will perform. If the manager of an offshore fund produced a better than average return in previous years, there is every chance that these superior investing skills will pull off a better – than – average performance in the coming ones. There is no guarantee that the manager will, of course; but someone with a good track record is a better bet than another who has done badly in the past.

There are a number of problems with this theory, however. Firstly, and most obvious, the individual fund manager could move elsewhere, and this does happen. Good managers are either poached by other investment houses or are promoted to manage larger or more important funds. Consistently bad managers will eventually get the sack.

The problem for the offshore investor, therefore, is keeping up to date with such personnel changes – a virtually impossible task and one which is not revealed by performance statistics. But this situation is not as bad as it seems. Most managers of offshore funds have to invest within strict guidelines, using certain analytical criteria drawn up by the fund management company for which they work. So just because an individual has stopped managing a particular fund does not mean that the fund will change direction dramatically. Usually the fund will continue to be managed in a broadly similar way – many are managed by a team of advisers, in any case – and therefore the problem of changing managers, although not unimportant, is not one on which to dwell too much when looking at performance statistics.

Risk and volatility

Of far more importance is an understanding of how a good track record has been achieved. Comparing an emerging market equity fund with one that invests primarily in US Treasury Bonds is a pointless exercise. Whatever happened to the performance of such funds in the past, it is far more important to know that the former takes high risks but is potentially highly rewarding and the latter is very low risk and low rewarding. For this reason funds are usually broken down into various sectors, as Micropal has segregated offshore funds into 193 sectors in the offshore performance tables in Part 4 of this guide.

The basic reason for doing this is that when looking at performance, an investor's key concern is to be able to compare similar funds with each other. If an investor has decided to buy into a high-risk fund such as one investing in emerging market equities – knowing the generally high risk/high return profile of such funds – then the investor's main consideration will be which emerging markets equity fund to go for.

But even within sectors of similarly invested funds, last year's top performing fund could have made its way to the top of the pile by taking larger risks than those taken by its peers. If things had turned out differently, such a fund could quite easily have found itself languishing at the bottom of its sector. It is, therefore, important to be able to spot such relatively higher risk funds. The reason for the outperformance of peers very often has less to do with the skill of their investment team and rather more to do with being lucky enough to be in the right place at the right time.

Take equity funds, for example. In a booming stock market, smaller company shares tend to do well. If a particular fund has a strategy of investing in more volatile smaller company shares; then with a booming (or bull) stock market such, a fund is likely to outperform those funds that invest more generally. But if the stock market turns sour (or bearish), such a fund is likely to trail its peers badly. So, if such a fund did well in the recent past, it is likely to do well in the future only if its investment environment stays broadly the same.

The performance of such funds tends to be more volatile than that of funds investing more generally. Some investors may prefer this volatility, but on the whole it is best to pick funds that consistently perform well compared with their peers, whatever the investment conditions.

It is possible to spot the volatile and consistent funds by looking at performance over a period of time. The performance periods chosen for this guide are one, three, five, and ten years to the end of 1996. Performances are shown as percentage increases (or decreases) on the original investment over each of the time periods.

The hare and the tortoise

Studying its performance periods carefully can reveal the basic nature of a fund. For example, the imaginary Hare and Tortoise Funds illustrated in the table below have both achieved an increase of 50 percent over five years. But they achieved this result in very different ways. The four-year performance of the Tortoise Fund showed 38 percent growth; over three years it had approximately 27 percent growth, over two years 18 percent and in the last year 7.5 percent growth. It can be seen that the performance of the tortoise fund over this period was fairly steady. In fact, the fund's year-on-year performance ranged between 7 percent and 10 percent – very low volatility and good consistency.

The Hare Fund, on the other hand, had 46 percent growth over four years, 22 percent growth over the three-year period, was down 19 percent over two years and had growth of 1.5 percent in the past year. Such a performance was highly volatile; indeed, the year-on-year performances ranged from a fall of 20 percent two years ago to a rise of 50 percent three years ago. An investor who had invested in such a fund two years ago on the basis of its one-year performance would have been in for a bit of a shock – up 50 percent one year and down 20 percent in the next. This type of performance is not untypical for a volatile fund.

The Hare and Tortoise Funds

	Performances (% increase)				
	1 year	2 years	3 years	4 years	5 years
Hare Fund	1.50	-18.80	22.80	46.20	50.00
Tortoise Fund	7.50	18.30	26.50	37.90	50.00

Volatility ratings

A short cut to spotting the consistent and volatile funds is to look at the Micropal Volatility Rating over three years. This is a measurement of the variability of a fund's investment return performance over the previous three years. In statistical terms, this is the standard deviation of monthly returns of the fund about its average; or in more simple terms, the volatility rating measures by how much a fund's monthly performance deviates from its average. The higher the number, the more volatile the fund has been.

A low number tends to indicate a low level of volatility and risk – for example, the low-risk US dollar money market funds have a volatility rating of less than 0.2. At the other end of the scale are warrant funds with, for example, some Japan warrant funds producing a rating of over 18. Most other investment sectors are somewhere in between, but within sectors the volatility ratings can vary quite markedly. Differences are more common with some asset types, such as equities, where the fund manager has a greater choice of investments.

The Risk Return Ratio

A useful aid to look at after volatility is the risk return ratio. The risk return ratio of a fund is calculated by dividing the three-year cumulative performance of the fund by its volatility ie what is the ratio between the fund's return and risk; the higher the ratio, the better. In Part 4 of the guide, we have ranked the funds according to this ratio and have added a twist. To get a rank the fund must have outperformed 90-day US Treasury Bills (effectively a risk-free investment) over a three year time period. Of those that do beat US Treasury Bills, the risk return ratio ratings are allocated as follows: the top 10 percent receive the number 5, the top 11 to 30 percent get number 4, the top 31 to 50 percent get number 3, the next 25 percent get number 2, and the bottom 25 percent receive the number 1.

Micropal Star Rating™

In Part 4 of the guide, as an extra performance aid, we have added the Micropal Star Rating™ for funds within each sector. The more stars a fund has, the greater its past ability to consistently outperform its sector peers.

The star rating is calculated using a fund's monthly performance relative to its sector average for each of the 36 months over the three years to date. The average and volatility of these 36 numbers is used to calculate a fund's star rating. The Micropal Star Rating is calculated by dividing the fund's average relative performance by the volatility of its relative performance. That most likely needs some explanation!

The relative performance of a fund is calculated by subtracting the sector average from its performance figure. Thus, if the fund rises by 6 percent in a month and its sector average rises by 4 percent in the same month, then the fund's relative performance is +2 percent. This number is calculated for each of the 36 months. By calculating the average of the fund's latest 36 relative performances, we are measuring its ability, on average, to out- or underperform the other funds in its sector. The higher the average, the more the fund has outperformed its peers over the 36 months.

Volatility (often known as the standard deviation) is a statistical method to measure how much a series of values deviates (how much it moves up and down) about its average. By calculating the volatility of the fund's 36 monthly relative performances, we are measuring how consistently the fund has out – or underperformed its peers. The higher the volatility, the less consistent.

Back to that formula. By dividing the fund's average relative performance by the volatility of its relative performance, we are measuring its ability not only to outperform its peers but also to do so consistently. The higher the ratio, the greater the fund's past ability to outperform its peers on a consistent basis.

Appendix 3 of this guide goes into greater detail about how the Micropal Star Rating works. Essentially, the allocation of the Star Rating is such that the more stars a fund has, the greater its ability consistently to outperform its peers. The top 10 percent of funds gain five stars, the next 20 percent are given four stars, the next 20 percent are given three stars, the next 25 percent have two stars, while the bottom 25 per cent have just one star.

The Micropal Star Rating system allows readers an easy way to spot the most consistently good performers. The more stars, the better.

Volatility and the two rating systems together

By using the risk return ratio and the Micropal Star rating together, you can gather a lot of information on the behaviour and performance of a fund. Ideally a fund should offer good return at an attractive level of risk and consistently outperform its peers. By looking at the risk return ratio, you can identify funds that have offered good return per unit of risk and which outperformed a risk-free investment (such as a US Treasury Bill). In reviewing the volatility (risk) of the fund and comparing it to other funds in the sector you can see how risky the fund is in relation to its peers. A 3.8 volatility figure is more risky than a 1.7 figure. The Micropal Star Rating™ identifies funds that have consistently outperformed their peers. A fund that exhibits good performance, a high risk return ratio, with low volatility in relation to its peers plus a high Micropal Star Rating™ should certainly be worthy of further consideration.

Rankings and quartiles

Another useful tool to use when looking at offshore fund performance is sector rankings. In part 4 these rankings are shown to the right of the performance returns. The rankings offer an understanding of a fund's performance relative to its peers within the sector.

But in looking just for top performers, a "No. 1" ranking is not always the best option. Because the top performers are very often more volatile funds than most of their peers (or very safe funds during difficult investment conditions), they can easily become one of the weakest performers in the coming year. Consequently, many investors look for those funds which have consistently been among the better ranked funds. A good way to do this is to divide the ranked funds into quartiles – the top 25 percent, the next 25 percent, the next 25 percent and the bottom 25 percent. Any fund that can maintain a top quartile ranking over a range of periods is an excellent performer. One that stays within the top two quartiles (top half) over a range of investment periods is also worth looking at. Those that occasionally dip into the bottom quartile are suspicious.

Laggards

The simplest form of analysis is to compare the absolute performance of a set of investment funds over a chosen period or periods. This is based on what one might call the horse racing theory: those in recently good form are naturally the favourites for winning the next race. Equally, of course, those funds which have of late trailed their peers may not be such a good bet for the future, particularly if their form has been consistently weak. An investor might ask: is the investment approach the manager taking here fundamentally flawed?

The odd bad patch for a fund, compared with its peers, is understandable, especially if that fund is inherently more risky or conservative in its make-up than those with which it is compared. But there are funds that do have problems and have consistently been poor performers. To identify the laggards, the sectors with the largest number of funds – such as Global equities, Global Mixed, Global Fixed Interest, UK equities and US equities – were chosen so as to avoid any statistical abnormalities in filtering. No UK equity laggards were found. The table below shows the 20 offshore funds which have found themselves consistently in the bottom quartile of their respective sectors in each of the past three years. Needless to say, these funds should be treated with the greatest caution.

1996 Offshore Laggards

	1996 % Return*	1995 % Return*	1994 % Return*
Global Equity			
W'Invest Excelle Gl Eq USD	3.90	7.86	-5.73
Royal Life/MBf Global Mgd	3.88	-8.47	-30.94
Buttress Equity Fund Ltd	2.45	5.24	-12.77
Jupiter Tyndall International	2.19	0.02	-7.88
MBf World Growth	1.32	0.75	-14.04
Contivest Actions Internat A	0.13	-2.12	-15.16
Jupiter Tyndall WUF Overseas	-0.44	5.21	-11.05
Abtrust World Growth	-2.22	-4.62	-11.75
Royal Life/MBf World Growth	-5.07	-1.26	-8.46
CL Asia Europe Equity Fund	-6.96	4.31	-11.12
ItalFortune Intl Banks & Insur	-8.04	-14.99	-14.29

	1996 % Return*	1995 % Return*	1994 % Return*
M-Fund Dollar Growth	-16.57	-6.77	-17.75
Plurigestion Plurivaleurs	-17.06	-29.63	-29.87
Global Mixed			
OMI (Ire) Dllr Special Mkt	0.63	2.03	-6.68
Dolphin IIS Contl Cap Builder	-11.10	8.77	-4.59
Global Fixed Interest			
RDS Global Intl Bond B	-2.54	5.70	-9.24
US Equity			
Clariden Emerging Gth	9.94	15.80	-13.58
Jupiter Tyndall GF Wall St	7.58	15.23	-6.84
Alliance Global Leisure Fund	4.39	10.74	-19.78
BanesFondo Intern. Dollars	3.80	11.56	-11.49

* US dollars, Offer-Offer, Gross Income Reinvested

Source: Micropal 4/97

The investment term

Should you always avoid volatile funds? The answer to this depends on the period of time in which you expect to hold your offshore fund investment. Over the long term the more risky, or courageous, funds are more likely to outperform their safety-conscious sector peers. If you can afford to sit on your investment for a while and ride through any bad times along the way without panicking and selling, then such funds can prove to be a good option and part of your portfolio of assets.

Just how long a time period you need to envisage for any particular fund depends on what it is invested in. The riskier the type of investment involved, the longer the time period you need to set the fund aside untouched. Broadly, this is at least three years for a managed equity fund or a single-country fixed interest fund, and at least five years for a single-country equity fund.

Consequently, when looking at performance figures you need to bear in mind the length of time you are likely to invest in any particular fund. For example, it would be imprudent to invest in a single-country equity fund on the basis of its one-year performance if you are likely to hold the investment for a number of years. That is not to say that its one-year performance should not be considered, but an investor should also look over other time periods to see if the fund has put on a consistently good showing.

Currency factors

We have presented the performance statistics in this book in US-dollar converted terms. This is the most popular currency denomination for offshore funds even though a large number of funds are in other currencies – deutschmarks, sterling and yen being the most popular. By converting performance into dollars, we are presenting the performance return experienced by an investor holding dollars as his base currency. This enables the reader to make comparisons between funds, while taking into account the effects of exchange rates. If the funds were left in the original denominations, comparisons would be meaningless.

Moving exchange rates have a big impact on a fund's performance and volatility, which sometimes may exceed the value changes of its underlying assets. For example, if the yen falls sharply against the dollar, the value of, say, Japanese equity funds will also fall – in dollar terms at least. This is naturally bad news for dollar-minded investors in such funds. But yen-minded investors will not be so worried, as the changing exchange rate will have had no impact on the value of their investments.

For this reason it is important to ascertain that the good performance of a fund is due mainly to the skill of the investment manager rather than to changing exchange rates. Currency movements need to be isolated when they are not part of the investment management function. In globally invested funds, taking advantage of exchange rates is part of the fund manager's role. In most other fund sectors outside of global ones the funds are mostly denominated in the same currency. But when investors compare sectors – say, US equities against Japanese equities – it is important to note that the different fortunes of the funds in each of these sectors often have much to do with exchange rate movements. In Part 4 of the guide which covers the performance of 5,500 funds, there is a column showing the currency in which a fund is denominated.

Where to find more performance information

Micropal is the leading source of offshore fund performance statistics which are listed in specialist investment publications such as *The International* and *Resident Abroad*. Other offshore statistics are published in the *Financial Times*, *The International Herald Tribune*, *International Fund Investment*, *Offshore Adviser*, *Investment International*, *The Wall Street Journal* (Europe and Asian editions), *International Money Marketing*, *International Fund Investment* and the *South China Morning Post* – in addition to the Micropal Website – micropal.com. See Appendix 4 for more detailed information on these publications.

Another source of information is the fund manager who should keep you up to date with events relating to the fund. At the bare minimum you can expect to receive an annual report and accounts, outlining performance and strategy over the year with a breakdown of the fund's holdings and charges. Depending on the manager, you will then get anything from a six-monthly to a monthly update on performance, holdings and market comment.

10. GETTING STARTED

You have read about investment strategies, types of funds, and the costs involved in investing in them. Now you want to get started.

First, choose how you want to invest. Lump-sum investments are common offshore and typically start at the $2,500 level. For a currency fund this can be even lower, but for an equity or bond fund a good general assumption is $5,000 to $10,000. Most unit trust /mutual funds have a programme to allow for pre-authorised purchased plans or regular investment schemes where you can invest, say, $500 a month or more. Once you have decided how much you wish to invest monthly or every three months, fill in the bank authorisation form which usually accompanies the application form. At the time specified the fund company will automatically purchase on your behalf the amount requested and accordingly debit your bank account. The beauty of this plan is that when the market declines, you will be able to purchase more units, lowering your average unit cost. Conversely, in rising markets your average cost per unit will rise. Over the long term your overall average cost should be below average and you should do well.

Going direct

There are two routes with open-ended funds, which the vast majority of individuals will buy. One is to go directly to the fund management company, particularly if you know which fund you want. A fax, letter, or telephone call will secure a prospectus outlining details of the fund. This should include the minimum investment, the investment strategy of the fund and its "benchmark" (the target it aims to beat), comment on past performance, and details of everyone involved in advising, safeguarding assets and day-to-day administration. The prospectus will also explain how to buy and how to redeem (sell) units.

As for cost, it will state the amount of the initial fee (including sales commission or fees), the annual management fee, and possibly a fee to switch between funds. In addition there may be custodian fees; but these may or may not be made clear in the prospectus, so ask if in any doubt.

The application form for purchasing the fund will require that the amount to be invested is specified and whether you are paying by cheque, draft or electronic transfer of funds. The form may give advice on payment: for instance, in the case of electronic transfer, the bank may have to send a fax to confirm that the payment has been made. The owner's name and address needs to be supplied. If you invest through a trust or company vehicle, the person authorised to deal must give their name and signature, and the name and address of the trust or company.

If there is the option, you will be asked whether you want dividends re-invested in the fund or paid out to yourself, to an agent or a bank. Some funds deal daily, so units will be purchased quickly. Others have a specific day or days in the month on which money will be invested (For an example of a typical application form, see Appendix 9.)

One advantage of going the direct route is that if you are investing a large sum, you may be able to negotiate lower sales charges.

Using an adviser

The second route is to use an adviser, particularly, if you need help in choosing the funds which meet your needs and are within your risk tolerance. This adviser may be your banker, accountant or a dedicated financial adviser. Whatever the case, ensure that she/he really is independent and that they explain exactly why a particular fund is being recommended and what advantages it has over others of its kind. After all, there are over 120 offshore funds investing in UK equities alone.

The adviser will work through the prospectus and application forms and will receive your money which is in turn passed on to the investment company. Make any cheques payable to the investment company, not to the adviser.

Once this procedure has been completed, the fund manager sends a contract note confirming the day of investment, the number of units bought, the initial charges paid, the exchange rate if necessary, plus a certificate proving your ownership. You can choose to have a "certificated" holding (where the certificate proving your ownership is sent) or an "uncertificated" holding (where just the contract note is sent). Later on, to sell the units you will need to hand over the certificate, or in the case of an uncertificated holding, the contract note plus a signed letter of instruction.

People who do not want the responsibility of holding on to certificates and contract notes can open a "nominee" account. Bear in mind that if you are in a regular savings scheme you may well receive a certificate for every payment. The units are held by a company set up by the fund manager, called a nominee company. Your relationship is with the nominee company, where you have an account number showing that you own the units. The nominee company takes care of all the paperwork, which makes dealing easier and faster. Many fund managers have free nominee services, or they charge a small annual fee. There is usually a section on the application form to apply for a nominee account (see Appendix 9).

Stock exchanges

An increasing trend is for mutual funds to be listed and traded through various stock exchanges around the world. This is also becoming a useful way for offshore funds to create additional exposure and liquidity for investors. Essentially, trust units or fund shares that are already issued by a particular fund can be bought or sold through independent market makers on these stock exchanges. This type of trading is classified as secondary market trading (as opposed to a primary market where units are bought or redeemed directly with the fund manager). For a small brokerage fee, units are bought or sold mainly at their net asset value (NAV).

As the table below shows, well over 50 percent of offshore funds are publicly listed. Many funds trade in frequently, but it is expected that this will change as more investors and financial intermediaries see the financial and regulatory benefits of trading through this market in preference to going direct to the funds.

Stock Exchange Listings of Offshore Investment Funds

	Quantity
Dublin Stock Exchange	560
Bourse de Luxembourg	2766
Cayman Stock Exchange	New
Bermuda Stock Exchange	62
London Stock Exchange	298
Hong Kong Stock Exchange	65
Total	3751

Purchase restrictions and tax

In many cases there are purchase restrictions within the articles of an offshore fund which prohibit or restrict the holding of shares or units by any person or company. For example, a fund may be domiciled in the Isle of Man and for various legal reasons it may not be sold to or owned by residents of the Isle of Man. More common, however, is the restriction on people designated as "United States persons", which has recently been clarified as referring to persons resident in the US. This restriction is imposed by certain funds to avoid becoming a "deemed public issuer within the US" and therefore subject to the rules and regulations of the Securities and Exchange Commission. In simplified terms if an offshore fund has over a hundred unit/shareholders who are designated to be "US persons", as defined in Regulation S of the US Securities Act of 1933, then that offshore fund if it is not registered with the SEC is deemed under the US Investment Company Act of 1940 to have unlawfully offered its share/units within the United States. In Canada, where the securities laws are provincially enacted, certain purchase restrictions may exist on funds due to the residence of the purchasers or their level of sophistication (exempt status). For more detailed information and examples of purchase restrictions as shown in a prospectus, see Appendix 7.

As each investor has differing taxation issues, it is not within the scope of this guide to deal with the various tax ramifications from investing offshore; and accordingly investors should consult with professionals skilled in tax areas.

Now on to the Investment Review of 1996.

Micropal

PART 2

Investment Review

with an update for the first quarter

Introduction

Surprise wove its way throughout the global investment world during 1996, to an even greater degree than investors could usually expect. Who would have bet on Italian bonds being one of the strongest fixed interest investments around or on Taiwanese equities powering ahead over the year after being openly threatened with all the military might of China?

But so it turned out, and investors who took the plunge into an offshore collective investment fund were able to participate in an diversity of surprises. Of the 5500 offshore funds reviewed by Micropal, the best ten grew by between 94.1 percent and 195.29 percent. For example warrant funds, which buy derivative instruments and the opportunity to buy the shares to which the warrant is attached, are two of the funds in Micropal's list of Top Performing Funds for 1996. Warrants amplify the underlying share price movement and the best return during 1996 – 195.29 percent from CIBC-CEF Hong Kong Warrant Fund, massively outperforming the Hong Kong Hang Seng's 33.48 percent rise. Throughout 1996, investment adviser Peter Chow heavily weighted the portfolio into banking and property development warrants, which turned out to be two of Hong Kong's most attractive sectors. Although the gearing is not extremely aggressive, at an average of three times the value invested, this is going to be a volatile fund. Three-year growth ran to just 53 percent.

The regional Invesco European Warrant Fund reached eighth position in Micropal's list of top performers by doubling its value in 1996. Investment adviser Rory Powell identifies growth stocks first and foremost. He will buy the attached warrant if it is technically attractive; but if not, he is happy to approach a third party institution and suggest terms under which they underwrite a 'covered' or third party warrant on that company. Gearing is as high as he can suitably achieve, and the fund invests in the $20bn continental European warrant market.

It was Eastern Europe which hoarded the

growth spotlight in 1996, accounting for eight of the Equity Growth sector top 10 funds. Four of these also appear in the overall list of top 10: Regent White Tiger Investment Company (150.46%), Mercury ST Eastern European (137.95%), Regent Blue Tiger Investment Company (137.53%), and Regent Red Tiger Investment Company (122.6%). The Mercury fund is regional, while the status of the three Regent funds reflects their two managers' strategy of investing in the Russian equity market.

A lone natural resources related fund made it into Micropal's top 10 performing funds, scoring an exceptional one-year growth of 147.86 percent. US Advisors GSF Precious Metals and Natural Resources is a specialist fund which mainly invests in the early stages of exploration and development of companies involved in mining. These can be small projects worth only a couple of million dollars, usually listed on specialist exchanges in London, USA and Canada. Investment adviser Victor Flores stresses that the fund is not a "commodity play" and relies instead on the skill of the manager and research team to back winning projects.

If the results of Micropal's research reveals a mixed bag of funds, this is then a fair reflection of the mixed fortunes surrounding global investment markets in 1996.

Top Performing Funds for 1996*

Fund	
CIBC-CEF HK Warrant	195.29%
Regent White Tiger	150.46%
US GSF Precious Metals	147.86%
Mercury ST Eastern European	137.95%
Regent Blue Tiger	137.53%
CIBC-CEF Pacific Venture	133.33%
Regent Red Tiger	122.60%
Invesco European Warrant	100.00%
Europa American Option	97.56%
Hansard/ Invesco European Warrant	94.10%

* US dollars, Offer-Offer, Gross Income Reinvested — Source: Micropal 4/97

United States

After a good 1995 when low inflation, moderate economic growth and falling interest rates pushed leading equity indices ahead by more than 30 percent, hopes for a follow-on into 1996 were not universally high at the start of the year. Against this early pessimism, the US equity market proved numerous forecasters wrong over the course of 1996.

The total return from the S&P 500 index, the broadest indicator of US equity performance, was 22.95 percent, and the Dow Jones index beat this with a climb of nearly 29 percent. Early on in 1996, market valuation for the S&P 500 stood around sixteen times price to earnings, but by the end of the year this had risen to around twenty times, a significant shift upwards in the value investors were prepared to put on corporate America. This was a solid effort, given initial worries that US equities would tread water in anticipation of the presidential election battle between President Clinton and Senator Robert Dole. Early on, the equity market was hampered by fears that the economy would weaken and cause earnings to contract.

By the second quarter some market predictions were being upgraded as evidence of reasonably strong economic growth filtered through. Allied to a lack of evidence that inflation might be creeping back in, this prompted strong rises on equity indices. Despite volatile quarter-by-quarter GDP figures (including a 4.7 percent second quarter jump which promptly brought inflation concerns flooding back) the broad trend was towards overall 2 to 3 percent GDP growth – not sluggish, yet also not too exciting a rate to worry the markets.

Indeed, signals of more moderate growth in the second half of the year were seen by some analysts as a justification for the Federal Reserve's decision not to raise interest rates at the September Open Market Committee meeting. Even so, pre-election nerves and concern about whether companies could sustain their earnings growth meant investors were not spared volatility. Once it became clear that President Clinton would stay in the White House and that the Republicans would keep their grip on Congress, the Dow Jones broke the 6,000 level in October and recorded its best monthly performance in five years. It increased by some 8 percent in November, while the S&P 500 went full steam ahead to hit 757.02 at month end.

However, the year ended with the US Federal Reserve chairman Alan Greenspan throwing cold water over investors. His warning in a speech on December 5 that "irrational exuberance" was unduly escalating US equities sent shudders through the hearts of many an investor: the Dow Jones reacted immediately by coming off 145 points and the S&P 500 came back in December to below 725.

As 1996 drew to a close the market was buoyed again by some positive economic statistics, but Mr Greenspan's comments were being pored over by investment professionals who could not decide whether he was simply trying to dampen down the threat of excessive speculation or whether he was really suspicious that if the Fed did not take action by tightening monetary policy, inflationary forces would nudge back into the economy.

Correlation – S&P 500 vs FTSE 100

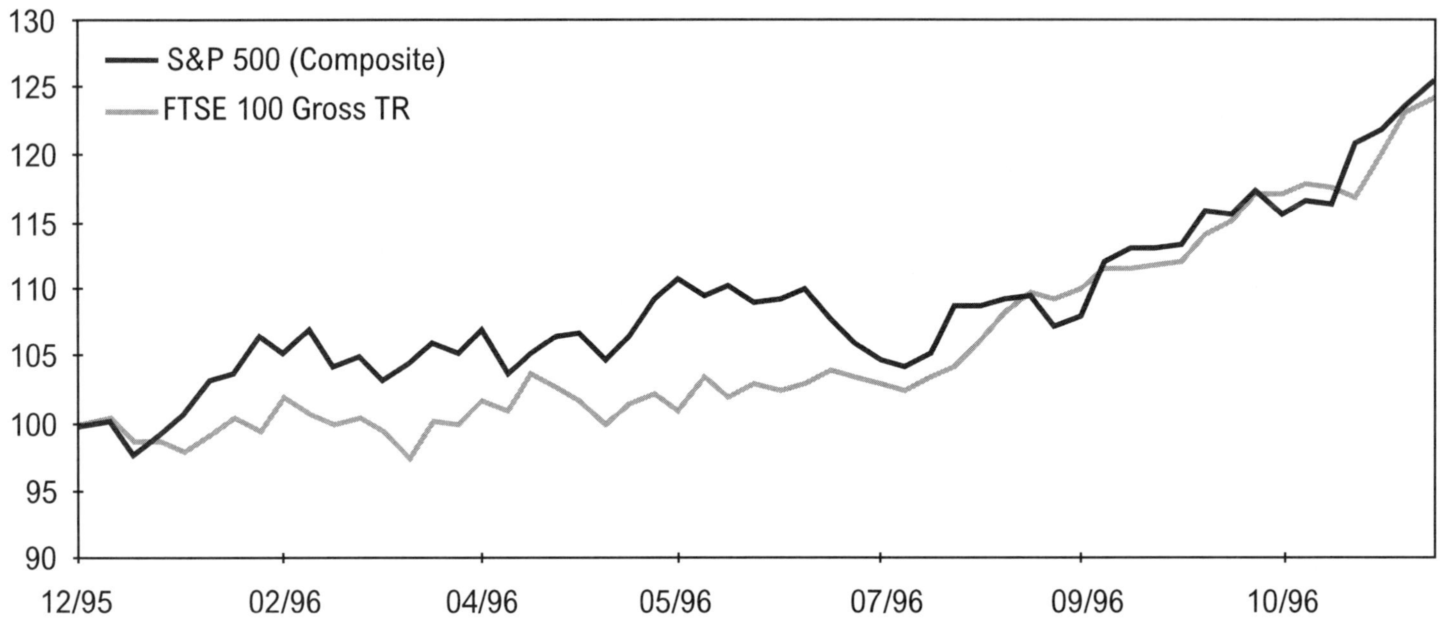

Source: Micropal 4/97 US dollars

United Kingdom

The UK continued to demonstrate that its equity market relies far more upon events in the US than on relations with its European Union partners. As was the case in the US, British equities continued to benefit from manageable inflation, falling unemployment and moderate economic growth. The FT-SE 100 registered a one-year gain of 23.04 percent compared to the FT-SE All Share's 28.58 percent.

Following a cautious Budget in November 1995, the market picked up early in the year when it became apparent that chancellor Kenneth Clarke was keeping reasonable fiscal stimulus under his hat. The FT-SE 100 reached 3,750 early on in the year, lost ground in March and broke the 3,800 level for the first time in April, buoyed up by expectations of healthy corporate earnings. Bond markets were firm, as they and many analysts looked forward to the first base rate cut in over two years, despite increases in public sector borrowing. This came at the end of June when Mr Clarke sliced 25 basis points off the base interest rate. Thus encouraged, the FT-SE 100 breached a new 4,000 high, but the autumn months saw problems arising as consumer spending figures and a spurt of activity in the housing market invoked the spectre of inflation once again. A lengthy stand-off about monetary policy between Eddie George, governor of the Bank of England, and Kenneth Clarke ended on October 3, when Mr Clarke hiked the base interest rate by 0.25 percent to 6 percent, the first rise for 18 months.

This change in direction sent the FT-SE 100 below 4,000, more because of worry about future upward moves than about the quarter point increase itself. In December Mr Greenspan's warnings of a stock market bubble quickly crossed the Atlantic, impacting on UK stocks. Even so, the FT-SE 100 managed to bounce back and close the year at 4,118, a 23 percent rise in dollar terms over the year.

Like their US counterparts, UK equity gains were too modest to put the funds up in the clouds with the more exotic offshore vehicles, although UK index trackers did well within their sector. Among actively managed funds, Jupiter Tyndall GF British Lions' 57.15 percent over one year put it in front of the UK equity pack. The fund is entirely stock driven, and the manager, Alan Miller, looks for well-managed companies with strong balance sheets based on cash flow and strong profits growth at not too demanding valuations. In 1996 these criteria tended to lead the fund towards smaller companies.

Fixed Interest

Latin American debt posted impressive returns among the fixed interest universe in 1996. The regional portion of JP Morgan's EMBI index indicated a basket of Latin American Brady bonds – typically a package of local currency defaulted debt plus some US debt – which generated a 34 percent total return. However, the yield spread over US treasuries debt instruments measured by the index shrank dramatically from a 10.7 percent risk premium to 5.42 percent.

This lessening yield spread is a symptom of the degree to which the risk perception of Latin American debt has improved since the government defaults of the early 1990s and the Mexican peso crisis in 1994. Recovery has been ongoing since then, aided by an improvement of economic fundamentals which carried onwards and upwards in 1996. In Brazil, for instance, the effect of the 1994 Real Plan was shown by inflation ending the year at 10 percent as against 900 percent two years earlier, and this was combined with economic growth at around 2 percent. In 1996 the government continued to make the right noises, announcing a raft of reforms to raise revenue through privatisation and reduce costs through employment reform. In the two other main debt markets, Argentinean inflation came down to a mere 0.6 percent, while Mexico's slid from 52 percent in 1995 to 28 percent.

General emerging market fixed interest funds snatched top places in the sector's top 10 performers, headed by the US dollar sub-fund LFM Emerging Market Capital Fund, a Luxembourg SICAV managed by the Dutch bank ING. The fund achieved a total return of 54.03 percent in 1996.

Allied to Latin America's improving economic fundamentals, was the global supply of liquidity searching for yield which served to drive forward Latin American bonds. Ecuador and Venezuela produced the strongest total returns of 67 percent and 61 percent respectively. Not surprisingly, Latin America also came through strongly in the offshore fixed interest sector. Sovereign High Yield, managed by Scudder, Stevens, & Clark of New York, achieved the most outstanding total return of 37.41 percent. The fund benefited from its major positions in Venezuelan and Brazilian debt.

Investors who opted for less thrilling European bonds did not do too badly at all. Those countries perceived as having a tendency to higher inflation, notably Italy and Spain, enjoyed the convergence effect as confidence accelerated that European Monetary Union would go ahead and harden up their inflation targets. Sniffing this prospect, investors flew the deutschmark bond market in favour of higher yielding markets. Italian government bonds saw some serious action throughout 1996, ten-year yields in lire starting the year at 10.8 percent, moving to 11.03 percent in late February and ending the year at 7.57 percent. By comparison, German ten-year bond yields edged from 6.03 percent to 5.77 percent.

In total, ten-year Italian bonds returned around 24 percent in local currency terms, translating into 29.62 percent for a dollar investor. That yield compares to dollar returns of 0.28 percent from German bonds, 5.87 from Japan and a mere 2.94 percent from US Treasuries. Bond weakness in the US arose from sporadic worries that interest rates must move upwards, despite a strong burst for US Treasuries in the last quarter when at the long end 30-year Treasury yields moved from 6.9 percent to 6.32 percent. Long dated sterling gilt prices followed a similar path, while ten-year yields hit 8.24 percent in May, declining to 7.5 percent at year end after expectations of interest rate rises moderated.

Continental Europe

Beneath the headline "21 percent rise" as measured by the Morgan Stanley Europe Capital index, continental Europe's bourses put in some varied and in some cases very encouraging performances. Individual MSCI indices show Italy lagged at 12.6 percent, while Scandinavian markets did particularly well within the region: Sweden returning 37.2 percent, Finland 33.9 percent and Norway 28.6 percent. However, Spain was the notable performer, boasting an excellent index return of 40.1 percent.

Central to these results were the continuing forecasts of declining inflation around the continent. With central banks nipping at interest rates to boost fluctuating economic growth, investors took themselves out of bonds and into equity markets. This was exacerbated by the quick march towards EMU getting even quicker, encouraging buyers to flock into non-core country bond markets. Dollar strength against most European currencies (Italian lire, Irish punts and sterling were notable exceptions) was another positive for continental European bourses. Germany, for example, has an economy of which over half is domestically oriented, whereas its stock market is more attuned to exports. The deutschmark lost 7.13 percent against the dollar over the year, and the MSCI German Index clocked a resulting stock market climb of 13.6 percent.

Against this general background, 1996 saw European corporates take a harder line on improving value to shareholders. For example, rather than recapitalising and rescuing, Daimler Benz's mid-year announcement that it would pull out of Fokker and put in place various costcutting measures was something of a landmark. The market's positive reaction sent Daimler's share price up immediately, a gain sustained throughout the year. Other German corporates such as Hoechst and Deutsche Bank followed suit, and the ripple effect saw French giant Elf's share price soar following statements about improving returns to investors.

While not in the top flight, numerous European equity funds make an appearance in Micropal's list of 350 top offshore funds for 1996. Two of the more successful vehicles are strictly stockpickers rather than slaves to economic indicators. Old Mutual International (Guernsey) European Stockmarket Fund posted a gain of 48.96 percent over one year, well above the regional average. To overweight Scandinavia was the primary reason for its success – and the fund increased its value as international investors grew to appreciate that Scandinavian companies' stock prices in preference to higher valued equivalent stocks in Netherlands and Germany were not reflecting the companies' efforts to improve shareholder value.

Invesco European Warrant's achievement in returning 100 percent to its investors deserves honourable mention. Its manager trained his strategy around companies which were able to grow despite the handicap of weak economies, noting that 1996 saw a widening valuation gap between attractive and poor companies on this basis.

Eastern Europe vs Global Emerging Markets

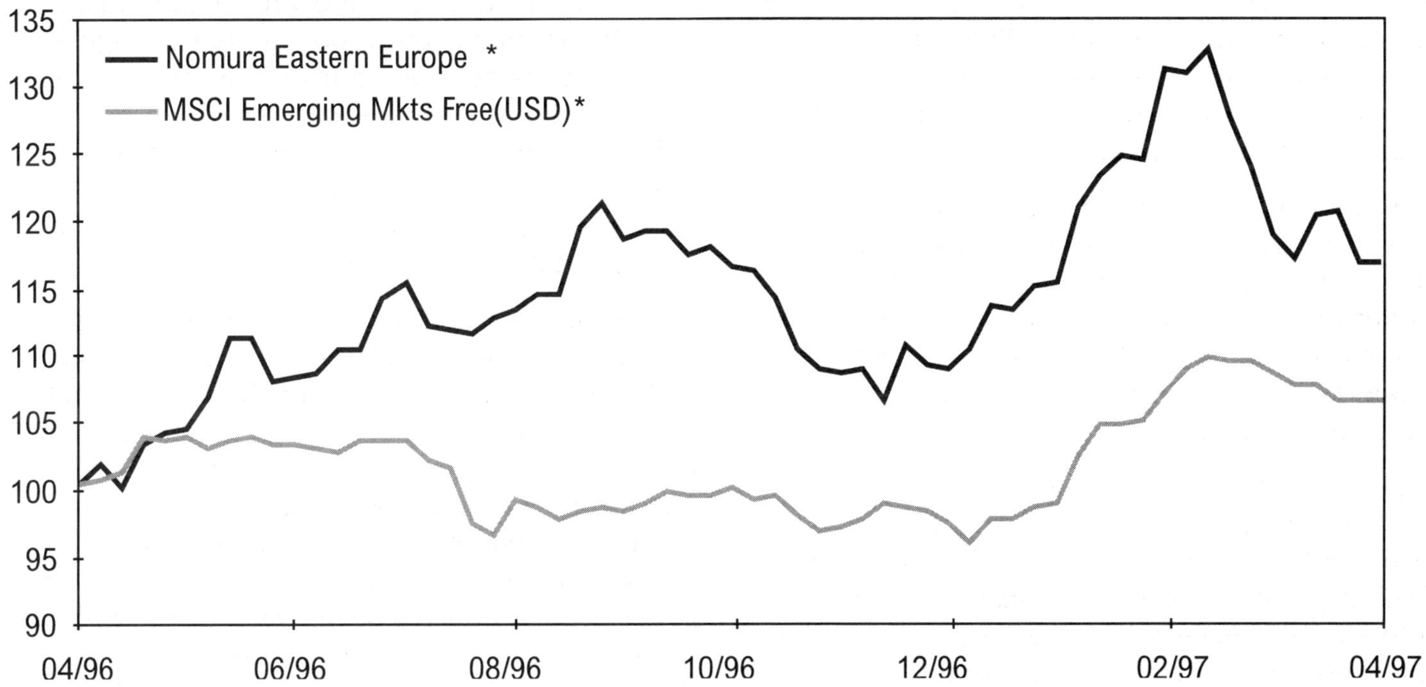

Source: Micropal 4/97 US dollars

Emerging Markets

Eastern European equity funds took eight places in the list of top 10 equity growth funds, four of them being Russian equities. The sector's top return, 150.46 percent, was produced by Regent Fund Management's White Tiger Investment Company, which together with Regent Blue Tiger and Regent Red Tiger focused entirely on Russia during the year. The funds' two managers took a positive view early on to fully invest in the market, and forecasted that Boris Yeltsin would stay in power because it is too hard to beat whoever has control of the Kremlin machine. Politics directed the market in 1996 – Russia began the year dogged by political worries in anticipation of the June election, following a good performance by the Communists in parliamentary elections at the end of 1995.

However, the market put on a strong run prior to the vote as Yeltsin's position strengthened, in anticipation of a post-election wall of foreign money. Economic fundamentals also improved significantly, as inflation was brought down from nearly 90 percent at the start of the year to around 13 percent. The introduction of American Depository Receipts, created by bundling domestically traded shares into internationally traded securities, generated foreign interest. Gazprom was allowed to issue an ADR in October 1996, placing $429m of its shares overseas.

MSCI figures show Hungary contributing 107.2 percent over one year, recognising what was essentially a turn-around year for the nascent stock market when it signed loan agreements with the IMF and received its first Standard & Poors investment rating. Poland's equity market contributed 58.9 percent growth, while the Czech Republic followed up with 30.5 percent.

All these markets enjoyed significant liquidity increases, as the annual January asset re-allocation forced international fund managers to reassess their eastern European weightings. The best placed regional fund in the list of equity growth top 10 performers is Mercury ST Eastern European, up 137.95 percent. The fund, a Luxembourg SICAV denominated in deutschmarks, aims to hunt down small and medium sized growth stocks.

Some Latin American stock markets were attention grabbers, notably Venezuela and Brazil. According to MSCI their respective indices returned 131.2 percent and 42.5 percent, while Chile and Peru, labouring under tighter monetary policy requirements, lagged with 13.5 percent and 0.5 percent gains.

However, indices can be deceptive, particularly in the emerging world. Significant rises on Brazil's main Bovespa (Sao Paulo Stock Exchange) index certainly attracted foreign interest, but these results were skewed towards a few giants like Telebras (telephone) and Electrobras (electric utility) which dominate the index, and major privatisations such as Light Participacoes (electric utility) in 1996. Venezuela's oil based economy, in particular, enjoyed the effects of a buoyant oil price and international recognition of its Agenda Venezuela reform programme, prompting a turnaround in international sentiment. This was illustrated in the huge oversubscription for the year's big sell-off of the government's remaining interest in "telecoms" company CANTV, worth over $1bn.

Regional Latin American funds took first and second place in the mixed growth sector, undoubtedly due to the attractive returns to be had from Latin American fixed interest securities as well as a number of equity markets. Latin America Income & Appreciation A was the top performing funds achieving 42.99 percent, while the second placed fund, Latinvest Value, managed by Peter Gruber, achieved 40.72 percent.

Canada

Following Quebec's failed attempt to win approval for secession in the referendum in 1995, perceptions of Canadian political risk were much improved in the following year. Indeed, Canada just managed to outrun its US neighbour in more ways than one during the year. While Canadian equities as measured by the Canada TSE 100 followed the same broad pattern as the S&P 500, the TSE 100's overall return was slightly better, returning 27.98 percent against the S&P 500's 22.95 percent.

A weak economic picture at the beginning of the year was encouraging for the bond markets and prompted a good run in gold-related stocks on the back of a gold price high of nearly US$420 an ounce in February. Attempting to inject life into a rather anaemic economy, manageable inflation allowed the Bank of Canada to cut short-term interest rates below those in the US in the second quarter of the year, a situation not seen in over twenty years. The JP Morgan Canadian bond index indicated that a dollar investor in Canadian ten-year bonds would have made a total gain of 15 percent over one year.

Japan

Japan continued on its seemingly endless cycle of raising analysts' hopes only to dash them. Early in 1996 forecasts proliferated, predicting that economic growth would improve noticeably and this prompted notable foreign buying.

However, a weak yen and other economic fundamentals did nothing to help the currency break out of a 5,000 point trading range for the year as a whole. A growth rate of 3 percent over 1996 in tandem with the miniscule headline "Bank of Japan discount rate of 0.5 percent" failed to spark much activity in the equity market. Although muted interest rates forced down bond yields to record lows, total bond returns were not looking tempting for foreign investors. A dollar investor in ten-year yen bonds would have been 5.8 percent down over the year.

On the equity market, the Nikkei 225 enjoyed a reasonably good run in the first quarter to scrape 23,000 but fell back after corporate profit hopes were downgraded in the second quarter. Even the September signs of recovery in industrial production and corporate profits could not breathe much life into the Nikkei. Crippled by a lack of investor confidence, the index drifted over the summer and then came back to the 20,000 level in December.

Yen weakness underpinned the strategy of funds which dodged a lot of the flak thrown at them in 1996. GAM Japan, run by Global Asset Management, achieved a creditable performance of .2 percent, creditable, that is, because the Nikkei 225 lost over 13.4 percent in dollar terms over the same 1996 period. The dollar denominated fund prudently opted to hedge yen exposure between 70 percent and 80 percent back into dollars for much of 1996.

Hong Kong

The Far East and Pacific equity markets (excluding Japan) really sprang some surprises on fund managers in 1996. Taiwan, Thailand and South Korea were all heavily tipped as the market to watch.

In the event, sharp divergence proved a lot of fund managers very wrong indeed. The key theme behind these differences was a drastic falling away of export growth. Sluggish demand from more developed economies hit earnings growth hard in 1996 as exports fell drastically. The yen's weakness against the US dollar also affected the competitiveness of these economies. Korea suffered particularly badly in its ship and car building industries from yen competitiveness. Thailand's export growth slumped to around 4 percent in 1996, a fall of 20 percent on the preceding year's form. Singapore

Top Performing Offshore Fund for 1996

US dollars, Offer-Offer, Gross Income Reinvested Source: Micropal 4/97

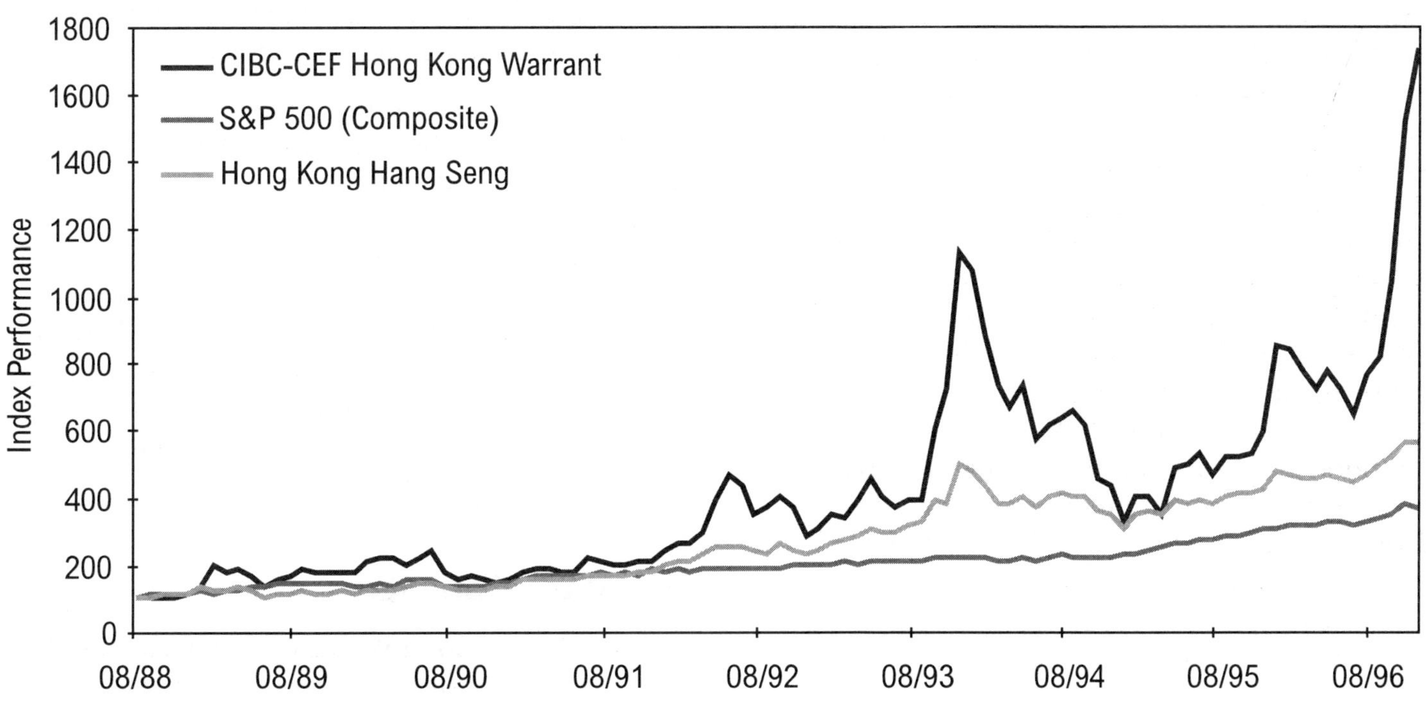

also stagnated due to a slowing down in the global technology industry. As a result, MSCI figures show South Korea and Thailand equities suffering damaging losses of 38.1 percent and 36.6 percent respectively, while Singapore ended the year 6.9 percent down.

In contrast, MSCI's Taiwan index increased by 40.3 percent even after the Chinese missile crisis devastated the stock market. Once this serious negative had passed, improvements in the liquidity situation and faint signs of economic improvement were enough to send the index leaping ahead.

As a result, regional fund managers who were caught out had a tough time in keeping up with the performance of the Hong Kong and/or China equity funds. Many of these made it into Micropal's list of 100 top offshore funds, among the best being HSBC GIF Chinese Equity's 76.21 percent and Schroder Asia China/Hong Kong Equity's 73.94 percent.

Hong Kong equities did particularly well, forging ahead in the third quarter on the back of a positive influences from the US to achieve a one-year 33.48 percent growth, as shown by the Hang Seng. The so-called "handover risk premium" appeared to mean little to investors whose sentiments were soothed by the election of Mr Tung Cheehwa as post-handover chief executive, seen as a respected figure by Chinese power brokers who are keen to safeguard Hong Kong's prosperity. Indeed, 1996 was notable for the substantial reweighting into Hong Kong in the second half of the year. In particular, the banking sector was highly favoured on the back of a buoyant property market and increasing mortgages, reflected in strong results from the major local banks. Over the border, China's stock markets reacted well to the government's confidence that its three-year austerity plan had succeeded in taming inflation sufficiently. Interest rate cuts in May and August also succeeded in freeing liquidity to boost the equity market.

Index Tracker Funds

In 1996 sterling appreciation versus the US dollar had much to do with the use of a UK benchmark by five of the top 10 index tracking funds. Dollar based investors were able to reap the benefits of rising indices and the strength of sterling. The best of the funds, Lazard SIT UK Index Fund, came in at third place with a gain of 33.29 percent in dollar terms. The fund tracks the FT-SE All-Share index, which registered a 16.66 percent climb during 1996 that translated into a 28.58 percent climb in US dollar terms. In contrast, the FT-SE 100, the top blue chip indicator, ended the year 23.04 percent higher in dollar terms. The next best UK index tracker fund, F&C RAF UK Equities, achieved growth of 27.37 percent for a dollar investor. The CMI GNF UK Equity Index Tracker, Scottish Amicable UK Index Tracker and CMI Ins Co UK Tracker generated marginally different variations on 26 percent.

Interestingly, Lazard SIT US Index Fund managed to noticeably outperform the S&P 500 index, which it attempted to reproduce by registering a one-year climb of 34.79 percent against the index's 22.9 percent. This is a sterling denominated fund, so again sterling strength lay behind its outperformance, dollar investors enjoying the 'double whammy' of rising equity values and currency strength.

However, the best performance was to be found from a rare beast, the Hang Seng Index Fund. Run by Hang Seng Investment Management, it grew 36.18 percent over the year, marginally outperforming the 33.48 percent rise on the Hang Seng index itself. As a sector, there was an increasing variety of index tracking options in addition to the major US and UK indices: it is possible to track, for example, a range of individual European equity markets or the region as a whole.

Derivatives/Warrants

CIBC-CEF Hong Kong Warrant Fund's excellent one-year growth of 195.29 percent elevates it to being the top offshore fund for 1996. After a sharp slump in its price in the first half, the real value of investing via a warrant, which amplifies the rise in the underlying security, came through in the second half of the year, reflecting a pickup in the underlying Hong Kong equity market.

Dire equity market performance bounced Japan warrant funds out of the sector's 1996 top 10 in favour of regional Asian funds such as MBf Pacific Warrants, Invesco Asia Tiger Warrant and Baring WUF Tristar Warrant. Given the surprises some Far East stock markets sprang on managers during the year, it is no surprise that their performance lagged behind that of the Hong Kong-focused fund, the best of the bunch being the MBf Pacific Warrant's 81.28 percent.

Bull-runs in a number of European markets pushed three European warrant funds into the sector's top 10. Invesco European Warrant ended the year by doubling its value, while Hansard/Invesco European Warrant, available through an offshore insurance-linked savings arrangement provided by the life insurer Hansard International, was close behind with 94.1 percent.

In the derivatives sector, returns were much diminished from those of 1995. However, George Soros' Quota fund managed the impressive feat of heading the sector for two years in a row. Having rewarded its investors with 160 percent in 1995, Quota put in a rise of 78.8 percent over 1996. In a sector where the average return was only 5.5 percent, investors did well to stick by Soros.

Top Performing Funds for 1996*

	1 year % Chg	3 years % Chg	5 years % Chg
Convertibles			
Alexandra Global Inv 1	34.58	-	-
Credit Lyonnais Convtbl Fd	18.60	26.19	60.75
Inc Ptnrs GSF Asian Conv Bond	18.14	-	-
Templeton GS Glbl Convertible	15.03	-	-
UBAM Emerging Growth Conv	13.24	8.55	-
Quilter Quad Gl Convertible	12.30	-	-
Star Series Convertible	12.16	-	-
GAM Bond US Dollar Spec	11.92	2.02	43.77
JF Global Convertibles	11.57	-6.57	46.76
Guinness Flight Glbl Conv	11.34	18.43	46.23

*US dollars, Offer-Offer, Gross Income Reinvested Source: Micropal 4/97

	1 year % Chg	3 years % Chg	5 years % Chg
Warrants			
CIBC-CEF Hong Kong Warrant	195.29	53.5	766.19
INVESCO European Warrant	100.00	45.60	219.30
Hansard\INVESCO European Warr	94.10	30.46	169.26
MBf Pacific Warrants	81.28	-10.81	150.19
Baring WUF Tristar Warrant	78.85	-33.14	223.67
Hansard\INVESCO Asia Tgr Warr	52.62	-8.76	197.68
INVESCO Asia Tiger Warrant	49.01	-19.57	211.24
GT Asian Warr & Derivatives B	28.27	154.28	202.70
GT Asian Warr & Derivatives A	27.60	153.05	200.85
Aragon Sv German Warrant	25.43	23.80	56.18

*US dollars, Offer-Offer, Gross Income Reinvested Source: Micropal 4/97

Top Performing Funds for 1996*

	1 year % Chg	3 years % Chg	5 years % Chg
Short Term Bonds			
AXA Eqty&Law IFM Total Income	17.32	36.80	26.67
Lazard Sterling Reserve	16.60	34.97	-
Abtrust Atlas Sterling	16.44	29.65	27.55
Beckman Reserve Assets	15.93	33.63	22.38
CMI Passport UK Curr Reserve	15.65	-	-
Swiss Life Proteus Reserve	15.24	31.42	-
Mercury IIT Reserve	14.61	29.64	18.59
Deltec Dollar Income	10.43	-	-
USD Floating Rate C	9.68	-	-
SSF Swedish Bonds	6.86	51.32	30.40
Physical Property			
Performa Real Estate Secs	30.39	-	-
American Phoenix US Real Est	27.68	-	-
Regent Undervalue Assets Prop	19.32	-	-
Rodamco NV	11.12	5.47	18.89
International Property Fund C	3.93	12.51	5.74
Cregem Immo Cap	-4.52	-	-
Immo Royal Immobiliere A	-6.10	23.23	14.55
Immocorp SICAV (m)	-11.82	4.93	-7.52
Physical Commodity			
Ermitage Global Mining	32.28	-	-
MORES	17.34	29.94	68.93
Samba Lux Islamic Trade Fin.	5.04	-	-
McD Financial Arbitrage	2.84	-22.59	18.43
MIMC MINT Ltd Ordinary	1.48	-30.66	-24.02
MIMC MINT Ltd Income	1.46	-31.78	-29.32
F&C RAF Gold	-1.10	-3.32	-
MIMC MINT Gtd Spcal Issue	-3.75	-25.42	-12.06
Luxor	-4.23	-5.01	3.16
Systemtrend Ltd	-8.02	-23.81	-19.08

*US dollars, Offer-Offer, Gross Income Reinvested Source: Micropal 4/97

	1 year % Chg	3 years % Chg	5 years % Chg
Money Market			
Lazard SIT UK Liquid Assets	20.09	38.12	19.77
DBIM Sterling Reserve	17.31	37.78	27.22
Lloyds Intl MMF NZD	17.21	54.94	78.28
Five Arrows CFL NZD	17.16	54.64	76.35
Five Arrows IRL NZD	17.07	53.96	75.67
CUCIM Trust	17.07	-	-
Fidelity NZD Currency Acc	16.89	53.48	75.24
RLI/Income Portfolio	16.84	31.72	-
Buttress Money Market GBP	16.62	-	-
Syfrets GI Stlg Money Mkt	16.57	33.24	-
Mixed Income			
F&C PF Sterling Dist	24.51	29.14	-
CU PP Monthly Income	21.58	23.73	47.88
Barclays Global Income	20.10	26.71	63.37
GAM Universal USD	18.25	20.48	80.15
PFC Stlg Inc & Gth Ptfl	17.74	27.97	48.57
Gartmore CSP Sterling M-T Bal	17.21	30.34	35.69
Royal Life/PFC Stlg Income	15.98	23.11	37.17
SBC Global USD Yield B	8.63	22.27	41.87
GAM Universal DEM Acc	7.88	34.80	99.77
GAM Universal DEM	7.46	34.32	98.98
Mixed Growth			
Latin America Income & App A	42.99	35.92	94.9
Latinvest Value	40.72	-	-
EDM International Strategy	32.86	45.18	44.95
M.Lynch Visionary Portf A	25.72	-	-
Bk of Ire Glbl Intl Stlg Gth	25.56	48.23	88.62
PRICOA WWIP European Growth	23.94	-	-
Eagle Star Stlg Blue Chip	23.61	40.26	43.86
World Invest Mixed	22.92	-	-
Royal Skandia Baring Stg Bal	22.91	28.58	47.50
Scot Prov GP Stlg Balanced	21.82	42.19	76.48

*US dollars, Offer-Offer, Gross Income Reinvested Source: Micropal 4/97

Top Performing Funds for 1996*

	1 year % Chg	3 years % Chg	5 years % Chg
Mixed			
Concept Fd Diversified Ptfl	31.20	-	-
Sun Life GP Distribution	22.36	40.38	-
Scot Eq (SEI) UK Deferrd Dist	22.20	-	-
Sun Life Deferred Dist	21.78	36.18	-
Ashburton Replica Sterling	21.06	31.76	54.63
Fidelity Fds Euro Balanced	18.79	-	-
Opportunity Brazil Balanced	18.71	63.91	-
Opportunity Balanced Ptfl Cls	18.00	-	-
Aetna IUF Latin American A	17.08	-2.31	-
Royal Skandia Gartmore STG Bal	16.19	28.27	-
Managed Currency			
North Star Intl Curr GBP	20.75	32.02	27.27
AXA Eqty&Law ILA Mgd Currency	15.99	20.61	29.16
PFC Lev Cross Ccy & Bd Stlg	15.71	-5.80	-
Hambros CF Sterling Managed	15.39	31.88	17.27
CitiLandmark Mgd Currency	15.08	20.01	26.83
Lloyds Intl MMF Managed GBP	14.73	33.31	22.05
North Star Intl Curr USD	14.53	20.12	32.21
Five Arrows IRL Mgd Sterling	13.84	27.43	25.98
Syfrets Gl Stlg Mgd Currency	12.96	24.70	-
AIB Grofund Sterling Mgd Curr	12.56	30.24	25.26
Fixed Interest			
LFM Emerg Mkt Cap Fd USD Cap	54.03	82.99	-
Morgan Stanley Emg Mkt Debt I	51.92	-	-
M.Lynch Americas Inc Portf A	51.6	-	-
Global Emerging Markets	47.69	-	-
Emerging Investments B	41.59	-	-
GT Emerging Markets Bond	40.58	47.02	-
M.Lynch Mex Inc Peso Portf A	38.39	-21.81	-
EPIC MF Emerging Market Debt	38.21	-	-
Sovereign High Yield A	37.41	36.55	82.88
AEB Worldfolio 14 Em Mkt Debt	37.30	-	-

*US dollars, Offer-Offer, Gross Income Reinvested Source: Micropal 4/97

	1 year % Chg	3 years % Chg	5 years % Chg
Equity Income			
Thornton Taiwan Equity Income	32.05	17.67	39.82
Prolific IF UK Equity Inc	31.34	64.55	101.67
Abtrust Atlas UK Gth of Inc	26.24	42.30	85.31
JF Pacific Income	25.83	3.87	95.71
INVESCO Amer Eqty Income	21.44	55.18	76.06
KB Int'l Equity Income	20.15	27.65	79.12
Thornton Oriental Income	11.98	6.24	56.96
Singer & Fried UK Equity Inc	11.04	-	-
Ippa Portf Belgian Immo B	-5.21	-	-
Equity Growth			
Regent White Tiger	150.46	-	-
US GSF Prec Met & Nat Res	147.86	634.62	-
Mercury ST Eastern European	137.95	-	-
Regent Blue Tiger Inv Co	137.53	-	-
The Bangladesh Fund	136.52	-	-
CIBC-CEF Pacific Venture	133.33	26.99	92.62
Regent Red Tiger	122.60	-	-
Eastern Capital	89.59	-	-
Vontobel Eastern Europe Eq A	87.77	-	-
Fleming FF Eastern European	80.17	-	-
Equity			
Lazard SIT UK Index	33.29	57.65	89.48
State Street American	31.07	47.22	89.62
Lazard Pan European	30.95	61.72	-
Pictet C.F. Valiber	30.85	58.71	31.01
RG America Fund	30.08	49.08	95.85
Genesis Condor	27.75	18.3	90.81
RG Europe Fund	26.68	47.69	94.56
TSB OIF UK Equity	25.17	55.06	171.53
Pictet C.F. Nedval	24.64	80.47	-
Lion Belgium Index	24.55	55.14	-

*US dollars, Offer-Offer, Gross Income Reinvested Source: Micropal 4/97

Top Performing Funds for 1996*

	1 year % Chg	3 years % Chg	5 years % Chg
Derivatives			
Europa American Option	97.56	121.13	165.48
Quota	78.80	327.15	851.64
Gain B	75.50	70.14	168.24
LPS Intl High Performance B	49.16	27.78	59.86
LPS Intl Australian Issue	45.14	7.05	-
AHL Currency	41.72	75.69	-
Quantum Emerging Gth	38.02	46.57	-
AHL Commodity	35.44	42.01	-
John Henry Gl Strategies D	33.45	-	-
SUN SUN Fund	33.17	0.37	-73.86

*US dollars, Offer-Offer, Gross Income Reinvested Source: Micropal 4/97

Update for the First Quarter of 1997

The first quarter of 1997 started well for many of the world's smaller markets. Morocco, Egypt, Greece, Zimbabwe, China, Turkey, Hungary, Brazil and Pakistan all managed gains of over 20 percent; but by far the best performing market in the first quarter of the this year has been Russia, climbing nearly 60 percent despite slipping in March. Of the larger, developed markets, Germany and Switzerland made the largest, double- digit gains but remained overshadowed by their emerging neighbours. In the UK, the run-up to the general election kept a lid on the market, whilst the US equity market experienced a very volatile quarter, ending on a decidedly downbeat note.

Given the above, it is hardly surprising to see the leading offshore investments for this period dominated by specialist funds investing in Russian securities and launched within the last 12-15 months. Despite the top three funds registering losses during March, overall, eight of the top 10 funds in the first quarter were Russian.

The leading performer is Brunswick Russian Growth, up 78.06 percent, managed by the London based Brunswick Capital Management, which currently has over US$60 million under management. The Russian Prosperity Fund placed second with a 76.31 percent rise. This is managed by the Stockholm based Westman and Leander Engstrom Investment Management Company, domiciled in Luxembourg, which currently has over US$100 million under management and is heavily weighted towards preferred shares. The largest of these three funds is Hermitage, in third position, having gained 75.76 percent It is managed by Bill Browdler of Hermitage Capital with over US$200 million under management. Like the two other funds, its current focus is purely on publicly traded Russian equities, although all of the funds can also invest in Russian debt securities such as GKOs, short term debentures of the Russian state treasury (T-Bill equivalents).

Top 10 Performing Offshore Funds During First Quarter 1997 *

Fund	Management Group	Three Month % Return	Rank	General Sector
Brunswick Russian Growth	Brunswick Capital Management	78.06	1	CIS Equity
Russian Prosperity	Westman & Leander-Engstrom Inv	76.31	2	CIS Equity
Hermitage	Hermitage Capital Mgmt	75.76	3	CIS Equity
Opportunity Brazil Value	Opportunity Asset Mgmt	68.27	4	Brazil Equity
Regent Red Tiger	Regent Pacific Group	63.83	5	CIS Equity
Regent White Tiger	Regent Pacific Group	62.20	6	CIS Equity
Regent Blue Tiger Inv Co	Regent Pacific Group	56.28	7	CIS Equity
Fleming Frontier Russia	Fleming Frontier	53.50	8	CIS Equity
Eastern Capital	Connor Asset Management Ltd	47.21	9	CIS Equity
CIBC-CEF Pacific Venture	CEF Capital Ltd	42.51	10	Far East & Pacific Equity

* US dollars, Offer-Offer, Gross Income Reinvested

Source: Micropal 4/97

Also ranked in the top 10 were Regent's three established Russian equity funds. Highest placed is Red Tiger Investment Company with a gain of 63.83 percent for the period. Next is White Tiger Investment Company with a 62.2 percent increment and then Blue Tiger, having risen 56.28 percent. The three funds are managed "collectively" (although each manager concentrates on one particular fund) by Jim Mellon, David Curl and Dominic Bokor-Ingram. Although the three funds mainly target Russian OTC equities, they have recently made moves into cash and GKOs because the managers viewed the market as likely to fall. The three funds can also diversify away from Moscow (Red Tiger into Central Asia, Blue Tiger into the Baltic countries and White Tiger into Siberia) but have yet to do so. Regent has gained a great deal of media exposure for the success of these funds (which take the top three slots over the year) and last year launched two Russian debt funds, an "undervalued assets" fund and a Ukraine fund. Profiles of the three "tiger" funds can be found in Part 3 of the guide.

Fleming Frontier Russia (ninth overall with a 53.5 percent rise) is similar to the leading three Russian funds in that it is one of the many new ones launched in 1996. Nevertheless, this small Luxembourg domiciled sub-fund of the Fleming Frontier Umbrella concentrates on blue-chip Russian equities (ie, the most actively traded, largest capitalisation companies) and does not seek to replicate any of the many Russian equity indices available. One place below, with a 47.21 percent gain, is Eastern Capital Fund Ltd, a BVI corporation managed by Benoit Meunier for fund managers Conner et Cie.

Sandwiched in-between these Russian funds is Opportunity Brazil Value. With its lead manager Carlos Eduardo Ramos, this small fund has achieved gains considerably ahead of the market benchmark. Most of the outperformance is due to the fund's style and preference for smaller companies. Another fund, Opportunity Brazil Aggressive Equities, made a 40.23 percent gain during this period to be placed just outside of the top 10. Rounding out the top 10 over the first quarter is CIBC-CEF Pacific Venture, a small volatile fund which invests in a number of Asian securities (including Japanese), especially warrants and other equity-linked instruments.

All of the above funds have shown well-above-average returns for the period, but the investment strategies these funds adopt make them volatile and not necessarily suitable for the smaller investor – indeed, many funds may not even entertain the idea of taking on investors who could not afford the risks the funds may take. Although the Russian market has made spectacular gains in the last twelve months, it is also prone to spectacular falls as a result of reductions in liquidity and political concerns. Although foreign and domestic capital inflows have eased some of the liquidity problems and the political situation appears relatively stable (in Russian terms!), the market is likely to exhibit "vertical take-off and landing" characteristics for some time to come.

The Brazilian market is another emerging one, much larger and relatively more mature than the Russian market which retains a great deal of inherent volatility. Similarly, the types of securities targeted by the CIBC-CEF fund ensure that it may exhibit far more volatility during its lifetime than a fund taking a more traditional approach.

In order to utilise these riskier strategies, many of the above funds are incorporated in the Caribbean, traditionally the location of sophisticated investment funds, such as hedge funds and similar vehicles. Likewise, few of the above funds (except where mentioned) are registered for sale into European countries and therefore cannot be marketed to investors in those countries, preferring to seek out institutional money and high networth individuals instead.

With Regent's White Tiger, Red Tiger and Blue Tiger taking the three top spots (up 354.59 percent, 322.95 percent and 311.10 percent respectively!) and Eastern Capital Fund in fourth with a modest-by-comparison gain of 224 percent, the Russian monopoly was broken by CIBC-CEF Pacific Venture in fifth (up 160.51 percent) and CIBC-CEF Hong Kong Warrant in sixth place, having gained 133.36 percent. This fund has outperformed the Hong Kong equity market by over 100 percent points in this period, despite having lost 13 percent during March 1997 – another reminder of the volatility of such vehicles.

Managed by the Paris-based FP Consult, FP Russian Equity also made the top 10. Again the focus was on Russian blue-chips, even though the fund does hold some second-tier stocks, mainly in the food and retail sectors. Opportunity Brazil Aggressive (up 120.29 percent), part of Opportunity's umbrella fund, is the highest ranked of three Opportunity Brazil equity funds to occupy places in the top 20 over the last 12 months, whilst Mercury ST Eastern European is the top placed East Europe regional fund (with an increase of 117.91 percent), reflecting the good performances of the East European market during 1996 and early 1997. As at 1996 year-end, this fund held nearly 9 percent of its assets in Lithuanian securities.

Placed seventh overall during the year and in the top place over three years, with a gain of 457.23 percent, is Quota Fund, a hedge fund of funds managed by the George Soros group. As with the quarter and one-year results, the three- five- and ten- year tables are dominated by sophisticated funds. With a gain of over 1,035 percent for the past five years, Quota Fund is the leader and the first of four Soros funds to make it into the five-year top 20 funds.

Other funds to feature prominently in the longer term rankings are: US GSF Precious Metals and Natural Resources Fund, an offshore fund targeting gold and exploration stocks whose impressive three-year gain of 424.41 percent is coming under pressure as the Bre-X scandal sees exploration stock prices fall; Lippo Indonesian Growth, a locally-managed fund which targets smaller companies in Indonesia, the fund has been in fourth place over three years (up 145.44 percent) and in third place over five years (up 389.90 percent); Deltec Latin American, a highly focused Latin American Brady-debt fund which has placed seventh over three years with a rise of 130.42 percent and fourth over five years with a 339 percent climb; and GT Asian Warrants & Derivatives, an exotic Asian fund with a 221.8 percent increase over three years (third place), and a 323 percent gain over five years (seventh place).

PART 3

The Top 350 Offshore Fund Performers for 1996

The following section details the outstanding performance of the top 350 offshore funds for 1996, ranked according to their absolute performance return converted into US dollars. From an original universe of 5500 offshore funds, 500 questionnaires for the fiscal year of 1996 were sent out to portfolio managers. Although information was not complete in all cases, conditions allowed for a subsequent selection of 350 top performers. Of the top 350 top performers in this edition 57 funds had the honour of being featured in last year's edition. As may be expected, over 50 percent of the offshore funds are domiciled in Luxembourg, and 52 percent of the funds are listed on a stock exchange.

In most cases the data is as of December 31, 1996 unless the fund had a different fiscal year-end, and then its most recent information was used. The asset size and performance returns for 1996 have been upgraded where possible to reflect Micropal's asset survey and performance returns as of March 31, 1997. The funds listed are predominately open-ended in nature – that is, shares in a given fund can normally either be purchased from, or sold back to, the fund at a price closely relating to the fund's net asset value per share.

Readers will note that some funds have different letters assigned alongside their entries. Alliance Middle East Opportunies Fund, for example, is followed by the letters A and B. Here, as elsewhere, attention is drawn to different share classes that may be available within the same fund. Though the lettering system is essentially generic in nature, the important consideration is that one share class may have a front-end load and no exit fee, whilst for another the reverse may be true. In addition, funds may have both accumulating and distributing income units or different minimum investment units. However, where a fund has a multiple number of units, data has been condensed, where practicable, to avoid information duplication. Investors who are interested in particular funds are urged to seek additional information to clarify the unit type.

Though most listed data items – such as fund name, domicile, currency, structure, total performance returns over discrete time periods, and so on – are largely self explanatory, one or two qualifications still need to be made. Firstly, where there is no yield listed for a particular fund, this means that the fund made no distribution in the twelve months to December 31, 1996. Yield, for purposes here, consists of income distributions as of the ex-dividend date or dates during the 12 months preceding December 31, 1996 divided by the net asset value. Secondly, in the top holdings column, there are occurrences where the holdings or their percentages have either not been listed, not been supplied, or are deemed not appropriate as in the case of certain hedge funds. In these cases, where possible, appropriate sector and/or country asset/currency allocations have been substituted instead.

More generally, two important concepts to be considered in evaluating data items are the expense ratio and the Micropal star rating given to funds.

The expense ratio is a particularly important evaluation concept because quoted annual management or advisory fees can be misleading, due to other expenses not having been factored into the equation. These may include custodian fees, administrative costs, marketing charges and other expenses incurred by a given fund. The net result is that total expenses charged to a fund may be marginally greater than the quoted annual fee. It is generally true, however, that the larger the investment fund's asset pool, the lower the level of annual expenses. Different methods of data presentation by fund managers unfortunately ensure that the task of comparing funds is rendered more difficult. In the absence, at present, of common industry guidelines on how source data should be presented, the likelihood is that this problem will continue to arise. Due to the inconsistencies in the survey data received, the portfolio turnover ratio and expense ratio have been removed from the statistics section.

Annual management or investment advisory fees are generally quoted as a fixed percentage of average net assets. By documenting a fund's total expenses over the same period and comparing this with the level of advisory fees paid, it will be possible to deduce the percentage of average daily net assets making up total fund charges.

This year in addition to volatility and the Risk Return Ratio we have included the new Micropal Star Rating™ performance measurement. In preference to the risk return ratio which evaluates a fund's return within its sector relative to the risk-free three-year return on 90-day US Treasury Bills, the new Micropal Star Rating™ measures the past ability of a fund to consistently outperform its sector peers. Based upon the last 36 months of performance returns this rating is calculated by dividing the funds average relative performance by the volatility of its relative performance. The higher the ratio, the greater the funds ability to outperform its peers on a consistent basis. The funds in the top 10% are accorded ✪✪✪✪✪, the top 11-30%, ✪✪✪✪, the 31-50%, ✪✪✪, the next 25%, ✪✪ and the bottom 25%, ✪. Note that the risk return ratio number is only assigned to funds that possess a minimum three year positive investment return.

The Top 350 Performers for 1996

(Based on US dollar conversion, on an offer to offer price basis with gross income reinvested)

Rank	Fund name	% Return
1	CIBC-CEF Hong Kong Warrant	195.29
2	Regent White Tiger	150.46
3	US GSF Prec Metal & Natural Resources	147.86
4	Mercury ST Eastern European Fund	137.95
5	Regent Blue Tiger Inv Co	137.53
6	CIBC-CEF Pacific Venture	133.33
7	Regent Red Tiger Inv Co	122.60
8	INVESCO European Warrant	100.00
9	Europa American Option	97.56
10	Hansard\INVESCO European Warrant	94.10
11	Vontobel Fund Eastern European Equity	87.77
12	Fleming FF Eastern European Fund	80.17
13	Barclays ASF China (PRC) Fund	78.89
14	Baring WUF Tristar Warrant	78.85
15	Quota Fund N.V.	78.80
16	ABN AMRO Eastern Europe Equity Fund	78.46
17	Opportunity Brazilian Aggressive Equities	77.20
18	Opportunity Brazilian Strategy	76.37
19	HSBC GIF Chinese Equity	76.21
20	Gain Limited B Share Fund	75.50
21	Schroders Asia China/HK Enterprise	73.94
22	Orbitex Dynamic	73.80
23	Schroder Eastern European Fund	72.98
24	FP Russian Equity Fund Limited	72.60
25	Everest Capital Frontier Fund Ltd	69.92
26	Opportunity Brazilian Equities	67.84
27	Sloane Robinson Europe	66.58
28	CMI GNF Greater China Equity	65.82
29	Fleming FF China Fund	65.47
30	ImPac AP Hong Kong	65.24
31	Julius Baer Multicooperation C Europe Stk	63.80
32	CMI Passport Greater China Eq	63.57
33	HYPO Osteuropa	62.59
34	Barclays ASF Hong Kong Fund	61.98
35	Thornton New Tiger Hong Kong	61.19
36	HSBC GIF Hong Kong Equity	60.38
37	Key BCM Emerging Value Inc.	60.33
38	Manulife Regent GF Global Resources	59.54
39	Everest Capital International	59.07
40	Indosuez Bangladesh Fund	58.08
41	JF China Trust	57.99
42	Pictet TF Eastern Europe	57.85
43	Jupiter Tyndall GF British Lion	57.15
44	Globalvest Value Fund LP	54.93
45	GT PRC A	54.90
46	LFM Emerg Mkt Cap Fd USD Cap	54.03
47	Nikko GUF Hong Kong	53.42
48	Schroders Asia Hong Kong	53.10
49	Schroder Brazil Fund	52.84
50	Hansard\INVESCO Asia Tiger Warrant	52.62
51	Credit Lyonnais China Growth Fund	52.44
52	SHK Middle Kingdom	52.06
53	Morgan Stanley SICAV Emerg Mkt Debt Fund	51.92
54	Dres Thornton ASF Hong Kong	51.31
55	Gartmore CSF UK Smaller Cos	50.95
56	GAM Brasilia Fund Inc.	50.57
57	M.Lynch Americas Income A	50.08
58	Prolific IF China Opportunities	49.91
59	Global Mgr HK Geared	49.85
60	Baring IUF Hong Kong	49.58
61	Morgan Grenfell American Entreprise Fund	49.37
62	Schroders Asia Hong Kong Sm Cos	49.23
63	Morgan Grenfell Euro Emg Mkts Fund	49.21
64	LPS Intl Ltd High Perform. B Share Fund	49.16
65	INVESCO Asia Tiger Warrant	49.01
66	OMI (Gnsy) Euro Stockmarket	48.96
67	SHK China	48.55
68	The Hansberger Global Fund PLC	48.47
69	Morgan Stanley SICAV Latin American Fund	48.17
70	Hansard Hong Kong	47.75
71	Gartmore CSF US Smaller Cos	47.75
72	Hansard\CL China Growth	47.48
73	Jupiter Tyndall GF UK Smaller Cos	47.23
74	Schroders Asia Energy	47.14
75	Dao Heng Hong Kong	46.65
76	Jupiter Tyndall GF China	46.39
77	Goldman Sachs Euro Small Cap	45.54
78	LPS Intl Ltd Australian Issue Share Fund	45.14
79	Jupiter Tyndall GF Europe Smaller Cos	45.08
80	Scot Prov ILA China Opportunities	44.11
81	Mercury ST UK Opportunities	43.32
82	Latin America Income & Appreciation Fd NV	42.99
83	Indosuez Hong Kong	42.92
84	Odey European Incorporated	42.71
85	Scot Prov ILA Special Sits	42.63
86	Guinness Flight Hong Kong	42.56
87	Patrimonio Corporate Inv	42.26
88	Genesis Malaysia Maju Fund	42.18
89	AHL Currency Fund	41.72
90	Alliance Middle East Opps A	41.52
91	EM Osteuropa Fonds (Lux)	41.35
92	GT Hong Kong Class A	41.35
93	Albany Intl UK Enterprise	41.32
94	Scontinvest Equity Fd North American Equity	41.05
95	M&G Island Gold	41.05
96	Fidelity Funds Hong Kong & China Fund	41.04
97	INVESCO PS Greater China Opportunities	41.03
98	BT IIS European Growth	41.01
99	Mercury ST European Opportunities Fund	40.96
100	IB Brazilian Leveraged Equities	40.88
101	Willerfunds-Willer Latinamerica	40.87
102	Nomura SF Hong Kong	40.84
103	Latinvest Fund Limited	40.72
104	Indosuez Shanghai	40.71
105	Pactual Eternity Fund Limited	40.67
106	GT Emerging Markets Bond	40.58
107	Five Arrows IE UK Smllr Cos	40.52
108	Lippo Indonesian Growth	40.28
109	Colonial Securities Hong Kong	40.27
110	M-Fund UK Performer	40.23
111	Fidelity Funds European Smaller Companies	39.91
112	Templeton GS China Fund	39.85
113	Brazilian Investment Company	39.84
114	Odey European USD Incorporated	39.79
115	Patrimonio New Fund Equity	39.57
116	Aetna UK Smaller Companies Class A	39.54
117	Von Ernst GP UK Smaller Cos Equity	39.33
118	Henderson HF UK Smaller Cos	39.28
119	Pactual Infinity Fund Limited	39.27
120	LOI Smaller European Cos	39.00
121	HYPO Greater China	38.69
122	CMI GNF Iberian Equity	38.64
123	Credis Equity Netherlands A/B	38.63
124	Fidelity Funds Nordic Fund	38.61
125	Orbitex Natural Resources	38.46
126	M.Lynch Mex Inc Peso Portf A	38.39
127	M-Fund Iberia Value	38.16
128	Quantum Emerging Growth Fund	38.02
129	Lazard SIT UK Active	37.93
130	Old Mutual Gnsy Euro Stockmarket	37.89
131	Albany Intl Euro Enterprise	37.71
132	Old Mutual Gnsy N Amer Stockmarket	37.70
133	Sovereign High Yield A	37.41
134	Carlson Fund Equity Nordic	37.39
135	Hansard EU Hong Kong Equity	37.37
136	CMI Passport Iberian Equity	37.32
137	AEB Worldfolio 14 Emerging Mkt Debt	37.30
138	GT Australian Sml Cos A Share	37.22
139	Hansard EU Latin America Equity	37.06
140	Fleming Frontier European Discovery	37.03
141	Credis Equity Hispano Iberia A	36.99
142	ABN AMRO China Equity Fund	36.72
143	Fonte Cindam Select	36.70
144	Samba Lux North America Equity	36.56
145	Global Emerging Value Fund	36.52
146	Vista Fixed Balanced Sub Fund	36.32
147	Aetna MF Dutch National Equity	36.28
148	Hansard\Fidelity Nordic	36.23
149	Global Mgr US Geared	36.22
150	Mansion House Hong Kong	36.11
151	Hansard\GT Healthcare	36.07
152	Regent Undervalued Assets Taiwan Fund	36.05
153	Dao Heng China	35.91
154	Albany Intl European Stlg	35.89
155	SSF Sweden Shares	35.87
156	Carlson Fund Equity Sweden	35.83
157	LFM Emerg Mkt Cap Fd DEM Cap/Dist	35.72
158	Lux Avantage1 A Cap	35.68
159	Value Partners A Fund	35.52
160	Morgan Grenfell Emerg Mkts Fixed Income Fd	35.48
161	Share Euro Selection	35.46
162	AHL Commodity Fund	35.44
163	Swiss Life Proteus UK Equity Fund	35.36
164	Thornton New Tiger China	35.33
165	Schroder Intl Sel Euro Sm Cos	35.31
166	Global Mgr German Geared	35.16
167	Mercury MOST European	35.07
168	Thornton New Tiger Malaysia	34.88
169	Lazard SIT US Index	34.79
170	Commercial Union PP Spanish Growth	34.46
171	Fidelity Funds Iberia	34.43
172	Inter Strategie Small Cap	34.36
173	Jupiter Tyndall GF Hong Kong	34.31
174	Credis Equity Small Cap USA	34.15
175	SBC Emeg Econ Portf Latin Am Bonds	34.08
176	Scudder GOF Emerg Markets Income A-2	34.02
177	Seahawk International Inc	33.98

Rank	Fund name	% Return
178	JF Malaysia Trust	33.88
179	Guinness Flight Global Privatisation	33.84
180	Generalpart	33.77
181	Multilink Finnish Equities	33.61
182	Ermitage UK Value Fund Ltd	33.56
183	G-Equity Fund G-Spanish Eq A/B	33.53
184	S-E-Banken Fund Sverige	33.52
185	GT European Smaller Companies Class A	33.46
186	Global Diversified Portfolio Series D	33.45
187	Thornton Taiwan Equity Growth	33.42
188	Fidelity Funds United Kingdom Fund	33.38
189	Momentum Stock Master	33.35
190	Lazard SIT UK Index	33.29
191	Quadrant European Equity Fund	33.27
192	Gartmore CSF HK & China	33.23
193	GT Healthcare A Share	33.16
194	Nestor Lateinamerika Fonds	33.15
195	AHL Diversified Guaranteed Ltd	32.90
196	EDM International Strategy	32.86
197	Europa American Equity	32.86
198	INVESCO PS European Enterprise	32.80
199	Allied Dunbar Europe	32.78
200	The Mexican Premium Income Portfolio NV	32.69
201	Danske NSS Nordic Equities	32.67
202	Global Mgr UK Geared	32.67
203	OMI (Gnsy) N.American Stockmarket	32.67
204	Caixa Funds Spanish Shares	32.62
205	Henderson HF European Smaller Cos	32.49
206	Govett GSIL European Equity	32.48
207	Five Arrows IE UK	32.44
208	Ermitage Emerging Markets Fund Ltd	32.35
209	Ermitage Global Mining Investment Fund Ltd	32.28
210	Friends Provident Stewardship	32.25
211	Hansard\Fidelity Iberia	32.14
212	Thornton Taiwan Equity Income	32.05
213	Credis Equity Small Cap Europe	31.98
214	Julius Baer Multistock Pacific Stock Fund A/B	31.97
215	Inter Strategie Australie	31.79
216	Allied Dunbar IB Europe	31.65
217	SSF Nordic	31.62
218	M-Fund Continental Europe	31.61
219	UBAM US Equity	31.60
220	Hansard\GT Newly Indusrialised Countries	31.56
221	CIBC-CEF Malaysia	31.51
222	Skandifond UK Equity	31.44
223	Prolific IF UK Equity Inc	31.34
224	Alfred Berg Norden SICAV Aktier	31.28
225	JF Hong Kong Trust	31.28
226	Skandifond Nordic Equity Fnd	31.22
227	Mosais SICAV Actiones Esp Et Port	31.18
228	Lion Fortune CL Latin Am Equity Fund	31.17
229	Irish Life International US Equity	31.09
230	Nikko GUF Oceania Fund	31.08
231	Aetna IUF UK Equity A	31.00
232	Scot Prov GP UK Equity	30.99
233	Lazard Pan European Fund	30.95
234	Financial and Metals Portfolio Series C	30.83
235	Hansard\Fidelity UK	30.82
236	Hansard UK Equity	30.78

Rank	Fund name	% Return
237	SHK Oriental Growth	30.77
238	Scot Prov ILA UK Blue Chip	30.77
239	Royal Life Intl Property	30.77
240	Parvest Holland B	30.72
241	Pictet CF Valiber	30.69
242	Dresdner Thornton ASF The China Fund	30.68
243	AIG Europe Small Companies Fund Plc	30.68
244	GT Newly Industrialised Countries Fund	30.65
245	Frontrunner Scandinavian Equities	30.58
246	GT Europe Fund A Share	30.57
247	Unifund Ltd Class A	30.53
248	DNB Investment Nordic Eq C	30.49
249	JF European Trust	30.49
250	Special Assets Pacific LP	30.48
251	Fleming Frontier Emerging Mkts Debt	30.46
252	Fleming FF European Smaller Companies Fd	30.43
253	Performa Real Estate Secs	30.39
254	Buchanan European & Atlantic	30.36
255	Parvest UK B	30.30
256	Manulife Regent GF American Growth	30.26
257	Mexican Investment Company	30.13
258	RG America Fund N.V.	30.08
259	VKAC Navigator Emerg. Mkts Fixed Inc Portf	30.08
260	GAM France Inc.	30.08
261	BT GAF Latin American Equity	30.07
262	Five Arrows GF Latin American Opps	29.97
263	Global Mgr HK Index	29.84
264	Friends Provident European Equity	29.82
265	Schroder Intl Sel Fund UK Equity	29.79
266	Morgan Grenfell Selector UK Fund	29.72
267	Paneurolife International Real Estate	29.72
268	Cregem Equities L-Compartiment Europe Cap	29.68
269	JF New Zealand Trust	29.61
270	Lux Privilege B	29.55
271	ABN AMRO Germany Equity Fund	29.54
272	Aetna IUF American Equity A	29.41
273	KB Lux Key Far East	29.41
274	Alliance Spanish Smaller Cos	29.41
275	CMI GNF Benelux Equity	29.27
276	Europa European Equity	29.27
277	Royal Life Intl European	29.20
278	The Ashburton International Equity Fund	29.10
279	EMIF Spain Index Plus B	29.08
280	Fleming FF America Fund	29.07
281	Mercury Energy International	29.05
282	Swissca Bond Invest ITL	28.96
283	Morgan Grenfell Latin America Fund	28.95
284	Gems Progressive Fd Ltd Class J Share	28.91
285	Vista Equity Sub Fund	28.80
286	Emerging Markets Bond Portfolio NV	28.79
287	Morgan Stanley SICAV US Equity Growth Fd	28.72
288	INVESCO PS UK Growth	28.65
289	Commercial Union PP UK Growth	28.63
290	Essex High Technology Ltd	28.61
291	Fleming FF UK Enterprise Fund	28.51
292	Morgan Grenfell European Fund	28.48
293	RBC Global Canadian Class	28.48
294	Fleming FF Continental European Fund	28.42
295	Enigma Convertible Fund Limited	28.40

Rank	Fund name	% Return
296	Fidelity Funds Latin America Fund	28.38
297	Newton UGF Continenetal Europe	28.38
298	HSBC GIF Malaysian Equity	28.37
299	JF American Growth Trust	28.32
300	Lion Fortune Interaction Europe	28.3
301	Hansard EU UK Equity	28.29
302	ING International-Latin American Equity Cap	28.27
303	Schroder Taiwan Fund	28.27
304	Formosa Fund	28.22
305	OMI (Gnsy) HK Stockmarket	28.19
306	CMI Passport Benelux Equity	28.18
307	Multilink Scandinavian Equities	28.10
308	Gartmore CSF Continental Europe	28.10
309	Aetna MF Hong Kong National Equity	28.08
310	Eagle Star European Equity	28.07
311	Scudder GOF Brazil Equity A-2	28.06
312	Comgest Europe	28.05
313	Govett Mexican Horizons Investment Co	28.04
314	Mosais SICAV Actiones Francaises	28.03
315	FIL Leveraged US Govt Bond	28.02
316	Credis Equity Italy A/B	28.02
317	KB Lux Bond ITL B	27.96
318	CMI GNF Canadian Equity	27.93
319	Luxlife Actions Francaises	27.89
320	Share Latin America	27.84
321	Sloane Robinson International	27.84
322	Perpetual Offshr Latin American Growth	27.83
323	American Phoenix US Real Est Sec Portf	27.77
324	Genesis Condor Fund Limited	27.75
325	Parvest Obli Lira A/B	27.73
326	UBS (Lux) Bond Invest ITL	27.67
327	AHL Athena Gtd Financials Capital Units	27.67
328	GT Japan Warr & Derivatives A	27.60
329	Turkish Growth Fund	27.54
330	Hamon Selected Asian Portfolio	27.47
331	INVESCO PS European Growth	27.45
332	Luxlife Actions Europeennes	27.44
333	SBC Bond Portfolio Italian Lira	27.41
334	Schroder Intl Sel Fund US Equity	27.39
335	Manulife Regent GF Euro Growth	27.38
336	Eagle Star UK Equity	27.37
337	BBL Renta Fund Lira C	27.35
338	SBC Equity Portfolio Canada	27.30
339	Credis Equity Euro Blue Chips A/B	27.27
340	Commercial Union PP Dutch Growth	27.23
341	Friends Provident UK Equity	27.23
342	CMI GNF Nordic Equity	27.21
343	Five Arrows Latin Amer Acc/Dist	27.21
344	CMI GNF UK Equity	27.19
345	Luxlife Actions Americaines	27.13
346	ABN AMRO Latin America Equity Fund	27.12
347	Guinness Flight Asian Sm Cos	27.02
348	Aragon SICAV Swedish Equities Selection Fd	27.01
349	GT Deutschland	26.95
350	Julius Baer Multistock US Stock A /B	26.90

Key to tables of Top 350 Performers

❶ Aetna IUF American Equity A

❸ **272/350**

❷ **Aetna Investment Management**
85 London Wall, London EC2M 7AD, United Kingdom
Tel 44-171-454-7949 Fax 44-171-628-9031
E mail aetna@dial.pipex.com

Contact: Joanne Philpot

❹ **Investment objective:**
The sub-fund aims at long-term capital growth through investment primarily in equities and equity-related instruments of corporations listed on the stock exchanges of the US. The top country allocations include the following: US (93.4%); UK (3.1%); Panama (1.8%); and Canada (0.6%).

❺ **Umbrella fund:** Aetna International Umbrella Fund
❻ **Launch date:** 01/04/87 ❼ **Domicile:** Luxembourg ❽ [UCITS]
❾ **Currency:** USD ❿ **Structure:** Open ended, SICAV
⓫ **Portfolio manager:** Steven L. Gold
Manager of Aetna International Umbrella Fund American Equity A/B since April 1996; graduate of Western U and MBA- Temple U; 12 years broad investment experience.

㉔ **Performance:**

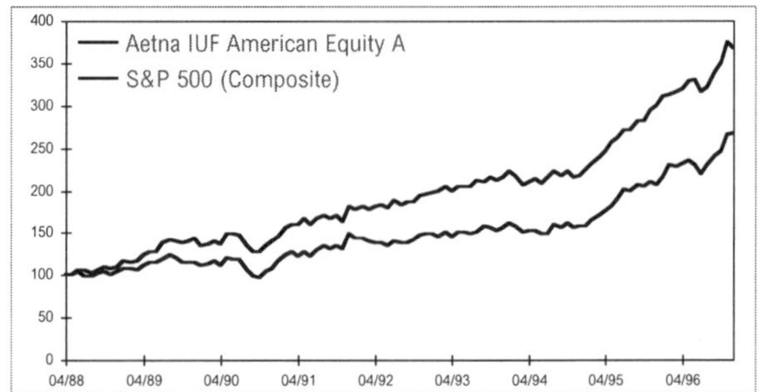

⓬ **Purchase:** Direct, Financial Advisor
⓭ **Minimum investment:** 2,500 USD
⓮ **Custodian:** Banque Internationale a Luxembourg
⓯ **Listed:** Luxembourg ⓰ **Dealings:** Daily
⓱ **Fund Sedol I.D.:** 4008 ⓲ **Published:** FT/SC/BZ
Fees ⓳ **Annual fee:** 1.25% ⓴ **Performance fee:** None
㉑ **Front end load:** Up to 6.00 ㉒ **Redemption fee:** None
㉓ **Switching fee:** 1.00%

㉕ **Top holdings:**

Bristol Myers Squibb	1.9%
British Petroleum	3.1%
Carnival Cruise Lines	1.8%
Chrysler	2.0%
Cigna	1.8%
Intel Corp	1.9%
McDonnell Douglas	1.9%
Texaco	2.3%
United Technologies	2.2%
Wallace Computer Services	2.1%

㉖ **TOTAL RETURNS %**

3 months 1997	1996	1995	1994	3 years	5 years
2.14	29.41	30.66	1.71	71.97	80.52

STATISTICS

㉗ Assets ($mil)	㉘ Current yield	㉙ Volatility	㉚ Risk return	㉛ Micropal Star Rating
5.48	—	3.27	4	✪✪✪✪✪

❶ Name of the fund, which may be abbreviated and may show various class of units or shares e.g. A/B/C or Capitalization/Distributing or USD, GBP.*

❷ Fund address and correspondent information.

❸ Ranking of fund among the other top 350 performers for 1996.

❹ Investment objectives of the fund.

❺ Name of umbrella fund.

❻ Date the fund was launched.

❼ Domicile: location where the fund has been legally organised or structure officially established.

❽ Designation allowing the fund to market in member states of the ECU.*

❾ Currency denomination of the fund, irrespective of the currency of its assets or what currencies the units may be sold in.

❿ The legal structure of the fund.

⓫ Fund investment manager(s) with a short bibliography or the name and address of the investment fund company.

⓬ How shares in the fund may be purchased.

⓭ Minimum value of investment, or units, required to purchase. Some classes of fund have different minimums, e.g. A – 2500 USD, B – 250,000 USD.*

⓮ Custodian's role is to safeguard the investor's assets and interests.

⓯ If the funds are traded on a stock exchange then this indicates the listing location(s).

⓰ Time when funds deal with the purchase/redemption of shares or units.

⓱ Unique number allocated to each fund by London Stock Exchange.*

⓲ Publications showing the fund's unit /share value.*

⓳ Annual fee charged to manage the fund; usually a percentage of the fund's assets.

⓴ Fee charged by the fund manager for having the fund's return performance being above a certain predetermined benchmark – usually calculated as a percentage of the increase in the net asset value of the fund.

㉑ Fee charged upon the initial purchase of the shares, usually includes a commission sales charge. This fee may be optional (CDSC) based on a rear load option.*

㉒ Sales charge that has been deferred (DSC) or charged when an investor sells or redeems units/shares. The fee may be contingent (CDSC) on the time the investor has held the fund (e.g. 4% in year 1 to 0% in year 6).

㉓ A flat or small percentage fee that may be charged by the fund manager when the investor wishes to exchange his units for units in another fund managed by the same manager.

㉔ Performance chart of fund with a comparative benchmark.

㉕ The top holdings of the fund are listed and may show their percentage allocation within the fund's portfolio. In the case of hedge funds long and short positions plus currency exposure may be presented.

㉖ Performance returns, USD converted, on an offer–offer basis with gross income reinvested over the time periods specified. 3 year and 5 year cumulative performances are given if available.

㉗ Fund asset size in USD millions as of December 31, 1996 or last fiscal period. Funds not disclosing their size are marked N/S (not supplied).

㉘ Percentage income yield of the fund based upon distributions for 12 months to December 31, 1996.

㉙ Measurement of the tendency of a security to rise or fall in value relative to the market. Ratings are calculated after 3 years of market pricing.

㉚ Risk Return Ratio rates a fund's risk-adjusted performance where rated funds can receive a ranking from one to five, five being best.

㉛ Micropal Star Rating™ : the more stars a fund has the greater its past ability to consistently outperform its sector peers.

**See Appendix 1 for abbreviations*

ABN AMRO China Equity Fund
142/350

ABN AMRO Investment Management
14 Rue Aldringen, L-1118 Luxembourg
Tel 352-42-42-29-54 Fax 352-42-42-65-00

Investment objective:
The primary objective of the sub-fund is to provide capital appreciation through investments listed in the China region of PRC, Hong Kong and Taiwan. The top sector allocations of the portfolio are the following: industry (24.0%); services (13.5%); finance (10.3%); and capital goods (9.5%).

Umbrella fund: ABN AMRO Funds
Launch date: 29/06/94 **Domicile:** Luxembourg [UCITS]
Currency: USD **Structure:** Open ended, SICAV
Portfolio manager: ABN AMRO Luxembourg Investment Management SA Manager of AAF China Equity Fund; located at 4, Rue Jean Monnet, L-2180 Luxembourg-Kirchberg.

Purchase: Direct
Minimum investment: 500 USD
Custodian: ABN AMRO Bank (Lux) S.A.
Listed: Luxembourg **Dealings:** Daily
Fund Sedol I.D.: 304353 **Published:** WSJ/HTE/BZ/LE/FE
Fees **Annual fee:** 1.20% **Performance fee:** None
Front end load: Up to 3.00% **Redemption fee:** None
Switching fee: 1.00%

Contact: Customer Services Department
Performance:

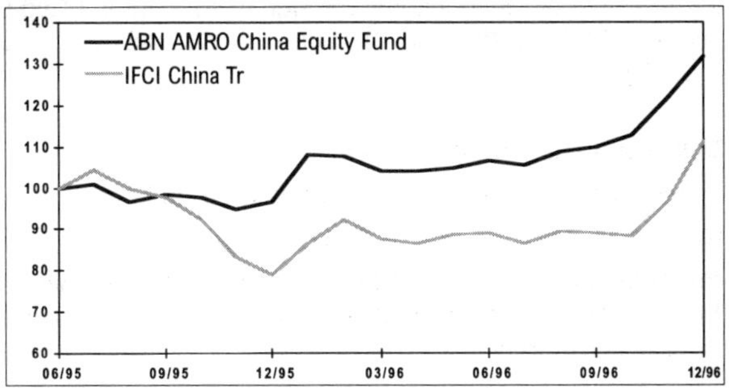

Top holdings:

Bank of East Asia	2.2%
Cheung Kong Infrastructure	2.8%
Cheung Kong	2.2%
Citic Pacific	5.3%
Guanqong Invest Ltd	2.5%
Guanqong Kelon Elec Hldg	2.2%
HSBC Holdings	3.8%
Huaneng Power Int. ADR	2.2%
Hutchison Whampoa	5.3%
New World Infrastructure	2.8%

TOTAL RETURNS %

3 months 1997	1996	1995	1994	3 years	5 years
1.87	36.72	N.A.	N.A.	N.A.	N.A.

STATISTICS

Assets ($mil)	Current yield	Volatility	Risk return	Micropal Star Rating
44.04	—	N.A.	—	———

ABN AMRO Eastern Europe Equity Fund
16/350

ABN AMRO Investment Management
14 Rue Aldringen, L-1118 Luxembourg
Tel 352-42-42-29-54 Fax 352-42-42-65-00

Investment objective:
The primary objective of the sub-fund is to provide long-term capital appreciation through investments in transferable securities which invest primarily in listed equities of central and eastern European companies. Currently, the top geographic allocation of the portfolio is Poland (30.1%).

Umbrella fund: ABN AMRO Funds
Launch date: 29/06/94 **Domicile:** Luxembourg [UCITS]
Currency: DEM **Structure:** Open ended, SICAV
Portfolio manager: ABN AMRO Luxembourg Investment Management SA Manager of AAF Eastern Europe Equity Fund; located at 4, Rue Jean Monnet, L-2180 Luxembourg-Kirchberg.

Purchase: Direct
Minimum investment: 1,000 DEM
Custodian: ABN AMRO Bank (Lux) S.A.
Listed: Luxembourg **Dealings:** Daily
Fund Sedol I.D.: 304351 **Published:** WSJ/HTE/BZ/LE/FE
Fees **Annual fee:** 1.20% **Performance fee:** None
Front end load: Up to 3.00% **Redemption fee:** None
Switching fee: 1.00%

Contact: Customer Services Department
Performance:

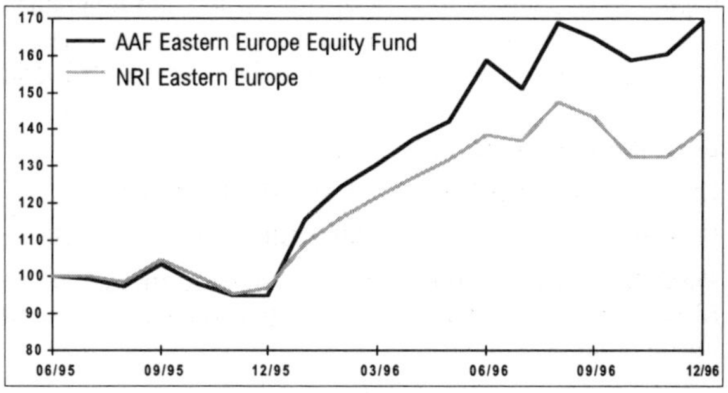

Top holdings:

Borsodchem GDR	2.7%
Computerland	2.5%
Debica	3.7%
Elektrim	4.7%
Komercni Banka	3.2%
LukOil	2.7%
Pannonplast	2.5%
Pliva	3.2%
Richter Gedeon	6.2%
SPT Telecom	5.5%

TOTAL RETURNS %

3 months 1997	1996	1995	1994	3 years	5 years
13.64	78.46	N.A.	N.A.	N.A.	N.A.

STATISTICS

Assets ($mil)	Current yield	Volatility	Risk return	Micropal Star Rating
144.82	—	N.A.	—	———

ABN AMRO Germany Equity Fund
271/350

ABN AMRO Investment Management
14 Rue Aldringen, L-1118 Luxembourg
Tel 352-42-42-29-54 Fax 352-42-42-65-00

Investment objective:
The primary objective of this sub-fund is to provide both capital appreciation and to a lesser extent dividend income through investment in listed German equities. The top sectors of this portfolio are allocated to industrial cyclical (26.1%); and finance (19.9%).

Umbrella fund: ABN AMRO Funds
Launch date: 29/06/94 **Domicile:** Luxembourg [UCITS]
Currency: DEM **Structure:** Open ended, SICAV
Portfolio manager: ABN AMBRO Luxembourg Investment Management SA Manager of AAF Germany Equity Fund; located at 4, Rue Jean Monnet, L-2180 Luxembourg-Kirchberg.

Purchase: Direct
Minimum investment: 1,000 DEM
Custodian: ABN AMRO Bank (Lux) S.A.
Listed: Luxembourg **Dealings:** Daily
Fund Sedol I.D.: 301626 **Published:** WSJ/HTE/BZ/LE/FE
Fees **Annual fee:** 0.72% **Performance fee:** None
Front end load: Up to 3.00% **Redemption fee:** None
Switching fee: 1.00%

Contact: Customer Services Department
Performance:

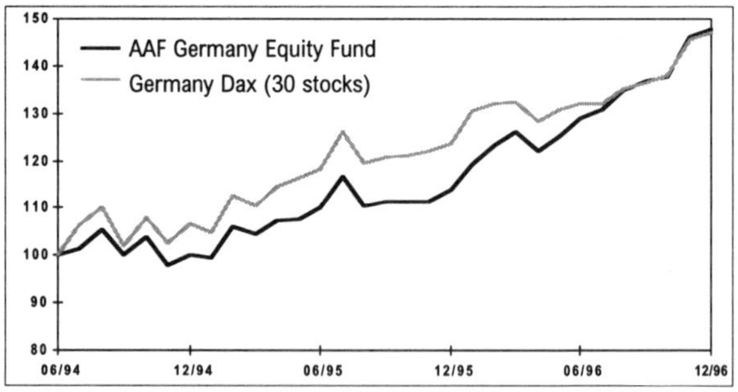

Top holdings:

Adidas	4.2%
Allianz Holding	4.1%
BASF	5.9%
Bayer	6.3%
Daimler Benz	7.3%
Hoechst	7.0%
Mannesmann	4.0%
SGL Carbon	4.2%
Veba	5.8%
Volkswagen	4.0%

TOTAL RETURNS %

3 months 1997	1996	1995	1994	3 years	5 years
11.77	29.54	13.87	N.A.	N.A.	N.A.

STATISTICS

Assets ($mil)	Current yield	Volatility	Risk return	Micropal Star Rating
27.56	—	N.A.	—	———

ABN AMRO Latin America Equity Fund
346/350

ABN AMRO Investment Management
14 Rue Aldringen, L-1118 Luxembourg
Tel 352-42-42-29-54 Fax 352-42-42-65-00

Investment objective:
The primary objective of this ABN AMRO (AAF) sub-fund is to provide long-term capital appreciation through investments in Latin American equities. The geographic allocations of this portfolio are in the following countries: Brazil (43.7%); Mexico (15.5%); Chile (11.8%); Argentina (9.2%) Peru (8.4%); and regionally (6.5%).

Umbrella fund: ABN AMRO Funds
Launch date: 29/06/94 **Domicile:** Luxembourg [UCITS]
Currency: USD **Structure:** Open ended, SICAV
Portfolio manager: ABN AMRO Luxembourg Investment Management SA Manager of AAF Latin American Equity Fund; located at 4, Rue Jean Monnet, L-2180 Luxembourg-Kirchberg.

Purchase: Direct
Minimum investment: 500 USD
Custodian: ABN AMRO Bank (Lux) S.A.
Listed: Luxembourg **Dealings:** Daily
Fund Sedol I.D.: 301627 **Published:** WSJ/HTE/BZ/LE/FE
Fees **Annual fee:** 0.96% **Performance fee:** None
Front end load: Up to 3.00% **Redemption fee:** None
Switching fee: 1.00%

Contact: Customer Services Department
Performance:

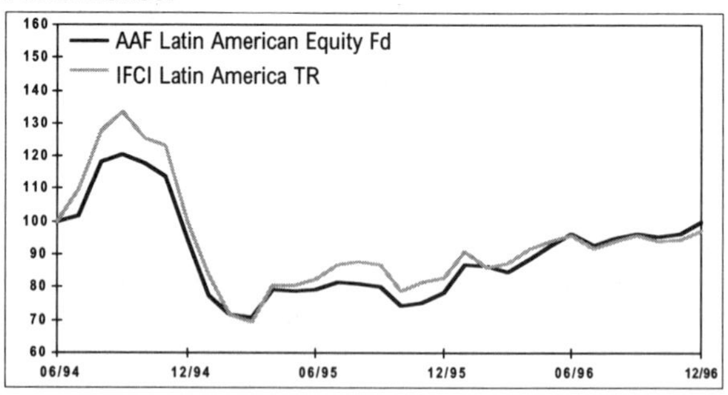

Top holdings:

Banco Itau	2.9%
Brahma	3.3%
Cemig	3.0%
Electrobas	4.5%
Light Participacoes	2.7%
Perez Companec	3.1%
Telebras	8.4%
Telefonico del Peru	3.1%
Telesp	3.0%

TOTAL RETURNS %

3 months 1997	1996	1995	1994	3 years	5 years
19.98	27.12	-17.04	N.A.	N.A.	N.A.

STATISTICS

Assets ($mil)	Current yield	Volatility	Risk return	Micropal Star Rating
120.88	—	N.A.	—	———

AEB Worldfolio 14 Emerging Mkt Debt
137/350

AEB Worldfolio Management Co
American Express Tower, World Financial Centre, New York, NY10285, United States
Tel 1-212-640-2958 Fax 1-212-640-9239

Investment objective:
The sub-fund of the American Express Bank seeks a higher rate of income and total return than standard debt instruments. Investments are in a broadly diversified range of transferable debt securities such as bonds, debentures, notes including warrants of Latin American, other emerging market governmental and private issuers.

Umbrella fund: AEB Worlfolio Mutual Funds
Launch date: 22/09/94 **Domicile:** Luxembourg [UCITS]
Currency: USD **Structure:** Open ended, FCP
Portfolio manager: Thomas K Flanagan CFA
Manager of America Express Bond Worldfolio 14 Emerging Market Debt since September 1994; Senior Portfolio Manager of Salomon Brothers Asset Management; MBA- U of Dartmouth.
Purchase: Direct, Through American Express Bank offices
Minimum investment: 10,000 USD
Custodian: Banque Internationale a Luxembourg
Listed: Luxembourg **Dealings:** Daily
Fund Sedol I.D.: 301578 **Published:** FT/IHT/SC
Fees **Annual fee:** 1.00% **Performance fee:** None
Front end load: Up to 3.00% **Redemption fee:** None
Switching fee: None

Contact: Susan Tannehill
Performance:

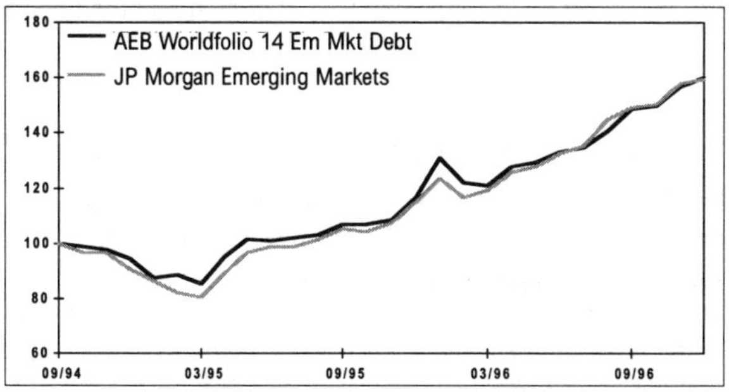

Top holdings:

Holding	%
Argentina FRB	13.8%
Bco Cen Uruguay	4.7%
Brazil A-L IDV	5.1%
Brazil Pars 2-I	6.2%
Ecuador	5.0%
Mexico - 11.5%	12.7%
Panama IRB	4.9%
Philippines	3.3%
Republic of Croatia First	3.5%
Russia Loan	6.3%

TOTAL RETURNS %

3 months 1997	1996	1995	1994	3 years	5 years
0.34	37.30	23.65	N.A.	N.A.	N.A.

STATISTICS

Assets ($mil)	Current yield	Volatility	Risk return	Micropal Star Rating
41.39	—	N.A.	—	———

Aetna IUF American Equity A
272/350

Aetna Investment Management
85 London Wall, London EC2M 7AD, United Kingdom
Tel 44-171-454-7949 Fax 44-171-628-9031
E mail aetna@dial.pipex.com

Investment objective:
The sub-fund aims at long-term capital growth through investment primarily in equities and equity-related instruments of corporations listed on the stock exchanges of the US. The top country allocations include the following: US (93.4%); UK (3.1%); Panama (1.8%); and Canada (0.6%).

Umbrella fund: Aetna International Umbrella Fund
Launch date: 01/04/87 **Domicile:** Luxembourg [UCITS]
Currency: USD **Structure:** Open ended, SICAV
Portfolio manager: Steven L. Gold
Manager of Aetna International Umbrella Fund American Equity A/B since April 1996; graduate of Western U and MBA- Temple U; 12 years broad investment experience.

Purchase: Direct, Financial Advisor
Minimum investment: 2,500 USD
Custodian: Banque Internationale a Luxembourg
Listed: Luxembourg **Dealings:** Daily
Fund Sedol I.D.: 400875 **Published:** FT/SC/BZ
Fees **Annual fee:** 1.25% **Performance fee:** None
Front end load: Up to 6.00 % **Redemption fee:** None
Switching fee: 1.00%

Contact: Joanne Philpot
Performance:

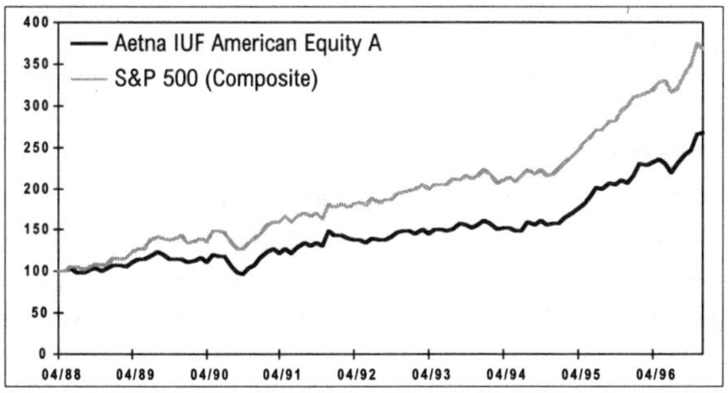

Top holdings:

Holding	%
Bristol Myers Squibb	1.9%
British Petroleum	3.1%
Carnival Cruise Lines	1.8%
Chrysler	2.0%
Cigna	1.8%
Intel Corp	1.9%
McDonnell Douglas	1.9%
Texaco	2.3%
United Technologies	2.2%
Wallace Computer Services	2.1%

TOTAL RETURNS %

3 months 1997	1996	1995	1994	3 years	5 years
2.14	29.41	30.66	1.71	71.97	80.52

STATISTICS

Assets ($mil)	Current yield	Volatility	Risk return	Micropal Star Rating
5.48	—	3.27	4	✪✪✪✪✪

Aetna IUF UK Equity A
231/350

Aetna Investment Management
85 London Wall, London EC2M 7AD, United Kingdom
Tel 44-171-454-7949 Fax 44-171-628-9031
E mail aetna@dial.pipex.com

Contact: Joanne Philpot

Investment objective:
The sub-fund seeks capital growth through investment primarily in equities and equity related instruments of UK corporations on the London Stock Exchange.

Umbrella fund: Aetna International Umbrella Fund

Launch date: 01/04/87 **Domicile:** Luxembourg [UCITS]

Currency: GBP **Structure:** Open ended, SICAV

Portfolio manager: Thomas Dobell
Manager of Aetna International Umbrella Fund United Kingdom Equity A sub-fund commenced April 1994; specialises in high income/ value stock of smaller companies; 10 years investment experience.

Purchase: Direct, Financial Advisor

Minimum investment: 2,500 USD

Custodian: Banque Internationale a Luxembourg

Listed: Luxembourg **Dealings:** Daily

Fund Sedol I.D.: 400880 **Published:** FT/SC/BZ

Fees **Annual fee:** 1.25% **Performance fee:** None
Front end load: Up to 6.00 % **Redemption fee:** None
Switching fee: 1.00%

Performance:

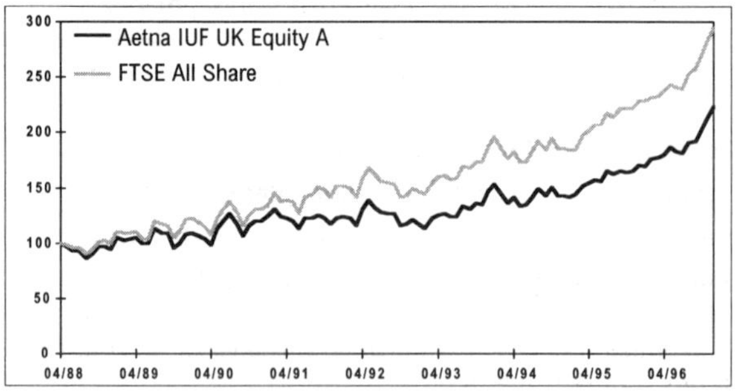

Top holdings:

Holding	%
Barclays PLC	2.6%
BAT Industries	2.4%
British Petroleum	3.7%
British Telecom	4.3%
Glaxo Wellcome	4.0%
HSBC Holdings	2.2%
Lasmo	1.9%
Lloyds TSB Group	4.2%
Rolls Royce	2.3%
Shell Transport & Trading	2.8%

TOTAL RETURNS %

3 months 1997	1996	1995	1994	3 years	5 years
1.02	31.00	19.41	-2.79	52.07	82.19

STATISTICS

Assets ($mil)	Current yield	Volatility	Risk return	Micropal Star Rating
7.32	2.30	3.69	3	✪✪✪✪

Aetna MF Dutch National Equity
147/350

Aetna Investment Management
85 London Wall, London EC2M 7AD, United Kingdom
Tel 44-171-454-7949 Fax 44-171-628-9031
E mail aetna@dial.pipex.com

Contact: Joanne Philpot

Investment objective:
The sub-fund seeks capital appreciation by investing primarily in equities and equity related securities quoted on the Amsterdam stock exchange. The asset allocations of the portfolio are 94.0% in equities and 6.0% cash/MM.

Umbrella fund: The Aetna Master Fund

Launch date: 01/02/90 **Domicile:** Luxembourg [UCITS]

Currency: NLG **Structure:** Open ended, SICAV

Portfolio manager: Amit Khandwala with Wright & Investors' Services Inc
Manager of Aetna MF Dutch National Equity commenced February 1990; BS – U of Bombay and MBA, investment/ corporate finance/ international finance/ marketing – U of Hartford.

Purchase: Direct, Financial Advisor

Minimum investment: 2,000 USD

Custodian: Banque Generale du Luxembourg

Listed: Luxembourg **Dealings:** Daily

Fund Sedol I.D.: 430053 **Published:** FT/IHT/SC

Fees **Annual fee:** 1.00% **Performance fee:** None
Front end load: 6.00% **Redemption fee:** Up to 4.50%
Switching fee: None

Performance:

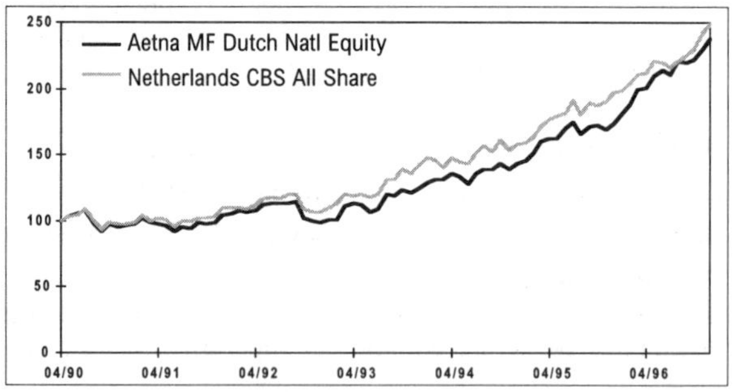

Top holdings:

Holding	%
ABN AMRO Holding	4.6%
AEGON	4.9%
Akzo Nobel	3.9%
Elsevier	4.7%
ING Groep	4.7%
KNP	4.3%
Philips Electronics	4.4%
Royal Dutch Petroleum	9.5%
Twentsche Kabel	4.6%
Unilever	9.6%

TOTAL RETURNS %

3 months 1997	1996	1995	1994	3 years	5 years
2.80	36.28	21.37	15.28	90.67	128.05

STATISTICS

Assets ($mil)	Current yield	Volatility	Risk return	Micropal Star Rating
3.63	—	2.84	4	✪✪✪✪

Aetna MF Hong Kong National Equity
309/350

Aetna Investment Management
85 London Wall, London EC2M 7AD, United Kingdom
Tel 44-171-454-7949 Fax 44-171-628-9031
E mail aetna@dial.pipex.com

Contact: Joanne Philpot

Investment objective:
The sub-fund seeks capital appreciation by investing primarily in equities and equity related securities quoted on the Hong Kong stock exchange. The asset allocations of the portfolio are 93.0% in equities and 7.0% in cash/MM.

Umbrella fund: The Aetna Master Fund
Launch date: 01/02/90 **Domicile:** Luxembourg [UCITS]
Currency: HKD **Structure:** Open ended, SICAV
Portfolio manager: Amit Khandwala with Wright & Investors' Services Inc.
Manager of Aetna MF Dutch National Equity commenced February 1990; BS – U of Bombay and MBA, investment/ corporate finance/ international finance/ marketing – U of Hartford.
Purchase: Direct, Financial Advisor
Minimum investment: 2,000 USD
Custodian: Banque Generale du Luxembourg
Listed: Luxembourg **Dealings:** Daily
Fund Sedol I.D.: 430059 **Published:** FT/IHT/SC
Fees **Annual fee:** 1.00% **Performance fee:** None
Front end load: 6.00% **Redemption fee:** Up to 4.50 %
Switching fee: None

Performance:

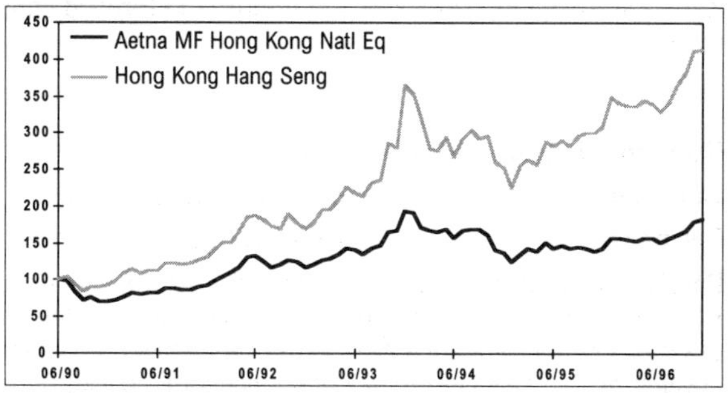

Top holdings:

Cathay Pacific	3.1%
Citic Pacific	5.1%
Hang Seng Bank	3.8%
Hong Kong Telecom	4.3%
HSBC Holdings	8.7%
Hutchison Whampoa	6.2%
New World Development	4.2%
Sun Hung Properties	6.8%
Swire Pacific	4.1%
Wheelock & Co	4.1%

TOTAL RETURNS %

3 months 1997	1996	1995	1994	3 years	5 years
-7.28	28.08	4.65	-29.33	-5.28	98.95

STATISTICS

Assets ($mil)	Current yield	Volatility	Risk return	Micropal Star Rating
1.63	—	5.01	—	✪

Aetna UK Smaller Companies Class A
116/350

Aetna Investment Management
85 London Wall, London EC2M 7AD, United Kingdom
Tel 44-171-454-7949 Fax 44-171-628-9031
E mail aetna@dial.pipex.com

Contact: Joanne Philpot

Investment objective:
The fund seeks long-term capital growth through investment primarily in equities and equity related instruments of UK corporations listed primarily on the London Stock Exchange typically with a market capitalization of below 250 million UK sterling. The top country allocations include the following: UK (95.6%); and Ireland (2.0%).

Umbrella fund: Aetna International Umbrella Fund
Launch date: 01/01/96 **Domicile:** Luxembourg [UCITS]
Currency: GBP **Structure:** Open ended, SICAV
Portfolio manager: Thomas Dobell
Manager of Aetna International Umbrella Fund United Kingdom Small Companies A sub-fund commenced January 1994; specialises in high income/value stock of smaller companies; 10 years investment experience.
Purchase: Direct, Financial Advisor
Minimum investment: 2,500 USD
Custodian: Banque Internationale a Luxembourg
Listed: Luxembourg **Dealings:** Daily
Fund Sedol I.D.: 400884 **Published:** FT/SC/BZ
Fees **Annual fee:** 1.25% **Performance fee:** None
Front end load: Up to 6.00% **Redemption fee:** None
Switching fee: 1.00%

Performance:

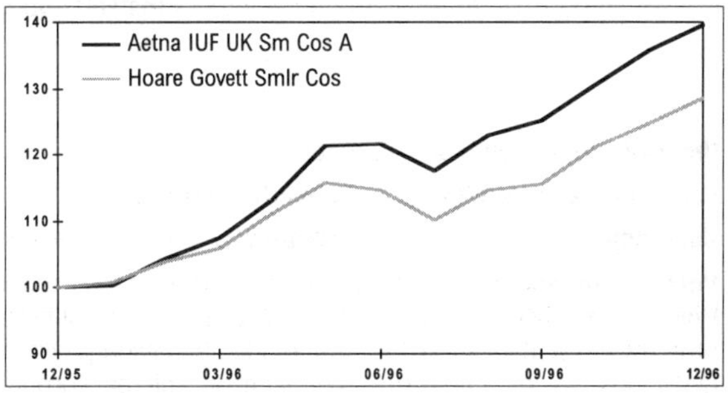

Top holdings:

Brands Hatch Leisure	2.4%
Chloride	2.4%
Corp Services	2.1%
Frost	2.1%
H&C Furnishing	2.3%
J.Bibby & Sons	2.2%
Kewill Systems	2.5%
Meggit	2.1%
Northern Leisure	3.1%
WS Atkins	2.4%

TOTAL RETURNS %

3 months 1997	1996	1995	1994	3 years	5 years
7.78	39.54	N.A.	N.A.	N.A.	N.A.

STATISTICS

Assets ($mil)	Current yield	Volatility	Risk return	Micropal Star Rating
7.63	2.63	N.A.	—	——

AHL Athena Gtd Financials Capital Units

327/350

ED&F Man Inv Products Ltd
Bahnhofstrasse 15, Pfaeffikon, 8808, Switzerland
Tel 41-55-415-3636 Fax 41-55-415-3637
http://www. manip.ch

Contact: Anthony Todd

Investment objective:
The fund seeks to achieve substantial capital appreciation through investment in Athena Trading Ltd, which deals in futures and forward contracts on the international markets.

Umbrella fund: This is a singular fund.

Launch date: 01/04/92 **Domicile:** Cayman Islands

Currency: USD **Structure:** Open ended, Investment Company

Portfolio manager: ED & F Management Investment Products Ltd
With David Huyton, Director with particular responsibility for research; at least 7 other professionals are involved in market behaviour, system refinements or product development – mostly from scientific/ economic backgrounds.

Purchase: Through the Registrar

Minimum investment: 10,000 USD

Custodian: ABN Trust Company N.V. Netherlands

Listed: None **Dealings:** Monthly

Fund Sedol I.D.: 200671 **Published:** FT/IHT

Fees **Annual fee:** 6.00% **Performance fee:** 15.00%
Front end load: None **Redemption fee:** Up to 5.00 %
Switching fee: None

Performance:

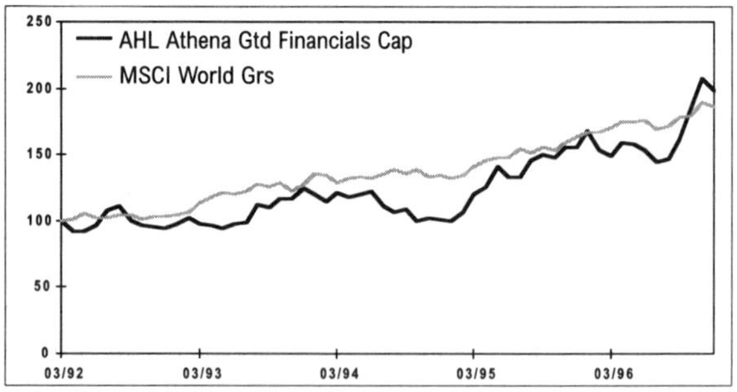

Top holdings:

Currencies & Interest rates	50.0%
Financials	50.0%

TOTAL RETURNS %

3 months 1997	1996	1995	1994	3 years	5 years
9.98	27.67	53.25	-18.49	59.49	N.A.

STATISTICS

Assets ($mil)	Current yield	Volatility	Risk return	Micropal Star Rating
5.72	—	6.28	2	✪✪✪✪

AHL Commodity Fund

162/350

ED&F Man Inv Products Ltd
Bahnhofstrasse 15, Pfaeffikon, 8808, Switzerland
Tel 41-55-415-3636 Fax 41-55-415-3637
http://www. manip.ch

Contact: Anthony Todd

Investment objective:
The fund seeks to achieve substantial medium-term capital appreciation by trading a diversified portfolio of the commodity futures markets though out the world.

Umbrella fund: AHL Funds Limited

Launch date: 12/08/93 **Domicile:** Bermuda

Currency: USD **Structure:** Open ended, Mutual Fund

Portfolio manager: ED & F Management Investment Products Ltd
With David Huyton, Director with particular responsibility for research; at least 7 other professionals are involved in market behaviour, system refinements or product development – mostly from scientific/ economic backgrounds

Purchase: Through the Registrar

Minimum investment: 30,000 USD

Custodian: Bermuda Commercial Bank Limited

Listed: None **Dealings:** Monthly

Fund Sedol I.D.: 256004 **Published:** FT/IHT

Fees **Annual fee:** 4.00% **Performance fee:** 20.00%
Front end load: None **Redemption fee:** Up to 5.00 %
Switching fee: None

Performance:

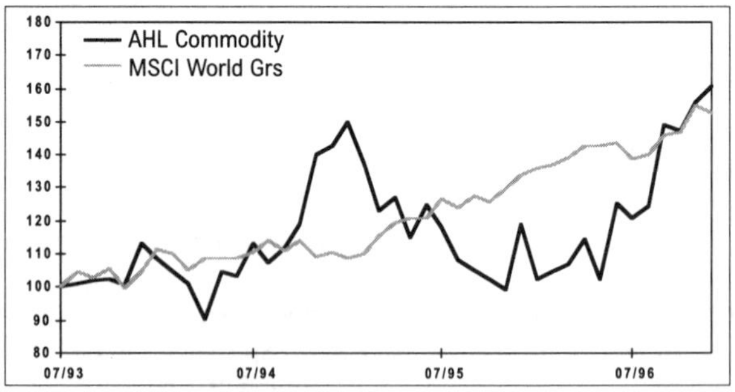

Top holdings:

Agriculturals	31.0%
Base metals	16.0%
Energy	19.0%
Precious Metals	16.0%
Soft Commodity	16.0%
Textiles	3.0%

TOTAL RETURNS %

3 months 1997	1996	1995	1994	3 years	5 years
8.27	35.44	-16.86	26.13	42.01	N.A.

STATISTICS

Assets ($mil)	Current yield	Volatility	Risk return	Micropal Star Rating
6.40	—	9.19	1	✪✪✪

AHL Currency Fund

89/350

ED&F Man Inv Products Ltd
Bahnhofstrasse 15, Pfaeffikon, 8808, Switzerland
Tel 41-55-415-3636 Fax 41-55-415-3637
http://www. manip.ch

Contact: Anthony Todd

Performance:

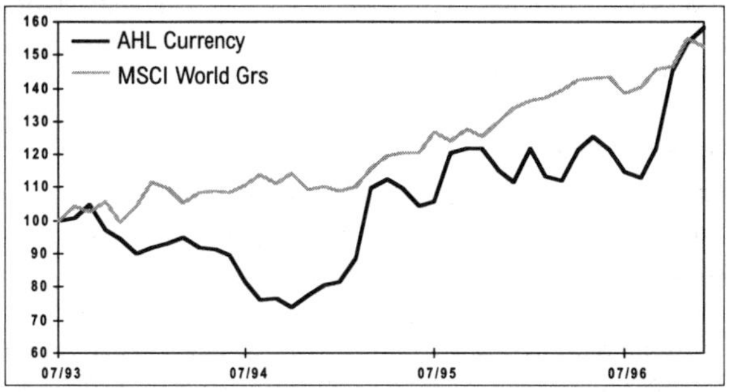

Top holdings:

Currencies	60.0%
Interest Rates	40.0%

Investment objective:
This fund's objective is to achieve substantial medium-term capital appreciation by trading a diversified portfolio of interbank currency markets and short-term interest rate futures markets.

Umbrella fund: AHL Funds Limited

Launch date: 12/08/93 **Domicile:** Bermuda

Currency: USD **Structure:** Open ended, Mutual Fund

Portfolio manager: ED & F Management Investment Products Ltd
With David Huyton, Director with particular responsibility for research; at least 7 other professionals are involved in market behaviour, system refinements or product development – mostly from scientific/ economic backgrounds.

Purchase: Through the Registrar

Minimum investment: 30,000 USD

Custodian: Bermuda Commercial Bank Limited

Listed: None **Dealings:** Monthly

Fund Sedol I.D.: 256005 **Published:** FT/IHT

Fees **Annual fee:** 4.00% **Performance fee:** 20.00%
Front end load: None **Redemption fee:** Up to 5.00%
Switching fee: None

TOTAL RETURNS %

3 months 1997	1996	1995	1994	3 years	5 years
7.26	41.72	38.76	-10.65	75.69	N.A.

STATISTICS

Assets ($mil)	Current yield	Volatility	Risk return	Micropal Star Rating
1.48	—	6.90	3	✪✪✪✪

AHL Diversified Guaranteed Ltd

195/350

ED&F Man Inv Products Ltd
Bahnhofstrasse 15, Pfaeffikon, 8808, Switzerland
Tel 41-55-415-3636 Fax 41-55-415-3637
http://www. manip.ch

Contact: Anthony Todd

Performance:

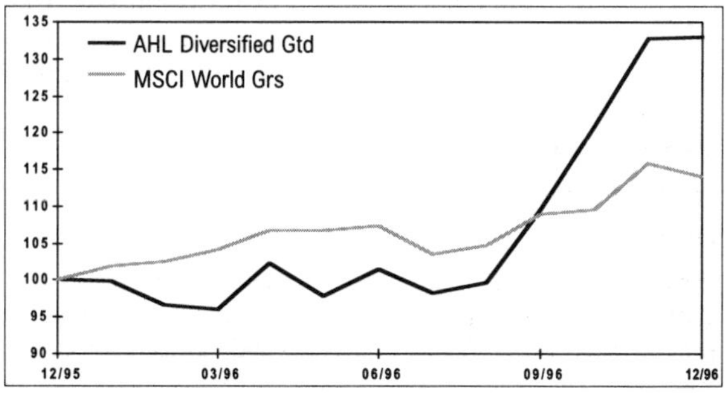

Top holdings:

Currencies	11.0%
Interests Rates	11.0%
Bonds	14.0%
Stock Markets	11.0%
Metals	9.0%
Energy	6.0%
Soft Commodity	5.0%
Agriculture	11.0%

Investment objective:
This fund seeks to achieve substantial medium-term growth by trading a diversified portfolio of international futures contracts.

Umbrella fund: This is a singular fund.

Launch date: 02/01/96 **Domicile:** Bermuda

Currency: USD **Structure:** Open ended, Investment Company

Portfolio manager: ED & F Management Investment Products Ltd
With David Huyton, Director with particular responsibility for research; at least 7 other professionals are involved in market behaviour, system refinements or product development – mostly from scientific/ economic backgrounds.

Purchase: Through the Registrar

Minimum investment: 30,000 USD

Custodian: Bermuda Commercial Bank Limited

Listed: None **Dealings:** Monthly

Fund Sedol I.D.: 305329 **Published:** FT/IHT

Fees **Annual fee:** 4.00% **Performance fee:** 20.00%
Front end load: None **Redemption fee:** Up to 3.00 %
Switching fee: None

TOTAL RETURNS %

3 months 1997	1996	1995	1994	3 years	5 years
8.74	32.90	N.A.	N.A.	N.A.	N.A.

STATISTICS

Assets ($mil)	Current yield	Volatility	Risk return	Micropal Star Rating
17.21	—	N.A.	—	———

AIG Europe Small Companies Fund Plc
243/350

AIG Asset Management Limited
AIG House, Merrion Road, Dublin 4, Ireland
Tel 353-1-283-7766 Fax 353-1-283-7820

Investment objective:
The fund seeks to achieve a high rate of return by making equity and equity related investments in small companies operating in economies of Europe. At present, the portfolio's main country allocation include the following: UK (38.0%); Germany (14.5%); Scandinavia (12.8%); and France (12.7%).

Umbrella fund: This is a singular fund.
Launch date: 12/12/92 **Domicile:** Ireland [UCITS]
Currency: USD **Structure:** Open ended, SICAV
Portfolio manager: David L Leary and John K Barden
Mr Leary, degree in economics/social studies- Manchester U; formerly with LO Intl Portfolio Mgt; joined AIG in 1988. Mr Barden, degree in economics- Manchester U; formerly with CMI Group as European Fund Mgr; joined AIG in 1992.
Purchase: Via the administrative agent
Minimum investment: 1share
Custodian: The Bank of Ireland
Listed: Dublin **Dealings:** Weekly
Fund Sedol I.D.: 2688 **Published:** IHT
Fees **Annual fee:** 1.25% **Performance fee:** None
Front end load: Up to 6.00% **Redemption fee:** None
Switching fee: None

Contact: Siobhan Warfield
Performance:

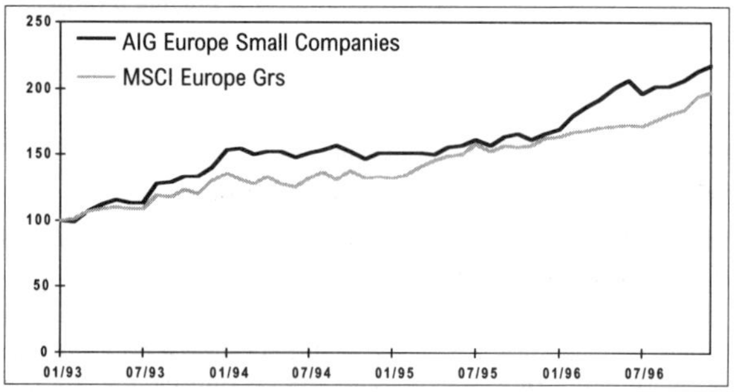

Top holdings:

Holding	%
Adidas Ag (DEM)	2.6%
Airtours (GBP)	2.2%
Cable + Wireless (GBP)	2.3%
Getronics (NLG)	2.6%
Hoganas AB-B (SEK)	3.0%
Konevanes Intl	4.1%
Manchester United (GBP)	2.6%
Sainsbury (GBP)	2.2%
Tarmac (GBP)	2.3%
Veba Ag (DEM)	3.1%

TOTAL RETURNS %

3 months 1997	1996	1995	1994	3 years	5 years
7.58	30.68	9.58	7.95	54.58	N.A.

STATISTICS

Assets ($mil)	Current yield	Volatility	Risk return	Micropal Star Rating
33.17	—	3.68	4	✪✪✪✪

Albany Intl Euro Enterprise
131/350

Albany International Assurance Ltd
St Mary's, The Parade, Castletown, Isle of Man
Tel 44-1624-823-262 Fax 44-1624-822-560

Investment objective:
This fund is designed to achieve long-term capital growth by investing in a concentrated portfolio of European smaller companies, including the United Kingdom. Currently, the portfolio is allocated to the following top six countries: UK (27.0%); Germany (10.0%); France (9.0%); Sweden (9.0%); Switzerland (8.0%); and Italy (6.0%).
Umbrella fund: This is a singular fund.
Launch date: 01/03/95 **Domicile:** Isle of Man
Currency: USD **Structure:** Open ended, Life Assurance Fund
Portfolio manager: Mercury Asset Management Plc
Investment management services to Albany International European Enterprise; located at 33 King William's Street, London EC4R 9AS.

Purchase: Via Albany International policies
Minimum investment: ILP
Custodian: Albany International Assurance Ltd
Listed: None **Dealings:** Daily
Fund Sedol I.D.: 1653 **Published:** FT/MM/RA
Fees **Annual fee:** 1.80% **Performance fee:** ILP
Front end load: ILP **Redemption fee:** ILP
Switching fee: ILP

Contact: Customer Services Department
Performance:

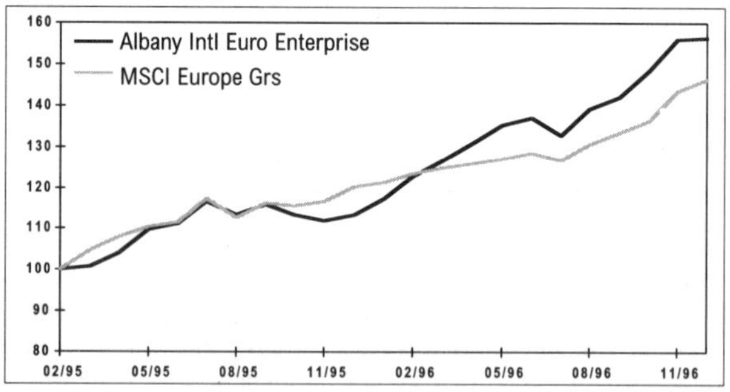

Top holdings:

Holding	%
Autoliv AB	2.0%
Apcoa Parking AG	1.8%
BASF	1.7%
British Biotech	1.9%
Capita Group	2.2%
Falck	1.9%
Hays	2.3%
Hoganas AB	2.5%
Schroders	1.9%
Stratec Holdings AG	1.9%

TOTAL RETURNS %

3 months 1997	1996	1995	1994	3 years	5 years
5.25	37.71	N.A.	N.A.	N.A.	N.A.

STATISTICS

Assets ($mil)	Current yield	Volatility	Risk return	Micropal Star Rating
N/S	—	N.A.	—	——

Albany Intl European Stlg
154/350

Albany International Assurance Ltd
St Mary's, The Parade, Castletown, Isle of Man
Tel 44-1624-823-262 Fax 44-1624-822-560

Investment objective:
The fund seeks long-term capital growth by investing primarily in the shares of European companies, but excluding UK companies. Currently the main country allocations of the portfolio include the following: France (26.0%); Germany (19.0%); Switzerland (14.0%); Netherlands (12.0%); Italy (9.0%); and Sweden (8.0%).

Umbrella fund: This is a singular fund.
Launch date: 04/02/87 **Domicile:** Isle of Man
Currency: GBP **Structure:** Open ended, Life Assurance Fund
Portfolio manager: Mercury Asset Management Plc
Investment management services to Albany International European Stlg; located at 33 King Williams Street, London EC4R 9AS.

Purchase: Via Albany International policies
Minimum investment: ILP
Custodian: Albany International Assurance Ltd
Listed: None **Dealings:** Daily
Fund Sedol I.D.: 1574 **Published:** FT/MM/RA
Fees **Annual fee:** 1.65% **Performance fee:** ILP
Front end load: ILP **Redemption fee:** ILP
Switching fee: ILP

Contact: Customer Services Department

Performance:

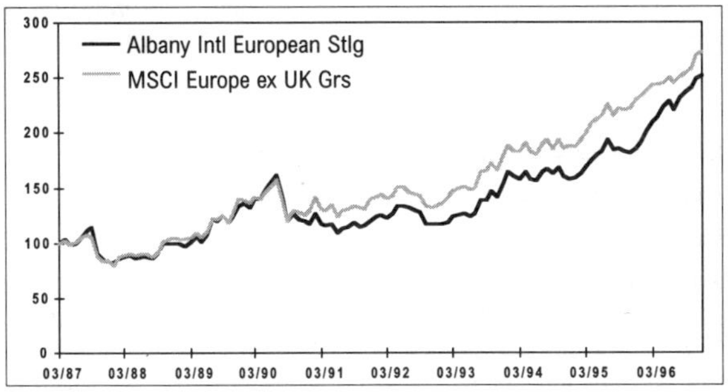

Top holdings:

Eaux Cie Generale	n/s
Adidas	n/s
Bayer	n/s
Dassault Systems	n/s
Gucci	n/s
Nutricia Verenegde	n/s
Pinault -Printemps	n/s
Roche Holdings	n/s
Sandoz	n/s
Total Oil	n/s

TOTAL RETURNS %

3 months 1997	1996	1995	1994	3 years	5 years
8.43	35.89	17.60	2.63	64.02	109.70

STATISTICS

Assets ($mil)	Current yield	Volatility	Risk return	Micropal Star Rating
N/S	—	3.11	4	✪✪✪✪✪

Albany Intl UK Enterprise
93/350

Albany International Assurance Ltd
St Mary's, The Parade, Castletown, Isle of Man
Tel 44-1624-823-262 Fax 44-1624-822-560

Investment objective:
The fund is designed to achieve long-term growth by investing in equities of UK smaller companies with potential for high growth. The following represent the top sector allocations of this portfolio; service (47.0%); general industrials; (24.0%); and finance (11.0%).

Umbrella fund: This is a singular fund.
Launch date: 01/03/95 **Domicile:** Isle of Man
Currency: GBP **Structure:** Open ended, Life Assurance Fund
Portfolio manager: Mercury Asset Management Plc
Investment management services to Albany International's range of funds: located at 33 King Williams Street, London EC4R 9AS.

Purchase: Via Albany International policies
Minimum investment: ILP
Custodian: Albany International Assurance Ltd
Listed: None **Dealings:** Daily
Fund Sedol I.D.: 1626 **Published:** FT/MM/RA
Fees **Annual fee:** 1.80% **Performance fee:** ILP
Front end load: ILP **Redemption fee:** ILP
Switching fee: ILP

Contact: Customer Services department

Performance:

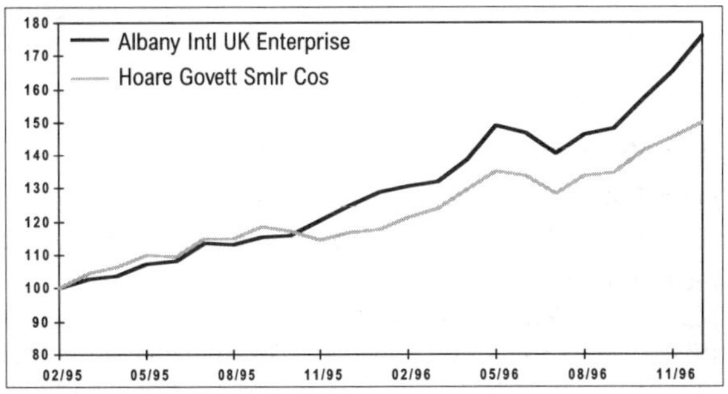

Top holdings:

AEA Technology	3.1%
City Sites Estates	2.8%
FI Group	3.2%
Global Group	3.2%
Hadleigh	3.3%
Harry Ramsden's	3.0%
Lorien	3.1%
MAM	2.7%
Tottenham Hotspur	3.4%
Whittard of Chelsea	2.9%

TOTAL RETURNS %

3 months 1997	1996	1995	1994	3 years	5 years
2.38	41.32	N.A.	N.A.	N.A.	N.A.

STATISTICS

Assets ($mil)	Current yield	Volatility	Risk return	Micropal Star Rating
N/S	—	N.A.	—	———

Alfred Berg Norden SICAV Aktier
224/350

Alfred Berg
26 route d'Arlon, L-1140 Luxembourg
Tel 352-45-20-30-291 Fax 352-45-20-30-405

Investment objective:
The fund seeks long term capital growth by selectively investing in the largest 250 companies listed on the Nordic exchanges . Currently, the geographic break down of the portfolio is Sweden (52.3%); Norway (17.6%); Finland (14.2%); and Denmark (13.1%).

Umbrella fund: Alfred Berg Norden SICAV
Launch date: 08/07/87 **Domicile:** Luxembourg
Currency: USD **Structure:** Open ended, SICAV
Portfolio manager: Niels Moller-Christensen with Alfred Berg Asset Management Managers of the fund; located in Stockholm; leading manager of Nordic equities and bonds; offers a wide range of funds and discretionary management solutions for institutional investors.
Purchase: Direct
Minimum investment: 1Unit
Custodian: Swiss Bank Corporation (Luxembourg) Ltd
Listed: Luxembourg **Dealings:** Daily
Fund Sedol I.D.: 301713 **Published:** IHT/SN
Fees **Annual fee:** 1.20% **Performance fee:** None
Front end load: Up to 5.00% **Redemption fee:** None
Switching fee: None

Contact: Frank Kuffer
Performance:

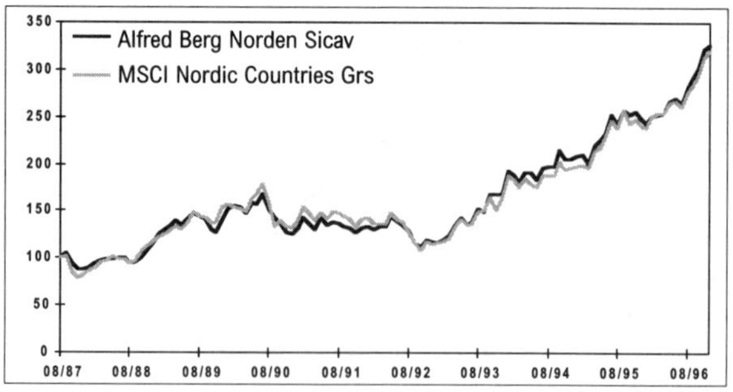

Top holdings:

Astra AB-A	7.8%
Atlas COPCO AB-A	3.0%
Autoliv AB	3.5%
Enso Oy	3.0%
Hennes & Mauritz AB	3.5%
Norsk Hydro As	5.1%
Novo-Nordiska As -B-	3.4%
Skandinaviska Enskilda Banken A	3.7%
Skanska AB	3.4%
Svenska Handelsbanken	8.2%

TOTAL RETURNS %

3 months 1997	1996	1995	1994	3 years	5 years
4.50	31.28	20.59	22.74	94.30	146.38

STATISTICS

Assets ($mil)	Current yield	Volatility	Risk return	Micropal Star Rating
43.45	—	4.63	3	✪✪✪✪

Alliance Middle East Opportunities A/B
90/350

Alliance Capital Management L.P.
35 Boulevard Prince Henri, L-1724 Luxembourg
Tel 352-22-66-93 Fax 352-22-68-93

Investment objective:
This fund seeks long-term appreciation from a portfolio of securities investing in the developing markets of the Middle East. Currently the portfolio is allocated in the following countries: Egypt (31.7%); Turkey (23.4%); Israel (13.5%); Morocco (10.7%); and Jordan (1.1%).

Umbrella fund: This is a singular fund.
Launch date: 31/01/95 **Domicile:** Luxembourg [UCITS]
Currency: USD **Structure:** Open ended, Mutual Fund
Portfolio manager: David L. Edgerly
Manager of New Alliance Middle East Opps A and VP – Emerging Markets Analyst; BA- Brown U and MBA in finance- NY U; previously managed a Fidelity affiliated UK unit trust; 13 years investment experience; 6 years with Alliance.
Purchase: Direct, Financial Advisor
Minimum investment: 2,000 USD
Custodian: Brown Brothers Harriman
Listed: Luxembourg **Dealings:** Daily
Fund Sedol I.D.: 301580 **Published:** FT/WS/AW
Fees **Annual fee:** 1.25% **Performance fee:** None
Front end load: Up to 6.25% **Redemption fee:** None
Switching fee: None

Contact: Customer Services Department
Performance:

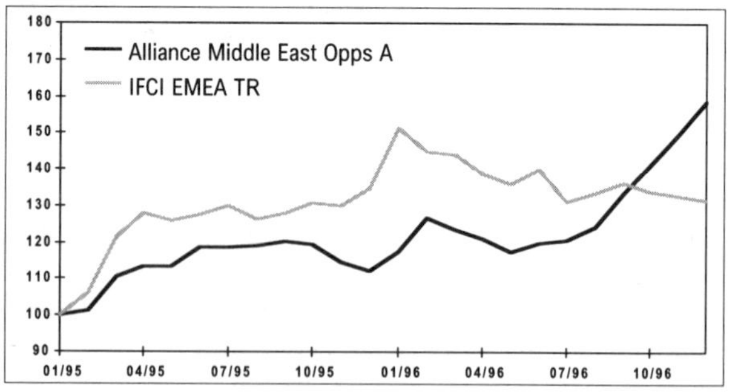

Top holdings:

Alexandria Cement	2.8%
Aselean AS	4.2%
Banque Commerciale du Maroc	4.2%
Commercial International Bank	2.6%
Egyptian Intern Pharm Invest	4.4%
Madinet Nasar City	13.1%
Migros	3.5%
Turk Sise ve CAM Fabrikalari	3.5%
Turkiye is Bankasi	2.9%
Usasucak Servisi AS	2.6%

TOTAL RETURNS %

3 months 1997	1996	1995	1994	3 years	5 years
18.23	41.52	N.A.	N.A.	N.A.	N.A.

STATISTICS

Assets ($mil)	Current yield	Volatility	Risk return	Micropal Star Rating
5.20	—	N.A.	—	——

Alliance Spanish Smaller Co

274/350

Alliance Capital Management L.P.
35 Boulevard Prince Henri, L-1724 Luxembourg
Tel 352-22-66-93 Fax 352-22-68-93

Investment objective:
The sub-fund aims at long-term capital growth through investment primarily in equities and equity-related instruments of corporations listed on the stock exchanges of Spain in Madrid, Barcelona, Valencia and the CATS system.

Umbrella fund: This is a singular fund.

Launch date: 31/10/91 **Domicile:** Luxembourg

Currency: USD **Structure:** Open ended, Mutual Fund

Portfolio manager: Mark H. Breedon
Senior VP of Alliance Capital Mgt and Director of Alliance Capital Ltd; BA Hons, economics- Lanchester Poly; previously with First National Bank responsible for Europe/UK investments; 19 years investment experience; 10 years with Alliance.

Purchase:

Minimum investment: 1 Unit

Custodian: Brown Brothers Harriman

Listed: Luxembourg **Dealings:** Monthly

Fund Sedol I.D.: 301872 **Published:** FT/IHT/SC

Fees **Annual fee:** 1.20% **Performance fee:** None
Front end load: Up to 6.25% **Redemption fee:** None
Switching fee: None

Contact: Customer Services Department

Performance:

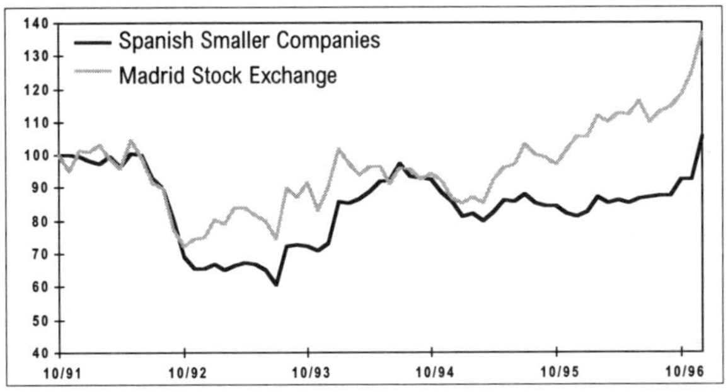

Top holdings:

Azucarera de Espana	4.4%
Banco de Galicia	46.5%
Campofrio Alimentacion SA	4.2%
Elecnor	4.2%
Electra de Viesgo SA	5.2%
EMP Ribagorzan SER B	7.7%
Faes ESP PROD QUIM	4.4%
Grupo Duro-Felguera SA	4.4%
Indo Internatinal	4.0%
Vidrala SA	4.4%

TOTAL RETURNS %

3 months 1997	1996	1995	1994	3 years	5 years
4.28	29.41	-4.97	17.10	44.01	5.43

STATISTICS

Assets ($mil)	Current yield	Volatility	Risk return	Micropal Star Rating
21.10	—	4.47	1	✪✪

Allied Dunbar Europe

199/350

Allied Dunbar International Fund Managers
Allied Dunbar International Centre, 43-51 Athol Street,
Douglas IM99 IET, Isle of Man
Tel 44-1624-661-551 Fax 44-1624-662-183

Investment objective:
The sub-fund invests primarily for capital growth through a portfolio of European equities. The portfolio is invested in the following countries: France (18.7%); Germany (17.3%); Sweden (10.6%); Netherlands (9.6%); Italy (7.8%); and Spain (7.3%).

Umbrella fund: Allied Dunbar International Funds

Launch date: 20/06/87 **Domicile:** Isle of Man

Currency: DEM **Structure:** Open ended, Investment Company

Portfolio manager: David Ballance
Manager of Allied Dunbar Europe commenced 1995; Honours degree in philosophy/ politics/ economics- Christchurch Oxford; previously with CSI and Provident Mutual; 9 years investment industry experience.

Purchase: Direct, Financial Advisor

Minimum investment: 6,000 DEM

Custodian: RBS (Isle of Man)

Listed: None **Dealings:** Daily

Fund Sedol I.D.: 1892 **Published:** FT

Fees **Annual fee:** 1.50% **Performance fee:** ILP
Front end load: ILP **Redemption fee:** ILP
Switching fee: ILP

Contact: Customer Services Department

Performance:

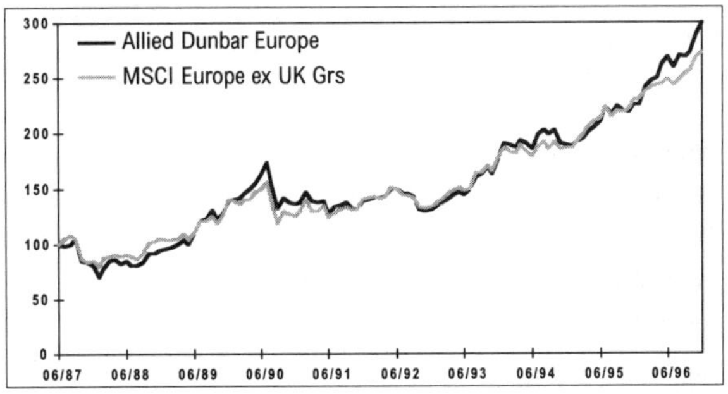

Top holdings:

Ahold Kon	1.7%
Carrefour	2.5%
Daimler Benz	1.7%
Gas Natural	1.8%
Norvatis Reg	3.2%
Porsche Pref	1.7%
Raision Tehtaat	2.2%
Roche Holdings	1.8%
Soendagsavisen	1.7%
Veba	1.8%

TOTAL RETURNS %

3 months 1997	1996	1995	1994	3 years	5 years
9.19	32.78	18.73	7.60	69.65	115.54

STATISTICS

Assets ($mil)	Current yield	Volatility	Risk return	Micropal Star Rating
39.22	—	3.31	4	✪✪✪✪✪

Allied Dunbar IB Europe

216/350

Allied Dunbar International Fund Managers
Allied Dunbar International Centre, 43-51 Athol Street, Douglas
IM99 IET, Isle of Man
Tel 44-1624-661-551 Fax 44-1624-662-183

Contact: Customer Services Department

Investment objective:
The insurance unit-linked sub-fund aims to invest primarily for capital growth through a portfolio of European equities. The top sector allocations of the portfolio are as follows: general manufacturers (31.5%); services (22.1%); consumer goods (18.3%); utilities (10.9%); and finance (10.5%).

Umbrella fund: This is a singular fund.

Launch date: 01/09/93 **Domicile:** Isle of Man

Currency: DEM **Structure:** Open ended, Insurance Fund

Portfolio manager: David Ballance
Manager of Allied IB Dunbar Europe commenced 1995; Honours degree in philosophy/ politics/ economics- Christchurch Oxford; previously with CSI and Provident Mutual; 9 years investment industry experience.

Purchase: Direct

Minimum investment: 5,000 GBP .

Custodian: Allied Dunbar International Assurance Ltd.

Listed: None **Dealings:** Daily

Fund Sedol I.D.: 3091 **Published:** FT

Fees **Annual fee:** 1.50% **Performance fee:** None
Front end load: 6.00% **Redemption fee:** None
Switching fee: None

Performance:

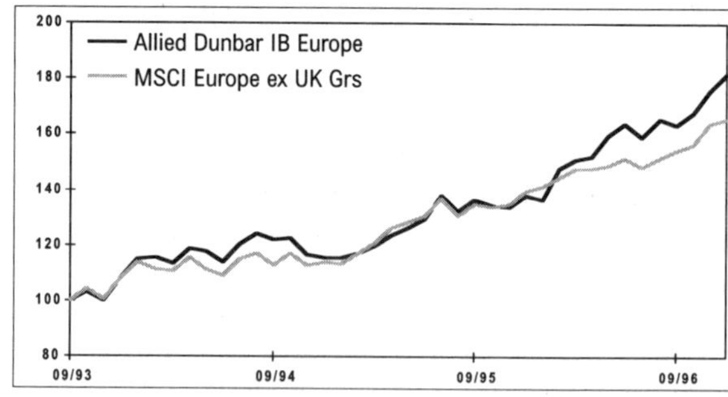

Top holdings:

Ahold Kon	1.7%
Carrefour	2.5%
Damler Benz	1.7%
Gas Natural	1.8%
Norvatis Reg	3.2%
Porsche Pref	1.7%
Raision Tehtaat	2.2%
Roche Holdings	1.8%
Soendagsavisen	1.7%
Veba	1.8%

TOTAL RETURNS %

3 months 1997	1996	1995	1994	3 years	5 years
9.36	31.65	19.32	7.07	68.19	N.A.

STATISTICS

Assets ($mil)	Current yield	Volatility	Risk return	Micropal Star Rating
15.71	—	3.08	5	✪✪✪✪✪

American Phoenix US Real Estate Securities Portfolio

323/350

American Phoenix
13 Rue Goethe, L-1637 Luxembourg
Tel 352-40-46-46-211 Fax 352-40-46-76

Contact: Sue Lee

Investment objective:
The sub-fund aims at long-term capital appreciation and income gain through a portfolio of real estate holdings. The portfolio is invested in the following US real estate sectors: commercial (23.9%); residential (29.7%); retail (22.7%); healthcare (6.11%); specialty (17.0); and the remainder being held in cash.

Umbrella fund: American Phoenix Investment Portfolios

Launch date: 02/01/95 **Domicile:** Luxembourg [UCITS]

Currency: USD **Structure:** Open ended, SICAV

Portfolio manager: Barbar Zubin and William Morris
Co-Managers of American Phoenix US Real Estate; Ms Zubin holds a BA- Williams College and MBA- U of Connecticut; Mr Morrill hold a BA- John Hopkins U and MBA-Harvard Business School.

Purchase: Direct, Financial Advisor

Minimum investment: 3,000 USD

Custodian: Bank of Bermuda (Lux) S.A.

Listed: Luxembourg **Dealings:** Daily

Fund Sedol I.D.: 403704 **Published:** FT/IHT

Fees **Annual fee:** 1.75% **Performance fee:** None
Front end load: Up to 8.25% **Redemption fee:** None
Switching fee: None

Performance:

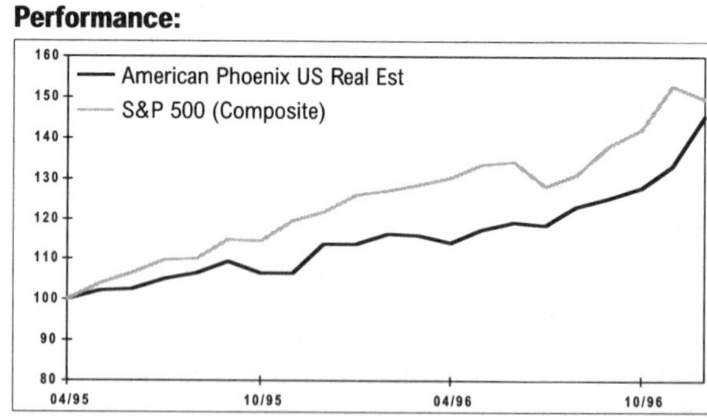

Top holdings:

Bay Apartment Comm	3.3%
Duke Realty	3.2%
Felcor Suite	3.3%
Highwoods Properties	4.6%
Merry Land & Industry	3.2%
Nationwide Healthcare Prop	3.3%
Patriot American Hospitality	5.0%
Simon de Bartolo	4.0%
Spicker Properties	4.0%
Taubman	3.2%

TOTAL RETURNS %

3 months 1997	1996	1995	1994	3 years	5 years
5.44	27.77	N.A.	N.A.	N.A.	N.A.

STATISTICS

Assets ($mil)	Current yield	Volatility	Risk return	Micropal Star Rating
8.11	—	N.A.	—	——

Aragon SICAV Swedish Equities Selection Fund

348/350

Investment objective:
The fund primarily invests in equities quoted on the Stockholm Stock Exchange. The top portfolio allocations by sectors are at present: finance (25%); consumer goods (20.0%); industrial cyclical (16.0%); health (15.0%); technology (7.0%); retail trade/services/utilities (each at 3.0%); and the remaining held in cash.

Umbrella fund: Aragon SICAV
Launch date: 17/10/89 **Domicile:** Luxembourg [UCITS]
Currency: SEK **Structure:** Open ended, SICAV
Portfolio manager: Ragnar Zetterberg
Manager of Aragon Sv Swedish E Aragon-Sicav commenced September 1993; joined Aragon 1987.

Purchase: Direct, Financial Advisor
Minimum investment: 50,000 SEK
Custodian: Banque Indosuez Luxembourg
Listed: None **Dealings:** Weekly
Fund Sedol I.D.: 300911 **Published:** SN/IN
Fees **Annual fee:** 1.00% **Performance fee:** None
Front end load: 1.00% **Redemption fee:** 1.00%
Switching fee: None

Aragon Fondkommission AB
PO Box 7794, Stockholm, 10396, Sweden
Tel 46-87-91-3500 Fax 46-86-11-2535
E mail fonder@aragon.se

Contact: Magnus Harning Nilsson

Performance:

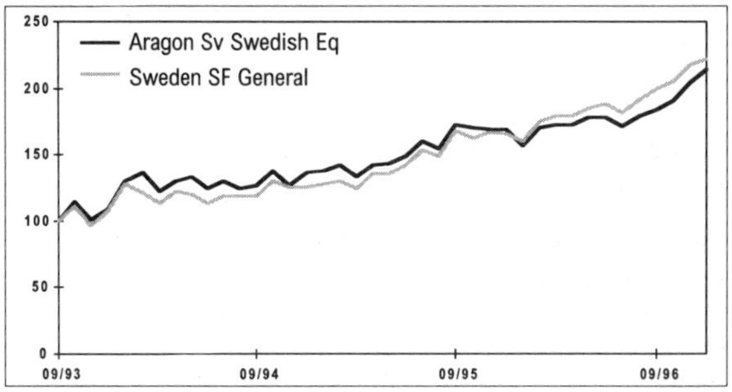

Top holdings:

Astra	9.0%
Ericsson	7.0%
Pharmacia Upjohn	5.0%
Skandia	4.0%
Svenska Handelsbank	5.0%
Volvo	5.0%
Wihlborg & Son	3.0%
WM Data B	3.0%
Zetterbergs Industries	4.0%

TOTAL RETURNS %

3 months 1997	1996	1995	1994	3 years	5 years
-0.78	27.01	23.74	25.60	97.39	N.A.

STATISTICS

Assets ($mil)	Current yield	Volatility	Risk return	Micropal Star Rating
15.30	—	6.03	2	✪✪

Barclays ASF China (PRC) Fund

13/350

Investment objective:
The sub-fund aims to provide investors with long-term capital growth from either direct investments in companies listed on stock exchanges in the People's Rep. of China (PRC) or indirect investments in the PRC through companies listed on the Hong Kong stock exchange. This portfolio is primarily allocated to the Hong Kong (70.1%) geographic sector.

Umbrella fund: Barclays Asian Selection Funds
Launch date: 04/09/92 **Domicile:** Jersey
Currency: USD **Structure:** Open ended, Investment Company
Portfolio manager: Raymond Chan
Manager of Barclays ASF China (PRC); MA- U of Exeter; formerly with Salomon Brothers Asset Management Asia Pacific and Credit Agricole Asset Management South East Asia; joined BSA in 1996.
Purchase: Direct, Financial Advisor, Life Companies
Minimum investment: 1,500 USD
Custodian: Barclays Private Bank & Trust Limited
Listed: Hong Kong **Dealings:** Daily
Fund Sedol I.D.: 8462 **Published:** FT/SC/IHT/HKET/HKEJ/JEP
Fees **Annual fee:** 1.75% **Performance fee:** None
Front end load: 5.00% **Redemption fee:** None
Switching fee: None

Barclays Fund Managers Limited
P.O.Box 152 Sutton House, 28-30 The Parade, St Helier, JE4 8RA, Jersey
Tel 44-1534-812-700 Fax 44-1534-608-910

Contact: David Johnson

Performance:

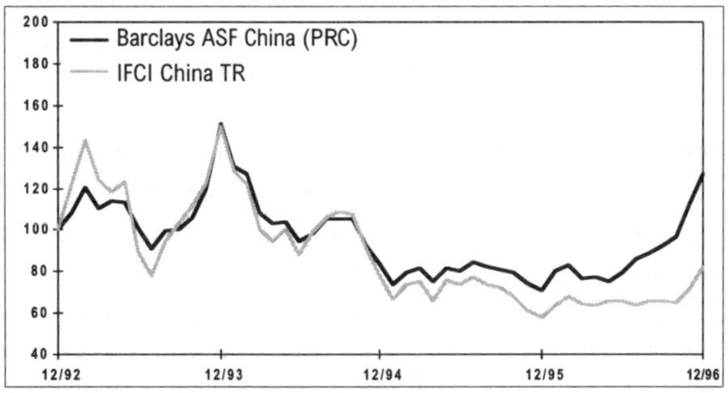

Top holdings:

China Resources Enterprises	5.6%
Citic Pacific	4.7%
Great Eagle Holdings	4.9%
Guangdong Kelon Elec.Hld	4.1%
Guangzhou Inv Ltd	4.2%
Hutchison Whampoa	3.4%
Kumagai Gumi (KH)	3.8%
Lai Sun Development	3.9%
Shanghai Industrial	3.5%
Shenzhen Fangda	5.8%

TOTAL RETURNS %

3 months 1997	1996	1995	1994	3 years	5 years
10.82	78.89	-15.82	-44.46	-16.37	N.A.

STATISTICS

Assets ($mil)	Current yield	Volatility	Risk return	Micropal Star Rating
14.27	—	7.64	—	✪✪✪

Barclays ASF Hong Kong Fund

34/350

Barclays Fund Managers Limited
P.O.Box 152 Sutton House, 28-30 The Parade, St Helier,
JE4 8RA, Jersey
Tel 44-1534-812-700 Fax 44-1534-608-910

Investment objective:
This sub-fund aims to provide investors with long-term capital growth from investments traded primarily on the Hong Kong stock market. At present, the assets of this portfolio are allocated to the following sectors: property (37.6%); commercial (40.9%); finance (15.0%); utilities (3.9%); and the remainder held in cash.

Umbrella fund: Barclays Asian Selection Funds
Launch date: 17/10/90 **Domicile:** Jersey
Currency: USD **Structure:** Open ended, Investment Company
Portfolio manager: Raymond Chang
Manager of the sub-fund and Associated Dir of BGI HK Ltd; BA Hons-economics- U of Durham and MA- U of Exeter; previously with Salomon Brokers Asset Mgt Asia Pacific Ltd et al; 7 years in the finance industry; 1 year with this sub-fund.
Purchase: Direct, Financial Advisor, Life Companies
Minimum investment: 1,500 USD
Custodian: Barclays Private Bank & Trust Limited
Listed: Hong Kong **Dealings:** Daily
Fund Sedol I.D.: 607801 **Published:** FT/SC/IHT/HKET/HKEJ/JEP
Fees **Annual fee:** 1.75% **Performance fee:** None
Front end load: 5.00% **Redemption fee:** None
Switching fee: None

Contact: David Johnson
Performance:

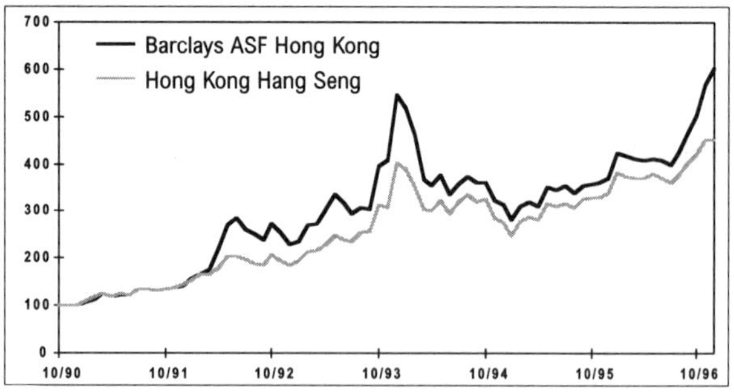

Top holdings:

Cheung Kong Holdings Ltd	6.0%
China Resources Enterprises	7.0%
Great Eagle Holdings	5.4%
Hang Seng Bank	4.7%
Henderson Land Development	6.5%
HSBC Holdings	7.1%
Hutchison Whampoa	6.3%
Lai Sun Development	4.9%
Shanghai Industrial	4.3%
SHK Properties	5.0%

TOTAL RETURNS %

3 months 1997	1996	1995	1994	3 years	5 years
0.88	61.98	19.02	-42.66	10.55	328.44

STATISTICS

Assets ($mil)	Current yield	Volatility	Risk return	Micropal Star Rating
11.86	—	7.41	—	✪✪

Baring IUF Hong Kong

60/350

Baring International Fund Managers (Ireland) Ltd
155 Bishopsgate, London EC2M 3XY, United Kingdom
Tel 44-171-628-6000 Fax 44-171-638-7928

Investment objective:
The primary objective of this sub-fund is to achieve long-term capital growth in the value of assets through investment in Hong Kong. The sector breakdown of investments at this time are as follows: property (35.5%); conglomerates (27.4%); finance (16.1%); commercial/industrial (13.9%); utilities (5.5%); and cash (1.6%).

Umbrella fund: Baring International Umbrella Fund
Launch date: 03/12/82 **Domicile:** Ireland
Currency: USD **Structure:** Open ended, Unit Trust
Portfolio manager: Sam Lau
Manager of the Baring Hong Kong Fund; 6 years investment experience; 4 years with Barings; previously with Sanwa Bank (HK), as an analyst; graduate – U of Hong Kong; specialises in the Pacific region and PRC companies.
Purchase: Direct, Financial Advisor
Minimum investment: 5,000 USD
Custodian: Baring Brothers (Ireland) LTD
Listed: Dublin **Dealings:** Daily
Fund Sedol I.D.: 42031 **Published:** RT/FT/SC/HKE
Fees **Annual fee:** 1.25% **Performance fee:** None
Front end load: 5.00% **Redemption fee:** None
Switching fee: None

Contact: Customer Services Department
Performance:

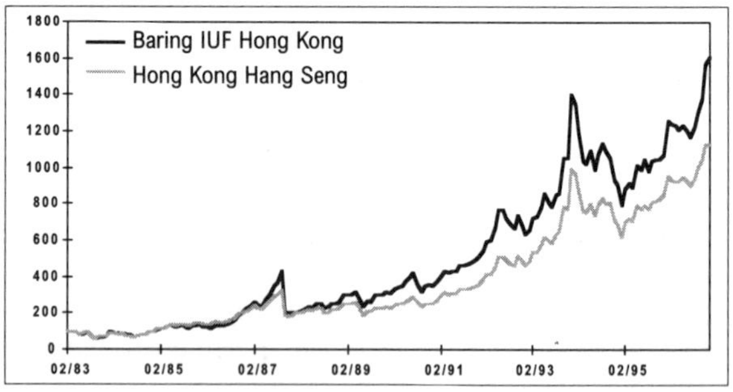

Top holdings:

Cheung Kong	4.9%
Cheung Kong Infra	2.9%
China Resources Enterprises	2.9%
Citic Pacific	3.9%
HSBC Holdings	7.1%
Hutchison Whampoa	7.8%
New World Development	5.7%
Sun Hung Kai Properties	7.2%
Swire Pacific "A"	2.8%

TOTAL RETURNS %

3 months 1997	1996	1995	1994	3 years	5 years
-5.55	49.58	18.11	-35.49	13.96	214.27

STATISTICS

Assets ($mil)	Current yield	Volatility	Risk return	Micropal Star Rating
69.76	—	7.31	—	✪✪

Baring WUF Tristar Warrant
14/350

Baring International Fund Managers (Ireland) Ltd
155 Bishopgate, London EC2M 3XY, United Kingdom
Tel 44-171-628-6000 Fax 44-171-628-7928

Investment objective:
This sub-fund seeks to achieve long-term growth in dollar terms, by investing in equity warrants issued by companies in the Asia Pacific region. At present this portfolio is allocated in the following countries: Hong Kong (71.1%); Malaysia (17.8%); Singapore (5.7%); Korea (0.3%); and with 5.1% held in cash.

Umbrella fund: Baring Warrant Umbrella Fund
Launch date: 24/07/89 **Domicile:** Ireland
Currency: USD **Structure:** Open ended, Unit Trust
Portfolio manager: John Payne CA
Manager of the fund; BA, business studies- Massey U-New Zealand; accountant; previously with INVESCO MIM as Fund Manager specialising in Asian equity markets and Australia; 11 years investment experience; 4 years with Barings.
Purchase: Direct, Financial Advisor
Minimum investment: 5,000 USD
Custodian: Baring Brothers (Ireland)Ltd
Listed: Dublin **Dealings:** Daily
Fund Sedol I.D.: 207782 **Published:** RT/FT/SC/HKE
Fees **Annual fee:** 1.50% **Performance fee:** None
Front end load: 5 .00% **Redemption fee:** None
Switching fee: None

Contact: Customer Services Department
Performance:

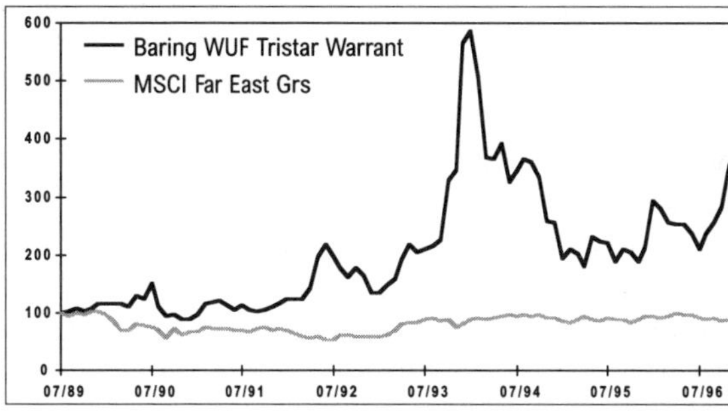

Top holdings:

Holding	%
BZW-HSBC Wts 03.10.97	4.1%
BZW-New World Developments Wts 10.97	4.6%
BZW-Sime Darby Wts 97	4.1%
Gamuda Wts 17.01.2000	4.4%
Hysan Dev Wts 98	4.8%
Peregrine Henderson Land Wts 27.11.97	5.5%
RF-Cheung Kong Wts 97	6.8%
RF-Hutchison Whampoa Wts 19.11.97	5.3%
RF-New World Dev Wts 97	7.1%
UBS-Citic Pacific Wts 97	5.8%

TOTAL RETURNS %

3 months 1997	1996	1995	1994	3 years	5 years
-22.57	78.85	-17.06	-54.92	-33.14	223.67

STATISTICS

Assets ($mil)	Current yield	Volatility	Risk return	Micropal Star Rating
15.24	—	13.78	—	✪✪✪

BBL Renta Fund Lira C
337/350

Banque Brussels Lambert
24 Avenue Marnix, Brussels, 1000, Belgium
Tel 32-27-386-776 Fax 32-27-386-376

Investment objective:
The primary objective of this fund is aimed at income growth through investment mainly in bonds denominated in Italian liras. At this time 96.6% of the asset allocation of this portfolio is held in bonds. The top country allocations of the portfolio include Italy (39.0%) and Germany (26.0%).

Umbrella fund: This is a singular fund.
Launch date: 31/03/94 **Domicile:** Luxembourg
Currency: ITL **Structure:** Open ended, SICAV
Portfolio manager: BBL (Bank Brussels Lambert)
Advisor to Bank Brussels Lambert Renta Lira; located at 24 Avenue Marnix, Brussels.

Purchase: Direct
Minimum investment: 1 Share
Custodian: Banque Brussels Lambert
Listed: None **Dealings:** Daily
Fund Sedol I.D.: 301776 **Published:** FT/IHT/SC
Fees **Annual fee:** 0.48% **Performance fee:** None
Front end load: None **Redemption fee:** None
Switching fee: None

Contact: Customer Services Department
Performance:

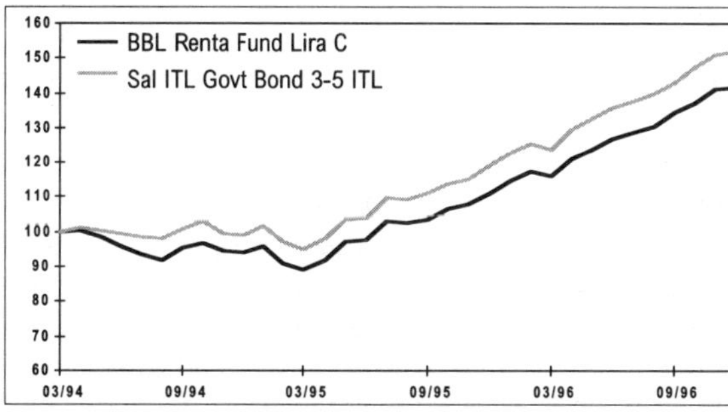

Top holdings:

Holding	%
Abbey National 10.7-97	3.7%
Bayeris Ver Bank 12%-97	5.0%
BTP 10.5% -3/05	10.6%
BTP 10.5% -4/05	16.0%
BTP 8.5% -2/06	4.0%
LKB Baden Nort 8-97	9.9%
Nordic Invest Bank 10.8%-03	10.6%
Rabobank 11.5 -97	2.5%
Swedish EXE Credit 11.7 -98	4.9%
Westo Landesbank 8%-03	10.6%

TOTAL RETURNS %

3 months 1997	1996	1995	1994	3 years	5 years
-9.17	27.35	18.20	N.A.	N.A.	N.A.

STATISTICS

Assets ($mil)	Current yield	Volatility	Risk return	Micropal Star Rating
20.98	—	N.A.	—	———

Brazilian Investment Company
113/350

F&C Emerging Markets Limited
Exchange House, Primrose Street, London EC2A 2NY, United Kingdom
Tel 44-171-628-1234 Fax 44-171-628-2283

Investment objective:
The fund seeks long-term capital appreciation and to be fully invested at all times. The fund provides investors resident outside of Brazil with an opportunity to participate in equities listed on Brazilian Stock Exchanges or acquired on other regulated markets organized by institutions and authorised by the Brazilian Securities and Exchange Commission.

Umbrella fund: This is a singular fund.

Launch date: 12/09/87 **Domicile:** Luxembourg [UCITS]

Currency: USD **Structure:** Open ended, SICAV

Portfolio manager: Josephine Ragni
Manager of the fund of Brazilian and Peru portfolios; read law/language- U of Buenos Aires; MSc, London School of Economics; joined Latin Am securities in 1993; manager of the fund since 1996.

Purchase: Direct, Financial Advisor, State Street Bank Luxembourg

Minimum investment: 5,000 USD

Custodian: State Street Bank (Lux) S.A.

Listed: None **Dealings:** Daily

Fund Sedol I.D.: 412111 **Published:** FT/IHT

Fees **Annual fee:** 2.50% **Performance fee:** None
Front end load: 5.00% **Redemption fee:** 0.50%
Switching fee: 5.50%

Contact: Jane Davies

Performance:

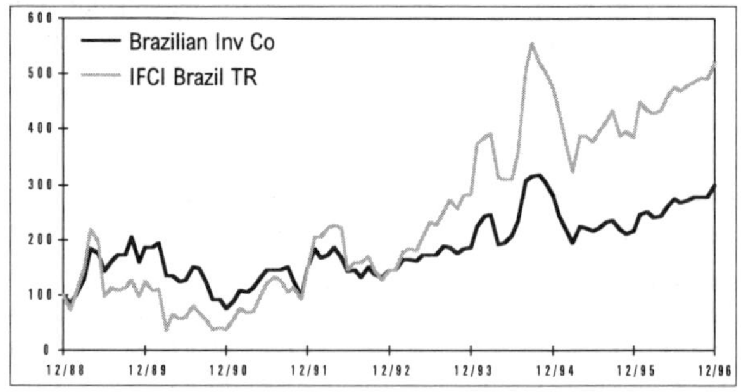

Top holdings:

Electrobas	10.1%
Petrobas	10.0%
Telebras	9.4%
Telee De Minas	4.7%
Telesp	9.6%

TOTAL RETURNS %

3 months 1997	1996	1995	1994	3 years	5 years
19.26	39.84	-23.80	50.91	60.81	104.15

STATISTICS

Assets ($mil)	Current yield	Volatility	Risk return	Micropal Star Rating
58.90	—	9.59	2	✪✪

BT GAF Latin American Equity
261/350

Bankers Trust Fund Managers Ireland Limited
80 Harcourt Street, Dublin 2, Ireland
Tel 353-1-790-2423 Fax 353-1-790-2410

Investment objective:
The primary objective of this fund is to achieve long-term growth through investment in the equity securities of companies domiciled in or doing business in Latin America that have the potential for above average growth in earnings. The top sectors of the portfolio are communications (17.6%); food/beverage (16.5%); industrials (16.3%); and electrical (10.9%).

Umbrella fund: BT Global Assets Funds

Launch date: 27/09/93 **Domicile:** Ireland [UCITS]

Currency: USD **Structure:** Open ended, Unit Trust

Portfolio manager: Maria-Elenar Carrion CFA and Emily Alejos CFA -Ms Carrion VP, Head of Latin Am Equities at Bankers Trust; previously with Latin Am Securities-London; MBA- Columbia U. Ms Alejos VP Portfolio Mgr; experienced with food/beverage/financial companies and Latin Am;; MBA- Stanford U; both joined BT in 1993.

Purchase: Financial Advisor, Banks or Brokers

Minimum investment: 10,000 USD

Custodian: BT Trustee Company

Listed: None **Dealings:** Daily

Fund Sedol I.D.: 8815 **Published:** FT

Fees **Annual fee:** 1.00% **Performance fee:** None
Front end load: 5.00% **Redemption fee:** None
Switching fee: None

Contact: Christina Frahm

Performance:

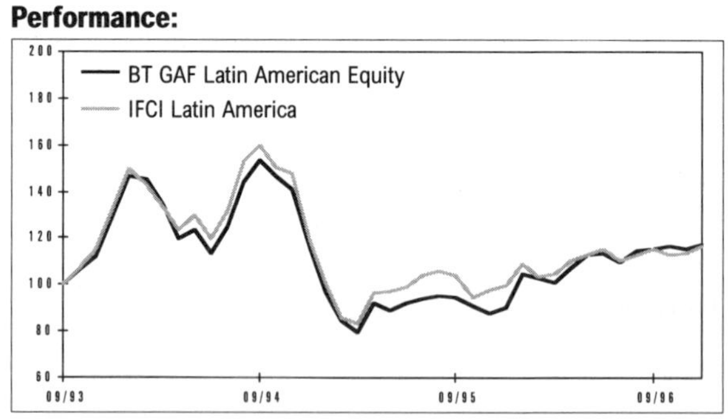

Top holdings:

Cemex	4.5%
Corp. San Luis	4.8%
CVRD	5.1%
Electrobas	6.4%
Fomento Economico	3.6%
Gruma	3.4%
Grupo Televisa	3.6%
Mavesa	3.7%
Petrobas	5.9%
Telebras	6.8%

TOTAL RETURNS %

3 months 1997	1996	1995	1994	3 years	5 years
14.13	30.07	-22.72	-9.99	-9.53	N.A.

STATISTICS

Assets ($mil)	Current yield	Volatility	Risk return	Micropal Star Rating
72.93	—	8.00	—	✪✪

BT IIS European Growth
98/350

Bankers Trust Fund Managers Ireland Limited
80 Harcourt Street, Dublin 2, Ireland
Tel 353-1-790-2400 Fax 353-1-790-2410

Investment objective:
The fund seeks long-term growth through investments in Western European stock markets. The fund invests in the equity securities of companies doing business in Germany, Netherlands, Switzerland, France, Sweden, UK, Italy and possibly other counties that are believed to be undervalued and have potential for significant earnings growth.

Umbrella fund: BT International Investment Series

Launch date: 02/11/92 **Domicile:** Ireland [UCITS]

Currency: USD **Structure:** Open ended, Unit Trust

Portfolio manager: Chris Selth
Manager of Bankers Trust IIS European Growth, Executive VP and Head of European Equities; BA Hons, economics- Sydney, Australia; previously with QBE, as assistant to the group Treasurer; joined Bankers Trust in 1987. 12 years experience.

Purchase: Financial Advisor, Banks or Brokers

Minimum investment: 10,000 USD

Custodian: BT Trustee Company

Listed: Dublin **Dealings:** Daily

Fund Sedol I.D.: 7157 **Published:** FT

Fees **Annual fee:** up to 2.00% **Performance fee:** None
Front end load: 5.00% **Redemption fee:** None
Switching fee: None

Contact: Christina Frahm

Performance:

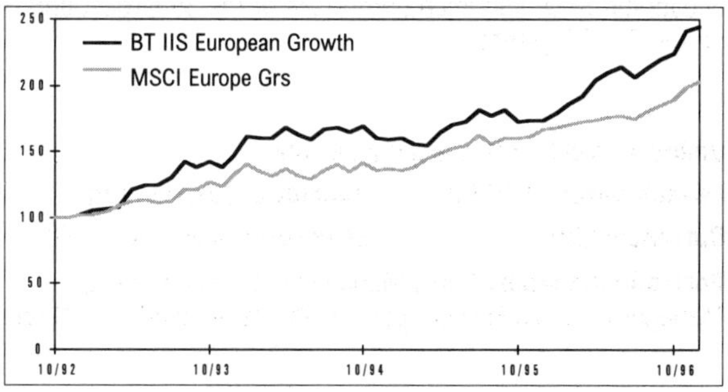

Top holdings:

Daimler Benz	1.3%
Elf Aquitaine	1.9%
Lagardere SCA	1.9%
Nordbanken	1.7%
Philips Electronics	1.4%
Prosegur Comp Seguridad	1.5%
Rolls Royce	1.8%
Stadshypotek A	1.4%
Vendex International	1.4%
Vodafone Group	1.3%

TOTAL RETURNS %

3 months 1997	1996	1995	1994	3 years	5 years
10.03	41.01	9.36	8.49	67.31	N.A.

STATISTICS

Assets ($mil)	Current yield	Volatility	Risk return	Micropal Star Rating
38.29	—	4.18	4	✪✪✪✪

Buchanan European & Atlantic
254/350

Buchanan Partners Ltd
6 Front Street, Hamilton, HM11, Bermuda
Tel 1-441-295-4000 Fax 1-441-295-6180

Investment objective:
The sub-fund seeks achievement of capital gains and appreciation in capital value in securities and derivatives of issuers domiciled, operating or traded on exchanges or over-the-counter markets in Europe, the Americas or which provide an exposure generally to these markets.

Umbrella fund: Buchanan Fund Ltd

Launch date: 29/05/92 **Domicile:** Bermuda

Currency: USD **Structure:** Open ended, Investment Company

Portfolio manager: Buchanan Team
Hon. Moncreiffe: MA, past MD of EF Hutton & Co- international capital market activities; Mr Hathorn: formerly with Prudential Portfolio Managers & Hill Samuel Investment Management; Mr Webb, CFA; Mr Cheung, CFA: formerly with KPMG.

Purchase: Financial Advisor

Minimum investment: 150,000 USD

Custodian: Bank of Bermuda

Listed: Dublin **Dealings:** Monthly

Fund Sedol I.D.: 214974 **Published:** FT/IHT/SC

Fees **Annual fee:** 2.00% **Performance fee:** 20.00%
Front end load: None **Redemption fee:** None
Switching fee: None

Contact: Adrian Collins

Performance:

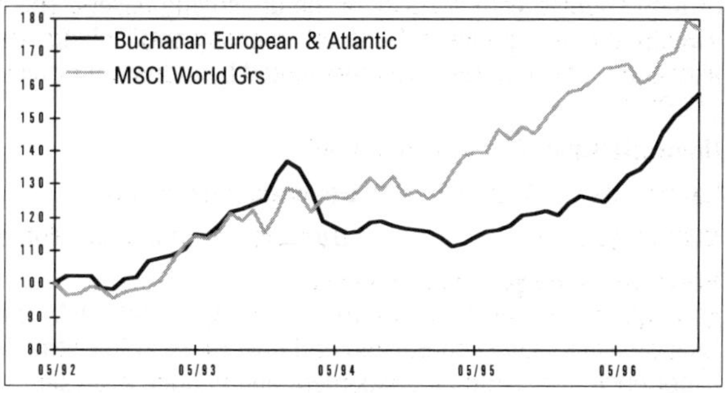

Top holdings:

Brazil C Bond 2014	5.4%
Brazil EIB 2006 - short	7.6%
Bulgaria Discha 2024	5.8%
Cardinal Health - short	3.7%
Federated Department - short	4.0%
Forajon Foramer	3.9%
GKO RER Note 53	3.9%
Owen Healthcare	3.4%
Russia MOF 2011 - short	12.6%
UAP	10.2%

TOTAL RETURNS %

3 months 1997	1996	1995	1994	3 years	5 years
6.79	30.36	3.96	-12.62	18.41	N.A.

STATISTICS

Assets ($mil)	Current yield	Volatility	Risk return	Micropal Star Rating
39.20	—	2.37	1	✪✪

Caixa Funds Spanish Shares
204/350

Societe Monegasque de Banque Privee
9 Boulevard d'Italie, 98000, Monaco
Tel 33-93-15-23-23 Fax 33-93-50-14-30

Investment objective:
The fund seeks capital appreciation by investing in the stocks of the Bourse Espagnole IBEX 35 which comprises of the 35 largest and most liquid stocks traded on the CATS System.

Umbrella fund: This is a singular fund.
Launch date: 19/10/92 **Domicile:** Luxembourg
Currency: ESP **Structure:** Open ended, SICAV
Portfolio manager: Caixa Management (Luxembourg)
Manager of Caixa Funds Spanish Shares; located at 2, Boulevard Royal, Luxembourg.

Contact: Josette Lellouche
Performance:

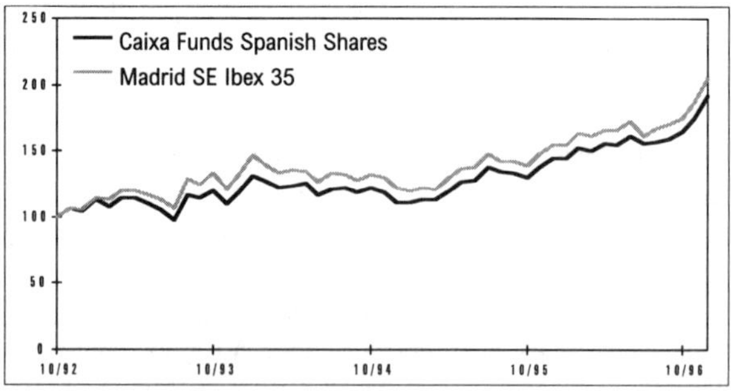

Purchase: Direct
Minimum investment: 50,000 ESP
Custodian: Banque Internationale a Luxembourg
Listed: None **Dealings:** Weekly
Fund Sedol I.D.: 300089 **Published:** FT/IHT/SC
Fees **Annual fee:** 1.50% **Performance fee:** None
Front end load: 1.50% **Redemption fee:** None
Switching fee: None

Top holdings:

Holding	%
Autriche 6.30% Bond	12.2%
Banco Bilbao Vizcaya	2.9%
Banco de Santander	3.1%
Banco Popular Esp	1.9%
E.I.B 6.22% Bond	14.5%
Empresa Nacion Endesa	5.4%
Gas Natural	2.9%
Iberdrola	4.2%
Repsol	3.9%
Telefonica de Espana	7.4%

TOTAL RETURNS %

3 months 1997	1996	1995	1994	3 years	5 years
-5.04	32.62	29.84	-6.50	61.00	N.A.

STATISTICS

Assets ($mil)	Current yield	Volatility	Risk return	Micropal Star Rating
10.56	—	4.15	4	✪✪✪

Carlson Fund Equity Nordic
134/350

Carlson Investment Management
PO Box 70379, Stockholm, S-10724, Sweden
Tel 46-8-700-6376 Fax 46-8-700-0019

Investment objective:
The main objective of this equity sub-fund is the realisation of long-term capital growth coupled with security of the underlying assets. This is accomplished through investments in equities in Denmark, Norway and Finland. The top two portfolio sector allocations for this fund are represented by industrial cyclical (31.0%) and services (17.0%).
Umbrella fund: Carlson Fund Equities
Launch date: 31/08/90 **Domicile:** Luxembourg
Currency: USD **Structure:** Open ended, Mutual Fund
Portfolio manager: Hans Johnsson
Manager of the sub-fund commenced in April 1994; BA- U of Lund; previously with Skandinaviska Enskilda Banken and now Carlson Investment Management; 7 years experience in portfolio management and finance analysis.

Contact: Hans Johnsson
Performance:

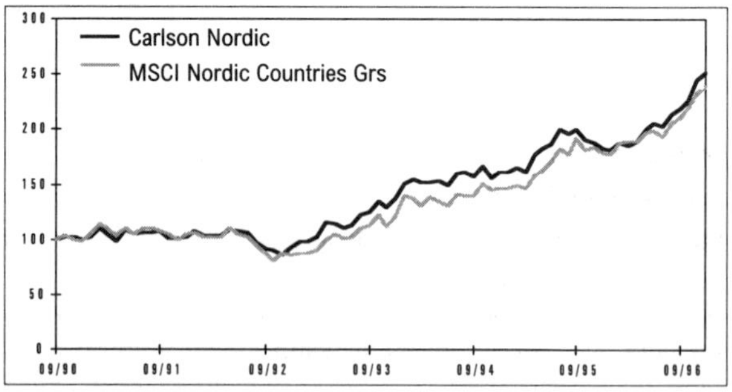

Purchase: Direct
Minimum investment: 5,000 USD
Custodian: Banque Indosuez
Listed: None **Dealings:** Weekly
Fund Sedol I.D.: 417534 **Published:** RT
Fees **Annual fee:** 1.25% **Performance fee:** None
Front end load: 5.00% **Redemption fee:** None
Switching fee: None

Top holdings:

Holding	%
Asko	4.2%
Bang Olufsen	4.0%
Merkantil Data	4.8%
Nokin	9.9%
Norsk Hydro As	7.6%
Norske Skogsind	4.6%
Orkla Ind	4.1%
Sampo	3.8%
Tele Denmark	6.2%
UPM Kymmene	3.8%

TOTAL RETURNS %

3 months 1997	1996	1995	1994	3 years	5 years
6.54	37.39	13.60	17.64	83.60	146.35

STATISTICS

Assets ($mil)	Current yield	Volatility	Risk return	Micropal Star Rating
6.46	—	4.00	4	✪✪✪

Carlson Fund Equity Sweden

156/350

Carlson Investment Management
6b route De Treves, Senningerberg, L-2633 Luxembourg
Tel 352-34-13-01 Fax 352-34-13-06

Investment objective:
The main objective of this equity sub-fund is the realisation of long-term capital growth coupled with security of the underlying assets. This is accomplished through investment in mainly blue chip Swedish companies. The top two portfolio sector allocations for this fund are represented by finance (18.0%) and technology (18.0%).

Umbrella fund: Carlson Fund Equities
Launch date: 31/08/90 **Domicile:** Luxembourg
Currency: SEK **Structure:** Open ended, Mutual Fund
Portfolio manager: Per Marinelle
Manager of this sub-fund since October 1995; MSc-KTH, Stockholm; 4 years experience in financial analysis and portfolio management at Carlson Investment Management.
Purchase: Direct
Minimum investment: 5,000 USD
Custodian: Banque Indosuez
Listed: None **Dealings:** Weekly
Fund Sedol I.D.: 417535 **Published:** RT
Fees **Annual fee:** 1.25% **Performance fee:** None
Front end load: 5.00% **Redemption fee:** None
Switching fee: None

Contact: Mrs Asa Hellsten

Performance:

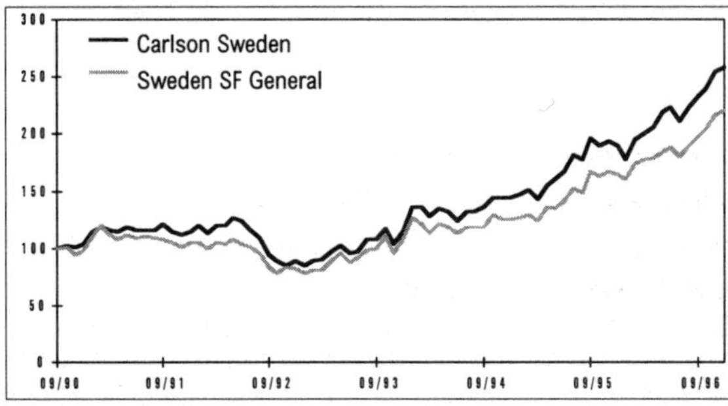

Top holdings:

Holding	%
Astra	9.0%
Autoliv	4.0%
Carlson Smabolag	5.0%
Ericsson	9.2%
Handelsbanken	4.2%
Scania	4.1%
SE Banken	4.7%
Skandia	3.9%
Stora Kopparberg	4.3%
WM Data	4.3%

TOTAL RETURNS %

3 months 1997	1996	1995	1994	3 years	5 years
1.11	35.83	31.92	25.97	125.72	126.57

STATISTICS

Assets ($mil)	Current yield	Volatility	Risk return	Micropal Star Rating
9.22	—	5.32	4	✪✪✪✪

CIBC-CEF Hong Kong Warrant

1/350

CEF Investment Management (Bermuda) Ltd
2nd Floor China Building, 29 Queens Road, Central, Hong Kong
Tel 852-2846-3688 Fax 852-2846-0634

Investment objective:
The stellar fund seeks capital appreciation by investing in the warrants of equity based companies. 100% of the portfolio's assets are country allocated to Hong Kong.

Umbrella fund: This is a singular fund.
Launch date: 15/08/88 **Domicile:** Bermuda
Currency: USD **Structure:** Open ended, Unit Trust
Portfolio manager: Peter Chau
Manager of the fund; Deputy Managing Director of CEF Investment Mgt Ltd; BA, mathematics- U of Waterloo; previously with Orion Royal Pacific Ltd and BNP Intl Fin. Services as a senior trader; 16 years in the finance industry; 10 years at CEF.
Purchase: Direct, Financial Advisor
Minimum investment: 3,000 USD
Custodian: The Bank of Butterfield Executor & Trustee Co
Listed: None **Dealings:** Daily
Fund Sedol I.D.: 615981 **Published:** SC/HKE
Fees **Annual fee:** 2.50% **Performance fee:** None
Front end load: 5.00% **Redemption fee:** 0.50%
Switching fee: 2.00%

Contact: Mr D. Chan

Performance:

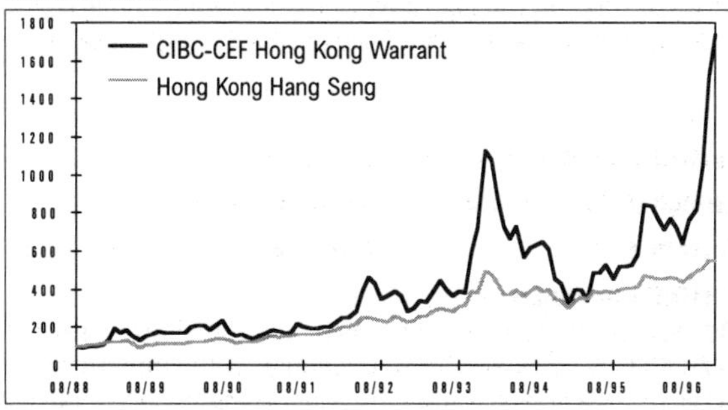

Top holdings:

Holding	%
Cheung Fong Wts 97	n/s
Cheung Kong Infrastructure Wts 97	n/s
Guangzhou Inv Wts 97	n/s
Hanny Hlds Wts 97	n/s
HSBC Wts 03.10.97	n/s
Hutchison Whampoa Wts 97	n/s
Hysan Dev Wts 98	n/s
Pacific Plywood Hlds Wts 98	n/s
Shanghai Ind. Wts 97	n/s
UBS-Cosco Pacific Wts 97	n/s

TOTAL RETURNS %

3 months 1997	1996	1995	1994	3 years	5 years
4.07	195.29	36.89	-62.03	53.50	766.19

STATISTICS

Assets ($mil)	Current yield	Volatility	Risk return	Micropal Star Rating
5.00	—	17.56	3	✪✪✪

CIBC-CEF Malaysia
221/350

CEF Investment Management (Bermuda) Ltd
2nd Floor China Building, 29 Queens Road, Central, Hong Kong
Tel 852-2846-3688 Fax 852-2846-0634

Investment objective:
The primary objective of the fund is to seek long-term capital growth. At present the portfolio allocates 83.0% of the assets to Malaysia.

Contact: Mr D Chan

Performance:

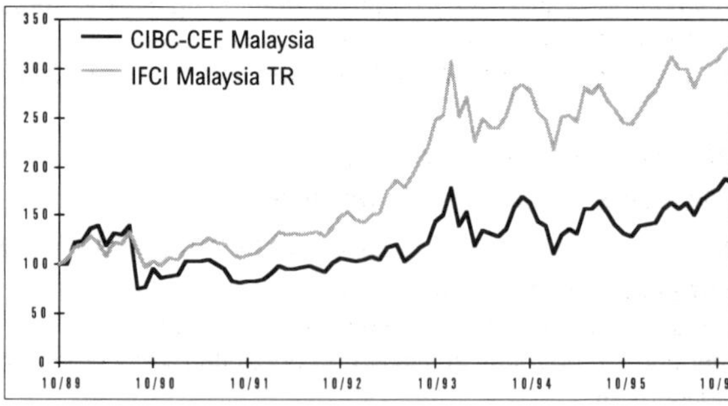

Umbrella fund: This is a singular fund.

Launch date: 16/10/89 **Domicile:** Bermuda

Currency: USD **Structure:** Open ended, Unit Trust

Portfolio manager: Teng Jee Hum
Manager of the fund since May 1995 and Executive Director responsible for investments in SE Asia and the Indian sub-continent; B of business admin- Singapore U; formerly with Merrill Lynch and Commodities Corporation; 14 years in the investment industry.

Purchase: Direct, Financial Advisor

Minimum investment: 3,000 USD

Custodian: The Bank of Butterfield Executor & Trustee Co

Listed: None **Dealings:** Daily

Fund Sedol I.D.: 615984 **Published:** SC/HKE

Fees **Annual fee:** 2.50% **Performance fee:** None
Front end load: 5.00% **Redemption fee:** 1.50%
Switching fee: 2.00%

Top holdings:

Angkasa Marketing	n/s
Cahya Mata Sarawak	n/s
Kelang Container Terminal	n/s
Landmarks Hlds	n/s
Malaysian Industrial Dev Finance	n/s
MBF Capital	n/s
MTD Capital	n/s
Sunway Building Technology	n/s
Tan Chong Motor	n/s
Time Engineering	n/s

TOTAL RETURNS %

3 months 1997	1996	1995	1994	3 years	5 years
21.87	31.51	-0.68	-21.81	2.13	115.73

STATISTICS

Assets ($mil)	Current yield	Volatility	Risk return	Micropal Star Rating
1.40	—	9.95	—	✪✪✪✪

CIBC-CEF Pacific Venture
6/350

CEF Investment Management (Bermuda) Ltd
2nd Floor China Building, 29 Queens Road, Central, Hong Kong
Tel 852-2846-3688 Fax 852-2846-0634

Investment objective:
The primary objective of the fund is to seek long-term capital growth. At present the portfolio's assets are allocated to the following countries: Hong Kong (81.0%); China (6.0%); Philippines (4.6%); Taiwan (4.4%); and Malaysia (2.0%).

Contact: Mr D Chan

Performance:

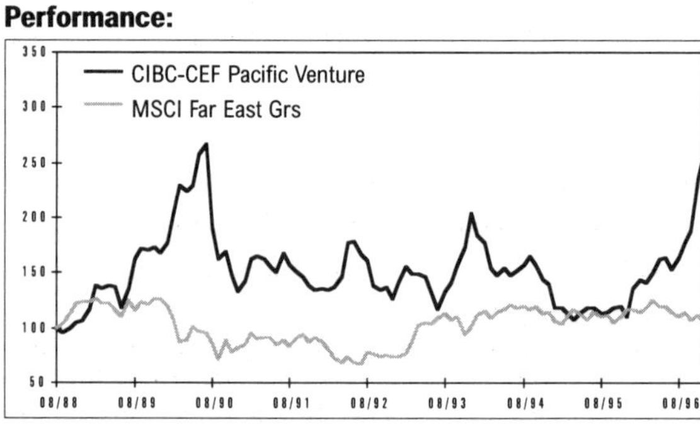

Umbrella fund: This is a singular fund.

Launch date: 02/08/88 **Domicile:** Bermuda

Currency: USD **Structure:** Open ended, Unit Trust

Portfolio manager: Peter Chau
Manager of the fund; Deputy Managing Director of CEF Investment Mgt Ltd; BA, mathematics- U of Waterloo; previously with Orion Royal Pacific Ltd and BNP Intl Fin. Services as a senior trader; 16 years in the finance industry; 10 years at CEF.

Purchase: Direct, Financial Advisor

Minimum investment: 3,000 USD

Custodian: The Bank of Butterfield Executor & Trustee Co

Listed: None **Dealings:** Daily

Fund Sedol I.D.: 615989 **Published:** SC/HKE

Fees **Annual fee:** 2.50% **Performance fee:** None
Front end load: 5.00% **Redemption fee:** 1.10%
Switching fee: 2.00%

Top holdings:

Anhui Express Way	n/s
China Resources	n/s
First Sign Intl	n/s
Goldlion	n/s
Hanny Holdings	n/s
Pacific Plywood	n/s
Pacific Plywood Hlds	n/s
Peregrine - Cheung Kong Infra Wts 97	n/s
Shanghai Industrial	n/s
Triplenic	n/s

TOTAL RETURNS %

3 months 1997	1996	1995	1994	3 years	5 years
42.51	133.33	-20.65	-31.42	26.99	92.62

STATISTICS

Assets ($mil)	Current yield	Volatility	Risk return	Micropal Star Rating
1.50	—	8.18	2	✪✪✪✪

CMI GNF Benelux Equity
275/350

CMI Asset Management (Lux) SA
166 Route d'Arlon, Strassen, L-8010 Luxembourg
Tel 352-317-831-1 Fax 352-317-831-500

Contact: Simon Friend

Investment objective:
The sub-fund aims to provide capital growth opportunities principally from investment in equity or equity related securities in Belgium, the Netherlands and Luxembourg. The sub-fund is denominated in Dutch guilders.

Umbrella fund: Universe-The CMI Global Network Fund
Launch date: 01/06/90 **Domicile:** Luxembourg [UCITS]
Currency: NLG **Structure:** Open ended, SICAV
Portfolio manager: Suez Nederland Asset Management
Fund Advisor to Clerical Medical International Global Network Fund Benelux Equity; located in Amsterdam, Holland.

Purchase: Direct, Financial Advisor
Minimum investment: 3,000 GBP
Custodian: Chase Manhattan Bank (Lux) S.A
Listed: Luxembourg **Dealings:** Daily
Fund Sedol I.D.: 415998 **Published:** FT
Fees **Annual fee:** 1.25% **Performance fee:** None
Front end load: Up to 2.00% **Redemption fee:** None
Switching fee: None

Performance:

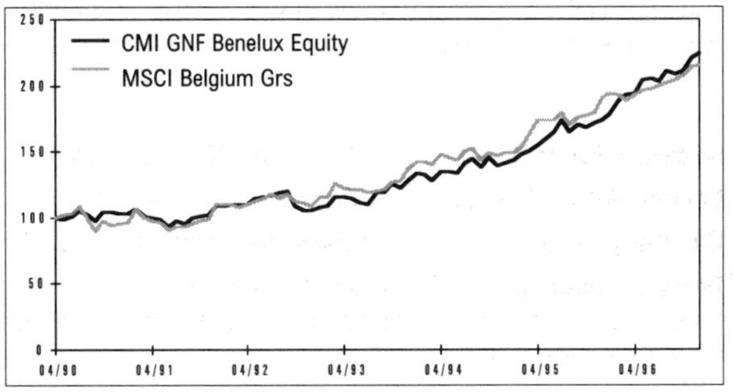

Top holdings:

ABN AMRO Holding	4.8%
Elsevier	3.7%
GIST Brocades	4.0%
ING Groep	4.9%
KNP	4.1%
Oce VDR Grinten	4.8%
Philips Electronics	4.0%
Royal Dutch Petroleum	5.4%
Stork	3.9%
Unilever	4.4%

TOTAL RETURNS %

3 months 1997	1996	1995	1994	3 years	5 years
5.65	29.27	22.76	10.49	75.35	106.28

STATISTICS

Assets ($mil)	Current yield	Volatility	Risk return	Micropal Star Rating
8.15	0.45	3.00	3	✪✪✪

CMI GNF Canadian Equity
318/350

CMI Asset Management (Lux) SA
166 Route d'Arlon, Strassen, L-8010 Luxembourg
Tel 352-317-831-1 Fax 352-317-831-500

Contact: Simon Friend

Investment objective:
The sub-fund seeks to provide capital growth opportunities principally from investment in equity related securities in Canada. The sub-fund is denominated in Canadian dollars.

Umbrella fund: Universe-The CMI Global Network Fund
Launch date: 01/06/90 **Domicile:** Luxembourg [UCITS]
Currency: CAD **Structure:** Open ended, SICAV
Portfolio manager: Jarislowsky, Fraser & Company
Fund Advisor to Clerical Medical International Global Network Fund Canadian Equity; located in Toronto, Canada.

Purchase: Direct, Financial Advisor
Minimum investment: 3,000 GBP
Custodian: Chase Manhattan Bank (Lux) S.A
Listed: Luxembourg **Dealings:** Daily
Fund Sedol I.D.: 415989 **Published:** FT
Fees **Annual fee:** 1.25% **Performance fee:** None
Front end load: Up to 2.00% **Redemption fee:** None
Switching fee: None

Performance:

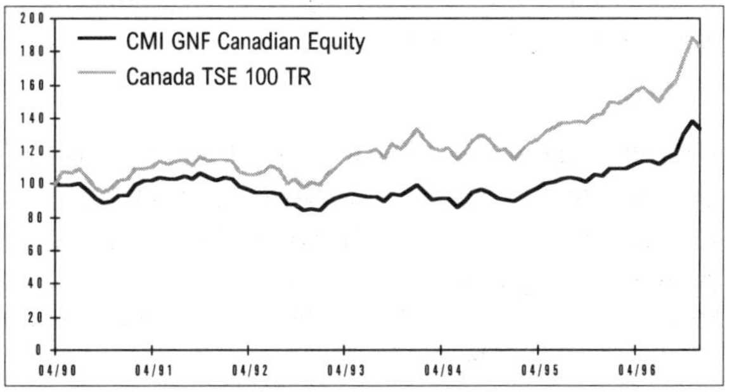

Top holdings:

Bank of Montreal	4.6%
Bombardier B	2.4%
Cdn Imp Bk Commerce	3.4%
Donohue CL A	2.6%
Imasco	2.4%
Northern Telecom	2.4%
Power Financial	2.3%
Royal Bank of Canada	5.7%
Seagram	3.2%
Shell Canada A	2.3%

TOTAL RETURNS %

3 months 1997	1996	1995	1994	3 years	5 years
4.44	27.93	15.71	-5.70	39.60	30.42

STATISTICS

Assets ($mil)	Current yield	Volatility	Risk return	Micropal Star Rating
3.33	—	3.37	4	✪✪✪

CMI GNF Greater China Equity
28/350

CMI Asset Management (Lux) SA
166 Route d'Arlon, Strassen, L-8010 Luxembourg
Tel 352-317-831-1 Fax 352-317-831-500

Investment objective:
The sub-fund aims to achieve capital growth through investment in Chinese equities and companies expected to grow in the Chinese economy. The sub-fund is denominated in US dollars.

Contact: Simon Friend

Performance:

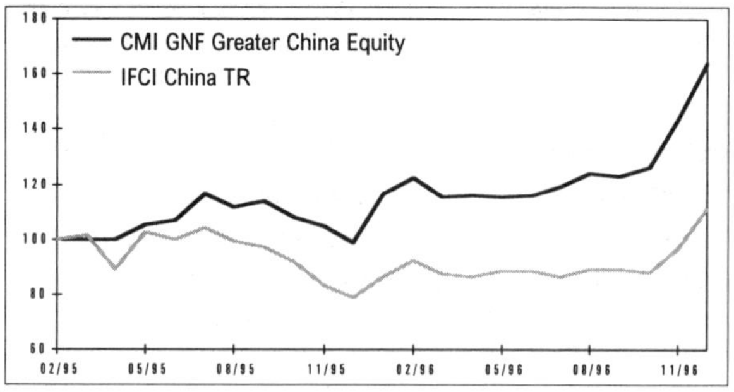

Umbrella fund: Universe-The CMI Global Network Fund
Launch date: 01/03/95 **Domicile:** Luxembourg [UCITS]
Currency: USD **Structure:** Open ended, SICAV
Portfolio manager: HSBC Asset Management
Fund Advisor to Clerical Medical International Global Network Fund Greater China Equity; located in Hong Kong.

Purchase: Direct, Financial Advisor
Minimum investment: 3,000 GBP
Custodian: Chase Manhattan Bank (Lux) S.A
Listed: Luxembourg **Dealings:** Daily
Fund Sedol I.D.: 423362 **Published:** FT
Fees **Annual fee:** 1.50% **Performance fee:** None
Front end load: Up to 2.00% **Redemption fee:** None
Switching fee: None

Top holdings:

Holding	%
China OS Land& Inv	6.4%
China Res Ent Rep	4.3%
Citic Pacific	3.9%
Eastern Comms B	3.4%
Guandong Kelon Elec.Hld	3.7%
New World Infrastructure	3.8%
NG Fung Kong Ltd	3.2%
Quingling Motors H Shares	3.5%
Shai Industrial	5.3%

TOTAL RETURNS %

3 months 1997	1996	1995	1994	3 years	5 years
6.64	65.82	N.A.	N.A.	N.A.	N.A.

STATISTICS

Assets ($mil)	Current yield	Volatility	Risk return	Micropal Star Rating
2.19	—	N.A.	—	———

CMI GNF Iberian Equity
122/350

CMI Asset Management (Lux) SA
166 Route d'Arlon, Strassen, L-8010 Luxembourg
Tel 352-317-831-1 Fax 352-317-831-500

Investment objective:
The sub-fund aims to provide capital growth opportunities principally from investment in equity, or equity related securities primarily in Spain. The sub-fund is denominated in Spanish peseta.

Contact: Simon Friend

Performance:

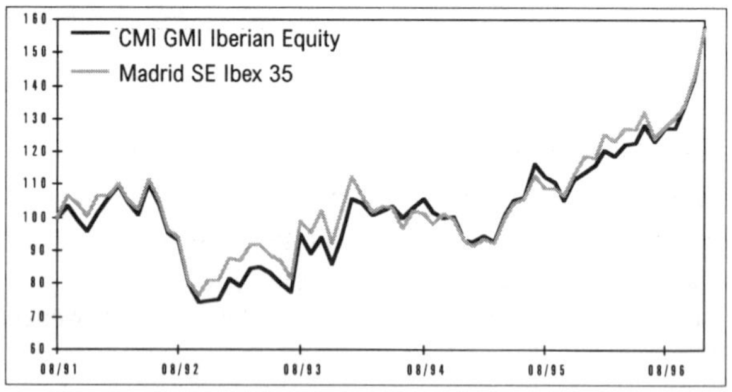

Umbrella fund: Universe-The CMI Global Network Fund
Launch date: 01/06/90 **Domicile:** Luxemboorg [UCITS]
Currency: ESP **Structure:** Open ended, SICAV
Portfolio manager: Beta Capital SA
Fund Advisor to Clerical Medical International Global Network Fund CMI GNF Iberian Equity; located in Madrid, Spain.

Purchase: Direct, Financial Advisor
Minimum investment: 3,000 GBP
Custodian: Chase Manhattan Bank (Lux) S.A
Listed: Luxembourg **Dealings:** Daily
Fund Sedol I.D.: 415995 **Published:** FT
Fees **Annual fee:** 1.25% **Performance fee:** None
Front end load: Up to 2.00% **Redemption fee:** None
Switching fee: None

Top holdings:

Holding	%
Bankinter R	6.1%
BNC Bilbao Vizcaya R	8.5%
BNC Santander R	8.5%
Corp Mapfre R	3.8%
Endesa	8.6%
Gas Natural SDG	3.8%
Inerdrola	4.8%
Puleva Unias	4.9%
Repsol	6.9%
Telefonica	9.3%

TOTAL RETURNS %

3 months 1997	1996	1995	1994	3 years	5 years
-0.98	38.64	21.90	-0.05	68.92	55.85

STATISTICS

Assets ($mil)	Current yield	Volatility	Risk return	Micropal Star Rating
4.18	0.20	4.51	3	✪✪✪✪

CMI GNF Nordic Equity
342/350

CMI Asset Management (Lux) SA
166 Route d'Arlon, Strassen, L-8010 Luxembourg
Tel 352-317-831-1 Fax 352-317-831-500

Investment objective:
The sub-fund aims to provide capital growth opportunities principally from investment in equity, or equity related securities in the Nordic countries. The sub-fund is denominated in Swedish krona.

Umbrella fund: Universe-The CMI Global Network Fund
Launch date: 01/06/90 **Domicile:** Luxembourg [UCITS]
Currency: SEK **Structure:** Open ended, SICAV
Portfolio manager: Nordbanken Asset Management
Fund Advisor to Clerical Medical International Global Network Fund Nordic Equity; located in Stockholm, Sweden.

Purchase: Direct, Financial Advisor
Minimum investment: 3,000 GBP
Custodian: Chase Manhattan Bank (Lux) S.A
Listed: Luxembourg **Dealings:** Daily
Fund Sedol I.D.: 415997 **Published:** FT
Fees **Annual fee:** 1.25% **Performance fee:** None
Front end load: Up to 2.00% **Redemption fee:** None
Switching fee: None

Contact: Simon Friend

Performance:

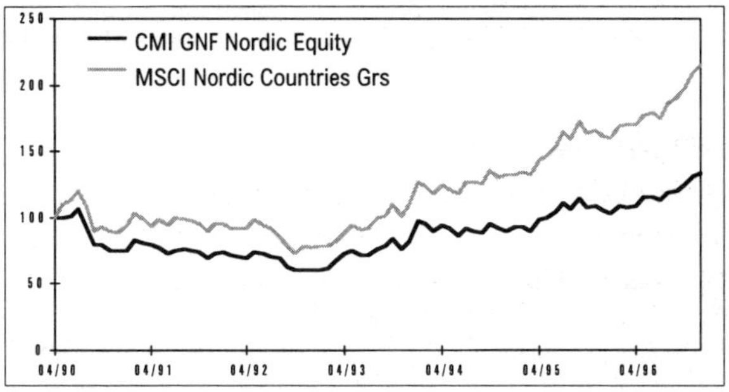

Top holdings:

Holding	%
ABB AB	2.8%
Astra AB-A	10.0%
Ericsson	8.1%
Hennes & Mauritz AB	3.5%
Nokia A	897.0%
Norsk Hydro As	3.2%
Novo-Nordiska As -B-	5.2%
Sophus Berendsen	2.8%
Stora Kopparberg	2.8%
Volvo	2.9%

TOTAL RETURNS %

3 months 1997	1996	1995	1994	3 years	5 years
5.96	27.21	16.50	10.09	63.16	82.13

STATISTICS

Assets ($mil)	Current yield	Volatility	Risk return	Micropal Star Rating
6.10	—	5.09	1	✪

CMI GNF UK Equity
344/350

CMI Asset Management (Lux) SA
166 Route d' Arlon, Strassen, L-8010 Luxembourg
Tel 352-317-831-1 Fax 352-317-831-500

Investment objective:
The sub-fund seeks to provide capital growth opportunities principally from investment in equity, or equity related securities in the United Kingdom. This sub-fund is denominated in UK sterling.

Umbrella fund: Universe-The CMI Global Network Fund
Launch date: 01/06/90 **Domicile:** Luxembourg [UCITS]
Currency: GBP **Structure:** Open ended, SICAV
Portfolio manager: CMI Asset Management
Manager of Clerical Medical International Global Network Fund ; located in London.

Purchase: Direct, Financial Advisor
Minimum investment: 3,000 GBP
Custodian: Chase Manhattan Bank (Lux) S.A
Listed: Luxembourg **Dealings:** Daily
Fund Sedol I.D.: 415987 **Published:** FT
Fees **Annual fee:** 1.25% **Performance fee:** None
Front end load: Up to 2.00% **Redemption fee:** None
Switching fee: None

Contact: Simon Friend

Performance:

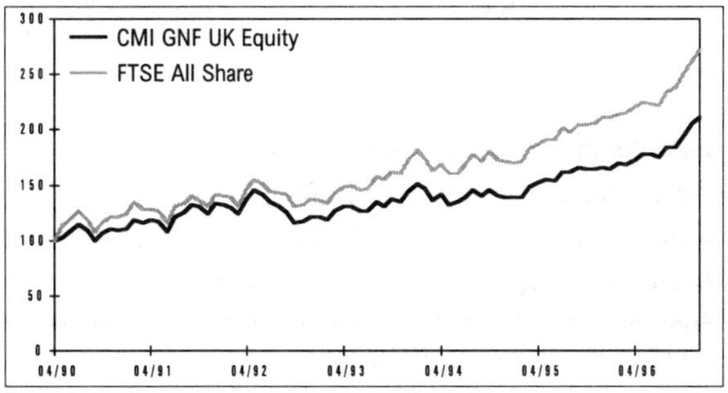

Top holdings:

Holding	%
Abbey National	3.0%
British Aerospace	3.0%
British Petroleum	4.5%
British Telecom	3.7%
Glaxo Wellcome	4.9%
HSBC Holdings	3.2%
Reuters Holdings	3.2%
Shell Transport & Trading	3.9%
Tesco	2.6%
Zeneca Group	3.6%

TOTAL RETURNS %

3 months 1997	1996	1995	1994	3 years	5 years
-0.36	27.19	19.65	-3.77	46.43	58.93

STATISTICS

Assets ($mil)	Current yield	Volatility	Risk return	Micropal Star Rating
51.83	1.81	3.30	3	✪✪

CMI Passport Benelux Equity
306/350

CMI Insurance Company Limited (Isle of Man)
Clerical Medical House, Victoria Road, Douglas IM99ILT,
Isle of Man
Tel 44-1624-638 888 Fax 44-1624-625-900

Contact: Customer Services Department

Investment objective:
The insurance sub-fund aims to provide capital growth opportunities principally from investment in equity or equity related securities in Belgium, the Netherlands and Luxembourg. The fund invests wholly via a fund-link into the CMI Global Network

Performance:

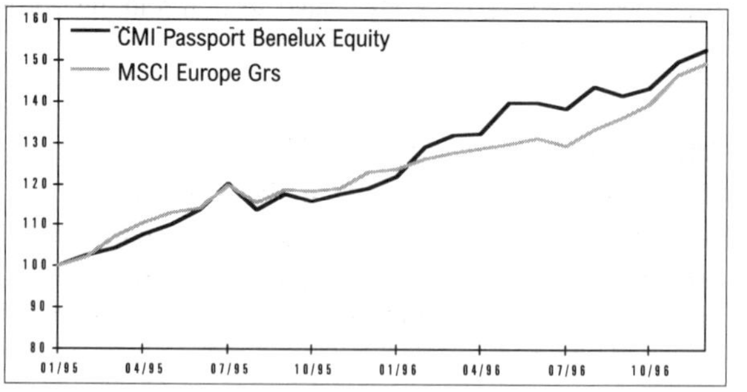

Umbrella fund: This is a singular fund.
Launch date: 16/01/95 **Domicile:** Isle of Man
Currency: NLG **Structure:** Open ended, Insurance Fund
Portfolio manager: Fund, Benelux Equity sub-fund.
Suez Nederland Asset Management
Fund Advisor to Clerical Medical International Global Network Fund Benelux Equity; located in Amsterdam, Holland.
Purchase: Through insurance products linked to this fund
Minimum investment: 7,500 GBP
Custodian: CMI Insurance Company Limited
Listed: None **Dealings:** Daily
Fund Sedol I.D.: 16944 **Published:** FT
Fees **Annual fee:** 1.25% **Performance fee:** None
Front end load: ILP **Redemption fee:** ILP
Switching fee: None

Top holdings:	
ABN AMRO Holding	4.8%
Elsevier	3.7%
Gist Brocades	4.0%
ING Groep	4.9%
KPN	4.1%
Oce VDR Grinten	4.8%
Philips Electronics	4.0%
Royal Dutch Petroleum	5.4%
Stork	3.9%
Unilever	4.4%

TOTAL RETURNS %

3 months 1997	1996	1995	1994	3 years	5 years
4.35	28.18	N.A.	N.A.	N.A.	N.A.

STATISTICS

Assets ($mil)	Current yield	Volatility	Risk return	Micropal Star Rating
0.17	—	N.A.	—	———

CMI Passport Greater China Eq
32/350

CMI Insurance Company Limited (Isle of Man)
Clerical Medical House, Victoria Road, Douglas IM99ILT,
Isle of Man
Tel 44-1624-638 888 Fax 44-1624-625-900

Contact: Customer Services Department

Investment objective:
The funds invests wholly into the Greater China Equity sub-fund of Universe, the Global Network Fund (Clerical Medical's Luxembourg Umbrella) which aims to achieve capital growth through Chinese Equities and companies exposed to the Chinese economy.

Performance:

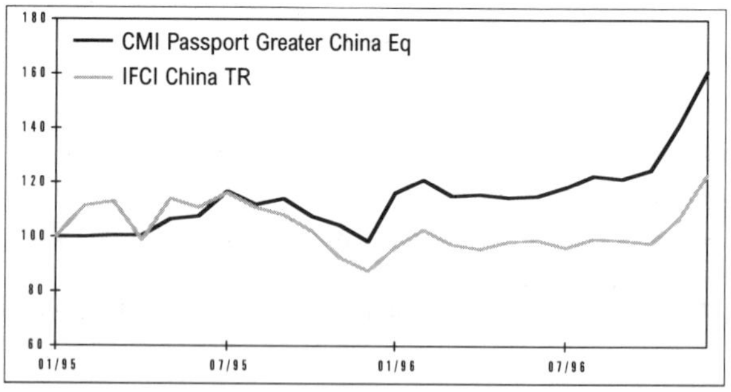

Umbrella fund: This is a singular fund.
Launch date: 16/01/95 **Domicile:** Isle of Man
Currency: USD **Structure:** Open ended, Insurance Fund
Portfolio manager: HSBC Asset Management
Fund Advisor to Clerical Medical International Global Network Fund Passport Greater China Equity; located in Hong Kong.

Purchase: Through insurance products linked to this fund
Minimum investment: 7,500 GBP
Custodian: CMI Insurance Company Limited
Listed: None **Dealings:** Daily
Fund Sedol I.D.: 16950 **Published:** FT
Fees **Annual fee:** 1.25% **Performance fee:** None
Front end load: ILP **Redemption fee:** ILP
Switching fee: None

Top holdings:	
China OS Land& Inv	6.4%
China Resources Enterprises	4.3%
Citic Pacific	3.9%
Eastern Comms B	3.4%
Guangdong Kelon H Shares	3.5%
New World Infrastructure	3.8%
NG Fung Kong Ltd	3.2%
Quingling Motors H Shares	3.5%
Shai Industrial	5.3%

TOTAL RETURNS %

3 months 1997	1996	1995	1994	3 years	5 years
6.30	63.57	N.A.	N.A.	N.A.	N.A.

STATISTICS

Assets ($mil)	Current yield	Volatility	Risk return	Micropal Star Rating
0.70	—	N.A.	—	———

CMI Passport Iberian Equity
136/350

CMI Insurance Company Limited (Isle of Man)
Clerical Medical House, Victoria Road, Douglas IM99ILT,
Isle of Man
Tel 44-1624-638 888 Fax 44-1624-625-900

Contact: Customer Services Department

Investment objective:
The fund invests wholly into the Iberian Equity sub-fund Universe (CMI Luxembourg Umbrella)seeking capital growth from equities, and equity based securities, primarily in Spain.

Umbrella fund: This is a singular fund.
Launch date: 16/01/95 **Domicile:** Isle of Man
Currency: ESP **Structure:** Open ended, Insurance Fund
Portfolio manager: Beta Capital SA, Madrid
Manager of Clerical Medical International Passport Iberia; located in Madrid.
The literature notes: CMI Asset Management (Lux) as the Investment Manager

Purchase: Through insurance products linked to this fund
Minimum investment: 7,500 GBP
Custodian: CMI Insurance Company Limited
Listed: None **Dealings:** Daily
Fund Sedol I.D.: 16957 **Published:** FT
Fees **Annual fee:** 1.25% **Performance fee:** None
Front end load: ILP **Redemption fee:** ILP
Switching fee: None

Performance:

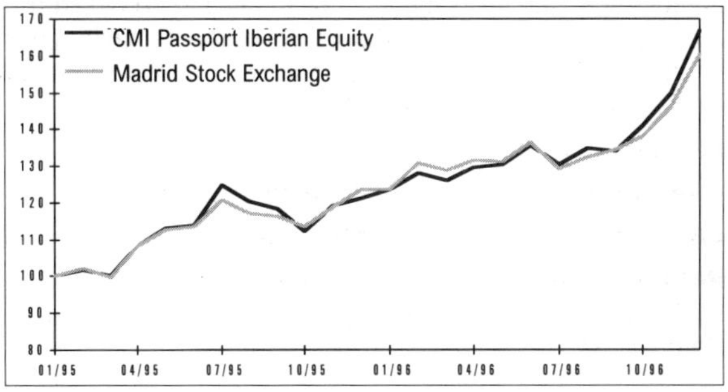

Top holdings:

Banco Bilbao Vizcaya	7.6%
Banco de Santander	8.5%
Bankinter	5.1%
Corp Mapfre	3.8%
Endesa	8.6%
Gas Natural SDG	3.8%
Iberdrola	4.8%
Puleva Union	4.9%
Repsol	6.9%
Telefonica	9.3%

TOTAL RETURNS %

3 months 1997	1996	1995	1994	3 years	5 years
-2.63	37.32	N.A.	N.A.	N.A.	N.A.

STATISTICS

Assets ($mil)	Current yield	Volatility	Risk return	Micropal Star Rating
0.01	—	N.A.	—	———

Colonial Securities Hong Kong
109/350

Panurgy Limited
1202 Tung Wah Mansion, 199-203 Hennessy Road, Wanchai,
Hong Kong
Tel 852-2511-4060 Fax 852-2519 -7536

Contact: Julian Bexon

Investment objective:
The fund invests principally in quoted securities in Hong Kong with the aim of achieving above average capital growth over the long-term. Currently, 97.6% of the fund has Hong Kong dollar exposure. The portfolio sector allocation is predominately in the following: real estate (30.0%); conglomerates (28.2%); and finance (21.3%).

Umbrella fund: This is a singular fund.
Launch date: 21/01/85 **Domicile:** Hong Kong
Currency: USD **Structure:** Open ended, Unit Trust
Portfolio manager: Mr J M A Bexon
Manager of Colonial Securities Hong Kong since January 1985; MA- Oxon; 24 years experience in the international finance industry.

Purchase: Direct, Financial Advisor
Minimum investment: 1,000 USD
Custodian: Bermuda Trust (Far East) Limited
Listed: None **Dealings:** Daily
Fund Sedol I.D.: 666944 **Published:** FT/SC
Fees **Annual fee:** 2.00% **Performance fee:** None
Front end load: 5.00% **Redemption fee:** None
Switching fee: None

Performance:

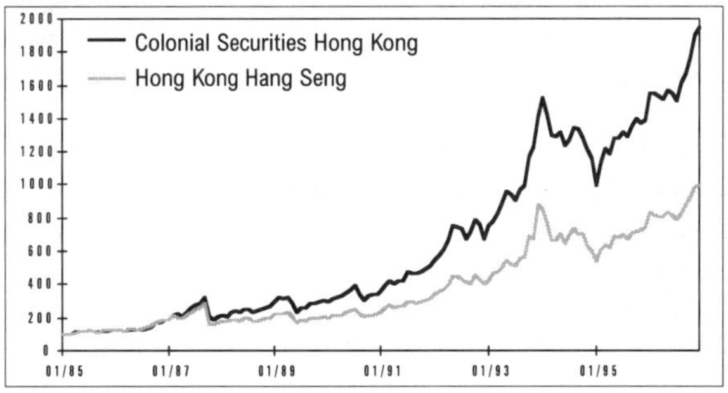

Top holdings:

Cheung Kong Holdings Ltd	8.0%
Citic Pacific	4.4%
Hang Seng Bank	6.9%
Henderson Land Development	6.9%
Hong Kong Telecom	4.5%
HSBC Holdings	12.0%
Hutchison Whampoa	9.6%
New World Development	4.6%
Sun Hung Kai Properties	9.2%
Wharf Holdings	3.8%

TOTAL RETURNS %

3 months 1997	1996	1995	1994	3 years	5 years
-7.13	40.27	20.24	-17.83	38.58	280.98

STATISTICS

Assets ($mil)	Current yield	Volatility	Risk return	Micropal Star Rating
11.15	—	5.74	4	✪✪✪✪✪

Comgest Europe
312/350

Comgest S.A.
39 allee Scheffer, L-2520 Luxembourg
Tel 352-47-67-2804 Fax 352-47-67-3661

Investment objective:
The primary objective of this fund is to achieve predictable and regular long-term appreciation with investments concentrated in European growth stocks. Typically only 20 to 25 stocks are held in the portfolio. The portfolio reflects the following top country allocations: UK (39.0%); France (23.0%); Switzerland (12.0%); Sweden (9.0%); and the Netherlands (8.0%).

Umbrella fund: This is a singular fund.

Launch date: 24/16/92 **Domicile:** Luxembourg [UCITS]

Currency: CHF **Structure:** Open ended, SICAV

Portfolio manager: Wedig von Gaudecker
Manager of Comgest Europe commenced May 1992 and Managing Director of Comgest SA.

Contact: Anne De Sahb

Performance:

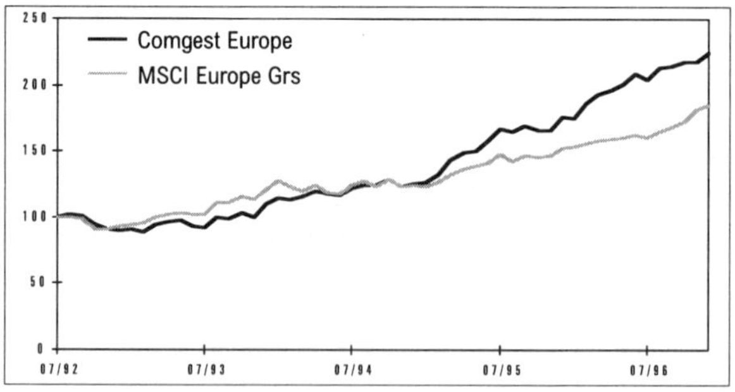

Purchase: Direct

Minimum investment: 1 Unit

Custodian: Banque Indosuez

Listed: None **Dealings:** Weekly

Fund Sedol I.D.: 300913 **Published:** FT/HTE/BZ

Fees **Annual fee:** 1.50% **Performance fee:** None
Front end load: None **Redemption fee:** None
Switching fee: None

Top holdings:

Holding	%
Carrefour	4.3%
Compass	5.3%
Electrocomponents	4.5%
L'Oreal	4.7%
Rentokil	6.2%
Reuters Holdings	6.6%
Sandoz	6.3%
Securitas	4.5%
Sodexho	6.5%
Wolters Kluwer	4.8%

TOTAL RETURNS %

3 months 1997	1996	1995	1994	3 years	5 years
-4.40	28.05	39.90	14.48	105.08	N.A.

STATISTICS

Assets ($mil)	Current yield	Volatility	Risk return	Micropal Star Rating
312.33	—	2.74	5	✪✪✪✪✪

Commercial Union PP Dutch Growth
340/350

Commercial Union Luxembourg SA
41 Avenue de la Gare, L-1013 Luxembourg
Tel 352-48-90-61 Fax 352-49-23-69
http://www. cupp.lu E mail cupp@cupp.lu

Investment objective:
The sub-fund seeks to achieve long-term capital appreciation by investing in equities of a range of shares and well established Dutch corporations. The sub-fund is denominated in Dutch guilders. The top sector allocations of the portfolio include the following: finance (14.8%); oil (15.2%); chemicals/ pharmaceuticals (7.2%); and finance (14.8%).

Umbrella fund: Commercial Union Privilege Portfolio Funds

Launch date: 01/06/90 **Domicile:** Luxembourg [UCITS]

Currency: NLG **Structure:** Open ended, Investment Company

Portfolio manager: Credit Suisse Investment Management – London, UK

Contact: Stephen Roberts

Performance:

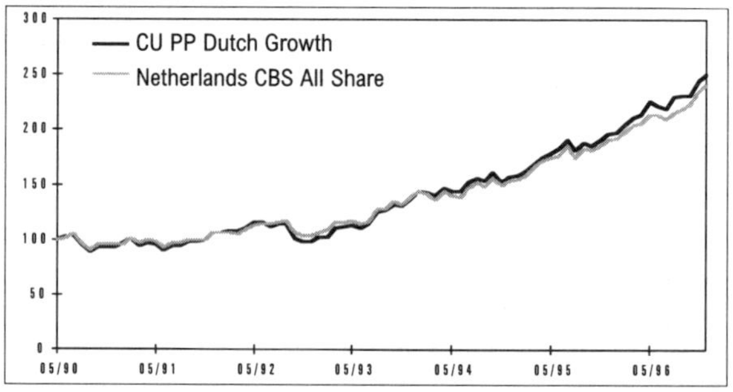

Purchase: Direct, Via appointed distributors

Minimum investment: 7,000 NLG

Custodian: Chase Manhattan Bank (Lux) S.A.

Listed: Luxembourg **Dealings:** Daily

Fund Sedol I.D.: 421206 **Published:** FT/LW

Fees **Annual fee:** 1.25% **Performance fee:** None
Front end load: Up to 6.00% **Redemption fee:** 1.00%
Switching fee: 1.00%

Top holdings:

Holding	%
ABN AMRO Holding	7.2%
Aegon	3.8%
Ahold Kon	4.0%
Akzo NV	4.6%
Doerdetsche Petrol	7.7%
ING Groep	6.7%
KNP	4.8%
Philips Electronics	4.2%
Royal Dutch Petroleum	7.5%
Unilever	8.1%

TOTAL RETURNS %

3 months 1997	1996	1995	1994	3 years	5 years
5.18	27.23	25.46	14.29	82.44	136.10

STATISTICS

Assets ($mil)	Current yield	Volatility	Risk return	Micropal Star Rating
14.24	—	3.07	2	✪

Commercial Union PP Spanish Growth

170/350

Commercial Union Luxembourg SA
41 Avenue de la Gare, L-1013 Luxembourg
Tel 352-48-90-61 Fax 352-49-23-69
http://www. cupp.lu E mail cupp@cupp.lu

Investment objective:
The sub-fund seeks to invest in a carefully selected portfolio of Spanish equities with the objective of achieving long-term capital growth. The sector allocations of the portfolio are the following: finance (29.8%); utilities (29.0%); communications (8.0%); oil (8.4%); and building/construction (6.6%).

Umbrella fund: Commercial Union Privilege Portfolio Funds
Launch date: 01/06/90 **Domicile:** Luxembourg [UCITS]
Currency: ESP **Structure:** Open ended, Investment Company
Portfolio manager: Bruno Berri
Manager of CU PP Spanish Growth with Commercial Union Investment Management Limited.

Purchase: Direct, Via appointed distributors
Minimum investment: 400,000 ESP
Custodian: Chase Manhattan Bank (Lux) S.A.
Listed: Luxembourg **Dealings:** Daily
Fund Sedol I.D.: 421202 **Published:** FT/LW
Fees **Annual fee:** 1.25% **Performance fee:** None
Front end load: Up to 6.00% **Redemption fee:** 1.00%
Switching fee: 1.00%

Contact: Stephen Roberts

Performance:

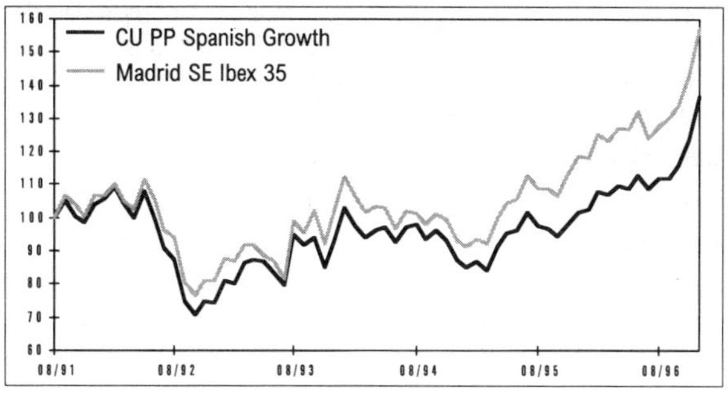

Top holdings:

Argentaria Banca de Espania	3.5%
Banco Bilbao Vizcaya	6.8%
Banco de Santander	5.1%
Banco Popular Esp	3.8%
Endesa	9.4%
Gas Natural	5.0%
Iberdrola	5.7%
Repsol	7.5%
Telefonica de Espana	8.0%
Union Electrica Fenosa	3.6%

TOTAL RETURNS %

3 months 1997	1996	1995	1994	3 years	5 years
-2.14	34.46	16.37	-5.60	47.71	31.47

STATISTICS

Assets ($mil)	Current yield	Volatility	Risk return	Micropal Star Rating
19.25	—	4.34	2	✪✪

Commercial Union PP UK Growth

289/350

Commercial Union Luxembourg SA
41 Avenue de la Gare, L-1013 Luxembourg
Tel 352-48-90-61 Fax 352-49-23-69
http://www. cupp.lu E mail cupp@cupp.lu

Investment objective:
The sub-fund primarily invests in the equities of UK blue chip companies with the objective of achieving capital growth. The base currency of the sub-fund is UK sterling.The top sector allocations of the portfolio include the following: banking (8.0%); chemicals/pharmaceuticals (8.6%); oil (8.1%); and retail (8.4%).

Umbrella fund: Commercial Union Privilege Portfolio Funds
Launch date: 01/06/90 **Domicile:** Luxembourg [UCITS]
Currency: GBP **Structure:** Open ended, Investment Company
Portfolio manager: Ian Ainscow
Manager of the CU PP UK Growth.

Purchase: Direct, Via appointed distributors
Minimum investment: 2,000 GBP
Custodian: Chase Manhattan Bank (Lux) S.A.
Listed: Luxembourg **Dealings:** Daily
Fund Sedol I.D.: 421200 **Published:** FT/LW
Fees **Annual fee:** 1.25% **Performance fee:** None
Front end load: Up to 6.00% **Redemption fee:** 1.00%
Switching fee: 1.00%

Contact: Stephen Roberts

Performance:

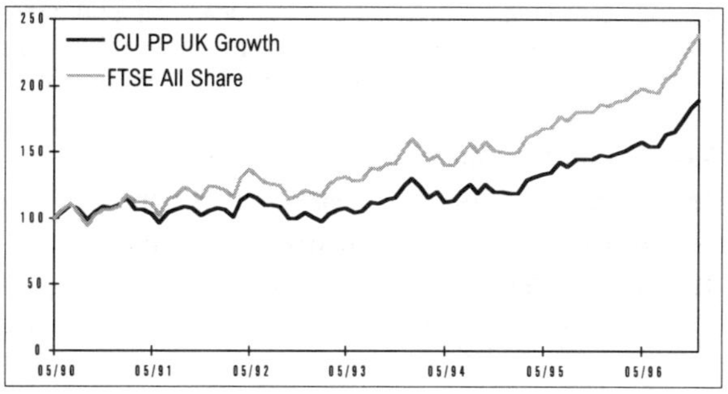

Top holdings:

Bass	1.6%
British Petroleum	4.4%
Eaglet Investment Trust	1.9%
Granada Group	2.0%
Legal & General	1.7%
Lloyds TSB Group	3.4%
Marks & Spencers	1.7%
Royal & Sun Alliance	2.0%
Shell Transport & Trading	3.2%

TOTAL RETURNS %

3 months 1997	1996	1995	1994	3 years	5 years
-0.29	28.63	23.03	-3.75	52.31	79.81

STATISTICS

Assets ($mil)	Current yield	Volatility	Risk return	Micropal Star Rating
10.42	—	3.72	3	✪✪✪✪

Credis Equity Euro Blue Chips A/B

339/350

Credis Equity Fund Managment Company
5 Rue Jean Monnet, L-2180 Luxembourg
Tel 352-43-61-61-610 Fax 352-42-38-86

Investment objective:
The sub-fund invests mainly in shares and, to a limited extent, convertible and warrant bonds issued by European blue chip companies denominated in any currency, ie leading European companies with a market capitalisation of at least 1 billion US dollars. The top sector allocations of the fund include the following: finance (19.0%); and energy (9.6%).

Umbrella fund: Credis Equity Fund

Launch date: 23/10/89 **Domicile:** Luxembourg [UCITS]

Currency: DEM **Structure:** Open ended, FCP

Portfolio manager: Credit Suisse Investment Management Ltd.
Investment advisor of the sub-fund; located at Beaufort House 15, St. Botolph Street, London EC3A 7JJ UK.

Contact: Fabrice Toussaint

Performance:

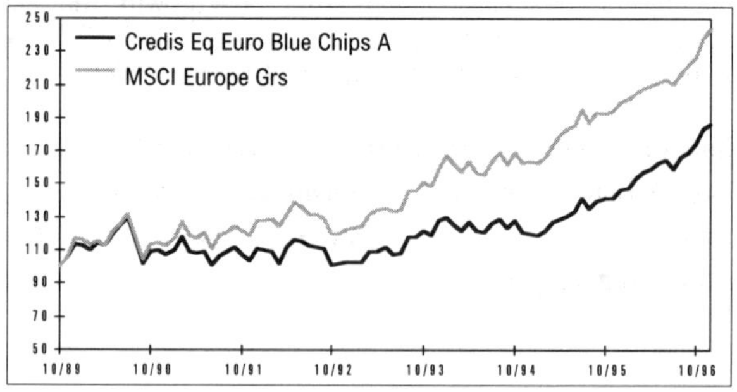

Purchase: Direct, Financial Advisor, Credit Suisse

Minimum investment: 1 Unit

Custodian: Credit Suisse (Luxembourg) S.A

Listed: Luxembourg **Dealings:** Daily

Fund Sedol I.D.: 301113 **Published:** FT/IHT/LW/NZZ/TK

Fees **Annual fee:** 1.92% **Performance fee:** None
Front end load: None **Redemption fee:** None
Switching fee: None

Top holdings:

Holding	%
Hoechst	2.0%
Iberdrola	2.1%
ING Groep	2.2%
NV Verenigd Bezit VNU	2.0%
Roche Holdings	2.3%
Sanofi	2.0%
Stet Spa	2.1%
Telefonica de Espana	2.3%
Total	2.0%
Vendex International	2.0%

TOTAL RETURNS %

3 months 1997	1996	1995	1994	3 years	5 years
2.09	27.27	22.09	-5.83	46.34	68.48

STATISTICS

Assets ($mil)	Current yield	Volatility	Risk return	Micropal Star Rating
49.81	—	3.02	2	✪✪✪

Credis Equity Hispano Iberia A

141/350

Credis Equity Fund Managment Company
5 Rue Jean Monnet, L-2180 Luxembourg
Tel 352-43-61-61-610 Fax 352-42-38-86

Investment objective:
The sub-fund invests mainly in shares, convertibles and warrant bonds issued by companies domiciled in Spain and Portugal. The fund concentrates on growth sectors, in particular companies set to profit especially from further economic integration within the EU. Currently the top sector allocations of the portfolio are finance (32.0%) and utilities (34.4%).

Umbrella fund: Credis Equity Fund

Launch date: 05/03/90 **Domicile:** Luxembourg [UCITS]

Currency: ESP **Structure:** Open ended, FCP

Portfolio manager: Credit Suisse Investment Management Ltd.
Investment advisor of the sub-fund; located at Beaufort House 15, St. Botolph Street, London EC3A 7JJ UK.

Contact: Fabrice Toussaint

Performance:

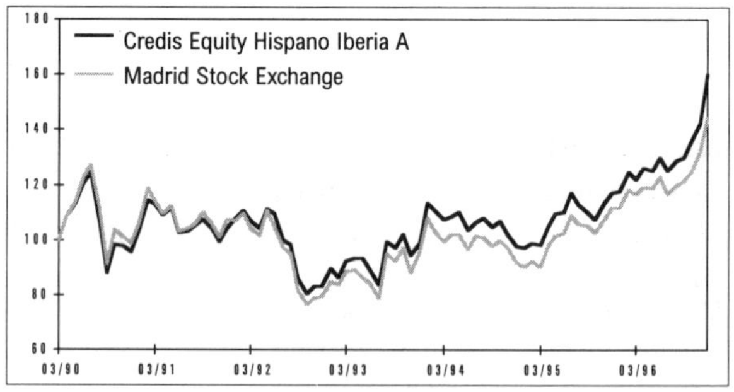

Purchase: Direct, Financial Advisor, Credit Suisse

Minimum investment: 1 Unit

Custodian: Credit Suisse (Luxembourg) S.A.

Listed: Luxembourg **Dealings:** Daily

Fund Sedol I.D.: 301115 **Published:** FT/IHT/LW/NZZ/TK

Fees **Annual fee:** 1.92% **Performance fee:** None
Front end load: None **Redemption fee:** None
Switching fee: None

Top holdings:

Holding	%
Argentaria Banca de Espania	3.8%
Banco Bilbao Vizcayna	6.5%
Bankinter	4.8%
BCo de Santander	7.8%
Empresa Nacional Electriciat	8.2%
Gas Natural	4.8%
Iberdrola	7.2%
Respol	4.6%
Telefonica de Espana	8.5%
Union Electrica Fenosa	3.6%

TOTAL RETURNS %

3 months 1997	1996	1995	1994	3 years	5 years
0.24	36.99	19.90	-1.26	62.18	53.80

STATISTICS

Assets ($mil)	Current yield	Volatility	Risk return	Micropal Star Rating
3.17	—	4.53	2	✪✪

Credis Equity Italy A/B

316/350

Credis Equity Fund Management Company
5 Rue Jean Monnet, L-2180 Luxembourg
Tel 352-43-61-61-610 Fax 352-42-38-86

Investment objective:
The sub-fund invests mainly in shares and to a limited extent, convertible and warrant bonds issued by companies domiciled in Italy. The sub-fund concentrates on growth sectors, in particular companies set to profit especially from further economic integration within the EU.

Umbrella fund: Credis Equity Fund
Launch date: 28/09/92 **Domicile:** Luxembourg [UCITS]
Currency: ITL **Structure:** Open ended, FCP
Portfolio manager: Credit Suisse Investment Management Ltd.
Investment advisor of the sub-fund; located at Beaufort House 15, St. Botolph Street, London EC3A 7JJ UK.

Purchase: Direct, Financial Advisor, Credit Suisse
Minimum investment: 1 Unit
Custodian: Credit Suisse (Luxembourg) S.A.
Listed: Luxembourg **Dealings:** Daily
Fund Sedol I.D.: 300267 **Published:** FT/IHT/LW/NZZ/TK
Fees **Annual fee:** 1.92% **Performance fee:** None
Front end load: None **Redemption fee:** None
Switching fee: None

Contact: Fabrice Toussaint

Performance:

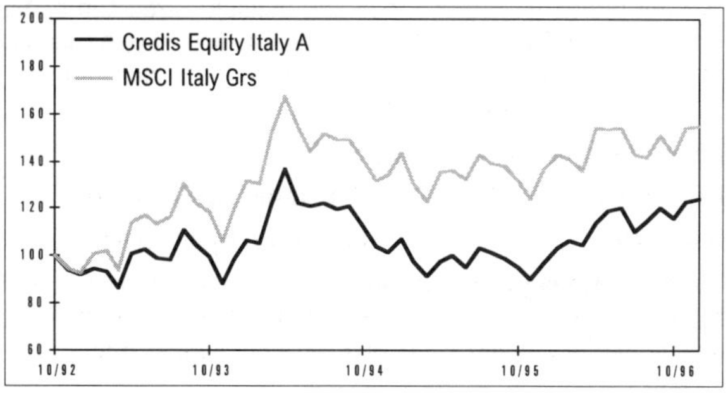

Top holdings:

ASSI Curazioni Generali	6.5%
Edison	4.4%
ENI SPA	9.4%
Istituto Mobiliare Italy	4.5%
Italglas spa	4.6%
Parmalat Finanziaria	4.2%
SAI SPA	3.6%
STET SPA	5.7%
Telecom Italia	7.7%
Telecom Italia Mobile	6.1%

TOTAL RETURNS %

3 months 1997	1996	1995	1994	3 years	5 years
2.39	28.02	-4.33	2.89	26.02	N.A.

STATISTICS

Assets ($mil)	Current yield	Volatility	Risk return	Micropal Star Rating
5.28	—	6.26	3	✪✪✪✪

Credis Equity Netherlands A/B

123/350

Credis Equity Fund Management Company
5 Rue Jean Monnet, L-2180 Luxembourg
Tel 352-43-61-61-610 Fax 352-42-38-86

Investment objective:
The sub-fund invests mainly in shares, convertible and warrant bonds issued by companies domiciled in the Netherlands. The sub-fund concentrates on growth sectors in particular companies set to profit especially from further economic integration within the EUC. The top sectors of the portfolio include: finance (29.0%); and technology (13.0%).

Umbrella fund: Credis Equity Fund
Launch date: 28/09/92 **Domicile:** Luxembourg [UCITS]
Currency: NLG **Structure:** Open ended, FCP
Portfolio manager: Credit Suisse Asset Management, Zurich
Manager of the sub-fund; Credit Suisse is the investment advisor to the sub-fund located at Paradeplatz 8 CH-8070 Zurich, Switzerland.

Purchase: Direct, Financial Advisor, Credit Suisse
Minimum investment: 1 Unit
Custodian: Credit Suisse (Luxembourg) S.A
Listed: Luxembourg **Dealings:** Daily
Fund Sedol I.D.: 300265 **Published:** FT/IHT/LW/NZZ/TK
Fees **Annual fee:** 1.92% **Performance fee:** None
Front end load: None **Redemption fee:** None
Switching fee: None

Contact: Fabrice Toussaint

Performance:

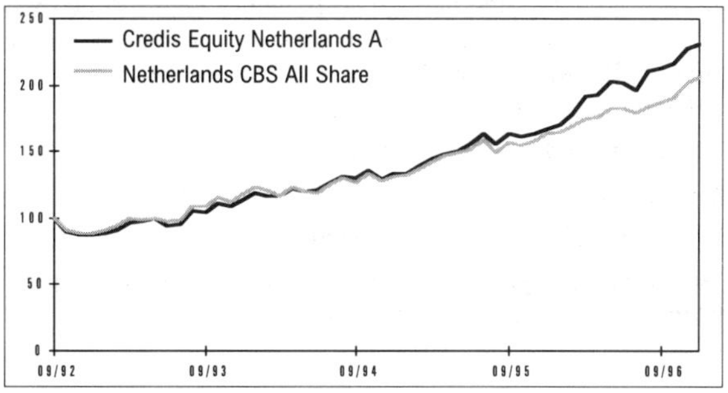

Top holdings:

ABN AMRO Holding	8.2%
Aegon	5.0%
Akzo NV	4.7%
Elsevier	5.3%
ING Groep	8.2%
Nutricia	5.0%
NV Verenigd Bezit VNU	4.5%
Oce-Van Der Grinten NV	4.6%
Royal Dutch Petroleum	4.5%
Unilever	7.4%

TOTAL RETURNS %

3 months 1997	1996	1995	1994	3 years	5 years
7.10	38.63	25.35	17.46	104.10	N.A.

STATISTICS

Assets ($mil)	Current yield	Volatility	Risk return	Micropal Star Rating
22.19	—	3.12	4	✪✪✪✪

Credis Equity Small Cap Europe
213/350

Credis Equity Fund Managment Company
5 Rue Jean Monnet, L-2180 Luxembourg
Tel 352-43-61-61-610 Fax 352-42-38-86

Investment objective:
The sub-fund invests mainly in shares and to a limited extent, convertible and warrant bonds issued by small and medium-sized companies domiciled in Europe (including the UK and Eastern Europe) which have a market capitalisation of no more than 3 billion German marks. The top country allocations of the portfolio are: Norway (23.4%); and Sweden (15.3%).

Umbrella fund: Credis Equity Fund

Launch date: 28/01/94 **Domicile:** Luxembourg [UCITS]

Currency: DEM **Structure:** Open ended, FCP

Portfolio manager: Credit Suisse Asset Management, Zurich
Manager of the sub-fund; Credit Suisse is the investment advisor to the sub-fund located at Paradeplatz 8 CH-8070 Zurich, Switzerland.

Contact: Fabrice Toussaint

Performance:

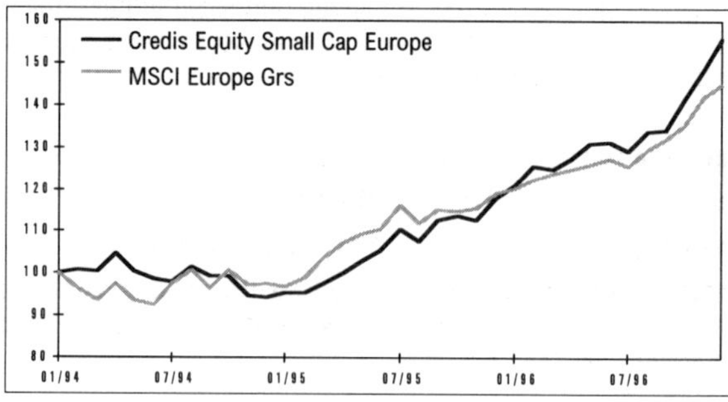

Purchase: Direct, Financial Advisor, Credit Suisse

Minimum investment: 1 Unit

Custodian: Credit Suisse (Luxembourg) S.A.

Listed: Luxembourg **Dealings:** Daily

Fund Sedol I.D.: 301545 **Published:** FT/IHT/LW/NZZ/TK

Fees **Annual fee:** 1.92% **Performance fee:** None
Front end load: None **Redemption fee:** None
Switching fee: None

Top holdings:

ARK AS	3.2%
Catena AB	3.5%
Elan Corp	2.2%
Euro De Telesecurite	4.6%
Getinge Industries	2.3%
LCI Computer	3.5%
Nera AS	2.5%
Tandberg	4.5%
Tege	2.4%
Tele Pizza	3.7%

TOTAL RETURNS %

3 months 1997	1996	1995	1994	3 years	5 years
16.21	31.98	25.24	N.A.	N.A.	N.A.

STATISTICS

Assets ($mil)	Current yield	Volatility	Risk return	Micropal Star Rating
99.69	—	N.A.	—	———

Credis Equity Small Cap USA
174/350

Credis Equity Fund Management Company
5 Rue Jean Monnet, L-2180 Luxembourg
Tel 352-43-61-61-610 Fax 352-42-38-86

Investment objective:
The sub-fund invests in shares of smaller US companies which have significantly greater growth potential than corporations with a large market capitalisation. The emphasis is on companies with a market capitalisation of less than 1 billion US dollars. The top sector allocations of the portfolio are energy (18.0%); technology (16.0%); and consumer goods (15.0%).

Umbrella fund: Credis Equity Fund

Launch date: 09/17/93 **Domicile:** Luxembourg [UCITS]

Currency: USD **Structure:** Open ended, FCP

Portfolio manager: Batterymarch Finance Management Inc
Manager of the sub-fund; located in Boston.

Contact: Fabrice Toussaint

Performance:

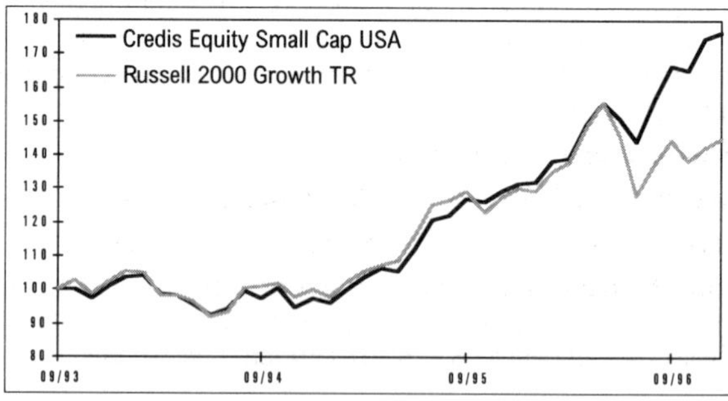

Purchase: Direct, Financial Advisor, Credit Suisse

Minimum investment: 1 Unit

Custodian: Credit Suisse (Luxembourg) S.A

Listed: Luxembourg **Dealings:** Daily

Fund Sedol I.D.: 301546 **Published:** FT/IHT/LW/NZZ/TK

Fees **Annual fee:** 1.92% **Performance fee:** None
Front end load: None **Redemption fee:** None
Switching fee: None

Top holdings:

Champion Enterprises Inc	1.5%
Cooper Cameron Corporation	2.1%
Lexmark Intl. Group Inc	1.4%
Marine Drilling Companies Inc	1.7%
Robert Half Intl Inc	1.4%
Ross Stores Inc	1.7%
Seacor Holdings	1.4%
SPX Corp	1.5%
Storage Technology Corp	1.5%
Union Texas Petroleum Hld Inc	1.9%

TOTAL RETURNS %

3 months 1997	1996	1995	1994	3 years	5 years
-4.54	34.15	35.17	-3.74	74.55	N.A.

STATISTICS

Assets ($mil)	Current yield	Volatility	Risk return	Micropal Star Rating
117.31	—	3.66	3	✪✪✪✪

Credit Lyonnais China Growth Fund
51/350

Credit Lyonnais International Asset Management (HK) Ltd
6 Floor Three Exchange Square, 8 Connaught Place, Central, Hong Kong
Tel 852-2846-7555 Fax 852-2868-4742
http://www. cliamasia.com.hk/cliam E mail cliamhk@hklink.net

Contact: Paul Mack and Deborah Leung

Investment objective:
This Credit Lyonnais sub-fund seeks long-term appreciation through investment in listed Chinese equities. A proportion of the sub-fund's assets may be invested in companies listed outside China, provided that the companies chosen have substantial investments in China.

Umbrella fund: Credit Lyonnais Equity Umbrella Fund PLC
Launch date: 20/05/92 **Domicile:** Ireland [UCITS]
Currency: USD **Structure:** Open ended, Mutual Fund
Portfolio manager: Timothy Greaton
Manager of Credit Lyonnais Equity Umbrella Fund Plc- Credit Lyonnais China Growth Fund; joined CLAIM HK in 1992; graduate of Middlebury College and Taiwan U; specialises in Taiwanese and emerging Chinese stock markets.
Purchase: Direct, Financial Advisor
Minimum investment: 1,000 USD
Custodian: Bermuda Trust (Dublin) Ltd
Listed: Dublin **Dealings:** Weekly
Fund Sedol I.D.: 424155 **Published:** SC/FT/RT/BG
Fees **Annual fee:** 1.50% **Performance fee:** None
Front end load: 5.00% **Redemption fee:** None
Switching fee: 2.00%

Performance:

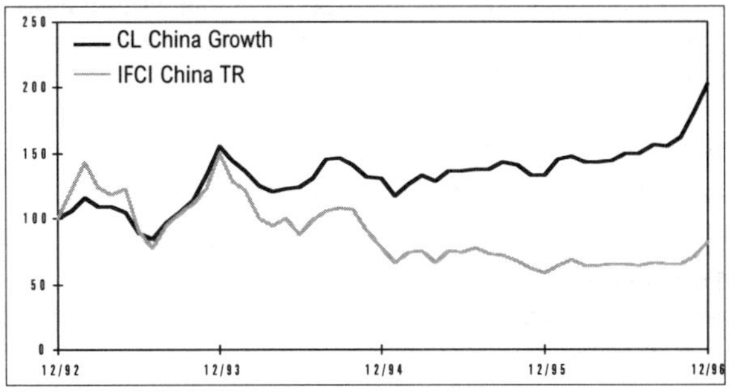

Top holdings:

Holding	
Cheung Kong Holdings Ltd	n/s
China Overseas Land & Invest Ltd	n/s
China Resources Enterprises	n/s
China Travel Intl Inv HK Ltd	n/s
Hutchison Whampoa	n/s
New World Infrastructure	n/s
Quingling Motors H Shares	n/s
Shanghai Industrial Hldg	n/s
Wan Hai Lines	n/s

TOTAL RETURNS %

3 months 1997	1996	1995	1994	3 years	5 years
6.76	52.44	1.84	-16.17	30.13	N.A.

STATISTICS

Assets ($mil)	Current yield	Volatility	Risk return	Micropal Star Rating
12.20	—	5.52	2	✪✪✪✪✪

Cregem Equities L-Compartiment Europe Cap
268/350

Credit Communal de Belgique
69 Route d'Esch, L-2953 Luxembourg
Tel 32-22-22-53-87 Fax 32-22-22-64-36

Contact: Romain Demeyer

Investment objective:
The fund seeks to achieve capital appreciation through investment in Europe. The The country allocation in the portfolio is as follows: Germany (17.5%); France (14.2%); UK (12.9%); Netherlands (8.3%); Italy (7.1%); and Spain (6.9%).The top sector allocations include the following: services (22.3%); consumer goods (21.0%); and finance (20.2%).
Umbrella fund: This is a singular fund.
Launch date: 01/02/90 **Domicile:** Luxembourg
Currency: BEF **Structure:** Open ended, SICAV
Portfolio manager: Romain Demeyer
Manager of the fund commenced December 1995; degrees in engineering and physics; experience in sciences, education and banking.

Purchase: Direct, Via Dexia Belgium
Minimum investment: 18,500 BEF
Custodian: Banque Internationale a Luxembourg
Listed: Luxembourg **Dealings:** Daily
Fund Sedol I.D.: 300414 **Published:** FT/IHT/SC
Fees **Annual fee:** 0.75% **Performance fee:** None
Front end load: 2.00% **Redemption fee:** None
Switching fee: None

Performance:

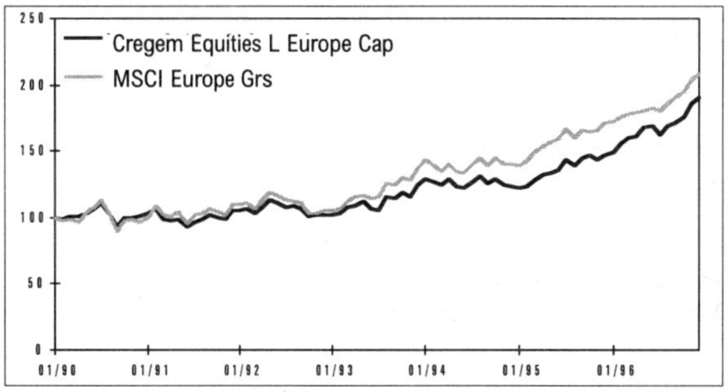

Top holdings:

Holding	
BASF	1.4%
Bayer	1.4%
British Petroleum	1.4%
Hoechst	1.9%
HSBC Holdings	1.4%
ING Groep	1.4%
Novartis	2.0%
Roche Holdings	1.5%
UCB	1.3%
Veba	2.5%

TOTAL RETURNS %

3 months 1997	1996	1995	1994	3 years	5 years
4.41	29.68	18.73	-0.40	53.35	80.60

STATISTICS

Assets ($mil)	Current yield	Volatility	Risk return	Micropal Star Rating
231.84	—	2.82	4	✪✪✪✪

Danske NSS Nordic Equities
201/350

Den Danske Bank International S.A.
2 Rue du Fosse, L-1536 Luxembourg
Tel 352-46-12-751 Fax 352-47-30-78

Investment objective:
The sub-fund pursues a growth orientated strategy focusing on the equities of individual companies that are expected to outperform a Nordic share index. The shares must be denominated in a Nordic currency and listed on one of the Nordic stock exchanges. The portfolio may have cash holdings or occasionally invest in short-term Nordic government bonds.

Umbrella fund: Danske Nordic Securities SICAV

Launch date: 05/05/90 **Domicile:** Luxembourg [UCITS]

Currency: ECU **Structure:** Open ended, SICAV

Portfolio manager: Danske Capital Management
Manager of Danske NSS Nordic Equities; located at 2, Rue du Fosse, L-1536, Luxembourg.

Contact: Lotte Svendsen

Performance:

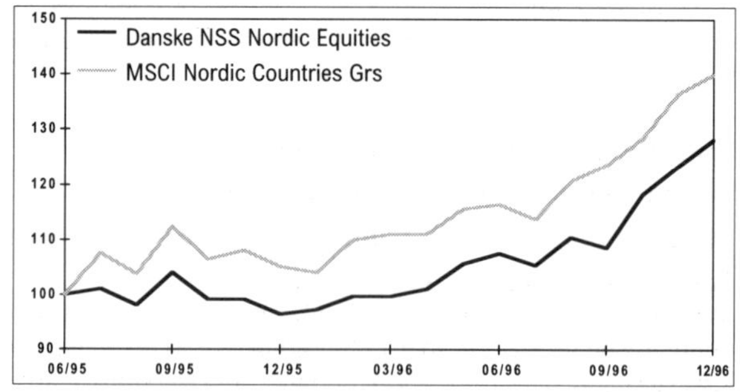

Purchase: Direct

Minimum investment: 100 Shares

Custodian: Den Danske Bank International S.A.

Listed: Luxembourg **Dealings:** Weekly

Fund Sedol I.D.: 301249 **Published:** LW

Fees **Annual fee:** 0.75% **Performance fee:** None
Front end load: Up to 3.00% **Redemption fee:** 1.00%
Switching fee: None

Top holdings:

Astra A Free	7.9%
D/S Svendborg A/S	5.0%
LM Ericsson	6.7%
Nokia A	9.9%
Norsk Hydro As	8.2%

TOTAL RETURNS %

3 months 1997	1996	1995	1994	3 years	5 years
4.63	32.67	N.A.	N.A.	N.A.	N.A.

STATISTICS

Assets ($mil)	Current yield	Volatility	Risk return	Micropal Star Rating
6.50	—	N.A.	—	———

Dao Heng China
153/350

Dao Heng Fund Management Ltd.
33 Floor Wu Chung House, 213 Queens Road East, Wanchai, Hong Kong
Tel 852-2831-7856 Fax 852-2831-7884

Investment objective:
The principal objective of the fund is to achieve long-term capital growth through investment primarily in equity securities of related companies in the People's Republic of China.

Umbrella fund: This is a singular fund.

Launch date: 01/08/92 **Domicile:** Hong Kong

Currency: USD **Structure:** Open ended, Unit Trust

Portfolio manager: Mr Peter Woo CFA and Ms. Wendy Yung
Managers of Dao Hang China.

Contact: Grace Li /Katie Wong

Performance:

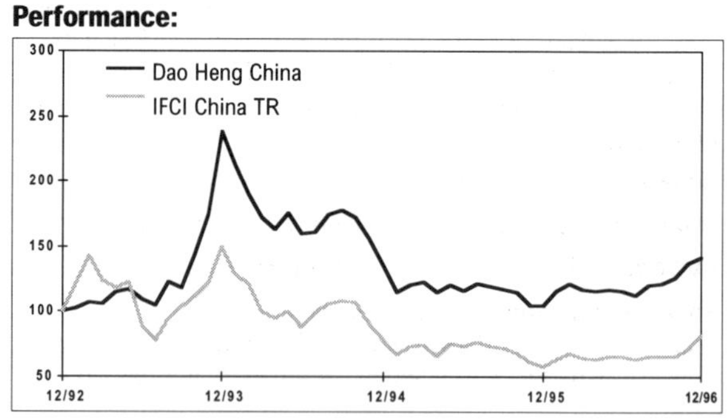

Purchase: Direct, Financial Advisor, Through Dao Heng /OTB Bank Branches in Hong Kong

Minimum investment: 5,000 USD

Custodian: Bank of Bermuda (Cayman) Ltd

Listed: None **Dealings:** Daily

Fund Sedol I.D.: 625470 **Published:** SC/HKEJ/HKET

Fees **Annual fee:** 1.50% **Performance fee:** None
Front end load: 4.00% **Redemption fee:** 1.00%
Switching fee: 1.00%

Top holdings:

China Resources Enterprises	n/s
China Travel Intl	n/s
Cosco Pacific	n/s
Guangzhon Investment	n/s
Shanghai Industrial Hldg	n/s

TOTAL RETURNS %

3 months 1997	1996	1995	1994	3 years	5 years
28.68	35.91	-22.27	-43.41	-40.22	N.A.

STATISTICS

Assets ($mil)	Current yield	Volatility	Risk return	Micropal Star Rating
1.10	—	6.55	—	✪

Dao Heng Hong Kong
75/350

Dao Heng Fund Management
33 Floor Wu Chung House, 213 Queens Road East, Wanchai, Hong Kong
Tel 852-2831-7856 Fax 852-2831-7884

Contact: Grace Li /Katie Wong

Investment objective:
The fund seeks to achieve long-term capital appreciation through principally investing into the Hong Kong stock market. At present the top sector allocations of the portfolio are property (50.0%); commercial conglomerate (19.7%); finance (16.2%); and hotels (2.5%).

Umbrella fund: This is a singular fund.
Launch date: 01/04/87 **Domicile:** Hong Kong
Currency: HKD **Structure:** Open ended, Unit Trust
Portfolio manager: Mr Peter Woo, CFA
Manager of the Dao Heng Hong Kong commenced July 1995.

Performance:

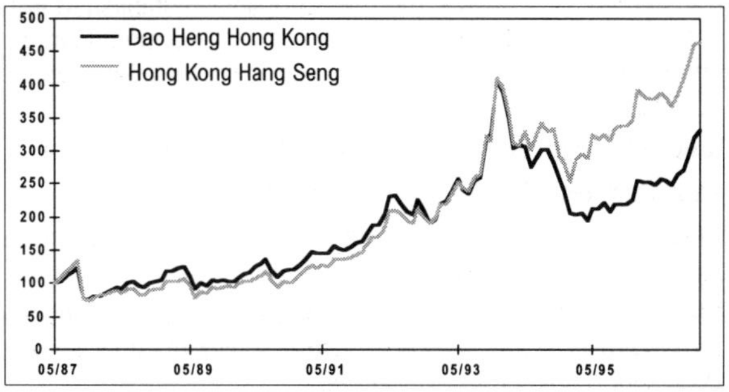

Purchase: Direct, Financial Advisor, Through Dao Heng/ DTB Bank branches in Hong Kong
Minimum investment: 10,000 Units
Custodian: Bermuda Trust (Far East) Ltd
Listed: None **Dealings:** Daily
Fund Sedol I.D.: 627297 **Published:** SC/HKEJ/HKET
Fees **Annual fee:** 1.00% **Performance fee:** None
Front end load: 3.00% **Redemption fee:** 1.00%
Switching fee: 1.00%

Top holdings:

Cheung Kong Holdings Ltd	n/s
HSBC Holdings	n/s
New World Development	n/s
Sun Hung Kai Properties	n/s
Swire Pacific	n/s

TOTAL RETURNS %

3 months 1997	1996	1995	1994	3 years	5 years
-7.43	46.65	-5.68	-41.23	-18.72	103.13

STATISTICS

Assets ($mil)	Current yield	Volatility	Risk return	Micropal Star Rating
3.62	—	6.31	—	✪

DNB Investment Nordic Eq C
248/350

Den Norske Bank
PB 1614 Vika, Oslo, 0119, Norway
Tel 47-22-94-8585 Fax 47-22-94-8494

Contact: Bjorn Andenas

Investment objective:
The sub-fund seeks broad diversification by being over weighted in the manufacturing industry in the Nordic market. The strategy is to invest in equities, convertible securities and, on an ancillary basis, in warrants of companies registered in and officially listed on a Scandinavian stock exchange or traded on another regulated Scandinavian market.
Umbrella fund: DNB Investment Fund SICAV
Launch date: 04/02/93 **Domicile:** Luxembourg
Currency: NOK **Structure:** Open ended, SICAV
Portfolio manager: Henrik Grassberg
Manager of the DNB Investment: Nordic Equity C commenced 1990; Sivilokonom, graduate level business and economics; experience in the investment industry since 1981.

Performance:

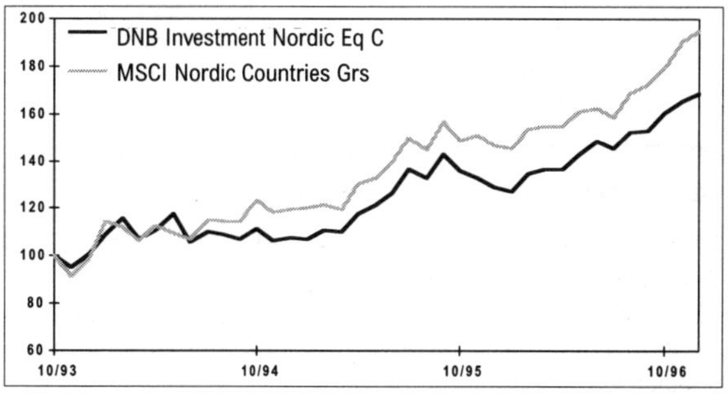

Purchase: Direct
Minimum investment: 100,000 NOK
Custodian: FETA
Listed: Luxembourg **Dealings:** Weekly
Fund Sedol I.D.: 304089 **Published:** FT/FV
Fees **Annual fee:** 1.50% **Performance fee:** None
Front end load: 5.25% **Redemption fee:** 0.75%
Switching fee: None

Top holdings:

Astra	3.4%
Autoliv	1.7%
Danisco	1.8%
Electrolux	2.5%
Finnlines	2.5%
Industriverden	1.7%
LM Ericsson	2.7%
Nokia A	3.6%
Sophus Berendsen	2.3%
UPM Kymmene	1.7%

TOTAL RETURNS %

3 months 1997	1996	1995	1994	3 years	5 years
4.48	30.49	20.16	6.69	67.29	N.A.

STATISTICS

Assets ($mil)	Current yield	Volatility	Risk return	Micropal Star Rating
20.49	—	4.35	2	✪✪

Dres Thornton ASF Hong Kong

54/350

Dresdner International Management Services Limited
International Financial Services Centre, La Touche House,
Dublin, Ireland
Tel 353-1-670-1444 Fax 353-1-670-1975

Contact: David Kanadagh /Marie McCrea

Investment objective:
The primary objective of the sub-fund is to achieve capital growth by investing in transferable securities issued by companies established in Hong Kong or companies established outside Hong Kong which derive a significant proportion of their revenue and/or profits from Hong Kong. The top sector allocation of the portfolio is: non-durables (26.0%).

Umbrella fund: Dresdner Thornton Asian Selection Fund

Launch date: 17/05/93 **Domicile:** Ireland [UCITS]

Currency: USD **Structure:** Open ended, Investment Company

Portfolio manager: Matthew Choi
Manager of Dres Thornton ASF Hong Kong; graduate, business administration-Simon Fraser U and Masters, business systems analysis and economics- City U and U of Kent; joined Thornton in 1987.

Purchase: Direct, Financial Advisor, Distributors

Minimum investment: 1,000 USD

Custodian: The Governor and Company of the Bank of Ireland (Ireland)

Listed: Dublin **Dealings:** Daily

Fund Sedol I.D.: 28191 **Published:** FT

Fees **Annual fee:** 1.75% **Performance fee:** None
Front end load: Up to 5.00% **Redemption fee:** None
Switching fee: None

Performance:

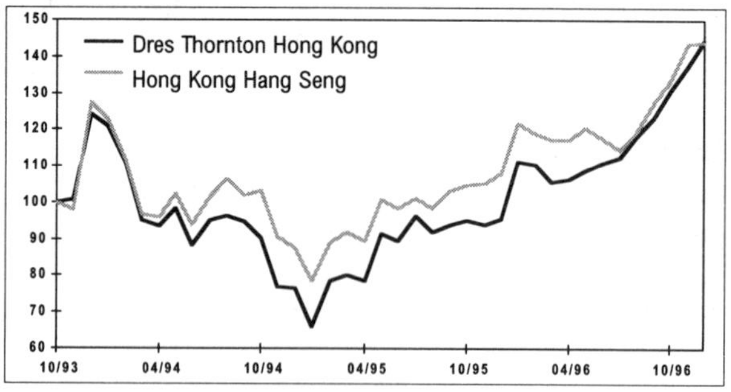

Top holdings:

Beijing Development	4.1%
China OS Land& Inv	4.1%
Cosco Pacific	4.2%
Great Eagle Holdings	4.1%
HKR International	4.7%
Lai Sun Development	6.7%
NG Fung Hong Ltd	4.6%
Peregrine Investments	4.1%
Tugyi (Cayman) Mgt	3.9%
Union Bank Hong Kong	3.8%

TOTAL RETURNS %

3 months 1997	1996	1995	1994	3 years	5 years
-1.59	51.31	25.00	-38.54	16.25	N.A.

STATISTICS

Assets ($mil)	Current yield	Volatility	Risk return	Micropal Star Rating
2.94	—	7.60	—	✪✪✪

Dresdner Thornton ASF The China Fund

242/350

Dresdner International Management Services Limited
International Financial Services Centre, La Touche House,
Dublin, Ireland
Tel 353-1-670-1444 Fax 353-1-670-1975

Contact: David Kanadagh /Marie McCrea

Investment objective:
The primary objective of the sub-fund is to achieve growth by investing in companies which are established in China or in companies established outside China which have interests in China. This is a US dollar denominated sub-fund. The top sector allocations of the fund include the following: technology (13.5%); services (10.3%); and utilities (9.3%).

Umbrella fund: Dresdner Thornton Asian Selection Fund

Launch date: 08/11/93 **Domicile:** Ireland [UCITS]

Currency: USD **Structure:** Open ended, Investment Company

Portfolio manager: Diahann Brown
Manager of Dres Thornton ASF China joined Thornton in 1992; previously with Robert Fleming Asset Management; started managing Asian funds in 1989; specialising in emerging markets.

Purchase: Direct, Financial Advisor, Distributors

Minimum investment: 1,000 USD

Custodian: The Governor and Company of the Bank of Ireland (Ireland)

Listed: Dublin **Dealings:** Daily

Fund Sedol I.D.: 28192 **Published:** FT

Fees **Annual fee:** 1.75% **Performance fee:** None
Front end load: Up to 5.00% **Redemption fee:** None
Switching fee: None

Performance:

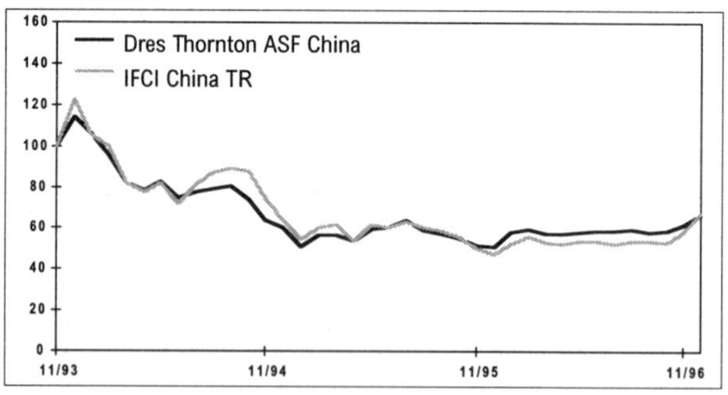

Top holdings:

Cheung Kong Infrastructure	3.5%
China OS Land& Inv	3.4%
China Resources	4.6%
Citic Pacific	3.4%
Cosco Pacific	3.0%
Guandong Invest Ltd	4.3%
Hutchison Whampoa	3.8%
New World Development	3.8%
New World Infrastructure	3.6%
Shanghai Industrial	3.8%

TOTAL RETURNS %

3 months 1997	1996	1995	1994	3 years	5 years
6.09	30.68	-14.88	-47.12	-41.17	N.A.

STATISTICS

Assets ($mil)	Current yield	Volatility	Risk return	Micropal Star Rating
81.61	—	6.83	—	✪

Eagle Star European Equity
310/350

Eagle Star International Life
4-6 Abbey Street, Reading, Berkshire, RG1 3BA, United Kingdom
Tel 44-1734-567-666 Fax 44-1734-585-186

Investment objective:
The fund seeks capital appreciation through investment in both EUC and non EUC countries. The majority of the portfolio is invested in larger quoted European companies including the UK and concentrates on the markets of Germany, France, Italy, Spain and Netherlands. Smaller companies showing strong growth potential may also be included from time to time.

Umbrella fund: This is a singular fund.

Launch date: 01/10/95 **Domicile:** Isle of Man

Currency: CHF **Structure:** Open ended, Life Assurance Fund

Portfolio manager: William Davies
Manager commenced 1993; BA Hons, economics; previously with Hambros Bank; 12 years experience in the finance industry.

Contact: Anna Radford

Performance:

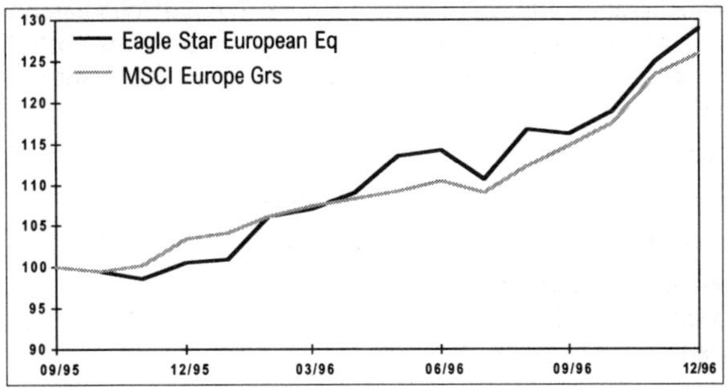

Purchase: Financial Advisor, Via a life product

Minimum investment: 1,000 GBP

Custodian: Chase Manhattan Bank

Listed: None **Dealings:** Daily

Fund Sedol I.D.: 29840 **Published:** FT

Fees **Annual fee:** 1.50% **Performance fee:** None
Front end load: ILP **Redemption fee:** ILP
Switching fee: None

Top holdings:

Altana	1.3%
British Petroleum	1.6%
Carrefour	1.5%
Fresenius Med. Care	1.3%
Glaxo Wellcome	1.6%
Norvatis Reg	1.5%
Raison Tehtaat	1.9%
Roche Holdings	1.3%
Safilo	1.5%
Shell Transport & Trading	1.5%

TOTAL RETURNS %

3 months 1997	1996	1995	1994	3 years	5 years
6.69	28.07	N.A.	N.A.	N.A.	N.A.

STATISTICS

Assets ($mil)	Current yield	Volatility	Risk return	Micropal Star Rating
5.19	—	N.A.	—	———

Eagle Star UK Equity
336/350

Eagle Star International Life
4-6 Abbey Street, Reading, Berkshire, RG1 3BA, United Kingdom
Tel 44-1734-567-666 Fax 44-1734-585-186

Investment objective:
The fund seeks capital growth through investment in large well established quoted UK companies and newer, smaller companies offering the opportunities for more exciting growth prospects.The top sector allocations of the portfolio are the following: services (26.6%); finances (19.3%); consumer goods (16.6%); and general manufacturers (15.9%).

Umbrella fund: This is a singular fund.

Launch date: 01/10/95 **Domicile:** Isle of Man

Currency: GBP **Structure:** Open ended, Life Assurance Fund

Portfolio manager: Jonathan Barber
Manager of Eagle Star UK Equity; commenced 1992; BSc in business administration; previously at Scottish Equitable for 2 years.

Contact: Anna Radford

Performance:

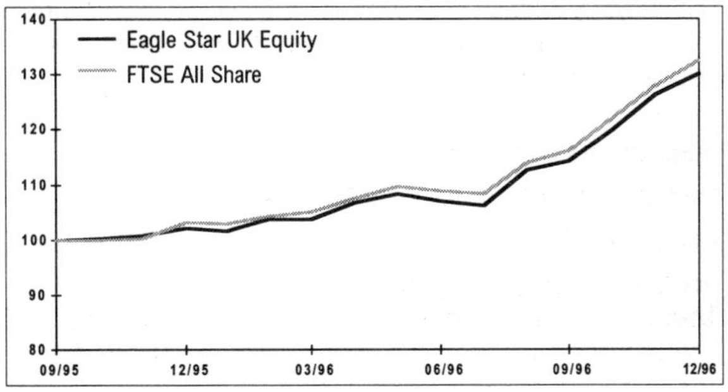

Purchase: Financial Advisor, Via a life product

Minimum investment: 1,000 GBP

Custodian: Chase Manhattan Bank

Listed: None **Dealings:** Daily

Fund Sedol I.D.: 29848 **Published:** FT

Fees **Annual fee:** 1.50% **Performance fee:** None
Front end load: ILP **Redemption fee:** ILP
Switching fee: None

Top holdings:

BI Group	1.9%
British Petroleum	4.5%
British Telecom	2.4%
Glaxo Wellcome	4.5%
HSBC Holdings	0.6%
Lloyds TSB Group	0.7%
Reuters Holdings	2.3%
Shell Transport & Trading	4.0%
Standard Chartered Bank	0.1%
Zeneca Group	3.4%

TOTAL RETURNS %

3 months 1997	1996	1995	1994	3 years	5 years
-0.14	27.37	N.A.	N.A.	N.A.	N.A.

STATISTICS

Assets ($mil)	Current yield	Volatility	Risk return	Micropal Star Rating
0.69	—	N.A.	—	———

EDM International Strategy
196/350

EDM Fund Management S.A
Diagonal 399, Barcelona, 08008, Spain
Tel 34-3-416-0143 Fax 34-3-416-0216
http://www. edm.es E mail edm@edm.es

Contact: Antoni Estabanell

Investment objective:
The fund seeks long-term capital growth by investing in European equities of high capitalization and liquid growth stocks. The portfolio has no specifications for country allocations. The top sector allocations of the portfolio are the following: services (23.0%); consumer goods (27.0%); retail trade (14.0%); and health (13.0%).

Umbrella fund: This is a singular fund.

Launch date: 01/10/90 **Domicile:** Luxembourg [UCITS]

Currency: ECU **Structure:** Open ended, SICAV

Portfolio manager: Joan Grau
Manager of EDM International Strategy since the fund's inception; 10 years experience in global markets.

Performance:

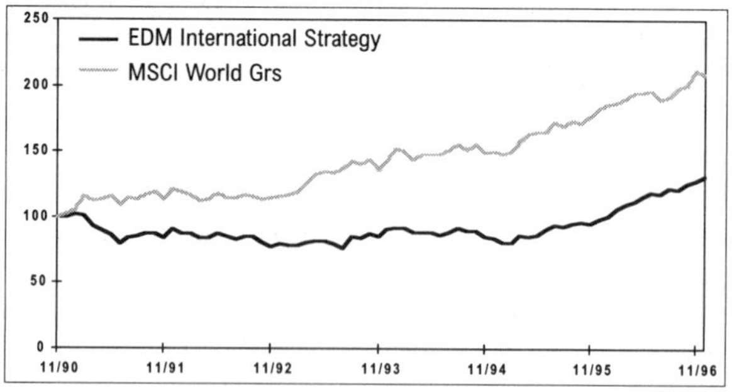

Purchase: Direct

Minimum investment: 1 Share

Custodian: Bank Internationale a Luxembourg

Listed: Luxembourg **Dealings:** Weekly

Fund Sedol I.D.: 304612 **Published:** JO/EP

Fees **Annual fee:** 2.50% **Performance fee:** None
Front end load: 2.00% **Redemption fee:** 0.25%
Switching fee: None

Top holdings:

Carrefour	4.0%
Compass	5.0%
Electrocomponents	4.0%
L'Oreal	5.0%
Novartis	7.0%
Rentokil	7.0%
Reuters Holdings	7.0%
Securitas	4.0%
Sodexho	6.0%
Wolters Kluwer	4.0%

TOTAL RETURNS %

3 months 1997	1996	1995	1994	3 years	5 years
-5.09	32.86	18.20	-7.56	45.18	44.95

STATISTICS

Assets ($mil)	Current yield	Volatility	Risk return	Micropal Star Rating
29.95	—	2.88	4	✪✪✪✪✪

EM Osteuropa Fonds (Lux)
91/350

Union Investment Lux SA
4 Rue Thomas Edison, L-1445 Luxembourg
Tel 352-45-98-66-232 Fax 352-44-33-88
http://www. unioninvest.lu E mail nicole@unioninvest.lu

Contact: Peter Tommerup

Investment objective:
The fund seeks capital appreciation by investing mainly in the equities and securities of Eastern European countries.The top country allocations of the portfolio include the following: Hungary (30.9%); Poland (27.9%); Czech Rep (21.1%); Russia (3.0%); Austria (2.7%); and Germany (2.6%).

Umbrella fund: This is a singular fund.

Launch date: 04/10/94 **Domicile:** Luxembourg [UCITS]

Currency: DEM **Structure:** Open ended, FCP

Portfolio manager: Herbert Schlembach
Manager of EM Osteuropa.

Performance:

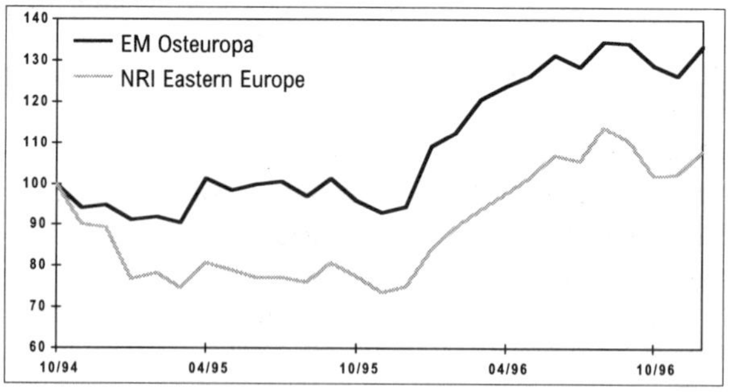

Purchase: Direct, Volksbanken & Raiffeisenbanken (FRG)

Minimum investment: None

Custodian: DG Bank Luxembourg S.A.

Listed: None **Dealings:** Daily

Fund Sedol I.D.: 973821 **Published:** TK/HB/BZ

Fees **Annual fee:** 1.50% **Performance fee:** None
Front end load: 5.00% **Redemption fee:** None
Switching fee: None

Top holdings:

Austria	2.7%
Czech Republic	21.1%
Germany	2.6%
Hungary	30.9%
Poland	27.9%
Russia	3.0%

TOTAL RETURNS %

3 months 1997	1996	1995	1994	3 years	5 years
16.19	41.35	-0.20	N.A.	N.A.	N.A.

STATISTICS

Assets ($mil)	Current yield	Volatility	Risk return	Micropal Star Rating
22.50	—	N.A.	—	——

Emerging Markets Bond Portfolio NV
286/350

LM Global Offshore Funds
4 Floor Picadilly Centre, George Town, Grand Cayman, Cayman Islands
Tel 305-443-0859 Fax 305-443-4885
http://www. lmglobal.com

Contact: Customer Services Department

Investment objective:
The fund seeks maximum total return, consisting of income and capital appreciation. The top country allocations of the portfolio are as follows: Brazil (25.0%); Argentina (19.0%); Mexico (15.0%) Russia (9.0%); and Ecuador (7.0%).

Performance:

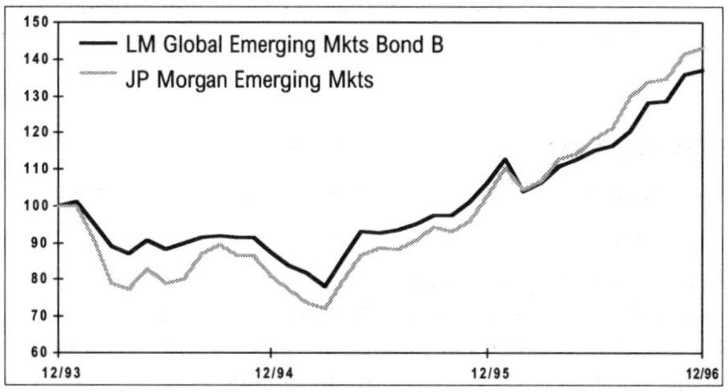

Umbrella fund: This is a singular fund.

Launch date: 11/04/91 **Domicile:** Netherlands Antilles

Currency: USD **Structure:** Open ended, Investment Company

Portfolio manager: Fouad Hashem
Head of Investment team at Western Asset Global Management; specialises in emerging markets with an emphasis on Latin America; MPhil degree, economics/ politics- Cambridge U and BSc, economics- Loughborough U.

Purchase: Direct, Financial Advisor

Minimum investment: 5,000 USD

Custodian: Boston Safe Deposit and Trust

Listed: None **Dealings:** Daily

Fund Sedol I.D.: 251417 **Published:** BG

Fees **Annual fee:** 1.00% **Performance fee:** None
Front end load: None **Redemption fee:** 5.00%
Switching fee: None

Top holdings:

Argentina FRB-PDI 6.492/05	14.3%
Brazil (DCB) SER:L FRN 6.562/12	5.0%
Brazil (EI) FRN 6.500/06	3.3%
Brazil (W.I.) C Bond 4.5/14	12.5%
Ecuador PDI Bear FRN 3.00/15	4.7%
Mexico Global Bond 11.5/26	8.9%
Morocco Tranch A Loan FRN 6.375/09	3.1%
Morocco Tranch A Loan FRN 6.437/09	3.1%
Venezuela DCB SER DL (FRN) 6.500/07	4.9%
Vneshekenombaux Loans 2020	8.9%

TOTAL RETURNS %

3 months 1997	1996	1995	1994	3 years	5 years
2.19	28.79	21.91	-12.67	37.11	87.29

STATISTICS

Assets ($mil)	Current yield	Volatility	Risk return	Micropal Star Rating
21.15	10.50	3.94	1	✪✪

EMIF Spain Index Plus B
279/350

CCF BHF HS KB BBV
Paseo de la Castellana 81, Madrid, 28046, Spain
Tel 34-1-374-61-47 Fax 34-1-374-62-89

Contact: Customer Services Department

Investment objective:
The objective of this sub-fund is to create appreciation through investments in Spanish equities. As a benchmark the Investment Manager's objective is to out perform the IBEX 35 Index which includes the largest and most liquid stocks traded on the CATS System.

Performance:

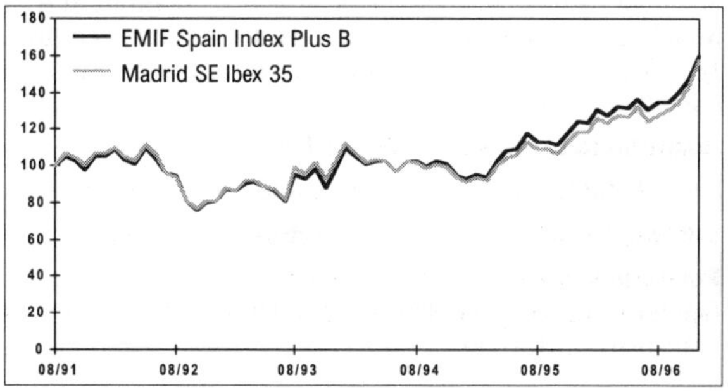

Umbrella fund: European Multi Index Fund

Launch date: 01/07/91 **Domicile:** Luxembourg [UCITS]

Currency: ESP **Structure:** Open ended, SICAV

Portfolio manager: Paloma Piqueinas of Banco Bilbao, Viscaya, Madrid
Manager of EMIF Spain Index Plus A/B, commenced May 1993.

Purchase: Direct, Financial Advisor

Minimum investment: 1 Unit

Custodian: Kredietbank S.A. Luxembourg

Listed: Luxembourg **Dealings:** Daily

Fund Sedol I.D.: 300469 **Published:** IHT

Fees **Annual fee:** 0.75% **Performance fee:** None
Front end load: Up to 8.50% **Redemption fee:** Up to 1.00%
Switching fee: None

Top holdings:

BBV	8.2%
Endesa	8.4%
Iberdrola	5.2%
Repsol	6.1%
Telefonica	8.5%

TOTAL RETURNS %

3 months 1997	1996	1995	1994	3 years	5 years
-4.71	29.08	31.52	-3.35	64.07	52.79

STATISTICS

Assets ($mil)	Current yield	Volatility	Risk return	Micropal Star Rating
1.73	—	4.56	3	✪✪✪✪

Enigma Convertible Fund Limited
295/350

Kornco/Folkes
Chelsea Wharf, 15 Lots Road, London SW10 0QJ,
United Kingdom
Tel 44-171-376-5437 Fax 44-171-351-1454

Investment objective:
Formerly Myrus International Fund, the fund seeks to achieve above average returns from diversified securities issued in private placements or public offerings.The country allocations of the portfolio are primarily held in the US (90.0%).

Contact: Patrick J.S. Folkes

Performance:

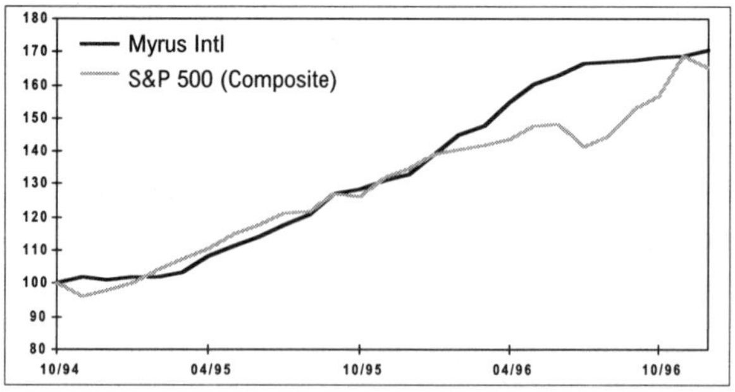

Top holdings:

US Convertibles- Others	70.0%
US Convertibles- Telcommunications	30.0%

Umbrella fund: This is a singular fund.
Launch date: 01/10/94 **Domicile:** Cayman Islands
Currency: USD **Structure:** Open ended, LLC
Portfolio manager: Sunder Advani
Manager, Director of the company and Chairman of Kernco Trust SA; graduate of Oxford U; specialises in emerging markets and managing global portfolios;over 20 years business experience managing international companies.
Purchase: Direct, Financial Advisor, Folkes Asset Management
Minimum investment: 250,000 USD
Custodian: Banque Scandinave (Geneva)
Listed: None **Dealings:** Monthly
Fund Sedol I.D.: 305258 **Published:** FT/IHT/SC
Fees **Annual fee:** 1.50% **Performance fee:** 20.00%
Front end load: 2.00% **Redemption fee:** None
Switching fee: None

TOTAL RETURNS %

3 months 1997	1996	1995	1994	3 years	5 years
2.70	28.40	31.52	N.A.	N.A.	N.A.

STATISTICS

Assets ($mil)	Current yield	Volatility	Risk return	Micropal Star Rating
6.00	—	N.A.	—	———

Ermitage Emerging Markets Fund Ltd
208/350

Ermitage Luxembourg SA
PO Box 1576, 68-70 Boulevard de la Petrusse, L-1015 Luxembourg
Tel 352-40-73-30 Fax 352-40-73-27
http://www. ermitage.lu E mail webmaster@ermitage.lu

Investment objective:
The fund seeks long-term capital appreciation through investment in select equity and debt funds in the newly industrializing countries in Asia, Latin America, the Middle East, Europe and Russia. Country allocations of the portfolio include: Russia (22.0%); Latin America (14.5%); Brazil (14.5%); Eastern Europe (10.5%); and South East Asia (6.5%).

Contact: D W Metcalf/M Baranowski

Performance:

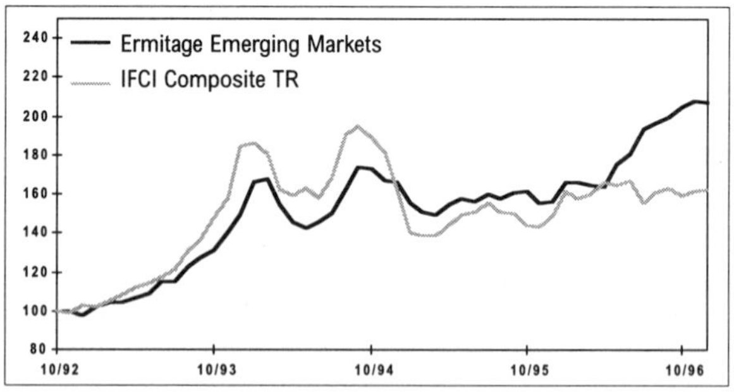

Top holdings:

Consulta Emerging Markets	12.0%
Croesus Russia	5.0%
Egypt Trust	4.5%
EMTR Fund SA	9.0%
Explorer fund	20.0%
FP Consult umbrella	7.5%
GT Emerging Markets Bond	4.5%
GT Orient	5.0%
Indosuez Asset Management	5.0%
WP Developing Markets Capital	6.0%

Umbrella fund: This is a singular fund.
Launch date: 29/11/91 **Domicile:** British Virgin Islands
Currency: USD **Structure:** Open ended, LLC
Portfolio manager: Matthew Ridley
Manager of Emerging Markets commenced 1991 and Investment advisor at Ermitage Management (UK)Ltd.

Purchase: Direct, Through administrative agent
Minimum investment: 10,000 USD
Custodian: Bank of Bermuda (Lux) S.A
Listed: None **Dealings:** Weekly
Fund Sedol I.D.: 429291 **Published:** FT/IHT/WS
Fees **Annual fee:** 1.00% **Performance fee:** None
Front end load: 5.00% **Redemption fee:** None
Switching fee: None

TOTAL RETURNS %

3 months 1997	1996	1995	1994	3 years	5 years
11.21	32.35	-5.95	11.46	38.74	N.A.

STATISTICS

Assets ($mil)	Current yield	Volatility	Risk return	Micropal Star Rating
16.35	—	4.03	3	✪✪✪✪✪

Ermitage Global Mining Investment Fund Ltd

209/350

Ermitage Luxembourg SA
PO Box 1576, 68-70 Boulevard de la Petrusse, L-1015 Luxembourg
Tel 352-40-73-30 Fax 352-40-73-27
http://www. ermitage.lu E mail webmaster@ermitage.lu

Investment objective:
This fund invests principally in equities with the aim of medium to long-term growth with a minimum of 70% invested in quoted equities of mining companies which have a market captialisation in excess of 50 million US dollars. Country allocations of this portfolio are as follows: Canada (57.6%); Australia (17.9%); US (13.4%); South Africa (5.7%); UK (2.7%); and Mexico (0.8%).

Umbrella fund: This is a singular fund.

Launch date: 26/09/95 **Domicile:** Bermuda

Currency: USD **Structure:** Open ended, LLC

Portfolio manager: Kjeld Thygesen
Investment manger of Ermitage Global Mining since 1995; Director of Lion Resources Management, London; previously with James Capel and Rothschild Asset Management; specialising in international mining.

Purchase: Through administrative agent

Minimum investment: 10,000 USD

Custodian: Bank of Bermuda (Lux) S.A

Listed: Dublin **Dealings:** Weekly

Fund Sedol I.D.: 232009 **Published:** FT/IHT/WS

Fees **Annual fee:** 1.50% **Performance fee:** 15.00%
Front end load: 5.00% **Redemption fee:** None
Switching fee: None

Contact: D W Metcalf/M Baranowski

Performance:

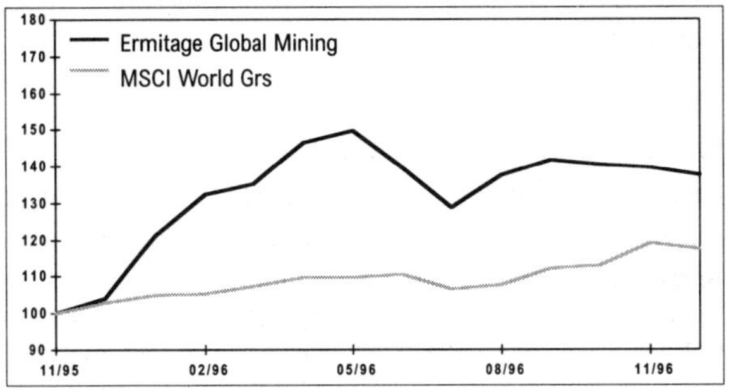

Top holdings:

Holding	%
Capral Aluminium	2.3%
City View	1.8%
Dayton Mining	2.2%
Freeport McMoran	1.9%
Gencor ADR	2.0%
Glenmore Highlands	2.2%
Minorca Resources	2.0%
Palmer Resources	2.5%
Western Mining Corp.	2.1%
Western Pacific Mining	1.8%

TOTAL RETURNS %

3 months 1997	1996	1995	1994	3 years	5 years
4.49	32.28	N.A.	N.A.	N.A.	N.A.

STATISTICS

Assets ($mil)	Current yield	Volatility	Risk return	Micropal Star Rating
45.40	—	N.A.	—	———

Ermitage UK Value Fund Ltd

182/350

Ermitage Luxembourg SA
PO Box 1576, 68-70 Boulevard de la Petrusse, L-1015 Luxembourg
Tel 352-40-73-30 Fax 352-40-73-27
http://www. ermitage.lu E mail webmaster@ermitage.lu

Investment objective:
This fund seeks long-term capital growth from a portfolio of UK transferable securities selected by the application of value-based research methods.
The top sector allocations of the portfolio are the following: services (28.0%); energy (17.0%); non-durables (15.0%); and finance (10.5%).

Umbrella fund: This is a singular fund.

Launch date: 09/01/95 **Domicile:** Bermuda

Currency: GBP **Structure:** Open ended, LLC

Portfolio manager: Colin McLean
Manager of Ermitage United Kingdom Value the fund commenced June 1995; Director of Scottish Value Management Ltd; previously with Templeton.

Purchase: Through administrative agent

Minimum investment: 10,000 GBP

Custodian: Bank of Bermuda (Bermuda) Ltd.

Listed: Dublin **Dealings:** Weekly

Fund Sedol I.D.: 230939 **Published:** FT/IHT/WS

Fees **Annual fee:** 1.50% **Performance fee:** 10.00%
Front end load: 5.00% **Redemption fee:** None
Switching fee: None

Contact: D W Metcalf/M Baranowski

Performance:

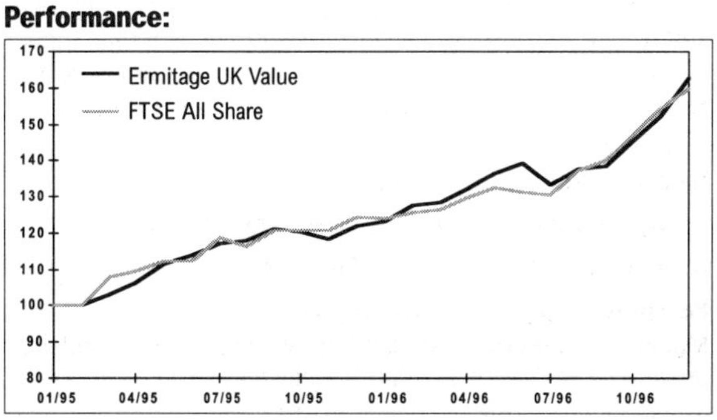

Top holdings:

Holding	%
Airtours (GBP)	5.0%
Beazer group	4.2%
British Aerospace	5.2%
Cairn Energy	15.8%
Go Ahead Group	5.0%
Lasmo	4.1%
Rail Track Group	5.4%
Sema Group	3.8%
Stagecoach Hldgs	4.7%
Zeneca Group	4.7%

TOTAL RETURNS %

3 months 1997	1996	1995	1994	3 years	5 years
6.53	33.56	N.A.	N.A.	N.A.	N.A.

STATISTICS

Assets ($mil)	Current yield	Volatility	Risk return	Micropal Star Rating
40.11	—	N.A.	—	———

Essex High Technology Ltd
290/350

Olympia Capital International Inc
Williams House, 20 Reid Street, Hamilton, HM 11, Bermuda
Tel 1-441-292-1018 Fax 1-441-295-2305

Investment objective:
The fund invests primarily in the equity securities of a broad range of US and foreign companies which develop, produce or provide services based on advanced high technology.

Umbrella fund: This is a singular fund.
Launch date: 01/09/95 **Domicile:** British Virgin Islands
Currency: USD **Structure:** Open ended, Investment Company
Portfolio manager: Joseph McNay, Essex Investment Management Company, Inc
Manager of the fund since 1995; Manager of Essex Investment Management Company, Inc; has managed equities since 1976.

Purchase: Direct, Financial Advisor
Minimum investment: 25,000 USD
Custodian: Morgan Stanley & Co Inc.
Listed: None **Dealings:** Monthly
Fund Sedol I.D.: 265687 **Published:** MP/BG/LP/TK
Fees **Annual fee:** 1.00% **Performance fee:** 15.00%
Front end load: None **Redemption fee:** None
Switching fee: None

Contact: Phillip Pedro
Performance:

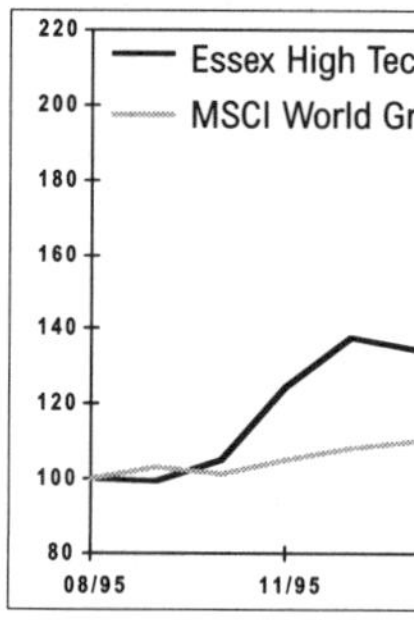

Top holdings:

Holding	%
Cash/MM - US	3.0%
Equities - US	99.7%

TOTAL RETURNS %

3 months 1997	1996	1995	1994	3 years	5 years
-3.71	28.61	N.A.	N.A.	N.A.	N.A.

STATISTICS

Assets ($mil)	Current yield	Volatility	Risk return	Micropal Star Rating
28.12	—	N.A.	—	———

Europa American Equity
197/350

Europa Funds Limited
527 Madison Avenue, New York, NY 10022, United States
Tel 1-212-838-7272 Fax 1-212-838-7824

Investment objective:
The sub-fund seeks capital appreciation through investments in quality growth stocks and to out perform the rate of return of conventional funds in the US. The portfolio consists of high quality steadily growing companies primarily in the US with minor holdings in the UK. The base currency of this sub-fund is in US dollars.

Umbrella fund: Europa Funds Limited
Launch date: 01/12/90 **Domicile:** Cayman Islands
Currency: USD **Structure:** Open ended, Investment Company
Portfolio manager: William P Stewart
Manager of Europa American Equity since 1990; founder of WP Stewart & Co; previously with Pyne Kendall & Hollister as CEO and Director of Research; 36 years of experience in the finance industry.
Purchase: Direct
Minimum investment: 100,000 USD
Custodian: Neuberger & Berman
Listed: Dublin **Dealings:** Daily
Fund Sedol I.D.: 232260 **Published:** IHT
Fees **Annual fee:** 2.00% **Performance fee:** None
Front end load: Up to 2.00% **Redemption fee:** 0.50%
Switching fee: None

Contact: Jeffery R Stewart
Performance:

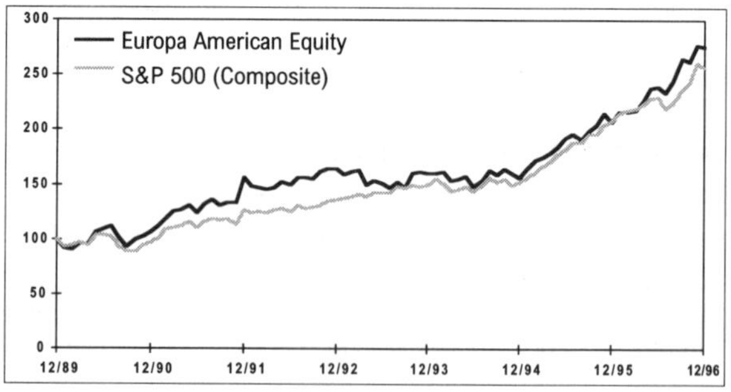

Top holdings:

Holding	%
Automatic Data Processing	11.6%
Autozone	6.2%
Disney	6.3%
Dollar General	6.4%
First Data Corp.	8.0%
Gillette	7.0%
Intel Corp.	8.2%
Mc Donalds	5.6%
Pfeizer	6.5%
Rentokil	7.7%

TOTAL RETURNS %

3 months 1997	1996	1995	1994	3 years	5 years
-0.07	32.86	33.23	-2.64	72.33	76.96

STATISTICS

Assets ($mil)	Current yield	Volatility	Risk return	Micropal Star Rating
4.00	—	3.41	4	✪✪✪✪

Europa American Option

9/350

Europa Funds Limited
527 Madison Avenue, New York, NY 10022, United States
Tel 1-212-838-7272 Fax 1-212-838-7824

Investment objective:
The sub-fund seeks aggressive growth through the investment of select call options in high quality growth US stocks while shorting the S & P Index (OEX) options, in order to achieve a rate of return superior to that generated by other conventional funds. The top sector allocations of this portfolio are as follows: retail trade (23.0%); and services (14.0%).

Umbrella fund: Europa Funds Limited
Launch date: 01/01/91 **Domicile:** Cayman Islands
Currency: USD **Structure:** Open ended, Investment Company
Portfolio manager: William P. Stewart, Jeffrey R. Stewart and Wedie von Gaudeker Co-Managers of Europa American Option.

Contact: Jeffery R Stewart

Performance:

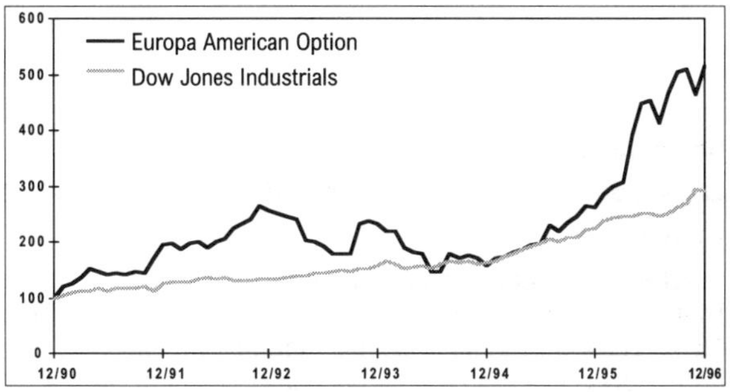

Purchase: Direct, Financial Advisor
Minimum investment: 100,000 USD
Custodian: Neuberger & Berman
Listed: Dublin **Dealings:** Daily
Fund Sedol I.D.: 232261 **Published:** IHT
Fees **Annual fee:** None **Performance fee:** 15.00%
Front end load: Up to 2.00% **Redemption fee:** 0.50%
Switching fee: None

Top holdings:

Holding	%
Autozone	7.0%
CUC International	5.0%
Dollar General	8.0%
General Electric	5.0%
Gillette	8.0%
Home Depot	3.0%
Mattel	3.0%
Mc Donalds	4.0%
Pfeizer	7.0%
Wal Mart	4.0%

TOTAL RETURNS %

3 months 1997	1996	1995	1994	3 years	5 years
-24.53	97.56	64.85	-32.10	121.13	165.48

STATISTICS

Assets ($mil)	Current yield	Volatility	Risk return	Micropal Star Rating
3.90	—	9.13	4	✪✪✪✪

Europa European Equity

276/350

Europa Funds Limited
527 Madison Avenue, New York, NY 10022, United States
Tel 1-212-838-7272 Fax 1-212-838-7824

Investment objective:
This sub-fund seeks capital appreciation through investments in high quality European growth stocks and to achieve a rate of return superior to that generated by other conventional funds in European equities. The top country allocations of the portfolio are as follows: UK (44.0%); France (22.0%); Germany (12.0%); Holland (10.0%); Sweden (10.0%); and Austria (2.0%).

Umbrella fund: Europa Funds Limited
Launch date: 01/01/93 **Domicile:** Cayman Islands
Currency: USD **Structure:** Open ended, Investment Company
Portfolio manager: Wedig non Gaudecker
Manager of Europa European Equity commenced January 1993; Managing Director of Comgest SA; MA, economics- U of Munich; 28 years of investment experience.

Contact: Jeffery R Stewart

Performance:

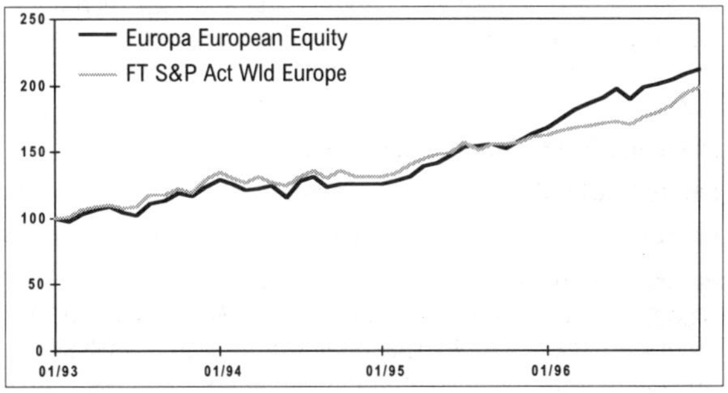

Purchase: Direct, Financial Advisor
Minimum investment: 100,000 USD
Custodian: Banque Indosuez (Luxembourg)
Listed: Dublin **Dealings:** Weekly
Fund Sedol I.D.: 232259 **Published:** IHT
Fees **Annual fee:** None **Performance fee:** 15.00%
Front end load: Up to 2.00% **Redemption fee:** 0.50%
Switching fee: None

Top holdings:

Holding	%
Carrefour	5.0%
Castorama	3.0%
Hornbach	5.0%
L'Oreal	5.0%
Roche Holdings	4.0%
Sapag	5.0%
Securitas	5.0%
Sodexho	6.0%
Wolford	2.0%
Wolters Kluwer	5.0%

TOTAL RETURNS %

3 months 1997	1996	1995	1994	3 years	5 years
-3.04	29.27	30.51	1.38	71.03	N.A.

STATISTICS

Assets ($mil)	Current yield	Volatility	Risk return	Micropal Star Rating
5.20	—	3.25	5	✪✪✪✪

Everest Capital Frontier Fund Ltd
25/350

Everest Capital Limited
PO Box HM 2458, Hamilton, HM JX, Bermuda
Tel 1-441-292-2200 Fax 1-441-292-2285
E mail everest@Intl.bm.

Investment objective:
The fund seeks to achieve superior absolute returns by investing in emerging markets.

Contact: Marko Dimitrijevic

Performance:

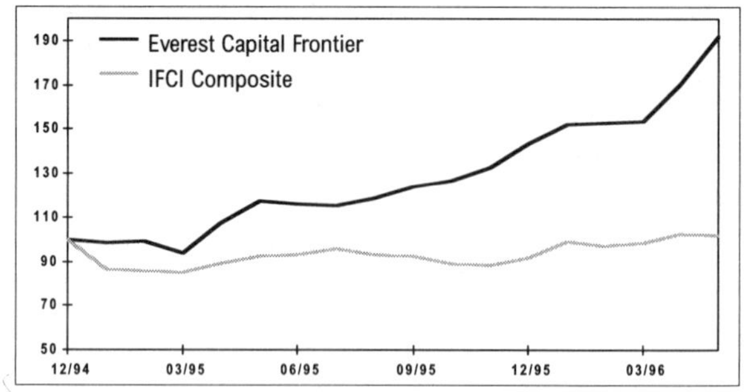

Top holdings: USD 100.0%

Umbrella fund: This is a singular fund.
Launch date: 01/01/95 **Domicile:** British Virgin Islands
Currency: USD **Structure:** Open ended, Investment Company
Portfolio manager: Marko Dimitrijevic CFA
Founder resident of Everest Capital Ltd; MBA- Stanford Grad Sch of Business; over 15 yr. experience in international mgt/ research analysis/ investment banking; previously with Compagie de Banque et de Credit SA, Paine Webber Inc et al.
Purchase: Direct
Minimum investment: 1,000,000 USD
Custodian: The Bank of Bermuda
Listed: None **Dealings:** Quarterly
Fund Sedol I.D.: 305369 **Published:** IHT/BG/WS/TK
Fees **Annual fee:** 1.50% **Performance fee:** 20.00%
Front end load: None **Redemption fee:** None
Switching fee: None

TOTAL RETURNS %

3 months 1997	1996	1995	1994	3 years	5 years
-2.37	69.92	43.40	N.A.	N.A.	N.A.

STATISTICS

Assets ($mil)	Current yield	Volatility	Risk return	Micropal Star Rating
165.00	—	N.A.	—	———

Everest Capital International
39/350

Everest Capital Limited
PO Box HM 2458, Hamilton, HM JX, Bermuda
Tel 1-441-292-2200 Fax 1-441-292-2285
E mail everest@Intl. hm.

Investment objective:
The fund seeks to achieve superior absolute returns while minimising the risk of loss of capital by using various hedging and arbitrage techniques. The fund invests globally using an opportunistic value approach focusing on debt and equity securities which it believes are neglected, distressed special situations or inefficiently priced.

Contact: Marko Dimitrijevic

Performance:

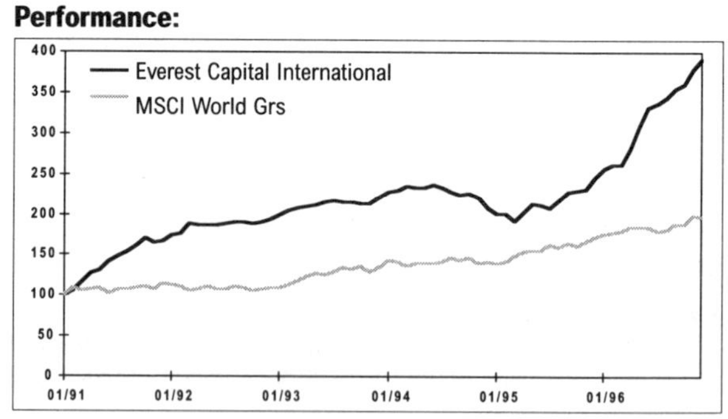

Top holdings: Not Supplied n/s

Umbrella fund: This is a singular fund.
Launch date: 01/01/92 **Domicile:** British Virgin Islands
Currency: USD **Structure:** Close ended, Investment Company
Portfolio manager: Marko Dimitrijevic CFA
Founder resident of Everest Capital Ltd; MBA- Stanford Grad Sch of Business; over 15 yrs experience in international mgt/ research analysis/ investment banking; previously with Compagie de Banque et de Credit SA, Paine Webber Inc et al.
Purchase: Direct
Minimum investment: 1,000,000 USD
Custodian: The Bank of Bermuda
Listed: None **Dealings:** Quarterly
Fund Sedol I.D.: 305390 **Published:** IHT/BG/WS/TK
Fees **Annual fee:** 1.50% **Performance fee:** 20.00%
Front end load: None **Redemption fee:** None
Switching fee: None

TOTAL RETURNS %

3 months 1997	1996	1995	1994	3 years	5 years
10.80	59.07	18.24	-6.32	76.20	133.11

STATISTICS

Assets ($mil)	Current yield	Volatility	Risk return	Micropal Star Rating
645.00	—	3.45	4	✪✪✪✪✪

Fidelity Funds European Smaller Companies
111/350

Fidelity Investments Luxembourg S.A.
Kansallis House, Place de l'Etoile, L-1021 Luxembourg
Tel 352-251-35-12-30 Fax 352-25-03-40
http://www. fid.intl.com

Investment objective:
The sub-fund provides long-term capital growth from an actively managed portfolio consisting of smaller companies listed in the UK and continental Europe. Smaller companies are defined as those with market capitalisation of less than 500 million US dollars. The top country allocations of this portfolio are UK (27.9%); Sweden (11.8%); France (10.5%); and Germany (6.3%).

Umbrella fund: Fidelity Funds
Launch date: 01/12/95 **Domicile:** Luxembourg [UCITS]
Currency: DEM **Structure:** Open ended, SICAV
Portfolio manager: Colin Stone
Manager of Fidelity Funds European Small Companies since October 1990; MA-Cambridge U; joined Fidelity in 1987.

Purchase: Direct, Financial Advisor, Institutional
Minimum investment: 2,500 USD
Custodian: Brown Brothers Harriman (Luxembourg) S.A.
Listed: None **Dealings:** Daily
Fund Sedol I.D.: 454712 **Published:** FT/HB/HF/NZZ/DS/HKE
Fees **Annual fee:** 1.50% **Performance fee:** None
Front end load: 5.25% **Redemption fee:** None
Switching fee: 1.00%

Contact: Customer Services Department
Performance:

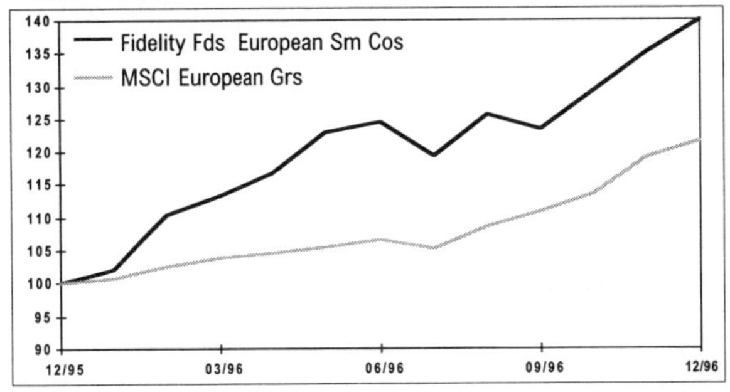

Top holdings:

Frontec	2.7%
Grandoptical Photolervia	2.3%
Kingspan Group	2.5%
NRZ	1.8%
Saes Gelten	1.9%

TOTAL RETURNS %

3 months 1997	1996	1995	1994	3 years	5 years
9.74	39.91	N.A.	N.A.	N.A.	N.A.

STATISTICS

Assets ($mil)	Current yield	Volatility	Risk return	Micropal Star Rating
135.74	—	N.A.	—	———

Fidelity Funds Hong Kong & China Fund
96/350

Fidelity Investments Luxembourg S.A.
Kansallis House, Place de l'Etoile, L-1021 Luxembourg
Tel 352-251-35-12-30 Fax 352-25-03-40
http://www. fid.intl.com

Investment objective:
The aim of the sub-fund is to provide long-term capital growth from an actively managed portfolio of companies listed primarily on the Hong Kong Stock Exchange, but also including shares and securities traded on the exchanges of China and elsewhere. The top geographic allocations of the assets are the following: Hong Kong (84.7%); and Singapore (2.3%).

Umbrella fund: Fidelity Funds
Launch date: 10/01/90 **Domicile:** Luxembourg [UCITS]
Currency: USD **Structure:** Open ended, SICAV
Portfolio manager: Joseph Tse
Manager of Fidelity Funds Hong Kong & China Fund since December 1993; MBA, business administration- U of Western Ontario; joined Fidelity, Hong Kong in 1990 as an investment analyst.

Purchase: Direct, Financial Advisor, Institutional
Minimum investment: 2,500 USD
Custodian: Brown Brothers Harriman (Luxembourg) S.A.
Listed: None **Dealings:** Daily
Fund Sedol I.D.: 434113 **Published:** FT/HB/HF/NZZ/DS/HKE
Fees **Annual fee:** 1.50% **Performance fee:** None
Front end load: 5.25% **Redemption fee:** None
Switching fee: 1.00%

Contact: Customer Services Department
Performance:

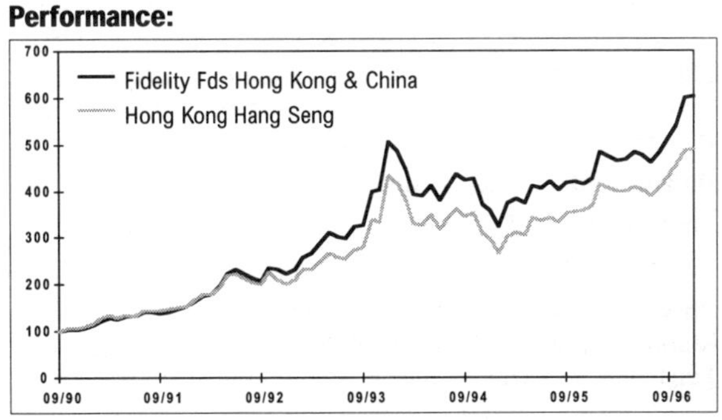

Top holdings:

Great Eagle Holdings	3.2%
Henderson Land Development	8.6%
HSBC Holdings	10.2%
Hutchison Whampoa	9.3%
Sun Hung Kai Properties	9.3%

TOTAL RETURNS %

3 months 1997	1996	1995	1994	3 years	5 years
-7.52	41.04	19.78	-29.17	19.67	294.12

STATISTICS

Assets ($mil)	Current yield	Volatility	Risk return	Micropal Star Rating
318.80	—	6.46	1	✪✪✪

Fidelity Funds Iberia

171/350

Fidelity Investments Luxembourg S.A.
Kansallis House, Place de l'Etoile, L-1021 Luxembourg
Tel 352-251-35-12-30 Fax 352-25-03-40
http://www. fid.intl.com

Investment objective:
The sub-fund seeks capital growth through investment in a diversified portfolio of primarily Spanish and Portuguese equities. The top sector allocations of the portfolio are the following: finance (31.1%); energy (22.9%); and services (21.6%). At this time the portfolio is divided between Spain (78.1%); Portugal (15.8%); and the remainder is held in cash (6.1%).

Umbrella fund: Fidelity Funds

Launch date: 01/10/90 **Domicile:** Luxembourg [UCITS]

Currency: ESP **Structure:** Open ended, SICAV

Portfolio manager: Frederic Gautier
Manager of Fidelity Funds Iberia and VP; MBA- ESLSCA Paris- economics/ finance; joined Fidelity in 1994.

Contact: Customer Services Department

Performance:

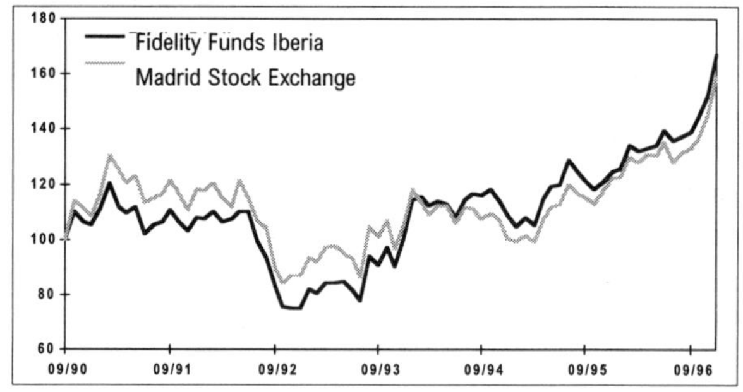

Purchase: Direct, Financial Advisor, Institutional

Minimum investment: 2,500 USD

Custodian: Brown Brothers Harriman (Luxembourg) S.A.

Listed: None **Dealings:** Daily

Fund Sedol I.D.: 434114 **Published:** FT/HB/HF/NZZ/DS/HKE

Fees **Annual fee:** 1.50% **Performance fee:** None
Front end load: 5.25% **Redemption fee:** None
Switching fee: 1.00%

Top holdings:

Banco Bilbao Vizcana	7.7%
Banco de Santander	6.3%
Endesa	5.5%
Iberdrola	6.9%
Telfonica de Espana	8.8%

TOTAL RETURNS %

3 months 1997	1996	1995	1994	3 years	5 years
2.48	34.43	14.34	8.47	66.72	55.20

STATISTICS

Assets ($mil)	Current yield	Volatility	Risk return	Micropal Star Rating
19.13	—	4.28	4	✪✪✪✪

Fidelity Funds Latin America Fund

296/350

Fidelity Investments Luxembourg S.A.
Kansallis House, Place de l'Etoile, L-1021 Luxembourg
Tel 352-251-35-12-30 Fax 352-25-03-40
http://www. fid.intl.com

Investment objective:
The sub-fund seeks to achieve long-term growth from a diversified and actively managed portfolio of securities of Latin America.The top country allocations of the portfolio are Brazil (42.6%); Mexico (23.8%); Argentina (11.6%); Chile (6.6%); and Peru (2.4%). The top sector allocations include the following: energy (17.9%); finance (14.8%); and services (21.1%).

Umbrella fund: Fidelity Funds

Launch date: 05/09/94 **Domicile:** Luxembourg [UCITS]

Currency: USD **Structure:** Open ended, SICAV

Portfolio manager: Patti Salterthwaite
Manager of Fidelity Funds Latin America commenced May 1994 and now VP; joined Fidelity as an analyst 1986.

Contact: Customer Services Department

Performance:

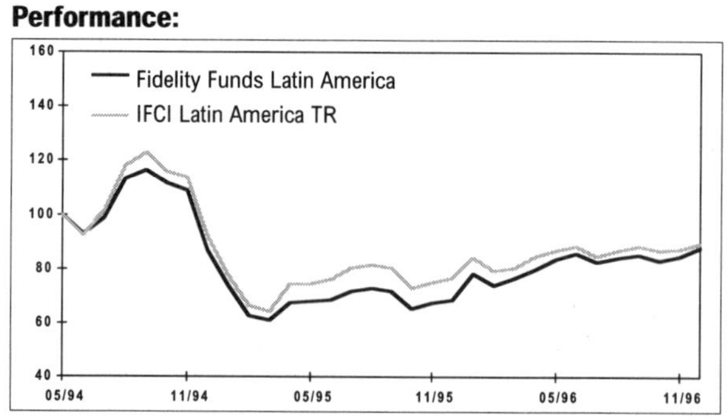

Purchase: Direct, Financial Advisor, Institutional

Minimum investment: 2,500 USD

Custodian: Brown Brothers Harriman (Luxembourg) S.A.

Listed: None **Dealings:** Daily

Fund Sedol I.D.: 439751 **Published:** FT/HB/HF/NZZ/DS/HKE

Fees **Annual fee:** 1.50% **Performance fee:** None
Front end load: 5.25% **Redemption fee:** None
Switching fee: 1.00%

Top holdings:

Electrobas	4.9%
Grupo Carso	3.9%
Telebras	6.2%
Telebras Preferred	3.8%
Telesp PN	3.7%

TOTAL RETURNS %

3 months 1997	1996	1995	1994	3 years	5 years
12.18	28.38	-21.38	N.A.	N.A.	N.A.

STATISTICS

Assets ($mil)	Current yield	Volatility	Risk return	Micropal Star Rating
60.00	—	N.A.	—	——

Fidelity Funds Nordic Fund
124/350

Fidelity Investments Luxembourg S.A.
Kansallis House, Place de l'Etoile, L-1021 Luxembourg
Tel 352-251-35-12-30 Fax 352-25-03-40
http://www. fid.intl.com

Investment objective:
The sub-fund seeks to provide long-term capital growth from investment primarily in the stock markets of Norway, Sweden, Denmark and Finland.The top sector allocation of the portfolio is as follows: capital equipment (25.5%); consumer goods (20.6%); services (17.5%); finance (14.7%); multi-industry (8.75); and materials (6.4%).

Umbrella fund: Fidelity Funds

Launch date: 10/01/90 **Domicile:** Luxembourg [UCITS]

Currency: SEK **Structure:** Open ended, SICAV

Portfolio manager: Colin Stone
Manager of Fidelity Funds Nordic Fund since October 1990; MA- Cambridge U; joined Fidelity in 1987 as an analyst.

Contact: Customer Services Department

Performance:

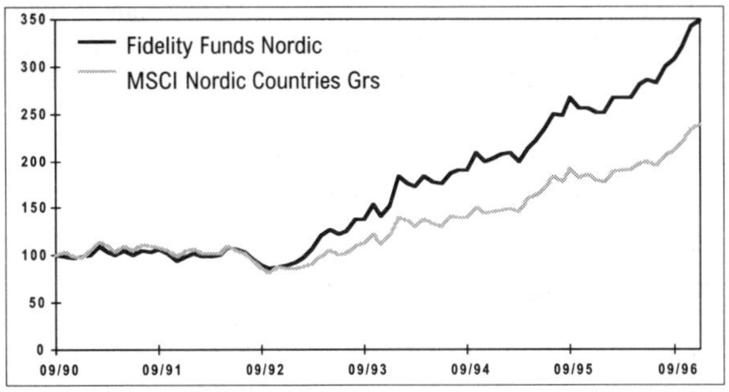

Purchase: Direct, Financial Advisor, Institutional

Minimum investment: 2,500 USD

Custodian: Brown Brothers Harriman (Luxembourg) S.A.

Listed: None **Dealings:** Daily

Fund Sedol I.D.: 434120 **Published:** FT/HB/HF/NZZ/DS/HKE

Fees **Annual fee:** 1.50% **Performance fee:** None
Front end load: 5.25% **Redemption fee:** None
Switching fee: 1.00%

Top holdings:	
ABB AB	4.3%
Astra	9.1%
Ericsson	9.3%
Nokia A	5.0%
Volvo	4.5%

TOTAL RETURNS %

3 months 1997	1996	1995	1994	3 years	5 years
6.21	38.61	23.91	33.50	129.30	252.00

STATISTICS

Assets ($mil)	Current yield	Volatility	Risk return	Micropal Star Rating
133.76	—	4.88	5	✪✪✪✪

Fidelity Funds United Kingdom Fund
188/350

Fidelity Investments Luxembourg S.A.
Kansallis House, Place de l'Etoile, L-1021 Luxembourg
Tel 352-251-35-12-30 Fax 352-25-03-40
http://www. fid.intl.com

Investment objective:
The sub-fund aims to achieve long-term capital growth primarily through the investment in shares listed in the United Kingdom.The country allocations of the portfolio include the following: UK (93.2%); Republic of Ireland (1.0%); and US (0.5%). The top sector allocations of the portfolio include the following: services (30.3%); consumer goods (15.4%); and finance (13.1%).

Umbrella fund: Fidelity Funds

Launch date: 10/01/90 **Domicile:** Luxembourg [UCITS]

Currency: GBP **Structure:** Open ended, SICAV

Portfolio manager: Anthony Bolton
Manager of Fidelity Funds United Kingdom Fund commenced October 1990; MD for Fidelity Investment Services; MA Hons, engineering and business studies-Cambridge U; joined Fidelity in 1979.

Contact: Customer Services Department

Performance:

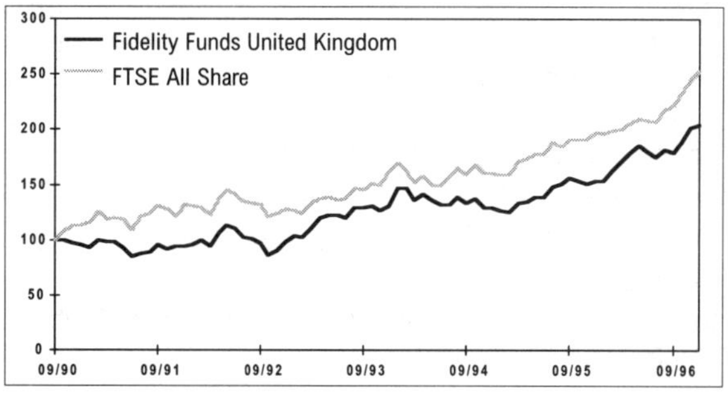

Purchase: Direct, Financial Advisor, Institutional

Minimum investment: 2,500 USD

Custodian: Brown Brothers Harriman (Luxembourg} S.A.

Listed: None **Dealings:** Daily

Fund Sedol I.D.: 434125 **Published:** FT/HB/HF/NZZ/DS/HKE

Fees **Annual fee:** 1.50% **Performance fee:** None
Front end load: 5.25% **Redemption fee:** None
Switching fee: 1.00%

Top holdings:	
British Petroleum	3.2%
London Insurance Market	3.2%
Misys	2.4%
Oriflame Intl	3.5%
Tongaat	3.5%

TOTAL RETURNS %

3 months 1997	1996	1995	1994	3 years	5 years
1.10	33.38	19.56	-1.92	56.40	116.75

STATISTICS

Assets ($mil)	Current yield	Volatility	Risk return	Micropal Star Rating
191.15	—	3.95	3	✪✪✪✪

FIL Leveraged US Govt Bond
315/350

First Investments Ltd (Bermuda)
1218 Two Pacific Place, 88 Queensway, Hong Kong
Tel 852-2868-1837 Fax 852-2877-6475
E mail 105307.130@ compuserve.com

Investment objective:
The fund seeks capital appreciation by investing in US government fixed income securities; mortgage related securities; interest rate swaps and options or contracts on any of the foregoing. The fund utilises a significant investment in research, computerised trading and hedging techniques, to generate an above average total return on shareholders' capital.

Umbrella fund: This is a singular fund.

Launch date: 01/10/92 **Domicile:** Bermuda

Currency: USD **Structure:** Open ended, Mutual Fund

Portfolio manager: Dr. Higgins MD and Dr. Knight, CEO
Co-Managers of the First Investments Limited Leveraged US Government Bond; both hold doctoral degrees in economics and are international portfolio analysts.

Purchase: Direct, Financial Advisor, Banks in Hong Kong

Minimum investment: 2,600 USD

Custodian: The Bank of Butterfield Executor & Trustee Co. Ltd

Listed: None **Dealings:** Weekly

Fund Sedol I.D.: 634101 **Published:** FT/WS/BG/SC

Fees **Annual fee:** 1.25% **Performance fee:** None
Front end load: 2.00% **Redemption fee:** None
Switching fee: 1.00%

Contact: Aster Chow/Leoff Mansfield

Performance:

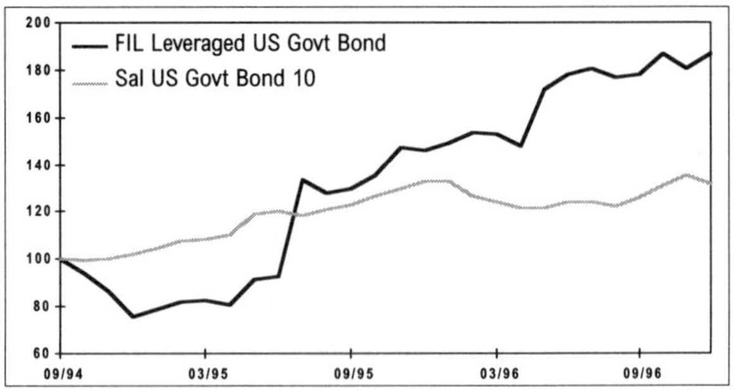

Top holdings:

Cash/MM	55.0%
Interest Rate Swaps - short	-10.0%
Leverage - short	-80.0%
US Treasury Bonds	135.0%

TOTAL RETURNS %

3 months 1997	1996	1995	1994	3 years	5 years
2.99	28.02	93.31	N.A.	N.A.	N.A.

STATISTICS

Assets ($mil)	Current yield	Volatility	Risk return	Micropal Star Rating
48.10	—	N.A.	—	———

Financial and Metals Portfolio Series C
234/350

John W Henry & Company Inc.
Rosebank Center, 11 Bermudiana Road, Pembroke, Bermuda
Tel 1-441-295-1111 Fax 1-441-295-6759
http://www. globalcapitalmgmt.com

Investment objective:
The fund is a Bermuda company that seeks capital appreciation and diversification through a disciplined investment in global futures and forwards markets. Series C is traded pursuant to JWH's Financial and Metals Portfolio, identifying and capitalising on intermediate and long-term price movements in financial and metal markets.

Umbrella fund: JWH Global Strategies Ltd

Launch date: 01/01/93 **Domicile:** Bermuda

Currency: USD **Structure:** Open ended, Investment Company

Portfolio manager: John W. Henry & Company Inc.
Manager of John Henry GI Strategies C; located in California, US; specialises in the managed futures industry.

Purchase: Direct

Minimum investment: 250,000 USD

Custodian: The Bank of Butterfield Executor and Trustee Co

Listed: None **Dealings:** Monthly

Fund Sedol I.D.: 239443 **Published:** IHT/WS

Fees **Annual fee:** 4.00% **Performance fee:** 15.00%
Front end load: 1.75% **Redemption fee:** None
Switching fee: None

Contact: Ms Paula Burt

Performance:

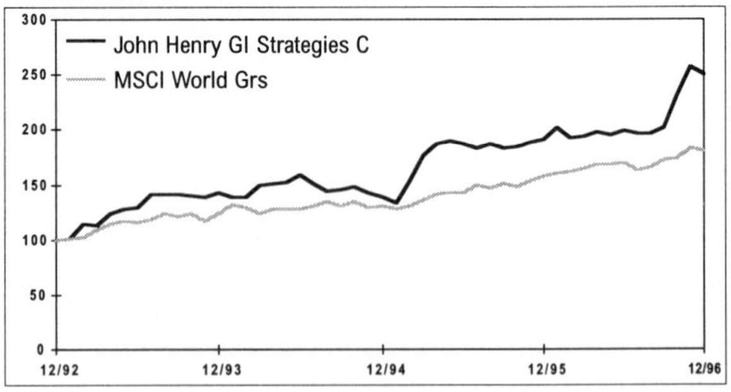

Top holdings:

European Interest Rates	21.0%
Foreign Exchange	24.3%
Metals	28.5%
Pacific Rim Interest Rates	13.4%
Stock Indices	7.6%
US Interest Rates	5.3%

TOTAL RETURNS %

3 months 1997	1996	1995	1994	3 years	5 years
2.15	30.83	38.41	-3.31	75.10	N.A.

STATISTICS

Assets ($mil)	Current yield	Volatility	Risk return	Micropal Star Rating
64.01	—	5.31	4	✪✪✪✪✪

Five Arrows GF Latin American Opps
262/350

Rothschild Asset Management
20 Boulevard Emmanuel Servais, L-2535 Luxembourg
Tel 352-47-93-46-282 Fax 352-47-29-86

Investment objective:
The sub-fund seeks to achieve long-term capital growth through active investment policy in Latin American securities and in ADR's of Latin American securities. Investments can also be made in the securities of Latin American country funds listed on international stock exchanges subject to certain restrictions.

Umbrella fund: Five Arrows Global Fund
Launch date: 20/05/94 **Domicile:** Luxembourg [UCITS]
Currency: USD **Structure:** Open ended, SICAV
Portfolio manager: Catherine Younger
Manager of the fund commenced in 1991; Senior Fund Manger for Latin America; studied history- Exeter U; Associate of the Institute of Investment Management and Research.
Purchase: Direct, Financial Advisor
Minimum investment: 1,000 USD
Custodian: Banque de Gestion Edmond de Rothschild (Lux) S.A.
Listed: Luxembourg **Dealings:** Daily
Fund Sedol I.D.: 418997 **Published:** FT/BZ
Fees **Annual fee:** 1.25% **Performance fee:** None
Front end load: 5.00% **Redemption fee:** None
Switching fee: None

Contact: Jean -Philippe Claessens
Performance:

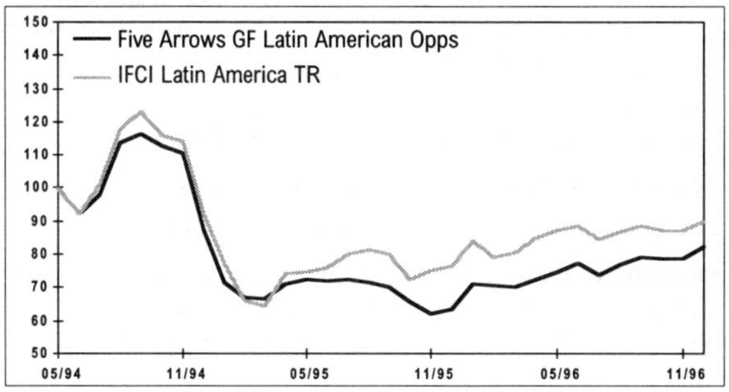

Top holdings:

Bufete	2.4%
Cemex	2.1%
Electrobas	6.8%
Five Arrows Chile	4.8%
ICA	2.2%
Imsa	2.2%
La Moderna	2.2%
Perez Companec	2.1%
Petrobas	2.4%
Telebras	9.8%

TOTAL RETURNS %

3 months 1997	1996	1995	1994	3 years	5 years
13.51	29.97	-27.38	N.A.	N.A.	N.A.

STATISTICS

Assets ($mil)	Current yield	Volatility	Risk return	Micropal Star Rating
5.59	—	N.A.	—	———

Five Arrows IE UK
207/350

Rothschild Asset Management
St Peter Port House, Sausmarez Street, St Peter Port,
GY1 3 PH, Guernsey
Tel 44-1481-719-700 Fax 44-1481-711-511

Investment objective:
The sub-fund aims to achieve capital growth and rising income by investing in all sectors of the UK economy. The top sector allocations of the portfolio include the following: pharmaceuticals (13.1%); finance (24.9%); and hotels/ leisure (8.1%).

Umbrella fund: Five Arrows International Equity Funds
Launch date: 15/09/93 **Domicile:** Guernsey
Currency: GBP **Structure:** Open ended, Unit Trust
Portfolio manager: Rothschild Asset Management (CI) Ltd
Manager of the sub-fund: located at PO Box 242, St Peter Port House, Sausmarez Street, St Peter Port Guernsey, Channel Islands GY1 3PH.

Purchase: Direct, Financial Advisor
Minimum investment: None
Custodian: Coutts (Guernsey) Limited
Listed: None **Dealings:** Daily
Fund Sedol I.D.: 74992 **Published:** FT
Fees **Annual fee:** 1.50% **Performance fee:** None
Front end load: 5.30% **Redemption fee:** None
Switching fee: None

Contact: Customer Services Department
Performance:

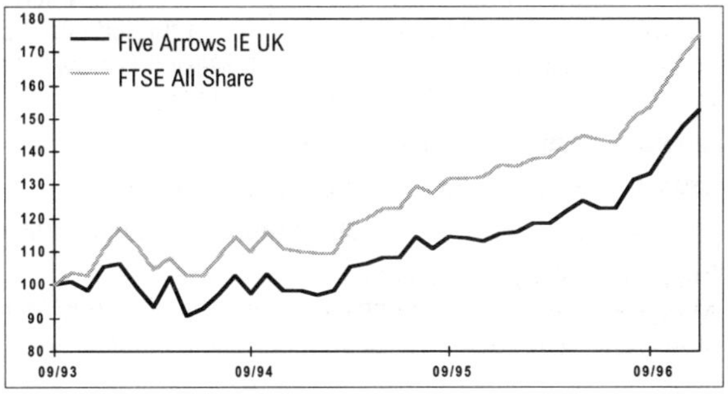

Top holdings:

British Biotech	2.6%
British Petroleum	4.2%
British Telecom	2.9%
Cattles	2.4%
Glaxo Wellcome	4.3%
HSBC Holdings	4.7%
Lloyds TSB Group	3.3%
Medeva	2.6%
Shell Transport & Trading	2.8%
STD Chartered	2.6%

TOTAL RETURNS %

3 months 1997	1996	1995	1994	3 years	5 years
1.06	32.44	17.33	-6.70	44.98	N.A.

STATISTICS

Assets ($mil)	Current yield	Volatility	Risk return	Micropal Star Rating
17.98	—	4.30	1	✪✪✪

Five Arrows IE UK Smllr Cos
107/350

Rothschild Asset Management
St Peter Port House, Sausmarez Street, St Peter Port,
GY1 3 PH, Guernsey
Tel 44-1481-719-700 Fax 44-1481-711-511

Contact: Customer Services Department

Investment objective:
The sub-fund aims at capital appreciation by investing in all sectors of the UK economy, principally in the ordinary and convertible shares of companies with a market capitalisation that would normally qualify them for inclusion in the Hoare Govett Smaller Cos Index.

Umbrella fund: Five Arrows International Equity Funds
Launch date: 15/09/93 **Domicile:** Guernsey
Currency: GBP **Structure:** Open ended, Unit Trust
Portfolio manager: Rothschild Asset Management (CI) Ltd
Manager of the sub-fund: located at PO Box 242, St Peter Port House, Sausmarez Street, St Peter Port Guernsey, Channel Islands GY1 3PH.

Purchase: Direct, Financial Advisor
Minimum investment: None
Custodian: Coutts (Guernsey) Limited
Listed: None **Dealings:** Daily
Fund Sedol I.D.: 74993 **Published:** FT
Fees **Annual fee:** 1.50% **Performance fee:** None
Front end load: 5.30% **Redemption fee:** None
Switching fee: None

Performance:

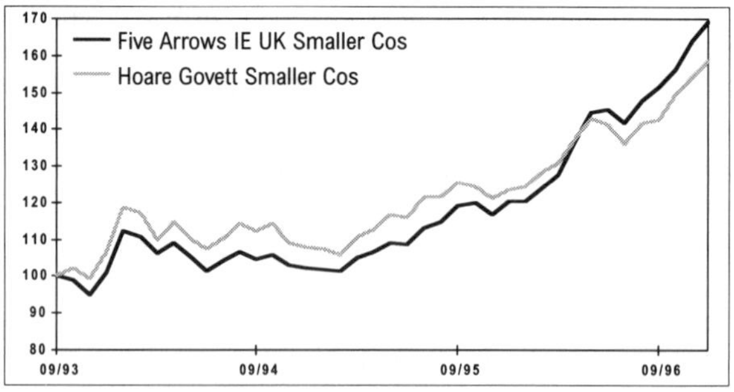

Top holdings:

American Port Services	3.1%
Bath Press	2.7%
Bodycote Intl	2.1%
Brit Borneo ptl	2.5%
Capita Group	4.3%
CRT Group	2.5%
Dixon Motors	2.1%
Gearhouse	2.7%
The Sage Group	3.5%
Ultra Electronics	2.3%

TOTAL RETURNS %

3 months 1997	1996	1995	1994	3 years	5 years
3.92	40.52	17.55	1.18	67.13	N.A.

STATISTICS

Assets ($mil)	Current yield	Volatility	Risk return	Micropal Star Rating
40.73	—	3.20	5	✪✪✪✪

Five Arrows Latin Amer Acc/Dist
343/350

Rothschild Asset Management
St Peter Port House, Sausmarez Street, St Peter Port,
GY1 3 PH, Guernsey
Tel 44-1481-726-331 Fax 44-1481-728-766

Contact: Alan Mahy

Investment objective:
The primary objective of the sub-fund is capital appreciation of Latin American equities through investment in the Five Arrows Latin American Distribution fund.The portfolio has 32.6% of its assets invested in the industrial cyclical sector and a geographic allocation of Brazil (41.7%); Mexico (27.5%); Argentina (11.4%); Chile (11.0%%); Venezuela (4.6%); and Peru (3.8%).
Umbrella fund: This is a singular fund.
Launch date: 30/09/92 **Domicile:** Guernsey [UCITS]
Currency: USD **Structure:** Open ended, Unit Trust
Portfolio manager: Catherine Younger
Manager of the fund commenced in 1991; Senior Fund Manger for Latin America; studied history- Exeter U; Associate of the Institute of Investment Management and Research.
Purchase: Direct
Minimum investment: None
Custodian: Coutts (Guernsey) Limited
Listed: None **Dealings:** Weekly
Fund Sedol I.D.: 75959 **Published:** FT
Fees **Annual fee:** 1.50% **Performance fee:** None
Front end load: 5.30% **Redemption fee:** None
Switching fee: None

Performance:

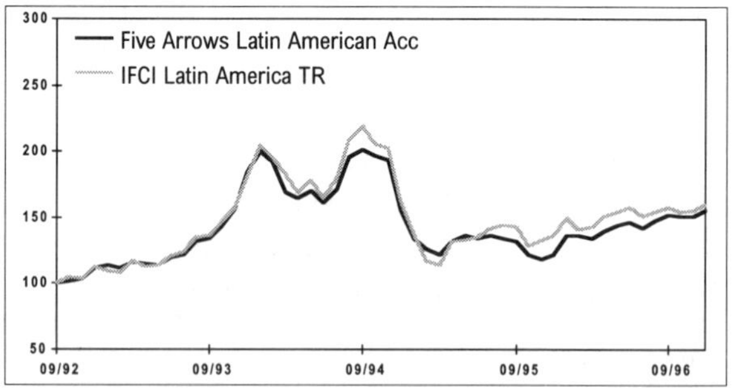

Top holdings:

Bufete	2.5%
Cemex	2.2%
Electrobas	6.8%
Five Arrows Chile	5.0%
ICA	2.2%
Imsa	2.1%
La Moderna	2.3%
Perez Companec	2.2%
Petrobas	2.5%
Telebras	9.8%

TOTAL RETURNS %

3 months 1997	1996	1995	1994	3 years	5 years
17.53	27.21	-22.29	-14.44	-15.42	N.A.

STATISTICS

Assets ($mil)	Current yield	Volatility	Risk return	Micropal Star Rating
4.40	—	6.48	—	✪

Fleming FF America Fund

280/350

Fleming Fund Management (Lux) S.A.
European Bank and Business Centre, 6 Route de Treves,
L-2663 Luxembourg
Tel 352-34-10-30-20 Fax 352-34-10-21-10
http://www. flemings.lu E mail info@flemings.lu

Contact: Hans Heller

Investment objective:
The sub-fund aims to achieve capital growth by investing in securities of North American companies, without sector or size specialisation. At this time the top sector allocations of the portfolio include the following: finance (30.9%); services (13.3%); and consumer goods (13.0%). Currently 100% of the sub-funds assets are allocated to US equities.

Umbrella fund: Fleming Flagship Fund

Launch date: 01/12/88 **Domicile:** Luxembourg [UCITS]

Currency: USD **Structure:** Open ended, SICAV

Portfolio manager: Jonathan Simon
Manager of Fleming FF America Fund since 1988; President of Fleming Capital Mgt; MA, mathematics- Oxford University; joined Flemings in 1980.

Performance:

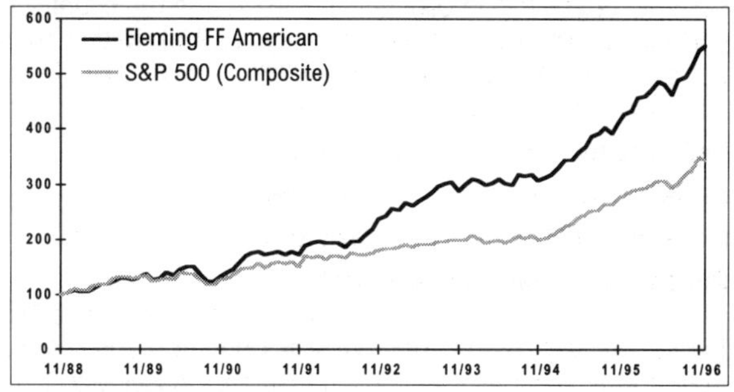

Purchase: Direct, Financial Advisor, Flemings Rapide (Internet Dealing)

Minimum investment: 2,000 USD

Custodian: Robert Fleming and Co Ltd (Luxembourg)

Listed: Luxembourg **Dealings:** Daily

Fund Sedol I.D.: 434291 **Published:** FT/RT

Fees **Annual fee:** 1.25% **Performance fee:** None
Front end load: 5.00% **Redemption fee:** 0.50%
Switching fee: 1.00%

Top holdings:

Bank of New York Co	2.9%
Brown Forman Corp	2.9%
Carlisle Cos Inc	3.4%
Clayton Homes Inc	4.0%
Gannett Co Inc	4.1%
Kimco Realty	3.8%
Maic Holdings Inc	2.9%
Marriott Intl	3.0%
Northern Trust Corp	3.3%
Williams Cos	4.2%

TOTAL RETURNS %

3 months 1997	1996	1995	1994	3 years	5 years
3.22	29.07	36.90	4.25	84.22	193.67

STATISTICS

Assets ($mil)	Current yield	Volatility	Risk return	Micropal Star Rating
615.86	—	2.68	5	✪✪✪✪✪

Fleming FF China Fund

29/350

Fleming Fund Management (Lux) S.A.
European Bank and Business Centre, 6 Route de Treves,
L-2633 Luxembourg
Tel 352-34-10-30-20 Fax 352-34-10-21-10
http://www. flemings.lu E mail info@flemings.lu

Contact: Hans Heller

Investment objective:
The sub-fund aims to provide capital growth through investment in a diversified portfolio of securities in the China region. The top sector allocations for the portfolio are general manufacturing (43.2%); services (21.4%); and finance (19.8%). The assets are primarily divided in the following countries: Hong Kong (47.0%); and China (48.5%).

Umbrella fund: Fleming Flagship Fund

Launch date: 04/07/94 **Domicile:** Luxembourg [UCITS]

Currency: USD **Structure:** Open ended, SICAV

Portfolio manager: Steve Luk
Manager of Fleming FF China since 1994; BSocSc, finance and accounting- U of Hong Kong and MBA- Columbia Business School; joined Jardine Fleming in 1990; 11 years experience in the finance industry.

Performance:

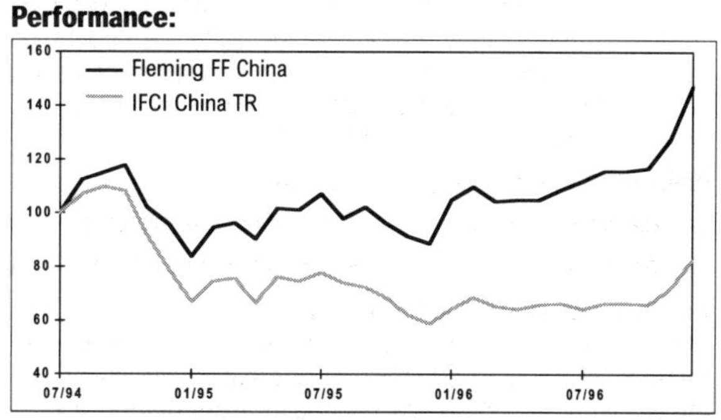

Purchase: Direct, Financial Advisor, Flemings Rapide (Internet Dealing)

Minimum investment: 2,000 USD

Custodian: Robert Fleming and Co Ltd (Luxembourg)

Listed: Luxembourg **Dealings:** Daily

Fund Sedol I.D.: 440535 **Published:** FT/RT

Fees **Annual fee:** 1.25% **Performance fee:** None
Front end load: 5.00% **Redemption fee:** 0.50%
Switching fee: 1.00%

Top holdings:

Cheung Kong Infrastructure	2.9%
Guangshen Railway	2.7%
Guangzhou Inv Ltd	3.2%
Harbin Power Equipment Co	4.1%
Maanshan Iron & Steel	5.4%
NG Fung Hong Ltd	3.6%
Shanghai Diesel Engine	4.3%
Shanghai Haixin Shipping	3.2%
Tineyi (Cayman) Holdings	4.3%
Zhenhai Refining Chemical	3.5%

TOTAL RETURNS %

3 months 1997	1996	1995	1994	3 years	5 years
2.72	65.47	-7.49	N.A.	N.A.	N.A.

STATISTICS

Assets ($mil)	Current yield	Volatility	Risk return	Micropal Star Rating
74.14	—	N.A.	—	———

Fleming FF Continental European Fund

294/350

Fleming Fund Management (Lux) S.A.
European Bank and Business Centre, 6 Route de Treves,
L-2622 Luxembourg
Tel 352-34-10-30-20 Fax 352-34-10-21-10
http://www. flemings.lu E mail info@flemings.lu
Contact: Hans Heller

Investment objective:
The sub-fund aims to provide capital growth through investment in a diversified portfolio of equities in continental Europe. The top country allocations of the portfolio are France (23.4%); Germany (15.2%); Netherlands (14.0%); Switzerland (11.8%); Italy (8.4%); and Spain (4.0%). General manufacturers (31.5%) is the main industry sector allocation of the fund.

Umbrella fund: Fleming Flagship Fund

Launch date: 01/12/88 **Domicile:** Luxembourg [UCITS]

Currency: DEM **Structure:** Open ended, SICAV

Portfolio manager: Richard Webb
Manager of Fleming FF Continental European Fund since 1995 and Dir of Fleming Investment Mgt; BA, history/ politics- Durham U and MA, European Mgt- Craufield Sch of Mgt; previously with Royal Insurance Asset Mgt, European Fund Manager.

Purchase: Direct, Financial Advisor, Flemings Rapide (Internet Dealing)

Minimum investment: 2,000 USD

Custodian: Robert Fleming and Co Ltd (Luxembourg)

Listed: Luxembourg **Dealings:** Daily

Fund Sedol I.D.: 434292 **Published:** FT/RT

Fees **Annual fee:** 1.25% **Performance fee:** None
Front end load: 5.00% **Redemption fee:** 0.50%
Switching fee: 1.00%

Performance:

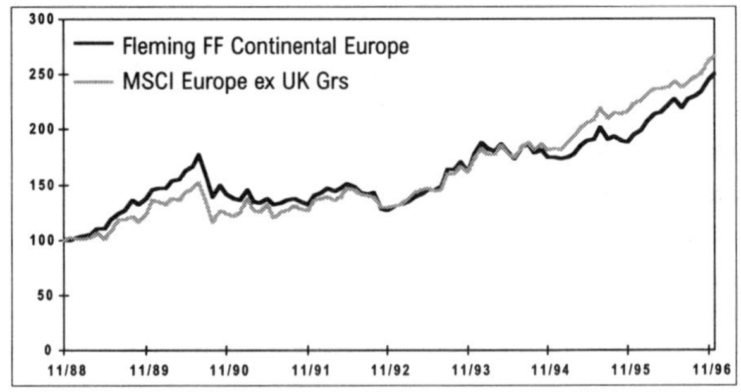

Top holdings:

Holding	%
EIF Aquitaine	1.7%
Fresenius Medical Care	1.9%
ING Groep	1.7%
Novartis AG	4.3%
Parmalat Finanziaria	2.0%
Pinault -Printemps	2.0%
Rexel	2.1%
Royal Dutch Petroleum	4.8%
Total	1.8%
Ver Nid Vitgeversbedr Ver Bezit NV	1.6%

TOTAL RETURNS %

3 months 1997	1996	1995	1994	3 years	5 years
5.96	28.42	11.63	-1.71	40.91	79.39

STATISTICS

Assets ($mil)	Current yield	Volatility	Risk return	Micropal Star Rating
100.94	—	3.05	2	✪

Fleming FF Eastern European Fund

12/350

Fleming Fund Management (Lux) S.A.
European Bank and Business Centre, 6 Route de Treves,
L-2633 Luxembourg
Tel 352-34-10-30-20 Fax 352-34-10-21-10
http://www. flemings.lu E mail info@flemings.lu
Contact: Hans Heller

Investment objective:
The sub-fund aims to achieve long-term capital appreciation through a portfolio of companies investing in the central and eastern European region. At present, the top sector allocation of the portfolio is general manufacturers (33.6%) followed by finance (15.9%). The top country allocations include the following: Poland (35.3%); Hungary (23.5%); and Russia (16.1%).

Umbrella fund: Fleming Flagship Fund

Launch date: 04/07/94 **Domicile:** Luxembourg [UCITS]

Currency: DEM **Structure:** Open ended, SICAV

Portfolio manager: Stefan Bottcher
Manager of Fleming FF Eastern European commenced in 1994; graduate of Fachbachschuleder Deutschen Bundesband; previously with Marcard, Stein & Co; joined Fleming 1990; 8 years in the investment industry.

Purchase: Direct, Financial Advisor, Flemings Rapide (Internet Dealing)

Minimum investment: 2,000 USD

Custodian: Robert Fleming and Co Ltd (Luxembourg)

Listed: Luxembourg **Dealings:** Daily

Fund Sedol I.D.: 440536 **Published:** FT/RT

Fees **Annual fee:** 1.25% **Performance fee:** None
Front end load: 5.00% **Redemption fee:** 0.50%
Switching fee: 1.00%

Performance:

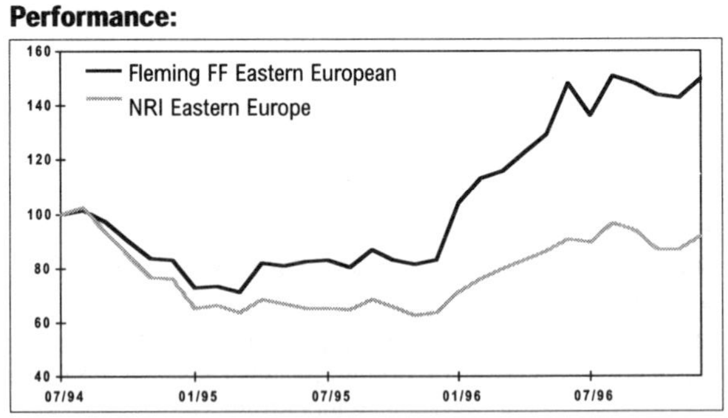

Top holdings:

Holding	%
Agros Holding	3.3%
Banka Przemyslowo Handlowy	4.5%
Computerland	3.2%
Elektrim	3.9%
Fleming Russia Securities Fund Ltd	3.8%
Gazprom	4.2%
Pliva	3.8%
Richter Gedeon	4.8%
Stomil Olsztyn	3.4%
Zagrebacka Banka	3.1%

TOTAL RETURNS %

3 months 1997	1996	1995	1994	3 years	5 years
17.18	80.17	0.09	N.A.	N.A.	N.A.

STATISTICS

Assets ($mil)	Current yield	Volatility	Risk return	Micropal Star Rating
231.27	—	N.A.	—	——

Fleming FF European Smaller Companies Fund

252/350

Fleming Fund Management (Lux) S.A.
European Bank and Business Centre, 6 Route de Treves,
L-2633 Luxembourg
Tel 352-34-10-30-20 Fax 352-34-10-21-10
http://www. flemings.lu E mail info@flemings.lu
Contact: Hans Heller

Investment objective:
The sub-fund aims to achieve long-term capital appreciation through investment in a diversified portfolio of smaller European companies. Country allocations of the portfolio are France (15.8%); UK (15.6%); Germany (11.1%); Italy (8.2%); Netherlands (7.9%); and Norway (7.6%). The main sector allocations of the fund are general manufacturing (37.8%); and services (29.2%).

Umbrella fund: Fleming Flagship Fund

Launch date: 18/04/94 **Domicile:** Luxembourg [UCITS]

Currency: DEM **Structure:** Open ended, SICAV

Portfolio manager: Peter Testa
Manager of Fleming FF European Smaller Companies Funds commenced 1994; BA, history-Davidson College; previously analyst in the UK research dept and Investment Manager with UK unit trust desk at Fleming; joined Fleming in 1989; 8 years in the investment industry.

Purchase: Direct, Financial Advisor, Flemings Rapide (Internet Dealing)

Minimum investment: 2,000 USD

Custodian: Robert Fleming and Co Ltd (Luxembourg)

Listed: Luxembourg **Dealings:** Daily

Fund Sedol I.D.: 440382 **Published:** FT/RT

Fees **Annual fee:** 1.25% **Performance fee:** None
Front end load: 5.00% **Redemption fee:** 0.50%
Switching fee: 1.00%

Performance:

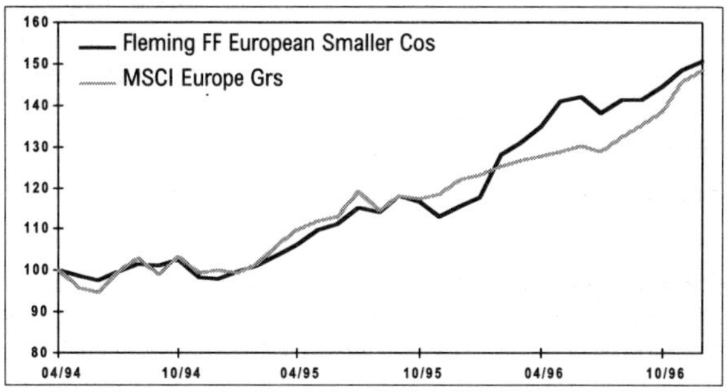

Top holdings:

Boss(Hugo)	1.8%
Cap Gemini NV	2.0%
Cardif SA	2.1%
Falck	2.4%
Fila Holdings SPA	1.8%
Fleming Frontier Fund	3.8%
Fresenius Medical Care	2.0%
Moebel Walther	2.1%
Tomra Systems ASA	2.5%

TOTAL RETURNS %

3 months 1997	1996	1995	1994	3 years	5 years
4.69	30.43	17.64	N.A.	N.A.	N.A.

STATISTICS

Assets ($mil)	Current yield	Volatility	Risk return	Micropal Star Rating
110.76	—	N.A.	—	———

Fleming FF UK Enterprise Fund

291/350

Fleming Fund Management (Lux) S.A.
European Bank and Business Centre, 6 Route de Treves,
L-2663 Luxembourg
Tel 352-34-10-30-20 Fax 352-34-10-21-10
http://www. flemings.lu E mail info@flemings.lu
Contact: Hans Heller

Investment objective:
The sub-fund aims to achieve capital growth through a rigorously researched portfolio of UK equities. The top sector allocations of the portfolio are finance (26.1%); services (23.5%); technology (10.5%); and energy (9.0%). The sub-fund is denominated in UK sterling.

Umbrella fund: Fleming Flagship Fund

Launch date: 04/01/92 **Domicile:** Luxembourg [UCITS]

Currency: GBP **Structure:** Open ended, SICAV

Portfolio manager: Andrew Spencer
Manager of Fleming FF UK Enterprise since 1994; Director of Fleming Investment Mgt Ltd; BA, economics- Nottingham U; previously and Investment Manager for the Save & Prosper Commodity Share Fund and three gold funds; joined Flemings in 1986.

Purchase: Direct, Financial Advisor, Flemings Rapide (Internet Dealing)

Minimum investment: 2,000 USD

Custodian: Robert Fleming and Co Ltd (Luxembourg)

Listed: Luxembourg **Dealings:** Daily

Fund Sedol I.D.: 438367 **Published:** FT/RT

Fees **Annual fee:** 1.25% **Performance fee:** None
Front end load: 5.00% **Redemption fee:** 0.50%
Switching fee: 1.00%

Performance:

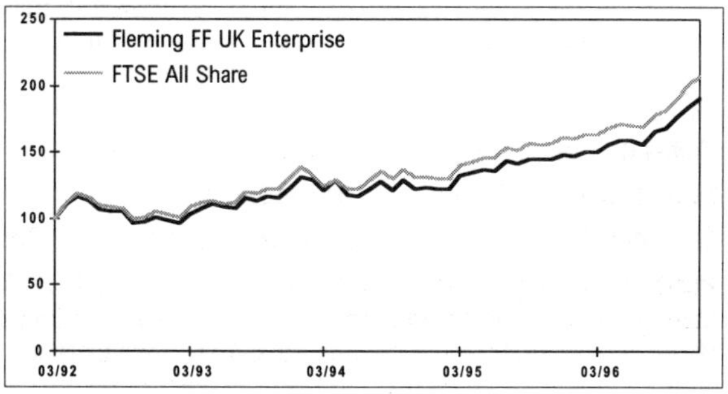

Top holdings:

British Aerospace	1.9%
British Petroleum	4.3%
HSBC Holdings	4.0%
Lloyds TSB Group	3.4%
National Westminster Bank	2.2%
Reuters Holdings	1.8%
S&P UK Smaller Cos	3.9%
Shell Transport & Trading	3.3%
Standard Chartered Bank	2.3%
Zeneca Group	2.8%

TOTAL RETURNS %

3 months 1997	1996	1995	1994	3 years	5 years
1.46	28.51	20.45	0.06	54.89	N.A.

STATISTICS

Assets ($mil)	Current yield	Volatility	Risk return	Micropal Star Rating
52.41	—	3.96	3	✪✪✪✪

Fleming Frontier Emerging Mkts Debt
251/350

Fleming Fund Management (Lux) S.A.
European Bank and Business Centre, 6 Route de Treves,
L-2633 Luxembourg
Tel 352-34-10-30-20 Fax 352-34-10-21-10
http://www. flemings.lu E mail info@flemings.lu

Contact: Hans Heller

Investment objective:
The sub-fund aims to provide high total return to be achieved principally though investment in fixed and where appropriate, variable rate instruments issued by multilateral organisations, governments and corporations in emerging markets. The Manager may also invest in US government treasury bonds, bill and notes.

Umbrella fund: Fleming Frontier Fund
Launch date: 23/08/95 **Domicile:** Luxembourg [UCITS]
Currency: USD **Structure:** Open ended, SICAV
Portfolio manager: Collective management -Fleming Fund Management
Managers of Fleming Frontier Emerging Markets Debt; located at the European Bank and Business Centre, 6 Route de Traeves, L-2633 Seningerberg, Luxembourg.

Performance:

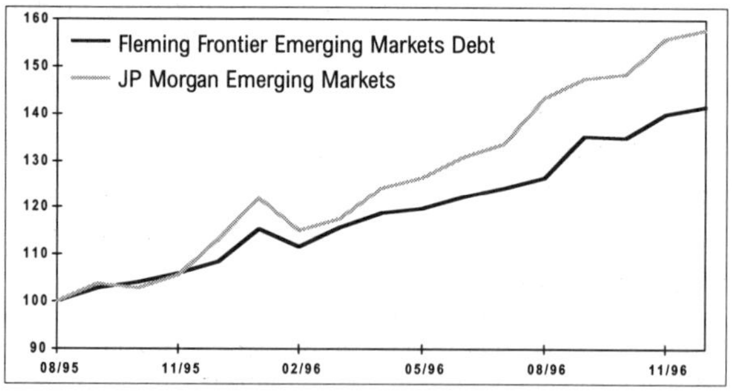

Purchase: Direct, Financial Advisor, Flemings Rapide (Internet Dealing)
Minimum investment: 10,000 USD
Custodian: Robert Fleming and Co Ltd (Luxembourg)
Listed: Luxembourg **Dealings:** Weekly
Fund Sedol I.D.: 457215 **Published:** FT/RT
Fees **Annual fee:** 0.75% **Performance fee:** None
Front end load: 5.00% **Redemption fee:** 0.50%
Switching fee: 1.00%

Top holdings:

Brazil	18.7%
Jordan	5.6%
Mexico	8.3%
Morocco	7.4%
Russia	20.9%
Venezuela	14.6%

TOTAL RETURNS %

3 months 1997	1996	1995	1994	3 years	5 years
5.20	30.46	N.A.	N.A.	N.A.	N.A.

STATISTICS

Assets ($mil)	Current yield	Volatility	Risk return	Micropal Star Rating
21.00	—	N.A.	—	———

Fleming Frontier European Discovery
140/350

Fleming Fund Management (Lux) S.A.
European Bank and Business Centre, 6 Route de Treves,
L-2633 Luxembourg
Tel 352-34-10-30-20 Fax 352-34-10-21-10
http://www. flemings.lu E mail info@flemings.lu

Contact: Hans Heller

Investment objective:
The sub-fund aims at capital appreciation through investment primarily in quoted equities of continental European companies below 150 million US dollars free floating market capitalisation. The sub-fund is denominated in US dollars.

Umbrella fund: Fleming Frontier Fund
Launch date: 13/03/95 **Domicile:** Luxembourg [UCITS]
Currency: USD **Structure:** Open ended, SICAV
Portfolio manager: Collective management-Fleming Fund Management
Managers of Fleming Frontier European Discovery; located at European Bank and Business Centre, 6 Route de Traeves, L-2633 Seningerberg, Luxembourg.

Performance:

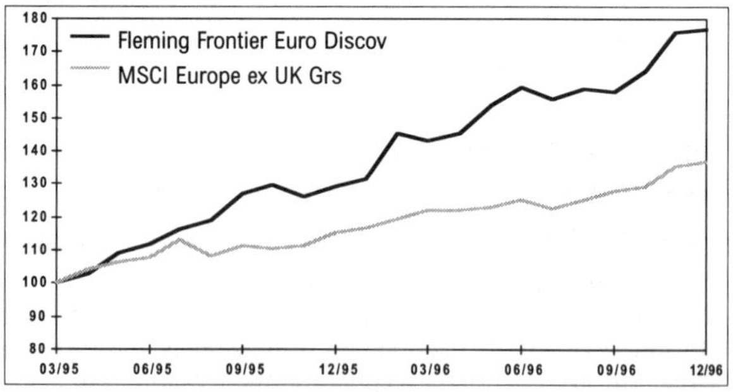

Purchase: Direct, Financial Advisor, Flemings Rapide (Internet Dealing)
Minimum investment: 10,000 USD
Custodian: Robert Fleming and Co Ltd (Luxembourg)
Listed: Luxembourg **Dealings:** Weekly
Fund Sedol I.D.: 481618 **Published:** FT/RT
Fees **Annual fee:** 1.50% **Performance fee:** None
Front end load: 5.00% **Redemption fee:** 0.50%
Switching fee: 1.00%

Top holdings:

Denmark	11.3%
France	21.7%
Italy	11.2%
Norway	12.2%
Spain	8.5%
Sweden	8.8%

TOTAL RETURNS %

3 months 1997	1996	1995	1994	3 years	5 years
13.49	37.03	N.A.	N.A.	N.A.	N.A.

STATISTICS

Assets ($mil)	Current yield	Volatility	Risk return	Micropal Star Rating
47.79	—	N.A.	—	———

Fonte Cindam Select
143/350

Banco Fonte Cindam
Av Presidente Wilson 231117, Centro Rio de Janeiro,
CEP 20030-021, Brazil
Tel 55-21-212-1800 Fax 55-21-240-3600
http://www. fontecindam.com.br

Investment objective:
The sub-fund invests in the stock of Brazilian companies considered to have greater growth potential. The fund's portfolio is to be concentrated in no more than 20 companies, with up to 40% being in stocks having lower liquidity. The top sectors are allocated to the following: communications (45.0%); energy (13.0%); oil (10%); home appliance (6.0%); and food (7.0%).

Umbrella fund: Fonte Cindam Brazil Fund

Launch date: 04/10/95 **Domicile:** Cayman Islands

Currency: USD **Structure:** Open ended, Unit Trust

Portfolio manager: Ricardo Amorim
Manager of Fonte Cindam Select commenced in 1995; degree in engineering; and specialises in options and future markets.

Contact: Bruno Scharfstein

Performance:

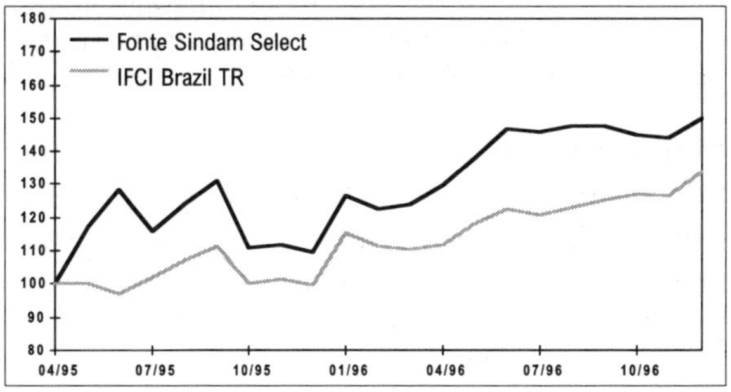

Top holdings:

Brazilian Equities	91.0%
Cash	9.0%

Purchase: Direct

Minimum investment: 50,000 USD

Custodian: Banco Fonte Cindam

Listed: None **Dealings:** Daily

Fund Sedol I.D.: 305115 **Published:** FT/IHT

Fees **Annual fee:** 1.50% **Performance fee:** 15.00%
Front end load: Up to 1.00% **Redemption fee:** None
Switching fee: None

TOTAL RETURNS %

3 months 1997	1996	1995	1994	3 years	5 years
25.03	36.70	N.A.	N.A.	N.A.	N.A.

STATISTICS

Assets ($mil)	Current yield	Volatility	Risk return	Micropal Star Rating
2.95	—	N.A.	—	———

Formosa Fund
304/350

Kwang Hua Securities Investment & Trust Co. Ltd
11 floor 76 Tun Hwa S. Road, Section 2, Tapei, 106,
Republic of China
Tel 886-2-708-8201 Fax 886-2-704-8014

Investment objective:
The fund aims to achieve long-term growth through investment in securities and monetary instruments issued by corporate and government entities in the Republic of China (Formosa). The top sectors held by this portfolio are as follows: electrical/ machinery (21.6%); finance (16.5%); and plastic/chemical (12.8%).

Umbrella fund: This is a singular fund.

Launch date: 07/03/86 **Domicile:** Republic of China [UCITS]

Currency: NTD **Structure:** Close ended, Investment Trust

Portfolio manager: Vincent Ho
Manager of Formosa Fund commenced 1995; MBA- National Taiwan U: previously Fund Manager at Kwang Hua and Kwang Hau Growth Fund; textile, chemical construction and cement analyst for the firm (1991-95).

Contact: Simon She

Performance:

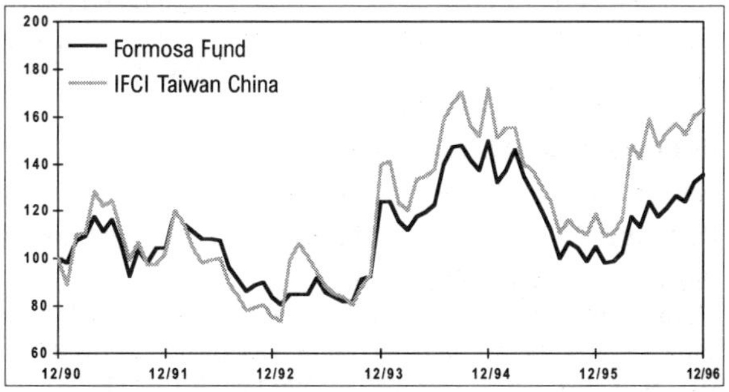

Top holdings:

Cathay Life Ins	6.1%
China Petrochemical	2.7%
China steel	3.4%
First Bank	5.5%
Formosa Plastic	3.1%
Hsing Ta Cement	2.8%
President Enterprise	2.9%
Siliconware	2.6%
Tatung	2.8%
Yageo	2.7%

Purchase: Direct, Financial Advisor

Minimum investment: 100 Shares

Custodian: Taipei Bank (Taiwan)

Listed: London **Dealings:** Daily

Fund Sedol I.D.: 34708 **Published:** FT

Fees **Annual fee:** 1.50% **Performance fee:** None
Front end load: 2.00% **Redemption fee:** None
Switching fee: None

TOTAL RETURNS %

3 months 1997	1996	1995	1994	3 years	5 years
18.93	28.22	-29.63	20.58	8.79	28.86

STATISTICS

Assets ($mil)	Current yield	Volatility	Risk return	Micropal Star Rating
503.60	—	6.48	—	✪✪

FP Russian Equity Fund Limited

24/350

Financial Portfolio Consulting S.A.
Canada Court, St Peter Port, GY1 3QE, Guernsey
Tel 33-1-44-35-52-00 Fax 33-1-42-89-34-01

Investment objective:
The FP Consult fund seeks to achieve long-term capital appreciation by investing in the equity or equity related investment instruments of Russian incorporated companies. In addition selected companies may be incorporated outside Russia but have more than 50% of their gross assets invested in Russia.

Umbrella fund: FP Umbrella Fund Limited

Launch date: 29/09/95 **Domicile:** Guernsey

Currency: USD **Structure:** Open ended, Investment Company

Portfolio manager: Francois Mereau
Manager of FP Russian Equity Fund Limited. FP Consult S.A., 90 Avenue des Champs Elysees,75008 Paris.

Purchase: Direct

Minimum investment: 100,000 USD

Custodian: Royal Bank of Canada (Channel Islands) Ltd

Listed: None **Dealings:** Monthly

Fund Sedol I.D.: 305207 **Published:** FT/IHT/SC

Fees **Annual fee:** 1.50% **Performance fee:** 20.00%
Front end load: Up to 1.00% **Redemption fee:** Up to 1.00%
Switching fee: None

Contact: Customer Services Department

Performance:

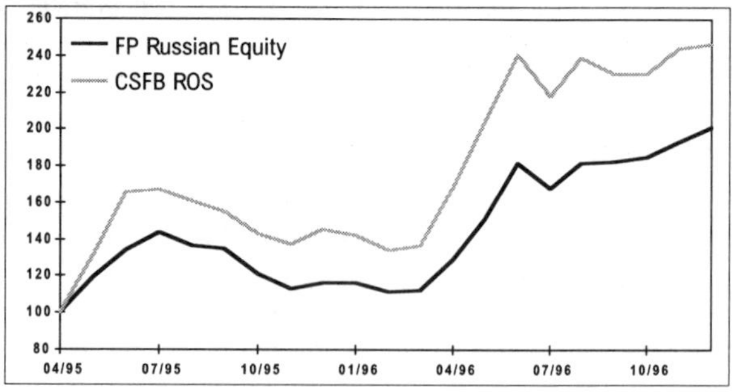

Top holdings:

Holding	%
Akron Fertilizer	7.1%
Aviastar	4.4%
CUM	5.0%
Gas Natural	4.8%
MMT	3.3%
Nizhnii Tagilskii Metal	2.8%
Oskolsky Electrometally	3.9%
Red October	4.4%
Sayansk Aluminium	4.5%
Sviazinform Nigni	4.5%

TOTAL RETURNS %

3 months 1997	1996	1995	1994	3 years	5 years
24.58	72.60	N.A.	N.A.	N.A.	N.A.

STATISTICS

Assets ($mil)	Current yield	Volatility	Risk return	Micropal Star Rating
4.79	—	N.A.	—	———

Friends Provident European Equity

264/350

Friends Provident Asset Managers
United Kingdom House, Castle Street, Salisbury, SP1 3SH, United Kingdom
Tel 44-1722-411-411 Fax 44-1722-332-005

Investment objective:
The fund seeks capital growth by investing in European stock market securities including European fixed interest securities excluding the UK. Although the bulk of investments take place in the major markets, smaller markets may also offer interesting opportunities. The top country allocations of the portfolio are as follows: Germany (19.0%); and France (18.5%).

Umbrella fund: This is a singular fund.

Launch date: 01/06/94 **Domicile:** Guernsey

Currency: GBP **Structure:** Open ended, Insurance Fund

Portfolio manager: Tony Zucker
Manager of Friends Provident European commenced 1993; previously overseas Director at Aetna, BP Pension Fund specialising in UK and European Markets and the Overseas Investment Manager at Sun Life of Canada.

Purchase: Financial Advisor

Minimum investment: 5,000 GBP

Custodian: Citicorp Trustee Company Limited

Listed: None **Dealings:** Daily

Fund Sedol I.D.: 35454 **Published:** FT

Fees **Annual fee:** 1.00% **Performance fee:** ILP
Front end load: 6.00% **Redemption fee:** ILP
Switching fee: 2 free switches- £25 per switch

Contact: Richard Duxbury

Performance:

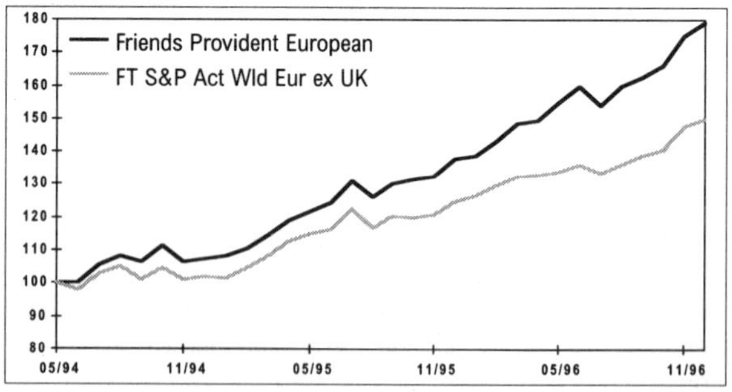

Top holdings:

Holding	%
Adidas	1.6%
Bayer AG	1.9%
Daimler Benz	1.7%
Hoechst	2.2%
Mannesmann	1.7%
Novartis	3.2%
SGL Carbon	1.6%
Sgs th Microelec	1.8%
Solmelia	1.6%
Vendex International	1.7%

TOTAL RETURNS %

3 months 1997	1996	1995	1994	3 years	5 years
7.95	29.82	28.37	N.A.	N.A.	N.A.

STATISTICS

Assets ($mil)	Current yield	Volatility	Risk return	Micropal Star Rating
3.89	—	N.A.	—	———

Friends Provident Stewardship

210/350

Friends Provident Asset Managers
United Kingdom House, Castle Street, Salisbury, SP1 3SH, United Kingdom
Tel 44-1722-411-411 Fax 44-1722-332-005

Investment objective:
The fund seeks long-term growth through investment in the ordinary shares of selected UK companies whose activities are considered to be of long-term benefit to society. Investment selection is made with advice from a committee of reference. Sector allocations of the portfolio include the following: services (41.0%); industrial cyclical (34.8%); and finance (11.8%).

Umbrella fund: This is a singular fund.

Launch date: 01/06/94 **Domicile:** Guernsey

Currency: GBP **Structure:** Open ended, Insurance Fund

Portfolio manager: Richard Lowman
Manager of Friends Provdent Stewardship; specialist in ethical investment commenced 1984; responsible for research of UK equities; previously with Lazard Securities and Prudential.

Purchase: Financial Advisor

Minimum investment: 5,000 GBP

Custodian: Citicorp Trustee Company Limited

Listed: None **Dealings:** Daily

Fund Sedol I.D.: 35447 **Published:** FT

Fees **Annual fee:** 1.00% **Performance fee:** ILP
Front end load: 6.00% **Redemption fee:** ILP
Switching fee: 2 free switches- £25 per switch

Contact: Richard Duxbury

Performance:

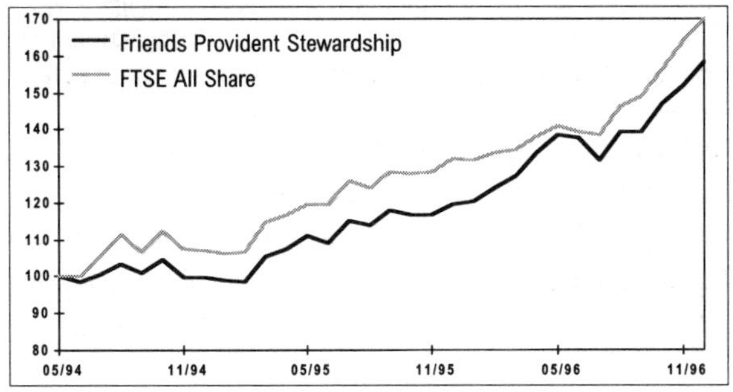

Top holdings:

Carpetright	1.4%
Cowie	2.5%
Entreprise Oil	1.9%
Eurotherm	1.4%
Forth Ports	1.4%
Go Ahead Group	1.8%
Halma plc ord	1.5%
Page Group	1.3%
St Nes plc	1.5%
Trinity Intl	2.1%

TOTAL RETURNS %

3 months 1997	1996	1995	1994	3 years	5 years
2.40	32.25	19.79	N.A.	N.A.	N.A.

STATISTICS

Assets ($mil)	Current yield	Volatility	Risk return	Micropal Star Rating
5.85	—	N.A.	—	———

Friends Provident UK Equity

341/350

Friends Provident Asset Managers
United Kingdom House, Castle Street, Salisbury, SP1 3SH, United Kingdom
Tel 44-1722-411-411 Fax 44-1722-332-005

Investment objective:
The fund invests primarily in well researched major UK companies listed on the London Stock Exchange which offer the best opportunities for capital growth and/or high and rising income. At present the top sectors of the portfolio are allocated to the following: services (21.7%); industrial cyclical (16.9%); consumer goods (16.2%); and finance (15.3%).

Umbrella fund: This is a singular fund.

Launch date: 01/06/94 **Domicile:** Guernsey

Currency: GBP **Structure:** Open ended, Insurance Fund

Portfolio manager: Greg Richmond
Manager of Friends Provdnt UK Equity commenced in 1986; member of the group's asset allocation committee; previously managed European equities, derivatives and fixed interest.

Purchase: Financial Advisor

Minimum investment: 5,000 GBP

Custodian: Citicorp Trustee Company Limited

Listed: None **Dealings:** Daily

Fund Sedol I.D.: 35456 **Published:** FT

Fees **Annual fee:** 1.00% **Performance fee:** ILP
Front end load: 6.00% **Redemption fee:** ILP
Switching fee: 2 free switches- £25 per switch

Contact: Richard Duxbury

Performance:

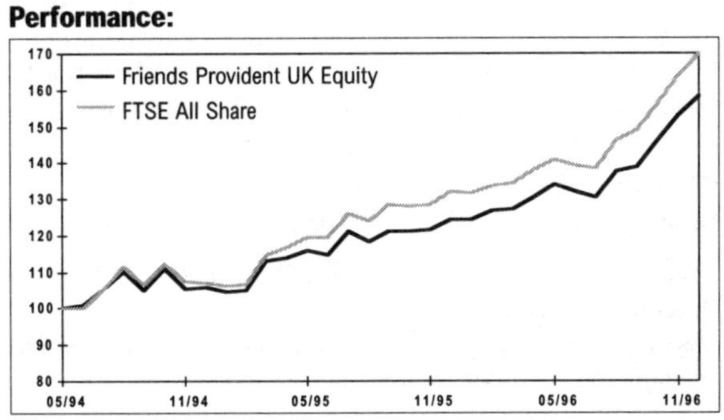

Top holdings:

Barclays PLC	1.6%
BAT Industries	1.9%
British Petroleum	2.4%
British Telecom	2.5%
FP Invest Small Co	4.9%
Glaxo Wellcome	4.0%
Grand Metro	1.8%
HSBC Holdings	2.0%
Marks & Spencers	1.6%
Natwest Bank	2.1%
Shell	4.4%

TOTAL RETURNS %

3 months 1997	1996	1995	1994	3 years	5 years
-0.07	27.23	17.69	N.A.	N.A.	N.A.

STATISTICS

Assets ($mil)	Current yield	Volatility	Risk return	Micropal Star Rating
3.47	—	N.A.	—	———

Frontrunner Scandinavian Equities
245/350

Frontrunner Management Company S.A.
672 Rue de Neudorf, Findel, L-2220 Luxembourg
Tel 352-43-39-50 Fax 352-43-39-40
E mail frontrunner@ibm.net

Investment objective:
The fund aims to preserve capital while providing an adequate rate of return. The fund invests in shares, convertible bonds and ancillary in warrants listed on a Scandinavian stock exchange. If possible, the investment strategy is based on the valuation principle of investing in companies whose current market value is substantially below the intrinsic business value.

Umbrella fund: Frontrunner 1 SICAV
Launch date: 04/05/92 **Domicile:** Luxembourg
Currency: ECU **Structure:** Open ended, SICAV
Portfolio manager: Frontrunner Management Company SA
Manager of Frontrunner Scandinavian Equities.

Contact: Customer Services Department

Performance:

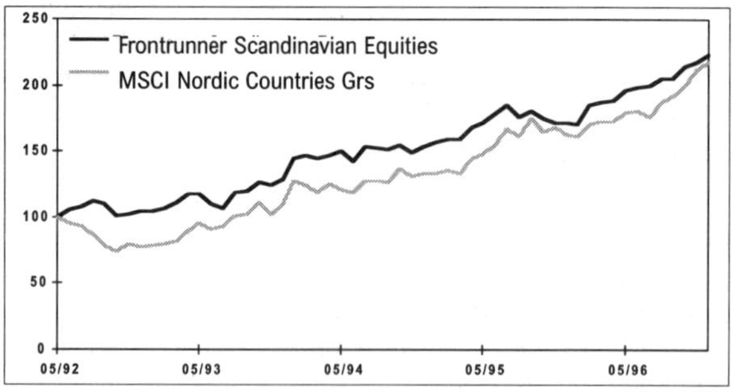

Purchase: Direct
Minimum investment: 5,000 ECU
Custodian: Unibank S.A. Luxembourg
Listed: None **Dealings:** Weekly
Fund Sedol I.D.: 300306 **Published:** FT/IHT/SC
Fees **Annual fee:** 1.00% **Performance fee:** None
Front end load: Up to 5.00% **Redemption fee:** None
Switching fee: Up to 1.00%

Top holdings:

Awilco Shipping b	2.5%
Bylock - Nordsoe Transport b	2.9%
F. Junckers Industrier	2.6%
Frontline	2.2%
Lemminkainen Oy	2.4%
Nordstjernan Construction	2.7%
Nycomed ASA A	2.6%
Partek Oyab	2.5%
Phonix Contractors C	2.8%
Spar Nord Holdings	2.8%

TOTAL RETURNS %

3 months 1997	1996	1995	1994	3 years	5 years
1.71	30.58	11.52	19.26	73.66	N.A.

STATISTICS

Assets ($mil)	Current yield	Volatility	Risk return	Micropal Star Rating
57.24	—	3.49	4	✪✪

G-Equity Fund G-Spanish Eq A/B
183/350

Generale Bank Asset Management
Montagne du Parc 3, Brussels, 1000, Belgium
Tel 32-2-565-5962 Fax 32-2-565-5036

Investment objective:
The sub-fund seeks to purchase equities listed on the Spanish Stock exchange which mirror or better the IBEX 35 Index. A low portfolio turnover is expected because of this method of tracking. The sector allocations of the portfolio are the following: energy/utilities (38.8%); finance (30.0%); and services (24.3%).

Umbrella fund: G-Equity Fund
Launch date: 28/03/93 **Domicile:** Luxembourg
Currency: ESP **Structure:** Open ended, SICAV
Portfolio manager: Didier Fourcroy
Manager of G-Equity Fund G-Spanish Eq B commenced January 1995; previously at Generale Bank; Fund Manager since 1988.

Contact: Freddy Cooresman

Performance:

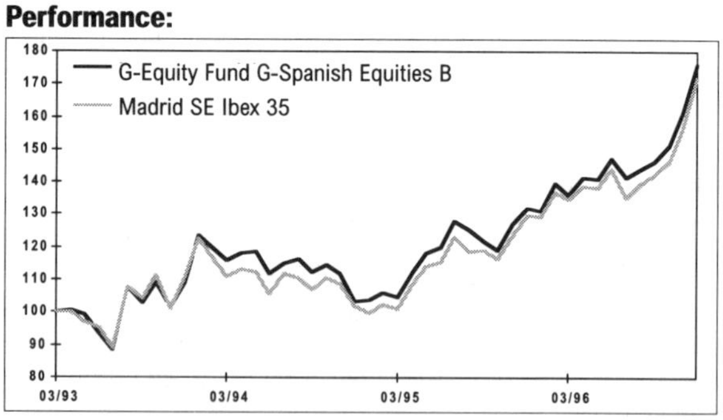

Purchase: Direct
Minimum investment: 5 Units
Custodian: Banque Generale du Luxembourg S.A. (Lux)
Listed: None **Dealings:** Daily
Fund Sedol I.D.: 300328 **Published:** LE/BP
Fees **Annual fee:** 0.75% **Performance fee:** None
Front end load: 3.00% **Redemption fee:** None
Switching fee: None

Top holdings:

BBV	5.0%
Endesa	5.9%
Iberdrola	5.1%
Repsol	5.1%
Telefonica	8.5%

TOTAL RETURNS %

3 months 1997	1996	1995	1994	3 years	5 years
-3.32	33.53	27.72	-5.34	61.42	N.A.

STATISTICS

Assets ($mil)	Current yield	Volatility	Risk return	Micropal Star Rating
10.26	—	4.43	3	✪✪✪

Gain Limited B Share Fund
20/350

LPS Futures Managers Ltd
832 Europort, Gibraltar
Tel 350-79120 Fax 350-78428

Investment objective:
The fund seeks long-term capital appreciation by trading a diversified portfolio of futures contracts through a systematic and technical methodology. The portfolio strategy successfully identifies low risk points for increasing exposure and higher risk points for reducing it. The markets traded at this time are US, UK, Germany, France and Singapore.

Umbrella fund: Gain Limited

Launch date: 01/10/91 **Domicile:** Bermuda

Currency: USD **Structure:** Open ended, Investment Company

Portfolio manager: Tim Ireton
Manager of Gain B; founder of LPS in 1986; experienced in accounting, dealing, brokering, systems research, creating, distributing and managing funds.

Contact: Tim Ireton

Performance:

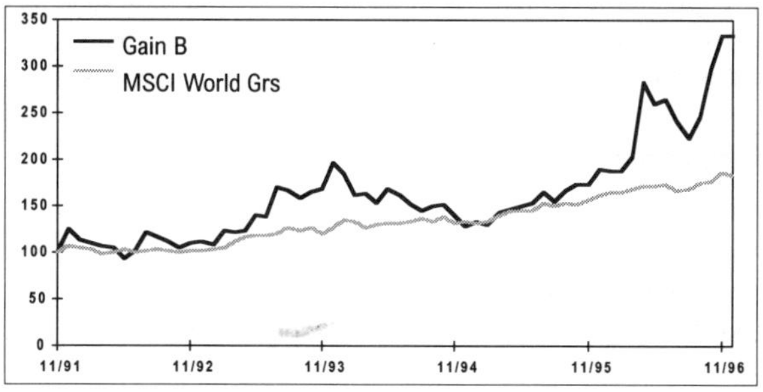

Purchase: Direct, Fin. Adv., Approved for purchase through CMI Offshore Ins. Bonds

Minimum investment: 30,000 USD

Custodian: Bank of Buitterfield Executor & Trustee Co. Ltd

Listed: None **Dealings:** Monthly

Fund Sedol I.D.: 305437 **Published:** MP/LP

Fees **Annual fee:** 3.00% **Performance fee:** 25.00%
Front end load: 5.00% **Redemption fee:** None
Switching fee: None

Top holdings:

Holding	%
Agriculture/Commodities Futures	26.0%
Base And Precious Metal Futures	10.0%
Currency Futures	10.0%
Energy Futures	6.0%
Government Bond Futures	6.0%
Short Term Interest Rate Futures	4.0%
Stock Index Futures	8.0%
Theoretical Maximum Initial Risk	70.0%
Typical Normal Initial Risk Exposure	35.0%

TOTAL RETURNS %

3 months 1997	1996	1995	1994	3 years	5 years
0.57	75.50	47.75	-34.38	70.14	168.24

STATISTICS

Assets ($mil)	Current yield	Volatility	Risk return	Micropal Star Rating
1.37	—	9.59	1	✪✪✪✪

GAM Brasilia Fund Inc.
56/350

Global Asset Management
11 Athol Street, Douglas IM99 1HH, Isle of Man
Tel 44-1624-632-777 Fax 44-1624-632-813
http://www. gam.com E mail info@gam.com

Investment objective:
The fund aims to achieve capital appreciation through investing primarily in a combination of equities and bonds in Brazil. The major holdings of the portfolio include the following: communications, utilities, electrical/gas; and energy sources. The fund is denominated in US dollars.

Umbrella fund: This is a singular fund.

Launch date: 23/11/94 **Domicile:** British Virgin Islands

Currency: USD **Structure:** Open ended, Investment Company

Portfolio manager: Daniel Dantas
Manager of GAM Brasilia and Director of Opportunity Asset Management located in Brazil; Post Doctorate degree, economics and finance- MIT; 13 years investment experience in Brazil.

Contact: Nikki Hague/Julian Crellin

Performance:

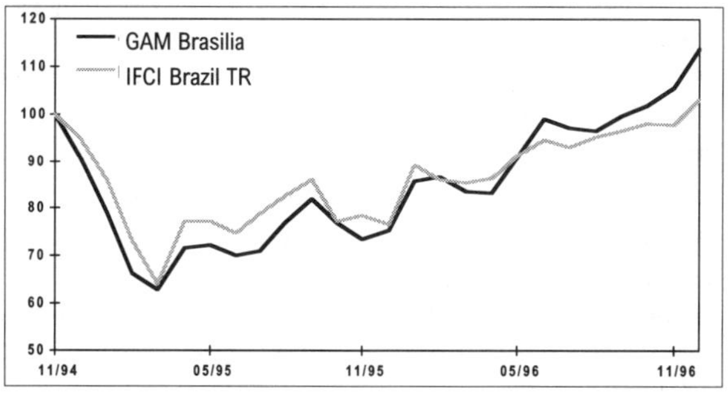

Purchase: Direct

Minimum investment: 15,000 USD

Custodian: Mees Pierson (Isle of Man) Ltd

Listed: None **Dealings:** Weekly

Fund Sedol I.D.: 237008 **Published:** FT/ WS/IHT/AW/BG/RT

Fees **Annual fee:** 1.00% **Performance fee:** 15.00%
Front end load: Up to 3.00% **Redemption fee:** None
Switching fee: None

Top holdings:

Holding	%
Electrobas	22.4%
Petrobas	22.5%
Telebras	49.1%
Telecom Rio de Janeiro	5.8%
Telecom Sao Paulo	4.3%

TOTAL RETURNS %

3 months 1997	1996	1995	1994	3 years	5 years
30.16	50.57	-16.62	N.A.	N.A.	N.A.

STATISTICS

Assets ($mil)	Current yield	Volatility	Risk return	Micropal Star Rating
11.80	—	N.A.	—	———

GAM France Inc.
260/350

Global Asset Management
11 Athol Street, Douglas IM99 1HH, Isle of Man
Tel 44-1624-632-777 Fax 44-1624-632-813
http://www. gam.com E mail info@gam.com

Investment objective:
The primary objective of the fund is to achieve capital appreciation, through investment in quoted securities in France. The fund may be invested in government bonds, other fixed interest securities, preferred stock and monetary instruments. The fund may also hold cash on deposit pending reinvestment.

Umbrella fund: This is a singular fund.
Launch date: 18/04/86 **Domicile:** British Virgin Islands
Currency: FRF **Structure:** Open ended, Investment Company
Portfolio manager: Guy de Mailly Nesle
Manager of GAM France Inc and associated with Rothschild & Compagnie Banque; located at 17 Avenue Matignon, 75008, Paris, France.

Contact: Nikki Hague/Julian Crellin
Performance:

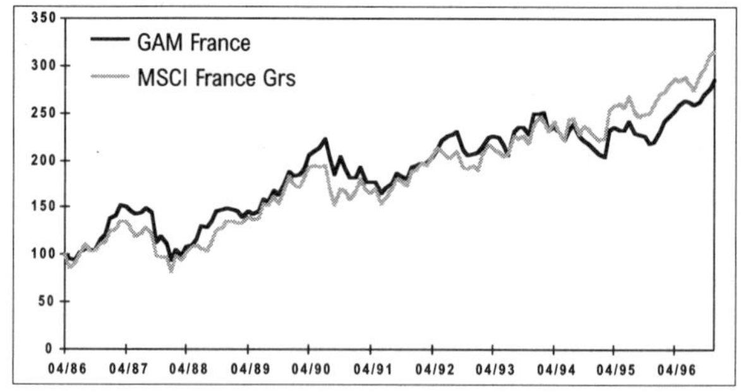

Purchase: Direct
Minimum investment: 100,000 FRF
Custodian: Mees Pierson (Isle of Man) Ltd
Listed: None **Dealings:** Weekly
Fund Sedol I.D.: 37306 **Published:** FT/ WS/IHT/AW/BG/RT
Fees **Annual fee:** 1.13% **Performance fee:** None
Front end load: Up to 3.00% **Redemption fee:** None
Switching fee: None

Top holdings:	
BIC	4.3%
Carrefour	4.7%
Cetelem	4.4%
L'Oreal	4.5%
Labinal	4.6%
LVMH	6.0%
Primagaz	4.2%
Saint-Gobain	5.1%
Sodexho	4.6%
Total Oil	5.1%

TOTAL RETURNS %

3 months 1997	1996	1995	1994	3 years	5 years
-0.34	30.08	3.26	-14.87	14.34	47.60

STATISTICS

Assets ($mil)	Current yield	Volatility	Risk return	Micropal Star Rating
3.97	—	3.66	—	✪

Gartmore CSF Continental Europe
308/350

Gartmore Fund Managers International Limited
45 La Motte Street, St Helier, JE4 8TF, Jersey
Tel 44-1534-886-688 Fax 44-1534-886-689

Investment objective:
The fund aims for a long-term total return in excess of the benchmark by investing in companies listed on continental European stock exchanges. There is no predetermined geographical set allocation, except that the fund is not normally invested in UK companies and that companies derive a significant proportion of their earnings from continental Europe.
Umbrella fund: Gartmore Capital Strategy Fund Limited
Launch date: 04/10/85 **Domicile:** Jersey
Currency: DEM **Structure:** Open ended, Investment Company
Portfolio manager: Roger Guy
Manager of Gartmore CSF Continental Europe; graduate, European finance analysis-Newcastle U; formerly with Eagle Star, responsible for European equity; joined Gartmore in 1993.

Contact: Nigel Parker
Performance:

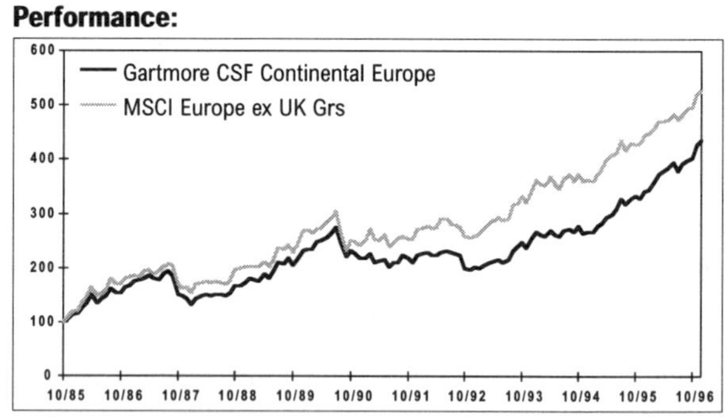

Purchase: Direct, Financial Advisor
Minimum investment: 2,500 USD
Custodian: The Chase Manhattan Bank
Listed: London **Dealings:** Daily
Fund Sedol I.D.: 36182 **Published:** FT/JE/SC/RT/HB
Fees **Annual fee:** 1.50% **Performance fee:** None
Front end load: 5.00% **Redemption fee:** None
Switching fee: None

Top holdings:	
Bayer	2.2%
Bayerische Mororen Werke	3.1%
Christian Dior	3.1%
Eaux (CIE Generale Des)	1.9%
Hoechst	2.8%
Novartis	3.9%
Roche Holdings	3.7%
Sanofi	2.7%
Total	2.3%
Volkswagen	2.2%

TOTAL RETURNS %

3 months 1997	1996	1995	1994	3 years	5 years
7.33	28.10	28.27	3.84	70.61	94.31

STATISTICS

Assets ($mil)	Current yield	Volatility	Risk return	Micropal Star Rating
113.10	0.50	2.72	5	✪✪✪✪✪

Gartmore CSF HK & China
192/350

Gartmore Fund Managers International Limited
45 La Motte Street, St Helier, JE4 8TF, Jersey
Tel 44-1534-886-688 Fax 44-1534-886-689

Investment objective:
The aim of the fund is to achieve long-term total return in excess of the Gartmore Hong Kong and China Composite Benchmark. The fund may invest in 'B' shares in Shanghai or Shenzhen, or other new stock exchanges in China as they open up, "H" shares (Chinese companies) and Hong Kong companies listed in Hong Kong.

Umbrella fund: Gartmore Capital Strategy Fund Limited
Launch date: 16/10/95 **Domicile:** Jersey
Currency: USD **Structure:** Open ended, Investment Company
Portfolio manager: Sean Kelly
Manager of Gartmore CSF HK & China; Honours degree, modern history- Oxford U; previously with Anderson Consulting and INVESCO Plc, head of the Far East desk; joined Gartmore as an Investment Manager in 1994.
Purchase: Direct, Financial Advisor
Minimum investment: 2,500 USD
Custodian: The Chase Manhattan Bank
Listed: London **Dealings:** Daily
Fund Sedol I.D.: 36084 **Published:** FT/JE/SC/RT/HB
Fees **Annual fee:** 1.50% **Performance fee:** None
Front end load: 5.00% **Redemption fee:** None
Switching fee: None

Contact: Nigel Parker
Performance:

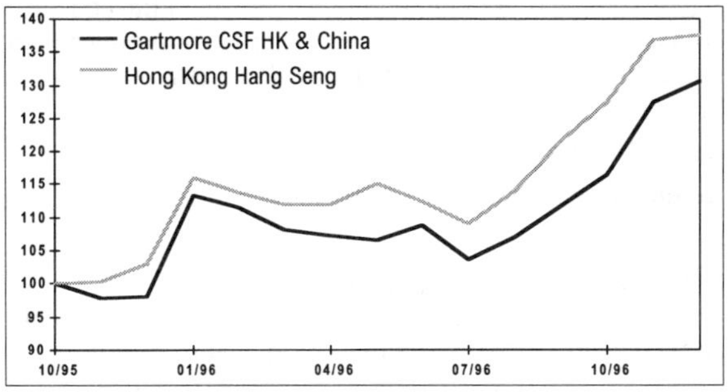

Top holdings:		
	Cheung Kong Holdings Ltd	5.3%
	Citic Pacific	3.2%
	Hang Seng Bank	2.9%
	Henderson Land Development	4.0%
	Hong Kong Land Holdings	2.7%
	HSBC Holdings	6.0%
	Hutchison Whampoa	4.3%
	New World Development	2.9%
	Sun Hung Kai Properties	3.7%
	Swire Pacific	3.4%

TOTAL RETURNS %

3 months 1997	1996	1995	1994	3 years	5 years
-2.69	33.23	N.A.	N.A.	N.A.	N.A.

STATISTICS

Assets ($mil)	Current yield	Volatility	Risk return	Micropal Star Rating
4.58	—	N.A.	—	———

Gartmore CSF UK Smaller Cos
55/350

Gartmore Fund Managers International Limited
45 La Motte Street, St Helier, JE4 8TF, Jersey
Tel 44-1534-886-688 Fax 44-1534-886-689

Investment objective:
The fund aims for long-term total return in excess of the FT-SE Small Cap (ex investment trusts) Index in sterling. This is achieved by investing in smaller companies listed on the London Stock Exchange or other stock exchanges where companies derive a significant proportion of their earnings from the UK.

Umbrella fund: Gartmore Capital Strategy Fund Limited
Launch date: 01/09/94 **Domicile:** Jersey
Currency: GBP **Structure:** Open ended, Investment Company
Portfolio manager: Frank Manduca
Manager of Gartmore CSF UK Small Companies since 1990; Honours, economic history- Kent U; previously with Laurence, Prust & Co, as investment analyst responsible for research of food manufacturing/retail sectors and small companies.
Purchase: Direct, Financial Advisor, Savings Scheme
Minimum investment: 2,500 USD
Custodian: The Chase Manhatten Bank
Listed: London **Dealings:** Daily
Fund Sedol I.D.: 36990 **Published:** FT/JE/SC/RT/HB
Fees **Annual fee:** 1.50% **Performance fee:** None
Front end load: 5.00% **Redemption fee:** None
Switching fee: None

Contact: Nigel Parker
Performance:

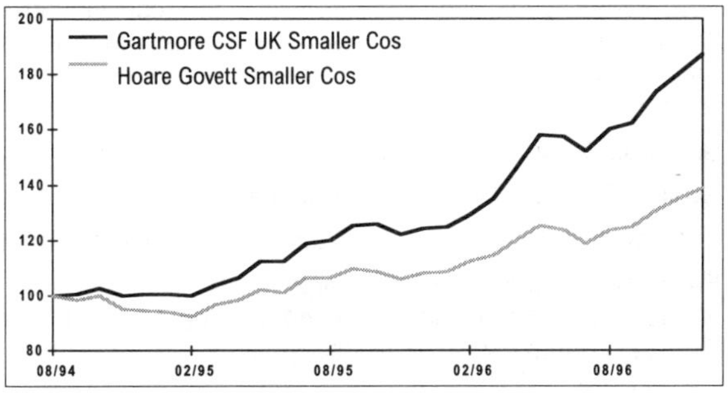

Top holdings:		
	Caspian Group	2.4%
	European Telecom	2.3%
	Go-Ahead Group	4.1%
	Meconic	2.4%
	Page (Michael) Group	3.2%
	Regent Inns Plc	3.5%
	Select Appointments	2.4%
	Southnews	3.0%
	Tinsley Robor	2.3%
	Wyevale Garden Centres	2.7%

TOTAL RETURNS %

3 months 1997	1996	1995	1994	3 years	5 years
7.67	50.95	23.32	N.A.	N.A.	N.A.

STATISTICS

Assets ($mil)	Current yield	Volatility	Risk return	Micropal Star Rating
16.39	—	N.A.	—	———

Gartmore CSF US Smaller Cos
71/350

Gartmore Fund Managers International Limited
45 La Motte Street, St Helier, JE4 8TF, Jersey
Tel 44-1534-886-688 Fax 44-1534-886-689

Investment objective:
The aim of the fund is to achieve a long-term total return in excess of the S & P 500 Index. The fund primarily invests in the equities of companies which comprise the bottom third of the major North American stock exchanges in terms of market capitalisation. The fund may also invest up to 15% in companies domiciled in Canada and Mexico.

Umbrella fund: Gartmore Capital Strategy Fund Limited

Launch date: 16/10/95 **Domicile:** Jersey

Currency: USD **Structure:** Open ended, Investment Company

Portfolio manager: Andrew Trower
Manager of Gartmore CSF US Small Companies since 1995; BA, business administration (finance and marketing)- Stetson U; previously at Schroders as Fund Manager; more than 10 years in the financial industry.

Purchase: Direct, Financial Advisor

Minimum investment: 2,500 USD

Custodian: The Chase Manhattan Bank

Listed: London **Dealings:** Daily

Fund Sedol I.D.: 36098 **Published:** FT/JE/SC/RT/HB

Fees **Annual fee:** 1.50% **Performance fee:** None
Front end load: 5.00% **Redemption fee:** None
Switching fee: None

Contact: Nigel Parker

Performance:

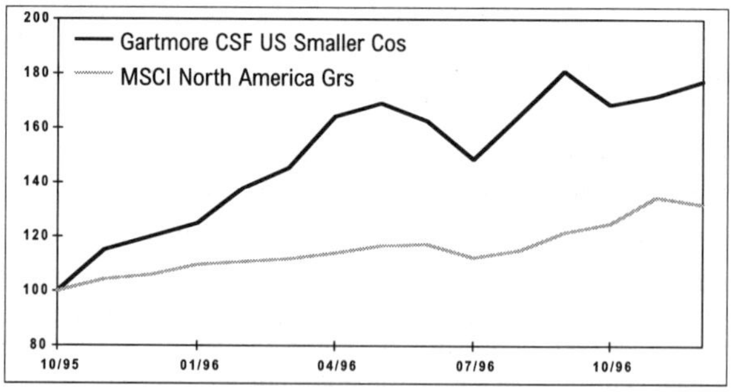

Top holdings:

Amresco	3.2%
Apache	2.4%
Avant	2.5%
CUC International	2.4%
Intergrated Systems	2.6%
Molecular Devices	2.5%
North Fork Bancorp	2.9%
Omnicare	2.4%
Periphonics	2.6%
Proxim	3.4%

TOTAL RETURNS %

3 months 1997	1996	1995	1994	3 years	5 years
-7.74	47.75	N.A.	N.A.	N.A.	N.A.

STATISTICS

Assets ($mil)	Current yield	Volatility	Risk return	Micropal Star Rating
12.32	—	N.A.	—	———

Gems Progressive Fund Limited Class J Share
284/350

Gems Management Ltd
4 Floor Russell House, Stokes Place St Stephen's Green, Dublin 2, Ireland
Tel 353-1-475-7601 Fax 353-1-475-7608
E mail ann.marie.okeeffe@meespierson.ie

Investment objective:
The principal focus of the fund's Class "J" shares is to realise above average long-term capital appreciation by co-investing and representing an investment in the Jaguar Fund NV managed by Tiger Management. In order to maximise its gain this fund takes short and long positions worldwide.

Umbrella fund: This is a singular fund.

Launch date: 01/06/92 **Domicile:** British Virgin Islands

Currency: USD **Structure:** Open ended, Investment Company

Portfolio manager: GEMS Management Ltd.
Manager of GEMS Progressive Fund, Limited, Class "J" shares since June 1992; formed December 1990 in the Bahamas.

Purchase: Financial Advisor

Minimum investment: 100,000 USD

Custodian: W & P Bank & Trust Co. Ltd

Listed: None **Dealings:** Monthly

Fund Sedol I.D.: 236351 **Published:** FT/IHT/SC

Fees **Annual fee:** 2.00% **Performance fee:** Up to 15.00%
Front end load: 5.00% **Redemption fee:** None
Switching fee: None

Contact: Ann-Marie O'Keeffe

Performance:

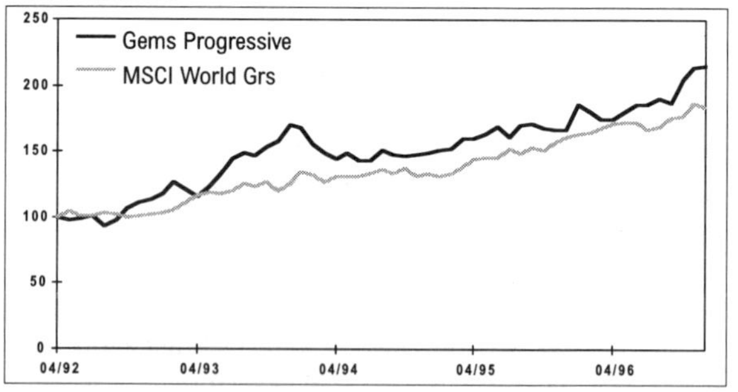

Top holdings:

AMR	n/s
Citicorp	n/s
Eurotunnel - short	n/s
General Motors	n/s

TOTAL RETURNS %

3 months 1997	1996	1995	1994	3 years	5 years
3.48	28.91	11.68	-12.01	26.67	N.A.

STATISTICS

Assets ($mil)	Current yield	Volatility	Risk return	Micropal Star Rating
7.64	—	3.79	1	✪✪✪

Generalpart
180/350

Banque Generale Du Luxembourg
50 JF Kennedy, L-2951 Luxembourg
Tel 352-42-42-32-04 Fax 352-42-42-26-75
http://www. bgl.lu E mail Info@bgl.lu

Investment objective:
The fund seeks to invest at least 75% assets in shares of fully taxable Luxembourg companies. Luxembourg tax payers resident in the Grand Duchy or in Belgium may claim a tax-free allowance of their investments in Generalpart. The main sector allocation of the portfolio is finance (50.2%).

Umbrella fund: This is a singular fund.
Launch date: 01/12/89 **Domicile:** Luxembourg
Currency: LUF **Structure:** Open ended, SICAV
Portfolio manager: Asset Management-BGL
Manager of Generalpart B; located at Banque Generale du Luxembourg SA, 50 Avenue JF Kennedy, L-2951 Lxembourg.

Purchase: Direct, Financial Advisor
Minimum investment: 1 Share
Custodian: Banque Generale Du Luxembourg
Listed: None **Dealings:** Daily
Fund Sedol I.D.: 301978 **Published:** LW
Fees **Annual fee:** 1.50% **Performance fee:** None
Front end load: 2.00% **Redemption fee:** 1.00%
Switching fee: None

Contact: Mrs Masset
Performance:

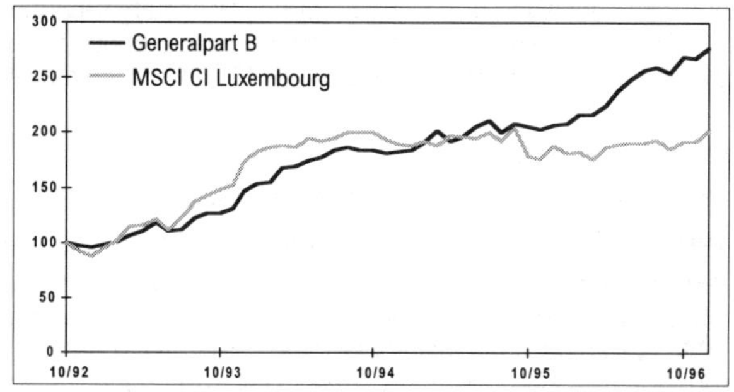

Top holdings:

Holding	%
Arbed	8.2%
ARES	0.2%
Audiofina	3.2%
Audiolux	3.4%
Banque Generale du Lux	13.0%
Banque Internationale Lux	12.8%
Cegedel	11.5%
Kleinwort Benson	13.0%
Luxempart	11.7%
Seo Lufpr	0.1%

TOTAL RETURNS %

3 months 1997	1996	1995	1994	3 years	5 years
2.36	33.77	13.43	24.41	88.79	178.94

STATISTICS

Assets ($mil)	Current yield	Volatility	Risk return	Micropal Star Rating
66.57	—	2.89	3	✪✪✪

Genesis Condor Fund Limited
324/350

Genesis Investment Management Limited
21 Knightsbridge, London SW1X 7LY, United Kingdom
Tel 44-171-235-5040 Fax 44-171-235-8065

Investment objective:
The primary object of the fund is to seek long-term capital growth and a growing dividend income by investing in the capital markets of Latin America. The top country allocations of the portfolio are Chile (23.9%); Brazil (18.3%); Central America (14.1%); Venezuela (9.8%); and Mexico (7.7%).The funds assets are held in equities (97.5%); and in cash/MM (2.5%).

Umbrella fund: This is a singular fund.
Launch date: 03/21/91 **Domicile:** Guernsey
Currency: USD **Structure:** Close ended, Investment Company
Portfolio manager: Richard Carss
Manager commenced March 1991; previously with Templeton Invest Mgt Ltd UK and JP Morgan Invest Mgt Pacific Ltd as MD and Vickers da Costa Ltd managed the international desk-South East Asia/ Brazil; plus 8 years in the oil industry.
Purchase: Direct
Minimum investment: None
Custodian: Bank of Bermuda (Guernsey) Ltd.
Listed: Dublin **Dealings:** N/A
Fund Sedol I.D.: 36349 **Published:** FT
Fees **Annual fee:** 1.50% **Performance fee:** None
Front end load: Up to 5.25% **Redemption fee:** None
Switching fee: None

Contact: Customer Services Department
Performance:

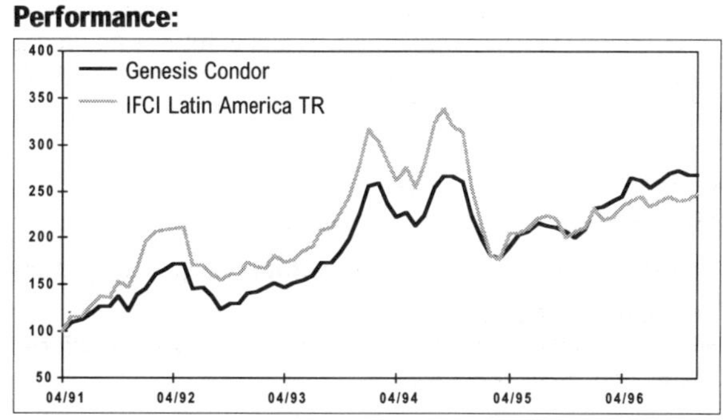

Top holdings:

Holding	%
Antofagasta Holdings	2.0%
Banco Itau	1.9%
Bardella	2.1%
Ceteco Ltd.	2.8%
Embotelladora Latin Americana	2.2%
Genesis Chile Fund Ltd.	23.0%
Greenstone Resources Ltd.	10.0%
Kimberly Clark de Mexico "A"	2.0%
Sivensa	1.8%
Venezolana	2.2%

TOTAL RETURNS %

3 months 1997	1996	1995	1994	3 years	5 years
13.45	27.75	-6.66	-0.78	18.30	90.81

STATISTICS

Assets ($mil)	Current yield	Volatility	Risk return	Micropal Star Rating
67.97	—	5.96	1	✪✪✪✪

Genesis Malaysia Maju Fund
88/350

Genesis
21 Knightsbridge, London SW1X 7LY, United Kingdom
Tel 44-171-235-5040 Fax 44-171-235-8065

Investment objective:
The fund seek long-term capital growth by investment in a professionally managed portfolio consisting of securities (principally equity securities) in Malaysia. The fund is primarily invested in small to medium-sized companies. The asset allocations of the portfolio are the following: equities (91.1%); and cash/MM (8.9%).

Umbrella fund: This is a singular fund.
Launch date: 02/12/90 **Domicile:** Guernsey
Currency: USD **Structure:** Close ended, Investment Company
Portfolio manager: Catherine Vlasto and Jonathan Points-Co-Managers. Ms Vlasto BA (Hons) Bristol U; experienced in SE Asia and natural resources; a fund manager since 1988; Mr Points a graduate of Oxford U; experienced in US, SE Asia and Latin America; formerly manager Kuwait Investment Office – London: 14 years in the finance industry.
Purchase: Direct
Minimum investment: None
Custodian: Bank of Bermuda (Guernsey) Ltd.
Listed: London **Dealings:** Annual
Fund Sedol I.D.: 36857 **Published:** FT
Fees **Annual fee:** 1.50% **Performance fee:** None
Front end load: Up to 5.25% **Redemption fee:** None
Switching fee: None

Contact: Richard Caryss
Performance:

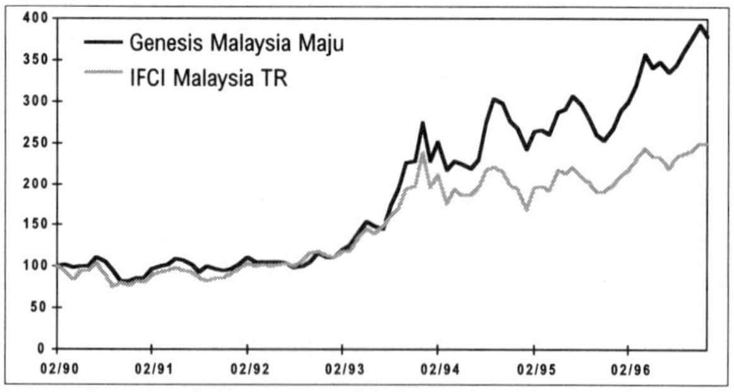

Top holdings:		
	Affin Holdings	3.5%
	Commerce Asset Holdings	3.6%
	John Hancock	3.4%
	London & Pacific	5.9%
	Muhibbah Engineering	3.0%
	Oriental	3.0%
	OYL Industries	8.6%
	Phileo Allied	4.9%
	Public Finance	2.8%
	Southern Bank	4.9%

TOTAL RETURNS %

3 months 1997	1996	1995	1994	3 years	5 years
13.85	42.18	-0.34	-2.72	37.84	293.40

STATISTICS

Assets ($mil)	Current yield	Volatility	Risk return	Micropal Star Rating
93.33	—	7.33	3	○○○○○

Global Diversified Portfolio Series D
186/350

John W Henry & Company Inc.
Rosebank Center, 11 Bermudiana Road, Pembroke, Bermuda
Tel 1-441-295-1111 Fax 1-441-295-6759
http://www. globalcapitalmgmt.com

Investment objective:
The fund is a Bermuda company that seeks capital appreciation and diversification through a disciplined investment in global futures and forwards markets. Series D is traded pursuant to JWH's Global Diversified Portfolio, identifying and capitalising on intermediate and long-term price movements in financial and non-financial markets.

Umbrella fund: JWH Global Strategies Ltd
Launch date: 01/01/94 **Domicile:** Bermuda
Currency: USD **Structure:** Open ended, Investment Company
Portfolio manager: John W. Henry & Company Inc.
Manager of John Henry GI Strategies D; located in California, US; specialises in the managed futures industry.

Purchase: Direct
Minimum investment: 250,000 USD
Custodian: The Bank of Butterfield Executor and Trustee Co
Listed: None **Dealings:** Monthly
Fund Sedol I.D.: 239444 **Published:** IHT/WS
Fees **Annual fee:** 4.00% **Performance fee:** 15.00%
Front end load: 1.75% **Redemption fee:** None
Switching fee: None

Contact: Ms Paula Burt
Performance:

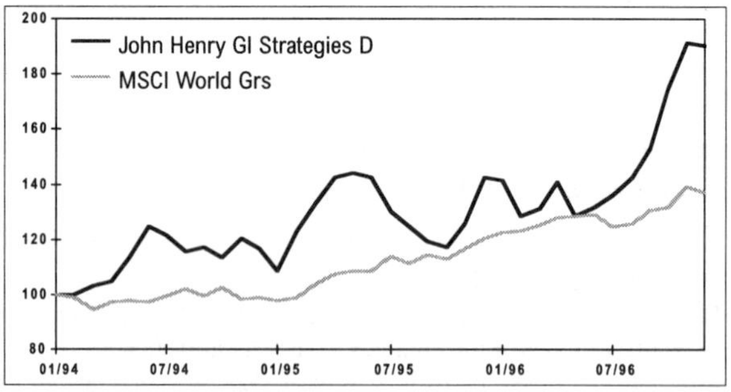

Top holdings:		
	Agricultural	11.6%
	Currencies	13.0%
	Energies	22.1%
	European Interest Rates	17.4%
	Metals	17.0%
	Pacific Rim Interest Rates	7.4%
	Stock Indices	7.0%
	US Interest Rates	4.5%

TOTAL RETURNS %

3 months 1997	1996	1995	1994	3 years	5 years
1.31	33.45	21.97	N.A.	N.A.	N.A.

STATISTICS

Assets ($mil)	Current yield	Volatility	Risk return	Micropal Star Rating
6.65	—	N.A.	—	———

Global Emerging Value Fund
145/350

Regent Fund Management (UK) Ltd
39 St James Street, London SW1A 1JQ, United Kingdom
Tel 44-171-316-0007 Fax 44-171-316-0010

Investment objective:
The fund seeks capital growth through investment in equity and equity related securities in emerging markets. At present the currency exposure of the portfolio is US dollar (21.%); and other (79.0%).

Umbrella fund: This is a singular fund.
Launch date: 23/02/94 **Domicile:** Cayman Islands
Currency: USD **Structure:** Open ended, Investment Company
Portfolio manager: Andrew Pegge CFA
Manager of Global Emerging Value Fund commenced in January 1996; BA, psychology/ cognitive studies and MBA; previously with Buchanan Emerging Markets Fd and Laurentian Fund Mgt; 10 years in the finance industry.
Purchase: Financial Advisor
Minimum investment: 100,000 USD
Custodian: Bermuda Trust (Far East) Limited.
Listed: Dublin **Dealings:** Weekly
Fund Sedol I.D.: 673014 **Published:** FT
Fees **Annual fee:** 1.00% **Performance fee:** 15.00%
Front end load: Up to 4.00% **Redemption fee:** None
Switching fee: None

Contact: Customer Services Department
Performance:

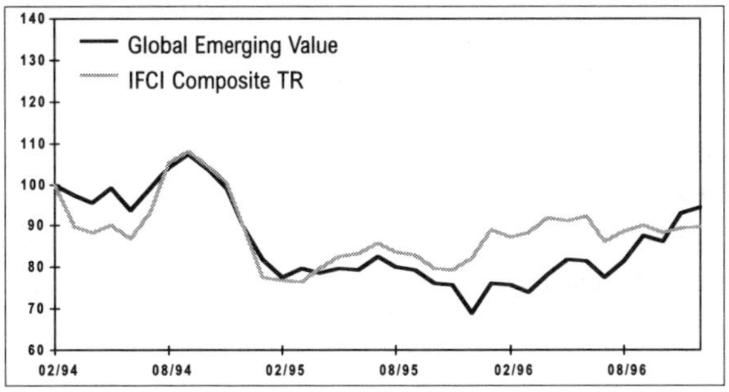

Top holdings:

Argentina	5.3%
Brazil	8.5%
Czech & Slovak	12.8%
India	5.0%
Indonesia	5.3%
Mexico	5.5%

TOTAL RETURNS %

3 months 1997	1996	1995	1994	3 years	5 years
10.40	36.52	-22.87	N.A.	N.A.	N.A.

STATISTICS

Assets ($mil)	Current yield	Volatility	Risk return	Micropal Star Rating
5.55	—	N.A.	—	———

Global Mgr German Geared
166/350

Bermuda International Investment Management Ltd
Compass Point, 9 Bermudiana Road, Hamilton, HM11, Bermuda
Tel 1-441-229-5600 Fax 1-441-229-6518
E mail bermudafunds@bankofbermuda.com

Investment objective:
The fund seeks to provide performance broadly double that of the relevant German index (DAX) by utilising both long and short option positions in DAX instruments. The fund is denominated in US dollars.

Umbrella fund: Global Manager Limited
Launch date: 01/09/94 **Domicile:** Bermuda
Currency: USD **Structure:** Open ended, Mutual Fund
Portfolio manager: BIIML (Bermuda International Investment Mgt Ltd)
The Manager of Global Manager German Geared; located at Bank of Bermuda Building, 6 Front Street, Hamilton HM11, Bermuda.

Purchase: Direct, Financial Advisor
Minimum investment: 25,000 USD
Custodian: Bank of Bermuda Limited
Listed: Dublin **Dealings:** Daily
Fund Sedol I.D.: 208874 **Published:** FT/RG
Fees **Annual fee:** 1.00% **Performance fee:** None
Front end load: Up to 5.00% **Redemption fee:** None
Switching fee: Up to 0.75%

Contact: Service Desk
Performance:

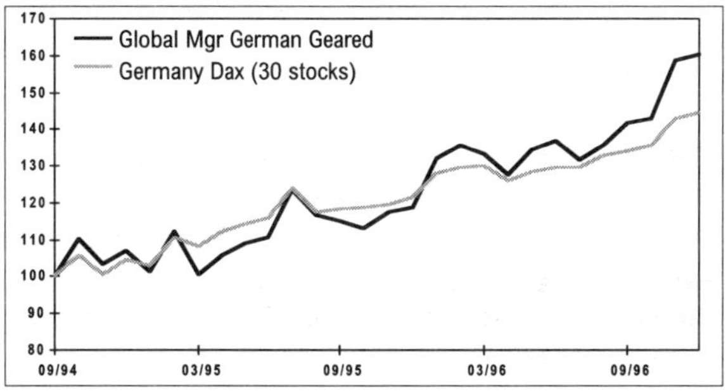

Top holdings:

Cash/MM	99.5%
Dax 2550 sept 96 Put	0.0%
Dax Sept 96 call	0.4%

TOTAL RETURNS %

3 months 1997	1996	1995	1994	3 years	5 years
27.69	35.16	11.03	N.A.	N.A.	N.A.

STATISTICS

Assets ($mil)	Current yield	Volatility	Risk return	Micropal Star Rating
0.20	—	N.A.	—	———

Global Mgr HK Geared
59/350

Bermuda International Investment Management Ltd
Compass Point, 9 Bermudiana Road, Hamilton, HM11, Bermuda
Tel 1-441-299-5600 Fax 1-441-229-6518
E mail bermudafunds@bankofbermuda.com

Investment objective:
The primary objective of this fund is to provide performance broadly double that of the Hang Seng Index. Fundamentally the Global Manager funds track their respective indexes without the pooling of stocks or bonds. Instead it uses financial futures to track the respective indexes. These instruments provide liquidity and cost effectiveness.

Umbrella fund: Global Manager Limited

Launch date: 01/09/94 **Domicile:** Bermuda

Currency: USD **Structure:** Open ended, Mutual Fund

Portfolio manager: BIIML (Bermuda International Investment Mgt Ltd)
The Manager of Global Manager Hong Kong Geared; located at Bank of Bermuda Building, 6 Front Street, Hamilton HM11, Bermuda.

Contact: Service Desk

Performance:

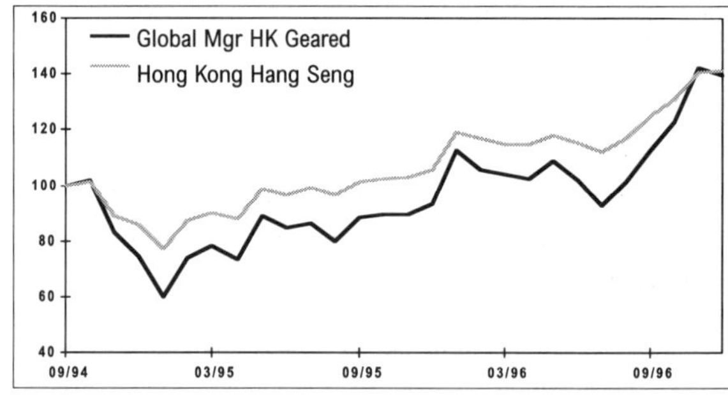

Top holdings:

Hang Seng July 96	-11.0%
Hang Seng 10800 Jul 96 Call	-16.0%
Hang Seng 8800 Jun 96 Put	-8.0%
Cash	10035.0%

Purchase: Direct, Financial Advisor

Minimum investment: 25,000 USD

Custodian: Bank of Bermuda Limited

Listed: Dublin **Dealings:** Daily

Fund Sedol I.D.: 208871 **Published:** FT/RG

Fees **Annual fee:** 1.00% **Performance fee:** None
Front end load: Up to 5.00% **Redemption fee:** None
Switching fee: Up to 0.75%

TOTAL RETURNS %

3 months 1997	1996	1995	1994	3 years	5 years
-17.86	49.85	25.01	N.A.	N.A.	N.A.

STATISTICS

Assets ($mil)	Current yield	Volatility	Risk return	Micropal Star Rating
0.30	—	N.A.	—	———

Global Mgr HK Index
263/350

Bermuda International Investment Management Ltd
Compass Point, 9 Bermudiana Road, Hamilton, HM11, Bermuda
Tel 1-441-299-5600 Fax 1-441-299-6518
E mail bermudafunds@bankofbermuda.com

Investment objective:
The sub-fund aims to provide a return mirroring the performance of the relevant index, Hang Seng Index. The funds maintains flexibility to alter the investment emphasis of holdings easily and quickly and to respond to changes in the economic or political climate as necessary.

Umbrella fund: Global Manager Limited

Launch date: 01/09/94 **Domicile:** Bermuda

Currency: USD **Structure:** Open ended, Mutual Fund

Portfolio manager: BIIML (Bermuda International Investment Mgt Ltd)
The Manager of Glbl Manager Hong Kong Index; located at Bank of Bermuda Building, 6 Front Street, Hamilton HM11, Bermuda.

Contact: Sevice Desk

Performance:

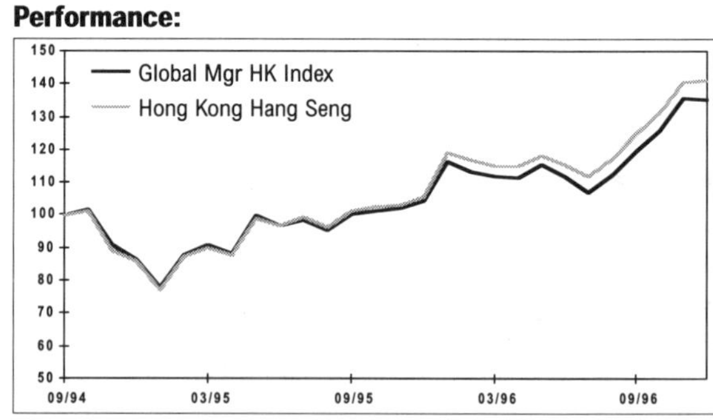

Top holdings:

Cash/MM	99.9%
Hang Seng July 96 Index	0.1%

Purchase: Direct, Financial Advisor

Minimum investment: 25,000 USD

Custodian: Bank of Bermuda Limited

Listed: Dublin **Dealings:** Daily

Fund Sedol I.D.: 208873 **Published:** FT/RG

Fees **Annual fee:** 1.00% **Performance fee:** None
Front end load: Up to 5.00% **Redemption fee:** None
Switching fee: Up to 0.75%

TOTAL RETURNS %

3 months 1997	1996	1995	1994	3 years	5 years
-8.09	29.84	20.47	N.A.	N.A.	N.A.

STATISTICS

Assets ($mil)	Current yield	Volatility	Risk return	Micropal Star Rating
0.90	—	N.A.	—	———

Global Mgr UK Geared
202/350

Bermuda International Investment Management Ltd
Compass Point, 9 Bermudiana Road, Hamilton, HM11, Bermuda
Tel 1-441-299-5600 Fax 1-441-299-6518
E mail bermudafunds@bankofbermuda.com

Investment objective:
The sub-fund seeks to provide performance broadly double that of the FTSE 100 Index. Fundamentally the Global Manager funds track their respective indexes without pooling of stocks or bonds. Instead, it uses financial futures to track the respective indexes. These instruments provide liquidity and cost effectiveness.

Contact: Service Desk

Performance:

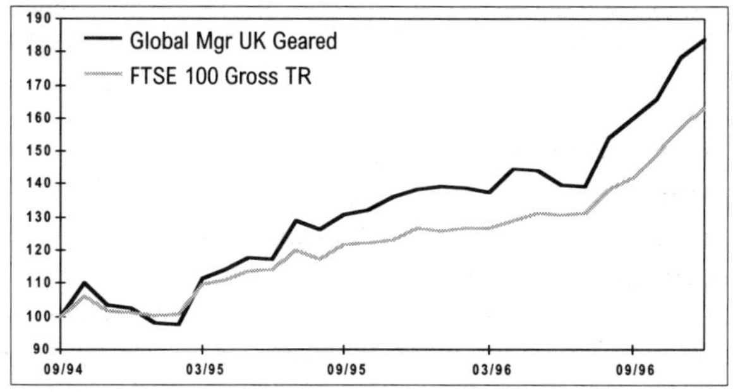

Umbrella fund: Global Manager Limited
Launch date: 01/09/94 **Domicile:** Bermuda
Currency: USD **Structure:** Open ended, Mutual Fund
Portfolio manager: BIIML (Bermuda International Investment Mgt Ltd)
The Manager of Global Manager United Kingdom Geared the fund located: Bank of Bermuda Building, 6 Front Street, Hamilton HM11, Bermuda.

Top holdings:

Cash/MM	101.9%
FTSE 100 Sept 96	-2.4%
FTSE 3025 Sept put	0.1%
FTSE 3850 Sept call	0.4%

Purchase: Direct, Financial Advisor
Minimum investment: 25,000 USD
Custodian: Bank of Bermuda Limited
Listed: Dublin **Dealings:** Daily
Fund Sedol I.D.: 208869 **Published:** FT/RG
Fees **Annual fee:** 1.00% **Performance fee:** None
Front end load: Up to 5.00% **Redemption fee:** None
Switching fee: Up to 0.75%

TOTAL RETURNS %

3 months 1997	1996	1995	1994	3 years	5 years
4.48	32.67	35.05	N.A.	N.A.	N.A.

STATISTICS

Assets ($mil)	Current yield	Volatility	Risk return	Micropal Star Rating
0.10	—	N.A.	—	———

Global Mgr US Geared
149/350

Bermuda International Investment Management Ltd
Compass Point, 9 Bermudiana Road, Hamilton, HM11, Bermuda
Tel 1-441-229-5600 Fax 1-441-299-6518
E mail bermudafunds@bankofbermuda.com

Investment objective:
The objective of the US Geared Index Fund is to provide performance probably double that of the S&P 500 Index. The fund management style allows for flexibility to alter investment emphasis of holdings easily and quickly while responding to changes in the economic or political climate.

Contact: Service Desk

Performance:

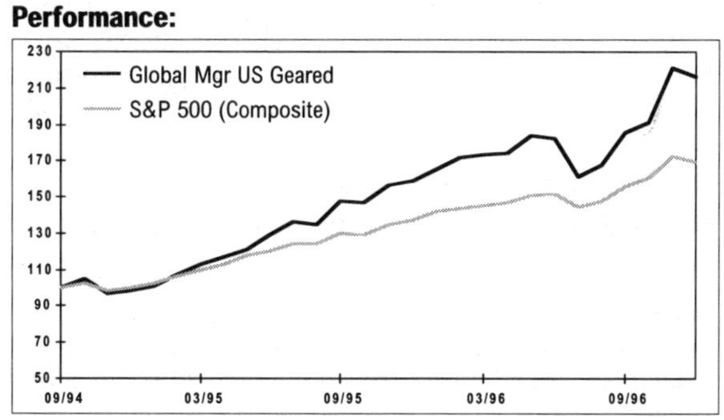

Umbrella fund: Global Manager Limited
Launch date: 01/09/94 **Domicile:** Bermuda
Currency: USD **Structure:** Open ended, Mutual Fund
Portfolio manager: BIIML (Bermuda International Investment Mgt Ltd)
The Manager of Global Manager US Geared; located at Bank of Bermuda Building, 6 Front Street, Hamilton HM11, Bermuda.

Top holdings:

Cash/MM	97.5%
S&P 500 Sept 96	2.4%
S&P 510 Sept put	0.1%

Purchase: Direct, Financial Advisor
Minimum investment: 25,000 USD
Custodian: Bank of Bermuda Limited
Listed: Dublin **Dealings:** Daily
Fund Sedol I.D.: 208860 **Published:** FT/RG
Fees **Annual fee:** 1.00% **Performance fee:** None
Front end load: Up to 5.00% **Redemption fee:** None
Switching fee: Up to 0.75%

TOTAL RETURNS %

3 months 1997	1996	1995	1994	3 years	5 years
7.74	36.22	61.10	N.A.	N.A.	N.A.

STATISTICS

Assets ($mil)	Current yield	Volatility	Risk return	Micropal Star Rating
0.30	—	N.A.	—	———

Globalvest Value Fund LP
44/350

Globalvest Management Co
4 The Cherries, Grange Wood, Rathfarnham, Dublin 16, Ireland
Tel 353-1-493-6282 Fax 353-1-493-6301

Investment objective:
The fund aims at a capital gain through an investment programme in emerging markets and under valued securities. The top country allocations of the fund are the following: Brazil (32.5%); Czech Rep (6.0%); Russia (33.0%); and Spain 15.0%.

Contact: John Lowry

Performance:

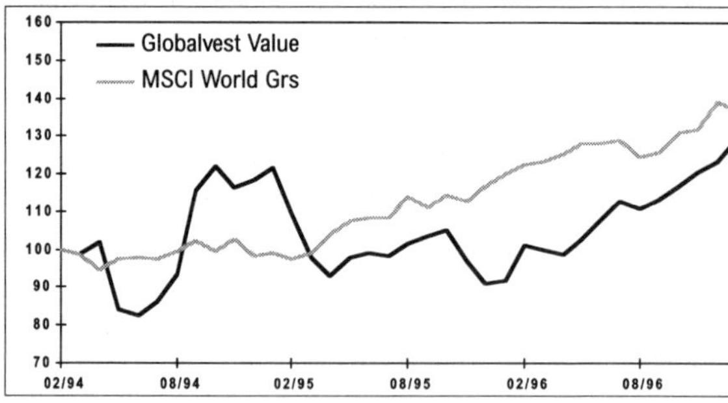

Umbrella fund: This is a singular fund.

Launch date: 01/01/94 **Domicile:** Cayman Islands

Currency: USD **Structure:** Open ended, Limited Partnership

Portfolio manager: Peter Gruber
Manager of Globalvest commenced January 1994 and President of Latinvest Mgt Co and Globalvest Management Company; specialises in Latin American and emerging market securities; active in the securities industry for over 20 years.

Purchase: Direct, Financial Advisor

Minimum investment: 1,000,000 USD

Custodian: Citibank

Listed: None **Dealings:** Monthly

Fund Sedol I.D.: 305569 **Published:** FT

Fees **Annual fee:** 1.50% **Performance fee:** 20.00%
Front end load: 3.50% **Redemption fee:** None
Switching fee: None

Top holdings:

Itaubanco	5.0%
Rostelecom	8.0%
Telebras ON	23.0%
Telefonica	7.0%
Unified EES Rosi	19.0%

TOTAL RETURNS %

3 months 1997	1996	1995	1994	3 years	5 years
26.26	54.93	-31.46	27.69	35.58	N.A.

STATISTICS

Assets ($mil)	Current yield	Volatility	Risk return	Micropal Star Rating
7.42	—	8.57	1	✪✪✪

Goldman Sachs Euro Small Cap
77/350

The Goldman Sachs Group LP
140 Fleet Street, London EC4 2BT, United Kingdom
Tel 44-171-774-5914 Fax 44-171-774-5193

Investment objective:
The sub-fund seeks long-term capital appreciation by investing in stocks of small European companies with public stock market capitalisation of 1 billion German marks or less at time of investment. The top portfolio country allocations are as follows: UK (27.1%); Germany (7.6%); Spain (7.1%); Italy (7.1%); and Netherlands (6.5%).

Contact: Claire Newson

Performance:

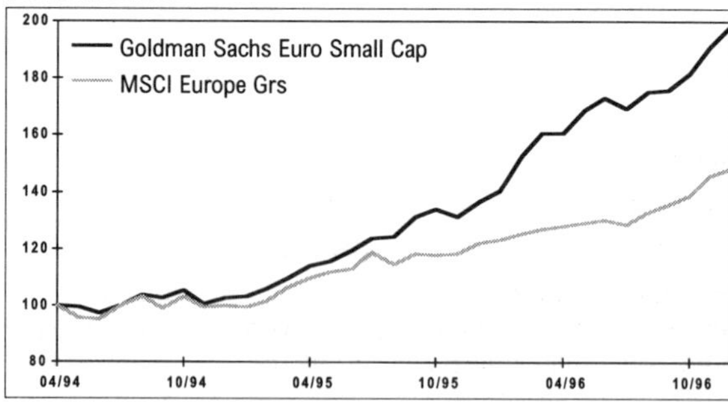

Umbrella fund: GS Equity Funds SICAV

Launch date: 02/05/94 **Domicile:** Luxembourg [UCITS]

Currency: DEM **Structure:** Open ended, SICAV

Portfolio manager: Roderick Jack and Marcel Jongen
Co-Managers of Goldman Sachs European Small Capitalisation both commenced in September 1992. Mr Jack has a MA in economics and Mr Jongen has a MA in public administration.

Purchase: Direct

Minimum investment: 2,500 DEM

Custodian: State Street Bank Luxembourg

Listed: Luxembourg **Dealings:** Daily

Fund Sedol I.D.: 441301 **Published:** FT/BZ/NZZ/SC

Fees **Annual fee:** 1.25% **Performance fee:** None
Front end load: 5.00% **Redemption fee:** None
Switching fee: None

Top holdings:

Corp Services	2.5%
Dahl International	3.1%
Fauck	2.8%
Konecranes	2.7%
Kuoni	2.7%
Moebel Waither	2.6%
OPG	2.4%
Partco	2.9%
Semapa	3.4%
Vidrala SA	2.5%

TOTAL RETURNS %

3 months 1997	1996	1995	1994	3 years	5 years
5.13	45.54	32.94	N.A.	N.A.	N.A.

STATISTICS

Assets ($mil)	Current yield	Volatility	Risk return	Micropal Star Rating
243.74	—	N.A.	—	———

Govett GSIL European Equity
206/350

John Govett (Channel Islands) Ltd
AIB House, Grenville Street, St Hellier, JE4 8WT, Jersey
Tel 44-1534-873-220 Fax 44-1534-888-422

Investment objective:
The sub-fund aims to achieve long-term capital growth with some income through investment in equities quoted in a variety of European equities including the United Kingdom. Preference is given to companies whose management pursue timely restructuring of their activities and by increasing returns on the equity capital employed in their business.

Umbrella fund: Global Stock Investment LTD

Launch date: 01/07/94 **Domicile:** Jersey

Currency: DEM **Structure:** Open ended, Investment Company

Portfolio manager: Peter Kysel
Manager, joined Govett as Director in 1994; graduate, economics/ management studies- Prague U and the Open U; previously with Touche Remnant, Lloyds Bank and as MD Komercni Bank investments division; 21 years in the finance industry.

Purchase: Direct, Financial Advisor

Minimum investment: 7,000 DEM

Custodian: Royal Bank of Scotland Trust Co (Jersey) Ltd

Listed: London **Dealings:** Daily

Fund Sedol I.D.: 37992 **Published:** FT/IHT/SC

Fees **Annual fee:** 1.50% **Performance fee:** None
Front end load: 5.50% **Redemption fee:** None
Switching fee: None

Contact: Chris Chambers

Performance:

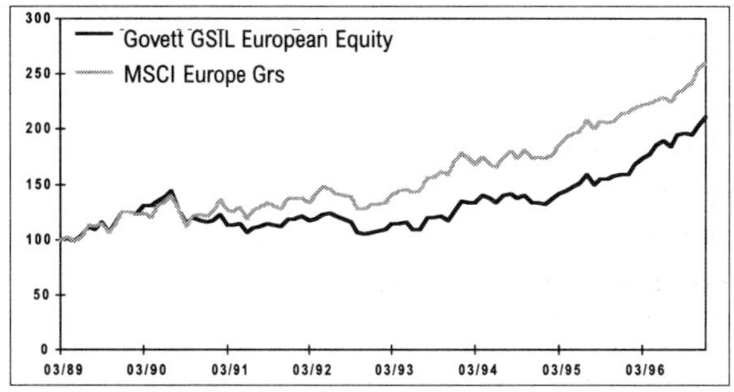

Top holdings:

Holding	%
Adecco	2.3%
Adidas	2.8%
Autoliv	1.7%
Bulgari	2.6%
Christian Dior	1.6%
Cofinec	2.3%
Elsevier	2.7%
Gucci	2.8%
Nutricia	1.8%
Porsche	1.9%

TOTAL RETURNS %

3 months 1997	1996	1995	1994	3 years	5 years
6.86	32.48	19.48	6.32	68.28	78.49

STATISTICS

Assets ($mil)	Current yield	Volatility	Risk return	Micropal Star Rating
4.12	1.08	3.11	5	✪✪✪✪✪

Govett Mexican Horizons Investment Co
313/350

John Govett (Channel Islands) Ltd
AIB House, Grenville Street, St Hellier, JE4 8WT, Jersey
Tel 44-1534-873-220 Fax 44-1534-888-422

Investment objective:
The fund aims to achieve long-term capital growth through investment in Mexican companies. The top sector allocations of the portfolio are as follows: industrial conglomerates (15.6%); food/ beverage/ tobacco (12.6%); metal/ mechanic (10.2%); finance (10.9%); retailing (9.9%); and communications (6.3%).

Umbrella fund: This is a singular fund.

Launch date: 27/07/94 **Domicile:** Jersey

Currency: USD **Structure:** Open ended, Investment Company

Portfolio manager: Caroline Lane
Director of Govett- 1994; graduate, economic history/ geography- Exeter U; formerly with Lloyds Bk Intl (Taiwan & Paris) and Crosby Securities (HK)- Head of Research for HK; joined Govett in 1990, specializing in Mexico/ Latin America.

Purchase: Direct, Financial Advisor

Minimum investment: 1,000 USD

Custodian: Royal Bank of Scotland Trust Co (Jersey) Ltd

Listed: Dublin **Dealings:** Daily

Fund Sedol I.D.: 38009 **Published:** FT/IHT/SC

Fees **Annual fee:** 1.50% **Performance fee:** None
Front end load: 5.50% **Redemption fee:** None
Switching fee: None

Contact: Chris Chambers

Performance:

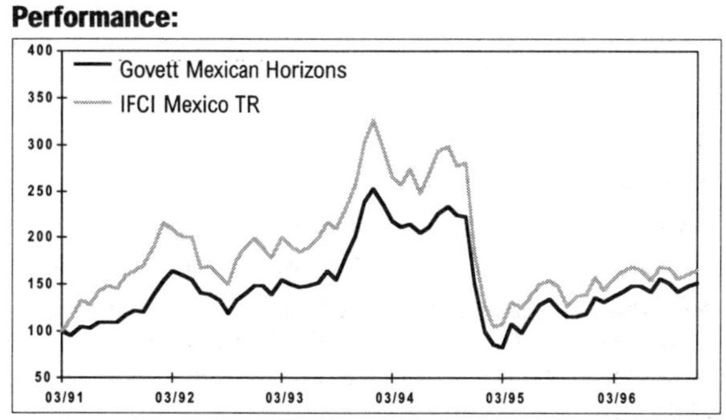

Top holdings:

Holding	%
Altos Hornos de Mexico B	3.3%
Cifra C	3.6%
Corp Geo	3.5%
Desc Soc De Fomento Ind	3.0%
Fin. Banacci 7% CNV 99	4.0%
Grupo Carso ADS	3.7%
Grupo Industrial Saltillo A	4.3%
Metalclad Corp Common US	3.0%
Nacional De Drogas B	2.9%

TOTAL RETURNS %

3 months 1997	1996	1995	1994	3 years	5 years
6.89	28.04	-21.76	-36.31	-36.19	25.34

STATISTICS

Assets ($mil)	Current yield	Volatility	Risk return	Micropal Star Rating
16.38	—	11.38	—	✪✪✪

GT Australian Small Cos A Share
138/350

GT Global
Alban Gate 14th Floor, 125 London Wall, London EC2Y 5AS, United Kingdom
Tel 44-171-626-4741 Fax 44-171-710-4600

Contact: European Marketing Department

Investment objective:
The aim of the sub-fund is to achieve long-term capital growth by investing in Australian small companies. The top sector allocations of the portfolio are finance (22.6%); multi industry (10.6%); gold mines/mining (10.0%); energy resources (5.8%); and construction/housing (5.3%).

Umbrella fund: GT Small Company Series
Launch date: 01/04/91 **Domicile:** Ireland [UCITS]
Currency: USD **Structure:** Open ended, Unit Trust
Portfolio manager: Tom Cottam
Manager of the sub-fund commenced June 1996; Diploma in Economics- London School of Economics; previously with LFT, Chief Investment Officer- Australia and Abu Dhabi Investment Authority, Senior Investment Manager- Japan and Pacific Rim.
Purchase: Direct, Financial Advisor, Duly appointed sales agent
Minimum investment: A-2,000: B-250,000 USD
Custodian: Chase Manhattan Bank (Ireland) Plc
Listed: Dublin **Dealings:** Daily
Fund Sedol I.D.: 37017 **Published:** FT/ WS
Fees **Annual fee:** 2.00% **Performance fee:** None
Front end load: 5.00% **Redemption fee:** None
Switching fee: 4.00%

Performance:

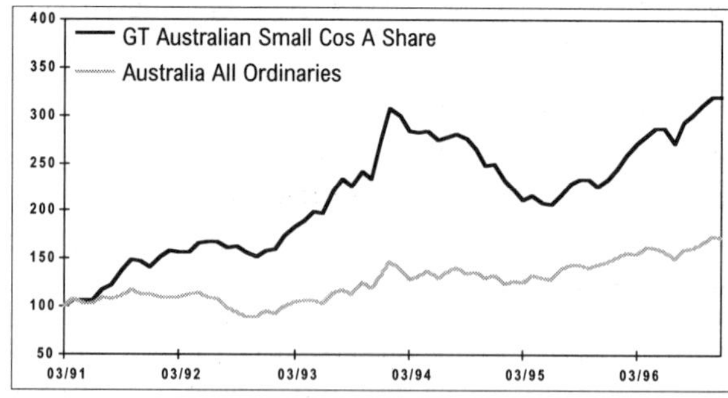

Top holdings:

Holding	%
Cochlear ltd	3.6%
Darling Park	3.8%
Gourmet Direct Investments	4.1%
MacMahon Holdings Ltd.	3.7%
Morgan and Banks ltd	4.8%
Novus Petroleum Ltd	4.7%
Reinsurance Australia	5.0%
Sons of Gwalia	4.5%
Spotless group	4.4%
Westralian Sands Ltd	3.8%

TOTAL RETURNS %

3 months 1997	1996	1995	1994	3 years	5 years
1.25	37.22	-6.35	-8.30	17.85	126.42

STATISTICS

Assets ($mil)	Current yield	Volatility	Risk return	Micropal Star Rating
35.00	—	4.36	3	✪✪✪

GT Deutschland
349/350

GT Global
Alban Gate 14th Floor, 125 London Wall, London EC2Y 5AS, United Kingdom
Tel 44-171-626-4741 Fax 44-171-710-4600

Contact: European Marketing Department

Investment objective:
The sub-fund seeks to achieve long-term capital growth by investment primarily in equity securities of German companies. The top sector allocations of the sub-fund are as follows: textiles/apparel (23.6%); business/public services (12.6%); chemicals (10.4%) electrical/ electrical equipment (7.2%); and finance (10.5%).

Umbrella fund: GT World Series
Launch date: 01/11/86 **Domicile:** Luxembourg [UCITS]
Currency: USD **Structure:** Open ended, Investment Company
Portfolio manager: Justin Thomson
Manager of GT World Series commenced December 1994; BA- Cambridge University; previously with LGT, as portfolio Manager and investment analyst, Europe.

Purchase: Direct, Financial Advisor, Duly appointed sales agent
Minimum investment: 1,000 USD
Custodian: Banque Internationale a Luxembourg
Listed: Luxembourg **Dealings:** Daily
Fund Sedol I.D.: 35896 **Published:** FT/ WS
Fees **Annual fee:** 1.00% **Performance fee:** None
Front end load: 5.00% **Redemption fee:** None
Switching fee: 4.00%

Performance:

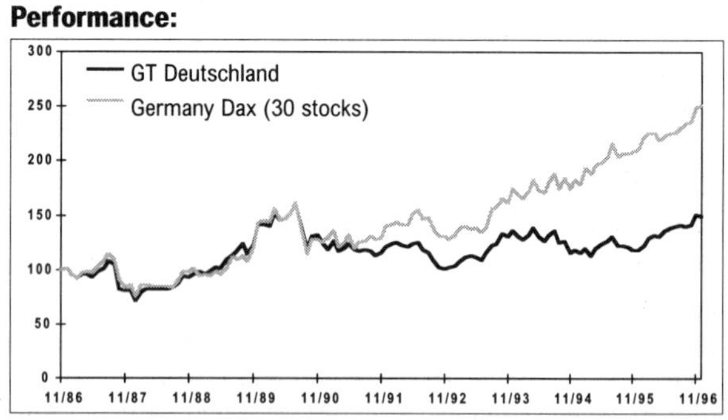

Top holdings:

Holding	%
Apcoa Parking AG	5.0%
BASF	6.3%
Bayerische Vereinsbank	4.1%
Berentzen Gruppe	4.5%
Biotest (Pref) 4.6%	4.6%
Eurobike AG	9.9%
Hoechst	4.6%
Koelnische Ruckversicherungs	3.8%
Moebel Walther	9.0%
Siemens	3.9%

TOTAL RETURNS %

3 months 1997	1996	1995	1994	3 years	5 years
3.54	26.95	-0.25	-13.27	9.82	23.80

STATISTICS

Assets ($mil)	Current yield	Volatility	Risk return	Micropal Star Rating
5.50	—	3.88	—	✪

GT Emerging Markets Bond
106/350

GT Global
Alban Gate 14th Floor, 125 London Wall, London EC2Y 5AS, United Kingdom
Tel 44-171-626-4741 Fax 44-171-710-4600

Investment objective:
The sub-fund's primary objective is to achieve a high income yield and long-term capital appreciation by investing in debt securities, loans and participation of issues in emerging countries. The top country allocations of this portfolio are as follows: Brazil (17.3%); Argentina (16.1%); Russia Fed (12.5%); Mexico (11.9%); Venezuela (8.4%); and Ecuador (5.4%).

Umbrella fund: GT World Bond Series

Launch date: 01/01/93 **Domicile:** Ireland

Currency: USD **Structure:** Open ended, Investment Company

Portfolio manager: Simon Nocera
Manager of GT World Bond Series since January 1994; Deputy Doctorate- State U of Milan; previously Putnam Companies, Senior VP Director of Global Fixed Income Research and International Monetary Fund, finance economist; joined LGT in 1994.

Purchase: Direct, Financial Advisor, Duly appointed sales agent

Minimum investment: 250,000 USD

Custodian: Chase Manhatton Bank (Ireland) Plc

Listed: Dublin **Dealings:** Daily

Fund Sedol I.D.: 35632 **Published:** FT/ WS

Fees **Annual fee:** 0.75% **Performance fee:** None
Front end load: 5.00% **Redemption fee:** None
Switching fee: 4.00%

Contact: European Marketing Department

Performance:

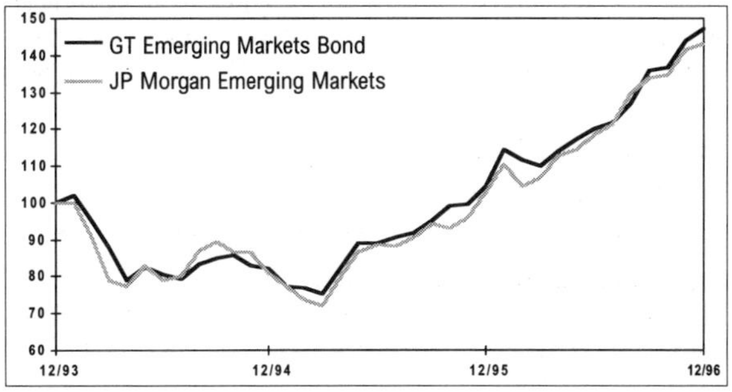

Top holdings:

Holding	%
Argentina Bocon 1/4/07	4.2%
Argentina Bocon 1/4/07 Euro	2.3%
Argentina FRN 31/3/23	9.3%
Brazil DCB L 15/4/12	10.5%
Brazil DCB L 15/4/12 (RG)	3.1%
Ecuador Euro 28/2/25	2.4%
Panama IRB 3.5% 17/7/14	3.7%
Venezuela DCB 18/12/07	8.3%
Vneshekonombank Loan	6.5%
Vneshekonombank Russia	2.0%

TOTAL RETURNS %

3 months 1997	1996	1995	1994	3 years	5 years
2.04	40.58	26.96	-17.63	47.02	N.A.

STATISTICS

Assets ($mil)	Current yield	Volatility	Risk return	Micropal Star Rating
127.00	6.17	4.61	2	✪✪

GT Europe Fund A Share
246/350

GT Global
Alban Gate 14th Floor, 125 London Wall, London EC2Y 5AS, United Kingdom
Tel 44-171-626-4741 Fax 44-171-710-4600

Investment objective:
The sub-fund aims to provide long-term capital growth through investment in a diversified portfolio of securities listed on any of the stock exchanges of Europe. Currently the top geographic allocations of the portfolio are UK (22.5%); France (14.1%); Sweden (11.5%); Germany (10.6%); Switzerland (9.1%); and Italy (7.2%).

Umbrella fund: GT World Series

Launch date: 01/01/84 **Domicile:** Luxembourg [UCITS]

Currency: USD **Structure:** Open ended, SICAV

Portfolio manager: Roger Yates
Manager of GT Europe Fund A/B commenced March 1995 and International CIO; Post Graduate research BA- Oxford U; previous experience CIO Pan Europe- LGT and CIO for UK pension fund- Morgan Grenfell Asset management.

Purchase: Direct, Financial Advisor, Duly appointed sales agent

Minimum investment: 2,000 USD

Custodian: Banque Internationale a Luxembourg

Listed: Luxembourg **Dealings:** Daily

Fund Sedol I.D.: 35801 **Published:** WS/FT/SC

Fees **Annual fee:** 1.50% **Performance fee:** None
Front end load: 5.00% **Redemption fee:** None
Switching fee: 4.00%

Contact: European Marketing Department

Performance:

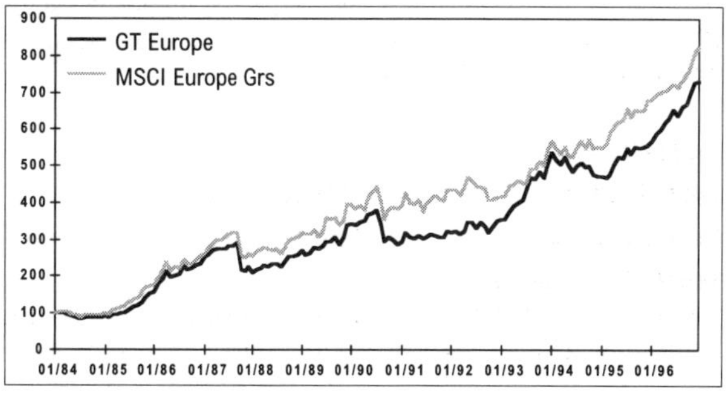

Top holdings:

Holding	%
Adecco	1.8%
Ahold Kon	2.1%
Astra	2.1%
Burton Group	2.5%
Dassault Systems	2.2%
Gehe	2.1%
Granada Group	2.7%
Novartis	4.0%
Sol Melia	1.8%
Tag Hever Intl SA	1.8%
Volkswagen	3.2%

TOTAL RETURNS %

3 months 1997	1996	1995	1994	3 years	5 years
5.97	30.57	18.67	-6.12	45.47	125.77

STATISTICS

Assets ($mil)	Current yield	Volatility	Risk return	Micropal Star Rating
262.00	—	3.03	2	✪✪✪

GT European Smaller Companies Class A
185/350

GT Global
Alban Gate 14th Floor, 125 London Wall, London EC2Y 5AS,
United Kingdom
Tel 44-171-626-4741 Fax 44-171-710-4600

Investment objective:
The sub-fund seeks long-term capital growth by investing in small companies incorporated in countries throughout Europe, but excluding the UK. The top country allocations of the portfolio are as follows: France (27.9%); Germany (12.5%); Switzerland (11.6%); Denmark (8.9%); Norway (8.8%); and Sweden (6.7%).

Umbrella fund: GT Small Company Series
Launch date: 01/10/84 **Domicile:** Ireland [UCITS]
Currency: USD **Structure:** Open ended, Unit Trust
Portfolio manager: Justin Thomson
Manager of GT European Smaller Companies Class A /B commenced April 1996; BA-Cambridge University; previously with LGT, as portfolio Manager and investment analyst, Europe.
Purchase: Direct, Financial Advisor, Duly appointed sales agent
Minimum investment: A-2,000: B-250,000 USD
Custodian: Chase Manhattan Bank (Ireland) Plc
Listed: Dublin **Dealings:** Daily
Fund Sedol I.D.: 438357 **Published:** FT/HKEJ/SC/WS
Fees **Annual fee:** 2.00% **Performance fee:** None
Front end load: 5.00% **Redemption fee:** None
Switching fee: 4.00%

Contact: European Marketing Department
Performance:

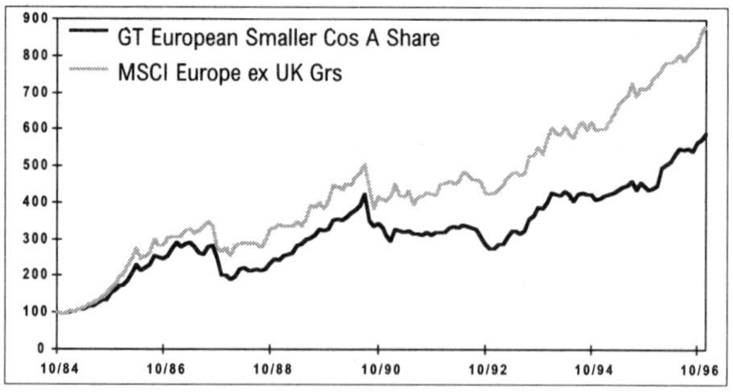

Top holdings:

Altrans Technologie	2.1%
Assa Abloy	3.8%
Dassault Systems	2.5%
Eurobike AG	2.2%
Moebel Walther	4.1%
Narvesen	2.0%
SIG Schweiz	2.4%
Stratec Holdings AG	2.5%
Tag Hever Intl SA	2.1%
Tele Pizza	2.4%

TOTAL RETURNS %

3 months 1997	1996	1995	1994	3 years	5 years
8.19	33.46	6.81	3.41	47.41	83.35

STATISTICS

Assets ($mil)	Current yield	Volatility	Risk return	Micropal Star Rating
158.00	—	3.03	2	✪✪✪

GT Healthcare A Share
193/350

GT Global
Alban Gate 14th Floor, 125 London Wall, London EC2Y 5AS,
United Kingdom
Tel 44-171-626-4741 Fax 44-171-710-4600

Investment objective:
The sub-fund seeks long-term capital growth by investing in healthcare companies throughout the world. The portfolio has the following sector allocations: Pharmaceuticals (25.0%); biotechnology (25.0%); devices/supplies (25.0%); and healthcare services (15.0%).

Umbrella fund: GT Pathfinder Series
Launch date: 01/06/82 **Domicile:** Ireland [UCITS]
Currency: USD **Structure:** Open ended, Unit Trust
Portfolio manager: Mike Yellen
Manager of GT Pathfinder Series since March 1994; BA- Stanford U; previously with Franklin Resources, senior securities analyst and LGT Healthcare as investment analyst.
Purchase: Direct, Financial Advisor, Duly appointed sales agent
Minimum investment: 2,000 USD
Custodian: Chase Manhattan Bank (Ireland) Plc
Listed: Dublin **Dealings:** Daily
Fund Sedol I.D.: 39298 **Published:** FT/ WS
Fees **Annual fee:** 2.00% **Performance fee:** None
Front end load: 5.00% **Redemption fee:** None
Switching fee: 4.00%

Contact: European MarketingDepartment
Performance:

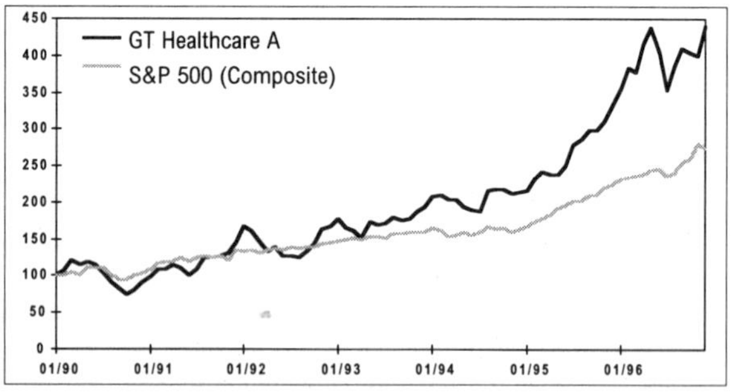

Top holdings:

Advanced Technology	3.3%
Amgen	5.4%
Mentor Corp.	3.0%
Protein Design Labs	6.8%
Sunrise Medical	5.0%
Theratech INC	5.2%
Visx Inc.	4.5%
Warner Lambert INC	6.3%
Watson Pharmaceuticals	3.9%

TOTAL RETURNS %

3 months 1997	1996	1995	1994	3 years	5 years
-3.11	33.16	54.50	10.15	126.61	202.15

STATISTICS

Assets ($mil)	Current yield	Volatility	Risk return	Micropal Star Rating
130.00	—	5.61	5	✪✪✪✪✪

GT Hong Kong Class A
92/350

GT Global
Alban Gate 14th Floor, 125 London Wall, London EC2Y 5AS, United Kingdom
Tel 44-171-626-4741 Fax 44-171-710-4600

Investment objective:
The sub-fund seeks long-term capital growth by investing in Hong Kong companies. The top sector allocations of the portfolio are: real estate (35.0%); finance (27.6%); multi industry (21.5%); and textiles/apparel (5.1%).

Umbrella fund: GT World Series
Launch date: 01/02/81 **Domicile:** Ireland [UCITS]
Currency: USD **Structure:** Open ended, Unit Trust
Portfolio manager: Billy Chan CA
Manager of GT Hong Kong Chase A/B commenced January 1997; BA- Cambridge U; previously with LGT (China and Taiwan) as portfolio Manager and investment analyst and Ernst & Young as a Chartered Accountant
Purchase: Direct, Financial Advisor, Duly appointed sales agent
Minimum investment: A-2,000: B-250,000 USD
Custodian: Chase Manhattan Bank (Ireland) Plc
Listed: Dublin **Dealings:** Daily
Fund Sedol I.D.: 37009 **Published:** FT/ WS/SC
Fees **Annual fee:** 1.50% **Performance fee:** None
Front end load: 5.00% **Redemption fee:** None
Switching fee: 4.00%

Contact: European Marketing Department
Performance:

Top holdings:

Cheung Kong	5.7%
Citic Pacific	4.0%
Guangzhou Investment	2.0%
Hang Seng Bank	7.1%
Henderson Land Development	5.3%
HSBC Holdings	9.5%
Hutchison Whampoa	5.4%
New World Development	4.8%
Sun Hung Kai Properties	4.4%
Swire Pacific	3.6%

TOTAL RETURNS %

3 months 1997	1996	1995	1994	3 years	5 years
-1.50	41.35	20.31	-36.53	7.94	186.61

STATISTICS

Assets ($mil)	Current yield	Volatility	Risk return	Micropal Star Rating
48.00	0.63	6.56	—	✪

GT Japan Warrants & Derivatives A
328/350

GT Global
Alban Gate 14th Floor, 125 London Wall, London EC2Y 5AS, United Kingdom
Tel 44-171-626-4741 Fax 44-171-710-4600

Investment objective:
Formerly, GT Asian Warrants & Derivatives, the sub-seeks to achieve capital growth superior to that obtainable by investment in an equivalent portfolio of Asia Pacific equities. This is achieved by investing actively in a portfolio of warrants and other derivative instruments.

Umbrella fund: GT World Series
Launch date: 01/10/91 **Domicile:** Ireland [UCITS]
Currency: USD **Structure:** Open ended, Unit Trust
Portfolio manager: Michael Lindsell
Manager of the fund since 1992 and Director of investment strategy, London; BSc Hons- Bristol U; previously Director-Warburg Asset Mgt and Senior Fund Manager, HK- Scimitar Asset Management; joined LGT in 1992; 14 years experience.
Purchase: Direct, Financial Advisor, Duly appointed sales agent
Minimum investment: A-2,000: B-250,000 USD
Custodian: Chase Manhattan Bank (Ireland)Plc
Listed: Dublin **Dealings:** Daily
Fund Sedol I.D.: 35625 **Published:** FT/WS
Fees **Annual fee:** 1.50% **Performance fee:** None
Front end load: 5.00% **Redemption fee:** None
Switching fee: 4.00%

Contact: European Marketing Department
Performance:

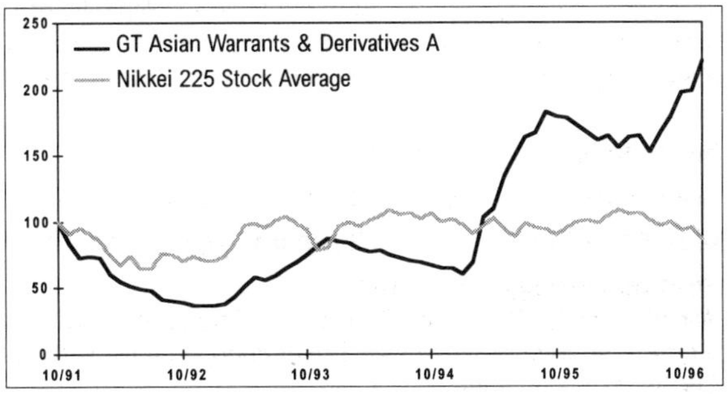

Top holdings:

BT Aust/News Corp Wts /97	3.0%
EximBank 2.875%/05 Euroyen Bonds	16.9%
IBRD 4.75%/04 Euroyen Bonds	7.6%
Industrial Finance Wts /97	3.0%
JGB/182 99.787 call options /96	2.4%
JGB/31 98.179 call options /96	3.0%
Natwest/Quantas Wts /97	3.1%
New Zealand 8%/04	27.6%
NZGB 8.33%/96 call options	3.6%
Yen/US$ Dec 1996-95 put options	2.9%

TOTAL RETURNS %

3 months 1997	1996	1995	1994	3 years	5 years
14.78	27.60	165.24	-25.24	153.05	200.85

STATISTICS

Assets ($mil)	Current yield	Volatility	Risk return	Micropal Star Rating
24.00	1.31	10.04	3	✪✪✪✪✪

GT Newly Industrialised Countries Fund
244/350

GT Global
Alban Gate 14th Floor, 125 London Wall, London EC2Y 5AS, United Kingdom
Tel 44-171-626-4741 Fax 44-171-710-4600

Contact: European Marketing Department

Investment objective:
The sub-fund aims to achieve long-term capital growth in dollar terms by investing in the Asian newly industrialised countries. The top country allocations of the portfolio are the following: Hong Kong (43.4%); Malaysia (32.5%); Philippines (10.7%); and Thailand (3.7%). The assets of the portfolio are allocated to equities (97.1%); and cash/MM (2.9%).

Umbrella fund: GT Emerging Markets Series
Launch date: 01/09/86 **Domicile:** Bermuda
Currency: USD **Structure:** Open ended, Investment Company
Portfolio manager: Christopher Wong
Manager of the sub-fund commenced August 1987; BA- U of Toronto; previously with Royal Bank of Canada as country analyst and Manager planning- Asia Pacific; joined LGT in 1987and now, MD and Senior Portfolio Manager Asia Pacific ex Japan;.
Purchase: Direct, Financial Advisor, Duly appointed sales agent
Minimum investment: 1,000 USD
Custodian: Bank of Bermuda
Listed: Bermuda **Dealings:** Daily
Fund Sedol I.D.: 35725 **Published:** FT/HKEJ/SC/WS
Fees **Annual fee:** 1.50% **Performance fee:** None
Front end load: 5.00% **Redemption fee:** None
Switching fee: 4.00%

Performance:

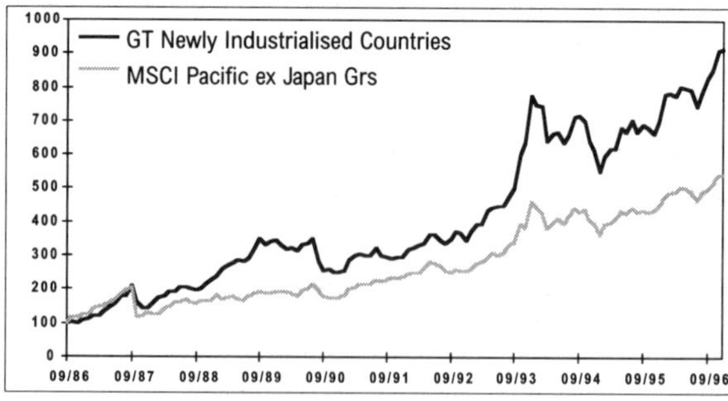

Top holdings:

Bank of East Asia	2.6%
Cheung Kong	3.2%
Hang Seng Bank	3.3%
Henderson Land Development	3.9%
Malaysian Resources	3.7%
Metro Bank	3.2%
New World Development	2.5%
Rashied Hussain Berhad	4.2%
Sun Hung Kai Properties	4.0%
United Engineers	2.9%

TOTAL RETURNS %

3 months 1997	1996	1995	1994	3 years	5 years
-0.04	30.65	13.73	-20.90	17.52	210.01

STATISTICS

Assets ($mil)	Current yield	Volatility	Risk return	Micropal Star Rating
626.00	—	5.54	2	✪✪✪✪✪

GT People's Republic of China A
45/350

GT Global
Alban Gate 14th Floor, 125 London Wall, London EC2Y 5AS, United Kingdom
Tel 44-171-626-4741 Fax 44-171-710-4600

Contact: European Marketing Department

Investment objective:
The sub-fund seeks to achieve long-term capital growth by investing in transferable securities of companies based in the People's Republic of China. The top sector allocations of the portfolio are as follows: conglomerates (22.2%); food (14.9%); machinery/engineering (14.9%); automotive (8.8%); and building materials (8.5%).

Umbrella fund: GT Emerging Markets Series
Launch date: 01/04/92 **Domicile:** Ireland
Currency: USD **Structure:** Open ended, Unit Trust
Portfolio manager: Billy Chan
Manager of GT PRC A since June 6, 1994; BA- Cambridge U; LGT (China and Taiwan) as Portfolio Manager and investment analyst , previously with Ernst & Young as Chartered Accountant.
Purchase: Direct, Financial Advisor, Duly appointed sales agent
Minimum investment: A-2,000: B-250,000 USD
Custodian: Chase Manhattan Bank (Ireland) Plc
Listed: Dublin **Dealings:** Daily
Fund Sedol I.D.: 35821 **Published:** FT/WS
Fees **Annual fee:** 2.00% **Performance fee:** None
Front end load: 5.00% **Redemption fee:** None
Switching fee: 4.00%

Performance:

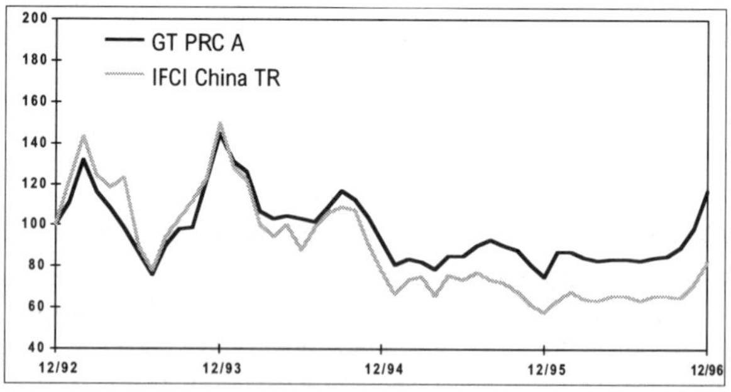

Top holdings:

China Everbright Intl	5.0%
Chongqing Changan Auto	4.1%
Cosco Pacific	4.2%
Guanghou Investments	5.7%
Guangnan Holdings	5.6%
Maanshan Iron Steel	5.6%
New World Development	4.7%
NG Fung Hong Ltd	5.6%
Qingling Motors	4.7%
Shanghai Erfangji	3.6%

TOTAL RETURNS %

3 months 1997	1996	1995	1994	3 years	5 years
17.67	54.90	-18.11	-36.24	-19.11	N.A.

STATISTICS

Assets ($mil)	Current yield	Volatility	Risk return	Micropal Star Rating
60.00	—	7.05	—	✪✪✪

Guinness Flight Asian Small Cos

347/350

Guinness Flight Global Asset Management Ltd
P O Box 250, La Plaiderie, St Peter Port, GY1 3QH, Guernsey
Tel 44-1481-710-404 Fax 44-1481-712-065

Investment objective:
The primary objective of the sub-fund is to achieve capital appreciation by investing in the quoted equity and equity related securities of small to medium sized Asian companies. Investment is primarily in established markets such as Hong Kong, Singapore, Malaysia and Thailand. A proportion of the fund's assets may be invested in the emerging markets in the region.

Umbrella fund: Guinness Flight Global Strategy Fund
Launch date: 29/09/95 **Domicile:** Guernsey
Currency: USD **Structure:** Open ended, Investment Company
Portfolio manager: Nerissa Lee
Manager of Guinness Flight Asian Small Companies.

Contact: Mr A.Le Prevost

Performance:

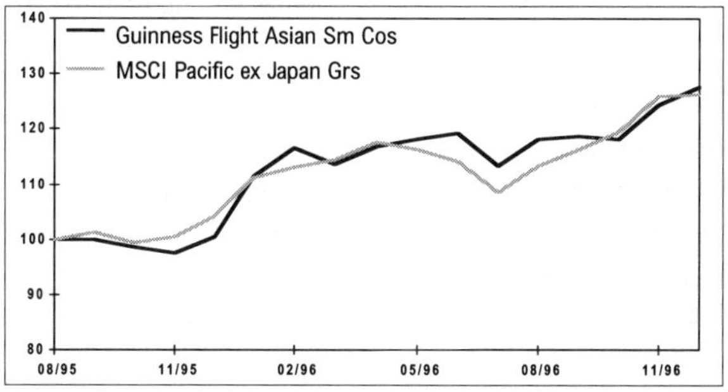

Purchase: Direct, Financial Advisor
Minimum investment: 7,500 USD
Custodian: Guinness Mahon Guernsey Limited
Listed: London **Dealings:** Daily
Fund Sedol I.D.: 39728 **Published:** FT
Fees **Annual fee:** 1.50% **Performance fee:** None
Front end load: 5.00% **Redemption fee:** None
Switching fee: None

Top holdings:

Datacraft Asia	2.0%
Elect & Eltek Intl.	3.0%
Gold Lion Hldgs	2.2%
Guahgnan Hldgs HK	3.5%
Huaneng Power ADR	3.2%
Moulin Intl Hldgs	2.2%
Pacific Concord	2.0%
Quingling Motors H Shares	2.5%
Texwinca Hldgs	2.3%
Venture MFG	2.0%

TOTAL RETURNS %

3 months 1997	1996	1995	1994	3 years	5 years
6.30	27.02	N.A.	N.A.	N.A.	N.A.

STATISTICS

Assets ($mil)	Current yield	Volatility	Risk return	Micropal Star Rating
28.29	0.26	N.A.	—	———

Guinness Flight Global Privatisation

179/350

Guinness Flight Global Asset Management Ltd
P O Box 250, La Plaiderie, St Peter Port, GY1 3QH, Guernsey
Tel 44-1481-710-404 Fax 44-1481-712-065

Investment objective:
The primary objective of the sub-fund is to provide capital appreciation primarily through investment in international equities. The portfolio is substantially invested in privatisation issues. A privatisation issue is defined as a publicly quoted company in which a government has, or has had, a significant share holding or influence.

Umbrella fund: Guinness Flight Global Strategy Fund
Launch date: 06/04/94 **Domicile:** Guernsey
Currency: USD **Structure:** Open ended, Investment Company
Portfolio manager: Andrew Couch
Manager of Guinness Flight Global Privatisation.

Contact: Mr A.Le Prevost

Performance:

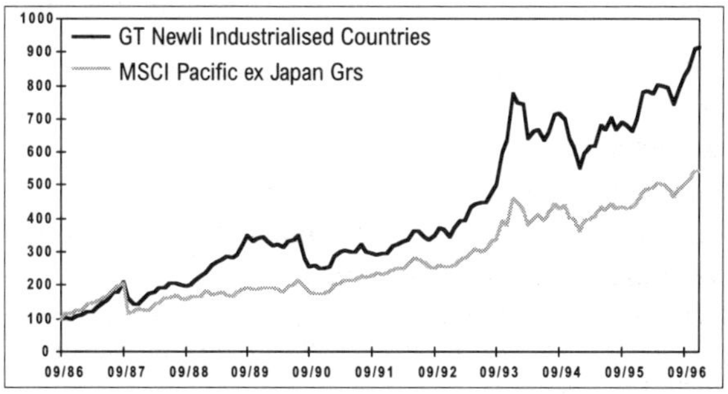

Purchase: Direct, Financial Advisor
Minimum investment: 7,500 USD
Custodian: Guinness Mahon Guernsey Limited
Listed: London **Dealings:** Daily
Fund Sedol I.D.: 39779 **Published:** FT
Fees **Annual fee:** 1.00% **Performance fee:** None
Front end load: 5.00% **Redemption fee:** None
Switching fee: None

Top holdings:

Ass Gen de France	2.7%
Elf Aquitaine	2.6%
Imispa	2.3%
Irish Life	2.3%
Mercury Euro Privat	2.3%
National Grid Group	3.0%
Nippon Tel & Telegraph	3.0%
Rhone Poulenc SA	3.1%
STET Di Risp	3.0%
Valmet	2.2%

TOTAL RETURNS %

3 months 1997	1996	1995	1994	3 years	5 years
7.13	33.84	13.35	N.A.	N.A.	N.A.

STATISTICS

Assets ($mil)	Current yield	Volatility	Risk return	Micropal Star Rating
46.21	1.13	N.A.	—	———

Guinness Flight Hong Kong
86/350

Guinness Flight Global Asset Management Ltd
P O Box 250, La Plaiderie, St Peter Port, GY1 3QH, Guernsey
Tel 44-1481-710-404 Fax 44-1481-712-065

Investment objective:
The sub-fund aims to achieve capital appreciation by investing in securities benefiting from the development of Hong Kong as an important centre for manufacturing and services for the Pacific Basin markets and its growth as a commercial gateway to China. The top sector allocations include properties (32.0%); conglomerates (23.0%); and finance (20.9%).

Umbrella fund: Guinness Flight Global Strategy Fund

Launch date: 26/11/90 **Domicile:** Guernsey

Currency: USD **Structure:** Open ended, Investment Company

Portfolio manager: Lynda Johnstone
Manager of Guinness Flight Hong Kong.

Contact: Mr A.Le Prevost

Performance:

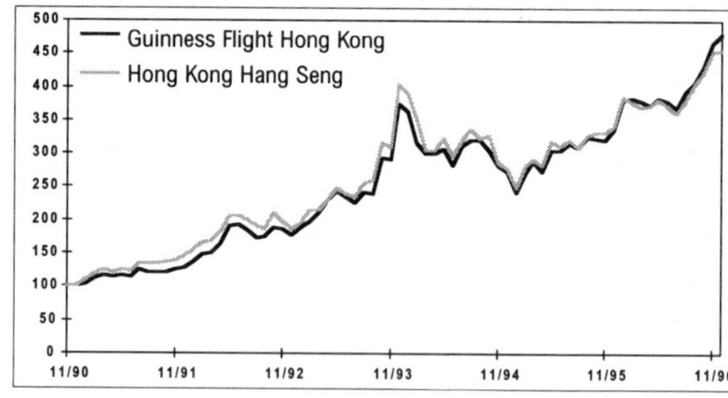

Purchase: Direct, Financial Advisor

Minimum investment: 7,500 USD

Custodian: Guinness Mahon Guernsey Limited

Listed: London **Dealings:** Daily

Fund Sedol I.D.: 78334 **Published:** FT

Fees **Annual fee:** 1.00% **Performance fee:** None
Front end load: 5.00% **Redemption fee:** None
Switching fee: None

Top holdings:

Holding	%
Cheung Kong Holdings Ltd	7.0%
Citic Pacific	4.0%
Hang Seng Bank	6.2%
Henderson Land Development	3.8%
Hong Kong Telecom	3.5%
HSBC Holdings	10.9%
Hutchison Whampoa	8.8%
New World Development	3.8%
Sun Hung Kai Properties	8.2%
Wharf Holdings	3.8%

TOTAL RETURNS %

3 months 1997	1996	1995	1994	3 years	5 years
-5.79	42.56	23.37	-27.05	28.29	273.25

STATISTICS

Assets ($mil)	Current yield	Volatility	Risk return	Micropal Star Rating
30.81	1.64	6.00	2	✪✪✪✪

Hamon Selected Asian Portfolio
330/350

Hamon Investment Group
2903-05 Alexandra House, 16-20 Charter Road, Central, Hong kong
Tel 852-2526-4268 Fax 852-2526-7277

Investment objective:
The primary objective of the fund is to achieve capital appreciation through strategic long-term equity investments in listed Asian (ex Japan) growth medium-sized companies. The fund concentrates on the characteristics of particular companies or industry sectors rather than the overall size or prospects of national economies or economic sector.

Umbrella fund: This is a singular fund.

Launch date: 01/12/89 **Domicile:** Hong Kong

Currency: USD **Structure:** Open ended, Unit Trust

Portfolio manager: Lawrence Lee
Manager of Hamon Selected Asian Portfolio commenced in 1994; experience in Asia and the US; 10 years experience in banking and investment management in Asian markets.

Contact: James Donald

Performance:

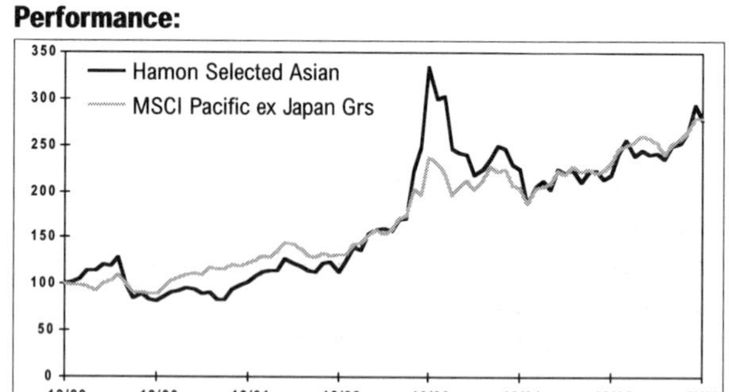

Purchase: Direct, Financial Advisor

Minimum investment: 5,000 USD

Custodian: Bermuda Trust (Far East) Limited.

Listed: None **Dealings:** Weekly

Fund Sedol I.D.: 640680 **Published:** FT/SC/HKEJ

Fees **Annual fee:** 1.50% **Performance fee:** None
Front end load: 5.00% **Redemption fee:** 1.00%
Switching fee: None

Top holdings:

Holding	%
Arab Malaysia Finance	2.3%
Bangkok Bank	2.2%
China Overseas	3.9%
Chung Hua Development	3.8%
CNPC (HK) Ltd	2.8%
D.C. Finance	4.0%
Gatek (MAL)	2.3%
Malaysian Resources	3.8%
Moulin International	5.0%
NG Fung Hong Ltd	2.7%

TOTAL RETURNS %

3 months 1997	1996	1995	1994	3 years	5 years
9.83	27.47	-2.79	-32.90	-16.85	171.39

STATISTICS

Assets ($mil)	Current yield	Volatility	Risk return	Micropal Star Rating
13.53	—	6.90	—	✪✪

Hansard EU Hong Kong Equity

135/350

Hansard Europe Ltd.
Enterprise House, Frascati Road, Dublin, Ireland
Tel 353-1-278-1488 Fax 353-1-278-1498
http://www. hansard.com

Investment objective:
The fund seeks to achieve capital growth through actively managed share portfolios predominately in the Hong Kong markets. The sub-fund is denominated in UK sterling.

Umbrella fund: This is a singular fund.
Launch date: 14/02/95 **Domicile:** Ireland
Currency: USD **Structure:** Open ended, Insurance Fund
Portfolio manager: Hansard Fund Managers
Managers of Hansard Europe Hong Kong; located in London.

Contact: Lorna Heavey

Performance:

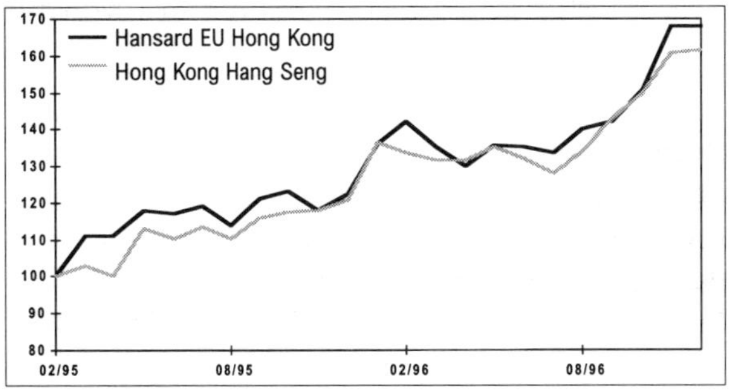

Top holdings: Fidelity Hong Kong 50.0%
GT Hong Kong 50.0%

Purchase: Via insurance policies sold by independent advisors
Minimum investment: ILP
Custodian: Midland Security Services
Listed: None **Dealings:** Weekly
Fund Sedol I.D.: 41126 **Published:** FT/FT Magazines
Fees **Annual fee:** 1.00% **Performance fee:** ILP
Front end load: ILP **Redemption fee:** ILP
Switching fee: ILP

TOTAL RETURNS %

3 months 1997	1996	1995	1994	3 years	5 years
-2.92	37.37	N.A.	N.A.	N.A.	N.A.

STATISTICS

Assets ($mil)	Current yield	Volatility	Risk return	Micropal Star Rating
N/S	—	N.A.	—	———

Hansard EU Latin America Equity

139/350

Hansard Europe Ltd.
Enterprise House, Frascati Road, Dublin, Ireland
Tel 353-1-278-1488 Fax 353-1-278-1498
http://www. hansard.com

Investment objective:
The primary objective of the fund is to achieve capital growth through actively managed share portfolios predominately in the Latin American markets.

Umbrella fund: This is a singular fund.
Launch date: 14/02/95 **Domicile:** Ireland
Currency: USD **Structure:** Open ended, Insurance Fund
Portfolio manager: Hansard Fund Managers
Managers of Hansard EU Latin America; located in London.

Contact: Lorna Heavey

Performance:

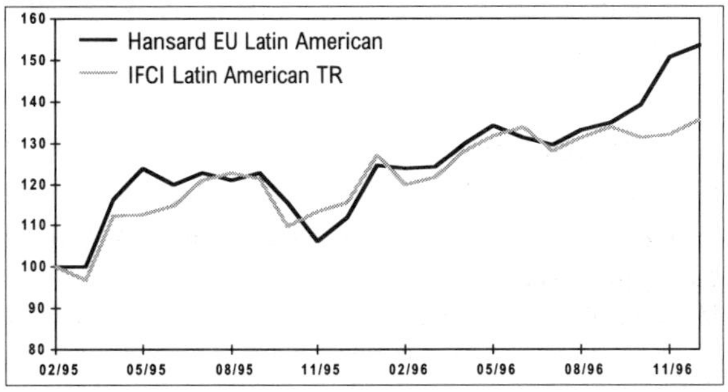

Top holdings: Fidelity Latin America 50.0%
GT Latin America 50.0%

Purchase: Via insurance policies sold by independent advisors
Minimum investment: ILP
Custodian: Midland Security Services
Listed: None **Dealings:** Weekly
Fund Sedol I.D.: 42313 **Published:** FT/FT Magazines
Fees **Annual fee:** 1.00% **Performance fee:** ILP
Front end load: ILP **Redemption fee:** ILP
Switching fee: ILP

TOTAL RETURNS %

3 months 1997	1996	1995	1994	3 years	5 years
11.07	37.06	N.A.	N.A.	N.A.	N.A.

STATISTICS

Assets ($mil)	Current yield	Volatility	Risk return	Micropal Star Rating
N/S	—	N.A.	—	———

Hansard EU UK Equity

301/350

Hansard Europe Ltd.
Enterprise House, Frascati Road, Dublin, Ireland
Tel 353-1-278-1488 Fax 353-1-278-1498
http://www. hansard.com

Investment objective:
The fund seeks to achieve capital growth through actively managed share portfolios predominately in the UK markets. The sub-fund is denominated in UK sterling.

Contact: Lorna Heavey

Performance:

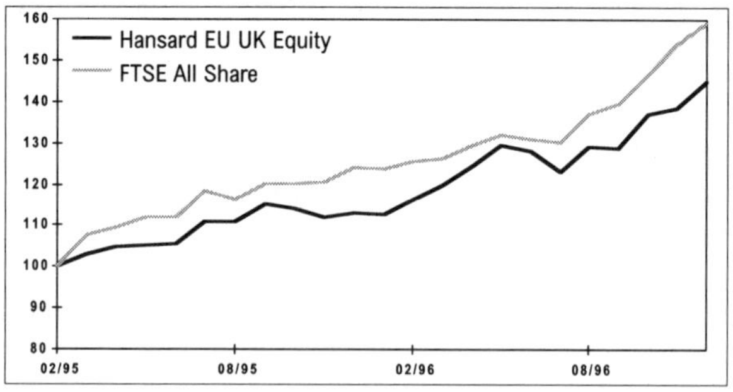

Umbrella fund: This is a singular fund.
Launch date: 14/02/95 **Domicile:** Ireland
Currency: GBP **Structure:** Open ended, Insurance Fund
Portfolio manager: Hansard Fund Managers
Managers of Hansard Europe UK Equity; located in London.

Top holdings:

Holding	%
Fidelity UK	50.0%
Flemings Flagship UK	50.0%

Purchase: Via insurance policies sold by independent advisors
Minimum investment: ILP
Custodian: Midland Security Services
Listed: None **Dealings:** Weekly
Fund Sedol I.D.: 41139 **Published:** FT/FT Magazines
Fees **Annual fee:** 1.00% **Performance fee:** ILP
Front end load: ILP **Redemption fee:** ILP
Switching fee: ILP

TOTAL RETURNS %

3 months 1997	1996	1995	1994	3 years	5 years
6.22	28.29	N.A.	N.A.	N.A.	N.A.

STATISTICS

Assets ($mil)	Current yield	Volatility	Risk return	Micropal Star Rating
N/S	—	N.A.	—	———

Hansard Hong Kong

70/350

Hansard International Ltd.
PO Box 192, Bank Hill, Douglas IM99 1QL, Isle of Man
Tel 44-1624-688-000 Fax 44-1624-688-008
http://www. hansard.com

Investment objective:
The insurance fund is denominated in US dollars and seeks to produce long-term gains from an actively managed portfolio of Hong Kong shares The assets allocation of the portfolio is equities (95.8%); and cash/MM (4.2%).

Contact: Paul Harwood

Performance:

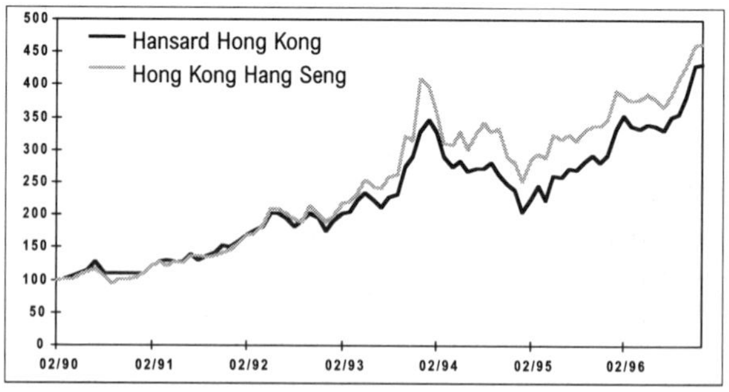

Umbrella fund: This is a singular fund.
Launch date: 01/04/88 **Domicile:** Isle of Man
Currency: USD **Structure:** Open ended, Insurance Fund
Portfolio manager: Jill Clark
Manager of Hansard Hong Kong.

Top holdings:

Holding	%
Hang Seng Bank	n/s
Henderson Land Development	n/s
HKR International	n/s
Hutchison Whampoa	n/s
New World Development	n/s

Purchase: Via insurance policies sold by independent advisors
Minimum investment: 50 GBP
Custodian: Royal Bank of Scotland (Isle of Man) Ltd
Listed: None **Dealings:** Weekly
Fund Sedol I.D.: 40885 **Published:** FT/RA
Fees **Annual fee:** ILP **Performance fee:** ILP
Front end load: ILP **Redemption fee:** ILP
Switching fee: ILP

TOTAL RETURNS %

3 months 1997	1996	1995	1994	3 years	5 years
-8.47	47.75	21.89	-27.11	31.28	186.76

STATISTICS

Assets ($mil)	Current yield	Volatility	Risk return	Micropal Star Rating
8.00	—	6.87	2	✪✪✪✪

Hansard UK Equity
236/350

Hansard International Ltd.
PO Box 192, Bank Hill, Douglas IM99 1QL, Isle of Man
Tel 44-1624-688-000 Fax 44-1624-688-008
http://www. hansard.com

Investment objective:
The primary objective of the funds is to achieve medium to long-term growth through investment in the equities of the United Kingdom. At present 94.2% of the portfolio's assets are allocated to equities, the remainder is held in cash/MM. The top sector allocations are the following: finance (17.5%); oil/ integrated (9.9%); and pharmaceuticals (6.9%).

Umbrella fund: This is a singular fund.

Launch date: 01/08/87 **Domicile:** Isle of Man

Currency: GBP **Structure:** Open ended, Insurance Fund

Portfolio manager: Hansard International Ltd
Manager of Hansard UK Equity.

Contact: Paul Harwood

Performance:

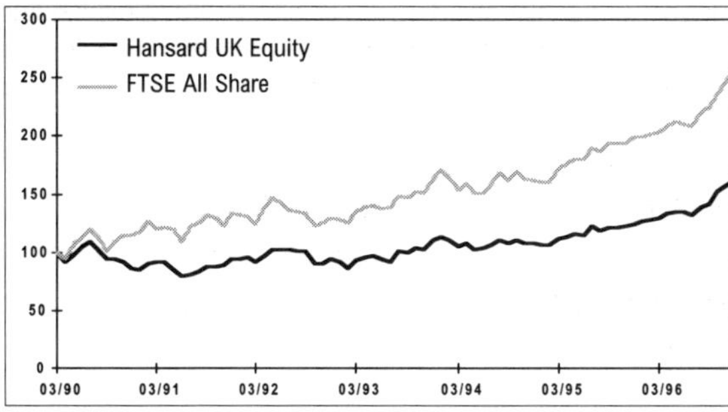

Purchase: Via insurance policies sold by independent advisors

Minimum investment: 50 GBP

Custodian: Royal Bank of Scotland (Isle of Man) Ltd

Listed: None **Dealings:** Weekly

Fund Sedol I.D.: 40812 **Published:** RA/FT

Fees **Annual fee:** ILP **Performance fee:** ILP
Front end load: ILP **Redemption fee:** ILP
Switching fee: ILP

Top holdings:

British Telecom	n/s
Burmah Castrol	n/s
Glaxo Wellcome	n/s
HSBC Holdings	n/s
Shell	n/s

TOTAL RETURNS %

3 months 1997	1996	1995	1994	3 years	5 years
1.03	30.78	15.53	-2.95	46.64	71.38

STATISTICS

Assets ($mil)	Current yield	Volatility	Risk return	Micropal Star Rating
5.92	—	2.91	4	✪✪

Hansard\CL China Growth
72/350

Hansard\Credit Lyonnais
PO Box 192, Bank Hill, Douglas IM88 1QL, Isle of Man
Tel 44-1624-688-000 Fax 44-1624-688-008
http://www. hansard.com

Investment objective:
With Credit Lyonnais the fund seeks long-term capital appreciation though investment in listed Chinese equities. A proportion of the fund's assets may be invested in companies listed outside China provided that the companies chosen have substantial investments in China. The country allocations of the portfolio are as follows: Hong Kong (49.1%); China (27.9%); Taiwan (17.0%); Malaysia (2.2%); and the remainder held in cash.

Umbrella fund: This is a singular fund.

Launch date: 29/10/92 **Domicile:** Isle of Man

Currency: USD **Structure:** Open ended, Insurance Fund

Portfolio manager: Hansard International Ltd
Manager of Hansard\CL China Growth.

Contact: Paul Harwood

Performance:

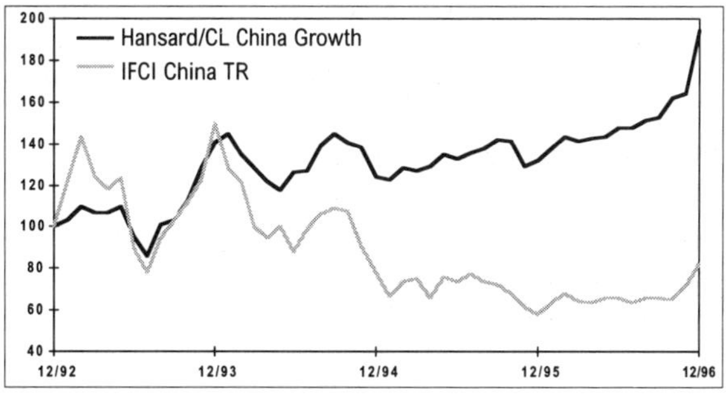

Purchase: Via insurance policies sold by independent advisors

Minimum investment: 50 GBP

Custodian: Royal Bank of Scotland (Isle of Man) Ltd

Listed: None **Dealings:** Weekly

Fund Sedol I.D.: 39939 **Published:** FT/RA

Fees **Annual fee:** ILP **Performance fee:** ILP
Front end load: ILP **Redemption fee:** ILP
Switching fee: ILP

Top holdings:

China Overseas Land	n/s
Hutchison Whampoa	n/s
New World Development	n/s
Quingling Motors H Shares	n/s

TOTAL RETURNS %

3 months 1997	1996	1995	1994	3 years	5 years
11.41	47.48	5.94	-11.33	38.53	N.A.

STATISTICS

Assets ($mil)	Current yield	Volatility	Risk return	Micropal Star Rating
3.73	—	5.08	3	✪✪✪✪

Hansard\Fidelity Iberia

211/350

Hansard\Fidelity
PO Box 192, Bank Hill, Douglas IM99 1QL, Isle of Man
Tel 44-1624-688-000 Fax 44-1624-688-008
http://www. hansard.com

Investment objective:
With Fidelity the primary objective of the fund is to achieve capital growth through investment in a diversified portfolio of primarily Spanish and Portuguese equities. Spain (78.1%); and Portugal (15.8%) represent the country allocations of the portfolio with the remainder held in cash.

Contact: Paul Harwood

Performance:

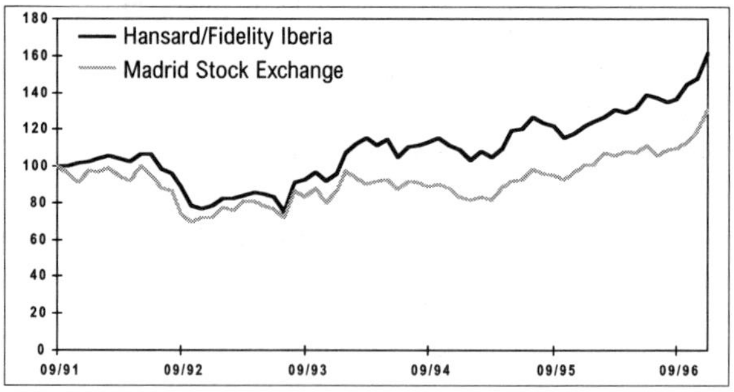

Umbrella fund: This is a singular fund.
Launch date: 31/10/91 **Domicile:** Isle of Man
Currency: ESP **Structure:** Open ended, Insurance Fund
Portfolio manager: Hansard International Ltd
Manager of Hansard\Fidelity Iberia.

Top holdings:		
	Banco Bilbao Vizcana	7.7%
	Banco de Santander	6.3%
	Endesa	5.5%
	Iberdola	6.9%
	Telefonica de Espana	8.8%

Purchase: Via insurance policies sold by independent advisors
Minimum investment: 50 GBP
Custodian: Royal Bank of Scotland (Isle of Man) Ltd
Listed: None **Dealings:** Weekly
Fund Sedol I.D.: 39962 **Published:** FT/RA
Fees **Annual fee:** ILP **Performance fee:** ILP
Front end load: ILP **Redemption fee:** ILP
Switching fee: ILP

TOTAL RETURNS %

3 months 1997	1996	1995	1994	3 years	5 years
1.59	32.14	12.27	13.20	67.94	57.30

STATISTICS

Assets ($mil)	Current yield	Volatility	Risk return	Micropal Star Rating
0.74	—	4.14	4	✪✪✪

Hansard\Fidelity Nordic

148/350

Hansard\Fidelity
PO Box 192, Bank Hill, Douglas IM99 1QL, Isle of Man
Tel 44-1624-688-000 Fax 44-1624-688-008
http://www. hansard.com

Investment objective:
With Fidelity the fund seeks to provide long-term capital growth from investment primarily in stock markets of Norway, Sweden, Denmark and Finland. At present, the country allocations of the portfolio are as follows: Sweden (52.0%); Finland (21.8%); Denmark (11.1%); Norway (11.0%); and US (1.3%) with the remainder held in cash.

Contact: Paul Harwood

Performance:

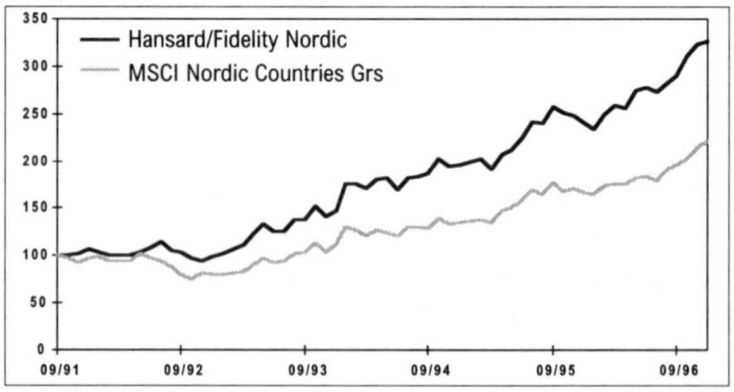

Umbrella fund: This is a singular fund.
Launch date: 30/07/92 **Domicile:** Isle of Man
Currency: SEK **Structure:** Open ended, Insurance Fund
Portfolio manager: Hansard International Ltd
Manager of Hansard\Fidelity Nordic.

Top holdings:		
	ABB AB	4.3%
	Astra	9.1%
	Ericsson	9.3%
	Nokia A	5.0%
	Volvo	4.5%

Purchase: Via insurance policies sold by independent advisors
Minimum investment: 50 GBP
Custodian: Royal Bank of Scotland (Isle of Man) Ltd
Listed: None **Dealings:** Weekly
Fund Sedol I.D.: 39911 **Published:** FT/RA
Fees **Annual fee:** ILP **Performance fee:** ILP
Front end load: ILP **Redemption fee:** ILP
Switching fee: ILP

TOTAL RETURNS %

3 months 1997	1996	1995	1994	3 years	5 years
6.01	36.23	22.57	32.61	121.42	204.55

STATISTICS

Assets ($mil)	Current yield	Volatility	Risk return	Micropal Star Rating
8.26	—	4.92	4	✪✪✪✪✪

Hansard\Fidelity UK
235/350

Hansard\Fidelity
PO Box 192, Bank Hill, Douglas IM99 1QL, Isle of Man
Tel 44-1624-688-000 Fax 44-1624-688-008
http://www. hansard.com

Investment objective:
With Fidelity the primary objective of the fund is to achieve long-term capital growth primarily through investment in shares listed in the UK which are considered to be 'special situations'. The country allocations for the portfolio are UK (93.2%); Republic of Ireland (1.0%); US (0.5%); and the remainder in cash.

Umbrella fund: This is a singular fund.
Launch date: 31/10/91 **Domicile:** Isle of Man
Currency: GBP **Structure:** Open ended, Insurance Fund
Portfolio manager: Hansard International Ltd
Manager of Hansard\Fidelity UK.

Contact: Paul Harwood
Performance:

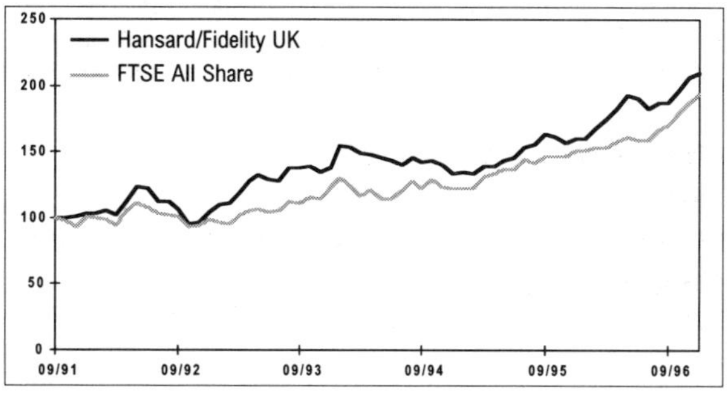

Purchase: Via insurance policies sold by independent advisors
Minimum investment: 50 GBP
Custodian: Royal Bank of Scotland (Isle of Man) Ltd
Listed: None **Dealings:** Weekly
Fund Sedol I.D.: 41105 **Published:** FT/RA
Fees **Annual fee:** ILP **Performance fee:** ILP
Front end load: ILP **Redemption fee:** ILP
Switching fee: ILP

Top holdings:

British Petroleum	3.2%
London Insurance Market	3.2%
Misys	2.4%
Oriflame Intl	3.5%
T&N	3.5%

TOTAL RETURNS %

3 months 1997	1996	1995	1994	3 years	5 years
3.34	30.82	19.94	-2.67	52.73	102.88

STATISTICS

Assets ($mil)	Current yield	Volatility	Risk return	Micropal Star Rating
1.27	—	3.43	4	✪✪✪

Hansard\GT Healthcare
151/350

Hansard\GT
PO Box 192, Bank Hill, Douglas IM99 1QL, Isle of Man
Tel 44-1624-688-000 Fax 44-1624-688-008
http://www. hansard.com

Investment objective:
With GT the primary objective of the insurance sub-fund is to seek long-term capital growth by investing in healthcare companies throughout the world. The sub-fund is denominated in US dollars.

Umbrella fund: This is a singular fund.
Launch date: 05/08/92 **Domicile:** Isle of Man
Currency: USD **Structure:** Open ended, Insurance Fund
Portfolio manager: Hansard International Ltd
Manager of Hansard/GT Biotech & Health.

Contact: Paul Harwood
Performance:

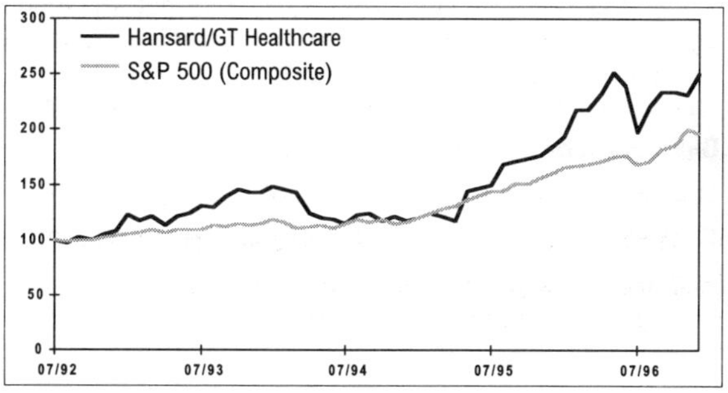

Purchase: Via insurance policies sold by independent advisors
Minimum investment: 50 GBP
Custodian: Royal Bank of Scotland (Isle of Man) Ltd
Listed: None **Dealings:** Weekly
Fund Sedol I.D.: 39932 **Published:** FT/RA
Fees **Annual fee:** ILP **Performance fee:** ILP
Front end load: ILP **Redemption fee:** ILP
Switching fee: ILP

Top holdings:

Advanced Technology	n/s
Amgen	n/s
Mentor Corp.	n/s
Protein Design Labs	n/s
Sunrise Medical	n/s
Theratech INC	n/s
Visx Inc.	n/s
Watson Pharmaceuticals	n/s
Zeneca Group	n/s

TOTAL RETURNS %

3 months 1997	1996	1995	1994	3 years	5 years
0.15	36.07	56.30	-17.53	75.39	N.A.

STATISTICS

Assets ($mil)	Current yield	Volatility	Risk return	Micropal Star Rating
5.67	—	6.92	1	✪✪✪

Hansard\GT Newly Indusrialised Countries

220/350

Hansard\GT
PO Box 192, Bank Hill, Douglas IM99 1QL, Isle of Man
Tel 44-1624-688-000 Fax 44-1624-688-008
http://www. hansard.com

Investment objective:
With GT the fund provides long-term capital growth through investment in the companies of the newly industrialised Asian countries. The top country allocations of the portfolio are as follows: Hong Kong (43.7%); Malaysia (32.6%); Philippines (11.2%); Thailand (3.7%); Singapore (2.6%); Indonesia (2.3%); and Korea (2.1%).

Umbrella fund: This is a singular fund.
Launch date: 26/09/91 **Domicile:** Isle of Man
Currency: USD **Structure:** Open ended, Insurance Fund
Portfolio manager: Hansard International Ltd
Manager of Hansard\GT Newly Ind Countries.

Contact: Paul Harwood

Performance:

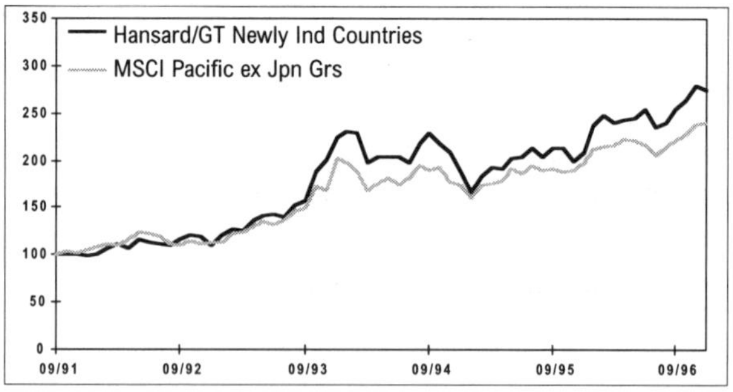

Purchase: Via insurance policies sold by independent advisors
Minimum investment: 50 GBP
Custodian: Royal Bank of Scotland (Isle of Man) Ltd
Listed: None **Dealings:** Weekly
Fund Sedol I.D.: 39947 **Published:** FT/RA
Fees **Annual fee:** ILP **Performance fee:** ILP
Front end load: ILP **Redemption fee:** ILP
Switching fee: ILP

Top holdings:

Holding	
Bank of East Asia	n/s
Cheung Kong	n/s
Henderson Land Development	n/s
Malaysian Resources	n/s
Metro Bank	n/s
Rashid Hussain Berhad	n/s
Sun Hung Kai Properties	n/s
United Engineers	n/s

TOTAL RETURNS %

3 months 1997	1996	1995	1994	3 years	5 years
2.16	31.56	10.59	-15.70	22.64	177.38

STATISTICS

Assets ($mil)	Current yield	Volatility	Risk return	Micropal Star Rating
8.41	—	6.02	3	✪✪✪✪

Hansard\INVESCO Asia Tiger Warrant

50/350

Hansard\INVESCO
PO Box 192, Bank Hill, Douglas IM99 1QL, Isle of Man
Tel 44-1624-688-000 Fax 44-1624-688-008
http://www. hansard.com

Investment objective:
With INVESCO the purpose of the fund is to achieve long-term capital growth from a highly geared investment in Asia equity warrants. The fund mainly invests in equity products issued on the Hong Kong, Singapore, Malaysia, Thailand and Korea stock exchanges. Certain other Asian markets issue warrants and are likely to be represented in the fund as their warrant markets develop.
Umbrella fund: This is a singular fund.
Launch date: 14/11/91 **Domicile:** Isle of Man
Currency: USD **Structure:** Open ended, Insurance Fund
Portfolio manager: Hansard International Ltd
Manager of Hansard\INVESCO Asia Tiger Warrants.

Contact: Paul Harwood

Performance:

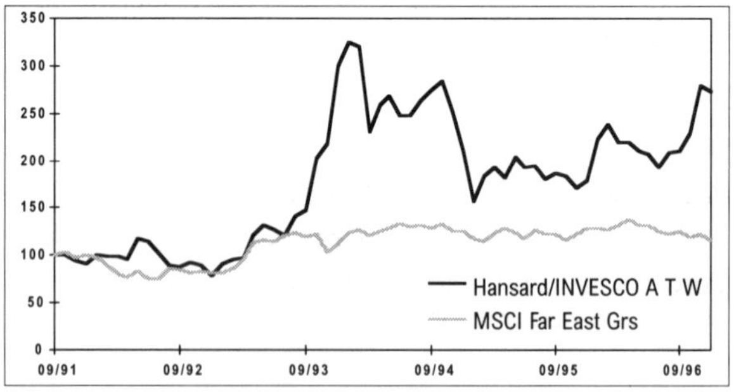

Purchase: Via insurance policies sold by independent advisors
Minimum investment: 50 GBP
Custodian: Royal Bank of Scotland (Isle of Man) Ltd
Listed: None **Dealings:** Weekly
Fund Sedol I.D.: 39946 **Published:** FT/RA
Fees **Annual fee:** ILP **Performance fee:** ILP
Front end load: ILP **Redemption fee:** ILP
Switching fee: ILP

Top holdings:

Holding	
Cheung Kong Infra. Wts 97	3.6%
Cheung Kong Wts 98	7.0%
Citic Pacific Wts 97	6.1%
City Dev Wts 98	5.1%
Commerce Asset Wts 98	5.3%
Gamada Wts 00	3.8%
Henderson Land Wts 98	5.6%
HSBC Wts 97	8.1%
Hutchison Wham. Wts 98	4.7%
New World Dev. Wts 97	3.6%

TOTAL RETURNS %

3 months 1997	1996	1995	1994	3 years	5 years
-0.10	52.62	-14.93	-29.72	-8.76	197.68

STATISTICS

Assets ($mil)	Current yield	Volatility	Risk return	Micropal Star Rating
3.92	—	10.92	—	✪✪✪✪

Hansard\INVESCO European Warrant
10/350

Hansard\INVESCO
PO Box 192, Bank Hill, Douglas IM99 1QL, Isle of Man
Tel 44-1624-688-000 Fax 44-1624-688-008
http://www. hansard.com

Investment objective:
With INVESCO the purpose of the fund is to provide shareholders with capital growth from a highly geared investment in the European equity markets through European equity warrants. The fund is mainly invested in equity warrants issued on the stock exchanges of Germany, France, Switzerland and the UK, although warrants issued on other European markets can be included in the portfolio.

Umbrella fund: This is a singular fund.

Launch date: 31/10/91 **Domicile:** Isle of Man

Currency: USD **Structure:** Open ended, Insurance Fund

Portfolio manager: Hansard International Ltd
Manager of Hansard\INVESCO European Warrants.

Contact: Paul Harwood

Performance:

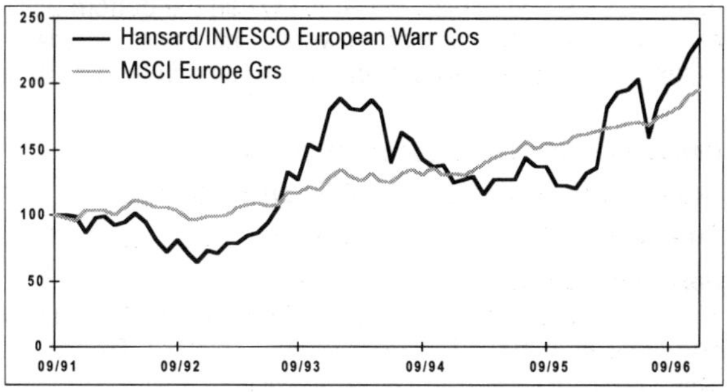

Purchase: Via insurance policies sold by independent advisors

Minimum investment: 50 GBP

Custodian: Royal Bank of Scotland (Isle of Man) Ltd

Listed: None **Dealings:** Weekly

Fund Sedol I.D.: 39957 **Published:** FT/RA

Fees **Annual fee:** ILP **Performance fee:** ILP
Front end load: ILP **Redemption fee:** ILP
Switching fee: ILP

Top holdings:

Holding	%
Astra Wts 98	4.6%
Bulgari Wts 98	4.2%
Carrefour Wts 97	6.4%
Christian Dior Wts 98	5.4%
Commerzbank Wts 99	4.7%
French Phor Cos Wts 98	6.0%
ING Groep Wts 97	4.4%
ING Groep Wts 98	5.7%
Sodexho Wts 04	4.2%
Swiss Re Wts 00	5.0%

TOTAL RETURNS %

3 months 1997	1996	1995	1994	3 years	5 years
38.88	94.10	-3.41	-30.41	30.46	169.26

STATISTICS

Assets ($mil)	Current yield	Volatility	Risk return	Micropal Star Rating
1.15	—	10.10	2	✪✪

Henderson HF European Smaller Cos
205/350

Henderson Investors
European Bank and Business Centre, 6D Route de Treves,
Senningerberg, L-2633 Luxembourg
Tel 352-34-66-22 Fax 352-34-65-55

Investment objective:
The sub-fund seeks long-term capital growth by investing in companies with a market capitalisation below 1 billion Dutch guilders or below the mean market capitalisation of each index. These are smaller companies quoted on European stock markets or dealt on regulated markets.

Umbrella fund: Henderson Horizon Fund

Launch date: 01/08/93 **Domicile:** Luxembourg [UCITS]

Currency: NLG **Structure:** Open ended, SICAV

Portfolio manager: Andrew McNally
Manager of Henderson Horizon Fund European Smaller Companies since 1995 and Manager of Horizon European Smaller Companies Fund; BA Hons, economics-Lancaster U; joined Henderson in 1995; 6 years of investment experience.

Contact: Celine Martine

Performance:

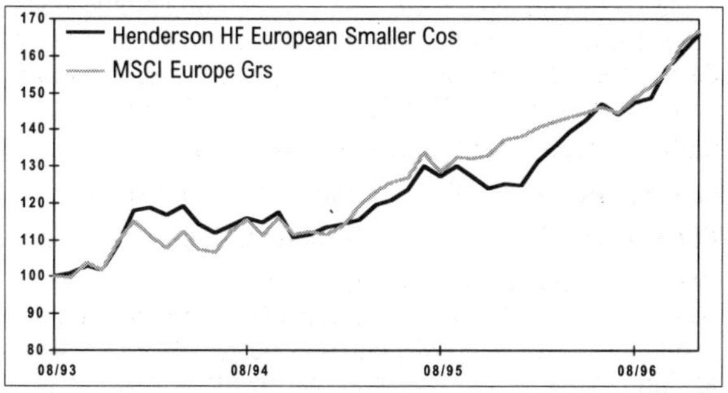

Purchase: Direct, Financial Advisor

Minimum investment: 2,500 USD

Custodian: Morgan Stanley Bank Luxembourg S.A.

Listed: Luxembourg **Dealings:** Daily

Fund Sedol I.D.: 443750 **Published:** FT/SC/MM

Fees **Annual fee:** 1.20% **Performance fee:** None
Front end load: 5.00% **Redemption fee:** None
Switching fee: 6 free - 1.00% thereafter

Top holdings:

Holding	%
Bure Investment	1.7%
CMG	1.7%
Ekorres	2.5%
Foreningsbanken	2.5%
Fokus Banken	2.1%
Kalmar Industries	2.2%
Moebel Walther	2.2%
Parily	1.7%
Pizza Express	1.7%
Pansse	1.8%

TOTAL RETURNS %

3 months 1997	1996	1995	1994	3 years	5 years
9.13	32.49	12.36	2.54	52.65	N.A.

STATISTICS

Assets ($mil)	Current yield	Volatility	Risk return	Micropal Star Rating
49.25	—	2.81	4	✪✪✪✪

Henderson HF UK Smaller Cos
118/350

Henderson Investors
European Bank and Business Centre, 6D Route de Treves,
Senningerberg, L-2633 Luxembourg
Tel 352-34-66-22 Fax 352-34-65-55

Investment objective:
The sub-fund seeks to achieve long-term capital growth by investing predominately in smaller UK companies, which fall within the bottom 25% by way of market capitalisation of the companies whose shares are included in the FTA All Share Index. The fund can invest from time to time in longer UK special situations stocks.

Umbrella fund: Henderson Horizon Fund
Launch date: 01/04/86 **Domicile:** Luxembourg [UCITS]
Currency: USD **Structure:** Open ended, SICAV
Portfolio manager: John Alexander
Manager of the Henderson Horizon Fund United Kingdom Smaller Companies commenced in 1993; MA Hons, modern history- Oxford U; joined Henderson in 1993;17 years of investment experience.
Purchase: Direct, Financial Advisor
Minimum investment: 2,500 USD
Custodian: Morgan Stanley Bank Luxembourg S.A.
Listed: Luxembourg **Dealings:** Daily
Fund Sedol I.D.: 42016 **Published:** FT/SC/MM
Fees **Annual fee:** 1.20% **Performance fee:** None
Front end load: 5.00% **Redemption fee:** None
Switching fee: 6 free - 1.00% thereafter

Contact: Celine Martin
Performance:

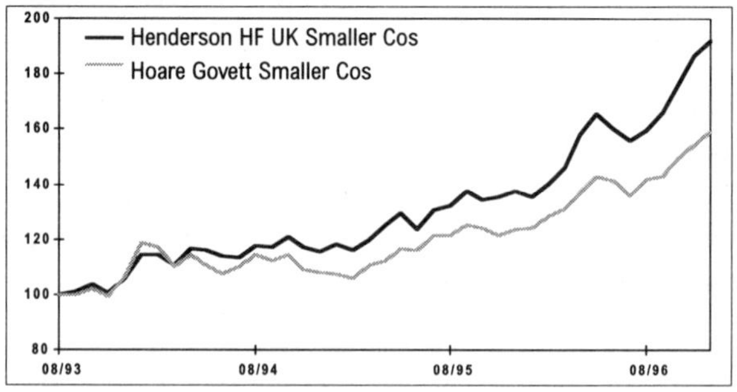

Top holdings:

Holding	%
Abbot Group	3.4%
Amberley Group	3.4%
Boxmore International	4.2%
BTG	5.0%
Caspian Group	6.4%
CMG	6.2%
Dixons Group	4.1%
Hamleys	3.5%
Jarvis	4.4%
Meconic	3.5%

TOTAL RETURNS %

3 months 1997	1996	1995	1994	3 years	5 years
6.26	39.28	19.45	8.80	81.01	N.A.

STATISTICS

Assets ($mil)	Current yield	Volatility	Risk return	Micropal Star Rating
9.78	—	3.36	5	✪✪✪✪✪

HSBC GIF Chinese Equity
19/350

HSBC Asset Management
7 Rue du Marche-aux-Herbes, L-1728 Luxembourg
Tel 352-47-68-121 Fax 352-47-55-69

Investment objective:
The main aim of the sub-fund is medium to long-term capital growth. This is achieved by investing in securities quoted on an official stock exchange or on a regulated market in China or related to companies whose activity is closely related to development and growth of economy of the PRC.The top asset allocations of the fund are Hong Kong (58.7%); and China (40.1%).
Umbrella fund: HSBC Global Investment Funds
Launch date: 25/06/92 **Domicile:** Luxembourg [UCITS]
Currency: USD **Structure:** Open ended, SICAV
Portfolio manager: Man Wing Chung
Manager of HSBC Global Investment Funds Chinese Equity since 1993; BA, economics- U of Pennsylvania; previously with East Asia Hamon Asset Management, as Fund Manager and Thornton Management (Asia) as economic researcher.
Purchase: Direct, Financial Advisor, Distributor & Agents of HSBC in UK/HK/Luxembourg
Minimum investment: 1,000 USD
Custodian: Banque Internationale a Luxembourg
Listed: Luxembourg **Dealings:** Daily
Fund Sedol I.D.: 493738 **Published:** FT/SC/RT
Fees **Annual fee:** 1.50% **Performance fee:** None
Front end load: 5.25% **Redemption fee:** None
Switching fee: Up to 1.00%

Contact: Stephen Cotterell
Performance:

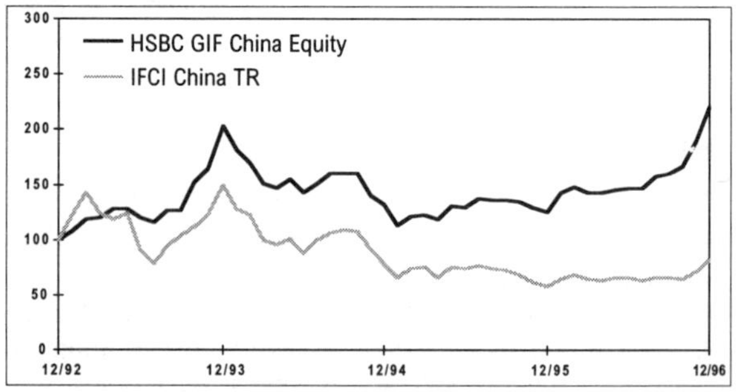

Top holdings:

Holding	%
Cheung Kong Holdings Ltd	3.9%
Cheung Kong Infrastructure	2.3%
China Resources Enterprises	5.6%
Citic Pacific	3.9%
Guandong Kelon Elec. Hldg	2.7%
Hutchison Whampoa	3.9%
New World Development	4.0%
NG Fung Hong Ltd	3.7%
Qingling Motors	3.0%
Shanghai Industrial	4.6%

TOTAL RETURNS %

3 months 1997	1996	1995	1994	3 years	5 years
7.29	76.21	-4.91	-35.09	8.77	N.A.

STATISTICS

Assets ($mil)	Current yield	Volatility	Risk return	Micropal Star Rating
38.97	—	7.15	—	✪✪✪✪

HSBC GIF Hong Kong Equity
36/350

HSBC Asset Management
7 Rue du Marche-aux-Herbes, L-1728 Luxembourg
Tel 352-47-68-121 Fax 352-47-55-69

Investment objective:
The sub-fund aims to provide capital appreciation though a managed portfolio of shares in companies quoted on the Hong Kong stock exchange. The top sector allocations of the portfolio are as follows: real estate (27.04%); diversified holding companies (18.6%); commercial/finance (12.6%); and diverse industrial (10.2%).

Umbrella fund: HSBC Global Investment Funds
Launch date: 16/01/84 **Domicile:** Luxembourg [UCITS]
Currency: USD **Structure:** Open ended, SICAV
Portfolio manager: Man Wing Chung
Manager of HSBC Global Investment Funds Hong Kong Equity since 1993; BA, economics- U of Pennsylvania; previously with East Asia Hamon Asset Management, as Fund Manager and Thornton Management (Asia) as economic researcher.
Purchase: Direct, Financial Advisor, Distributor & Agents of HSBC in UK/HK/Luxembourg
Minimum investment: 1,000 USD
Custodian: Banque Internationale a Luxembourg
Listed: Luxembourg **Dealings:** Daily
Fund Sedol I.D.: 93908 **Published:** FT/SC/RT
Fees **Annual fee:** 1.00% **Performance fee:** None
Front end load: 5.25% **Redemption fee:** None
Switching fee: Up to 1.00%

Contact: Stephen Cotterell
Performance:

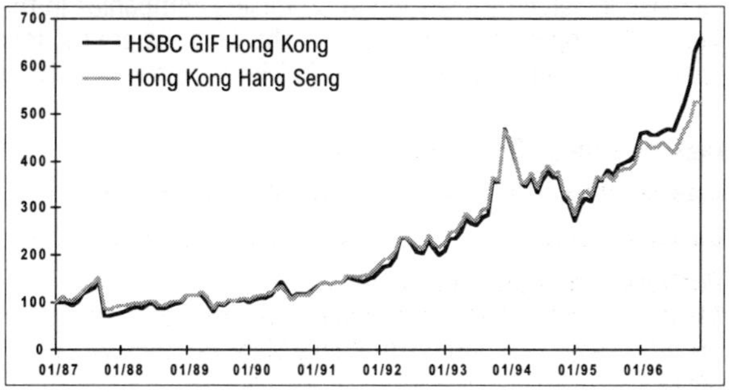

Top holdings:

Holding	%
Cheung Kong	5.1%
China Resources	5.8%
Citic Pacific	3.9%
Hang Seng Bank	4.0%
HSBC Holdings	6.7%
Hutchison Whampoa	7.5%
New World Development	4.2%
Shanghai Industrial	3.4%
Swire Pacific	2.9%
Wharf Holdings	4.0%

TOTAL RETURNS %

3 months 1997	1996	1995	1994	3 years	5 years
0.20	60.38	32.13	-33.26	41.42	328.32

STATISTICS

Assets ($mil)	Current yield	Volatility	Risk return	Micropal Star Rating
97.75	—	6.89	3	✪✪✪✪✪

HSBC GIF Malaysian Equity
298/350

HSBC Asset Management
7 Rue du Marche-aux-Herbes, L-1728 Luxembourg
Tel 352-47-68-121 Fax 352-47-55-69

Investment objective:
The sub-fund seeks to provide long-term capital appreciation from a portfolio of traded investments in the equity markets of Malaysia. The top sector allocations of the portfolio are as follows: diverse industrial (21.1%); real estate (16.9%); diversified holding companies (11.7%); and finance (11.1%).

Umbrella fund: HSBC Global Investment Funds
Launch date: 16/01/87 **Domicile:** Luxembourg [UCITS]
Currency: USD **Structure:** Open ended, SICAV
Portfolio manager: Rosanna Lam
Manager of HSBC Global Investment Malaysian Equity and Director of HSBC Asset Management; previously with Royal Trust Asia and Citicorp as Senior Fund Manager; 17 years experience in the finance industry.
Purchase: Direct, Financial Advisor, Distributor & Agents of HSBC in UK/HK/Luxembourg
Minimum investment: 1,000 USD
Custodian: Banque Internationale a Luxembourg
Listed: Luxembourg **Dealings:** Daily
Fund Sedol I.D.: 93910 **Published:** FT/SC/RT
Fees **Annual fee:** 1.00% **Performance fee:** None
Front end load: 5.25% **Redemption fee:** None
Switching fee: Up to 1.00%

Contact: Stephen Cotterell
Performance:

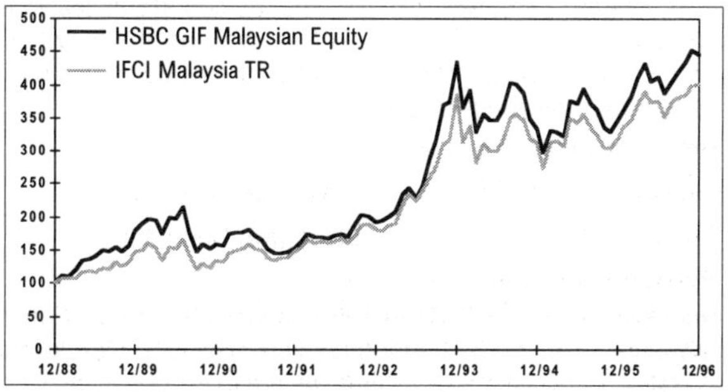

Top holdings:

Holding	%
Bolton Properties Berhad	6.3%
Genting Berhad	3.8%
IOI Corporation	6.2%
Magnum Corp	3.3%
Malayan Bank Berhad	6.1%
Malaysian Resources	7.0%
MBF Capital	4.6%
Oriental	4.0%
OYL Industries	3.0%
Rashid Hussain Berhad	5.8%

TOTAL RETURNS %

3 months 1997	1996	1995	1994	3 years	5 years
5.93	28.37	4.11	-23.07	2.80	194.36

STATISTICS

Assets ($mil)	Current yield	Volatility	Risk return	Micropal Star Rating
14.47	—	7.24	—	✪✪✪

HYPO Greater China
121/350

Foreign & Colonial Management
4 Rue Alphonse Weiker, L-2721 Luxembourg
Tel 352-42-12-04-52 Fax 352-42-19-82
E mail kgehlen@hypo-invest.lu

Investment objective:
The primary objective of the fund is to achieve long-term growth and a strong increase in value by investing in promising companies in the People's Republic of China. The top sector allocations of the portfolio are the following; energy (28.8%); finance (18.5%); and technology (6.7%).

Umbrella fund: This is a singular fund.
Launch date: 01/09/94 **Domicile:** Luxembourg
Currency: DEM **Structure:** Open ended, FCP
Portfolio manager: Stephanie Wu
Manager of HYPO Greater China commenced January 1997; BSc and MSc- LSE; joined Foreign & Colonial Emerging Markets 1994 as a Fund Manager on the Asian desk.
Purchase: Direct
Minimum investment: 1 Unit
Custodian: HYPO-Bank Luxembourg
Listed: None **Dealings:** Daily
Fund Sedol I.D.: 973716 **Published:** FT/HB/FA
Fees **Annual fee:** 1.90% **Performance fee:** None
Front end load: 5.00% **Redemption fee:** None
Switching fee: None

Contact: Kerstein Gehlen
Performance:

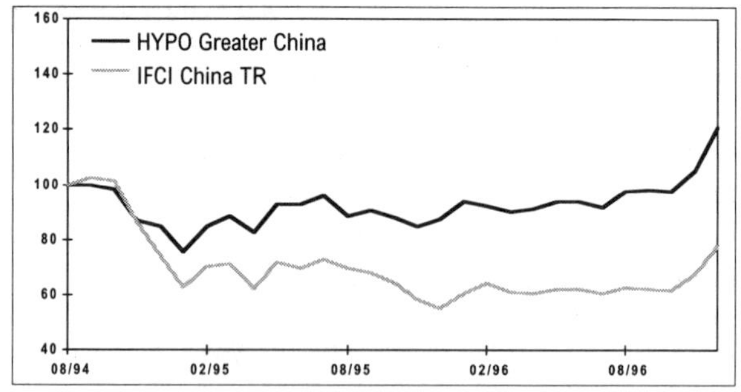

Top holdings:

Holding	%
Cheung Kong Infrastructure	2.8%
Dah Sing Financial	3.2%
Guangdong Investment	4.8%
Heilong Jiang Motors	8.7%
Huaneng Power Int. ADR	5.1%
Qingling Motors	8.8%
Shanghai Petrochemicals	4.9%
Taiwan Index Wts	3.2%
Yizheng Chemical	7.0%
Zhenhai Refining Chemical	5.3%

TOTAL RETURNS %

3 months 1997	1996	1995	1994	3 years	5 years
0.85	38.69	2.85	N.A.	N.A.	N.A.

STATISTICS

Assets ($mil)	Current yield	Volatility	Risk return	Micropal Star Rating
25.74	—	N.A.	—	———

HYPO Osteuropa
33/350

Foreign & Colonial Management
4 Rue Alphonse Weiker, L-2721 Luxembourg
Tel 352-42-12-04-52 Fax 352-42-19-82
E mail kgehlen@hypo-invest.lu

Investment objective:
The fund seeks a long-term and strong increase in value by investing in companies from Eastern European markets. The top country allocations of the portfolio are as follows: Poland (38.9%); Russia (19.2%); and Hungary (15.6%). In addition the top sector allocations are represented by the following: finance (15.8%); and health/pharmaceutical (12.6%).
Umbrella fund: This is a singular fund.
Launch date: 03/04/95 **Domicile:** Luxembourg
Currency: DEM **Structure:** Open ended, FCP
Portfolio manager: Isabel Knight
Commenced with FCEM in 1995, responsible for East European investments; graduate, economics- London U; previously with Morgan Stanley and Morgan Stanley; investment speciality areas are in Europe, N Africa, Far/ Middle East.
Purchase: Direct
Minimum investment: 1 Unit
Custodian: HYPO-Bank Luxembourg
Listed: None **Dealings:** Daily
Fund Sedol I.D.: 973916 **Published:** FT/HB/FA
Fees **Annual fee:** 1.75% **Performance fee:** None
Front end load: 5.00% **Redemption fee:** None
Switching fee: None

Contact: Kerstein Gehlen
Performance:

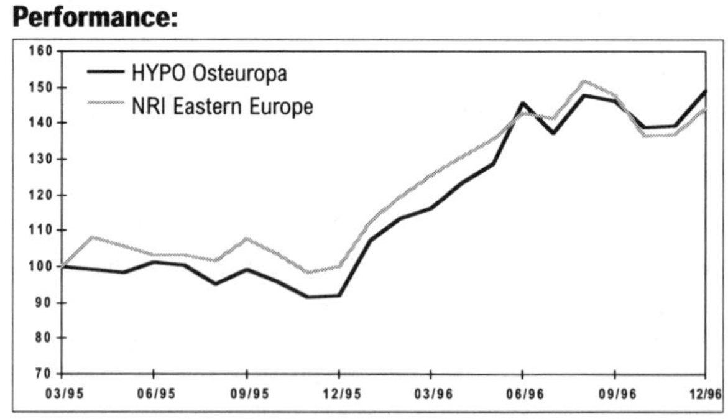

Top holdings:

Holding	%
Bank Slaski	4.3%
Daruibius Hotel	3.3%
Eleektrobudowa	3.4%
Elektrim	3.6%
Lukoil	4.4%
Mosenergo	4.2%
Pliva	4.4%
Polifarb Wraclaw	3.6%
Rostelekom	3.2%
Zagrebacka Banka	3.3%

TOTAL RETURNS %

3 months 1997	1996	1995	1994	3 years	5 years
17.25	62.59	N.A.	N.A.	N.A.	N.A.

STATISTICS

Assets ($mil)	Current yield	Volatility	Risk return	Micropal Star Rating
21.40	—	N.A.	—	———

IB Brazilian Leveraged Equities
100/350

Banco Icatu SA
Avenue President Wilson, 231-9 andar, Rio de Janiero,
20030-021, Brazil
Tel 55-21-217-1308 Fax 55-21-262-6007
http://www. icatu.com.br E mail mcukierm@icatu.com.br
Contact: Marcelo Cukierman

Investment objective:
The fund is invested primarily in the equities of publicly traded Brazilian companies on the Rio de Janeiro and San Paulo exchanges in order to seek capital gains. The top sectors of the portfolio include the following: communications (70.0%); consumer goods (9.0%); industrial cyclical (5.0%); and energy (2.0%).

Umbrella fund: This is a singular fund.
Launch date: 10/08/95 **Domicile:** Cayman Islands
Currency: USD **Structure:** Open ended, Investment Company
Portfolio manager: Banco Icatu SA
Manager of IB Brazilian Leveraged Equity.

Performance:

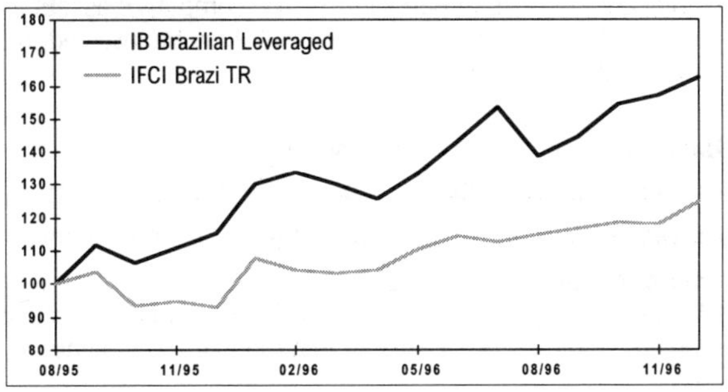

Purchase: Direct, Swiss Bank and Trust
Minimum investment: 50,000 USD
Custodian: Swiss Bank and Trust
Listed: None **Dealings:** Daily
Fund Sedol I.D.: 305427 **Published:** N/A
Fees **Annual fee:** 1.00% **Performance fee:** 15.00%
Front end load: None **Redemption fee:** 0.25%
Switching fee: None

Top holdings:

Brasmotor PN	6.0%
CSN ON	2.5%
Livraria Saraiva	5.0%
Odebrecht	3.5%
Petroneo E Ipiranga	2.0%
Telebras PN	45.0%
Telemig PNB	5.0%
Telesp pn	17.0%

TOTAL RETURNS %

3 months 1997	1996	1995	1994	3 years	5 years
28.20	40.88	N.A.	N.A.	N.A.	N.A.

STATISTICS

Assets ($mil)	Current yield	Volatility	Risk return	Micropal Star Rating
18.16	—	N.A.	—	———

ImPac AP Hong Kong
30/350

ImPac Fund Managers (BVI) Ltd
1205 Universal Trade Center, 3 Arbuthnot Street,
Central, Hong Kong
Tel 852-2869-6168 Fax 852-2810-5563
http://www. thepress.com/impac E mail impac@impac.com.hk
Contact: Julian Wong

Investment objective:
The fund seeks average returns from investments in Hong Kong with a minimum of 50% invested in liquid large-cap stocks.The investment style is mainly top-down, although stock selections from medium-sized and smaller companies are important. Due to the up coming re-union with China, a maximum of 25% of its net assets may be invested in "B" Shares and GDR's.
Umbrella fund: ImPac Asia Pacific Funds Limited
Launch date: 31/10/95 **Domicile:** Cayman Island
Currency: USD **Structure:** Open ended, Investment Company
Portfolio manager: Gary Ting, CFA
Manager joined ImPac Asia Pacific HK as a Director 1995; BSc, Ind engineering- U of HK, MBA- Wharton School; formerly with DICAM (HK) CO, established Chariot Industries Holdings; 10 years fund mgt experience; 5 yrs manufacturing engineering.
Purchase: Direct, Financial Advisor
Minimum investment: 5,000 USD
Custodian: Bank of Bermuda (Cayman) Limited
Listed: None **Dealings:** Daily
Fund Sedol I.D.: 305266 **Published:** HKET/HKEJ/AW/SC/FT
Fees **Annual fee:** 1.25% **Performance fee:** None
Front end load: 5.00% **Redemption fee:** 0.50%
Switching fee: 2.00%

Performance:

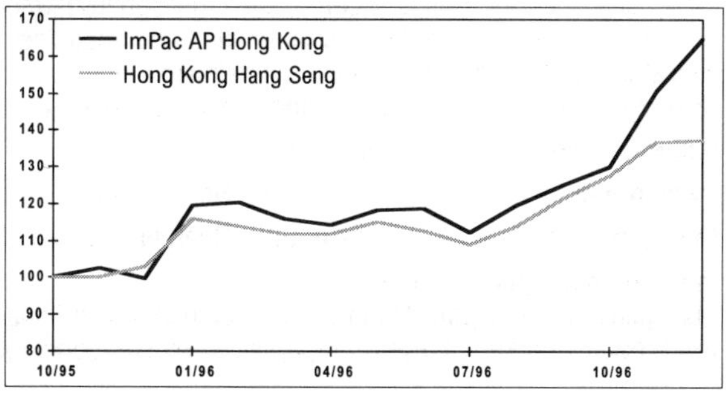

Top holdings:

Basket Properties Wts 97	4.0%
Basket Red Chips 9771	5.0%
China Overseas	4.0%
Citic Pacific	6.0%
Dao Heng Bank	4.0%
Dongfang Electric	5.0%
First Pacific	6.0%
Guangdong Investment	4.0%
Hopewell Holdings	6.0%
Hutchison Whampoa	5.0%

TOTAL RETURNS %

3 months 1997	1996	1995	1994	3 years	5 years
-8.84	65.24	N.A.	N.A.	N.A.	N.A.

STATISTICS

Assets ($mil)	Current yield	Volatility	Risk return	Micropal Star Rating
2.27	—	N.A.	—	———

Indosuez Bangladesh Fund
40/350

Indosuez Asset Management Asia
Suite 2606-2608, One Exchange Square, 8 Connaught Place, Hong Kong
Tel 852-2521-4231 Fax 852-2877-2163

Investment objective:
The fund seeks capital appreciation through investment in companies in or with significant interests in Bangladesh. The company's assets are invested principally in equity related instruments. 25% of NAV may be invested in unlisteds. The fund is denominated in US dollars.

Umbrella fund: This is a singular fund.
Launch date: 01/07/94 **Domicile:** Cayman Islands
Currency: USD **Structure:** Close ended, Investment Company
Portfolio manager: Ayaz Ebrahim
Manager of Indosuez Bangladesh; BSc, accounting; specialises in emerging equity markets; 10 years experience in institutional investments.

Purchase: Direct, Market Maker
Minimum investment: None
Custodian: Banque Indosuez Luxembourg
Listed: Dublin **Dealings:** Weekly
Fund Sedol I.D.: 7113 **Published:** AW/FT/IHT/SC/HKE/RT
Fees **Annual fee:** 1.50% **Performance fee:** None
Front end load: None **Redemption fee:** None
Switching fee: None

Contact: Marketing Department
Performance:

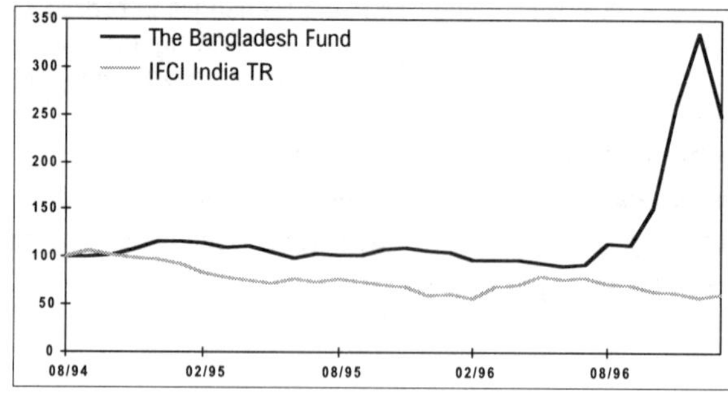

Top holdings:

Apex Footwear	n/s
Apex Tannery	n/s
Bata Shoes	n/s
Beximco Pharma	n/s
Meghna Cement	n/s
Monno Ceramic	n/s
Monno Fabrics	n/s
Padma Textile Mills	n/s
Shine Pukur Holdings	n/s
Square Pharmaceutical	n/s

TOTAL RETURNS %

3 months 1997	1996	1995	1994	3 years	5 years
30.40	58.08	-7.96	N.A.	N.A.	N.A.

STATISTICS

Assets ($mil)	Current yield	Volatility	Risk return	Micropal Star Rating
37.22	—	N.A.	—	———

Indosuez Hong Kong
83/350

Indosuez Asset Management Asia
Suite 2606-2608, One Exchange Square, 8 Connaught Place, Hong Kong
Tel 852-2521-4231 Fax 852-2877-2163

Investment objective:
The fund aims to achieve the maximum capital appreciation consistent with reasonable security. This is accomplished through investment mainly in leading Hong Kong equities, with limited exposure to smaller companies. The top sectors allocations of the portfolio include the following: real estate (39.0%); finance (20.0%); multi industry (21.0%); and consumer goods (6.0%).
Umbrella fund: This is a singular fund.
Launch date: 13/01/86 **Domicile:** Hong Kong
Currency: USD **Structure:** Open ended, Unit Trust
Portfolio manager: Husan Pai
Manager of the Indosuez Hong Kong; BBA, economics/ finance; specialises in North Asian equity markets; 10 years experience in institutional investments.

Purchase: Direct
Minimum investment: 1,500 USD
Custodian: Banque Indosuez Luxembourg
Listed: None **Dealings:** Daily
Fund Sedol I.D.: 36197 **Published:** FT/IHT/SC/HKEJ/HKET/RT
Fees **Annual fee:** 1.80% **Performance fee:** None
Front end load: None **Redemption fee:** None
Switching fee: 1.00%

Contact: Marketing Department
Performance:

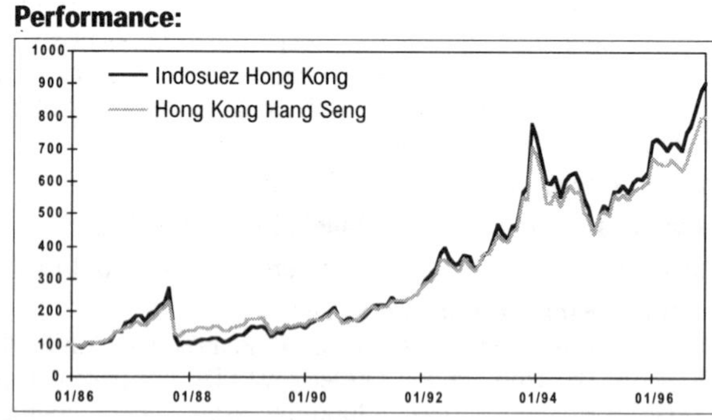

Top holdings:

Chaifa Holdings	5.1%
Cheung Kong	11.8%
HSBC Holdings	10.5%
Hutchison Whampoa	7.6%
Sun Hung Kai Properties	5.3%

TOTAL RETURNS %

3 months 1997	1996	1995	1994	3 years	5 years
-8.72	42.92	22.34	-33.69	15.94	257.54

STATISTICS

Assets ($mil)	Current yield	Volatility	Risk return	Micropal Star Rating
23.19	—	6.74	—	✪✪

Indosuez Shanghai
104/350

Indosuez Asser Management Asia
39 Allee Scheffer, L-2520 Luxembourg
Tel 352-476-74-89 Fax 352-47-67-55-1

Investment objective:
The fund seeks long-term capital appreciation through China and China related securities. The fund can invest up to 15% of its total net assets in unlisted securities. The top sector allocations are electrical/ electronics (13.0%); real estate (12.0%); and capital equipment (12.0%). The assets are in Hong Kong (71.1%); Shanghai (16.5%); and Shenzhen (11.4%).

Umbrella fund: This is a singular fund.

Launch date: 01/06/92 **Domicile:** Cayman Islands

Currency: USD **Structure:** Open ended, Investment Company

Portfolio manager: Husan Pai
Manager of the Indosuez Hong Kong; BBA, economics and finance; specialises in North Asian equity markets; 10 years experience in institutional investments.

Purchase: Direct

Minimum investment: 100,000 USD

Custodian: Banque Indosuez Luxembourg

Listed: London **Dealings:** Weekly

Fund Sedol I.D.: 645919 **Published:** FT/IHT/SC/HKEJ/HKET/RT

Fees **Annual fee:** 1.50% **Performance fee:** None

Front end load: None **Redemption fee:** None

Switching fee: None

Contact: Brian Dunne

Performance:

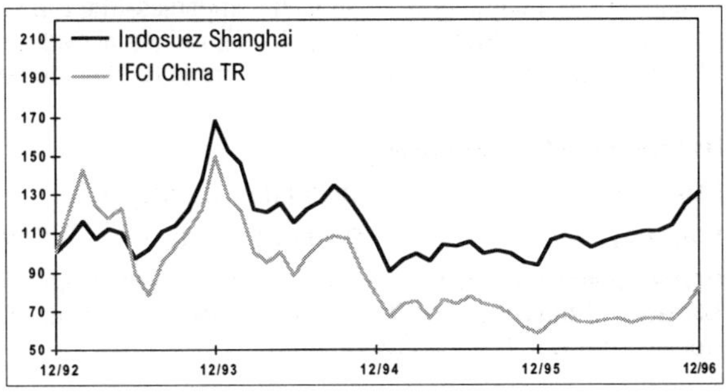

Top holdings:

Chaifa Holdings	n/s
Changchou Co	n/s
Cheung Kong	n/s
Cosco Pacific	n/s
Guangzhou Inv Ltd	n/s
HSBC Holdings	n/s
New World Development	n/s
Union Bank Hong Kong	n/s
Weifu Fuel Injection	n/s

TOTAL RETURNS %

3 months 1997	1996	1995	1994	3 years	5 years
7.59	40.71	-11.76	-37.29	-22.13	N.A.

STATISTICS

Assets ($mil)	Current yield	Volatility	Risk return	Micropal Star Rating
16.75	—	6.51	—	✪✪

ING International-Latin American Equity Cap
302/350

ING Investment Management
227 Route D'Arlon, Strassen, L-8010 Luxembourg
Tel 352-31-66-111 Fax 352-31-8433
http://www. ingbank.com
E mail 100664.3026@compuserve.com

Investment objective:
The objective of the sub-fund is to realise long-term capital growth by investment in a diversified portfolio of shares traded on the stock exchanges of countries in Latin America and the Caribbean. The top country allocations of the portfolio are as follows: Brazil (38.0%); Mexico (23.0%); Chile (14.2%); Argentina (10.4%); and Peru (2.7%).

Umbrella fund: ING International

Launch date: 24/05/94 **Domicile:** Luxembourg [UCITS]

Currency: USD **Structure:** Open ended, SICAV

Portfolio manager: Matthew Linsey
Manager of ING International Latin American Equity Cap commenced April 1994; MBA, marketing/ finance- U of Michigan.

Purchase: Financial Advisor

Minimum investment: 500 USD

Custodian: ING Bank (Luxembourg) S.A.

Listed: Luxembourg **Dealings:** Daily

Fund Sedol I.D.: 301837 **Published:** EB/GN

Fees **Annual fee:** 1.35% **Performance fee:** None

Front end load: 3.00% **Redemption fee:** None

Switching fee: None

Contact: Ria Claes /Anne Molitor

Performance:

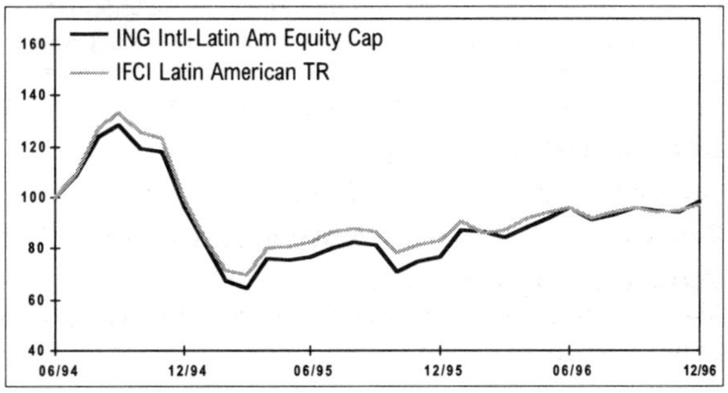

Top holdings:

Banamex	1.9%
Banco Edwards	2.3%
Cemex CPO	2.1%
Electrobas	2.3%
Grupo Televisa	2.1%
Petrobas	3.4%
Telebras	3.8%
Telmex	5.7%
Vale de Riodoce	2.3%
YPF	2.1%

TOTAL RETURNS %

3 months 1997	1996	1995	1994	3 years	5 years
14.43	28.27	-20.80	N.A.	N.A.	N.A.

STATISTICS

Assets ($mil)	Current yield	Volatility	Risk return	Micropal Star Rating
19.47	—	N.A.	—	———

Inter Strategie Australie

215/350

Banque Nationale de Paris
BP 1243, L-1012 Luxembourg
Tel 352-47-64-1 Fax 352-22-64-80

Investment objective:
The primary objective of the sub-fund is to generate medium-term gains through investment in the equity of Australian companies. The top sector allocations of the portfolio are as follows: services (34.7%); industrial cyclical (32.8%); finance (18.4%); consumer goods (7.9%); retail trade (5.1%); and energy (1.4%).

Umbrella fund: Inter Strategie
Launch date: 13/10/94 **Domicile:** Luxembourg [UCITS]
Currency: USD **Structure:** Open ended, SICAV
Portfolio manager: BNP Investment Management (Australia)Ltd
Manager of Inter Strategie Australie commenced October 1994; located at 22, Boulevard Royal, L-2952 Luxembourg.

Purchase: Direct, From the BNP network
Minimum investment: 1 Share
Custodian: Banque Nationale de Paris (Lux)
Listed: Luxembourg **Dealings:** Weekly
Fund Sedol I.D.: 411780 **Published:** FT
Fees **Annual fee:** 1.30% **Performance fee:** None
Front end load: 2.50% **Redemption fee:** None
Switching fee: None

Contact: Mr Dufour
Performance:

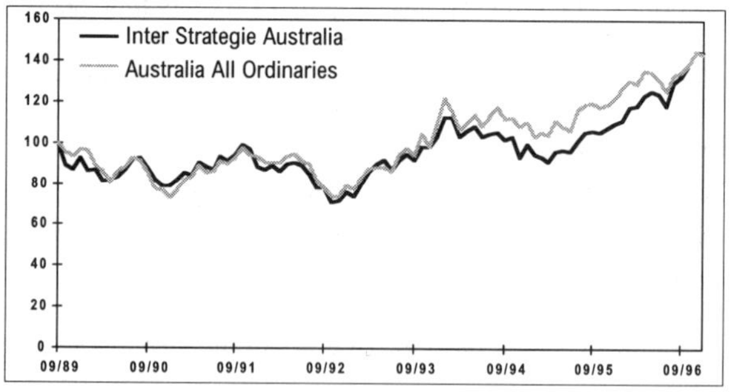

Top holdings:

Holding	%
ANZ Banking Group Ltd	4.1%
Atkins Carlyle	2.0%
Broken Hill Properties	7.2%
Commonwealth Bk of Australia	2.2%
CRA Ltd	3.2%
Mayne Nickless	3.0%
National Australia Bank	6.5%
North Ltd	2.0%
The News Corp	2.7%
Western Mining	2.6%

TOTAL RETURNS %

3 months 1997	1996	1995	1994	3 years	5 years
2.11	31.79	9.50	-3.17	39.73	63.22

STATISTICS

Assets ($mil)	Current yield	Volatility	Risk return	Micropal Star Rating
20.42	—	4.24	4	✪✪✪

Inter Strategie Small Cap

172/350

Banque Nationale de Paris
BP 1243, L-1012 Luxembourg
Tel 352-47-64-1 Fax 352-22-64-80

Investment objective:
The primary objective of the sub-fund is to generate medium-term gains through equity investment in small and medium capitalisation US companies. The top sector allocations of the portfolio are as follows: industrial cyclical (48.2%); services (15.9%); energy (15.5%); and finance (11.1%). The portfolio's assets are divided between equities (92.8%) and cash/MM (7.2%).
Umbrella fund: Inter Strategie
Launch date: 20/10/94 **Domicile:** Luxembourg [UCITS]
Currency: USD **Structure:** Open ended, SICAV
Portfolio manager: Neuburger & Berman
Managed by Neuburger & Berman and in turn managed by Ms Hahn commenced October 1996.

Purchase: Direct, From the BNP network
Minimum investment: 1 Share
Custodian: Banque Nationale de Paris (Lux)
Listed: None **Dealings:** Weekly
Fund Sedol I.D.: 300178 **Published:** FT
Fees **Annual fee:** 1.50% **Performance fee:** None
Front end load: 2.50% **Redemption fee:** None
Switching fee: None

Contact: Mr Dufour
Performance:

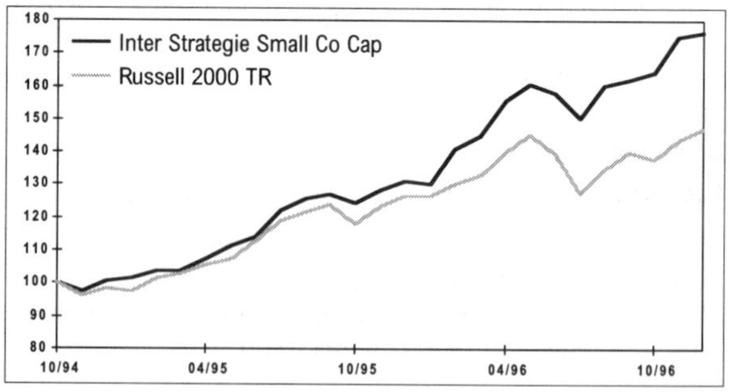

Top holdings:

Holding	%
AAR Corp	1.8%
Apache Corp	2.1%
Apogee Enterprises	2.3%
Dallas Semi Conductor	2.2%
Dreco Energy Serv	2.0%
Nabors Industries	2.6%
Pride Petroleum	2.5%
SCI Systems	2.0%
Texas Industries	2.2%
Thiokol Corp	2.2%

TOTAL RETURNS %

3 months 1997	1996	1995	1994	3 years	5 years
0.77	34.36	30.69	N.A.	N.A.	N.A.

STATISTICS

Assets ($mil)	Current yield	Volatility	Risk return	Micropal Star Rating
16.34	—	N.A.	—	——

INVESCO Asia Tiger Warrant

65/350

INVESCO International Ltd
PO Box 271, Grenville Street, St Helier, JE4 8TD, Jersey
Tel 44-1534-814-000 Fax 44-1534-814-100
http://www. invesco.com E mail ifa-mail@jer.invesco.com

Contact: Janice Hook

Investment objective:
The fund seeks to achieve long-term capital growth from highly geared investments in Asian equity warrants. The fund principally invests in equity warrants invested on the stock exchanges of Hong Kong; Singapore; Malaysia; Thailand and Korea.

Umbrella fund: This is a singular fund.

Launch date: 22/01/90 **Domicile:** Luxembourg [UCITS]

Currency: USD **Structure:** Open ended, SICAV

Portfolio manager: Sam Lau
Manager of INVESCO Asia Tiger Warrant; MBA, Chinese U of Hong Kong; specialises in Taiwan, China, and Hong Kong; joined INVESCO in 1994.

Purchase: Direct, Financial Advisor

Minimum investment: 5,000 USD

Custodian: Chase Manhattan Bank S.A

Listed: Luxembourg **Dealings:** Daily

Fund Sedol I.D.: 55489 **Published:** FT/IHT/SC

Fees **Annual fee:** 2.45% **Performance fee:** None
Front end load: 6.00% **Redemption fee:** 1.00%
Switching fee: 1.00%

Performance:

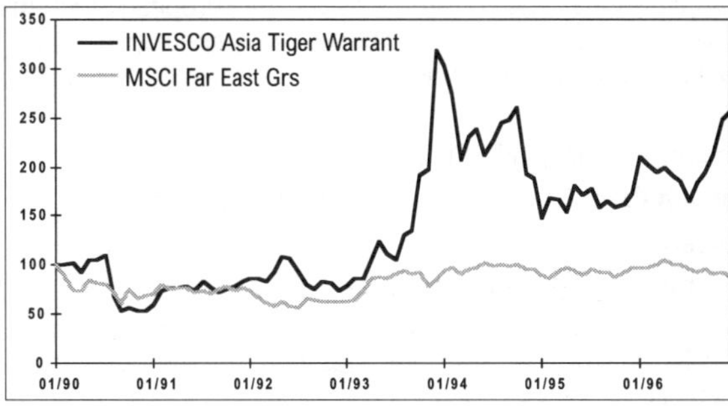

Top holdings:

Cheung Kong Infra. Wts 97	3.6%
Cheung Kong Wts 98	7.0%
Citic Pacific Wts 97	6.1%
City Dev Wts 98	5.1%
Commerce Asset Wts 98	5.3%
Gamuda Wts 17.01.2000	3.8%
Henderson Land Dev. Wts 98	5.6%
HSBC Wts 97	8.1%
Hutchison Whampoa Wts 97	4.7%
New World Dev Wts 97	3.6%

TOTAL RETURNS %

3 months 1997	1996	1995	1994	3 years	5 years
-4.75	49.01	-8.31	-41.13	-19.57	211.24

STATISTICS

Assets ($mil)	Current yield	Volatility	Risk return	Micropal Star Rating
32.50	—	10.80	—	✪✪✪

INVESCO European Warrant

8/350

INVESCO International Ltd
PO Box 271, Grenville Street, St Helier, JE4 8TD, Jersey
Tel 44-1534-814-000 Fax 44-1534-814-100
http://www. invesco.com E mail ifa-mail@jer.invesco.com

Contact: Janice Hook

Investment objective:
The fund seeks to achieve long-term capital growth from highly geared investments in equity warrants. The fund primarily invests in equity warrants issued on the stock exchanges of Germany, France, Switzerland and UK.The top country allocations of the portfolio are Germany (29.9%); Netherlands (13.6%); France (25.0%); and Switzerland (17.2%).

Umbrella fund: This is a singular fund.

Launch date: 22/01/90 **Domicile:** Luxembourg [UCITS]

Currency: USD **Structure:** Open ended, SICAV

Portfolio manager: Rory Powe
Manager of INVESTCO European Warrant and Head of European Equities Team; BA Hons, modern history- Trinity College; joined INVESCO in 1986.

Purchase: Direct, Financial Advisor

Minimum investment: 5,000 USD

Custodian: Chase Manhattan Bank S.A

Listed: Luxembourg **Dealings:** Daily

Fund Sedol I.D.: 55623 **Published:** FT/IHT/SC

Fees **Annual fee:** 1.50% **Performance fee:** None
Front end load: 6.00% **Redemption fee:** 1.00%
Switching fee: 1.00%

Performance:

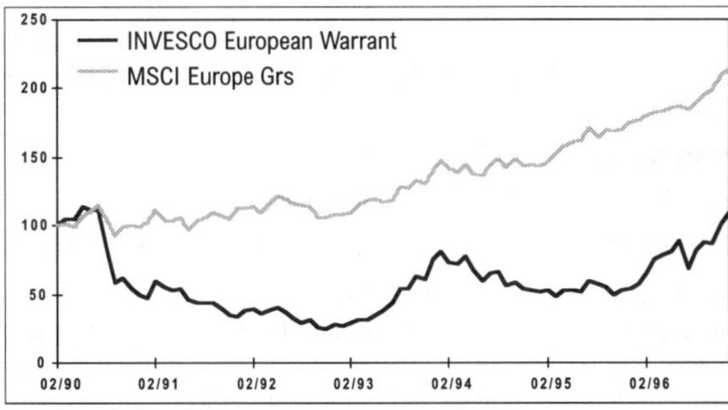

Top holdings:

Astra	4.6%
Bulgari	4.2%
Carrefour	6.4%
Christian Dior	5.4%
Commerzbank	4.7%
French Pharmaceuticals	6.0%
ING Groep	5.7%
Sodexho	4.2%
Swiss Re	5.0%

TOTAL RETURNS %

3 months 1997	1996	1995	1994	3 years	5 years
40.66	100.00	3.80	-29.87	45.60	219.30

STATISTICS

Assets ($mil)	Current yield	Volatility	Risk return	Micropal Star Rating
27.40	—	9.43	3	✪✪✪

INVESCO PS European Enterprise

198/350

Invesco International Limited
PO Box 271, Grenville Street, St Helier, JE4 8TD, Jersey
Tel 44-1534-814-000 Fax 44-1534-814-100
http://www. invesco.com E mail ifa-mail@jer.invesco.com

Contact: Janice Hook

Investment objective:
The sub-fund seeks long-term capital growth through investments in smaller companies and special situations on any European stock market. Investments are made where the freely traded portion of share capital has a market value under 150 million UK sterling generally.

Umbrella fund: INVESCO Premier Select
Launch date: 02/01/91 **Domicile:** Luxembourg [UCITS]
Currency: USD **Structure:** Open ended, SICAV
Portfolio manager: Claire Griffiths
Manager of INVESCO PS European Enterprise; specialises in continental European smaller companies; MA Hons, classics- St John's College; commenced in the financial industry in 1989.
Purchase: Direct, Financial Advisor
Minimum investment: 1,000 USD
Custodian: Chase Manhattan Bank S.A
Listed: Luxembourg **Dealings:** Daily
Fund Sedol I.D.: 448801 **Published:** FT/IHT/SC
Fees **Annual fee:** 1.50% **Performance fee:** None
Front end load: 6.00% **Redemption fee:** None
Switching fee: 1.00%

Performance:

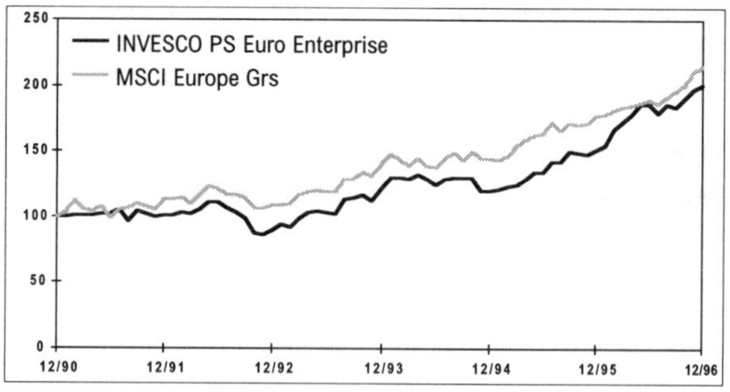

Top holdings:	
Bulgari	2.2%
Coloplast	1.6%
Distronic	1.5%
Eurobike AG	1.6%
Grandoptical Photolervia	1.6%
Heidenij	1.6%
Penoville Polyserv	1.5%
Robert Half Intl Inc	1.4%
Saloman	1.6%
Scandic Hotels	1.4%

TOTAL RETURNS %

3 months 1997	1996	1995	1994	3 years	5 years
8.07	32.80	26.63	-2.13	64.59	99.21

STATISTICS

Assets ($mil)	Current yield	Volatility	Risk return	Micropal Star Rating
37.83	—	3.03	4	✪✪✪✪✪

INVESCO PS European Growth

331/350

Invesco International Limited
PO Box 271, Grenville Street, St Helier, JE4 8TD, Jersey
Tel 44-1534-814-000 Fax 44-1534-814-100
http://www. invesco.com E mail ifa-mail@jer.invesco.com

Contact: Janice Hook

Investment objective:
The sub-fund aims to achieve long-term capital growth through investment in the equity markets of Europe (including the UK) with an emphasis on larger companies with above average growth prospects. Emphasis is placed on investment in companies which are able to grow earnings consistently even in weak operating environments.

Umbrella fund: INVESCO Premier Select
Launch date: 02/01/91 **Domicile:** Luxembourg [UCITS]
Currency: USD **Structure:** Open ended, SICAV
Portfolio manager: Steven Chamberlain
Manager of INVESTCO PS European Growth; BA Hons, geology- Kingston Polytechnic; prior fund management, worked in the INVESCO Dealing Room on the European Desk; commenced his investment career in 1989.
Purchase: Direct, Financial Advisor
Minimum investment: 1,000 USD
Custodian: Chase Manhattan Bank S.A
Listed: Luxembourg **Dealings:** Daily
Fund Sedol I.D.: 448800 **Published:** FT/IHT/SC
Fees **Annual fee:** 1.50% **Performance fee:** None
Front end load: 6.00% **Redemption fee:** None
Switching fee: 1.00%

Performance:

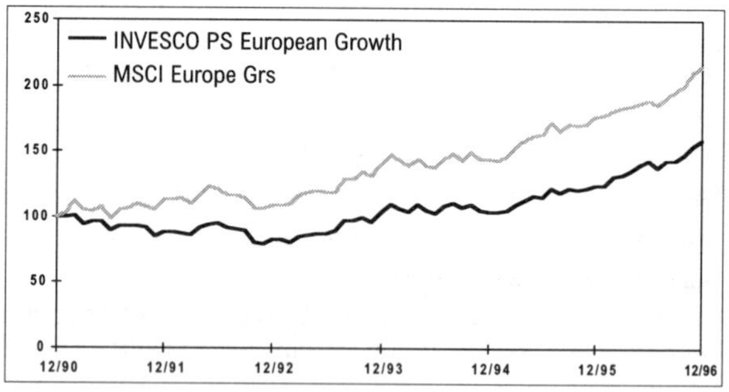

Top holdings:	
Adidas	1.9%
Bulgari	2.1%
Cimpor	1.8%
Compass	1.8%
Fresenius Med. Care	2.6%
Gucci	1.6%
Sage Group	1.7%
Scala	1.9%
Tomra Systems ASA	2.1%
Wolford	1.6%

TOTAL RETURNS %

3 months 1997	1996	1995	1994	3 years	5 years
6.93	27.45	19.58	-0.57	51.53	79.64

STATISTICS

Assets ($mil)	Current yield	Volatility	Risk return	Micropal Star Rating
41.46	—	2.94	3	✪✪✪✪

INVESCO PS Greater China Opportunities

97/350

Invesco International Limited
PO Box 271, Grenville Street, St Helier, JE4 8TD, Jersey
Tel 44-1534-814-000 Fax 44-1534-814-100
http://www. invesco.com E mail ifa-mail@jer.invesco.com

Contact: Janice Hook

Investment objective:
The sub-fund aims to achieve long-term capital growth from investments in the equity markets of Hong Kong and mainland China with an emphasis upon larger companies with average growth prospects. At this time the portfolio is allocated between Hong Kong (85.8%); and China (6.1%) with the remainder held in cash.

Umbrella fund: INVESCO Premier Select
Launch date: 15/07/92 **Domicile:** Luxembourg [UCITS]
Currency: USD **Structure:** Open ended, SICAV
Portfolio manager: Adrian Au
Manager of the INVESCO Greater China Opportunities; BA, engineering science-Cambridge U; specialises in the markets of Hong Kong, China and Taiwan; joined INVESCO in September 1994.
Purchase: Direct, Financial Advisor
Minimum investment: 1,000 USD
Custodian: Chase Manhattan Bank S.A
Listed: Luxembourg **Dealings:** Daily
Fund Sedol I.D.: 444609 **Published:** FT/IHT/SC
Fees **Annual fee:** 1.50% **Performance fee:** None
Front end load: 6.00% **Redemption fee:** None
Switching fee: 1.00%

Performance:

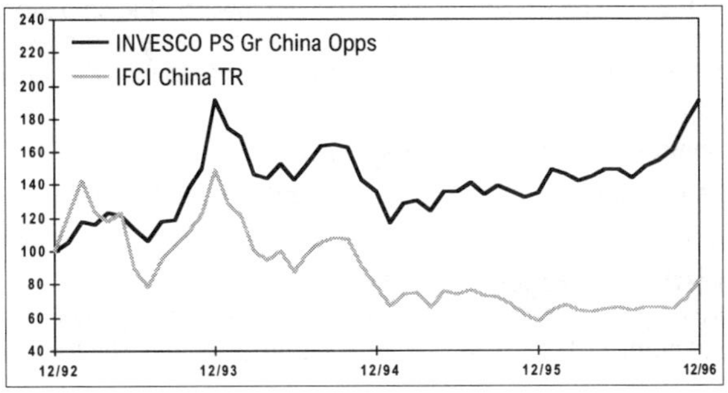

Top holdings:

Cheung Kong Holdings Ltd	7.3%
Cheung Kong Infra	4.2%
China Everbright INTL	3.7%
China Resources Enterprises	5.1%
Citic Pacific	5.9%
Henderson Land Development	5.2%
HSBC Holdings	6.4%
Hutchison Whampoa	6.0%
New World Development	5.2%
Sun Hung Kai Properties	6.3%

TOTAL RETURNS %

3 months 1997	1996	1995	1994	3 years	5 years
1.44	41.03	-0.30	-29.26	-0.53	N.A.

STATISTICS

Assets ($mil)	Current yield	Volatility	Risk return	Micropal Star Rating
10.67	—	6.36	—	✪✪✪✪

INVESCO PS UK Growth

288/350

Invesco International Limited
PO Box 271, Grenville Street, St Helier, JE4 8TD, Jersey
Tel 44-1534-814-000 Fax 44-1534-814-100
http://www. invesco.com E mail ifa-mail@jer.invesco.com

Contact: Janice Hook

Investment objective:
The sub-fund seeks long-term capital growth from investment in the shares of companies operating in the UK. These range from major multi-nationals, with widely spread international interests, through to smaller companies that are leaders in their area of business. The top sector allocations of the portfolio are services (32.1%)and consumer goods (22.1%).

Umbrella fund: INVESCO Premier Select
Launch date: 01/04/93 **Domicile:** Luxembourg [UCITS]
Currency: GBP **Structure:** Open ended, SICAV
Portfolio manager: Tim Mann
Manager of INVESCO PS UK Growth since 1989; BA Hons, chemical engineering-Cambridge U; commenced his investment career in 1987; specialises in UK equities.

Purchase: Direct, Financial Advisor
Minimum investment: 500 GBP
Custodian: Chase Manhattan Bank S.A
Listed: Luxembourg **Dealings:** Daily
Fund Sedol I.D.: 444259 **Published:** FT/IHT/SC
Fees **Annual fee:** 1.50% **Performance fee:** None
Front end load: 6.00% **Redemption fee:** None
Switching fee: 1.00%

Performance:

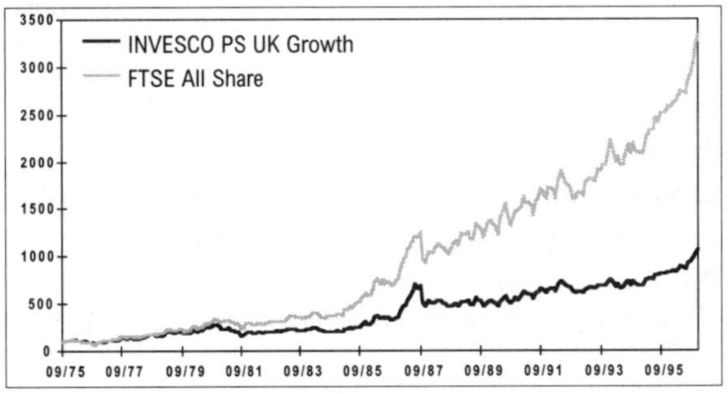

Top holdings:

British Petroleum	3.1%
Cable + Wireless (GBP)	2.0%
Glaxo Wellcome	2.5%
HSBC Holdings	2.5%
Lloyds TSB Group	2.5%
Marks & Spencers	2.1%
Sage Group	2.2%
Shell Transport & Trading	2.1%
Siebe	2.3%
Smithkline Beecham Beecham	2.0%

TOTAL RETURNS %

3 months 1997	1996	1995	1994	3 years	5 years
0.88	28.65	19.84	-5.90	45.07	66.70

STATISTICS

Assets ($mil)	Current yield	Volatility	Risk return	Micropal Star Rating
16.27	—	3.65	2	✪✪

Irish Life International US Equity
229/350

Irish Life International
Irish Life Centre, Lower Abbey Street, Dublin 1, Ireland
Tel 353-1704-1508 Fax 353-1704-1922

Investment objective:
The insurance fund seeks capital growth by investing in shares of companies quoted in the US stock markets and is biased toward blue chip stocks. The fund holds a diversified portfolio of industries which are likely to out perform over the coming 12 to 18 months. The top sectors of this portfolio include consumer goods (31.0%) and capital goods (21.0%).

Umbrella fund: This is a singular fund.

Launch date: 01/10/94 **Domicile:** Ireland

Currency: USD **Structure:** Open ended, Insurance Fund

Portfolio manager: Gareth Maher
Manager of Irish Life International US Equity commenced in 1990; Master's degree, economics- U College Dublin; joined Irish Life in 1987 as an investment analyst.

Purchase: Direct

Minimum investment: ILP

Custodian: Irish Life Assurance

Listed: None **Dealings:** Daily

Fund Sedol I.D.: 46768 **Published:** FT/IHT/SC

Fees **Annual fee:** 1.35% **Performance fee:** ILP
Front end load: ILP **Redemption fee:** ILP
Switching fee: ILP

Contact: Nick Reid

Performance:

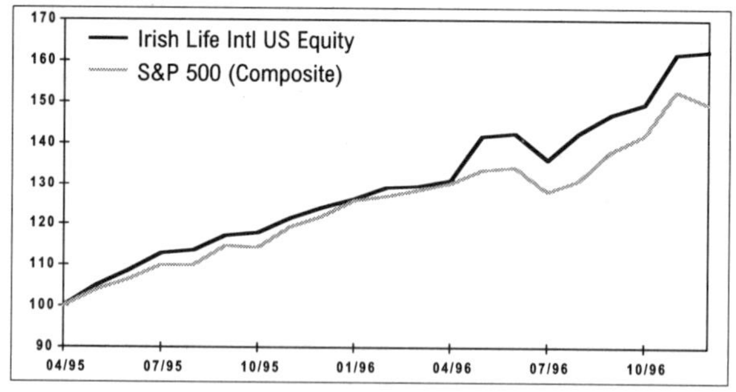

Top holdings:

Citicorp	4.2%
IBM	4.8%
McDonalds	3.8%
United Healthcare	3.3%
Wal Mart	4.2%

TOTAL RETURNS %

3 months 1997	1996	1995	1994	3 years	5 years
6.09	31.09	N.A.	N.A.	N.A.	N.A.

STATISTICS

Assets ($mil)	Current yield	Volatility	Risk return	Micropal Star Rating
12.72	—	N.A.	—	———

JF American Growth Trust
299/350

Jardine Fleming
37 Floor Jardine House, 1 Connaught Place, Central, Hong Kong
Tel 852-2843-8888 Fax 852-2845-2421

Investment objective:
The fund seeks to achieve long-term capital growth in US dollar terms. The portfolio consists primarily of equities of companies, operating principally in the US or primarily linked either directly or indirectly to the American economy. The top sector allocations of the portfolio are as follows: finance (24.5%); energy (11.1%); consumer services (8.8%); and insurance (7.6%).

Umbrella fund: This is a singular fund.

Launch date: 07/07/83 **Domicile:** British Virgin Islands

Currency: USD **Structure:** Open ended, Unit Trust

Portfolio manager: Jonathan Simon
Manager of JF American Growth commenced 1991 and President of Fleming Capital Management- New York; specialises in North American securities; joined Fleming 12 years ago.

Purchase: Direct

Minimum investment: 2,000 USD

Custodian: East Asia International Trustees Ltd

Listed: Hong Kong **Dealings:** Daily

Fund Sedol I.D.: 47094 **Published:** FT/SC/HKEJ/CT/EDN

Fees **Annual fee:** 1.50% **Performance fee:** None
Front end load: Up to 5.00% **Redemption fee:** 0.50%
Switching fee: None

Contact: Customer Services Department

Performance:

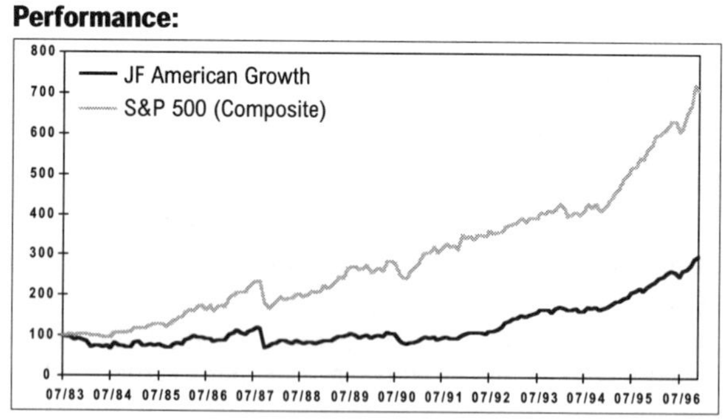

Top holdings:

Bank of New York Co	2.7%
Carlisle Cos inc	3.6%
Clayton Homes Inc	3.5%
Gannett Co Inc	3.8%
Kimco Realty	3.8%
Maic Holdings inc	3.6%
Marriott inc	2.7%
Northern Trust Corp	3.0%
Providian Corp	2.7%
Williams Cos	3.8%

TOTAL RETURNS %

3 months 1997	1996	1995	1994	3 years	5 years
5.26	28.32	35.88	0.63	75.46	187.68

STATISTICS

Assets ($mil)	Current yield	Volatility	Risk return	Micropal Star Rating
69.46	—	2.73	5	✪✪✪✪✪

JF China Trust

41/350

Jardine Fleming
37 Floor Jardine House, 1 Connaught Place, Central, Hong Kong
Tel 852-2843-8888 Fax 852-2845-2421

Investment objective:
The fund seeks long-term capital growth in US dollar terms. The portfolio consists primarily of securities listed on the Shenzhen Stock Exchange, Shanghai Securities Exchange and other stock exchanges as may be established in China, or shares of companies listed elsewhere but which trade with or invest significantly in China.

Umbrella fund: This is a singular fund.
Launch date: 18/05/92 **Domicile:** Cayman Islands
Currency: USD **Structure:** Open ended, Unit Trust
Portfolio manager: D Eu
Manager of Jardine Fleming China.

Contact: Customer Services Department

Performance:

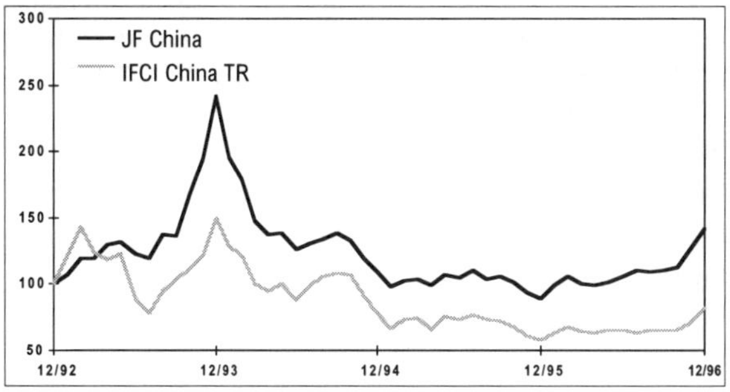

Purchase: Direct
Minimum investment: 2,000 USD
Custodian: HSBC Trustee (Cayman) Ltd
Listed: None **Dealings:** Daily
Fund Sedol I.D.: 646738 **Published:** FT/SC/HKEJ/CT/EDN
Fees **Annual fee:** 1.50% **Performance fee:** None
Front end load: Up to 5.00% **Redemption fee:** 0.50%
Switching fee: None

Top holdings:

Holding	%
Cheung Kong Holdings Ltd	4.9%
Guandong Provincial Expressary	2.9%
Guangshen Railway	4.0%
HuangchunTourism Developement	5.0%
Hutchison Whampoa	75.0%
New World Development	6.9%
Qingling Motors	3.1%
Seapower International	2.8%
Shanghai Diesel Engine	3.4%
Swire Pacific	2.8%

TOTAL RETURNS %

3 months 1997	1996	1995	1994	3 years	5 years
4.58	57.99	-18.02	-54.71	-41.34	N.A.

STATISTICS

Assets ($mil)	Current yield	Volatility	Risk return	Micropal Star Rating
32.51	—	7.40	—	✪

JF European Trust

249/350

Jardine Fleming
37 Floor Jardine House, 1 Connaught Place, Central, Hong Kong
Tel 852-2843-8888 Fax 852-2845-2421

Investment objective:
The fund aims to secure long-term capital growth in US dollar terms primarily from continental Europe or the UK. The top country allocations of the portfolio are as follows: UK (32.0%); France (16.7%); Germany (11.6%); and Netherlands (9.3%). At present the currency exposure is UK sterling (32.0%); German marks (11.6%); and Switzerland franc (5.2%).

Umbrella fund: This is a singular fund.
Launch date: 02/10/85 **Domicile:** Cayman Islands
Currency: USD **Structure:** Open ended, Unit Trust
Portfolio manager: J Fisher
Manager of Jardine Fleming European.

Contact: Customer Services Department

Performance:

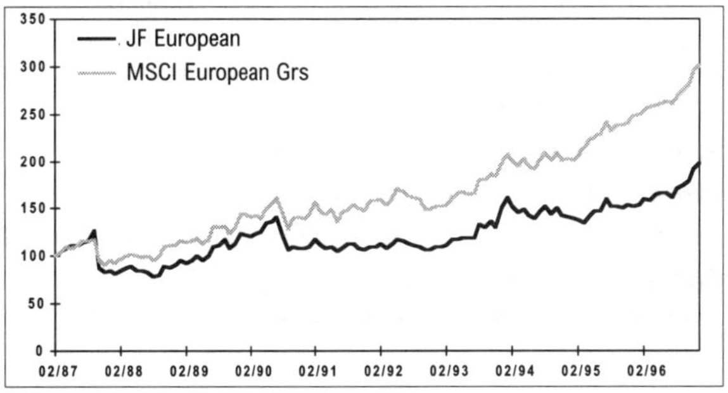

Purchase: Direct
Minimum investment: 2,000 USD
Custodian: Royal Bank of Canada Trust Co (Cayman) Ltd
Listed: None **Dealings:** Daily
Fund Sedol I.D.: 47117 **Published:** FT/SC/HKEJ/CT/EDN
Fees **Annual fee:** 1.50% **Performance fee:** None
Front end load: Up to 5.00% **Redemption fee:** 0.50%
Switching fee: None

Top holdings:

Holding	%
British Aerospace	2.7%
British Land	2.0%
Granada Group	2.4%
Next Ord	2.7%
Nokia A	4.4%
Pinault -Printemps	3.9%
Saipem	2.1%
Standard Chartered	2.2%
Total B Shares	2.0%
3i Group PL	2.6%

TOTAL RETURNS %

3 months 1997	1996	1995	1994	3 years	5 years
5.42	30.49	7.31	-5.94	31.71	81.13

STATISTICS

Assets ($mil)	Current yield	Volatility	Risk return	Micropal Star Rating
28.36	—	3.91	1	✪✪

JF Hong Kong Trust

225/350

Jardine Fleming
37 Floor Jardine House, 1 Connaught Place, Central, Hong Kong
Tel 852-2843-8888 Fax 852-2845-2421

Investment objective:
The fund seeks to secure long-term capital growth in US dollar terms. The investment focus consists mainly of securities of companies with a significant proportion of their business in Hong Kong. The top sector allocations for the portfolio are as follows: property/real estate (44.8%); conglomerate (21.5%); finance (21.3%); and utilities (6.3%).

Umbrella fund: This is a singular fund.

Launch date: 31/12/73 **Domicile:** British West Indies

Currency: USD **Structure:** Open ended, Unit Trust

Portfolio manager: D Eu
Manager of Jardine Fleming Hong Kong.

Contact: Customer Services Department

Performance:

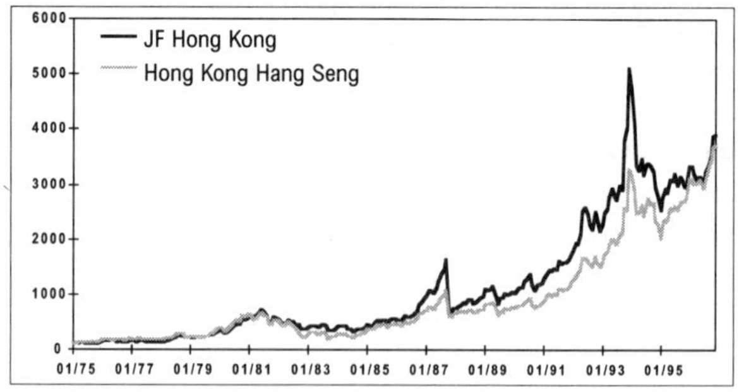

Purchase: Direct

Minimum investment: 2,000 USD

Custodian: HSBC Trustee (Cayman) Ltd

Listed: Hong Kong **Dealings:** Daily

Fund Sedol I.D.: 47076 **Published:** FT/SC/HKEJ/CT/EDN

Fees **Annual fee:** 1.50% **Performance fee:** None
Front end load: Up to 5.00% **Redemption fee:** 0.50%
Switching fee: None

Top holdings:

Cheung Kong Holdings Ltd	8.1%
Hang Seng Bank	4.7%
Henderson Land Dev. Wts 98	5.3%
HK Telecommunications	4.5%
HSBC Holdings	9.6%
Hutchison Whampoa	8.8%
New World Development	8.1%
Sun Hung Kai Properties	4.8%
Swire Pacific	6.5%
The Wharf Holdings Ltd	5.2%

TOTAL RETURNS %

3 months 1997	1996	1995	1994	3 years	5 years
-8.40	31.28	7.02	-45.66	-23.65	131.64

STATISTICS

Assets ($mil)	Current yield	Volatility	Risk return	Micropal Star Rating
71.29	—	6.68	—	✪

JF Malaysia Trust

178/350

Jardine Fleming
37 Floor Jardine House, 1 Connaught Place, Central, Hong Kong
Tel 852-2843-8888 Fax 852-2845-2421

Investment objective:
The fund aims to provide capital growth through investing primarily in securities listed on the Malaysian Stock Exchange or companies listed elsewhere, but which trade or invest significantly in Malaysia.The country allocations of the portfolio is divided between Malaysia (99.0%); and Australia (1.0%). The top sector allocation is commercial/industrial (41.3%).

Umbrella fund: This is a singular fund.

Launch date: 12/12/89 **Domicile:** Cayman Islands

Currency: USD **Structure:** Open ended, Unit Trust

Portfolio manager: C Yew
Manager of Jardine Fleming Malaysia.

Contact: Customer Services Department

Performance:

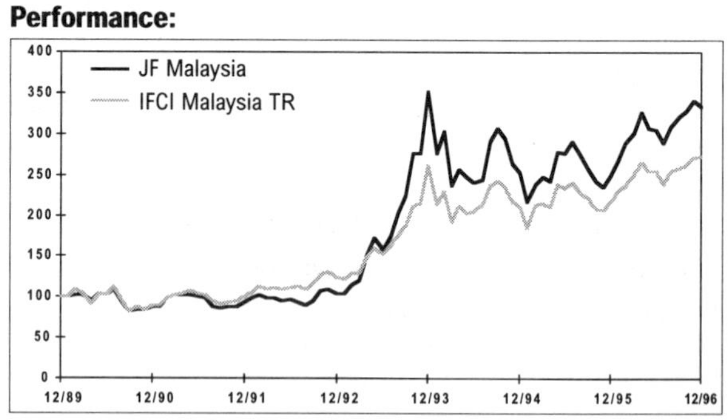

Purchase: Direct

Minimum investment: 2,000 USD

Custodian: HSBC Trustee (Cayman) Ltd

Listed: None **Dealings:** Daily

Fund Sedol I.D.: 647130 **Published:** FT/SC/HKEJ/CT/EDN

Fees **Annual fee:** 1.50% **Performance fee:** None
Front end load: Up to 5.00% **Redemption fee:** 0.50%
Switching fee: None

Top holdings:

Berjaja Sports Toto Berhad	4.7%
Dialog Group	2.4%
Gata Sarawak	3.9%
Gooleh Malaysian Berhad	6.8%
Kuantan Corp	2.4%
Kwong Yik Bank	5.1%
Lityan Holdings	2.6%
Malayan Bank Berhad	8.4%
MBF Capital	3.8%

TOTAL RETURNS %

3 months 1997	1996	1995	1994	3 years	5 years
13.61	33.88	-1.25	-27.92	-4.70	256.08

STATISTICS

Assets ($mil)	Current yield	Volatility	Risk return	Micropal Star Rating
85.60	—	8.68	—	✪✪

JF New Zealand Trust
269/350

Jardine Fleming
37 Floor Jardine House, 1 Connaught Place, Central, Hong Kong
Tel 852-2843-8888 Fax 852-2845-2421

Contact: Customer Services Department

Investment objective:
The fund aims to provide capital growth through investment primarily in securities listed on the New Zealand Stock Exchange or companies listed elsewhere but which trade or invest significantly in New Zealand. The top sector allocations of the portfolio are as follows: energy (15.2%); utilities (9.4%); communications (8.2%); building materials (7.6%); and finance (7.4%).

Umbrella fund: This is a singular fund.

Launch date: 20/10/89 **Domicile:** Cayman Islands

Currency: USD **Structure:** Open ended, Unit Trust

Portfolio manager: SK Lim
Manager of Jardine Fleming New Zealand.

Performance:

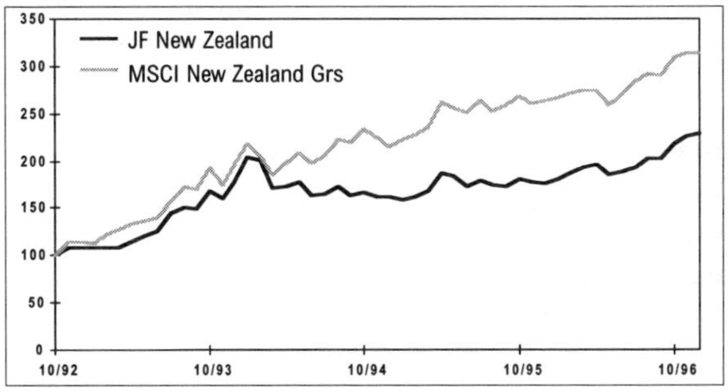

Purchase: Direct

Minimum investment: 2,000 USD

Custodian: HSBC Trustee (Cayman) Ltd

Listed: None **Dealings:** Daily

Fund Sedol I.D.: 647208 **Published:** FT/SC/HKEJ/CT/EDN

Fees **Annual fee:** 1.50% **Performance fee:** None
Front end load: Up to 5.00% **Redemption fee:** 0.50%
Switching fee: None

Top holdings:

Holding	%
Brierley Investments Ltd	3.5%
Carter Holt Harvey Ltd	7.2%
Fletcher Challenge Building	4.7%
Fletcher Challenge Energy	3.7%
Hellaby Holdings	4.0%
Natural Gas Corp	4.0%
Nuplex Industries	5.5%
Telecom Corp of NZ	8.2%
Trustpower Ltd	3.6%
Wilson & Horton	6.2%

TOTAL RETURNS %

3 months 1997	1996	1995	1994	3 years	5 years
-4.14	29.61	8.87	-9.02	28.37	168.56

STATISTICS

Assets ($mil)	Current yield	Volatility	Risk return	Micropal Star Rating
7.91	—	5.06	3	✪✪✪

Julius Baer Multicooperation Central Europe Stk
31/350

Julius Baer Investment Fund Services
50 Boulevard J.F Kennedy, L-2951 Luxembourg
Tel 352-42-42-27-72 Fax 352-42-42-20-92
http://www. juliusbaer.com

Contact: Customer Services Department

Investment objective:
The objective of this Julius Baer fund is to achieve a long-term capital gain by investing in a portfolio of high quality shares of companies domiciled in Central European countries. Up to a third of the net assets may be invested in securities, convertible bonds and warrant issues.The top country allocations held by the portfolio are in Poland and Hungary.

Umbrella fund: Julius Baer Multicooperation SICAV

Launch date: 31/10/94 **Domicile:** Luxembourg [UCITS]

Currency: ATS **Structure:** Open ended, SICAV

Portfolio manager: Gunter Mandl
Mr Mandl commenced managing the Julius Baer Multicooperation Central Europe October 1994; located in Vienna.

Performance:

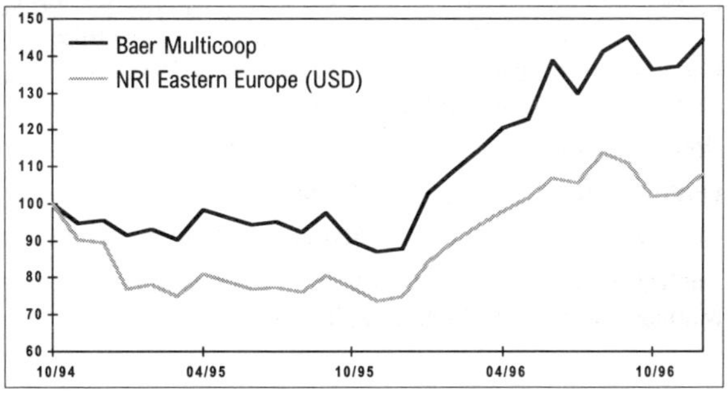

Purchase: Financial Advisor, Call 41-1-287-5319 for most suitable bank connection

Minimum investment: 5,000 CHF

Custodian: Banque Generale du Luxembourg S.A.

Listed: None **Dealings:** Daily

Fund Sedol I.D.: 301075 **Published:** FT/IHT/SC

Fees **Annual fee:** 1.50% **Performance fee:** None
Front end load: Up to 5.00% **Redemption fee:** None
Switching fee: Up to 1.00%

Top holdings:

Holding	%
Agros Holding	3.8%
BIG Bk Inicjatyw Gospodd	4.9%
Borsodhem RT	3.2%
Gedeon Richter	3.8%
Komercni Banka AS	3.8%
OTP Bank	3.4%
Polfa Kutno	4.4%
Tiszai Vegyi Kombinet RT	3.4%

TOTAL RETURNS %

3 months 1997	1996	1995	1994	3 years	5 years
15.31	63.80	-7.69	N.A.	N.A.	N.A.

STATISTICS

Assets ($mil)	Current yield	Volatility	Risk return	Micropal Star Rating
14.56	—	N.A.	—	———

Julius Baer Multistock Pacific Stock Fund A/B

214/350

Investment objective:
This Julius Baer fund seeks to achieve long-term growth by investing in carefully selected dividend bearing securities issued by companies domiciled in Pacific Rim countries (excluding Japan). Up to a maximum of 25% of the fund's assets can be invested in convertible bonds and in warrant linked bonds.

Umbrella fund: This is a singular fund.

Launch date: 01/10/91 **Domicile:** Luxembourg

Currency: USD **Structure:** Open ended, SICAV

Portfolio manager: Lawrence Yip, LGT Asia Hong Kong Manager of Baer Multistock Pacific Stock.

Purchase: Financial Advisor

Minimum investment: 5,000 CHF

Custodian: Banque Generale Du Luxembourg

Listed: None **Dealings:** Daily

Fund Sedol I.D.: 301375 **Published:** FT/IHT/SC

Fees **Annual fee:** 1.50% **Performance fee:** None
Front end load: Up to 5.00 % **Redemption fee:** None
Switching fee: Up to 1.00 %

Bank Julius Baer
50 boulevard J.F.Kennedy, L-2951 Luxembourg
Tel 352-42-42-27-72 Fax 352-42-42-2092
http://www. julisbaer.com

Contact: Customer Services Department

Performance:

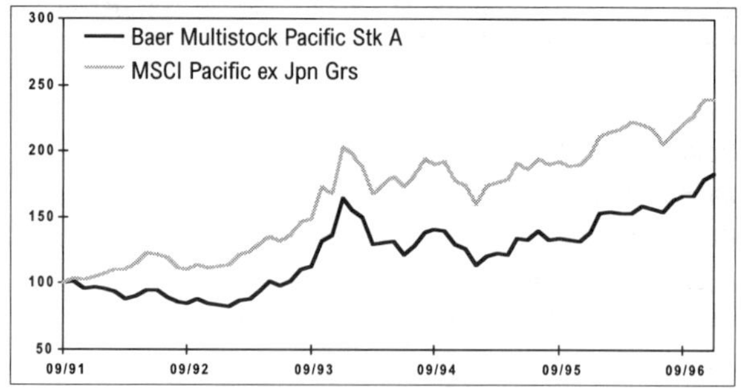

Top holdings:

Cheung Kong Holdings Ltd	4.8%
Ekran BHD	3.5%
Henderson Land Development	4.0%
Hutchison Whampoa	3.3%
New World Development	6.3%
NG Fung Hong Ltd	4.1%
PWE Industries BHD	4.1%
Rashid Hussain Berhad	3.5%

TOTAL RETURNS %

3 months 1997	1996	1995	1994	3 years	5 years
-1.30	31.97	9.94	-23.38	11.15	88.31

STATISTICS

Assets ($mil)	Current yield	Volatility	Risk return	Micropal Star Rating
212.25	—	5.18	—	✪✪✪✪✪

Julius Baer Multistock US Stock A /B

350/350

Investment objective:
The primary objective of this Julius Baer sub-fund is to achieve long-term capital growth by investing in carefully selected dividend-bearing securities issued by companies in the US and up to a maximum of one third of the funds assets in Canada.The top sector allocations of the portfolio include: pharmaceuticals (18.0%); electronics (15.0%); and finance (11.0%).

Umbrella fund: Julius Baer Multistock SICAV

Launch date: 01/07/90 **Domicile:** Luxembourg [UCITS]

Currency: USD **Structure:** Open ended, SICAV

Portfolio manager: Fayez Sarofim International Management Company Manager of Baer Multistock US Stock A; located in Houston, USA.

Purchase: Financial Advisor, Call 41-1-287-5319 for most suitable bank connection

Minimum investment: 5,000 CHF

Custodian: Banque Generale du Luxembourg S.A

Listed: None **Dealings:** Daily

Fund Sedol I.D.: 301202 **Published:** FT/IHT/SC

Fees **Annual fee:** 1.50% **Performance fee:** None
Front end load: Up to 5.00 % **Redemption fee:** None
Switching fee: Up to 1.00%

Julius Baer Investment Fund Services
50 Boulevard J.F.Kennedy, L-2951 Luxembourg
Tel 352-42-42-27-72 Fax 352-42-42-20-92
http://www. juliusbaer.com

Contact: Customer Services Department

Performance:

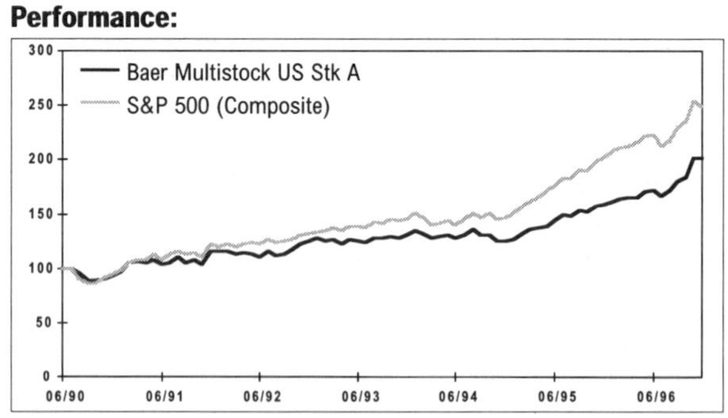

Top holdings:

Coca-Cola Co.	5.2%
General Electric Co.	3.9%
Intel Corp.	4.0%
Johnson & Johnson	3.1%
Merck & Co. Inc.	3.7%
Pfizer Inc.	2.8%
Philip Morris Cos. Inc.	5.2%
Procter & Gamble Co.	3.0%

TOTAL RETURNS %

3 months 1997	1996	1995	1994	3 years	5 years
4.54	26.90	26.36	-3.36	54.97	74.57

STATISTICS

Assets ($mil)	Current yield	Volatility	Risk return	Micropal Star Rating
52.15	—	2.81	3	✪✪

Jupiter Tyndall GF British Lion
43/350

Jupiter Tyndall (Luxembourg) S.A.
Knightsbridge House, 195-197 Knightsbridge, London SW7 1RB, United Kingdom
Tel 44-171-412-0703 Fax 44-171-412-7719

Contact: Alexander Odd

Investment objective:
This sub-fund seeks capital growth through investment primarily in ordinary shares of companies quoted on the London Stock Exchange. These companies are undervalued and exhibit superior profits growth arising from committed management, quality products or services, high barriers to entry and exceptionally strong free cash flow.

Umbrella fund: Jupiter Tyndall Global Funds SICAV

Launch date: 30/11/90 **Domicile:** Luxembourg [UCITS]

Currency: GBP **Structure:** Open ended, SICAV

Portfolio manager: Alan Miller
Manager of the sub-fund and Director of Jupiter Asset Mgt Ltd; previously with Hermes Investment Mgt Ltd- London, managed part of the UK equity portfolio and Gartmore, managing UK equity portfolios; accountant; joined Jupiter in 1994.

Purchase: Direct

Minimum investment: 2,500 GBP

Custodian: Bank of Bermuda (Luxembourg) S.A

Listed: Luxembourg **Dealings:** Daily

Fund Sedol I.D.: 490879 **Published:** FT/SC/HKEJ

Fees **Annual fee:** 1.25% **Performance fee:** 15.00%
Front end load: 5.00% **Redemption fee:** None
Switching fee: 1.00%

Performance:

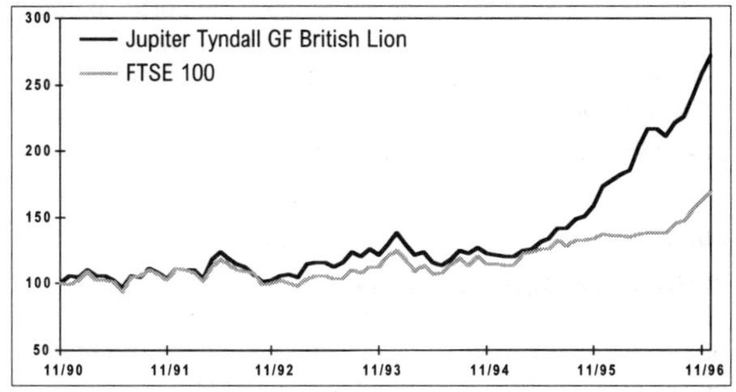

Top holdings:

Carlton Comm	2.3%
Caspian Group	4.9%
Colleagues G	3.1%
Exeter Inv.	2.3%
Glaxo Wellcome	3.4%
Jarvis	2.2%
Mentmore Abbey	2.2%
Pace Mico Tech	2.0%
Store House	2.2%
Tottenham Hotspur	2.2%

TOTAL RETURNS %

3 months 1997	1996	1995	1994	3 years	5 years
3.28	57.15	42.17	-6.47	108.96	143.63

STATISTICS

Assets ($mil)	Current yield	Volatility	Risk return	Micropal Star Rating
22.87	—	4.06	5	✪✪✪✪✪

Jupiter Tyndall GF China
76/350

Jupiter Tyndall (Luxembourg) S.A.
Knightsbridge House, 195-197 Knightsbridge, London SW7 1RB, United Kingdom
Tel 44-171-412-0703 Fax 44-171-412-7719

Contact: Alexander Odd

Investment objective:
The fund seeks capital growth through investments in the publicly listed shares available to foreigners. The assets of the portfolio are divided between Hong Kong (52.9%); China (40.9%); Taiwan (5.3%); and US (0.08%). The top sector allocations for the portfolio are as follows: industrial cyclical (38.2); services (11.2%); and consumer goods (8.8%).

Umbrella fund: Jupiter Tyndall Global Funds SICAV

Launch date: 01/05/92 **Domicile:** Luxembourg [UCITS]

Currency: USD **Structure:** Open ended, SICAV

Portfolio manager: Peter Adderson
Manager of the fund and Director of Jupiter Intl Grp Plc and MD of Jupiter Asset Mgt (Asia) Ltd based in Hong Kong; joined Jupiter in 1994; specialises in Asian stock markets; over 20 years experience in investment management.

Purchase: Direct

Minimum investment: 2,500 GBP

Custodian: Bank of Bermuda (Luxembourg) S.A

Listed: Luxembourg **Dealings:** Daily

Fund Sedol I.D.: 490863 **Published:** FT/SC/HKEJ

Fees **Annual fee:** 1.75% **Performance fee:** 15.00%
Front end load: 5.00% **Redemption fee:** None
Switching fee: 1.00%

Performance:

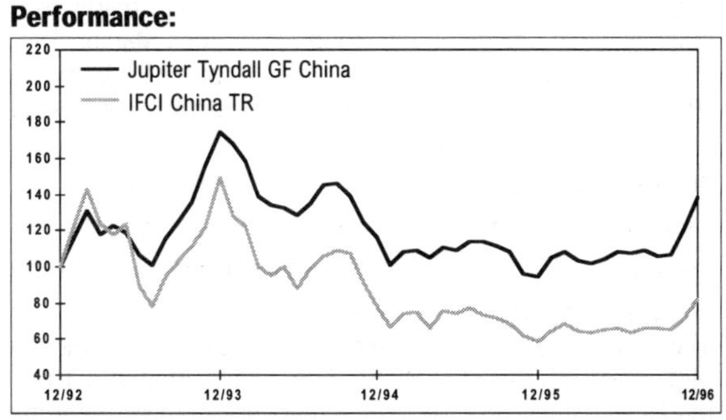

Top holdings:

Citic Pacific	3.7%
Guandong Kelcon	2.9%
Hutchison Land	4.2%
Ka Wah Bank	4.4%
Marn Shan	3.5%
Shang Che	3.3%
Shang Dong Huan	2.8%
Shanghai T&R	2.9%
Taiwan Investment	4.8%
Tsang Kuen Ent	3.8%

TOTAL RETURNS %

3 months 1997	1996	1995	1994	3 years	5 years
13.61	46.39	-19.17	-33.15	-20.89	N.A.

STATISTICS

Assets ($mil)	Current yield	Volatility	Risk return	Micropal Star Rating
4.19	—	6.45	—	✪✪

Jupiter Tyndall GF Europe Smaller Cos
79/350

Jupiter Tyndall (Luxembourg) S.A.
Knightsbridge House, 195-197 Knightsbridge, London SW7 1RB, United Kingdom
Tel 44-171-412-0703 Fax 44-171-412-7719

Contact: Alexander Odd

Investment objective:
The fund seeks to achieve capital growth investment in European smaller companies listed on their relevant stock exchanges. The portfolio country allocations are: France (21.6%); Austria (13.6%); Italy (12.9%); Norway (6.7%); and Switzerland (4.2%). The top sector allocations include the following: trade and service (33.7%); and industrial cyclical (10.4%).

Umbrella fund: Jupiter Tyndall Global Funds SICAV

Launch date: 07/12/93 **Domicile:** Luxembourg [UCITS]

Currency: GBP **Structure:** Open ended, SICAV

Portfolio manager: Richard Pease
Manager of the fund and Jupiter European Invest Trust; previously at the Central Board of Finance-Church of England and Windsor Investment Mgt to run the European Unit Trust; joined Jupiter in 1990 to set up and run the European dept.

Purchase: Direct

Minimum investment: 2,500 GBP

Custodian: Bank of Bermuda (Luxembourg) S.A.

Listed: Luxembourg **Dealings:** Daily

Fund Sedol I.D.: 448092 **Published:** FT/SC/HKEJ

Fees **Annual fee:** 1.50% **Performance fee:** 15.00%
Front end load: 5.00% **Redemption fee:** None
Switching fee: 1.00%

Performance:

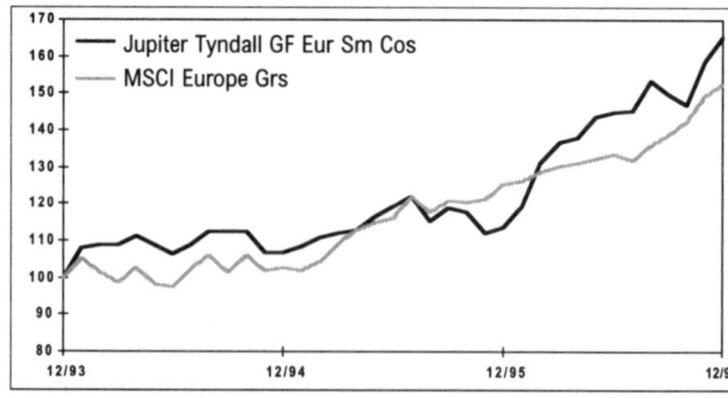

Top holdings:

Holding	%
Cie Euro P Telese	3.0%
Cipe	3.7%
Fokus Bank	3.8%
Maffai Spa	2.8%
Near Medic	12.7%
Shes Getters	3.1%
Siunit	5.1%
Spir Commonicat	2.9%
Tybring Gjedde	3.7%
Verwalt Private Bk	3.4%

TOTAL RETURNS %

3 months 1997	1996	1995	1994	3 years	5 years
-4.67	45.08	6.52	6.72	64.93	N.A.

STATISTICS

Assets ($mil)	Current yield	Volatility	Risk return	Micropal Star Rating
16.05	—	3.44	4	✪✪✪✪

Jupiter Tyndall GF Hong Kong
173/350

Jupiter Tyndall (Luxembourg) S.A.
Knightsbridge House, 195-197 Knightsbridge, London SW7 1RB, United Kingdom
Tel 44-171-412-0703 Fax 44-171-412-7719

Contact: Alexander Odd

Investment objective:
The sub-fund seeks to achieve capital growth primarily through investment in publicly listed shares on the Hong Kong Stock Market. The assets of the portfolio are divided between Hong Kong (90.4%); China (3.5%); and Vietnam (4.2). The top sector allocations of the portfolio are as follows: real estate (28.9%); finance (28.2%); and industrial cyclical (18.0%).

Umbrella fund: Jupiter Tyndall Global Funds SICAV

Launch date: 18/07/94 **Domicile:** Luxembourg [UCITS]

Currency: USD **Structure:** Open ended, SICAV

Portfolio manager: Peter Adderson
Manager of the fund and Director of Jupiter Intl Grp Plc and MD of Jupiter Asset Mgt (Asia) Ltd based in Hong Kong; joined Jupiter in 1994; specialises in the stock markets of Asia; over 20 years experience in investment management.

Purchase: Direct

Minimum investment: 2,500 GBP

Custodian: Bank of Bermuda (Luxembourg) S.A.

Listed: Luxembourg **Dealings:** Daily

Fund Sedol I.D.: 454420 **Published:** FT/SC/HKEJ

Fees **Annual fee:** 1.75% **Performance fee:** 15.00%
Front end load: 5.00% **Redemption fee:** None
Switching fee: 1.00%

Performance:

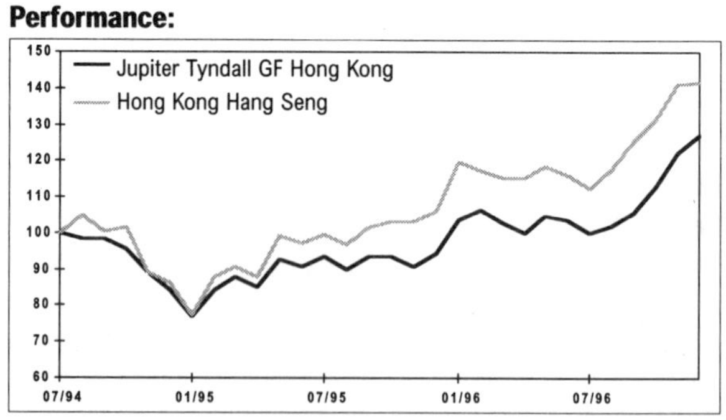

Top holdings:

Holding	%
Beta Mekong	4.2%
Cheung Kong	3.4%
China Resources	3.5%
Citic Pacific	4.3%
Hang Seng Bank	4.6%
Henderson Land Development	3.8%
HSBC Holdings	8.1%
Hutchison Whampoa	9.1%
New World Development	5.1%
Sun Hung Kai Properties	9.5%

TOTAL RETURNS %

3 months 1997	1996	1995	1994	3 years	5 years
-1.46	34.31	12.09	N.A.	N.A.	N.A.

STATISTICS

Assets ($mil)	Current yield	Volatility	Risk return	Micropal Star Rating
0.78	—	N.A.	—	———

Jupiter Tyndall GF UK Smaller Cos
73/350

Jupiter Tyndall (Luxembourg) S.A.
Knightsbridge House, 195-197 Knightsbridge, London SW7 1RB, United Kingdom
Tel 44-171-412-0703 Fax 44-171-412-7719

Investment objective:
The sub-fund aims to achieve capital growth through investment primarily in UK Smaller Companies listed on the London Stock Exchange. The top sector allocations of the portfolio include the following: industrial cyclical (23.5%); energy (17.9); services (15.1%); finance (9.5%); and retail trade (8.1%).

Umbrella fund: Jupiter Tyndall Global Funds SICAV
Launch date: 01/06/93 **Domicile:** Luxembourg [UCITS]
Currency: GBP **Structure:** Open ended, SICAV
Portfolio manager: Edward Bonham Carter
Manager of the fund and Dir of Jupiter Asset Mgt; previously with Schroder Invest Mgt, analysing UK and US equities and Electra Invest as a Portfolio Mgr; joined Jupiter to manage high performance funds; started his career in the early 1980's.
Purchase: Direct
Minimum investment: 2,500 GBP
Custodian: Bank of Bermuda (Luxembourg) S.A.
Listed: Luxembourg **Dealings:** Daily
Fund Sedol I.D.: 451818 **Published:** FT/SC/HKEJ
Fees **Annual fee:** 1.50% **Performance fee:** 15.00%
Front end load: 5.00% **Redemption fee:** None
Switching fee: 1.00%

Contact: Alexander Odd
Performance:

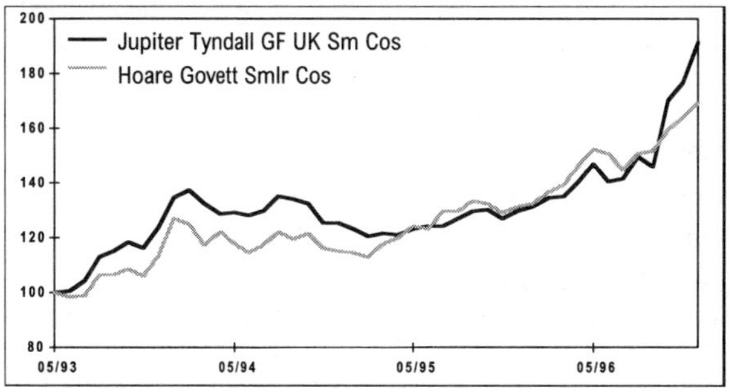

Top holdings:

Holding	%
Brit Tech	2.5%
Car Group	3.3%
Dawson Holdings	2.6%
Games Work Shop	3.1%
Great West Res	8.2%
Independent Ins	3.4%
London Clubs Int	3.8%
Pictronic Comte	6.9%
Sage Group	2.7%
Vanguard Media	3.0%

TOTAL RETURNS %

3 months 1997	1996	1995	1994	3 years	5 years
4.34	47.23	3.78	1.11	54.50	N.A.

STATISTICS

Assets ($mil)	Current yield	Volatility	Risk return	Micropal Star Rating
8.88	—	4.01	3	✪✪✪

KB Lux Bond ITL B
317/350

Kredietbank Luxembourg
43 Boulevard Royal, L-2955 Luxembourg
Tel 352-47-97-22-72 Fax 352-47-97-45-60

Investment objective:
The sub-fund seeks growth by investing in transferable securities (mainly bonds issued by issuers of first quality); and denominated in Italian lira. The asset allocations of the portfolio are the following: cash/MM (8.4%); and bond (91.6%).

Umbrella fund: KBLux Bond Fund
Launch date: 28/03/88 **Domicile:** Luxembourg [UCITS]
Currency: ITL **Structure:** Open ended, SICAV
Portfolio manager: Lawrence Jodogne
Manager of KB Luxembourg Bond Italy B; commenced Portfolio Manager in 1989.

Purchase: Direct
Minimum investment: 1 Share
Custodian: Kredietbank Luxembourg
Listed: Luxembourg **Dealings:** Daily
Fund Sedol I.D.: 304411 **Published:** LW/LE/FE
Fees **Annual fee:** 0.30% **Performance fee:** None
Front end load: 6.00% **Redemption fee:** None
Switching fee: None

Contact: A Eren
Performance:

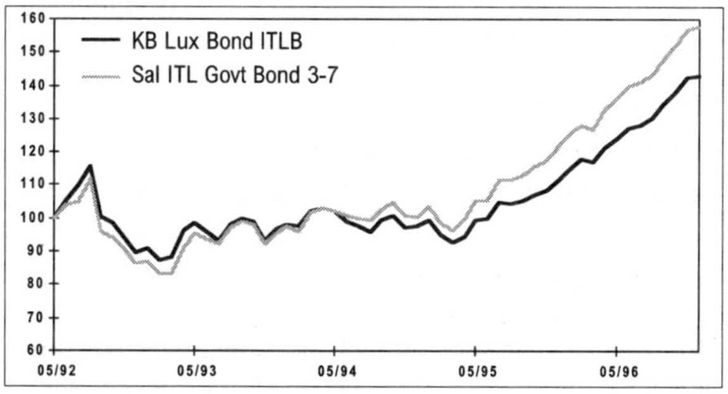

Top holdings:

Holding	%
EIB 10.875 % 95/05	9.3%
EIB 7.55 % 96/01	6.9%
Eurofima 10.75% 93/03	6.5%
Helaba 8.75% 96/99	5.0%
HYPO FIN 9.1% 96/99	10.0%
IADB 7.7% 94/4	14.7%
KFW 7.625% 96/02	4.4%
LBK Hessen 0% 93/03	4.5%
Rabobank 7.70% 94/04	5.4%
SEK 12.0% 93/98	10.1%

TOTAL RETURNS %

3 months 1997	1996	1995	1994	3 years	5 years
-9.66	27.96	14.62	1.00	48.15	N.A.

STATISTICS

Assets ($mil)	Current yield	Volatility	Risk return	Micropal Star Rating
12.45	—	2.33	3	✪✪✪

KB Lux Key Far East
273/350

Kredietbank Luxembourg
43 Boulevard Royal, L-2955 Luxembourg
Tel 352-47-97-22-72 Fax 352-47-97-45-60

Investment objective:
The sub-fund seeks capital growth through investment mainly in Far East equities. The top holding of this portfolio is GT Newly Industrialised Countries Fund. This sub-fund currently allocates 98.2% of the sub-fund's assets to the finance sector.

Contact: A Eren

Performance:

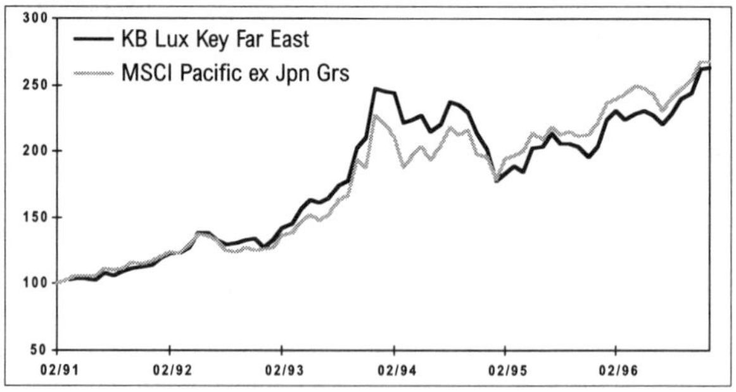

Top holdings: GT Newly Ind. Countries Fund 98.2%

Umbrella fund: KBLux Key Fund

Launch date: 23/09/94 **Domicile:** Luxembourg

Currency: USD **Structure:** Open ended, FCP

Portfolio manager: Jean Luc Neyens
Manager of the fund; commenced his career as Portfolio Manager in 1995; specialising in the fund of fund structure and in the selection of individual stocks; graduate, marketing- IESN, Nomura; joined Credit Bank Trust 10 years ago.

Purchase: Direct

Minimum investment: 1Share

Custodian: Kredietbank Luxembourg

Listed: None **Dealings:** Daily

Fund Sedol I.D.: 304430 **Published:** LW

Fees **Annual fee:** 0.25% **Performance fee:** None
Front end load: 2.25% **Redemption fee:** None
Switching fee: 0.50%

TOTAL RETURNS %

3 months 1997	1996	1995	1994	3 years	5 years
0.10	29.41	0.80	-18.27	6.61	132.21

STATISTICS

Assets ($mil)	Current yield	Volatility	Risk return	Micropal Star Rating
57.49	—	4.77	—	✪✪✪✪

Key BCM Emerging Value Inc.
37/350

Bennett Capital Management
Block 1 Harcourt Centre, Harcourt Street, Dublin 2, Ireland
Tel 353-1-707-5000 Fax 353-1-475-7756

Investment objective:
The sub-fund seeks to achieve strong capital appreciation by investing in the emerging markets of Europe, the Middle East and Africa. The investment Manager implements a bottom-up strategy and invests primarily in medium sized listed companies. Stocks are selected following an in depth fundamental research and frequent company visits.

Contact: Susan Byrne

Performance:

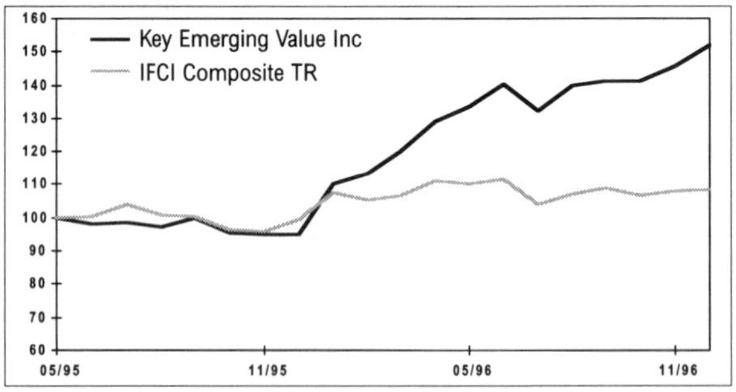

Top holdings:

Czech & Slovak	7.0%
Egypt	8.0%
Hungary	8.0%
Israel	16.0%
Poland	13.0%
Russia	14.0%

Umbrella fund: This is a singular fund.

Launch date: 15/05/95 **Domicile:** British Virgin Islands

Currency: USD **Structure:** Open ended, Investment Company

Portfolio manager: Peter M Bennett
Manager of Key BCM Emerging Value Inc commenced May 1995; formerly with Morgan Stanley Asset Management (London); responsible for investing US dollars in emerging markets of Europe, the Middle East and Africa.

Purchase: From Administrator

Minimum investment: 500,000 USD

Custodian: Northern Trust

Listed: Dublin **Dealings:** Monthly

Fund Sedol I.D.: 49086 **Published:** IHT

Fees **Annual fee:** 2.00% **Performance fee:** 20.00%
Front end load: None **Redemption fee:** None
Switching fee: None

TOTAL RETURNS %

3 months 1997	1996	1995	1994	3 years	5 years
21.97	60.33	N.A.	N.A.	N.A.	N.A.

STATISTICS

Assets ($mil)	Current yield	Volatility	Risk return	Micropal Star Rating
45.00	—	N.A.	—	———

Latin America Income & Appreciation Fund NV

82/350

Scudder Stevens & Clark
8th Floor New London House, 6 London Street, London EC3R 7BE, United Kingdom
Tel 44-171-265-0077 Fax 44-171-265-0099
http://www. ny.scudder.com/ E mail jenny.brundit@scudder.com
Contact: David McConnell and Jenny Brundit

Investment objective:
The fund seeks long-term capital appreciation and high interest income through investment in Latin American equity and debt makets. The top sector allocations of the portfolio are the following: communications (26.5%); utilities (23.2%); finance (20.5%); and steel (8.1%). The primary country allocation of the fund is Brazil (83.9%).

Umbrella fund: This is a singular fund.

Launch date: 02/12/91 **Domicile:** Netherlands Antilles

Currency: USD **Structure:** Open ended, Investment Company

Portfolio manager: Isabel Saltzman
Manager/Product Leader, principal Senior Portfolio Manager of the Emerging Markets/High Yield Bond Group; MIA, School of International Affairs- Columbia U; previously with JP Morgan; 17 years experience in the finance industry.

Purchase: Financial Advisor

Minimum investment: 5,000 USD

Custodian: State Street Bank Curacao

Listed: Dublin **Dealings:** Daily

Fund Sedol I.D.: 278231 **Published:** FT/IHT/SC

Fees **Annual fee:** 1.00% **Performance fee:** None
Front end load: Up to 5.50% **Redemption fee:** None
Switching fee: None

Performance:

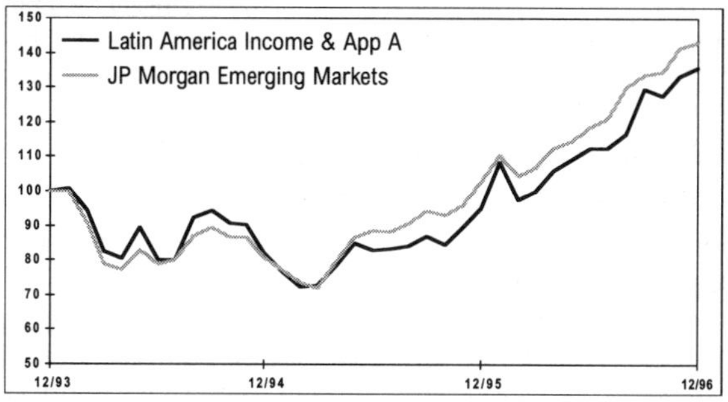

Top holdings:

Argentina FRB	n/s
Argentina PAR	n/s
Brazil C	n/s
Brazil Discount	n/s
Brazil EI	n/s
Chilean Peso Time Deposit	n/s
Mexico Discount	n/s
Mexico Par	n/s
Panama IRB	n/s
Venezeula DCB	n/s

TOTAL RETURNS %

3 months 1997	1996	1995	1994	3 years	5 years
6.92	42.99	15.63	-17.79	35.92	94.90

STATISTICS

Assets ($mil)	Current yield	Volatility	Risk return	Micropal Star Rating
13.96	11.68	6.79	2	✪✪✪

Latinvest Fund Limited

103/350

Globavest Management Co
4 The Cherries, Grange Wood, Rathfarnham, Dublin 16, Ireland
Tel 353-1-493-6282 Fax 353-1-493-6301
Contact: John Lowry

Investment objective:
The fund seeks long-term capital appreciation and high interest income through investment in Latin American equity and debt markets. The top sector allocations of the portfolio are the following: communications (26.5%); utilities (23.2%); finance (20.5); and steel (8.1%). The primary country allocation of the fund is Brazil (83.9%).

Umbrella fund: This is a singular fund.

Launch date: 01/10/91 **Domicile:** Bahamas

Currency: USD **Structure:** Open ended, Investment Company

Portfolio manager: Peter Gruber
Manager of Latinvest, commenced January 1994 and President of Latinvest Management Co and Globalvest Mgt Co; specialises in Latin American securities and emerging markets; more than 20 years experience in the securities industry.

Purchase: Direct, Financial Advisor

Minimum investment: 250,000 USD

Custodian: Citibank

Listed: None **Dealings:** Monthly

Fund Sedol I.D.: 305567 **Published:** FT

Fees **Annual fee:** 1.00% **Performance fee:** 20.00%
Front end load: 3.50% **Redemption fee:** None
Switching fee: None

Performance:

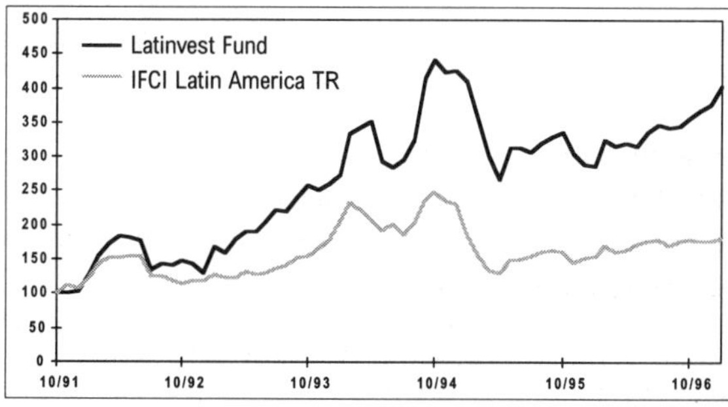

Top holdings:

Banco Real	3.2%
Bradesco	3.3%
Electricidad	2.6%
Electrobas PNB	9.7%
Electrobras ON	9.2%
Gerdau PN	2.1%
Itaubanco-PN	3.6%
Petrobras-PN	4.6%
Telebras ON	11.9%
Telebras PN	10.7%

TOTAL RETURNS %

3 months 1997	1996	1995	1994	3 years	5 years
4.97	40.72	-30.25	50.82	61.36	47.74

STATISTICS

Assets ($mil)	Current yield	Volatility	Risk return	Micropal Star Rating
214.10	—	8.78	4	✪✪✪✪✪

Lazard Pan European Fund

233/350

Lazard Brothers Investment Funds plc.
20/22 Lower Hatch Street, Dublin2, Ireland
Tel 353-1-790-5068 Fax 353-1-790-5010

Investment objective:
The fund seeks long-term capital growth by investing in a portfolio of continental European and UK equities. The fund aims at closely matching the capital performance of the FT/S&P World Europe ex UK Index. The top sector of the portfolio is consumer goods (47.6%). Assets of Lazard Greater Europe Fund were merged into this fund at the end of June, 1996.

Umbrella fund: Lazard Brothers Global Equity Fund Plc

Launch date: 21/01/92 **Domicile:** Ireland [UCITS]

Currency: DEM **Structure:** Open ended, Investment Company

Portfolio manager: Dino Fuschillo
Advisor;BEng Hons, French- Bath U; specialises in research and security analysis of Germany, Switzerland, Italy, Spain and Belgium; previously with Hill Samuel, as European Fund Mgr; joined Lazard in 1989; 18 years investment experience.

Purchase: Direct

Minimum investment: 2,000 DEM

Custodian: BT Trustee Company (Ireland) Limited

Listed: Dublin **Dealings:** Daily

Fund Sedol I.D.: 50954 **Published:** FT

Fees **Annual fee:** 1.50% **Performance fee:** None
Front end load: Up to 7.00% **Redemption fee:** 2.00%
Switching fee: Up to 1.00%

Contact: Customer Services Department

Performance:

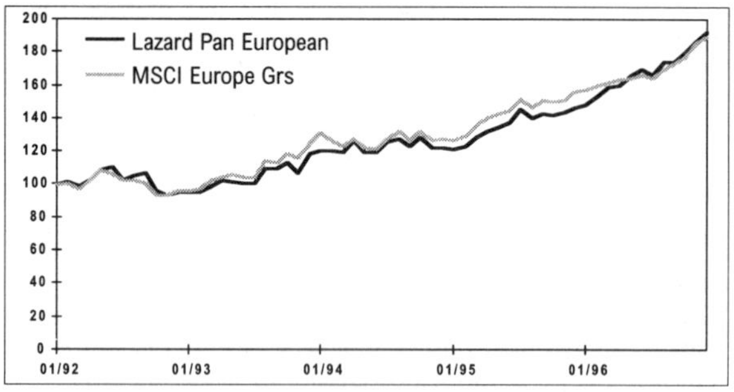

Top holdings:

Holding	%
Barclays PLC	2.0%
British Telecom	1.8%
Generales des Eaux	1.8%
Novartis	1.9%
Sanofi	2.0%
Shell	2.0%
Telecom Italia	1.9%
Unilever	1.7%
Viag	1.8%
VNU	1.9%

TOTAL RETURNS %

3 months 1997	1996	1995	1994	3 years	5 years
2.54	30.95	20.15	2.79	61.72	N.A.

STATISTICS

Assets ($mil)	Current yield	Volatility	Risk return	Micropal Star Rating
9.60	—	2.86	4	✪✪✪✪✪

Lazard SIT UK Active

129/350

Lazard Fund Managers (CI) Ltd
Sarnia House, Le Truchot, St Peter Port, GY1 4EN, Guernsey
Tel 44-1481-724-983 Fax 44-1481-727-344

Investment objective:
The fund seeks to invest in UK equities with above average yield and to achieve capital growth. The fund is actively managed and the overall long-term performance objective is to exceed the returns of the FT-Actuaries All Share Index. The asset allocations of the portfolio are the following: equities (99.4%); and cash/MM (0.6%).

Umbrella fund: This is a singular fund.

Launch date: 13/02/89 **Domicile:** Guernsey

Currency: GBP **Structure:** Open ended, Investment Company

Portfolio manager: Tim Russell
Advisor to the fund and Director in charge of UK equities; PPE degree- Oxford U; previously with UBS Philips & Drew and Merrill Lynch; joined Lazard in 1992; 16 years investment experience.

Purchase: Direct, Financial Advisor

Minimum investment: 5,000 USD

Custodian: Lloyds Bank International (Guernsey) Ltd

Listed: London **Dealings:** Weekly

Fund Sedol I.D.: 50913 **Published:** FT

Fees **Annual fee:** 1.50% **Performance fee:** None
Front end load: 5.00% **Redemption fee:** None
Switching fee: Up to 1.00%

Contact: Charlotte Musgrove

Performance:

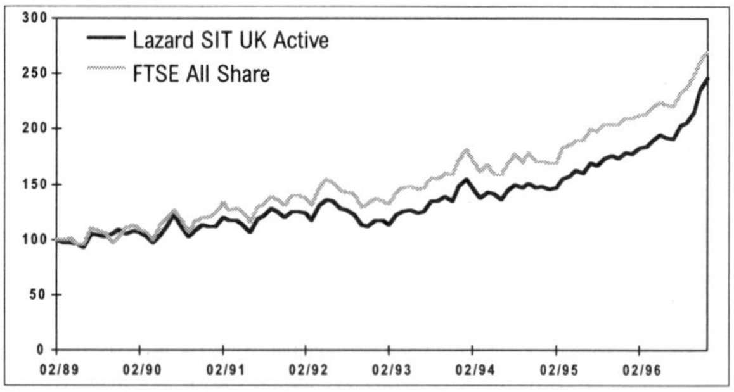

Top holdings:

Holding	%
Abbey National	2.6%
Barclays PLC	2.5%
BAT Industries	3.1%
British Telecom	2.8%
BTR	2.5%
Glaxo Wellcome	3.4%
HSBC Holdings	2.6%
Lazard UK Smaller Companies	4.6%
Lloyds TSB Group	4.2%
Shell Transport & Trading	4.9%

TOTAL RETURNS %

3 months 1997	1996	1995	1994	3 years	5 years
3.41	37.93	21.10	-0.81	65.69	97.68

STATISTICS

Assets ($mil)	Current yield	Volatility	Risk return	Micropal Star Rating
65.38	2.76	3.38	4	✪✪✪✪

Lazard SIT UK Index

190/350

Lazard Fund Managers (CI) Ltd
Sarnia House, Le Truchot, St Peter Port, GY1 4EN, Guernsey
Tel 44-1481-724-983 Fax 44-1481-727-344

Investment objective:
The fund seeks to match closely the capital performance of the FT Actuaries All Share Index. The fund is currently invested in 200 companies represented in the Index and the anticipated tracking error is of the order of 1%.

Umbrella fund: This is a singular fund.
Launch date: 13/02/89 **Domicile:** Guernsey
Currency: GBP **Structure:** Open ended, Investment Company
Portfolio manager: Guy Dunham
Advisor to the fund; MA, mathematics- Cambridge U; previously with Towers Perrin as an actuarial pension consultant; joined Lazard in 1992; specialises in quantitative analysis and derivative strategies; 5 years investment experience.
Purchase: Direct, Financial Advisor
Minimum investment: 10,000 GBP
Custodian: Lloyds Bank International (Guernsey) Ltd
Listed: London **Dealings:** Weekly
Fund Sedol I.D.: 50915 **Published:** FT
Fees **Annual fee:** 1.50% **Performance fee:** None
Front end load: 5.00% **Redemption fee:** None
Switching fee: Up to 1.00%

Contact: Charlotte Musgrove

Performance:

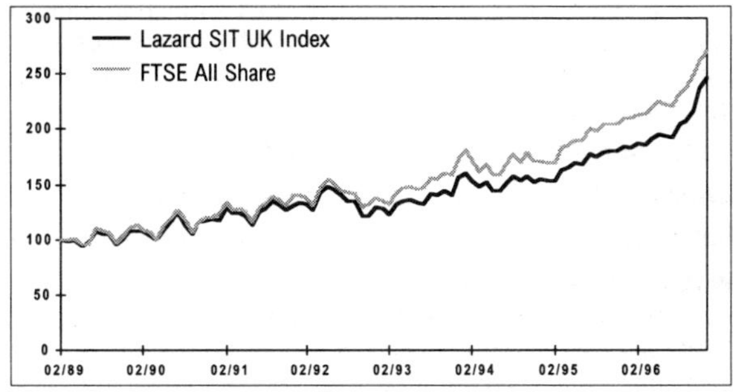

Top holdings:

Barclays PLC	1.9%
British Petroleum	4.1%
British Telecom	2.9%
Glaxo Wellcome	3.6%
HSBC Holdings	2.3%
Lloyds TSB Group	2.2%
Marks & Spencers	1.6%
Shell Transport & Trading	3.5%
Smithkline Beecham	1.9%
Zeneca Group	1.7%

TOTAL RETURNS %

3 months 1997	1996	1995	1994	3 years	5 years
0.77	33.29	19.79	-1.26	57.65	89.48

STATISTICS

Assets ($mil)	Current yield	Volatility	Risk return	Micropal Star Rating
65.45	3.05	3.18	4	✪✪✪✪

Lazard SIT US Index

169/350

Lazard Fund Managers (CI) Ltd
Sarnia House, Le Truchot, St Peter Port, GY1 4EN, Guernsey
Tel 44-1481-724-983 Fax 44-1481-727-344

Investment objective:
The sub-fund seeks to closely match the S & P Composite Index, which consists of stocks in 500 companies. The fund is currently invested in 170 companies represented in the Index and the anticipated tracking error is in the order of 1%. The fund is denominated in UK sterling.

Umbrella fund: This is a singular fund.
Launch date: 13/02/89 **Domicile:** Guernsey
Currency: GBP **Structure:** Open ended, Investment Company
Portfolio manager: Guy Dunham
Advisor to the fund; MA, mathematics- Cambridge U; previously with Towers Perrin as an actuarial pension consultant; joined Lazard in 1992; specialises in quantitative analysis and derivative strategies; 5 years investment experience.
Purchase: Direct, Financial Advisor
Minimum investment: 10,000 GBP
Custodian: Lloyds Bank International (Guernsey) Ltd
Listed: London **Dealings:** Weekly
Fund Sedol I.D.: 50917 **Published:** FT
Fees **Annual fee:** 1.50% **Performance fee:** None
Front end load: 5.00% **Redemption fee:** None
Switching fee: Up to 1.00%

Contact: Charlotte Musgrove

Performance:

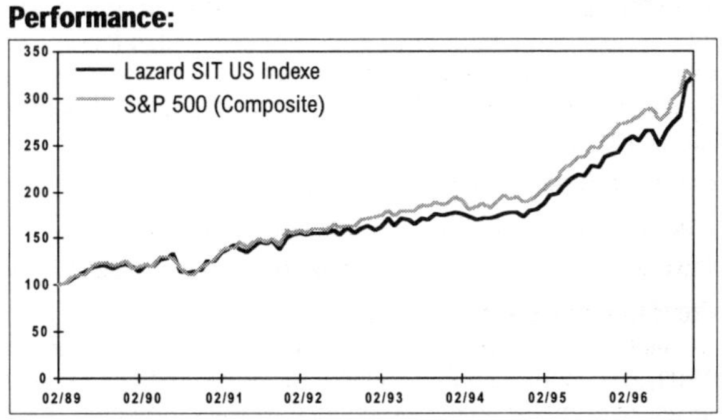

Top holdings:

AT&T	1.3%
Coca-Cola Co.	2.0%
Exxon Corp	1.9%
General Electric Co.	2.1%
IBM	1.7%
Intel Corp.	2.1%
Merck & Co. Inc.	1.7%
Microsoft	1.8%
Philip Morris	1.6%
Royal Dutch Petroleum	2.4%

TOTAL RETURNS %

3 months 1997	1996	1995	1994	3 years	5 years
3.03	34.79	33.95	1.80	83.80	114.88

STATISTICS

Assets ($mil)	Current yield	Volatility	Risk return	Micropal Star Rating
8.58	1.00	3.05	5	✪✪✪✪

LFM Emerg Mkt Cap Fd DEM Cap/Dist
157/350

Baring Asset Management/ING Investment Management
224 Route D'Arlon, Strassen, L-8010 Luxembourg
Tel 352-316-61-11 Fax 352-31-84-33
http://www. ingbank.com
E mail 100664.3026@compuserve.com
Contact: Mrs Ria Claes/ Anne Molitor

Investment objective:
The sub-fund denominated in German marks seeks to invest almost exclusively in interest-bearing instruments and securities which include fixed rate bonds, floating rate bonds, cum warrant bonds, convertible bonds, bonds resulting from restructured syndicated loans (ie.Brady bonds); and subordinated bonds issued by issuers domiciled in emerging countries.

Umbrella fund: LFM Emerging Markets Capital Fund
Launch date: 12/02/93 **Domicile:** Luxembourg
Currency: DEM **Structure:** Open ended, SICAV
Portfolio manager: Simon Romyn
Manager of LFM Emerging Market Capital Fund USD Cap commenced December 1991; BSc Hons, Dip Acc- Fellow Securities Institute of Australia; 15 years investment management experience; 6 years emerging markets debt experience.
Purchase: Financial Advisor
Minimum investment: 5,000 DEM
Custodian: ING Bank (Luxembourg) S.A
Listed: Luxembourg **Dealings:** Weekly
Fund Sedol I.D.: 301635 **Published:** FD/EB/FE
Fees **Annual fee:** 1.25% **Performance fee:** 10.00%
Front end load: 2.50% **Redemption fee:** None
Switching fee: None

Performance:

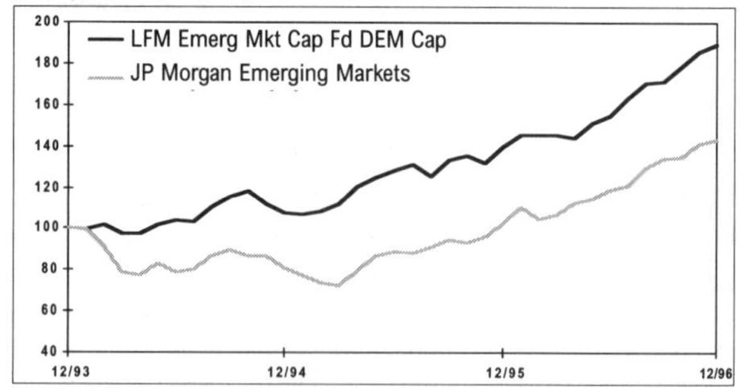

Top holdings:

Holding	%
Algeria Repro A/1	4.6%
Argentina Discounts	6.0%
Argentina PAR	5.3%
Brazil C Bond 2014	19.1%
Ecuador PDI	4.8%
Ivory Coast Loans	5.0%
Mexico 11% 2016	9.2%
Morocco A Loans	3.4%
Russia Loan - Other	13.2%
Russia Min Finance IV	4.9%

TOTAL RETURNS %

3 months 1997	1996	1995	1994	3 years	5 years
-1.53	35.72	30.13	7.29	89.49	N.A.

STATISTICS

Assets ($mil)	Current yield	Volatility	Risk return	Micropal Star Rating
57.16	—	3.23	4	✪✪✪✪

LFM Emerg Mkt Cap Fd USD Cap
46/350

Baring Asset Management/ING Investment Management
224 Route D'Arlon, Strassen, L-8010 Luxembourg
Tel 352-316-61-11 Fax 352-31-84-33
http://www. ingbank.com
E mail 100664.3026@compuserve.com
Contact: Mrs Ria Claes/Anne Molitor

Investment objective:
The sub-fund denominated in US dollars seeks to invest almost exclusively in interest-bearing instruments and securities which include fixed rate bonds, floating rate bonds, cum warrant bonds, convertible bonds, bonds resulting from restructured syndicated loans (ie Brady bonds); and subordinated bonds issued by issuers domiciled in emerging countries.

Umbrella fund: LFM Emerging Markets Capital Fund
Launch date: 12/02/93 **Domicile:** Luxembourg
Currency: USD **Structure:** Open ended, SICAV
Portfolio manager: Simon Romyn
Manager of LFM Emerging Market Capital Fund USD Cap commenced December 1991; BSc Hons, Dip Acc- Fellow Securities Institute of Australia; 15 years investment management experience; 6 years emerging markets debt experience.
Purchase: Financial Advisor
Minimum investment: 5,000 USD
Custodian: ING Bank (Luxembourg) S.A
Listed: Luxembourg **Dealings:** Weekly
Fund Sedol I.D.: 301633 **Published:** FD/EB/FE
Fees **Annual fee:** 1.25% **Performance fee:** 10.00%
Front end load: 2.50% **Redemption fee:** None
Switching fee: None

Performance:

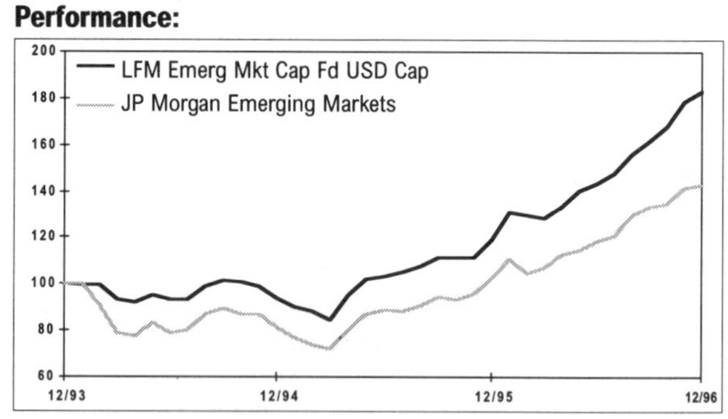

Top holdings:

Holding	%
Algeria Repro A/1	4.6%
Argentina Discounts	6.0%
Argentina PAR	5.3%
Brazil C Bond 2014	19.1%
Ecuador PDI	4.8%
Ivory Coast Loans	5.0%
Mexico 11% 2016	9.2%
Morocco A Loans	3.4%
Russia Loan - Other	13.2%
Russia Min Finance IV	4.9%

TOTAL RETURNS %

3 months 1997	1996	1995	1994	3 years	5 years
5.70	54.03	26.91	-6.38	82.99	N.A.

STATISTICS

Assets ($mil)	Current yield	Volatility	Risk return	Micropal Star Rating
36.72	—	4.07	3	✪✪✪✪✪

Lion Fortune CL Latin Am Equity Fund
228/350

Credit Lyonnais Paris
26A Boulevard Royal, L-2094 Luxembourg
Tel 352-47-68-31-1 Fax 352-47-68-31-440
http://www. creditlyonnais.lu

Contact: Olivier Gillot

Investment objective:
The main investment objective of the sub-fund is to offer to its shareholders the highest possible appreciation of the invested funds through investments in selected securities issued by Latin American corporations. Stocks are mostly diversified both geographically and by economic sectors. The top country allocation of the portfolio is Brazil (94.1%).

Umbrella fund: SICAV-Lion Fortune
Launch date: 21/02/94 **Domicile:** Luxembourg
Currency: USD **Structure:** Open ended, SICAV
Portfolio manager: Credit Lyonnais SA
Managers of Lion Fortune Credit Lyonnais Latin American Equity A; ; located at Paris 19, Boulevard de Italiens, F-750002, Paris, France.

Purchase: Direct
Minimum investment: 2,500 USD
Custodian: Credit Lyonnais Luxembourg SA
Listed: None **Dealings:** Weekly
Fund Sedol I.D.: 301962 **Published:** TK/RT
Fees **Annual fee:** 1.50% **Performance fee:** None
Front end load: Up to 5.00% **Redemption fee:** None
Switching fee: None

Performance:

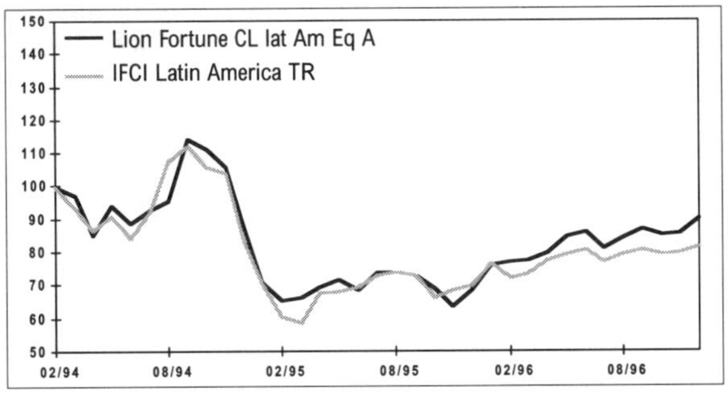

Top holdings:

Holding	%
ACT Electrobas Cent Ele	3.5%
ACT Telebras	4.1%
ADR Cemig	3.3%
ADR Telefonica de Argent-B	2.9%
ADR Telmex SP (20-L)	3.8%
ADR YPF SA SP-D	3.3%
PRV Banco Itau SA	62.3%
PRV CIA Vale d Rio Doce	3.5%
PRV Petrobas	4.2%
PRV Unibanco	2.7%

TOTAL RETURNS %

3 months 1997	1996	1995	1994	3 years	5 years
20.19	31.17	-22.50	N.A.	N.A.	N.A.

STATISTICS

Assets ($mil)	Current yield	Volatility	Risk return	Micropal Star Rating
26.39	—	N.A.	—	———

Lion Fortune Interaction Europe
300/350

Credit Lyonnais Paris
26A Boulevard Royal, L-2094 Luxembourg
Tel 352-47-68-31-1 Fax 352-47-68-31-440
http://www. creditlyonnais.lu

Contact: Olivier Gillot

Investment objective:
The fund seeks to maximise net asset value through selective investments mainly in the equities of European companies. The top country allocations of the portfolio are as follows: UK (29.2%); France (12.9%); Switzerland (7.6%); Germany (8.8%); Italy (4.7%); Sweden (4.6%); Spain (6.4%); Norway (3.6%); and Netherlands (8.7%).

Umbrella fund: SICAV-Lion Interaction
Launch date: 09/03/89 **Domicile:** Luxembourg
Currency: ECU **Structure:** Open ended, SICAV
Portfolio manager: Credit Lyonnais SA
Managers of Lion Interaction Europe; located at Paris 19, Boulevard de Italiens, F-750002, Paris, France.

Purchase: Direct
Minimum investment: 100 ECU
Custodian: Credit Lyonnais Luxembourg SA
Listed: Luxembourg **Dealings:** Weekly
Fund Sedol I.D.: 422757 **Published:** TK/RT
Fees **Annual fee:** 1.00% **Performance fee:** None
Front end load: 2..00% **Redemption fee:** 0.50%
Switching fee: None

Performance:

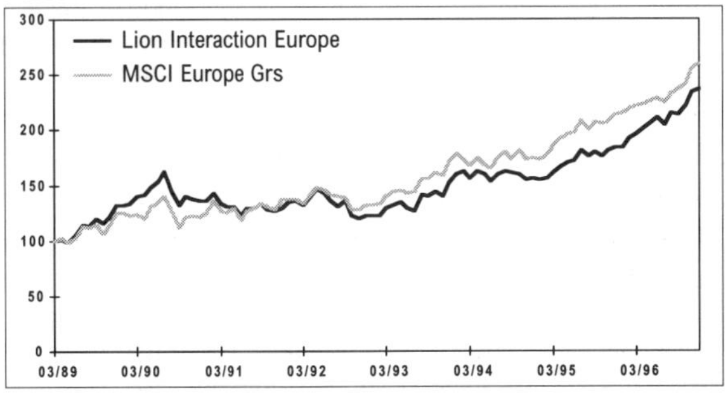

Top holdings:

Holding	%
Accor	1.6%
AGF	1.6%
Carrefour Supermarket	1.5%
Cetelem	1.4%
Compass	1.4%
Kon Ahold	1.4%
Novartis	1.4%
Saint-Gobain	1.4%
Storebrand	1.3%
Svenska Cellulosa -B	1.4%

TOTAL RETURNS %

3 months 1997	1996	1995	1994	3 years	5 years
5.90	28.30	18.03	2.75	55.59	83.22

STATISTICS

Assets ($mil)	Current yield	Volatility	Risk return	Micropal Star Rating
25.70	—	2.74	4	✪✪✪✪

Lippo Indonesian Growth
108/350

Lippo Investments
43 Floor Lippo Tower, Lippo Centre, 89 Queensway, Hong Kong
Tel 852-2867-6818 Fax 852-2596-0388
E mail lippo@hk.supernet

Investment objective:
The sub-fund seeks long-term capital growth from a diversified and actively managed portfolio of equity securities with primary focus on investment in companies whose equity securities are listed on an Indonesia Stock Exchange. The top sector allocations include the following: consumer goods (22.6%); industrial cyclical (18.9%); and utilities (12.4%).

Umbrella fund: Lippo Global Investment Funds

Launch date: 18/03/92 **Domicile:** Cayman Islands

Currency: USD **Structure:** Open ended, Unit Trust

Portfolio manager: Roland Haas
Manager of Lippo Indonesian Growth commenced January 1994; MBA- U San Francisco; previously with LGT Management as Regional Fund Manager; located in Jakarta, Indonesia.

Purchase: Direct, Financial Advisor, Standard Chartered Bank, Hong Kong Chinese Bank

Minimum investment: 2,000 USD

Custodian: Bermuda Trust (Far East) Limited

Listed: Jakarta **Dealings:** Weekly

Fund Sedol I.D.: 251921 **Published:** IHT/AW/RT/BG

Fees **Annual fee:** 2.00% **Performance fee:** None
Front end load: 5.00% **Redemption fee:** None
Switching fee: 1.00%

Contact: Mary Ann Chan/Terry Lok

Performance:

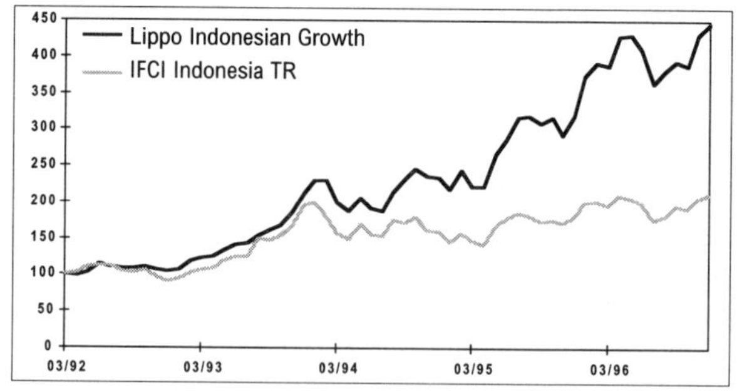

Top holdings:

Holding	%
Darya Varia	4.8%
Gudang Garam	7.9%
HM Sampoerna	8.3%
Indocement	3.6%
Indofood	5.2%
Indosat	5.1%
Lippo Bank	4.2%
Semen Gresik	5.1%
Telkom	7.4%

TOTAL RETURNS %

3 months 1997	1996	1995	1994	3 years	5 years
9.72	40.28	36.20	9.98	110.12	N.A.

STATISTICS

Assets ($mil)	Current yield	Volatility	Risk return	Micropal Star Rating
41.10	—	7.97	3	✪✪✪✪✪

LOI Smaller European Cos
120/350

Lombard Odier International Portfolio Management Ltd
47 Boulevard Royal, L-2449 Luxembourg
Tel 352-46-40-10 Fax 352-46-36-31

Investment objective:
The sub-fund aims at capital appreciation by investing primarily in equity securities of smaller European companies with a capitalisation of the equivalent of up to 2 billion US dollars quoted on recognised stock exchanges in Europe. The top sector allocations of the portfolio are as follows: capital goods (12.9%); services (15.7%); and non-durable (10.3%).

Umbrella fund: Lombard Odier Invest

Launch date: 15/02/94 **Domicile:** Luxembourg [UCITS]

Currency: DEM **Structure:** Open ended, SICAV

Portfolio manager: Neil Worsley
Manager of the fund commenced February 1994 and Director of UK equities; previously with Windsor Trust Manager, UK Equity Manager and National Westminster Bank; joined Lombard Odier in 1990; 18 years investment experience.

Purchase: Direct, Financial Advisor, Yes

Minimum investment: 5,000 USD

Custodian: State Street Luxembourg

Listed: None **Dealings:** Daily

Fund Sedol I.D.: 300915 **Published:** FT/IHT/WS/NZZ/JG

Fees **Annual fee:** 1.00% **Performance fee:** None
Front end load: Up to 3.00% **Redemption fee:** None
Switching fee: 50 USD

Contact: Jean Fouchet

Performance:

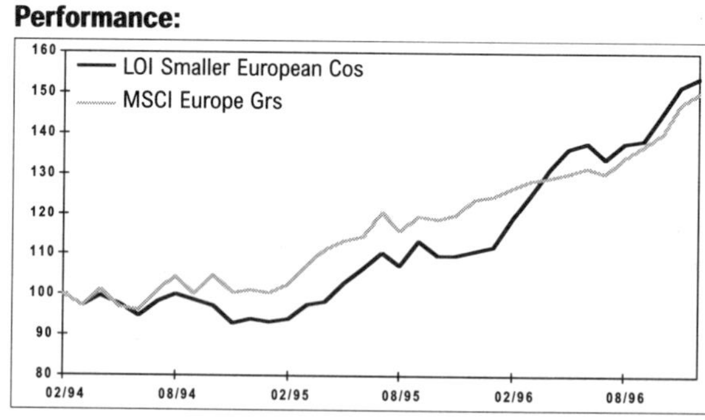

Top holdings:

Holding	%
BBA Group	2.8%
British Borneo Petroleum	2.4%
FKI	2.4%
Henlys Group	3.1%
Hugo Boss (Priv.)	2.3%
Medeva	2.7%
Premier Farnell	2.9%
Rexel	2.2%
Stagecoach Holdings	2.4%
Ultra Electronic Holdings	2.6%

TOTAL RETURNS %

3 months 1997	1996	1995	1994	3 years	5 years
1.48	39.00	18.00	N.A.	N.A.	N.A.

STATISTICS

Assets ($mil)	Current yield	Volatility	Risk return	Micropal Star Rating
43.54	—	N.A.	—	——

LPS International Ltd Australian Issue Share Fund

78/350

LPS Futures Managers Ltd
832 Europort, Gibraltar
Tel 350-79-120 Fax 350-78-428

Contact: Tim Ireton

Investment objective:
The sub-fund seeks long-term capital growth through a systematic and technical program both, providing long and short exposure, to energy, metal, commodities and currencies, as well as equity, bond and interest rate markets. This is an aggressively managed futures/hedge fund designed for Australian investors.

Umbrella fund: LPS International Ltd
Launch date: 01/10/93 **Domicile:** Bermuda
Currency: AUD **Structure:** Open ended, Investment Company
Portfolio manager: Tim Ireton
Manager or LPS International Ltd High Performance B Share Fund, founder of LPS in 1986; experienced in accounting, dealing, broking, systems research, creating, distributing and managing funds.
Purchase: Direct, Financial Advisor
Minimum investment: 10,000 AUD
Custodian: Bank of Butterfield Executor & Trustee Co ltd, Bermuda
Listed: None **Dealings:** Monthly
Fund Sedol I.D.: 252512 **Published:** MP/LP
Fees **Annual fee:** 3.00% **Performance fee:** 20.00%
Front end load: 5.00% **Redemption fee:** None
Switching fee: None

Performance:

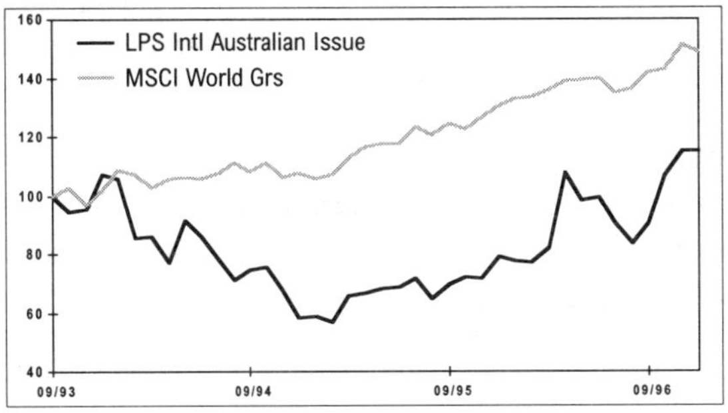

Top holdings:	
Agriculture/Commodities Futures	20.0%
Base And Precious Metal Futures	10.0%
Currency Futures	10.0%
Energy Futures	6.0%
Government Bond Futures	6.0%
Livestock Futures	6.0%
Short Term Interest Rate Futures	4.0%
Stock Index Futures	8.0%
Theoretical Maximum Initial Risk	70.0%
Typical Normal Initial Risk Exposure	35.0%

TOTAL RETURNS %

3 months 1997	1996	1995	1994	3 years	5 years
0.19	45.14	36.51	-45.97	7.05	N.A.

STATISTICS

Assets ($mil)	Current yield	Volatility	Risk return	Micropal Star Rating
0.36	—	9.95	—	✪✪✪

LPS International Ltd High Performance B Share Fund

64/350

LPS Futures Managers Ltd
832 Europort, Gibraltar
Tel 350-79-120 Fax 350-78-428

Contact: Tim Ireton

Investment objective:
The sub-fund objective is long-term capital growth through a diversified trading programme systematic and technical, providing long and short exposure to energy, metal, commodities and currencies, as well as equity, bond and interest rate market. A portfolio volatility strategy, introduced in February 1996 identifies low risk points for increasing exposure and higher risk points for reducing it.
Umbrella fund: LPS International Ltd
Launch date: 01/10/91 **Domicile:** Bermuda
Currency: USD **Structure:** Open ended, Investment Company
Portfolio manager: Tim Ireton
Manager or LPS International Ltd High Performance B Share Fund, founder of LPS in 1986; experienced in accounting, dealing, broking, systems research, creating, distributing and managing funds.
Purchase: Direct, Fin. Adv., Approved for purchase through CMI Offshore Ins. Funds
Minimum investment: 50,000 USD
Custodian: Bank of Butterfield Executor & Trustee Co. ltd,Bermuda
Listed: None **Dealings:** Monthly
Fund Sedol I.D.: 252516 **Published:** MP/LP
Fees **Annual fee:** 3.00% **Performance fee:** 20.00%
Front end load: 5.00% **Redemption fee:** None
Switching fee: None

Performance:

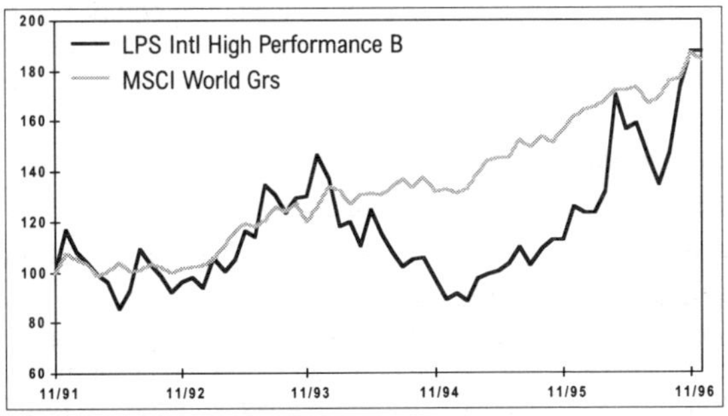

Top holdings:	
Agriculture/Commodities Futures	20.0%
Base And Precious Metal Futures	10.0%
Currency Futures	10.0%
Energy Futures	6.0%
Government Bond Futures	6.0%
Livestock Futures	6.0%
Short Term Interest Rate Futures	4.0%
Stock Index Futures	8.0%
Theoretical Maximum Initial Risk	70.0%
Typical Normal Initial Risk Exposure	35.0%

TOTAL RETURNS %

3 months 1997	1996	1995	1994	3 years	5 years
0.05	49.16	41.33	-39.39	27.78	59.86

STATISTICS

Assets ($mil)	Current yield	Volatility	Risk return	Micropal Star Rating
1.40	—	8.59	1	✪✪✪

Lux Avantage1 A Cap
158/350

Banque et Caisse D'Epargne de L'Etat
1 Place de Mete, L - 2954 Luxembourg
Tel 352-40-15-54-55 Fax 352-40-15-54-60
http://www. bcee.lu

Investment objective:
The sub-fund aims to invest at least 75% of the net assets in equities of Luxembourg companies. Lux-Avantage offers the possibility to Luxembourg residents to benefit from tax advantages. The top sector allocations of the portfolio include finance (57.8%)and energy (9.7%).The fund assets are divided into equities (66.9%); cash/MM (24.3%) and preferred (8.8%).

Umbrella fund: Lux-Advantage

Launch date: 28/12/93 **Domicile:** Luxembourg

Currency: LUF **Structure:** Open ended, SICAV

Portfolio manager: Lux-Avantage Advisory SA
Manager of Lux Avantage 1 A Cap; located at 1, Place de Metz, L-1930 Luxembourg.

Contact: Norbert Nickels

Performance:

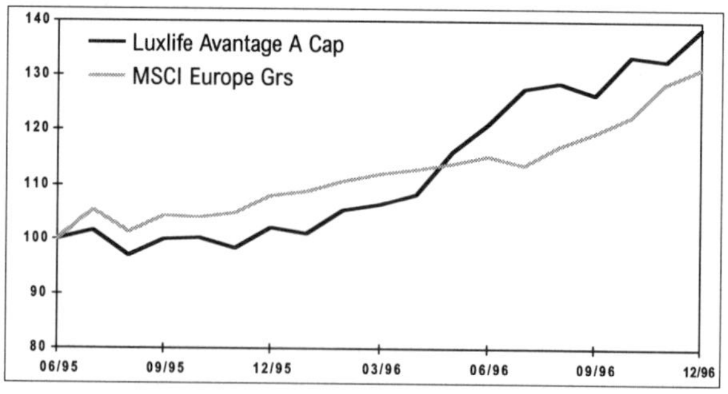

Purchase: Direct, Financial Advisor

Minimum investment: 1 Share

Custodian: Banque et Caisse D'Epargne De L'Etat

Listed: None **Dealings:** Weekly

Fund Sedol I.D.: 304373 **Published:** LW/IN

Fees **Annual fee:** 0.50% **Performance fee:** None
Front end load: Up to 2.50 % **Redemption fee:** None
Switching fee: None

Top holdings:

Arbed	0.8%
Audiofina	4.8%
Audiolux	0.9%
BGL	14.8%
BIL	14.6%
Cegedel	9.7%
KBL	6.0%
KBL Priv.	8.8%
Luxempart	13.7%
Millicom International	1.8%

TOTAL RETURNS %

3 months 1997	1996	1995	1994	3 years	5 years
-2.09	35.68	N.A.	N.A.	N.A.	N.A.

STATISTICS

Assets ($mil)	Current yield	Volatility	Risk return	Micropal Star Rating
85.22	—	N.A.	—	———

Lux Privilege B
270/350

Societe Europeenne de Banque
18-21 Boulevard Prince Henri, L-1724 Luxembourg
Tel 352-46-14-11-251 Fax 352-22-15-91

Investment objective:
The fund seeks growth through a portfolio where 75% minimum of the assets are invested in securities or rights of Luxembourg companies and a minimum of 20% in liquidity and in money market instruments. The top sector allocations of the fund include the following: finance (68.7%); energy (5.9%); and cash (24.3%).

Umbrella fund: This is a singular fund.

Launch date: 31/01/94 **Domicile:** Luxembourg

Currency: LUF **Structure:** Open ended, SICAV

Portfolio manager: Michel Janiak
Manager and Directeur-Adjoint, Le Foyer Assurances and the Chairman of LuxiPrivlege Conseil SA; responsible for the financial market activities and portfolio management; 13 years banking experience; joined the firm in 1990.

Contact: Burgen - Catrysse

Performance:

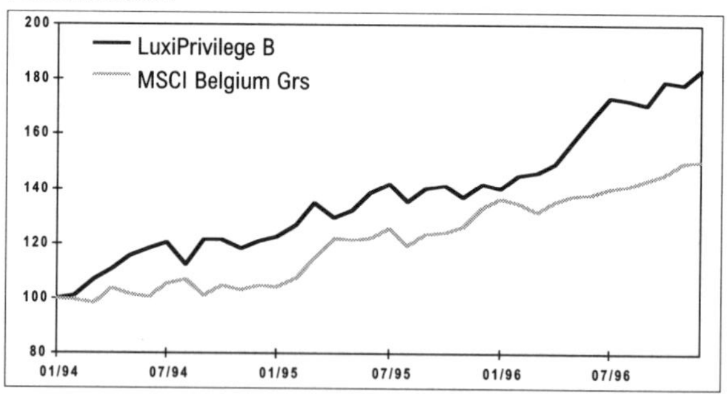

Purchase: Direct

Minimum investment: None

Custodian: Societe Europeenne De Banque

Listed: None **Dealings:** Bi-Monthly

Fund Sedol I.D.: 304228 **Published:** FT/IHT/SC

Fees **Annual fee:** 0.75% **Performance fee:** None
Front end load: 3.00% **Redemption fee:** 0.50%
Switching fee: None

Top holdings:

Arbed	9.5%
Audiolux	9.5%
BGL	9.4%
BIL	11.5%
Cegedel	6.0%
CLT 'B'	1.0%
KB Lux Priva	1.4%
Luxempart	1.4%

TOTAL RETURNS %

3 months 1997	1996	1995	1994	3 years	5 years
1.76	29.55	17.55	N.A.	N.A.	N.A.

STATISTICS

Assets ($mil)	Current yield	Volatility	Risk return	Micropal Star Rating
4.00	—	N.A.	—	———

Luxlife Actions Americaines
345/350

Luxlife
4 Rue du Fort Rheinstein, L-2017 Luxembourg
Tel 352-25-27-71 Fax 352-25-27-79
E mail luxlife@pt.lu

Investment objective:
The fund aims at capital appreciation through investments in US equities. The top sector allocations of the portfolio are as follows: finance (31.0%); consumer goods (13.0%); services (13.0%); retail trade (7.0%); and energy (7.0%).The fund is denominated in US dollars.

Umbrella fund: This is a singular fund.
Launch date: 01/10/94 **Domicile:** Luxembourg
Currency: USD **Structure:** Open ended, Insurance Fund
Portfolio manager: Luxlife-Luxembourg Life and Capitalisation Company Manager of Luxlife Actions Americaines; located at 4 Rue de Fort Rheinsheim, BP 723, L-2017, Luxembourg.

Purchase: Direct
Minimum investment: 7,500 USD
Custodian: Luxembourg Life and Capitalisation Company
Listed: None **Dealings:** Weekly
Fund Sedol I.D.: 304395 **Published:** FT/IHT/SC
Fees **Annual fee:** ILP **Performance fee:** ILP
Front end load: ILP **Redemption fee:** ILP
Switching fee: ILP

Contact: Customer Services Department
Performance:

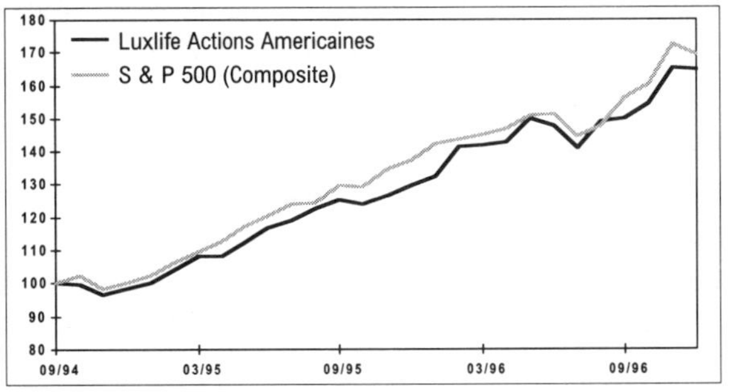

Top holdings:

Carlisle Cos Inc	n/s
Clayton Homes Inc	n/s
Ganett Co.Inc.	n/s
Kim Co. Realty	n/s
Northern Trust Corp	n/s
Williams Cos	n/s

TOTAL RETURNS %

3 months 1997	1996	1995	1994	3 years	5 years
5.07	27.13	31.60	N.A.	N.A.	N.A.

STATISTICS

Assets ($mil)	Current yield	Volatility	Risk return	Micropal Star Rating
471.40	—	N.A.	—	———

Luxlife Actions Europeennes
332/350

Luxlife
4 Rue du Fort Rheinstein, L-2017 Luxembourg
Tel 352-52-27-71 Fax 352-25-27-79
E mail luxlife@pt.lu

Investment objective:
The principle aim of the fund is to achieve capital growth through a diversified portfolio of equities quoted in Europe. The top country allocations of the portfolio are as follows: UK, France, Sweden, Germany and Switzerland.

Umbrella fund: This is a singular fund.
Launch date: 01/10/94 **Domicile:** Luxembourg
Currency: ECU **Structure:** Open ended, Insurance Fund
Portfolio manager: Luxlife-Luxembourg Life and Capitalisation Company Manager of Luxlife Actions Europeennes; located at 4 Rue de Fort Rheinsheim, BP 723, L-2017, Luxembourg.

Purchase: Direct
Minimum investment: 7,500 USD
Custodian: Luxembourg Life and Capitalisation Company
Listed: None **Dealings:** Weekly
Fund Sedol I.D.: 304389 **Published:** FT/IHT/SC
Fees **Annual fee:** ILP **Performance fee:** ILP
Front end load: ILP **Redemption fee:** ILP
Switching fee: ILP

Contact: Customer Services Department
Performance:

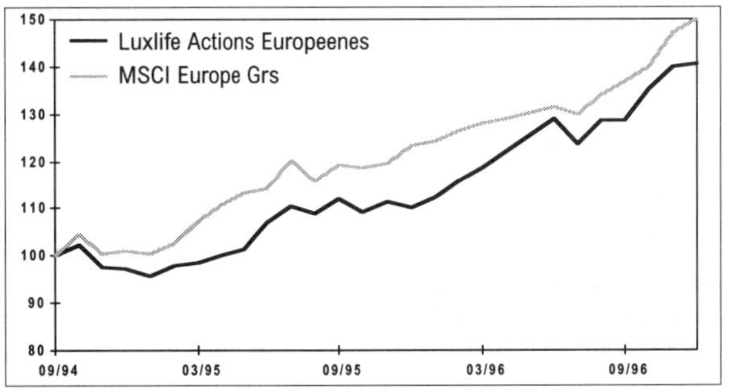

Top holdings:

Ahold	2.2%
Astra	2.1%
Burton Group	2.5%
Ciba Geigy	4.3%
Dassault Systems	2.4%
Gehe	2.2%
Granada Group	2.8%
Volkswagen	3.2%

TOTAL RETURNS %

3 months 1997	1996	1995	1994	3 years	5 years
3.30	27.44	13.51	N.A.	N.A.	N.A.

STATISTICS

Assets ($mil)	Current yield	Volatility	Risk return	Micropal Star Rating
225.05	—	N.A.	—	———

Luxlife Actions Francaises
319/350

Luxlife
4 Rue du Fort Rheinstein, L-2017 Luxembourg
Tel 352-25-27-71 Fax 352-25-27-79
E mail luxlife@pt.lu

Investment objective:
The principle aim of the fund is to achieve capital growth through a diversified portfolio of equities quoted in France. The top sector allocations of the portfolio are as follows: retail trade (22.0%); consumer goods (19.0%); services (14.0%); and finance (10.0%). The top country allocations include: the UK, France, Sweden, German and Switzerland.

Umbrella fund: This is a singular fund.

Launch date: 01/10/94 **Domicile:** Luxembourg

Currency: FRF **Structure:** Open ended, Insurance Fund

Portfolio manager: Luxlife-Luxembourg Life and Capitalisation Company
Manager of Luxlife Actions Francaises; located at 4 Rue de Fort Rheinsheim, BP 723, L-2017, Luxembourg.

Contact: Customer Services Department

Performance:

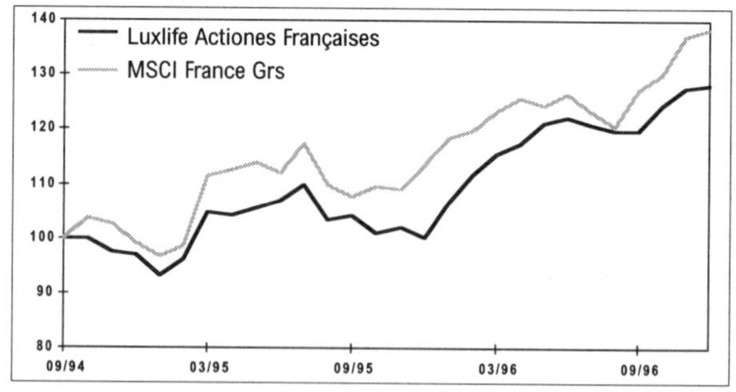

Purchase: Direct

Minimum investment: 40,000 FRF

Custodian: Luxembourg Life and Capitalisation Company

Listed: None **Dealings:** Weekly

Fund Sedol I.D.: 304390 **Published:** FT/IHT/SC

Fees **Annual fee:** ILP **Performance fee:** ILP
Front end load: ILP **Redemption fee:** ILP
Switching fee: ILP

Top holdings:

Holding	%
Ahold	2.2%
Astra	2.1%
Burton Group	2.5%
Ciba Geigy	4.3%
Dassault Systems	2.4%
Gehe	2.1%
Granada Group	2.8%
Volkswagen	3.2%

TOTAL RETURNS %

3 months 1997	1996	1995	1994	3 years	5 years
1.39	27.89	3.25	N.A.	N.A.	N.A.

STATISTICS

Assets ($mil)	Current yield	Volatility	Risk return	Micropal Star Rating
533.84	—	N.A.	—	———

M&G Island Gold
95/350

M&G (Island)
PO Box 44, The Grange, St Peter Port, GY1 3BG, Guernsey
Tel 44-1481-722-663 Fax 44-1481-716-762

Investment objective:
The fund seeks consistent growth of both capital and income mainly by investing in equities listed in the UK, although overseas holdings may be considered. The top country allocations of the portfolio are as follows: Canada (36.2%); Australia (27.9%); South Africa/Africa (17.2%); and the US (10.3%).

Umbrella fund: This is a singular fund.

Launch date: 01/04/75 **Domicile:** Guernsey

Currency: GBP **Structure:** Open ended, Unit Trust

Portfolio manager: Graham French
Manager of M&G Island Gold commenced in 1989; Honours degree, geography-Durham U; associate of the Institute of Investment Management & Research.

Contact: Brenda Hallett

Performance:

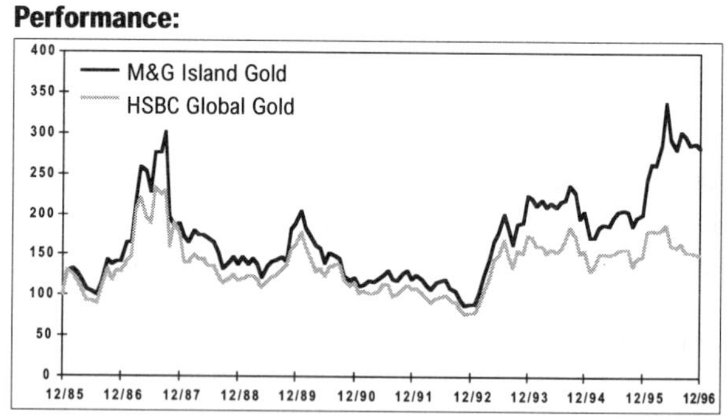

Purchase: Direct, Financial Advisor

Minimum investment: 1,000 GBP

Custodian: Kleinwort Benson (Guernsey) Limited

Listed: None **Dealings:** Daily

Fund Sedol I.D.: 54953 **Published:** FT

Fees **Annual fee:** 1.00% **Performance fee:** None
Front end load: 5.00% **Redemption fee:** None
Switching fee: 2.50%

Top holdings:

Holding	%
AUR Resources	2.6%
Barrick Gold	4.0%
Black Swan Gold Mines	4.6%
Contour Mining	2.6%
Equinox Resources	4.4%
Euro-Nevada	4.9%
Franco-Nevada	4.9%
Freeport McMoran	3.1%
Gold Mines of Sardinia	2.6%
Rand Gold & Exploration	2.8%

TOTAL RETURNS %

3 months 1997	1996	1995	1994	3 years	5 years
-4.94	41.05	-1.20	-9.12	26.64	135.29

STATISTICS

Assets ($mil)	Current yield	Volatility	Risk return	Micropal Star Rating
18.40	0.37	7.35	1	✪✪✪✪

M-Fund Continental Europe

218/350

Banco Mello
20 Boulevard Emmanuel Servais, L-2535 Luxembourg
Tel 352-47-93-46-280 Fax 352-47-29-86

Investment objective:
The sub-fund aims at long-term capital growth through an active investment policy in European equities-with the exception of the UK and Ireland. The top country allocations of the portfolio are as follows: Germany (25.0%); France (21.0%); Netherlands (15.0%); and Italy (9.0%).

Umbrella fund: M-Fund SICAV
Launch date: 02/11/94 **Domicile:** Luxembourg
Currency: DEM **Structure:** Open ended, SICAV
Portfolio manager: Mr Chamberlain
Adviser of M-Fund Continental Europe commenced January 1994; Bsc-Kingston U – London; previously Manager in INVESCO 1987-89; 10 years in the finance industry.

Purchase: Direct
Minimum investment: None
Custodian: Banque de Gestion Edmond de Rothschild
Listed: Luxembourg **Dealings:** Weekly
Fund Sedol I.D.: 300001 **Published:** MP/RT/TK/FT
Fees **Annual fee:** 1.25% **Performance fee:** None
Front end load: 5.00% **Redemption fee:** 1.00%
Switching fee: None

Contact: Carole Hansay
Performance:

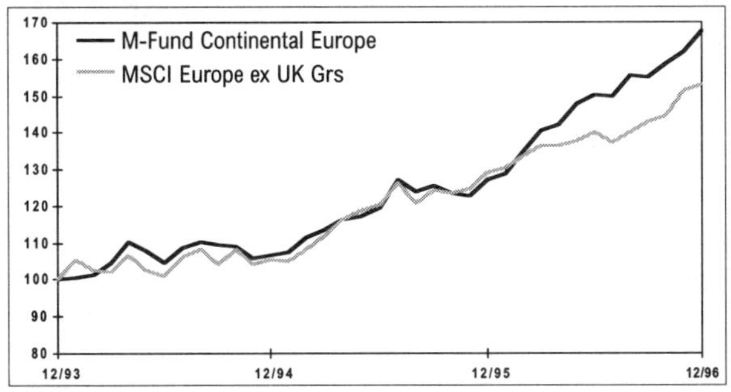

Top holdings:

Adidas	2.5%
Bulgari	2.8%
Gucci	2.3%
Saloman	2.7%
SAP AG	2.2%

TOTAL RETURNS %

3 months 1997	1996	1995	1994	3 years	5 years
9.05	31.61	19.42	6.63	67.58	N.A.

STATISTICS

Assets ($mil)	Current yield	Volatility	Risk return	Micropal Star Rating
26.27	—	2.35	5	✪✪✪✪

M-Fund Iberia Value

127/350

Banco Mello
20 Boulevard Emmanuel Servais, L-2535 Luxembourg
Tel 352-47-93-46-280 Fax 352-47-29-86

Investment objective:
The sub-fund seeks to achieve long-term capital growth through an active management policy in Spanish and Portuguese equities. The top sector allocations of the portfolio are the following: finance (30.0%); energy (25.0%); and transport (8.0%). At this time the country allocation of assets are divided between Spain (70.0%); and Portugal (19.0%).
Umbrella fund: M-Fund SICAV
Launch date: 02/11/94 **Domicile:** Luxembourg
Currency: PTE **Structure:** Open ended, SICAV
Portfolio manager: Mr Borbosa
Advisor of M-Fund Iberia Value commenced November 1994; degree in economics and Masters, finance; experience in capital markets.

Purchase: Direct
Minimum investment: None
Custodian: Banque de Gestion Edmond de Rothschild
Listed: Luxembourg **Dealings:** Weekly
Fund Sedol I.D.: 300003 **Published:** MP/RT/TK/FT
Fees **Annual fee:** 1.25% **Performance fee:** None
Front end load: 5.00% **Redemption fee:** 1.00%
Switching fee: None

Contact: Carole Hansay
Performance:

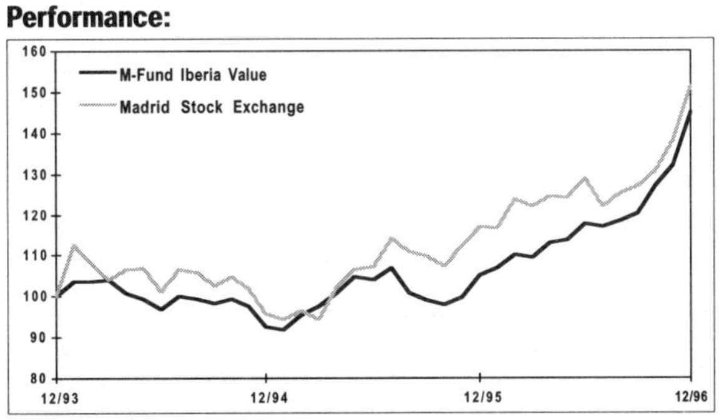

Top holdings:

Acerinox	6.1%
Banco Bilbao Vizcana	9.3%
Banco Popular Esp	4.2%
Bankinjer	5.5%
Endesa	4.1%
Fenosa	5.7%
Iberdola	6.1%
Repsol	6.1%
Telefonica de Espana	7.6%

TOTAL RETURNS %

3 months 1997	1996	1995	1994	3 years	5 years
0.04	38.16	13.55	-7.56	45.01	N.A.

STATISTICS

Assets ($mil)	Current yield	Volatility	Risk return	Micropal Star Rating
4.64	—	3.11	3	✪

M-Fund UK Performer
110/350

Banco Mello
20 Boulevard Emmanuel Servais, L-2535 Luxembourg
Tel 352-47-93-46-280 Fax 352-47-29-86

Investment objective:
The sub-fund seeks to achieve long-term growth through an active investment policy in UK and Irish equities. The top sector allocations for the portfolio are finance (17.0%) and transportation (13.0%). The assets of the sub-fund are divided between the UK (71.0%) and Ireland (13.0%) with the remainder held in cash.

Umbrella fund: M-Fund SICAV
Launch date: 02/11/94 **Domicile:** Luxembourg
Currency: GBP **Structure:** Open ended, SICAV
Portfolio manager: David J. Leary – AIG Global Investment Corp. (Europe) Ltd. Manager of M-Fund United Kingdom Performer; Degree in economic/ social studies-Manchester U; previously with Lombard Odier,equity administration department 1986-88; joined AIG European equity team in 1988 as analyst and fund manager.
Purchase: Direct
Minimum investment: None
Custodian: Banque de Gestion Edmond de Rothschild
Listed: Luxembourg **Dealings:** Weekly
Fund Sedol I.D.: 300005 **Published:** MP/RT/TK/FT
Fees **Annual fee:** 1.25% **Performance fee:** None
Front end load: 5.00% **Redemption fee:** 1.00%
Switching fee: None

Contact: Carole Hansay
Performance:

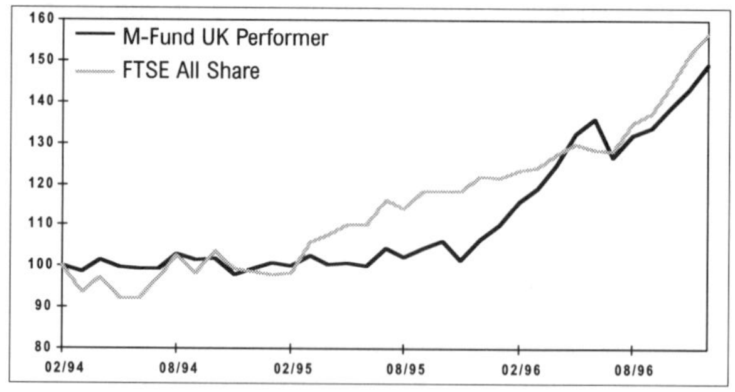

Top holdings:

Holding	%
Adam & Harvey Group	4.0%
Airtours	6.9%
Grafton Group	4.9%
Manchester United	6.3%
Marley	3.6%
Polypipe	4.4%
Pressac Holdings	5.8%
Stanley Leisure Org	3.6%
Videologic Group	3.5%
Waddington Plc	7.0%

TOTAL RETURNS %

3 months 1997	1996	1995	1994	3 years	5 years
3.27	40.23	7.26	N.A.	N.A.	N.A.

STATISTICS

Assets ($mil)	Current yield	Volatility	Risk return	Micropal Star Rating
3.48	—	N.A.	—	———

Merrill Lynch Americas Income A
57/350

Merrill Lynch Asset Management
800 Scudders Mill Road, Plainsboro, New Jersey, 08536, USA
Tel 1-609-282-2454 Fax 1-609-282-1045

Investment objective:
The fund seeks a high level of current income and secondarily, capital appreciation consistent with reasonable investment risk by investing in US dollar denominated debt securities of issuers domiciled primarily in the western hemisphere. The asset allocations of the portfolio include the following: Brady Bonds (75.7%); bonds (23.8%); and cash/MM (0.5%).
Umbrella fund: This is a singular fund.
Launch date: 02/04/94 **Domicile:** Cayman Islands
Currency: USD **Structure:** Open ended, Mutual Fund
Portfolio manager: Paolo Valle
Manager of the fund commenced April 1994; MBA- U of Pittsburgh School of Business; extensive experience in Latin American debt reconstructing; formerly with PNC Financial Corp as banking /investment/loan manager; 15 years- finance industry.
Purchase: Merrill Lynch Financial Consultant
Minimum investment: 1,000 USD
Custodian: Brown Brothers Harriman & Co
Listed: None **Dealings:** Daily
Fund Sedol I.D.: 305320 **Published:** FT/IHT/WS
Fees **Annual fee:** 0.55% **Performance fee:** None
Front end load: Up to 3.00% **Redemption fee:** None
Switching fee: 0.50%

Contact: John Caddetta
Performance:

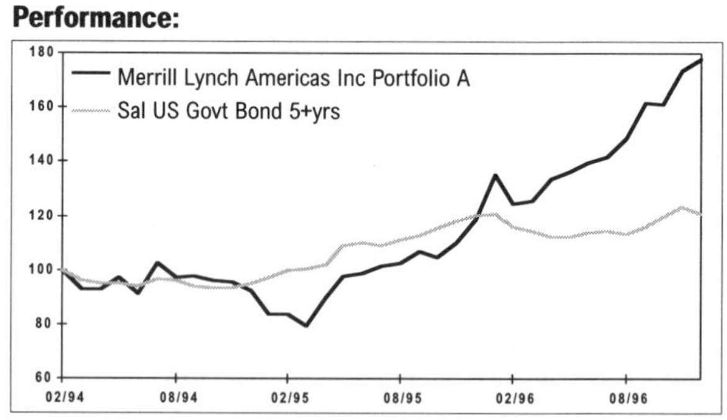

Top holdings:

Holding	%
Argentina Par 'L' 5.0%/23	5.0%
Brazil C Bond 8.00%/14	6.3%
Brazil Debt FRB 'L' 6.563%/12	6.6%
Ecuador 6.063%/15	4.8%
Ecuador 6.063%/15	3.4%
Mexico - 11.5% / 26	12.8%
Panama FRB 6.75%/16	2.3%
Venezuela FRB 6.375%/07	3.4%
Venezuela FRB 6.5%/07	8.6%
Vnesheconombank 3.25%/96	10.3%

TOTAL RETURNS %

3 months 1997	1996	1995	1994	3 years	5 years
-0.72	50.08	28.53	N.A.	N.A.	N.A.

STATISTICS

Assets ($mil)	Current yield	Volatility	Risk return	Micropal Star Rating
30.16	—	N.A.	—	———

Merrill Lynch Mex Inc Peso Portfolio A
126/350

Merrill Lynch Asset Management
800 Scudders Mill Road, Plainsboro, New Jersey, 08536, USA
Tel 1-609-282-2454 Fax 1-609-282-1045

Investment objective:
The fund seeks to achieve high current income primarily through investment in Mexican peso denominated income or debt securities.

Umbrella fund: This is a singular fund.
Launch date: 30/07/92 **Domicile:** Cayman Islands
Currency: USD **Structure:** Open ended, Mutual Fund
Portfolio manager: Paolo Valle
Manager of the fund commenced April 1994; MBA- U of Pittsburgh School of Business; extensive experience in Latin American debt reconstructing; formerly with PNC Financial Corp as banking /investment/loan manager; 15 years- finance industry.
Purchase: Merrill Lynch Financial Consultant
Minimum investment: 100 Shares
Custodian: Banque Internationale a Luxembourg
Listed: None **Dealings:** Daily
Fund Sedol I.D.: 301505 **Published:** FT/IHT/WS
Fees **Annual fee:** 0.75% **Performance fee:** None
Front end load: 2.00% **Redemption fee:** None
Switching fee: 0.50%

Contact: John Caddetta
Performance:

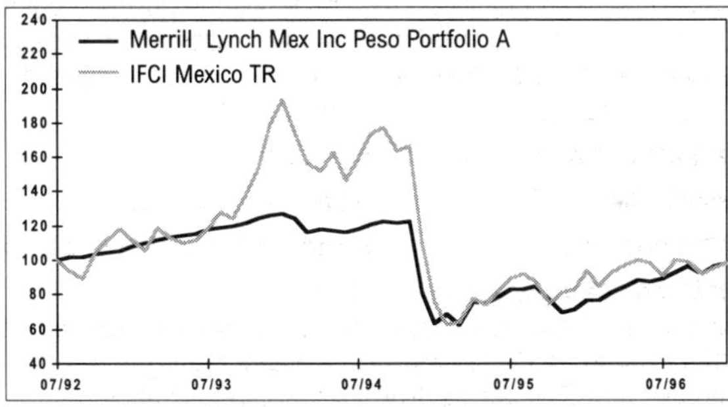

Top holdings:

Holding	%
110.0 MXN Cetes 27.55%/97	7.2%
133.0 MXN Cetes 34.48%/97	9.6%
191.0 MXN Cetes 32.9%/97	12.7%
218.46 MXN Cetes 32.48%/97	15.5%
317.58 MXN Cetes 42.83%/97	24.0%
40.5 MXN Cetes 31.6%/96	3.3%
50.0 MXN Cetes 36.618%/97	3.9%
50.0 MXN Cetes 44.5%/97	3.7%
71.12 MXN Banamex 28.5%/96	5.8%
86.36 Invermex Casade Bolsa 32.2% / 96	7.0%

TOTAL RETURNS %

3 months 1997	1996	1995	1994	3 years	5 years
6.03	38.39	-12.48	-35.44	-21.81	N.A.

STATISTICS

Assets ($mil)	Current yield	Volatility	Risk return	Micropal Star Rating
62.43	—	8.30	—	✪✪

Mansion House Hong Kong
150/350

Mansion House Investment Management Services
37A Bank of China Tower, 1 Garden Road, Central, Hong Kong
Tel 852-2843-1486 Fax 852-2537-8158

Investment objective:
The fund seeks to achieve capital growth through investment in the Hong Kong market. The top sector allocations of the portfolio are the following: properties (31.2%); conglomerates (30.1%); finance (13.6%); utilities (10.4%); and consumer goods (4.8%).

Umbrella fund: This is a singular fund.
Launch date: 01/01/87 **Domicile:** Hong Kong
Currency: HKD **Structure:** Open ended, Unit Trust
Portfolio manager: Norman C Lone
Manager of Mansion House Hong Kong commenced in 1996.

Purchase: Direct, Financial Advisor
Minimum investment: 1,000 Units
Custodian: HSBC Trustee (HK) Ltd
Listed: None **Dealings:** Weekly
Fund Sedol I.D.: 656370 **Published:** FT/IHT/SC
Fees **Annual fee:** 1.50% **Performance fee:** None
Front end load: 5.00% **Redemption fee:** None
Switching fee: None

Contact: Pearl Chon /Eric Lowe
Performance:

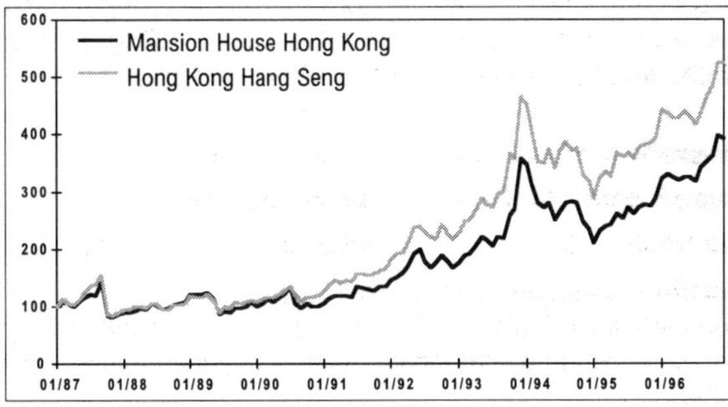

Top holdings:

Holding	%
Cheung Kong	7.0%
Citic Pacific	9.1%
Guangdong Holdings	5.3%
HKR International	5.6%
HSBC Holdings	7.2%
Hutchison Whampoa	6.2%
New World Development	4.9%
SHK Properties	6.2%
Swire Pacific "A"	4.9%
Wheelock & Co	4.5%

TOTAL RETURNS %

3 months 1997	1996	1995	1994	3 years	5 years
N.A.	36.11	23.03	-34.54	9.60	191.48

STATISTICS

Assets ($mil)	Current yield	Volatility	Risk return	Micropal Star Rating
6.36	—	6.11	—	✪✪

Manulife Regent GF American Growth
256/350

Manulife Regent Investment Corporation
Suite 1305 13 Floor, 9 Queen's Road, Central, Hong Kong
Tel 852-2501-9100 Fax 852-2810-9510
http://www. mfdirect.com E mail invest@mfdirect.com

Investment objective:
The fund aims to achieve capital growth from a portfolio of North American equities with the main emphasis on the US. While the portfolio consists mainly of securities of major companies, smaller or medium-sized companies are also included. Sector allocations of the portfolio are as follows: consumer goods (34.0%); technology (18.0%); finance 16.0%); and energy (9.0%).

Umbrella fund: Manulife Regent Global Fund

Launch date: 10/09/87 **Domicile:** Luxembourg

Currency: USD **Structure:** Open ended, SICAV

Portfolio manager: Gavin Rennie CA
Director, US Equities -Abbey Life; previously with Pannell Kerr Foster, Glasgow and Arthur Young McClellan Moore, Assistant Manager and Ivory & Sime, Investment Manager and Director for North American portfolios.

Purchase: Direct

Minimum investment: 5,000 HKD

Custodian: Bank of Bermuda (Luxembourg) SA

Listed: None **Dealings:** Daily

Fund Sedol I.D.: 517 **Published:** FT/IHT/SC

Fees **Annual fee:** 1.50% **Performance fee:** 8.00%
Front end load: None **Redemption fee:** Up to 1.00%
Switching fee: None

Contact: Dennis Lau

Performance:

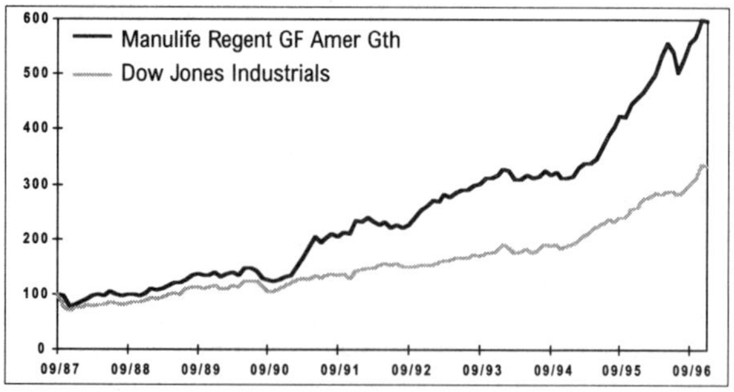

Top holdings:

American Home Products	n/s
Atlantic Richfield	n/s
Bankers Trust	n/s
Baxter International	n/s
Browning Ferris	n/s
Chase Manhattan Bk	n/s
Occidental Petroleum	n/s
Philip Morris	n/s
Texaco	n/s
United Technologies	n/s

TOTAL RETURNS %

3 months 1997	1996	1995	1994	3 years	5 years
1.80	30.26	47.01	-2.09	87.48	154.24

STATISTICS

Assets ($mil)	Current yield	Volatility	Risk return	Micropal Star Rating
10.00	—	3.25	5	✪✪✪✪✪

Manulife Regent GF Euro Growth
335/350

Manulife Regent Investment Corporation
Suite 1305 13 Floor, 9 Queen's Road, Central, Hong Kong
Tel 852-2501-9100 Fax 852-2810-9510
http://www. mfdirect.com E mail invest@mfdirect.com

Investment objective:
The sub-fund aims at capital growth from a diversified portfolio of equities in mainly larger companies quoted on stock markets in Europe. The top country allocations of the portfolio are France (23.0%); Germany (16.0%); Switzerland (11.0%); Netherlands (10.0%); Sweden (10.0%); and Spain (7.0%).

Umbrella fund: Manulife Regent Global Fund

Launch date: 01/10/87 **Domicile:** Luxembourg

Currency: USD **Structure:** Open ended, SICAV

Portfolio manager: Carolyn Dearling
Fund Manager, European Equities; graduate of London U; previously with James Capel managing discretionary portfolios; joined the European team at Abbey Life in 1990.

Purchase: Direct

Minimum investment: 5,000 HKD

Custodian: Bank of Burmuda (Luxembourg) S.A.

Listed: None **Dealings:** Daily

Fund Sedol I.D.: 525 **Published:** FT/IHT/SC

Fees **Annual fee:** 1.50% **Performance fee:** 8.00%
Front end load: None **Redemption fee:** Up to 1.00%
Switching fee: None

Contact: Dennis Lau

Performance:

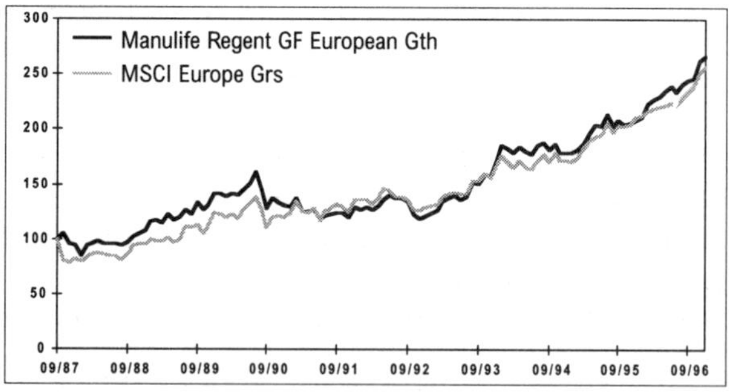

Top holdings:

Bayer	n/s
Ciba Geigy	n/s
Elf Aquitaine	n/s
Hoechst	n/s
Inwear Group	n/s
Roche Holdings	n/s
Rhone Poulenc	n/s
SGS Thomson	n/s
Total	n/s
Volkswagen	n/s

TOTAL RETURNS %

3 months 1997	1996	1995	1994	3 years	5 years
7.09	27.38	17.10	3.43	54.28	106.50

STATISTICS

Assets ($mil)	Current yield	Volatility	Risk return	Micropal Star Rating
9.50	—	3.01	3	✪✪✪✪

Manulife Regent GF Global Resources
38/350

Manulife Regent Investment Corporation
Suite 1305 13 Floor, 9 Queen's Road, Central, Hong Kong
Tel 852-2501-9100 Fax 852-2810-9510
http://www. mfdirect.com E mail invest@mfdirect.com

Investment objective:
The sub-fund seeks capital growth by investing principally in international securities of companies engaged in natural resource industries and industries supportive of companies engaged in the natural resources sector. The top sector allocations of the portfolio are as follows: gold/silver (13.0%); base metals (27.0%); oil/gas (41.0%); and forest products (7.0%).

Umbrella fund: Manulife Regent Global Fund

Launch date: 01/12/93 **Domicile:** Luxembourg

Currency: USD **Structure:** Open ended, SICAV

Portfolio manager: David F Taylor CFA, Altamira Management Ltd.
Manager of the fund commenced June 1995 and VP of Canadian equities, research analyst and portfolio Manager of Altamira Mgt Ltd; previously with Ontario Teachers Pension Plan Board as Portfolio Manager; joined Altamira 1995; 9 years experience.

Purchase: Direct

Minimum investment: 5,000 HKD

Custodian: Bank of Burmuda (Luxembourg) S.A.

Listed: None **Dealings:** Daily

Fund Sedol I.D.: 473379 **Published:** FT/IHT/SC

Fees **Annual fee:** 1.50% **Performance fee:** 8.00%
Front end load: None **Redemption fee:** Up to 1.00%
Switching fee: None

Contact: Dennis Lau

Performance:

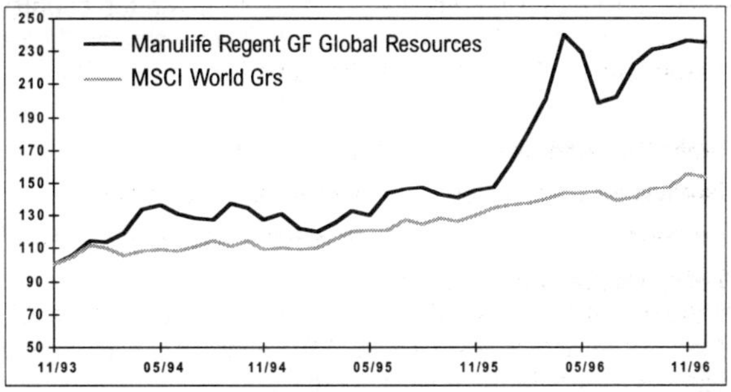

Top holdings:

Botsana	n/s
Canadian 88 Energy	n/s
Epic Energy	n/s
Falconbridge	n/s
General Mineral	n/s
Getchell Gold	n/s
Kerr-McGee	n/s
Pacalta Dodge	n/s
Remington	n/s
Serenpet Inc	n/s

TOTAL RETURNS %

3 months 1997	1996	1995	1994	3 years	5 years
-0.64	59.54	12.87	23.39	122.19	N.A.

STATISTICS

Assets ($mil)	Current yield	Volatility	Risk return	Micropal Star Rating
22.00	—	6.37	3	✪✪✪✪✪

Mercury Energy International
281/350

Mercury Asset Management
Forum House, Grenville Street, St Helier, JE4 8RL, Jersey
Tel 44-1534-600-719 Fax 44-1534-600-687

Investment objective:
The fund aims for maximum long-term returns by investing internationally in securities of companies involved in the exploration, development, production, transport and marketing of hydrocarbons and other sources of energy. The sector allocation of the portfolio is primarily energy (59.4%). The top country allocations are US (30.0%); and Netherlands (14.0%).

Umbrella fund: This is a singular fund.

Launch date: 01/03/69 **Domicile:** Netherlands Antilles

Currency: USD **Structure:** Open ended, Investment Company

Portfolio manager: Mercury Asset Mgt Channel Is Ltd & Lehman Bro. Global Asset Mgt Inc Mercury Asset Mgt CI; located at Forum House, Grenville Street, St Helier, Jersey JE4 8RL, Channel Islands- non US equities. Lehman Brothers Global Asset Mgt Inc; located at 3 World Financial Center, New York, NY 10285 US- US equities.

Purchase: Direct, Financial Advisor

Minimum investment: 5,000 USD

Custodian: SG. Warburg & Co (Jersey) Ltd.

Listed: Luxembourg **Dealings:** Daily

Fund Sedol I.D.: 76475 **Published:** FT/NZZ/RT

Fees **Annual fee:** 1.50% **Performance fee:** None
Front end load: 5.00% **Redemption fee:** None
Switching fee: None

Contact: Myra Alletson

Performance:

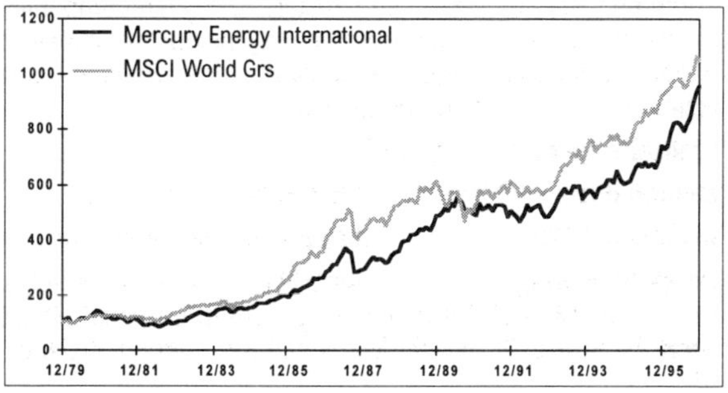

Top holdings:

Baker Hughes	3.5%
British Petroleum	8.0%
Norsk Hydro As	n/s
Phillips Petroleum	4.0%
Pool Energy Services	2.8%
Royal Dutch Petroleum	12.3%
Texaco	3.4%
Total Oil	4.0%
Trimac	3.5%
Weatherford Enterra	4.0%

TOTAL RETURNS %

3 months 1997	1996	1995	1994	3 years	5 years
2.22	29.05	22.56	7.59	70.15	89.74

STATISTICS

Assets ($mil)	Current yield	Volatility	Risk return	Micropal Star Rating
87.70	—	3.22	4	✪✪✪✪✪

Mercury MOST European
167/350

Mercury Asset Management
BP 1058, L-1010 Luxembourg
Tel 352-34-20-10-1 Fax 352-34-20-10-3

Investment objective:
The sub-fund seeks to achieve long-term capital growth by investing primarily in the shares of European companies (except UK). The top country allocations of the portfolio are the following: France (25.4%); Germany (18.8%); Switzerland (14.8%); Netherlands (11.8%); Italy (8.7%); and Sweden (7.9%).

Umbrella fund: Mercury Offshore Sterling Trust
Launch date: 01/11/86 **Domicile:** Luxembourg
Currency: GBP **Structure:** Open ended, SICAV
Portfolio manager: M Legros
Manager Mercury OST European commenced in 1993; MBA- ESSEC, France; joined Mercury Asset Management in 1991; previously with a merchant bank, European team; 11 years in the finance industry.
Purchase: Direct, Financial Advisor
Minimum investment: 1,000 GBP
Custodian: S.G. Warburg & Co. Ltd (Luxembourg)
Listed: Luxembourg **Dealings:** Daily
Fund Sedol I.D.: 93850 **Published:** Mercury Messenger
Fees **Annual fee:** 1.38% **Performance fee:** None
Front end load: 5.00% **Redemption fee:** None
Switching fee: 6 Free switchings within a calender year

Contact: Customer Services Department
Performance:

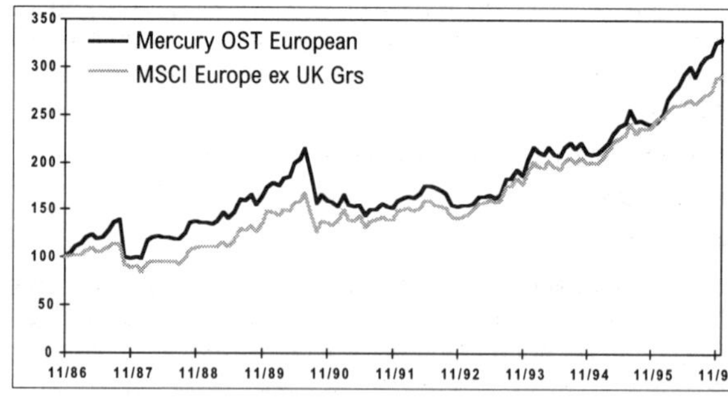

Top holdings:

Adidas	2.8%
Bayer	2.8%
Dassault Systems	2.6%
Eaux (CIE Generale Des)	3.3%
Gucci	4.1%
Novartis	4.3%
Nutricia Verenigde	2.4%
Pinault Printemps	3.7%
Roche Holdings	3.1%
Total Oil	2.7%

TOTAL RETURNS %

3 months 1997	1996	1995	1994	3 years	5 years
9.26	35.07	17.04	2.81	62.53	105.74

STATISTICS

Assets ($mil)	Current yield	Volatility	Risk return	Micropal Star Rating
29.82	—	3.08	4	✪✪✪✪

Mercury ST Eastern European Fund
4/350

Mercury Asset Management
BP 1058, L-1010 Luxembourg
Tel 352-34-20-10-1 Fax 352-34-20-10-3

Investment objective:
The sub-fund aims to provide long-term capital growth by investing primarily in quoted equities of Central and Eastern European companies, including those in the former Soviet Union. The portfolio may include companies from the developed markets which have significant business operations in the region. The currency exposure is normally left unhedged.
Umbrella fund: Mercury Select Trust
Launch date: 29/12/95 **Domicile:** Luxembourg [UCITS]
Currency: DEM **Structure:** Open ended, Investment Company
Portfolio manager: Mercury Asset Management Channel Islands Ltd.
Investment Manager of Mercury ST Eastern European; located at Forum House, Grenville Street, St. Helier, Jersey JE4 8RL, Channel Islands.

Purchase: Direct, Financial Advisor
Minimum investment: 5,000 USD
Custodian: S.G. Warburg & Co. Ltd (Luxembourg)
Listed: Luxembourg **Dealings:** Daily
Fund Sedol I.D.: 500160 **Published:** FT/NZZ/SC/RT
Fees **Annual fee:** 1.50% **Performance fee:** None
Front end load: 5.00% **Redemption fee:** None
Switching fee: 6 Free switchings within a calender year

Contact: Jean Michel Rasquin
Performance:

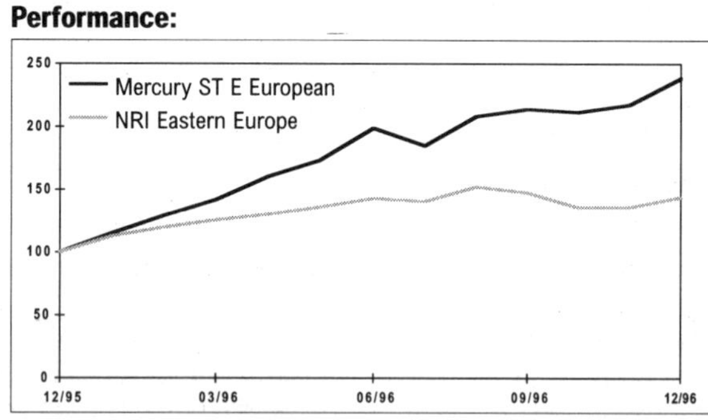

Top holdings:

Borsodchem RT	3.9%
Exbud	3.6%
Mostostal Zabrze	4.8%
Pannonplast	3.8%
Pliva	2.5%
Richter Gedeon Vegyeszeti	4.2%
Scala	2.6%
Tatneft	2.9%
Vilniaus Bankas	4.8%
Zagrebacka Banka	2.8%

TOTAL RETURNS %

3 months 1997	1996	1995	1994	3 years	5 years
29.56	137.95	N.A.	N.A.	N.A.	N.A.

STATISTICS

Assets ($mil)	Current yield	Volatility	Risk return	Micropal Star Rating
94.82	—	N.A.	—	———

Mercury ST European Opportunities Fund

99/350

Mercury Asset Management
BP 1058, L-1010 Luxembourg
Tel 352-34-20-10-1 Fax 352-34-20-10-3

Investment objective:
The sub-fund seeks capital growth by investing primarily in quoted equities of companies based in Europe. The top sector allocations of the portfolio are as follows: services (25.2%); capital equipment (19.3%); consumer goods (17.9%); finance (16.2%). The top country allocations of the fund include the following: UK (23.8%); France (9.8%); Italy (8.8%); and Switzerland (9.7%).

Umbrella fund: Mercury Select Trust

Launch date: 01/05/87 **Domicile:** Luxembourg [UCITS]

Currency: USD **Structure:** Open ended, SICAV

Portfolio manager: James Hordern
Manager of Mercury Select Trust European Opportunities Fund commenced January 1993; joined MAM in 1990; responsible for European specialist portfolios.

Contact: Jean Michel Rasquin

Performance:

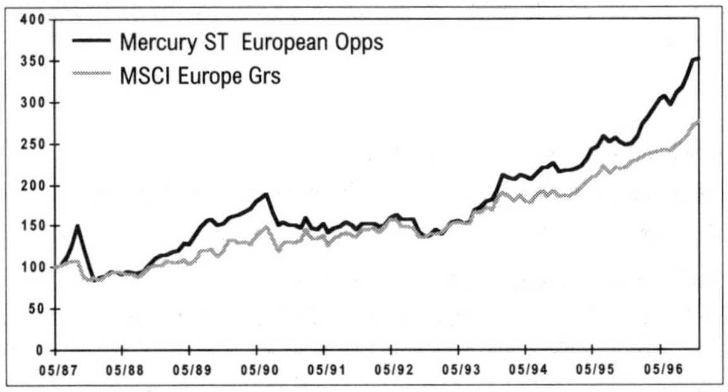

Purchase: Direct, Financial Advisor

Minimum investment: 5,000 USD

Custodian: S.G. Warburg & Co. Ltd (Luxembourg)

Listed: Luxembourg **Dealings:** Daily

Fund Sedol I.D.: 93892 **Published:** FT

Fees **Annual fee:** 1.50% **Performance fee:** None
Front end load: 5.00% **Redemption fee:** None
Switching fee: 6 Free switchings within a calender year

Top holdings:

Aalberts Industie	1.9%
Capita Group	2.0%
Gucci	1.8%
Halma plc ord	1.9%
Hays	2.4%
Hoganas AB	1.6%
Kuoni Reisen Hldg	1.9%
Sondagavisen	2.2%
Stratec Holdings AG	2.6%
TT Tietto	1.4%

TOTAL RETURNS %

3 months 1997	1996	1995	1994	3 years	5 years
4.94	40.96	15.50	12.55	83.25	131.67

STATISTICS

Assets ($mil)	Current yield	Volatility	Risk return	Micropal Star Rating
176.01	—	2.97	5	✪✪✪✪✪

Mercury ST UK Opportunities

81/350

Mercury Asset Management
BP 1058, L-1010 Luxembourg
Tel 352-34-20-10-1 Fax 352-34-20-10-3

Investment objective:
The sub-fund aims to invest primarily in quoted equities of UK companies, typically with a market value of less than 200 million UK sterling. The top sector allocations of the portfolio are the followings: services (45.0%); general manufacturers (31.5%); consumer goods (7.8%); finances (7.5%); and mineral extraction (4.7%).

Umbrella fund: Mercury Select Trust

Launch date: 01/02/93 **Domicile:** Luxembourg [UCITS]

Currency: GBP **Structure:** Open ended, SICAV

Portfolio manager: David Boyle
Manager of Mercury ST UK Opportunities commenced February 1993 and Director of Mercury Asset Management; previously with a Merchant Bank as Pension Fund Manager; joined MAM in 1982; 20 years finance industry experience.

Contact: Jean Michel Rasquin

Performance:

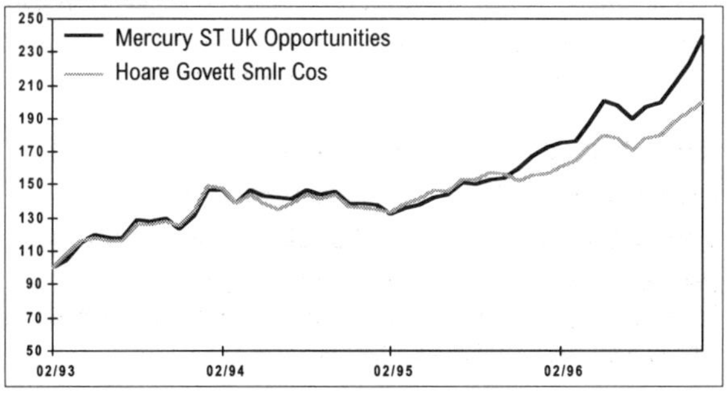

Purchase: Direct, Financial Advisor

Minimum investment: 5,000 USD

Custodian: S.G. Warburg & Co. Ltd (Luxembourg)

Listed: Luxembourg **Dealings:** Daily

Fund Sedol I.D.: 94035 **Published:** FT

Fees **Annual fee:** 1.50% **Performance fee:** None
Front end load: 5.00% **Redemption fee:** None
Switching fee: 6 Free switchings within a calender year

Top holdings:

AEA Technology	3.0%
Benson Group	2.4%
City Sites Estates	2.4%
FI Group	2.6%
Global Group	2.6%
Harry Ramsden's	2.5%
Lorien	2.7%
Ramco Energy	2.6%
Tyzack Precision	2.6%
Whittard of Chelsea	2.4%

TOTAL RETURNS %

3 months 1997	1996	1995	1994	3 years	5 years
1.63	43.32	20.19	5.98	82.56	N.A.

STATISTICS

Assets ($mil)	Current yield	Volatility	Risk return	Micropal Star Rating
39.89	—	3.76	5	✪✪✪✪✪

Mexican Investment Company
257/350

F&C Emerging Mkts Limited
Exchange House, Primrose Street, London EC2A 2NY, United Kingdom
Tel 44-171-628-1234 Fax 44-171-628-2283

Investment objective:
The fund seeks to provide a medium through which investors outside of Mexico may participate in the Mexican stock or future exchanges. The fund is denominated in US dollars.

Contact: Jane Davis

Performance:

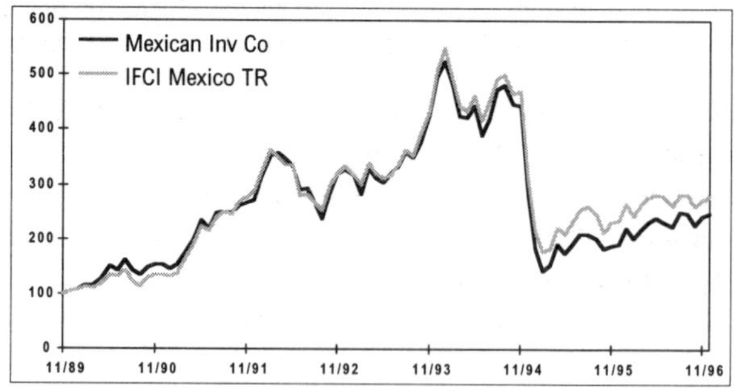

Umbrella fund: This is a singular fund.
Launch date: 06/11/89 **Domicile:** Luxembourg
Currency: USD **Structure:** Open ended, SICAV
Portfolio manager: Veroncia Berger Collins
Manager of Mexican Inv Co fund, FCEM's Argentinean and Colombian portfolios; read law/ languages- U of Buenos Aires; previously research analyst with Credit Suisse First Boston, London; joined Foreign & Colonial Emerging Markets 1992.
Purchase: Direct, Financial Advisor
Minimum investment: 5,000 USD
Custodian: State Street Bank Luxembourg S.A.
Listed: Luxembourg **Dealings:** Daily
Fund Sedol I.D.: 412142 **Published:** FT/IHT
Fees **Annual fee:** 2.25% **Performance fee:** None
Front end load: 5.00% **Redemption fee:** 0.50%
Switching fee: 5.50%

Top holdings:

Grupo Carso	8.3%
Grupo Industrial Maseca	6.9%
Grupo Modelo	5.9%
Kimberely Clark	8.3%
Telmex	10.0%

TOTAL RETURNS %

3 months 1997	1996	1995	1994	3 years	5 years
6.28	30.13	-32.47	-43.37	-50.23	-8.76

STATISTICS

Assets ($mil)	Current yield	Volatility	Risk return	Micropal Star Rating
28.98	—	12.41	—	✪✪

Momentum Stock Master
189/350

Momentum Asset Mgmt Ltd
140 Brompton Road, London SW3 1NY, United Kingdom
Tel 44-171-581-5841 Fax 44-171-581-5545
http://www. mbp_momentumuk.com

Investment objective:
The sub-fund seeks aggressive capital appreciation through hedged portfolio of global stocks, bonds, commodities and currencies. The sub-fund invests primarily with Julian Jaguar Fund which uses a macro-economic approach to global markets and a bottom-up approach to equity investment.

Contact: Mark Barker

Performance:

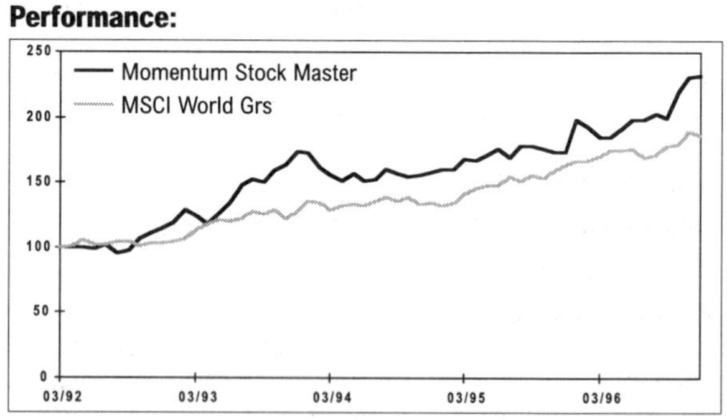

Umbrella fund: Momentum Performance Strategies Ltd
Launch date: 31/03/92 **Domicile:** Bermuda
Currency: USD **Structure:** Open ended, Mutual Fund
Portfolio manager: Momentum Advisory Ltd
Manager of Momentum Stock Master; located at Bank of Bermuda Building, 6 Front Street, Hamilton HM11, Bermuda.

Purchase: Direct, Financial Advisor
Minimum investment: 25,000 USD
Custodian: Bank of Bermuda
Listed: None **Dealings:** Monthly
Fund Sedol I.D.: 305352 **Published:** FT/IHT/TK/RT
Fees **Annual fee:** 1.25% **Performance fee:** 7.50%
Front end load: 5.00% **Redemption fee:** None
Switching fee: None

Top holdings:

AMR Corp	n/s
Barclays PLC	n/s
Cie Generale Des eaux	n/s
Citicorp	n/s
General Motors	n/s
Intel Corp.	n/s
Novartis AG	n/s
Tosco Corp	n/s
USAir Group	n/s
Wells Fargo	n/s

TOTAL RETURNS %

3 months 1997	1996	1995	1994	3 years	5 years
3.22	33.35	10.44	-9.29	33.60	N.A.

STATISTICS

Assets ($mil)	Current yield	Volatility	Risk return	Micropal Star Rating
24.35	—	3.87	1	✪✪✪

Morgan Grenfell American Enterprise Fund
61/350

Morgan Grenfell Asset Management (Irl) Ltd
George's Dock House, IFSC, Dublin 1, Ireland
Tel 353-1-607-6300 Fax 353-1-607-6491

Investment objective:
The sub-fund aims to provide long-term capital appreciation by investing primarily in the common shares of small and medium-sized US companies that are early in their life cycle but have the potential to become major enterprises. Such shares are generally traded over-the-counter and quoted on the NASDAQ. The fund may also invest in debt securities.

Umbrella fund: Morgan Grenfell Funds Plc
Launch date: 27/10/93 **Domicile:** Ireland [UCITS]
Currency: USD **Structure:** Open ended, VCIC
Portfolio manager: Audrey M T Jones, CFA
Manager of Morgan Grenfell American Enterprise Fund.

Contact: Orla Young /Catrina Dowling
Performance:

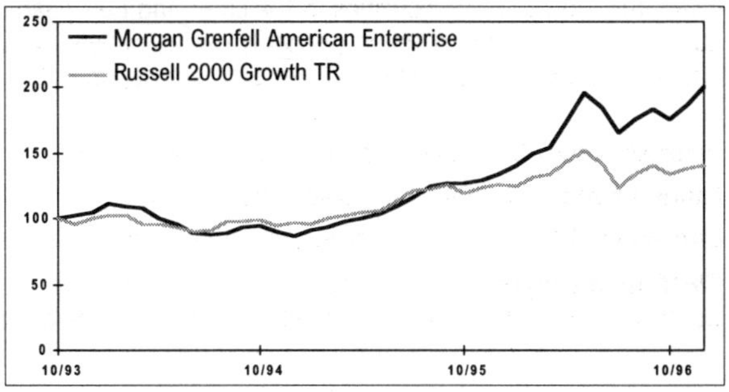

Purchase: Direct, Financial Advisor
Minimum investment: 75,000 USD
Custodian: Morgan Grenfell Custodial Services (Ireland) Ltd
Listed: Dublin **Dealings:** Weekly
Fund Sedol I.D.: 459189 **Published:** FT
Fees **Annual fee:** 1.50% **Performance fee:** None
Front end load: Up to 6.00% **Redemption fee:** None
Switching fee: 2.00%

Top holdings:

Capital Goods	27.8%
Cash	6.4%
Consumer Goods	23.3%
Energy	7.9%
Finance	9.8%
Materials	3.5%
Multi Indusrial	1.4%
Services	19.9%

TOTAL RETURNS %

3 months 1997	1996	1995	1994	3 years	5 years
-3.48	49.37	55.40	-17.04	92.56	N.A.

STATISTICS

Assets ($mil)	Current yield	Volatility	Risk return	Micropal Star Rating
17.70	—	5.34	2	✪✪✪✪

Morgan Grenfell Emerging Markets Fixed Income Fund
160/350

Morgan Grenfell Asset Management (Irl) Ltd
George's Dock House, IFSC, Dublin 1, Ireland
Tel 353-1-607-6300 Fax 353-1-607-6491

Investment objective:
The sub-fund aims for capital growth from investments in fixed income securities of any credit quality issuers located in countries with emerging securities markets. The top country allocations of the portfolio are the following: Brazil (27.9%); Russia (16.9%); Argentina (16.9%); Venezuela (10.0%); Equator (4.6); and Morocco (3.4%).

Umbrella fund: Morgan Grenfell Fixed Income Fund Plc
Launch date: 17/02/94 **Domicile:** Ireland [UCITS]
Currency: USD **Structure:** Open ended, VCIC
Portfolio manager: David Dowjett
Manager of Morgan Grenfell Emerging Market Fixed Income.

Contact: Orla Young /Catrina Dowling
Performance:

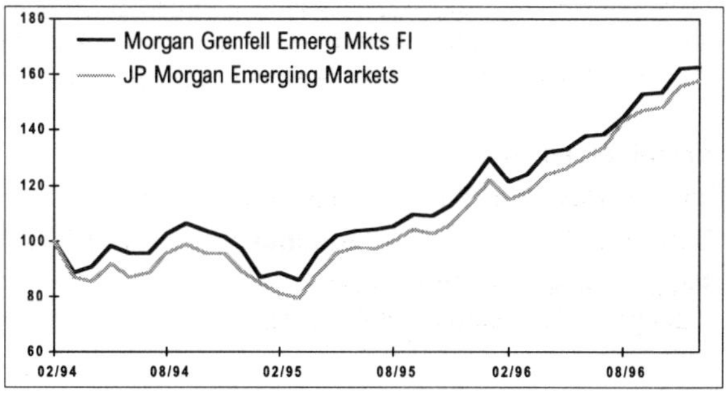

Purchase: Direct, Financial Advisor
Minimum investment: 300,000 USD
Custodian: Morgan Grenfell Custodial Services (Ireland) Ltd
Listed: Dublin **Dealings:** Weekly
Fund Sedol I.D.: 60478 **Published:** FT
Fees **Annual fee:** 1.40% **Performance fee:** None
Front end load: Up to 6.00% **Redemption fee:** None
Switching fee: 2.00%

Top holdings:

Argentina Disc. Bd 03/23	5.7%
Argentina FRB-PDI 6.492/05	4.6%
Brazil C-Bonds	4.3%
Brazil Disc. 04/24	5.2%
Brazil Mydfa FRN	4.1%
Brazil NMB 94 FRN	7.1%
Brazil PAR 04/24	6.9%
Mexico 6.25% USD-A	6.1%
Russia USD Loan	13.4%
Venezeula Discounts	4.3%

TOTAL RETURNS %

3 months 1997	1996	1995	1994	3 years	5 years
3.59	35.48	23.88	N.A.	N.A.	N.A.

STATISTICS

Assets ($mil)	Current yield	Volatility	Risk return	Micropal Star Rating
20.80	—	N.A.	—	———

Morgan Grenfell Euro Emerging Mkts Fund
63/350

Morgan Grenfell Asset Management (Irl) Ltd
George's Dock House, IFSC, Dublin 1, Ireland
Tel 353-1-607-6300 Fax 353-1-607-6491

Investment objective:
The sub-fund aims to achieve long-term capital growth through investments in a diversified portfolio of securities in the emerging European equity markets. Emerging European in this context refers primarily to the markets of Greece, Portugal, Turkey, Poland, Hungary, Czech Republic and Slovakia Republic.

Umbrella fund: Morgan Grenfell Fixed Income Fund Plc
Launch date: 02/08/94 **Domicile:** Ireland
Currency: GBP **Structure:** Open ended, VCIC
Portfolio manager: Chris Turner and Daniel Salter
Co-Managers of the Morgan Grenfell European Emerging Market Fund.

Contact: Orla Young /Catrina Dowling
Performance:

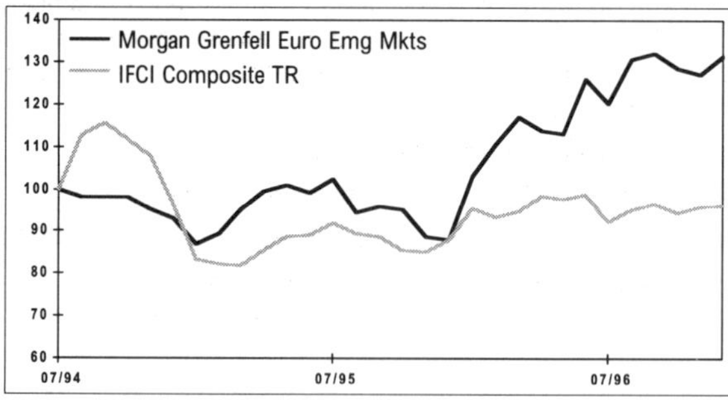

Purchase: Direct, Financial Advisor
Minimum investment: 1,000 GBP
Custodian: Morgan Grenfell Custodial Services (Ireland) Ltd
Listed: Dublin **Dealings:** Weekly
Fund Sedol I.D.: 60489 **Published:** FT
Fees **Annual fee:** 1.50% **Performance fee:** None
Front end load: Up to 6.00% **Redemption fee:** Up to 2%
Switching fee: 2.00%

Top holdings:

Ardem	4.7%
Bkapramysl	2.9%
Bohemia	3.9%
Debica	3.4%
Egis & Yes	4.8%
Elektrim	4.8%
Pliva	4.3%
Richter Gedeon	4.9%
Valifav Kiral	3.9%
Zagrebalka Banka	4.7%

TOTAL RETURNS %

3 months 1997	1996	1995	1994	3 years	5 years
9.23	49.21	-5.28	N.A.	N.A.	N.A.

STATISTICS

Assets ($mil)	Current yield	Volatility	Risk return	Micropal Star Rating
8.97	—	N.A.	—	———

Morgan Grenfell European Fund
292/350

Morgan Grenfell Asset Management (Irl) Ltd
George's Dock House, IFSC, Dublin 1, Ireland
Tel 353-1-607-6300 Fax 353-1-607-6491

Investment objective:
The sub-fund seeks to provide a means by which investors can invest in a professionally managed well diversified portfolio of continental European equities. The top country allocations of the portfolio are as follows: Sweden (20.6%); France (17.7%); Netherlands (13.8%); Germany (9.5%); Denmark (9.0%); and Italy (8.1%).

Umbrella fund: Morgan Grenfell Profunds Plc
Launch date: 03/01/93 **Domicile:** Ireland
Currency: GBP **Structure:** Open ended, VCIC
Portfolio manager: Katrina Mitchell
Manager of Morgan Grenfell PF European Fund commenced February 1996.

Contact: Orla Young /Catrina Dowling
Performance:

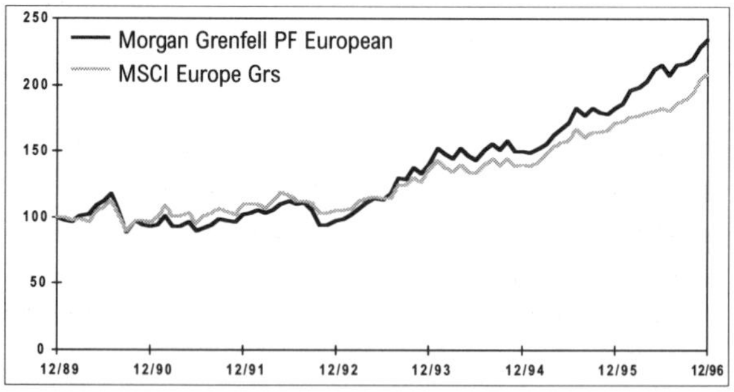

Purchase: Direct, Financial Advisor
Minimum investment: 50,000 GBP
Custodian: Morgan Grenfell Custodial Services (Ireland) Ltd
Listed: Dublin **Dealings:** Daily
Fund Sedol I.D.: 458948 **Published:** FT
Fees **Annual fee:** 0.50% **Performance fee:** None
Front end load: Up to 6.00% **Redemption fee:** None
Switching fee: 2.00%

Top holdings:

Assa Abloy	2.9%
BIC	3.3%
Carrefour	3.3%
Elsevier	2.7%
Falck	2.8%
Gucci	3.3%
Novartis	2.7%
Novo-Nordiska As -B-	3.7%
Securitas	3.2%
Wolters Kluwer	2.9%

TOTAL RETURNS %

3 months 1997	1996	1995	1994	3 years	5 years
4.59	28.48	21.39	6.94	66.80	130.13

STATISTICS

Assets ($mil)	Current yield	Volatility	Risk return	Micropal Star Rating
546.05	—	3.23	4	✪✪✪✪✪

Morgan Grenfell Latin America Fund
283/350

Morgan Grenfell Asset Management (Irl) Ltd
George's Dock House, IFSC, Dublin 1, Ireland
Tel 353-1-607-6300 Fax 353-1-607-6491

Investment objective:
The sub-fund aims to achieve long-term appreciation through investment in Latin American securities. The top country allocations of the portfolio include the following: Brazil (42.0%); Mexico (25.%); Argentina (11.0%); and Chile (9.0%).

Umbrella fund: Morgan Grenfell Funds Plc
Launch date: 22/06/93 **Domicile:** Ireland [UCITS]
Currency: GBP **Structure:** Open ended, VCIC
Portfolio manager: Richard Lamb
Manager of Morgan Grenfell Latin American.

Purchase: Direct, Financial Advisor
Minimum investment: 10,000 GBP
Custodian: Morgan Grenfell Custodial Services (Ireland) Ltd
Listed: Dublin **Dealings:** Weekly
Fund Sedol I.D.: 60467 **Published:** FT
Fees **Annual fee:** 0.75% **Performance fee:** None
Front end load: Up to 6.00% **Redemption fee:** None
Switching fee: 2.00%

Contact: Orla Young /Catrina Dowling

Performance:

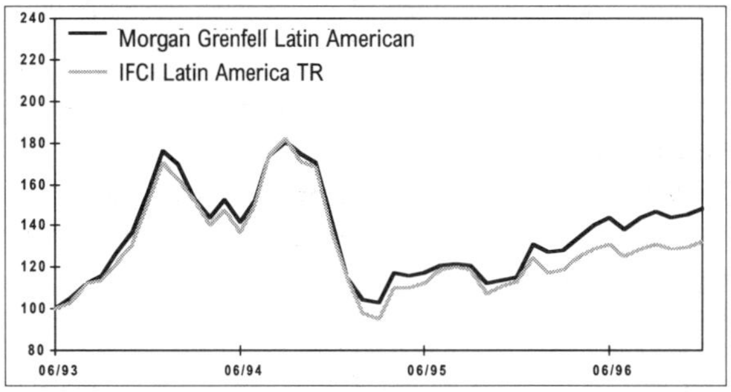

Top holdings:

Electrobas	2.4%
GPO Carso SA DE CV	2.1%
Perez Company SA	1.9%
Petrol Brazil	2.0%
Telebras Telec Braspon	7.7%
Telecom de Chile	2.0%
Telefonas de Mexico	3.8%
Usiminas - USI SD	2.2%
Vale Rio Doce	2.5%
YPF SA Spon ADR	2.5%

TOTAL RETURNS %

3 months 1997	1996	1995	1994	3 years	5 years
18.20	28.95	-18.58	-9.05	-4.51	N.A.

STATISTICS

Assets ($mil)	Current yield	Volatility	Risk return	Micropal Star Rating
30.45	—	7.44	—	✪✪✪

Morgan Grenfell Selector UK Fund
266/350

Morgan Grenfell Asset Management (Irl) Ltd
George's Dock House, IFSC, Dublin 1, Ireland
Tel 353-1-607-6300 Fax 353-1-607-6491

Investment objective:
The sub-fund aims for capital appreciation through investment in UK equities quoted on the London Stock Exchange. The top sector allocations of the portfolio are as follows: services (31.1%); finance (19.2%); industrial cyclical (18.7%); and consumer goods (10.6%).

Umbrella fund: Morgan Grenfell International Funds Plc
Launch date: 12/06/93 **Domicile:** Ireland [UCITS]
Currency: GBP **Structure:** Open ended, VCIC
Portfolio manager: Charles Curtis
Manager of Morgan Grenfell Selector United Kingdom commenced June 1993.

Purchase: Direct, Financial Advisor
Minimum investment: 1,000 GBP
Custodian: Morgan Grenfell Custodial Services (Ireland) Ltd
Listed: Dublin **Dealings:** Daily
Fund Sedol I.D.: 460725 **Published:** FT
Fees **Annual fee:** 1.50% **Performance fee:** None
Front end load: Up to 5.50% **Redemption fee:** None
Switching fee: 2.00%

Contact: Orla Young /Catrina Dowling

Performance:

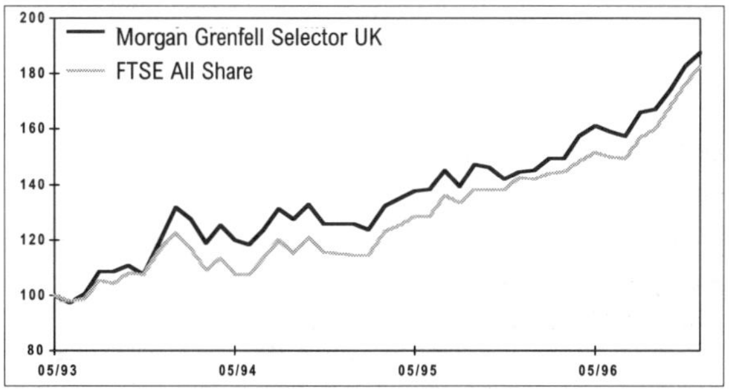

Top holdings:

Barclays PLC	2.9%
British Petroleum	3.5%
British Telecom	2.7%
Glaxo Wellcome	3.9%
Lloyds TSB Group	4.0%
Royal +Sun Alliance	2.2%
Royal Bank of Scotland	2.0%
Shell Transport & Trading	2.2%
Waste Recycled	2.0%
Zeneca Group	2.0%

TOTAL RETURNS %

3 months 1997	1996	1995	1994	3 years	5 years
0.06	29.72	15.21	5.72	58.00	N.A.

STATISTICS

Assets ($mil)	Current yield	Volatility	Risk return	Micropal Star Rating
119.60	—	3.93	4	✪✪✪✪

Morgan Stanley SICAV Emerging Market Debt Fund
53/350

Morgan Stanley Asset Management
6c Route de Treves, Senningerberg, L-2633 Luxembourg
Tel 352-34-64-60-00 Fax 352-34-64-62-22

Investment objective:
The sub-fund invests in countries that have fundamentally attractive debt bond prospects and a positive rate of change both politically and economically. The goal is to establish positions when market sentiment is negative, creating under-valuation, and lighten or eliminate holdings as countries become more economically mature and stable. Fee share class: IN- Institutional, A- Front-end load, B- Back-end load.

Umbrella fund: Morgan Stanley SICAV
Launch date: 01/04/95 **Domicile:** Luxembourg [UCITS]
Currency: USD **Structure:** Open ended, SICAV
Portfolio manager: Paol Ghaffari
Manager of the fund and MD of the Firm; MS, foreign service- Georgetown U; previously VP of fixed income division of emerging markets sales and trading at Morgan Stanley & Co; joined Morgan Stanley Asset Management in 1993.
Purchase: Direct, Financial Advisor
Minimum investment: IN- 2,500,000; A/B- 10, 000 USD
Custodian: Morgan Stanley Bank Luxembourg SA.
Listed: None **Dealings:** Daily
Fund Sedol I.D.: 300545 **Published:** SC/BZ/DS/CS/IS/FT/BG/RT
Fees **Annual fee:** Up to 1.40% **Performance fee:** None
Front end load: Up to 4.00% **Redemption fee:** CDSC up to 4.00%
Switching fee: None

Contact: Customer Services Department
Performance:

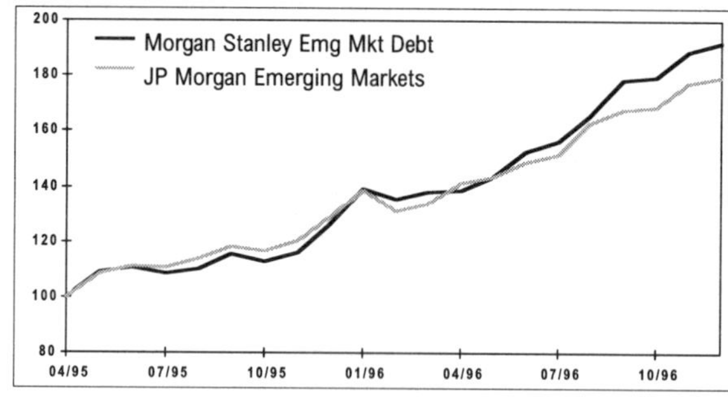

Top holdings:

Holding	%
Argentina Pre 3 Ser 2	4.2%
Argentina Ser.L Euro	8.0%
Brazil C-Bonds Euro	9.5%
Bulgaria Interest Arrears Bond	4.7%
Bulgaria USD Series A	4.3%
Ecuador PDI	5.7%
Mexico Disc Bonds Ser A Euro	3.8%
Morocco Restruct & Cons ADR	3.8%
Russia BFEA Loan Agreements	6.1%
Venzuela Ser A Euro	3.9%

TOTAL RETURNS %

3 months 1997	1996	1995	1994	3 years	5 years
5.64	51.92	N.A.	N.A.	N.A.	N.A.

STATISTICS

Assets ($mil)	Current yield	Volatility	Risk return	Micropal Star Rating
17.30	—	N.A.	—	———

Morgan Stanley SICAV Latin American Fund
69/350

Morgan Stanley Asset Management
6c Route de Treves, Senningerberg, L-2633 Luxembourg
Tel 352-34-64-60-00 Fax 352-34-64-62-22

Investment objective:
The sub-fund aims to achieve superior returns through investment in a diversified portfolio of Latin American issuers. The investment discipline of the sub-fund is growth driven. The fund seeks to capitalise on positive economic developments using both a top-down and a bottom-up approach. Fee share class: IN- Institutional, A- Front-end load, B- Back-end load.

Umbrella fund: Morgan Stanley SICAV
Launch date: 01/08/94 **Domicile:** Luxembourg [UCITS]
Currency: USD **Structure:** Open ended, SICAV
Portfolio manager: Robert Meyer CFA
Manager of Morgan Stanley Latin American and MD of Morgan Stanley & Co; BA, economics/political science- Yale U and JD- Harvard Law School; joined Morgan Stanley Asset Management in 1989.
Purchase: Direct, Financial Advisor
Minimum investment: IN- 2,500,000; A/B- 10, 000 USD
Custodian: Morgan Stanley Bank Luxembourg SA.
Listed: None **Dealings:** Daily
Fund Sedol I.D.: 301996 **Published:** SC/BZ/DS/CS/IS/FT/BG/RT
Fees **Annual fee:** Up to 1.50% **Performance fee:** None
Front end load: Up to 5.75% **Redemption fee:** CDSC up to 4.00%
Switching fee: None

Contact: Customer Services Department
Performance:

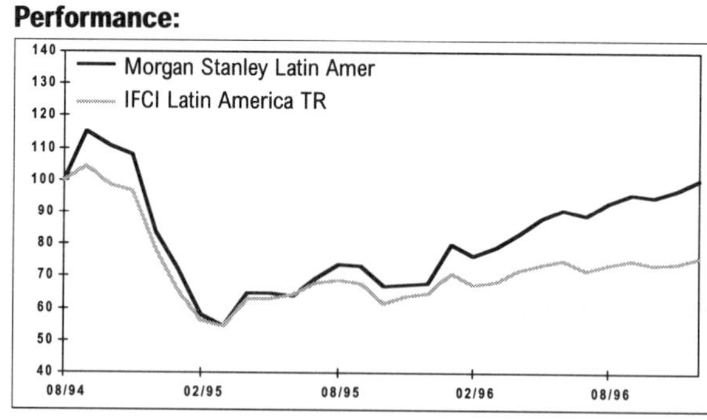

Top holdings:

Holding	%
Banco De Colombia	2.5%
Telefonas Venezuela	4.0%
Centrias Electrias Brasilieras	5.3%
Fomento Economico Mexico	5.9%
Grupo Televisa	3.9%
Losas Renner	2.8%
Petroleo Brasiliero	2.5%
Telecommunication Brasilieras	10.7%
Telefonica De Argentina	6.3%
Tubos De Acero Mexico	2.7%

TOTAL RETURNS %

3 months 1997	1996	1995	1994	3 years	5 years
17.79	48.17	-19.07	N.A.	N.A.	N.A.

STATISTICS

Assets ($mil)	Current yield	Volatility	Risk return	Micropal Star Rating
11.49	—	N.A.	—	———

Morgan Stanley SICAV US Equity Growth Fund

287/350

Morgan Stanley Asset Management
6c Route de Treves, Senningerberg, L-2633 Luxembourg
Tel 352-34-64-60-00 Fax 352-34-64-62-22

Investment objective:
The sub-fund seeks long-term capital appreciation by investing primarily in common stocks of medium to large capitalisation US companies with sustainable earnings growth or earnings momentum. The investment process is bottom-up and driven by fundamental equity research. The top sector allocation is consumer goods (55.1%). Fee share class: IN- Institutional, A- Front-end load, B- Back-end load.

Umbrella fund: Morgan Stanley SICAV

Launch date: 01/08/92 **Domicile:** Luxembourg [UCITS]

Currency: USD **Structure:** Open ended, SICAV

Portfolio manager: Kurt Feuerman and Margaret Johnson
Co-Managers of the fund commenced July 1993. Mr Feuerman, specialises in emerging growth stock/ gaming/ restaurants/ tobacco MA- Syracuse U; previously MD of Drexel Burnham Lambert; 13 years finance industry experience.

Purchase: Direct, Financial Advisor

Minimum investment: IN- 2,500,000; A/B- 10, 000 USD

Custodian: Morgan Stanley Bank Luxembourg SA

Listed: None **Dealings:** Daily

Fund Sedol I.D.: 301990 **Published:** SC/BZ/DS/CS/IS/FT/BG/RT

Fees **Annual fee:** Up to 1.20% **Performance fee:** None
Front end load: Up to 5.75% **Redemption fee:** CDSC up to 4.00%
Switching fee: None

Contact: Customer Services Department

Performance:

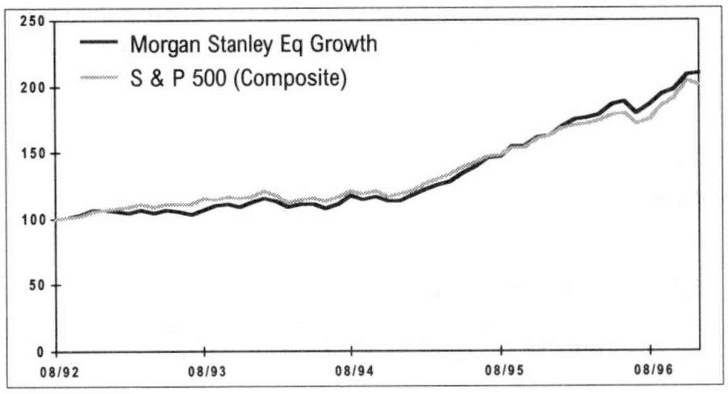

Top holdings:

Holding	%
Campbell Soup Co	3.7%
Clear Channel Communications	2.5%
Gtech Hldg	3.2%
HFS Inc	6.7%
International Game Technology	2.6%
K-III Communications	2.9%
Philip Morris	5.6%
RJR Nabisco	8.2%
United Technologies	3.1%
Wells Fargo	2.9%

TOTAL RETURNS %

3 months 1997	1996	1995	1994	3 years	5 years
4.12	28.72	42.97	1.76	87.26	N.A.

STATISTICS

Assets ($mil)	Current yield	Volatility	Risk return	Micropal Star Rating
57.01	—	2.79	5	✪✪✪✪✪

Mosais SICAV Actiones Espagnoles Et Portugaises

227/350

Credit Agricole
13 Avenue Porte-Neuve, L-1223 Luxembourg
Tel 352-46-808-267 Fax 352-46-52-50

Investment objective:
The sub-fund aims at obtaining medium-term capital appreciation through active management by investing in a portfolio of Spanish and Portuguese transferable securities. The top sector allocations of the portfolio are the following: energy (35.7%); finance (23.2%); and services (14.4%). The base currency of the fund is Spanish pesetas.

Umbrella fund: Mosais SICAV

Launch date: 12/02/90 **Domicile:** Luxembourg [UCITS]

Currency: ESP **Structure:** Open ended, SICAV

Portfolio manager: Segespar SA
Management company of Credit Agricole Group commenced managing the sub-fund January 1990; located at 90, Boulevard Pasteur, F-75015, Paris, France.

Purchase: Direct, Financial Advisor, Credit Agricole Subsidiaries & Caisses Regionales

Minimum investment: 1,500 ECU

Custodian: Credit Agricole Luxembourg S.A

Listed: Luxembourg **Dealings:** Daily

Fund Sedol I.D.: 301329 **Published:** TR/RT/TK

Fees **Annual fee:** 0.80% **Performance fee:** None
Front end load: Up to 4.50% **Redemption fee:** None
Switching fee: None

Contact: Frank Gimel

Performance:

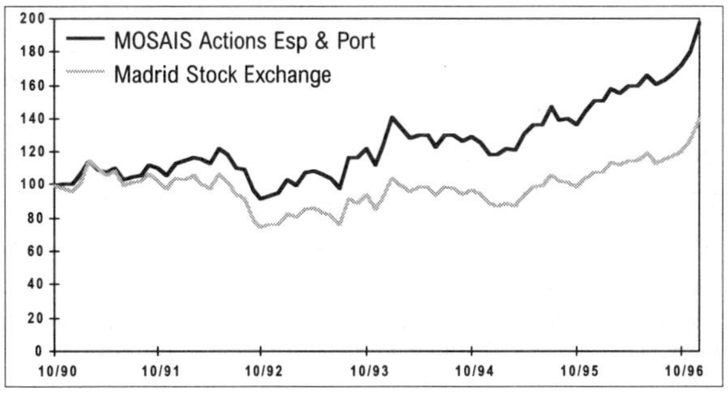

Top holdings:

Holding	%
Agnes de Barcelona	2.7%
Aumar	3.1%
Autopisto Concesion	3.8%
Banco Bilbao Vizcana	3.8%
Banco de Santander	6.9%
Banco Popular Esp	3.1%
Empresa Nacion Endessa	8.8%
Iberdola	8.6%
Repsol	6.3%
Telefonica de Espana	6.1%

TOTAL RETURNS %

3 months 1997	1996	1995	1994	3 years	5 years
-2.43	31.18	27.16	-4.45	59.38	75.03

STATISTICS

Assets ($mil)	Current yield	Volatility	Risk return	Micropal Star Rating
17.58	—	4.39	1	✪

Mosais SICAV Actiones Francaises

314/350

Credit Agricole
13 Avenue Porte-Neuve, L-1223 Luxembourg
Tel 352-46-808-267 Fax 352-46-52-50

Investment objective:
The sub-fund seeks to obtain medium-term capital appreciation through active management. The portfolio is invested in French transferable securities. Currently the asset allocations of the portfolio are as follows: equities (79.1%); bonds (10.9%); and cash/MM (9.2%).

Umbrella fund: Mosais SICAV
Launch date: 12/02/90 **Domicile:** Luxembourg [UCITS]
Currency: FRF **Structure:** Open ended, SICAV
Portfolio manager: Segespar SA
Management company of Credit Agricole Group commenced managing the sub-fund January 1990; located at 90, Boulevard Pasteur, F-75015, Paris, France.

Purchase: Direct, Financial Advisor, Credit Agricole Subsidiaries & Caisses Regionales
Minimum investment: 1,500 ECU
Custodian: Credit Agricole Luxembourg S.A
Listed: Luxembourg **Dealings:** Daily
Fund Sedol I.D.: 301328 **Published:** TR/RT/TK
Fees **Annual fee:** 0.80% **Performance fee:** None
Front end load: Up to 4.50% **Redemption fee:** None
Switching fee: None

Contact: Frank Gimel

Performance:

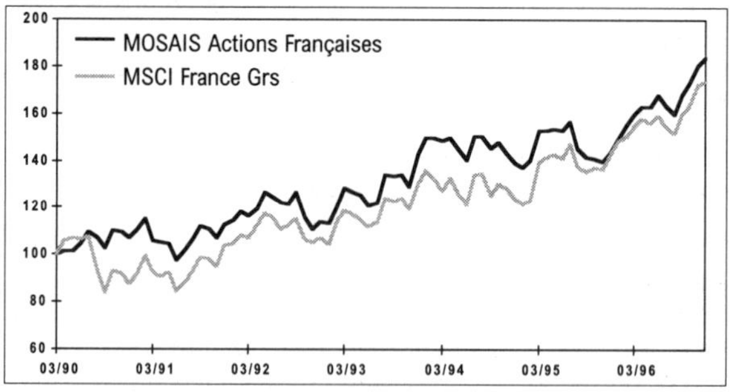

Top holdings:

Consumer Goods	10.1%
Energy	11.7%
Finance	14.9%
Government	11.7%
Retail Trade	11.5%
Telecommunications	9.2%

TOTAL RETURNS %

3 months 1997	1996	1995	1994	3 years	5 years
6.69	28.03	2.81	-2.29	28.61	62.60

STATISTICS

Assets ($mil)	Current yield	Volatility	Risk return	Micropal Star Rating
26.13	—	3.37	3	✪✪✪✪

Multilink Finnish Equities

181/350

Skandia Life Assurance(Holdings) Ltd
11 Boulevard Grande-Duchesse Charlotte, L-1331 Luxembourg
Tel 352-25-47-01-255 Fax 352-25-47-01-500

Investment objective:
The sub-fund invests its assets in equities quoted mainly on the Finnish markets. Only 10% of its net assets are invested in non-quoted shares if the quotations are expected to begin in less than 1 year. The top sector allocations of the portfolio are the following: forest products/paper (12.0%); electronics/electrical (9.2%); and heavy industries (8.1%).
Umbrella fund: Multilink
Launch date: 01/10/93 **Domicile:** Luxembourg [UCITS]
Currency: FIM **Structure:** Open ended, SICAV
Portfolio manager: Skandia Advisory Company SA
Investment Advisor of MultiLink Finnish Equities: located at Skandia Advisory Company SA -69, Route d'Esch, L-1470 Luxembourg.

Purchase: Direct, Financial Advisor
Minimum investment: 10,000 SEK
Custodian: Banque Internationale (Luxembourg)
Listed: Luxembourg **Dealings:** Daily
Fund Sedol I.D.: 300514 **Published:** None
Fees **Annual fee:** 1.00% **Performance fee:** None
Front end load: Up to 5.00% **Redemption fee:** None
Switching fee: None

Contact: Marc Vanmansart

Performance:

Top holdings:

Finnlines	4.2%
Huhtamaeki	4.7%
Kemira	3.9%
Kesko	6.0%
Nokia A	5.1%
Nokia K	4.1%
Orion	5.7%
Rautaruukki	4.3%
UPM Kymmene	9.1%
Valmet	7.0%

TOTAL RETURNS %

3 months 1997	1996	1995	1994	3 years	5 years
3.03	33.61	-9.02	22.02	48.33	N.A.

STATISTICS

Assets ($mil)	Current yield	Volatility	Risk return	Micropal Star Rating
14.99	—	6.09	2	✪✪

Multilink Scandinavian Equities
307/350

Skandia Life Assurance(Holdings) Ltd
11 Boulevard Grande-Duchesse Charlotte, L-1331 Luxembourg
Tel 352-25-47-01-255 Fax 352-25-47-01-500

Investment objective:
The sub-fund seeks to invest its assets in equities quoted mainly on the Scandinavian Stock Exchange. Only 10% of the fund's net assets are invested in non-quoted shares if the quotations are expected to begin in less than 1 year. The top sector allocations of the portfolio are the following: electronics/electrical (19.9%); pharmaceuticals (14.1%); and finance (7.6%).

Umbrella fund: Multilink

Launch date: 01/12/90 **Domicile:** Luxembourg [UCITS]

Currency: SEK **Structure:** Open ended, SICAV

Portfolio manager: Skandia Advisory Company SA
Investment Advisor of MultiLink Finnish Equities: located at Skandia Advisory Company SA -69, Route d'Esch, L-1470 Luxembourg.

Contact: Marc Vanmansart

Performance:

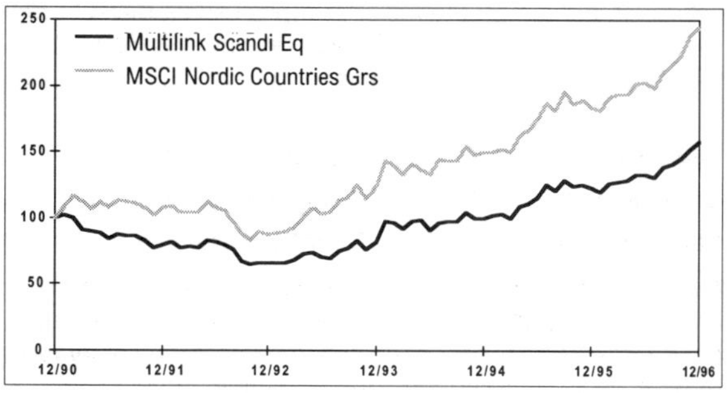

Purchase: Direct, Financial Advisor

Minimum investment: 10,000 SEK

Custodian: Banque Internationale (Luxembourg)

Listed: Luxembourg **Dealings:** Daily

Fund Sedol I.D.: 481228 **Published:** None

Fees **Annual fee:** 1.00% **Performance fee:** None
Front end load: Up to 5.00% **Redemption fee:** None
Switching fee: None

Top holdings:

Holding	%
Astra	9.7%
Dampskibssels B	2.4%
Nokia A	6.3%
Norsk Hydro As	4.1%
Orion B	2.5%
Stadshypotek A	2.2%
Telefon AB L M Ericisson	9.0%
UPM Kymmene	2.1%
Volvo B	2.5%

TOTAL RETURNS %

3 months 1997	1996	1995	1994	3 years	5 years
5.18	28.10	23.07	21.71	91.88	98.80

STATISTICS

Assets ($mil)	Current yield	Volatility	Risk return	Micropal Star Rating
25.65	—	4.82	3	✪✪✪✪

Nestor Lateinamerika Fonds
194/350

Nestor Investment Mgt SA
Friedrichstr. 76, Krouberg, 61476, Germany
Tel 49-6173-94-0405 Fax 49-6173-94-0406
E mail nestor.funds@online.de

Investment objective:
The sub-fund aims at capital growth through investment in shares of Latin American companies selling at substantial discounts from intrinsic value. The top sector allocations of the portfolio are the following: technology (20.9%); finance (18.4%); energy (17.4%); utilities (14.6%); and services 13.5%). This fund is primarily invested in Brazil (66.4%) and Mexico (12.1).

Umbrella fund: Nestor Fonds

Launch date: 19/01/94 **Domicile:** Luxembourg [UCITS]

Currency: DEM **Structure:** Open ended, Unit Trust

Portfolio manager: Peter J. Gruber
Manager of Nestor Lateinamerika since fund inception, 1994 and Manager of Latinvest Fund; over 20 years investment experience in Latin American equity and emerging markets.

Contact: Dr Klaus Kaposi

Performance:

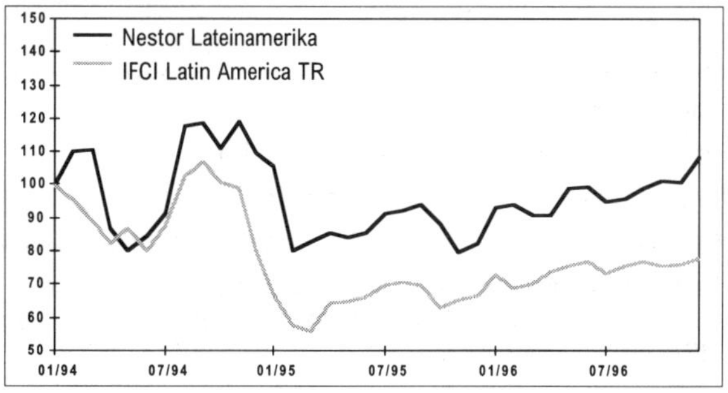

Purchase: Direct, Financial Advisor, M.H. Warburg Bank Lux /Hamburg /Frankfurt

Minimum investment: 10,000 DEM

Custodian: M.M. Warburg Bank (Luxembourg)

Listed: None **Dealings:** Weekly

Fund Sedol I.D.: 972881 **Published:** BZ/FAZ

Fees **Annual fee:** 1.35% **Performance fee:** 12.50%
Front end load: 5.00% **Redemption fee:** None
Switching fee: 1.00%

Top holdings:

Holding	%
Banco Itau	6.2%
Bco Bradesco	5.0%
Bco Del Pacifico	3.1%
Cementos De Mexico	3.3%
Electrobas	10.4%
Ipiranga Petrol	4.2%
Petrobas	5.8%
Telebras	10.9%
Telefonas de Mexico	3.2%
Venezuela FPN 2007	5.4%

TOTAL RETURNS %

3 months 1997	1996	1995	1994	3 years	5 years
9.62	33.15	-24.89	N.A.	N.A.	N.A.

STATISTICS

Assets ($mil)	Current yield	Volatility	Risk return	Micropal Star Rating
7.72	—	N.A.	—	———

Newton UGF Continental Europe
297/350

Newton Fund Mgrs (C.I.) Ltd
PO Box 548 Newton House, Bath Street, St Helier, JE4 8UH, Jersey
Tel 44-1534-285-707 Fax 44-1534-285-751

Investment objective:
The sub-fund seeks long-term capital growth though investment in a selection of securities quoted on the major European stock markets excluding the UK. Emphasis is placed on the markets of France, Holland, Germany, Italy and Switzerland but may include exposure to other markets such as Spain and Austria.

Umbrella fund: Newton Universal Growth Fund

Launch date: 01/03/88 **Domicile:** Jersey

Currency: USD **Structure:** Open ended, Investment Company

Portfolio manager: Kelran Gallagher of Newton Fund Management (CI)Ltd
Manager of Newton UGF Continental Europe; MA Hons, economics- U Canterbury; previously with Sunlife assurance, the European equity desk; joined the European desk at Newton Investment Management in 1993.

Purchase: Direct, Financial Advisor

Minimum investment: 5,000 GBP

Custodian: Royal Bank of Scotland Trust Company (Jersey) Ltd

Listed: None **Dealings:** Daily

Fund Sedol I.D.: 17410 **Published:** FT/IHT/SC

Fees **Annual fee:** 1.25% **Performance fee:** None
Front end load: 5.50% **Redemption fee:** None
Switching fee: None

Contact: Wendy Herve

Performance:

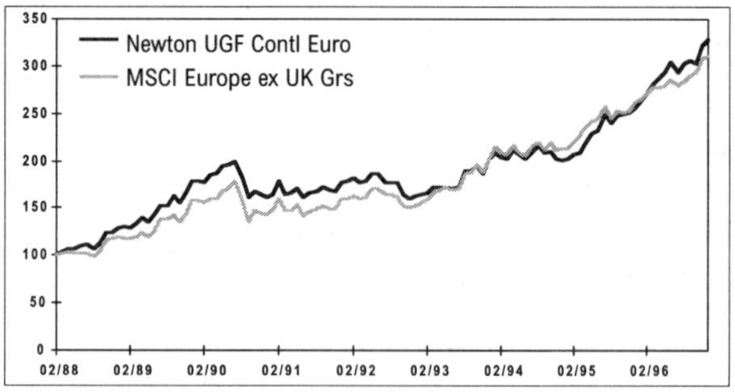

Top holdings:

Holding	%
Adidas	3.2%
Bure Investment	3.1%
Elf Aquitaine	3.5%
Lufthansa	3.0%
Nokia A	3.6%
SAP AG	3.1%
Sligos	3.5%
Societe Generale	3.0%
Telecel	3.0%
Telecom Italia Mobile	3.5%

TOTAL RETURNS %

3 months 1997	1996	1995	1994	3 years	5 years
6.93	28.38	27.25	-1.15	61.48	85.60

STATISTICS

Assets ($mil)	Current yield	Volatility	Risk return	Micropal Star Rating
21.90	—	2.80	5	✪✪✪✪

Nikko GUF Hong Kong
47/350

Nikko Bank Luxembourg
16 Boulevard Royal, PO Box 14, L-2010 Luxembourg
Tel 352-46-23-84 Fax 352-46-23-83

Investment objective:
The fund aims to out perform the benchmark of the Hang Seng Index. This is done through a core portfolio investing in listed stocks, combined with a satellite portfolio investing in high growth, small capitalisation issues and certain non-listed issues of the market. The top sector allocations of the portfolio are: holdings/finance (68.0%) and real estate companies (13.0%).

Umbrella fund: Nikko Global Umbrella Fund

Launch date: 01/03/93 **Domicile:** Luxembourg [UCITS]

Currency: USD **Structure:** Open ended, SICAV

Portfolio manager: Nikko Capital Management (Singapore)Ltd
Investment Advisor of Nikko Hong Kong Fund; located at 80 Raffles Place, 44-02 UOB Plaza 1, Singapore 0104.

Purchase: Direct

Minimum investment: 5,000 USD

Custodian: Nikko Bank (Luxembourg) SA

Listed: Luxembourg **Dealings:** Daily

Fund Sedol I.D.: 301511 **Published:** BL/RT

Fees **Annual fee:** 1.00% **Performance fee:** None
Front end load: Up to 5.00% **Redemption fee:** Up to 1.50%
Switching fee: None

Contact: Customer Services Department

Performance:

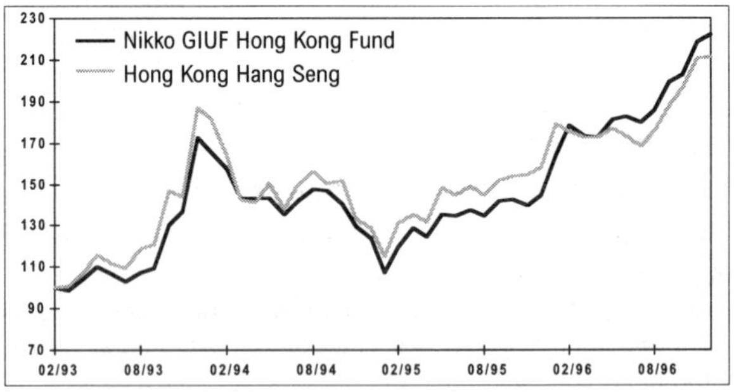

Top holdings:

Holding	%
Cheung Kong Holdings Ltd	4.8%
Citic Pacific	8.1%
Guandong Invest Ltd	5.4%
Hang Seng Bank	7.7%
HSBC Holdings	8.1%
Hutchison Whampoa	7.8%
New World Development	4.6%
Sun Hung Kai Properties	7.7%
Swire Pacific	4.5%
Wharf Holdings	3.4%

TOTAL RETURNS %

3 months 1997	1996	1995	1994	3 years	5 years
-6.61	53.42	17.23	-28.31	28.94	N.A.

STATISTICS

Assets ($mil)	Current yield	Volatility	Risk return	Micropal Star Rating
2.20	—	5.76	3	✪✪✪✪

Nikko GUF Oceania Fund
230/350

Nikko Bank Luxembourg
16 Boulevard Royal, PO Box 14, L-2010 Luxembourg
Tel 352-46-23-84 Fax 352-46-23-83

Investment objective:
The fund seeks to out perform the market benchmark of the Australia All Ordinaries Share Index. This is accomplished by investing in listed stocks, combined with a satellite portfolio investing in high growth, small capitalisation issues and certain non-listed issues in the Australian market.

Umbrella fund: Nikko Global Umbrella Fund
Launch date: 01/03/93 **Domicile:** Luxembourg [UCITS]
Currency: USD **Structure:** Open ended, SICAV
Portfolio manager: Nikko Capital Management (Singapore)Ltd
Investment Advisor of Nikko Oceania Fund; located at 80 Raffles Place, 44-02 UOB Plaza 1, Singapore 0104.

Purchase: Direct
Minimum investment: 5,000 USD
Custodian: Nikko Bank (Luxembourg) SA
Listed: Luxembourg **Dealings:** Daily
Fund Sedol I.D.: 301517 **Published:** RT/BL
Fees **Annual fee:** 1.00% **Performance fee:** None
Front end load: Up to 5.00% **Redemption fee:** Up to 1.50%
Switching fee: None

Contact: Customer Services Department

Performance:

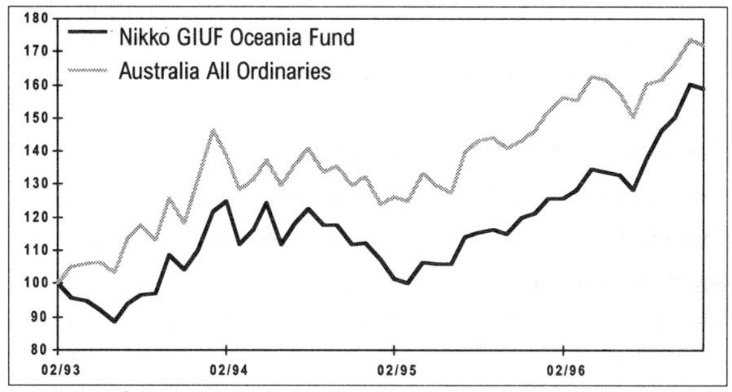

Top holdings:

Holding	%
AMP Office Trust	3.7%
ANZ Banking Group Ltd	3.8%
Commonwealth Bk of Australia	3.3%
CRA Ltd	4.5%
National Australia Bank	7.6%
Oil Search	5.7%
Orogen Minerals	4.3%
Reinsurance Australia	8.8%
South Corp Holdings	5.2%
WMC ltd	7.9%

TOTAL RETURNS %

3 months 1997	1996	1995	1994	3 years	5 years
2.39	31.08	8.01	2.00	44.41	N.A.

STATISTICS

Assets ($mil)	Current yield	Volatility	Risk return	Micropal Star Rating
1.51	—	4.70	3	✪✪✪✪

Nomura SF Hong Kong
102/350

Nomura Trust (Cayman) Ltd.
20th Floor, 3 Garden Road, Central, Hong Kong
Tel 852-2536-1111 Fax 852-2536-1922

Investment objective:
The sub-fund aims to invest primarily in major listed Hong Kong companies. However, a proportion of its assets may be invested in warrants or in smaller listed companies.

Umbrella fund: Nomura Selection Funds
Launch date: 28/12/95 **Domicile:** Cayman Islands
Currency: USD **Structure:** Open ended, Unit Trust
Portfolio manager: Nomura Trust (Cayman) Limited
Manager of Nomura SF China; located at 20th Floor, 3 Garden Road, Hong Kong.

Purchase: Direct, The manager.
Minimum investment: 5,000 USD
Custodian: Bermuda Trust (Far East)Ltd (HK)
Listed: Hong Kong **Dealings:** Daily
Fund Sedol I.D.: 664789 **Published:** SCMP/HKEJ
Fees **Annual fee:** 1.25% **Performance fee:** None
Front end load: None **Redemption fee:** Up to 1.50%
Switching fee: 0.50%

Contact: Mr T Nakumara or Ms C Lau

Performance:

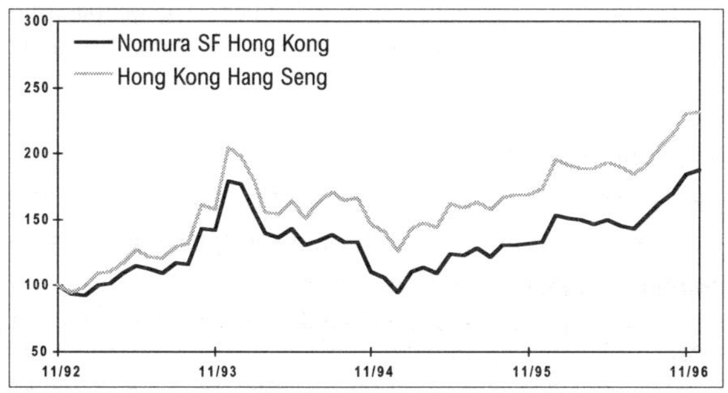

Top holdings:

Holding	%
Amoy Properties	n/s
Citic Pacific Ltd	n/s
Guangdong Invest Ltd	n/s
HSBC Holdings Ltd	n/s
Hutchison Whampoa	n/s
Hysan Development Co Ltd	n/s
New World Development	n/s
New World Infrastructure	n/s
Sino Land Company	n/s
Wing Hang Bank	n/s

TOTAL RETURNS %

3 months 1997	1996	1995	1994	3 years	5 years
-8.80	40.84	25.36	-40.57	4.93	N.A.

STATISTICS

Assets ($mil)	Current yield	Volatility	Risk return	Micropal Star Rating
1.28	—	7.09	—	✪

Odey European Incorporated

84/350

Odey Asset Management
12 Upper Grosvenor Street, London W1X 9PA, United Kingdom
Tel 44-171-208-1400 Fax 44-171-208-1401
E mail a.king@odey.co.uk

Investment objective:
The fund aims at capital appreciation in German marks through investment, long and short-term, in European equities bonds and currencies. The top country allocations of the portfolio are as follows: France (38.5%); UK (7.0%); Germany (6.0%); Spain (5.5%); Netherlands (4.%) and Switzerland (2.5%).

Umbrella fund: This is a singular fund.
Launch date: 01/05/92 **Domicile:** British Virgin Islands
Currency: DEM **Structure:** Open ended, Investment Company
Portfolio manager: Crispin Odey
Manager of the fund and commenced as Director of Odey Asset Mgt in 1991.; degrees in history/economics/law; previously with Baring Asset Management, Director and Framlington, Fund Manager; 14 years in the finance industry.
Purchase: Financial Advisor, Yes
Minimum investment: 250,000 DEM
Custodian: Morgan Stanley & Co International
Listed: None **Dealings:** Weekly
Fund Sedol I.D.: 65643 **Published:** FT/MM/RA
Fees **Annual fee:** 1.00% **Performance fee:** 20.00%
Front end load: Up to 5.00% **Redemption fee:** None
Switching fee: None

Contact: Andrew King
Performance:

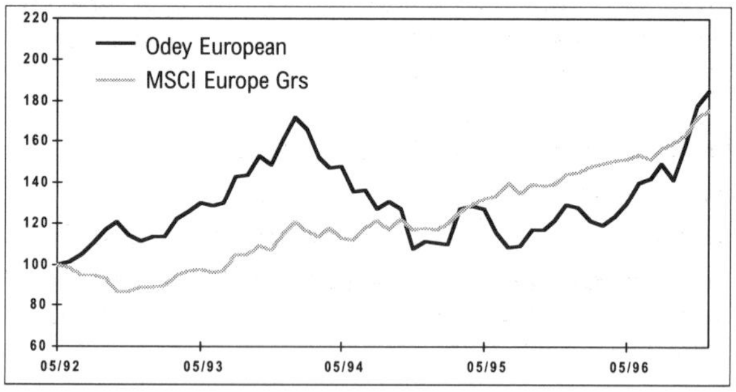

Top holdings:

Barclays PLC	9.8%
BIC	3.7%
Boiron - short	2.5%
British Steel - short	8.7%
Cipe France	5.8%
Danka - short	6.0%
Dauphin	3.2%
Granada Group - short	2.8%
Renault - short	3.3%
Volkswagen	4.1%

TOTAL RETURNS %

3 months 1997	1996	1995	1994	3 years	5 years
3.12	42.71	16.53	-31.16	14.49	N.A.

STATISTICS

Assets ($mil)	Current yield	Volatility	Risk return	Micropal Star Rating
24.32	—	6.39	—	✪✪

Odey European USD Incorporated

114/350

Odey Asset Management
12 Upper Grosvenor Street, London W1X 9PA, United Kingdom
Tel 44-171-208-1400 Fax 44-171-208-1401
E mail a.king@odey.co.uk

Investment objective:
This feeder fund invests for long-term capital appreciation, through investment in shares of Odey European Inc. The fund aims at capital appreciation in German marks through investment, long and short-term, in European equities bonds and currencies.

Umbrella fund: This is a singular fund.
Launch date: 21/02/94 **Domicile:** British Virgin Islands
Currency: USD **Structure:** Open ended, Investment Company
Portfolio manager: Crispin Odey
Manager of the fund commenced May 1993 and a Director of Odey Asset Management since 1991; degrees in history/economics/law; previously with Baring Asset Management, Director and Framlington, Fund Manager; 14 years in the finance industry.
Purchase: Financial Advisor, Yes
Minimum investment: 150,000 USD
Custodian: Morgan Stanley & Co International
Listed: None **Dealings:** Weekly
Fund Sedol I.D.: 65629 **Published:** FT/MM/TI
Fees **Annual fee:** 1.00% **Performance fee:** 20.00%
Front end load: Up to 5.00% **Redemption fee:** None
Switching fee: None

Contact: Andrew King
Performance:

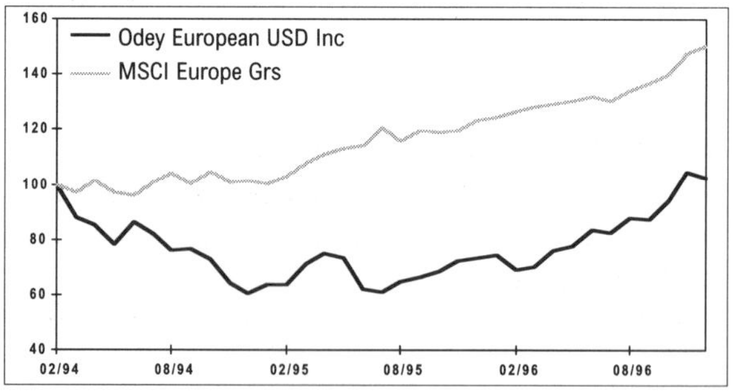

Top holdings:

Barclays PLC	9.8%
BIC	3.7%
Boiron - short	2.5%
British Steel - short	8.7%
Cipe France	5.8%
Danka - short	6.0%
Dauphin	3.2%
Granada Group - short	2.8%
Renault - short	3.3%
Volkswagen	4.1%

TOTAL RETURNS %

3 months 1997	1996	1995	1994	3 years	5 years
14.97	39.79	20.93	N.A.	N.A.	N.A.

STATISTICS

Assets ($mil)	Current yield	Volatility	Risk return	Micropal Star Rating
4.55	—	N.A.	—	———

Old Mutual Gnsy Euro Stockmarket
130/350

Old Mutual Guernsey
Fairbairn House, PO Box 121 Rohais, St Peter Port,
GY1 3HE, Guernsey
Tel 44-1481-726-726 Fax 44-1481-700-523

Contact: Martin Sines

Investment objective:
The insurance fund aims to generate long-term capital growth from the active management of a portfolio of investments giving diversified international exposure to continental European equity markets. The top sector allocations of the portfolio are the following: consumer goods (21.1%); finance (13.1%); services (12.0%) energy (10.5%); and technology (10.4%).

Umbrella fund: This is a singular fund.

Launch date: 02/01/96 **Domicile:** Guernsey

Currency: GBP **Structure:** Open ended, Insurance Fund

Portfolio manager: Talal Shakerchi CFA
Manager of the fund commenced February 1991; previously with National Bank of Kuwait as European Equities Portfolio Manager and British Petroleum Pension Fund as UK equities analyst; 10 years experience with the fund management industry.

Purchase: Financial Advisor, Tied Sales Forces

Minimum investment: ILP

Custodian: Credit Suisse

Listed: Various **Dealings:** Weekly

Fund Sedol I.D.: 66259 **Published:** FT/IHT/SC

Fees **Annual fee:** 1.25% **Performance fee:** None
Front end load: 7.00% **Redemption fee:** None
Switching fee: 25 GBP

Performance:

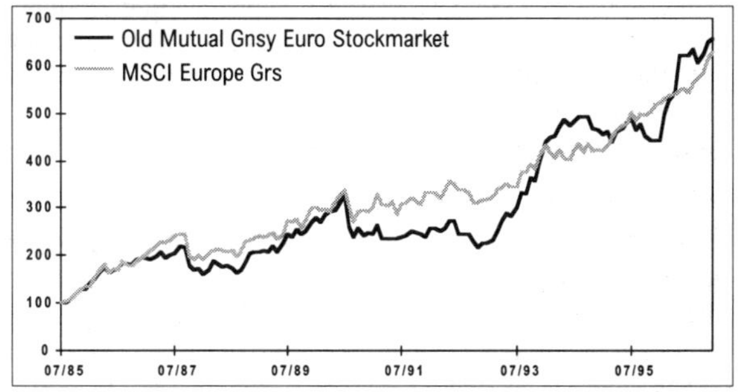

Top holdings:

Holding	%
Elf Aquitaine	2.9%
Genset	4.9%
ICB Shipping	4.4%
Nedlloyd	3.7%
Olivetti & Spa	5.3%
Orkla A	6.1%
Raisian Tehtaat	4.3%
SAS Norge ASA	2.6%
Tornet Fastigh	3.4%
UPM Kymmene	2.5%

TOTAL RETURNS %

3 months 1997	1996	1995	1994	3 years	5 years
7.38	37.89	N.A.	N.A.	N.A.	N.A.

STATISTICS

Assets ($mil)	Current yield	Volatility	Risk return	Micropal Star Rating
9.32	—	N.A.	—	———

Old Mutual Gnsy N Amer Stockmarket
132/350

Old Mutual Guernsey
Fairbairn House, PO Box 121 Rohais, St Peter Port,
GY1 3HE, Guernsey
Tel 44-1481-726-726 Fax 44-1481-700-523

Contact: Martin Sines

Investment objective:
The insurance fund aims to provide investors with capital growth from a diverse portfolio of quoted US, Canadian and Mexican equities. Investment in stock index futures, equity options and equity warrants is permitted. The top sector allocations of the portfolio are as follows: finance (34.0%); technology (28.3%); consumer goods (14.0%); and energy (5.0%).

Umbrella fund: This is a singular fund.

Launch date: 02/01/96 **Domicile:** Guernsey

Currency: USD **Structure:** Open ended, Insurance Fund

Portfolio manager: Carol Judd
Manager of Old Mutual Guernsey North American Stock Market commenced 1995; a quantitative analysis based fund manager; 9 years finance industry experience.

Purchase: Financial Advisor, Tied Sales Forces

Minimum investment: ILP

Custodian: Credit Suisse

Listed: Various **Dealings:** Weekly

Fund Sedol I.D.: 65799 **Published:** FT/IHT/SC

Fees **Annual fee:** 1.25% **Performance fee:** None
Front end load: 7.00% **Redemption fee:** None
Switching fee: 25 GBP

Performance:

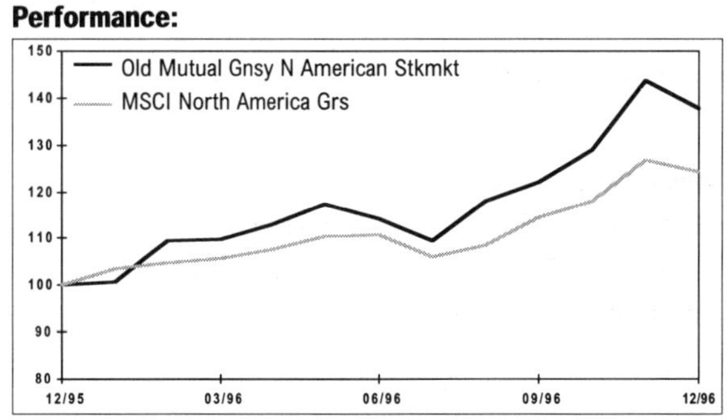

Top holdings:

Holding	%
American International	3.7%
Bank America Corp.	3.5%
Bristol Myers	3.0%
Citicorp	3.1%
Coca-Cola Co.	6.9%
Du Pont	5.1%
IBM	4.0%
Intel Corp.	7.2%
Microsoft	5.3%
Nations Bank	3.8%

TOTAL RETURNS %

3 months 1997	1996	1995	1994	3 years	5 years
9.66	37.70	N.A.	N.A.	N.A.	N.A.

STATISTICS

Assets ($mil)	Current yield	Volatility	Risk return	Micropal Star Rating
0.13	—	N.A.	—	———

OMI (Gnsy) Euro Stockmarket
66/350

Old Mutual Intl (Gnsy)
Fairbairn House, PO Box 121 Rohais, St Peter Port,
GY1 3HE, Guernsey
Tel 44-1481-726-726 Fax 44-1481-700-523

Investment objective:
The insurance fund aims to generate long-term capital growth from the active management of a portfolio of investments giving diversified international exposure to continental European equity markets. The top sector allocations of the portfolio are the following: consumer goods (21.1%); finance (13.1%); services (12.0%); and technology (10.45).

Umbrella fund: This is a singular fund.

Launch date: 23/07/85 **Domicile:** Guernsey

Currency: GBP **Structure:** Open ended, Insurance Fund

Portfolio manager: Talal Shakerchi CFA
Manager of the fund commenced May 1991; previously with National Bank of Kuwait as European equities Portfolio Manager and British Petroleum Pension Fund as UK equities analyst; 10 years experience with the fund management industry.

Purchase: Financial Advisor, Tied Sales Forces

Minimum investment: ILP

Custodian: Credit Suisse

Listed: Various **Dealings:** Weekly

Fund Sedol I.D.: 70780 **Published:** FT/MM

Fees **Annual fee:** 1.25% **Performance fee:** None
Front end load: 7.00% **Redemption fee:** None
Switching fee: 25 GBP

Contact: Martin Sines

Performance:

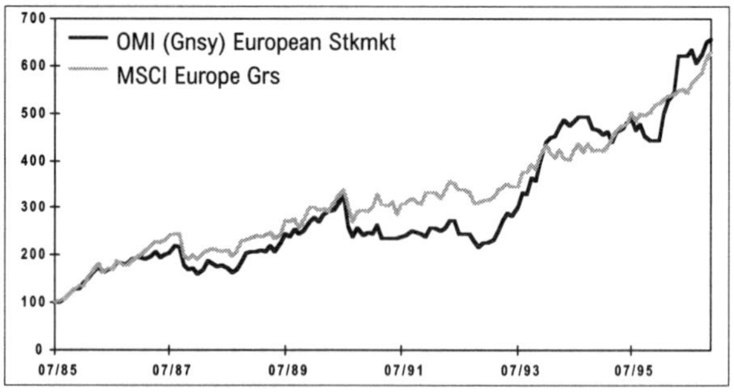

Top holdings:

Elf Aquitaine	2.9%
Genset	4.9%
ICB Shipping	4.4%
Nedlloyd	3.7%
Olivetti & Spa	5.3%
Orkla A	6.1%
Raisian Tehtaat	4.3%
SAS Norge ASA	2.6%
Tornet Fastigh	3.4%
UPM Kymmene	2.5%

TOTAL RETURNS %

3 months 1997	1996	1995	1994	3 years	5 years
7.41	48.96	-5.14	16.23	64.24	176.60

STATISTICS

Assets ($mil)	Current yield	Volatility	Risk return	Micropal Star Rating
102.71	—	4.42	2	✪✪✪✪

OMI (Gnsy) HK Stockmarket
305/350

Old Mutual Intl (Gnsy)
Fairbairn House, PO Box 121 Rohais, St Peter Port,
GY1 3HE, Guernsey
Tel 44-1481-726-726 Fax 44-1481-700-523

Investment objective:
The insurance fund aims to generate growth from a portfolio of quoted Hong Kong equities and appropriate Hong Kong derivatives. It can also invest up to 15% of its asset value in Chinese stocks. The top sector allocations of the portfolio are the following: property (34.8%); industrial cyclical (33.7); finance (22.9%); and utilities (8.4%).

Umbrella fund: This is a singular fund.

Launch date: 23/07/85 **Domicile:** Guernsey

Currency: USD **Structure:** Open ended, Insurance Fund

Portfolio manager: Ashok Shah
Manager of OMI (Gnsy)HK Stockmarket; qualified actuary; managing funds since 1985; started in the industry 1973.

Purchase: Financial Advisor, Tied Sales Forces

Minimum investment: ILP

Custodian: Credit Suisse

Listed: Various **Dealings:** Weekly

Fund Sedol I.D.: 70785 **Published:** FT/MM

Fees **Annual fee:** 1.25% **Performance fee:** None
Front end load: 7.00% **Redemption fee:** None
Switching fee: 25 GBP

Contact: Martin Sines

Performance:

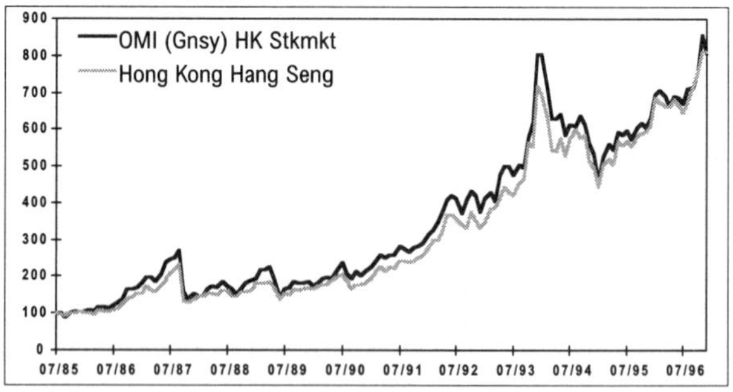

Top holdings:

Cheung Kong Holdings Ltd	7.9%
Hang Seng Bank	4.6%
Henderson Land Development	5.5%
Hong Kong & China Cos.	4.7%
HSBC Holdings	9.4%
Hutchison Whampoa	4.4%
New World Development	5.4%
Sun Hung Kai Properties	8.9%
Swire Pacific	4.2%
Wharf Holdings	4.6%

TOTAL RETURNS %

3 months 1997	1996	1995	1994	3 years	5 years
-1.24	28.19	18.13	-33.63	0.51	179.47

STATISTICS

Assets ($mil)	Current yield	Volatility	Risk return	Micropal Star Rating
10.38	—	6.61	—	✪

OMI (Gnsy) N.American Stockmarket
203/350

Old Mutual Intl (Gnsy)
Fairbairn House, PO Box 121 Rohais, St Peter Port,
GY1 3HE, Guernsey
Tel 44-1481-726-726 Fax 44-1481-700-523

Contact: Martin Sines

Investment objective:
The insurance fund aims to provide investors with capital growth from a diverse portfolio of quoted US, Canadian and Mexican equities. The top sector allocations of the portfolio are as follows: finance (34.0%); technology (28.3%); and consumer goods (14.0%). Currently, 98.0% of the portfolio assets are allocated to the US.

Umbrella fund: This is a singular fund.
Launch date: 11/05/82 **Domicile:** Guernsey
Currency: USD **Structure:** Open ended, Insurance Fund
Portfolio manager: Carole Judd
Manager of OMI (Guernsey) North American Stock Market commenced in 1995; Quantitative analysis based expert; 9 years experience in the finance industry.

Purchase: Financial Advisor, Tied Sales Forces
Minimum investment: ILP
Custodian: Credit Suisse
Listed: Various **Dealings:** Weekly
Fund Sedol I.D.: 70706 **Published:** FT/MM
Fees **Annual fee:** 1.25% **Performance fee:** None
Front end load: 7.00% **Redemption fee:** None
Switching fee: 25 GBP

Performance:

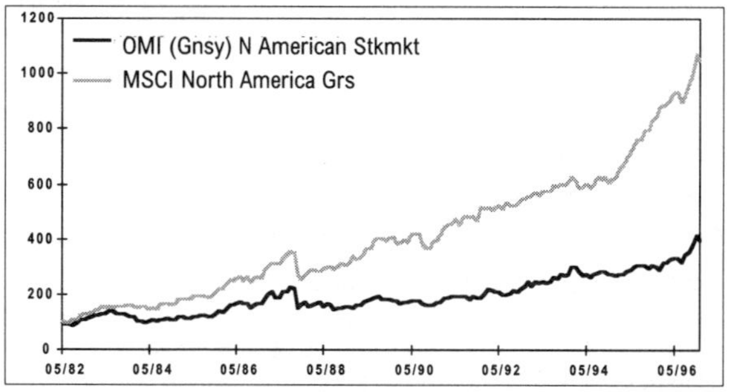

Top holdings:

American International	3.7%
Bank America Corp.	3.5%
Bristol Myers	3.0%
Citicorp	3.1%
Coca-Cola Co.	6.9%
Du Pont	5.1%
IBM	4.0%
Intel Corp.	7.2%
Microsoft	5.3%
Nations Bank	3.8%

TOTAL RETURNS %

3 months 1997	1996	1995	1994	3 years	5 years
9.33	32.67	10.26	-0.78	45.14	113.41

STATISTICS

Assets ($mil)	Current yield	Volatility	Risk return	Micropal Star Rating
5.41	—	3.96	1	✪✪

Opportunity Brazilian Aggressive Equities
17/350

Opportunity Asset Mgmt
231 Avenue Presidente Wilson, 28th Floor, Rio de Janeiro,
RJ-20-030-021, Brazil
Tel 55-21-532-1000 Fax 55-21-532-2880

Contact: Carlos Rodenburg

Investment objective:
The fund seeks to achieve long-term capital gains, through investing primarily in Brazilian equity securities, equity derivatives and arbitrage. The fund may also invest in Brazilian fixed income instruments and it may be leveraged up to twice the net asset value.

Umbrella fund: This is a singular fund.
Launch date: 15/08/94 **Domicile:** Cayman Islands
Currency: USD **Structure:** Open ended, Mutual Fund
Portfolio manager: Dorio Ferman
Manager of the fund and founder of Ferman DTVM later became Logica DTVM and subsequently Banco Opportunity of which he is the President; electrical engineer; Master's degree, economics- Fundacao Getulio Vargas- Rio de Janeiro.
Purchase: Direct
Minimum investment: 50,000 USD
Custodian: N/S
Listed: None **Dealings:** Daily
Fund Sedol I.D.: 305024 **Published:** FT
Fees **Annual fee:** 1.00% **Performance fee:** 25.00%
Front end load: None **Redemption fee:** 1.50%
Switching fee: None

Performance:

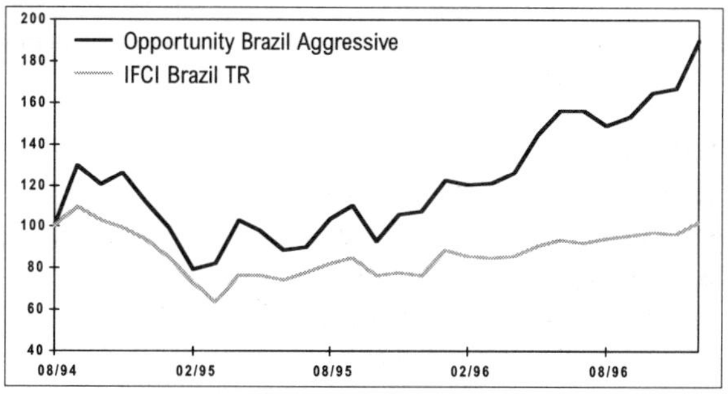

Top holdings:

Oil	28.0%
Telecommunications	46.0%
Utilities	26.0%

TOTAL RETURNS %

3 months 1997	1996	1995	1994	3 years	5 years
40.23	77.20	-4.10	N.A.	N.A.	N.A.

STATISTICS

Assets ($mil)	Current yield	Volatility	Risk return	Micropal Star Rating
12.17	—	N.A.	—	———

Opportunity Brazilian Equities
26/350

Opportunity Asset Mgmt
231 Avenue Presidente Wilson, 28th Floor, Rio de Janeiro, RJ-20-030-021, Brazil
Tel 55-21-532-1000 Fax 55-21-532-2880

Contact: Carlos Rodenburg

Investment objective:
The sub-fund seeks to achieve long-term capital gains through investing in a diversified portfolio of publicly traded equities of Brazilian companies both state owned and private, that offer superior potential growth.

Umbrella fund: This is a singular fund.

Launch date: 08/01/93 **Domicile:** Cayman Islands

Currency: USD **Structure:** Open ended, Mutual Fund

Portfolio manager: Dorio Ferman
Manager of the fund and founder of Ferman DTVM later became Logica DTVM and subsequently Banco Opportunity of which he is the President; electrical engineer; Master's degree, economics- Fundacao Getulio Varga.

Purchase: Direct

Minimum investment: 50,000 USD

Custodian: N/S

Listed: None **Dealings:** Daily

Fund Sedol I.D.: 305028 **Published:** FT

Fees **Annual fee:** 1.50% **Performance fee:** 15.00%
Front end load: None **Redemption fee:** 1.50%
Switching fee: None

Performance:

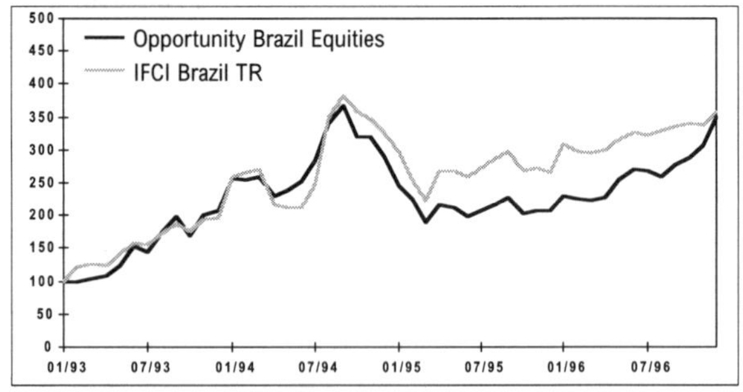

Top holdings:

Oil	21.0%
Telecommunications	51.0%
Transport	2.0%
Utilities	26.0%

TOTAL RETURNS %

3 months 1997	1996	1995	1994	3 years	5 years
31.94	67.84	-28.31	39.23	67.53	N.A.

STATISTICS

Assets ($mil)	Current yield	Volatility	Risk return	Micropal Star Rating
66.99	—	9.17	3	✪✪✪

Opportunity Brazilian Strategy
18/350

Opportunity Asset Mgmt
Avenue Presidente Wilson 231, 28th Floor, Rio De Janeiro, RJ-20-030-021, Brazil
Tel 55-21-532-1000 Fax 55-21-532-2880

Contact: Carlos Rodenburg

Investment objective:
The sub-fund seeks to achieve long-term capital growth by investing primarily, although not exclusively, in equities of publicly traded Brazilian companies. The fund focuses on the equities of companies which are state owned or has been privatized. This fund is closed to new subscribers.

Umbrella fund: This is a singular fund.

Launch date: 28/03/93 **Domicile:** Cayman Islands

Currency: USD **Structure:** Open ended, Mutual Fund

Portfolio manager: Dorio Ferman
Manager of the fund and founder of Ferman DTVM later became Logica DTVM and subsequently Banco Opportunity of which he is the President; electrical engineer; Master's degree, economics- Fundacao Getulio Varga.

Purchase: Direct

Minimum investment: 50,000 USD

Custodian: N/S

Listed: None **Dealings:** Daily

Fund Sedol I.D.: 305032 **Published:** FT

Fees **Annual fee:** 1.50% **Performance fee:** 15.00%
Front end load: None **Redemption fee:** 1.50%
Switching fee: None

Performance:

Top holdings: Brazilian Equities 100.0%

TOTAL RETURNS %

3 months 1997	1996	1995	1994	3 years	5 years
28.11	76.37	-12.98	33.99	105.63	N.A.

STATISTICS

Assets ($mil)	Current yield	Volatility	Risk return	Micropal Star Rating
3.05	—	10.31	4	✪✪✪✪

Orbitex Dynamic
22/350

Orbitex Management Ltd
Maritime House, Frederick Street, Nassau, N-9932, Bahamas
Tel 1-809-356-6456 Fax 1-809-356-5866
http://www. orbitex.com

Investment objective:
The fund seeks exceptional growth of capital by taking higher risks investing in common shares of North American securities of select small to medium capitalised companies; companies whose real asset values have not been recognised in terms of market pricing or may be in new issues.

Umbrella fund: This is a singular fund.
Launch date: 01/08/95 **Domicile:** Canada
Currency: USD **Structure:** Open ended, Unit Trust
Portfolio manager: Ian Ainsworth CFA, Altamira Management Ltd.
Manager commenced June 1995; joined Altamira Management Ltd as VP of foreign equities in 1992; MBA, finance- Dalhousie U; previously with BGH Central Investment Mgt Ltd, MD and Guardian Capital Enterprises Ltd, VP; 19 years- finance industry.
Purchase: Direct
Minimum investment: 50,000 CAN
Custodian: State Street /CIBC Trust
Listed: None **Dealings:** Daily
Fund Sedol I.D.: 305408 **Published:** FT/IHT/WS
Fees **Annual fee:** 4.50% **Performance fee:** None
Front end load: Up to 10.00% **Redemption fee:** Up to 2.00%
Switching fee: Negotiable

Contact: Customer Services Department
Performance:

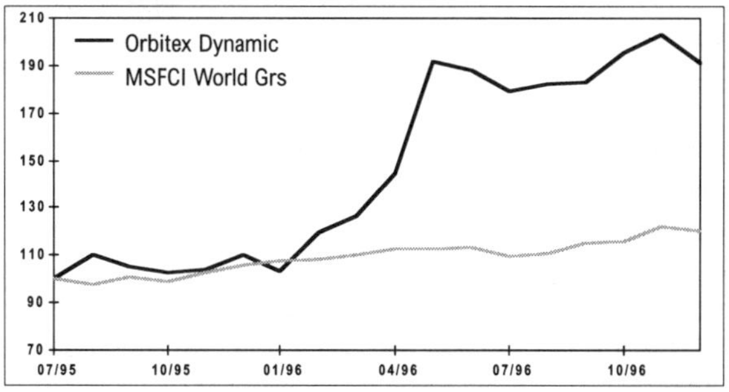

Top holdings:

Holding	%
BBN Corp.	30.4%
Cognos Incorporated	1.1%
Harmonic Lightwaves	7.0%
Millennium Pharma	2.1%
Psinet Inc.	7.5%
Synaptic Pharm Corp.	5.7%

TOTAL RETURNS %

3 months 1997	1996	1995	1994	3 years	5 years
-20.92	73.80	N.A.	N.A.	N.A.	N.A.

STATISTICS

Assets ($mil)	Current yield	Volatility	Risk return	Micropal Star Rating
6.40	—	N.A.	—	———

Orbitex Natural Resources
125/350

Orbitex Management Ltd
Box 452, Gartenstrasse 19, Zurich, CH-8027, Switzerland
Tel 41-1-201-4710 Fax 41-1-201-0391
http://www. orbitex.com

Investment objective:
The fund seeks to achieve capital growth through a flexible policy of investing in stock and debt obligations of companies engaged in natural resource industries, with primary emphasis on securities of Canadian companies engaged in such industries. The top country allocations of the portfolio are Canada (67.7%) and US (8.3%).

Umbrella fund: This is a singular fund.
Launch date: 15/06/86 **Domicile:** Canada
Currency: CAD **Structure:** Open ended, Unit Trust
Portfolio manager: David F Taylor CFA, Altamira Management Ltd.
Manager of the fund commenced June 1995 and VP of Canadian equities, research analyst and portfolio Manager of Altamira Mgt Ltd; previously with Ontario Teachers Pension Plan Board as Portfolio Manager; joined Altamira 1995; 9 years finance industry experience.
Purchase: Direct
Minimum investment: 50,000 CAN
Custodian: CIBC Trust Corp
Listed: None **Dealings:** Daily
Fund Sedol I.D.: 402174 **Published:** FT
Fees **Annual fee:** 2.50% **Performance fee:** None
Front end load: Up to 10.00% **Redemption fee:** Up to 2.00%
Switching fee: Negotiable

Contact: Customer Services Department
Performance:

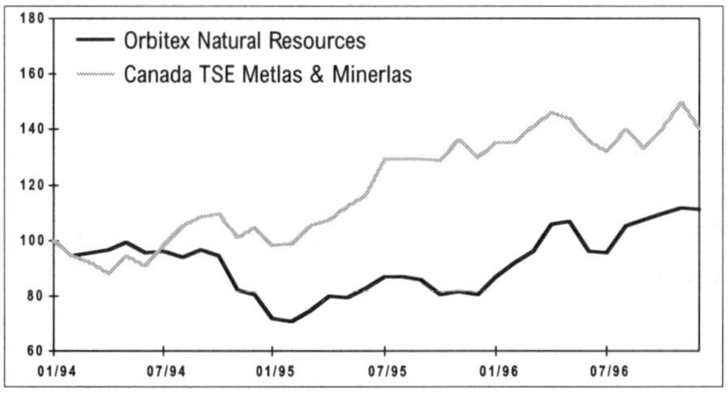

Top holdings:

Holding	%
Cabre Exploration	3.1%
Canadian 88 Energy	4.4%
General Minerals	5.0%
Indochina	2.6%
Metallica Resources	2.8%
Ocelot Energy	3.9%
Remington Energy	4.8%
Seven Seas Pete	2.4%
Teck Corp.	2.7%
Wascana Energy Inc.	5.1%

TOTAL RETURNS %

3 months 1997	1996	1995	1994	3 years	5 years
-3.85	38.46	-0.59	-15.65	16.11	139.59

STATISTICS

Assets ($mil)	Current yield	Volatility	Risk return	Micropal Star Rating
109.74	—	5.21	—	✪✪✪

Pactual Eternity Fund Limited
105/350

Banco Pactual
Avenue Republica do Chile 230, 29 Andar Centro, Rio de Janeiro, 20031-170, Brazil
Tel 55-21-272-1179 Fax 55-21-272-1331

Contact: Adriana Vilhena/ Malu Marino

Performance:

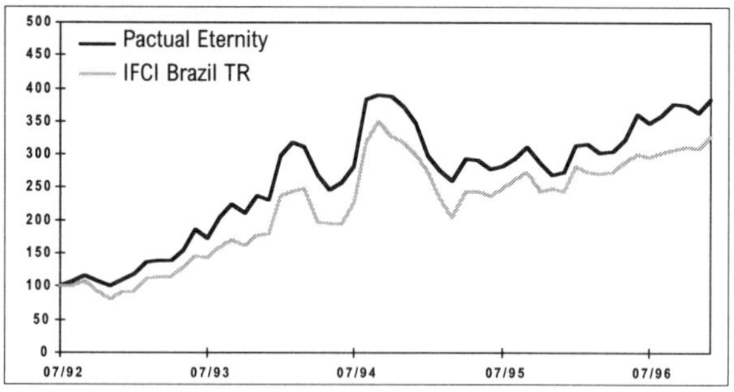

Investment objective:
This Pactual Eternity Fund seeks capital appreciation by investments in the Brazilian equity markets, using active asset allocation between stocks and fixed income to counter balance the markets high volatility. The top sector allocations for the fund include the following: energy (30.5%); communication (20.8%); retail trade (10.9%).

Umbrella fund: This is a singular fund.

Launch date: 31/07/92 **Domicile:** Cayman Islands

Currency: USD **Structure:** Open ended, LLC

Portfolio manager: Florian Bartunek
Manager for the fund since December 1994 and partner; BS, business administration- Catholic U, Rio de Janeiro; joined Pactual 1990 as an investment analyst.

Purchase: Direct, Financial Advisor, Euroclear/Cedel

Minimum investment: 1,000,000 USD

Custodian: Pactual Overseas Bank and Trust Limited

Listed: Brazil **Dealings:** Daily

Fund Sedol I.D.: 207952 **Published:** FT/HTE

Fees **Annual fee:** 1.25% **Performance fee:** 15.00%
Front end load: None **Redemption fee:** Up to 1.50%
Switching fee: None

Top holdings:

Holding	%
Belgo Mineira	6.0%
Continental	5.0%
COPEL	13.0%
CPFL	12.0%
CRT	10.0%
Itausa	6.0%
Larapva	9.0%
Petrobas	9.0%
Sabesp	5.0%
Telemig	7.0%

TOTAL RETURNS %

3 months 1997	1996	1995	1994	3 years	5 years
36.52	40.67	-21.38	50.24	66.16	N.A.

STATISTICS

Assets ($mil)	Current yield	Volatility	Risk return	Micropal Star Rating
54.18	—	10.08	2	✪✪

Pactual Infinity Fund Limited
119/350

Banco Pactual
Avenue Republica do Chile 230, 29 Andar Centro, Rio de Janeiro, 20031-170, Brazil
Tel 55-21-272-1179 Fax 55-21-272-1331

Contact: Adrianna Vilhena /Malu Marinho

Performance:

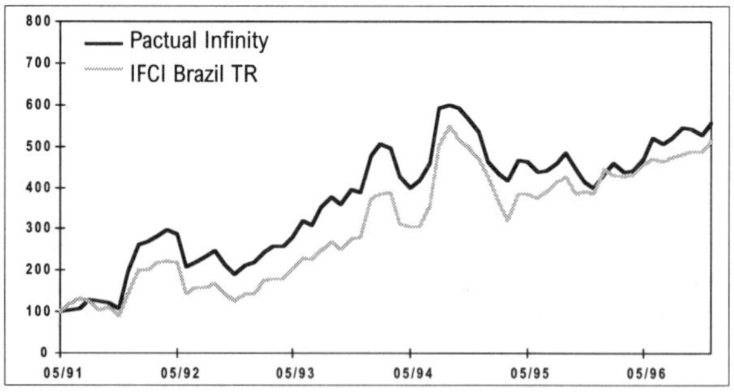

Investment objective:
The fund seeks capital appreciation by investing in Brazilian equity markets, using active asset allocation between stocks and fixed income to counter balance the markets high volatility. The top sector allocations of the portfolio are as follows: energy (30.5%); retail trade (11.0%); oil (11.0%); communications (20.7%); mining (7.3%); and finance (7.3%).

Umbrella fund: This is a singular fund.

Launch date: 31/05/91 **Domicile:** Cayman Islands

Currency: USD **Structure:** Open ended, LLC

Portfolio manager: Florian Barunek
Manager of Pactual Infinity Fund Ltd commenced December 1994.

Purchase: Direct, Financial Advisor, Bank of Butterfield/Euroclear

Minimum investment: 50,000 USD

Custodian: Pactual Overseas Bank and Trust Limited

Listed: Brazil **Dealings:** Daily

Fund Sedol I.D.: 266805 **Published:** FT/IHT

Fees **Annual fee:** 1.38% **Performance fee:** 15.00%
Front end load: None **Redemption fee:** Up to 1.50%
Switching fee: None

Top holdings:

Holding	%
Belgo Mineira	6.0%
Continental	5.0%
COPEL	13.0%
CPFL	12.0%
CRT	10.0%
Itausa	6.0%
Larapva	9.0%
Petrobas	9.0%
Sabesp	5.0%
Telemig PNB	7.0%

TOTAL RETURNS %

3 months 1997	1996	1995	1994	3 years	5 years
33.50	39.27	-25.30	37.14	42.67	182.04

STATISTICS

Assets ($mil)	Current yield	Volatility	Risk return	Micropal Star Rating
73.83	—	8.76	1	✪

Paneurolife International Real Estate
267/350

Pan European Life
7 Rue De La Chapelle, L-1325 Luxembourg
Tel 352-45-67-30-1 Fax 352-45-67-34
http://www. paneurolife.lu
E mail paneuro.lu@pophost.eunet.lu
Contact: Beatrice Dessauger

Investment objective:
The fund seeks regular income through a portfolio of shares in property or property related investments globally. Investments are spread internationally with the top country allocations as follows: Hong Kong (46.0%); Great Britain (19.0%); USA (11.0%); Japan (10.0%); Cayman Islands (8.0%); and Singapore (7.0%).

Umbrella fund: This is a singular fund.
Launch date: 19/02/91 **Domicile:** Luxembourg
Currency: ECU **Structure:** Open ended, Insurance Fund
Portfolio manager: Thierry Charon
Manager of Paneurolife International Real Estate commenced 1991.

Performance:

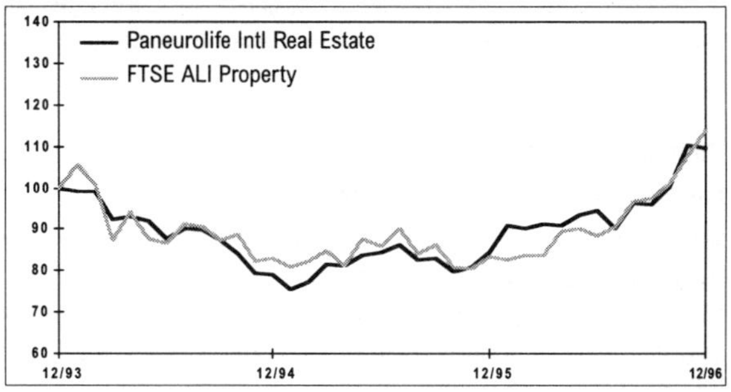

Purchase: Financial Advisor
Minimum investment: 6,000 GBP
Custodian: N/S
Listed: None **Dealings:** Weekly
Fund Sedol I.D.: 304798 **Published:** FT/ LEB/ JF
Fees **Annual fee:** 0.45% **Performance fee:** None
Front end load: None **Redemption fee:** Up to 0.10%
Switching fee: 1.00%

Top holdings:

Holding	%
Cheung Kong	11.6%
Henderson Land Dev. Wts 98	3.7%
HKR International	6.4%
Hysan Development Wts 98	3.8%
Land Securities	3.7%
Medusa (USA)	2.9%
New World Development	4.6%
Sun Hung Kai Properties	7.4%
The British Land (GB)	4.7%
The Wharf Holdings Ltd	6.8%

TOTAL RETURNS %

3 months 1997	1996	1995	1994	3 years	5 years
-3.61	29.72	6.95	-21.00	9.60	57.61

STATISTICS

Assets ($mil)	Current yield	Volatility	Risk return	Micropal Star Rating
6.27	—	3.72	—	✪✪✪

Parvest Holland B
240/350

Paribas Asset Management
41 Avenue de l'Opera, Paris, France
Tel 33-1-42-98-43-40 Fax 33-1-42-98-62-56
http://www. parvest.com
E mail paneuro.lu@pophost.eunet.lu
Contact: Customer Services Department

Investment objective:
The sub-fund seeks to out perform the MSCI Netherlands Index over the medium-term. The top sector allocations of the portfolio are as follows: finance (32.4%); services (25.6%); energy (18.4%); consumer goods (12.2%); and industrial cyclical (12.0%).

Umbrella fund: Parvest
Launch date: 16/07/90 **Domicile:** Luxembourg [UCITS]
Currency: NLG **Structure:** Open ended, SICAV
Portfolio manager: Olivier Rudigoz
Manager of Parvest Holland A/B; MBA Ecole des Hautes Etudes Commerciales (HEC); and a law degree- Paris University; joined Paribas in 1987.

Performance:

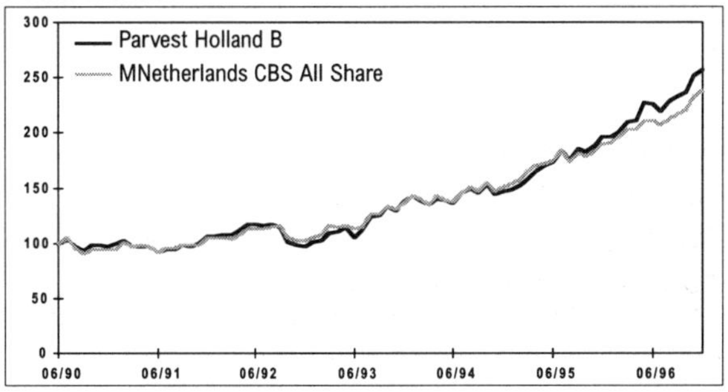

Purchase: Financial Advisor, Paribas Private Banking and other financial intermediaries
Minimum investment: 1Unit
Custodian: Banque Paribas Luxembourg
Listed: None **Dealings:** Daily
Fund Sedol I.D.: 300157 **Published:** IHT/FAZ/HB/MF/LEB/JG
Fees **Annual fee:** 1.50% **Performance fee:** None
Front end load: Up to 4.00% **Redemption fee:** None
Switching fee: None

Top holdings:

Holding	%
ABN AMRO Holding	7.5%
Akzo NV	4.5%
Dordtsche Petroleum	4.5%
Elsevier	5.9%
Ing cert NV	8.9%
Koninklijke Ahold	4.6%
Philips Electronics	5.4%
Royal Dutch United	4.7%
Unilever	4.7%
Wolters Kluwer	4.7%

TOTAL RETURNS %

3 months 1997	1996	1995	1994	3 years	5 years
6.04	30.72	33.25	7.70	87.59	140.80

STATISTICS

Assets ($mil)	Current yield	Volatility	Risk return	Micropal Star Rating
48.14	—	3.33	1	✪✪✪

Parvest Obli Lira A/B

325/350

Paribas Asset Management
41 Avenue de l'Opera, Paris, France
Tel 33-1-42-98-43-40 Fax 33-1-42-98-62-56
http://www. parvest.com
E mail paneuro.lu@pophost.eunet.lu
Contact: Customer Services Department

Investment objective:
The sub-fund seeks to maximise returns over the medium-term by investing in Italian lira denominated bonds issued by governments and companies. The benchmark of this fund is the JP Morgan 5-7 year Italian Government Bond Traded Index.

Umbrella fund: Parvest
Launch date: 20/07/93 **Domicile:** Luxembourg [UCITS]
Currency: ITL **Structure:** Open ended, SICAV
Portfolio manager: Jacques Rachi
Manager of Parvest Obli Lira A/B; Master degree, economics and advanced Masters degree, finance- U Paris; previously at Banque San Paolo, Paris in charge of the fixed income department; joined Paribas in 1993.
Purchase: Financial Advisor, Paribas Private Banking and other financial intermediaries
Minimum investment: 1Unit
Custodian: Banque Paribas Luxembourg
Listed: None **Dealings:** Daily
Fund Sedol I.D.: 300184 **Published:** IHT/FAZ/HB/MF/LEB/JG
Fees **Annual fee:** 1.50% **Performance fee:** None
Front end load: 4.00% **Redemption fee:** None
Switching fee: None

Performance:

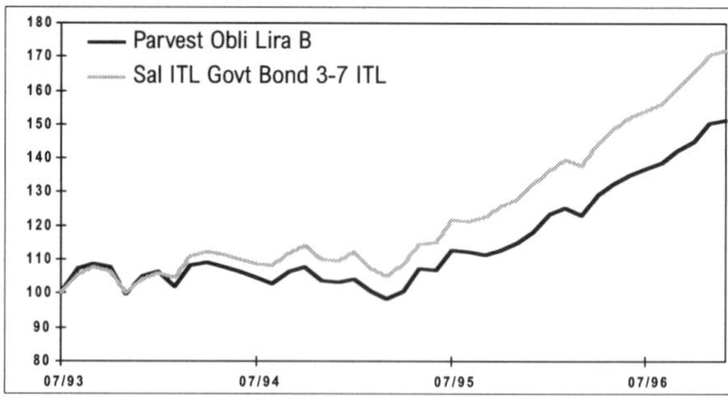

Top holdings:	
DSL Finance 8.37%	n/s
EIB 12.75%	n/s
Italy 10.5%	n/s
Italy 11.5%	n/s
Italy BTP 10.5%	n/s
Italy BTP 9.5%	n/s
LKB Baden Wurt 11.62%	n/s
Shinhan Bank	n/s
Westdeutsche LB 10%	n/s

TOTAL RETURNS %

3 months 1997	1996	1995	1994	3 years	5 years
-10.87	27.73	14.45	-1.78	43.59	N.A.

STATISTICS

Assets ($mil)	Current yield	Volatility	Risk return	Micropal Star Rating
21.92	—	2.60	2	✪✪✪

Parvest UK B

255/350

Paribas Asset Management
41 Avenue de l'Opera, Paris, France
Tel 33-1-42-98-43-40 Fax 33-1-42-98-62-56
http://www. parvest.com
E mail paneuro.lu@pophost.eunet.lu
Contact: Customer Services Department

Investment objective:
The sub-fund seeks to out perform the MSCI UK Index over the medium-term. The top sector allocations of the portfolio are as follows: services (26.9%); finance (24.3%); consumer goods (22.2%); industrial cyclical (13.7%); and energy (7.1%).

Umbrella fund: Parvest
Launch date: 12/01/94 **Domicile:** Luxembourg [UCITS]
Currency: GBP **Structure:** Open ended, SICAV
Portfolio manager: Claude Guillaume
Manager of Parvest UK A/B; graduate- Ecole Centrale de Paris, the Institut D'Etudes Politiques de Paris and economics/law- U of Paris; joined Paribas in 1983.

Purchase: Financial Advisor, Paribas Private Banking and other financial intermediaries
Minimum investment: 1Unit
Custodian: Banque Paribas Luxembourg
Listed: None **Dealings:** Daily
Fund Sedol I.D.: 300196 **Published:** IHT/FAZ/HB/MF/LEB/JG
Fees **Annual fee:** 1.50% **Performance fee:** None
Front end load: 4.00% **Redemption fee:** None
Switching fee: None

Performance:

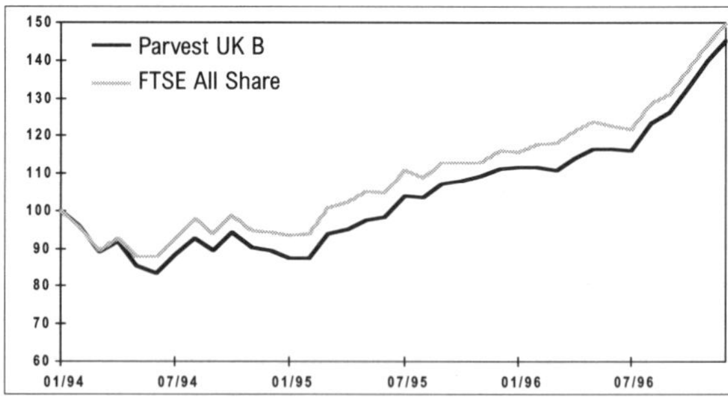

Top holdings:	
Barclays PLC	3.2%
British Petroleum	5.9%
British Telecom	4.1%
BTR	3.7%
Glaxo Wellcome	5.9%
HSBC Holdings	6.4%
Kingfisher	3.5%
Reed International	3.9%
Smithkline Beecham Beecham	3.8%
TSB Group	4.9%

TOTAL RETURNS %

3 months 1997	1996	1995	1994	3 years	5 years
0.27	30.30	24.52	N.A.	N.A.	N.A.

STATISTICS

Assets ($mil)	Current yield	Volatility	Risk return	Micropal Star Rating
43.81	—	N.A.	—	———

Patrimonio Corporate Investments
87/350

Banco Patrimonio S.A.
Avenue Brigadeiro Faria Lima, 2000 - 4 Andar, Sao Paulo, SP, Brazil
Tel 55-11-3039-3885 Fax 55-11-3039-1900
http://www. patrimonio.com
E mail fund.info@patrimonio.com
Contact: Renata Lopes Kotscho

Investment objective:
The sub-fund seeks to maximises investment return by investing in stocks of small capital companies with market capitalization up to 50 million UK sterling, in Brazil with strong growth potential and low valuations. The top sector allocations include the following: industrial cyclical (25.6%); consumer goods (22.9%); retail (21.4%); transportation (7.3%); and energy (3.0%).

Umbrella fund: Patrimonio Funds Inc
Launch date: 09/04/92 **Domicile:** Cayman Islands
Currency: USD **Structure:** Open ended, Investment Company
Portfolio manager: Flavio Teles de Menezes
Manager of Patrimonio Corporate Inv; MBA- Chicago U; former equity analyst and specializes in Latin American areas.

Performance:

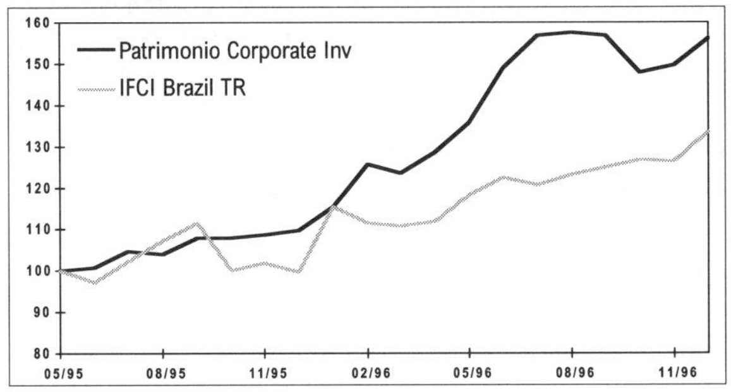

Purchase: Direct, Financial Advisor, Euroclear/Cedel
Minimum investment: 50,000 USD
Custodian: Bank of Boston
Listed: Bovespa **Dealings:** Daily
Fund Sedol I.D.: 305252 **Published:** BZ/RT/LP
Fees **Annual fee:** 1.50% **Performance fee:** 15.00%
Front end load: None **Redemption fee:** None
Switching fee: None

Top holdings:

Holding	%
Arno PN	7.0%
BIC Caloi Convertibles	9.9%
CO Patrimonio Overseas	6.5%
H Renner PN	12.8%
Inentex PN	8.6%
Lorenz PR	11.2%
Magnesia PNA	5.0%
Money Market	5.6%
Tam PR	7.3%
Tectoy PN	6.4%

TOTAL RETURNS %

3 months 1997	1996	1995	1994	3 years	5 years
12.26	42.26	N.A.	N.A.	N.A.	N.A.

STATISTICS

Assets ($mil)	Current yield	Volatility	Risk return	Micropal Star Rating
12.20	—	N.A.	—	———

Patrimonio New Fund Equity
115/350

Banco Patrimonio S.A.
Avenue Brigadeiro Faria Lima, 2000 - 4 Andar, Sao Paulo, SP, Brazil
Tel 55-11-3039-3885 Fax 55-11-3039-1900
http://www. patrimonio.com
E mail fund.info@patrimonio.com
Contact: Renata Lopes Kotscho

Investment objective:
The sub-fund seeks to maximise long-term capital growth by investing primarily in stocks traded on the San Paulo and Rio de Janeiro Stock Exchanges. The top sector allocations of the portfolio are the following: communications (36.9%); energy (18.4%); industrial cyclical (10.9%); and non-durable (7.4%). At this time the portfolio's assets are located in Brazil.

Umbrella fund: Patrimonio Funds Inc
Launch date: 09/04/92 **Domicile:** Cayman Islands
Currency: USD **Structure:** Open ended, Investment Company
Portfolio manager: Flavio Teles de Menezes
Manager of Patrimonio New Fund Equity commenced in 1992; MBA- Chicago U; former equity analyst and specializes in Latin American areas.

Performance:

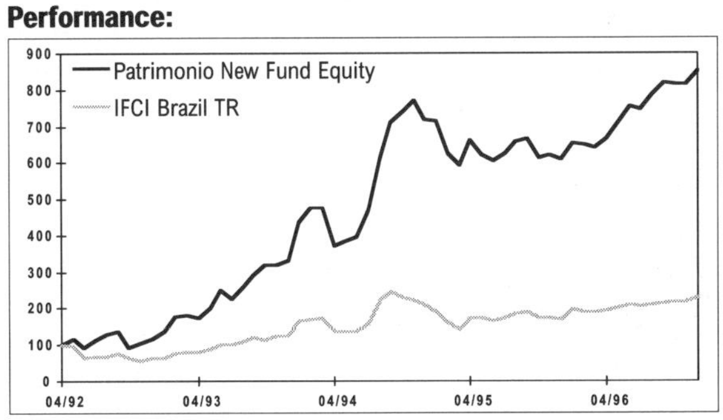

Purchase: Direct, Financial Advisor, Euroclear/Cedel
Minimum investment: 50,000 USD
Custodian: Bank of Boston
Listed: Bovespa **Dealings:** Daily
Fund Sedol I.D.: 305251 **Published:** BZ/RT/LP
Fees **Annual fee:** 2.00% **Performance fee:** 15.00%
Front end load: None **Redemption fee:** Up to 5.00%
Switching fee: None

Top holdings:

Holding	%
Arno PN	n/s
BCN PN	n/s
Brahma PN	n/s
Cemig-PN	n/s
Electrobras ON	n/s
Lojas Arapua	n/s
Petrobas-PN	n/s
Telebras ON	n/s
Telebras PN	n/s
Telesp PN	n/s

TOTAL RETURNS %

3 months 1997	1996	1995	1994	3 years	5 years
20.92	39.57	-14.81	117.77	158.92	N.A.

STATISTICS

Assets ($mil)	Current yield	Volatility	Risk return	Micropal Star Rating
7.50	—	10.05	4	✪✪✪✪

Performa Real Estate Securities
253/350

Performa Investment Advisors
14 Rue Aldringen, L-1118 Luxembourg
Tel 41-75-232-2748 Fax 41-75-233-2758

Investment objective:
The fund aims to provide diversification and super total returns by investing in US real estate securities. The sector allocations of the portfolio include real estate securities (95.6%); and the remainder held in cash (4.4%). The asset allocations are equities (86.5%); convertibles (9.1%); and cash (4.4%).

Umbrella fund: This is a singular fund.
Launch date: 01/07/94 **Domicile:** Luxembourg
Currency: USD **Structure:** Open ended, SICAV
Portfolio manager: Cydney C. Donnell
Investment Committee Member for Performa Real Estate Securities; 10 years in the financial industry.

Purchase: Direct
Minimum investment: None
Custodian: Banque Generale du Luxembourg
Listed: Luxembourg **Dealings:** Weekly
Fund Sedol I.D.: 300584 **Published:** BZ/HZ
Fees **Annual fee:** None **Performance fee:** None
Front end load: 0.50% **Redemption fee:** None
Switching fee: None

Contact: Alfons Thony
Performance:

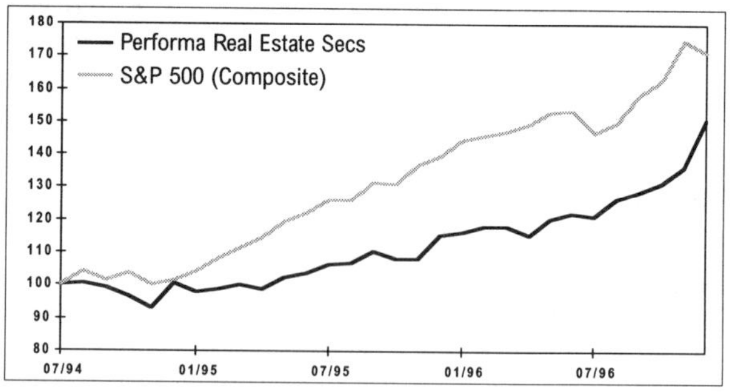

Top holdings:

Holding	%
Carr America Realty	4.0%
Crescent Real Estate	3.4%
Kimco Realty	2.9%
Liberty Properties	3.5%
Macerich Co.	3.1%
Patriot American	3.2%
Rouse Company	3.1%
Security Capital	2.9%
Simon de Bartolo	3.8%
Starwood Lodging	4.0%

TOTAL RETURNS %

3 months 1997	1996	1995	1994	3 years	5 years
3.69	30.39	15.12	N.A.	N.A.	N.A.

STATISTICS

Assets ($mil)	Current yield	Volatility	Risk return	Micropal Star Rating
63.78	—	N.A.	—	———

Perpetual Offshr Latin American Growth
322/350

Perpetual
D'Hauteville Chambers, Seale Street, St Helier, JE4 8WS, Jersey
Tel 44-1534-607-600 Fax 44-1534-38-918

Investment objective:
The fund seeks to achieve capital growth in Latin America by investing mainly in shares of companies in South and Central America (including Mexico) and the Caribbean. The fund may include other Latin America related investments that the Manager considers appropriate. The fund may also hold cash.

Umbrella fund: This is a singular fund.
Launch date: 31/01/95 **Domicile:** Jersey
Currency: USD **Structure:** Open ended, Investment Company
Portfolio manager: Mark Turner
Manager of Perpetual Offshore Latin American Growth commenced February 1993; studied at Cardiff U; 5 years at GRE Asset Management; 8 years investment industry experience.
Purchase: Direct, Financial Advisor
Minimum investment: 2,000 USD
Custodian: Royal Bank of Scotland Trust Company (Jersey) Limited
Listed: None **Dealings:** Daily
Fund Sedol I.D.: 68272 **Published:** FT/IHT/JE
Fees **Annual fee:** 1.50% **Performance fee:** None
Front end load: 5.25% **Redemption fee:** None
Switching fee: None

Contact: Julie Legg
Performance:

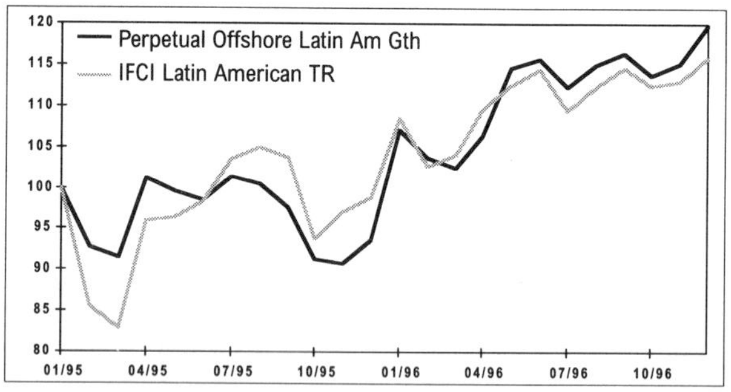

Top holdings:

Holding	%
Bufete Industrial	2.5%
Cernex SA	2.0%
Cesp Cia Energy	2.3%
Electrobas	2.2%
Embraer	3.1%
Grupo Televisa	3.8%
Petrol Brasiliero	2.2%
Telebras Telec Braspon	3.0%
Telerej-Tel Pro Jan	2.1%
Telex Tel S.Paulo	2.1%

TOTAL RETURNS %

3 months 1997	1996	1995	1994	3 years	5 years
9.57	27.83	N.A.	N.A.	N.A.	N.A.

STATISTICS

Assets ($mil)	Current yield	Volatility	Risk return	Micropal Star Rating
9.60	—	N.A.	—	———

Pictet CF Valiber
241/350

Pictet Gestion (Luxembourg) S.A.
17 Cote d'Eich, L-1450 Luxembourg
Tel 352-46-71-71-1 Fax 352-46-69-95
http://www. pictet.com

Contact: Pascal Chauvaux

Investment objective:
This sub-fund seeks capital appreciation by investing in Spanish equities for at least 85% of the fund and the remaining part in Portuguese equities. The fund is comprised of two distinct parts: one managed in line with the Ibex 35 Index and the other actively managed. The base currency of this fund is in Spanish pesetas.

Umbrella fund: Pictet Country Fund
Launch date: 01/11/88 **Domicile:** Luxembourg
Currency: ESP **Structure:** Open ended, SICAV
Portfolio manager: Herve Gaudart
Manager of Pictet CF Valiber commenced 1992; financial analyst; graduate, accounting- U of Columbia.

Purchase: Direct, Financial Advisor
Minimum investment: None
Custodian: Banque Pictet (Luxembourg) S.A.
Listed: Luxembourg **Dealings:** Weekly
Fund Sedol I.D.: 301845 **Published:** RT/IHT/FT/BZ
Fees **Annual fee:** 1.00% **Performance fee:** None
Front end load: 1.00% **Redemption fee:** 1.00%
Switching fee: 1.00%

Performance:

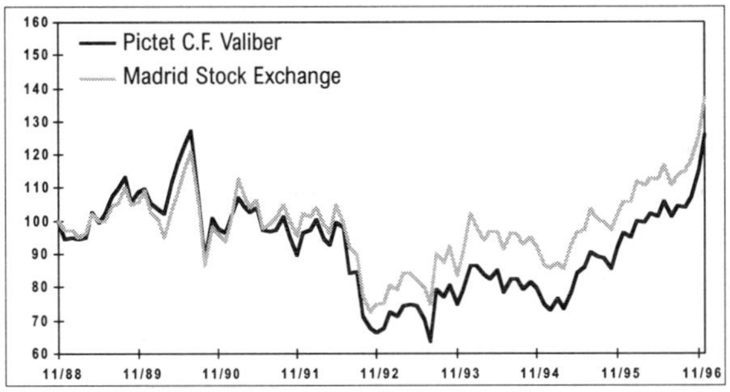

Top holdings:

Argentaria Banca de Espania	2.0%
Banco Bilbao Vizcaya	9.9%
Banco Central Hispano	1.9%
Banco de Santander	8.7%
Banco Popular Esp	3.6%
Endesa	12.7%
Gas Natural	6.5%
Iberdola	16.3%
Respol	7.9%
Telefonica	14.9%

TOTAL RETURNS %

3 months 1997	1996	1995	1994	3 years	5 years
0.95	30.69	28.94	-5.81	58.71	31.01

STATISTICS

Assets ($mil)	Current yield	Volatility	Risk return	Micropal Star Rating
7.54	—	4.44	1	✪✪

Pictet TF Eastern Europe
42/350

Pictet Gestion (Luxembourg) S.A.
17 Cote d'Eich, L-1450 Luxembourg
Tel 352-46-71-71-1 Fax 352-46-69-95
http://www. pictet.com

Contact: Pascal Chauvaux

Investment objective:
The sub-fund seeks long-term capital growth in Eastern Europe equities, mainly the Visegrad markets. The portfolio is primarily allocated into the following countries: Hungary (22.7%); Russia (22.2%); Poland (22.1%); and Czech Republic (14.0%).

Umbrella fund: Pictet Targeted Fund
Launch date: 01/06/95 **Domicile:** Luxembourg [UCITS]
Currency: DEM **Structure:** Open ended, FCP
Portfolio manager: Yves Kuhn
Manager of Pictet Targeted Funds- Eastern Europe commenced June 1995; graduate- Swiss Federal Institute of Technology.

Purchase: Direct, Financial Advisor
Minimum investment: None
Custodian: Banque Pictet (Luxembourg) S.A.
Listed: Luxembourg **Dealings:** Weekly
Fund Sedol I.D.: 304332 **Published:** RT/IHT/FT/BZ
Fees **Annual fee:** 2.00% **Performance fee:** None
Front end load: 2.00% **Redemption fee:** 2.00%
Switching fee: 2.00%

Performance:

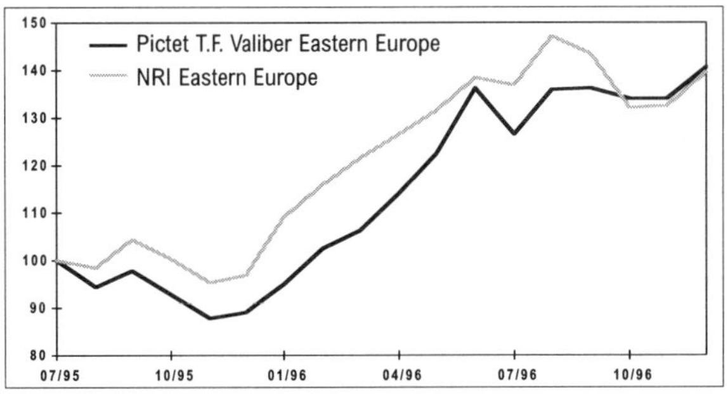

Top holdings:

Danubis Hotels	2.2%
Elektrim	2.8%
Kormercui Banka	2.6%
Lukoil Holdings	2.6%
Magyar Olaf Es Gas	3.6%
Pliva	2.7%
Rostelecom	3.3%
SPT Telecom	2.6%
United Energy Systems	4.0%
Zagrebacka Banka	3.2%

TOTAL RETURNS %

3 months 1997	1996	1995	1994	3 years	5 years
26.31	57.85	N.A.	N.A.	N.A.	N.A.

STATISTICS

Assets ($mil)	Current yield	Volatility	Risk return	Micropal Star Rating
99.72	—	N.A.	—	——

Prolific IF China Opportunities

58/350

Prolific Intl Mangement (Ire) Ltd.
53 Fitzwilliam Square, Dublin 2, Ireland
Tel 353-1-676-8836 Fax 353-1-676-2136
http://www. iii.co.uk./prolific
E mail customer.services@prolific.co.uk
Contact: Customer Services Department

Investment objective:
The insurance fund aims for capital growth by investing in companies which are domiciled in China or companies that either invest or trade with China. The top sector allocations are as follows: capital goods (16.6%); consumer goods (16.5); services (15.3%); and finance (11.5%).

Umbrella fund: Prolific International Fund Plc
Launch date: 28/03/92 **Domicile:** Ireland [UCITS]
Currency: GBP **Structure:** Open ended, Investment Company
Portfolio manager: Sean Darby
Fund Manager Prolific IF China Opportunities commenced December 1994; graduate Exeter U 1985, post graduate course Japanese – Stirling U: previous experience corporate finance department of Japanese Investment house.
Purchase: Direct, Financial Advisor
Minimum investment: 1,500 GBP
Custodian: RBS Securities Services (Ire) Ltd
Listed: None **Dealings:** Daily
Fund Sedol I.D.: 440215 **Published:** FT/SC
Fees **Annual fee:** 1.50% **Performance fee:** None
Front end load: 5.00% **Redemption fee:** None
Switching fee: None

Performance:

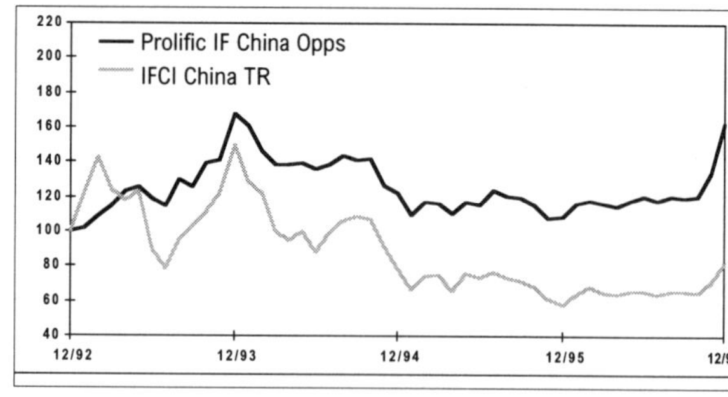

Top holdings:

Cheung Kong Infra	3.2%
China Resources Enterprises	3.4%
China Travel Intl	3.1%
Clipsal Inds.	3.0%
Dazhong Taxi	2.9%
Guandong Kelon	3.8%
Lung Kee (Bermuda)	2.9%
Qingling Motors	3.2%
Shanghai Post & Tel	3.4%
Zhenhai Refining Chemical	2.9%

TOTAL RETURNS %

3 months 1997	1996	1995	1994	3 years	5 years
3.56	49.91	-11.47	-27.18	-3.36	N.A.

STATISTICS

Assets ($mil)	Current yield	Volatility	Risk return	Micropal Star Rating
12.15	—	5.96	—	✪✪✪✪

Prolific IF UK Equity Inc

223/350

Prolific Intl Mangement (Ire) Ltd.
53 Fitzwilliam Square, Dublin 2, Ireland
Tel 353-1-676-8836 Fax 353-1-676-2136
http://www. iii.co.uk/prolific
E mail customer.services@prolific.co.uk
Contact: Customer Services Department

Investment objective:
The sub-fund seeks high and growing income together with capital growth from investment in the ordinary shares of UK companies. The top sector allocations are as follows: general industrials (29.0%); mineral extraction (5.5%); consumer (10.2%); finance (19.1); and services (26.5%).

Umbrella fund: Prolific International Fund Plc
Launch date: 17/03/89 **Domicile:** Ireland [UCITS]
Currency: GBP **Structure:** Open ended, Investment Company
Portfolio manager: Neil Tyson
Senior Fund Manager of Prolific IF UK Equity Inc; 12 years investment experience; specialises in income equities and smaller companies.

Purchase: Direct, Financial Advisor
Minimum investment: 1,500 GBP
Custodian: RBS Securities Services (Ire) Ltd
Listed: None **Dealings:** Daily
Fund Sedol I.D.: 440222 **Published:** FT/SC
Fees **Annual fee:** 1.50% **Performance fee:** None
Front end load: 5.00% **Redemption fee:** None
Switching fee: None

Performance:

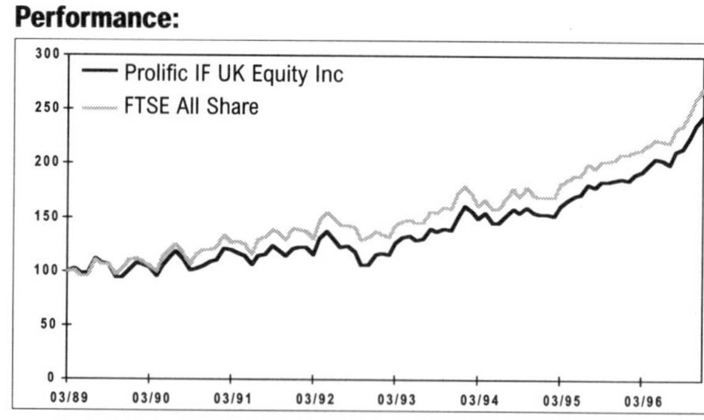

Top holdings:

Abbey National	2.3%
Bodycote Intl	1.8%
British Petroleum	3.4%
EMI	2.1%
Ladbroke Group	1.8%
Nestor BNA	1.9%
Prudential	1.8%
Siebe	1.9%
Smiths Inds	1.8%
Zeneca Group	2.8%

TOTAL RETURNS %

3 months 1997	1996	1995	1994	3 years	5 years
-1.81	31.34	21.35	3.24	64.55	101.67

STATISTICS

Assets ($mil)	Current yield	Volatility	Risk return	Micropal Star Rating
111.46	2.80	3.25	5	✪✪✪✪✪

Quadrant European Equity Fund
191/350

Quilter International Management Limited
19/21 Circular Road, Douglas IM99 1EZ, Isle of Man
Tel 44-1624-622-699 Fax 44-1624-627-515
E mail rhr@enterprise.net

Investment objective:
The sub-fund aims to maximise capital appreciation in US dollars terms by investing in continental European equities. The top sector allocations of the portfolio are as follows: consumer goods (20.2%); industrial cyclical (22.3%); health (12.6%); and services (11.9%). The assets of the portfolio are primarily allocated to Germany (24.9%); France (20.1%); Switzerland (14.4%); Sweden (10.3%); and Holland (9.1%).

Umbrella fund: Quadrant Fund (IOM) Ltd

Launch date: 07/09/94 **Domicile:** Isle of Man

Currency: USD **Structure:** Open ended, Investment Company

Portfolio manager: Guy Breeden
Manager of Quadrant European Equity Fund commenced October 1990; Baccalaureate, business management degree- HEC Lausanne,

Contact: Jenny Croskery

Performance:

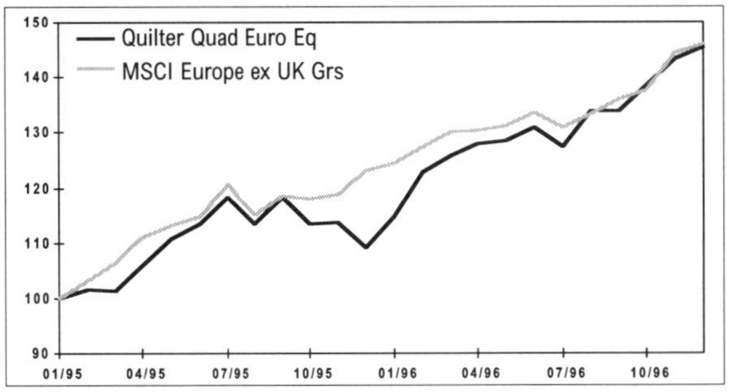

Purchase: Direct, Financial Advisor

Minimum investment: None

Custodian: Royal Bank of Scotland

Listed: None **Dealings:** Weekly

Fund Sedol I.D.: 72086 **Published:** FT/MP

Fees **Annual fee:** 1.00% **Performance fee:** None
Front end load: 5.00% **Redemption fee:** None
Switching fee: None

Top holdings:

Holding	%
ABB	2.9%
Adidas	3.3%
Banco Santander	3.8%
Ericsson	2.8%
Fresenius	2.8%
L'Oreal	2.8%
LVMH	2.9%
Mannesmann	3.0%
STET	3.5%
Veba	3.4%

TOTAL RETURNS %

3 months 1997	1996	1995	1994	3 years	5 years
3.95	33.27	N.A.	N.A.	N.A.	N.A.

STATISTICS

Assets ($mil)	Current yield	Volatility	Risk return	Micropal Star Rating
12.32	—	N.A.	—	———

Quantum Emerging Growth Fund
128/350

Soros Fund Mgmt
14 Ryder Street, St James's, London SW1Y 6QB, United Kingdom
Tel 44-171-925-2555 Fax 44-171-925-2625

Investment objective:
The fund seeks capital appreciation by investing globally in common and preferred stocks, warrants and convertible debt securities-dividend. The fund focuses on emerging growth concepts and securities markets that have recently become accessible to international investors or securities markets in developing countries.

Umbrella fund: This is a singular fund.

Launch date: 02/01/92 **Domicile:** Netherlands Antilles

Currency: USD **Structure:** Open ended, LLC

Portfolio manager: Soros Fund Management LLC
Principal investment advisor; located at 888 Seventh Avenue, New York, NY 10106 US.

Contact: John Denny/Mark Knapen

Performance:

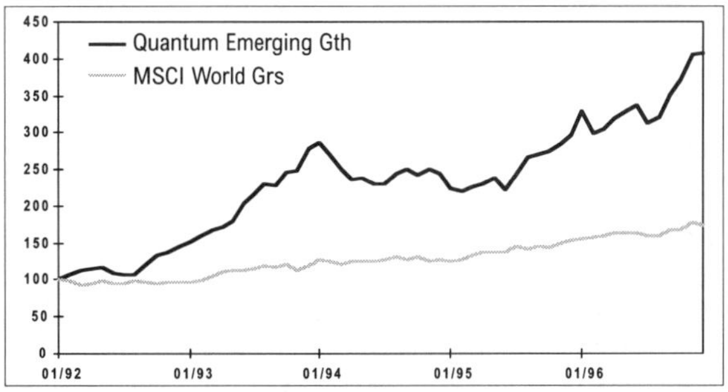

Purchase: Direct, Selected Agents-Worldwide

Minimum investment: 1,000 Shares

Custodian: Arnhold and S. Bleichroeder

Listed: None **Dealings:** Daily

Fund Sedol I.D.: 271615 **Published:** IHT/HT

Fees **Annual fee:** 1.00% **Performance fee:** 20.00%
Front end load: Variable **Redemption fee:** Variable
Switching fee: Variable

Top holdings:

Holding	
108.0m Brazil Disc Bond Ser. Z-L 4.25% 4/15/24	n/s
140.0m Brazil Par.Bond Ser. Z-L 4.25% 4/15/24	n/s
74.9m CIBC Wood Gundy 5.48% repo 9/30/97	n/s
50.5m Daiwa Securities 5.27% repo 7/31/97	n/s
41.2m Daiwa Securities 5.30% repo 12/31/96	n/s
62.0m Deutsche Bank 5.00% repo 9/30/97	n/s
50.6m Deutsche Bank 5.35% repo 7/31/97	n/s
16.3m Hong Kong & China Gas	n/s
14.0m Hong Kong Land Holdings	n/s
121.7m US TBill 7/11/96	n/s

TOTAL RETURNS %

3 months 1997	1996	1995	1994	3 years	5 years
17.57	38.02	21.56	-12.64	46.57	N.A.

STATISTICS

Assets ($mil)	Current yield	Volatility	Risk return	Micropal Star Rating
1876.00	—	8.68	2	✪✪✪✪

Quota Fund N.V.
15/350

Soros Fund Mgmt
14 Ryder Street, St James's, London SW1Y 6QB, United Kingdom
Tel 44-171-925-2555 Fax 44-171-925-2625

Investment objective:
The fund's prime objective is to seek capital appreciation. The fund invests worldwide in equity, debt, commodity and currency markets. In addition, the fund conducts trading transactions in markets for commodities and currencies, for both hedging and speculative purposes.

Umbrella fund: This is a singular fund.
Launch date: 02/01/92 **Domicile:** Netherlands Antilles
Currency: USD **Structure:** Open ended, LLC
Portfolio manager: Soros Fund Management LLC
Principal investment advisor; located at 888 Seventh Avenue, New York, NY 10106 USA.

Purchase: Direct, Selected Agents-Worldwide
Minimum investment: 1,000 Shares
Custodian: Arnhold and S. Bleichroeder
Listed: None **Dealings:** Daily
Fund Sedol I.D.: 305064 **Published:** IHT/FT
Fees **Annual fee:** 1.00% **Performance fee:** 20.00%
Front end load: Variable **Redemption fee:** Variable
Switching fee: Variable

Contact: John Denny/Mark Knapen
Performance:

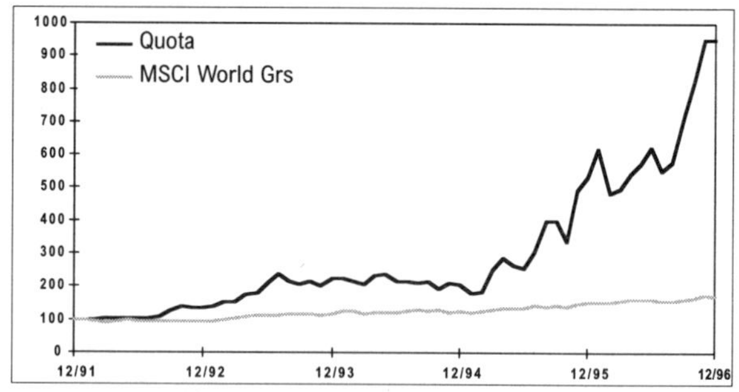

Top holdings:

Holding	
1.12bn US Treasury Bill 08/22 96	n/s
1.1m Burlington Northern Santa Fe Corp	n/s
1.25bn US Treasury Bill 11/30/97	n/s
100m Argentina par Bond 4.25% 3/31/23	n/s
2.8m Newmont Mining Corp	n/s
225m South Africa series 153.13% 08/31/10	n/s
3.9bn DM due 01/22/96 Short	n/s
305.49bn Japenese Yen 01/03/96 Short	n/s
402m Venezuela DCB Bond Ser-DL/FRN12/18/23	n/s
73m US Treasury Bond 05/23/96	n/s

TOTAL RETURNS %

3 months 1997	1996	1995	1994	3 years	5 years
21.52	78.80	160.56	-8.31	327.15	851.64

STATISTICS

Assets ($mil)	Current yield	Volatility	Risk return	Micropal Star Rating
2250.80	—	13.92	5	✪✪✪✪✪

RBC Global Canadian Class
293/350

Royal Bank of Canada Offshore Fund Managers
PO Box 246, Canada Court, St Peter Port, GY1 3QE, Guernsey
Tel 44-1481-723-021 Fax 44-1481-715-976
http://www. royalbankci.com

Investment objective:
The sub-fund seeks to achieve long-term capital appreciation from a portfolio of Canadian shares. The top sector allocations of the portfolio are as follows: industrial cyclical (35.0%); consumer goods (15.1%); finance (13.3%); energy (12.9%); and services (7.6%).

Umbrella fund: RBC Global Funds
Launch date: 20/11/95 **Domicile:** Guernsey
Currency: CAD **Structure:** Open ended, Unit Trust
Portfolio manager: Michael Fulton
VP – Manager of Royal Bank Canada Global Investment Canadian commenced 1991; BSc, geology and graduate Dip, business administration- McGill U; previously with McLean Budden Ltd, Portfolio Manager; 34 years in the finance industry.
Purchase: Direct, Financial Advisor, Global Private Banking Network
Minimum investment: 10,000 USD
Custodian: Royal Bank of Canada (CI) Limited
Listed: None **Dealings:** Weekly
Fund Sedol I.D.: 74902 **Published:** FT/SC/GE
Fees **Annual fee:** 1.50% **Performance fee:** None
Front end load: None **Redemption fee:** None
Switching fee: None

Contact: F.J Bourget/John Renouf
Performance:

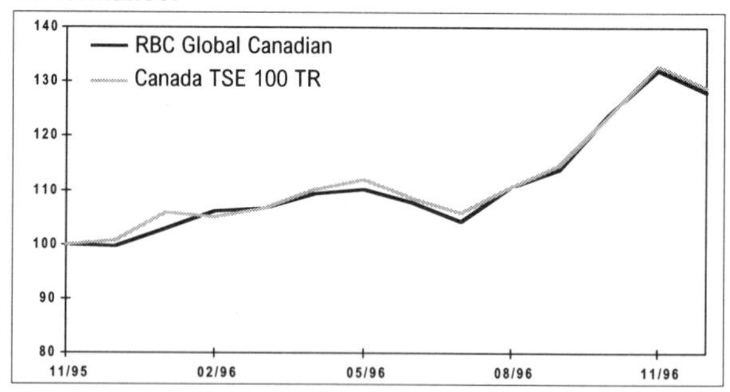

Top holdings:

Holding	
Alcan Aluminium	2.4%
Bank of Montreal	2.0%
Bank of Nova Scotia	2.9%
BCE Inc.	2.8%
Canadian Pacific	2.1%
CIBC	2.7%
Northern Telecom	2.2%
Royal Bank of Canada	3.0%
Seagram Co	2.6%
Toronto Dominion Bank	2.2%

TOTAL RETURNS %

3 months 1997	1996	1995	1994	3 years	5 years
4.66	28.48	N.A.	N.A.	N.A.	N.A.

STATISTICS

Assets ($mil)	Current yield	Volatility	Risk return	Micropal Star Rating
12.44	—	N.A.	—	———

Regent Blue Tiger Inv Co
5/350

Regent Fund Management Ltd
39 St James's Street, London SW1A 1JQ, United Kingdom
Tel 44-171-316-0007 Fax 44-171-316-0008

Investment objective:
The fund aims to invest in Russian equities, up to 20% of the assets can be invested in the Baltic states. The top sector allocations are the following: utilities (38.0%); consumer goods (37.0%); communications (17.0%); and metals (1.0%). The assets of the portfolio are divided between equities (93.0%); cash/MM (5.0%); and bonds (2.0%). Share redemptions conditional.

Umbrella fund: This is a singular fund.

Launch date: 10/08/95 **Domicile:** Cayman Islands

Currency: USD **Structure:** Close ended, Investment Company

Portfolio manager: Dominic Boker Ingram
Manager of Regent Blue Tiger Investment Company commenced January 1995.

Contact: Christy York

Performance:

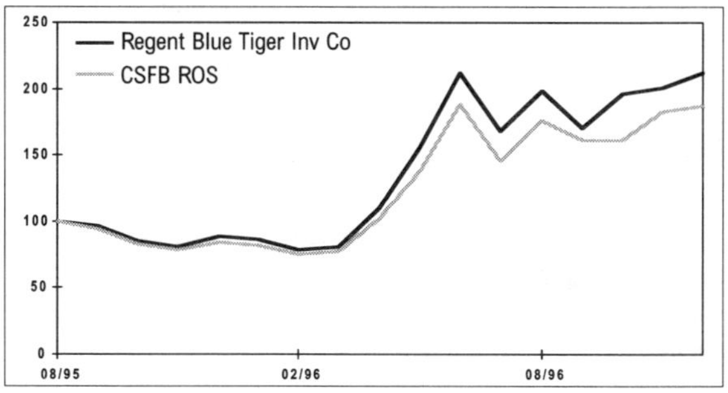

Purchase: Market makers

Minimum investment: 100,000 USD

Custodian: Bermuda Trust Far East Ltd

Listed: Dublin **Dealings:** N/A

Fund Sedol I.D.: 274222 **Published:** FT/IHT/SC

Fees **Annual fee:** 1.50% **Performance fee:** Up to 15.00%
Front end load: Up to 5.00% **Redemption fee:** None
Switching fee: None

Top holdings:

Holding	%
Irkutsk	8.3%
LukOil	7.9%
LukOil (Pref)	4.6%
Mosenergo	11.7%
Noralsk Nickel	2.8%
Rostelekom	13.4%
Russian Govt Bonds	3.4%
Surgut (Pref)	5.7%
Surgut Neftegaz	6.9%
Unified Energy	19.0%

TOTAL RETURNS %

3 months 1997	1996	1995	1994	3 years	5 years
56.28	137.53	N.A.	N.A.	N.A.	N.A.

STATISTICS

Assets ($mil)	Current yield	Volatility	Risk return	Micropal Star Rating
54.18	—	N.A.	—	———

Regent Red Tiger Inv Co
7/350

Regent Fund Management Ltd
39 St James's Street, London SW1A 1JQ, United Kingdom
Tel 44-171-316-0007 Fax 44-171-316-0008

Investment objective:
The fund seeks to invest in companies based throughout Russia, predominately who are based in Moscow and St. Petersburg. Up to 20% of the portfolio may be invested in companies in the central Asian republics although this is currently not the intention. At least 75.0% of the assets are invested in companies traded through a stock exchange or over-the-counter.

Umbrella fund: This is a singular fund.

Launch date: 19/12/94 **Domicile:** Cayman Islands

Currency: USD **Structure:** Close ended, Investment Company

Portfolio manager: Dominic Bokor-Ingram
Manager of Regent Red Tiger.

Contact: Christy York

Performance:

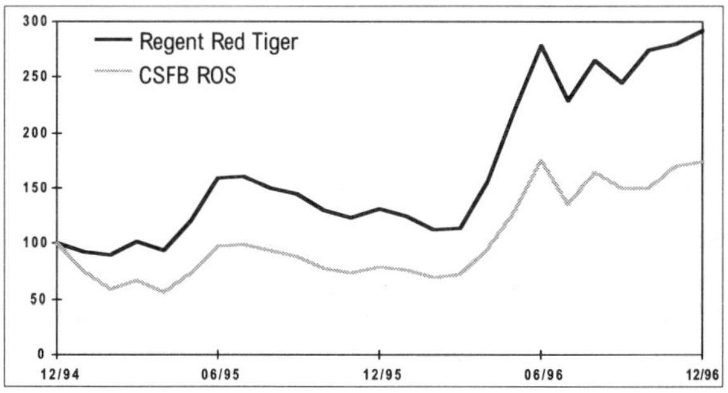

Purchase: Direct, Market Makers

Minimum investment: 100,000 USD

Custodian: Bermuda Trust Far East Ltd

Listed: Dublin **Dealings:** Monthly

Fund Sedol I.D.: 275627 **Published:** BZ/FT/IHT

Fees **Annual fee:** 1.50% **Performance fee:** Up to 15.00%
Front end load: Up to 5.00% **Redemption fee:** None
Switching fee: None

Top holdings:

Holding	%
Irkutsk Energo	10.4%
Lukoil (Pref)	5.6%
Mosenergo	15.2%
Neftyanaya Kompaniya Lukoil	0.9%
Permneft (Pref)	2.3%
Rostelekom	17.9%
Russia T/B-GKO 22036 MRFS 0%/96	3.7%
Surgut Neftegaz	6.9%
Unified Energy Systems	23.6%
Yuganskneftegas	4.6%

TOTAL RETURNS %

3 months 1997	1996	1995	1994	3 years	5 years
63.83	122.60	31.40	N.A.	N.A.	N.A.

STATISTICS

Assets ($mil)	Current yield	Volatility	Risk return	Micropal Star Rating
54.20	—	N.A.	—	———

Regent Undervalued Assets Taiwan Fund

152/350

Regent Fund Management Ltd
39 St Jame's Street, London SW1A 1JQ, United Kingdom
Tel 44-171-316-0007 Fax 44-171-316-0008

Investment objective:
The fund seeks to take advantage of the significant discount at which the listed shares of Taiwanese on-shore closed-end funds trade in relation to their net asset value and to profit from both the capital appreciation of the underlying assets in the funds and from any narrowing of those discounts.

Umbrella fund: This is a singular fund.

Launch date: 21/09/94 **Domicile:** Cayman Islands

Currency: USD **Structure:** Close ended, Investment Company

Portfolio manager: David Curl
Manager of Regent Undervalued Assets Taiwan Series 3 Fund commenced September 1994.

Purchase: Direct, Financial Advisor

Minimum investment: 100,000 USD

Custodian: Bermuda Trust Far East Ltd

Listed: Dublin **Dealings:** Monthly

Fund Sedol I.D.: 272786 **Published:** FT/IHT/SC

Fees **Annual fee:** 1.00% **Performance fee:** Up to 15.00%
Front end load: 4.00% **Redemption fee:** None
Switching fee: None

Contact: Christy York

Performance:

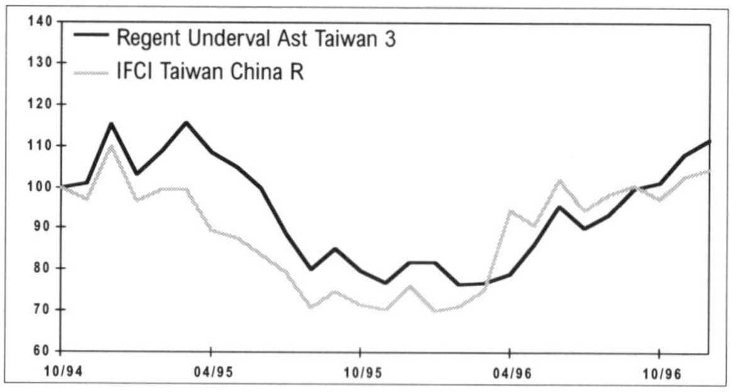

Top holdings:

Holding	%
China Growth Fund	21.1%
China Sucess Fund	13.2%
Citizen Fund	6.2%
Core Pacific Pioneer	8.5%
Diamond Mutual	11.0%
Grand Pacific	5.9%
Jardine Flemming Fund	3.4%
Kwang Hua Fund	3.5%
Masterlink Fund	14.5%
NITC FuYuan Fund	16.4%

TOTAL RETURNS %

3 months 1997	1996	1995	1994	3 years	5 years
13.25	36.05	-28.91	N.A.	N.A.	N.A.

STATISTICS

Assets ($mil)	Current yield	Volatility	Risk return	Micropal Star Rating
43.48	—	N.A.	—	———

Regent White Tiger

2/350

Regent Fund Management Ltd
39 St Jame's Street, London SW1A 1JQ, United Kingdom
Tel 44-171-316-0007 Fax 44-171-316-0008

Investment objective:
The sub-fund seeks capital growth through investment in Russian listed or over the counter securities. The top sector allocations of the portfolio are as follows: consumer goods (38.0%); utilities (38.0%); communications (16.0%) and finance (1.0%). At present, 92.0% of the assets are held in equities 7% in cash/MM and the remaining 1% in bonds.

Umbrella fund: This is a singular fund.

Launch date: 01/09/94 **Domicile:** Cayman Islands

Currency: USD **Structure:** Open ended, Investment Company

Portfolio manager: David Curl
Manager of Regent White Tiger commenced September 1994.

Purchase: Direct, Institutional /Professional / Accredited investors only

Minimum investment: 100,000 USD

Custodian: Bermuda Trust Far East Ltd

Listed: Dublin **Dealings:** Monthly

Fund Sedol I.D.: 273449 **Published:** FT/IHT/SC

Fees **Annual fee:** 1.50% **Performance fee:** Up to 15.00%
Front end load: Up to 5.00% **Redemption fee:** None
Switching fee: None

Contact: Christy York

Performance:

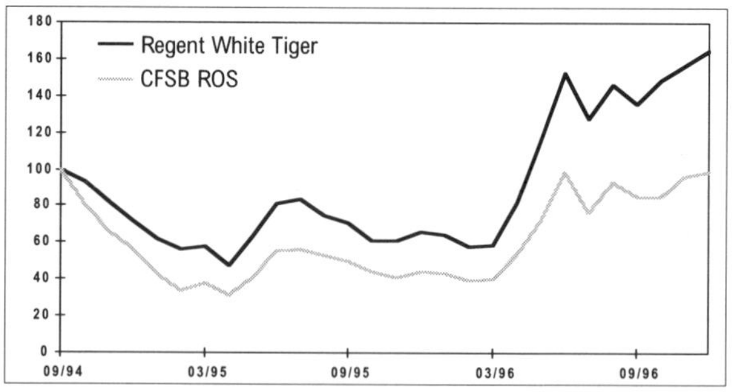

Top holdings:

Holding	%
Noyabrskneftegaz Pref	0.6%
Permneft Pref	0.8%
Rostelekom	14.4%
Sberbank	0.3%
Surgut Holdings	8.8%
Surgut Neftegaz	7.6%
Tatneft	2.6%
Tzum	0.2%
Unified Energy Systems	21.8%
Unified Energy Systems Pref	0.6%

TOTAL RETURNS %

3 months 1997	1996	1995	1994	3 years	5 years
62.20	150.46	-7.71	N.A.	N.A.	N.A.

STATISTICS

Assets ($mil)	Current yield	Volatility	Risk return	Micropal Star Rating
103.47	—	N.A.	—	———

RG America Fund N.V.

258/350

Robeco Administrative Maatschappij N.V.
Coolsingel 120, Rotterdam, NL-3000 AZ, Netherlands
Tel 31-10-224-1224 Fax 31-10-224-1224
http://www. robeco.nl
E mail robeco.advies@ robeco.nl

Contact: Customer Services Department

Performance:

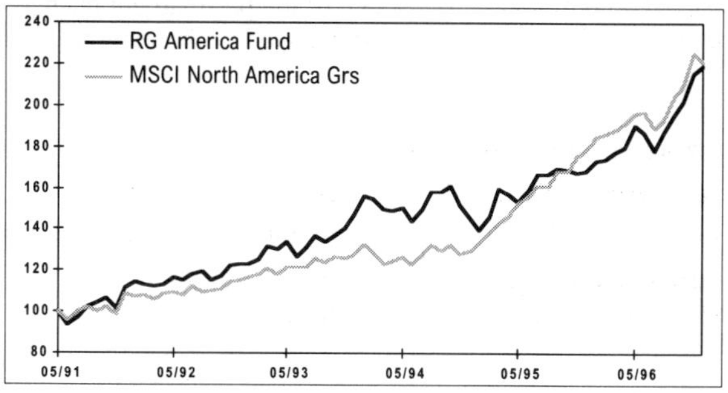

Investment objective:
The fund aims for capital appreciation and dividend yield through investment in North and Latin American shares. The country allocation of the portfolio is US (87.0%); Canada (8.0%); Brazil (3.0%); and Mexico (2.0%). The top sector allocations are as follows: technology (20.0%); finance (16.0); health (15.0%); and consumer goods (11.0%).

Umbrella fund: This is a singular fund.

Launch date: 19/02/91 **Domicile:** Netherlands [UCITS]

Currency: NLG **Structure:** Open ended, Invsetment Company

Portfolio manager: Mamix Vriezen
Senior Portfolio Manager of North American equities and Product Manager of RG America Fund, RG SelfSelect Countryfund, and Mean Reversion & Trending Fund; PhD- U of Amsterdam; joined Robeco in 1989.

Purchase: Direct, Financial Advisor

Minimum investment: 1,000 NLG

Custodian: Robeco Bank (Luxembourg) S.A.

Listed: None **Dealings:** Daily

Fund Sedol I.D.: 474383 **Published:** FT/IHT/SC

Fees **Annual fee:** 0.50% **Performance fee:** None
Front end load: None **Redemption fee:** None
Switching fee: 0.50%

Top holdings:

Citicorp	3.0%
Coca-Cola Co.	4.0%
Exxon Corp	4.0%
General Electric	5.0%
Gillette	3.0%
Intel Corp.	4.0%
Merck & Co. Inc.	3.0%
Microsoft	4.0%
Pfeizer	3.0%
Procter & Gamble Co.	3.0%

TOTAL RETURNS %

3 months 1997	1996	1995	1994	3 years	5 years
10.73	30.08	16.17	-1.35	49.08	95.85

STATISTICS

Assets ($mil)	Current yield	Volatility	Risk return	Micropal Star Rating
75.06	—	3.64	2	✪✪

Royal Life Intl European

277/350

Royal Life International
Royal Court, Castletown, IM9 IRA, Isle of Man
Tel 44-1624-821-212 Fax 44-1624-824-405
http://www. rlii.com

Contact: Mike Haywood

Performance:

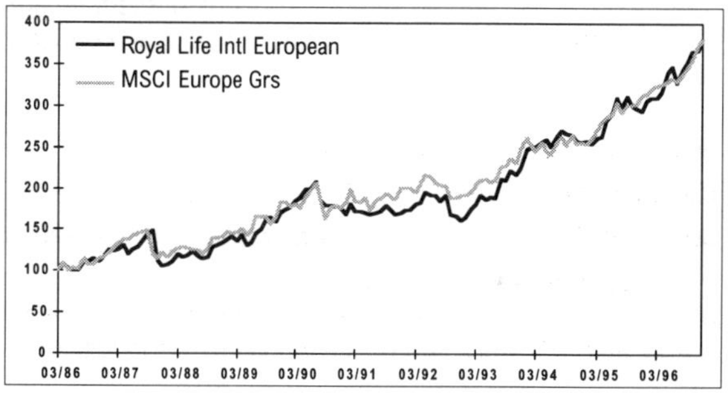

Investment objective:
This insurance sub-fund aims at maximising capital growth through investment in a portfolio of ordinary shares in European markets. At this time the top country allocations of the portfolio are follows: France (19.8%); Germany (14.8%); Switzerland (13.5%); Netherlands (13.1%); Sweden (9.7%); and Italy (7.4%).

Umbrella fund: This is a singular fund.

Launch date: 01/03/86 **Domicile:** Isle of Man

Currency: GBP **Structure:** Open ended, Insurance Fund

Portfolio manager: Royal Life International
Manager of Royal Life International Europe.

Purchase: Insurance Policy

Minimum investment: ILP

Custodian: Royal Life International

Listed: None **Dealings:** Weekly

Fund Sedol I.D.: 52288 **Published:** FT/IHT/SC

Fees **Annual fee:** 1.20% **Performance fee:** None
Front end load: 7.00% **Redemption fee:** None
Switching fee: None

Top holdings:

ABN AMRO Holding	1.8%
Carrefour	1.8%
Elf Aquitaine	2.4%
Ericsson	2.0%
Novartis	2.9%
Raison Tehtaat	1.9%
Roche Holdings	2.8%
Royal Dutch Petroleum	2.3%
SGS Thomson	2.1%
UCB	1.8%

TOTAL RETURNS %

3 months 1997	1996	1995	1994	3 years	5 years
7.09	29.20	14.94	12.93	67.70	123.42

STATISTICS

Assets ($mil)	Current yield	Volatility	Risk return	Micropal Star Rating
14.45	—	3.27	4	✪✪✪✪

Royal Life International Property
239/350

Royal Life International
Royal Court, Castletown, IM9 IRA, Isle of Man
Tel 44-1624-821-212 Fax 44-1624-824-405
http://www. rlii.com

Investment objective:
The insurance fund seeks to provide long-term capital growth by investing in UK property companies. The assets of the portfolio are divided into equities (92.5%); and cash/MM. The fund is denominated in UK sterling.

Umbrella fund: This is a singular fund.
Launch date: 01/02/82 **Domicile:** Isle of Man
Currency: GBP **Structure:** Open ended, Insurance Fund
Portfolio manager: Peter O'Reilly
Manager of Royal Life International Property.

Purchase: Insurance Policy
Minimum investment: ILP
Custodian: Royal Life International
Listed: None **Dealings:** Weekly
Fund Sedol I.D.: 75783 **Published:** FT/IHT/SC
Fees **Annual fee:** 1.20% **Performance fee:** None
Front end load: 7.00% **Redemption fee:** None
Switching fee: None

Contact: Mike Haywood
Performance:

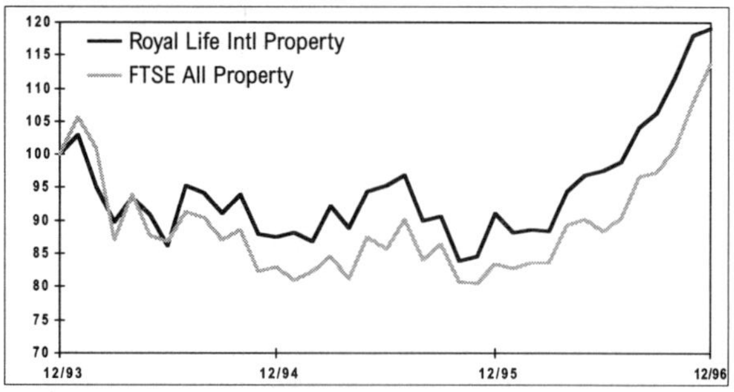

Top holdings:

Holding	%
Argant Group	5.8%
British land	11.2%
Burford Holdings	6.2%
Frogmere Estates	4.4%
Great Portland	5.3%
Hammerson	8.8%
Land Securities	23.1%
MSPC Ord	11.4%
PSII Ord	4.6%
Slough Estates	8.2%

TOTAL RETURNS %

3 months 1997	1996	1995	1994	3 years	5 years
2.94	30.77	3.97	-12.42	19.07	44.70

STATISTICS

Assets ($mil)	Current yield	Volatility	Risk return	Micropal Star Rating
1.61	—	4.54	2	✪✪✪✪

S-E-Banken Fund Sverige
184/350

Skandinaviska Enskilda Banken
PO Box 487, L-2014 Luxembourg
Tel 352-46-17-17-239 Fax 352-22-55-50
http://www. sebank.se/fonder

Investment objective:
The main objective of the sub-fund is long-term capital growth with investments in Swedish equities. The top sector allocations of the fund are the following: technology (24.8%); finance (17.3%); health/pharmaceutical products (16.0%); and utilities/others (10.3%).

Umbrella fund: S.E Banken Fund
Launch date: 25/09/93 **Domicile:** Luxembourg [UCITS]
Currency: SEK **Structure:** Open ended, Mutual Fund
Portfolio manager: Patrik Tigershlold
Manager of S-E-Banken Fund Sverige commenced October 1993; specialising in the Nordic area; 11 years experience in the finance industry

Purchase: Direct, S-E-Banken Group
Minimum investment: 2,500 USD
Custodian: S.E Banken Luxembourg
Listed: Luxembourg **Dealings:** Daily
Fund Sedol I.D.: 301790 **Published:** IHT
Fees **Annual fee:** 1.50% **Performance fee:** None
Front end load: 1.00% **Redemption fee:** None
Switching fee: 1.00%

Contact: Mr E Kremer
Performance:

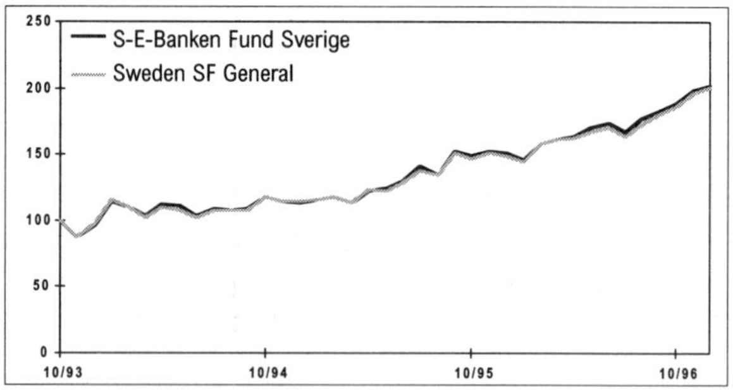

Top holdings:

Holding	%
ABB AB	3.0%
Astra	9.5%
Electrolux	3.5%
Ericsson	9.9%
Investor	3.8%
S-E-Banken	3.5%
Sandvik	4.3%
Skanska AB	3.8%
Svenska Handelsbanken	3.0%
Volvo	6.1%

TOTAL RETURNS %

3 months 1997	1996	1995	1994	3 years	5 years
4.68	33.52	33.89	17.31	109.71	N.A.

STATISTICS

Assets ($mil)	Current yield	Volatility	Risk return	Micropal Star Rating
142.38	—	5.44	3	✪✪✪

Samba Lux North America Equity

144/350

Samba Investment Management (Luxembourg) S.A
Nightingale House, 65 Curzon Street, London W1Y 7PE, United Kingdom
Tel 44-171-355-4411 Fax 44-171-355-4412
E mail ghulum.mohatarem@citicorp.com

Contact: Richard P. Keigher

Investment objective:
The sub-fund seeks long-term capital growth through investments in the US, Canadian and Mexican markets. At present the portfolio is fully allocated to the US. The top sector allocations of the portfolio include technology (37.4%); consumer goods (33.2%); capital goods (8.8%); basic industry (6.6%); and finance (1.7%).

Umbrella fund: This is a singular fund.
Launch date: 01/01/95 **Domicile:** Luxembourg [UCITS]
Currency: USD **Structure:** Open ended, Mutual Fund
Portfolio manager: Richard P. Keigher
Manager of Samba Lux North America Equity commenced in 1988; previously with Mellon Bank, Pittsburgh, Continental Bank, Chicago and KID, Kuwait; Senior Investment Officer with 30 years experience of managing US dollar equities.
Purchase: Direct, Saudi American Bank Branches /Samba Finance S.A. Geneva
Minimum investment: 10,000 USD
Custodian: Citibank (Luxembourg) S.A.
Listed: None **Dealings:** Weekly
Fund Sedol I.D.: 301299 **Published:** FT/IHT/SC
Fees **Annual fee:** 1.75% **Performance fee:** None
Front end load: Up to 5.00% **Redemption fee:** None
Switching fee: 0.25%

Performance:

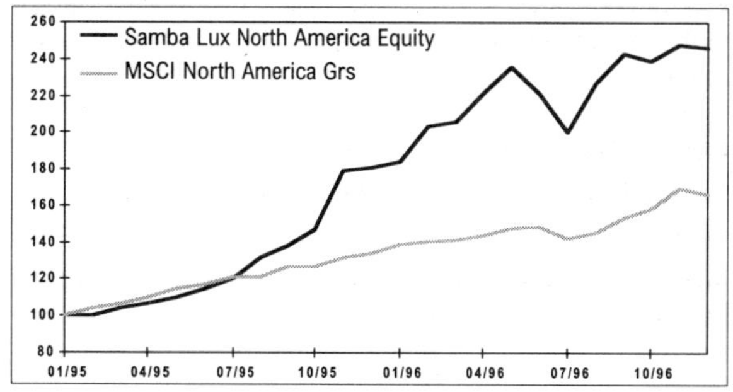

Top holdings:

Holding	%
Dupont Photomasks	2.4%
Duracell	n/s
Estee Lauder	3.5%
General Motors	2.4%
Hewlett - Packard	2.6%
Lucent Technologies	2.9%
Robert Half	2.5%
Sabre Group	2.9%
Whitman - Hart	2.7%
Wind River Systems	2.5%

TOTAL RETURNS %

3 months 1997	1996	1995	1994	3 years	5 years
-5.63	36.56	N.A.	N.A.	N.A.	N.A.

STATISTICS

Assets ($mil)	Current yield	Volatility	Risk return	Micropal Star Rating
9.52	—	N.A.	—	———

SBC Bond Portfolio Italian Lira

333/350

SBC Bond Portfolio Management Company SA
26 route d'Arlon, L-2010 Luxembourg
Tel 352-45-20-30-291 Fax 352-45-20-30-405

Contact: Customer Services Department

Investment objective:
The sub-fund seeks capital appreciation by investing in a diversified basis in bonds of high-quality borrowers in Italian Lira. In order to guarantee the high quality level, the credit rating of all securities held by the fund is checked regularly.

Umbrella fund: SBC Bond Portfolio
Launch date: 08/07/94 **Domicile:** Luxembourg
Currency: ITL **Structure:** Open ended, FCP
Portfolio manager: Schweiz Bankverein (Luxembourg)AG
Manager of Swiss Bank Corporation Bond Portfolio -Italian Lira A/B.

Purchase: Direct
Minimum investment: 1 Unit
Custodian: Schweiz Bankverein (Luxembourg) AG
Listed: Luxembourg **Dealings:** Daily
Fund Sedol I.D.: 301829 **Published:** WS/FT/IHT/GN
Fees **Annual fee:** 0.72% **Performance fee:** None
Front end load: 1.00% **Redemption fee:** None
Switching fee: None

Performance:

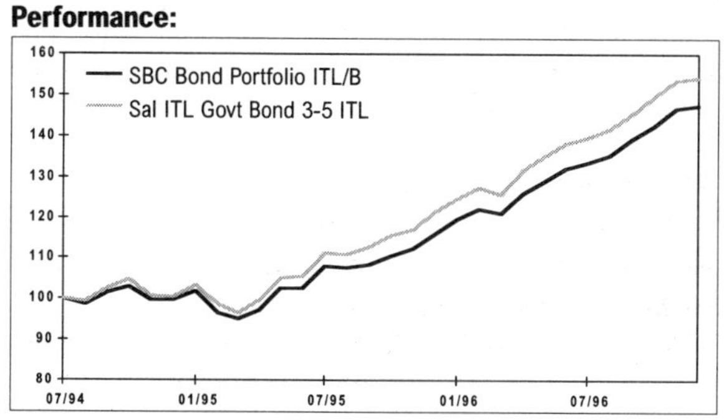

Top holdings:

Structure of bond maturities	
Bonds 1-3 years	16.0%
Bonds 3-5 years	21.7%
Over 5 years	32.2%
Key ratios	
Theoretical yield on maturity (net)	6.3%
Modified duration	3.8 years
Average remaining maturity	5.2 years

TOTAL RETURNS %

3 months 1997	1996	1995	1994	3 years	5 years
-10.09	27.41	16.06	N.A.	N.A.	N.A.

STATISTICS

Assets ($mil)	Current yield	Volatility	Risk return	Micropal Star Rating
168.07	—	N.A.	—	———

SBC Emeg Econ Portf Latin Am Bonds
175/350

SBC Bond Portfolio Management Company SA
26 Route d'Arlon, L-2010 Luxembourg
Tel 352-45-20-30-291 Fax 352-45-20-30-405

Investment objective:
The sub-fund seeks capital appreciation through investing in the US dollar bonds of Latin American issuers. Based on the not inconsiderable debtor risk the yield is higher than the rates of first-class US dollar bonds with significant price fluctuations to be taken into account.

Umbrella fund: SBC Emerging Economies Portfolio
Launch date: 21/02/95 **Domicile:** Luxembourg
Currency: USD **Structure:** Open ended, FCP
Portfolio manager: Schweiz Bankverein (Luxembourg)AG
Manager of Swiss Bank Corporation Emerging Economies Portfolio -Latin American Bonds.

Purchase: Direct
Minimum investment: 1 Unit
Custodian: Schweiz Bankverein (Luxembourg) AG
Listed: Luxembourg **Dealings:** Daily
Fund Sedol I.D.: 301231 **Published:** FT/WS/IHT/GN
Fees **Annual fee:** 1.50% **Performance fee:** None
Front end load: 1.00% **Redemption fee:** None
Switching fee: None

Contact: Customer Services Department
Performance:

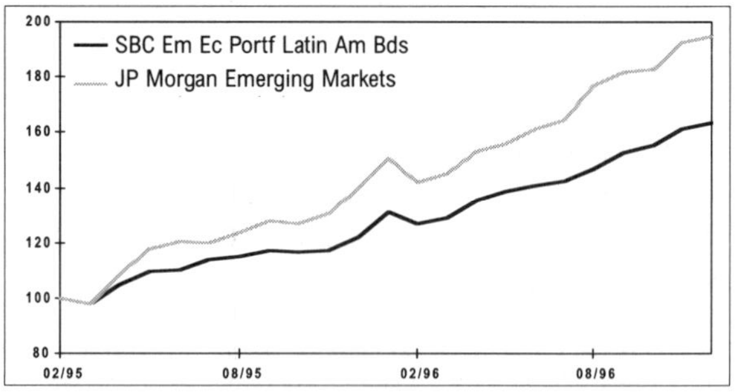

Top holdings:

Structure of bond maturities	
Up to 1 year	8.1%
1-3 years	11.6%
3-5 years	5.4%
Over 5yrs	70.5%
Key ratios	
Theoretical yield on maturity (net)	8.2%
Modified duration	6.4 years
Average remaining maturity	12.4 years

TOTAL RETURNS %

3 months 1997	1996	1995	1994	3 years	5 years
2.93	34.08	N.A.	N.A.	N.A.	N.A.

STATISTICS

Assets ($mil)	Current yield	Volatility	Risk return	Micropal Star Rating
218.96	—	N.A.	—	———

SBC Equity Portfolio Canada
338/350

SBC Equity Portfolio Management Company SA
26 Route d'Arlon, L-2010 Luxembourg
Tel 352-45-20-30-291 Fax 352-45-20-30-405

Investment objective:
The sub-fund seeks capital appreciation by following an investment style based on a strong orientation to the MSCI Canadian Market Index. There is scope for active investment decisions which can be used to over-and under-weight individual stock positions. The top sector allocations of the portfolio are utilities (13.0%) and food/beverages/tobacco (11.5).

Umbrella fund: SBC Equity Portfolio
Launch date: 22/04/93 **Domicile:** Luxembourg
Currency: CAD **Structure:** Open ended, FCP
Portfolio manager: Brinson Partners Ltd, Chicago
Managers of Swiss Bank Corporation Equity Portfolio -Canada.

Purchase: Direct
Minimum investment: 1 Unit
Custodian: Schweiz Bankverein (Luxembourg) AG
Listed: Luxembourg **Dealings:** Daily
Fund Sedol I.D.: 301648 **Published:** FT/WS/IHT/GN
Fees **Annual fee:** 1.20% **Performance fee:** None
Front end load: 1.00% **Redemption fee:** None
Switching fee: None

Contact: Customer Services Department
Performance:

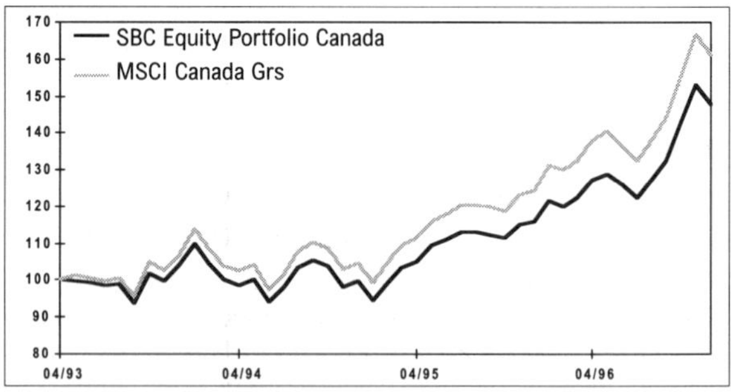

Top holdings:

Alcan Aluminium	3.8%
Bank of Montreal	4.0%
Barrick Gold	3.5%
BCE INC	6.0%
Canadian Pacific	4.4%
Imperial Oil	3.8%
Northern Telecom	6.0%
Royal Bank of Canada	4.8%
Seagram	5.8%
Thomson Corp	5.3%

TOTAL RETURNS %

3 months 1997	1996	1995	1994	3 years	5 years
-0.14	27.30	16.39	-4.15	42.02	N.A.

STATISTICS

Assets ($mil)	Current yield	Volatility	Risk return	Micropal Star Rating
208.94	—	3.67	3	✪✪✪✪

Schroder Brazil Fund
49/350

Schroder Investment Management (Guernsey) Ltd
PO Box 255, St Peters Port, GY1 3QH, Guernsey
Tel 44-1481-710-651 Fax 44-1481-710-285

Investment objective:
The primary aim of the fund is long-term capital appreciation through investment in equity, equity related and debt securities benefiting from the economic growth in Brazil. The top sector allocations of the portfolio are the following: utilities (54.4%); finance (12.1%); basic materials (10.5%); and consumer goods (10.1%).

Umbrella fund: This is a singular fund.

Launch date: 29/09/94 **Domicile:** Guernsey

Currency: USD **Structure:** Open ended, Unit Trust

Portfolio manager: Robert Davy CA
Manager, Director of Schroder Latin Am Fund & Schroder Brazil Fund and Director of Schroder Capital Mgt; graduate- Cambridge U; joined Schroder UK research department in 1986 transferring to the US desk; also specialises in Latin Am.

Purchase: Direct, Financial Advisor

Minimum investment: 10,000 USD

Custodian: Chase Manhattan Bank

Listed: Dublin **Dealings:** Weekly

Fund Sedol I.D.: 79129 **Published:** FT

Fees **Annual fee:** 1.25% **Performance fee:** None
Front end load: None **Redemption fee:** None
Switching fee: None

Contact: Renee McLeuer

Performance:

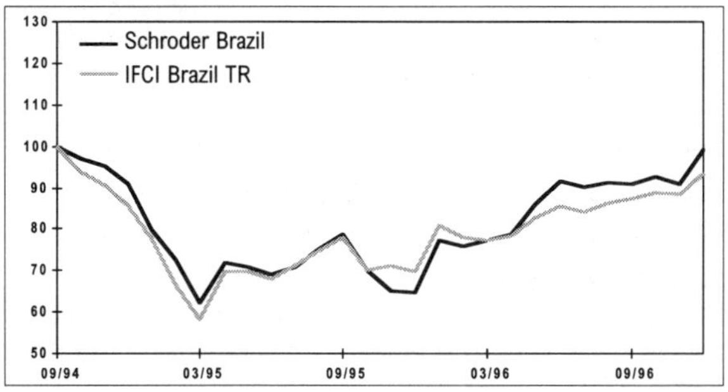

Top holdings:

Banco Itau	3.6%
Cemig	5.0%
Electrobas	10.0%
Forca Luz-Cia Paul	4.6%
Petroleo Brasil	6.0%
Rio Bradesco	6.5%
Telec Brasileiras	6.3%
Telepar	5.6%
Telesp Sao Paulo	9.8%
Vale Rio Doce	6.1%

TOTAL RETURNS %

3 months 1997	1996	1995	1994	3 years	5 years
19.76	52.84	-28.76	N.A.	N.A.	N.A.

STATISTICS

Assets ($mil)	Current yield	Volatility	Risk return	Micropal Star Rating
49.87	—	N.A.	—	———

Schroder Eastern European Fund
23/350

Schroder Investment Management (Guernsey) Ltd
PO Box 255, St Peters Port, GY1 3QH, Guernsey
Tel 44-1481-710-651 Fax 44-1481-710-285

Investment objective:
The fund aims at long-term capital appreciation through investment in equity, equity related and debt securities benefiting from the economic growth of Eastern Europe. The top country allocations of the portfolio are as follows: Poland (45.9%); Hungary (19.7%); Russia (10.6%); Czech Rep (8.6%); Croatia Rep (7.5%); and Slovakia Rep (4.3%).

Umbrella fund: This is a singular fund.

Launch date: 12/14/94 **Domicile:** Guernsey

Currency: USD **Structure:** Open ended, Unit Trust

Portfolio manager: Isabel Goiri
Director, Schroder Investment Mgt.; MBA – Imperial College; responsible for stock selection/ European asset allocations and European emerging markets in both the Mediterranean/ Eastern European areas; joined Schroder in 1990.

Purchase: Direct, Financial Advisor

Minimum investment: 10,000 USD

Custodian: Chase Manhattan Bank

Listed: Dublin **Dealings:** Weekly

Fund Sedol I.D.: 79169 **Published:** FT

Fees **Annual fee:** 1.25% **Performance fee:** None
Front end load: None **Redemption fee:** None
Switching fee: None

Contact: Renee Mcleuer

Performance:

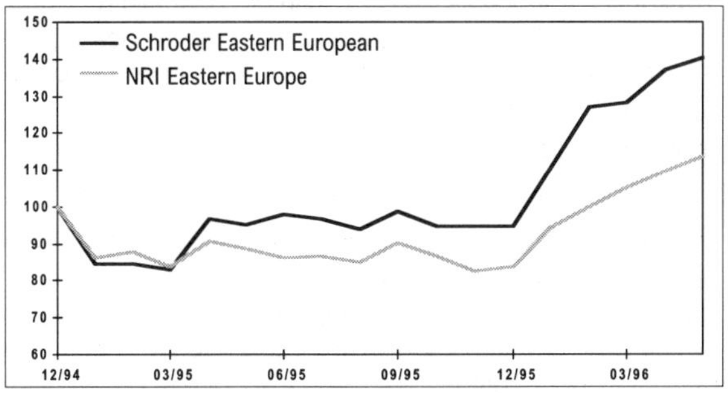

Top holdings:

Bank Razouju Eksport	4.3%
Bank Slaski	4.7%
Debica	3.3%
Elecktrim	5.3%
Gorazdze	3.6%
LukOil	4.4%
Pliva Do	6.8%
Rao Gazpam	3.6%
Richter Gedeon	5.0%
Stomil Olsztyn	3.7%

TOTAL RETURNS %

3 months 1997	1996	1995	1994	3 years	5 years
9.55	72.98	-5.48	N.A.	N.A.	N.A.

STATISTICS

Assets ($mil)	Current yield	Volatility	Risk return	Micropal Star Rating
143.20	—	N.A.	—	———

Schroder Intl Sel Euro Small Cos

165/350

Schroders Investment Management Limited
5 Rue Hohenhoff, L-1736 Luxembourg
Tel 352-341-342-212 Fax 352-341-342-344

Investment objective:
The primary objective of the sub-fund is to provide capital growth through investment in smaller companies listed on the principal European exchanges and in the securities of companies listed on the small European exchange markets such as those of Austria, Portugal and Greece.

Umbrella fund: Schroders International Selection Fund
Launch date: 08/10/94 **Domicile:** Luxembourg [UCITS]
Currency: ECU **Structure:** Open ended, SICAV
Portfolio manager: Ton Tjia
Manager of Schroder International Select European Small Companies and Director; degree in economics- U Amsterdam; previously with Pierson, Heldring and Pierson; joined Schroder 1987.
Purchase: Direct, Financial Advisor
Minimum investment: 6,000 ECU
Custodian: Bank of Bermuda (Luxembourg) S.A.
Listed: Luxembourg **Dealings:** Daily
Fund Sedol I.D.: 475872 **Published:** BZ/DS/CS/LEB/FT/NZZ
Fees **Annual fee:** 1.00% **Performance fee:** None
Front end load: 5.00% **Redemption fee:** None
Switching fee: None

Contact: William Cullen/Ramona Murrell

Performance:

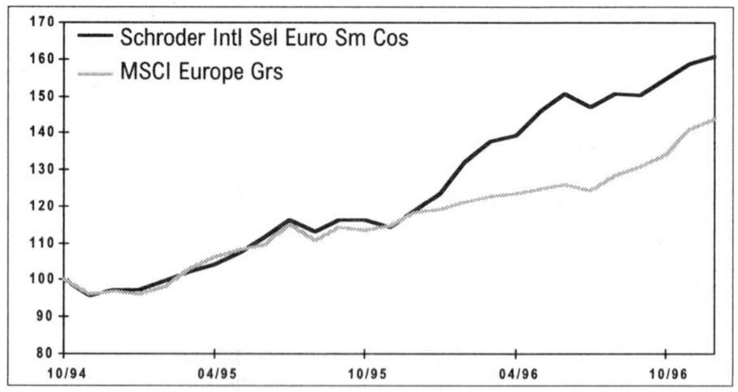

Top holdings:

Adecco	1.9%
ADT	1.8%
Berentzen Gruppe	1.5%
Endemol Entertainment	2.7%
Hagemeyer	1.5%
KBB	1.7%
Ole-Van Der Grinten	1.5%
Primagaz	3.5%
SGL Carbon	1.6%
Volker Stevin	1.9%

TOTAL RETURNS %

3 months 1997	1996	1995	1994	3 years	5 years
5.66	35.31	21.85	N.A.	N.A.	N.A.

STATISTICS

Assets ($mil)	Current yield	Volatility	Risk return	Micropal Star Rating
39.98	—	N.A.	—	———

Schroder Intl Sel Fund UK Equity

265/350

Schroders Investment Management Limited
5 Rue Hohenhoff, L-1736 Luxembourg
Tel 352-341-342-212 Fax 352-341-342-344

Investment objective:
The sub-fund aims to achieve capital growth through investment in UK equities. Investment is in a balanced portfolio of good quality companies. The top sector allocations of the portfolio are the following: services (23.2%); finances (19.4%); general manufacturers (17.4%); consumer goods (14.0%); mineral extraction (11.3%); and utilities (9.1%).
Umbrella fund: Schroders International Selection Fund
Launch date: 12/03/93 **Domicile:** Luxembourg [UCITS]
Currency: GBP **Structure:** Open ended, SICAV
Portfolio manager: David Rowe
Manager of Schroder International Selection Fund UK Equity since 1993 and Director; Honours degree, economics- Exeter U; joined Schroder Investment Management in 1986.
Purchase: Direct, Financial Advisor
Minimum investment: 3,000 GBP
Custodian: Bank of Bermuda (Luxembourg) S.A.
Listed: Luxembourg **Dealings:** Daily
Fund Sedol I.D.: 479138 **Published:** BZ/DS/CS/LEB/FT/NZZ
Fees **Annual fee:** 1.00% **Performance fee:** None
Front end load: 5.00% **Redemption fee:** None
Switching fee: None

Contact: William Cullen/Ramara Murrell

Performance:

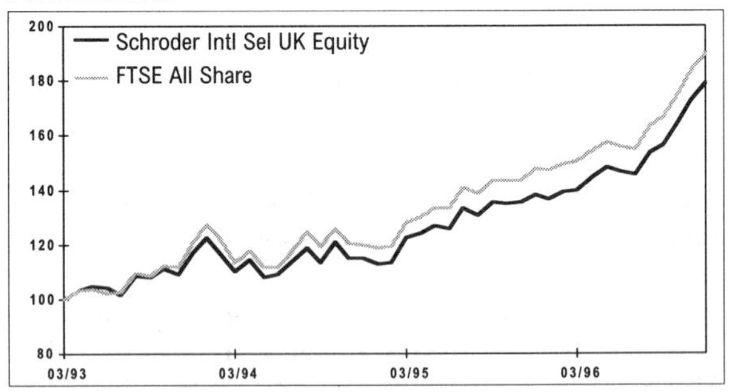

Top holdings:

Barclays PLC	2.6%
BAT Industries	2.1%
British Petroleum	3.9%
British Telecom	2.4%
Cable + Wireless (GBP)	2.2%
Glaxo Wellcome	3.7%
HSBC Holdings	2.8%
Lloyds TSB Group	2.2%
Schroder UK Smaller Companies	4.1%
Shell Transport & Trading	3.8%

TOTAL RETURNS %

3 months 1997	1996	1995	1994	3 years	5 years
1.29	29.79	20.30	-2.14	52.79	N.A.

STATISTICS

Assets ($mil)	Current yield	Volatility	Risk return	Micropal Star Rating
72.32	1.58	3.62	3	✪✪✪✪

Schroder Intl Sel Fund US Equity
334/350

Schroders Investment Management Limited
5 Rue Hohenhoff, L-1736 Luxembourg
Tel 352-341-342-212 Fax 352-341-342-344

Investment objective:
The sub-fund seeks to provide capital growth through investment in securities of companies listed on the principal stock exchanges in the US and securities quoted on the over-the-counter markets of the US. The top sector allocations of the portfolio are the following: finance (14.3%); technology (12.6%); capital goods (12.1%); and consumer staples (10.7%).

Umbrella fund: Schroders International Selection Fund

Launch date: 02/08/93 **Domicile:** Luxembourg [UCITS]

Currency: USD **Structure:** Open ended, SICAV

Portfolio manager: Michael Grant
Manager of Schroder International Selection Fund US Equity since March 1995, Director; business graduate- U Alberta; previously Metropolitan Money Mgt; joined Schroder Asia, HK; 8 years of finance industry experience.

Purchase: Direct, Financial Advisor

Minimum investment: 5,000 USD

Custodian: Bank of Bermuda (Luxembourg) S.A

Listed: Luxembourg **Dealings:** Daily

Fund Sedol I.D.: 78103 **Published:** BZ/DS/CS/LEB/FT/NZZ

Fees **Annual fee:** 1.00% **Performance fee:** None
Front end load: 5.00% **Redemption fee:** None
Switching fee: None

Contact: William Cullen/Ramara Murrell

Performance:

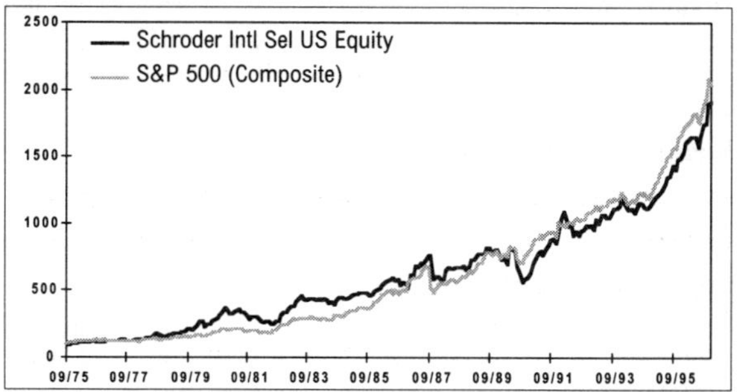

Top holdings:

Allied Signal	3.9%
American International	3.1%
Bank America Corp.	3.4%
Columbia/HCA Healthcare	3.3%
Conagra Incorporated	3.9%
Exxon Corp	3.4%
FPL Group	3.3%
IBM	3.5%
Intel Corp.	3.2%
Rockwell International	3.3%

TOTAL RETURNS %

3 months 1997	1996	1995	1994	3 years	5 years
3.16	27.39	32.31	-0.11	68.37	110.07

STATISTICS

Assets ($mil)	Current yield	Volatility	Risk return	Micropal Star Rating
83.24	0.15	3.00	3	✪✪✪✪

Schroder Taiwan Fund
303/350

Schroder Investment Management (Guernsey) Ltd
PO Box 255, St Peters Port, GY1 3QH, Guernsey
Tel 44-1481-710-651 Fax 44-1481-710-285

Investment objective:
The fund seeks long-term capital appreciation though investment in equity, equity related and debt securities benefiting from the economic growth in Taiwan. The top sector allocations of the portfolio are the following: finance (30.1%); electric/electronic (29.1%); plastics/chemicals (17.1%); and construction (9.4%).

Umbrella fund: This is a singular fund.

Launch date: 07/06/96 **Domicile:** Guernsey

Currency: USD **Structure:** Open ended, Unit Trust

Portfolio manager: Ho Hsiu Mei
Manager of Taiwan Fund; joined Schroder(HK) in 1990 to promote unit trusts business in Taiwan; graduate, economics- National Taiwan U and MBA- U of California; formerly at the China Development Corp, Taiwan; 7 years financial experience.

Purchase: Direct, Financial Advisor

Minimum investment: 10,000 USD

Custodian: Schroder Investment Management

Listed: Dublin **Dealings:** Weekly

Fund Sedol I.D.: 79070 **Published:** FT

Fees **Annual fee:** 1.50% **Performance fee:** None
Front end load: None **Redemption fee:** None
Switching fee: None

Contact: Renee McLeuer

Performance:

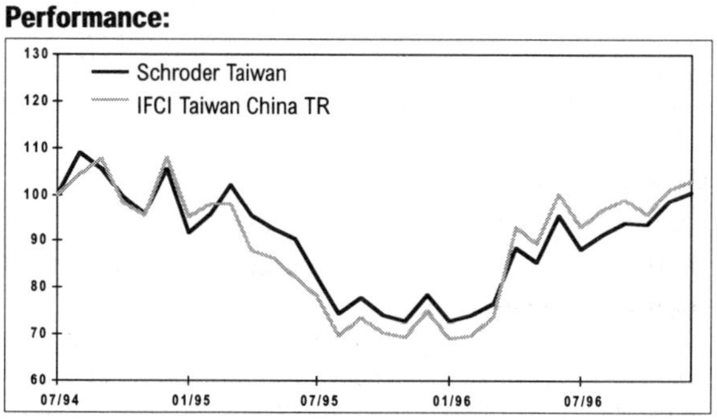

Top holdings:

Arer Peripherals	2.9%
Cathay Construction	3.9%
Cathay Life Ins	7.4%
China Development	3.9%
Clevo Company	3.6%
Formosa Chemicals	2.9%
Formosa Plastic	4.4%
ICBC Bank	2.8%
Nan Ya Plastics	2.8%
Shinkong Life Insurance	2.8%

TOTAL RETURNS %

3 months 1997	1996	1995	1994	3 years	5 years
17.80	28.27	-25.57	N.A.	N.A.	N.A.

STATISTICS

Assets ($mil)	Current yield	Volatility	Risk return	Micropal Star Rating
207.86	—	N.A.	—	———

Schroders Asia China/HK Enterprise
21/350

Schroder Investment Mgmt (HK)
19 th Floor, Two Exchange Square, Central, Hong Kong
Tel 852-2521-1633 Fax 852-2524-7094

Investment objective:
The fund invests in quoted securities connected with the economies of the China and Hong Kong. The selection of stocks in Hong Kong is not limited exclusively to companies with close connections to China. Up to 75% of the fund's assets may be invested in securities listed in China. The top country allocations are Hong Kong (57.0%) and Malaysia (17.0%).

Umbrella fund: This is a singular fund.

Launch date: 01/02/94 **Domicile:** Cayman Islands

Currency: HKD **Structure:** Open ended, Unit Trust

Portfolio manager: Tina Ho
Manager of Schroder Asian Fund commenced 1995; graduate of U of British Columbia; joined Schroder as an Assistant Director; 9 years experience as investment analyst and manager.

Purchase: Direct, Financial Advisor, Banks

Minimum investment: 5,000 HKD

Custodian: Bank of Bermuda (Cayman) Ltd

Listed: None **Dealings:** Daily

Fund Sedol I.D.: 677961 **Published:** FT/IHT/SC

Fees **Annual fee:** 1.50% **Performance fee:** None
Front end load: 5.00% **Redemption fee:** None
Switching fee: 1.00%

Contact: Unit Trust Marketing

Performance:

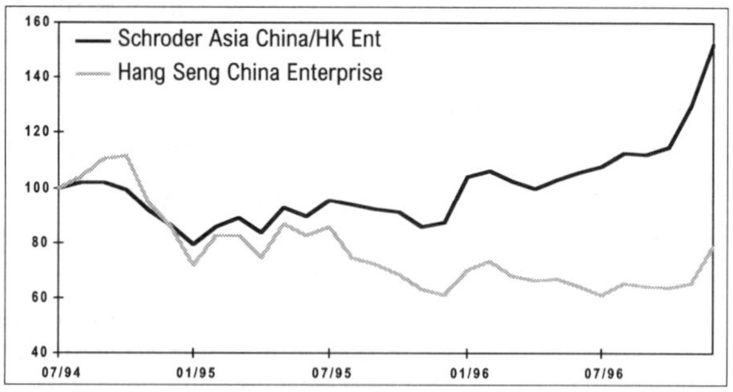

Top holdings:

Holding	%
Cheung Kong	3.4%
Citic Pacific	3.0%
Dongfang Electric	3.0%
Guangdong Investment	2.8%
Guangshen Railway	3.2%

TOTAL RETURNS %

3 months 1997	1996	1995	1994	3 years	5 years
5.11	73.94	1.27	N.A.	N.A.	N.A.

STATISTICS

Assets ($mil)	Current yield	Volatility	Risk return	Micropal Star Rating
36.02	—	N.A.	—	———

Schroders Asia Energy
74/350

Schroder Investment Mgmt (HK)
19 th Floor, Two Exchange Square, Central, Hong Kong
Tel 852-2521-1633 Fax 852-2524-7094

Investment objective:
The fund invests in quoted securities worldwide of companies connected with the production and provision of energy. Typically the fund holds investments in utility companies, coal mining, oil and gas businesses active in all the major economies of the world including Asia. The Manager seeks to sustain capital growth though an active investment policy.

Umbrella fund: This is a singular fund.

Launch date: 01/09/87 **Domicile:** Cayman Islands

Currency: USD **Structure:** Open ended, Unit Trust

Portfolio manager: Elizabeth Scott
Manager of Schroder Asia Energy and assistant Director; graduate of Edinburgh U; previous experience at a Scottish life assurance company as research analyst and a North American investment management company; joined Schroder 1992.

Purchase: Direct, Financial Advisor, Banks

Minimum investment: 1,000 USD

Custodian: Bank of Bermuda (Cayman) Ltd

Listed: None **Dealings:** Daily

Fund Sedol I.D.: 78745 **Published:** FT/IHT/SC

Fees **Annual fee:** 1.00% **Performance fee:** None
Front end load: 5.00% **Redemption fee:** None
Switching fee: 1.00%

Contact: Unit Trust Marketing

Performance:

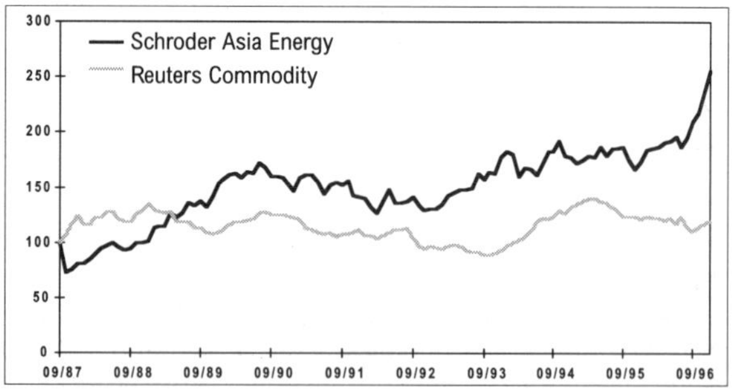

Top holdings:

Holding	%
Calor	8.3%
Clyde Petroleum	13.0%
Discovery Petroleum	5.5%
Entreprise Oil	7.9%
Railtrack	5.4%

TOTAL RETURNS %

3 months 1997	1996	1995	1994	3 years	5 years
-1.87	47.14	-2.33	0.47	44.38	80.73

STATISTICS

Assets ($mil)	Current yield	Volatility	Risk return	Micropal Star Rating
7.59	—	4.53	3	✪✪✪✪

Schroders Asia Hong Kong
48/350

Schroder Investment Mgmt (HK)
19 th Floor, Two Exchange Square, Central, Hong Kong
Tel 852-2521-1633 Fax 852-2524-7094

Investment objective:
The fund invests mainly in quoted securities connected with the economy of Hong Kong. The Manager believes that the superior economic growth rate of Hong Kong will be sustained and that there are sound opportunities for long-term capital growth through investment.

Umbrella fund: This is a singular fund.
Launch date: 01/01/88 **Domicile:** Cayman Islands
Currency: HKD **Structure:** Open ended, Unit Trust
Portfolio manager: Kingson Lee CFA
Manager of Schroder Asia Hong Kong commenced January 1995 and Assistant Director; graduate and post-graduate diploma- London School of Economics; joined Schroders in 1993 and 13 years experience in the financial industry.
Purchase: Direct, Financial Advisor, Banks
Minimum investment: 5,000 HKD
Custodian: Bank of Bermuda (Cayman)Ltd
Listed: None **Dealings:** Daily
Fund Sedol I.D.: 677958 **Published:** FT/IHT/SC
Fees **Annual fee:** 1.25% **Performance fee:** None
Front end load: 5.00% **Redemption fee:** None
Switching fee: 1.00%

Contact: Unit Trust Marketing
Performance:

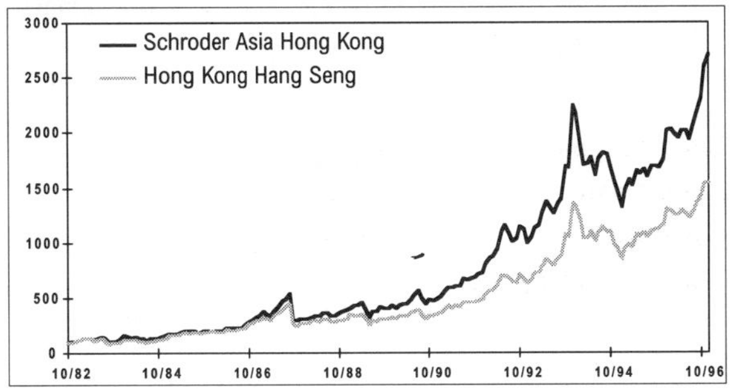

Top holdings:

Cheung Kong Infra	6.9%
Henderson Land Development	6.2%
HSBC Holdings	5.5%
Hutchison Whampoa	7.1%
Sun Hung Kai Properties	7.2%

TOTAL RETURNS %

3 months 1997	1996	1995	1994	3 years	5 years
-3.15	53.10	20.54	-34.91	20.12	269.88

STATISTICS

Assets ($mil)	Current yield	Volatility	Risk return	Micropal Star Rating
54.75	—	6.57	1	✪✪✪

Schroders Asia Hong Kong Small Cos
62/350

Schroder Investment Mgmt (HK)
19 th Floor, Two Exchange Square, Central, Hong Kong
Tel 852-2521-1633 Fax 852-2524-7094

Investment objective:
The fund invests in quoted securities of smaller Hong Kong companies. Investments are concentrated in companies in the bottom half of the stock exchange index in terms of cumulative market capitalisations. Such companies are likely to have a market capitalisation of less than 4 billion Hong Kong dollars. Companies are selected for their growth potential.
Umbrella fund: This is a singular fund.
Launch date: 01/09/92 **Domicile:** Cayman Islands
Currency: HKD **Structure:** Open ended, Unit Trust
Portfolio manager: Matthew Lam
Manager of Schroder Asia Hong Kong Small Companies commenced January 1995; BA, economics- U of Manitoba; joined Schroder in 1994 and has 7 years of investment management experience.
Purchase: Direct, Financial Advisor
Minimum investment: 5,000 HKD
Custodian: Bank of Bermuda (Cayman) Ltd
Listed: None **Dealings:** Daily
Fund Sedol I.D.: 677903 **Published:** FT/IHT/SC
Fees **Annual fee:** 1.50% **Performance fee:** None
Front end load: 5.00% **Redemption fee:** None
Switching fee: 1.00%

Contact: Unit Trust Marketing
Performance:

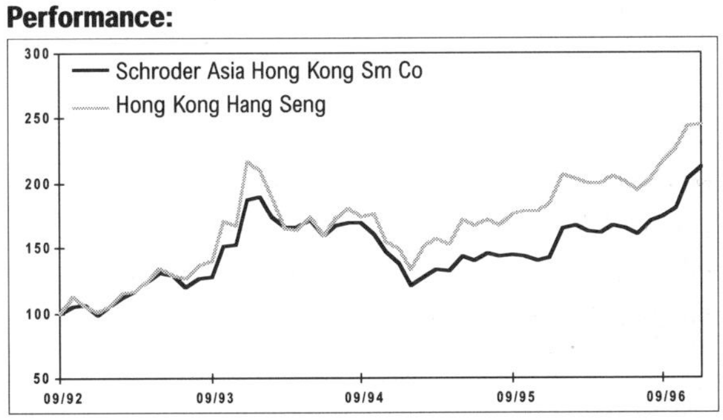

Top holdings:

China Travel Intl	4.0%
Guangzhon Investment	4.0%
Harbour Centre	6.9%
Tian Teck Land	5.0%
Wing Hang Bank	4.9%

TOTAL RETURNS %

3 months 1997	1996	1995	1994	3 years	5 years
-3.28	49.23	3.19	-26.53	13.14	N.A.

STATISTICS

Assets ($mil)	Current yield	Volatility	Risk return	Micropal Star Rating
7.12	—	5.61	—	✪✪

Scontinvest Equity Fd North American Equity
94/350

Scontinvest
18 Boulevard Royal, L-2449 Luxembourg
Tel 352-22-80-07-1 Fax 352-46-03-09

Investment objective:
The sub-fund aims to achieve capital growth by investing in US equities. The top sector allocations of the portfolio are the following: finance (31.0%); technology (19.9%); energy (16.5%); and consumer goods (10.4%). Currency exposure of this portfolio is 100% US dollars.

Umbrella fund: Scontinvest Equity Fund
Launch date: 28/02/92 **Domicile:** Luxembourg [UCITS]
Currency: USD **Structure:** Open ended, Mutual Fund
Portfolio manager: Scontinvest Equity Fund Management Company SA
Manager of Scontinvest Equity North America Equity.

Contact: Mr J. Benzeno

Performance:

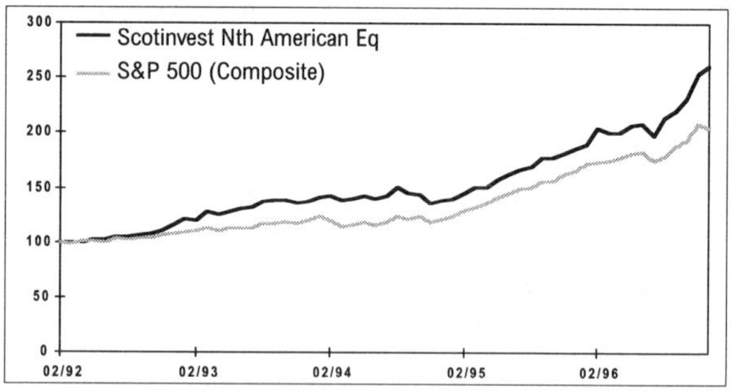

Purchase: Direct, Financial Advisor
Minimum investment: 5,000 USD
Custodian: Discount Bank S.A Luxembourg
Listed: Luxembourg **Dealings:** Weekly
Fund Sedol I.D.: 301650 **Published:** IHT/FT/FW
Fees **Annual fee:** 1.20% **Performance fee:** None
Front end load: Up to 5.00% **Redemption fee:** Up to 1.00%
Switching fee: 1.00%

Top holdings:

Bear Stearns	3.8%
IBM	5.6%
Mitchell Energy & Development Corp	3.0%
Nuevo Energy	3.7%
Philip Morris Cos. Inc.	7.4%
Providian Corp	3.5%
Reliastar	3.5%
Seagull Energy	3.4%
Travelers Group	5.2%
US Life	4.4%

TOTAL RETURNS %

3 months 1997	1996	1995	1994	3 years	5 years
3.06	41.05	33.97	1.19	91.22	N.A.

STATISTICS

Assets ($mil)	Current yield	Volatility	Risk return	Micropal Star Rating
65.16	—	3.36	5	✪✪✪✪✪

Scot Prov GP UK Equity
232/350

Scottish Provident International Life Assurance
Provident House, Ballacottier Business Park, Douglas IM2 2SP, Isle of Man
Tel 44-1624-681-681 Fax 44-1624-677-336

Investment objective:
The fund aims for long-term capital growth through investment directly or otherwise in a portfolio of UK companies. The balance between large blue chip medium-sized and smaller companies in the portfolio reflect the investment climate. The top sector allocations of the portfolio are the following: services (26.0%); industrial cyclical (25.0%); and finance (17.0%).
Umbrella fund: This is a singular fund.
Launch date: 01/09/91 **Domicile:** Isle of Man
Currency: GBP **Structure:** Open ended, Life Assurance Fund
Portfolio manager: Scottish Provident International
Manager of Scot Prov GP UK Equity.

Contact: Sam Bowman

Performance:

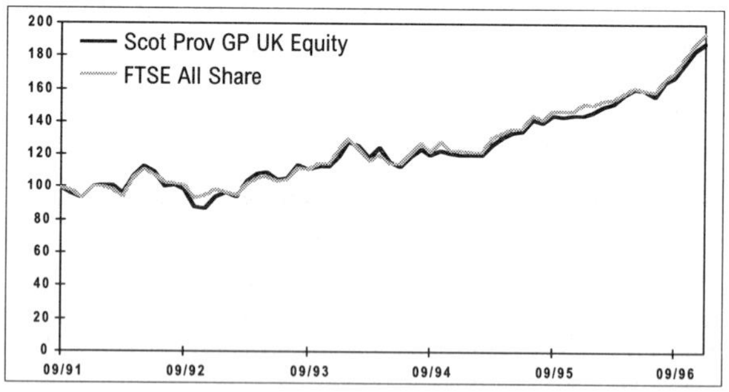

Purchase: Financial Advisor
Minimum investment: ILP
Custodian: Citibank
Listed: None **Dealings:** Daily
Fund Sedol I.D.: 40208 **Published:** FT
Fees **Annual fee:** 2.00% **Performance fee:** ILP
Front end load: ILP **Redemption fee:** ILP
Switching fee: ILP

Top holdings:

Abbey National	2.3%
Bodycote Intl	2.0%
EMI	2.4%
Grand Metro	2.1%
Laporte	1.8%
Nestor BNA	1.9%
Safeway	1.8%
Siebe	2.0%
Smiths Inds	1.9%
Zeneca	2.8%

TOTAL RETURNS %

3 months 1997	1996	1995	1994	3 years	5 years
-2.03	30.99	19.93	0.97	58.62	87.07

STATISTICS

Assets ($mil)	Current yield	Volatility	Risk return	Micropal Star Rating
45.67	—	3.13	4	✪✪✪✪✪

Scot Prov ILA China Opportunities

80/350

Scottish Provident International Life Assurance
Provident House, Ballacottier Business Park, Douglas IM2 2SP, Isle of Man
Tel 44-1624-681-681 Fax 44-1624-677-336

Contact: Sam Bowman

Investment objective:
The fund aims for capital growth by investing in companies which are domiciled in China or either invest or trade with China. The country allocations of the portfolio are the following: (Hong Kong (51.0%); China (36.0%); Singapore (5.0%); US (3.0%); and the remainder held in cash (5.0%).

Umbrella fund: This is a singular fund.
Launch date: 01/10/95 **Domicile:** Isle of Man
Currency: USD **Structure:** Open ended, Life Assurance Fund
Portfolio manager: Scottish Provident International
Manager of Scot Prov ILA China Opportunities.

Performance:

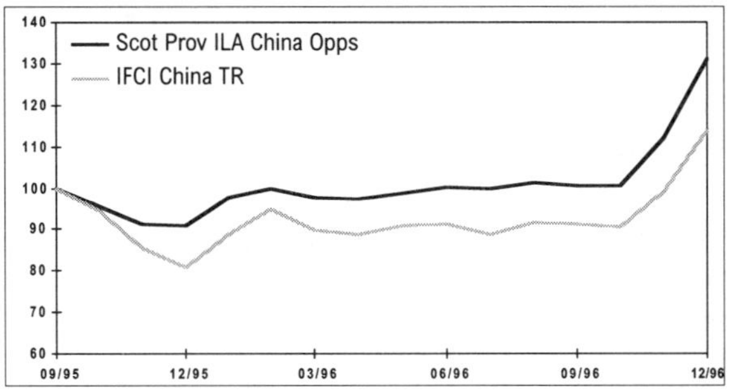

Purchase: Financial Advisor
Minimum investment: ILP
Custodian: Citibank
Listed: None **Dealings:** Daily
Fund Sedol I.D.: 78236 **Published:** FT
Fees **Annual fee:** 2.50% **Performance fee:** ILP
Front end load: ILP **Redemption fee:** ILP
Switching fee: ILP

Top holdings:

Cheung Kong	3.1%
China Resources	3.7%
Clipsal Inds.	3.1%
Cosco Pacific	4.8%
Dazhong Taxi	3.1%
Guangdong Kelon H Shares	3.2%
Lung Kee (Bermuda)	3.1%
Quingling Motors H Shares	3.2%
Shanghai Post & Tel	3.5%
Zhenhai Refining Chemical	3.1%

TOTAL RETURNS %

3 months 1997	1996	1995	1994	3 years	5 years
11.34	44.11	N.A.	N.A.	N.A.	N.A.

STATISTICS

Assets ($mil)	Current yield	Volatility	Risk return	Micropal Star Rating
1.00	—	N.A.	—	———

Scot Prov ILA Special Situations

85/350

Scottish Provident International Life Assurance
Provident House, Ballacottier Business Park, Douglas IM2 2SP, Isle of Man
Tel 44-1624-681-681 Fax 44-1624-677-336

Contact: Sam Bowman

Investment objective:
The fund aims to maximise capital growth from a portfolio of UK securities which the advisors believe offer excellent scope for capital appreciation. Currently, the portfolio has the following sector allocations: industrial cyclical (42.0%); service (37.0%); finance (9.0%); consumer goods (5.0%) mineral extract (3.0%); and utilities (2.0%).
Umbrella fund: This is a singular fund.
Launch date: 01/01/96 **Domicile:** Isle of Man
Currency: GBP **Structure:** Open ended, Life Assurance Fund
Portfolio manager: Scottish Provident International
Manager of Scot Prov Special Situations

Performance:

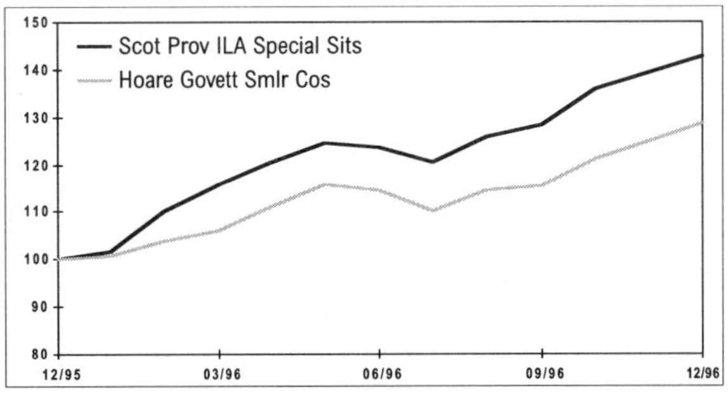

Purchase: Financial Advisor
Minimum investment: ILP
Custodian: Citibank
Listed: None **Dealings:** Daily
Fund Sedol I.D.: 78445 **Published:** FT
Fees **Annual fee:** 2.25% **Performance fee:** ILP
Front end load: ILP **Redemption fee:** ILP
Switching fee: ILP

Top holdings:

Baynes Charles	2.4%
Bodycote Intl	2.0%
Brammer	1.8%
BTG	1.8%
Cairn Energy	2.3%
Chelsfield	2.4%
CRH	1.9%
Finelist	2.3%
Nestor BNA	2.1%
Sema	2.2%

TOTAL RETURNS %

3 months 1997	1996	1995	1994	3 years	5 years
0.62	42.63	N.A.	N.A.	N.A.	N.A.

STATISTICS

Assets ($mil)	Current yield	Volatility	Risk return	Micropal Star Rating
2.88	—	N.A.	—	———

Scot Prov ILA UK Blue Chip

238/350

Scottish Provident International Life Assurance
Provident House, Ballacottier Business Park, Douglas IM2 2SP, Isle of Man
Tel 44-1624-681-681 Fax 44-1624-677-336

Contact: Sam Bowman

Investment objective:
The fund seeks above average investment return of capital growth and income, by investing in well known UK companies primarily constituents of the FTSE 100 Index and other companies considered to be blue chip. Sector allocations of the portfolio are (24.0%); industrial cyclical (23.0%); finance (21.0%); and consumer goods (13.0%).

Umbrella fund: This is a singular fund.

Launch date: 01/10/95 **Domicile:** Isle of Man

Currency: GBP **Structure:** Open ended, Life Assurance Fund

Portfolio manager: Scottish Provident International
Manager of Scot Prov ILA UK Blue Chip.

Performance:

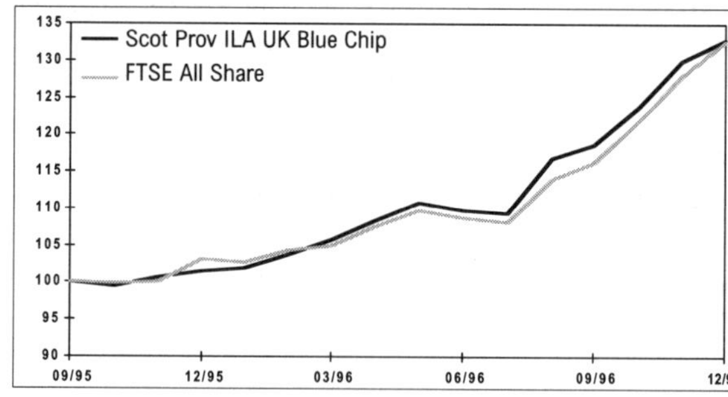

Purchase: Financial Advisor

Minimum investment: ILP

Custodian: Citibank

Listed: None **Dealings:** Daily

Fund Sedol I.D.: 78250 **Published:** FT

Fees **Annual fee:** 2.00% **Performance fee:** ILP
Front end load: ILP **Redemption fee:** ILP
Switching fee: ILP

Top holdings:

British Petroleum	3.6%
British Telecom	2.2%
Cable + Wireless (GBP)	2.0%
Glaxo Wellcome	3.2%
HSBC Holdings	3.0%
Lloyds TSB Group	3.8%
Shell Transport & Trading	3.1%
Siebe	2.5%
Smithkline Beecham	2.8%
Zeneca Group	2.5%

TOTAL RETURNS %

3 months 1997	1996	1995	1994	3 years	5 years
1.34	30.77	N.A.	N.A.	N.A.	N.A.

STATISTICS

Assets ($mil)	Current yield	Volatility	Risk return	Micropal Star Rating
15.06	—	N.A.	—	———

Scudder GOF Brazil Equity A-2

311/350

Scudder Stevens & Clark Inc.
8 Floor New London House, 6 London Street, London EC3R 7BE, UK
Tel 44-171-265-0077 Fax 44-171-265-0099
http://www. ny.scudder.com
E mail jenny_brundit@scudder.com

Contact: David McConnell/Jenny Brundit

Investment objective:
The sub-fund seeks to achieve long-term growth of capital through investment primarily in equity securities of Brazilian issuers. The top sector allocations of the portfolio are as follows: utilities (26.4%); manufacturing (16.8%); communications (16.6%); finance (13.4%); metals/minerals (10.9%); consumer staples (7.4%); and energy (6.4%).

Umbrella fund: Scudder Global Opportunities Funds

Launch date: 09/01/95 **Domicile:** Luxembourg [UCITS]

Currency: USD **Structure:** Open ended, SICAV

Portfolio manager: Paul H. Rogers
Manager of the fund joining Scudder's Global Equity Grp in 1995; BA, political science- U Vermont and MBA, finance- New York U; formerly with Scudder's Emerging Markets, Latin American bonds and Chemical Bank, Latin American Group.

Performance:

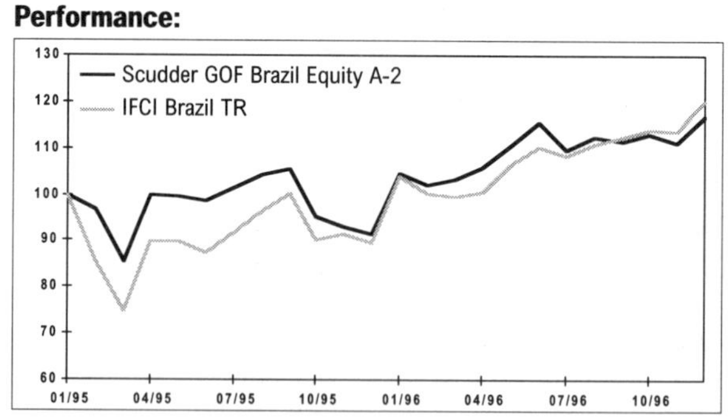

Purchase: Financial Advisor

Minimum investment: 5,000 USD

Custodian: State Street Bank Luxembourg

Listed: Luxembourg **Dealings:** Daily

Fund Sedol I.D.: 478185 **Published:** FT/IHT/SC

Fees **Annual fee:** 1.40% **Performance fee:** None
Front end load: Up to 5.50% **Redemption fee:** None
Switching fee: None

Top holdings:

Cemig-PN	4.7%
Central Electric	5.9%
Electrobras PN	5.3%
Forca Luz-Cia Paul	6.5%
Itaubanco-PN	4.8%
Petrobras-PN	6.4%
Telebras PN	4.9%
Telepar	6.5%
Telesp PN	4.9%
Usiminas Uni	5.3%

TOTAL RETURNS %

3 months 1997	1996	1995	1994	3 years	5 years
16.39	28.06	N.A.	N.A.	N.A.	N.A.

STATISTICS

Assets ($mil)	Current yield	Volatility	Risk return	Micropal Star Rating
0.41	—	N.A.	—	———

Scudder GOF Emerg Markets Income A-2

176/350

Scudder Stevens & Clark Inc.
8 Floor New London House, 6 London Street, London EC3R 7BE, UK
Tel 44-171-265-0077 Fax 44-171-265-0099
http://www. ny.scudder.com
E mail jenny_brundit@scudder.com

Contact: David McConnell/Jenny Brundit

Investment objective:
The sub-fund seeks to achieve high capital appreciation primarily through investment in a diversified portfolio of Latin American, Asian and other emerging market equities. The top country allocations of the portfolio are the following: Poland (17.3%); Brazil (12.2%); Philippines (10.1%); Peru (9.3%); Egypt (8.6%); and Indonesia (4.9%).

Umbrella fund: Scudder Global Opportunities Funds

Launch date: 14/04/93 **Domicile:** Luxembourg [UCITS]

Currency: USD **Structure:** Open ended, SICAV

Portfolio manager: Isabel Saltzman and Susan Grey (refer to Sovereign High Yield A) Product Leader, Senior Portfolio Manager of the Emerging Markets/High Yield Bond Group;BA -Tufts U, MIA, School of International Affairs- Columbia U; previously with JP Morgan; 17 years experience in the finance industry

Purchase: Financial Advisor

Minimum investment: 5,000 USD

Custodian: State Street Bank Luxembourg

Listed: Luxembourg **Dealings:** Daily

Fund Sedol I.D.: 478604 **Published:** FT/IHT/SC

Fees **Annual fee:** 1.00% **Performance fee:** None
Front end load: Up to 5.50% **Redemption fee:** None
Switching fee: None

Performance:

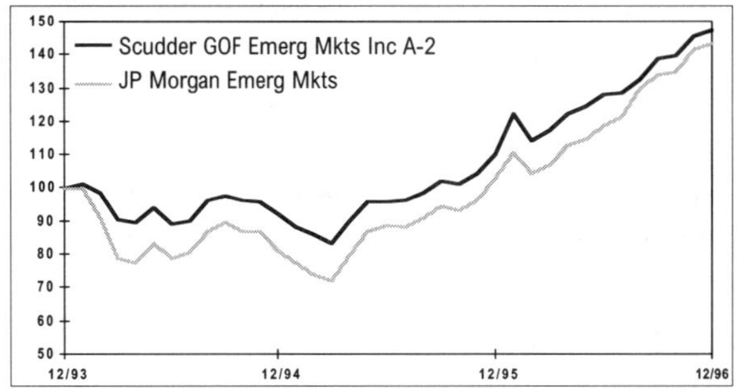

Top holdings:

Holding	%
Argentina FRN	10.3%
Argentina PAR	11.2%
Brazil Discount Bond	4.1%
Brazil FLIRB Bearer	4.7%
Morocco Tranch A	5.6%
Panama IRB	6.5%
Rep of Brazil Exit Bond	4.0%
United Mexican States	4.7%
Venezuelan Debt Conversion FRN	8.8%
Vnesheconombank USSR	3.7%

TOTAL RETURNS %

3 months 1997	1996	1995	1994	3 years	5 years
3.65	34.02	19.43	-7.84	47.51	N.A.

STATISTICS

Assets ($mil)	Current yield	Volatility	Risk return	Micropal Star Rating
15.30	—	4.14	2	✪✪✪

Seahawk International Inc

177/350

Seahawk International Inc
British American Centre Phase 3, Dr Roy's Drive, George Town, Grand Cayman
Tel 1-345-949-7942 Fax 1-345-949-8340

Contact: Craig F. Magher

Investment objective:
The primary objective the fund is to achieve substantial long-term capital appreciation by buying and selling common equities listed on US securities exchanges. It utilises trading techniques which include purchasing securities on margin, selling securities short, purchasing put and call options of securities, finance market indices.

Umbrella fund: This is a singular fund.

Launch date: 01/02/92 **Domicile:** Cayman Islands

Currency: USD **Structure:** Open ended, Investment Company

Portfolio manager: T Garic Moran
Manager of Seahawk International Inc commenced July 1991 and co-founder of Hawkeye Partners LP; graduate, economics- Washington & Lee U; previously with Smith Barney (VP), Harris Upham & Co; over 11 years in the financial industry.

Purchase: Direct

Minimum investment: 500,000 USD

Custodian: MeesPierson (Cayman) Ltd

Listed: Dublin **Dealings:** Monthly

Fund Sedol I.D.: 279058 **Published:** FT/IHT/SC

Fees **Annual fee:** 1.50% **Performance fee:** 20.00%
Front end load: None **Redemption fee:** None
Switching fee: None

Performance:

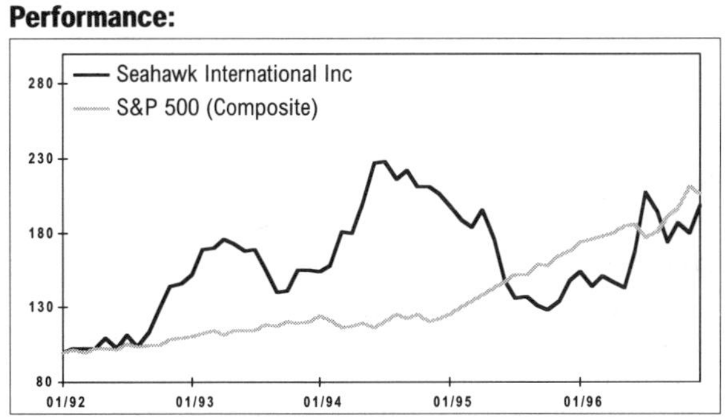

Top holdings:

Holding	
Cascade Communications Corp	n/s
Chase Manhattan Corp	n/s
First USA Inc.	n/s
Louisana Land & Exploration	n/s
MBNA Corp	n/s
Microsoft Corp	n/s
Oracle Systems Corp	n/s
Peoplesoft Inc.	n/s
Petsmart Inc.	n/s
Worldcom Inc.	n/s

TOTAL RETURNS %

3 months 1997	1996	1995	1994	3 years	5 years
2.99	33.98	-28.26	33.03	27.85	N.A.

STATISTICS

Assets ($mil)	Current yield	Volatility	Risk return	Micropal Star Rating
32.35	—	8.33	1	✪✪

Share Euro Selection
161/350

Bearbull
39 Allee Scheffer, L-2520 Luxembourg
Tel 41-22-799-9555 Fax 41-22-788-2920
E mail b.claeyssens@bearbull.ch

Investment objective:
The primary objective of the sub-fund is growth through investment in European equities only. The top country allocations of the portfolio are the following: UK (35.6%); France (21.3%); Switzerland (12.3%); Sweden (12.3%); and Netherlands (7.6%). The main sector allocations of the portfolio are: service (20.5%); health (15.7%); and consumer goods (15.6%).

Umbrella fund: Share
Launch date: 01/11/93 **Domicile:** Luxembourg [UCITS]
Currency: DEM **Structure:** Open ended, SICAV
Portfolio manager: Kempf Yves
Manager of Share Euroselection commenced November 1993; senior partner of Bearbull since 1970.

Contact: Muller/Schoen/Belvallette
Performance:

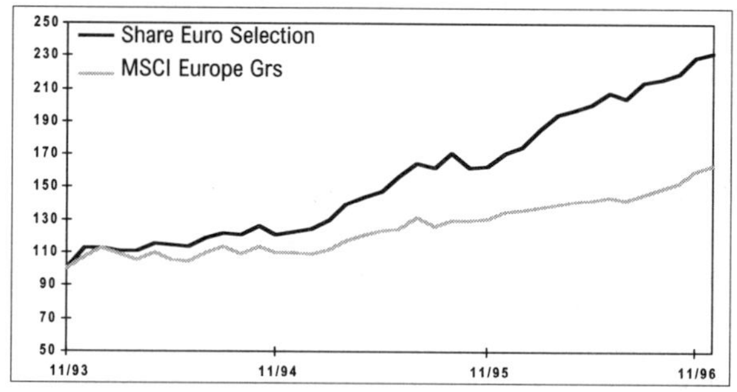

Purchase: Direct
Minimum investment: 1 Unit
Custodian: Banque Indosuez
Listed: None **Dealings:** Weekly
Fund Sedol I.D.: 301686 **Published:** BG
Fees **Annual fee:** 1.50% **Performance fee:** None
Front end load: 2.75% **Redemption fee:** 0.75%
Switching fee: 1.50%

Top holdings:

Holding	%
Carrefour	4.6%
Compass	5.5%
Electrocomponents	4.9%
L'Oreal	4.8%
Novartis	7.1%
Rentokil Initial	6.7%
Reuters Holdings	7.0%
Securitas B Free	4.4%
Sodexho SA	6.6%
Wolters Kluwer	5.0%

TOTAL RETURNS %

3 months 1997	1996	1995	1994	3 years	5 years
-3.04	35.46	39.38	8.59	105.02	N.A.

STATISTICS

Assets ($mil)	Current yield	Volatility	Risk return	Micropal Star Rating
120.26	—	2.96	5	✪✪✪✪✪

Share Latin America
320/350

Bearbull
39 Allee Scheffer, L-2520 Luxembourg
Tel 41-22-799-95-55 Fax 41-22-788-29-20
E mail b.claeyssens@bearbull.ch

Investment objective:
The sub-fund seeks growth through investment in Latin American equities only. The top country allocations of the portfolio are the following: Brazil (38.0%); Mexico (30.1%); Argentina (12.7%); and Chile (11.9%). The top sector allocations of the portfolio are as follows: services (24.5%); finance (18.1%); industrial cyclical (13.4%); and utilities (10.8%).

Umbrella fund: Share
Launch date: 01/05/90 **Domicile:** Luxembourg [UCITS]
Currency: USD **Structure:** Open ended, SICAV
Portfolio manager: Kempf Yves
Manager of Share Latin America commenced May 1990; senior partner of Bearbull since 1970.

Contact: Muller/ Schoen/Belvallette
Performance:

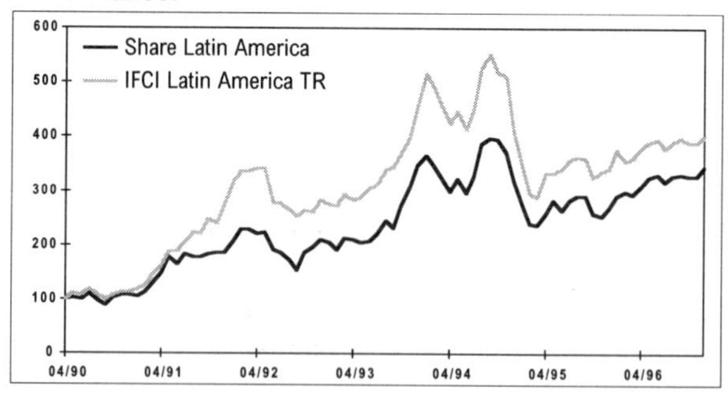

Purchase: Direct
Minimum investment: 1 Unit
Custodian: Banque Indosuez
Listed: None **Dealings:** Weekly
Fund Sedol I.D.: 410235 **Published:** BG
Fees **Annual fee:** 1.50% **Performance fee:** None
Front end load: 2.75% **Redemption fee:** 1.25%
Switching fee: 1.50%

Top holdings:

Holding	%
Banco Itau	3.8%
Cemex	5.6%
Cemig	3.3%
CIA Telecom Chili	5.3%
Electrobas	4.3%
Kimberley Clark MEX	2.6%
Perez Company ARG	5.1%
Tear B-1 Vote	3.3%
Telebras	4.6%
Telecom Brasileiras	7.1%

TOTAL RETURNS %

3 months 1997	1996	1995	1994	3 years	5 years
16.85	27.84	-15.91	-7.51	-0.57	85.84

STATISTICS

Assets ($mil)	Current yield	Volatility	Risk return	Micropal Star Rating
7.05	—	7.40	—	✪✪✪

SHK China
67/350

HK
3rd Floor Tower Two, Admirality Centre, Hong Kong
Tel 852-2822-5783 Fax 852-2822-5730

Investment objective:
The fund invests primarily in quoted equity securities of the People's Republic of China. These securities are normally listed on a stock exchange in China.The Manager may also invest up to 15% of the fund in securities which are unlisted but expected to be listed on an exchange in China within one year. The top country allocation of the portfolio is Hong Kong (60.6%).

Umbrella fund: This is a singular fund.

Launch date: 22/06/92 **Domicile:** Cayman Islands

Currency: USD **Structure:** Open ended, Unit Trust

Portfolio manager: Christopher Lai Mun Kit
Manager of SHK China; BA, business administration; previously with Wardley Investment Services Ltd and DBS Asset Management; 10 years of fund management experience.

Purchase: Direct, Financial Advisor

Minimum investment: 10,000 USD

Custodian: Bermuda Trust (Far East) Ltd

Listed: None **Dealings:** Daily

Fund Sedol I.D.: 679508 **Published:** SC/AW/HKET/HKEJ

Fees **Annual fee:** 1.50% **Performance fee:** None
Front end load: 5.00% **Redemption fee:** None
Switching fee: 1.00%

Contact: Sandy Cheng

Performance:

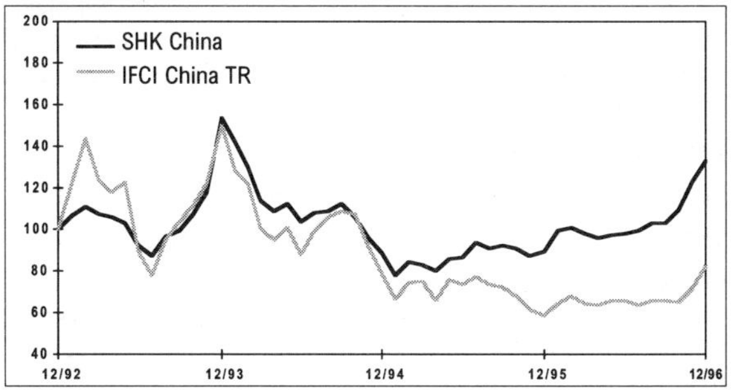

Top holdings:

Cheung KG Infra	11.2%
Eastern Comms B	6.8%
RF-HSBC Wts 97	7.0%
Shen Fangda B	7.8%
SHK China Ind	9.3%

TOTAL RETURNS %

3 months 1997	1996	1995	1994	3 years	5 years
5.45	48.55	1.17	-42.58	-13.70	N.A.

STATISTICS

Assets ($mil)	Current yield	Volatility	Risk return	Micropal Star Rating
6.53	—	6.18	—	✪✪✪

SHK Middle Kingdom
52/350

SHK
3rd Floor Tower Two, Admirality Centre, Hong Kong
Tel 852-2822-5783 Fax 852-2822-5730

Investment objective:
The primary objective of the fund is to achieve capital growth. This is accomplished by investing in publicly quoted equity or equity linked securities of companies within the Pacific region whose business selection relates substantially to the People's Republic of China.The top sector allocations of the portfolio are property (30.1%); and finance (18.4%).

Umbrella fund: This is a singular fund.

Launch date: 10/05/89 **Domicile:** Hong Kong

Currency: HKD **Structure:** Open ended, Unit Trust

Portfolio manager: Christopher Lai Mun Kit
Manager of SHK Middle Kingdom; BA, business administration; previously with Wardley Investment Services Ltd and DBS Asset Management; 10 years of fund management experience.

Purchase: Direct, Financial Advisor

Minimum investment: 5,000 HKD

Custodian: Bermuda Trust (Far East) Ltd

Listed: None **Dealings:** Daily

Fund Sedol I.D.: 676376 **Published:** SC/AW/HKET/HKEJ

Fees **Annual fee:** 1.75% **Performance fee:** None
Front end load: 5.00% **Redemption fee:** None
Switching fee: 1.00%

Contact: Sandy Cheng

Performance:

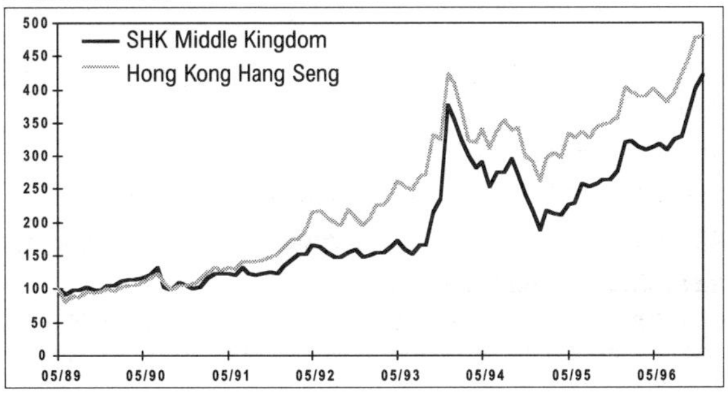

Top holdings:

Cheung Kong Infra	7.2%
Citic Pacific	7.9%
Eastern Comms B	6.0%
Hon Kwok Land Holdings	5.8%
Hutchison Whampoa	7.4%

TOTAL RETURNS %

3 months 1997	1996	1995	1994	3 years	5 years
-3.66	52.06	27.20	-42.10	11.99	238.71

STATISTICS

Assets ($mil)	Current yield	Volatility	Risk return	Micropal Star Rating
1.48	—	7.45	—	✪✪

SHK Oriental Growth
237/350

SHK
3rd Floor Tower Two, Admirality Centre, Hong Kong
Tel 852-2822-5783 Fax 852-2822-5730

Investment objective:
The fund seeks blue chip exposure to the economies of Hong Kong, Singapore and Malaysia. Investments are made in equities or equity linked securities of companies included in Hang Seng Index in Hong Kong, the Overseas Chinese Banking Corp Index in Singapore and the Kuala Lumpur Stock Exchange Composite Index in Malaysia.

Umbrella fund: This is a singular fund.

Launch date: 10/05/89 **Domicile:** Cayman Islands

Currency: HKD **Structure:** Open ended, Unit Trust

Portfolio manager: Christopher Lai Mun Kit
Manager of SHK Oriental Growth; BA, business administration; previously with Wardley Investment Services Ltd and DBS Asset Management; 10 years of fund management experience.

Purchase: Direct, Financial Advisor

Minimum investment: 5,000 HKD

Custodian: Bermuda Trust (Far East) Ltd

Listed: None **Dealings:** Daily

Fund Sedol I.D.: 676377 **Published:** SC/AW/HKET/HKEJ

Fees **Annual fee:** 1.75% **Performance fee:** None
Front end load: 5.00% **Redemption fee:** None
Switching fee: 1.00%

Contact: Sandy Cheng

Performance:

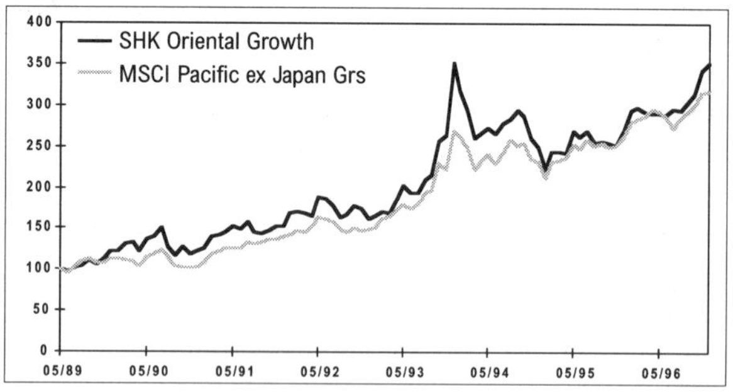

Top holdings:

Bank of East Asia	5.1%
Citic Pacific	9.9%
Hutchison Whampoa	8.5%
New World Development	9.6%
UOB-Foreign	4.9%

TOTAL RETURNS %

3 months 1997	1996	1995	1994	3 years	5 years
-7.19	30.77	7.66	-29.08	-0.16	129.93

STATISTICS

Assets ($mil)	Current yield	Volatility	Risk return	Micropal Star Rating
3.51	—	5.49	—	✪✪✪

Skandifond Nordic Equity Fund
226/350

Skandiaviska Enskilda Banken
PO Box 487, L-2014 Luxembourg
Tel 352-46-17-17-239 Fax 352-22-55-50
http://www. sebank.se/fonder

Investment objective:
The main objective of the sub-fund is the realisation of long-term capital growth coupled with security of the underlying assets, with emphasis on the investments in the equities of Denmark, Norway, Sweden and Finland. At present, the currency exposure of the portfolio is as follows: Swedish krones (51.0%); Finnish marks (19.0%); and Norwegian kronor (17.0%).

Umbrella fund: Skandifond Equity Fund

Launch date: 06/12/88 **Domicile:** Luxembourg [UCITS]

Currency: USD **Structure:** Open ended, Mutual Fund

Portfolio manager: Patrik Tigershlold
Manager of S-E-Banken Fund Sverige commenced October 1993; located in Stockholm; specialising in the Nordic area; 11 years experience in the finance industry.

Purchase: Direct, S.E Banken Group / Luxembourg

Minimum investment: 2,500 USD

Custodian: S-E-Banken Luxembourg S.A.

Listed: Luxembourg **Dealings:** Daily

Fund Sedol I.D.: 476293 **Published:** FT/IHT

Fees **Annual fee:** 1.50% **Performance fee:** None
Front end load: 1.00% **Redemption fee:** None
Switching fee: 1.00%

Contact: Mr E. Kremer

Performance:

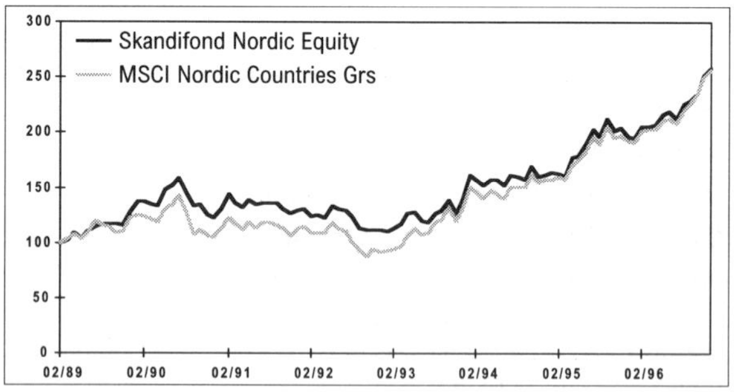

Top holdings:

ABB AB	2.9%
Astra	9.5%
Ericsson	10.0%
Merita	2.5%
Nokia A	7.1%
Norsk Hydro As	5.3%
Novo-Nordiska As -B-	2.6%
Saevik Supply	2.9%
Svenska Handelsbanken	2.5%
Volvo	3.1%

TOTAL RETURNS %

3 months 1997	1996	1995	1994	3 years	5 years
4.46	31.22	22.02	16.46	86.47	99.87

STATISTICS

Assets ($mil)	Current yield	Volatility	Risk return	Micropal Star Rating
15.70	—	4.77	2	✪✪✪

Skandifond UK Equity
222/350

Skandiaviska Enskilda Banken
PO Box 487, L-2014 Luxembourg
Tel 352-46-17-17-239 Fax 352-22-55-50
http://www. sebank.se/fonder

Investment objective:
The sub-fund seeks the realisation of long-term capital growth coupled with security of underlying assets. The emphasis is placed on investments in transferable securities in the UK. The fund is denominated in UK sterling.

Umbrella fund: Skankifond Equity Funds
Launch date: 06/12/88 **Domicile:** Luxembourg [UCITS]
Currency: GBP **Structure:** Open ended, Mutual Fund
Portfolio manager: Stephan Webster
Manager of Skandifond UK Equity; located in London; 14 years experience in the finance industry.

Purchase: Direct, S.E Banken Group / Luxembourg
Minimum investment: 2,500 USD
Custodian: S-E-Banken Luxembourg S.A.
Listed: Luxembourg **Dealings:** Daily
Fund Sedol I.D.: 476295 **Published:** FT/IHT
Fees **Annual fee:** 1.50% **Performance fee:** None
Front end load: 1.00% **Redemption fee:** None
Switching fee: 1.00%

Contact: Mr E. Kremer
Performance:

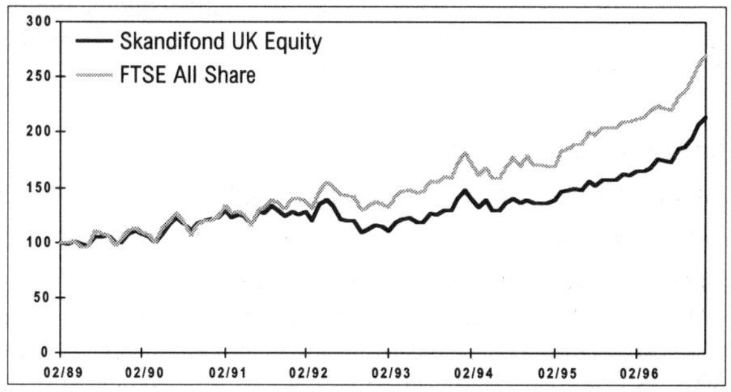

Top holdings:

Abbey National	4.1%
BP	3.9%
British Airways	4.5%
General Electric	4.5%
Glaxo Wellcome	4.2%
Granada Group	5.0%
National Westminster Bank	5.0%
Scottish + Newcastle	4.5%
Shell Transport & Trading	6.5%
Siebe	5.9%

TOTAL RETURNS %

3 months 1997	1996	1995	1994	3 years	5 years
-0.61	31.44	20.50	-3.20	53.32	68.05

STATISTICS

Assets ($mil)	Current yield	Volatility	Risk return	Micropal Star Rating
34.63	—	3.38	4	✪✪✪✪

Sloane Robinson Europe
27/350

Sloane Robinson Investment Management
Bermuda House, St Julians Avenue, St Peter Port,
GY1 3NF, Guernsey
Tel 44-1481-707-000 Fax 44-1481-726-295

Investment objective:
The Sloane Robinson sub-fund seeks to achieve and preserve above average capital returns through a policy of investing in quoted European securities and their derivatives. The funds foreign currency exposure is actively managed. The top sector allocations of the portfolio are the following: finance (27.1%); industrial cyclical (22.6%); services (16.6%); and retail trade (11.5%).
Umbrella fund: SR Global Fund
Launch date: 01/01/94 **Domicile:** British Virgin Islands
Currency: USD **Structure:** Open ended, Investment Company
Portfolio manager: Stephen Pearson
Manager of Sloane Robinson Europe commenced January 1994; graduate, classics-Oxford U; previously with GT Management, UK capital goods analyst, UK Fund Manager.
Purchase: Direct
Minimum investment: 250,000 USD
Custodian: Bank of Bermuda
Listed: Dublin **Dealings:** Monthly
Fund Sedol I.D.: 305221 **Published:** FT/IHT
Fees **Annual fee:** 1.00% **Performance fee:** 15.00%
Front end load: None **Redemption fee:** None
Switching fee: None

Contact: Stephan Woernle
Performance:

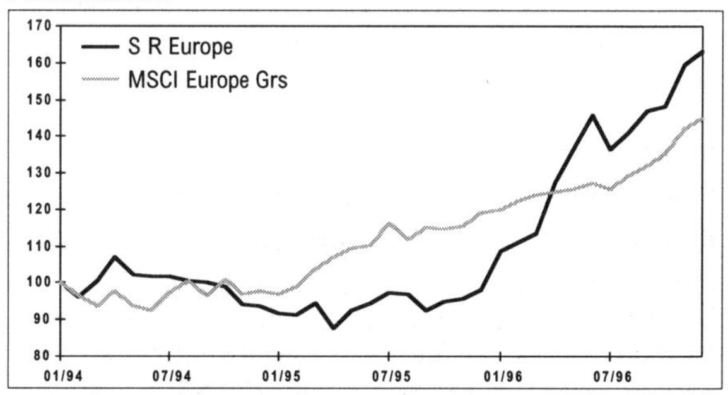

Top holdings:

Bank of Ireland	1.9%
BG Bank	3.2%
Elksop	2.5%
ENI SPA	2.7%
Miquel Costas	3.4%
Nordbanken	3.6%
SE Banken	2.9%
Short FTSE Index	-51.3%
Swedbank	3.9%
Tornet Fastigh	2.0%

TOTAL RETURNS %

3 months 1997	1996	1995	1994	3 years	5 years
11.02	66.58	4.81	N.A.	N.A.	N.A.

STATISTICS

Assets ($mil)	Current yield	Volatility	Risk return	Micropal Star Rating
42.00	—	N.A.	—	———

Sloane Robinson International

321/350

Sloane Robinson Investment Management
Bermuda House, St Julians Avenue, St Peter Port,
GY1 3NF, Guernsey
Tel 44-1481-707-087 Fax 44-1481-726-273

Contact: Stephan Woernle

Investment objective:
The Sloane Robinson sub-fund aims to provide long-term capital growth through investment in Europe and Asia.The top country allocations of the portfolio are long following: China (19.3%); Sweden (12.0%); Russia (8.9%); Hong Kong (7.6%); Italy (7.5%); and short Japan (-17.5%).

Umbrella fund: SR Global Fund

Launch date: 01/01/94 **Domicile:** British Virgin Islands

Currency: USD **Structure:** Open ended, Investment Company

Portfolio manager: Hugh Sloane
Manager of Sloane Robinson International commenced January 1994; graduate, economics/politics- U Bristol and MPhil, economics- Oxford U; previously with GT Mgt, as Asian economist investment and Director of GT Japan.

Purchase: Direct

Minimum investment: 1,000,000 USD

Custodian: Bank of Bermuda

Listed: Dublin **Dealings:** Monthly

Fund Sedol I.D.: 305222 **Published:** FT

Fees **Annual fee:** 1.00% **Performance fee:** 15.00%
Front end load: None **Redemption fee:** None
Switching fee: None

Performance:

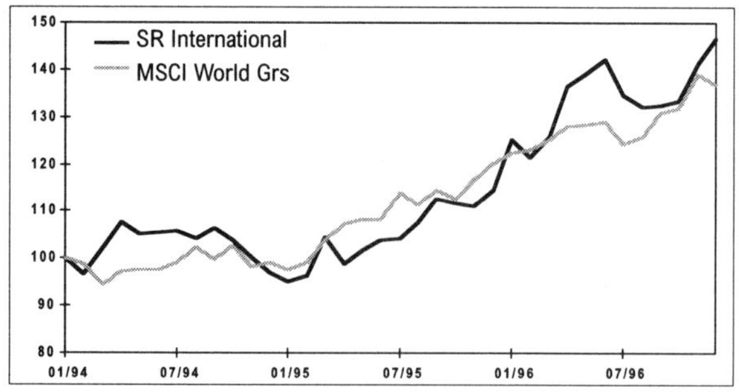

Top holdings:

Holding	%
China Overseas	5.5%
Mosenergo	2.3%
NEC Corp	2.9%
Nikkei Simex - short	29.0%
Nordbanken	3.4%
Petroz	2.3%
Quingling Motors H Shares	2.8%
SE Banken	3.8%
Sino Land	3.7%
Valmet	2.3%

TOTAL RETURNS %

3 months 1997	1996	1995	1994	3 years	5 years
19.81	27.84	18.37	N.A.	N.A.	N.A.

STATISTICS

Assets ($mil)	Current yield	Volatility	Risk return	Micropal Star Rating
91.40	—	N.A.	—	———

Sovereign High Yield A

133/350

Scudder Stevens & Clark
8th Floor New London House, 6 London St., London EC3R 7BE, UK
Tel 44-171-265-0077 Fax 44-171-265-0099
http://www. ny.scudder.com/
E mail jenny_brundit@scudder.com

Contact: David McConnell and Jenny Brundit

Investment objective:
The investment fund seeks high current income with capital appreciation being a secondary objective through investment in a diversified portfolio of US dollar denominated bonds, issued or guaranteed by primarily Latin American Governments.

Umbrella fund: This is a singular fund.

Launch date: 29/11/89 **Domicile:** Netherlands Antilles

Currency: USD **Structure:** Open ended, Investment Company

Portfolio manager: Susan Gray & Isabel Saltzman (refer to Scudder GOF Emg Mkt Inc A-2)
Susan Gray Senior co-manager and market strategist for the Emerging Markets/High Yield Bond Group; BA, East Asian studies and government- Colby College; previously with the Japan Fund; joined the Emerging Markets group in 1990.

Purchase: Financial Advisor

Minimum investment: 5,000 USD

Custodian: State Street Bank (Curacao)

Listed: Dublin **Dealings:** Daily

Fund Sedol I.D.: 278234 **Published:** FT/IHT/SC

Fees **Annual fee:** 2.00% **Performance fee:** None
Front end load: Up to 5.50% **Redemption fee:** None
Switching fee: None

Performance:

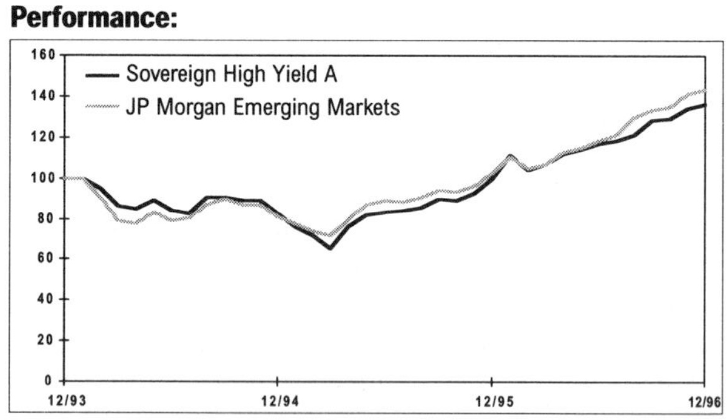

Top holdings:

Holding	%
Argentina FRB	n/s
Argentina Par	n/s
Brazil C	n/s
Brazil Discount	n/s
Brazil IDU	n/s
Morocco Tranch A	n/s
Panama FRN	n/s
United Mexican States / 26	n/s
Venezuela DCB	n/s
Venezuela FLIRB	n/s

TOTAL RETURNS %

3 months 1997	1996	1995	1994	3 years	5 years
3.68	37.41	20.54	-17.56	36.55	82.88

STATISTICS

Assets ($mil)	Current yield	Volatility	Risk return	Micropal Star Rating
325.18	11.98	6.13	1	✪✪

Special Assets Pacific LP
250/350

Special Assets Limited
6 Floor Terrace, 8 Duddell Street, Central, Hong Kong
Tel 852-2593-0588 Fax 852-28-45-5517
E mail Salhk@hk.super.net

Investment objective:
The fund seeks long-term investment in a concentrated portfolio of superior, excellently managed, cash flowing, undervalued publicly listed special companies in the Asian Pacific region. Special companies are monopolies and other companies dominant in their market niche with pricing power.

Umbrella fund: This is a singular fund.
Launch date: 03/06/94 **Domicile:** Cayman Islands
Currency: USD **Structure:** Open ended, Limited Partnership
Portfolio manager: Robert L Meyer
Manager of Special Assets Pacific L.P commenced June 1985 and co-founder, Special Assets Group (1985) and First Pacific Co. Ltd (1981).

Purchase: Direct
Minimum investment: 100,000 USD
Custodian: Bermuda Trust (Far East) Limited
Listed: None **Dealings:** Monthly
Fund Sedol I.D.: 305037 **Published:** AW/WS
Fees **Annual fee:** 1.00% **Performance fee:** 20.00%
Front end load: None **Redemption fee:** None
Switching fee: None

Contact: Robert L. Meyer
Performance:

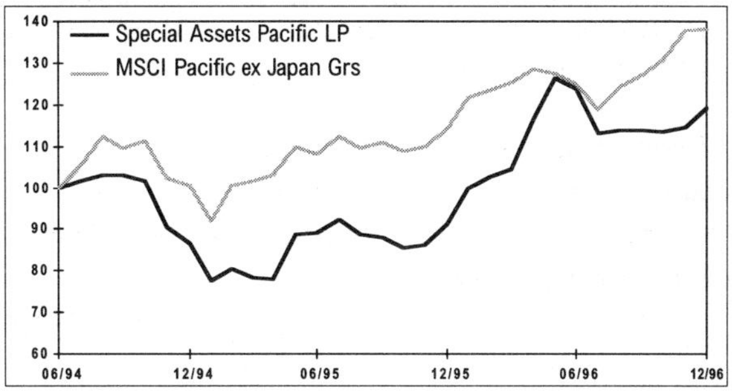

Top holdings:

Consumer Goods	45.5%
Financial Services	3.1%
Health	5.5%
Industrial Cyclical	2.0%
Insurance	10.8%
Non-Durable	12.1%
Others	5.1%
Retail Trade	8.8%
Technology	7.1%

TOTAL RETURNS %

3 months 1997	1996	1995	1994	3 years	5 years
8.43	30.48	5.57	N.A.	N.A.	N.A.

STATISTICS

Assets ($mil)	Current yield	Volatility	Risk return	Micropal Star Rating
36.11	—	N.A.	—	———

SSF Nordic
217/350

Svenska Handelsbanken
146 Boulevard de la Petrusse, L-2330 Luxembourg
Tel 352-49-98-11-1 Fax 352-499-811-314

Investment objective:
The sub-fund seeks capital appreciation by investment in Nordic countries including Sweden, Norway, Denmark and Finland. The fund is denominated in Swedish kronor. The top sectors of the portfolio include the following: consumer goods (30.0%); finance (10.2%); and health (8.9%).

Umbrella fund: Svenska Selection Fund
Launch date: 01/06/94 **Domicile:** Luxembourg [UCITS]
Currency: SEK **Structure:** Open ended, SICAV
Portfolio manager: Christina Holmberg and Arne Lindman
Co-Managers of Svenska Selection Fund Nordic; Mr Lindman commenced in 1989 and is the head of investment policies.

Purchase: Direct, Financial Advisor
Minimum investment: 1,000 SEK
Custodian: Handelsbanken Luxembourg
Listed: Luxembourg **Dealings:** Daily
Fund Sedol I.D.: 301659 **Published:** FT
Fees **Annual fee:** 1.50% **Performance fee:** None
Front end load: Up to 5.00% **Redemption fee:** None
Switching fee: 1.00%

Contact: Pierre Jean-Marc
Performance:

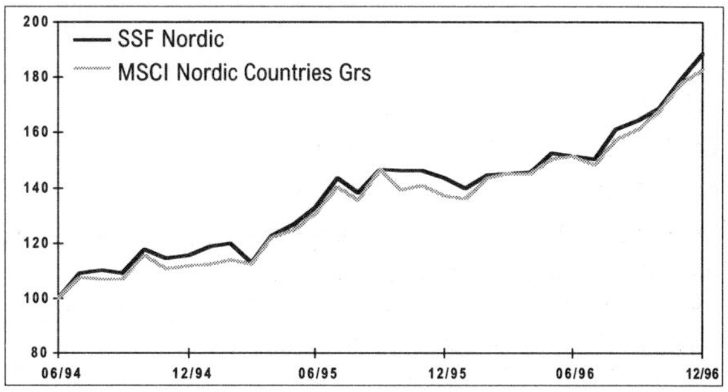

Top holdings:

Astra A Free	8.9%
Diligentia	5.0%
Enator - short	3.2%
Enso Oy	6.1%
Ericsson B Free	9.4%
Netcom Sys B - short	3.1%
Nokia A	8.5%
S-E-Banken	3.3%
SHB A	3.2%
SSAB A	4.2%

TOTAL RETURNS %

3 months 1997	1996	1995	1994	3 years	5 years
2.01	31.62	23.95	N.A.	N.A.	N.A.

STATISTICS

Assets ($mil)	Current yield	Volatility	Risk return	Micropal Star Rating
12.55	—	N.A.	—	———

SSF Sweden Shares
155/350

Svenska Handelsbanken
146 Boulevard de la Petrusse, L-2330 Luxembourg
Tel 352-49-98-11-1 Fax 352-499-811-314

Investment objective:
The primary objective of the sub-fund is to seek capital appreciation through Swedish investments. The top sector allocations of the portfolio are the following: consumer goods (17.0%); electrical/electronics (13.9%); finance (12.2%); health (9.8%); building/materials (9.0%); and energy (5.4%).

Umbrella fund: Svenska Selection Fund
Launch date: 30/06/95 **Domicile:** Luxembourg
Currency: SEK **Structure:** Open ended, SICAV
Portfolio manager: Gustav Sjogren
Manager of SSF Shares (Sweden) commenced May 1996; best investor in 1996, Sweden.

Purchase: Direct, Financial Advisor
Minimum investment: 1,000 SEK
Custodian: Handelsbanken Luxembourg
Listed: Luxembourg **Dealings:** Daily
Fund Sedol I.D.: 301661 **Published:** FT
Fees **Annual fee:** 1.50% **Performance fee:** None
Front end load: Up to 5.00% **Redemption fee:** None
Switching fee: 1.00%

Contact: Jean-Marc Pierre
Performance:

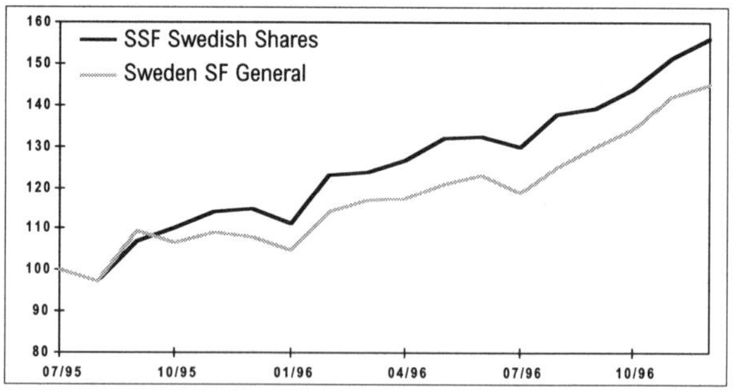

Top holdings:

Holding	%
Astra A Free	9.8%
Autoliv AB	3.9%
Diligentia	3.7%
Enator - short	3.7%
Ericsson B Free	10.1%
Investor B Free	4.9%
NCC B Free	4.3%
S-E-Banken	3.3%
Trygg Hansa B - short	2.8%
Volvo B	4.0%

TOTAL RETURNS %

3 months 1997	1996	1995	1994	3 years	5 years
-2.84	35.87	N.A.	N.A.	N.A.	N.A.

STATISTICS

Assets ($mil)	Current yield	Volatility	Risk return	Micropal Star Rating
26.88	—	N.A.	—	———

Swiss Life Proteus UK Equity Fund
163/350

Swiss Life Investment Management
Swiss Life House, 24-26 South Park, Sevenoaks, TN13 1BG , United Kingdom
Tel 44-1732-582-000 Fax 44-1732-582-012

Investment objective:
The sub-fund actively seek long-term growth by investing in transferable securities with the aim of spreading investment risk. The sub-fund selects UK companies, both large and small, which have greater than average growth potential. The sector allocations of the portfolio are services (34.7%); general industrials (21.7%); finance (18.3%); and consumer goods (14.5%).
Umbrella fund: Swiss Life Investment Fund Plc - Proteus
Launch date: 15/11/91 **Domicile:** Ireland [UCITS]
Currency: GBP **Structure:** Open ended, SICAV
Portfolio manager: Mark Amery
Manager of Proteus UK Equity Fund commenced 1994; previously at Hill Samuel; 14 years experience in the finance industry.

Purchase: Direct, Financial Advisor
Minimum investment: 2,500 GBP
Custodian: The Governors & the Bank of Ireland (Dublin)
Listed: None **Dealings:** Weekly
Fund Sedol I.D.: 485712 **Published:** FT/VW/NZZ
Fees **Annual fee:** 1.25% **Performance fee:** None
Front end load: 5.25% **Redemption fee:** None
Switching fee: None

Contact: George Pavlou
Performance:

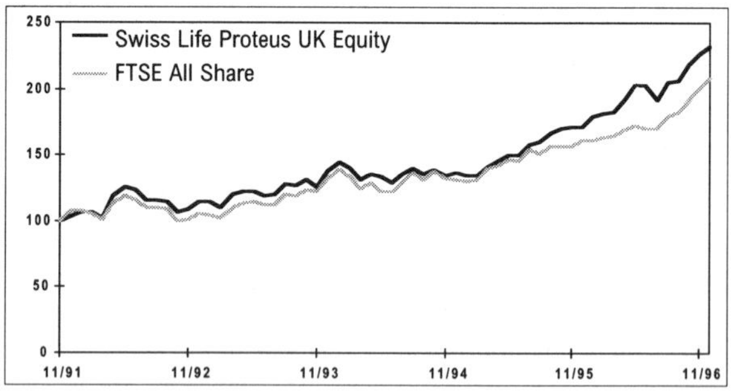

Top holdings:

Holding	%
British Aerospace	3.2%
British Petroleum	2.4%
Glaxo Wellcome	3.7%
Standard Chartered	3.0%
Zeneca Group	2.7%

TOTAL RETURNS %

3 months 1997	1996	1995	1994	3 years	5 years
5.82	35.36	25.06	-0.72	68.05	125.63

STATISTICS

Assets ($mil)	Current yield	Volatility	Risk return	Micropal Star Rating
201.98	—	3.42	5	✪✪✪✪✪

Swissca Bond Invest ITL
282/350

Swissca Bond Invest Mgt Co S.A
1 Place De Metz, L-2954 Luxembourg
Tel 352-40-15-5370 Fax 352-40-15-5361
http://www. swissca.ch

Investment objective:
The sub-fund seeks capital appreciation, capital security and liquidity. Investments focus on the principle of spreading risk, mainly in bonds issued by first-class borrowers and those guaranteed by first-class underwriters and listed on a stock exchange or traded in some other regulated market (ECU).

Umbrella fund: Swissca Bond Invest
Launch date: 12/04/94 **Domicile:** Luxembourg
Currency: ITL **Structure:** Open ended, UnitTrust
Portfolio manager: David Byrne
Manager of Swissca bond Invest LIT; previously with Wardley Investment Service Intl Ltd, Fund Manager responsible for a multi-currently fund and Hill Samuel Investment Mgt Ltd, responsible for the UK fixed interest department; joined Swissca in 1991.
Purchase: Direct
Minimum investment: 1 Unit
Custodian: Banque et Caisse d'Espargne de l'Etat Luxembourg
Listed: Luxembourg **Dealings:** Daily
Fund Sedol I.D.: 300646 **Published:** BG/TK/RT/NZZ/JG
Fees **Annual fee:** 0.50% **Performance fee:** None
Front end load: 1.00% **Redemption fee:** None
Switching fee: None

Contact: Jean-Marie Hermann

Performance:

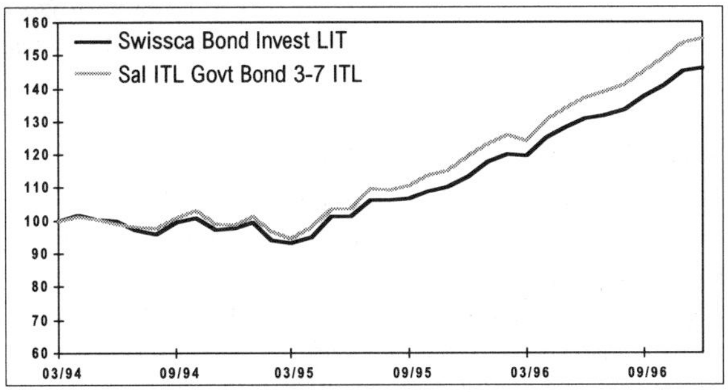

Top holdings:

Holding	%
BEI 10.75%/05	14.9%
Berd 9.75%/05	15.4%
BNG 10.5% /03	2.6%
Eurofima 10.40%/99	14.7%
IFC 10.625%/99	4.5%
KFW Intern 11.625%/98	7.6%
Schweden 10%/01	3.8%
Suedwestdeutsche 8%/04	9.1%
Westdeutsche 8.65%/03	8.5%

TOTAL RETURNS %

3 months 1997	1996	1995	1994	3 years	5 years
-10.28	28.96	16.14	N.A.	N.A.	N.A.

STATISTICS

Assets ($mil)	Current yield	Volatility	Risk return	Micropal Star Rating
10.27	—	N.A.	—	———

Templeton GS China Fund
112/350

Templeton Asset Management Ltd
Saltire Court, 20 Castle Terrace, Edinburgh, EH1 2EH, Scotland
Tel 44-131-469-4000 Fax 44-131-228-4506

Investment objective:
The sub-fund seeks long-term capital appreciation by investing in companies that are located in China, Hong Kong and Taiwan or have business with these emerging economies. The assets of the portfolio are divided between the following country allocations: Hong Kong (74.9%); and China (25.1%).

Umbrella fund: Templeton Global Strategy
Launch date: 01/09/94 **Domicile:** Luxembourg [UCITS]
Currency: USD **Structure:** Open ended, SICAV
Portfolio manager: Mark Mobius
Manager Templeton Global Strategy Funds commenced January 1987; MA- Boston U and Phd, economics/ political science- MIT.

Purchase: Direct, Financial Advisor
Minimum investment: 5,000 USD
Custodian: Chase Manhattan Bank Luxembourg
Listed: Luxembourg **Dealings:** Daily
Fund Sedol I.D.: 488184 **Published:** FT/HB/ WS/IHT/SC
Fees **Annual fee:** 1.75% **Performance fee:** None
Front end load: 5.75% **Redemption fee:** None
Switching fee: None

Contact: Catrona McRae

Performance:

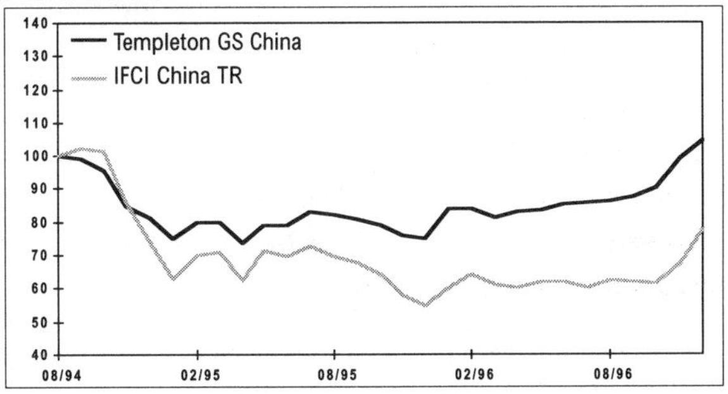

Top holdings:

Holding	%
Cheung Kong Holdings Ltd	4.9%
Hang Lung Development	2.7%
Hong Kong Electric Holdings	3.8%
Hopewell Holdings	4.7%
HSBC Holdings	4.9%
New World Development	5.0%
NG Fung Hong Ltd	2.1%
Sun Hung Kai Properties	4.8%
Wheelock Holdings	2.8%
Yue Yuen Industrial	4.7%

TOTAL RETURNS %

3 months 1997	1996	1995	1994	3 years	5 years
-1.73	39.85	-7.77	N.A.	N.A.	N.A.

STATISTICS

Assets ($mil)	Current yield	Volatility	Risk return	Micropal Star Rating
13.56	—	N.A.	—	———

The Ashburton International Equity Fund
278/350

Ashburton (Isle of Man) Ltd
4th Floor Victory House, Prospect Hill, Douglas Isle of Man
Tel 44-1624-620-097 Fax 44-1624-672-338

Investment objective:
The sub-fund invests in a portfolio of international equities with a view to maximise capital growth. The top country allocations of the portfolio are US (44.0%); SE Asia (15.0%); UK (11.0%); Germany (5.0%); Netherlands (5.0%); and Italy (3.0%).

Umbrella fund: Ashburton Global Funds Ltd
Launch date: 01/01/92 **Domicile:** Isle of Man [UCITS]
Currency: GBP **Structure:** Open ended, Investment Company
Portfolio manager: Nicholas Lee
Manager of The Ashburton International Equity Fund (Jersey) commenced January 1992; joined Ashburton 8 years ago; previously with Barclays de Zoete Wedd Investment Management as an analyst/Fund Manager; 18 years industry experience.
Purchase: Direct
Minimum investment: 25,000 GBP
Custodian: Royal Bank of Scotland (Isle of Man) Ltd.
Listed: None **Dealings:** Weekly
Fund Sedol I.D.: 4927 **Published:** FT
Fees **Annual fee:** 2.00% **Performance fee:** None
Front end load: 4.00% **Redemption fee:** None
Switching fee: None

Contact: Tony Edmonds/Paul Barlow
Performance:

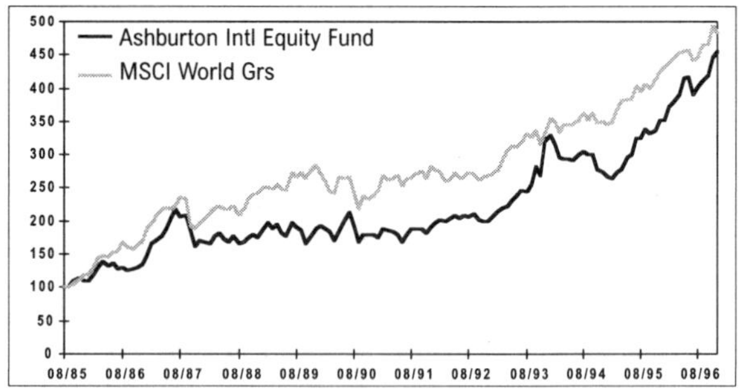

Top holdings:

Abbey National Plc	2.7%
Aspect Telecommunications	2.3%
AT&T Corp	2.4%
British Aerospace Plc	2.3%
Brown & Sharp Manuf Co	2.7%
Cheung Kong Infrastructure	2.3%
China Travel Intl	2.9%
IMC Global Inc	2.7%
Kumpulan Jetson Berhad	2.4%
Morgan Stanley Group Inc	2.2%

TOTAL RETURNS %

3 months 1997	1996	1995	1994	3 years	5 years
4.93	29.10	28.67	-14.56	41.92	137.59

STATISTICS

Assets ($mil)	Current yield	Volatility	Risk return	Micropal Star Rating
35.98	—	3.56	3	✪✪✪✪

The Hansberger Global Fund PLC
68/350

Hansberger Global Investors
SIS East Las Olas Boulevard, Suite 1300, Fort Lauderdale, FL33301, United States
Tel 1-954-522-5150 Fax 1-954-790-3700

Investment objective:
The sub-fund aims to achieve long-term capital growth through investment primarily in emerging global equity securities which the Investment Manager believes to be under valued. The top country allocations for the portfolio are as follows: Russia (13.3%); Hong Kong (11.5%); China (11.3%); Brazil (8.8%) Singapore (5.0%); and Slovakia Rep (3.8%).
Umbrella fund: This is a singular fund.
Launch date: 22/12/94 **Domicile:** Ireland
Currency: USD **Structure:** Close ended, Investment Company
Portfolio manager: Tom Hansberger
Manager of The Hansberger Global Fund Plc commenced December 1994; has been a Global Portfolio Manager since 1969; previously President and CEO of Templeton Worldwide.
Purchase: Direct, Financial Advisor, no
Minimum investment: 350,000 USD
Custodian: Chase Manhattan Bank (Ireland) Plc
Listed: Dublin **Dealings:** Monthly
Fund Sedol I.D.: 305116 **Published:** N/A
Fees **Annual fee:** None **Performance fee:** None
Front end load: None **Redemption fee:** None
Switching fee: None

Contact: Dave Lamanski
Performance:

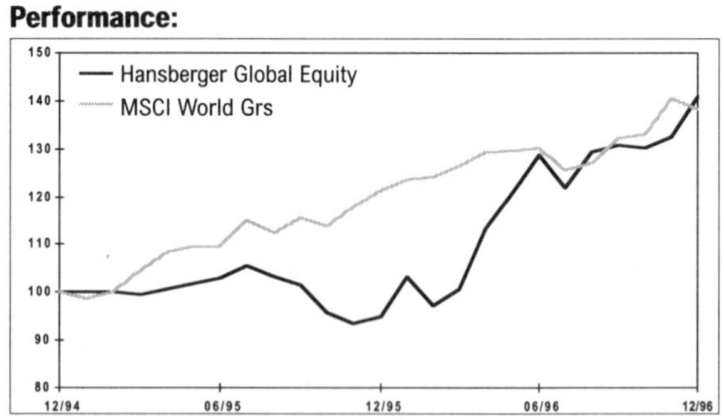

Top holdings:

AO Mosenergo	2.4%
HSBC Holdings	2.6%
Louyang Glass Co	2.6%
Lukoil	2.8%
Peregrine Wts 27/11/97	2.1%
Pliva	2.1%
Rostelekom	2.5%
Shanghai Hai Xing Ship	2.0%
Sivensa	2.3%
YPF Sociedad Anonima	2.0%

TOTAL RETURNS %

3 months 1997	1996	1995	1994	3 years	5 years
14.55	48.47	-5.10	N.A.	N.A.	N.A.

STATISTICS

Assets ($mil)	Current yield	Volatility	Risk return	Micropal Star Rating
4.37	—	N.A.	—	———

The Mexican Premium Income Portfolio NV

200/350

LM Global Offshore Funds
4 Floor Picadilly Centre, George Town, Grand Cayman, Cayman Islands
Tel 305-443-0859 Fax 305-443-4885
http://www. lmglobal.com

Contact: Customer Services Department

Investment objective:
The primarily objective of the fund is to achieve high current income and to assume the foreign exchange risk of exposure to the Mexican peso. The fund invests primarily in high quality, peso denominated debt obligations of the Mexican government and its agencies, commercial banks and major corporations.

Umbrella fund: This is a singular fund.
Launch date: 08/06/90 **Domicile:** Netherlands Antilles
Currency: USD **Structure:** Open ended, Investment Company
Portfolio manager: Western Asset Global Management-London
Yturbe, Laborde y Asociados S.C. ,a Mexico city based investment advisory firm specializing in Mexican fixed income investments, has served as Sub-Manager of the fund since June 1990.
Purchase: Direct, Financial Advisor
Minimum investment: 5,000 USD
Custodian: Boston Safe Deposit and Trust
Listed: None **Dealings:** Daily
Fund Sedol I.D.: 250977 **Published:** BG
Fees **Annual fee:** 0.88% **Performance fee:** None
Front end load: None **Redemption fee:** 5.00%
Switching fee: None

Performance:

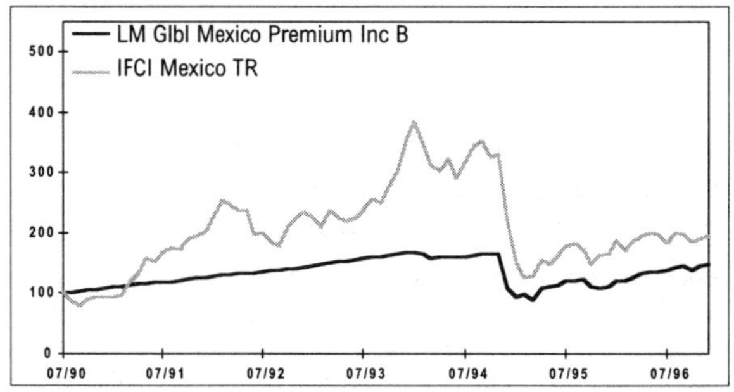

Top holdings:

Holding	%
Bond	40.2%
Cash/MM	5.4%
Fixed Income Bonds	54.4%

TOTAL RETURNS %

3 months 1997	1996	1995	1994	3 years	5 years
4.26	32.69	3.70	-35.04	-10.61	17.59

STATISTICS

Assets ($mil)	Current yield	Volatility	Risk return	Micropal Star Rating
19.39	22.50	7.61	—	✪✪✪

Thornton New Tiger China

164/350

Thornton Management (Asia) Ltd
25 Floor Jardine House, One Connaught Place, Hong Kong
Tel 852-826-8835 Fax 852-877-2566

Contact: Customer Services Department

Investment objective:
The fund aims at providing investors with capital appreciation by investing in companies in the People's Republic of China and companies located elsewhere which have significant interest in China.

Umbrella fund: Thornton New Tiger Selections Fund
Launch date: 01/07/92 **Domicile:** Bermuda
Currency: USD **Structure:** Open ended, Mutual Fund
Portfolio manager: Diahann Brown and Diana Dai
Ms Brown joined Thornton in 1992; previously with Robert Fleming Asset Mgt and Goldman Sachs; managing Asian funds since 1989; specialising in emerging markets. Ms Dai joined Thornton in 1996; MA, English- U of Massachusetts.
Purchase: Direct
Minimum investment: 2,000 USD
Custodian: The Bank of Bermuda (Far East) Ltd
Listed: None **Dealings:** Daily
Fund Sedol I.D.: 89049 **Published:** IHT/FT/SC/HKEJ
Fees **Annual fee:** 2.00% **Performance fee:** None
Front end load: 5.00% **Redemption fee:** None
Switching fee: Up to 2.00%

Performance:

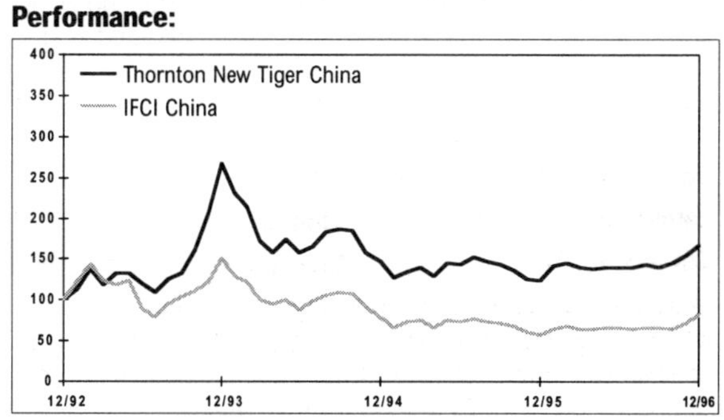

Top holdings:

Holding	
Gold Lion hdgs	n/s
Harbin Power Equipment Co	n/s
Luoyang Glass	n/s
Maanshan Iron Steel	n/s
Qingling Motors	n/s
Shanghai Jin Jiang Tower	n/s
Shanghai Petrochemicals	n/s
Shanghai Refrigerator Compressor	n/s
Shanghai Yaohua Pilkinton	n/s
Zhenhai Refining Chemical	n/s

TOTAL RETURNS %

3 months 1997	1996	1995	1994	3 years	5 years
4.78	35.33	-16.36	-45.03	-37.78	N.A.

STATISTICS

Assets ($mil)	Current yield	Volatility	Risk return	Micropal Star Rating
9.58	—	7.84	—	✪

Thornton New Tiger Hong Kong
35/350

Thornton Management (Asia) Ltd
25 Floor Jardine House, One Connaught Place, Hong Kong
Tel 852-826-8835 Fax 852-877-2566

Investment objective:
This open-ended fund seeks to provide investors with capital appreciation from a portfolio of securities invested principally in Hong Kong. The base currency of this fund is Hong Kong dollars.

Contact: Customer Services Department

Performance:

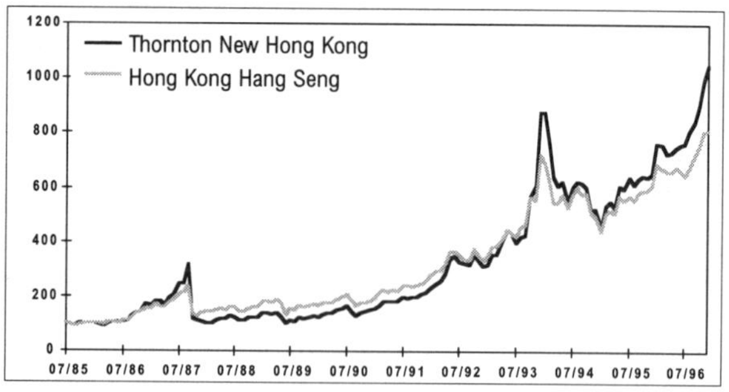

Umbrella fund: Thornton New Tiger Selections Fund
Launch date: 01/07/85 **Domicile:** Bermuda
Currency: USD **Structure:** Open ended, Mutual Fund
Portfolio manager: Diahann Brown, Matthew Choi and Diana Dai
Ms. Brown joined Thornton in 1992; specialising in emerging markets. Matthew Choi joined Thornton in 1987; Masters, business systems analysis- City U and Masters, economics- U of Kent. Ms Dai joined Thornton in 1996; MA, English- U of Mass.
Purchase: Direct
Minimum investment: 2,000 USD
Custodian: The Bank of Bermuda (Far East) Ltd
Listed: None **Dealings:** Daily
Fund Sedol I.D.: 88976 **Published:** IHT/FT/SC/HKEJ
Fees **Annual fee:** 2.00% **Performance fee:** None
Front end load: 5.00% **Redemption fee:** None
Switching fee: Up to 2.00%

Top holdings:

Beijing Land Ltd	n/s
Cheung Kong Infra	n/s
China Everbright INTL	n/s
Cosco Pacific	n/s
Great Eagle Holdings	n/s
JGG Holdings	n/s
Lai Sun Development	n/s
NG Fung Hong Ltd	n/s
Peregrine Investments	n/s
Ting Yi Holdings	n/s

TOTAL RETURNS %

3 months 1997	1996	1995	1994	3 years	5 years
-4.40	61.19	25.35	-40.57	20.07	384.45

STATISTICS

Assets ($mil)	Current yield	Volatility	Risk return	Micropal Star Rating
44.32	—	8.16	1	✪✪✪

Thornton New Tiger Malaysia
168/350

Thornton Management (Asia) Ltd
25 Floor Jardine House, One Connaught Place, Hong Kong
Tel 852-826-8835 Fax 852-877-2566

Investment objective:
The fund aims at providing investors with capital appreciation by investing in Malaysian securities. The base currency of this fund is US dollars.

Contact: Customer Services Department

Performance:

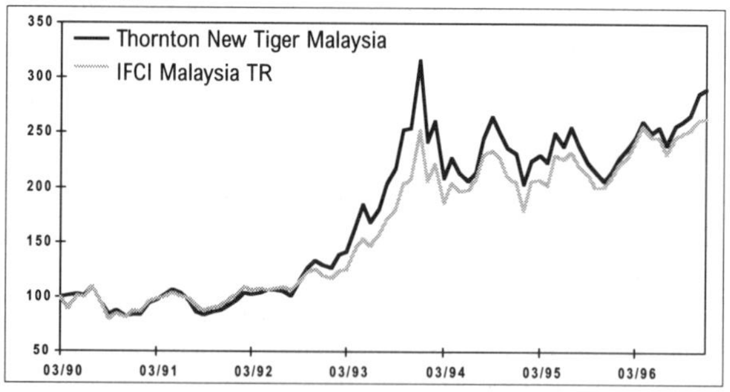

Umbrella fund: Thornton New Tiger Selections Fund
Launch date: 01/03/90 **Domicile:** Bermuda
Currency: USD **Structure:** Open ended, Mutual Fund
Portfolio manager: Diahann Brown and Ian Lui
Ms Brown joined Thornton in 1992; previously with Robert Fleming Asset Mgt; specialising in emerging markets. Mr Lui joined Thornton in 1994; MBA- Chinese U of HK; formerly with Daiwa Investment Advisors; specialising in Asian markets.
Purchase: Direct
Minimum investment: 2,000 USD
Custodian: The Bank of Bermuda (Far East) Ltd
Listed: None **Dealings:** Daily
Fund Sedol I.D.: 88828 **Published:** IHT/FT/SC/HKEJ
Fees **Annual fee:** 2.00% **Performance fee:** None
Front end load: 5.00% **Redemption fee:** None
Switching fee: Up to 2.00%

Top holdings:

Affin Holdings	n/s
AMMB Holdings	n/s
Commercial Asset Holdings Wts 98	n/s
Litrak	n/s
Malayan Bank Berhad	n/s
Sime Darby	n/s
Star Public	n/s
Telecom Malaysia	n/s
Tenaga	n/s
United Engineers	n/s

TOTAL RETURNS %

3 months 1997	1996	1995	1994	3 years	5 years
3.17	34.88	-6.88	-26.97	-8.27	218.78

STATISTICS

Assets ($mil)	Current yield	Volatility	Risk return	Micropal Star Rating
14.65	—	8.17	—	✪✪

Thornton Taiwan Equity Growth

187/350

Thornton Investment Management Ltd
Swan House, 33 Queen Street, London EC4R 1AX,
United Kingdom
Tel 44-171-246-3001 Fax 44-171-246-3003

Investment objective:
The fund seeks to provide investors with capital appreciation by investing in Taiwanese securities. The fund is not authorised in Hong Kong and is not available to Hong Kong residents. The base currency of this fund is US dollars.

Umbrella fund: Thornton Taiwan Fund Limited
Launch date: 01/08/91 **Domicile:** Cayman Islands
Currency: USD **Structure:** Open ended, Investment Company
Portfolio manager: Diahann Brown
Manager of Thornton Taiwan Equity Income joined Thornton in 1992; previously with Robert Fleming Asset Management and Goldman Sachs; started managing Asian funds in 1989; specialising in emerging markets.
Purchase: Direct
Minimum investment: 50,000 USD
Custodian: The Bank of Bermuda (Far East) Ltd
Listed: Hong Kong **Dealings:** Weekly
Fund Sedol I.D.: 688928 **Published:** IHT/FT/SC/HKEJ
Fees **Annual fee:** 1.50% **Performance fee:** None
Front end load: 5.00% **Redemption fee:** 0.50%
Switching fee: 2.00%

Contact: Customer Services Department

Performance:

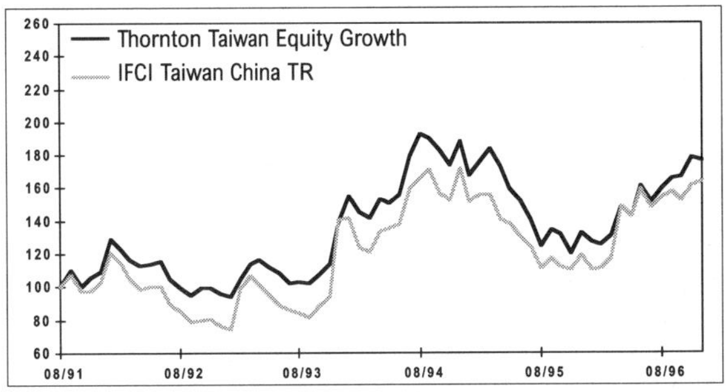

Top holdings:

Cathay Construction	n/s
Cathay Life Ins	n/s
Chang Hwa Bank	n/s
China Development	n/s
China Trust	n/s
Far East Department Stores	n/s
Kindom Construction	n/s
Taichung Machinery	n/s
UTD World C Comm Bank	n/s
Yue Loong Motor	n/s

TOTAL RETURNS %

3 months 1997	1996	1995	1994	3 years	5 years
24.15	33.42	-29.60	35.54	27.31	61.29

STATISTICS

Assets ($mil)	Current yield	Volatility	Risk return	Micropal Star Rating
52.98	—	7.29	3	✪✪✪✪✪

Thornton Taiwan Equity Income

212/350

Thornton Investment Management Ltd
Swan House, 33 Queen Street, London EC4R 1AX,
United Kingdom
Tel 44-171-246-3001 Fax 44-171-246-3003

Investment objective:
The fund seeks to provide investors with both income and capital appreciation by investing in Taiwanese securities. The fund is not authorised in Hong Kong and is not available to Hong Kong residents. The base currency of this fund is US dollars.

Umbrella fund: Thornton Taiwan Fund Limited
Launch date: 01/08/91 **Domicile:** Cayman Islands
Currency: USD **Structure:** Open ended, Investment Company
Portfolio manager: Diahann Brown
Manager of Thornton \new Tiger Selections Fund- China joining Thornton in 1992; previously with Robert Fleming Asset Management and started managing Asian funds in 1989; specialising in emerging markets.
Purchase: Direct
Minimum investment: 51,000 USD
Custodian: The Bank of Bermuda (Far East) Ltd
Listed: Hong Kong **Dealings:** Weekly
Fund Sedol I.D.: 688927 **Published:** IHT/FT/SC/HKEJ
Fees **Annual fee:** 1.50% **Performance fee:** None
Front end load: 5.00% **Redemption fee:** 0.50%
Switching fee: 2.00%

Contact: Customer Services Department

Performance:

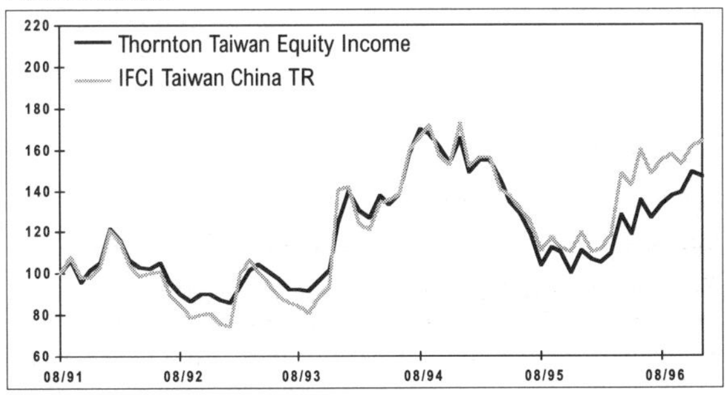

Top holdings:

Cathay Construction	n/s
Cathay Life Ins	n/s
Chang Hwa Bank	n/s
China Development	n/s
China Trust	n/s
Far East Department Stores	n/s
ICBC Bank	n/s
Kindom Construction	n/s
Taichung Machinery	n/s
UTD World C Comm Bank	n/s

TOTAL RETURNS %

3 months 1997	1996	1995	1994	3 years	5 years
23.07	32.05	-32.91	32.82	17.67	39.82

STATISTICS

Assets ($mil)	Current yield	Volatility	Risk return	Micropal Star Rating
5.75	—	7.41	2	✪✪✪✪

Turkish Growth Fund

329/350

Alliance Capital Mgmt L.P.
35 Boulevard Prince Henri, L-1724 Luxembourg
Tel 352-22-66-93 Fax 352-22-68-93

Investment objective:
This fund seeks long-term capital appreciation by investing principally in a portfolio of equity and/or equity related securities of Turkish companies which are traded on the Istanbul Stock Exchange or any other over-the-counter exchanges in Turkey. The base currency of this fund in US dollars.

Umbrella fund: This is a singular fund.

Launch date: 28/02/94 **Domicile:** Luxembourg [UCITS]

Currency: USD **Structure:** Close ended, Mutual Fund

Portfolio manager: David L. Edgerly
Vice President, Emerging Markets Analyst; BA- Brown U and MBA in finance- New York U; previously managed a Fidelity affiliated UK unit trust; 13 years investment experience; 5 years with Alliance.

Purchase: Direct

Minimum investment: None

Custodian: Brown Brothers Harriman

Listed: Luxembourg **Dealings:** N/A

Fund Sedol I.D.: 301813 **Published:** FT

Fees **Annual fee:** 1.25% **Performance fee:** None
Front end load: None **Redemption fee:** None
Switching fee: None

Contact: Customer Services Department

Performance:

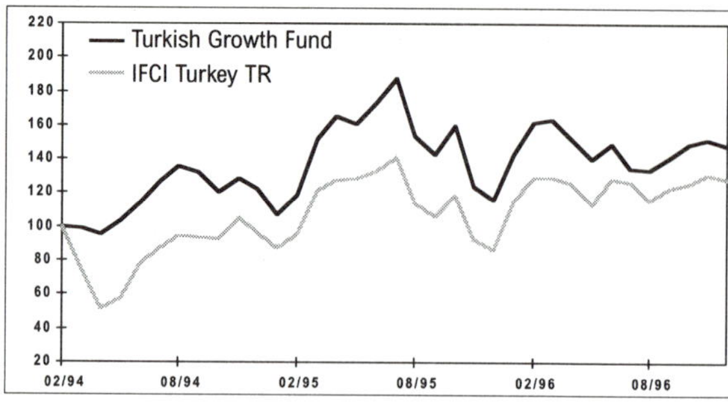

Top holdings:

Arcelik	3.9%
Eczacibasi ILAC	3.7%
Izmir Demir Celik	4.2%
Turkiye is Bankasi	4.3%
Yapi Ve Kredi Bankasi A.S	3.6%

TOTAL RETURNS %

3 months 1997	1996	1995	1994	3 years	5 years
20.51	27.54	-4.68	N.A.	N.A.	N.A.

STATISTICS

Assets ($mil)	Current yield	Volatility	Risk return	Micropal Star Rating
69.70	—	N.A.	—	———

UBAM US Equity

219/350

UBAM International Services (Lux)
11 Rue Aldringen, L-2960 Luxembourg
Tel 352-46-81-91 Fax 352-46-54-52

Investment objective:
The sub-fund seeks capital appreciation by a 'Top-down' approach for individual stock selection and economic sectors. The asset allocation among various US sectors is based on macro-economic forecasts and interest rates outlook. The selection of individual assets relies on fundamental analysis. The use of derivatives is permitted only for hedging purposes.

Umbrella fund: UBAM SICAV

Launch date: 01/12/89 **Domicile:** Luxembourg

Currency: USD **Structure:** Open ended, SICAV

Portfolio manager: Alliance Capital Management
Manager of UBAM-US Equity commenced July 1995; Minneapolis based investment company, founded in 1978 and is a part of the Alliance Group.

Purchase: Direct

Minimum investment: 1 Share

Custodian: Kredietbank S.A.(Luxembourg)

Listed: Luxembourg **Dealings:** Weekly

Fund Sedol I.D.: 301420 **Published:** FT/IHT/JG/NZZ

Fees **Annual fee:** 1.50% **Performance fee:** None
Front end load: 5.75% **Redemption fee:** 0.50%
Switching fee: 1.00%

Contact: Claudy Toussaint

Performance:

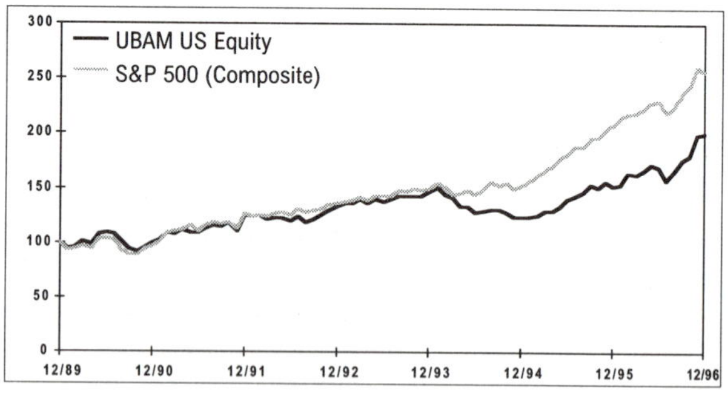

Top holdings:

Cisco System Inc	4.4%
Federal National	4.9%
Home Depot	3.2%
Intel Corp.	7.3%
MBNA Corp	3.6%
Merck & Co. Inc.	4.7%
Pepsico Inc	3.4%
Philip Morris	6.8%
UAL Corp	3.3%
Walt Disney Co	4.0%

TOTAL RETURNS %

3 months 1997	1996	1995	1994	3 years	5 years
-1.22	31.60	22.76	-15.02	37.30	59.90

STATISTICS

Assets ($mil)	Current yield	Volatility	Risk return	Micropal Star Rating
23.95	—	3.72	1	✪

UBS (Lux) Bond Invest ITL
326/350

UBS Investment Funds
Bahnhofstrasse 45, Zurich, CH-8021, Switzerland
Tel 41-1-235-36-36 Fax 41-1-234-93-20
http://www. ubs.com

Investment objective:
The sub-fund aims for high regular income with due consideration to capital security and liquidity of assets in Italian bonds. The sector allocations of the portfolio are 66.3%-government and public sector and 37.7%-international organisations.

Umbrella fund: UBS(Lux) Bond Invest
Launch date: 01/05/93 **Domicile:** Luxembourg [UCITS]
Currency: ITL **Structure:** Open ended, FCP
Portfolio manager: Jung Lutz
Manager of UBS (Lux) Bond Invest-ITL.

Purchase: Direct, Financial Advisor
Minimum investment: 1 Unit
Custodian: UBS(Luxembourg) S.A.
Listed: Luxembourg **Dealings:** Daily
Fund Sedol I.D.: 301654 **Published:** IHT/NZZ/IN
Fees **Annual fee:** None **Performance fee:** None
Front end load: 1.00% **Redemption fee:** None
Switching fee: None

Contact: Fund Hotline
Performance:

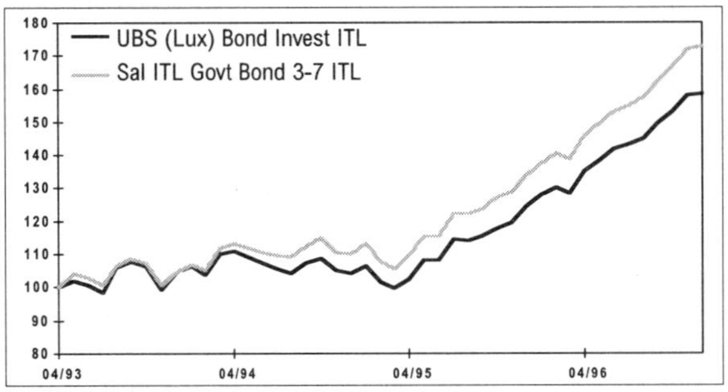

Top holdings:

Bonds Maturity 1-3 years	22.8%
Bonds Maturity 3-5 years	39.8%
Bonds Maturity 5-7 years	13.6%
Bonds Maturity 7-10 years	11.8%
Bonds Maturity over ten years	12.0%

TOTAL RETURNS %

3 months 1997	1996	1995	1994	3 years	5 years
-9.93	27.67	19.10	-0.39	51.47	N.A.

STATISTICS

Assets ($mil)	Current yield	Volatility	Risk return	Micropal Star Rating
84.20	—	2.59	3	✪✪✪✪

Unifund Ltd Class A
247/350

Unibanco Asset Managment
Av das Nacoes Unidas 1255/21, Brooklin Novo, Sao Paulo, SP-04578-903, Brazil
Tel 55-11-3043-7605 Fax 55-11-3043-7608

Investment objective:
The fund seeks capital appreciation with the objective of aggressive trading. The fund invests primarily in Brazil Class"A" shares and may invest in futures contracts and options. At present the currency exposure of the portfolio is 50% US dollars and 50% Brazil reals.

Umbrella fund: Unifund
Launch date: 21/02/94 **Domicile:** Cayman Islands
Currency: USD **Structure:** Open ended, Investment Company
Portfolio manager: Ulysses Duniz and Ronalto Patch
Managers of Unifund Ltd Class A" commenced November 1995.

Purchase: Primary Dealer
Minimum investment: 50,000 USD
Custodian: Unibanco
Listed: None **Dealings:** Daily
Fund Sedol I.D.: 305474 **Published:** MP/FT/LP
Fees **Annual fee:** 1.50% **Performance fee:** None
Front end load: Up to 5.00% **Redemption fee:** None
Switching fee: None

Contact: Laurie Rezende
Performance:

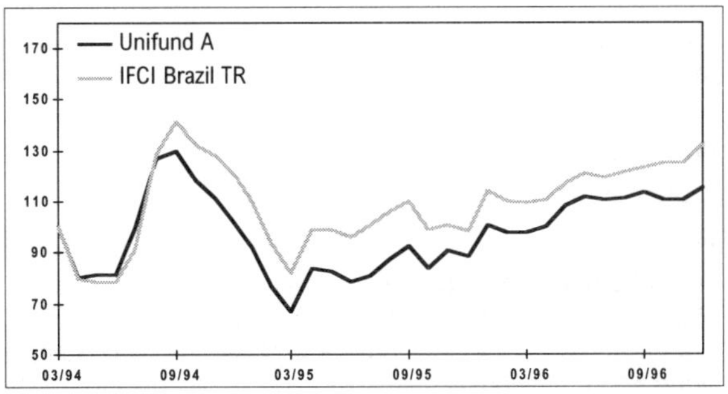

Top holdings: Brazil 100.0%

TOTAL RETURNS %

3 months 1997	1996	1995	1994	3 years	5 years
26.43	30.53	-13.35	N.A.	N.A.	N.A.

STATISTICS

Assets ($mil)	Current yield	Volatility	Risk return	Micropal Star Rating
12.55	—	N.A.	—	———

US GSF Prec Metal & Natural Resources

3/350

US Advisors (Guernsey) Ltd
Butterfield House, The Grange, St. Peters Port,
GY1 3NQ, Guernsey
Tel 44-1481-720-321 Fax 44-1481-716-117

Investment objective:
The sub-fund seeks capital appreciation by investing primarily in shares of companies that mine gold and precious metals world-wide. The sub-fund also invests a portion of its assets in gold bullion. The country allocations of the portfolio are as follows: Canada (45.8%); Mexico (12.2%); Russia (7.9%); China (6.9%); and Khazakstan (5.7%).

Umbrella fund: U.S. Global Strategies Fund Ltd

Launch date: 02/09/93 **Domicile:** Guernsey

Currency: USD **Structure:** Open ended, Investment Company

Portfolio manager: Victor Flores CFA
Manager of the fund commenced February 1994 and CIO of United Services Advisors, Inc; BSc, geological sciences and MA, energy/mineral resources management- U Texas; previously Portfolio Manager- US Global Resource Fund.

Purchase: Direct, Financial Advisor

Minimum investment: 25,000 USD

Custodian: Bank of Butterfield Intl (Guernsey) Ltd

Listed: None **Dealings:** Daily

Fund Sedol I.D.: 91971 **Published:** FT/IHT

Fees **Annual fee:** 2.00% **Performance fee:** 20.00%
Front end load: 4.00% **Redemption fee:** None
Switching fee: None

Contact: Sue Queripel

Performance:

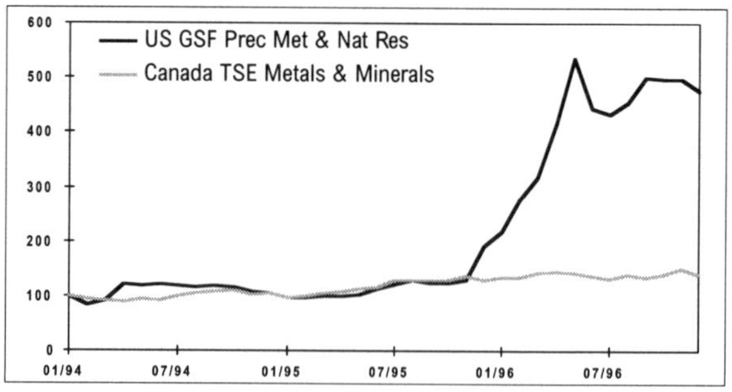

Top holdings:

Holding	%
Amarc Resources	5.5%
Andoraq Resources	4.6%
Ausrailia/ Indian Resources	3.4%
Farallon Resources	5.5%
Newfoundland Cap Corp	4.7%
Norcal Resources	2.7%
Romarco Resources	3.7%
Santa Catalina Mining	3.3%
Vedcon Gold	3.3%

TOTAL RETURNS %

3 months 1997	1996	1995	1994	3 years	5 years
1.61	147.86	84.95	60.25	634.62	N.A.

STATISTICS

Assets ($mil)	Current yield	Volatility	Risk return	Micropal Star Rating
8.46	—	15.59	5	✪✪✪✪✪

Value Partners A Fund

159/350

Value Partners Ltd
5 Floor Devon House, 979 King's Road, Quarry Bay, Hong Kong
Tel 852-2880-9263 Fax 852-2564-8487
E mail vpl@hk.linkage.net

Investment objective:
The fund seeks capital appreciation through a value and growth driven style with bottom-up approach and value investing in Asian securities. Concentrating on out-of-favour stocks and shares of medium to small-sized companies which offer a wide margin of safety because they are under researched and over looked by the market.

Umbrella fund: This is a singular fund.

Launch date: 01/04/93 **Domicile:** Cayman Islands

Currency: USD **Structure:** Open ended, Unit Trust

Portfolio manager: Cheah Cheng Hye
Manager of the fund commenced April 1993 and MD and CIO of Value Partners Ltd; Graduate, law- Columbia U; previously with Morgan Grenfell's proprietary trading in Hong Kong; previously the banking and finance editor of the Asia Wall Street Journal.

Purchase: Direct, Financial Advisor

Minimum investment: 100,000 USD

Custodian: The Bank of Bermuda Ltd (HK)

Listed: Dublin **Dealings:** Weekly

Fund Sedol I.D.: 92923 **Published:** FT/AW/HKEJ/HKET

Fees **Annual fee:** 0.75% **Performance fee:** 15.00%
Front end load: 1.00% **Redemption fee:** 1.50%
Switching fee: None

Contact: Winnie Sze

Performance:

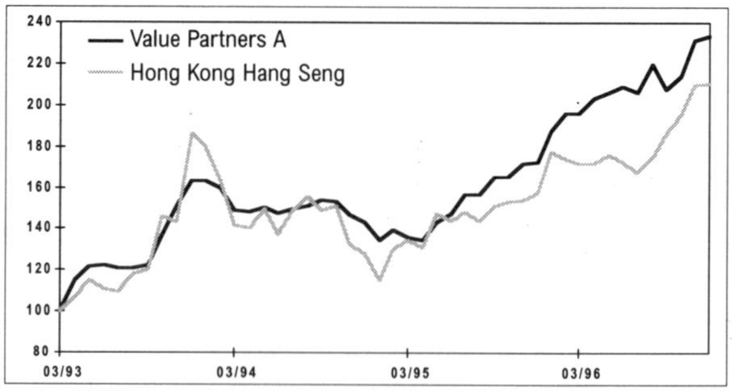

Top holdings:

Holding	%
Fountainslet	9.2%
K-wan	3.7%
Kumagai Gumi (KH)	6.4%
La Sanda	6.3%
Lin Chong Hing Investment	3.9%
Lin Hong Kong Bank	5.5%
TSL Fewardling	3.4%
Vtech	7.6%
Won Kee	7.0%

TOTAL RETURNS %

3 months 1997	1996	1995	1994	3 years	5 years
-0.34	35.52	20.36	-11.97	43.59	N.A.

STATISTICS

Assets ($mil)	Current yield	Volatility	Risk return	Micropal Star Rating
70.78	—	3.73	5	✪✪✪✪

Vista Equity Sub Fund
285/350

Banco Boavista S.A.
Praca Pio X 118, 10th Floor, Centro, Rio de Janeiro, Brazil
Tel 55-21-211-2150 Fax 55-21-233-9137
http://www. boavista.com.br

Investment objective:
The sub-fund seeks long-term capital appreciation through investing primarily in equity securities of Brazilian publicly traded companies. The fund is denominated in US dollars.

Contact: Veronica Medeiros Nieckele

Performance:

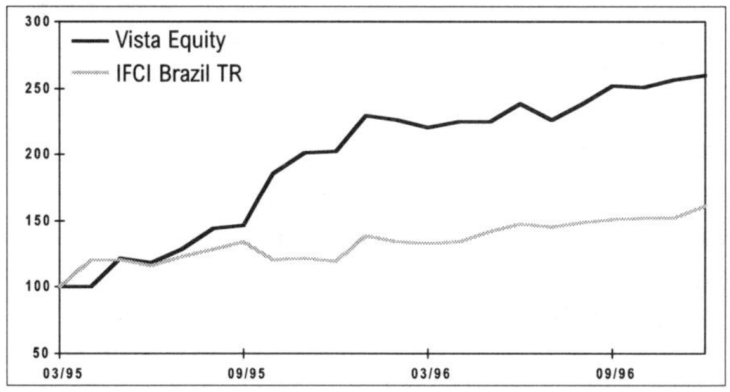

Top holdings:

Consumer Goods	10.0%
Energy	60.0%
Industrial	20.0%
Technology	10.0%

Umbrella fund: Vistafund
Launch date: 20/03/95 **Domicile:** Cayman Islands
Currency: USD **Structure:** Open ended, Investment Fund
Portfolio manager: Carlos Alberto Villapuerte Oyola
Manager of Vista Equity Sub-Fund commenced March 1995 and currently Director of the international investments division; previously in charge of the administration of local funds; a nine year veteran of Banco Boavista.
Purchase: Financial Advisor, Private Banks
Minimum investment: 20,000 USD
Custodian: Boavista Banking Limited
Listed: None **Dealings:** Daily
Fund Sedol I.D.: 207338 **Published:** FT
Fees **Annual fee:** 1.75% **Performance fee:** 20.00%
Front end load: None **Redemption fee:** None
Switching fee: None

TOTAL RETURNS %

3 months 1997	1996	1995	1994	3 years	5 years
24.21	28.80	N.A.	N.A.	N.A.	N.A.

STATISTICS

Assets ($mil)	Current yield	Volatility	Risk return	Micropal Star Rating
20.20	—	N.A.	—	———

Vista Fixed Balanced Sub Fund
146/350

Banco Boavista S.A.
Praco Pio X 118, 10th Floor, Centro, Rio de Janeiro, Brazil
Tel 55-21-211-2150 Fax 55-21-233-9131
http://www. boavista.com.br

Investment objective:
The sub-fund seeks capital appreciation by investing principally in sovereign debt and fixed income instruments of Brazilian issuers traded outside Brazil. The fund is denominated in US dollars.

Contact: Veronica Medeiros Nieckele

Performance:

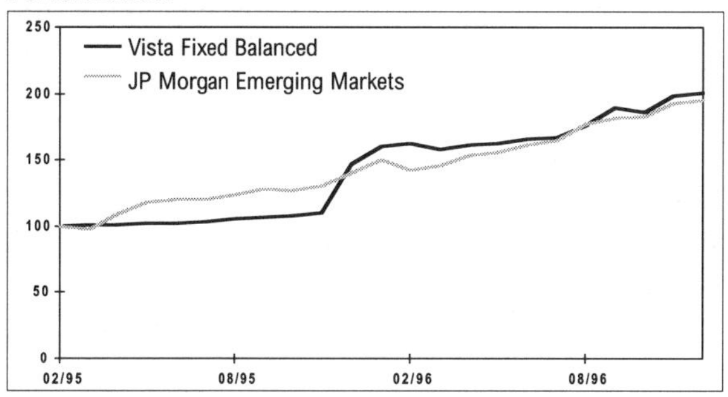

Top holdings:

Bond	70.0%
Cash/MM	30.0%

Umbrella fund: Vistafund
Launch date: 02/02/95 **Domicile:** Cayman Islands
Currency: USD **Structure:** Open ended, Investment Fund
Portfolio manager: Carlos Alberto Villapuerte Oyola
Manager of Fixed Balanced Sub-Fund and currently Director of the international investments division; previously in charge of the administration of local funds; a nine year veteran of Banco Boavista.
Purchase: Financial Advisor, Private Banks
Minimum investment: 20,000 USD
Custodian: Boavista Banking Limited
Listed: None **Dealings:** Daily
Fund Sedol I.D.: 207337 **Published:** FT
Fees **Annual fee:** 1.50% **Performance fee:** 15.00%
Front end load: None **Redemption fee:** None
Switching fee: None

TOTAL RETURNS %

3 months 1997	1996	1995	1994	3 years	5 years
4.25	36.32	N.A.	N.A.	N.A.	N.A.

STATISTICS

Assets ($mil)	Current yield	Volatility	Risk return	Micropal Star Rating
3.80	—	N.A.	—	———

VKAC Navigator Emerg. Markets Fixed Inc Portf

259/350

Van Kampen American Capital Investment Advisory Corp
One Parkview Plaza, Oakbrook Terrace, Illinois, IL 60181, United States
Tel 1-630-684-6000 Fax 1-630-684-6587

Investment objective:
The Fixed Income sub-fund seeks primarily to provide a high level of current income from a portfolio of debt securities issued by public or private entities located in emerging market countries, with a secondary objective of capital appreciation. The top country allocations for the portfolio include: Brazil (15.2%); Ecuador (11.2%); Venezuela (1.3%); and Argentina (5.0%).

Umbrella fund: Van Kampen American Capital Navigator Fund
Launch date: 27/06/95 **Domicile:** Luxembourg
Currency: USD **Structure:** Open ended, SICAV
Portfolio manager: Paul Ghaffari
Manager of Van Kampen American Capital Navigator Emerging Markets Fixed Income Portfolio commenced July 1996; BA, international relations- Pamana College and MS foreign studies- Georgetown U.
Purchase: Direct, Financial Advisor
Minimum investment: 5,000 USD
Custodian: State Street Bank Luxembourg
Listed: None **Dealings:** Daily
Fund Sedol I.D.: 305406 **Published:** FT/IHT/SC
Fees **Annual fee:** 1.50% **Performance fee:** None
Front end load: 6.25% **Redemption fee:** None
Switching fee: None

Contact: Teresa Daggett
Performance:

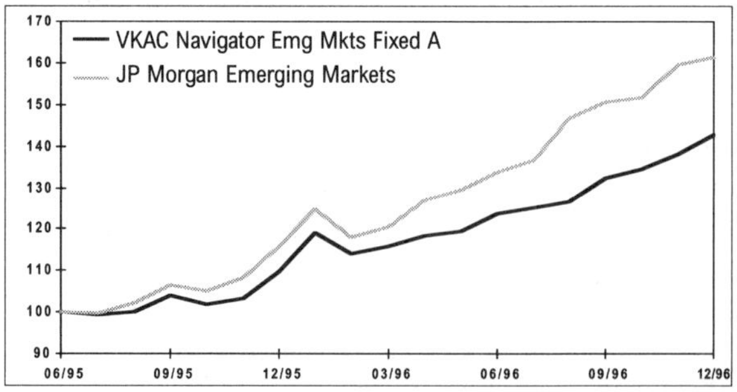

Top holdings:

Holding	%
Argentina (Rep of)	4.0%
BCO Central Costa	3.5%
Brazil (Fed Rep of)	10.0%
Bulgaria (Nat Rep)	4.4%
Ecuador (Rep of)	4.3%
Ecuador (Rep of)	4.0%
Lebanon (Rep of)	3.2%
Mexico (UTD MEX ST)	4.6%
Russia Interest Arrears	4.2%
Venezuela (Rep of)	10.3%

TOTAL RETURNS %

3 months 1997	1996	1995	1994	3 years	5 years
2.94	30.08	N.A.	N.A.	N.A.	N.A.

STATISTICS

Assets ($mil)	Current yield	Volatility	Risk return	Micropal Star Rating
4.16	8.64	N.A.	—	———

Von Ernst GP UK Smaller Cos Equity

117/350

Bank Von Ernst GP
PO Box 5325, Berne, CH-3001, Switzerland
Tel 41-31-329-1111 Fax 41-31-311-6391

Investment objective:
The sub-fund seeks capital growth by investing in the equities of small companies in the UK. The top sector allocations of the portfolio are the following: general manufacturing (43.4%); services (36.0%); finance (6.8%); and consumer goods (6.3%).

Umbrella fund: Von Ernst Globel Porte
Launch date: 01/12/89 **Domicile:** Luxembourg [UCITS]
Currency: GBP **Structure:** Open ended, SICAV
Portfolio manager: Board of Directors of the fund
Manager of Von Ernst GP UK Small Companies Equity.

Purchase: Direct, Financial Advisor
Minimum investment: 5,000 GBP
Custodian: Kredietbank Luxembourg
Listed: Luxembourg/Berne **Dealings:** Daily
Fund Sedol I.D.: 442690 **Published:** FT/NZZ
Fees **Annual fee:** 1.00% **Performance fee:** None
Front end load: 5.00% **Redemption fee:** None
Switching fee: None

Contact: George Hemmer
Performance:

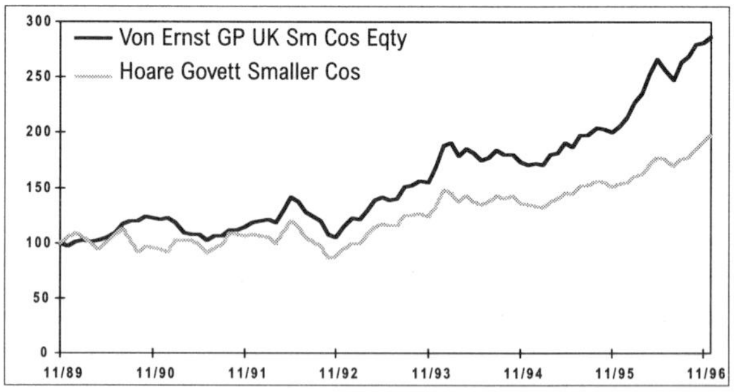

Top holdings:

Holding	%
Alexon Group Plc	2.8%
API Group	2.2%
Bellway Plc	24.5%
Charles Baynes	2.1%
Denby Group	2.2%
Mayflower Corp	2.4%
More Group	2.4%
Regent Inns Plc	2.7%
Transtec Plc	2.4%
Westbury	2.3%

TOTAL RETURNS %

3 months 1997	1996	1995	1994	3 years	5 years
-0.03	39.33	20.16	0.65	68.50	141.12

STATISTICS

Assets ($mil)	Current yield	Volatility	Risk return	Micropal Star Rating
18.47	—	3.75	4	✪✪✪✪

Vontobel Fund Eastern European Equity
11/350

Bank J. Vontobel
European Bank and Business Centre, 6D Route De Treves,
L-2633 Luxembourg
Tel 352-34-66-22-240 Fax 352-34-65-55
http://www. vontobel.ch

Contact: Customer Service Department

Investment objective:
The sub-fund aims to achieve the highest possible capital growth from investment in Eastern European companies whilst respecting the principle of risk diversification. The portfolio country allocation is mainly divided into the following: Hungary (42.3%); Poland (28.1%); Russia (12.1%); Czech Rep (6.8%); and Croatia Rep (4.3%).

Umbrella fund: Vontobel Fund

Launch date: 22/08/94 **Domicile:** Luxembourg

Currency: DEM **Structure:** Open ended, SICAV

Portfolio manager: Arpad Pongracz
Manager of Vontobel Fund Eastern European Equity commenced August 1994.

Performance:

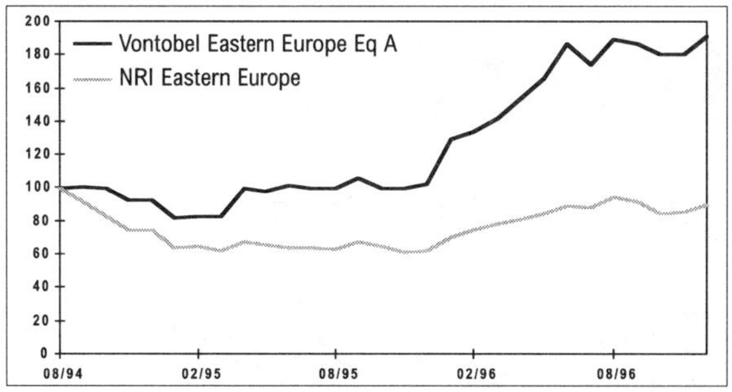

Purchase: Direct, Bank Vontobel Zurich – Schweizer Verband der Raiffeisenbanken CH9001

Minimum investment: 5,000 CHF

Custodian: Morgan Stanley Bank Luxembourg S.A.

Listed: Luxembourg **Dealings:** Daily

Fund Sedol I.D.: 301602 **Published:** NZZ/FW/BZ/HB/DS/CH/MF

Fees **Annual fee:** 1.25% **Performance fee:** None
Front end load: None **Redemption fee:** Up to 5.00%
Switching fee: None

Top holdings:

Holding	%
Danubius Hotels	4.2%
Egis G Yes	4.4%
Graboplast Textiles	4.0%
Magyar Olaj Es Gaz	3.6%
Pannonplast	4.8%
Pliva	4.2%
Richter Gedeon Vegyes	4.3%
Scala (Overseas)	3.8%
Tiszai Vegyi Kombinat RT	3.8%
WBK	3.7%

TOTAL RETURNS %

3 months 1997	1996	1995	1994	3 years	5 years
15.68	87.77	10.52	N.A.	N.A.	N.A.

STATISTICS

Assets ($mil)	Current yield	Volatility	Risk return	Micropal Star Rating
168.27	—	N.A.	—	——

Willerfunds-Willer Latinamerica
101/350

Willerfunds Management Co.
11 Rue Aldringen, L-1118 Luxembourg
Tel 352-021-264-876 Fax 352-021-269-562
http://www. willerfunds.com
E mail wilfunds@wilfunds.ch

Contact: Massimo Catemario Di Quadri

Investment objective:
The sub-fund seeks capital growth by investing mainly in shares and international certificates of companies listed in the finance markets of South America and Central America. It may also invest in straight and convertible bonds, denominated in any currency, issued or guaranteed by the above countries, their public entities or companies incorporated.

Umbrella fund: Willerfunds

Launch date: 01/03/95 **Domicile:** Luxembourg [UCITS]

Currency: USD **Structure:** Open ended, Unit Trust

Portfolio manager: Willerfund Management Co.
Manager of the Willerfunds-Willer Latinamerica.

Performance:

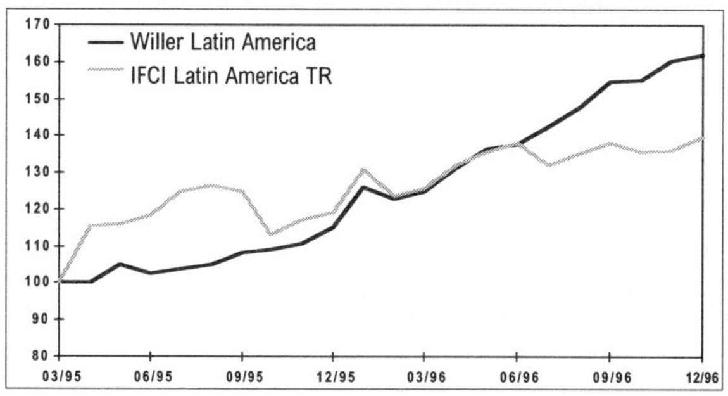

Purchase: Financial Advisor

Minimum investment: 1,000 USD

Custodian: Kredietbank SA (Luxembourg)

Listed: Luxembourg **Dealings:** Weekly

Fund Sedol I.D.: 301169 **Published:** IHT/CS/IS/IG

Fees **Annual fee:** 2.00% **Performance fee:** None
Front end load: 0.50% **Redemption fee:** 0.50%
Switching fee: 1.00%

Top holdings:

Holding	%
Argentine SER L/05	8.1%
Argentine SER L/23	4.0%
Brazil (W.I.) C Bond/14	10.8%
Brazil SER L /09	9.2%
Ceval Alimentos SA	3.5%
Ecuador IEB/04	7.1%
Ecuadorian 25.4.97/Zero	3.0%
Panama FRN/02	5.1%
Venezuela 6.75%/20	4.7%
Venezuela Sie DL/07	2.7%

TOTAL RETURNS %

3 months 1997	1996	1995	1994	3 years	5 years
4.81	40.87	N.A.	N.A.	N.A.	N.A.

STATISTICS

Assets ($mil)	Current yield	Volatility	Risk return	Micropal Star Rating
15.61	—	N.A.	—	——

PART 4

Offshore Fund Performance Tables and Statistics

Describing a typical offshore fund is like trying to describe a typical person. There is no such thing. Offshore funds come in every shape and size, have differing objectives and go about achieving these in diverse and numerous ways.

What most offshore investors want to know is, What is the best offshore fund? Just because a particular fund has achieved a better return than another does not mean it is a better fund in which to invest. It could be that the better performing fund manager took more risks; that the better performing fund manager invested heavily in a specialist area of investment, for example, smaller companies based in Latin America. It would hardly be surprising if such a fund beat one that invested mainly in ultra-safe US Treasury Bills. Offshore fund investors need guidance as to how performances are achieved.

If offshore funds are all so different, how can you compare them? How do you find out which is the best? In essence, you give up on the idea of the "best fund" and try to find the best from among those that could reasonably be considered to be peers, that is, those funds which invest in similar types of investment.

Micropal segregates all offshore funds into 193 sectors, and within each sector it becomes possible to compare "near-like" funds. For example, the United Kingdom equities sector lists all those funds that invest at least 70 per cent of their assets in shares listed on the UK stock market. While all UK equity fund managers may approach their job differently, it is reasonable to suggest that the fund that produces the highest returns over a reasonably long investment period has been the best fund in that sector.

For the purposes of such comparisons, offshore funds have been divided in two ways. Firstly, they are divided by the type of asset invested in. This breaks down into eight broad categories: equities, fixed interest stocks (bonds) including laufzeitfonds, money markets, convertible bonds, short-term bonds, warrants, specialist funds and mixed funds. Secondly, most of these categories have been broken down further with a geographical split. For example, the large equities category is broken down into 61 geographic areas; some are regions, such as Europe or the Far East and the Pacific, while others cover a single country, be that a large market like Japan or a small one like Columbia.

Some funds remain difficult to compare, even within these sectors. Readers should be very wary of a fund which dramatically outperforms or underperforms the other funds in its sector. It could be that the fund manager has a rather different investment philosophy to most other fund managers in the sector. This underlines the importance of offshore fund investors checking with the promoters of any particular fund to establish exactly what the fund investment philosophy is. For there may be little point in investing in last year's top performer if it turns out that the manager achieved success by taking some unacceptable risks (which could, none the less, be the philosophy of the fund). Likewise, some funds may not be aimed at out-and-out performance. Some will put an emphasis on income from dividends, from a safety-first approach, or they will attempt to produce a performance which replicates a relevant investment index.

The offshore performance statistics provided are the 1–, 3–, 5– and 10–year performance gross income returns (US dollar-converted terms) to the end of 1996. In addition the three-month performance figures for the first quarter of 1997 are listed in the tables. The volatility and risk return ratio based on the three-year performance returns is also featured with the popular Micropal Star Rating™.

(For more information on how to review fund performance statistics see Chapter 9: Analysing Offshore Fund Performance in Part 1.)

OFFSHORE FUND SECTOR INDEX

Key to Offshore Fund tables

1 Global Equity

Funds investing in excess of 70% in Global equities or related instruments. Such funds may have an objective of capital and/or income growth, or to track a specified index or perform inversely to a given index. Funds in this category may leverage or gear by a maximum of 20% of total assets.

		2 CCY	Fund Size ($mil) 3	4 Fund Name	5 Manager Code	6 Fund Start Date	7 Domicile Code	8 3 Mths 97 % Chg	3 Mths 97 Rank	1 Year % Chg	1 Year Rank	Micropal Star Rating 3 Years 9 Volatility	3 Years % Chg	3 Years Rank	10 Rating	11 Risk Return Rating	5 Years % Chg	5 Years Rank	10 Years % Chg	10 Years Rank
12			**80.05**	**Mean/Count**				**1.03**		**12.04**	**302**	**2.98**	**23.18**	**216**		**1**	**56.17**	**155**	**144.56**	**49**
	▲	USD	4.46	Abtrust Atlas Global Capital	A002	31/03/88	LUX	1.31	132	12.98	128	2.91	17.98	144	✪✪	1	48.29	94	N.A.	
		USD	8.43	Abtrust International Equity	A003	30/07/82	GU	4.61	39	19.76	34	2.88	26.07	100	✪✪✪	2	66.63	46	116.14	31
		USD	0.89	Abtrust World Growth	A003	31/07/87	GU	3.79	54	-2.22	293	4.47	-17.70	210	✪		24.80	136	N.A.	
		GBP	4.79	Accelerated Gth Portfolio A	C020	14/04/95	IRL	-0.17	213	14.31	102	N.A.	N.A.				N.A.		N.A.	
		USD	21.86	ACMGI Global Growth Trends AX	A005	31/10/91	LUX	-2.94	306	14.43	101	4.02	72.34	3	✪✪✪✪✪	5	125.12	4	N.A.	
		USD	22.43	ACMGI Intl Health Care Ptf AX	A005	29/07/83	LUX	3.73	59	2.18	277	4.16	70.40	5	✪✪✪✪✪	5	50.47	86	473.20	1
		USD	9.60	ACMGI Intl Privatn Portf A	A005	30/06/94	LUX	6.29	23	17.47	58	N.A.	N.A.				N.A.		N.A.	
	▲	USD	21.64	AEB Worldfolio 7 Global Eq	A009	31/12/85	LUX	-0.54	236	11.86	158	2.72	37.93	33	✪✪✪✪✪	4	43.50	106	95.85	37
		BEF	34.35	AGAM Strategy Inter Equities C	A013	28/04/95	LUX	0.02	203	13.42	120	N.A.	N.A.				N.A.		N.A.	
	▲	IEP	5.15	AIB Offs Inst Intl Equity Mgd	A016	31/10/89	GU	0.41	179	13.14	124	2.44	30.93	66	✪✪✪✪	3	46.37	100	N.A.	
	▲	IEP	2.67	AIB Offs Intl Equity Mgd	A016	31/10/89	GU	-0.05	209	14.02	112	2.47	33.83	48	✪✪✪✪	4	49.63	88	N.A.	
12	▲	GBP	9.42	AIB Offs Stlg Intl Equity Mgd	A016	29/05/81	GU	2.93	77	14	113	2.48	36.19	36	✪✪✪✪	4	49.64	87	64.36	45
		USD	67.40	AIS Worldwide	O008	31/05/95	CA	4.46	45	13.35	122	N.A.	N.A.				N.A.		N.A.	
		DEM	80.37	Aktien Global Fonds	T011	31/12/93	LUX	4.79	36	18.04	52	2.53	55.39	9	✪✪✪✪✪	5	N.A.		N.A.	
13	●	USD	0	Albany Intl Global Dllr	A018	31/03/87	IOM	-0.94	256	14.13	109	2.81	25.87	102	✪✪✪	2	57.68	63	N.A.	

1 Asset sector and definition.

2 Currency denomiation of the fund. The code used for the currencies is explained in Appendix 1.*

3 Fund size in US dollar millions as of December 31, 1996 or at last fiscal period. Some funds do not disclose their size and are marked N.S. (not supplied).

4 The funds are listed in alphabetical order under their sector headings. Some fund names have been abbreviated to 29 characters.*

5 See Part 5: Management Directory for listing of fund manager name and contact details.

6 Date the fund was launched or commenced operations.

7 The location where the funds are principally registered.

8 Two columns are shown under each time period. The left column shows the result of funds invested over the time period shown, with price changes analysed on an offer-to-offer price (or change in net asset value) basis, with gross income reinvested. The right column shows the fund's particular ranking against other funds within the sector – with 1 being the top performing fund in the sector over the time shown.

9 Measurement of the tendency of a fund to rise or fall in value relative to the market. Volatility ratings are calculated after 3 years of market pricing.

10 Micropal Star Rating™ : the more stars a fund has the greater its past ability to consistently outperform its sector peers.

11 Risk Return Ratio rates a fund's risk-adjusted performance where rated funds can receive a ranking from one to five, five being best.

12 The bold figures at the top of each table show the average performance of the funds in the sector over the time period, and the number of funds in the sector.

13 Triangle indicates funds that have been approved for sale by the SIB in the UK.

14 Circle indicates insurance linked investment fund.

**See Appendix 1 for abbreviations*

CONVERTIBLE BOND FUNDS

Generally, a convertible bond or debenture is an unsecured loan of a corporation which may be exchanged for ordinary shares in the company, in most cases at the discretion of the holder of the bond. As an investment convertible bond funds tend to work in part like an equity and in part like a bond. When the share price of the company in question rises above the conversion price of the bond, the price of the bond tends to move in line with the price of the underlying shares. But should the share price be below that of the conversion price, then, as they pay interest and have a limited life, convertible bond funds act more like bonds. All this tends to make their performance over time lie somewhere between that of equities and fixed interest stocks (bonds).

This has great appeal for investors looking for investment growth while being unwilling to take on too much risk. A portfolio of convertible bonds gives an investor a stake in a rising stock market – as convertible bond prices go in tandem with share prices – while allowing protection from the bad times, when the bonds continue to pay out interest.

Convertible bonds are not a big area for offshore investment, indeed, only 33 such funds are listed. The majority of convertible bond funds are invested globally, although there are area specific funds, such as those investing mainly in the convertible bond markets of Japan, the Far East, the UK and Switzerland.

The Micropal definition of a fund in one of its convertible bond sectors is that it should have at least 70 per cent of its assets in convertible bonds and preference shares. Preference shares are fixed income shares whose holders have the right to receive dividends before ordinary shareholders.

As one might suspect, convertible bond funds on the whole produce returns somewhere between those of pure equity funds and pure bond funds. The average dollar-converted annual return over the past five years for the offshore global convertible bond funds has been over 10.5 per cent.

Far East & Pacific Ex Japan Convertible Bonds

Funds investing predominantly (70%) in convertible bonds and preference shares of companies in Far East & Pacific excluding Japan.

	CCY	Fund Size ($mil)	Fund Name	Manager Code	Fund Start Date	Domicile Code	3 Mths 97 % Chg	3 Mths 97 Rank	1 Year % Chg	1 Year Rank	Micropal Star Rating 3 Years Volatility	3 Years % Chg	3 Years Rank	3 Years Rating	Risk Return Rating	5 Years % Chg	5 Years Rank	10 Years % Chg	10 Years Rank
		19.10	**Mean/Count**				**-1.75**	**7**	**10.51**	**5**	**0**	**0**	**0**			**0**	**0**	**0**	**0**
	USD	0.75	ImPac AP Convertible Bond	I005	31/05/96	CA	0.99	1	N.A.		N.A.	N.A.				N.A.		N.A.	
	USD	61	Inc Ptnrs GSF Asian Conv Bond	I006	07/04/95	CA	-3.75	6	18.14	1	N.A.	N.A.				N.A.		N.A.	
▲	USD	9.30	INVESCO PS Asian Conv Bond	I014	28/04/95	LUX	-5.33	7	7.25	5	N.A.	N.A.				N.A.		N.A.	
▲	USD	12.57	Nikko GIUF Asia Convertible	N007	29/07/94	LUX	0.56	2	8.13	3	N.A.	N.A.				N.A.		N.A.	
	USD	28.29	Parworld Asian Convertible B	B037	13/01/95	LUX	-2.77	5	11.16	2	N.A.	N.A.				N.A.		N.A.	
	CHF	N.S.	RMF Convertibles Far East	R008	05/01/96	LUX	-0.51	3	N.A.		N.A.	N.A.				N.A.		N.A.	
▲	USD	2.66	Schroder Intl Sel Asia Conv	S010	21/10/94	LUX	-1.45	4	7.88	4	N.A.	N.A.				N.A.		N.A.	

Global Convertible Bonds

Funds investing predominantly (70%) in Global convertible bonds and preference shares.

	CCY	Fund Size ($mil)	Fund Name	Manager Code	Fund Start Date	Domicile Code	3 Mths 97 % Chg	3 Mths 97 Rank	1 Year % Chg	1 Year Rank	Micropal Star Rating 3 Years Volatility	3 Years % Chg	3 Years Rank	3 Years Rating	Risk Return Rating	5 Years % Chg	5 Years Rank	10 Years % Chg	10 Years Rank
		20.64	**Mean/Count**				**-0.05**	**21**	**6.17**	**22**	**2.33**	**12.63**	**16**			**52.48**	**11**	**99.49**	**2**
	CHF	33.42	Baer Multibond Convert Bond A	J007	29/10/93	LUX	0.94	8	5.31	14	2.29	13.05	9	✪✪		N.A.		N.A.	
	USD	15.58	BAII Interportf Convertible	B003	31/05/93	LUX	5.38	1	6.33	12	2.43	4.87	11	✪✪		N.A.		N.A.	
	DEM	9.88	BBL & MC Fund Convertibles D	B052	24/11/95	LUX	-3.13	19	-6.89	22	N.A.	N.A.				N.A.		N.A.	
	LUF	23.44	BR Fund Convertible	B070	30/06/88	LUX	-3.39	20	1.96	17	2.43	17.45	8	✪✪✪	1	83.33	1	N.A.	
	FRF	2.68	Capital Gestion Convertibles	C009	20/10/95	LUX	-2.81	18	4.65	15	N.A.	N.A.				N.A.		N.A.	
●	ECU	48.88	Credit Lyonnais Convtbl Fd	C062	30/11/90	LUX	4.38	2	18.60	1	1.90	26.19	2	✪✪✪✪	4	60.75	2	N.A.	
	USD	0	Cresvale Managed Convertible	C066	30/09/93	LUX	2.66	4	7.50	11	2.18	-2.44	15	✪		N.A.		N.A.	
▲	USD	38.22	Fleming FF Global Convertible	F020	30/11/88	LUX	1.06	7	9.73	8	2.42	3.21	13	✪		54.22	4	N.A.	
	USD	22.20	GAM Bond US Dollar Spec	G002	29/11/85	IOM	1.56	5	11.92	3	3.28	2.02	14	✪		43.77	10	109.80	1
▲	USD	1.82	Guinness Flight Glbl Conv	G019	30/06/87	GU	0.21	10	11.34	5	2.19	18.43	6	✪✪✪	1	46.23	8	N.A.	
	DEM	56.10	International Conv Expert Cap	F018	30/06/95	LUX	-1.08	14	2.37	16	N.A.	N.A.				N.A.		N.A.	
	USD	4.50	JF Global Convertibles	J004	31/10/88	HK	0.46	9	11.57	4	2.74	-6.57	16	✪		46.76	6	N.A.	
▲	USD	25.26	Lloyds IP Convertible	L016	30/11/90	LUX	-0.38	11	0.06	19	2.97	4.51	12	✪✪		46.36	7	N.A.	
	CHF	61.24	LO Obliflex 29 Convertibles	L019	31/12/93	JER	-4.13	21	-3.85	20	2.75	26.40	1	✪✪✪✪	2	N.A.		N.A.	
	USD	55.10	LO Obliflex R Convertibles	L019	30/04/87	JER	1.56	6	10.24	7	1.71	25.78	3	✪✪✪✪✪	4	60.22	3	N.A.	
	USD	10.36	M.Lynch Convert Securities O	M023	29/08/86	LUX	-0.48	12	8.22	10	1.58	19.76	5	✪✪✪✪	3	45.16	9	89.17	2
	FRF	9.95	MOSAIS Oblig Convtbls Int	C058	31/12/90	LUX	-1.89	15	5.75	13	1.98	23	4	✪✪✪✪	3	46.92	5	N.A.	
	CHF	4.66	Pleiade Intl Convertible Bds	B039	29/10/93	LUX	-2.02	16	-4.70	21	2.57	8.81	10	✪✪		N.A.		N.A.	
	GBP	3.96	Quilter Quad Gl Convertible	Q003	13/01/95	IOM	-0.97	13	10.77	6	N.A.	N.A.				N.A.		N.A.	
	LUF	22.12	Safei Globalise	G022	29/11/91	LUX	N.A.	—	8.45	9	1.93	17.66	7	✪✪✪	2	43.51	11	N.A.	
▲	USD	1.56	Templeton GS Glbl Convertible	T001	30/06/94	LUX	3.26	3	15.03	2	N.A.	N.A.				N.A.		N.A.	
	USD	3.18	The Interallianz Convert Grwth	I010	28/02/95	LUX	-2.22	17	1.47	18	N.A.	N.A.				N.A.		N.A.	

▲ SIB Approved ● Insurance Fund **Values in US Dollars, on an offer to offer price basis with gross income reinvested** Data Source Micropal™

Global Emerging Markets Convertible Bonds

Funds investing predominantly (70%) in convertible bonds and preference shares of companies in Emerging Markets.

		Fund Size		Manager	Fund Start	Domicile	3 Mths 97		1 Year		Micropal Star Rating 3 Years				Risk Return	5 Years		10 Years	
	CCY	($mil)	Fund Name	Code	Date	Code	% Chg	Rank	% Chg	Rank	Volatility	% Chg	Rank	Rating	Rating	% Chg	Rank	% Chg	Rank
		45.17	**Mean/Count**				**2.01**	**1**	**13.24**	**1**	**2.85**	**8.55**	**1**			**0**	**0**	**0**	**0**
	USD	45.17	UBAM Emerging Growth Convert	U010	30/11/93	LUX	2.01	1	13.24	1	2.85	8.55	1	✪✪✪		N.A.		N.A.	

Japan Convertible Bonds

Funds investing predominantly (70%) in Japanese convertible bonds and preference shares.

		Fund Size		Manager	Fund Start	Domicile	3 Mths 97		1 Year		Micropal Star Rating 3 Years				Risk Return	5 Years		10 Years	
	CCY	($mil)	Fund Name	Code	Date	Code	% Chg	Rank	% Chg	Rank	Volatility	% Chg	Rank	Rating	Rating	% Chg	Rank	% Chg	Rank
		7.33	**Mean/Count**				**-5.55**	**4**	**-14.88**	**3**	**3.67**	**3.36**	**3**			**28.91**	**2**	**72.15**	**1**
▲	CHF	9.37	Coutts GF Japanese Convertible	C052	29/06/90	IRL	-6.71	3	-13.14	1	3.73	15.59	1	✪✪✪✪		42.56	1	N.A.	
	GBP	8.12	INVESCO Japan Inc & Gth	I013	08/07/83	JER	-4.67	2	-14.55	2	3.27	-6.49	3	✪✪		15.25	2	72.15	1
	CHF	N.S.	RMF Convertibles Japan	R008	16/02/96	LUX	-2.77	1	N.A.		N.A.	N.A.				N.A.		N.A.	
▲	CHF	4.49	Schroder Intl Sel Japan Conv	S010	31/07/92	LUX	-8.06	4	-16.94	3	4.02	0.98	2	✪✪✪		N.A.		N.A.	

Switzerland Convertible Bonds

Funds investing predominantly (70%) in Swiss convertible bonds and preference shares

		Fund Size		Manager	Fund Start	Domicile	3 Mths 97		1 Year		Micropal Star Rating 3 Years				Risk Return	5 Years		10 Years	
	CCY	($mil)	Fund Name	Code	Date	Code	% Chg	Rank	% Chg	Rank	Volatility	% Chg	Rank	Rating	Rating	% Chg	Rank	% Chg	Rank
		17.76	**Mean/Count**				**-8.36**	**1**	**-15.22**	**1**	**3.57**	**1.52**	**1**			**18.78**	**1**	**0**	**0**
	CHF	17.76	CS Sfr Convert Bd Fd (A)	S023	29/11/91	LUX	-8.36	1	-15.22	1	3.57	1.52	1	✪✪✪		18.78	1	N.A.	

▲ SIB Approved ● Insurance Fund Values in US Dollars, on an offer to offer price basis with gross income reinvested Data Source Micropal™

EQUITY FUNDS

The largest number of offshore funds invest primarily in equities and equity-related instruments. They account for over 50 per cent of the total offshore funds.

These funds can be as diverse as the companies they invest in. Some funds will specialise in smaller companies based in a single country; others only invest in the blue chip shares of major multi-national corporations.

For the purposes of comparison, Micropal has segregated the nearly 2,000 equity offshore funds into over 60 geographical sectors. Sectors may be single countries, others may be regions. To be included within a specific sector, at least 70 per cent of a fund's assets must be invested in equities from the named area.

For example, there is both a North America equity sector and a USA equity sector. Funds over 70 per cent invested in US equities are in the USA sector. Those funds with more than the maximum of 30 per cent of their assets outside the US, into Canada and Mexico, are in the North America sector. The reason for this division is that investors need to know what markets they are being exposed to. If, for example, the US stock market booms at a time when the Canadian one does less well, then the mainly US funds will do well regardless of the fund management expertise of the more generally invested funds.

Underlying a stock market are the individual equity funds. Fund managers have different investment agendas. Some will specialise in smaller companies, which tend to be riskier than those of larger blue chip companies but, over the long term, usually produce better returns. Alternatively, a fund manager may attempt to produce a high level of income, so will concentrate on shares paying good dividends. Some managers will invest mainly in one sector of the economy, such as shares of information technology companies. Others, with index tracking funds, will attempt to replicate stock market trends by aligning their asset mix to that of a relevant index, such as the Dow Jones Industrial Average. Many investors prefer equity funds because, over the long term at least, they can produce returns well in advance of bank deposits. While the actual level of income such funds earn is comparatively low, this is more than compensated for by significant capital appreciation. Naturally, potential high returns come with potential high risks. The value of an equity fund investment can, in the short term, rise or fall quite dramatically, so investors should consider their equity funds as medium- to long-term investments (that is, at least three years) – in order to appreciate the growth potential. Those of a nervous disposition who are likely to jump ship at the slightest downward movement should stick to money market funds.

There may be 61 equity sectors but the key ones are those covering the world's largest and most sophisticated stock markets. These are equity sectors in Japan, North America, the United States of America and the United Kingdom. Other large and important sectors include those in Europe, the Far East and Pacific, and the Far East and Pacific excluding Japan equity and global equity. Global equity covers all those funds that aim to produce capital growth or income by investing in any or all of the world's stock markets. Some fund managers will attempt to spread their assets evenly across all markets, while others will take a more aggressive stance and move their investments around the world, pursuing the best returns, wherever they may be.

Some of the best returns can be made by investing in the shares of companies from the emerging economies of the world, be that Latin America, Africa, Eastern Europe or Southeast Asia. The global emerging markets sector is for those funds specialising in this type of equity investment. Most of the funds in this sector have only been in existence for a few years. It is a high risk, high return sector and represents a more speculative part to any portfolio.

Argentina Equity

Funds investing in excess of 70% in Argentinean equities or related instruments. Such funds may have an objective of capital and/or income growth, or to track a specified index or perform inversely to a given index. Funds in this category may leverage or gear by a maximum of 20% of total assets.

	CCY	Fund Size ($mil)	Fund Name	Manager Code	Fund Start Date	Domicile Code	3 Mths 97 % Chg	3 Mths 97 Rank	1 Year % Chg	1 Year Rank	Micropal Star Rating 3 Years Volatility	3 Years % Chg	3 Years Rank	Rating	Risk Return Rating	5 Years % Chg	5 Years Rank	10 Years % Chg	10 Years Rank
		38.80	**Mean/Count**				**12.09**	**1**	**14.35**	**1**	**8.63**	**-19.14**	**1**			**-24.70**	**1**	**0**	**0**
▲	USD	38.80	Argentinia Inv Co	F002	31/01/91	LUX	12.09	1	14.35	1	8.63	-19.14	1	✪✪✪		-24.70	1	N.A.	

ASEAN Equity

Funds investing in excess of 70% in ASEAN (Singapore,Thailand, Malaysia, Indonesia, Vietnam, Brunei) equities or related instruments. Such funds may have an objective of capital and/or income growth, or to track a specified index or perform inversely to a given index. Funds in this category may leverage or gear by a maximum of 20% of total assets.

	CCY	Fund Size ($mil)	Fund Name	Manager Code	Fund Start Date	Domicile Code	3 Mths 97 % Chg	3 Mths 97 Rank	1 Year % Chg	1 Year Rank	Micropal Star Rating 3 Years Volatility	3 Years % Chg	3 Years Rank	Rating	Risk Return Rating	5 Years % Chg	5 Years Rank	10 Years % Chg	10 Years Rank
		83.82	**Mean/Count**				**0.96**	**19**	**4.49**	**16**	**5.71**	**-6.66**	**11**			**141.94**	**8**	**440.55**	**2**
	USD	N.S.	AB Asean Growth	A027	31/08/93	BVI	2.37	9	3.10	10	2.95	3.43	2	✪✪✪		N.A.		N.A.	
	USD	13.11	Barclays ASF ASEAN	B044	31/05/96	JER	-2.10	14	N.A.		N.A.	N.A.				N.A.		N.A.	
▲	USD	542.50	Fidelity Fds ASEAN	F011	28/09/90	LUX	-3.47	17	-6.28	15	6.84	-22.01	10	✪		138.34	4	N.A.	
▲●	USD	107.76	Groupe Indosuez ASEAN	G017	31/12/90	LUX	-5.42	19	2.98	11	6.01	-15.31	9	✪✪		156.68	3	N.A.	
▲	USD	193	GT ASEAN A Share	G018	31/01/79	IRL	3.34	7	17.11	2	6.46	-8.31	7			105.20	7	352.62	2
▲	USD	46.47	Guinness Flight ASEAN	G019	30/11/90	GU	-2.50	15	2.33	12	5.23	3.31	3	✪✪✪✪✪		132.27	5	N.A.	
●	USD	9.23	Hamon ASEAN	H007	22/12/95	IRL	5.80	2	-5.29	14	N.A.	N.A.				N.A.		N.A.	
●	USD	1.10	Hansard\GT ASEAN	H016	08/07/94	IOM	5.76	3	17.01	3	N.A.	N.A.				N.A.		N.A.	
●	USD	2.84	Hansard\JF ASEAN	H019	08/07/94	IOM	5.19	4	9.87	5	N.A.	N.A.				N.A.		N.A.	
	USD	7.43	ImPac AP ASEAN	I005	31/10/95	CA	-1.36	12	-12.56	16	N.A.	N.A.				N.A.		N.A.	
	USD	78.40	INVESCO ASEAN Dev	A010	29/06/90	BVI	6.08	1	3.49	9	6.33	-2.14	5	✪✪✪		234.77	1	N.A.	
	USD	426.48	JF ASEAN	J004	29/07/83	HK	2.39	8	10.70	4	6.72	-22.47	11	✪		161.45	2	528.48	1
	USD	31.86	LM Glbl Asian Dragon B	L005	29/03/96	NL	-1.95	13	N.A.		N.A.	N.A.				N.A.		N.A.	
▲	USD	5.50	Newton UGF South East Asia	N006	29/06/90	JER	-2.56	16	-1.61	13	5.88	-10.21	8	✪✪		108.03	6	N.A.	
	USD	22.42	Parvest ASEAN B	B037	18/11/94	LUX	-4.92	18	4.47	7	N.A.	N.A.				N.A.		N.A.	
●	USD	5.90	RLI/GT Asean	R025	31/08/90	IOM	3.94	6	17.92	1	6.71	-7.06	6	✪✪		98.79	8	N.A.	
	USD	3.42	Sogelux Fd Equities Emerg Asia	S037	21/06/96	LUX	4.82	5	N.A.		N.A.	N.A.				N.A.		N.A.	
	USD	1.45	Thornton Managed S.E Asia	T006	31/12/93	CA	1.18	11	3.78	8	4.67	6.80	1	✪✪✪✪		N.A.		N.A.	
	USD	9.91	Thornton SSF ASEAN Growth	T006	29/10/93	CA	1.75	10	4.85	6	5.02	0.68	4	✪✪✪✪		N.A.		N.A.	

Asian Subcontinent Equity

Funds investing in excess of 70% in Asian Subcontinent (India, Pakistan, Bangladesh, Sri Lanka, Nepal, Bhutan) equities or related instruments. Such funds may have an objective of capital and/or income growth, or to track a specified index or perform inversely to a given index. Funds in this category may leverage or gear by a maximum of 20% of total assets.

	CCY	Fund Size ($mil)	Fund Name	Manager Code	Fund Start Date	Domicile Code	3 Mths 97 % Chg	3 Mths 97 Rank	1 Year % Chg	1 Year Rank	Micropal Star Rating 3 Years Volatility	3 Years % Chg	3 Years Rank	Rating	Risk Return Rating	5 Years % Chg	5 Years Rank	10 Years % Chg	10 Years Rank
		19.63	**Mean/Count**				**0.42**	**3**	**-7.69**	**3**	**0**	**0**	**0**			**0**	**0**	**0**	**0**
	USD	37.22	Indosuez Bangladesh	I007	29/07/94	CA	30.40	1	58.08	1	N.A.	N.A.				N.A.		N.A.	
	USD	18.35	Regent Moghul	R005	31/03/94	CA	20.09	2	-39.33	2	N.A.	N.A.				N.A.		N.A.	
	USD	3.32	Regent South Asia	R005	22/07/94	CA	-49.24	3	-41.82	3	N.A.	N.A.				N.A.		N.A.	

▲ SIB Approved ● Insurance Fund

Values in US Dollars, on an offer to offer price basis with gross income reinvested

Data Source Micropal™

Australasia Equity

Funds investing in excess of 70% in Australian equities or related instruments. Such funds may have an objective of capital and/or income growth, or to track a specified index or perform inversely to a given index. Funds in this category may leverage or gear by a maximum of 20% of total assets.

	CCY	Fund Size ($mil)	Fund Name	Manager Code	Fund Start Date	Domicile Code	3 Mths 97 % Chg	3 Mths 97 Rank	1 Year % Chg	1 Year Rank	Micropal Star Rating 3 Years Volatility	3 Years % Chg	3 Years Rank	Rating	Risk Return Rating	5 Years % Chg	5 Years Rank	10 Years % Chg	10 Years Rank
		31.87	**Mean/Count**				**-0.30**	**8**	**18.83**	**8**	**4.35**	**29.07**	**6**		**1**	**72.99**	**5**	**242.22**	**1**
	AUD	1.92	Aetna MF Australasian Natl Eq	A012	31/07/90	LUX	-0.27	4	19.31	5	3.56	29.02	4	✪✪	3	42.12	5	N.A.	
▲	AUD	5.97	CMI GNF Australasian Equity	C042	30/04/90	LUX	-0.07	3	23.33	2	4.34	41.65	2	✪✪✪✪	4	61.86	3	N.A.	
●	USD	2	CMI Ins Co Australasian Eqty	C043	31/12/90	IOM	-1.30	7	22.18	3	4.52	34.90	3	✪✪✪	2	45.57	4	N.A.	
●	AUD	0	CMI Passport Australasian Eq	C044	20/01/95	IOM	-0.36	5	21.78	4	N.A.	N.A.				N.A.		N.A.	
▲	USD	12.38	Dres Thornton ASF Aus & NZ	D015	31/01/94	IRL	1.77	2	7.97	7	N.A.	N.A.				N.A.		N.A.	
▲	USD	21.51	Mercury ST Australia & NZ	M021	29/05/87	LUX	-0.73	6	18.49	6	4.74	23.56	5	✪✪	1	92.49	2	N.A.	
▲	USD	1.51	Nikko GIUF Oceania Fund	N007	26/02/93	LUX	2.39	1	31.08	1	4.70	44.41	1	✪✪✪✪	3	N.A.		N.A.	
	USD	209.66	Pictet T.F. Australasia	P016	29/11/85	LUX	-3.81	8	6.48	8	4.22	0.90	6	✪		122.90	1	242.22	1

Australia Equity

Funds investing in excess of 70% in Australian and New Zealand equities or related instruments. Such funds may have an objective of capital and/or income growth, or to track a specified index or perform inversely to a given index. Funds in this category may leverage or gear by a maximum of 20% of total assets.

	CCY	Fund Size ($mil)	Fund Name	Manager Code	Fund Start Date	Domicile Code	3 Mths 97 % Chg	3 Mths 97 Rank	1 Year % Chg	1 Year Rank	Micropal Star Rating 3 Years Volatility	3 Years % Chg	3 Years Rank	Rating	Risk Return Rating	5 Years % Chg	5 Years Rank	10 Years % Chg	10 Years Rank
		20.02	**Mean/Count**				**-0.94**	**14**	**23.53**	**14**	**4.56**	**31.92**	**12**		**1**	**84.32**	**11**	**69**	**5**
▲	AUD	1.91	Aetna IUF Australian Eqty A	A011	29/04/88	LUX	-1.65	9	17.20	13	5.08	34.85	7	✪✪✪	2	58.27	10	N.A.	
▲	GBP	3.91	Barclays Australian Equity	B046	31/12/71	JER	-1.80	10	18.46	11	4.59	35.42	6	✪✪	2	63.41	8	89.45	2
	USD	30.86	Baring IUF Australia	B049	31/12/81	IRL	-2.70	13	25.60	5	4.63	38.57	4	✪✪✪✪	3	113.03	2	112.17	1
▲	AUD	40.17	Fidelity Fds Australia	F011	31/12/91	LUX	-0.80	7	23.94	7	4.17	40.71	1	✪✪✪✪✪	5	78.97	6	N.A.	
	USD	3.50	GAM Australia	G003	31/07/85	IOM	-3.07	14	24.87	6	4.45	35.53	5	✪✪	3	93.32	5	77.74	3
▲	USD	5	GT Australia A Share	G018	30/03/79	IRL	-0.55	4	18.92	10	4.16	25.93	10	✪✪	2	52.61	11	57.31	4
	USD	35	GT Australian Sml Cos A Share	G018	29/03/91	IRL	1.25	2	37.22	1	4.36	17.85	11			126.42	1	N.A.	
●	USD	1.12	Hansard\Baring Australia	H012	27/09/91	IOM	-2.12	12	23.93	8	4.50	40.56	2	✪✪✪✪	4	109.54	3	N.A.	
●	USD	0.31	Hansard\JF Australia	H019	08/07/94	IOM	-0.99	8	22.17	9	N.A.	N.A.				N.A.		N.A.	
▲	USD	20.42	Inter Strategie Australie	B069	29/09/89	LUX	2.11	1	31.79	2	4.24	39.73	3	✪✪✪	4	63.22	9	N.A.	
	USD	42.05	JF Australia	J004	30/06/81	HK	-0.73	6	26.40	3	5.47	17.12	12	✪	1	73.75	7	8.32	5
	USD	11.29	KB Lux Key Australia	K011	30/09/94	LUX	-1.85	11	26.11	4	N.A.	N.A.				N.A.		N.A.	
●	USD	1.80	Royal Life/Baring Australia	R022	30/10/87	IOM	0.36	3	17.43	12	4.73	30.18	8	✪✪	2	95	4	N.A.	
▲	AUD	82.98	SBC Equity Portfolio Austral	S007	30/09/93	LUX	-0.67	5	15.32	14	4.38	26.57	9	✪	1	N.A.		N.A.	

Austria Equity

Funds investing in excess of 70% in Austrian equities or related instruments. Such funds may have an objective of capital and/or income growth, or to track a specified index or perform inversely to a given index. Funds in this category may leverage or gear by a maximum of 20% of total assets.

	CCY	Fund Size ($mil)	Fund Name	Manager Code	Fund Start Date	Domicile Code	3 Mths 97 % Chg	3 Mths 97 Rank	1 Year % Chg	1 Year Rank	Micropal Star Rating 3 Years Volatility	3 Years % Chg	3 Years Rank	Rating	Risk Return Rating	5 Years % Chg	5 Years Rank	10 Years % Chg	10 Years Rank
		3.72	**Mean/Count**				**-0.89**	**3**	**1.38**	**3**	**3.29**	**1.67**	**3**			**9.38**	**3**	**0**	**0**
	ATS	1.11	Aetna MF Austrian Natl Equity	A012	30/04/90	LUX	-4.87	3	-7.37	3	2.54	-11.85	3	✪✪		-22.43	3	N.A.	
	ATS	4.89	Callander Fund Austrian	C005	31/10/89	LUX	1.61	1	5.40	2	3.56	0.69	2	✪✪✪		2.41	2	N.A.	
▲	ATS	5.17	Swiss Life Proteus Aust Share	S056	29/11/91	IRL	0.60	2	6.12	1	3.79	16.18	1	✪✪✪✪		48.16	1	N.A.	

▲ SIB Approved ● Insurance Fund **Values in US Dollars, on an offer to offer price basis with gross income reinvested** Data Source Micropal™

Belgium Equity

Funds investing in excess of 70% in Belgian equities or related instruments. Such funds may have an objective of capital and/or income growth, or to track a specified index or perform inversely to a given index. Funds in this category may leverage or gear by a maximum of 20% of total assets.

	CCY	Fund Size ($mil)	Fund Name	Manager Code	Fund Start Date	Domicile Code	3 Mths 97 % Chg	3 Mths 97 Rank	1 Year % Chg	1 Year Rank	Micropal Star Rating 3 Years Volatility	3 Years % Chg	3 Years Rank	Rating	Risk Return Rating	5 Years % Chg	5 Years Rank	10 Years % Chg	10 Years Rank
		31.42	**Mean/Count**				**4.64**	**14**	**15.69**	**11**	**2.86**	**51.82**	**5**			**82.32**	**3**	**0**	**0**
	BEF	1.03	Aetna MF Belgian/Lux Natl Eq	A012	31/07/90	LUX	3.24	13	19.07	3	2.49	57.54	1	✪✪✪	4	81.52	2	N.A.	
	BEF	122.41	BBL (L) Invest Equi-Fix 1	B052	30/09/93	LUX	-4.51	14	6.93	11	2.78	42.48	5	✪	1	N.A.		N.A.	
	BEF	40.79	Cera Invest BEL20-1	C018	30/06/94	LUX	8.09	1	16.53	5	N.A.	N.A.				N.A.		N.A.	
	BEF	26.62	Cera Invest BEL20-2	C018	30/11/94	LUX	3.26	12	9.98	10	N.A.	N.A.				N.A.		N.A.	
	BEF	16.92	Cera Invest BEL20-3	C018	07/07/95	LUX	7.79	3	13.53	8	N.A.	N.A.				N.A.		N.A.	
	BEF	54.24	Cera Invest BEL20-4	C018	01/03/96	LUX	6.55	4	N.A.		N.A.	N.A.				N.A.		N.A.	
	BEF	11.92	Cera Invest BEL20-5	C018	19/04/96	LUX	7.85	2	N.A.		N.A.	N.A.				N.A.		N.A.	
	BEF	41.52	Cregem Equities L Bel 20	C059	19/07/95	LUX	6.09	6	21.20	2	N.A.	N.A.				N.A.		N.A.	
	BEF	31.45	Cregem Equities L Bel 20/2	C059	31/10/95	LUX	6.22	5	18.68	4	N.A.	N.A.				N.A.		N.A.	
▲	BEF	7.95	CU PP Belgian Growth	C070	31/05/90	LUX	3.33	11	11.51	9	2.95	47.26	4	✪✪	2	75.92	3	N.A.	
	BEF	25.04	EMIF Belgium Index Plus B	C015	31/05/90	LUX	3.80	9	16.06	6	2.86	56.70	2	✪✪✪✪	3	89.51	1	N.A.	
	BEF	20.47	Lion Belgium Index	C060	30/07/93	LUX	4.21	8	24.55	1	3.24	55.14	3	✪✪✪	3	N.A.		N.A.	
	BEF	31.56	Parvest Belgium B	B037	29/09/95	LUX	3.75	10	14.60	7	N.A.	N.A.				N.A.		N.A.	
	BEF	7.89	Portefeuille BG Act Belgique	B063	26/01/96	LUX	5.36	7	N.A.		N.A.	N.A.				N.A.		N.A.	

Benelux Equity

Funds investing in excess of 70% in Belgian, Luxembourg and the Netherlands equities or related instruments. Such funds may have an objective of capital and/or income growth, or to track a specified index or perform inversely to a given index. Funds in this category may leverage or gear by a maximum of 20% of total assets.

	CCY	Fund Size ($mil)	Fund Name	Manager Code	Fund Start Date	Domicile Code	3 Mths 97 % Chg	3 Mths 97 Rank	1 Year % Chg	1 Year Rank	Micropal Star Rating 3 Years Volatility	3 Years % Chg	3 Years Rank	Rating	Risk Return Rating	5 Years % Chg	5 Years Rank	10 Years % Chg	10 Years Rank
		15.46	**Mean/Count**				**5.49**	**4**	**28.88**	**5**	**3.15**	**71.14**	**2**		**1**	**99.06**	**2**	**0**	**0**
	LUF	62.43	BIL Luxpart C	B067	29/12/95	LUX	N.A.	—	23.59	5	N.A.	N.A.				N.A.		N.A.	
▲	NLG	8.15	CMI GNF Benelux Equity	C042	30/04/90	LUX	5.65	2	29.27	2	3	75.35	1	✪✪✪	3	106.28	1	N.A.	
●	GBP	1.86	CMI Ins Co Benelux Equity	C043	31/01/91	IOM	3.41	4	28.68	3	3.31	66.93	2	✪✪	2	91.85	2	N.A.	
●	NLG	0.17	CMI Passport Benelux Equity	C044	20/01/95	IOM	4.35	3	28.18	4	N.A.	N.A.				N.A.		N.A.	
▲●	NLG	4.72	TGA Benelux Eq	T009	30/06/95	LUX	8.57	1	34.69	1	N.A.	N.A.				N.A.		N.A.	

Brazil Equity

Funds investing in excess of 70% in Brazilian equities or related instruments. Such funds may have an objective of capital and/or income growth, or to track a specified index or perform inversely to a given index. Funds in this category may leverage or gear by a maximum of 20% of total assets.

	CCY	Fund Size ($mil)	Fund Name	Manager Code	Fund Start Date	Domicile Code	3 Mths 97 % Chg	3 Mths 97 Rank	1 Year % Chg	1 Year Rank	Micropal Star Rating 3 Years Volatility	3 Years % Chg	3 Years Rank	Rating	Risk Return Rating	5 Years % Chg	5 Years Rank	10 Years % Chg	10 Years Rank
		17.90	**Mean/Count**				**24.64**	**32**	**40.59**	**23**	**9.98**	**85.93**	**7**			**143.10**	**2**	**0**	**0**
▲	USD	58.90	Brazilian Inv Co	F002	31/12/87	LUX	19.26	23	39.84	10	9.59	60.81	6	✪✪	2	104.15	2	N.A.	
	USD	54.18	Eternity	B014	31/07/92	CA	36.52	3	40.67	8	10.08	66.16	5	✪✪	2	N.A.		N.A.	
●	USD	2.95	Fonte Cindam Select	F025	14/04/95	CA	25.03	15	36.70	15	N.A.	N.A.				N.A.		N.A.	
	USD	11.80	GAM Brasilia	G002	25/11/94	IOM	30.16	6	50.57	5	N.A.	N.A.				N.A.		N.A.	
●	USD	0.50	Hansard Multiplic Brazil	H011	29/04/94	IOM	23.39	18	40.15	9	N.A.	N.A.				N.A.		N.A.	
	USD	5.82	IB Brazilian Equities	I001	28/10/94	CA	16.93	26	34.19	16	N.A.	N.A.				N.A.		N.A.	
	USD	18.16	IB Brazilian Leveraged Eq	I001	11/08/95	CA	28.20	9	40.88	7	N.A.	N.A.				N.A.		N.A.	
	USD	73.83	Infinity	B014	31/05/91	CA	33.50	4	39.27	13	8.76	42.67	7	✪	1	182.04	1	N.A.	

▲ SIB Approved ● Insurance Fund **Values in US Dollars, on an offer to offer price basis with gross income reinvested** Data Source Micropal™

Brazil Equity

continued

	CCY	Fund Size ($mil)	Fund Name	Manager Code	Fund Start Date	Domicile Code	3 Mths 97 % Chg	Rank	1 Year % Chg	Rank	Micropal Star Rating 3 Years Volatility	% Chg	Rank	Rating	Risk Return Rating	5 Years % Chg	Rank	10 Years % Chg	Rank
		17.90	**Mean/Count**				**24.64**	**32**	**40.59**	**23**	**9.98**	**85.93**	**7**			**143.10**	**2**	**0**	**0**
	USD	0.69	Jupiter Tyndall SF Brazil	J011	10/02/95	BER	25.42	14	26.88	20	N.A.	N.A.				N.A.		N.A.	
	USD	1.09	Liberal S.A.F.E.	L010	17/11/95	BAH	28.27	8	38.99	14	N.A.	N.A.				N.A.		N.A.	
	USD	1.03	Liberal S.T.I.B.	L010	17/11/95	BAH	17.75	24	39.78	11	N.A.	N.A.				N.A.		N.A.	
▲	USD	2	Morgan Grenfell Brazil	M038	12/07/95	IRL	20.66	21	24.05	22	N.A.	N.A.				N.A.		N.A.	
	USD	12.17	Opportunity Brazil Aggressive	O010	19/08/94	CA	40.23	2	77.20	1	N.A.	N.A.				N.A.		N.A.	
	USD	66.99	Opportunity Brazil Equities	O010	29/01/93	CA	31.94	5	67.84	3	9.17	67.53	4	✪✪✪	3	N.A.		N.A.	
	USD	3.05	Opportunity Brazil Strategy	O010	30/06/93	CA	28.11	10	76.37	2	10.31	105.63	2	✪✪✪✪	4	N.A.		N.A.	
	USD	0.77	Opportunity Brazil Value	O010	12/07/93	CA	68.27	1	12.34	23	11.87	99.80	3	✪✪✪	3	N.A.		N.A.	
	USD	12.20	Patrimonio Corporate Inv	B015	26/05/95	CA	12.26	30	42.26	6	N.A.	N.A.				N.A.		N.A.	
	USD	7.50	Patrimonio New Fund Equity	B015	30/04/92	CA	20.92	20	39.57	12	10.05	158.92	1	✪✪✪✪	4	N.A.		N.A.	
	USD	49.87	Schroder Brazil	S008	30/09/94	GU	19.76	22	52.84	4	N.A.	N.A.				N.A.		N.A.	
	USD	0.41	Scudder GOF Brazil Equity A-2	S019	06/01/95	LUX	16.39	27	28.06	19	N.A.	N.A.				N.A.		N.A.	
	USD	6.44	The Logus Fund	A030	31/10/94	BAH	6.41	32	25.81	21	N.A.	N.A.				N.A.		N.A.	
	USD	6.55	UAM Columbus Index	U004	31/10/96	CA	27.88	11	N.A.		N.A.	N.A.				N.A.		N.A.	
	USD	12.55	Unifund A	U004	31/03/94	CA	26.43	12	30.53	17	N.A.	N.A.				N.A.		N.A.	
	USD	20.20	Vista Equity	B010	24/03/95	CA	24.21	17	28.80	18	N.A.	N.A.				N.A.		N.A.	

Canada Equity

Funds investing in excess of 70% in Canadian equities or related instruments. Such funds may have an objective of capital and/or income growth, or to track a specified index or perform inversely to a given index. Funds in this category may leverage or gear by a maximum of 20% of total assets.

	CCY	Fund Size ($mil)	Fund Name	Manager Code	Fund Start Date	Domicile Code	3 Mths 97 % Chg	Rank	1 Year % Chg	Rank	Micropal Star Rating 3 Years Volatility	% Chg	Rank	Rating	Risk Return Rating	5 Years % Chg	Rank	10 Years % Chg	Rank
		41.31	**Mean/Count**				**3.71**	**6**	**26.71**	**6**	**3.49**	**38.47**	**3**		**1**	**26.54**	**2**	**0**	**0**
▲	CAD	3.33	CMI GNF Canadian Equity	C042	30/04/90	LUX	4.44	4	27.93	2	3.37	39.60	2	✪✪✪	4	30.42	1	N.A.	
●	USD	0.30	CMI Ins Co Canadian Equity	C043	28/02/91	IOM	4.58	3	26.61	4	3.44	33.79	3	✪✪	2	22.66	2	N.A.	
●	CAD	0	CMI Passport Canadian Equity	C044	20/01/95	IOM	4.90	1	26.40	5	N.A.	N.A.				N.A.		N.A.	
	CAD	22.84	Pictet C.F. Valcanada	P016	30/06/94	LUX	3.83	5	23.54	6	N.A.	N.A.				N.A.		N.A.	
▲	CAD	12.44	RBC GI Canadian	R003	24/11/95	GU	4.66	2	28.48	1	N.A.	N.A.				N.A.		N.A.	
▲	CAD	208.94	SBC Equity Portfolio Canada	S007	30/04/93	LUX	-0.14	6	27.30	3	3.67	42.02	1	✪✪✪✪	3	N.A.		N.A.	

Chile Equity

Funds investing in excess of 70% in Chilean equities or related instruments. Such funds may have an objective of capital and/or income growth, or to track a specified index or perform inversely to a given index. Funds in this category may leverage or gear by a maximum of 20% of total assets.

	CCY	Fund Size ($mil)	Fund Name	Manager Code	Fund Start Date	Domicile Code	3 Mths 97 % Chg	Rank	1 Year % Chg	Rank	Micropal Star Rating 3 Years Volatility	% Chg	Rank	Rating	Risk Return Rating	5 Years % Chg	Rank	10 Years % Chg	Rank
		248.20	**Mean/Count**				**8.74**	**2**	**-16.85**	**2**	**6.92**	**27.27**	**2**		**2**	**107.20**	**2**	**0**	**0**
	USD	419.40	Genesis Chile	G010	30/11/89	GU	17.64	1	-14.44	1	7.37	37.20	1	✪✪✪	3	135.17	1	N.A.	
	USD	77	GT Chile Growth	G018	28/02/90	CA	-0.16	2	-19.26	2	6.47	17.34	2	✪✪	2	79.24	2	N.A.	

▲ SIB Approved ● Insurance Fund Values in US Dollars, on an offer to offer price basis with gross income reinvested Data Source Micropal™

China Equity

Funds investing in excess of 70% in Chinese equities or related instruments. Such funds may have an objective of capital and/or income growth, or to track a specified index or perform inversely to a given index. Funds in this category may leverage or gear by a maximum of 20% of total assets. Funds in this category include "China-play" funds, i.e., funds which seek to gain by economic growth in China by investing in companies listed outside of China but which operate in China and derive a considerable degree of revenue from these activities.

	CCY	Fund Size ($mil)	Fund Name	Manager Code	Fund Start Date	Domicile Code	3 Mths 97 % Chg	3 Mths 97 Rank	1 Year % Chg	1 Year Rank	Micropal Star Rating 3 Years Volatility	3 Years % Chg	3 Years Rank	Rating	Risk Return Rating	5 Years % Chg	5 Years Rank	10 Years % Chg	10 Years Rank
		20.77	**Mean/Count**				**7.26**	**28**	**49.93**	**24**	**6.76**	**-15.54**	**16**			**0**	**0**	**0**	**0**
▲	USD	44.04	AAF China Equity Fund	A001	16/06/95	LUX	1.87	23	36.72	20	N.A.	N.A.				N.A.		N.A.	
	USD	14.27	Barclays ASF China (PRC)	B044	30/04/92	JER	10.82	8	78.89	1	7.64	-16.37	7	✪✪✪		N.A.		N.A.	
▲	USD	12.20	CL China Growth	C063	29/05/92	CA	6.76	11	52.44	9	5.52	30.13	2	✪✪✪✪✪	2	N.A.		N.A.	
▲	USD	2.19	CMI GNF Greater China Equity	C042	28/02/95	LUX	6.64	12	65.82	4	N.A.	N.A.				N.A.		N.A.	
●	USD	0.70	CMI Passport Greater China Eq	C044	20/01/95	IOM	6.30	13	63.57	6	N.A.	N.A.				N.A.		N.A.	
	USD	1.10	Dao Heng China	D005	31/08/92	HK	28.68	1	35.91	21	6.55	-40.22	13	✪		N.A.		N.A.	
▲	USD	81.61	Dres Thornton ASF China	D015	30/11/93	IRL	6.09	14	30.68	23	6.83	-41.17	14	✪		N.A.		N.A.	
▲	USD	74.14	Fleming FF China	F020	01/07/94	LUX	2.72	21	65.47	5	N.A.	N.A.				N.A.		N.A.	
	USD	60	GT PRC A	G018	31/03/92	IRL	17.67	3	54.90	8	7.05	-19.11	8	✪✪✪		N.A.		N.A.	
▲	USD	14.60	Guinness Flight Sel China	G021	12/01/96	IRL	14.42	4	N.A.		N.A.	N.A.				N.A.		N.A.	
	USD	3.73	Hansard\CL China Growth	H013	31/07/92	IOM	11.41	6	47.48	12	5.08	38.53	1	✪✪✪✪	3	N.A.		N.A.	
▲	USD	38.97	HSBC GIF Chinese Equity	H033	30/06/92	LUX	7.29	10	76.21	2	7.15	8.77	3	✪✪✪✪		N.A.		N.A.	
	DEM	25.74	HYPO Greater China	H024	31/08/94	LUX	0.85	26	38.69	19	N.A.	N.A.				N.A.		N.A.	
	USD	2.84	ImPac AP Greater China	I005	31/05/96	CA	-1.24	27	N.A.		N.A.	N.A.				N.A.		N.A.	
	USD	16.75	Indosuez Shanghai	I007	30/06/92	CA	7.59	9	40.71	17	6.51	-22.13	10	✪✪		N.A.		N.A.	
▲	USD	10.67	INVESCO PS Gr China Opps	I014	31/07/92	LUX	1.44	25	41.03	16	6.36	-0.53	4	✪✪✪✪		N.A.		N.A.	
	USD	32.51	JF China	J004	30/06/92	CA	4.58	18	57.99	7	7.40	-41.34	15	✪		N.A.		N.A.	
▲	USD	4.19	Jupiter Tyndall GF China	J010	30/04/92	LUX	13.61	5	46.39	14	6.45	-20.89	9	✪✪		N.A.		N.A.	
	HKD	17.19	LG SC China	L013	31/07/92	BER	20.59	2	47.26	13	6.77	-28	11	✪✪		N.A.		N.A.	
	USD	0.93	Nomura SF China	N010	31/08/93	CA	1.63	24	26.47	24	8.82	-41.40	16	✪✪		N.A.		N.A.	
	USD	35	Parvest Greater China B	B037	15/11/96	LUX	3.13	20	N.A.		N.A.	N.A.				N.A.		N.A.	
▲	GBP	12.15	Prolific IF China Opps	P027	30/04/92	IRL	3.56	19	49.91	10	5.96	-3.36	5	✪✪✪✪		N.A.		N.A.	
	HKD	36.02	Schroder Asia China/HK Ent	S011	31/01/94	CA	5.11	16	73.94	3	N.A.	N.A.				N.A.		N.A.	
	USD	1	Scot Prov ILA China Opps	S014	29/09/95	IOM	11.34	7	44.11	15	N.A.	N.A.				N.A.		N.A.	
	USD	6.53	SHK China	S024	30/06/92	HK	5.45	15	48.55	11	6.18	-13.70	6	✪✪✪		N.A.		N.A.	
	USD	9.23	Sogelux Fd Equities China	S037	21/06/96	LUX	2.02	22	N.A.		N.A.	N.A.				N.A.		N.A.	
▲	USD	13.56	Templeton GS China	T001	31/08/94	LUX	-1.73	28	39.85	18	N.A.	N.A.				N.A.		N.A.	
	USD	9.58	Thornton New Tiger China	T007	31/07/92	BER	4.78	17	35.33	22	7.84	-37.78	12	✪		N.A.		N.A.	

CIS Equity

Funds investing in excess of 70% in Commonwealth of Independent States equities or related instruments. Such funds may have an objective of capital and/or income growth, or to track a specified index or perform inversely to a given index. Funds in this category may leverage or gear by a maximum of 20% of total assets.

	CCY	Fund Size ($mil)	Fund Name	Manager Code	Fund Start Date	Domicile Code	3 Mths 97 % Chg	3 Mths 97 Rank	1 Year % Chg	1 Year Rank	Micropal Star Rating 3 Years Volatility	3 Years % Chg	3 Years Rank	Rating	Risk Return Rating	5 Years % Chg	5 Years Rank	10 Years % Chg	10 Years Rank
		34.18	**Mean/Count**				**57.65**	**10**	**99.40**	**6**	**0**	**0**	**0**			**0**	**0**	**0**	**0**
	USD	N.S.	Brunswick Russian Growth	B075	31/07/96	CA	78.06	1	N.A.		N.A.	N.A.				N.A.		N.A.	
	USD	3.80	Eastern Capital	C050	30/12/94	BVI	47.21	8	89.59	4	N.A.	N.A.				N.A.		N.A.	
	USD	7.47	Fleming Frontier Russia	F021	20/09/96	LUX	53.50	7	N.A.		N.A.	N.A.				N.A.		N.A.	
	USD	4.79	FP Russian Equity	F029	28/04/95	GU	24.58	10	72.60	5	N.A.	N.A.				N.A.		N.A.	
	USD	N.S.	Hermitage	H029	26/04/96	GU	75.76	3	N.A.		N.A.	N.A.				N.A.		N.A.	
	USD	11.34	Magnum Russia	M002	30/11/94	BVI	38.76	9	23.61	6	N.A.	N.A.				N.A.		N.A.	

▲ SIB Approved ● Insurance Fund **Values in US Dollars, on an offer to offer price basis with gross income reinvested** Data Source Micropal™

CIS Equity

continued

CCY	Fund Size ($mil)	Fund Name	Manager Code	Fund Start Date	Domicile Code	3 Mths 97 % Chg	3 Mths 97 Rank	1 Year % Chg	1 Year Rank	Micropal Star Rating 3 Years Volatility	3 Years % Chg	3 Years Rank	3 Years Rating	Risk Return Rating	5 Years % Chg	5 Years Rank	10 Years % Chg	10 Years Rank
	34.18	**Mean/Count**				**57.65**	**10**	**99.40**	**6**	**0**	**0**	**0**			**0**	**0**	**0**	**0**
USD	54.18	Regent Blue Tiger Inv Co	R005	31/08/95	CA	56.28	6	137.53	2	N.A.	N.A.				N.A.		N.A.	
USD	54.20	Regent Red Tiger	R005	16/12/94	CA	63.83	4	122.60	3	N.A.	N.A.				N.A.		N.A.	
USD	103.47	Regent White Tiger	R005	16/09/94	CA	62.20	5	150.46	1	N.A.	N.A.				N.A.		N.A.	
USD	N.S.	Russian Prosperity	W003	20/09/96	CA	76.31	2	N.A.		N.A.	N.A.				N.A.		N.A.	

Columbia Equity

Funds investing in excess of 70% in Columbian equities or related instruments. Such funds may have an objective of capital and/or income growth, or to track a specified index or perform inversely to a given index. Funds in this category may leverage or gear by a maximum of 20% of total assets.

CCY	Fund Size ($mil)	Fund Name	Manager Code	Fund Start Date	Domicile Code	3 Mths 97 % Chg	3 Mths 97 Rank	1 Year % Chg	1 Year Rank	Micropal Star Rating 3 Years Volatility	3 Years % Chg	3 Years Rank	3 Years Rating	Risk Return Rating	5 Years % Chg	5 Years Rank	10 Years % Chg	10 Years Rank
	37.01	**Mean/Count**				**16**	**1**	**-1.79**	**1**	**8.16**	**-16.14**	**1**			**0**	**0**	**0**	**0**
USD	37.01	Colombian Inv Co	F002	29/05/92	LUX	16	1	-1.79	1	8.16	-16.14	1	✪✪✪		N.A.		N.A.	

Czech & Slovak Republics Equity

Funds investing in excess of 70% in Czech and Slovak Republics equities or related instruments. Such funds may have an objective of capital and/or income growth, or to track a specified index or perform inversely to a given index. Funds in this category may leverage or gear by a maximum of 20% of total assets.

CCY	Fund Size ($mil)	Fund Name	Manager Code	Fund Start Date	Domicile Code	3 Mths 97 % Chg	3 Mths 97 Rank	1 Year % Chg	1 Year Rank	Micropal Star Rating 3 Years Volatility	3 Years % Chg	3 Years Rank	3 Years Rating	Risk Return Rating	5 Years % Chg	5 Years Rank	10 Years % Chg	10 Years Rank
	7.68	**Mean/Count**				**-8.07**	**2**	**0.84**	**2**	**0**	**0**	**0**			**0**	**0**	**0**	**0**
DEM	3.39	CF Czech Fund	C067	29/04/94	LUX	-11.90	2	-14.99	2	N.A.	N.A.				N.A.		N.A.	
ATS	11.97	IA Tschechien & Slovakei	E002	31/05/94	LUX	-4.24	1	16.66	1	N.A.	N.A.				N.A.		N.A.	

Denmark Equity

Funds investing in excess of 70% in Danish equities or related instruments. Such funds may have an objective of capital and/or income growth, or to track a specified index or perform inversely to a given index. Funds in this category may leverage or gear by a maximum of 20% of total assets.

CCY	Fund Size ($mil)	Fund Name	Manager Code	Fund Start Date	Domicile Code	3 Mths 97 % Chg	3 Mths 97 Rank	1 Year % Chg	1 Year Rank	Micropal Star Rating 3 Years Volatility	3 Years % Chg	3 Years Rank	3 Years Rating	Risk Return Rating	5 Years % Chg	5 Years Rank	10 Years % Chg	10 Years Rank
	16.53	**Mean/Count**				**4.09**	**1**	**21.30**	**1**	**3.17**	**38.45**	**1**		**3**	**52.54**	**1**	**0**	**0**
DKK	16.53	Danske Danish Eq Mngd	D003	31/12/90	LUX	4.09	1	21.30	1	3.17	38.45	1	✪✪✪	3	52.54	1	N.A.	

▲ SIB Approved ● Insurance Fund Values in US Dollars, on an offer to offer price basis with gross income reinvested Data Source Micropal™

East Europe Equity

Funds investing in excess of 70% in Eastern European (Czech Republic, Slovakia, Poland, Hungary, Baltics, Romania, Bulgaria, Slovenia and former Soviet Union (including Central Asia) equities or related instruments. Such funds may have an objective of capital and/or income growth, or to track a specified index or perform inversely to a given index. Funds in this category may leverage or gear by a maximum of 20% of total assets.

	CCY	Fund Size ($mil)	Fund Name	Manager Code	Fund Start Date	Domicile Code	3 Mths 97 % Chg	3 Mths 97 Rank	1 Year % Chg	1 Year Rank	Micropal Star Rating 3 Years Volatility	3 Years % Chg	3 Years Rank	3 Years Rating	Risk Return Rating	5 Years % Chg	5 Years Rank	10 Years % Chg	10 Years Rank
		76.96	**Mean/Count**				17.23	15	66.07	11	0	0	0			0	0	0	0
▲	DEM	144.82	AAF Eastern Europe Equity Fund	A001	16/06/95	LUX	13.64	13	78.46	4	N.A.	N.A.				N.A.		N.A.	
▲	USD	14.83	Aetna IUF Emerging Europe A	A011	29/12/95	LUX	18.97	4	19.48	11	N.A.	N.A.				N.A.		N.A.	
	ATS	14.56	Baer Multicoop Central Eur A	J007	31/10/94	LUX	15.31	12	63.80	6	N.A.	N.A.				N.A.		N.A.	
	USD	54.53	Baring GUF Eastern Europe	B049	27/09/96	IRL	25.88	3	N.A.		N.A.	N.A.				N.A.		N.A.	
●	DEM	48.10	DBIM DB Osteuropa	D006	10/11/95	LUX	4.80	15	24.34	10	N.A.	N.A.				N.A.		N.A.	
	DEM	22.50	EM Osteuropa	U012	31/10/94	LUX	16.19	8	41.35	9	N.A.	N.A.				N.A.		N.A.	
▲	DEM	231.27	Fleming FF Eastern European	F020	01/07/94	LUX	17.18	6	80.17	3	N.A.	N.A.				N.A.		N.A.	
	DEM	21.40	HYPO Osteuropa	H024	31/03/95	LUX	17.25	5	62.59	7	N.A.	N.A.				N.A.		N.A.	
	USD	8.45	JF Eastern European Trust	J004	14/06/96	CA	15.41	11	N.A.		N.A.	N.A.				N.A.		N.A.	
	DEM	11.03	KB Lux Key Eastern Europe	K011	06/12/96	LUX	15.53	10	N.A.		N.A.	N.A.				N.A.		N.A.	
▲	DEM	94.82	Mercury ST Eastern European	M021	29/12/95	LUX	29.56	1	137.95	1	N.A.	N.A.				N.A.		N.A.	
	DEM	99.72	Pictet T.F. Eastern Europe	P016	31/07/95	LUX	26.31	2	57.85	8	N.A.	N.A.				N.A.		N.A.	
	USD	143.20	Schroder Eastern European	S008	16/12/94	GU	9.55	14	72.98	5	N.A.	N.A.				N.A.		N.A.	
	DEM	168.27	Vontobel Eastern Europe Eq A	B017	31/08/94	LUX	15.68	9	87.77	2	N.A.	N.A.				N.A.		N.A.	

Europe Equity

Funds investing in excess of 70% in European equities or related instruments. Such funds may have an objective of capital and/or income growth, or to track a specified index or perform inversely to a given index. Funds in this category may leverage or gear by a maximum of 20% of total assets.

	CCY	Fund Size ($mil)	Fund Name	Manager Code	Fund Start Date	Domicile Code	3 Mths 97 % Chg	3 Mths 97 Rank	1 Year % Chg	1 Year Rank	Micropal Star Rating 3 Years Volatility	3 Years % Chg	3 Years Rank	3 Years Rating	Risk Return Rating	5 Years % Chg	5 Years Rank	10 Years % Chg	10 Years Rank
		60.68	**Mean/Count**				4.59	156	23.89	145	2.94	45.75	102		1	75.88	66	174.34	8
▲	USD	37.49	AAF Europe Equity Fund	A001	25/11/94	LUX	6.58	41	24.72	49	N.A.	N.A.				N.A.		N.A.	
▲	USD	64.60	AEB Worldfolio 10 Euro Eqs	A009	30/03/90	LUX	3.49	92	19.63	98	3.09	44.68	47	✪✪✪	2	63.91	44	N.A.	
●	FRF	42.10	AGF Euroinvest	A014	31/01/95	LUX	0.14	145	14.63	133	N.A.	N.A.				N.A.		N.A.	
▲	USD	6.28	AIG Europe	A017	29/01/93	IRL	4.94	63	22.70	64	4.14	45.03	45	✪✪✪	2	N.A.		N.A.	
▲	USD	33.17	AIG Europe Small Companies	A017	29/01/93	IRL	7.58	29	30.68	24	3.68	54.58	18	✪✪✪✪	4	N.A.		N.A.	
	USD	N.S.	Albany Intl Euro Enterprise	A018	28/02/95	IOM	5.25	56	37.71	16	N.A.	N.A.				N.A.		N.A.	
	DEM	18.54	Alfred Berg Sicav Europe	A019	31/01/95	LUX	4.14	83	20.35	89	N.A.	N.A.				N.A.		N.A.	
	ECU	7	Alpha Europe	A023a	29/06/90	BVI	-1.87	149	11.92	139	2.36	12.87	102	✪		21.33	66	N.A.	
▲	ECU	10.16	American Phoenix Euro Multi	A025	29/01/93	LUX	4.72	66	23.79	57	2.98	66.82	9	✪✪✪✪✪	5	N.A.		N.A.	
	ECU	214.99	Baer Multistock Eur Stk A	J007	29/06/90	LUX	3.52	91	24.92	47	2.78	51.14	26	✪✪✪✪	4	69.74	39	N.A.	
	ECU	3.37	BanesFondo Intern. Europa	B030	28/06/91	LUX	2.50	115	21.98	70	2.50	21.96	98	✪	1	27.11	65	N.A.	
▲	GBP	115.25	Barclays (Lux) Euro Equity	B047	31/07/87	LUX	4.71	67	26.73	40	3.15	64.58	13	✪✪✪✪✪	4	102.65	9	N.A.	
	GBP	15.06	Baring Europe Select Feeder	B049	28/06/96	IRL	8.81	21	N.A.		N.A.	N.A.				N.A.		N.A.	
	USD	42.39	Baring IUF Europa	B049	30/04/87	IRL	3.53	89	22.17	68	2.91	40.34	62	✪✪	2	78.49	28	N.A.	
	LUF	43.66	BBL (L) Invest Europe C	B052	29/01/88	LUX	2.36	118	17.83	116	2.91	38.08	69	✪	1	63.41	45	N.A.	
	DEM	13.29	Bcilux Established Europe	B007	26/07/96	LUX	0.44	142	N.A.		N.A.	N.A.				N.A.		N.A.	
	USD	26.50	Bermuda Eqty European	B066	30/11/90	BER	9.57	13	12.81	137	3	26.85	95	✪	1	71.81	34	N.A.	
	LUF	32.17	BIL Europe Growth All Mkts C	B067	31/01/90	LUX	-0.60	147	17.64	118	2.75	31.17	89	✪	1	45.64	61	N.A.	
●	ECU	106.08	BL Equities Europe B	B025	28/09/90	LUX	4.33	78	25.81	44	2.41	55.01	17	✪✪✪✪	5	76.64	31	N.A.	
	LUF	N.S.	BR & A European	B019	24/11/95	LUX	3.41	95	14.15	135	N.A.	N.A.				N.A.		N.A.	
	ECU	25.83	BSS Universal Eurosec ECU	B029	28/06/91	LUX	3.63	87	21.65	71	2.87	40.90	59	✪✪	2	84.27	18	N.A.	
▲	USD	38.29	BT IIS European Growth	B077	30/10/92	IRL	10.03	10	41.01	10	4.18	67.31	8	✪✪✪✪	4	N.A.		N.A.	
	ECU	5.63	Caixa Funds European Shares	C004	29/11/91	LUX	6.23	42	15	131	2.35	39.07	65	✪✪	3	30.49	64	N.A.	

▲ SIB Approved **● Insurance Fund** **Values in US Dollars, on an offer to offer price basis with gross income reinvested** Data Source Micropal™

Europe Equity

continued

	CCY	Fund Size ($mil)	Fund Name	Manager Code	Fund Start Date	Domicile Code	3 Mths 97 % Chg	3 Mths 97 Rank	1 Year % Chg	1 Year Rank	Micropal Star Rating 3 Years Volatility	3 Years % Chg	3 Years Rank	3 Years Rating	Risk Return Rating	5 Years % Chg	5 Years Rank	10 Years % Chg	10 Years Rank
		60.68	**Mean/Count**				**4.59**	**156**	**23.89**	**145**	**2.94**	**45.75**	**102**		**1**	**75.88**	**66**	**174.34**	**8**
	ECU	0	CCF/Fram Euro Smllr Cos A	C015	30/09/87	LUX	7.86	28	18.21	114	2.83	49.35	30	✪✪✪	3	50.17	58	N.A.	
▲●	USD	158.98	Chase Vista Europe Eq	C019	30/09/87	LUX	4.61	70	21.36	79	2.82	43.50	52	✪✪	2	55.24	55	N.A.	
	CHF	5.63	CIBC PCF European Equity	C021	30/04/93	GU	6	44	10.40	142	2.19	31.18	88	✪	2	N.A.		N.A.	
	USD	10.21	Citimarkets European Equity A	C034	29/09/95	LUX	2.74	110	18.70	110	N.A.	N.A.				N.A.		N.A.	
●	USD	16.31	Citimarkets European Equity B	C034	30/09/87	LUX	3.15	101	20.61	84	2.71	44.47	48	✪✪✪	3	89.93	14	N.A.	
●	ECU	115.61	Clariden Europe Multi Manager	C039	14/07/95	CA	0.46	141	20.51	86	N.A.	N.A.				N.A.		N.A.	
▲	CHF	312.33	Comgest Europe	C045	31/07/92	LUX	-4.40	155	28.05	34	2.74	105.08	2	✪✪✪✪✪	5	N.A.		N.A.	
●	DEM	49.81	Credis Eq Euro Blue Chips A	C056	31/10/89	LUX	2.09	122	27.27	38	3.02	46.34	40	✪✪✪	2	68.48	40	N.A.	
●	DEM	99.69	Credis Equity Small Cap Eur	C056	31/01/94	LUX	16.21	2	31.98	22	N.A.	N.A.				N.A.		N.A.	
	BEF	231.84	Cregem Equities L Europe Cap	C059	31/01/90	LUX	4.41	75	29.68	28	2.82	53.35	20	✪✪✪✪	4	80.60	24	N.A.	
▲	NOK	9.22	DNB Investment Euro Equities A	D013	31/10/94	LUX	5.41	53	20.08	91	N.A.	N.A.				N.A.		N.A.	
	CHF	5.19	Eagle Star European Eq	E001	29/09/95	IOM	6.69	40	28.07	33	N.A.	N.A.				N.A.		N.A.	
	CHF	N.S.	Eagle Star European Smaller Co	E001	27/09/96	IOM	N.A.	—	N.A.		N.A.	N.A.				N.A.		N.A.	
	USD	N.S.	EPIC MF Euro Equities	A024	20/10/95	LUX	3.62	88	19.68	97	N.A.	N.A.				N.A.		N.A.	
	ECU	65.72	Esprit Sicav	B024	30/05/86	LUX	4.35	77	19.27	100	2.51	36.35	76	✪	2	48.95	60	103.70	8
▲	ECU	72.46	Eufinvest Cap	E012	30/04/90	LUX	5.38	54	20.96	81	2.81	41.20	57	✪✪	2	60.42	48	N.A.	
	DEM	41.15	EuroAction	U012	17/11/95	LUX	N.A.	—	24.52	51	N.A.	N.A.				N.A.		N.A.	
	USD	5.20	Europa European Equity	E013	29/01/93	CA	-3.04	152	29.27	29	3.25	71.03	5	✪✪✪✪	5	N.A.		N.A.	
	USD	31.90	European Financial Equities	E010	31/03/93	IRL	9.12	16	22.27	67	2.68	51.37	25	✪✪✪	4	N.A.		N.A.	
	DEM	11.82	European Growth Fund	B067	28/02/90	LUX	2.93	107	20.64	83	2.89	37.25	74	✪✪	1	60.34	49	N.A.	
	ECU	17.75	Europhenix B	B037	31/07/87	LUX	9.61	12	18.71	109	2.79	35.23	81	✪	1	65	43	N.A.	
▲	ECU	4.01	F&C PF Euro Sm Cos Equity	F001	29/03/96	LUX	0.09	146	N.A.		N.A.	N.A.				N.A.		N.A.	
	DEM	135.74	Fidelity Fds European Sm Cos	F011	29/12/95	LUX	9.74	11	39.91	12	N.A.	N.A.				N.A.		N.A.	
	CHF	N.S.	Fiduciary European Equity	F014	03/01/97	IRL	N.A.		N.A.		N.A.	N.A.				N.A.		N.A.	
	CHF	N.S.	Five Arrows IMP Euro Cap Gth	R015	31/07/96	GU	0.15	144	N.A.		N.A.	N.A.				N.A.		N.A.	
	USD	37.76	Five Arrows IP European	R016	30/12/94	GU	2.26	119	21.56	75	N.A.	N.A.				N.A.		N.A.	
▲	DEM	110.76	Fleming FF Euro Sm Cos	F020	29/04/94	LUX	4.69	68	30.43	27	N.A.	N.A.				N.A.		N.A.	
▲	DEM	70.03	Fleming FF European	F020	30/11/88	LUX	5.60	50	24.73	48	3.04	48.39	34	✪✪✪	3	81.74	21	N.A.	
●	ECU	118.72	Frontrunner European Equities	F032	29/09/89	LUX	1.86	124	12.13	138	2.33	39.98	63	✪✪	3	78.31	29	N.A.	
	ECU	15.29	Fructilux Actions Europeennes	B043	29/01/93	LUX	5.37	55	19.80	95	2.36	52.85	22	✪✪✪✪	5	N.A.		N.A.	
▲	DEM	16.14	GAM Europa Fonds	G002	30/10/92	IOM	1.03	134	19	104	2.67	40.48	60	✪✪	2	N.A.		N.A.	
	DEM	65.14	GAM Multi-Europe DM	G003	30/06/92	IOM	2.39	117	18.98	105	2.68	32.17	84	✪	1	N.A.		N.A.	
	USD	162	GAM Multi-Europe USD	G003	31/10/91	IOM	8.90	19	24.43	52	2.63	16.61	100	✪		60.19	50	N.A.	
	CHF	23.80	GAM Pan Europa Fonds	G002	18/11/94	IOM	2.97	104	19.39	99	N.A.	N.A.				N.A.		N.A.	
	USD	184.20	GAM Pan European	G002	18/11/94	IOM	3.27	98	18.89	106	N.A.	N.A.				N.A.		N.A.	
▲	DEM	8.44	Gartmore CSF Europe	G007	13/10/95	JER	4.01	84	25.99	43	N.A.	N.A.				N.A.		N.A.	
	DEM	243.74	Goldman Sachs Euro Small Cap	G013	29/04/94	LUX	5.13	58	45.54	6	N.A.	N.A.				N.A.		N.A.	
	DEM	4.12	Govett GSIL European Equity	G015	31/03/89	JER	6.86	39	32.48	21	3.11	68.28	6	✪✪✪✪✪	5	78.49	27	N.A.	
▲	USD	262	GT Europe	G018	31/01/84	LUX	5.97	46	30.57	25	3.03	45.47	44	✪✪✪	2	125.77	5	213.40	3
▲	GBP	10.21	Guinness Fl IF Euro Equity	G020	30/06/88	GU	2.19	121	22.83	63	2.99	50.69	28	✪✪✪✪	3	88.37	15	N.A.	
▲	DEM	7.55	Hambros Eqty Sel Euro Gth	H003	30/04/87	GU	2.25	120	25.17	46	2.75	50.40	29	✪✪✪✪	4	77.35	30	N.A.	
●	USD	1.82	Hansard\Baring Europa	H012	27/09/91	IOM	6.16	43	19.27	101	2.58	36.10	77	✪✪	1	71.39	36	N.A.	
▲	NLG	49.25	Henderson HF European Sllr Cos	H025	31/08/93	LUX	9.13	15	32.49	20	2.81	52.65	23	✪✪✪✪	4	N.A.		N.A.	
	ECU	23.87	Hermes European	H028	29/05/92	BER	-2.82	150	10.97	141	2.32	30.24	90	✪	1	N.A.		N.A.	
▲	GBP	16.09	Hill Samuel OS European	H030	31/05/85	JER	11.20	8	15.62	125	2.58	37.91	70	✪✪	2	70.32	38	136.47	7
	USD	18.90	HSBC Euro Countries Tactical	H034	31/12/92	BAH	3	103	16.74	120	2.43	31.26	87	✪	1	N.A.		N.A.	
▲	USD	25.17	HSBC GIF Pan-European Equity	H033	30/11/93	LUX	5.18	57	23.50	58	2.90	48.78	32	✪✪✪	3	N.A.		N.A.	
	DEM	44.95	HYPO New Europe	H024	30/04/90	LUX	3.89	86	21.51	77	2.56	38.20	68	✪	2	71.54	35	N.A.	
▲	DEM	21.83	Indosuez European Smaller Cos	B033	30/12/94	LUX	5.81	48	20.50	87	N.A.	N.A.				N.A.		N.A.	
▲	DEM	70.54	Inter Strategie Europe Centre	B069	29/09/89	LUX	N.A.	—	11.53	140	2.45	37.70	72	✪✪	2	84.38	17	N.A.	
	LUF	154.62	Interselex Europa B	G009	31/08/94	LUX	4.25	79	18.51	111	N.A.	N.A.				N.A.		N.A.	
▲	USD	37.83	INVESCO PS Euro Enterprise	I014	31/12/90	LUX	8.07	26	32.80	19	3.03	64.59	12	✪✪✪✪✪	4	99.21	10	N.A.	
▲	USD	41.46	INVESCO PS European Gth	I014	31/12/90	LUX	6.93	38	27.45	35	2.94	51.53	24	✪✪✪✪	3	79.64	26	N.A.	
	LUF	41.90	Ippa Portf Stock Yield B	B035	31/03/92	LUX	5.07	60	18.16	115	2.65	37.30	73	✪	2	N.A.		N.A.	
	USD	28.36	JF European	J004	27/02/87	HK	5.42	52	30.49	26	3.91	31.71	86	✪✪	1	81.13	23	N.A.	
●	DEM	0.51	JRIA European	J002	29/01/93	IRL	0.53	139	20.33	90	2.60	23.59	97	✪	1	N.A.		N.A.	
	DEM	5.34	JRIA/Greater European DM	J002	30/12/94	IRL	0.55	138	20.36	88	N.A.	N.A.				N.A.		N.A.	

▲ SIB Approved ● Insurance Fund **Values in US Dollars, on an offer to offer price basis with gross income reinvested**

Data Source Micropal™

Europe Equity

continued

	CCY	Fund Size ($mil)	Fund Name	Manager Code	Fund Start Date	Domicile Code	3 Mths 97 % Chg	3 Mths 97 Rank	1 Year % Chg	1 Year Rank	Micropal Star Rating 3 Years Volatility	3 Years % Chg	3 Years Rank	3 Years Rating	Risk Return Rating	5 Years % Chg	5 Years Rank	10 Years % Chg	10 Years Rank
		60.68	**Mean/Count**				**4.59**	**156**	**23.89**	**145**	**2.94**	**45.75**	**102**		**1**	**75.88**	**66**	**174.34**	**8**
▲	GBP	16.05	Jupiter Tyndall GF Eur Sm Cos	J010	31/12/93	LUX	-4.67	156	45.08	7	3.44	64.93	11	✪✪✪✪	4	N.A.		N.A.	
	DEM	109.09	KB Lux Equity Noveurope	K011	29/12/89	LUX	4.53	72	19.85	94	2.40	38.48	67	✪	3	60.05	51	N.A.	
	DEM	19.23	KB Lux Key Euro Smaller Cies	K011	19/07/96	LUX	4.83	65	N.A.		N.A.	N.A.				N.A.		N.A.	
▲	DEM	9.60	Lazard Pan European	L002	31/01/92	GU	2.54	114	30.95	23	2.86	61.72	15	✪✪✪✪✪	4	N.A.		N.A.	
	ECU	25.70	Lion Interaction Europe	C062	31/03/89	LUX	5.90	47	28.30	32	2.74	55.59	16	✪✪✪✪	4	83.22	20	N.A.	
▲	ECU	149.22	Lloyds IP European Equity	L016	31/03/92	LUX	2.40	116	22.53	65	2.39	47.16	38	✪✪✪	4	N.A.		N.A.	
	USD	4.68	LM Glbl European Equity B	L005	29/03/96	NL	2.94	106	N.A.		N.A.	N.A.				N.A.		N.A.	
	DEM	43.54	LOI Smaller European Cos	L019	28/02/94	LUX	1.48	128	39	14	N.A.	N.A.				N.A.		N.A.	
	ECU	225.05	Luxlife Actions Europeennes	L024	23/09/94	LUX	3.30	96	27.44	36	N.A.	N.A.				N.A.		N.A.	
	USD	30.11	M.Lynch Euro Equity Portf O	M023	31/08/90	LUX	7.27	34	23.36	59	3.16	45.02	46	✪✪✪	2	84.66	16	N.A.	
▲	USD	9.50	Manulife Regent GF Euro Gth	M006	30/09/87	LUX	7.09	36	27.38	37	3.01	54.28	19	✪✪✪✪	3	106.50	7	N.A.	
	DEM	0	MeesPierson UF Eur Large Cap	M012	01/03/96	LUX	1.64	125	N.A.		N.A.	N.A.				N.A.		N.A.	
	DEM	N.S.	MeesPierson UF Eur Small Cap	M012	01/03/96	LUX	-3.72	154	N.A.		N.A.	N.A.				N.A.		N.A.	
	DEM	4.58	Merck Finck Invest EuroLux A	M014	29/10/93	LUX	-3.13	153	15.54	127	2.71	35.93	79	✪✪	2	N.A.		N.A.	
▲	USD	119.51	Mercury ST European	M021	30/11/93	LUX	4.15	82	26.07	42	2.93	47.70	36	✪✪✪✪	3	N.A.		N.A.	
▲	USD	176.01	Mercury ST European Opps	M021	29/05/87	LUX	4.94	62	40.96	11	2.97	83.25	4	✪✪✪✪✪	5	131.67	3	N.A.	
▲	GBP	33.43	Midland ICF European Growth	M028	28/02/90	LUX	N.A.	—	23.22	60	2.91	47.74	35	✪✪✪	3	75.86	32	N.A.	
▲	USD	10.80	Midland ICF European Opps	M028	29/03/91	LUX	N.A.	—	24.08	56	3.01	48.66	33	✪✪✪✪	3	92.02	13	N.A.	
▲	DEM	452.48	Morgan Grenfell Euro Cap Gth	M038	06/09/96	IRL	9.08	17	N.A.		N.A.	N.A.				N.A.		N.A.	
▲	GBP	546.05	Morgan Grenfell PF European	M038	29/12/89	IRL	4.59	71	28.48	31	3.23	66.80	10	✪✪✪✪✪	4	130.13	4	N.A.	
	ECU	134.88	Morgan Stanley Euro Equity	M039	29/03/91	LUX	4.91	64	21.46	78	2.80	49.09	31	✪✪✪	3	103.32	8	N.A.	
	USD	15.83	MultiLink European Equities	I011	20/09/96	LUX	12.44	7	N.A.		N.A.	N.A.				N.A.		N.A.	
	DEM	10.61	Nestor Europa	N002	31/12/93	LUX	14.82	5	13.91	136	2.36	37.84	71	✪✪	4	N.A.		N.A.	
	DEM	24.32	Odey European	O002	29/05/92	IOM	3.12	102	42.71	9	6.39	14.49	101	✪✪		N.A.		N.A.	
▲	DEM	3.30	Odey European Growth	O002	31/12/92	IRL	0.51	140	15.13	130	2.97	17.47	99	✪	1	N.A.		N.A.	
	USD	4.55	Odey European USD Inc	O002	25/02/94	BVI	14.97	4	39.79	13	N.A.	N.A.				N.A.		N.A.	
	GBP	9.32	Old Mutual Gnsy Euro Stkmkt	O003	29/12/95	GU	7.38	32	37.89	15	N.A.	N.A.				N.A.		N.A.	
	GBP	2.28	Old Mutual HK European Stkmkt	O004	28/04/95	HK	7.27	33	49.08	3	N.A.	N.A.				N.A.		N.A.	
	GBP	102.71	OMI (Gnsy) European Stkmkt	O005	31/07/85	GU	7.41	30	48.96	4	4.42	64.24	14	✪✪✪✪	2	176.60	1	238.69	1
	USD	1.47	OMI (Ire) Dllr Euro Stkmkt	O006	15/07/94	IRL	8.65	23	43	8	N.A.	N.A.				N.A.		N.A.	
▲	USD	66.17	OMI Galileo Euro Stkmkt	O007	31/05/94	IRL	7.40	31	48	5	N.A.	N.A.				N.A.		N.A.	
	USD	9.46	OYSTER Europe Value	B067	31/01/94	LUX	21.09	1	17.74	117	N.A.	N.A.				N.A.		N.A.	
	ECU	202.72	Parvest Europe B	B037	30/09/85	LUX	2.95	105	22.51	66	2.78	46.77	39	✪✪✪	3	81.59	22	145.23	6
	ECU	66.31	Parvest Europe Mid Cap B	B037	14/06/96	LUX	3.18	100	N.A.		N.A.	N.A.				N.A.		N.A.	
	USD	N.S.	PCP Europe	P007	15/03/96	CA	1.05	133	N.A.		N.A.	N.A.				N.A.		N.A.	
	ECU	44.49	Performa European Equity	P009	31/12/91	LUX	7.19	35	21.57	73	2.60	32	85	✪	1	59.60	52	N.A.	
	USD	N.S.	Permal Europe Ltd USD	P010	31/08/89	BVI	0.58	137	-3.26	145	3.71	28.42	93	✪✪	1	60.47	47	N.A.	
	USD	67.60	Perpetual Offshr European Gth	P011	28/11/86	JER	7.90	27	15.40	128	3.01	43.29	55	✪✪	2	83.88	19	175.95	4
	ECU	139.98	Pictet T.F. Euroval	P016	31/01/80	LUX	3.90	85	20.94	82	2.61	43.34	54	✪✪	3	75.14	33	157.59	5
	ECU	7.66	Pleiade Europe Equities	B039	26/02/93	LUX	8.77	22	18.84	108	2.47	45.52	43	✪✪✪	4	N.A.		N.A.	
	DEM	28.12	Portefeuille BG Actions Europe	B063	23/06/95	LUX	2.73	111	19.72	96	N.A.	N.A.				N.A.		N.A.	
	ECU	18.58	Prime Lipper Europe	P023	28/02/92	LUX	-1.18	148	21.56	74	2.48	42.25	56	✪✪	3	N.A.		N.A.	
	ECU	4.75	Proton IF European Equities	P024	29/09/95	BVI	1.88	123	22.85	61	N.A.	N.A.				N.A.		N.A.	
	USD	36.05	Quaestor Equity Europe	Q001	29/06/90	IRL	1.38	130	18.33	112	4.96	41.14	58	✪✪	2	70.90	37	N.A.	
	CHF	50.49	Raiffeisen Euro Actions A	F024	31/03/94	LUX	1.59	127	21.65	72	N.A.	N.A.				N.A.		N.A.	
▲	NLG	211.42	RG Europe Fund	R009	31/05/91	EN	9.13	14	26.68	41	2.89	47.69	37	✪✪✪	3	94.56	11	N.A.	
	GBP	4.91	RLI/Morgan Grenfell Euro Gth	R033	11/08/95	IOM	8.58	24	7.26	144	N.A.	N.A.				N.A.		N.A.	
●	GBP	14.45	Royal Life Intl European	R020	31/03/86	IOM	7.09	37	29.20	30	3.27	67.70	7	✪✪✪✪	4	123.42	6	223.67	2
	USD	53.91	S-E-Banken Fund Europa	S001	29/10/93	LUX	2.85	108	21.29	80	2.77	34.04	83	✪	1	N.A.		N.A.	
	USD	18.27	Samba Lux European Equity	S006	31/01/95	LUX	5.07	59	24.36	53	N.A.	N.A.				N.A.		N.A.	
▲	ECU	0.22	SanPaolo Ecu Actions	S004	28/02/90	LUX	1.40	129	18.32	113	2.40	43.47	53	✪✪	4	57.40	53	N.A.	
▲	CHF	3.96	Sarasin EuroSar SICAV	B038	28/06/91	LUX	4.48	73	19.98	93	2.79	44.16	49	✪✪✪	2	80.50	25	N.A.	
▲	ECU	31.92	SBC Eq Ptf Small & Mid Europe	S007	31/01/95	LUX	3.29	97	24.08	55	N.A.	N.A.				N.A.		N.A.	
▲	ECU	241.09	SBC Equity Portfolio Europe	S007	31/08/90	LUX	3.53	90	20.06	92	2.92	36.05	78	✪	1	62.48	46	N.A.	
	USD	33.97	Schroder Asia European	S011	31/03/88	HK	1.62	126	20.60	85	3.32	45.76	42	✪✪✪	2	93.36	12	N.A.	
▲	ECU	58.53	Schroder Intl Sel Eur Mkt Cap	S010	01/12/95	LUX	4.36	76	22.84	62	N.A.	N.A.				N.A.		N.A.	
▲	ECU	74.04	Schroder Intl Sel Euro Eqty	S010	30/07/93	LUX	5.49	51	25.20	45	2.59	50.85	27	✪✪✪✪	4	N.A.		N.A.	

▲ SIB Approved ● Insurance Fund Values in US Dollars, on an offer to offer price basis with gross income reinvested Data Source Micropal™

Europe Equity

continued

	CCY	Fund Size ($mil)	Fund Name	Manager Code	Fund Start Date	Domicile Code	3 Mths 97 % Chg	3 Mths 97 Rank	1 Year % Chg	1 Year Rank	Micropal Star Rating 3 Years Volatility	3 Years % Chg	3 Years Rank	Rating	Risk Return Rating	5 Years % Chg	5 Years Rank	10 Years % Chg	10 Years Rank
		60.68	**Mean/Count**				**4.59**	**156**	**23.89**	**145**	**2.94**	**45.75**	**102**		**1**	**75.88**	**66**	**174.34**	**8**
▲	ECU	39.98	Schroder Intl Sel Euro Sm Cos	S010	31/10/94	LUX	5.66	49	35.31	18	N.A.	N.A.				N.A.		N.A.	
	ECU	106.02	Scontinvest Euroval Euro Eq	S012	30/11/92	LUX	3.43	94	24.63	50	2.72	52.93	21	✪✪✪✪	4	N.A.		N.A.	
●	DEM	2.52	Scot Amicable Euro Tracker	S015	30/06/94	IRL	8.21	25	16.26	123	N.A.	N.A.				N.A.		N.A.	
▲	ECU	10.53	Scot Equitable IF Euro Equity	S017	31/07/92	LUX	3.21	99	17.49	119	3.16	36.48	75	✪✪	1	N.A.		N.A.	
	DEM	120.26	Share Euro Selection	B053	30/11/93	LUX	-3.04	151	35.46	17	2.96	105.02	3	✪✪✪✪✪	5	N.A.		N.A.	
	BEF	N.S.	Small Cap European Cap	B026	30/04/90	LUX	8.82	20	26.94	39	2.77	44.10	50	✪✪✪	3	53.30	56	N.A.	
	ECU	13.81	Sogelux Fd Equities Europe	S037	31/05/88	LUX	2.76	109	14.53	134	2.64	34.82	82	✪	1	51.75	57	N.A.	
	ECU	48.56	Sogenal Europe	S037	29/09/89	LUX	4.64	69	15.64	124	2.15	28.99	92	✪	1	49.51	59	N.A.	
	USD	25.08	Southern Intl European EQ	S041	04/10/96	LUX	0.84	135	N.A.		N.A.	N.A.				N.A.		N.A.	
	DEM	N.S.	SR Europe DEM	S031	29/02/96	BVI	5.98	45	N.A.		N.A.	N.A.				N.A.		N.A.	
	USD	42	SR Europe USD	S031	31/01/94	BVI	11.02	9	66.58	1	N.A.	N.A.				N.A.		N.A.	
	GBP	13.92	Sun All Intl Stlg Gl Mgd	S051	31/10/95	GU	2.58	113	14.99	132	N.A.	N.A.				N.A.		N.A.	
▲	ECU	2.45	Sun Life GP European Gth	S052	31/03/88	LUX	4.20	81	21.55	76	3.81	27.39	94	✪✪	1	38.95	62	N.A.	
▲	ECU	15.67	Svecia Euro Top 100 Sel III	S054	30/04/92	LUX	N.A.	—	16.64	121	2.21	29.23	91	✪	1	N.A.		N.A.	
▲	GBP	3.32	SVM European Gth	S018	30/09/93	IRL	14.07	6	50.30	2	5.86	151.86	1	✪✪✪✪✪	5	N.A.		N.A.	
▲	GBP	5.26	Swiss Life Proteus Euro Eq	S056	29/11/91	IRL	0.39	143	7.51	143	2.75	25.28	96	✪	1	33.79	63	N.A.	
	DEM	10.35	Syfrets Gl European Eq	S060	10/11/95	CA	0.68	136	15.37	129	N.A.	N.A.				N.A.		N.A.	
▲	CHF	10.36	Templeton GS European	T001	30/04/91	LUX	2.67	112	19.13	102	2.89	45.96	41	✪✪✪	3	66.30	41	N.A.	
▲	GBP	38.74	TSB OIF European	T013	30/04/90	JER	8.90	18	19.04	103	3.19	43.88	51	✪✪✪	2	142.67	2	N.A.	
	DEM	73.01	UBAM European Equity	U010	24/11/95	LUX	3.47	93	18.87	107	N.A.	N.A.				N.A.		N.A.	
	DEM	59.11	UBS (Lux) Equity Invst Europe	U001	31/07/90	LUX	4.24	80	16.38	122	2.71	35.93	80	✪	1	56.83	54	N.A.	
	DEM	305.42	UniEuropa	U012	30/11/92	LUX	5	61	24.21	54	2.59	38.57	66	✪	2	N.A.		N.A.	
	ECU	124.42	Vontobel Fund European Eq A	B017	29/11/91	LUX	1.33	131	22.13	69	3.12	40.35	61	✪✪	1	65.04	42	N.A.	
	ECU	22.79	Willerequity Europe	W004	31/07/92	LUX	4.46	74	15.58	126	2.63	39.56	64	✪✪	2	N.A.		N.A.	

Europe Central Equity

Funds investing in excess of 70% in developed Central Europe (Germany, Austria, Netherlands, France, Belgium, Luxembourg) equities or related instruments. Such funds may have an objective of capital and/or income growth, or to track a specified index or perform inversely to a given index. Funds in this category may leverage or gear by a maximum of 20% of total assets.

CCY	Fund Size ($mil)	Fund Name	Manager Code	Fund Start Date	Domicile Code	3 Mths 97 % Chg	3 Mths 97 Rank	1 Year % Chg	1 Year Rank	Micropal Star Rating 3 Years Volatility	3 Years % Chg	3 Years Rank	Rating	Risk Return Rating	5 Years % Chg	5 Years Rank	10 Years % Chg	10 Years Rank
	0	**Mean/Count**				**5.12**	**1**	**0**	**0**	**0**	**0**	**0**			**0**	**0**	**0**	**0**
CHF	N.S.	UBS (Lux) Equity I Central Eur	U001	30/09/96	LUX	5.12	1	N.A.		N.A.	N.A.				N.A.		N.A.	

▲ SIB Approved ● Insurance Fund

Data Source Micropal™

Europe (Mediterranean) Equity

Funds investing in excess of 70% in Southern European (Italy, Spain, Greece) equities or related instruments. Such funds may have an objective of capital and/or income growth, or to track a specified index or perform inversely to a given index. Funds in this category may leverage or gear by a maximum of 20% of total assets.

	CCY	Fund Size ($mil)	Fund Name	Manager Code	Fund Start Date	Domicile Code	3 Mths 97 % Chg	3 Mths 97 Rank	1 Year % Chg	1 Year Rank	Micropal Star Rating 3 Years Volatility	3 Years % Chg	3 Years Rank	3 Years Rating	Risk Return Rating	5 Years % Chg	5 Years Rank	10 Years % Chg	10 Years Rank
		10.32	**Mean/Count**				**2**	**3**	**21.60**	**3**	**4.22**	**32.41**	**3**		**3**	**25.80**	**3**	**0**	**0**
●	USD	4.66	Carlson Mediterranean	C011	28/09/90	LUX	-0.97	3	21.29	2	4.37	28.66	2	✪✪✪	3	30.93	1	N.A.	
▲	ECU	20.79	Inter Strategie Europe du Sud	B069	29/09/89	LUX	1.78	2	25.15	1	4.15	45.47	1	✪✪✪✪	4	28.15	2	N.A.	
▲	USD	5.52	Skandifond Mediterranean Eq	S030	28/02/89	LUX	5.17	1	18.37	3	4.13	23.10	3	✪✪	2	18.31	3	N.A.	

Europe Excluding UK Equity

Funds investing in excess of 70% in Europe (excluding the United Kingdom) equities or related instruments. Such funds may have an objective of capital and/or income growth, or to track a specified index or perform inversely to a given index. Funds in this category may leverage or gear by a maximum of 20% of total assets.

	CCY	Fund Size ($mil)	Fund Name	Manager Code	Fund Start Date	Domicile Code	3 Mths 97 % Chg	3 Mths 97 Rank	1 Year % Chg	1 Year Rank	Micropal Star Rating 3 Years Volatility	3 Years % Chg	3 Years Rank	3 Years Rating	Risk Return Rating	5 Years % Chg	5 Years Rank	10 Years % Chg	10 Years Rank
		120.09	**Mean/Count**				**6.43**	**63**	**22.54**	**54**	**2.92**	**47.93**	**43**		**2**	**83.34**	**35**	**154.08**	**14**
▲	DEM	7.75	Abtrust Atlas Contl Europe	A002	31/03/88	LUX	6.89	31	20.44	35	2.89	42.67	29	✪✪	2	73.91	25	N.A.	
	USD	4.65	Abtrust European Equity	A003	31/01/84	GU	8.69	15	19.53	39	3.51	32.20	39	✪✪	1	74.23	24	121.17	8
▲	USD	6.86	Aetna IUF European Eqty A	A011	29/04/88	LUX	4.89	46	19.88	38	2.94	47.59	21	✪✪✪	3	89.91	13	N.A.	
●	USD	0	Albany Intl European Dllr	A018	31/03/87	IOM	4.70	48	25.05	19	2.85	46.17	24	✪✪	3	73.79	26	N.A.	
●	GBP	0	Albany Intl European Stlg	A018	31/03/87	IOM	8.43	16	35.89	2	3.11	64.02	6	✪✪✪✪✪	4	109.70	3	N.A.	
▲	DEM	39.22	Allied Dunbar Europe	A020	30/06/87	IOM	9.19	11	32.78	6	3.31	69.65	2	✪✪✪✪✪	4	115.54	2	N.A.	
●	DEM	15.71	Allied Dunbar IB Europe	A021	30/09/93	IOM	9.36	8	31.65	7	3.08	68.19	3	✪✪✪✪✪	5	N.A.		N.A.	
	GBP	5.29	Apollo European	H023	17/05/96	GU	2.92	57	N.A.		N.A.	N.A.				N.A.		N.A.	
	GBP	0.85	AXA Eqty&Law IFM Euro Eqty	A039	29/11/85	IOM	7.50	24	20.81	33	2.50	46.48	23	✪✪	3	65.11	30	108.69	11
●	GBP	8.97	AXA Eqty&Law ILA Euro Eqty	A040	31/10/85	IOM	6.38	38	21.95	30	2.42	50.73	18	✪✪✪	4	77.26	23	120.57	9
●	USD	16.43	Carlson Continental Europe	C011	28/09/90	LUX	4.81	47	20.66	34	2.39	44.52	25	✪✪	3	81.41	19	N.A.	
▲	ECU	188.48	Citi PF Contntl Euro Eq	C036	30/09/88	LUX	6.42	37	21.50	32	2.84	43.79	27	✪✪	2	78.29	22	N.A.	
	GBP	15.83	Continental Euro Sentinel	I009	26/05/95	BAH	-5.38	63	4.74	53	N.A.	N.A.				N.A.		N.A.	
▲	ECU	76.94	Coutts GF Cont European Eq	C052	31/05/93	IRL	5.61	42	11.34	52	2.91	32.84	38	✪	1	N.A.		N.A.	
▲	ECU	17.01	CU PP European Growth	C070	31/05/90	LUX	6.12	39	12.88	50	2.78	30.47	40	✪	1	56.79	34	N.A.	
●	DEM	213.73	Dit Lux Europa Aktien RB	D017	31/01/94	LUX	0.03	62	12.91	49	N.A.	N.A.				N.A.		N.A.	
	DEM	1.28	F&C RAF Contl Euro Eqtys	F003	29/05/92	JER	7.82	21	14.51	48	2.95	35.64	34	✪✪	1	N.A.		N.A.	
▲	DEM	610.66	Fidelity Fds Europe	F011	28/09/90	LUX	9.35	9	23.77	23	3.02	64.25	5	✪✪✪✪	4	107.77	4	N.A.	
	GBP	0.73	Finistere European Life	F016	31/05/84	GU	5.56	43	21.82	31	3.37	49.02	19	✪✪✪	2	82.63	18	96.29	13
	DEM	4.48	Five Arrows IE Europe	R014	30/09/93	GU	2.54	58	26.13	16	2.86	55.15	14	✪✪✪✪	3	N.A.		N.A.	
▲	DEM	100.94	Fleming FF Continental Euro	F020	30/11/88	LUX	5.96	41	28.42	10	3.05	40.91	30	✪	2	79.39	21	N.A.	
	USD	47.79	Fleming Frontier Euro Discov	F021	10/03/95	LUX	13.49	1	37.03	1	N.A.	N.A.				N.A.		N.A.	
	GBP	3.89	Friends Provdnt European	F031	31/05/94	GU	7.95	19	29.82	9	N.A.	N.A.				N.A.		N.A.	
▲	DEM	113.10	Gartmore CSF Cont'l Europe	G007	31/10/85	JER	7.33	25	28.10	12	2.72	70.61	1	✪✪✪✪✪	5	94.31	10	160.86	7
▲●	ECU	76.57	Groupe Indosuez Contl Euro	G017	31/12/90	LUX	4.91	45	24.61	20	2.81	59.35	11	✪✪✪✪	4	91.61	12	N.A.	
▲	USD	158	GT European Smllr Cos A Share	G018	31/10/84	IRL	8.19	17	33.46	4	3.03	47.41	22	✪✪✪	2	83.35	17	113.99	10
▲	USD	72.82	Guinness Flight European	G019	31/01/85	GU	4.13	51	22.86	28	2.93	52.97	17	✪✪✪	3	86.71	15	178.95	5
●	CHF	N.S.	Hansard EU European	H010	17/02/95	IRL	12.09	2	18.91	42	N.A.	N.A.				N.A.		N.A.	
●	FRF	2.46	Hansard European Growth	H011	26/02/93	IOM	9.80	6	19.30	40	3.60	40	31	✪✪	1	N.A.		N.A.	
●	CHF	11.81	Hansard European Managed	H011	28/02/90	IOM	6.43	36	23.36	25	2.67	38.68	32	✪✪	2	87.07	14	N.A.	
▲	DEM	12.93	HCIC European	H026	30/12/94	IOM	4.37	50	19.09	41	N.A.	N.A.				N.A.		N.A.	
▲	USD	10.09	Henderson HF European	H025	29/06/84	LUX	7.10	28	25.76	17	3.79	42.75	28	✪✪	1	66.87	28	90.58	14
	USD	36.10	Investissements Atlantiques	I015	31/05/84	LUX	0.72	61	25.52	18	3.68	59.37	10	✪✪✪	2	116.22	1	222.86	2
	GBP	7.80	Irish Life Intl Euro Equity	I017	30/09/94	IRL	3.45	56	24.15	22	N.A.	N.A.				N.A.		N.A.	
	USD	17.34	JF Continental European	J004	31/10/85	HK	6.61	34	24.38	21	3.30	22.37	43	✪	1	58.98	33	106.29	12
▲	GBP	8.95	Jupiter Tyndall GF European	J010	31/12/90	LUX	1.78	59	23.49	24	2.76	43.99	26	✪✪	3	79.46	20	N.A.	
▲	DEM	6.52	KB Continental European	K007	30/11/89	GU	6.51	35	16.28	46	2.59	34.88	35	✪	2	56.63	35	N.A.	
▲	DEM	N.S.	Lazard European DEM	L002	31/01/85	IRL	3.92	53	23.16	26	2.64	54.50	15	✪✪✪✪	4	97.46	6	224.33	1
▲	USD	N.S.	Lazard European USD	L002	31/01/85	GU	3.88	54	22.19	29	2.93	53.28	16	✪✪✪	3	95.81	9	220.92	3

▲ SIB Approved ● Insurance Fund Values in US Dollars, on an offer to offer price basis with gross income reinvested Data Source Micropal™

Europe Excluding UK Equity

continued

	CCY	Fund Size ($mil)	Fund Name	Manager Code	Fund Start Date	Domicile Code	3 Mths 97 % Chg	Rank	1 Year % Chg	Rank	Micropal Star Rating 3 Years Volatility	% Chg	Rank	Rating	Risk Return Rating	5 Years % Chg	Rank	10 Years % Chg	Rank
		120.09	**Mean/Count**				**6.43**	**63**	**22.54**	**54**	**2.92**	**47.93**	**43**		**2**	**83.34**	**35**	**154.08**	**14**
▲	GBP	5.04	Lazard SIT Europe Index	L001	28/02/89	GU	6.01	40	26.15	15	2.59	56.68	13	✪✪✪	4	96.06	8	N.A.	
	DEM	26.27	M-Fund Continental Europe	B013	31/12/93	LUX	9.05	12	31.61	8	2.35	67.58	4	✪✪✪✪	5	N.A.		N.A.	
	GBP	3673.82	Mercury IIT Continental Eur	M018	31/08/72	JER	4.45	49	26.60	14	2.65	57.17	12	✪✪✪✪	4	97.38	7	178.42	6
▲	GBP	29.82	Mercury OST European	M020	28/11/86	LUX	9.26	10	35.07	3	3.08	62.53	7	✪✪✪✪	4	105.74	5	213.15	4
▲	USD	21.90	Newton UGF Contl Euro	N006	29/02/88	JER	6.93	29	28.38	11	2.80	61.48	9	✪✪✪✪	5	85.60	16	N.A.	
	ECU	126.14	Pictet T.F. Euro Opportunity	P016	31/01/91	LUX	7.10	27	17.41	44	2.67	27.77	42	✪	1	68.34	27	N.A.	
▲	GBP	55.25	Prolific IF European Gth	P027	30/04/92	IRL	7.73	23	20.22	36	2.98	36.28	33	✪	1	N.A.		N.A.	
	USD	12.32	Quilter Quad Euro Eq	Q003	13/01/95	IOM	3.95	52	33.27	5	N.A.	N.A.				N.A.		N.A.	
▲	DEM	9.71	RBC GI Cont'l European	R003	24/11/95	GU	0.88	60	15.61	47	N.A.	N.A.				N.A.		N.A.	
	USD	1.40	RLI/GT European Smllr Cos	R025	19/01/96	IOM	8.88	14	N.A.		N.A.	N.A.				N.A.		N.A.	
	ECU	19.82	Scot Prov GP European Equity	S014	30/09/91	IOM	9.38	7	17.91	43	2.70	34	37	✪	2	63.43	31	N.A.	
▲	GBP	80.18	Singer & Fried European Gth	S027	30/04/93	IRL	3.82	55	23.14	27	3.22	61.73	8	✪✪✪✪	3	N.A.		N.A.	
▲	USD	298.83	Skandifond Contl Euro Equity	S030	30/12/88	LUX	6.93	30	16.67	45	2.71	29.65	41	✪	1	65.92	29	N.A.	
	CHF	4.13	Swiss Life Proteus HC Gth Cos	S056	20/10/95	IRL	10.52	4	-2.44	54	N.A.	N.A.				N.A.		N.A.	
▲	DEM	56.31	TGA European Eq	T009	28/02/89	LUX	9.84	5	27.46	13	3.19	47.79	20	✪✪✪	2	91.83	11	N.A.	
▲	DEM	49.53	TGA European Smaller Cos	T009	12/07/96	LUX	7.77	22	N.A.		N.A.	N.A.				N.A.		N.A.	
	FRF	57.96	UAP European Securities	U009	31/01/94	LUX	6.62	33	19.92	37	N.A.	N.A.				N.A.		N.A.	
▲	DEM	34.19	Von Ernst GP European Eqty	B021	30/11/89	LUX	7.90	20	11.93	51	2.19	34.05	36	✪	2	62.45	32	N.A.	

Far East & Pacific Equity

Funds investing in excess of 70% in Far Eastern equity or related instruments. Such funds may have an objective of capital and/or income growth, or to track a specified index or perform inversely to a given index. Funds in this category may leverage or gear by a maximum of 20% of total assets.

	CCY	Fund Size ($mil)	Fund Name	Manager Code	Fund Start Date	Domicile Code	3 Mths 97 % Chg	Rank	1 Year % Chg	Rank	Micropal Star Rating 3 Years Volatility	% Chg	Rank	Rating	Risk Return Rating	5 Years % Chg	Rank	10 Years % Chg	Rank
		49.79	**Mean/Count**				**-1.41**	**81**	**4.74**	**82**	**4.30**	**-6.76**	**61**			**64.64**	**48**	**199.37**	**16**
	USD	1.12	Abtrust Pacific Enterprise	A003	31/07/87	GU	-5.04	60	6.50	33	4.92	-16.72	48	✪✪		41.15	34	N.A.	
▲	USD	44.57	AEB Worldfolio 11 Pacific Eqs	A009	30/03/90	LUX	-6.79	70	-1.03	58	3.64	-2.69	29	✪✪✪		19.73	43	N.A.	
▲	USD	62.20	Allied Dunbar Far East	A020	31/05/84	IOM	-3.73	53	8.96	23	3.79	15.61	3	✪✪✪✪✪		126.27	4	263.81	4
●	USD	18.38	Allied Dunbar IB Far East	A021	30/09/93	IOM	-1.63	33	7.21	29	3.52	14.79	4	✪✪✪✪✪		N.A.		N.A.	
	USD	4.42	Alpha Pacific	A023a	29/12/89	BVI	6.43	5	-1.46	60	2.53	-24.94	53	✪		22.14	42	N.A.	
	USD	2.84	Asia Equity Dynamic 90's	B067	30/04/90	LUX	-4.57	57	10.06	17	3.41	-12.37	42	✪		34.01	39	N.A.	
	USD	2.25	Asia Pacific Capital Strat	P014	30/06/94	BER	-3.20	48	-13.72	79	N.A.	N.A.				N.A.		N.A.	
	USD	585.80	Asian Capital Holdings	M011	31/03/93	LUX	N.A.	—	N.A.		N.A.	N.A.		✪		N.A.		N.A.	
	USD	12.19	Asian Technology Portfolio A	A005	31/07/96	LUX	-1.67	34	N.A.		N.A.	N.A.				N.A.		N.A.	
●	USD	0.45	AXA Eqty&Law IFM F East Eqty	A039	29/11/85	IOM	-5.97	64	1.42	46	3.38	6.03	16	✪✪✪✪		39.36	35	95.46	14
●	USD	8.90	AXA Eqty&Law ILA F East Eqty	A040	31/10/85	IOM	-6.56	66	0.21	50	3.30	4.23	20	✪✪✪		49.18	32	106.26	13
	USD	79.71	Baring IUF Pacific	B049	30/11/78	IRL	-7.21	72	12.68	9	5.78	-17.34	49	✪✪		94.09	10	369.13	1
▲	USD	96.62	BT IIS Asian Growth	B077	30/10/92	IRL	5.82	6	3.86	41	4.30	-9.22	35	✪✪		N.A.		N.A.	
	USD	9	Buttress Asia	B080	31/07/90	BER	1.41	18	9.94	18	7.15	-16.02	47	✪✪		99.48	7	N.A.	
	USD	8.80	CIBC PCF Far East	C021	29/04/94	GU	1	20	3.81	42	N.A.	N.A.				N.A.		N.A.	
	USD	1.50	CIBC-CEF Pacific Venture	C017	31/08/88	BER	42.51	1	133.33	1	8.18	26.99	1	✪✪✪✪	2	92.62	12	N.A.	
▲	USD	14.90	CL Pacific Growth	C063	30/06/88	HK	1.92	16	16.32	7	4.61	-3.73	30	✪✪✪		161.31	1	N.A.	
	USD	30.62	Comgest Asia	C045	31/05/93	LUX	0.81	22	17.37	5	4.36	0.18	24	✪✪✪		N.A.		N.A.	
	USD	7.03	EDM International Asia	E009	30/06/94	LUX	-0.69	28	12.48	10	N.A.	N.A.				N.A.		N.A.	
	USD	N.S.	EPIC MF Pacific Basin Equities	A024	20/10/95	LUX	-6.26	65	-2.31	62	N.A.	N.A.				N.A.		N.A.	
	USD	7	Europa Asian Equity	E013	31/12/92	CA	2.08	15	9.46	21	2.52	7.53	12	✪✪✪✪		N.A.		N.A.	
▲	USD	75.20	Fidelity Fds Pacific	F011	31/01/94	LUX	-6.72	68	-3.30	68	N.A.	N.A.				N.A.		N.A.	
	USD	17.93	Five Arrows IP Asia Pacific	R016	30/12/94	GU	-3.12	44	12.32	11	N.A.	N.A.				N.A.		N.A.	
▲	USD	271.14	Fleming FF Pacific	F020	30/11/88	LUX	3.62	11	-5.89	69	4.53	-28.84	55	✪		50.56	31	N.A.	

▲ SIB Approved ● Insurance Fund **Values in US Dollars, on an offer to offer price basis with gross income reinvested** Data Source Micropal™

Far East & Pacific Equity

continued

	CCY	Fund Size ($mil)	Fund Name	Manager Code	Fund Start Date	Domicile Code	3 Mths 97 % Chg	3 Mths 97 Rank	1 Year % Chg	1 Year Rank	Micropal Star Rating: Volatility	3 Years % Chg	3 Years Rank	Rating	Risk Return Rating	5 Years % Chg	5 Years Rank	10 Years % Chg	10 Years Rank
		49.79	**Mean/Count**				**-1.41**	**81**	**4.74**	**82**	**4.30**	**-6.76**	**61**			**64.64**	**48**	**199.37**	**16**
	GBP	2.59	Friends Provdnt Far East	F031	31/05/94	GU	-5.41	62	9.33	22	N.A.	N.A.				N.A.		N.A.	
▲	DEM	59.86	GAM Orient Fonds	G002	30/09/91	IOM	-1.92	37	-0.14	51	3.44	14.40	5	✪✪✪✪✪		70.57	22	N.A.	
	USD	295.20	GAM Pacific	G003	30/11/83	IOM	-2.44	40	0.86	48	3.47	12.95	6	✪✪✪✪✪		68.02	23	274.33	3
	USD	71	GT Asia A Share	G018	28/11/75	IRL	-2.44	39	8.74	26	4.15	5.34	17	✪✪✪✪		37.05	37	227.88	7
▲	USD	33.14	Guinness Flight Jap & Pacific	G019	31/01/85	GU	-3.20	47	-0.41	52	3.23	-0.84	25	✪✪✪		71.16	21	225.72	8
▲	USD	2.92	Hambros Super Asean Japan Gth	H004	29/11/91	GU	-7.55	74	9.72	19	5.85	-23.72	51	✪		81.33	15	N.A.	
●	USD	N.S.	Hansard EU US Dllr Pac Mgd	H010	17/02/95	IRL	-1.76	35	5.68	35	N.A.	N.A.				N.A.		N.A.	
●	USD	17.04	Hansard Pacific Managed	H011	28/02/90	IOM	-4.88	59	9.55	20	3.40	8.24	11	✪✪✪✪✪		73.84	20	N.A.	
●	USD	1.32	Hansard\JF Pacific Smllr Cos	H019	08/07/94	IOM	4.74	7	4.33	40	N.A.	N.A.				N.A.		N.A.	
▲	USD	18.16	HCIC Pacific & Far East	H026	30/12/94	IOM	-5.60	63	-0.97	56	N.A.	N.A.				N.A.		N.A.	
	USD	41.69	Hermes Asian	H028	30/04/92	BER	2.69	14	-0.62	54	2.54	-13.09	44	✪		N.A.		N.A.	
▲	GBP	8.63	Hill Samuel OS Far Eastern	H030	31/08/90	JER	-7.43	73	-3.21	67	4.05	12.59	8	✪✪✪✪		52.10	29	N.A.	
	HKD	22.68	Indosuez Pacific	I007	28/02/77	HK	-4.28	55	6.31	34	4.40	-2.33	28	✪✪✪		92.20	13	154.99	11
	USD	11.61	JF Masterfund Asia Gth	J004	20/10/95	HK	-1.59	32	-15.58	81	N.A.	N.A.				N.A.		N.A.	
	USD	0.79	JF Nomura Asia	J004	31/08/87	HK	-1.16	30	-3.15	66	6	-46.47	59	✪		24.49	41	N.A.	
	USD	63.57	JF Pacific Income	J004	31/10/80	HK	-3.24	49	25.83	2	4.43	3.87	21	✪✪✪✪		95.71	9	248.43	6
	USD	219.06	JF Pacific Securities	J004	26/05/78	HK	4.14	8	-8.75	74	5.32	-34.26	58	✪		93.21	11	250.21	5
	USD	36.59	JF Pacific Smaller Companies	J004	31/05/93	CA	-0.13	26	5.44	39	5.50	-54.63	61	✪		N.A.		N.A.	
	USD	2.74	LG Intl Fund Asian Growth	L014	31/01/96	LUX	0.41	24	N.A.		N.A.	N.A.				N.A.		N.A.	
▲	USD	2.63	Liberty NW-Newport Pacific	L011	08/12/95	LUX	-7.87	75	-7.20	71	N.A.	N.A.				N.A.		N.A.	
	USD	23.85	Lion Interaction Asie Pac	C062	31/03/89	LUX	-7.95	76	-12.61	78	3.62	-14.01	46	✪✪		9.85	46	N.A.	
	USD	3.29	LM Glbl Pacific Equity B	L005	29/03/96	NL	-6.72	69	N.A.		N.A.	N.A.				N.A.		N.A.	
●	USD	343.10	Luxlife Actions Pacifique	L024	23/09/94	LUX	3.45	12	-10.54	76	N.A.	N.A.				N.A.		N.A.	
	USD	4.75	M-Fund Pacific Rim	B013	31/12/93	LUX	0.74	23	8.62	27	4.20	4.75	19	✪✪✪✪		N.A.		N.A.	
	USD	44.70	M.Lynch Pacific EQ Portf A	M023	31/08/94	LUX	3.09	13	6.58	32	N.A.	N.A.				N.A.		N.A.	
▲	USD	9.38	Manulife Regent GF Pac Basin	M006	30/09/87	LUX	-2.92	43	-12.40	77	4.23	-23.81	52	✪		76.45	18	N.A.	
▲	USD	2.52	MBf Pacific Enterprise	M010	31/03/87	HK	-8.66	80	10.75	15	4.96	-11.31	39	✪✪		58.55	25	N.A.	
	USD	11.17	Mega Pacific	M013	31/08/89	HK	N.A.	—	25.69	3	6.53	-12.07	41	✪✪		77.04	17	N.A.	
	USD	5.14	New Asian Fund Portfolio -A-	B067	31/01/90	LUX	-2.52	42	-1.89	61	3.39	-9.69	36	✪✪		27.02	40	N.A.	
▲	USD	13.68	Newport Pacific USD	N005	29/04/83	BER	-10.16	81	5.62	37	4.59	-0.93	26	✪✪✪		62.21	24	115.89	12
	USD	20.50	Northgate Pacific	N011	30/04/82	JER	6.63	4	10.14	16	4.39	-11.48	40	✪✪		57.54	27	78.27	15
	USD	2.13	Old Mutual Gnsy Pacific Stmkt	O003	29/12/95	GU	-8.57	79	-3.10	65	N.A.	N.A.				N.A.		N.A.	
	USD	1.47	Old Mutual HK Pacific Stkmkt	O004	28/04/95	HK	-8.32	77	-0.95	55	N.A.	N.A.				N.A.		N.A.	
	USD	39.11	OMI (Gnsy) Pacific Stkmkt	O005	31/05/82	GU	-8.53	78	-1.02	57	3.65	-9.19	34	✪✪		77.53	16	159.34	10
	USD	35.30	Orbitex Asia Pacific	O014	30/09/93	BAH	-1.48	31	0.26	49	4.29	-26.71	54	✪		N.A.		N.A.	
	USD	5.70	Pacific Nies Fund	E015	30/12/88	LUX	0.13	25	-7.13	70	5.41	-32.11	57	✪		16.30	44	N.A.	
	USD	48.80	Perpetual Offshr Far East Gth	P011	28/11/86	JER	-3.18	46	11.36	13	3.65	17.45	2	✪✪✪✪✪	3	149.19	2	366.51	2
	USD	24	Pierson Asia Pacific Growth	M011	29/06/90	LUX	N.A.	—	-7.48	72	3.79	-32.02	56	✪		-3.73	48	N.A.	
	USD	4.20	Pleiade Asia Pacific Equities	B039	30/11/93	LUX	-0.96	29	10.76	14	4.93	5.09	18	✪✪✪		N.A.		N.A.	
▲	USD	47.58	PRICOA WWIP Pacific Growth	P022	31/01/92	LUX	-3.57	51	3.28	44	3.52	-1.12	27	✪✪✪		N.A.		N.A.	
	LUF	N.S.	Puilaetco Quality Fd Pacific	P031	31/05/91	LUX	N.A.	—	-16.40	82	3.57	1.01	23	✪✪✪		9.58	47	N.A.	
	USD	1.61	Quilter Quad Far East Eq	Q003	13/01/95	IOM	-3.61	52	-0.43	53	N.A.	N.A.				N.A.		N.A.	
	JPY	1.76	RDS Global Pacific Basin B	R004	31/10/94	LUX	-6.80	71	-10	75	N.A.	N.A.				N.A.		N.A.	
	USD	28.79	Regent Discover Asia	R005	30/06/94	CA	15.90	2	-13.81	80	N.A.	N.A.				N.A.		N.A.	
▲	NLG	437.17	RG Pacific Fund	R009	31/05/91	EN	-3.75	54	-2.95	64	3.74	11.90	9	✪✪✪✪		58.37	26	N.A.	
●	USD	12.10	Royal Life/Baring Pacific	R022	30/10/87	IOM	-4.79	58	13.47	8	6.15	-12.44	43	✪✪		83.40	14	N.A.	
	USD	24.87	Schroder Asia FE Gth	S011	31/01/90	HK	-2.37	38	6.62	31	4.43	-13.81	45	✪✪		109.95	5	N.A.	
	USD	8.82	Schroder Asia Pacific Growth	S011	31/01/90	HK	-5.24	61	7.81	28	4.47	-6.06	32	✪✪✪		74.99	19	N.A.	
	USD	25	Scot Prov GP Far East Equity	S014	30/09/91	IOM	-2.46	41	5.64	36	3.55	7.47	13	✪✪✪✪		51.63	30	N.A.	
	HKD	10.04	SHK Pacific	S024	31/05/89	HK	-4.29	56	8.94	24	4.67	-10.34	38	✪✪		96.68	8	N.A.	
	USD	318	SR Asia	S031	31/01/94	BVI	13.02	3	17.01	6	N.A.	N.A.				N.A.		N.A.	
	USD	5.78	Stewart Asia	B072	06/01/95	CA	1.88	17	8.80	25	N.A.	N.A.				N.A.		N.A.	
▲	JPY	5.56	Sun Life GP Far East Growth	S052	31/03/88	LUX	-3.53	50	5.46	38	4.30	-9.75	37	✪✪		38.80	36	N.A.	
	USD	3.80	Syfrets GI Pacific Equity	S060	30/11/93	CA	-1.91	36	6.79	30	2.92	-5.77	31	✪✪✪		N.A.		N.A.	
	USD	155	Templeton Asia	T002	31/12/90	LUX	N.A.	—	25.09	4	5.16	12.73	7	✪✪✪✪		105.97	6	N.A.	
	USD	0.95	Thornton Eastern Crusader	T006	29/05/87	BER	1.23	19	1.25	47	6.05	-54	60	✪		14.31	45	N.A.	
	USD	1.08	Thornton Managed Far East	T006	31/12/93	CA	0.97	21	3.76	43	4.25	8.55	10	✪✪✪✪		N.A.		N.A.	

▲ SIB Approved ● Insurance Fund **Values in US Dollars, on an offer to offer price basis with gross income reinvested** Data Source Micropal™

Far East & Pacific Equity

continued

	CCY	Fund Size ($mil)	Fund Name	Manager Code	Fund Start Date	Domicile Code	3 Mths 97 % Chg	3 Mths 97 Rank	1 Year % Chg	1 Year Rank	Micropal Star Rating 3 Years Volatility	3 Years % Chg	3 Years Rank	3 Years Rating	Risk Return Rating	5 Years % Chg	5 Years Rank	10 Years % Chg	10 Years Rank
		49.79	**Mean/Count**				**-1.41**	**81**	**4.74**	**82**	**4.30**	**-6.76**	**61**			**64.64**	**48**	**199.37**	**16**
	USD	5.22	Thornton Oriental Income	T006	31/10/85	BER	3.87	10	11.98	12	3.20	6.24	14	✪✪✪✪		56.96	28	179.02	9
▲	GBP	74.21	Thornton Pacific Investment	T006	29/05/87	LUX	-3.13	45	2.32	45	3.54	-7.64	33	✪✪		41.76	33	N.A.	
▲	GBP	19.45	TSB OIF Far Eastern	T013	30/04/90	JER	-6.58	67	-2.94	63	3.74	2.53	22	✪✪✪✪		127.41	3	N.A.	
	CHF	11.52	Von Ernst Crossbow Far East	B020	28/02/79	CH	N.A.	—	-8.28	73	4.85	6.24	15	✪✪✪		35.28	38	74.68	16
	USD	17.50	Winchester Eastern Dragon	0008	29/10/93	BVI	-0.31	27	-1.30	59	2.68	-17.63	50	✪		N.A.		N.A.	

Far East & Pacific Ex Japan Equity

Funds investing in excess of 70% in Far Eastern equity or related instruments excluding Japan. Such funds may have an objective of capital and/or income growth, or to track a specified index or perform inversely to a given index. Funds in this category may leverage or gear by a maximum of 20% of total assets.

	CCY	Fund Size ($mil)	Fund Name	Manager Code	Fund Start Date	Domicile Code	3 Mths 97 % Chg	3 Mths 97 Rank	1 Year % Chg	1 Year Rank	Micropal Star Rating 3 Years Volatility	3 Years % Chg	3 Years Rank	3 Years Rating	Risk Return Rating	5 Years % Chg	5 Years Rank	10 Years % Chg	10 Years Rank
		101.49	**Mean/Count**				**-1.02**	**205**	**10.93**	**190**	**5.26**	**-7.19**	**135**			**114.98**	**94**	**348.33**	**19**
	DEM	19.53	A.L.S.A. Asian Tiger	A007	28/02/95	LUX	-2.86	120	-2.98	179	N.A.	N.A.				N.A.		N.A.	
▲	USD	73.81	AAF Asian Tigers Equity Fund	A001	25/11/94	LUX	-1.28	85	19.57	33	N.A.	N.A.				N.A.		N.A.	
▲	USD	13.17	Abtrust Atlas Pacific	A002	31/03/88	LUX	-2.34	108	15.27	58	4.38	5.75	22	✪✪✪✪		148.03	20	N.A.	
	USD	6.09	Abtrust Pacific Equity	A003	30/07/82	GU	-0.83	77	13.55	67	4.17	3.99	27	✪✪✪		60.11	84	100.07	19
●	USD	11.20	ACL Asian Growth	F017	28/02/94	BVI	0.89	51	5.53	140	N.A.	N.A.				N.A.		N.A.	
▲	USD	30.24	AEB Worldfolio 13 Asian Grwth	A009	30/11/94	LUX	-0.51	71	17.27	47	N.A.	N.A.				N.A.		N.A.	
▲	USD	53.25	Aetna IUF Asian Equity A	A011	29/04/88	LUX	-0.11	66	21.18	31	6.05	2.43	32	✪✪✪✪		184.53	7	N.A.	
▲	USD	19.88	Aetna IUF Emerging Asia A	A011	29/12/95	LUX	9.15	8	1.79	160	N.A.	N.A.				N.A.		N.A.	
▲	USD	276.42	AIG South East Asia	A017	31/07/91	IRL	-1.15	80	7.28	129	5.15	-6.50	74	✪✪		138.49	26	N.A.	
	USD	28	Al Kharejiyah GSF Pacific Eq	K005	31/10/89	GU	-3.13	128	3.47	152	5.48	-18.19	108	✪		107.13	51	N.A.	
●	USD	0	Albany Intl Pacific Basin Dllr	A018	31/07/87	IOM	-3.57	136	6.42	134	5.87	-28.19	127	✪		92.08	64	N.A.	
●	GBP	0	Albany Intl Pacific Basin Stlg	A018	31/07/87	IOM	-3.55	135	5.37	142	5.71	-23.18	119	✪		90.79	66	N.A.	
	USD	77.09	Alfred Berg Sicav Far East	A019	30/10/92	LUX	-0.98	78	9.60	109	4.48	-1.52	50	✪✪✪		N.A.		N.A.	
●	USD	11.19	Allied Dunbar IB Emerg Asia	A021	30/09/93	IOM	0.50	56	-1.64	177	4.46	-21.39	117	✪		N.A.		N.A.	
●	USD	438.30	Allied Dunbar IS Emerg Asia	A022	12/07/93	IOM	-1.63	93	0	174	4.58	-22	118	✪		N.A.		N.A.	
	GBP	16.51	Apollo Tiger	H023	29/04/94	GU	-0.82	76	13.61	65	N.A.	N.A.				N.A.		N.A.	
	USD	8.68	Asia Growth Fund	B067	31/05/90	LUX	-5.32	181	13.24	73	7.25	-20.12	113	✪✪		67.49	79	N.A.	
	USD	39.49	Asia Pacific Performance	D011	10/02/95	LUX	N.A.	—	N.A.		N.A.	N.A.				N.A.		N.A.	
	USD	17.27	Asia Plus Fund	C058	19/07/96	LUX	1.63	43	N.A.		N.A.	N.A.				N.A.		N.A.	
●	USD	0	AsiaInvest South East Asia	A036	28/06/91	BVI	N.A.	—	-5.66	182	7.38	-48.20	134	✪		2.55	93	N.A.	
	USD	212.25	Baer Multistock Pacific Stk A	J007	30/09/91	LUX	-1.30	86	31.97	1	5.18	11.15	9	✪✪✪✪✪		88.31	72	N.A.	
▲	GBP	73.36	Barclays (Lux) Pacific Equity	B047	29/02/72	LUX	-1.58	91	21.33	27	5.64	-5.20	70	✪✪✪		112.16	45	210.83	16
	USD	216.66	Barclays ASF S E Asia	B044	31/10/90	JER	-4.16	158	12.49	83	5.98	-17.85	107	✪		237.21	2	N.A.	
	USD	305.04	Baring IUF Octopus	B049	30/01/87	IRL	-6.32	190	13.54	68	6	-8.17	80	✪✪		102.71	55	N.A.	
	USD	13.50	Bermuda Eqty Pacific Rim	B066	30/11/90	BER	-5.38	182	17.12	48	4.54	24.64	1	✪✪✪✪✪	4	100.09	56	N.A.	
	USD	65.85	BSS Universal Far East	B029	30/04/92	LUX	-6.99	196	19.32	35	4.55	-1.74	53	✪✪✪		N.A.		N.A.	
●	USD	11.92	Carlson Eq Asian Small Cap	C011	31/05/95	LUX	4.12	31	19.30	36	N.A.	N.A.				N.A.		N.A.	
●	USD	93.74	Carlson Far East	C011	28/09/90	LUX	-2.37	109	9.53	110	4.17	-0.38	48	✪✪✪		111.66	46	N.A.	
	USD	18.49	CCF Sam EMF Asia Indx Track C	C015	30/06/95	LUX	-0.35	68	1.25	166	N.A.	N.A.				N.A.		N.A.	
▲●	USD	101.63	Chase Vista SE Asia Eq	C019	30/03/90	LUX	-4.15	157	15.94	55	4.91	-4.48	67	✪✪✪		89.26	71	N.A.	
	USD	0.04	CIBC-CEF Asian Consumer Trust	C017	31/05/91	BER	-4.52	168	-9.11	185	5.93	-71.44	135	✪		-47.47	94	N.A.	
	USD	17.10	CIBC-CEF Emerging Pac Mkts	C017	30/09/88	BER	7.62	14	2.03	159	6.41	-24.12	123	✪		87.58	73	N.A.	
	USD	2.30	CIBC-CEF Golden Buddha	C017	30/03/90	BER	-6.67	193	-17.96	189	8.69	-31.58	129	✪✪		93.20	62	N.A.	
	USD	2.10	CIBC-CEF Indonesia-Philippne	C017	28/02/90	BER	0	61	2.78	155	7.32	-34.51	130	✪		60.87	83	N.A.	
	USD	1.65	CIBC-CEF Thai-Philippine	C017	28/02/90	BER	-7.46	200	-19.94	190	7.02	-42.22	133	✪		35.87	92	N.A.	
	USD	20.13	Citi Asian Equity	C027	31/12/93	HK	-3.76	142	7.29	128	5.13	-4.30	66	✪✪✪		N.A.		N.A.	
▲	USD	301.33	Citi PF Emrng Asian Mkts Eq	C036	31/08/90	LUX	-1.51	90	1.53	164	6.51	-21.20	116	✪		91.55	65	N.A.	

▲ **SIB Approved** ● **Insurance Fund** **Values in US Dollars, on an offer to offer price basis with gross income reinvested** Data Source Micropal™

Far East & Pacific Ex Japan Equity

continued

	CCY	Fund Size ($mil)	Fund Name	Manager Code	Fund Start Date	Domicile Code	3 Mths 97 % Chg	3 Mths 97 Rank	1 Year % Chg	1 Year Rank	Micropal Star Rating 3 Years Volatility	3 Years % Chg	3 Years Rank	3 Years Rating	Risk Return Rating	5 Years % Chg	5 Years Rank	10 Years % Chg	10 Years Rank
		101.49	**Mean/Count**				**-1.02**	**205**	**10.93**	**190**	**5.26**	**-7.19**	**135**			**114.98**	**94**	**348.33**	**19**
▲	USD	136.32	Citi PF Ind Asia Pac Ex Japan	C036	30/09/88	LUX	-8.61	204	23.40	21	4.86	16.30	4	✪✪✪✪✪		106.41	52	N.A.	
	USD	5.05	Citicorp Super Asia Infra	C028	31/12/91	LUX	N.A.	—	1.56	163	5.10	-9.28	81	✪✪		82.25	75	N.A.	
▲	USD	5.90	CL Asian Smaller Companies	C063	29/01/93	CA	6.29	21	25.39	13	4.36	0.51	40	✪✪✪		N.A.		N.A.	
▲	USD	39.30	CL Asian Special Situations	C063	30/06/88	HK	1.19	49	17.32	46	5.06	-10.61	85	✪✪		105.76	53	N.A.	
●	USD	53.26	Clariden Asia Pacific	C039	31/12/90	CA	-8.49	203	19.17	39	4.56	-3.97	62	✪✪✪		89.72	69	N.A.	
●	USD	13.63	Clariden Asian Emerging Mkts	C039	29/04/94	GU	-5.73	185	-5.14	181	N.A.	N.A.				N.A.		N.A.	
▲	USD	2.19	CMI GNF Emerging Asia Equity	C042	28/02/95	LUX	7.38	15	4.02	148	N.A.	N.A.				N.A.		N.A.	
▲	USD	52.14	CMI GNF S E Asian Equity	C042	30/04/90	LUX	-3.84	145	13.45	69	5.56	5.46	25	✪✪✪✪		147.80	21	N.A.	
●	USD	33.30	CMI Ins Co SE Asian Equity	C043	31/12/90	IOM	-5.03	177	12.40	85	5.54	3.24	29	✪✪✪✪		137.09	28	N.A.	
●	USD	1	CMI Passport Emerging Asia Eq	C044	20/01/95	IOM	7.09	17	2.86	154	N.A.	N.A.				N.A.		N.A.	
●	USD	1.50	CMI Passport S E Asian Equity	C044	20/01/95	IOM	-4.09	153	12.12	86	N.A.	N.A.				N.A.		N.A.	
▲	USD	131.56	Coutts GF Pacific Basin Eqty	C052	31/05/93	IRL	-6.47	191	9.14	114	4.98	6.19	21	✪✪✪✪		N.A.		N.A.	
▲	USD	19.84	CSFB PIP II (Asia Pacific)	C069	30/10/92	LUX	-2.96	123	19.29	37	6.26	-6.57	75	✪✪		N.A.		N.A.	
▲	USD	6.54	CSFB PIP III (Emerging Asia)	C069	30/06/94	LUX	1.71	41	23.05	23	N.A.	N.A.				N.A.		N.A.	
▲	USD	55.09	CU PP Far Eastern	C070	31/10/88	LUX	-4.44	166	21.87	25	4.84	3.17	30	✪✪✪✪		112.85	44	N.A.	
	USD	5.50	Dao Heng Asia	D005	30/10/87	HK	-1.46	88	21.24	30	5.94	-6.80	77	✪✪		117.46	41	N.A.	
●	DEM	669.30	DBIM Mandarin Fonds	D006	30/04/93	LUX	1.03	50	8.79	119	4.53	1.81	37	✪✪✪✪		N.A.		N.A.	
●	DEM	182.48	DBIM Tigerfund	D006	30/11/89	LUX	0.66	54	6.07	135	4.49	1.61	39	✪✪✪		97.76	58	N.A.	
	DEM	166.73	DekaLux Pazifik	D009	30/06/94	LUX	-5.02	176	10.78	97	N.A.	N.A.				N.A.		N.A.	
	USD	3.12	Eagle Star Pacific Basin Eq	E001	29/09/95	IOM	-4.14	156	13.40	70	N.A.	N.A.				N.A.		N.A.	
	DEM	9.64	EM Fernost	U012	31/10/94	LUX	6.81	18	-5.80	183	N.A.	N.A.				N.A.		N.A.	
	USD	N.S.	EPIC MF Emerging Asian Eqs	A024	20/10/95	LUX	0.16	58	16.95	49	N.A.	N.A.				N.A.		N.A.	
	USD	N.S.	EV Medallion Gr China Gth B	E003	18/11/94	CA	-2.64	116	13.31	71	N.A.	N.A.				N.A.		N.A.	
▲	USD	11.79	F&C PF Emer Asian Equity	F001	29/09/89	LUX	2.95	34	-7.29	184	4.58	-19.71	111	✪		65.91	80	N.A.	
▲	USD	63.20	Fidelity Fds Asian Spec Sits	F011	30/09/94	LUX	-2.23	107	13.15	74	N.A.	N.A.				N.A.		N.A.	
▲	USD	602.80	Fidelity Fds South East Asia	F011	28/09/90	LUX	-4.86	175	16.58	50	5.46	6.76	19	✪✪✪✪✪		153.19	18	N.A.	
▲●	USD	34.31	Five Arrows GF Asian Opps	R011	31/07/92	LUX	-4.62	171	11.10	91	5.35	-2.31	54	✪✪✪✪		N.A.		N.A.	
▲●	USD	4.43	Five Arrows GF Asian Sm Cos	R011	29/04/94	LUX	4.47	27	24.79	14	N.A.	N.A.				N.A.		N.A.	
	USD	4.60	Five Arrows IE Asia	R014	30/09/93	GU	-3.90	149	10	105	5.35	-3.97	61	✪✪✪		N.A.		N.A.	
	USD	N.S.	Five Arrows IMP Asia Cap Gth	R015	31/07/96	GU	-1.81	97	N.A.		N.A.	N.A.				N.A.		N.A.	
	USD	75.27	FL Trust Asia	B031	29/01/93	LUX	-1.61	92	23.87	19	5.30	10.07	12	✪✪✪✪		N.A.		N.A.	
▲	USD	17.69	Fleming FF Asian Smllr Cos	F020	01/07/94	LUX	-3.88	147	19.14	40	N.A.	N.A.				N.A.		N.A.	
▲	USD	302.78	Fleming FF Eastern Opps	F020	31/08/89	LUX	-2.73	119	12.53	82	5.46	-13.81	96	✪		108	50	N.A.	
●	ECU	19.65	Frontrunner Far East Equities	F032	31/01/94	LUX	-10.82	205	2.27	157	N.A.	N.A.				N.A.		N.A.	
	USD	257.10	GAM ASEAN	G003	29/05/87	IOM	N.A.	—	1.14	168	5.07	-17.78	106	✪		119.89	38	N.A.	
▲	DEM	36.97	GAM Asia Fonds	G002	07/10/94	IOM	-2.53	114	0.73	170	N.A.	N.A.				N.A.		N.A.	
	USD	42.40	GAM Asian Developing Mkts	G003	29/12/95	BVI	5.11	25	5.53	141	N.A.	N.A.				N.A.		N.A.	
	USD	40.30	GAM East Asia	G003	31/07/85	PAN	-4.45	167	-3.97	180	4.83	-23.72	121	✪		134.56	31	365.92	7
▲	USD	40.49	Gartmore CSF Asia Pacific	G007	31/05/84	JER	-3.31	131	7.86	122	5.47	-2.87	57	✪✪✪		115.49	43	113.03	18
	USD	228.20	Goldman Sachs Asia	G013	31/05/94	LUX	-3.89	148	8.99	115	N.A.	N.A.				N.A.		N.A.	
	USD	17.89	Govett GSIL Far East Equity	G015	31/03/89	JER	1.62	44	14.89	59	5.33	0.32	41	✪✪✪✪		145.69	23	N.A.	
▲●	USD	72.11	Groupe Indosuez Asia Pac	G017	31/12/90	LUX	-2.88	121	14.20	61	5.82	-1.60	52	✪✪✪✪		135.17	30	N.A.	
▲	USD	140	GT Asian Small Cos A Share	G018	31/07/92	IRL	-2.97	124	15.61	57	4.42	-13.99	97	✪✪		N.A.		N.A.	
	USD	626	GT Newly Industrialised Ctrys	G018	30/09/86	BER	-0.04	62	30.65	4	5.54	17.52	3	✪✪✪✪✪	2	210.01	6	739.21	1
▲	USD	28.29	Guinness Flight Asian Sm Cos	G019	31/08/95	GU	6.30	20	27.02	8	N.A.	N.A.				N.A.		N.A.	
▲	USD	N.S.	Hambros Asian Korea Advantage	H006	12/01/96	IRL	-6.74	195	N.A.		N.A.	N.A.				N.A.		N.A.	
▲	USD	37.89	Hambros Eqty Sel SE Asian	H003	31/05/84	GU	-6.21	189	19.25	38	6.05	-7.18	78	✪✪		164.35	12	423.30	6
	USD	5.43	Hamon Asian Market Leaders	H007	22/12/95	IRL	8.18	13	11.31	90	N.A.	N.A.				N.A.		N.A.	
	USD	13.53	Hamon Selected Asian	H007	29/12/89	HK	9.83	7	27.47	7	6.90	-16.85	103	✪✪		171.39	9	N.A.	
●	USD	N.S.	Hansard EU SE Asia	H010	17/02/95	IRL	4.13	30	12.66	81	N.A.	N.A.				N.A.		N.A.	
●	USD	12.87	Hansard South East Asia	H011	31/07/92	IOM	-0.39	69	7.53	124	5.11	5.57	24	✪✪✪		N.A.		N.A.	
	USD	3.15	Hansard\CL Asian Special Sits	H013	31/07/92	IOM	6.40	19	13.55	66	4.65	-13.25	94	✪✪		N.A.		N.A.	
●	USD	8.41	Hansard\GT Newly Ind Countries	H016	27/09/91	IOM	2.16	37	31.56	2	6.02	22.64	2	✪✪✪✪	3	177.38	8	N.A.	
▲	USD	25.06	Henderson HF Pacific	H025	31/07/85	LUX	-1.27	84	9.33	112	5.55	-15.95	101	✪		142.24	25	313.95	11
	USD	53.30	HSBC Asian Countries Tactical	H034	31/12/92	BAH	-2.23	106	5.82	138	4.46	7.21	17	✪✪✪✪		N.A.		N.A.	
▲	USD	274.40	HSBC GIF Asian Equity	H033	31/07/74	LUX	-3.83	144	11.53	89	5.31	0.07	44	✪✪✪✪		146.16	22	598.28	2
	USD	3553	IBJ Asian Equity	I002	28/02/94	LUX	1.86	39	17.93	45	N.A.	N.A.				N.A.		N.A.	

▲ **SIB Approved** ● **Insurance Fund** **Values in US Dollars, on an offer to offer price basis with gross income reinvested** Data Source Micropal™

Far East & Pacific Ex Japan Equity

continued

	CCY	Fund Size ($mil)	Fund Name	Manager Code	Fund Start Date	Domicile Code	3 Mths 97 % Chg	3 Mths 97 Rank	1 Year % Chg	1 Year Rank	Micropal Star Rating Volatility	3 Years % Chg	3 Years Rank	3 Years Rating	Risk Return Rating	5 Years % Chg	5 Years Rank	10 Years % Chg	10 Years Rank
		101.49	**Mean/Count**				**-1.02**	**205**	**10.93**	**190**	**5.26**	**-7.19**	**135**			**114.98**	**94**	**348.33**	**19**
	USD	18.12	ImPac AP Asia	I005	31/10/95	CA	-7.32	199	1.47	165	N.A.	N.A.				N.A.		N.A.	
	USD	8.57	ImPac AP Asia Green Chips	I005	31/10/95	CA	12.74	5	26.74	9	N.A.	N.A.				N.A.		N.A.	
	USD	176.90	Indosuez Asian Growth	I007	31/10/84	HK	-1.70	94	12.05	88	5.56	-3.01	58	✪✪✪		168.01	11	325.92	10
	USD	175.13	Indosuez Asian Growth Fund	B033	31/10/84	LUX	-2.37	110	12.82	79	5.67	-2.54	56	✪✪✪		161.27	14	328.86	9
	USD	19.46	ING Intl-New Asia Equity Cap	I008	30/06/94	LUX	-6.05	188	6.01	136	N.A.	N.A.				N.A.		N.A.	
	USD	45.01	Inter Multi Inv Sud Est Asia	B069	31/12/90	LUX	-4.40	164	12.46	84	5.39	-2.43	55	✪✪✪		115.94	42	N.A.	
▲	USD	122.02	Inter Strategie Sud Est Asia	B069	31/01/90	LUX	-1.77	96	13.03	76	5.86	-3.02	59	✪✪✪		118.33	39	N.A.	
	USD	18	INVESCO Asia	A010	30/06/87	HK	8.74	11	21.92	24	6.11	-0.23	46	✪✪✪		235.29	4	N.A.	
	USD	10.50	INVESCO Asia Powerful	I013	31/08/89	LUX	-6.74	194	7.43	127	5.12	0.22	42	✪✪✪✪		108.50	49	N.A.	
	USD	6.90	INVESCO Asia Super Growth	I013	31/08/87	LUX	-1.02	79	21.27	29	5.68	2.06	35	✪✪✪✪		127.37	35	N.A.	
▲	USD	63	INVESCO PS Asia Tiger Gth	I014	31/12/90	LUX	-0.76	74	16.04	54	5.08	10.29	11	✪✪✪✪✪		157.93	15	N.A.	
	USD	167.50	JF Asia Select Limited	J004	29/12/89	CA	4.76	26	7.69	123	4.37	-6.15	73	✪✪		60	85	N.A.	
	USD	42.63	JF Asian Emerging Mkts Tst	J004	07/10/94	CA	13.47	3	0.60	171	N.A.	N.A.				N.A.		N.A.	
	USD	572.03	JF Eastern	J004	26/02/71	HK	-2.63	115	15.92	56	5.62	-5.20	71	✪✪✪		219.28	5	538.86	3
	USD	86.03	JF Eastern Smaller Companies	J004	31/12/91	HK	-0.05	63	23.56	20	4.81	-10.99	88	✪✪		302.96	1	N.A.	
●	USD	3.90	JRIA Far Eastern	J002	29/01/93	IRL	-4	151	-0.03	175	5.09	-20.42	114	✪		N.A.		N.A.	
	GBP	3.04	JRIA/Far East Stlg	J002	30/12/94	IRL	-4.77	174	8.92	117	N.A.	N.A.				N.A.		N.A.	
▲	USD	18.73	Jupiter Tyndall GF Asian Spec	J010	05/01/96	LUX	-1.20	81	N.A.		N.A.	N.A.				N.A.		N.A.	
▲	GBP	2.98	Jupiter Tyndall GF Tiger	J010	31/12/90	LUX	-2.01	102	-2.26	178	4.17	-26.89	126	✪		68.01	78	N.A.	
▲	USD	12.62	Jupiter Tyndall WUF Tiger	J008	31/01/84	BER	-3.33	132	2.92	153	4.08	-20.50	115	✪		61.48	82	230.18	14
▲	USD	54.48	KB Far East	K007	27/02/76	GU	-3.61	138	12.95	78	4.70	1.76	38	✪✪✪✪		118.05	40	233.26	13
	USD	57.49	KB Lux Key Far East	K011	28/02/91	LUX	0.10	59	29.41	6	4.77	6.61	20	✪✪✪✪		132.21	32	N.A.	
▲	USD	15.30	KB SEL Emerging Asia	K008	28/02/90	LUX	-0.78	75	9.92	107	5	14	7	✪✪✪✪✪		142.61	24	N.A.	
▲	USD	N.S.	Lazard Asia Pacific	L002	31/01/92	GU	-3.12	127	7.25	130	5.43	-17.13	104	✪		N.A.		N.A.	
	USD	22.99	LG Asian Smaller Companies	L013	30/06/92	BER	7.20	16	10.92	95	4.02	-6.60	76	✪✪		N.A.		N.A.	
▲	USD	16.41	Liberty NW-Newport Tiger	L011	31/10/95	LUX	-7	197	10.43	101	N.A.	N.A.				N.A.		N.A.	
	USD	0.12	Lion Fortune CL Asian Growth C	C062	23/08/96	LUX	1.76	40	N.A.		N.A.	N.A.				N.A.		N.A.	
▲	USD	164.27	Lloyds IP Pacific Equity	L016	31/03/92	LUX	-1.27	83	10.08	103	5.35	-5.21	72	✪✪		N.A.		N.A.	
	USD	38.40	LOI Pacific Rim	L019	29/07/94	LUX	-0.29	67	12.96	77	N.A.	N.A.				N.A.		N.A.	
	USD	81.10	M.Lynch Dragon Portfolio O	M023	29/05/92	LUX	-3.80	143	16.19	53	5.25	1.88	36	✪✪✪✪		N.A.		N.A.	
▲	USD	10.39	Manulife Regent GF Tiger	M006	31/03/93	LUX	-2	101	-15.81	188	3.50	-39.56	131	✪		N.A.		N.A.	
	USD	0.74	MBf Oriental Growth	M010	30/11/87	HK	-1.21	82	2.78	156	5.84	-26.68	125	✪		46.11	90	N.A.	
	USD	N.S.	MeesPierson UF Asian Pacific	M012	01/03/96	LUX	-5.24	179	N.A.		N.A.	N.A.				N.A.		N.A.	
	GBP	2058.34	Mercury IIT Pacific	M018	28/06/85	JER	-1.71	95	9.90	108	4.33	-1.31	49	✪✪✪		99.91	57	220.65	15
▲	GBP	28.18	Mercury OST Pacific	M020	28/11/86	LUX	-4.01	152	5.84	137	5.71	-23.45	120	✪		90.69	67	176.99	17
	USD	36.02	Mercury Pacific Opportunities	M017	31/05/90	JER	-3.15	130	13.30	72	6.10	-7.19	79	✪✪		136.13	29	N.A.	
▲	USD	9.47	Mercury ST Asian Opps	M021	29/02/96	LUX	0.66	53	N.A.		N.A.	N.A.				N.A.		N.A.	
▲	USD	58.03	Mercury ST Pacific	M021	29/05/87	LUX	-4.11	154	6.80	133	5.88	-28.20	128	✪		90.52	68	N.A.	
▲	GBP	31.18	Midland ICF Pacific Growth	M028	28/02/90	LUX	-4.56	169	13.10	75	5.07	12.79	8	✪✪✪✪✪		111.20	47	N.A.	
▲	USD	6.90	Morgan Grenfell Asian Sm Cos	M038	29/10/93	IRL	-0.60	72	19.84	32	3.93	-4.10	63	✪✪		N.A.		N.A.	
▲	GBP	894.69	Morgan Grenfell Pacific	M038	30/04/81	IRL	-5.08	178	25.66	12	4.79	8.08	15	✪✪✪✪✪		153.48	17	536.03	4
	USD	228.70	Morgan Stanley Asian Equity	M039	31/10/91	LUX	-3.87	146	4.26	146	5.30	-4.71	68	✪✪✪		149.64	19	N.A.	
	USD	76.66	MOSAIS Actions Bassin Pac	C058	30/03/90	LUX	-3.03	125	6.87	131	4.66	-9.74	83	✪✪		127.99	34	N.A.	
	USD	7.66	MultiLink Far East Eqs	I011	30/11/93	LUX	-4.59	170	18.74	43	4.97	-12.74	93	✪✪		N.A.		N.A.	
	USD	111.90	National Mutual Pacific	N001	31/07/87	HK	5.98	23	25.73	11	5.37	5.43	26	✪✪✪✪✪		236	3	N.A.	
	DEM	7.59	Nestor Fernost	N002	31/01/94	LUX	5.47	24	24	18	N.A.	N.A.				N.A.		N.A.	
	USD	0.33	New Asian Fund Portfolio -B-	B067	31/01/90	LUX	N.A.	—	2.08	158	4.21	-15.66	100	✪		51.67	86	N.A.	
▲	USD	12.94	Newport Tiger USD	N005	31/12/92	BER	-7.72	201	8.96	116	5.27	3.76	28	✪✪✪✪		N.A.		N.A.	
▲	USD	33	Newton UGF Asian Growth	N006	29/02/88	JER	-3.63	139	1.73	161	5.38	-11.59	90	✪✪		92.13	63	N.A.	
▲	USD	15.48	Nikko GIUF Asia Pacific Fund	N007	26/02/93	LUX	-4.18	159	26.27	10	4.99	14.63	6	✪✪✪✪✪		N.A.		N.A.	
	USD	17	NM ASF Pacific Opps	N001	07/06/96	IRL	9.04	10	N.A.		N.A.	N.A.				N.A.		N.A.	
	USD	10.21	Nomura SF Asia	N010	30/11/92	CA	-0.71	73	4.20	147	6.12	-20.05	112	✪		N.A.		N.A.	
	USD	2.83	Nomura SF Asia Emerging Mkts	N010	30/11/92	CA	9.12	9	-12.47	186	6.10	-41.20	132	✪		N.A.		N.A.	
	USD	5.37	Old Mutual Gnsy Emer Asia Stmk	O003	29/12/95	GU	-2.65	117	1.70	162	N.A.	N.A.				N.A.		N.A.	
	USD	2.07	Old Mutual HK Em Asian Stkmkt	O004	28/04/95	HK	-2.89	122	1.23	167	N.A.	N.A.				N.A.		N.A.	
	USD	103.15	OMI (Gnsy) Emerg Asian Stkmkt	O005	30/06/89	GU	-2.66	118	1.08	169	5.03	-11.03	89	✪✪		120.98	37	N.A.	
▲	USD	9.34	OMI Galileo Emerging Asian Eq	O007	29/12/95	IRL	3.32	33	-12.60	187	N.A.	N.A.				N.A.		N.A.	

▲ SIB Approved ● Insurance Fund

Values in US Dollars, on an offer to offer price basis with gross income reinvested

Data Source Micropal™

Far East & Pacific Ex Japan Equity

continued

	CCY	Fund Size ($mil)	Fund Name	Manager Code	Fund Start Date	Domicile Code	3 Mths 97 % Chg	3 Mths 97 Rank	1 Year % Chg	1 Year Rank	Micropal Star Rating 3 Years Volatility	Micropal Star Rating 3 Years % Chg	Micropal Star Rating 3 Years Rank	Micropal Star Rating Rating	Risk Return Rating	5 Years % Chg	5 Years Rank	10 Years % Chg	10 Years Rank
		101.49	**Mean/Count**				**-1.02**	**205**	**10.93**	**190**	**5.26**	**-7.19**	**135**			**114.98**	**94**	**348.33**	**19**
	USD	117.28	Parvest Asian Growth B	B037	30/03/90	LUX	-4.77	173	13.69	64	5.60	-5.02	69	✪✪✪		50.35	87	N.A.	
	USD	N.S.	PCP Asian Growth	P007	29/03/96	CA	-3.08	126	N.A.		N.A.	N.A.				N.A.		N.A.	
	USD	6.12	Peregrine Asian Gth Opps	P008	31/03/93	CA	-5.91	187	3.89	150	6.56	-3.12	60	✪✪✪		N.A.		N.A.	
	USD	22.47	Peregrine Premier Asia	P008	29/09/95	CA	-4.29	162	-0.28	176	N.A.	N.A.				N.A.		N.A.	
	USD	88.80	Perpetual Offshr Asian Sm Mkts	P011	31/03/93	JER	0.06	60	16.21	52	5.70	-1.57	51	✪✪✪		N.A.		N.A.	
	USD	8.50	Portefeuille BG Actions Asie	B063	23/06/95	LUX	-0.10	65	7.50	125	N.A.	N.A.				N.A.		N.A.	
▲	GBP	74.41	Prolific IF Asia Pacific	P027	30/04/92	IRL	-4.12	155	13.80	62	4.77	9.69	13	✪✪✪✪		N.A.		N.A.	
	USD	5.84	Proton IF Asian Equities	P024	29/09/95	BVI	1.28	48	9.23	113	N.A.	N.A.				N.A.		N.A.	
▲	USD	23.60	RBC Gl Asian Gth	R003	24/11/95	GU	-2.21	104	10.85	96	N.A.	N.A.				N.A.		N.A.	
	USD	4.50	RLI/Barclays AS SE Asia	R021	30/04/93	IOM	-3.49	134	11.06	94	5.54	-13.27	95	✪✪		N.A.		N.A.	
●	USD	9.80	RLI/Baring Octopus	R022	31/08/90	IOM	-2.42	112	10.62	99	5.94	-4.22	64	✪✪		89.28	70	N.A.	
●	USD	0.90	RLI/JF Asian Emerging Markets	R030	11/08/95	IOM	13.49	2	0.35	173	N.A.	N.A.				N.A.		N.A.	
	USD	3.10	RLI/JF Eastern Trust	R030	14/07/95	IOM	-0.09	64	13.72	63	N.A.	N.A.				N.A.		N.A.	
	USD	2.80	RLI/Thornton Little Dragons	R037	31/08/90	IOM	16.74	1	10.53	100	5.47	-24.20	124	✪		104.62	54	N.A.	
	USD	3.30	RLI/Thornton Tiger	R037	31/01/90	IOM	-2.53	113	6.83	132	5.22	-18.60	110	✪		81.22	76	N.A.	
●	USD	0.30	Royal Life/MBf Pacific Ent	R032	29/09/89	HK	-8.06	202	4.83	144	4.78	-16.33	102	✪✪		38.89	91	N.A.	
	USD	61.63	S-E-Banken Fund Fjarran Ostrn	S001	29/10/93	LUX	-4.36	163	8.81	118	4.88	-0.36	47	✪✪✪		N.A.		N.A.	
	USD	11.77	Samba Lux Far Eastern Equity	S006	31/01/95	LUX	-0.42	70	23.09	22	N.A.	N.A.				N.A.		N.A.	
	USD	303.71	Schroder Asian	S011	30/04/74	HK	-4.43	165	21.82	26	4.93	10.56	10	✪✪✪✪✪		162.64	13	495.47	5
	USD	25.44	Schroder Asian Emer Mkts	S011	29/09/95	HK	4.43	29	8	121	N.A.	N.A.				N.A.		N.A.	
	USD	19.66	Schroder Asian Smllr Cos	S011	30/06/93	HK	2.26	36	24.44	15	5.57	-9.95	84	✪✪		N.A.		N.A.	
▲	USD	197.17	Schroder Intl Sel Pacific Eqty	S010	29/10/93	LUX	-1.95	100	24.08	17	5.40	14.81	5	✪✪✪✪✪		N.A.		N.A.	
	USD	352	SCI Asian Hedge Net Prf Ind	S039	31/03/89	BVI	4.47	28	18.84	42	4.94	9.45	14	✪✪✪✪		154.76	16	N.A.	
	USD	65.55	Scontinvest Pacific Equity	S012	30/07/93	LUX	-5.46	183	3.95	149	5.59	-10.76	86	✪✪		N.A.		N.A.	
	USD	3.20	Scot Prov ILA Far East	S014	29/09/95	IOM	-3.14	129	11.08	93	N.A.	N.A.				N.A.		N.A.	
	LUF	21.44	Sen Mon Fund Grow Asia	P013	30/11/93	LUX	-1.83	98	5.02	143	4.16	-15.20	99	✪		N.A.		N.A.	
	USD	120.34	Share Pacific	B053	31/10/88	LUX	-1.93	99	24.20	16	5.42	5.66	23	✪✪✪✪		168.96	10	N.A.	
	HKD	2.26	SHK Oriental Emerg Economies	S024	31/05/89	HK	3.44	32	4.29	145	4.73	-17.42	105	✪		62.87	81	N.A.	
	HKD	3.51	SHK Oriental Growth	S024	31/05/89	HK	-7.19	198	30.77	3	5.49	-0.16	45	✪✪✪		129.93	33	N.A.	
▲●	GBP	60.90	Singer & Fried Tai Pan	S027	30/11/93	IRL	1.98	38	18.99	41	4.04	7.66	16	✪✪✪✪		N.A.		N.A.	
▲	USD	365.85	Skandifond Far East	S030	30/06/86	LUX	-3.94	150	10.04	104	5.04	0.14	43	✪✪✪✪		138.12	27	364.59	8
	USD	4.03	Sogelux Fd Equities Pacific	S037	21/06/96	LUX	-4.69	172	N.A.		N.A.	N.A.				N.A.		N.A.	
	USD	15.39	Southern Intl Far East Exc Jap	S041	04/10/96	LUX	-1.49	89	N.A.		N.A.	N.A.				N.A.		N.A.	
	USD	36.11	Special Assets Pacific LP	S042	30/06/94	CA	8.43	12	30.48	5	N.A.	N.A.				N.A.		N.A.	
	USD	0.90	Sun Life Aggressive Dllr	S053	30/06/94	IOM	1.69	42	8.74	120	N.A.	N.A.				N.A.		N.A.	
	GBP	3.72	Sun Life Aggressive Stlg	S053	29/01/93	IOM	0.42	57	9.97	106	5.99	-12.58	92	✪✪		N.A.		N.A.	
▲	USD	78.73	Swiss Life Proteus Pacific	S056	27/09/96	IRL	-1.32	87	N.A.		N.A.	N.A.				N.A.		N.A.	
▲	USD	41.93	Templeton GS Asian Growth	T001	28/06/91	LUX	1.46	47	19.51	34	3.87	-10.96	87	✪✪		49.51	89	N.A.	
▲	USD	8.55	Templeton GS Asian Smallr Cos	T001	05/05/95	LUX	2.67	35	0.47	172	N.A.	N.A.				N.A.		N.A.	
▲	USD	60.55	TGA Pac Basin Eq	T009	28/02/89	LUX	-4.24	160	14.45	60	4.98	2.75	31	✪✪✪✪		110.56	48	N.A.	
	USD	7.39	The Interallianz Asian Equity	I010	30/06/95	LUX	1.47	46	10.20	102	N.A.	N.A.				N.A.		N.A.	
	USD	36.56	Thornton Asian Infrastructure	T006	29/09/95	CA	1.49	45	5.64	139	N.A.	N.A.				N.A.		N.A.	
	USD	69.67	Thornton Little Dragons	T006	27/02/87	BER	12.92	4	16.49	51	5.86	-18.31	109	✪		124.58	36	N.A.	
	DEM	246.01	Thornton Lux Tiger Fund	D017	31/10/89	LUX	-5.47	184	10.66	98	5.55	-4.29	65	✪✪		94.71	59	N.A.	
	USD	93	Thornton Tiger	T006	30/05/86	BER	-3.74	141	11.08	92	5.61	-14.28	98	✪✪		94.12	60	302.92	12
	DEM	105.03	Trinkaus Asia Fonds	T011	28/02/94	LUX	-3.60	137	7.47	126	N.A.	N.A.				N.A.		N.A.	
	USD	44.14	UAP Pacific Securities	U009	30/06/93	LUX	-3.64	140	21.30	28	4.99	6.89	18	✪✪✪✪		N.A.		N.A.	
	USD	74.76	UBAM South Pacific & Asia	U010	31/12/91	LUX	-3.45	133	3.73	151	4.79	-24.08	122	✪		85.94	74	N.A.	
	DEM	154.96	UniAsia	U012	31/01/90	LUX	-2.42	111	9.40	111	4.83	2.11	34	✪✪✪✪		49.52	88	N.A.	
▲	USD	15.05	Von Ernst GP Pacific Bas Eqty	B021	30/11/89	LUX	-5.28	180	12.11	87	3.99	2.12	33	✪✪✪		79.64	77	N.A.	
	USD	55.63	Willerequity South East Asia	W004	30/11/90	LUX	0.51	55	18.29	44	4.96	-12.05	91	✪✪		93.94	61	N.A.	
	USD	7	Worldsec Dynasty	W007	30/06/92	HK	0.87	52	12.78	80	4.43	-9.39	82	✪✪		N.A.		N.A.	

▲ SIB Approved ● Insurance Fund Values in US Dollars, on an offer to offer price basis with gross income reinvested Data Source Micropal™

Finland Equity

Funds investing in excess of 70% in Finish equities or related instruments. Such funds may have an objective of capital and/or income growth, or to track a specified index or perform inversely to a given index. Funds in this category may leverage or gear by a maximum of 20% of total assets.

	CCY	Fund Size ($mil)	Fund Name	Manager Code	Fund Start Date	Domicile Code	3 Mths 97 % Chg	Rank	1 Year % Chg	Rank	Micropal Star Rating 3 Years Volatility	% Chg	Rank	Rating	Risk Return Rating	5 Years % Chg	Rank	10 Years % Chg	Rank
		31.30	**Mean/Count**				**2.97**	**2**	**29.79**	**2**	**6.19**	**50.04**	**2**		**2**	**103.01**	**1**	**0**	**0**
	FIM	47.61	Merita Private Fund	M022	30/11/88	LUX	2.92	2	25.97	2	6.28	51.75	1	✪✪✪	3	103.01	1	N.A.	
	FIM	14.99	MultiLink Finnish Eqs	I011	29/10/93	LUX	3.03	1	33.61	1	6.09	48.33	2	✪✪	2	N.A.		N.A.	

France Equity

Funds investing in excess of 70% in French equities or related instruments. Such funds may have an objective of capital and/or income growth, or to track a specified index or perform inversely to a given index. Funds in this category may leverage or gear by a maximum of 20% of total assets.

	CCY	Fund Size ($mil)	Fund Name	Manager Code	Fund Start Date	Domicile Code	3 Mths 97 % Chg	Rank	1 Year % Chg	Rank	Micropal Star Rating 3 Years Volatility	% Chg	Rank	Rating	Risk Return Rating	5 Years % Chg	Rank	10 Years % Chg	Rank
		51.18	**Mean/Count**				**4.78**	**29**	**22.26**	**28**	**3.64**	**22.90**	**24**		**1**	**47.79**	**20**	**105.28**	**2**
	FRF	2.11	Aetna MF French Natl Equity	A012	30/04/90	LUX	-2.84	29	27.12	4	3.40	36.02	2	✪✪✪✪✪	4	77.98	1	N.A.	
▲	FRF	3.29	Baring CF French Growth	B049	21/10/94	IRL	5.92	11	24.16	10	N.A.	N.A.				N.A.		N.A.	
	FRF	70.19	BIL Equities France C	B067	30/06/94	LUX	5.07	16	18.29	25	N.A.	N.A.				N.A.		N.A.	
	FRF	2.46	CIC Euroleaders Sicav (France)	C022	30/09/92	LUX	0.20	26	19.24	22	3.57	16.57	19	✪✪		N.A.		N.A.	
▲	FRF	31.73	Citi PF French Equity	C036	31/08/90	LUX	5.50	12	19.27	21	3.70	18.89	15	✪	2	45.65	11	N.A.	
▲	FRF	11.75	CMI GNF French Equity	C042	30/04/90	LUX	5.39	13	22.91	11	3.80	26.93	8	✪✪✪	2	56.89	7	N.A.	
●	GBP	3.72	CMI Ins Co French Equity	C043	31/01/91	IOM	2.84	23	22.12	14	3.75	22.25	11	✪✪✪	2	48.02	8	N.A.	
●	FRF	0.06	CMI Passport French Equity	C044	20/01/95	IOM	3.86	21	21.54	15	N.A.	N.A.				N.A.		N.A.	
●	FRF	30.59	Credis Equity France A	C056	28/06/91	LUX	0.89	25	25.55	7	3.90	27.43	7	✪✪✪✪	3	36.78	15	N.A.	
▲	FRF	10	CU PP French Growth	C070	31/05/90	LUX	5.99	10	18.37	24	3.77	13.38	21	✪		32.91	17	N.A.	
	FRF	42.91	EMIF France Index Plus B	C015	31/05/90	LUX	7.66	5	22.38	12	4.77	12.05	23	✪		28.96	19	N.A.	
▲	FRF	88.16	Fidelity Fds France	F011	28/09/90	LUX	8.44	3	19.63	18	3.36	13.29	22	✪		67.29	3	N.A.	
	FRF	18.74	France Privatisations	B037	29/10/93	LUX	N.A.	—	26.54	6	3.13	29.70	4	✪✪✪✪	4	N.A.		N.A.	
	FRF	10.13	Fructilux Actions Francaises	B043	31/03/92	LUX	7.27	6	26.64	5	3.47	28.90	5	✪✪✪✪	3	N.A.		N.A.	
	FRF	70.75	G-Equity Fund G-French Eq B	G009	31/03/93	LUX	5.99	9	17.89	27	3.74	17.78	17	✪✪	1	N.A.		N.A.	
	FRF	3.97	GAM France	G003	30/04/86	IOM	-0.34	27	30.08	1	3.66	14.34	20	✪		47.60	9	136.17	1
	FRF	19.70	Green Line France	C058	31/03/87	LUX	8.44	4	21	16	3.28	23.59	10	✪✪✪	3	58.07	6	N.A.	
▲●	FRF	17.50	Groupe Indosuez France	G017	31/01/91	LUX	5.09	15	18.58	23	3.91	19.14	14	✪✪	1	30.77	18	N.A.	
●	FRF	0.37	Hansard\Fidelity France	H014	27/09/91	IOM	4.20	20	19.78	17	3.53	16.98	18	✪✪	1	41.39	13	N.A.	
	FRF	34.09	Independance & Expansion	S028	28/09/90	LUX	13.11	1	19.36	19	4.45	55.21	1	✪✪✪✪✪	5	59.61	5	N.A.	
▲	FRF	29.87	Inter Strategie France	B069	29/09/89	LUX	6.68	8	18.29	26	3.30	18.03	16	✪✪	2	42.61	12	N.A.	
	FRF	533.84	Luxlife Actions Francaises	L024	23/09/94	LUX	1.39	24	27.89	3	N.A.	N.A.				N.A.		N.A.	
	FRF	26.13	MOSAIS Actions Francaises	C058	30/03/90	LUX	6.69	7	28.03	2	3.37	28.61	6	✪✪✪✪	3	62.60	4	N.A.	
	FRF	367.14	Parvest France B	B037	31/10/91	LUX	-0.47	28	24.75	9	3.89	34.40	3	✪✪✪✪	4	71.64	2	N.A.	
	FRF	57.69	Pictet C.F. Valfrance	P016	30/04/86	LUX	5.27	14	22.23	13	3.80	20.68	12	✪✪✪	2	47.60	10	74.40	2
▲	ECU	0.95	SanPaolo Ecu Actions France	S004	28/02/90	LUX	2.92	22	25.21	8	2.33	24.55	9	✪✪✪	4	27.65	20	N.A.	
	FRF	14	Scontinvest French Equity	S012	24/05/96	LUX	4.43	19	N.A.		N.A.	N.A.				N.A.		N.A.	
	FRF	1.82	Share France	B053	31/10/88	LUX	4.94	17	19.28	20	3.87	19.37	13	✪✪	1	38.66	14	N.A.	
	FRF	12.43	Sogelux Fd Equities France	S037	21/06/96	LUX	4.81	18	N.A.		N.A.	N.A.				N.A.		N.A.	
	FRF	19.29	UAP French securities	U009	31/03/88	LUX	9.38	2	17.10	28	3.57	11.45	24	✪		33.16	16	N.A.	

▲ SIB Approved ● Insurance Fund **Values in US Dollars, on an offer to offer price basis with gross income reinvested** Data Source Micropal™

Germany Equity

Funds investing in excess of 70% in German equities or related instruments. Such funds may have an objective of capital and/or income growth, or to track a specified index or perform inversely to a given index. Funds in this category may leverage or gear by a maximum of 20% of total assets.

	CCY	Fund Size ($mil)	Fund Name	Manager Code	Fund Start Date	Domicile Code	3 Mths 97 % Chg	3 Mths 97 Rank	1 Year % Chg	1 Year Rank	Micropal Star Rating 3 Years Volatility	3 Years % Chg	3 Years Rank	Rating	Risk Return Rating	5 Years % Chg	5 Years Rank	10 Years % Chg	10 Years Rank
		35.18	**Mean/Count**				**9.09**	**44**	**13.39**	**41**	**3.35**	**32.44**	**26**		**1**	**49.56**	**19**	**48.91**	**1**
▲	DEM	27.56	AAF Germany Equity Fund	A001	30/06/94	LUX	11.77	5	29.54	2	N.A.	N.A.				N.A.		N.A.	
	DEM	1.93	Aetna MF German Natl Equity	A012	30/04/90	LUX	5.80	36	15.88	15	3.26	19.88	24	✪	1	24.66	18	N.A.	
	DEM	7.84	Alfred Berg Sicav Germany	A019	31/07/89	LUX	9.82	14	12.70	27	3.32	27.04	19	✪✪	1	46.45	12	N.A.	
	DEM	128.30	Baer Multistock German Stk A	J007	31/12/93	LUX	8.83	21	24.25	5	3.01	65.50	1	✪✪✪✪✪	5	N.A.		N.A.	
	DEM	57.61	Baer Multistock Sp Ger Stk A	J007	30/04/96	LUX	9.78	15	N.A.		N.A.	N.A.				N.A.		N.A.	
	DEM	66.45	BIL Equities Allemagne C	B067	30/06/94	LUX	9.69	16	14.05	25	N.A.	N.A.				N.A.		N.A.	
	DEM	67.92	CAMCO Fonds DM-Aktien	C006	15/12/95	LUX	8.97	20	8.90	33	N.A.	N.A.				N.A.		N.A.	
	DEM	4.56	Capital Gestion Actions Allem	C009	20/10/95	LUX	4.89	37	7.76	34	N.A.	N.A.				N.A.		N.A.	
	DEM	30.39	CB Lux Portfolio DM Aktien	A007	31/03/93	LUX	10.54	10	14.90	22	3.59	36.24	9	✪✪✪	3	N.A.		N.A.	
▲	DEM	61.49	Citi PF German Equity	C036	31/07/90	LUX	10.79	7	15.20	19	3.21	29.40	17	✪✪	2	47.73	10	N.A.	
▲	DEM	26.05	CMI GNF German Equity	C042	30/04/90	LUX	11.33	6	15.14	20	3.52	35.02	13	✪✪✪	2	55.97	7	N.A.	
●	GBP	3.72	CMI Ins Co German Equity	C043	30/11/90	IOM	7.42	30	15.44	18	3.64	30.51	15	✪✪	1	34.36	15	N.A.	
●	DEM	0.45	CMI Passport DEM Enhanced Mgd	C044	20/01/95	IOM	-0.68	42	4.95	36	N.A.	N.A.				N.A.		N.A.	
●	DEM	172.97	CMI Passport DEM G'teed Gth	C044	20/01/95	IOM	-6.34	43	-1.53	38	N.A.	N.A.				N.A.		N.A.	
●	DEM	0.19	CMI Passport German Equity	C044	20/01/95	IOM	8.29	26	14.88	23	N.A.	N.A.				N.A.		N.A.	
●	DEM	56.60	Credis Equity Germany A	C056	28/02/91	LUX	12.34	4	17.15	14	3.36	29.45	16	✪✪	2	44.68	14	N.A.	
●	DEM	6.81	Credis Equity Small Cap Ger	C056	31/08/94	LUX	8.98	19	-7	39	N.A.	N.A.				N.A.		N.A.	
▲	DEM	16.18	CU PP German Growth	C070	29/06/90	LUX	8.02	28	17.99	11	3.41	36.42	8	✪✪✪✪	3	67.03	3	N.A.	
	DEM	53.70	EMIF Germany Index plus B	C015	31/05/90	LUX	8.48	24	15.01	21	3.50	32.03	14	✪✪	2	57.57	5	N.A.	
▲	DEM	56.65	Fidelity Fds Germany	F011	28/09/90	LUX	8.39	25	18.48	10	3.37	35.63	11	✪✪✪✪	3	67.83	2	N.A.	
	DEM	54.27	G-Equity Fund G-German Eq B	G009	31/03/93	LUX	8.68	22	17.16	13	3.18	36.68	7	✪✪✪✪	4	N.A.		N.A.	
	USD	0.70	Glbl Mgr German Bear	B066	30/09/94	BER	-22.18	44	-25.84	41	N.A.	N.A.				N.A.		N.A.	
	USD	0.20	Glbl Mgr German Geared	B066	30/09/94	BER	27.69	2	35.16	1	N.A.	N.A.				N.A.		N.A.	
	USD	0.70	Glbl Mgr German Index	B066	30/09/94	BER	9.31	18	14.53	24	N.A.	N.A.				N.A.		N.A.	
▲●	DEM	14.81	Groupe Indosuez Germany	G017	31/05/91	LUX	9.60	17	10.57	31	3.35	28.54	18	✪✪	2	47.15	11	N.A.	
	USD	5.50	GT Deutschland	G018	28/11/86	LUX	3.54	39	26.95	3	3.88	9.82	26	✪		23.80	19	48.91	1
●	DEM	0.46	Hansard\Fidelity Germany	H014	27/09/91	IOM	6.01	34	15.77	16	3.02	22.10	22	✪✪	1	49.47	9	N.A.	
	USD	233.08	HYPO Deutschland Garant 12/99	H024	19/07/96	LUX	5.97	35	N.A.		N.A.	N.A.				N.A.		N.A.	
	DEM	10.92	JF Germany	J004	31/01/90	HK	7.41	31	26.90	4	3.39	35.20	12	✪✪✪	3	60.88	4	N.A.	
	DEM	18.33	Lux Linea	M034	31/12/91	LUX	10.39	12	19.40	8	4.07	49.90	2	✪✪✪✪	4	91.03	1	N.A.	
	DEM	26.57	Luxlife Actions Allemandes	L024	23/12/94	LUX	2.95	40	12.90	26	N.A.	N.A.				N.A.		N.A.	
	DEM	17.62	MOSAIS Actions Allemandes	C058	31/10/90	LUX	10.05	13	21.15	7	3.54	39.08	4	✪✪✪✪	4	57.16	6	N.A.	
	DEM	28.30	Multiscor Demshares	S013	31/01/90	LUX	10.62	9	11.78	29	3.05	26.02	20	✪	2	46.15	13	N.A.	
	DEM	12.02	Oppenheim Aktien D Protect	O009	07/07/95	LUX	4.63	38	4.63	37	N.A.	N.A.				N.A.		N.A.	
	DEM	4.95	Oppenheim Turnaround Werte	O009	29/04/94	LUX	16.90	3	-11.62	40	N.A.	N.A.				N.A.		N.A.	
	DEM	162.09	Parvest Germany B	B037	30/06/93	LUX	8.66	23	24.12	6	3.71	48.90	3	✪✪✪✪✪	4	N.A.		N.A.	
	DEM	36.46	Pictet C.F. Germaval	P016	28/02/90	LUX	6.34	33	19.30	9	3.38	37.54	6	✪✪✪	4	55.95	8	N.A.	
▲	DEM	0.08	SanPaolo Ecu Actions Allemgne	S004	31/12/93	LUX	1.89	41	10.30	32	2.25	36.23	10	✪✪✪	5	N.A.		N.A.	
	DEM	7.88	Sogelux Fd Equities Germany	S037	21/06/96	LUX	10.63	8	N.A.		N.A.	N.A.				N.A.		N.A.	
	DEM	11.73	The Interallianz German Equity	I010	28/02/95	LUX	70.60	1	11.47	30	N.A.	N.A.				N.A.		N.A.	
	DEM	0.45	Thornton Dres ES Germany	T008	31/05/90	BER	8.26	27	11.79	28	3.26	21.21	23	✪	1	33.75	16	N.A.	
	DEM	0.14	Thornton Dres ES New Germany	T008	31/05/90	BER	6.76	32	17.60	12	3.46	24.95	21	✪	1	30.03	17	N.A.	
	DEM	24.47	Unico UF DEM Aktien	U006	31/12/92	LUX	7.87	29	5.70	35	2.77	12.46	25	✪		N.A.		N.A.	
	DEM	28.99	Vereins Lux Portf DM Aktien	A007	31/03/93	LUX	10.44	11	15.56	17	3.69	37.80	5	✪✪✪✪	3	N.A.		N.A.	

▲ SIB Approved ● Insurance Fund Values in US Dollars, on an offer to offer price basis with gross income reinvested Data Source Micropal™

Global Equity

Funds investing in excess of 70% in Global equities or related instruments. Such funds may have an objective of capital and/or income growth, or to track a specified index or perform inversely to a given index. Funds in this category may leverage or gear by a maximum of 20% of total assets.

	CCY	Fund Size ($mil)	Fund Name	Manager Code	Fund Start Date	Domicile Code	3 Mths 97 % Chg	3 Mths 97 Rank	1 Year % Chg	1 Year Rank	Micropal Star Rating 3 Years Volatility	3 Years % Chg	3 Years Rank	3 Years Rating	Risk Return Rating	5 Years % Chg	5 Years Rank	10 Years % Chg	10 Years Rank
		80.05	**Mean/Count**				**1.03**		**12.04**	**302**	**2.98**	**23.18**	**216**		**1**	**56.17**	**155**	**144.56**	**49**
▲	USD	4.46	Abtrust Atlas Global Capital	A002	31/03/88	LUX	1.31	132	12.98	128	2.91	17.98	144	✪✪	1	48.29	94	N.A.	
	USD	8.43	Abtrust International Equity	A003	30/07/82	GU	4.61	39	19.76	34	2.88	26.07	100	✪✪✪	2	66.63	46	116.14	31
	USD	0.89	Abtrust World Growth	A003	31/07/87	GU	3.79	54	-2.22	293	4.47	-17.70	210	✪		24.80	136	N.A.	
	GBP	4.79	Accelerated Gth Portfolio A	C020	14/04/95	IRL	-0.17	213	14.31	102	N.A.	N.A.				N.A.		N.A.	
	USD	21.86	ACMGI Global Growth Trends AX	A005	31/10/91	LUX	-2.94	306	14.43	101	4.02	72.34	3	✪✪✪✪✪	5	125.12	4	N.A.	
	USD	22.43	ACMGI Intl Health Care Ptf AX	A005	29/07/83	LUX	3.73	59	2.18	277	4.16	70.40	5	✪✪✪✪✪	5	50.47	86	473.20	1
	USD	9.60	ACMGI Intl Privatn Portf A	A005	30/06/94	LUX	6.29	23	17.47	58	N.A.	N.A.				N.A.		N.A.	
▲	USD	21.64	AEB Worldfolio 7 Global Eq	A009	31/12/85	LUX	-0.54	236	11.86	158	2.72	37.93	33	✪✪✪✪✪	4	43.50	106	95.85	37
	BEF	34.35	AGAM Strategy Inter Equities C	A013	28/04/95	LUX	0.02	203	13.42	120	N.A.	N.A.				N.A.		N.A.	
▲	IEP	5.15	AIB Offs Inst Intl Equity Mgd	A016	31/10/89	GU	0.41	179	13.14	124	2.44	30.93	66	✪✪✪✪	3	46.37	100	N.A.	
▲	IEP	2.67	AIB Offs Intl Equity Mgd	A016	31/10/89	GU	-0.05	209	14.02	112	2.47	33.83	48	✪✪✪✪	4	49.63	88	N.A.	
▲	GBP	9.42	AIB Offs Stlg Intl Equity Mgd	A016	29/05/81	GU	2.93	77	14	113	2.48	36.19	36	✪✪✪✪	4	49.64	87	64.36	45
	USD	67.40	AIS Worldwide	O008	31/05/95	CA	4.46	45	13.35	122	N.A.	N.A.				N.A.		N.A.	
	DEM	80.37	Aktien Global Fonds	T011	31/12/93	LUX	4.79	36	18.04	52	2.53	55.39	9	✪✪✪✪✪	5	N.A.		N.A.	
●	USD	0	Albany Intl Global Dllr	A018	31/03/87	IOM	-0.94	256	14.13	109	2.81	25.87	102	✪✪✪	2	57.68	63	N.A.	
●	GBP	0	Albany Intl Global Stlg	A018	31/03/87	IOM	2.26	90	12.30	148	2.77	24.89	108	✪✪✪	2	46	102	N.A.	
	USD	79.14	Alfred Berg Sicav Global	A019	31/08/87	LUX	3.52	64	10.96	180	2.57	29.50	75	✪✪✪✪	3	56.35	68	N.A.	
	USD	12.63	Alliance Intl Technology I	A005	30/03/84	LUX	-9.42	329	17.99	53	5.85	115.65	1	✪✪✪✪✪	5	180.92	1	373.53	2
●	USD	11.01	Allied Dunbar IB Wwide Equity	A021	30/09/93	IOM	1.97	105	11.55	163	2.47	31.70	62	✪✪✪✪	3	N.A.		N.A.	
▲	USD	101.40	Allied Dunbar Wwide Equity	A020	31/05/84	IOM	1.50	122	12.61	141	2.80	33.85	47	✪✪✪✪	3	60.56	58	145.70	18
	USD	65.61	Alpha Global	A023a	30/09/88	BVI	7.32	17	12.13	152	2.71	3.59	189	✪		51.14	84	N.A.	
▲	ECU	18.16	American Phoenix Global Multi	A025	29/01/93	LUX	2.55	83	16.33	66	2.97	55.32	10	✪✪✪✪✪	5	N.A.		N.A.	
	USD	15.60	Anchor International	B066	30/07/76	BER	-0.73	283	2.57	273	3.36	7.51	181	✪		47.48	97	86.55	40
	DEM	25.72	ApoAesculap	U012	31/03/94	LUX	9.64	8	8.37	218	N.A.	N.A.				N.A.		N.A.	
	USD	31.70	Aragon Sv-Global Eq Select	A028	31/01/90	LUX	4.08	50	20.53	25	2.94	51.66	12	✪✪✪✪✪	5	119.01	9	N.A.	
●	CHF	86.29	Argus Fund Equity Portfolio	S022	30/12/94	LUX	4.51	41	11.60	161	N.A.	N.A.				N.A.		N.A.	
▲	GBP	35.98	Ashburton Intl Equity Fd	A034	30/08/85	IOM	4.93	33	29.10	6	3.56	41.92	22	✪✪✪✪	3	137.59	3	237.87	5
	GBP	1.78	AXA Eqty&Law IFM Global Eqty	A039	31/10/86	IOM	-0.77	248	12.97	129	2.56	34.75	43	✪✪✪✪	4	63.11	53	137.73	20
	GBP	4.79	Bachmann GIF Global Eqty	B001	30/09/93	GU	-1.08	263	9.50	204	2.54	19.59	138	✪✪	1	N.A.		N.A.	
	USD	N.S.	Bachmann GIF Intl Eq Index	B001	17/02/95	GU	-0.30	222	10.83	182	N.A.	N.A.				N.A.		N.A.	
	ESP	0.01	BanesFondo Intern. Global	B030	28/06/91	LUX	-0.44	232	14.44	100	2.15	31.28	65	✪✪✪	4	-9.73	153	N.A.	
▲	GBP	35.34	Barclays (Lux) Intl Equity	B047	31/12/71	LUX	0.13	195	14.80	95	2.69	33.78	49	✪✪✪✪	3	60.67	57	82.11	41
	GBP	N.S.	Barclays Intl FF Gth Mgr Stlg	B045	30/08/96	JER	0.01	204	N.A.		N.A.	N.A.				N.A.		N.A.	
	USD	N.S.	Barclays Intl FF Gth Mgr USD	B045	30/08/96	JER	1.18	137	N.A.		N.A.	N.A.				N.A.		N.A.	
	USD	9.01	BBL (L) Invest Food&Bev'rage C	B052	30/08/96	LUX	3.40	67	N.A.		N.A.	N.A.				N.A.		N.A.	
	USD	27.63	BBL (L) Invest HealthCare C	B052	14/06/96	LUX	4.32	47	N.A.		N.A.	N.A.				N.A.		N.A.	
	USD	30.75	BBL (L) Invest Tlcom & Media C	B052	17/11/95	LUX	-0.38		7.12	244	N.A.	N.A.				N.A.		N.A.	
	LUF	18.10	BBL (L) Invest World C	B052	28/09/90	LUX	-0.25	221	8.82	212	2.71	25.28	105	✪✪✪	2	40.08	118	N.A.	
	USD	13.77	Bcilux Dollar Equity	B007	26/07/96	LUX	-0.13	212	N.A.		N.A.	N.A.				N.A.		N.A.	
	ECU	0.99	Bermuda Intl Eqty ECU	B066	31/07/91	BER	0.78	150	-0.02	289	3.31	24.39	112	✪✪	1	40.71	116	N.A.	
	GBP	3.38	Bermuda Intl Eqty GBP	B066	31/07/91	BER	0.27	190	2.84	270	3.24	23.40	117	✪✪	1	30.38	133	N.A.	
	USD	86	Bermuda Intl Eqty USD	B066	30/09/83	BER	0.34	185	1.26	285	2.52	15.96	157	✪✪		39.98	120	59.73	47
	BEF	47.68	BIL Delta Fund Croissance C	B067	28/02/94	LUX	-1.12	265	5.20	257	N.A.	N.A.				N.A.		N.A.	
	GBP	326.24	Bk of Ire Glbl Intl Equity	B018	30/04/87	IOM	1.44	127	25.08	12	3.37	51.39	13	✪✪✪✪✪	4	103.34	12	N.A.	
	USD	26.55	BSS Universal Global USD	B029	30/12/88	LUX	0.96	146	5.28	256	3.01	10.89	172	✪		58.10	62	N.A.	
▲	USD	95.18	BT IIS International Growth	B077	30/10/92	IRL	6.63	21	18.73	45	3.70	33.40	51	✪✪✪✪	2	N.A.		N.A.	
●	USD	10.90	Buttress Equity Fund Ltd	B080	30/09/75	BER	0.66	160	2.45	274	2.95	-5.96	202	✪		18.56	142	64.12	46
	CHF	63.15	Cantrade Invest Capital Gain	C007	28/02/92	LUX	4.49	42	11.06	177	2.57	35.80	37	✪✪✪✪	4	N.A.		N.A.	
	USD	1.70	Capel-Cure Myers Dllr Growth	C008	29/05/87	LUX	0.77	152	16.10	71	2.57	27.08	87	✪✪✪	2	26.15	134	N.A.	
	GBP	8.29	Capel-Cure Myers Stlg Growth	C008	29/05/87	LUX	-2.33	297	20.57	24	3	31.71	61	✪✪✪	2	44.04	105	N.A.	
	USD	783.96	Capital International	C010	31/12/69	LUX	3.82	53	11.75	160	2.75	35.09	41	✪✪✪✪	4	75.32	32	197.38	8
●	USD	21.83	Carlson Global Equity	C011	28/09/90	LUX	1.37	130	7.51	234	2.39	22.35	125	✪✪	2	57.48	64	N.A.	
	USD	N.S.	Carnegie Worldwide	C012	05/01/96	LUX	1.49	123	N.A.		N.A.	N.A.				N.A.		N.A.	
	BEF	18.23	Cera Invest World Basket	C018	01/12/95	LUX	-1.45	276	14.84	94	N.A.	N.A.				N.A.		N.A.	
●	USD	2.25	Citi Intl Equity A	C032	30/06/94	CA	-1.90	284	2.08	279	N.A.	N.A.				N.A.		N.A.	
	USD	6.29	Citimarkets Global Equity A	C034	29/09/95	LUX	-0.35	227	5.89	252	N.A.	N.A.				N.A.		N.A.	
●	USD	23.25	Citimarkets Global Equity B	C034	30/09/86	LUX	0.05	202	7.60	232	2.60	22.33	126	✪✪	1	39.91	121	135.16	21

▲ SIB Approved ● Insurance Fund Values in US Dollars, on an offer to offer price basis with gross income reinvested Data Source Micropal™

Global Equity

continued

	CCY	Fund Size ($mil)	Fund Name	Manager Code	Fund Start Date	Domicile Code	3 Mths 97 % Chg	3 Mths 97 Rank	1 Year % Chg	1 Year Rank	Micropal Star Rating 3 Years Volatility	3 Years % Chg	3 Years Rank	3 Years Rating	Risk Return Rating	5 Years % Chg	5 Years Rank	10 Years % Chg	10 Years Rank
		80.05	**Mean/Count**				**1.03**		**12.04**	**302**	**2.98**	**23.18**	**216**		**1**	**56.17**	**155**	**144.56**	**49**
▲●	USD	178.15	Citinvest VIP Selector	C035	31/07/87	LUX	-7.50	325	1.40	283	4.55	6.09	183	✪✪		67.76	44	N.A.	
▲●	USD	2.59	CL Asia Europe Equity Fund	C062	30/06/89	LUX	-8.13	326	-6.96	299	3.01	-13.74	207	✪		8.21	148	N.A.	
▲●	ECU	4.76	CL Earth Fund C	C062	30/11/90	LUX	-3.26	309	11.44	169	3.27	6.87	182	✪		11.41	147	N.A.	
●	GBP	57.18	CMI Ins Co GBP Opportunity	C043	29/01/88	IOM	-3.25	308	15.34	86	2.75	32.88	52	✪✪✪✪	3	56.78	66	N.A.	
●	USD	17.30	CMI Ins Co USD Opportunity	C043	29/01/88	IOM	-2.01	286	9.60	201	2.55	22.19	127	✪✪	1	44.40	104	N.A.	
▲	GBP	64.72	CMI Intl Equity	C041	29/05/87	LUX	-0.30	224	15.66	78	2.77	35.02	42	✪✪✪✪	3	64.81	48	N.A.	
●	GBP	0.68	CMI Passport Global Equity	C044	20/01/95	IOM	-2.11	291	15.04	91	N.A.	N.A.				N.A.		N.A.	
	USD	29.29	Consulta Capital	C051	31/12/91	GU	3.06	76	17.44	59	2.96	15.46	159	✪✪	2	36.72	127	N.A.	
	USD	419.10	Contivest Actions Internat A	B023	30/06/93	LUX	8.69	12	0.13	288	3.18	-16.86	209	✪		N.A.		N.A.	
▲	CHF	14.53	Coutts GF Global Equity	C052	31/12/73	IRL	0.16	193	7.99	226	2.99	32.09	60	✪✪✪	2	42.77	109	95.56	38
▲	USD	89.49	Coutts GF Small Cap Eq	C052	31/03/95	IRL	2.10	96	15.10	90	N.A.	N.A.				N.A.		N.A.	
●	DEM	2.87	Credis Equity Oeko Protec A	C056	31/10/90	LUX	1.77	108	4.90	258	2.33	8.47	179	✪		1.82	152	N.A.	
	BEF	77.86	Cregem Equities L Triple	C059	12/01/96	LUX	N.A.	—	N.A.		N.A.	N.A.				N.A.		N.A.	
	DEM	54.17	CS Portfolio Gth DM	C068	30/06/93	LUX	-0.83	251	4.21	262	2.22	18.27	143	✪✪	1	N.A.		N.A.	
	CHF	119.82	CS Portfolio Gth SFR	C068	30/06/93	LUX	0.32	188	-2.53	294	2.40	15.49	158	✪✪		N.A.		N.A.	
	USD	30.61	CS Portfolio Gth USD	C068	30/06/93	LUX	1.17	138	4.79	260	2.14	14.36	162	✪		N.A.		N.A.	
	ECU	5.17	Danske Intl Equities Mgd	D003	29/01/93	LUX	0.66	162	17.79	55	2.87	33.74	50	✪✪✪✪	3	N.A.		N.A.	
	USD	0.70	Dao Heng Gl Balanced Gth	D005	11/10/96	HK	9.17	9	N.A.		N.A.	N.A.				N.A.		N.A.	
	USD	1	Dao Heng Gl Equity	D005	11/10/96	HK	3.37	68	N.A.		N.A.	N.A.				N.A.		N.A.	
●	USD	491.49	Dean Witter World Wide Invest	D008	30/08/85	LUX	-2.08	289	6.08	249	2.37	2.09	192	✪		13.04	145	67.62	44
	USD	30.09	Deltec Fund	D010	30/04/87	BVI	11.33	6	39.12	3	4.67	68.59	7	✪✪✪✪	4	140.66	2	N.A.	
▲	USD	13.62	DNB Investment Worldwide A	D013	31/10/94	LUX	-0.90	254	8.04	225	N.A.	N.A.				N.A.		N.A.	
▲	USD	0.68	Dolphin IIS International	D014	31/05/89	LUX	-2.31	296	8.98	210	4.16	5.44	186	✪		12.32	146	N.A.	
	USD	8.26	Eagle Star Dllr Adventurous	E001	29/02/88	IOM	0.57	168	14.22	105	2.64	26.78	90	✪✪✪	2	51.51	82	N.A.	
●	GBP	21.74	Eagle Star Eagle Adventurous	E001	29/02/88	IOM	0.78	151	15.32	87	2.73	28.33	79	✪✪✪✪	2	52.32	81	N.A.	
●	GBP	5.47	Eagle Star Stlg Adventurous	E001	29/02/88	IOM	0.69	156	15.46	84	2.79	29.19	78	✪✪✪✪	2	54.72	74	N.A.	
	ECU	63.44	Ecuscor Actiscor	S013	31/10/90	LUX	0.01	205	11.24	171	2.40	35.79	38	✪✪✪✪	4	60.74	56	N.A.	
●	USD	42.40	Enviromental Investment Co	E006	30/04/93	JER	N.A.	—	21.98	18	3.77	4.59	187	✪		N.A.		N.A.	
	USD	N.S.	EPIC MF World Equities	A024	20/10/95	LUX	0.50	174	6.55	247	N.A.	N.A.				N.A.		N.A.	
	USD	42.24	Equity Investment Fund	D002	31/01/90	LUX	-3.10	307	6.02	250	4.36	-7.71	205	✪		24.66	137	N.A.	
	USD	28.12	Essex High Technology	O008	31/08/95	BVI	-3.71	313	28.61	7	N.A.	N.A.				N.A.		N.A.	
	USD	N.S.	EV Medallion Info Age B	E003	10/11/95	CA	-2.01	287	13.25	123	N.A.	N.A.				N.A.		N.A.	
	DEM	23.47	F&V International Inv	F004	12/07/91	LUX	-1.32	269	10.64	186	2.52	19.78	137	✪✪	1	53.63	79	N.A.	
▲	USD	249.20	Fidelity Fds International	F011	31/12/91	LUX	0.45	177	17.19	61	2.64	39.69	26	✪✪✪✪✪	4	78.60	27	N.A.	
	USD	1.10	Fidelity Global Selection	F012	30/06/88	LUX	-8.97	328	7.68	230	3.40	-1.84	197	✪		68.16	43	N.A.	
	USD	9.50	Fidelity World	F012	31/07/73	LUX	4.12	48	13.78	119	3.13	22.95	121	✪✪	1	70.11	39	177.01	11
●	GBP	0.88	Finistere Dllr Equity Life	F016	31/12/81	GU	7.44	15	20.41	27	2.85	46.93	16	✪✪✪✪	4	79.28	25	166.78	14
	USD	8.09	Five Arrows IE Global Equity	R014	30/09/93	GU	-0.74	247	10.64	187	2.60	23.39	118	✪✪	2	N.A.		N.A.	
	GBP	5.89	Five Arrows IMP Intl Cap Stlg	R015	30/12/94	GU	-0.48	234	11.13	175	N.A.	N.A.				N.A.		N.A.	
	USD	1.41	Five Arrows IMP Intl Cap USD	R015	30/12/94	GU	-0.85	252	10.29	192	N.A.	N.A.				N.A.		N.A.	
	GBP	4.11	Five Arrows IMP UK Cap Gth	R015	30/12/94	GU	-1.28	268	18.82	43	N.A.	N.A.				N.A.		N.A.	
▲	DEM	108.17	Fleming FF International Eqty	F020	30/11/88	LUX	-0.72	243	11.92	156	2.80	19.92	135	✪✪	1	55	73	N.A.	
	USD	5.52	Fleming Frontier Gl Equity	F021	22/12/95	LUX	0.60	167	10.45	190	N.A.	N.A.				N.A.		N.A.	
	USD	N.S.	Fleming Oasis Intl Equity	F022	02/02/96	LUX	-0.24	218	N.A.		N.A.	N.A.				N.A.		N.A.	
	GBP	7.22	Friends Provdnt Global Eq	F031	31/05/94	GU	1.22	135	14.96	92	N.A.	N.A.				N.A.		N.A.	
	USD	713.40	GAM Diversity	G003	29/12/89	IOM	7.17	18	15.29	88	2.73	16.57	154	✪✪		92.19	18	N.A.	
	USD	2.10	GAM Dollar And International	G003	31/12/96	BVI	0.90	147	N.A.		N.A.	N.A.				N.A.		N.A.	
	CHF	13.79	GAM Franc Val	G003	31/01/85	IOM	-1.83	282	0.43	287	2.74	24.81	109	✪✪	2	60.04	60	130.61	24
	USD	54.90	GAM Worldwide	G003	31/05/83	IOM	3.33	69	15.59	80	2.84	34.37	45	✪✪✪	3	93.90	17	216.95	6
	DEM	123.27	Gamax Funds-Maxifonds Int. A	G004	31/07/92	LUX	5.08	31	6.02	251	3.37	4.02	188	✪		N.A.		N.A.	
	DEM	40.75	Gamax Funds-Top 100 A	G004	22/09/95	LUX	1.69	113	13.06	126	N.A.	N.A.				N.A.		N.A.	
▲	USD	85.70	Gartmore CSF Global Equity	G007	31/05/84	JER	-1.32	270	12.15	151	2.41	16.62	152	✪		46.36	101	112.06	33
●	GBP	9.79	Gartmore CSP Sterling Mgd Eq	G007	30/04/86	JER	-1.35	272	20.40	28	3.16	32.46	57	✪✪✪	2	64.06	52	117.51	30
●	USD	1.97	Gartmore CSP US Dllr Mgd Eq	G007	28/02/92	JER	-0.61	238	10.81	183	2.54	24.24	113	✪✪✪	2	N.A.		N.A.	
	DEM	39.58	Generalinvest Croissance B	B064	31/01/95	LUX	1.78	107	9.51	203	N.A.	N.A.				N.A.		N.A.	
	DEM	19.30	Global Advantage Major Mkts	S047	31/05/93	LUX	2.03	101	12.73	139	2.09	36.75	35	✪✪✪✪	5	N.A.		N.A.	
	GBP	15.51	Global Portfolio Solution A	C020	14/04/95	IRL	-0.97	257	12.30	147	N.A.	N.A.				N.A.		N.A.	

▲ SIB Approved ● Insurance Fund Values in US Dollars, on an offer to offer price basis with gross income reinvested Data Source Micropal™

Global Equity

continued

	CCY	Fund Size ($mil)	Fund Name	Manager Code	Fund Start Date	Domicile Code	3 Mths 97 % Chg	3 Mths 97 Rank	1 Year % Chg	1 Year Rank	Micropal Star Rating 3 Years Volatility	3 Years % Chg	3 Years Rank	3 Years Rating	Risk Return Rating	5 Years % Chg	5 Years Rank	10 Years % Chg	10 Years Rank
		80.05	**Mean/Count**				**1.03**		**12.04**	**302**	**2.98**	**23.18**	**216**		**1**	**56.17**	**155**	**144.56**	**49**
	USD	7.42	Globalvest Value	A023b	30/07/93	BVI	26.26	1	54.93	1	8.57	35.58	39	✪✪✪	1	N.A.		N.A.	
	USD	60	Goldman Sachs Global Equity	G013	31/12/92	LUX	3.32	5	21.72	22	2.80	42.31	21	✪✪✪✪✪	4	N.A.		N.A.	
▲●	USD	13.01	Groupe Indosuez Intl	G017	31/12/90	LUX	-2.29	294	10.47	189	2.50	14.61	161	✪		38.46	124	N.A.	
	USD	27.63	GT Global	G018	31/12/87	LUX	0.07	201	18.36	48	3.18	23.33	119	✪✪	1	64.70	50	N.A.	
	USD	29	GT Global Smaller Companies	G018	30/09/87	BER	-0.34	225	21.86	20	2.78	20.27	132	✪✪	1	102.44	14	N.A.	
▲	USD	280	GT Investment	G018	30/09/75	LUX	0.97	145	20.30	29	2.97	43.15	19	✪✪✪✪✪	4	120.59	7	259.53	4
▲	USD	101	GT Telecommunications A	G018	30/06/92	IRL	-2.54	301	9.23	207	4.54	13.47	164	✪✪		N.A.		N.A.	
▲	USD	21.01	Guinness FI IF Intl Equity	G020	30/06/88	GU	2.19	94	10.03	196	2.53	27.41	84	✪✪✪	3	72.69	37	N.A.	
▲	USD	152.81	Guinness Flight Glbl Equity	G019	31/01/85	GU	2.27	89	9.83	198	2.52	25.18	106	✪✪✪	2	71.07	38	191.34	9
▲	USD	2.75	Guinness Flight Glbl Leisure	G019	31/01/85	GU	-0.45	233	14.28	103	2.66	23.04	120	✪✪	1	64.70	49	187.34	10
▲	USD	46.21	Guinness Flight Glbl Priv	G019	31/03/94	GU	7.13	19	33.84	4	N.A.	N.A.				N.A.		N.A.	
▲	GBP	3.65	Hambros Eqty Sel Managed	H003	30/11/77	GU	-1.35	273	12.93	133	3.01	34.57	44	✪✪✪✪	3	54.49	75	114.25	32
	GBP	3.50	Hambros Global Growth	H005	11/10/96	JER	0.11	197	N.A.		N.A.	N.A.				N.A.		N.A.	
●	GBP	N.S.	Hansard EU Intl Gth	H010	17/02/95	IRL	3.77	55	15.55	82	N.A.	N.A.				N.A.		N.A.	
●	GBP	N.S.	Hansard EU UK Stlg Gth	H010	17/02/95	IRL	5.33	28	21.97	19	N.A.	N.A.				N.A.		N.A.	
●	USD	N.S.	Hansard EU US Dllr Gth	H010	17/02/95	IRL	4.48	43	16.73	65	N.A.	N.A.				N.A.		N.A.	
●	GBP	47.53	Hansard International Growth	H011	30/04/90	IOM	2.06	99	13.82	117	2.71	28.25	80	✪✪✪	2	68.51	42	N.A.	
●	GBP	3.55	Hansard UK Sterling Growth	H011	22/01/93	IOM	1.45	126	22	17	2.84	42.80	20	✪✪✪✪	4	N.A.		N.A.	
●	USD	2.13	Hansard US Dollar Growth	H011	22/01/93	IOM	0.29	189	21.73	21	3	41.65	23	✪✪✪✪	4	N.A.		N.A.	
●	USD	0.25	Hansard\GF GSF Glbl Leisure	H017	31/07/92	IOM	-2.43	300	14.79	96	2.02	19.04	140	✪✪	2	N.A.		N.A.	
●	USD	2.50	Hansard\GF GSF Glbl Priv	H017	08/07/94	IOM	7.01	20	30.76	5	N.A.	N.A.				N.A.		N.A.	
●	USD	5.51	Hansard\GT Telecommunications	H016	31/07/92	IOM	-3.40	310	12.97	130	4.36	20.77	129	✪✪	1	N.A.		N.A.	
●	USD	4.37	Hansberger Global Equity	H020	30/12/94	IRL	14.55	3	48.47	2	N.A.	N.A.				N.A.		N.A.	
▲	GBP	2.55	HCIC Global Mgd	H026	30/12/94	IOM	0.33	187	20.12	32	N.A.	N.A.				N.A.		N.A.	
	USD	N.S.	Henderson HF Gl Technology	H025	18/10/96	LUX	-2.37	298	N.A.		N.A.	N.A.				N.A.		N.A.	
	USD	20.91	Henderson HF Glbl Sm Cos	H025	11/10/96	LUX	-0.09	210	N.A.		N.A.	N.A.				N.A.		N.A.	
	USD	11.01	Henderson IF USD Bal Ptfl	H027	18/08/95	LUX	-0.18	215	8.72	214	N.A.	N.A.				N.A.		N.A.	
▲	GBP	17.31	Hill Samuel OS International	H030	28/02/91	JER	1.27	133	7.17	241	2.26	17.13	149	✪✪	1	40.59	117	N.A.	
▲	USD	11.15	HSBC GIF Intl Managed Equity	H033	30/11/90	LUX	-0.17	214	8.06	224	2.51	26.66	93	✪✪✪	2	38.23	125	N.A.	
	DEM	40.13	Hypo Dynamik	H024	29/10/93	LUX	1.92	106	5.32	255	2.07	16.61	153	✪		N.A.		N.A.	
	DEM	41.60	HYPO Eco Tech	H024	30/04/90	LUX	-4.20	318	8.80	213	2.77	24.07	115	✪✪	1	53.72	78	N.A.	
▲	USD	12.14	Indosuez Multimedia Fund	B033	29/07/94	LUX	-8.31	327	-6.46	298	N.A.	N.A.				N.A.		N.A.	
	FRF	17.73	Inter Multi Inv Privatisatns	B069	30/04/92	LUX	3.26	71	7.45	235	2.79	5.52	185	✪		N.A.		N.A.	
	USD	22.06	Inter Multi Inv Telecom	B069	31/12/93	LUX	1.07	141	14.14	108	2.77	26.17	99	✪✪✪	2	N.A.		N.A.	
▲	USD	31.40	Inter Strategie Global	B069	28/02/94	LUX	2.05	100	14.95	93	N.A.	N.A.				N.A.		N.A.	
	LUF	60.71	Interselex World B	G009	31/01/91	LUX	-0.25	220	11.16	173	2.80	39.23	30	✪✪✪✪	4	57.34	65	N.A.	
	USD	8.70	INVESCO Okasan Glbl Stgy	I013	31/03/86	LUX	0.66	161	9.74	199	2.67	24.44	111	✪✪	2	40.75	115	100.72	36
▲	USD	14.40	INVESCO PS Global Gth	I014	31/12/90	LUX	0.27	191	12.46	145	2.68	30.51	68	✪✪✪✪	3	48.59	92	N.A.	
▲	USD	14.90	INVESCO PS Global Leisure	I014	30/09/94	LUX	-0.94	255	11.16	172	N.A.	N.A.				N.A.		N.A.	
	USD	6.16	Investec Global Gth	I016	15/03/96	BVI	0.67	157	N.A.		N.A.	N.A.				N.A.		N.A.	
	LUF	5.64	Ippa Portf Stock Market B	B035	31/05/94	LUX	-1.36	274	9.92	197	N.A.	N.A.				N.A.		N.A.	
	USD	8.63	Irish Life Intl Gth Mgd Dllr	I017	30/09/94	IRL	2.07	98	17.03	62	N.A.	N.A.				N.A.		N.A.	
	GBP	6.21	Irish Life Intl Gth Mgd Stlg	I017	21/04/95	IRL	2.37	88	19.74	35	N.A.	N.A.				N.A.		N.A.	
	LUF	N.S.	Isis Global Assets Eq High C	B026	29/01/93	LUX	0.53	172	9.37	206	2.02	26.70	92	✪✪✪	4	N.A.		N.A.	
	USD	0.22	ItalFortune Intl Banks & Insur	F015	30/07/93	LUX	-10.58	331	-8.04	300	3.02	-32.99	213	✪		N.A.		N.A.	
	USD	2.34	ItalFortune Intl Global Equity	F015	29/06/90	LUX	-6.37	324	14.77	97	2.15	26.55	95	✪✪	3	34.05	128	N.A.	
	USD	41.35	JF Global Securities	J004	30/04/74	HK	2.11	95	18.88	40	3.20	1.70	193	✪		76.10	30	121.42	28
	USD	7.25	JF Masterfund Intl Gth	J004	20/10/95	CA	1.76	109	5.37	254	N.A.	N.A.				N.A.		N.A.	
●	GBP	48.89	JRIA/GAM Stlg Mgd	J002	30/12/94	IRL	6.20	24	16.32	67	N.A.	N.A.				N.A.		N.A.	
●	USD	13.90	JRIA/GAM US Dllr Mgd	J002	30/12/94	IRL	7.32	16	16.74	64	N.A.	N.A.				N.A.		N.A.	
●	GBP	20.47	JRIA/M&G Stlg Mgd	J002	30/12/94	IRL	-2.01	288	14.09	110	N.A.	N.A.				N.A.		N.A.	
●	GBP	17.42	JRIA/Scot Am Stlg Mgd	J002	30/12/94	IRL	-1.34	271	7.45	236	N.A.	N.A.				N.A.		N.A.	
●	GBP	89.25	JRIA/SJP Stlg Mgd	J002	30/12/94	IRL	1.61	120	27.83	9	N.A.	N.A.				N.A.		N.A.	
▲	GBP	4.75	Jupiter Tyndall GF Intl	J010	30/11/90	LUX	-2.57	303	-3.62	296	4.59	1.64	194	✪		42.33	110	N.A.	
	GBP	13.70	Jupiter Tyndall International	J009	31/10/75	JER	5.28	30	2.19	276	2.51	-5.84	201	✪		16.72	144	57.12	48
▲	USD	10.44	Jupiter Tyndall WUF Overseas	J008	31/01/84	BER	-1.75	279	-0.44	290	4.32	-6.82	203	✪		22.53	139	72.32	43
	ECU	5.66	Kaupthing Global Equity Class	K002	18/10/96	LUX	-1.99	285	N.A.		N.A.	N.A.				N.A.		N.A.	

▲ SIB Approved ● Insurance Fund **Values in US Dollars, on an offer to offer price basis with gross income reinvested** Data Source Micropal™

Global Equity

continued

	CCY	Fund Size ($mil)	Fund Name	Manager Code	Fund Start Date	Domicile Code	3 Mths 97 % Chg	3 Mths 97 Rank	1 Year % Chg	1 Year Rank	Micropal Star Rating: Volatility	3 Years % Chg	3 Years Rank	3 Years Rating	Risk Return Rating	5 Years % Chg	5 Years Rank	10 Years % Chg	10 Years Rank
		80.05	**Mean/Count**				**1.03**		**12.04**	**302**	**2.98**	**23.18**	**216**		**1**	**56.17**	**155**	**144.56**	**49**
▲	GBP	57.07	KB Int'l Equity Income	K007	30/12/83	JER	0	208	20.15	31	2.65	27.65	82	✪✪✪	2	79.12	26	199.24	7
	DEM	33.24	KB Lux Interequity	K011	29/12/89	LUX	0.64	163	7.30	238	2.50	-0.41	195	✪		21.76	140	N.A.	
▲	FIM	6.39	KB SEL Kansallis World	K008	28/09/90	LUX	3.77	57	13.40	121	2.65	29.59	74	✪✪✪	3	46.43	99	N.A.	
▲	GBP	24.53	KB Strategic Investment	K007	31/01/91	GU	1.74	112	18.84	42	2.74	30.01	72	✪✪✪✪	3	56.64	67	N.A.	
	DEM	20.81	KD Fonds Oeko Invest	U006	30/08/91	LUX	-0.99	259	-0.99	292	2.02	13	166	✪		5.98	150	N.A.	
	USD	24.94	Lazard Freres Global Equity	L003	29/01/93	GU	N.A.	—	12.25	150	2.30	35.50	40	✪✪✪✪	4	N.A.		N.A.	
▲	USD	N.S.	Lazard International Equity	L002	30/09/77	GU	1.02	143	10.87	181	2.81	23.47	116	✪✪	1	37.79	126	77.47	42
▲	GBP	18.86	Lazard SIT Global Active	L001	28/02/89	GU	-1.22	267	15.23	89	3.04	32.66	56	✪✪✪	2	50.71	85	N.A.	
	USD	69.70	Lehman Glbl Advisors Ptfl 1 B	L008	31/03/93	NL	1.75	111	19.46	37	2.68	14.68	160	✪✪		N.A.		N.A.	
	USD	22.29	Leicom Fund	L004	28/06/91	LUX	-0.90	253	10.41	191	3.30	3.20	190	✪		51.17	83	N.A.	
▲	USD	20.46	Liberty NW-Newport Global Oppo	L011	31/03/92	LUX	-0.35	228	17.49	57	2.56	32.77	54	✪✪✪✪	3	N.A.		N.A.	
	USD	86.11	Lion Fortune CL Global Gth C	C062	31/07/91	LUX	-4.11	317	10.17	194	3.37	30.62	67	✪✪✪	2	87.14	20	N.A.	
	USD	12.37	Lion Interaction CL Gbl Eq Fd	C062	31/03/89	LUX	14.46	4	0.75	286	3.27	18.75	142	✪✪	1	39.57	122	N.A.	
▲	USD	71.57	Lloyds IP World Equity	L016	31/03/92	LUX	4.86	35	1.98	280	2.94	22.86	122	✪✪	1	N.A.		N.A.	
	DEM	60.06	Lux Equity DEM/LUF	C002	30/06/95	LUX	2.26	91	11.57	162	N.A.	N.A.				N.A.		N.A.	
	DEM	25.60	Luxinvest OekoLux	B061	28/02/92	LUX	-3.83	315	7.89	229	2.49	13.98	163	✪		N.A.		N.A.	
	USD	242.80	Luxlife Actions Internat.	L024	23/09/94	LUX	0.63	165	17.94	54	N.A.	N.A.				N.A.		N.A.	
▲	GBP	50.55	M&G Island Global	M001	30/09/75	GU	0.51	173	10.98	178	2.72	26.92	88	✪✪✪✪	2	48.26	95	139.22	19
	USD	4.60	M-Fund Dollar Growth	B013	31/03/93	LUX	-3.51	311	-16.57	301	3.96	-36.02	215	✪		N.A.		N.A.	
	USD	6.56	M.Lynch Global Equity Portf O	M023	28/02/89	LUX	2.38	87	4.71	261	2.90	20.28	131	✪✪	1	23.56	138	N.A.	
	USD	6.65	M.Lynch Global SmallCap A	M023	30/11/94	LUX	0.09	198	12.54	143	N.A.	N.A.				N.A.		N.A.	
	USD	183	Malabar International	M003	31/05/90	BER	5.97	25	7.63	231	3.24	17.62	145	✪✪	1	103.09	13	N.A.	
▲	USD	3.46	Manulife Regent GF Intl Gth	M006	30/09/87	LUX	-0.83	250	7.15	242	4.33	-2.22	198	✪		32.81	129	N.A.	
	USD	0.44	MBf Global Managed	M010	31/01/85	HK	-1.77	280	14.44	99	5.47	-27.32	212	✪		3.77	151	-22.15	49
	USD	2.25	MBf World Growth	M010	31/10/86	HK	-0.73	244	1.32	284	4.92	-12.25	206	✪		40.08	119	118.98	29
	DEM	18.64	MC International Fund B	M009	31/08/94	LUX	-2.85	305	3.68	267	N.A.	N.A.				N.A.		N.A.	
	DEM	N.S.	MeesPierson UF Global Equity	M012	01/03/96	LUX	0.42	178	N.A.		N.A.	N.A.				N.A.		N.A.	
	DEM	6.37	Mega Invest	M034	31/03/93	LUX	N.A.	—	10.09	195	2.24	29.66	73	✪✪✪	4	N.A.		N.A.	
▲	GBP	23.26	Mercury OST Global	M020	28/11/86	LUX	1.76	110	11.47	168	2.79	24.19	114	✪✪✪	1	46.83	98	128.13	25
▲	GBP	6.77	Mercury OST Overseas	M020	30/11/79	LUX	2.09	97	11.94	154	2.74	24.46	110	✪✪✪	2	48.64	91	111	34
▲	USD	16.34	Mercury ST Glbl Opportunities	M021	29/02/96	LUX	-3.86	316	N.A.		N.A.	N.A.				N.A.		N.A.	
▲●	USD	30.90	Mercury ST Global Equity	M021	31/12/71	LUX	-2.29	293	14.19	107	2.85	26.01	101	✪✪✪	2	56.28	69	90.21	39
	DEM	142.39	Merita Intl Equity	M022	29/02/88	LUX	0.71	154	16.76	63	2.42	27.23	85	✪✪✪	3	67.71	45	N.A.	
	USD	176.40	MFS Meridian Global Equity	M026	31/01/89	CA	0.33	186	19.83	33	3.11	38.40	32	✪✪✪✪✪	4	72.97	35	N.A.	
	USD	82.30	MFS Meridian World Gth	M026	23/12/94	CA	-0.39	231	14.20	106	N.A.	N.A.				N.A.		N.A.	
	USD	77.10	MLBS (B) WW Equity	M024	30/09/94	LUX	1.65	115	7.93	227	N.A.	N.A.				N.A.		N.A.	
▲	GBP	21.14	Morgan Grenfell O'seas Assets	M038	31/07/78	IRL	0.55	170	14.22	104	2.94	32.34	58	✪✪✪✪	3	55.70	70	124.63	27
	USD	373.46	Morgan Stanley Global Equity	M039	31/10/89	LUX	2.03	102	20.17	30	2.79	51.25	14	✪✪✪✪✪	5	121.37	6	N.A.	
	ECU	22.18	Morgan Stanley Intl SmCap	M039	30/11/93	LUX	3.25	72	15.51	83	3.10	25.86	103	✪✪	1	N.A.		N.A.	
	FRF	6.02	MOSAIS Actions Int Divers	C058	30/03/90	LUX	2.75	80	22.23	16	2.84	37.84	34	✪✪✪✪	4	54.20	76	N.A.	
	GBP	16.71	MultiLink Aaron Balanced Mgd	I011	31/07/96	LUX	-2.08	290	N.A.		N.A.	N.A.				N.A.		N.A.	
	USD	179.60	National Mutual Global	N001	28/02/90	HK	-0.53	235	11.87	157	2.58	27.50	83	✪✪✪	2	59.74	61	N.A.	
	USD	6.23	New World Dynamic Fund	B067	31/07/92	LUX	-2.84	304	8.35	220	2.40	17.53	146	✪✪	1	N.A.		N.A.	
▲	USD	10.30	Newton UGF Intl Ptfl	N006	29/02/88	JER	5.96	26	18.27	50	2.79	32.69	55	✪✪✪✪	3	48.64	90	N.A.	
▲	GBP	4.23	Norwich Un JIP Int'l Equity	N013	28/02/90	JER	1.23	134	12.90	135	2.53	31.61	63	✪✪✪✪	3	61.62	55	N.A.	
	USD	2.34	Old Mutual Gnsy Intl Stkmkt	0003	29/12/95	GU	1.40	129	7.30	239	N.A.	N.A.				N.A.		N.A.	
	USD	0.89	Old Mutual HK Intl Stkmkt	0004	28/04/95	HK	2.51	84	9.20	208	N.A.	N.A.				N.A.		N.A.	
	USD	34	OMI (Gnsy) Intl Stkmkt	0005	31/05/82	GU	1.62	118	9.47	205	2.74	13.45	165	✪✪		72.96	36	132.82	22
	USD	0.42	OMI (Ire) Dllr Intl Stkmkt	0006	29/10/93	IRL	3.73	60	8.96	211	2.58	17.31	147	✪✪	1	N.A.		N.A.	
	DEM	0.29	OMI (Ire) Dmark Intl Stkmkt	0006	29/10/93	IRL	3.59	62	9.67	200	2.48	26.24	97	✪✪✪	2	N.A.		N.A.	
	GBP	0.44	OMI (Ire) Stlg Intl Stkmkt	0006	29/10/93	IRL	1.62	119	13.02	127	2.63	21.45	128	✪✪	1	N.A.		N.A.	
	USD	190.60	Oppenheim Pharma/wHealth	0009	30/11/93	LUX	3.77	56	18.69	47	4.04	72.31	4	✪✪✪✪	5	N.A.		N.A.	
	USD	885.37	Orbis Global Equity	0013	29/12/89	BER	3.55	63	13.78	118	3.58	51.96	11	✪✪✪✪✪	4	99.44	16	N.A.	
	USD	1011.23	Orbis Optimal Equity	0013	29/12/89	BER	0.63	164	3.98	263	1.90	22.46	123	✪✪	3	62.40	54	N.A.	
	USD	13.20	Orbitex Comm&Info Technology	0014	30/09/94	BAH	-10.25	330	6.09	248	N.A.	N.A.				N.A.		N.A.	
	USD	2.10	Orbitex Global Discovery	0014	31/10/94	BAH	1.08	140	15.58	81	N.A.	N.A.				N.A.		N.A.	
	USD	10.20	Orbitex Health & Enviromental	0014	31/10/91	BAH	-0.30	223	2.74	272	4.33	26.21	98	✪✪	1	48.16	96	N.A.	

▲ SIB Approved **● Insurance Fund** **Values in US Dollars, on an offer to offer price basis with gross income reinvested** Data Source Micropal™

Global Equity

continued

	CCY	Fund Size ($mil)	Fund Name	Manager Code	Fund Start Date	Domicile Code	3 Mths 97 % Chg	3 Mths 97 Rank	1 Year % Chg	1 Year Rank	Micropal Star Rating 3 Years Volatility	3 Years % Chg	3 Years Rank	3 Years Rating	Risk Return Rating	5 Years % Chg	5 Years Rank	10 Years % Chg	10 Years Rank
		80.05	**Mean/Count**				**1.03**		**12.04**	**302**	**2.98**	**23.18**	**216**		**1**	**56.17**	**155**	**144.56**	**49**
	USD	2.22	OYSTER World Opportunities	B067	13/09/96	LUX	8.27	176	N.A.		N.A.	N.A.				N.A.		N.A.	
	LUF	47.81	Panelfund World LUF Cap	A037	31/05/90	LUX	0.39	181	11.54	165	2.35	30.14	71	✪✪✪✪	4	39.10	123	N.A.	
	NLG	52.60	Panelfund World NLG Cap	A037	29/04/94	LUX	0.55	171	11.54	164	N.A.	N.A.				N.A.		N.A.	
	USD	N.S.	PCP Glbl Mgd Aggressive	P007	31/05/96	CA	0.39	199	N.A.		N.A.	N.A.				N.A.		N.A.	
	USD	4.34	Peregrine Global Equity	P008	31/05/96	CA	3.45	65	N.A.		N.A.	N.A.				N.A.		N.A.	
	USD	137	Perpetual Offshr Emerging Cos	P011	30/04/85	JER	-1.39	275	12.57	142	2.67	20.44	130	✪✪	1	123.72	5	346.21	3
	USD	127.80	Perpetual Offshr Intl Growth	P011	31/01/83	JER	1.46	125	11.93	155	2.76	26.45	96	✪✪✪	2	81.39	23	158.21	16
	USD	11.64	PFC Specialist Growth	P014	30/04/85	HK	1.63	117	7.91	228	2.92	11.59	169	✪		76.62	29	148.58	17
	USD	57.90	Pictet T.F. Intl Small Cap	P016	31/05/89	LUX	1.35	131	9.55	202	2.86	-0.84	196	✪		42.22	111	N.A.	
	DEM	N.S.	Pioneer Global Equity	P017	18/08/95	IRL	3.75	58	18.70	46	N.A.	N.A.				N.A.		N.A.	
	USD	2.58	Pleiade Enviroment Equities	B039	26/02/93	LUX	5.29	29	3.21	268	3.16	-2.76	199	✪		N.A.		N.A.	
	FRF	0.66	Plurigestion Plurivaleurs	M040	31/07/91	LUX	-14.37	332	-17.06	302	4.92	-59.07	216	✪		-74.98	155	N.A.	
	DEM	49.04	Postbank Dynamik Global	P019	31/05/95	LUX	7.89	14	10.66	185	N.A.	N.A.				N.A.		N.A.	
	BEF	7.51	Privalux Global Invest	C003	31/10/89	LUX	1.40	128	8.30	221	2.91	-6.98	204	✪		6.07	149	N.A.	
▲	GBP	93.53	Prolific IF Global Growth	P027	31/03/89	IRL	4.64	38	8.54	216	3.17	10.62	174	✪		49.13	89	N.A.	
	USD	13.56	Prolific IF Technology	P027	12/04/96	IRL	-5.83	323	N.A.		N.A.	N.A.				N.A.		N.A.	
	LUF	N.S.	Puilaetco Quality Fd Global EQ	P031	31/05/91	LUX	1.14	139	25.18	11	2.39	65.71	8	✪✪✪✪✪	5	85.10	21	N.A.	
	USD	N.S.	Putnam Embassy Global Gth A	P033	31/03/94	CA	1.61	121	13.84	115	N.A.	N.A.				N.A.		N.A.	
	USD	N.S.	Putnam Embassy Global Gth B	P033	31/03/94	CA	1.48	124	12.96	131	N.A.	N.A.				N.A.		N.A.	
	USD	20.66	Putnam International	P032	29/02/84	LUX	0.15	194	12.79	138	2.31	26.75	91	✪✪✪	3	55.59	71	126.39	26
	DEM	60.83	Q Discount	Q004	30/04/92	LUX	3.86	52	16.16	69	2.37	29.38	76	✪✪✪	3	N.A.		N.A.	
	DEM	32.94	Q Turn-Around	Q004	29/10/93	LUX	9.08	10	-2.54	295	2.44	2.13	191	✪		N.A.		N.A.	
	NLG	4.96	Rabobank Select Equity	R001	19/04/96	LUX	-4.36	319	N.A.		N.A.	N.A.				N.A.		N.A.	
▲	USD	33.50	RBC Gl Dllr Intl Cap	R003	24/11/95	GU	-2.38	299	10.97	179	N.A.	N.A.				N.A.		N.A.	
▲	GBP	10.15	RBC Gl Stlg Intl Cap	R003	24/11/95	GU	-2.54	302	12.65	140	N.A.	N.A.				N.A.		N.A.	
	USD	0.83	RDS Global Intl Equity B	R004	31/12/93	LUX	3.63	61	2.77	271	3.61	-3.98	200	✪		N.A.		N.A.	
	USD	105.05	Regent Undervalued Assets	R005	28/06/91	CA	10.03	7	4.85	259	2.50	10.89	173	✪		119.31	8	N.A.	
	GBP	1.05	Restricted Risk Portfolio A	C020	14/04/95	IRL	-0.97	258	11.82	159	N.A.	N.A.				N.A.		N.A.	
●	GBP	0.85	RLI/Equity Plus	R020	15/12/95	IOM	8.81	11	3.68	266	N.A.	N.A.				N.A.		N.A.	
●	USD	4.30	RLI/GF GSF Global Equity	R026	31/08/90	IOM	4.08	49	7.31	237	2.42	19.07	139	✪✪	1	60.35	59	N.A.	
▲	NLG	6085.96	Robeco N.V	R009	31/12/76	EN	1.66	114	19.16	39	2.68	43.36	18	✪✪✪✪✪	5	80.19	24	161.93	15
▲	NLG	3303.10	Rolinco N.V	R009	31/12/76	EN	1.07	142	16.02	75	2.93	41.25	24	✪✪✪✪✪	4	73.47	34	169.38	13
●	GBP	22.16	Royal Life Intl Intl Growth	R020	30/10/87	IOM	-1.54	277	15.60	79	2.84	34.13	46	✪✪✪✪	3	64.55	51	N.A.	
●	GBP	8.63	Royal Life/Gart Intl Growth	R024	30/10/87	IOM	0.69	155	11.98	153	2.47	16.41	156	✪✪		45.47	103	N.A.	
●	USD	0.06	Royal Life/MBf Barracuda	R032	29/09/89	HK	-0.62	239	-0.49	291	6.23	-25.55	211	✪		32.63	131	N.A.	
●	USD	0.06	Royal Life/MBf Global Mgd	R032	29/09/89	HK	4.02	51	3.88	265	5.21	-34.34	214	✪		-15.84	154	N.A.	
●	USD	0.20	Royal Life/MBf World Growth	R032	29/09/89	HK	4.46	44	-5.07	297	4.64	-14.20	208	✪		20.36	141	N.A.	
●	USD	20.20	Royal Life/Perp Emerging Cos	R034	30/10/87	IOM	2.72	81	11.24	170	2.68	17.15	148	✪✪	1	108.91	10	N.A.	
●	USD	24.40	Royal Life/Perp Intl Gth	R034	30/10/87	IOM	6.52	22	7.56	233	2.26	20.18	134	✪✪	1	69.44	41	N.A.	
	GBP	119.88	Royal Skandia Perpetual Agg ST	R038	28/02/92	IOM	0.12	196	12.28	149	2.81	30.27	70	✪✪✪	2	N.A.		N.A.	
	USD	31.13	Royal Skandia Perpetual Agg US	R038	28/02/92	IOM	-0.21	217	5.79	253	2.90	27.95	81	✪✪✪	2	N.A.		N.A.	
	USD	99.48	S-E-Banken Fund Global	S001	30/06/93	LUX	0.90	148	12.92	134	2.64	26.56	94	✪✪✪	2	N.A.		N.A.	
	USD	78.52	S-E-Banken Fund Lakemedel	S001	29/10/93	LUX	2.43	86	18.86	41	5.40	69.89	6	✪✪✪✪	4	N.A.		N.A.	
	USD	11.17	S-E-Banken Fund Miljo	S001	29/10/93	LUX	0.76	153	16.02	74	3.48	11.43	170	✪✪		N.A.		N.A.	
	USD	44.30	S-E-Banken Fund Teknologi	S001	29/10/93	LUX	-5.30	321	19.72	36	6.36	99.78	2	✪✪✪✪✪	4	N.A.		N.A.	
	USD	35.50	Samba Lux Global Equity	S006	31/01/95	LUX	-1.68	278	11.52	166	N.A.	N.A.				N.A.		N.A.	
	DEM	9.88	Santander Invest Global Equity	B011	30/11/93	LUX	4.97	32	18.13	51	2.81	38.86	31	✪✪✪✪	4	N.A.		N.A.	
	GBP	N.S.	Sarasin Equisar	S005	31/07/96	GU	4.51	40	N.A.		N.A.	N.A.				N.A.		N.A.	
▲	CHF	75.20	Sarasin TecSar SICAV	B038	07/07/95	LUX	-3.82	314	2.22	275	N.A.	N.A.				N.A.		N.A.	
	USD	20.29	Scala Intl Blue Chips B	B006	09/02/96	LUX	N.A.	—	N.A.		N.A.	N.A.				N.A.		N.A.	
	USD	36.92	Schroder Asia International	S011	31/01/72	HK	-1.12	79	17.34	60	3.22	16.99	151	✪✪	1	73.98	33	131.86	23
▲	USD	106.62	Schroder Intl Sel Global Eqty	S010	30/06/93	LUX	2.91	207	12.53	144	2.61	31.42	64	✪✪✪✪	3	N.A.		N.A.	
▲	GBP	62.28	Schroder Intl Sel Portfolio	S010	30/09/94	LUX	0	73	19.35	38	N.A.	N.A.				N.A.		N.A.	
	USD	38.48	Scontinvest Technology	S012	29/03/96	LUX	3.21	295	N.A.		N.A.	N.A.				N.A.		N.A.	
●	JPY	2.46	Scot Amicable Gl Bal FE	S015	16/06/95	IRL	-2.30	281	8.43	217	N.A.	N.A.				N.A.		N.A.	
●	GBP	6.18	Scot Amicable Gl Bal UK	S015	16/06/95	IRL	-1.79	200	11.15	174	N.A.	N.A.				N.A.		N.A.	
●	USD	2.35	Scot Amicable Gl Bal US	S015	16/06/95	IRL	0.09	237	15.68	77	N.A.	N.A.				N.A.		N.A.	

▲ SIB Approved ● Insurance Fund **Values in US Dollars, on an offer to offer price basis with gross income reinvested** Data Source Micropal™

Global Equity

continued

	CCY	Fund Size ($mil)	Fund Name	Manager Code	Fund Start Date	Domicile Code	3 Mths 97 % Chg	Rank	1 Year % Chg	Rank	Micropal Star Rating 3 Years Volatility	% Chg	Rank	Rating	Risk Return Rating	5 Years % Chg	Rank	10 Years % Chg	Rank
		80.05	**Mean/Count**				**1.03**		**12.04**	**302**	**2.98**	**23.18**	**216**		**1**	**56.17**	**155**	**144.56**	**49**
	GBP	3.72	Scot Eq (SEI) Intl Equity	S016	23/06/95	LUX	-0.59	260	7.19	240	N.A.	N.A.				N.A.		N.A.	
▲	ECU	33.58	Scot Equitable IF Intl Equity	S017	31/07/92	LUX	-0.99	46	13.07	125	2.73	30.43	69	✪✪✪	3	N.A.		N.A.	
	GBP	7.95	Scot Prov GP Global Growth	S014	30/08/91	IOM	4.37	37	8.35	219	3.14	10.46	175	✪		32.77	130	N.A.	
	USD	12.50	Scot Prov GP World Equity	S014	30/09/91	IOM	4.70	322	7.14	243	2.98	8.62	177	✪		41.31	112	N.A.	
	USD	5.90	Scot Prov ILA Technology	S014	29/09/95	IOM	-5.83	184	12.89	136	N.A.	N.A.				N.A.		N.A.	
	USD	25.82	Scottish World Fund	M008	31/01/89	LUX	0.35	78	12.84	137	2.64	25.40	104	✪✪✪	2	54.09	77	N.A.	
	USD	131.82	Scudder GOF Str Gl Themes A-2	S019	30/04/93	LUX	2.92	104	12.95	132	2.36	32.30	59	✪✪✪✪	4	N.A.		N.A.	
▲●	GBP	29.43	Singer & Fried Investment Tst	S027	31/05/95	IRL	1.98	144	18.73	44	N.A.	N.A.				N.A.		N.A.	
▲	USD	197.16	Skandifond Global	S030	30/12/88	LUX	1.01	240	12.43	146	2.69	26.88	89	✪✪✪	2	41.24	113	N.A.	
	USD	16.87	Sogelux Fd Equities Intl Gth	S037	31/05/88	LUX	-0.62	158	25.50	10	4.01	19.87	136	✪✪	1	65.98	47	N.A.	
	USD	6.29	Sogelux Fd Equities World	S037	31/05/88	LUX	0.67	85	13.89	114	2.55	29.24	77	✪✪✪	3	53.43	80	N.A.	
	USD	22.32	Southern Intl Global Equities	S041	31/07/96	LUX	2.50	2	N.A.		N.A.	N.A.				N.A.		N.A.	
	USD	91.40	SR International	S031	31/01/94	BVI	19.81	93	27.84	8	N.A.	N.A.				N.A.		N.A.	
	USD	7.97	Strider	O016	30/09/92	CA	2.19	34	15.42	85	1.70	8.85	176	✪		N.A.		N.A.	
	USD	22.37	Sun All Intl US Dllr Gl Mgd	S051	31/10/95	GU	4.89	211	8.17	222	N.A.	N.A.				N.A.		N.A.	
▲	DEM	5.94	Sun Life GP Ecological	S052	31/12/92	LUX	-0.11	249	14.57	98	2.63	8.59	178	✪		N.A.		N.A.	
▲	USD	16.72	Sun Life GP Global Masters	S052	31/03/88	LUX	-0.80	246	10.29	193	2.61	20.20	133	✪✪	1	43.37	107	N.A.	
▲	USD	5.97	Sun Life GP Global Recovery	S052	31/03/88	LUX	-0.74	182	9.02	209	3.20	11.34	171	✪✪		25.85	135	N.A.	
	CHF	59.82	Swissca Portfolio Equity	S059	31/03/95	LUX	3.11	75	13.84	116	N.A.	N.A.				N.A.		N.A.	
	USD	21.02	Syfrets Gl Global Equity	S060	30/11/93	CA	-1.05	264	8.11	223	1.72	12.66	167	✪		N.A.		N.A.	
	FRF	5.63	SynalFund Actions Internat.	S061	31/07/90	LUX	-1.11	242	2.16	278	2.02	17.11	150	✪✪	1	18.25	143	N.A.	
▲	DEM	164.25	Templeton GS DM Global Growth	T001	30/04/91	LUX	-0.66	226	14.02	111	2.27	39.69	27	✪✪✪✪✪	5	87.18	19	N.A.	
	USD	5.25	Templeton GS Glbl Prop Sec	T001	15/03/96	LUX	-0.34	219	N.A.		N.A.	N.A.				N.A.		N.A.	
▲	USD	4.72	Templeton GS Glbl Utilities	T001	30/06/94	LUX	-0.24	192	16.13	70	N.A.	N.A.				N.A.		N.A.	
▲	USD	359.66	Templeton GS Global Growth	T001	28/02/91	LUX	0.24	116	15.94	76	2.33	39.26	29	✪✪✪✪✪	5	78.10	28	N.A.	
▲	USD	4.73	Templeton GS Infra & Comm	T001	31/08/94	LUX	1.63	27	16.21	68	N.A.	N.A.				N.A.		N.A.	
▲	USD	50.12	Templeton GS Smaller Cos	T001	31/07/91	LUX	5.57	216	22.51	15	2.84	32.85	53	✪✪✪✪	3	69.98	40	N.A.	
▲	USD	4.67	TGA Intl Eqty	T009	22/03/96	LUX	-0.21	74	N.A.		N.A.	N.A.				N.A.		N.A.	
	USD	40.06	The Establishment Trust	T003	28/02/89	LUX	3.19	312	11.47	167	3.08	12.62	168	✪		75.44	31	N.A.	
	GBP	5.45	The Ivory Growth Fund	R019	30/08/85	JER	-3.64	66	18.35	49	3.63	39.93	25	✪✪✪	3	84.64	22	174	12
	USD	2.80	The M*A*R*S Fund Cl A	B074	30/06/93	LUX	N.A.	—	6.74	246	1.49	8.16	180	✪		N.A.		N.A.	
	ECU	26.69	The Sailor's-Internat Equity	B005	31/05/91	LUX	3.41	92	10.69	184	2.17	27.12	86	✪✪✪	3	43.08	108	N.A.	
	DEM	N.S.	The Stafford Fund	C025	29/01/93	BVI	2.20	320	16.03	73	2.07	39.48	28	✪✪✪✪✪	5	N.A.		N.A.	
	ESP	25.30	Top Fund World Equities	F008	30/09/94	IRL	-5.24	169	1.70	282	N.A.	N.A.				N.A.		N.A.	
	GBP	19.74	TSB Island Pension	T012	27/02/87	JER	0.55	175	20.51	26	3.39	46.57	17	✪✪✪✪	4	107.23	11	N.A.	
▲	GBP	41.61	TSB OIF Intl Equity	T013	30/04/90	JER	0.49	159	10.49	188	3.30	22.38	124	✪✪	1	102.27	15	N.A.	
▲	GBP	42.80	TSB OIF Island Equity	T013	13/01/95	JER	0.67	149	21.22	23	N.A.	N.A.				N.A.		N.A.	
	USD	70.92	UBAM Intl. Growth Equity	U010	27/10/95	LUX	0.89	241	22.65	14	N.A.	N.A.				N.A.		N.A.	
	USD	N.S.	UBS (Lux) Equity I Biotech	U001	30/09/96	LUX	-0.65	183	N.A.		N.A.	N.A.				N.A.		N.A.	
▲	GBP	6.26	Ulster Bank Gl Equity	U003	17/03/95	IOM	0.37	292	17.79	56	N.A.	N.A.				N.A.		N.A.	
	DEM	25.31	Unico Equity	U006	31/08/87	LUX	-2.17	206	8.62	215	2.93	18.86	141	✪✪	1	32.05	132	N.A.	
▲	USD	1.80	Von Ernst GP Global Equity	B021	30/11/89	LUX	0	136	6.94	245	2.56	16.42	155	✪		40.90	114	N.A.	
	USD	4.30	W'Invest Excelle Gl Eq USD	W006	31/05/79	JER	1.19	166	3.90	264	3.24	5.64	184	✪		55.14	72	109.73	35
	USD	30.49	Willer Telecom	W004	28/02/94	LUX	0.61	82	1.78	281	N.A.	N.A.				N.A.		N.A.	
▲	ECU	132.70	Win GF Intl Diversified	W005	19/08/94	LUX	2.71	103	23.81	13	N.A.	N.A.				N.A.		N.A.	
▲	ECU	34.51	Win GF Intl Equity	W005	31/01/91	LUX	1.99	229	11.06	176	2.63	25.10	107	✪✪✪	2	48.29	93	N.A.	
	ECU	135.42	Winchester Gl Healthcare Op	O008	31/12/93	BVI	-0.36	262	3.02	269	2.16	48.16	15	✪✪✪✪	5	N.A.		N.A.	
	ECU	21.32	World Invest Share	B022	24/02/95	LUX	-1.08	332	16.09	72	N.A.	N.A.				N.A.		N.A.	

▲ **SIB Approved** ● **Insurance Fund** **Values in US Dollars, on an offer to offer price basis with gross income reinvested** Data Source Micropal™

Global Emerging Markets Equity

Funds investing in excess of 70% in Global Emerging Market equities or related instruments. Such funds may have an objective of capital and/or income growth, or to track a specified index or perform inversely to a given index. Funds in this category may leverage or gear by a maximum of 20% of total assets.

	CCY	Fund Size ($mil)	Fund Name	Manager Code	Fund Start Date	Domicile Code	3 Mths 97 % Chg	3 Mths 97 Rank	1 Year % Chg	1 Year Rank	Micropal Star Rating 3 Years Volatility	3 Years % Chg	3 Years Rank	Rating	Risk Return Rating	5 Years % Chg	5 Years Rank	10 Years % Chg	10 Years Rank
		115.65	**Mean/Count**				**10.18**	**99**	**11.07**	**86**	**4.66**	**-8.49**	**45**			**54.72**	**15**	**0**	**0**
	USD	11.12	Ace Emerging Markets	A004	19/08/94	LUX	7.59	66	5.43	61	N.A.	N.A.				N.A.		N.A.	
	USD	38.43	ACMGI Dev. Regional Mkts A	A005	30/10/92	LUX	9.24	16	20	14	5.15	-7.80	21	✪✪✪		N.A.		N.A.	
●	GBP	0	Albany Intl Emerging Mkts	A018	31/08/93	IOM	13.75	57	22.95	9	5.16	3.77	6	✪✪✪✪		N.A.		N.A.	
	USD	291.46	Baring Chrysalis Undiluted	B050	29/11/91	CA	9.93	53	7.84	47	5.16	-23.72	39	✪		19.94	14	N.A.	
	USD	184.86	Baring EMUF Global Emerg Mkts	B049	28/02/92	IRL	10.26	50	8.51	46	5.73	-26.72	41	✪		N.A.		N.A.	
▲	GBP	16.70	Baring GUF Emerging World	B049	29/04/94	IRL	10.42	86	2.87	75	N.A.	N.A.				N.A.		N.A.	
	USD	23.86	BT Emerging World	B078	31/05/94	IRL	14.98	12	4.80	65	N.A.	N.A.				N.A.		N.A.	
	USD	1311.25	Capital Intl Emerging Markets	C010	29/06/90	LUX	10.75	24	14.44	25	4.86	1.50	11	✪✪✪✪		101.67	2	N.A.	
	USD	N.S.	Capital Intl Latin American	C010	07/06/96	LUX	12.24	80	N.A.		N.A.	N.A.				N.A.		N.A.	
	GBP	68.17	Cazenove Gl Emerging Mkt Ptfl	C014	22/09/95	JER	7.72	56	9.80	42	N.A.	N.A.				N.A.		N.A.	
	USD	191	CCF Sam EMF World Emer Eq C	C015	30/09/93	LUX	10.01	95	6.37	57	5.25	-11.45	25	✪✪		N.A.		N.A.	
	LUF	11.99	Cera Invest Emerging Markets C	C018	30/06/94	LUX	0.17	69	17.29	19	N.A.	N.A.				N.A.		N.A.	
●	USD	15.04	Citimarkets Glbl Emerg Mkts A	C034	31/03/93	LUX	9.12	62	2.51	77	4.90	-2.87	17	✪✪✪		N.A.		N.A.	
●	USD	35.34	Citimarkets Glbl Emerg Mkts B	C034	31/03/93	LUX	9.48	55	4.05	69	4.91	0.45	14	✪✪✪		N.A.		N.A.	
▲	USD	4	CL Developing Markets	C063	31/12/90	HK	10.07	7	5.95	58	5.33	-4.62	18	✪✪✪		110.29	1	N.A.	
●	USD	711.41	Credis Equity Emerging Mkts	C056	30/09/93	LUX	16.01	92	7.39	51	4.95	-17.63	35	✪✪		N.A.		N.A.	
	BEF	19.22	Cregem Equities L Emerg Mkts C	C059	24/06/94	LUX	3.89	72	3.05	72	N.A.	N.A.				N.A.		N.A.	
▲	USD	67.65	CU PP Emerging Countries	C070	30/11/93	LUX	8.95	5	3.15	71	4.75	-28.84	43	✪		N.A.		N.A.	
	USD	36.28	Deltec Emerging Mkts Eq	D010	28/02/94	BVI	16.41	27	29.32	5	N.A.	N.A.				N.A.		N.A.	
	GBP	N.S.	Edinburgh Glbl Emerging Mkts	E008	31/05/94	IRL	11.92	19	9.97	39	N.A.	N.A.				N.A.		N.A.	
	DEM	28.29	Emerging Fund	T011	31/01/95	LUX	12.90	1	18.15	18	N.A.	N.A.				N.A.		N.A.	
	DEM	3.21	Emerging Markets Quant	O008	29/02/96	BVI	25.27	36	N.A.		N.A.	N.A.				N.A.		N.A.	
	USD	16.35	Ermitage Emerging Markets	E011	30/10/92	BVI	11.21	70	32.35	4	4.03	38.74	1	✪✪✪✪✪	3	N.A.		N.A.	
	USD	N.S.	EV Medallion Emerging Mkts B	E003	21/04/95	CA	9	79	24.32	8	N.A.	N.A.				N.A.		N.A.	
▲	USD	184	Fidelity Fds Emerging Markets	F011	29/10/93	LUX	7.95	85	4.10	68	3.77	-23.60	38	✪		N.A.		N.A.	
●	USD	2.70	FIL Developing Markets	F017	31/01/94	BER	6.49	34	8.71	44	N.A.	N.A.				N.A.		N.A.	
	USD	9.23	Five Arrows IP Emerging Mkts	R016	30/12/94	GU	11.40	35	9.68	43	N.A.	N.A.				N.A.		N.A.	
▲	USD	26.10	Fleming FF Emerging Mkts	F020	29/04/94	LUX	11.38	87	7.66	49	N.A.	N.A.				N.A.		N.A.	
	USD	25.33	FP Gl Emerging Equities	F029	29/10/93	LUX	5.90	11	1.92	80	3.23	4.13	5	✪✪✪		N.A.		N.A.	
	USD	110.70	GAM Emerging Mkts Multi-Fund	G003	31/03/92	IOM	15	39	24.52	7	3.89	10.65	4	✪✪✪✪✪		N.A.		N.A.	
▲	USD	11.11	Gartmore CSF Emerging Mkts	G007	29/05/87	JER	11	76	5.38	62	4.90	-27.37	42	✪		18.41	15	N.A.	
	USD	14.85	Generalinvest Emerg Mkt B	B064	19/04/96	LUX	8.07	6	N.A.		N.A.	N.A.				N.A.		N.A.	
	USD	472.22	Genesis Emerging Markets	G010	31/07/89	GU	16.22	71	20.26	13	4.10	10.75	3	✪✪✪✪✪		90.76	3	N.A.	
	DEM	37.32	Global Advantage Emerg. Mkts	S047	31/12/93	LUX	8.95	47	14.14	26	4.07	22.09	2	✪✪✪✪✪	2	N.A.		N.A.	
▲	USD	20.80	Global Emerging Mkts Inv Co	F002	30/06/94	LUX	10.59	52	9.82	41	N.A.	N.A.				N.A.		N.A.	
	USD	5.55	Global Emerging Value	R005	28/02/94	CA	10.40	58	36.52	3	N.A.	N.A.				N.A.		N.A.	
▲●	USD	38.05	Groupe Indosuez Dev Mkts	G017	31/01/91	LUX	9.85	22	3.83	70	5.17	-32.71	44	✪		27.95	12	N.A.	
	USD	20.30	GT Africa A Share	G018	24/11/95	BER	12.59	33	14.77	23	N.A.	N.A.				N.A.		N.A.	
▲	USD	329	GT Emerging Markets A Share	G018	29/06/90	IRL	11.47	93	2.68	76	4.51	-14.31	32	✪✪		42.15	10	N.A.	
▲	USD	54	GT Emerging Mkts Small Cos A	G018	30/11/93	IRL	3.20	32	4.42	67	3.92	-12.94	30	✪✪		N.A.		N.A.	
▲	USD	20.87	Guinness Flight Emerging Mkts	G019	30/06/94	GU	11.59	45	5.31	63	N.A.	N.A.				N.A.		N.A.	
●	USD	1.32	Hansard\Gartmore CSF Em Mkts	H015	31/07/92	IOM	10.63	15	5.57	60	5.06	-22.18	37	✪		N.A.		N.A.	
●	USD	6.41	Hansard\GT Emerging Markets	H016	27/09/91	IOM	13.89	68	1.35	81	4.81	-9.76	24	✪✪		40	11	N.A.	
▲	USD	25.96	Henderson HF Glbl Emerg Mkts	H025	31/08/93	LUX	9.13	20	14.54	24	5.49	-14.54	33	✪✪		N.A.		N.A.	
	USD	29.12	Hermes Emerging Markets	H028	29/05/92	BER	12.72	37	21.43	10	4.01	1.39	12	✪✪✪✪		N.A.		N.A.	
▲	USD	47.73	HSBC GIF Intl Emerging Mkt	H033	18/11/94	LUX	11.11	88	11.18	35	N.A.	N.A.				N.A.		N.A.	
	USD	183.02	HYPO Emerging Markets Garantie	H024	19/07/96	LUX	5.87	38	N.A.		N.A.	N.A.				N.A.		N.A.	
	DEM	114.92	HYPO New Horizon	H024	31/07/91	LUX	11.04		12.11	30	4.73	-12.95	31	✪✪		26.70	13	N.A.	
	GBP	17.25	INVESCO Pioneer Markets	I013	31/07/87	JER	11.73	29	4.59	66	5	-9.56	23	✪✪✪		57.45	6	N.A.	
▲	USD	21.90	INVESCO PS Glbl Emer Mkts	I014	31/12/90	LUX	9.82	61	6.87	55	4.65	-19.51	36	✪		46.28	8	N.A.	
	USD	4.53	Irish Life Intl Emg Mkts Eq	I017	30/09/94	IRL	9.52	48	18.20	17	N.A.	N.A.				N.A.		N.A.	
	GBP	139.42	KB Emerging Markets	K007	28/02/92	GU	10.49	44	13.70	27	4.56	2.01	9	✪✪✪✪		N.A.		N.A.	
▲	USD	8.40	KB SEL Emerging Mkts	K008	28/02/94	LUX	10.65	3	7.64	50	N.A.	N.A.				N.A.		N.A.	
	USD	45	Key Emerging Value Inc	B056	19/05/95	CA	21.97	17	60.33	1	N.A.	N.A.				N.A.		N.A.	
	USD	40.58	Lazard Emerging World	L002	29/04/94	GU	13.68	74	11.67	33	N.A.	N.A.				N.A.		N.A.	
	USD	32.95	LG Antenna	L013	30/04/92	BER	8.76	31	12.44	29	3.81	-6.93	19	✪✪✪		N.A.		N.A.	
	USD	439.10	Luxlife Marches Emergents	L024	23/09/94	LUX	11.64	73	-2.22	84	N.A.	N.A.				N.A.		N.A.	

▲ SIB Approved ● Insurance Fund **Values in US Dollars, on an offer to offer price basis with gross income reinvested** Data Source Micropal™

Global Emerging Markets Equity

continued

	CCY	Fund Size ($mil)	Fund Name	Manager Code	Fund Start Date	Domicile Code	3 Mths 97 % Chg	3 Mths 97 Rank	1 Year % Chg	1 Year Rank	Micropal Star Rating 3 Years Volatility	3 Years % Chg	3 Years Rank	Rating	Risk Return Rating	5 Years % Chg	5 Years Rank	10 Years % Chg	10 Years Rank
		115.65	**Mean/Count**				**10.18**	**99**	**11.07**	**86**	**4.66**	**-8.49**	**45**			**54.72**	**15**	**0**	**0**
	USD	4.40	M.Lynch Emerg Mkts Portf A	M023	31/05/94	CA	8.82	98	6.43	56	N.A.	N.A.				N.A.		N.A.	
	USD	0.41	MBf Venture Portfolio	M010	28/02/92	CA	-4.72	83	-19.19	85	5.99	-47.99	45	✪		N.A.		N.A.	
	USD	N.S.	MeesPierson UF Global Emerg	M012	01/03/96	LUX	7.18	14	N.A.		N.A.	N.A.				N.A.		N.A.	
▲	USD	109.42	Mercury ST Emerging Markets	M021	30/11/93	LUX	14.50	67	20.91	11	5.20	1.21	13	✪✪✪✪		N.A.		N.A.	
▲	GBP	8.97	Morgan Grenfell Euro Emg Mkts	M038	29/07/94	IRL	9.23	51	49.21	2	N.A.	N.A.				N.A.		N.A.	
▲	GBP	591.72	Morgan Grenfell Gl Emerg Mkts	M038	08/03/96	IRL	10.41	28	N.A.		N.A.	N.A.				N.A.		N.A.	
	USD	145.30	Morgan Stanley Emg Markets	M039	30/07/93	LUX	11.76	23	11.80	32	5.02	-11.66	26	✪✪		N.A.		N.A.	
	USD	0.60	Old Mutual Gnsy Emerg Stkmkt	O003	29/12/95	GU	12.49	25	0.10	82	N.A.	N.A.				N.A.		N.A.	
	USD	17.90	Olympia Stars Emerging Mkts	O008	31/12/93	BVI	12.22	21	16.39	20	3.27	-7.22	20	✪✪✪		N.A.		N.A.	
	USD	8.15	OMI (Gnsy) Emerging Stkmkt	O005	08/07/94	GU	12.62	26	2.50	78	N.A.	N.A.				N.A.		N.A.	
	USD	0.57	OMI (Ire) Emerging Stkmkt	O006	15/07/94	IRL	12.13	54	2.25	79	N.A.	N.A.				N.A.		N.A.	
▲	USD	16.77	OMI Galileo Emer Mkt Equity	O007	31/05/94	IRL	10.11	78	7.01	54	N.A.	N.A.				N.A.		N.A.	
▲	USD	2.47	OMI Galileo South African Eq	O007	03/11/95	IRL	7.96	94	-20.83	86	N.A.	N.A.				N.A.		N.A.	
	LUF	7.23	Panelfund Emerg Mkts LUF Cap	A037	11/11/94	LUX	0.46	96	16.08	21	N.A.	N.A.				N.A.		N.A.	
	USD	7.37	Panelfund Emerg Mkts USD Cap	A037	11/11/94	LUX	0.14	30	16.03	22	N.A.	N.A.				N.A.		N.A.	
	USD	23.97	Partner Emerg Mkts Global	B062	29/01/93	LUX	11.66	18	3.03	74	3.96	-16.37	34	✪		N.A.		N.A.	
	USD	N.S.	PCP Emerging Markets	P007	31/05/96	CA	13.15	60	N.A.		N.A.	N.A.				N.A.		N.A.	
	USD	8.88	PFC Emerging Markets Ptfl	P014	30/11/90	CA	9.73	9	18.22	16	5	-7.99	22	✪✪✪		54.82	7	N.A.	
	USD	461.75	Pictet T.F. Emerging Markets	P016	30/09/91	LUX	15.42	89	10.60	36	4.05	-11.98	28	✪✪		67.18	5	N.A.	
	USD	7.02	Power Capital Navigator	P020	30/09/96	BVI	5.82	84	N.A.		N.A.	N.A.				N.A.		N.A.	
	CHF	26.25	Pro Fonds Lux Emerging Markets	P018	31/01/94	LUX	6.81	13	5.88	59	N.A.	N.A.				N.A.		N.A.	
	USD	1.48	Proton IF Emerg Mkts Equity	P024	29/09/95	BVI	14.54	4	7.34	52	N.A.	N.A.				N.A.		N.A.	
▲	NLG	181.05	RG Emerging Markets Fund	R009	30/11/94	LUX	19.61	10	9.92	40	N.A.	N.A.				N.A.		N.A.	
	USD	1.60	RLI/GT Emerging Markets	R025	27/10/95	IOM	15.23	99	7.72	48	N.A.	N.A.				N.A.		N.A.	
	CHF	N.S.	RMF Emerging Markets Equity	R008	23/08/96	LUX	-5.09	41	N.A.		N.A.	N.A.				N.A.		N.A.	
●	GBP	2.37	Royal Life/INVESCO PioneerMkt	R029	30/10/87	IOM	10.80	81	5.05	64	6.05	-12.71	29	✪✪		43.98	9	N.A.	
	ECU	168.52	Sarasin Emergingsar	B038	07/06/96	LUX	7.65	42	N.A.		N.A.	N.A.				N.A.		N.A.	
	USD	1911.21	Schroder Emerging Markets	S008	30/04/92	GU	10.76	64	7.06	53	4.68	-1.34	15	✪✪✪✪		N.A.		N.A.	
▲	USD	131.09	Schroder Intl Sel Emer Mkts	S010	31/03/94	LUX	9.45	8	10.29	38	N.A.	N.A.				N.A.		N.A.	
	USD	1.90	Scot Prov ILA Emerging Mkts	S014	29/12/95	IOM	15.52	40	12.10	31	N.A.	N.A.				N.A.		N.A.	
	USD	16.03	Scudder GOF Emerg Mkt Gth A-2	S019	30/04/93	LUX	10.86	65	26.10	6	4.73	1.93	10	✪✪✪✪		N.A.		N.A.	
	USD	12.37	Sestertium	C071	29/10/93	BVI	9.35	63	13.61	28	4.46	3.06	7	✪✪✪✪		N.A.		N.A.	
▲	USD	65.68	Skandifond Emerging Mkts USD	S030	31/03/92	LUX	9.46	2	8.52	45	5.28	-24.68	40	✪		N.A.		N.A.	
	USD	44.67	SR Emerging	S031	29/02/96	BVI	24.32	49	N.A.		N.A.	N.A.				N.A.		N.A.	
	USD	1.76	Syfrets Gl Emerging Mkts	S060	30/11/93	CA	10.43	75	11.48	34	3.39	-2.80	16	✪✪✪		N.A.		N.A.	
▲	USD	453.31	Templeton GS Emerging Mkts	T001	28/02/91	LUX	8.43	46	20.88	12	3.96	2.93	8	✪✪✪✪		73.30	4	N.A.	
	USD	349.89	The Emerging Mkts Strategic C	B065	28/02/94	LUX	10.61	97	3.03	73	N.A.	N.A.				N.A.		N.A.	
	ESP	2.10	Top Fund Emerging Markets	F008	30/09/94	IRL	-0.97	90	-1.20	83	N.A.	N.A.				N.A.		N.A.	
	USD	1.88	VKAC Navigator Emg Mkts Eq A	V002	30/06/95	LUX	4.63	77	19.32	15	N.A.	N.A.				N.A.		N.A.	
	USD	102.91	Vontobel Fund Emerging Mkts A	B017	30/11/92	LUX	7.96	91	10.57	37	4.61	-11.81	27	✪✪		N.A.		N.A.	

▲ SIB Approved ● Insurance Fund Values in US Dollars, on an offer to offer price basis with gross income reinvested Data Source Micropal™

Holland Equity

Funds investing in excess of 70% in Dutch equities or related instruments. Such funds may have an objective of capital and/or income growth, or to track a specified index or perform inversely to a given index. Funds in this category may leverage or gear by a maximum of 20% of total assets.

	CCY	Fund Size ($mil)	Fund Name	Manager Code	Fund Start Date	Domicile Code	3 Mths 97 % Chg	3 Mths 97 Rank	1 Year % Chg	1 Year Rank	Micropal Star Rating 3 Years Volatility	3 Years % Chg	3 Years Rank	3 Years Rating	Risk Return Rating	5 Years % Chg	5 Years Rank	10 Years % Chg	10 Years Rank
		52.27	**Mean/Count**				**5.40**	**14**	**28.67**	**9**	**3.04**	**87.08**	**8**		**1**	**134.98**	**3**	**0**	**0**
	NLG	3.63	Aetna MF Dutch Natl Equity	A012	30/04/90	LUX	2.80	14	36.28	2	2.84	90.67	2	✪✪✪✪	4	128.05	3	N.A.	
	NLG	47.93	BIL Equities Pays-Bas C	B067	30/06/94	LUX	4.16	11	21.73	9	N.A.	N.A.				N.A.		N.A.	
	NLG	23.49	Cera Invest EOE Click1	C018	07/06/96	LUX	6.58	3	N.A.		N.A.	N.A.				N.A.		N.A.	
●	NLG	22.19	Credis Equity Netherlands A	C056	30/09/92	LUX	7.10	2	38.63	1	3.12	104.10	1	✪✪✪✪	4	N.A.		N.A.	
▲	NLG	14.24	CU PP Dutch Growth	C070	31/05/90	LUX	5.18	5	27.23	4	3.07	82.44	7	✪	2	136.10	2	N.A.	
	NLG	40.20	EMIF Netherlands Index Plus B	C015	31/12/92	LUX	4.97	7	26.49	5	3.07	83.09	5	✪✪	2	N.A.		N.A.	
	NLG	45.61	G-Equity Fund G-Dutch Eq B	G009	31/03/93	LUX	4.59	10	25.76	7	2.70	82.67	6	✪✪	3	N.A.		N.A.	
	NLG	0	MeesPierson UF Dutch Equity	M012	01/03/96	LUX	4.63	9	N.A.		N.A.	N.A.				N.A.		N.A.	
	NLG	48.14	Parvest Holland B	B037	29/06/90	LUX	6.04	4	30.72	3	3.33	87.59	3	✪✪✪	1	140.80	1	N.A.	
	NLG	31.58	Pictet C.F. Nedval	P016	30/11/93	LUX	3.26	12	25.76	6	3.11	81.68	8	✪	1	N.A.		N.A.	
	NLG	4.34	Rabobank Holland Dutch EQ	R001	19/04/96	LUX	2.99	13	N.A.		N.A.	N.A.				N.A.		N.A.	
▲	NLG	345.85	SBC Equity Portfolio Nthlands	S007	30/04/93	LUX	4.94	8	25.40	8	3.07	84.42	4	✪✪✪	3	N.A.		N.A.	

Hong Kong Equity

Funds investing in excess of 70% in Hong Kong equities or related instruments. Such funds may have an objective of capital and/or income growth, or to track a specified index or perform inversely to a given index. Funds in this category may leverage or gear by a maximum of 20% of total assets.

	CCY	Fund Size ($mil)	Fund Name	Manager Code	Fund Start Date	Domicile Code	3 Mths 97 % Chg	3 Mths 97 Rank	1 Year % Chg	1 Year Rank	Micropal Star Rating 3 Years Volatility	3 Years % Chg	3 Years Rank	3 Years Rating	Risk Return Rating	5 Years % Chg	5 Years Rank	10 Years % Chg	10 Years Rank
		27.43	**Mean/Count**				**-4.34**	**41**	**38.94**	**38**	**6.40**	**15.40**	**27**			**230.60**	**19**	**534.73**	**9**
	HKD	1.63	Aetna MF Hong Kong Natl Eqty	A012	29/06/90	LUX	-7.28	30	28.08	34	5.01	-5.28	24	✪		98.95	19	N.A.	
	USD	11.86	Barclays ASF Hong Kong	B044	31/10/90	JER	0.88	3	61.98	2	7.41	10.55	19	✪✪		328.44	2	N.A.	
	USD	69.76	Baring IUF Hong Kong	B049	28/02/83	IRL	-5.55	24	49.58	10	7.31	13.96	16	✪✪		214.27	11	605.82	3
	USD	14.40	Citi Hong Kong Equity	C027	31/12/93	HK	-8.15	34	40.88	19	6.31	31.30	5	✪✪✪✪	3	N.A.		N.A.	
●	HKD	0	CMI Passport HKD Enhanced Mgd	C044	20/01/95	IOM	-0.55	8	2.40	37	N.A.	N.A.				N.A.		N.A.	
	USD	11.15	Colonial Securities Hong Kong	P004	31/01/85	HK	-7.13	29	40.27	21	5.74	38.58	4	✪✪✪✪✪	4	280.98	5	921.99	1
	HKD	3.62	Dao Heng Hong Kong	D005	29/05/87	HK	-7.43	31	46.65	13	6.31	-18.72	25	✪		103.13	18	N.A.	
▲	USD	2.94	Dres Thornton ASF Hong Kong	D015	29/10/93	IRL	-1.59	14	51.31	8	7.60	16.25	13	✪✪✪		N.A.		N.A.	
▲	USD	318.80	Fidelity Fds Hong Kong & China	F011	28/09/90	LUX	-7.52	32	41.04	18	6.46	19.67	12	✪✪✪	1	294.12	4	N.A.	
	GBP	0.42	Finistere Hong Kong Life	F016	28/02/83	GU	-0.07	6	34.33	26	6.99	22.14	9	✪✪✪	2	249.40	9	487.70	5
	USD	N.S.	GAM Hong Kong	G003	31/12/96	BVI	-4.98	23	N.A.		N.A.	N.A.				N.A.		N.A.	
▲	USD	4.58	Gartmore CSF HK & China	G007	13/10/95	JER	-2.69	15	33.23	28	N.A.	N.A.				N.A.		N.A.	
	USD	0.60	Glbl Mgr HK Bear	B066	30/09/94	BER	8.96	1	-25.77	38	N.A.	N.A.				N.A.		N.A.	
	USD	0.30	Glbl Mgr HK Geared	B066	30/09/94	BER	-17.86	41	49.85	9	N.A.	N.A.				N.A.		N.A.	
	USD	0.90	Glbl Mgr HK Index	B066	30/09/94	BER	-8.09	33	29.84	31	N.A.	N.A.				N.A.		N.A.	
	USD	5.66	Govett Hong Kong Safeguard A	G016	29/03/96	JER	-7	28	N.A.		N.A.	N.A.				N.A.		N.A.	
▲	USD	48	GT Hong Kong A Share	G018	30/03/84	IRL	-1.50	13	41.35	17	6.56	7.94	21	✪✪		186.61	14	416.89	7
▲	USD	30.81	Guinness Flight Hong Kong	G019	30/11/90	GU	-5.79	25	42.56	16	6	28.29	8	✪✪✪✪	2	273.25	6	N.A.	
	HKD	73.66	Hang Seng Index Fund	H008	25/08/95	CA	-6.80	27	36.18	23	N.A.	N.A.				N.A.		N.A.	
●	USD	N.S.	Hansard EU Hong Kong	H010	17/02/95	IOM	-2.92	16	37.37	22	N.A.	N.A.				N.A.		N.A.	
●	USD	8	Hansard Hong Kong	H011	28/02/90	IOM	-8.47	36	47.75	12	6.87	31.28	6	✪✪✪✪	2	186.76	13	N.A.	
▲	USD	97.75	HSBC GIF Hong Kong Equity	H033	30/01/87	LUX	0.20	5	60.38	4	6.89	41.42	3	✪✪✪✪✪	3	328.32	3	N.A.	
	HKD	12.86	HSBC Guaranteed	H034	28/06/96	HK	0.31	4	N.A.		N.A.	N.A.				N.A.		N.A.	
	USD	2.27	ImPac AP Hong Kong	I005	31/10/95	CA	-8.84	39	65.24	1	N.A.	N.A.				N.A.		N.A.	
	USD	23.19	Indosuez Hong Kong	I007	31/01/86	HK	-8.72	37	42.92	15	6.74	15.94	14	✪✪		257.54	8	445.17	6

▲ SIB Approved ● Insurance Fund **Values in US Dollars, on an offer to offer price basis with gross income reinvested** Data Source Micropal™

Hong Kong Equity

continued

	CCY	Fund Size ($mil)	Fund Name	Manager Code	Fund Start Date	Domicile Code	3 Mths 97 % Chg	3 Mths 97 Rank	1 Year % Chg	1 Year Rank	Micropal Star Rating 3 Years Volatility	3 Years % Chg	3 Years Rank	Rating	Risk Return Rating	5 Years % Chg	5 Years Rank	10 Years % Chg	10 Years Rank
		27.43	**Mean/Count**				**-4.34**	**41**	**38.94**	**38**	**6.40**	**15.40**	**27**			**230.60**	**19**	**534.73**	**9**
	USD	71.29	JF Hong Kong	J004	31/12/73	HK	-8.40	35	31.28	30	6.68	-23.65	26	✪		131.64	17	309.63	9
▲	USD	0.78	Jupiter Tyndall GF Hong Kong	J010	15/07/94	LUX	-1.46	12	34.31	27	N.A.	N.A.				N.A.		N.A.	
	HKD	6.36	Mansion House Hong Kong	M005	30/01/87	HK	N.A.	—	36.11	24	6.11	9.60	20	✪✪		191.48	12	N.A.	
	USD	0.92	MBf Hong Kong Sp Sits	M010	28/02/92	CA	-4.46	22	15.25	36	5.62	-23.87	27	✪		N.A.		N.A.	
▲	USD	2.20	Nikko GIUF Hong Kong Fund	N007	26/02/93	LUX	-6.61	26	53.42	5	5.76	28.94	7	✪✪✪✪	3	N.A.		N.A.	
	USD	1.28	Nomura SF Hong Kong	N010	30/11/92	CA	-8.80	38	40.84	20	7.09	4.93	22	✪		N.A.		N.A.	
	USD	0.26	Old Mutual Gnsy HK Stkmkt	O003	29/12/95	GU	-1.10	9	26.70	35	N.A.	N.A.				N.A.		N.A.	
	USD	0.57	Old Mutual HK HK Stkmkt	O004	28/04/95	HK	-3.16	18	28.74	32	N.A.	N.A.				N.A.		N.A.	
	USD	10.38	OMI (Gnsy) HK Stkmkt	O005	31/07/85	GU	-1.24	10	28.19	33	6.61	0.51	23	✪		179.47	16	375.27	8
▲	USD	7.23	OMI Galileo HK Stockmarket	O007	31/01/96	IRL	-9.65	40	N.A.		N.A.	N.A.				N.A.		N.A.	
●	USD	3.42	Royal Life/Baring Hong Kong	R022	30/10/87	IOM	1.59	2	43.63	14	7.30	15.22	15	✪✪		184.04	15	N.A.	
	HKD	54.75	Schroder Asia Hong Kong	S011	29/10/82	HK	-3.15	17	53.10	6	6.57	20.12	10	✪✪✪	1	269.88	7	742.71	2
	HKD	7.12	Schroder Asia Hong Kong Sm Co	S011	30/09/92	HK	-3.28	19	49.23	11	5.61	13.14	17	✪✪		N.A.		N.A.	
	HKD	1.48	SHK Middle Kingdom	S024	31/05/89	HK	-3.66	20	52.06	7	7.45	11.99	18	✪✪		238.71	10	N.A.	
	USD	44.32	Thornton New Tiger Hong Kong	T007	31/07/85	BER	-4.40	21	61.19	3	8.16	20.07	11	✪✪✪	1	384.45	1	507.35	4
	USD	70.78	Value Partners A	V001	31/03/93	CA	-0.34	7	35.52	25	3.73	43.59	1	✪✪✪✪	5	N.A.		N.A.	
	USD	70.96	Value Partners A (Grs Pf Fee)	V001	31/03/93	CA	-1.32	11	32.88	29	3.92	41.90	2	✪✪✪✪	4	N.A.		N.A.	

Hungary Equity

Funds investing in excess of 70% in Hungarian equities or related instruments. Such funds may have an objective of capital and/or income growth, or to track a specified index or perform inversely to a given index. Funds in this category may leverage or gear by a maximum of 20% of total assets.

	CCY	Fund Size ($mil)	Fund Name	Manager Code	Fund Start Date	Domicile Code	3 Mths 97 % Chg	3 Mths 97 Rank	1 Year % Chg	1 Year Rank	Micropal Star Rating 3 Years Volatility	3 Years % Chg	3 Years Rank	Rating	Risk Return Rating	5 Years % Chg	5 Years Rank	10 Years % Chg	10 Years Rank
		126.08	**Mean/Count**				**16.26**	**1**	**60.12**	**1**	**6.92**	**32.03**	**1**		**3**	**20.49**	**1**	**0**	**0**
	USD	126.08	Hungarian Investment Co Ltd	G014	31/01/90	JER	16.26	1	60.12	1	6.92	32.03	1	✪✪✪	3	20.49	1	N.A.	

Iberia Equity

Funds investing in excess of 70% in Iberian (Spain and Portugal) equities or related instruments. Such funds may have an objective of capital and/or income growth, or to track a specified index or perform inversely to a given index. Funds in this category may leverage or gear by a maximum of 20% of total assets.

	CCY	Fund Size ($mil)	Fund Name	Manager Code	Fund Start Date	Domicile Code	3 Mths 97 % Chg	3 Mths 97 Rank	1 Year % Chg	1 Year Rank	Micropal Star Rating 3 Years Volatility	3 Years % Chg	3 Years Rank	Rating	Risk Return Rating	5 Years % Chg	5 Years Rank	10 Years % Chg	10 Years Rank
		6.41	**Mean/Count**				**-0.49**	**9**	**35.29**	**9**	**4.26**	**61.78**	**8**		**2**	**53.74**	**7**	**0**	**0**
▲	ESP	4.18	CMI GNF Iberian Equity	C042	30/04/90	LUX	-0.98	6	38.64	1	4.51	68.92	1	✪✪✪✪	3	55.85	3	N.A.	
●	GBP	0.68	CMI Ins Co Iberian Equity	C043	31/01/91	IOM	-3.64	9	38.07	3	4.64	65.34	4	✪✪✪	2	48.03	6	N.A.	
●	ESP	0.01	CMI Passport Iberian Equity	C044	20/01/95	IOM	-2.63	8	37.32	4	N.A.	N.A.				N.A.		N.A.	
●	ESP	3.17	Credis Eqty Hispano Iberia A	C056	30/03/90	LUX	0.24	4	36.99	5	4.53	62.18	5	✪✪	2	53.80	5	N.A.	
▲	ESP	19.13	Fidelity Fds Iberia	F011	28/09/90	LUX	2.48	1	34.43	6	4.28	66.72	3	✪✪✪✪	4	55.20	4	N.A.	
●	ESP	0.74	Hansard\Fidelity Iberia	H014	27/09/91	IOM	1.59	2	32.14	7	4.14	67.94	2	✪✪✪	4	57.30	2	N.A.	
	PTE	4.64	M-Fund Iberia Value	B013	31/12/93	LUX	0.04	5	38.16	2	3.11	45.01	8	✪	3	N.A.		N.A.	
	ESP	17.58	MOSAIS Actions Esp & Port	C058	31/10/90	LUX	-2.43	7	31.18	8	4.39	59.38	6	✪	1	75.03	1	N.A.	
	ESP	7.54	Pictet C.F. Valiber	P016	30/11/88	LUX	0.95	3	30.69	9	4.44	58.71	7	✪✪	1	31.01	7	N.A.	

▲ SIB Approved ● Insurance Fund Values in US Dollars, on an offer to offer price basis with gross income reinvested Data Source Micropal™

India Equity

Funds investing in excess of 70% in Indian equities or related instruments. Such funds may have an objective of capital and/or income growth, or to track a specified index or perform inversely to a given index. Funds in this category may leverage or gear by a maximum of 20% of total assets.

	CCY	Fund Size ($mil)	Fund Name	Manager Code	Fund Start Date	Domicile Code	3 Mths 97 % Chg	3 Mths 97 Rank	1 Year % Chg	1 Year Rank	Micropal Star Rating 3 Years Volatility	3 Years % Chg	3 Years Rank	3 Years Rating	Risk Return Rating	5 Years % Chg	5 Years Rank	10 Years % Chg	10 Years Rank
		40.18	**Mean/Count**				**11.66**	**31**	**-8.50**	**21**	**7.65**	**-44.29**	**6**			**48.95**	**1**	**0**	**0**
	USD	N.S.	CIAM Cazenove Indian Ptfl	C014	10/05/96	KP	8	23	N.A.		N.A.	N.A.				N.A.		N.A.	
▲	USD	11.70	CL Indian Subcontinent	C063	31/01/94	HK	10.13	19	-1.95	3	N.A.	N.A.				N.A.		N.A.	
●	USD	6.84	Clariden India	C039	07/10/94	GU	5.36	25	-26.08	21	N.A.	N.A.				N.A.		N.A.	
	USD	N.S.	Credis Equity Trust India	C056	31/10/96	LUX	11.81	16	N.A.		N.A.	N.A.				N.A.		N.A.	
▲	USD	5.33	Dresdner Thornton India	D016	27/01/95	IRL	13.71	13	-17.47	19	N.A.	N.A.				N.A.		N.A.	
	USD	N.S.	EV Medallion Greater India B	E003	18/11/94	CA	5.12	26	-7.86	12	N.A.	N.A.				N.A.		N.A.	
▲●	USD	10.02	Five Arrows GF India	R011	22/12/95	LUX	11.93	15	-7.38	8	N.A.	N.A.				N.A.		N.A.	
▲	USD	101.72	Fleming FF India	F020	31/08/95	LUX	16.29	5	-4.40	5	N.A.	N.A.				N.A.		N.A.	
	USD	13.11	Govett India	G014	29/10/93	JER	9.97	22	-18.90	20	8.01	-46.90	3	✪✪		N.A.		N.A.	
▲	USD	19	GT Indian Small Cos A	G018	02/12/94	IRL	14.32	11	-2.95	4	N.A.	N.A.				N.A.		N.A.	
▲	USD	15.30	Guinness Flight Sel Madr Ind	G021	10/11/95	IRL	13.33	14	-9.39	14	N.A.	N.A.				N.A.		N.A.	
	USD	1.91	Hansard\CL Indian S'continent	H013	31/03/94	IOM	18.57	3	-7.70	11	N.A.	N.A.				N.A.		N.A.	
▲	USD	11.51	HSBC GIF Indian Equity	H033	29/02/96	LUX	16.06	6	N.A.		N.A.	N.A.				N.A.		N.A.	
	USD	10.13	HTR India	H027	15/07/94	LUX	15.90	7	-8.08	13	N.A.	N.A.				N.A.		N.A.	
	USD	11.95	India Focus Fund	C028	31/08/94	LUX	11.17	17	-13.94	18	N.A.	N.A.				N.A.		N.A.	
	USD	51.59	India Liberalisation A	A005	31/12/93	LUX	15.42	8	-10.20	15	6.11	-38.95	2	✪✪✪✪		N.A.		N.A.	
	USD	133.80	Indian Inv Co	F002	30/09/93	LUX	14.18	12	-10.42	16	7.58	-51.80	5	✪		N.A.		N.A.	
	USD	143.72	JF India	J004	30/11/89	HK	21.30	2	-7.44	9	8.87	-48.24	4	✪✪✪		48.95	1	N.A.	
▲	USD	20.80	KB India Eq Gth	K007	29/02/96	IRL	14.66	10	N.A.		N.A.	N.A.				N.A.		N.A.	
	USD	37.91	LG India	L013	31/08/93	KP	6.61	24	-6.49	7	7.17	-27.99	1	✪✪✪✪		N.A.		N.A.	
▲	USD	15.20	Morgan Grenfell India	M038	15/09/95	IRL	17.72	4	0.01	2	N.A.	N.A.				N.A.		N.A.	
	USD	18.70	Peregrine Indian Smaller Cos	P008	31/08/94	CA	3.24	29	-6.46	6	N.A.	N.A.				N.A.		N.A.	
	USD	39.95	Pictet C.F. Indiaval	P016	28/06/96	LUX	10.05	21	N.A.		N.A.	N.A.				N.A.		N.A.	
●	USD	84.60	RLI/JF India	R030	31/12/93	IOM	28.71	1	-13.07	17	8.14	-51.83	6	✪✪		N.A.		N.A.	
	USD	193.67	Schroder India	S008	10/03/95	GU	10.11	20	9.22	1	N.A.	N.A.				N.A.		N.A.	
	USD	1.20	Scot Prov ILA Indian	S014	29/09/95	IOM	1.88	31	-7.51	10	N.A.	N.A.				N.A.		N.A.	
	USD	4.59	Thornton New Tiger Sel India	T007	14/06/96	BER	10.24	18	N.A.		N.A.	N.A.				N.A.		N.A.	

Indonesia Equity

Funds investing in excess of 70% in Indonesian equities or related instruments. Such funds may have an objective of capital and/or income growth, or to track a specified index or perform inversely to a given index. Funds in this category may leverage or gear by a maximum of 20% of total assets.

	CCY	Fund Size ($mil)	Fund Name	Manager Code	Fund Start Date	Domicile Code	3 Mths 97 % Chg	3 Mths 97 Rank	1 Year % Chg	1 Year Rank	Micropal Star Rating 3 Years Volatility	3 Years % Chg	3 Years Rank	3 Years Rating	Risk Return Rating	5 Years % Chg	5 Years Rank	10 Years % Chg	10 Years Rank
		17.22	**Mean/Count**				**7.17**	**15**	**15.43**	**13**	**7.06**	**-12.64**	**9**			**54.50**	**5**	**0**	**0**
	USD	13.43	Barclays ASF Indonesia	B044	31/10/90	JER	14.85	2	15.29	7	7.37	-18.64	3	✪✪✪✪		75.99	2	N.A.	
▲	USD	5	CL Indonesian Growth	C063	31/03/89	HK	12.28	4	19.15	4	6.85	-19.72	4	✪✪✪		98.35	1	N.A.	
▲	USD	12.10	Dres Thornton ASF Indonesia	D015	31/05/93	IRL	8.45	8	3.31	13	7.18	-37.95	8	✪		N.A.		N.A.	
▲	USD	32.20	Fidelity Fds Indonesia	F011	02/12/94	LUX	7.93	9	10.39	8	N.A.	N.A.				N.A.		N.A.	
	USD	0.76	Hansard\CL Indonesian Growth	H013	31/07/92	IOM	15.37	1	18.41	5	7.02	-8.17	2	✪✪✪✪		N.A.		N.A.	
	USD	0.94	ImPac AP Indonesia	I005	31/10/95	CA	13.29	3	21.91	2	N.A.	N.A.				N.A.		N.A.	
	USD	82.60	JF Indonesia	J004	31/03/89	HK	-1.27	14	16.30	6	5.88	-33.47	6	✪✪		60.20	3	N.A.	
	USD	25.13	JF Indonesia Trust	J004	14/10/94	CA	3.83	12	21.24	3	N.A.	N.A.				N.A.		N.A.	
	USD	41.10	Lippo Indonesian Growth	L012	31/03/92	CA	9.72	5	40.28	1	7.97	110.12	1	✪✪✪✪✪	3	N.A.		N.A.	
	USD	0.71	MBf Indonesian Growth	M010	31/05/89	HK	-6.54	15	10.31	9	6.90	-44.85	9	✪		-18.94	5	N.A.	
▲	USD	12.70	Morgan Grenfell Indonesian	M038	30/09/94	IRL	4.47	11	6.53	12	N.A.	N.A.				N.A.		N.A.	
▲	USD	0.97	Nikko GIUF Indonesia Fund	N007	26/02/93	LUX	0.25	13	7.41	11	6.59	-26.15	5	✪✪✪		N.A.		N.A.	
	USD	7	NM ASF Indonesian	N001	14/06/96	IRL	6.73	10	N.A.		N.A.	N.A.				N.A.		N.A.	
	USD	0.30	RLI/Lippo Indonesian Gth	R031	12/07/96	IOM	8.76	7	N.A.		N.A.	N.A.				N.A.		N.A.	
	USD	23.40	Thornton New Tiger Indonesia	T007	30/03/90	BER	9.40	6	10.07	10	7.77	-34.94	7	✪✪		56.91	4	N.A.	

▲ SIB Approved ● Insurance Fund **Values in US Dollars, on an offer to offer price basis with gross income reinvested** Data Source Micropal™

Ireland Equity

Funds investing in excess of 70% in Irish equities or related instruments. Such funds may have an objective of capital and/or income growth, or to track a specified index or perform inversely to a given index. Funds in this category may leverage or gear by a maximum of 20% of total assets.

		Fund			Fund						Micropal Star Rating				Risk				
		Size		Manager	Start	Domicile	3 Mths 97		1 Year		3 Years				Return	5 Years		10 Years	
	CCY	($mil)	Fund Name	Code	Date	Code	% Chg	Rank	% Chg	Rank	Volatility	% Chg	Rank	Rating	Rating	% Chg	Rank	% Chg	Rank
		0.47	**Mean/Count**				**2.96**	**2**	**23.97**	**2**	**3.38**	**58.23**	**1**		**1**	**20.39**	**1**	**0**	**0**
▲	IEP	0.94	CMI GNF Irish Equity	C042	31/05/91	LUX	3.63	1	24.80	1	3.38	58.23	1	✪✪✪	3	20.39	1	N.A.	
●	IEP	0	CMI Passport Irish Equity	C044	20/01/95	IOM	2.30	2	23.14	2	N.A.	N.A.				N.A.		N.A.	

Israel Equity

Funds investing in excess of 70% in Israel equities or related instruments. Such funds may have an objective of capital and/or income growth, or to track a specified index or perform inversely to a given index. Funds in this category may leverage or gear by a maximum of 20% of total assets.

		Fund			Fund						Micropal Star Rating				Risk				
		Size		Manager	Start	Domicile	3 Mths 97		1 Year		3 Years				Return	5 Years		10 Years	
	CCY	($mil)	Fund Name	Code	Date	Code	% Chg	Rank	% Chg	Rank	Volatility	% Chg	Rank	Rating	Rating	% Chg	Rank	% Chg	Rank
		12.62	**Mean/Count**				**7.26**	**2**	**-2.90**	**2**	**0**	**0**	**0**			**0**	**0**	**0**	**0**
▲	USD	10.99	Israel 2000	C023	29/07/94	LUX	6.88	2	-6.72	2	N.A.	N.A.				N.A.		N.A.	
	USD	14.25	Scontinvest Mid East Israval	S012	31/01/95	LUX	7.65	1	0.93	1	N.A.	N.A.				N.A.		N.A.	

Italy Equity

Funds investing in excess of 70% in Italian equities or related instruments. Such funds may have an objective of capital and/or income growth, or to track a specified index or perform inversely to a given index. Funds in this category may leverage or gear by a maximum of 20% of total assets.

		Fund			Fund						Micropal Star Rating				Risk				
		Size		Manager	Start	Domicile	3 Mths 97		1 Year		3 Years				Return	5 Years		10 Years	
	CCY	($mil)	Fund Name	Code	Date	Code	% Chg	Rank	% Chg	Rank	Volatility	% Chg	Rank	Rating	Rating	% Chg	Rank	% Chg	Rank
		13.24	**Mean/Count**				**1.13**	**22**	**16.85**	**17**	**5.63**	**18.66**	**12**			**-5.86**	**8**	**0**	**0**
	ITL	0.93	Aetna MF Italian Natl Eqty	A012	30/04/90	LUX	-1.43	19	20.39	7	5.22	26.94	3	✪✪✪	3	-3.27	5	N.A.	
▲	ITL	28.75	Citi PF Italian Equity	C036	30/06/95	LUX	0.88	13	14.24	12	N.A.	N.A.				N.A.		N.A.	
▲	ITL	3.63	CMI GNF Italian Equity	C042	30/04/90	LUX	-1.45	20	10.57	13	6.63	1.88	11	✪		-19.49	6	N.A.	
●	GBP	0.68	CMI Ins Co Italian Equity	C043	28/02/91	IOM	2.83	3	6.23	16	6.47	-6.89	12	✪		-43.34	8	N.A.	
●	ITL	0.01	CMI Passport Italian Equity	C044	20/01/95	IOM	2.74	4	6.88	15	N.A.	N.A.				N.A.		N.A.	
●	ITL	5.28	Credis Equity Italy A	C056	30/10/92	LUX	2.39	6	28.02	1	6.26	26.02	5	✪✪✪✪	3	N.A.		N.A.	
▲	ITL	3.76	CU PP Italian Growth	C070	31/05/90	LUX	1.81	8	14.54	11	6.95	17.49	7	✪✪✪	1	8.35	2	N.A.	
	ITL	4	EMIF Italy Index Plus B	C015	31/01/94	LUX	4.19	2	17.26	10	N.A.	N.A.				N.A.		N.A.	
▲	ITL	90.17	Fidelity Fds Italy	F011	28/09/90	LUX	1.96	7	24.42	2	6.10	32.15	2	✪✪✪✪	4	28.75	1	N.A.	
	ITL	17.68	G-Equity Fund G-Italian Eq B	G009	31/03/94	LUX	0.70	15	20.08	8	N.A.	N.A.				N.A.		N.A.	
▲●	ITL	13.13	Groupe Indosuez Italy	G017	22/03/96	LUX	1.43	10	N.A.		N.A.	N.A.				N.A.		N.A.	
●	ITL	0.04	Hansard\Fidelity Italy	H014	27/09/91	IOM	0.59	16	23.94	3	4.17	9.61	9	✪✪		-22.90	7	N.A.	
	ITL	36.08	ItalFortune Intl Aggr Gwth Ita	F015	31/08/93	LUX	-1.88	21	6.23	17	3.54	16.04	8	✪✪		N.A.		N.A.	
	ITL	5.67	MOSAIS Actions Italiennes	C058	31/10/90	LUX	0.96	12	17.72	9	5.81	18.62	6	✪✪	2	-2.66	4	N.A.	
	ITL	1.32	OYSTER Italian Opportunities	B067	13/09/96	LUX	5.40	1	N.A.		N.A.	N.A.				N.A.		N.A.	
	ITL	42.44	Parvest Italy B	B037	30/09/94	LUX	1.39	11	22.86	4	N.A.	N.A.				N.A.		N.A.	
	ITL	3.24	Pictet C.F. Valitalia	P016	31/07/89	LUX	0.76	14	22.82	5	6.49	26.69	4	✪✪✪	2	7.69	3	N.A.	
▲	ITL	0.11	SanPaolo Ecu Actions Italie	S004	30/04/93	LUX	-2	22	22.77	6	4.45	47.46	1	✪✪✪✪✪	4	N.A.		N.A.	
	ITL	4.61	Schroder Intl Sel Italian Eq	S010	03/05/96	LUX	-0.18	17	N.A.		N.A.	N.A.				N.A.		N.A.	
	ITL	3.85	Sogelux Fd Equities Italy	S037	21/06/96	LUX	-0.20	18	N.A.		N.A.	N.A.				N.A.		N.A.	
	ITL	12.68	Willerequity Italy	W004	30/10/92	LUX	2.46	5	7.52	14	5.53	7.89	10	✪		N.A.		N.A.	

▲ SIB Approved ● Insurance Fund Values in US Dollars, on an offer to offer price basis with gross income reinvested Data Source Micropal™

Japan Equity

Funds investing in excess of 70% in Japanese equities or related instruments. Such funds may have an objective of capital and/or income growth, or to track a specified index or perform inversely to a given index. Funds in this category may leverage or gear by a maximum of 20% of total assets.

	CCY	Fund Size ($mil)	Fund Name	Manager Code	Fund Start Date	Domicile Code	3 Mths 97 % Chg	3 Mths 97 Rank	1 Year % Chg	1 Year Rank	Micropal Star Rating: Volatility	3 Years % Chg	3 Years Rank	Rating	Risk Return Rating	5 Years % Chg	5 Years Rank	10 Years % Chg	10 Years Rank
		52.22	**Mean/Count**				**-10.59**	**198**	**-15.61**	**182**	**5.17**	**-7.33**	**136**			**-7.23**	**104**	**67.48**	**36**
▲	USD	90.02	AAF Japan Equity Fund	A001	25/11/94	LUX	-6.60	29	-9.17	22	N.A.	N.A.				N.A.		N.A.	
▲	GBP	5.13	Abtrust Atlas Japan	A002	31/03/88	LUX	-5.58	21	-11.48	32	4.38	-8.41	72	✪✪		-16.50	74	N.A.	
▲	JPY	21.66	Aetna IUF Japanese Eqty A	A011	29/04/88	LUX	-10.07	100	-19.74	148	5.12	-9.16	76	✪✪		-13.60	62	N.A.	
	JPY	1.91	Aetna MF Japanese Natl Eqty	A012	31/05/93	LUX	-9.14	74	-18.35	129	5.14	-10.22	83	✪✪		N.A.		N.A.	
▲	USD	19.13	AIG Japan	A017	31/07/91	IRL	-9.28	77	-15.75	90	6.11	-17.78	113	✪		-19.51	82	N.A.	
	USD	48.83	AIG Japan Sm Cos	A017	31/12/93	IRL	-17.32	180	-17.66	119	5.91	0.91	30	✪✪✪✪		N.A.		N.A.	
●	USD	0	Albany Intl Japan Dllr	A018	31/03/87	IOM	-4.76	19	-9.35	25	5.05	-3.82	56	✪✪✪		-13.70	63	N.A.	
	USD	N.S.	Albany Intl Japan Enterprise	A018	28/02/95	IOM	-8.75	68	-8.20	18	N.A.	N.A.				N.A.		N.A.	
●	GBP	0	Albany Intl Japan Stlg	A018	31/03/87	IOM	-7.07	38	-15.12	78	5.36	-11.82	90	✪✪		-20.13	83	N.A.	
	JPY	9.78	Alfred Berg Sicav Japan	A019	26/02/93	LUX	-10.19	110	-16.63	105	5.21	-2.05	47	✪✪✪		N.A.		N.A.	
	GBP	6.80	Apollo Japan Fund	H023	10/02/95	GU	-11.65	128	-23.85	173	N.A.	N.A.				N.A.		N.A.	
	JPY	64.67	Asia Fund	S037	30/03/90	LUX	-9.62	88	-13.51	52	4.56	1.20	28	✪✪✪✪		20.31	6	N.A.	
	USD	11.55	Asia Nies Japan Fund	G018	31/10/88	LUX	-5.68	23	8.77	1	4.98	-5.31	60	✪✪		57.37	1	N.A.	
	JPY	119.40	Baer Multistock Japan Stock A	J007	31/03/93	LUX	-4.44	15	-14.48	65	4.84	-5.94	62	✪✪✪		N.A.		N.A.	
	USD	23.27	Barclays ASF Japan	B044	31/05/93	JER	-12.01	136	-16.25	97	5.02	-26.50	133	✪		N.A.		N.A.	
▲	USD	24.70	Baring GUF Jap Sm Cos	B049	19/01/96	IRL	-12.71	144	N.A.		N.A.	N.A.				N.A.		N.A.	
	USD	40.87	Baring IUF Japan	B049	30/04/76	IRL	-8.06	52	-10.79	30	4.28	-4.65	59	✪✪✪		-10.25	56	16.29	29
	USD	32.20	Bermuda Eqty Japanese	B066	30/11/90	BER	-10.60	114	-20.33	159	5.44	-17.32	111	✪		-21.48	89	N.A.	
	JPY	28.84	BIL Equities Japon C	B067	31/01/90	LUX	-5.96	25	-14.73	71	3.89	-12.89	98	✪		-15.58	70	N.A.	
	JPY	64.45	BSS Universal Japan	B029	30/04/92	LUX	-9.51	81	-19.39	140	5.40	-12.85	97	✪✪		N.A.		N.A.	
●	JPY	34.19	Carlson Japan	C011	28/09/90	LUX	-10.15	107	-19.94	151	5.01	-1.87	45	✪✪✪✪		18.31	9	N.A.	
●	JPY	16.75	Carlson Japan Regional	C011	15/07/94	LUX	-16.32	174	-20.14	157	N.A.	N.A.				N.A.		N.A.	
▲●	USD	68.55	Chase Vista Japan Eq	C019	31/12/86	LUX	0.56	2	-14.51	67	4.06	-4.03	57	✪✪✪		-4.26	39	-5.46	35
▲●	USD	22.58	Chase Vista Japan Sm Cap Eq	C019	13/10/95	LUX	-4.11	12	-17.68	120	N.A.	N.A.				N.A.		N.A.	
▲	JPY	34.50	Citi PF Jap Small Cap Gth Stk	C036	30/11/94	LUX	-14.47	160	-22.93	170	N.A.	N.A.				N.A.		N.A.	
▲	JPY	147.82	Citi PF Japanese Equity	C036	30/09/88	LUX	-11.18	122	-17.03	110	5.13	-7.03	66	✪✪✪		-15.38	68	N.A.	
	USD	0.75	Citifunds Japan Equity	C031	31/12/87	JER	-6.55	28	-15.46	83	4.65	-1.24	40	✪✪✪		-8.84	50	N.A.	
●	JPY	58.98	Clariden Japan Investments	C039	31/01/86	CA	-9.85	92	-13.82	55	4.74	-9.61	80	✪✪		-11.22	57	13.70	32
▲	JPY	11.42	CMI GNF Japan Eqty Index Tr	C042	30/04/90	LUX	-11.09	120	-13.71	54	5.37	-0.67	36	✪✪✪✪		-15.38	69	N.A.	
▲	JPY	26.45	CMI GNF Japanese Equity	C042	30/04/90	LUX	-8.26	57	-16.34	99	5.05	-13.42	100	✪		-22.50	93	N.A.	
●	GBP	8.46	CMI Ins Co Japan Tracker	C043	31/05/90	IOM	-12.25	141	-14.62	69	4.89	2.21	21	✪✪✪✪		-8.76	49	N.A.	
●	USD	7.40	CMI Ins Co Japanese Equity	C043	31/12/90	IOM	-10.15	108	-17.40	117	4.90	-18.76	116	✪		-25.38	96	N.A.	
●	JPY	0.15	CMI Passport Japanese Equity	C044	20/01/95	IOM	-9.26	76	-17.36	116	N.A.	N.A.				N.A.		N.A.	
●	JPY	0.17	CMI Passport Japanese Index	C044	20/01/95	IOM	-11.75	132	-15.26	80	N.A.	N.A.				N.A.		N.A.	
▲	JPY	93.74	Coutts GF Japan Eqty	C052	31/05/93	IRL	-9.58	84	-16.30	98	5.06	-3.34	54	✪✪✪		N.A.		N.A.	
●	JPY	0.18	Credis Eqty Japan Megatrend	C056	31/03/93	LUX	-7.55	44	-15.78	93	4.86	-18.28	115	✪		N.A.		N.A.	
●	JPY	3.07	Credis Equity Small Cap Jap	C056	31/08/94	LUX	-19.39	192	-26.12	177	N.A.	N.A.				N.A.		N.A.	
▲	USD	4.05	CSFB PIP I (Japan)	C069	30/10/92	LUX	-8.96	73	-14.27	61	4.68	0.07	31	✪✪✪✪		N.A.		N.A.	
▲	JPY	26.44	CU PP Japanese Growth	C070	31/05/90	LUX	-8.38	62	-14.06	58	5.23	-9	73	✪✪		-21.12	88	N.A.	
	JPY	26.78	Daiwa Dites	D001	31/08/89	CA	-9.56	82	-16.49	103	4.87	17.76	4	✪✪✪✪✪	1	33.02	3	N.A.	
	JPY	10.40	Daiwa TAA Japan	D001	10/05/96	CA	-12.99	149	N.A.		N.A.	N.A.				N.A.		N.A.	
	DEM	238.17	DekaLux Japan	D009	30/11/93	LUX	-8.30	60	-18.47	131	5.01	-3	53	✪✪✪		N.A.		N.A.	
	JPY	1.77	Eagle Star Japanese Eq	E001	29/09/95	IOM	-7.31	43	-13.99	57	N.A.	N.A.				N.A.		N.A.	
	JPY	N.S.	Eagle Star Japanese Smaller Co	E001	27/09/96	IOM	-13.19	151	N.A.		N.A.	N.A.				N.A.		N.A.	
▲	JPY	4.19	F&C PF Jap Sm Cos Equity	F001	28/09/79	LUX	-19.56	193	-22.74	169	5.95	-11.94	92	✪✪		-15.60	71	28.15	25
	JPY	0.97	F&C RAF Japanese Eq	F003	31/03/87	JER	-9.29	78	-16.72	107	6.06	-1.18	39	✪✪✪		-20.63	86	N.A.	
	USD	31.20	Fidelity Far East	F012	29/02/80	LUX	-8.27	58	-13.24	49	4.29	-12.91	99	✪		-9.05	51	39.36	19
▲	JPY	285.02	Fidelity Fds Japan	F011	28/09/90	LUX	-6.88	36	-11.06	31	5.12	-1.97	46	✪✪✪✪		-4.69	41	N.A.	
▲	JPY	97.55	Fidelity Fds Japan Smaller Co	F011	31/12/91	LUX	-15.32	168	-23.50	171	5.47	-21.95	124	✪		2.80	21	N.A.	
	USD	17.30	Fidelity Orient	F012	30/04/82	LUX	-8.89	71	-14.79	73	4.22	-13.90	103	✪		-8.38	48	54.25	16
	USD	13.30	Fidelity Special Growth	F012	31/03/83	LUX	-9.36	80	-1.02	4	3.58	4.26	15	✪✪✪✪		14.62	14	66.84	13
	GBP	0.17	Finistere Jap Smllr Cos Life	F016	31/05/84	GU	-19.74	194	-15.52	87	4.93	-2.22	49	✪✪✪		-1.45	33	178.43	4

▲ SIB Approved ● Insurance Fund

Values in US Dollars, on an offer to offer price basis with gross income reinvested

Data Source Micropal™

Japan Equity

continued

	CCY	Fund Size ($mil)	Fund Name	Manager Code	Fund Start Date	Domicile Code	3 Mths 97 % Chg	3 Mths 97 Rank	1 Year % Chg	1 Year Rank	Micropal Star Rating Volatility	3 Years % Chg	3 Years Rank	3 Years Rating	Risk Return Rating	5 Years % Chg	5 Years Rank	10 Years % Chg	10 Years Rank
		52.22	**Mean/Count**				**-10.59**	**198**	**-15.61**	**182**	**5.17**	**-7.33**	**136**			**-7.23**	**104**	**67.48**	**36**
	GBP	0.19	Finistere Tokyo Life	F016	31/12/85	GU	-10.28	111	-8.29	19	3.99	5.41	12	✪✪✪✪		-2.14	35	44.64	18
▲●	USD	17.34	Five Arrows GF Japan Rec	R011	17/07/92	LUX	-11.79	133	-18.42	130	5.28	-8.38	70	✪✪		N.A.		N.A.	
▲●	USD	2.35	Five Arrows GF Japan Sm Cos	R011	31/05/93	LUX	-18.90	186	-22.19	167	5.81	-23.37	126	✪		N.A.		N.A.	
	USD	1.31	Five Arrows IE Jap Smllr Cos	R014	30/09/93	GU	-18.59	185	-17.35	115	5.36	-18.80	117	✪		N.A.		N.A.	
	USD	6.42	Five Arrows IE Japan	R014	30/09/93	GU	-9.94	95	-17.22	113	5.17	-11.90	91	✪✪		N.A.		N.A.	
	USD	29	Five Arrows IP Japan	R016	30/12/94	GU	-9.84	91	-16.54	104	N.A.	N.A.				N.A.		N.A.	
▲	USD	155.16	Fleming FF Japanese	F020	30/11/88	LUX	-9.84	90	-22.36	168	5.76	-19.13	119	✪		-17.84	78	N.A.	
▲	USD	29.17	Fleming FF Japanese Smllr Cos	F020	01/07/94	LUX	-18.99	188	-21.78	166	N.A.	N.A.				N.A.		N.A.	
	USD	868	GAM Japan	G003	31/07/85	IOM	-0.93	3	0.20	3	3.90	26.67	2	✪✪✪✪✪	3	41.28	2	296.25	2
▲	DEM	187.88	GAM Tokyo Fonds	G002	31/03/92	IOM	-6.79	33	-7.01	12	3.85	35.61	1	✪✪✪✪✪	4	N.A.		N.A.	
▲	JPY	5.49	Gartmore CSF Jap Sm Cos	G007	13/10/95	JER	-18.98	187	-19.39	139	N.A.	N.A.				N.A.		N.A.	
▲	JPY	110.29	Gartmore CSF Japan	G007	31/05/84	JER	-9.62	89	-19	134	5.73	4.73	13	✪✪✪✪✪		20.14	7	33.63	24
	USD	0.10	Glbl Mgr Japan Bear	B066	30/09/94	BER	-4.42	14	-15.20	79	N.A.	N.A.				N.A.		N.A.	
	USD	5	Glbl Mgr Japan Geared	B066	30/09/94	BER	-19.03	190	-18.17	127	N.A.	N.A.				N.A.		N.A.	
	USD	1.60	Glbl Mgr Japan Index	B066	30/09/94	BER	-11.80	134	-14.58	68	N.A.	N.A.				N.A.		N.A.	
	USD	4.68	Govett GSIL Japan Smaller Cos	G015	31/03/89	JER	-15.05	166	-20.11	155	4.98	-25.11	128	✪		-23.51	95	N.A.	
	USD	2.83	Govett Japan Safeguard A	G016	29/03/96	JER	-1.53	5	N.A.		N.A.	N.A.				N.A.		N.A.	
▲●	JPY	59.53	Groupe Indosuez Japan	G017	31/12/90	LUX	-7.81	49	-19.18	136	5.82	-1.40	41	✪✪✪✪		2.47	24	N.A.	
▲	USD	36	GT Berry Japan A	G018	30/09/75	IRL	-4.38	13	-7.20	13	3.38	1.02	29	✪✪✪		-15.27	67	11.24	33
▲	USD	80	GT Honshu Pathfinder A Share	G018	30/11/82	IRL	-10.01	98	-11.98	37	5.70	-13.88	101	✪✪		-9.78	55	65.04	14
▲	USD	32	GT Japan OTC Stock A	G018	29/12/89	IRL	-7.69	45	-14.17	60	6.15	-12.79	96	✪✪		-6.96	45	N.A.	
▲	USD	110	GT Japan Small Companies A	G018	30/04/80	IRL	-8.53	65	-8.77	20	5.64	-8.05	69	✪✪		-6.33	44	81.98	8
▲	USD	23.10	Guinness Flight Japan	G019	30/11/90	GU	-8.10	53	-12.32	43	4.94	1.29	27	✪✪✪✪		-2.43	36	N.A.	
▲	USD	8.13	Guinness Flight Japan Sm Cos	G019	30/11/90	GU	-17.32	179	-20.94	162	5.66	-6.39	63	✪✪✪		-1.21	32	N.A.	
▲	USD	12.84	Hambros Eqty Sel Japan	H003	31/12/76	GU	-10.11	103	-16.64	106	5.50	-10.88	87	✪✪		-15.98	72	75.50	11
	USD	3.76	Hambros Japanese OTC	H004	31/05/90	GU	-15.84	172	-14.41	62	4.71	-13.90	102	✪✪		-21.98	92	N.A.	
▲	USD	5.76	Hambros Japanese Smllr Cos	H004	28/06/85	GU	-11.71	130	-27.04	178	5.51	-25.79	132	✪		-37.41	101	35	23
●	USD	4.88	Hamon Japan Recovery	H007	22/12/95	IRL	-1.88	6	-23.61	172	N.A.	N.A.				N.A.		N.A.	
●	JPY	N.S.	Hansard EU Japan	H010	17/02/95	IRL	-8.64	67	-14.11	59	N.A.	N.A.				N.A.		N.A.	
●	JPY	4.25	Hansard Japan	H011	28/02/90	IOM	-6.03	26	-9.22	24	3.78	2.52	18	✪✪✪		-3.42	37	N.A.	
●	USD	0.93	Hansard\Baring Jap Sm Cos	H012	27/09/91	IOM	-11.86	135	-14.44	64	4.42	-25.38	129	✪		-21.62	90	N.A.	
●	USD	1.84	Hansard\GT Honshu Pathfinder	H016	27/09/91	IOM	-9.62	87	-11.77	33	4.40	-15.10	104	✪✪		-14.23	65	N.A.	
	JPY	0	Heisei Japan	A023a	31/01/90	BVI	3.12	1	-31.55	180	6.91	-48.66	136	✪		-47.67	103	N.A.	
▲	USD	4.62	Henderson HF Japanese	H025	31/07/85	LUX	-12.07	138	-16.01	96	5.05	-9.83	82	✪✪		-8.17	47	14.68	31
▲	USD	133.33	Henderson HF Japanese Sm Cos	H025	30/08/85	LUX	-17.18	178	-14.42	63	5.82	1.88	24	✪✪✪✪		10.08	16	208.93	3
▲	USD	61.18	HSBC GIF Japanese Equity	H033	30/01/87	LUX	-8.19	54	-15.77	92	5.67	-0.17	33	✪✪✪✪		3.70	20	N.A.	
	USD	3.20	HSBC Japanese Eqty Tactical	H034	31/07/96	BAH	-14.13	157	N.A.		N.A.	N.A.				N.A.		N.A.	
	USD	90.52	HYPO Japan Garantie 6/2000	H024	19/07/96	LUX	-1.96	7	N.A.		N.A.	N.A.				N.A.		N.A.	
	DEM	117.44	HYPO Nippon	H024	30/09/92	LUX	-11.20	123	-19.67	146	5.14	4.63	14	✪✪✪✪✪		N.A.		N.A.	
	USD	25.97	Indosuez Japan	I007	31/10/77	HK	-9.57	83	-21.04	164	5.48	-10.67	86	✪✪		-6.25	43	79.31	9
	JPY	10.03	Indosuez Japan Regional Gth	I007	29/06/90	HK	-12.12	139	-17.77	121	5.72	-10.45	85	✪✪		-11.81	59	N.A.	
▲	JPY	77.44	Inter Strategie Japan	B069	29/09/89	LUX	-7.76	48	-15.51	86	5.19	-4.35	58	✪✪✪		-4.44	40	N.A.	
	USD	5.20	INVESCO Mount Fuji	A010	28/11/86	HK	-11.26	126	-19.60	143	5.23	-8.41	71	✪✪		-14.88	66	18.52	28
▲	USD	11.90	INVESCO PS Nippon Enterprise	I014	31/12/90	LUX	-13.96	154	-16.89	108	5.23	-12.79	95	✪✪		-11.98	60	N.A.	
▲	USD	15.80	INVESCO PS Nippon Gth	I014	31/12/90	LUX	-9.31	79	-19.83	149	5.37	-9.62	81	✪✪		-19.14	81	N.A.	
	GBP	5.67	Irish Life Intl Jap Equity	I017	30/09/94	IRL	-8.31	61	-5.52	9	N.A.	N.A.				N.A.		N.A.	
	USD	N.S.	Japan Diversified	M011	29/05/87	LUX	-10.44	113	N.A.		N.A.	N.A.		✪		N.A.		N.A.	
	JPY	15.17	Japan Dynamic Fund	I003	31/01/90	LUX	-10.07	101	-19.43	141	5.91	-9.43	78	✪✪		-15.99	73	N.A.	
	GBP	13.47	Japanese Sentinel	I009	26/05/95	BAH	-17.07	177	-12.26	41	N.A.	N.A.				N.A.		N.A.	
	GBP	200.29	JF Fledgeling Japan Limited	J004	31/10/86	BER	-14.83	162	-20.15	158	6.16	1.75	25	✪✪✪✪		-5.30	42	148.54	5
	JPY	198.65	JF Japan	J004	29/08/69	HK	-8.82	70	-20.08	154	6.50	-9.37	77	✪✪✪		-20.73	87	92.18	7
	JPY	62.10	JF Japan OTC	J004	28/06/91	HK	-23.65	198	-35.56	182	6.58	-25.56	130	✪		19.50	8	N.A.	
	JPY	67.51	JF Japan Smaller Companies	J004	29/08/80	HK	-15.74	170	-19.99	153	7.21	-19.10	118	✪✪		-26.57	98	67.36	12
	JPY	64.90	JF Japan Technology	J004	29/05/81	HK	-8.03	51	-25.35	174	8.54	2.46	20	✪✪✪✪		10.02	17	60.29	15
●	USD	2.60	JRIA Japan	J002	29/01/93	IRL	-2.16	8	-1.10	5	4.09	20.32	3	✪✪✪✪✪	2	N.A.		N.A.	
▲	GBP	2.81	Jupiter Tyndall GF Japan	J010	30/11/90	LUX	-8.90	72	-17.96	122	4.80	-9.12	75	✪✪		-18.98	80	N.A.	
▲	USD	42.85	KB Japanese	K007	31/10/89	GU	-3.90	11	-9	21	4.72	5.42	11	✪✪✪✪✪		1.99	25	N.A.	

▲ **SIB Approved** ● **Insurance Fund** **Values in US Dollars, on an offer to offer price basis with gross income reinvested** Data Source Micropal™

Japan Equity

continued

	CCY	Fund Size ($mil)	Fund Name	Manager Code	Fund Start Date	Domicile Code	3 Mths 97 % Chg	3 Mths 97 Rank	1 Year % Chg	1 Year Rank	Micropal Star Rating Volatility	3 Years % Chg	3 Years Rank	Rating	Risk Return Rating	5 Years % Chg	5 Years Rank	10 Years % Chg	10 Years Rank
		52.22	**Mean/Count**				**-10.59**	**198**	**-15.61**	**182**	**5.17**	**-7.33**	**136**			**-7.23**	**104**	**67.48**	**36**
	JPY	70.20	KB Lux Equity Japan	K011	31/05/93	LUX	-10.16	109	-20.53	160	5.90	-9.08	74	✪✪✪		N.A.		N.A.	
▲	USD	N.S.	Lazard Japan	L001	30/03/84	GU	-9.97	96	-15.37	82	5.06	1.99	23	✪✪✪✪		2.76	22	77.01	10
▲	USD	N.S.	Lazard Japan USD (Dublin)	L002	31/01/92	GU	-10.14	106	-18	123	4.88	-7.22	68	✪✪✪		N.A.		N.A.	
▲	GBP	11.08	Lazard SIT Japan Index	L001	28/02/89	GU	-12.88	148	-6.24	11	5.31	12.08	7	✪✪✪✪✪		0.62	28	N.A.	
	USD	1.37	LG Japan	L013	24/06/94	IRL	-10.67	115	-13.38	51	N.A.	N.A.				N.A.		N.A.	
▲	JPY	99.42	Lloyds IP Japan Equity	L016	31/03/92	LUX	-8.28	59	-17.01	109	5.02	-1.75	43	✪✪✪		N.A.		N.A.	
	JPY	119.55	LOI Japan OTC	L019	28/04/95	LUX	-14.40	158	-15.81	94	N.A.	N.A.				N.A.		N.A.	
	DEM	15.52	Luxinvest Japan	B061	30/06/94	LUX	-19.03	189	-19.69	147	N.A.	N.A.				N.A.		N.A.	
	JPY	4.27	M-Fund Japan Profit	B013	30/11/94	LUX	-13.08	150	-19.28	137	N.A.	N.A.				N.A.		N.A.	
▲	USD	2.37	Manulife Regent GF Jap Gth	M006	30/09/87	LUX	-3.85	10	-5.60	10	6.37	-16.77	110	✪✪		-34.24	100	N.A.	
	JPY	N.S.	MeesPierson UF Jap Large Cap	M012	01/03/96	LUX	-12.88	147	N.A.		N.A.	N.A.				N.A.		N.A.	
	GBP	577	Mercury IIT Japan	M018	28/06/85	JER	-3.81	9	0.65	2	4.19	14.96	6	✪✪✪✪✪		14.73	13	23.39	26
▲	GBP	13.80	Mercury OST Japan	M020	28/11/86	LUX	-6.60	30	-15.73	89	5.36	-12.22	93	✪✪		-20.36	84	-4.07	34
▲	USD	42.90	Mercury ST Japan	M021	31/12/85	LUX	-5.16	20	-9.43	26	5.10	-3.60	55	✪✪✪✪		-14.18	64	14.96	30
▲	USD	42.75	Mercury ST Japan Opps	M021	29/05/87	LUX	-9.22	75	-8.07	17	5.35	2.03	22	✪✪✪✪		21.30	5	N.A.	
▲	GBP	15.55	Midland ICF Japan Growth	M028	28/02/90	LUX	-11.52	127	-15.09	77	4.78	-11.44	89	✪✪		-17.97	79	N.A.	
▲	USD	5.74	Midland ICF Japanese Opps	M028	29/03/91	LUX	-12.04	137	-19.05	135	5.80	-0.35	35	✪✪✪✪		0.02	29	N.A.	
▲	DEM	0	Morgan Grenfell Jap Bullet DM	M038	31/03/92	IRL	-15.80	171	-19.51	142	4.91	-19.23	120	✪		N.A.		N.A.	
▲	JPY	62.68	Morgan Grenfell Jap Cap Gth	M038	13/10/95	IRL	-6.94	37	-15.76	91	N.A.	N.A.				N.A.		N.A.	
▲	GBP	23.51	Morgan Grenfell Jap Emerg Cos	M038	29/04/94	IRL	-16.72	176	-13.63	53	N.A.	N.A.				N.A.		N.A.	
▲	GBP	240.55	Morgan Grenfell Jap Small Cos	M038	31/05/84	IRL	-14.89	164	-18.66	132	5.07	-15.42	105	✪		2.67	23	324.46	1
▲	GBP	116.21	Morgan Grenfell Japan Bullet	M038	31/01/92	IRL	-15.33	169	-19.37	138	4.97	-19.31	121	✪		N.A.		N.A.	
▲	GBP	255.94	Morgan Grenfell PF Japan	M038	29/12/89	IRL	-7.73	47	-12.09	39	4.61	4.10	16	✪✪✪✪✪		17.11	10	N.A.	
	JPY	75.10	Morgan Stanley Japanese Eq	M039	31/05/93	LUX	-4.59	16	-12.29	42	4.57	-0.04	32	✪✪✪✪		N.A.		N.A.	
	JPY	11.17	MOSAIS Actions Japonaises	C058	30/03/90	LUX	-11.10	121	-14.73	72	4.48	-6.87	65	✪✪		1.03	27	N.A.	
	JPY	3.72	MultiLink Jap Eq	I011	31/12/90	LUX	-7.90	50	-12.90	47	4.97	-17.61	112	✪		-21.63	91	N.A.	
	DEM	5.53	Nestor Japan	N002	31/01/94	LUX	-9.97	97	-26.05	176	N.A.	N.A.				N.A.		N.A.	
▲	USD	16.80	Newton UGF Japanese	N006	29/02/88	JER	-4.71	18	-5.45	8	5.09	5.49	10	✪✪✪✪✪		5.87	18	N.A.	
▲	JPY	24.65	NICAM Japan Return Reversal	N009	28/02/92	GU	-11.09	119	-18.19	128	5.54	-1.74	42	✪✪✪✪		N.A.		N.A.	
	USD	2.10	NICAM New Generation	N009	30/04/84	GU	-12.85	145	-16.35	100	5.03	-15.86	106	✪✪		-17.81	77	38.76	20
▲	JPY	30.76	Nikko GIUF Japan Rtn Reversal	N007	31/10/94	LUX	-11.26	125	-17.33	114	N.A.	N.A.				N.A.		N.A.	
▲	JPY	7.92	Nikko GIUF Jasdaq A YEN	N007	27/10/95	LUX	-18.46	184	-20.96	163	N.A.	N.A.				N.A.		N.A.	
▲	JPY	0.06	Nikko GIUF Jasdaq B USD	N007	27/10/95	LUX	-17.55	181	-18.12	126	N.A.	N.A.				N.A.		N.A.	
▲	JPY	6.94	Nikko GIUF Jasdaq B YEN	N007	27/10/95	LUX	-12.22	140	-7.60	14	N.A.	N.A.				N.A.		N.A.	
	USD	30.39	Nippon Fund	C027	30/09/75	HK	-6.85	34	-15.59	88	4.69	-1.78	44	✪✪✪		-11.37	58	20.15	27
	USD	7.47	Nomura SF Japan	N010	30/11/92	CA	-20.06	196	-31.81	181	6.28	-40.59	135	✪		N.A.		N.A.	
	USD	36.38	Nomura SF Japan Growth Opps	N010	31/03/95	CA	-15.28	167	-21.49	165	N.A.	N.A.				N.A.		N.A.	
	USD	0.49	Old Mutual Gnsy Japan Stkmkt	O003	29/12/95	GU	-14.97	165	-7.80	15	N.A.	N.A.				N.A.		N.A.	
	USD	0.39	Old Mutual HK Japan Stkmkt	O004	28/04/95	HK	-14.47	159	-9.88	28	N.A.	N.A.				N.A.		N.A.	
	USD	13.14	OMI (Gnsy) Japan Stkmkt	O005	30/01/87	GU	-14.81	161	-4.74	7	4.47	10.91	8	✪✪✪✪		15.31	12	N.A.	
	USD	18.30	Orbitex Japan	O014	31/03/94	BAH	-14.01	155	-10.04	29	N.A.	N.A.				N.A.		N.A.	
	JPY	140.86	Parvest Japan B	B037	30/03/90	LUX	-7.73	46	-20.90	161	5.69	-9.45	79	✪✪		-20.51	85	N.A.	
	JPY	0.01	Parvest Japan Small Cap A	B037	11/10/96	LUX	-19.95	195	N.A.		N.A.	N.A.				N.A.		N.A.	
	JPY	9.13	Parvest Japan Small Cap B	B037	11/10/96	LUX	-8.52	64	N.A.		N.A.	N.A.				N.A.		N.A.	
	USD	N.S.	PCP Japan	P007	31/05/96	CA	-13.80	153	N.A.		N.A.	N.A.				N.A.		N.A.	
	USD	40.60	Perpetual Offshr Japanese Gth	P011	29/11/91	JER	-11.71	131	-25.47	175	6.01	-15.95	107	✪		-0.45	31	N.A.	
	JPY	4.17	Portefeuille BG Actions Japon	B063	23/06/95	LUX	-10.68	116	-15.50	84	N.A.	N.A.				N.A.		N.A.	
▲	GBP	53.39	Prolific IF Japan Growth	P027	30/04/92	IRL	-17.97	183	-17.06	111	5.30	-7.20	67	✪✪✪		N.A.		N.A.	
	USD	80.38	Prospect Japan	P028	16/12/94	GU	-8.20	56	-17.42	118	N.A.	N.A.				N.A.		N.A.	
	USD	0.85	Proton IF Japan	P024	29/09/95	BVI	-10.14	105	-11.92	36	N.A.	N.A.				N.A.		N.A.	
	USD	80.26	Quaestor Equity Japan	Q001	30/06/92	IRL	-8.76	69	-16.38	101	6.06	-2.28	50	✪✪✪		N.A.		N.A.	
▲	JPY	14.81	RBC GI Japan	R003	24/11/95	GU	-6.52	27	-13.97	56	N.A.	N.A.				N.A.		N.A.	
●	USD	0.70	Royal Life/Baring Japan Tech	R022	30/10/87	IOM	-17.82	182	-9.49	27	4.88	-25.01	127	✪		-13.34	61	N.A.	
●	USD	8.40	Royal Life/Hend Japan Sm Cos	R027	30/10/87	IOM	-22.73	197	-9.18	23	5.02	-0.29	34	✪✪✪		13.40	15	N.A.	
●	USD	2.30	Royal Life/Indosuez Japan	R028	30/10/87	IOM	-14.05	156	-18	124	4.45	-10.98	88	✪✪		-6.99	46	N.A.	
	JPY	15.19	S-E-Banken Fund Japan	S001	29/10/93	LUX	-6.71	31	-15.08	76	4.83	-22.23	125	✪		N.A.		N.A.	
	USD	19.59	Samba Lux Japan Equity	S006	31/01/95	LUX	-11.20	124	-12.21	40	N.A.	N.A.				N.A.		N.A.	

▲ **SIB Approved** ● **Insurance Fund** **Values in US Dollars, on an offer to offer price basis with gross income reinvested**

Data Source Micropal™

Japan Equity

continued

	CCY	Fund Size ($mil)	Fund Name	Manager Code	Fund Start Date	Domicile Code	3 Mths 97 % Chg	3 Mths 97 Rank	1 Year % Chg	1 Year Rank	Micropal Star Rating 3 Years Volatility	3 Years % Chg	3 Years Rank	3 Years Rating	Risk Return Rating	5 Years % Chg	5 Years Rank	10 Years % Chg	10 Years Rank
		52.22	**Mean/Count**				**-10.59**	**198**	**-15.61**	**182**	**5.17**	**-7.33**	**136**			**-7.23**	**104**	**67.48**	**36**
▲	JPY	60.12	SBC Eq Ptf Small & Mid Japan	S007	31/01/95	LUX	-19.28	191	-19.63	144	N.A.	N.A.				N.A.		N.A.	
	USD	12.18	Schroder Asia Nippon	S011	28/02/94	CA	-5.86	24	-12.42	44	N.A.	N.A.				N.A.		N.A.	
▲	JPY	77.74	Schroder Intl Sel Jap Sm Cos	S010	29/10/93	LUX	-16.67	175	-18.06	125	4.64	-10.37	84	✪✪		N.A.		N.A.	
▲	JPY	259.29	Schroder Intl Sel Japan Eqty	S010	30/07/93	LUX	-7.25	41	-12.07	38	5.02	7.40	9	✪✪✪✪✪		N.A.		N.A.	
	USD	962.17	Schroder Japan	S011	29/04/77	HK	-6.88	35	-8.05	16	5.25	16.22	5	✪✪✪✪✪		25.49	4	116.67	6
	JPY	8.32	Scontinvest Japan Equity	S012	28/06/96	LUX	-13.78	152	N.A.		N.A.	N.A.				N.A.		N.A.	
	USD	0.60	Scot Prov GP Jap Safeguard C	S014	31/05/96	IOM	-1.23	4	N.A.		N.A.	N.A.				N.A.		N.A.	
	USD	1.30	Scot Prov ILA Japan Gth	S014	29/12/95	IOM	-9.90	93	-17.20	112	N.A.	N.A.				N.A.		N.A.	
	LUF	42.06	Sen Mon Fund Japanese Growth	P013	30/11/83	LUX	-10.81	118	-14.50	66	4.26	-2.21	48	✪✪✪		-1.92	34	50.87	17
	JPY	39.73	Share Japan	B053	31/01/89	LUX	-7.19	40	-12.73	46	5.82	3.36	17	✪✪✪✪		1.58	26	N.A.	
	HKD	1.57	SHK Japan	S024	30/03/90	HK	-10.09	102	-19.92	150	4.55	-17.86	114	✪		-28.75	99	N.A.	
▲	GBP	47.70	Singer & Fried Samurai	S027	30/04/93	IRL	-8.54	66	-4.42	6	6.96	-29.66	134	✪		N.A.		N.A.	
▲	JPY	112.10	Skandifond Japan Equity	S030	30/06/88	LUX	-6.72	32	-15.50	85	5.14	-20.28	123	✪		-17.46	76	N.A.	
	JPY	21.86	Sogelux Fd Equities Japan	S037	31/05/88	LUX	-10.07	99	-13.29	50	4.49	2.47	19	✪✪✪✪		17.10	11	N.A.	
	USD	23.62	Southern Intl Japan EQ	S041	30/09/96	LUX	-9.60	85	N.A.		N.A.	N.A.				N.A.		N.A.	
▲	JPY	3.03	Sun Life GP Japan Growth	S052	31/03/88	LUX	-8.47	63	-18.84	133	5.31	-16.13	108	✪		-26.20	97	N.A.	
	JPY	35.94	Swiss Life Proteus Japan	S056	27/09/96	IRL	-10.28	112	N.A.		N.A.	N.A.				N.A.		N.A.	
▲	JPY	58.30	TGA Jap Eqty	T009	28/02/89	LUX	-7.28	42	-14.83	74	5.33	-2.85	52	✪✪✪✪		-9.44	53	N.A.	
▲	JPY	153.59	TGA Jap SmCos Eq	T009	30/11/95	LUX	-12.86	146	-12.56	45	N.A.	N.A.				N.A.		N.A.	
	JPY	26.33	The Interallianz Nippon Equity	I010	30/07/93	LUX	-9.92	94	-15.36	81	4.61	-1.17	38	✪✪✪		N.A.		N.A.	
	USD	4.79	Thornton New Tiger Japan	T007	28/09/84	BER	-5.61	22	-16.47	102	4.90	-20.24	122	✪		-49.08	104	-33.74	36
	JPY	146.40	Transpacific Fund	N003	31/03/89	LUX	-4.70	17	-12.96	48	5.14	-2.78	51	✪✪✪✪		-3.59	38	N.A.	
	JPY	71.92	UAP Japanese Securities	U009	31/01/94	LUX	-8.19	55	-15.90	95	N.A.	N.A.				N.A.		N.A.	
	JPY	19.38	UBAM Japanese Equity	U010	31/10/86	LUX	-9.61	86	-14.65	70	6.53	-16.56	109	✪✪		-22.51	94	37.88	22
▲	JPY	19.77	Von Ernst GP Japanese Eqty	B021	30/11/89	LUX	-11.65	129	-19.67	145	5.26	-5.89	61	✪✪✪		-9.68	54	N.A.	
	JPY	87.56	Vontobel Fund Japanese Eq A	B017	29/11/91	LUX	-10.76	117	-19.96	152	5.23	-12.58	94	✪		-17.11	75	N.A.	
	JPY	17.57	WFNIA Japan Index	B081	30/05/86	GU	-15.88	173	-11.80	34	5.29	1.36	26	✪✪✪		-0.12	30	38.36	21
	JPY	23.77	Willerequity Japan	W004	30/11/90	LUX	-7.16	39	-14.85	75	4.72	-0.97	37	✪✪✪✪		4.52	19	N.A.	
	CHF	89.17	World Invest Nippon	B022	29/03/91	LUX	-10.12	104	-28.64	179	4.93	-25.68	131	✪		-41.29	102	N.A.	
	USD	6.80	Yamaichi ISS	Y001	29/06/90	GU	-12.52	142	-20.12	156	5.17	-6.47	64	✪✪✪		-9.22	52	N.A.	
	USD	4.66	Zipangu	B072	06/01/95	CA	-14.88	163	-11.88	35	N.A.	N.A.				N.A.		N.A.	

Korea Equity

Funds investing in excess of 70% in Korean equities or related instruments. Such funds may have an objective of capital and/or income growth, or to track a specified index or perform inversely to a given index. Funds in this category may leverage or gear by a maximum of 20% of total assets.

	CCY	Fund Size ($mil)	Fund Name	Manager Code	Fund Start Date	Domicile Code	3 Mths 97 % Chg	3 Mths 97 Rank	1 Year % Chg	1 Year Rank	Micropal Star Rating 3 Years Volatility	3 Years % Chg	3 Years Rank	3 Years Rating	Risk Return Rating	5 Years % Chg	5 Years Rank	10 Years % Chg	10 Years Rank
		20.57	**Mean/Count**				**-6.32**	**25**	**-32.85**	**24**	**6.90**	**-37.28**	**13**			**-23.20**	**7**	**0**	**0**
	USD	14.68	Baer Multistock Korea Stock A	J007	31/12/93	LUX	-5.51	10	-34.85	16	5.51	-51.72	13	✪		N.A.		N.A.	
	USD	7.92	Barclays ASF Korea	B044	31/10/90	JER	-6.58	12	-37.76	22	7.08	-45.53	11	✪		-26.62	5	N.A.	
	USD	46.88	Baring Korea Feeder Fund	B049	31/10/88	IRL	-4.63	8	-31.95	9	7.37	-27.54	3	✪✪✪✪		-14.79	1	N.A.	
	USD	21.17	Bordier Korea	B071	31/10/89	BVI	1.40	3	-32.46	14	6.50	-25.64	2	✪✪✪✪✪		-18.42	3	N.A.	
	USD	N.S.	Citi Korea Equity	C026	28/02/94	IRL	-1.85	4	-36.05	18	N.A.	N.A.				N.A.		N.A.	
	USD	17.14	Clemente Korea Emerging Gth	R005	30/04/92	LUX	-5.57	11	-28.82	3	5.63	-41.03	8	✪✪		N.A.		N.A.	
●	USD	0.20	CMI Passport Korean Equity	C044	20/01/95	IOM	-15.12	24	-32.98	15	N.A.	N.A.				N.A.		N.A.	
▲	USD	23.03	Dres Thornton ASF Korea	D015	30/11/93	IRL	-8.28	17	-32.38	13	5.74	-50.40	12	✪		N.A.		N.A.	
▲	USD	33.20	Fidelity Fds Korea	F011	03/11/95	LUX	-3.45	5	-29.36	5	N.A.	N.A.				N.A.		N.A.	
	USD	15.90	GT Korea	G018	31/10/89	BER	-6.79	14	-39	23	9.27	-44.33	10	✪✪		-37.36	7	N.A.	
●	USD	1.80	Hansard\Baring Korea	H012	30/08/91	IOM	-9.08	20	-30.78	7	7.19	-20.83	1	✪✪✪✪		-16.48	2	N.A.	

▲ SIB Approved ● Insurance Fund **Values in US Dollars, on an offer to offer price basis with gross income reinvested** Data Source Micropal™

Korea Equity

continued

	CCY	Fund Size ($mil)	Fund Name	Manager Code	Fund Start Date	Domicile Code	3 Mths 97 % Chg	3 Mths 97 Rank	1 Year % Chg	1 Year Rank	Micropal Star Rating Volatility	3 Years % Chg	3 Years Rank	3 Years Rating	Risk Return Rating	5 Years % Chg	5 Years Rank	10 Years % Chg	10 Years Rank
		20.57	**Mean/Count**				**-6.32**	**25**	**-32.85**	**24**	**6.90**	**-37.28**	**13**			**-23.20**	**7**	**0**	**0**
	USD	33.57	Indosuez Korea	I007	31/12/91	BLUX	-5.18	9	-32.08	10	5.90	-30.04	4	✪✪✪✪		-20.80	4	N.A.	
	USD	71.88	JF Korea	J004	31/12/91	CA	7.49	1	-36.64	19	10.20	-41.24	9	✪✪✪		-27.90	6	N.A.	
▲	USD	18.49	Jupiter Tyndall GF Korea Vis	J010	31/12/92	LUX	-8.67	19	-37.55	21	6.97	-34.47	6	✪✪✪		N.A.		N.A.	
	USD	23.94	Jupiter Tyndall SF KoreaSmCos	J011	25/11/94	BER	3.08	2	-30.85	8	N.A.	N.A.				N.A.		N.A.	
	USD	6.77	LG Korea	L013	15/07/94	IRL	-3.72	6	-36.80	20	N.A.	N.A.				N.A.		N.A.	
	USD	12.57	NICAM Asia Pacific UF Korea	N007	31/01/94	LUX	-6.67	13	-35.33	17	N.A.	N.A.				N.A.		N.A.	
	USD	23.60	NM First Korean	N001	22/09/95	IRL	-7.74	16	-32.10	11	N.A.	N.A.				N.A.		N.A.	
	USD	12.50	Peregrine Korea Preferred	P008	12/05/95	CA	-20	25	-47.65	24	N.A.	N.A.				N.A.		N.A.	
	USD	23.07	Regent New Korea Gth	R005	31/05/93	CA	-9.40	21	-27.88	2	5.67	-39.03	7	✪✪		N.A.		N.A.	
	USD	0.20	RLI/Baring Korea	R022	12/07/96	IOM	-7.38	15	N.A.		N.A.	N.A.				N.A.		N.A.	
	USD	38.82	Scudder GOF Greater Korea A-2	S019	21/04/95	LUX	-8.43	18	-28.96	4	N.A.	N.A.				N.A.		N.A.	
▲	USD	6.62	Templeton GS Korean	T001	05/05/95	LUX	-4.10	7	-13.56	1	N.A.	N.A.				N.A.		N.A.	
	USD	14.98	Thornton Korea	T006	30/04/92	FRA	-9.84	22	-32.32	12	6.64	-32.84	5	✪✪✪		N.A.		N.A.	
	USD	24.63	Thornton New Tiger Korea	T007	31/01/94	BER	-11.88	23	-30.25	6	N.A.	N.A.				N.A.		N.A.	

Latin America Equity

Funds investing in excess of 70% in Latin American equities or related instruments. Such funds may have an objective of capital and/or income growth, or to track a specified index or perform inversely to a given index. Funds in this category may leverage or gear by a maximum of 20% of total assets.

	CCY	Fund Size ($mil)	Fund Name	Manager Code	Fund Start Date	Domicile Code	3 Mths 97 % Chg	3 Mths 97 Rank	1 Year % Chg	1 Year Rank	Micropal Star Rating Volatility	3 Years % Chg	3 Years Rank	3 Years Rating	Risk Return Rating	5 Years % Chg	5 Years Rank	10 Years % Chg	10 Years Rank
		45.52	**Mean/Count**				**15.25**	**62**	**22.91**	**55**	**6.94**	**-1.86**	**24**			**74.36**	**10**	**0**	**0**
▲	USD	120.88	AAF Latin American Equity Fd	A001	30/06/94	LUX	19.98	6	27.12	16	N.A.	N.A.				N.A.		N.A.	
	USD	15.03	AIG Latin America	A017	29/01/93	IRL	11.02	53	20.85	34	6.73	-3.92	11	✪✪		N.A.		N.A.	
	USD	13.74	Alpha Latin America	A023a	29/11/91	BVI	8.30	60	26.41	18	6.16	55.75	1	✪✪✪✪✪	4	171.44	1	N.A.	
	USD	0.68	BanesFondo Intern. 1992 Discov	B030	31/10/91	LUX	11.81	50	16.94	44	3.30	27.44	3	✪✪✪✪	3	27.29	10	N.A.	
	USD	54.94	Baring EMUF Latin America	B049	31/03/93	IRL	16.01	31	26.24	19	8.08	-9.60	15	✪✪		N.A.		N.A.	
	USD	188.87	Baring Puma	B050	29/03/91	CA	15.07	39	20.34	37	7.10	-3.62	10	✪✪✪		73.16	5	N.A.	
	USD	37.47	BSS Universal Latin America	B029	31/03/93	LUX	15.49	38	17.85	43	8.52	-23.77	22	✪✪		N.A.		N.A.	
▲	USD	72.93	BT GAF Latin American Eqty	B076	30/09/93	IRL	14.13	43	30.07	6	8	-9.53	14	✪✪		N.A.		N.A.	
	USD	N.S.	Capital Intl Emerg Countries	C010	07/07/95	LUX	9.31	59	13.53	48	N.A.	N.A.				N.A.		N.A.	
	USD	32.24	CCF Sam EMF Lat Am Indx Tr C	C015	30/06/95	LUX	16.30	28	16.62	45	N.A.	N.A.				N.A.		N.A.	
▲●	USD	31.85	Chase Vista Latin Am Eq	C019	28/02/92	LUX	14.23	42	22.38	31	4.76	29.86	2	✪✪✪✪✪	3	N.A.		N.A.	
	USD	14.61	Citimarkets Lat Amer Equity A	C034	05/07/96	LUX	15.72	36	N.A.		N.A.	N.A.				N.A.		N.A.	
▲	USD	14.86	CMI GNF Latin American Eqty	C042	29/04/94	LUX	19.02	7	25	23	N.A.	N.A.				N.A.		N.A.	
●	USD	0.40	CMI Passport Lat American Eq	C044	20/01/95	IOM	17.60	17	23.39	29	N.A.	N.A.				N.A.		N.A.	
●	USD	64.18	Credis Equity Latin America	C056	31/03/94	LUX	13.75	44	18.40	42	N.A.	N.A.				N.A.		N.A.	
●	DEM	71.76	DBIM Latinamerika	D006	31/05/94	LUX	16.72	25	25.40	22	N.A.	N.A.				N.A.		N.A.	
▲	USD	15.80	DSB Thornton LAS Conquistador	D018	31/05/94	IRL	18.02	12	22.36	32	N.A.	N.A.				N.A.		N.A.	
	USD	N.S.	Eagle Star Latin American Equi	E001	27/09/96	IOM	17.71	15	N.A.		N.A.	N.A.				N.A.		N.A.	
	DEM	6.43	EM Latinamerika	U012	31/10/94	LUX	15.50	37	13.22	49	N.A.	N.A.				N.A.		N.A.	
▲	USD	60	Fidelity Fds Latin America	F011	31/05/94	LUX	12.18	48	28.38	9	N.A.	N.A.				N.A.		N.A.	
▲●	USD	5.59	Five Arrows GF Latin Am Opps	R011	27/05/94	LUX	13.51	45	29.97	7	N.A.	N.A.				N.A.		N.A.	
	USD	4.40	Five Arrows Latin Amer Acc	R018	30/09/92	GU	17.53	19	27.21	15	6.48	-15.42	19	✪		N.A.		N.A.	
▲	USD	27.21	Five Arrows Latin Amer Dist	R018	30/09/92	GU	17.55	18	27.52	14	6.51	-14.82	18	✪		N.A.		N.A.	
▲	USD	124.23	Fleming FF Latin American	F020	29/05/92	LUX	17.18	23	20.25	39	6.99	-16.58	20	✪		N.A.		N.A.	
▲	USD	3.15	Gartmore CSF Latin America	G007	13/10/95	JER	20.69	2	19.55	40	N.A.	N.A.				N.A.		N.A.	
	USD	67.97	Genesis Condor	G010	30/04/91	GU	13.45	46	27.75	13	5.96	18.30	4	✪✪✪✪	1	90.81	3	N.A.	
▲	USD	92	GT Latin America A	G018	30/04/91	IRL	10.10	56	24.89	25	7.99	-5.71	13	✪✪✪		30.49	9	N.A.	
	USD	N.S.	Hansard EU Latin America	H010	17/02/95	IRL	11.07	52	37.06	3	N.A.	N.A.				N.A.		N.A.	

▲ **SIB Approved** ● **Insurance Fund** **Values in US Dollars, on an offer to offer price basis with gross income reinvested** Data Source Micropal™

Latin America Equity

continued

	CCY	Fund Size ($mil)	Fund Name	Manager Code	Fund Start Date	Domicile Code	3 Mths 97 % Chg	3 Mths 97 Rank	1 Year % Chg	1 Year Rank	Micropal Star Rating 3 Years Volatility	3 Years % Chg	3 Years Rank	Rating	Risk Return Rating	5 Years % Chg	5 Years Rank	10 Years % Chg	10 Years Rank
		45.52	**Mean/Count**				**15.25**	**62**	**22.91**	**55**	**6.94**	**-1.86**	**24**			**74.36**	**10**	**0**	**0**
●	USD	1.71	Hansard Latin America	H011	31/07/92	IOM	12.03	49	25.54	21	7.93	-1.02	9	✪✪✪		N.A.		N.A.	
●	USD	2.98	Hansard\GT Latin America	H016	30/08/91	IOM	10.97	54	25.80	20	9.26	0.88	7	✪✪✪✪		34.79	7	N.A.	
	USD	20.93	Indosuez Latin America C	B033	29/04/94	LUX	15.96	34	16.41	46	N.A.	N.A.				N.A.		N.A.	
	USD	19.47	ING Intl-Latin Am Equity Cap	I008	30/06/94	LUX	14.43	41	28.27	10	N.A.	N.A.				N.A.		N.A.	
▲	USD	4.82	Jupiter Tyndall GF Latin Amer	J010	15/07/94	LUX	17.71	16	21.52	33	N.A.	N.A.				N.A.		N.A.	
	USD	28.18	KB Lux Key Latin America	K011	28/02/92	LUX	12.81	47	20.71	36	7	-9.87	16	✪✪		N.A.		N.A.	
▲	USD	11.95	Latin American Inv Co	F002	30/06/92	LUX	15.96	35	24.13	26	7.59	-10.48	17	✪✪		N.A.		N.A.	
▲	USD	N.S.	Lazard Latin American	L002	30/06/92	GU	17.35	22	20.72	35	7.87	-33.11	24	✪		N.A.		N.A.	
	USD	26.39	Lion Fortune CL Lat Am Eq A	C062	28/02/94	LUX	20.19	4	31.17	5	N.A.	N.A.				N.A.		N.A.	
▲	USD	52.49	Lloyds IP Latin Am Eq	L016	17/05/96	LUX	17.48	20	N.A.		N.A.	N.A.				N.A.		N.A.	
	USD	3.73	LM Glbl Latin American Eqty B	L005	29/03/96	NL	16.08	30	N.A.		N.A.	N.A.				N.A.		N.A.	
	USD	4.77	LM Glbl Mercosur Equity B	L005	29/03/96	NL	15.07	40	N.A.		N.A.	N.A.				N.A.		N.A.	
	USD	48.81	M.Lynch Latin Amer Portf O	M023	29/11/91	LUX	18.02	11	18.92	41	6.40	-17.43	21	✪		30.78	8	N.A.	
▲	USD	10.07	Mercury ST Latin America	M021	31/03/94	LUX	16.09	29	26.83	17	N.A.	N.A.				N.A.		N.A.	
▲	GBP	30.45	Morgan Grenfell Latin American	M038	30/06/93	IRL	18.20	10	28.95	8	7.44	-4.51	12	✪✪✪		N.A.		N.A.	
	USD	11.49	Morgan Stanley Latin Amer	M039	31/08/94	LUX	17.79	13	48.17	1	N.A.	N.A.				N.A.		N.A.	
	DEM	7.72	Nestor Lateinamerika	N002	31/01/94	LUX	9.62	57	33.15	4	N.A.	N.A.				N.A.		N.A.	
	USD	0.17	Old Mutual Gnsy Lat Am Stkmkt	O003	29/12/95	GU	21.01	1	3.30	55	N.A.	N.A.				N.A.		N.A.	
	USD	0.34	Old Mutual HK Latin Am Stkmkt	O004	28/04/95	HK	20.43	3	9.94	52	N.A.	N.A.				N.A.		N.A.	
	USD	8.93	OMI (Gnsy) Latin Am Stkmkt	O005	31/03/92	GU	19	8	9.53	53	7.87	-25.09	23	✪		N.A.		N.A.	
	USD	9.60	Perpetual Offshr Latin Am Gth	P011	13/01/95	JER	9.57	58	27.83	12	N.A.	N.A.				N.A.		N.A.	
	USD	2.02	Portefeuille BG Act Am Latine	B063	23/06/95	LUX	17.73	14	22.90	30	N.A.	N.A.				N.A.		N.A.	
	USD	N.S.	RBC Gl Latin America	R003	27/09/96	GU	N.A.	—	N.A.		N.A.	N.A.				N.A.		N.A.	
	USD	N.S.	River & Merc Latin American	R007	20/10/95	LUX	7.66	61	6.64	54	N.A.	N.A.				N.A.		N.A.	
	USD	0.95	RLI/Schroder Latin Am	R036	27/10/95	IOM	20.05	5	11.80	51	N.A.	N.A.				N.A.		N.A.	
	USD	854.04	Schroder Latin American	S008	31/12/90	GU	18.98	9	24.91	24	7.38	10.99	6	✪✪✪✪		138.22	2	N.A.	
	USD	0.50	Scot Prov ILA Latin America	S014	29/12/95	IOM	10.59	55	23.70	28	N.A.	N.A.				N.A.		N.A.	
	USD	21.39	Scudder GOF Latin America A-2	S019	29/04/94	LUX	15.97	33	23.82	27	N.A.	N.A.				N.A.		N.A.	
	USD	7.05	Share Latin America	B053	30/04/90	LUX	16.85	24	27.84	11	7.40	-0.57	8	✪✪✪		85.84	4	N.A.	
▲●	GBP	13.03	Singer & Fried Aztec	S027	29/04/94	IRL	15.98	32	12.36	50	N.A.	N.A.				N.A.		N.A.	
	USD	3.32	Sogelux Fd Equities Latin Am	S037	21/06/96	LUX	16.40	27	N.A.		N.A.	N.A.				N.A.		N.A.	
▲	USD	7.49	Templeton GS Latin American	T001	28/02/91	LUX	11.58	51	15.14	47	3.94	17.08	5	✪✪✪✪	2	60.76	6	N.A.	
▲	USD	177.57	TGA Latin Am Eq	T009	17/11/95	LUX	17.41	21	20.26	38	N.A.	N.A.				N.A.		N.A.	
	USD	15.61	Willer Latin America	W004	31/03/95	LUX	4.81	62	40.87	2	N.A.	N.A.				N.A.		N.A.	

Luxembourg Equity

Funds investing in excess of 70% in Luxembourg equities or related instruments. Such funds may have an objective of capital and/or income growth, or to track a specified index or perform inversely to a given index. Funds in this category may leverage or gear by a maximum of 20% of total assets.

CCY	Fund Size ($mil)	Fund Name	Manager Code	Fund Start Date	Domicile Code	3 Mths 97 % Chg	3 Mths 97 Rank	1 Year % Chg	1 Year Rank	Micropal Star Rating 3 Years Volatility	3 Years % Chg	3 Years Rank	Rating	Risk Return Rating	5 Years % Chg	5 Years Rank	10 Years % Chg	10 Years Rank
	24.12	**Mean/Count**				**0.94**	**4**	**31.66**	**2**	**2.89**	**88.79**	**1**		**1**	**178.94**	**1**	**0**	**0**
LUF	66.57	Generalpart B	B064	31/01/91	LUX	2.36	1	33.77	1	2.89	88.79	1	✪✪✪	3	178.94	1	N.A.	
BEF	1.78	KB Lux Luxinvest C	K011	04/10/96	LUX	0.06	3	N.A.		N.A.	N.A.				N.A.		N.A.	
LUF	4	LuxiPrivilege B	S036	31/01/94	LUX	1.76	2	29.55	2	N.A.	N.A.				N.A.		N.A.	

▲ SIB Approved ● Insurance Fund Values in US Dollars, on an offer to offer price basis with gross income reinvested Data Source Micropal™

Malaysia Equity

Funds investing in excess of 70% in Malaysian equities or related instruments. Such funds may have an objective of capital and/or income growth, or to track a specified index or perform inversely to a given index. Funds in this category may leverage or gear by a maximum of 20% of total assets.

	CCY	Fund Size ($mil)	Fund Name	Manager Code	Fund Start Date	Domicile Code	3 Mths 97 % Chg	3 Mths 97 Rank	1 Year % Chg	1 Year Rank	Micropal Star Rating 3 Years Volatility	3 Years % Chg	3 Years Rank	3 Years Rating	Risk Return Rating	5 Years % Chg	5 Years Rank	10 Years % Chg	10 Years Rank
		40.22	**Mean/Count**				**7.32**	**14**	**28.35**	**14**	**7.75**	**0.48**	**12**			**196.56**	**11**	**0**	**0**
	USD	5.53	Barclays ASF Malaysia	B044	31/10/90	JER	5.42	8	26.10	10	7.65	-9.03	10	✪		220.81	4	N.A.	
	USD	1.40	CIBC-CEF Malaysia	C017	31/10/89	BER	21.87	1	31.51	5	9.95	2.13	5	✪✪✪✪		115.73	11	N.A.	
▲	USD	78	Fidelity Fds Malaysia	F011	28/09/90	LUX	-2.51	14	24.71	12	7.42	5.19	3	✪✪✪✪		261.28	2	N.A.	
	USD	93.33	Genesis Malaysia Maju	G010	28/02/90	GU	13.85	2	42.18	2	7.33	37.84	1	✪✪✪✪✪	3	293.40	1	N.A.	
●	USD	2.42	Hansard\Fidelity Malaysia	H014	27/09/91	IOM	4.73	10	24.79	11	7.01	10	2	✪✪✪		180.09	7	N.A.	
▲	USD	14.47	HSBC GIF Malaysian Equity	H033	30/01/87	LUX	5.93	7	28.37	6	7.24	2.80	4	✪✪✪		194.36	6	N.A.	
	USD	0.64	ImPac AP Malaysia	I005	31/10/95	CA	12.25	4	15.47	13	N.A.	N.A.				N.A.		N.A.	
	USD	85.60	JF Malaysia	J004	29/12/89	HK	13.61	3	33.88	4	8.68	-4.70	8	✪✪		256.08	3	N.A.	
	USD	208.91	Malaysia Equity	D001	29/12/89	CA	8.60	5	26.21	8	7.02	-10.15	11	✪		165.20	8	N.A.	
	USD	N.S.	Malaysian Emerging Cos Gth	P015	30/06/94	BVI	7.42	6	45.13	1	N.A.	N.A.				N.A.		N.A.	
	USD	0.39	MBf Malaysian	M010	31/05/90	HK	4.50	11	9.66	14	6.55	-16.48	12	✪		124.97	10	N.A.	
▲	USD	0.56	Nikko GIUF Malaysia Fund	N007	26/02/93	LUX	-1.25	13	26.15	9	8.29	-2.12	7	✪✪✪		N.A.		N.A.	
	USD	16.90	The Malaysia Capital Fund	M011	30/03/90	CA	4.88	9	27.83	7	7.69	-1.50	6	✪✪		131.47	9	N.A.	
	USD	14.65	Thornton New Tiger Malaysia	T007	30/03/90	BER	3.17	12	34.88	3	8.17	-8.27	9	✪✪		218.78	5	N.A.	

Malaysia & Singapore Equity

Funds investing in excess of 70% in Malaysian and Singaporean equities or related instruments. Such funds may have an objective of capital and/or income growth, or to track a specified index or perform inversely to a given index. Funds in this category may leverage or gear by a maximum of 20% of total assets.

	CCY	Fund Size ($mil)	Fund Name	Manager Code	Fund Start Date	Domicile Code	3 Mths 97 % Chg	3 Mths 97 Rank	1 Year % Chg	1 Year Rank	Micropal Star Rating 3 Years Volatility	3 Years % Chg	3 Years Rank	3 Years Rating	Risk Return Rating	5 Years % Chg	5 Years Rank	10 Years % Chg	10 Years Rank
		18.60	**Mean/Count**				**2.50**	**8**	**15.97**	**8**	**6.70**	**7.30**	**8**			**169.79**	**8**	**503.79**	**3**
	USD	69.27	Baring IUF Malaysia & Sing	B049	30/04/80	IRL	-1.55	8	19.41	5	6.77	4.29	5	✪✪		160.32	4	659.92	2
	USD	2.10	Dao Heng Malaysia & Singapore	D005	31/05/91	HK	7.91	1	20.11	3	5.80	22.16	1	✪✪✪✪	3	104.76	8	N.A.	
	GBP	0.19	Finistere Sing & Malay Life	F016	31/05/84	GU	1.55	5	2.25	8	6.44	-0.35	7	✪		125.47	7	173.56	3
	USD	25.20	GAM Singapore/Malaysia	G003	31/07/85	IOM	1.06	6	5.12	7	5.13	11.25	3	✪✪✪		220.47	2	677.90	1
●	USD	7.11	Hansard\Baring Malay & Sing	H012	27/09/91	IOM	2.88	4	15.51	6	7.10	8.73	4	✪✪✪		149.09	6	N.A.	
	USD	22.87	Indosuez Singapore & Malay	I007	30/01/87	HK	-0.78	7	23.30	1	6.08	21.37	2	✪✪✪✪	2	268.70	1	N.A.	
▲	USD	14.47	Mercury ST Singapore & Malay	M021	29/05/87	LUX	5.41	2	22.21	2	8.83	-12.05	8	✪		178.77	3	N.A.	
●	USD	7.60	Royal Life/Baring Malay&Sing	R022	30/10/87	IOM	3.48	3	19.86	4	7.42	3.01	6	✪✪		150.77	5	N.A.	

Mexico Equity

Funds investing in excess of 70% in Mexican equities or related instruments. Such funds may have an objective of capital and/or income growth, or to track a specified index or perform inversely to a given index. Funds in this category may leverage or gear by a maximum of 20% of total assets.

	CCY	Fund Size ($mil)	Fund Name	Manager Code	Fund Start Date	Domicile Code	3 Mths 97 % Chg	3 Mths 97 Rank	1 Year % Chg	1 Year Rank	Micropal Star Rating 3 Years Volatility	3 Years % Chg	3 Years Rank	3 Years Rating	Risk Return Rating	5 Years % Chg	5 Years Rank	10 Years % Chg	10 Years Rank
		15.27	**Mean/Count**				**6.17**	**3**	**24.36**	**3**	**11.89**	**-43.21**	**2**			**8.29**	**2**	**0**	**0**
▲	USD	16.38	Govett Mexican Horizons	G014	29/03/91	JER	6.89	1	28.04	2	11.38	-36.19	1	✪✪✪		25.34	1	N.A.	
	USD	0.46	Jupiter Tyndall SF Mexico	J011	10/02/95	BER	5.34	3	14.91	3	N.A.	N.A.				N.A.		N.A.	
▲	USD	28.98	Mexican Inv Co	F002	30/11/89	LUX	6.28	2	30.13	1	12.41	-50.23	2	✪✪		-8.76	2	N.A.	

▲ SIB Approved ● Insurance Fund **Values in US Dollars, on an offer to offer price basis with gross income reinvested**

Data Source Micropal™

Middle East Equity

Funds investing in excess of 70% in Middle Eastern equities or related instruments. Such funds may have an objective of capital and/or income growth, or to track a specified index or perform inversely to a given index. Funds in this category may leverage or gear by a maximum of 20% of total assets.

	CCY	Fund Size ($mil)	Fund Name	Manager Code	Fund Start Date	Domicile Code	3 Mths 97 % Chg	3 Mths 97 Rank	1 Year % Chg	1 Year Rank	Micropal Star Rating 3 Years Volatility	3 Years % Chg	3 Years Rank	3 Years Rating	Risk Return Rating	5 Years % Chg	5 Years Rank	10 Years % Chg	10 Years Rank
		5.20	**Mean/Count**				**18.23**	**1**	**41.52**	**1**	**0**	**0**	**0**			**0**	**0**	**0**	**0**
	USD	5.20	Alliance Middle East Opps A	A005	31/01/95	LUX	18.23	1	41.52	1	N.A.	N.A.				N.A.		N.A.	

New Zealand Equity

Funds investing in excess of 70% in New Zealand equities or related instruments. Such funds may have an objective of capital and/or income growth, or to track a specified index or perform inversely to a given index. Funds in this category may leverage or gear by a maximum of 20% of total assets.

	CCY	Fund Size ($mil)	Fund Name	Manager Code	Fund Start Date	Domicile Code	3 Mths 97 % Chg	3 Mths 97 Rank	1 Year % Chg	1 Year Rank	Micropal Star Rating 3 Years Volatility	3 Years % Chg	3 Years Rank	3 Years Rating	Risk Return Rating	5 Years % Chg	5 Years Rank	10 Years % Chg	10 Years Rank
		4.03	**Mean/Count**				**-4.12**	**2**	**27.57**	**2**	**5.06**	**28.37**	**1**		**1**	**168.56**	**1**	**0**	**0**
●	USD	0.15	Hansard\JF New Zealand	H019	08/07/94	IOM	-4.10	1	25.54	2	N.A.	N.A.				N.A.		N.A.	
	USD	7.91	JF New Zealand	J004	31/10/89	HK	-4.14	2	29.61	1	5.06	28.37	1	✪✪✪	3	168.56	1	N.A.	

North America Equity

Funds investing in excess of 70% in North American (Canada and the USA) equities or related instruments. Such funds may have an objective of capital and/or income growth, or to track a specified index or perform inversely to a given index. Funds in this category may leverage or gear by a maximum of 20% of total assets.

	CCY	Fund Size ($mil)	Fund Name	Manager Code	Fund Start Date	Domicile Code	3 Mths 97 % Chg	3 Mths 97 Rank	1 Year % Chg	1 Year Rank	Micropal Star Rating 3 Years Volatility	3 Years % Chg	3 Years Rank	3 Years Rating	Risk Return Rating	5 Years % Chg	5 Years Rank	10 Years % Chg	10 Years Rank
		35.60	**Mean/Count**				**1.27**	**105**	**19.90**	**102**	**3.23**	**49.76**	**80**		**1**	**87.16**	**66**	**222.55**	**23**
▲	USD	30.97	AAF North American Equity Fd	A001	30/06/94	LUX	0.56	70	20.36	49	N.A.	N.A.				N.A.		N.A.	
	USD	4.58	Abtrust North American Equity	A003	30/07/82	GU	6.69	6	24.19	25	3.02	52.84	37	✪✪✪	3	81.02	33	149.10	21
▲	USD	5.48	Aetna IUF American Equity A	A011	29/04/88	LUX	2.14	49	29.41	10	3.27	71.97	7	✪✪✪✪✪	4	80.52	34	N.A.	
	USD	N.S.	Albany Intl N Amer Enterprise	A018	28/02/95	IOM	-6.41	102	25.86	13	N.A.	N.A.				N.A.		N.A.	
●	USD	0	Albany Intl N American Dllr	A018	31/03/87	IOM	3.26	32	22.38	41	2.78	82.94	4	✪✪✪✪✪	5	155.58	3	N.A.	
●	GBP	0	Albany Intl N American Stlg	A018	31/03/87	IOM	3.07	35	25.69	14	2.91	55.67	30	✪✪✪	3	87.24	26	N.A.	
	USD	22.31	Alfred Berg Sicav-Nth America	A019	29/03/91	LUX	4.86	14	17.33	68	2.56	49.36	45	✪✪	4	65.22	52	N.A.	
●	USD	5.83	Allied Dunbar IB N American	A021	30/09/93	IOM	2.49	42	24.41	24	2.92	60.67	19	✪✪✪✪	4	N.A.		N.A.	
▲	USD	25.30	Allied Dunbar N American Gth	A020	31/05/84	IOM	3.16	33	24.54	22	3.17	61.60	17	✪✪✪✪	3	60.41	55	256.10	5
	USD	7.27	Alpha Short	A023a	30/03/90	BVI	1.73	52	-9.17	102	4.87	-30.05	80	✪		-43.90	66	N.A.	
	USD	12.69	Alpha Tilldale	A023a	31/07/90	BVI	-0.91	81	14.90	79	1.72	37.38	64	✪✪	4	65.62	50	N.A.	
	GBP	20.91	American Sentinel	I009	26/05/95	BAH	3.01	37	18.67	59	N.A.	N.A.				N.A.		N.A.	
●	USD	0.37	AXA Eqty&Law IFM N Amer Eqty	A039	29/11/85	IOM	-3.89	91	16.78	73	3.79	55.16	33	✪✪✪	2	71.60	42	173.53	16
●	USD	5.90	AXA Eqty&Law ILA N Amer Eqty	A040	31/10/85	IOM	-3.96	92	16.87	72	3.72	55.59	31	✪✪✪	2	86.20	27	200.38	13
▲	USD	50.16	Barclays (Lux) N American Eqty	B047	30/09/75	LUX	2.94	39	16.91	71	3.19	52.89	36	✪✪✪	3	122.35	10	218.53	8
	USD	47.73	Baring IUF North America	B049	29/01/82	IRL	4.75	18	25.66	15	3.53	49.58	44	✪✪	2	76.41	37	230.79	7
	USD	36	Bermuda Eqty North American	B066	30/11/90	BER	4.54	22	13	88	2.62	45.21	53	✪✪	2	54.69	60	N.A.	
	USD	68.90	BIL Equities USA C	B067	31/01/90	LUX	0.13	72	16.17	74	2.82	41.81	61	✪✪	2	43.81	64	N.A.	
●	USD	16.42	BL Equities Amer Du Nord B	B025	31/01/92	LUX	-0.08	76	15.82	75	3.51	44.43	56	✪✪	1	N.A.		N.A.	
●	USD	26.76	Carlson North America	C011	28/09/90	LUX	-0.74	79	23.96	28	3	56.41	25	✪✪✪	3	71.56	43	N.A.	
▲	USD	78.72	Citi PF N.America Equity	C036	30/09/88	LUX	1.21	62	12.79	90	3	46.47	48	✪✪	2	60.77	54	N.A.	
●	USD	71.67	Clariden North American	C039	31/01/86	CA	1.71	53	24.84	20	3.38	39.67	62	✪	1	57.48	56	160.91	18
▲	USD	49.70	Coutts GF North American Eqty	C052	31/05/93	IRL	3.90	28	12.48	92	3.21	31.21	71	✪	1	N.A.		N.A.	
●	USD	26.23	Credis Equity North America A	C056	28/06/91	LUX	5.37	11	18.75	58	3.16	45.42	52	✪✪	2	76.12	38	N.A.	

▲ SIB Approved **● Insurance Fund** **Values in US Dollars, on an offer to offer price basis with gross income reinvested** Data Source Micropal™

North America Equity

continued

	CCY	Fund Size ($mil)	Fund Name	Manager Code	Fund Start Date	Domicile Code	3 Mths 97 % Chg	3 Mths 97 Rank	1 Year % Chg	1 Year Rank	Micropal Star Rating: Volatility	3 Years % Chg	3 Years Rank	Rating	Risk Return Rating	5 Years % Chg	5 Years Rank	10 Years % Chg	10 Years Rank
		35.60	**Mean/Count**				**1.27**	**105**	**19.90**	**102**	**3.23**	**49.76**	**80**		**1**	**87.16**	**66**	**222.55**	**23**
▲	USD	25.02	CU PP American Growth	C070	31/05/90	LUX	3.13	34	22.81	37	2.91	59.91	20	✪✪✪✪	4	85	29	N.A.	
	USD	0.84	Eagle Star N American Eq	E001	29/09/95	IOM	-5.44	96	21.74	45	N.A.	N.A.				N.A.		N.A.	
	USD	4	Europa American Equity	E013	29/12/89	CA	-0.07	75	32.86	6	3.41	72.33	6	✪✪✪✪	4	76.96	36	N.A.	
▲	USD	124.80	F&C PF Amer Sm Cos Equity	F001	31/07/81	LUX	0.08	73	18.92	56	2.78	62.06	16	✪✪✪✪	4	153.07	5	391.16	2
	USD	1.10	Fidelity Frontier	F012	31/08/83	LUX	-0.04	74	15.39	77	4.52	30.37	72	✪	1	52.12	62	188.96	14
	USD	7.43	Five Arrows IE America	R014	30/09/93	GU	2.46	43	18.21	62	2.86	45.45	51	✪✪	2	N.A.		N.A.	
	USD	63.85	Five Arrows IP North America	R016	30/12/94	GU	1.37	58	22.16	43	N.A.	N.A.				N.A.		N.A.	
	GBP	1.03	Friends Provdnt North American	F031	31/05/94	GU	4.36	23	24.44	23	N.A.	N.A.				N.A.		N.A.	
	USD	30	GAM GAMCO	G003	30/10/87	IOM	5.06	13	20.36	50	2.66	42.42	59	✪✪	2	119.59	13	N.A.	
	DEM	11.64	GAM Multi-US DEM	G003	29/12/95	IOM	2.45	44	8.82	97	N.A.	N.A.				N.A.		N.A.	
	USD	33.80	GAM Multi-US USD	G003	29/12/95	IOM	2.16	48	13.57	85	N.A.	N.A.				N.A.		N.A.	
▲	USD	40.14	Gartmore CSF North America	G007	31/05/84	JER	0.76	67	24.96	18	3.23	56.05	26	✪✪✪✪	3	87.55	24	158.29	20
▲	USD	12.32	Gartmore CSF US Sm Cos	G007	13/10/95	JER	-7.74	104	47.75	1	N.A.	N.A.				N.A.		N.A.	
▲●	USD	34.58	Groupe Indosuez N.America	G017	31/12/90	LUX	0.50	71	23.31	32	3.32	50	43	✪✪	2	70.34	44	N.A.	
▲	USD	42	GT North America A	G018	30/09/75	IRL	2.96	38	15.67	76	2.88	52.68	38	✪✪	3	104.66	17	211.46	11
▲	USD	7.63	Guinness Flight Amer Sm Cos	G019	31/01/85	GU	-3.75	90	14.38	81	4.36	55.74	29	✪✪✪	1	84.42	30	169.59	17
▲	USD	4.63	Hambros Eqty Sel N.Amer Gth	H003	29/09/89	GU	-5.53	97	18.27	61	4.35	63.11	14	✪✪✪✪	2	91.28	20	N.A.	
▲	USD	5.25	HCIC North American	H026	30/12/94	IOM	3.74	30	23.12	35	N.A.	N.A.				N.A.		N.A.	
▲	USD	40.38	Henderson HF American Sm Cos	H025	31/08/93	LUX	-4.68	95	25.97	12	4.25	78.42	5	✪✪✪✪✪	3	N.A.		N.A.	
	USD	8.27	Hermes North America	H028	30/04/92	BER	1.39	57	13.83	84	2.14	38.54	63	✪	3	N.A.		N.A.	
▲	GBP	8.83	Hill Samuel OS North American	H030	31/08/90	JER	-0.77	80	20.29	51	2.77	50.79	41	✪✪✪	4	72.53	41	N.A.	
▲	USD	7.02	HSBC GIF N American Equity	H033	30/01/87	LUX	1.43	56	17.69	64	2.73	31.61	70	✪	1	55.19	58	N.A.	
	DEM	10.70	HYPO America	H024	30/11/92	LUX	4.25	25	12.34	94	3.14	36.25	65	✪	1	N.A.		N.A.	
▲	USD	28.56	Inter Strategie Amer du Nord	B069	30/11/89	LUX	2.50	40	23.84	30	2.93	63.13	13	✪✪✪✪	4	108.11	15	N.A.	
	GBP	14.89	INVESCO Amer Eqty Income	I013	20/11/81	JER	3.94	27	21.44	47	2.42	55.18	32	✪✪✪	4	76.06	39	206.59	12
▲	USD	8.70	INVESCO PS Amer Enterprise	I014	31/12/90	LUX	-6.24	100	17.37	67	4.67	35.26	67	✪✪	1	75.83	40	N.A.	
▲	USD	16.30	INVESCO PS American Gth	I014	31/12/90	LUX	0.73	68	15.36	78	2.80	34.97	68	✪	1	56.74	57	N.A.	
●	USD	1.40	JRIA North American	J002	29/01/93	IRL	1.20	63	12.76	91	2.60	29.45	74	✪	1	N.A.		N.A.	
●	USD	3.50	JRIA/North America Dllr	J002	30/12/94	IRL	1.22	61	12.83	89	N.A.	N.A.				N.A.		N.A.	
▲	USD	6.01	Jupiter Tyndall WUF Nth Amer	J008	31/01/84	BER	-3.15	88	9.58	95	3.23	3.74	79	✪		20.47	65	143.25	22
	USD	26.82	KB Lux Equity Amercan	K011	31/05/93	LUX	4.09	26	18.62	60	2.96	22.62	77	✪	1	N.A.		N.A.	
▲	USD	35.68	KB North American	K007	30/11/89	GU	0.97	65	23.14	34	2.80	62.26	15	✪✪✪✪✪	4	90.64	22	N.A.	
▲	USD	N.S.	Lazard North American	L002	30/06/83	GU	3.88	29	17.07	70	3.03	67.25	11	✪✪✪✪	4	79.21	35	179.50	15
	USD	23.70	Lion Interaction Amerique	C062	31/03/89	LUX	5.67	9	22.53	40	3.13	60.97	18	✪✪✪✪	4	123.33	9	N.A.	
▲	USD	61.98	Lloyds IP North American Eq	L016	31/03/92	LUX	2.44	45	4.50	99	2.74	26.29	76	✪	1	N.A.		N.A.	
▲	USD	29.77	Lloyds IP Small Cos	L016	30/11/90	LUX	-2.33	87	24.80	21	4.29	31.93	69	✪	1	66.94	47	N.A.	
▲	USD	10	Manulife Regent GF Amer Gth	M006	30/09/87	LUX	1.80	51	30.26	8	3.25	87.48	2	✪✪✪✪✪	5	154.24	4	N.A.	
	GBP	404.12	Mercury IIT N. America	M018	31/07/74	JER	4.66	20	25.21	16	2.91	69.62	9	✪✪✪✪✪	4	106.54	16	287.48	4
▲	GBP	17.59	Mercury OST North American	M020	28/11/86	LUX	1.49	55	25.97	11	2.92	55.79	28	✪✪✪	3	88.01	23	214.85	9
▲	USD	58.18	Mercury ST N American Opps	M021	29/05/87	LUX	-7.45	103	23.06	36	3.90	59.20	21	✪✪✪✪	2	120.62	12	N.A.	
▲	USD	127.87	Mercury ST North American	M021	31/12/85	LUX	1.94	50	24.16	27	2.76	86.17	3	✪✪✪✪✪	5	132.42	7	315.61	3
▲	USD	7.74	Midland ICF American Opps	M028	29/03/91	LUX	5.77	8	23.55	31	2.66	54.34	34	✪✪✪	4	82.53	31	N.A.	
▲	GBP	12.21	Midland ICF N American Growth	M028	28/02/90	LUX	2.37	46	17.26	69	2.80	42.82	58	✪✪	2	61.76	53	N.A.	
▲	GBP	154.10	Morgan Grenfell PF N.American	M038	29/12/89	IRL	4.83	15	19.12	55	2.66	58.27	22	✪✪✪✪	4	90.71	21	N.A.	
	USD	11.87	MOSAIS Actions Nord Americ	C058	30/03/90	LUX	1.54	54	13.38	86	2.79	30.27	73	✪	1	54.70	59	N.A.	
	USD	154.95	N American Capital Corp NV	E016	31/01/84	NL	1.21	82	34.56	5	2.89	71.50	8	✪✪✪✪	5	85.87	28	213.26	10
	USD	11.88	New York Small Cap Fund	S047	14/04/95	LUX	-3.23	89	9.01	96	N.A.	N.A.				N.A.		N.A.	
	USD	13.49	New York Value Fund	S047	14/04/95	LUX	4.35	24	25.09	17	N.A.	N.A.				N.A.		N.A.	
▲	USD	30.70	Newton UGF N American	N006	29/02/88	JER	1.25	60	22.80	38	3.47	52.13	39	✪✪✪	2	52.67	61	N.A.	
	USD	0.13	Old Mutual Gnsy N Amer Stkmkt	O003	29/12/95	GU	9.66	2	37.70	3	N.A.	N.A.				N.A.		N.A.	
	USD	2.08	Olympia Amerique	O008	31/03/95	LUX	-4.58	94	4.89	98	N.A.	N.A.				N.A.		N.A.	
	USD	5.41	OMI (Gnsy) N.American Stkmkt	O005	31/05/82	GU	9.33	3	32.67	7	3.96	45.14	54	✪✪	1	113.41	14	138.58	23
●	USD	9.10	Orbitex Growth	O014	31/12/86	BAH	-9.10	105	0.50	100	5.51	11.03	78	✪		66.43	48	160.24	19
	USD	179	Orion Fund Ltd	O015	31/07/90	BER	4.61	21	12.48	93	2.13	57.37	23	✪✪✪	5	140.14	6	N.A.	
	USD	N.S.	PCP North America	P007	15/03/96	CA	5.38	10	N.A.		N.A.	N.A.				N.A.		N.A.	
	USD	232	Perpetual Offshr American Gth	P011	30/04/84	JER	-2.02	85	21.53	46	3.17	53.19	35	✪✪✪	3	122.28	11	513.73	1
	USD	5.20	Pleiade Nth America Equities	B039	26/02/93	LUX	1.36	59	13.03	87	2.56	46.09	49	✪✪	3	N.A.		N.A.	

▲ SIB Approved ● Insurance Fund **Values in US Dollars, on an offer to offer price basis with gross income reinvested** Data Source Micropal™

North America Equity

continued

	CCY	Fund Size ($mil)	Fund Name	Manager Code	Fund Start Date	Domicile Code	3 Mths 97 % Chg	3 Mths 97 Rank	1 Year % Chg	1 Year Rank	Micropal Star Rating 3 Years Volatility	3 Years % Chg	3 Years Rank	3 Years Rating	Risk Return Rating	5 Years % Chg	5 Years Rank	10 Years % Chg	10 Years Rank
		35.60	**Mean/Count**				**1.27**	**105**	**19.90**	**102**	**3.23**	**49.76**	**80**		**1**	**87.16**	**66**	**222.55**	**23**
	USD	13.48	Portefeuille BG Act Am du Nord	B063	23/06/95	LUX	0.59	69	24.17	26	N.A.	N.A.				N.A.		N.A.	
	USD	0.06	ProntoFund US & CAD Eq B	B006	09/02/96	LUX	-2.04	86	N.A.		N.A.	N.A.				N.A.		N.A.	
	USD	2.71	Proton IF North American Eqs	P024	29/09/95	BVI	2.31	47	23.90	29	N.A.	N.A.				N.A.		N.A.	
	USD	4.55	Quilter Quad N American Eq	Q003	13/01/95	IOM	4.78	16	17.40	66	N.A.	N.A.				N.A.		N.A.	
▲	NLG	75.06	RG America Fund	R009	31/05/91	EN	10.73	1	30.08	9	3.64	49.08	46	✪✪	2	95.85	18	N.A.	
●	USD	1.90	RLI/Fidelity American Assets	R023	31/08/90	IOM	8.33	4	14.01	83	2.66	45.73	50	✪✪	3	66.12	49	N.A.	
	USD	13.42	S-E-Banken Fund Nordamerika	S001	29/10/93	LUX	4.67	19	22.74	39	3.16	50.76	42	✪✪✪	3	N.A.		N.A.	
	USD	9.52	Samba Lux North America Equity	S006	31/01/95	LUX	-5.63	99	36.56	4	N.A.	N.A.				N.A.		N.A.	
	USD	15.03	Schroder Asia North American	S011	30/10/87	HK	3.42	31	19.71	53	3.56	26.63	75	✪	1	65.36	51	N.A.	
	USD	65.16	Scontinvest Nth American Eq	S012	28/02/92	LUX	3.06	36	41.05	2	3.36	91.22	1	✪✪✪✪✪	5	N.A.		N.A.	
	USD	19.20	Scot Prov GP N American Eqty	S014	30/09/91	IOM	6.15	7	20.69	48	3.27	46.65	47	✪✪	2	128.46	8	N.A.	
	USD	1.10	Scot Prov ILA American Opps	S014	29/12/95	IOM	7.53	5	14.20	82	N.A.	N.A.				N.A.		N.A.	
▲	GBP	66.65	Singer & Fried American Gth	S027	31/03/94	IRL	4.76	17	17.61	65	N.A.	N.A.				N.A.		N.A.	
▲	USD	131.63	Skandifond N.American Eq	S030	28/02/89	LUX	5.32	12	22.33	42	3.26	51.17	40	✪✪	2	87.37	25	N.A.	
	USD	11.79	Sogelux Fd Equities N.America	S037	31/05/88	LUX	-1.76	84	18.83	57	3.04	35.41	66	✪	1	69.26	45	N.A.	
	USD	17.65	Sun Life American Gth	S053	31/08/95	IOM	2.49	41	24.87	19	N.A.	N.A.				N.A.		N.A.	
▲	USD	35.75	Swiss Life Proteus American	S056	29/11/91	IRL	-5.59	98	19.45	54	4.33	66.27	12	✪✪✪✪	2	188.38	2	N.A.	
▲	USD	133.41	TGA North Am Eq	T009	28/02/89	LUX	1	64	21.90	44	3.08	57.13	24	✪✪✪✪	3	92.03	19	N.A.	
▲	USD	45.73	TGA North American Sm Cos	T009	19/07/96	LUX	-6.26	101	N.A.		N.A.	N.A.				N.A.		N.A.	
▲	GBP	34.68	TSB OIF Pan American	T013	30/04/90	JER	-1.37	83	23.18	33	3.60	55.83	27	✪✪✪	2	265.05	1	N.A.	
	USD	18.16	UAP North American Securities	U009	31/03/88	LUX	-0.35	77	17.98	63	3.24	42.97	57	✪	1	81.25	32	N.A.	
▲	USD	18.14	Von Ernst GP N American Eqty	B021	30/11/89	LUX	-0.59	78	19.84	52	2.82	42.35	60	✪	2	50.25	63	N.A.	
	USD	13.22	Willerequity North America	W004	31/07/92	LUX	0.88	66	14.54	80	2.74	69.04	10	✪✪✪✪	5	N.A.		N.A.	
	USD	39.10	Winchester Frontier Ltd	O008	31/05/85	BER	-4.44	93	-5.15	101	6.33	44.87	55	✪✪	1	67.79	46	236.70	6

Pakistan Equity

Funds investing in excess of 70% in Pakistan equities or related instruments. Such funds may have an objective of capital and/or income growth, or to track a specified index or perform inversely to a given index. Funds in this category may leverage or gear by a maximum of 20% of total assets.

	CCY	Fund Size ($mil)	Fund Name	Manager Code	Fund Start Date	Domicile Code	3 Mths 97 % Chg	3 Mths 97 Rank	1 Year % Chg	1 Year Rank	Micropal Star Rating 3 Years Volatility	3 Years % Chg	3 Years Rank	3 Years Rating	Risk Return Rating	5 Years % Chg	5 Years Rank	10 Years % Chg	10 Years Rank
		2.74	**Mean/Count**				**19.16**	**4**	**-24.46**	**4**	**7.65**	**-55.55**	**2**			**-50.28**	**1**	**0**	**0**
▲	USD	4.20	CL Pakistan Growth	C063	29/11/91	CA	17.58	3	-16.89	2	7.24	-57.27	2	✪✪		-50.28	1	N.A.	
	USD	0.26	Hansard\CL Pakistan Growth	H013	31/07/92	IOM	15.40	4	-13.03	1	8.05	-53.84	1	✪✪✪		N.A.		N.A.	
	USD	5.82	JF Pakistan Trust	J004	31/01/94	CA	21.59	2	-20.25	3	N.A.	N.A.				N.A.		N.A.	
	USD	0.67	Thornton New Tiger Pakistan	T007	02/09/94	BER	22.10	1	-47.67	4	N.A.	N.A.				N.A.		N.A.	

▲ SIB Approved ● Insurance Fund Values in US Dollars, on an offer to offer price basis with gross income reinvested Data Source Micropal™

Peru Equity

Funds investing in excess of 70% in Peruvian equities or related instruments. Such funds may have an objective of capital and/or income growth, or to track a specified index or perform inversely to a given index. Funds in this category may leverage or gear by a maximum of 20% of total assets.

	CCY	Fund Size ($mil)	Fund Name	Manager Code	Fund Start Date	Domicile Code	3 Mths 97 % Chg	3 Mths 97 Rank	1 Year % Chg	1 Year Rank	Micropal Star Rating 3 Years Volatility	3 Years % Chg	3 Years Rank	Rating	Risk Return Rating	5 Years % Chg	5 Years Rank	10 Years % Chg	10 Years Rank
		27.35	**Mean/Count**				**16.51**	**1**	**2.39**	**1**	**7.44**	**20.68**	**1**		**3**	**0**	**0**	**0**	**0**
	USD	27.35	Peruvian Inv Co	F002	30/04/93	LUX	16.51	1	2.39	1	7.44	20.68	1	✪✪✪	3	N.A.		N.A.	

Philippines Equity

Funds investing in excess of 70% in Philippine equities or related instruments. Such funds may have an objective of capital and/or income growth, or to track a specified index or perform inversely to a given index. Funds in this category may leverage or gear by a maximum of 20% of total assets.

	CCY	Fund Size ($mil)	Fund Name	Manager Code	Fund Start Date	Domicile Code	3 Mths 97 % Chg	3 Mths 97 Rank	1 Year % Chg	1 Year Rank	Micropal Star Rating 3 Years Volatility	3 Years % Chg	3 Years Rank	Rating	Risk Return Rating	5 Years % Chg	5 Years Rank	10 Years % Chg	10 Years Rank
		22	**Mean/Count**				**2.44**	**8**	**18.03**	**6**	**7.86**	**-13.02**	**4**			**228.89**	**3**	**526.60**	**2**
	USD	6.47	Barclays ASF Philippines	B044	31/10/90	JER	1.95	6	16.22	4	7.42	-17.34	4	✪		160.90	3	N.A.	
●	USD	0.44	Hansard\JF Philippine	H019	08/07/94	IOM	4.73	2	24.72	2	N.A.	N.A.				N.A.		N.A.	
	USD	127.30	JF Philippine	J004	31/07/74	HK	3.31	4	23.44	3	7.17	-14.78	3	✪✪		208.03	2	729.17	1
▲	USD	0.97	Jupiter Tyndall GF Ph'ppines	J010	11/11/94	LUX	3.26	5	10.84	5	N.A.	N.A.				N.A.		N.A.	
▲	USD	0.08	Nikko GIUF Philippines Fund	N007	26/02/93	LUX	-1.50	7	7.29	6	8.56	-10.19	2	✪✪✪		N.A.		N.A.	
	USD	0.20	RLI/Thornton New Tiger Phil	R037	12/07/96	IOM	5.24	1	N.A.		N.A.	N.A.				N.A.		N.A.	
	USD	18.57	Thornton New Tiger Philippine	T007	30/06/86	BER	4.11	3	25.67	1	8.30	-9.77	1	✪✪✪		317.74	1	324.04	2

Scandinavia Equity

Funds investing in excess of 70% in Scandinavian (Denmark, Sweden, Finland, Norway) equities or related instruments. Such funds may have an objective of capital and/or income growth, or to track a specified index or perform inversely to a given index. Funds in this category may leverage or gear by a maximum of 20% of total assets.

	CCY	Fund Size ($mil)	Fund Name	Manager Code	Fund Start Date	Domicile Code	3 Mths 97 % Chg	3 Mths 97 Rank	1 Year % Chg	1 Year Rank	Micropal Star Rating 3 Years Volatility	3 Years % Chg	3 Years Rank	Rating	Risk Return Rating	5 Years % Chg	5 Years Rank	10 Years % Chg	10 Years Rank
		21.64	**Mean/Count**				**4.72**	**19**	**31.20**	**16**	**4.66**	**84.57**	**13**		**1**	**127.62**	**11**	**160.24**	**1**
	USD	43.45	Alfred Berg Norden Sicav	A019	31/08/87	LUX	4.50	10	31.28	8	4.63	94.30	4	✪✪✪✪	3	146.38	3	N.A.	
	SEK	9.09	Aragon Sv-Nordic Eq Select	A028	31/01/90	LUX	13.16	1	25.13	16	5.70	66.49	11	✪✪	1	130.77	5	N.A.	
	SEK	N.S.	BSS Universal Nordic Equities	B029	01/03/96	LUX	4.07	13	N.A.		N.A.	N.A.				N.A.		N.A.	
●	USD	6.46	Carlson Nordic	C011	28/09/90	LUX	6.54	2	37.39	2	4	83.60	7	✪✪✪	4	146.35	4	N.A.	
	USD	N.S.	Carnegie Nordic Markets	C012	05/04/96	LUX	3.49	15	N.A.		N.A.	N.A.				N.A.		N.A.	
▲	SEK	6.10	CMI GNF Nordic Equity	C042	30/04/90	LUX	5.96	5	27.21	13	5.09	63.16	12	✪	1	82.13	10	N.A.	
●	GBP	3.72	CMI Ins Co Nordic Equity	C043	31/01/91	IOM	3.95	14	26.31	14	5.02	54.87	13	✪	1	54.22	11	N.A.	
●	SEK	0.04	CMI Passport Nordic Equity	C044	20/01/95	IOM	4.83	7	25.32	15	N.A.	N.A.				N.A.		N.A.	
	ECU	7.66	Danske Nordic Eq Mngd	D003	31/12/90	LUX	3	16	32.18	6	3.85	67.38	9	✪	2	90.60	9	N.A.	
	ECU	6.50	Danske NSS Nordic Equities	D003	23/06/95	LUX	4.63	9	32.67	5	N.A.	N.A.				N.A.		N.A.	
▲	NOK	20.49	DNB Investment Nordic Eq C	D013	29/10/93	LUX	4.48	11	30.49	11	4.35	67.29	10	✪✪	2	N.A.		N.A.	
▲	SEK	133.76	Fidelity Fds Nordic	F011	28/09/90	LUX	6.21	3	38.61	1	4.88	129.30	1	✪✪✪✪	5	252	1	N.A.	
●	ECU	57.24	Frontrunner Scandinavian Eqs	F032	29/05/92	LUX	1.71	18	30.58	10	3.49	73.66	8	✪✪	4	N.A.		N.A.	
●	SEK	8.26	Hansard\Fidelity Nordic	H014	27/09/91	IOM	6.01	4	36.23	3	4.92	121.42	2	✪✪✪✪✪	4	204.55	2	N.A.	
	SEK	25.65	MultiLink Scandi Eq	I011	31/12/90	LUX	5.18	6	28.10	12	4.82	91.88	5	✪✪✪✪	3	98.80	7	N.A.	
	SEK	9.58	Parvest Scandinavia B	B037	04/10/96	LUX	4.82	8	N.A.		N.A.	N.A.				N.A.		N.A.	
▲	USD	15.70	Skandifond Nordic Equity	S030	28/02/89	LUX	4.46	12	31.22	9	4.77	86.47	6	✪✪✪	2	99.87	6	N.A.	
▲	SEK	12.55	SSF Nordic	S055	30/06/94	LUX	2.01	17	31.62	7	N.A.	N.A.				N.A.		N.A.	
▲	GBP	1.59	Unibank Scandinavian	U005	30/08/85	IOM	0.77	19	34.92	4	5.01	99.54	3	✪✪✪	3	98.19	8	160.24	1

▲ SIB Approved ● Insurance Fund **Values in US Dollars, on an offer to offer price basis with gross income reinvested** Data Source Micropal™

Singapore (CPF Basic) Equity

Funds investing in excess of 70% in Singapore equities or related instruments. Such funds may have an objective of capital and/or income growth, or to track a specified index or perform inversely to a given index. Funds in this category may leverage or gear by a maximum of 20% of total assets.

	CCY	Fund Size ($mil)	Fund Name	Manager Code	Fund Start Date	Domicile Code	3 Mths 97 % Chg	3 Mths 97 Rank	1 Year % Chg	1 Year Rank	Micropal Star Rating 3 Years Volatility	3 Years % Chg	3 Years Rank	3 Years Rating	Risk Return Rating	5 Years % Chg	5 Years Rank	10 Years % Chg	10 Years Rank
		21.25	**Mean/Count**				**-2.82**	**8**	**4.43**	**8**	**6.44**	**1.70**	**8**			**98.63**	**5**	**0**	**0**
	USD	6.08	Barclays ASF Singapore	B044	31/10/90	JER	-4.79	6	8.12	2	6.20	19.87	1	✪✪✪✪	3	90.96	3	N.A.	
▲	USD	20.76	Dres Thornton ASF Singapore	D015	31/05/93	IRL	-2.96	4	7.91	3	5.32	-3.27	6	✪		N.A.		N.A.	
▲	USD	47.80	Fidelity Fds Singapore	F011	28/09/90	LUX	-8.46	7	3.24	5	6.27	2.29	4	✪✪✪		112.98	2	N.A.	
●	USD	0.70	Hansard\Fidelity Singapore	H014	27/09/91	IOM	-3.57	5	2.93	6	6.64	6.73	3	✪✪✪		69.15	5	N.A.	
▲	USD	10.41	HSBC GIF Singaporean Equity	H033	30/01/87	LUX	-2.18	3	0.37	7	6.16	-1.11	5	✪✪		76.89	4	N.A.	
▲	USD	3.59	Nikko GIUF Singapore Fund	N007	26/02/93	LUX	-11.17	8	6.36	4	6.85	10.95	2	✪✪✪✪		N.A.		N.A.	
	USD	69.21	Singapore Sesdaq Ltd	G014	31/10/89	JER	12.19	1	-3.89	8	7.91	-17.77	8	✪✪		143.17	1	N.A.	
	USD	11.42	Thornton New Tiger Singapore	T007	31/07/92	BER	-1.58	2	10.38	1	6.19	-4.11	7	✪		N.A.		N.A.	

Spain Equity

Funds investing in excess of 70% in Spanish equities or related instruments. Such funds may have an objective of capital and/or income growth, or to track a specified index or perform inversely to a given index. Funds in this category may leverage or gear by a maximum of 20% of total assets.

	CCY	Fund Size ($mil)	Fund Name	Manager Code	Fund Start Date	Domicile Code	3 Mths 97 % Chg	3 Mths 97 Rank	1 Year % Chg	1 Year Rank	Micropal Star Rating 3 Years Volatility	3 Years % Chg	3 Years Rank	3 Years Rating	Risk Return Rating	5 Years % Chg	5 Years Rank	10 Years % Chg	10 Years Rank
		7.38	**Mean/Count**				**-1.90**	**11**	**29.82**	**8**	**4.22**	**51.02**	**8**		**2**	**27.90**	**6**	**0**	**0**
	ESP	0.57	Aetna MF Spanish Natl Eqty	A012	31/05/90	LUX	-1.68	5	18.56	8	3.19	34.06	7	✪	2	5.25	6	N.A.	
	ESP	10.56	Caixa Funds Spanish Shares	C004	30/10/92	LUX	-5.04	11	32.62	4	4.15	61	4	✪✪✪	4	N.A.		N.A.	
	ESP	2.03	Callander Fund Spanish	C005	31/10/88	LUX	-3.24	8	21.39	7	3.99	25.91	8	✪	1	10.16	4	N.A.	
▲	ESP	19.25	CU PP Spanish Growth	C070	31/05/90	LUX	-2.14	6	34.46	2	4.34	47.71	5	✪✪	2	31.47	3	N.A.	
	ESP	1.73	EMIF Spain Index Plus B	C015	31/07/91	LUX	-4.71	10	29.08	6	4.56	64.07	2	✪✪✪✪	3	52.79	2	N.A.	
	ESP	10.26	G-Equity Fund G-Spanish Eq B	G009	31/03/93	LUX	-3.32	9	33.53	3	4.43	61.42	3	✪✪✪	3	N.A.		N.A.	
▲●	ESP	3.99	Groupe Indosuez Spain	G017	22/03/96	LUX	-1.21	3	N.A.		N.A.	N.A.				N.A.		N.A.	
	ESP	3.90	Sogelux Fd Equities Spain	S037	21/06/96	LUX	-1.42	4	N.A.		N.A.	N.A.				N.A.		N.A.	
	USD	21.10	Spanish Smaller Companies	A005	31/10/91	LUX	4.28	1	29.41	5	4.47	44.01	6	✪✪	1	5.43	5	N.A.	
	DEM	0.36	Thornton Dres ES Spain	T008	31/05/90	BER	0.77	2	39.50	1	4.60	69.96	1	✪✪✪✪	4	62.33	1	N.A.	

Sri Lanka Equity

Funds investing in excess of 70% in Sri Lankan equities or related instruments. Such funds may have an objective of capital and/or income growth, or to track a specified index or perform inversely to a given index. Funds in this category may leverage or gear by a maximum of 20% of total assets.

	CCY	Fund Size ($mil)	Fund Name	Manager Code	Fund Start Date	Domicile Code	3 Mths 97 % Chg	3 Mths 97 Rank	1 Year % Chg	1 Year Rank	Micropal Star Rating 3 Years Volatility	3 Years % Chg	3 Years Rank	3 Years Rating	Risk Return Rating	5 Years % Chg	5 Years Rank	10 Years % Chg	10 Years Rank
		11.98	**Mean/Count**				**4.77**	**3**	**-20.52**	**3**	**8**	**-54.88**	**1**			**0**	**0**	**0**	**0**
	USD	9.57	Regent Sri Lanka	R005	30/11/93	CA	6.77	2	-17.63	2	8	-54.88	1	✪✪✪		N.A.		N.A.	
	USD	25.76	Sri Lanka Growth	C011	28/02/94	CA	6.86	1	-13.08	1	N.A.	N.A.				N.A.		N.A.	
	USD	0.60	Thornton New Tiger Sri Lanka	T007	31/05/94	BER	0.67	3	-30.86	3	N.A.	N.A.				N.A.		N.A.	

▲ SIB Approved ● Insurance Fund **Values in US Dollars, on an offer to offer price basis with gross income reinvested** Data Source Micropal™

Sweden Equity

Funds investing in excess of 70% in Swedish equities or related instruments. Such funds may have an objective of capital and/or income growth, or to track a specified index or perform inversely to a given index. Funds in this category may leverage or gear by a maximum of 20% of total assets.

	CCY	Fund Size ($mil)	Fund Name	Manager Code	Fund Start Date	Domicile Code	3 Mths 97 % Chg	3 Mths 97 Rank	1 Year % Chg	1 Year Rank	Micropal Star Rating 3 Years Volatility	3 Years % Chg	3 Years Rank	Rating	Risk Return Rating	5 Years % Chg	5 Years Rank	10 Years % Chg	10 Years Rank
		48.45	**Mean/Count**				**0.54**	**4**	**33.06**	**4**	**5.60**	**110.94**	**3**		**2**	**126.57**	**1**	**0**	**0**
	SEK	15.30	Aragon Sv Swedish Eq	A028	30/09/93	LUX	-0.78	3	27.01	4	6.03	97.39	3	✪✪	2	N.A.		N.A.	
●	SEK	9.22	Carlson Sweden	C011	28/09/90	LUX	1.11	2	35.83	2	5.32	125.72	1	✪✪✪✪	4	126.57	1	N.A.	
	SEK	142.38	S-E-Banken Fund Sverige	S001	29/10/93	LUX	4.68	1	33.52	3	5.44	109.71	2	✪✪✪	3	N.A.		N.A.	
▲	SEK	26.88	SSF Swedish Shares	S055	07/07/95	LUX	-2.84	4	35.87	1	N.A.	N.A.				N.A.		N.A.	

Switzerland Equity

Funds investing in excess of 70% in Swiss equities or related instruments. Such funds may have an objective of capital and/or income growth, or to track a specified index or perform inversely to a given index. Funds in this category may leverage or gear by a maximum of 20% of total assets.

	CCY	Fund Size ($mil)	Fund Name	Manager Code	Fund Start Date	Domicile Code	3 Mths 97 % Chg	3 Mths 97 Rank	1 Year % Chg	1 Year Rank	Micropal Star Rating 3 Years Volatility	3 Years % Chg	3 Years Rank	Rating	Risk Return Rating	5 Years % Chg	5 Years Rank	10 Years % Chg	10 Years Rank
		21.39	**Mean/Count**				**7.23**	**23**	**-0.23**	**19**	**3.47**	**26.49**	**10**		**1**	**92.03**	**8**	**0**	**0**
▲	CHF	13.36	AAF Switzerland Equity Fund	A001	16/06/95	LUX	6.81	13	-0.32	8	N.A.	N.A.				N.A.		N.A.	
	CHF	4.50	Alfred Berg Sicav-Switzerland	A019	29/12/89	LUX	6.20	16	0.08	7	3.47	35.11	3	✪✪✪✪	4	97.50	3	N.A.	
	CHF	58.57	Baer Multistock Sp Swiss Sk A	J007	30/04/92	LUX	7.03	11	-3.06	14	2.97	12.19	10	✪		N.A.		N.A.	
	CHF	125.94	Baer Multistock Swiss Stock A	J007	29/11/91	LUX	6.87	12	-0.40	9	3.49	36.79	2	✪✪✪✪✪	4	118.41	2	N.A.	
	CHF	5.49	Callander Fund Swiss Growth	C005	30/03/90	LUX	9.14	6	-9.91	19	3.44	21.76	8	✪✪	1	40.56	8	N.A.	
▲	CHF	9.02	CMI GNF Swiss Equity	C042	30/04/90	LUX	7.71	10	-2.54	12	3.51	22.34	7	✪✪	2	94.15	4	N.A.	
●	GBP	5.41	CMI Ins Co Swiss Equity	C043	30/11/90	IOM	4.30	20	-3.31	15	3.58	17.37	9	✪	1	77.62	7	N.A.	
●	CHF	0.15	CMI Passport Swiss Equity	C044	20/01/95	IOM	6.21	15	-3.78	17	N.A.	N.A.				N.A.		N.A.	
	CHF	N.S.	Coutts GF Swiss Equity	C052	13/12/96	IRL	9.22	5	N.A.		N.A.	N.A.				N.A.		N.A.	
	CHF	4.40	EMIF Switzerland Index Plus B	C015	31/01/94	LUX	10.43	4	-0.67	10	N.A.	N.A.				N.A.		N.A.	
▲	CHF	16.75	Fidelity Fds Switzerland	F011	10/02/95	LUX	8.31	9	8.91	2	N.A.	N.A.				N.A.		N.A.	
	CHF	N.S.	Fiduciary Swiss Equity	F014	03/01/97	IRL	N.A.		N.A.		N.A.	N.A.				N.A.		N.A.	
	CHF	55.80	FL Trust Switzerland	B031	31/07/90	LUX	13.05	1	-2.33	11	3.59	26.63	5	✪✪✪	3	92.86	5	N.A.	
▲●	CHF	9.84	Groupe Indosuez Switzerland	G017	31/12/90	LUX	3.19	22	0.97	6	3.90	30.96	4	✪✪✪	3	92.16	6	N.A.	
	CHF	3.52	Helvetia	B032	17/03/95	LUX	1.10	23	-3.54	16	N.A.	N.A.				N.A.		N.A.	
▲	CHF	8.72	Lloyds IP Swiss Eq	L016	14/06/96	LUX	3.80	21	N.A.		N.A.	N.A.				N.A.		N.A.	
	CHF	4.51	MOSAIS Actions Suisses	C058	31/03/95	LUX	11.89	2	12.80	1	N.A.	N.A.				N.A.		N.A.	
	CHF	1	OYSTER Helvetic Opportunities	B067	13/09/96	LUX	8.50	8	N.A.		N.A.	N.A.				N.A.		N.A.	
	CHF	28.53	Parvest Switzerland B	B037	31/01/95	LUX	10.90	3	4.56	3	N.A.	N.A.				N.A.		N.A.	
	CHF	76.17	Raiffeisen Swiss Actions A	F024	31/03/94	LUX	5.87	18	-2.89	13	N.A.	N.A.				N.A.		N.A.	
▲	CHF	12.33	Schroder Intl Sel Swiss Eq	S010	15/12/95	LUX	6.20	17	2.52	5	N.A.	N.A.				N.A.		N.A.	
	CHF	3.69	Sogelux Fd Equities Switzerl.	S037	21/06/96	LUX	4.37	19	N.A.		N.A.	N.A.				N.A.		N.A.	
	CHF	16.95	UAP Swiss Securities	U009	31/07/90	LUX	8.84	7	3.52	4	3.49	37.55	1	✪✪✪✪	5	123.02	1	N.A.	
	CHF	5.89	Von Ernst GP Swiss Equity	B021	31/08/93	LUX	6.28	14	-4.99	18	3.31	24.25	6	✪✪	2	N.A.		N.A.	

▲ SIB Approved ● Insurance Fund **Values in US Dollars, on an offer to offer price basis with gross income reinvested** Data Source Micropal™

Taiwan Equity

Funds investing in excess of 70% in Taiwanese equities or related instruments. Such funds may have an objective of capital and/or income growth, or to track a specified index or perform inversely to a given index. Funds in this category may leverage or gear by a maximum of 20% of total assets.

	CCY	Fund Size ($mil)	Fund Name	Manager Code	Fund Start Date	Domicile Code	3 Mths 97 % Chg	Rank	1 Year % Chg	Rank	Micropal Star Rating 3 Years Volatility	% Chg	Rank	Rating	Risk Return Rating	5 Years % Chg	Rank	10 Years % Chg	Rank
		76.76	**Mean/Count**				**21.82**	**17**	**25.77**	**12**	**7.11**	**10.60**	**9**			**38.36**	**7**	**689.25**	**2**
●	NTD	503.60	Formosa Fund	F026	18/07/86	TW	18.93	11	28.22	5	6.48	8.79	6	✪✪		28.86	5	683.30	2
	USD	N.S.	Govett Taiwan OTC	G014	09/08/96	JER	21.47	7	N.A.		N.A.	N.A.				N.A.		N.A.	
	USD	71.20	GT Taiwan	G018	28/06/91	CA	17.11	14	25.55	9	7.25	-3.63	8	✪		18.98	6	N.A.	
●	USD	1.62	Hansard\INVESCO Taiwan Gth	H018	08/07/94	IOM	20.96	8	17.05	11	N.A.	N.A.				N.A.		N.A.	
	USD	5.38	ImPac AP Taiwan	I005	31/05/96	CA	35.47	2	N.A.		N.A.	N.A.				N.A.		N.A.	
▲	USD	59.10	INVESCO Taiwan Growth	I013	31/10/91	LUX	15.90	16	18.53	10	6.80	13.63	4	✪✪✪		48.10	3	N.A.	
	NTD	14.01	JF Taipei Trust	J004	28/02/91	CA	29.03	3	10.82	12	8.66	1.73	7	✪✪		13.87	7	N.A.	
	USD	27.35	JF Taiwan Trust	J004	01/03/96	CA	35.78	1	N.A.		N.A.	N.A.				N.A.		N.A.	
▲	USD	9.08	Jupiter Tyndall GF Taiwan	J010	29/01/93	LUX	17.84	12	26.84	7	6.03	-8.02	9	✪		N.A.		N.A.	
	USD	55.10	NM ASF Taiwan	N001	07/06/96	IRL	19.06	10	N.A.		N.A.	N.A.				N.A.		N.A.	
	USD	43.48	Regent Underval Ast Taiwan 3	R005	07/10/94	CA	13.25	17	36.05	1	N.A.	N.A.				N.A.		N.A.	
	USD	0.10	RLI/Thornton Taiwan Eq Gth	R037	05/07/96	IOM	16.97	15	N.A.		N.A.	N.A.				N.A.		N.A.	
	USD	207.86	Schroder Taiwan	S008	29/07/94	GU	17.80	13	28.27	4	N.A.	N.A.				N.A.		N.A.	
	NTD	26.52	Taipei Fund NAV	P029	28/11/86	TW	20.76	9	26.85	6	6.81	27.53	1	✪✪✪✪	4	57.58	2	695.21	1
	USD	145.02	Taiwan Capital	G014	31/12/93	JER	23.31	5	25.64	8	7.24	10.39	5	✪✪✪		N.A.		N.A.	
	USD	52.98	Thornton Taiwan Equity Growth	T006	02/08/91	CA	24.15	4	33.42	2	7.29	27.31	2	✪✪✪✪✪	3	61.29	1	N.A.	
	USD	5.75	Thornton Taiwan Equity Income	T006	02/08/91	CA	23.07	6	32.05	3	7.41	17.67	3	✪✪✪✪	2	39.82	4	N.A.	

Thailand Equity

Funds investing in excess of 70% in Thai equities or related instruments. Such funds may have an objective of capital and/or income growth, or to track a specified index or perform inversely to a given index. Funds in this category may leverage or gear by a maximum of 20% of total assets.

	CCY	Fund Size ($mil)	Fund Name	Manager Code	Fund Start Date	Domicile Code	3 Mths 97 % Chg	Rank	1 Year % Chg	Rank	Micropal Star Rating 3 Years Volatility	% Chg	Rank	Rating	Risk Return Rating	5 Years % Chg	Rank	10 Years % Chg	Rank
		30.88	**Mean/Count**				**-13.17**	**15**	**-36.32**	**12**	**7.29**	**-45.43**	**11**			**64.33**	**9**	**0**	**0**
	USD	17.02	Barclays ASF Thailand	B044	31/10/90	JER	-6.05	2	-42.17	11	8	-47.55	7	✪✪✪		73.62	6	N.A.	
	USD	2.90	CIBC-CEF Thai	C017	31/08/89	BER	-12.69	8	-39.91	7	7.95	-56.35	9	✪✪		3.08	7	N.A.	
▲	USD	4.64	Dres Thornton ASF Thailand	D015	31/05/93	IRL	-4.87	1	-39.39	6	6.79	-47.07	6	✪✪		N.A.		N.A.	
▲	USD	122.40	Fidelity Fds Thailand	F011	28/09/90	LUX	-11.34	6	-34.92	5	7.93	-34.59	3	✪✪✪✪✪		109.05	3	N.A.	
●	USD	5.72	Hansard\Fidelity Thailand	H014	27/09/91	IOM	-13.81	10	-31.98	3	7.40	-24.27	1	✪✪✪✪		131.39	2	N.A.	
	USD	13	HSBC Thai Equity	H034	12/04/96	HK	-16.16	12	N.A.		N.A.	N.A.				N.A.		N.A.	
	USD	3.19	ImPac AP Thailand	I005	31/10/95	CA	-24.62	15	-40.28	9	N.A.	N.A.				N.A.		N.A.	
	USD	165.87	JF Thailand	J004	31/08/89	HK	-10	5	-28.29	2	6.96	-34.25	2	✪✪✪✪		157.79	1	N.A.	
	USD	0.82	MBf Thailand	M010	31/03/88	CA	-19.40	13	-43.29	12	5.88	-65.56	11	✪		-42.92	8	N.A.	
	USD	N.S.	MFC Invesco Thailand	I013	31/05/96	CA	-11.70	7	N.A.		N.A.	N.A.				N.A.		N.A.	
▲	USD	0.69	Nikko GIUF Thailand Fund	N007	26/02/93	LUX	-6.90	4	-40.53	10	8.62	-49.81	8	✪✪		N.A.		N.A.	
●	USD	0.20	RLI/JF Thailand Trust	R030	05/07/96	IOM	-15.40	11	N.A.		N.A.	N.A.				N.A.		N.A.	
●	USD	0.30	Royal Life/MBf Thailand	R032	29/09/89	HK	-24.48	14	-40.02	8	5.66	-63.47	10	✪		-44.97	9	N.A.	
	USD	67.92	Siam Fund (Cayman) Ltd	I007	29/01/88	CA	-13.75	9	-20.74	1	7.70	-39.15	5	✪✪✪		87.53	5	N.A.	
	USD	27.68	Thornton New Tiger Thailand	T007	30/03/90	BER	-6.36	3	-34.29	4	7.24	-37.64	4	✪✪✪		104.40	4	N.A.	

▲ SIB Approved ● Insurance Fund **Values in US Dollars, on an offer to offer price basis with gross income reinvested** Data Source Micropal™

Turkey Equity

Funds investing in excess of 70% in Turkish equities or related instruments. Such funds may have an objective of capital and/or income growth, or to track a specified index or perform inversely to a given index. Funds in this category may leverage or gear by a maximum of 20% of total assets.

	CCY	Fund Size ($mil)	Fund Name	Manager Code	Fund Start Date	Domicile Code	3 Mths 97 % Chg	3 Mths 97 Rank	1 Year % Chg	1 Year Rank	Micropal Star Rating 3 Years Volatility	3 Years % Chg	3 Years Rank	Rating	Risk Return Rating	5 Years % Chg	5 Years Rank	10 Years % Chg	10 Years Rank
		69.70	**Mean/Count**				**20.51**	**1**	**27.54**	**1**	**0**	**0**	**0**			**0**	**0**	**0**	**0**
	USD	69.70	Turkish Growth Fund	A005	28/02/94	LUX	20.51	1	27.54	1	N.A.	N.A.				N.A.		N.A.	

United Kingdom Equity

Funds investing in excess of 70% in British equities or related instruments. Such funds may have an objective of capital and/or income growth, or to track a specified index or perform inversely to a given index. Funds in this category may leverage or gear by a maximum of 20% of total assets.

	CCY	Fund Size ($mil)	Fund Name	Manager Code	Fund Start Date	Domicile Code	3 Mths 97 % Chg	3 Mths 97 Rank	1 Year % Chg	1 Year Rank	Micropal Star Rating 3 Years Volatility	3 Years % Chg	3 Years Rank	Rating	Risk Return Rating	5 Years % Chg	5 Years Rank	10 Years % Chg	10 Years Rank
		31.86	**Mean/Count**				**0.78**	**121**	**27**	**115**	**3.53**	**48.36**	**79**		**1**	**72.61**	**63**	**191.13**	**22**
▲	GBP	7.32	Abtrust Atlas UK Gth of Inc	A002	31/03/88	LUX	1.27	41	26.24	53	3.48	42.30	55	✪✪	2	85.31	14	N.A.	
	GBP	5.48	Abtrust UK Equity	A003	29/01/82	GU	3.63	15	24.40	74	3.06	26.31	73	✪	1	44.73	58	139.49	19
▲	GBP	7.32	Aetna IUF UK Equity A	A011	29/04/88	LUX	1.02	49	31	25	3.69	52.07	25	✪✪✪✪	3	82.19	16	N.A.	
▲	GBP	7.63	Aetna IUF UK Sm Cos A	A011	29/12/95	LUX	7.78	1	39.54	10	N.A.	N.A.				N.A.		N.A.	
	GBP	0.58	Aetna MF UK Natl Equity	A012	31/05/90	LUX	-0.20	80	20.44	102	3.26	25.36	74	✪	1	24.65	62	N.A.	
●	GBP	0	Albany Intl UK Blue Chip Stlg	A018	31/07/87	IOM	0.58	64	26.66	49	3.79	49.09	33	✪✪✪	2	76.72	21	N.A.	
●	USD	0	Albany Intl UK Dllr	A018	31/03/87	IOM	0.21	73	25.97	57	3.57	44.56	49	✪✪	2	74.30	24	N.A.	
	GBP	N.S.	Albany Intl UK Enterprise	A018	28/02/95	IOM	2.38	26	41.32	7	N.A.	N.A.				N.A.		N.A.	
●	GBP	0	Albany Intl UK Stlg	A018	31/03/87	IOM	1.67	30	23.78	83	3.61	46.97	40	✪✪✪	2	58.69	45	N.A.	
●	GBP	12.74	Allied Dunbar IB UK Cap Gth	A021	30/09/93	IOM	0.84	56	25.01	65	2.99	51.22	27	✪✪✪✪	4	N.A.		N.A.	
▲	GBP	91.35	Allied Dunbar UK Capital Gth	A020	30/06/87	IOM	0.43	65	25.89	59	3.29	52.58	23	✪✪✪✪	4	75.14	22	N.A.	
●	GBP	0.93	AXA Eqty&Law IFM UK Equity	A039	29/11/85	IOM	0.88	54	24.27	76	3.40	44.17	51	✪✪	2	69.48	30	216.76	8
	GBP	15.82	AXA Eqty&Law ILA UK Equity	A040	31/10/85	IOM	0.58	63	24.84	66	3.20	47	39	✪✪	3	81.52	17	248.95	4
▲	GBP	76.43	Barclays (Lux) UK Equity	B047	28/09/84	LUX	0.74	59	26.72	47	3.35	42	56	✪	2	63.97	38	159.82	15
	GBP	3.92	BIL Equities Grand-Bretagne C	B067	30/06/94	LUX	2.64	21	23.70	86	N.A.	N.A.				N.A.		N.A.	
●	GBP	9.10	Carlson UK Equity	C011	28/09/90	LUX	1.35	38	24.41	72	3.81	41.61	59	✪✪	1	58.03	47	N.A.	
●	GBP	14.38	Cater Allen Equity Growth	C013	31/10/79	JER	-0.32	85	16.82	110	3.96	49.68	32	✪✪✪	3	63.78	39	190.70	11
	GBP	6.72	Chameleon UK Equity	A031	28/02/92	BVI	-2.41	113	17.85	107	2.24	25.34	75	✪	1	N.A.		N.A.	
▲	GBP	24.60	Citi PF UK Equity	C036	30/09/88	LUX	-1.41	104	24.60	70	3.29	36.74	68	✪	1	42.36	61	N.A.	
▲	GBP	56.11	CMI GNF UK Eqty Index Tr	C042	30/04/90	LUX	0.73	60	26.85	45	3.83	49.94	31	✪✪✪	2	74.08	25	N.A.	
▲	GBP	51.83	CMI GNF UK Equity	C042	30/04/90	LUX	-0.36	89	27.19	42	3.30	46.43	44	✪✪	3	58.93	44	N.A.	
●	GBP	17.25	CMI Ins Co UK Equity	C043	31/01/91	IOM	-2.53	116	25.89	58	3.49	41.67	58	✪✪	2	42.92	60	N.A.	
●	GBP	34.51	CMI Ins Co UK Tracker	C043	31/05/90	IOM	-1.03	100	26.39	52	3.66	48.16	37	✪✪✪	3	73.29	26	N.A.	
●	GBP	1.52	CMI Passport GBP Enhanced Mgd	C044	20/01/95	IOM	1.04	47	9.19	113	N.A.	N.A.				N.A.		N.A.	
●	GBP	279.96	CMI Passport GBP G'teed Gth	C044	20/01/95	IOM	-2.50	115	18.23	106	N.A.	N.A.				N.A.		N.A.	
●	GBP	0.34	CMI Passport UK Equity	C044	20/01/95	IOM	-1.53	105	25.65	62	N.A.	N.A.				N.A.		N.A.	
●	GBP	0.68	CMI Passport UK Index	C044	20/01/95	IOM	-0.24	81	26.09	56	N.A.	N.A.				N.A.		N.A.	
▲	GBP	69.36	Coutts GF United Kingdom Eqty	C052	31/01/79	IRL	0.94	52	23.38	88	3.54	43.50	53	✪✪	2	56.11	48	207.65	9
●	GBP	4.42	Credis Equity UK A	C056	28/06/91	LUX	-1.05	101	22.89	91	3.69	40.57	61	✪	1	46.54	55	N.A.	
▲	GBP	10.42	CU PP UK Growth	C070	31/05/90	LUX	-0.29	83	28.63	34	3.72	52.31	24	✪✪✪✪	3	79.81	18	N.A.	
	GBP	1.39	Duncan Lawrie Sterling	D019	29/01/82	GU	1.05	46	16.37	111	3.59	38.66	63	✪✪	1	22.34	63	136.80	21
	GBP	0.69	Eagle Star UK Equity	E001	29/09/95	IOM	-0.14	79	27.37	40	N.A.	N.A.				N.A.		N.A.	
	GBP	26.25	EMIF UK Index Plus B	C015	31/05/90	LUX	1	50	23.70	85	3.46	46.78	41	✪✪	3	64.37	37	N.A.	
	GBP	40.11	Ermitage UK Value	E011	06/01/95	LUX	6.53	6	33.56	16	N.A.	N.A.				N.A.		N.A.	
	GBP	5.58	F&C RAF UK Equities	F003	18/07/86	JER	1.65	31	27.37	39	3.88	50.36	30	✪✪✪	2	74.90	23	259.12	2
	GBP	2.20	F&C RAF UK Neg Equity	F003	29/05/92	JER	-6.86	119	2.79	114	3.81	7.59	79	✪		N.A.		N.A.	
▲	GBP	191.15	Fidelity Fds United Kingdom	F011	28/09/90	LUX	1.10	44	33.38	17	3.95	56.40	15	✪✪✪✪	3	116.75	6	N.A.	
	GBP	0.19	Finistere Special Sits Life	F016	31/05/84	GU	7.20	3	23.95	80	4.50	16.42	78	✪		51.31	50	127.92	22
●	GBP	1.01	Finistere Stlg Equity Life	F016	31/12/81	GU	2.53	23	22.94	90	3.41	46.51	43	✪✪	3	78.44	19	147.73	17
	GBP	17.98	Five Arrows IE UK	R014	30/09/93	GU	1.06	45	32.44	21	4.30	44.98	48	✪✪✪	1	N.A.		N.A.	
	GBP	40.73	Five Arrows IE UK Smllr Cos	R014	30/09/93	GU	3.92	14	40.52	8	3.20	67.13	7	✪✪✪✪	5	N.A.		N.A.	

▲ **SIB Approved** ● **Insurance Fund** **Values in US Dollars, on an offer to offer price basis with gross income reinvested** Data Source Micropal™

United Kingdom Equity

continued

	CCY	Fund Size ($mil)	Fund Name	Manager Code	Fund Start Date	Domicile Code	3 Mths 97 % Chg	Rank	1 Year % Chg	Rank	Micropal Star Rating: 3 Years Volatility	3 Years % Chg	Rank	Rating	Risk Return Rating	5 Years % Chg	Rank	10 Years % Chg	Rank
		31.86	**Mean/Count**				**0.78**	**121**	**27**	**115**	**3.53**	**48.36**	**79**		**1**	**72.61**	**63**	**191.13**	**22**
	USD	36.52	Five Arrows IP UK Equity	R016	30/12/94	GU	-1.54	106	25.79	60	N.A.	N.A.				N.A.		N.A.	
▲	GBP	52.41	Fleming FF UK Enterprise	F020	31/03/92	LUX	1.46	37	28.51	36	3.96	54.89	17	✪✪✪✪	3	N.A.		N.A.	
	GBP	5.85	Friends Provdnt Stewardship	F031	31/05/94	GU	2.40	25	32.25	22	N.A.	N.A.				N.A.		N.A.	
	GBP	3.47	Friends Provdnt UK Equity	F031	31/05/94	GU	-0.07	78	27.23	41	N.A.	N.A.				N.A.		N.A.	
	GBP	48.57	G-Equity Fund G-British Eq B	G009	31/03/93	LUX	1.54	34	24.01	79	3.54	47.38	38	✪✪✪	3	N.A.		N.A.	
▲	GBP	16.39	Gartmore CSF UK Smllr Cos	G007	31/08/94	JER	7.67	2	50.95	2	N.A.	N.A.				N.A.		N.A.	
▲	GBP	108.50	Gartmore CSF United Kingdom	G007	31/05/84	JER	-2.44	114	22.12	94	3.69	37	66	✪	1	66.44	35	241.62	5
	USD	0.60	Glbl Mgr UK Bear	B066	30/09/94	BER	-7.66	120	0.81	115	N.A.	N.A.				N.A.		N.A.	
	USD	0.10	Glbl Mgr UK Geared	B066	30/09/94	BER	4.48	12	32.67	20	N.A.	N.A.				N.A.		N.A.	
	USD	1	Glbl Mgr UK Index	B066	30/09/94	BER	0.77	58	24.83	69	N.A.	N.A.				N.A.		N.A.	
	GBP	23.72	Govett UK Safeguard A	G016	15/03/96	JER	-1.02	99	N.A.		N.A.	N.A.				N.A.		N.A.	
▲●	GBP	20.52	Groupe Indosuez UK	G017	31/01/91	LUX	1.57	33	24.84	68	3.65	41.99	57	✪✪	1	67.77	33	N.A.	
▲	GBP	50.03	Guinness Flight UK	G019	31/01/85	GU	0.25	71	24.05	78	3.69	50.52	29	✪✪✪	3	86.87	13	274.11	1
▲	GBP	28.44	Hambros Eqty Sel UK Growth	H003	31/01/72	GU	-0.30	84	24.42	71	3.50	43.75	52	✪✪	2	82.86	15	220.84	7
	GBP	3.37	Hambros Equity Income	H005	30/09/75	JER	-0.45	91	23.09	89	3.37	36.78	67	✪	2	48.16	54	164.92	14
	GBP	N.S.	Hansard EU UK Equity	H010	17/02/95	IRL	6.22	8	28.29	37	N.A.	N.A.				N.A.		N.A.	
●	GBP	5.92	Hansard UK Equity	H011	30/03/90	IOM	1.03	48	30.78	28	2.91	46.64	42	✪✪	4	71.38	28	N.A.	
●	GBP	1.27	Hansard\Fidelity UK	H014	27/09/91	IOM	3.34	17	30.82	27	3.43	52.73	22	✪✪✪	4	102.88	7	N.A.	
▲	GBP	10.52	HCIC Income	H026	27/10/95	IOM	-0.33	86	19.40	105	N.A.	N.A.				N.A.		N.A.	
▲	GBP	5.07	HCIC UK Gth	H026	30/12/94	IOM	0.88	53	24.29	75	N.A.	N.A.				N.A.		N.A.	
▲	USD	9.78	Henderson HF UK Smllr Cos	H025	31/08/93	LUX	6.26	7	39.28	12	3.36	81.01	4	✪✪✪✪✪	5	N.A.		N.A.	
▲	GBP	32.65	Hill Samuel OS British	H030	30/04/79	JER	-0.25	82	26.48	51	3.66	51.58	26	✪✪✪✪	4	71.23	29	184.76	12
▲	GBP	33.54	Inter Strategie Eur du Nord	B069	29/09/89	LUX	1.12	43	25.67	61	2.98	51.20	28	✪✪✪	4	68.09	31	N.A.	
▲	GBP	16.27	INVESCO PS UK Growth	I014	30/09/75	LUX	0.88	55	28.65	33	3.65	45.07	47	✪✪	2	66.70	34	196.78	10
	GBP	7.70	Irish Life Intl UK Equity	I017	30/09/94	IRL	1.50	35	26.16	54	N.A.	N.A.				N.A.		N.A.	
	GBP	4.26	JRIA UK Tracker	J002	29/01/93	IRL	0.43	66	26.11	55	3.68	44.43	50	✪✪	2	N.A.		N.A.	
▲	GBP	22.87	Jupiter Tyndall GF Brit Lion	J010	30/11/90	LUX	3.28	18	57.15	1	4.06	108.96	2	✪✪✪✪✪	5	143.63	2	N.A.	
▲	GBP	8.88	Jupiter Tyndall GF UK Sm Cos	J010	31/05/93	LUX	4.34	13	47.23	4	4.01	54.50	18	✪✪✪	3	N.A.		N.A.	
▲	GBP	18.27	Jupiter Tyndall WUF UK Sm Cos	J008	28/07/95	BER	6.76	5	21.33	95	N.A.	N.A.				N.A.		N.A.	
▲	GBP	7.41	KB British	K007	31/01/91	GU	2.90	20	27.15	43	3.64	36.27	69	✪	1	60.98	41	N.A.	
▲	GBP	65.38	Lazard SIT UK Active	L001	28/02/89	GU	3.41	16	37.93	13	3.38	65.69	8	✪✪✪✪	4	97.68	9	N.A.	
▲	GBP	65.45	Lazard SIT UK Index	L001	28/02/89	GU	0.77	57	33.29	18	3.18	57.65	14	✪✪✪✪	4	89.48	11	N.A.	
▲	GBP	N.S.	Lazard UK Equity GBP	L002	28/06/96	IRL	1.49	36	N.A.		N.A.	N.A.				N.A.		N.A.	
▲	USD	N.S.	Lazard UK Equity USD	L002	28/06/96	IRL	1.13	42	N.A.		N.A.	N.A.				N.A.		N.A.	
▲	GBP	43.14	Lloyds IP UK Equities	L016	30/11/90	LUX	0.03	76	24.41	73	3.21	41.01	60	✪✪	2	51.09	51	N.A.	
	GBP	26.05	Luxlife Actions Anglaises	L024	07/07/95	LUX	0.98	51	24.16	77	N.A.	N.A.				N.A.		N.A.	
▲	GBP	64.96	M&G Island UK	M001	30/09/75	GU	0.67	61	20.68	99	3.32	37.08	65	✪	1	77.28	20	222.93	6
	GBP	3.48	M-Fund UK Performer	B013	28/02/94	LUX	3.27	19	40.23	9	N.A.	N.A.				N.A.		N.A.	
▲	USD	7.85	Manulife Regent GF UK Gth	M006	30/09/87	LUX	-1.83	111	28.20	38	3.60	31.92	71	✪	1	53.97	49	N.A.	
▲	GBP	20.79	Mercury OST United Kingdom	M020	28/11/86	LUX	1.71	29	25.35	63	3.60	48.91	34	✪✪✪	3	59.16	43	153.03	16
▲	GBP	39.89	Mercury ST UK Opportunities	M021	26/02/93	LUX	1.63	32	43.32	5	3.76	82.56	3	✪✪✪✪✪	5	N.A.		N.A.	
▲	USD	32.41	Mercury ST United Kingdom	M021	31/12/85	LUX	-0.55	92	26.86	44	3.56	45.62	46	✪✪	2	71.68	27	175.08	13
▲	GBP	20.38	Midland ICF UK Growth	M028	28/02/90	LUX	-0.81	96	23.91	82	3.45	42.70	54	✪✪	2	60.30	42	N.A.	
	GBP	14.04	Monument Growth	M037	07/04/95	GU	6.84	4	34.87	15	N.A.	N.A.				N.A.		N.A.	
▲	GBP	119.60	Morgan Grenfell Selector UK	M038	31/05/93	IRL	0.06	75	29.72	32	3.93	58	13	✪✪✪✪	4	N.A.		N.A.	
	GBP	8.04	MOSAIS Actions Anglaises	C058	31/10/90	LUX	-0.59	93	26.48	50	3.78	40.50	62	✪	1	45.51	56	N.A.	
▲	GBP	21.31	Newton UGF UK Equity	N006	29/02/88	JER	2.57	22	20.92	97	3.48	38.66	64	✪	1	48.79	52	N.A.	
	GBP	0.46	Old Mutual Gnsy UK Stkmkt	O003	29/12/95	GU	1.94	28	23.56	87	N.A.	N.A.				N.A.		N.A.	
	GBP	14.43	OMI (Gnsy) UK Stkmkt	O005	31/05/82	GU	0.40	67	23.75	84	3.13	34.29	70	✪	1	58.37	46	144.23	18
	GBP	43.81	Parvest UK B	B037	31/01/94	LUX	0.27	70	30.30	30	N.A.	N.A.				N.A.		N.A.	
	USD	270.90	Perpetual Offshr UK Growth	P011	30/10/87	JER	0.22	72	24.84	67	3.39	62.65	10	✪✪✪✪✪	4	130.16	4	N.A.	
	GBP	110.24	Pictet C.F. UK Val	P016	28/02/85	LUX	-1.64	109	23.91	81	3.33	60.88	11	✪✪✪✪	4	93.14	10	252.09	3
▲	GBP	111.46	Prolific IF UK Equity Inc	P027	31/03/89	IRL	-1.81	110	31.34	24	3.25	64.55	9	✪✪✪✪✪	5	101.67	8	N.A.	
▲	GBP	4.06	RBC GI UK Equity	R003	24/11/95	GU	-1.15	103	20.73	98	N.A.	N.A.				N.A.		N.A.	
●	GBP	5.75	RLI/Perpetual Mgd Equity	R034	15/12/95	IOM	0.27	69	20.65	100	N.A.	N.A.				N.A.		N.A.	
●	GBP	8.97	RLI/UK Index Tracker	R020	31/10/90	IOM	5.20	10	22.29	93	3.14	48.33	36	✪✪✪	4	62.87	40	N.A.	
●	GBP	8.97	Royal Life Intl UK Equity	R020	31/03/86	IOM	2.21	27	21.02	96	3.20	52.95	20	✪✪✪	4	48.17	53	139.45	20

▲ SIB Approved **● Insurance Fund** **Values in US Dollars, on an offer to offer price basis with gross income reinvested**

Data Source Micropal™

United Kingdom Equity

continued

	CCY	Fund Size ($mil)	Fund Name	Manager Code	Fund Start Date	Domicile Code	3 Mths 97 % Chg	3 Mths 97 Rank	1 Year % Chg	1 Year Rank	Micropal Star Rating 3 Years Volatility	3 Years % Chg	3 Years Rank	3 Years Rating	Risk Return Rating	5 Years % Chg	5 Years Rank	10 Years % Chg	10 Years Rank
		31.86	**Mean/Count**				**0.78**	**121**	**27**	**115**	**3.53**	**48.36**	**79**		**1**	**72.61**	**63**	**191.13**	**22**
▲	GBP	72.32	Schroder Intl Sel UK Equity	S010	31/03/93	LUX	1.29	40	29.79	31	3.62	52.79	21	✪✪✪✪	3	N.A.		N.A.	
●	GBP	43.44	Scot Amicable UK Equity Stg	S015	30/06/94	IRL	-1.58	107	19.59	104	N.A.	N.A.				N.A.		N.A.	
●	GBP	10.79	Scot Amicable UK Index Track	S015	30/06/94	IRL	0.37	68	26.70	48	N.A.	N.A.				N.A.		N.A.	
	GBP	45.67	Scot Prov GP UK Equity	S014	30/09/91	IOM	-2.03	112	30.99	26	3.13	58.62	12	✪✪✪✪✪	4	87.07	12	N.A.	
●	GBP	5.24	Scot Prov GP UK Safeguard C	S014	31/05/96	IOM	-1.08	102	N.A.		N.A.	N.A.				N.A.		N.A.	
	GBP	2.88	Scot Prov ILA Special Sits	S014	29/12/95	IOM	0.62	62	42.63	6	N.A.	N.A.				N.A.		N.A.	
	GBP	15.06	Scot Prov ILA UK Blue Chip	S014	29/09/95	IOM	1.34	39	30.77	29	N.A.	N.A.				N.A.		N.A.	
	GBP	N.S.	Singer & Fried AIM	S027	26/04/96	IRL	-0.87	97	N.A.		N.A.	N.A.				N.A.		N.A.	
▲	GBP	25.88	Singer & Fried UK Emer Ldrs	S027	28/10/94	IRL	-3.96	117	20.04	103	N.A.	N.A.				N.A.		N.A.	
▲●	GBP	52.27	Singer & Fried UK Equity Inc	S027	31/05/95	IRL	-0.88	98	11.04	112	N.A.	N.A.				N.A.		N.A.	
▲	GBP	50.41	Singer & Fried UK Growth	S027	30/04/93	IRL	-1.60	108	20.58	101	3.45	21.26	77	✪	1	N.A.		N.A.	
▲	GBP	34.63	Skandifond UK Equity	S030	28/02/89	LUX	-0.61	94	31.44	23	3.38	53.32	19	✪✪✪✪	4	68.05	32	N.A.	
	GBP	2.72	Sogelux Fd Equities UK	S037	21/06/96	LUX	-0.38	90	N.A.		N.A.	N.A.				N.A.		N.A.	
▲	GBP	3.67	Sun Life GP UK Growth	S052	31/03/88	LUX	-0.66	95	22.60	92	3.30	26.46	72	✪	1	43.76	59	N.A.	
	GBP	0.90	Sun Life Intl Equity	S053	31/08/95	IOM	N.A.	—	32.90	19	N.A.	N.A.				N.A.		N.A.	
▲	GBP	21.26	SVM UK Gth	S018	30/09/93	IRL	5	11	50.56	3	3.71	125.38	1	✪✪✪✪✪	5	N.A.		N.A.	
▲	GBP	201.98	Swiss Life Proteus UK Equity	S056	29/11/91	IRL	5.82	9	35.36	14	3.42	68.05	6	✪✪✪✪✪	5	125.63	5	N.A.	
▲	GBP	57.84	TGA UK Equity	T009	28/02/89	LUX	0.08	74	26.76	46	3.65	45.91	45	✪✪	2	65.31	36	N.A.	
▲	GBP	113.17	TSB OIF UK Equity	T013	30/04/90	JER	2.43	24	25.17	64	4.15	55.06	16	✪✪✪✪	2	171.53	1	N.A.	
	GBP	34.85	UAP UK Securities	U009	31/08/93	LUX	-0.34	88	28.58	35	3.66	48.72	35	✪✪✪	3	N.A.		N.A.	
	GBP	19.28	UK Sentinel	I009	26/05/95	BAH	-4.55	118	17.43	109	N.A.	N.A.				N.A.		N.A.	
▲	GBP	9.27	Von Ernst GP UK Equity	B021	30/11/89	LUX	-0.33	87	17.71	108	3.63	23.18	76	✪	1	44.76	57	N.A.	
▲	GBP	18.47	Von Ernst GP UK Sm Cos Eqty	B021	30/11/89	LUX	-0.03	77	39.33	11	3.75	68.50	5	✪✪✪✪	4	141.12	3	N.A.	

United States Of America Equity

Funds investing in excess of 70% in American equities or related instruments. Such funds may have an objective of capital and/or income growth, or to track a specified index or perform inversely to a given index. Funds in this category may leverage gear by a maximum of 20% of total assets.

	CCY	Fund Size ($mil)	Fund Name	Manager Code	Fund Start Date	Domicile Code	3 Mths 97 % Chg	3 Mths 97 Rank	1 Year % Chg	1 Year Rank	Micropal Star Rating 3 Years Volatility	3 Years % Chg	3 Years Rank	3 Years Rating	Risk Return Rating	5 Years % Chg	5 Years Rank	10 Years % Chg	10 Years Rank
		50.31	**Mean/Count**				**-0.91**	**151**	**18.16**	**131**	**3.77**	**56.61**	**84**		**1**	**97.89**	**60**	**264.31**	**19**
▲	USD	10.16	Abtrust Atlas United States	A002	31/03/88	LUX	4.68	23	25.34	27	3.01	59.15	39	✪✪✪	3	85.95	36	N.A.	
	USD	11.24	Ace Healthcare Reform USD	A004	23/06/95	LUX	-6.43	125	0.20	126	N.A.	N.A.				N.A.		N.A.	
	USD	26.36	ACMGI American Growth Ptf A	A005	28/02/92	LUX	2.86	55	19.42	65	3.89	55.68	42	✪✪✪	2	N.A.		N.A.	
▲	USD	22.13	AEB Worldfolio 8 US Cons Eqs	A009	31/05/93	LUX	2.50	66	23.64	37	3.23	65.78	27	✪✪✪✪	3	N.A.		N.A.	
▲	USD	30.58	AEB Worldfolio 9 US Aggr Eqs	A009	31/05/93	LUX	-7.99	130	26.25	21	4.07	72.78	19	✪✪✪✪	2	N.A.		N.A.	
▲	USD	9.26	Aetna IUF Am Sm Cos A	A011	29/12/95	LUX	-8.92	133	7.02	111	N.A.	N.A.				N.A.		N.A.	
	USD	44.80	AIS Arbitrage	O008	29/12/95	CA	1.13	77	9.28	105	N.A.	N.A.				N.A.		N.A.	
	USD	2.17	Alliance Global Leisure Fund	A005	28/09/90	LUX	0.44	84	4.39	115	3.79	-7.27	83	✪		26.14	56	N.A.	
	USD	12.82	America Index Plus Fund B	C015	30/06/94	LUX	2.60	62	25.49	26	N.A.	N.A.				N.A.		N.A.	
	USD	1.40	American Partners Spec Tech	O008	30/04/96	BVI	-23.38	149	N.A.		N.A.	N.A.				N.A.		N.A.	
▲	USD	9.14	American Phoenix US Grwth Cos	A025	28/04/95	LUX	-5.44	121	19.90	60	N.A.	N.A.				N.A.		N.A.	
	USD	2	American Quant	S039	29/03/91	BVI	7.59	4	19.83	62	2.68	62.80	33	✪✪✪	4	114.29	18	N.A.	
	USD	52.15	Baer Multistock US Stk A	J007	29/06/90	LUX	4.54	25	26.90	19	2.81	54.97	43	✪✪	3	74.57	41	N.A.	
	USD	3.80	BanesFondo Intern. Dollars	B030	30/06/93	LUX	-3.44	107	3.80	117	1.56	2.50	82	✪		N.A.		N.A.	
	USD	93	BEM International	B054	30/03/90	BER	-4.79	117	13.59	92	2.85	36.19	66	✪	1	116.94	13	N.A.	
	USD	3	Berkshire Arista Bio-Med Gth	B058	30/06/95	CA	-10.30	139	-15.71	131	N.A.	N.A.				N.A.		N.A.	
	USD	13.50	Berkshire Arista Capital Gth	B058	30/09/94	CA	-12.94	142	7.50	109	N.A.	N.A.				N.A.		N.A.	
	USD	10	Berkshire Arista High Tec Gth	B058	05/04/96	CA	-26.90	150	N.A.		N.A.	N.A.				N.A.		N.A.	
▲	USD	112.11	BT GAF US Smaller Cos	B076	12/05/95	IRL	-9.56	136	12.20	99	N.A.	N.A.				N.A.		N.A.	

▲ **SIB Approved** ● **Insurance Fund** **Values in US Dollars, on an offer to offer price basis with gross income reinvested** Data Source Micropal™

United States Of America Equity

continued

	CCY	Fund Size ($mil)	Fund Name	Manager Code	Fund Start Date	Domicile Code	3 Mths 97 % Chg	3 Mths 97 Rank	1 Year % Chg	1 Year Rank	Micropal Star Rating 3 Years Volatility	3 Years % Chg	3 Years Rank	3 Years Rating	Risk Return Rating	5 Years % Chg	5 Years Rank	10 Years % Chg	10 Years Rank
		50.31	**Mean/Count**				**-0.91**	**151**	**18.16**	**131**	**3.77**	**56.61**	**84**		**1**	**97.89**	**60**	**264.31**	**19**
	USD	2.41	Callander Emerging Growth	C005	30/06/86	LUX	-4.38	115	6.90	112	3.80	27.40	72	✪	1	17.10	59	98.24	18
	USD	21.87	Callander Fund Asset	C005	30/11/88	LUX	3.28	45	17.78	77	2.76	47.96	58	✪✪	2	103.62	23	N.A.	
	USD	1.79	Callander Fund US Healthcare	C005	31/12/91	LUX	3.08	49	-3.28	129	10.17	-23.60	84	✪		-39.57	60	N.A.	
	USD	7.34	CB Lux Portfolio US Aktien	A007	31/03/93	LUX	4.44	27	22.89	41	2.72	69.69	22	✪✪✪✪	4	N.A.		N.A.	
	BEF	13.45	Cera Invest Dollar Plus	C018	07/07/95	LUX	6.73	9	-1.42	128	N.A.	N.A.				N.A.		N.A.	
▲●	USD	75.27	Chase Vista US Large Cap Eq	C019	31/12/86	LUX	2.63	59	19.66	63	2.40	50.44	53	✪✪	3	81.81	39	144.93	16
▲●	USD	69.72	Chase Vista US Mid Cap Eq	C019	31/12/93	LUX	-1.05	92	22.78	43	2.96	51.81	51	✪✪	2	N.A.		N.A.	
▲	USD	30.84	Citi PF US Earnings Growth	C036	12/07/96	LUX	-7.68	128	N.A.		N.A.	N.A.				N.A.		N.A.	
▲	USD	28.17	Citi PF US Small Caps Stock	C036	07/06/96	LUX	-16.59	147	N.A.		N.A.	N.A.				N.A.		N.A.	
●	USD	35.40	Citi US Equity A	C032	24/06/94	CA	-0.64	91	12.22	98	N.A.	N.A.				N.A.		N.A.	
●	USD	13.76	Clariden Emerging Gth	C039	30/08/91	CA	4.93	17	9.94	104	4.24	10.02	80	✪		64.15	47	N.A.	
▲	USD	127.96	CMI GNF US Eqty Index Tr	C042	30/04/90	LUX	2.95	54	24.23	33	2.82	65.64	29	✪✪✪✪	4	93.72	30	N.A.	
▲	USD	37.61	CMI GNF US Equity	C042	30/04/90	LUX	3.23	46	20.81	57	3.04	73.93	17	✪✪✪✪	4	102.69	24	N.A.	
●	USD	4.10	CMI Ins Co US Equity	C043	29/03/91	IOM	2.51	65	19.58	64	2.90	68.50	23	✪✪✪✪	4	96.17	29	N.A.	
●	GBP	5.75	CMI Ins Co US Tracker	C043	31/05/90	IOM	2.96	53	25.66	24	3.01	65.74	28	✪✪✪✪	3	99.19	26	N.A.	
●	USD	0.20	CMI Passport US Equity	C044	20/01/95	IOM	3.46	41	19.27	66	N.A.	N.A.				N.A.		N.A.	
●	USD	0.60	CMI Passport US Index	C044	20/01/95	IOM	3.94	38	24.56	29	N.A.	N.A.				N.A.		N.A.	
●	USD	1.70	CMI Passport USD Enhanced Mgd	C044	20/01/95	IOM	-0.21	89	3.54	118	N.A.	N.A.				N.A.		N.A.	
●	USD	50.10	CMI Passport USD G'teed Gth	C044	20/01/95	IOM	1.42	74	6.29	113	N.A.	N.A.				N.A.		N.A.	
●	USD	117.31	Credis Equity Small Cap USA	C056	30/09/93	LUX	-4.54	116	34.15	7	3.66	74.55	14	✪✪✪✪	3	N.A.		N.A.	
	USD	N.S.	Eagle Star US Smaller Companie	E001	27/09/96	IOM	N.A.	—	N.A.		N.A.	N.A.				N.A.		N.A.	
	USD	7.04	Emerge Capital	L023	31/10/94	LUX	-9.73	137	13.51	94	N.A.	N.A.				N.A.		N.A.	
	USD	N.S.	EPIC MF US Large Cos Equities	A024	27/10/95	LUX	0.88	80	22.28	48	N.A.	N.A.				N.A.		N.A.	
	USD	N.S.	EPIC MF US Small Cos Equities	A024	10/11/95	LUX	-8.42	132	1.62	123	N.A.	N.A.				N.A.		N.A.	
	USD	0.98	F&C RAF US Equities	F003	31/01/86	JER	4.16	31	23.82	36	2.85	64.80	30	✪✪✪✪	3	91.15	32	262.77	7
	USD	30.99	Falcon International Inc	F005	31/12/90	CA	-1.51	95	30.40	13	5.26	58.41	40	✪✪✪	1	55.91	49	N.A.	
▲	USD	442.20	Fidelity Fds America	F011	28/09/90	LUX	-0.56	90	17.28	81	2.95	57.25	41	✪✪✪	3	73.60	42	N.A.	
	USD	N.S.	Fiduciary US Core Equity	F014	03/01/97	IRL	N.A.		N.A.		N.A.	N.A.				N.A.		N.A.	
	USD	0.26	Five Arrows IE Amer Smllr Cos	R014	30/09/93	GU	-2.06	98	17.75	78	3.26	43.02	62	✪	1	N.A.		N.A.	
▲	USD	271.21	Fleming FF Amer Fledgeling	F020	28/09/84	LUX	-5.25	119	18.44	71	3.75	53.93	48	✪✪	2	109.65	22	282.40	5
▲	USD	615.86	Fleming FF American	F020	30/11/88	LUX	3.22	47	29.07	14	2.68	84.22	10	✪✪✪✪✪	5	193.67	5	N.A.	
▲	USD	241.25	Fleming FF US Discovery	F020	30/11/88	LUX	-2.53	101	17.81	76	3.42	49.71	56	✪✪	2	137.94	9	N.A.	
	USD	108.70	GAM Arbitrage	G003	31/01/84	IOM	2.32	67	13.06	95	0.83	39.38	63	✪	5	87	35	195.12	14
	USD	66.10	GAM Science Inc	G003	09/02/96	BVI	-14.67	143	N.A.		N.A.	N.A.				N.A.		N.A.	
	USD	118.40	GAM Selection	G003	31/05/84	IOM	-3.74	113	17.86	75	3.24	19.56	77	✪	1	98.87	27	355.99	2
	USD	2.50	GAM Tyche	G003	31/03/83	IOM	7.50	5	3.19	119	4.32	30.96	69	✪	1	64.83	46	246.47	9
	USD	24.10	GAM US	G003	18/07/86	IOM	7.33	6	24.59	28	2.64	67.19	25	✪✪✪	4	54.61	50	258.24	8
	USD	59.40	GAMerica	G003	31/05/83	IOM	2.27	68	17	83	3.47	53.95	46	✪✪	2	115.68	15	240.66	11
	USD	1.60	Glbl Mgr US Bear	B066	30/09/94	BER	-3.48	108	-13.61	130	N.A.	N.A.				N.A.		N.A.	
	USD	0.30	Glbl Mgr US Geared	B066	30/09/94	BER	7.74	3	36.22	3	N.A.	N.A.				N.A.		N.A.	
	USD	0.80	Glbl Mgr US Index	B066	30/09/94	BER	4.29	29	22.56	45	N.A.	N.A.				N.A.		N.A.	
	USD	18.66	Govett GSIL US Smaller Cos	G015	31/03/89	JER	-16.10	146	18.16	74	6.59	98.47	7	✪✪✪✪	2	176.92	7	N.A.	
	USD	17.84	Govett US Safeguard A	G016	15/03/96	JER	2.58	63	N.A.		N.A.	N.A.				N.A.		N.A.	
	USD	147.50	GSAM Oracle	G003	30/06/94	IOM	-1.22	93	1.70	121	N.A.	N.A.				N.A.		N.A.	
	USD	130	GT Healthcare A	G018	31/01/90	IRL	-3.11	105	33.16	9	5.61	126.61	3	✪✪✪✪✪	5	202.15	4	N.A.	
▲	USD	81	GT Technology A Share	G018	28/09/79	IRL	-3.20	106	24.37	32	5.68	121.60	4	✪✪✪✪✪	5	118.88	12	355.15	3
▲	USD	54	GT US Smaller Companies	G018	31/12/86	LUX	-14.83	144	14.90	90	4.31	59.72	36	✪✪✪	2	115.87	14	272.16	6
▲	USD	11.06	Guinness Flight Amer B'Chip	G019	30/11/90	GU	4.60	24	21.21	52	2.80	50.30	54	✪✪	3	68.45	44	N.A.	
●	USD	N.S.	Hansard EU USD Stockmkt	H010	17/02/95	IRL	4.83	18	22.27	49	N.A.	N.A.				N.A.		N.A.	
●	USD	14.25	Hansard US Momentum	H011	29/04/94	IOM	-1.67	96	9.04	107	N.A.	N.A.				N.A.		N.A.	
●	USD	2.74	Hansard US Stock Market	H011	28/02/90	IOM	0.04	88	22.53	46	3.62	53.49	49	✪✪	2	82.27	38	N.A.	
●	USD	5.67	Hansard\GT Healthcare	H016	31/07/92	IOM	0.15	87	36.07	4	6.92	75.39	13	✪✪✪	1	N.A.		N.A.	
●	USD	3.98	Hansard\GT Technology	H016	31/07/92	IOM	-5.21	118	24.54	30	5.64	149.30	2	✪✪✪✪✪	5	N.A.		N.A.	
●	USD	4.10	Hansard\GT US Smaller Cos	H016	27/09/91	IOM	-12.19	141	13.76	91	4.46	60.14	35	✪✪✪	2	126.08	11	N.A.	
▲	USD	16.34	Inter Strategie Small Co Cap	B069	31/10/94	LUX	0.77	81	34.36	6	N.A.	N.A.				N.A.		N.A.	
	USD	12.72	Irish Life Intl US Equity	I017	28/04/95	IRL	6.09	12	31.09	11	N.A.	N.A.				N.A.		N.A.	
	USD	69.46	JF American Growth	J004	29/07/83	HK	5.26	14	28.32	16	2.73	75.46	12	✪✪✪✪✪	5	187.68	6	229.49	12

▲ SIB Approved ● Insurance Fund **Values in US Dollars, on an offer to offer price basis with gross income reinvested** Data Source Micropal™

United States Of America Equity

continued

	CCY	Fund Size ($mil)	Fund Name	Manager Code	Fund Start Date	Domicile Code	3 Mths 97 % Chg	3 Mths 97 Rank	1 Year % Chg	1 Year Rank	Micropal Star Rating 3 Years Volatility	3 Years % Chg	3 Years Rank	3 Years Rating	Risk Return Rating	5 Years % Chg	5 Years Rank	10 Years % Chg	10 Years Rank
		50.31	Mean/Count				-0.91	151	18.16	131	3.77	56.61	84		1	97.89	60	264.31	19
▲	GBP	1.12	Jupiter Tyndall GF Wall St	J010	30/11/90	LUX	-3.11	104	7.58	108	2.67	15.49	79	✪		29.36	54	N.A.	
▲	GBP	8.58	Lazard SIT US Index	L001	28/02/89	GU	3.03	50	34.79	5	3.05	83.80	11	✪✪✪✪	5	114.88	17	N.A.	
	USD	9.90	LM Glbl US Appreciation B	L005	29/03/96	NL	-2.21	100	N.A.		N.A.	N.A.				N.A.		N.A.	
	USD	34.10	LOI The North America Fund	L019	31/03/94	LUX	-2.20	99	25.57	25	N.A.	N.A.				N.A.		N.A.	
	USD	15.86	Luxembourg Europ & American Fd	L023	29/11/91	LUX	0.29	85	16.13	87	3.22	51.83	50	✪✪	2	82.75	37	N.A.	
	USD	471.40	Luxlife Actions Americaines	L024	23/09/94	LUX	5.07	15	27.13	18	N.A.	N.A.				N.A.		N.A.	
	USD	43.90	M.Lynch Basic Value Portf O	M023	30/03/90	LUX	4.02	37	18.59	70	2.60	59.19	37	✪✪✪	4	110.25	20	N.A.	
	USD	13.50	M.Lynch Technology Portf A	M023	31/03/95	LUX	2.52	64	4.04	116	N.A.	N.A.				N.A.		N.A.	
	USD	2	McD Merger Arbitrage	A032	30/11/83	BER	3.42	44	12.13	100	1.40	34.91	68	✪	4	74.66	40	169.49	15
	USD	4.30	McD US Equity	A032	29/12/89	BER	8.01	2	22.06	50	2.76	71.43	21	✪✪✪	4	114.89	16	N.A.	
	USD	N.S.	MeesPierson UF US Large Cap	M012	01/03/96	LUX	4.74	20	N.A.		N.A.	N.A.				N.A.		N.A.	
	USD	N.S.	MeesPierson UF US Small Cap	M012	01/03/96	LUX	2.96	52	N.A.		N.A.	N.A.				N.A.		N.A.	
	USD	8.23	MFS Intl Fds US Emerg Gth B1	M026	30/06/94	LUX	-2.91	102	15.65	88	N.A.	N.A.				N.A.		N.A.	
	USD	4.15	MFS Intl Fds US Equity B1	M026	27/08/93	LUX	1.77	73	23.84	35	2.60	60.47	34	✪✪✪	4	N.A.		N.A.	
	USD	N.S.	MFS Meridian Research	M026	02/02/96	CA	-2.95	103	N.A.		N.A.	N.A.				N.A.		N.A.	
	USD	516.10	MFS Meridian US Emerging Gth	M026	31/12/91	CA	-6.28	124	16.81	86	5.65	74.17	16	✪✪✪✪	2	157.66	8	N.A.	
	USD	112.20	MFS Meridian US Equity	M026	31/08/92	CA	2.84	57	20.92	55	3.19	54.50	44	✪✪	3	N.A.		N.A.	
	USD	17	Momentum Navellier	M036	31/12/93	BER	-18.17	148	15.17	89	6.08	26.36	73	✪✪	1	N.A.		N.A.	
	USD	1	Momentum ValueMaster	M035	28/04/95	BER	4.29	28	7.44	110	N.A.	N.A.				N.A.		N.A.	
▲	GBP	11.67	Morgan Grenfell Am Sm Cos	M038	12/05/95	IRL	-5.92	123	19.84	61	N.A.	N.A.				N.A.		N.A.	
▲●	USD	17.70	Morgan Grenfell Amer E'prise	M038	29/10/93	IRL	-3.48	109	49.37	2	5.34	92.56	8	✪✪✪✪	2	N.A.		N.A.	
▲	GBP	25.88	Morgan Grenfell PF US Sm Cos	M038	31/08/88	IRL	-6.76	127	26.39	20	4.07	73.51	18	✪✪✪✪	3	92.27	31	N.A.	
	USD	6.70	Morgan Stanley Emg Growth	M039	30/08/91	LUX	-8.99	134	4.79	114	3.95	36.50	65	✪	1	24.23	57	N.A.	
	USD	57.01	Morgan Stanley Eq Growth	M039	31/08/92	LUX	4.12	33	28.72	15	2.79	87.26	9	✪✪✪✪✪	5	N.A.		N.A.	
	USD	6.84	Morgan Stanley US SmCap Val	M039	31/05/94	LUX	2.03	71	21.31	51	N.A.	N.A.				N.A.		N.A.	
	USD	27.13	Morgan Stanley US Value Eq	M039	31/05/94	LUX	2.85	56	18.38	72	N.A.	N.A.				N.A.		N.A.	
	USD	34.08	MultiLink US Eq	I011	31/12/90	LUX	2.60	61	22.47	47	2.83	63.51	32	✪✪✪	3	98.79	28	N.A.	
	USD	38.06	Multiscor Dolshares	S013	31/01/90	LUX	3.46	42	10.59	103	2.03	25.60	75	✪	1	40.83	52	N.A.	
	USD	N.S.	Nicholas-Applegate Flex Gth	A023a	30/06/92	BVI	-9.01	135	10.62	102	5.70	35.98	67	✪✪	1	N.A.		N.A.	
	USD	64.93	Parvest USA B	B037	30/03/90	LUX	2.62	60	25.77	23	3.39	53.93	47	✪✪	2	64.94	45	N.A.	
	USD	N.S.	Permal Growth	P010	29/04/83	BVI	-9.99	138	20.78	58	3.99	47.72	59	✪✪	1	49.52	51	195.46	13
	USD	N.S.	Permal Media&Communication	P010	31/08/89	BVI	-5.42	120	0.61	125	5.52	25.86	74	✪	1	32.08	53	N.A.	
	USD	55.21	Pictet C.F. Noramval	P016	29/06/84	LUX	4.09	34	21.16	53	2.47	51.64	52	✪✪	3	73.32	43	138.60	17
	USD	87.40	Pictet T.F.2 Biotech	P016	31/01/94	LUX	1.80	72	-0.80	127	N.A.	N.A.				N.A.		N.A.	
▲	USD	34.38	PRICOA WWIP US Growth	P022	31/01/92	LUX	1.31	75	19.13	67	2.35	59.15	38	✪✪✪	4	N.A.		N.A.	
▲	GBP	44.91	Prolific IF American	P027	30/04/92	IRL	4.99	16	24.38	31	3.28	49.99	55	✪✪	2	N.A.		N.A.	
	USD	4.27	Proton IF US Small Caps	P024	29/09/95	BVI	-5.90	122	13.54	93	N.A.	N.A.				N.A.		N.A.	
	USD	N.S.	Putnam Embassy US Growth A	P033	31/03/94	CA	-3.58	111	18.17	73	N.A.	N.A.				N.A.		N.A.	
	USD	N.S.	Putnam Embassy US Growth B	P033	31/03/94	CA	-3.78	114	17.23	82	N.A.	N.A.				N.A.		N.A.	
	USD	25.28	Putnam Emerging Health Science	P032	30/12/83	LUX	4.47	26	1.70	122	6.05	19.17	78	✪	1	21.68	58	311.61	4
	USD	127.16	Putnam Emerging Info Science	P032	31/05/85	LUX	-15.23	145	12.95	97	7.44	154.34	1	✪✪✪✪✪	3	342.25	1	925.51	1
	USD	36.62	Quaestor Equity America	Q001	29/06/90	IRL	6.53	10	21.11	54	5.71	63.68	31	✪✪✪	4	90.55	33	N.A.	
▲	USD	22.90	RBC GI USA	R003	24/11/95	GU	4.72	21	20.85	56	N.A.	N.A.				N.A.		N.A.	
	USD	0.35	RLI/Schroder US Sm Cos	R036	01/12/95	IOM	1.07	78	11.47	101	N.A.	N.A.				N.A.		N.A.	
●	USD	10.80	Royal Life/Perp American Gth	R034	30/10/87	IOM	2.12	70	16.84	85	3.58	46.77	61	✪✪	1	113.69	19	N.A.	
▲	USD	54.22	SBC Eq Ptf Small & Mid USA	S007	31/01/95	LUX	0.91	79	13	96	N.A.	N.A.				N.A.		N.A.	
	USD	18	Schroder Capital US Equity	S009	30/09/75	BVI	4.02	36	1.38	124	5.14	6.91	81	✪		26.98	55	93.82	19
▲	USD	83.24	Schroder Intl Sel US Equity	S010	30/09/75	LUX	3.16	48	27.39	17	3	68.37	24	✪✪✪✪	3	110.07	21	245.74	10
▲	USD	171.98	Schroder Intl Sel US Sm Cos	S010	31/07/89	LUX	0.63	82	18.79	69	3.18	74.35	15	✪✪✪✪✪	4	214.47	2	N.A.	
●	USD	2.28	Scot Amicable US Index Track	S015	30/06/94	IRL	4.75	19	22.59	44	N.A.	N.A.				N.A.		N.A.	
	USD	1.20	Scot Prov GP US Safeguard C	S014	31/05/96	IOM	2.16	69	N.A.		N.A.	N.A.				N.A.		N.A.	
	USD	35.75	Scudder GOF US Growth A-2	S019	30/04/93	LUX	4.13	32	18.91	68	2.76	48.67	57	✪✪	2	N.A.		N.A.	
	USD	32.35	Seahawk International Inc	S021	31/01/92	CA	2.99	51	33.98	8	8.33	27.85	71	✪✪	1	N.A.		N.A.	
	USD	5.18	State Street American	S048	31/12/90	LUX	-6.54	126	31.07	12	3.41	47.22	60	✪✪	2	89.62	34	N.A.	
▲	USD	19.60	Sun Life GP American Growth	S052	31/03/88	LUX	2.70	58	23.52	39	3.52	100.54	6	✪✪✪✪✪	5	208.35	3	N.A.	
▲	USD	2.70	Svecia USA Select III	S054	30/04/92	LUX	N.A.	—	9.05	106	3.24	23.43	76	✪	1	N.A.		N.A.	
	USD	N.S.	Templeton GS American A	T001	30/09/96	LUX	0.49	83	N.A.		N.A.	N.A.				N.A.		N.A.	

▲ SIB Approved ● Insurance Fund

Values in US Dollars, on an offer to offer price basis with gross income reinvested

Data Source Micropal™

United States Of America Equity

continued

	CCY	Fund Size ($mil)	Fund Name	Manager Code	Fund Start Date	Domicile Code	3 Mths 97 % Chg	3 Mths 97 Rank	1 Year % Chg	1 Year Rank	Micropal Star Rating 3 Years Volatility	3 Years % Chg	3 Years Rank	3 Years Rating	Risk Return Rating	5 Years % Chg	5 Years Rank	10 Years % Chg	10 Years Rank
		50.31	**Mean/Count**				**-0.91**	**151**	**18.16**	**131**	**3.77**	**56.61**	**84**		**1**	**97.89**	**60**	**264.31**	**19**
	USD	N.S.	Templeton GS American B	T001	30/09/96	LUX	0.26	86	N.A.		N.A.	N.A.				N.A.		N.A.	
	DEM	6.17	Thieme Fonds	T004	30/06/94	LUX	-1.80	97	3.10	120	N.A.	N.A.				N.A.		N.A.	
	USD	23.95	UBAM US Equity	U010	29/12/89	LUX	-1.22	94	31.60	10	3.72	37.30	64	✪	1	59.90	48	N.A.	
	USD	125.44	UBS (Lux) Small Cap Invst USA	U001	30/09/92	LUX	-3.50	110	16.93	84	4.23	29.52	70	✪	1	N.A.		N.A.	
	USD	32.30	US Financial Equities	E010	04/11/94	IRL	10.39	1	26	22	N.A.	N.A.				N.A.		N.A.	
	USD	8.50	Veco Capital Growth	B058	30/08/96	CA	-28.15	151	N.A.		N.A.	N.A.				N.A.		N.A.	
	USD	19.43	Vereins Lux Portf US Aktien	A007	31/03/93	LUX	6.10	11	23.13	40	2.96	71.47	20	✪✪✪✪	4	N.A.		N.A.	
	USD	0.11	VKAC Navigator US Quality Eq	V002	30/06/95	LUX	4.21	30	17.68	79	N.A.	N.A.				N.A.		N.A.	
▲	USD	24.74	Von Ernst GP US Sm Cos Eqty	B021	30/11/89	LUX	-7.91	129	22.88	42	4.47	101.76	5	✪✪✪✪✪	4	136.61	10	N.A.	
	USD	144.53	Vontobel Fund US Select Eq A	B017	30/10/92	LUX	-3.60	112	17.50	80	3.06	54.47	45	✪✪✪	2	N.A.		N.A.	
	USD	80.25	Vontobel Fund US Value Eq A	B017	29/11/91	LUX	5.85	13	19.97	59	2.84	66.26	26	✪✪✪	4	100.77	25	N.A.	
	USD	N.S.	Voyager Select IPO	V003	31/05/96	BER	1.24	76	N.A.		N.A.	N.A.				N.A.		N.A.	
	USD	30.55	Wellington MP US Eq Resrch A	W001	30/06/94	LUX	3.53	40	24.12	34	N.A.	N.A.				N.A.		N.A.	
	USD	15.99	Wellington MP US Eq Resrch B	W001	30/06/94	LUX	3.44	43	23.60	38	N.A.	N.A.				N.A.		N.A.	
	USD	N.S.	World Invest Tech	B022	08/11/96	LUX	-10.41	140	N.A.		N.A.	N.A.				N.A.		N.A.	
	USD	4.50	Zanett Lombadier	L020	07/01/00	CA	6.81	8	64.56	1	N.A.	N.A.				N.A.		N.A.	

▲ SIB Approved ● Insurance Fund **Values in US Dollars, on an offer to offer price basis with gross income reinvested** Data Source Micropal™

FIXED INTEREST STOCK (BOND) FUNDS

Offshore funds in the fixed interest stock sector are those which invest in fixed interest securities – alternatively known as bonds – with a maturity of three years or more. This is an important sector among offshore funds. After equity funds, fixed interest funds are more numerous than any other type of offshore fund — over 1,000 of them are listed.

The term fixed interest security covers a wide range of investment instruments, including government treasury bonds, corporate and municipal bonds. Such investments are relatively risk free, the main risk being that the bond issuers (effectively the government or organisation that has borrowed the money) will be unable to repay it. With stable governments this risk is usually acceptable. Because of their lack of creditworthiness, bonds to Third World governments and corporations naturally have more risk. The riskier the bond issuer, the higher yield rate on its debt.

The value of fixed interest stocks tends to run in the opposite direction of the interest rates in the economy in which the instrument is denominated. For example, a bond with a nominal value of $100 may pay 10 per cent interest ($10) a year. But it is not worth $100 if the current rates of interest are at just 5 per cent. Investors therefore only expect a 5 per cent return on their fixed interest investments so would be willing to pay up to $200 for a 10 per cent coupon bond. Such calculations are complicated by the length of time the bond has to maturity, but in essence the value of the bond goes up and down in an inverse relationship to the interest rate.

Micropal segregates fixed interest stock funds into 33 sectors. Most of these cover a single country, but there are some that are less geographically specific such as global fixed interest, global emerging markets, fixed interest and European-based sectors. The common theme is that at least 70 per cent of the assets of such funds must be invested in fixed interest securities with a maturity of three years or more.

By far the largest sector is global fixed interest. By investing in the funds in this sector, offshore investors can gain a diversified mix of fixed interest securities. Such diversification is useful, as picking the best individual markets can be difficult. Low inflation, low interest rate economies are unfavourable to a fixed interest investor, due to the poor rates of return available on fixed interest stocks. On the other hand, investing in fixed interest stocks from economies with more generous rates of interest may also suffer from a weaker currency. Unless it is important to the investor that the income produced by the fixed income fund is denominated in a certain currency, it is often best to consider a diversified global fixed interest fund.

Offshore investors select fixed interest funds due to their lower risk and the high levels of income such funds can achieve.

Australian Dollar Fixed Interest

Funds investing in excess of 70% in Australian Dollar denominated fixed interest securities (corporate, government, index-linked) with a maturity of three years or greater.

CCY	Fund Size ($mil)	Fund Name	Manager Code	Fund Start Date	Domicile Code	3 Mths 97 % Chg	Rank	1 Year % Chg	Rank	Micropal Star Rating 3 Years Volatility	% Chg	Rank	Rating	Risk Return Rating	5 Years % Chg	Rank	10 Years % Chg	Rank
	29.66	**Mean/Count**				**-2.07**	**9**	**17.95**	**9**	**2.56**	**41.07**	**5**		**1**	**52.01**	**3**	**0**	**0**
▲ AUD	2.43	Aetna IUF Aus Dllr Bond A	A011	29/04/88	LUX	-1.45	2	14.92	9	1.97	36.06	5	✪	4	39.35	3	N.A.	
AUD	1.25	BBL Renta Fd Australian Dlr C	B052	30/06/95	LUX	-2.18	6	17.39	6	N.A.	N.A.				N.A.		N.A.	
● AUD	23.05	Credis Bond AUD A	C054	28/02/92	LUX	-2.06	4	20.03	1	3.44	45.10	1	✪✪✪✪	3	N.A.		N.A.	
▲ AUD	1.19	Hambros EMMA Austr Dllr Bond	H002	29/04/88	GU	-2.16	5	18.06	5	2.56	39.37	4	✪✪	1	56.99	2	N.A.	
AUD	2.12	KB Lux Bond AUD B	K011	30/09/94	LUX	-2.02	3	15.99	8	N.A.	N.A.				N.A.		N.A.	
▲ AUD	36.05	Lloyds IP AUD Bond	L016	19/08/94	LUX	-2.42	7	19.59	2	N.A.	N.A.				N.A.		N.A.	
AUD	2.77	M.Lynch Global Curr AUS A	M023	28/04/89	LUX	-2.62	9	17.04	7	2.50	41.37	3	✪✪✪	2	59.70	1	N.A.	
▲ AUD	185.20	SBC Bond Portfolio AusD /B	S007	30/04/92	LUX	-1.27	1	19.25	4	2.36	43.44	2	✪✪✪	3	N.A.		N.A.	
AUD	12.83	Swissca Bond Invest AUD	S057	31/03/94	LUX	-2.44	8	19.30	3	N.A.	N.A.				N.A.		N.A.	

Austrian Schilling Fixed Interest

Funds investing in excess of 70% in Austrian Schilling denominated fixed interest securities (corporate, government, index-linked) with a maturity of three years or greater.

CCY	Fund Size ($mil)	Fund Name	Manager Code	Fund Start Date	Domicile Code	3 Mths 97 % Chg	Rank	1 Year % Chg	Rank	Micropal Star Rating 3 Years Volatility	% Chg	Rank	Rating	Risk Return Rating	5 Years % Chg	Rank	10 Years % Chg	Rank
	115.98	**Mean/Count**				**-6.08**	**3**	**-2.26**	**3**	**2.42**	**31.04**	**3**		**3**	**44.63**	**3**	**0**	**0**
ATS	202.69	Baer Multibond Austro Bond A	J007	29/11/91	LUX	-6.58	3	0.11	2	2.36	36.41	2	✪✪✪	3	51.69	1	N.A.	
ATS	143.46	KB Lux Bond ATS B	K011	31/03/89	LUX	-6.46	2	0.27	1	2.37	37.24	1	✪✪✪✪	4	50.45	2	N.A.	
▲ ATS	1.80	Swiss Life Proteus Aust Bond	S056	29/11/91	IRL	-5.21	1	-7.15	3	2.53	19.48	3	✪✪	2	31.75	3	N.A.	

BEF/LUF Fixed Interest

Funds investing in excess of 70% in Belgian and Luxembourg Franc denominated fixed interest securities (corporate, government, index-linked etc) with a maturity of three years or greater.

CCY	Fund Size ($mil)	Fund Name	Manager Code	Fund Start Date	Domicile Code	3 Mths 97 % Chg	Rank	1 Year % Chg	Rank	Micropal Star Rating 3 Years Volatility	% Chg	Rank	Rating	Risk Return Rating	5 Years % Chg	Rank	10 Years % Chg	Rank
	135.22	**Mean/Count**				**-7.03**	**38**	**0.82**	**33**	**2.38**	**39.12**	**26**		**1**	**55.87**	**23**	**153.80**	**2**
BEF	81.67	AGAM Strategy Bonds BEF Cap	A013	31/12/93	LUX	-7.34	24	2.81	2	2.32	43.53	3	✪✪✪✪	5	N.A.		N.A.	
BEF	N.S.	Astrobal Belgian Bonds B	B036	28/06/96	LUX	-7.16	14	N.A.		N.A.	N.A.				N.A.		N.A.	
BEF	N.S.	Bacob Luxinvest Short Term Cap	B002	08/12/95	LUX	-6.10	3	-4.71	33	N.A.	N.A.				N.A.		N.A.	
BEF	642.29	BBL Renta Fund Lux C	B052	31/12/85	LUX	-7.03	9	1.40	17	2.41	44.77	1	✪✪✪✪✪	4	63.12	2	198.73	1
LUF	581.59	Belicav B	C018	31/01/89	LUX	-7.08	10	2.14	7	2.46	42.09	6	✪✪✪✪	4	59.59	6	N.A.	
LUF	162.75	Belubond Fund LUF Cap	A037	29/01/88	LUX	-7.18	16	1.88	9	2.30	43.95	2	✪✪✪✪✪	5	56.51	12	N.A.	
LUF	193.88	BIL Bonds Francs C	B067	31/08/90	LUX	-7.27	19	-1.03	29	2.47	36.42	23	✪	1	48.67	21	N.A.	
● LUF	133.66	BL Multi Tst Bd FB FLUX B	B025	31/01/89	LUX	-7.42	28	1.65	14	2.34	39.63	15	✪✪	2	53.10	18	N.A.	
BEF	45.29	Cera Invest Capital Fix-1	C018	31/03/95	LUX	-7.78	35	1.76	11	N.A.	N.A.				N.A.		N.A.	
BEF	42.53	Contivest Obli Belux Long-T A	B023	30/11/94	LUX	-7.85	37	-1.36	31	N.A.	N.A.				N.A.		N.A.	
BEF	1.20	Cregem Bonds Beluf Cap	C059	31/01/89	LUX	-7.14	12	0.29	24	2.36	40.46	11	✪✪✪	3	54.87	15	N.A.	
LUF	N.S.	Demeter Francs Belges Cap	B026	30/04/90	LUX	-7.31	22	1.82	10	2.39	38.52	19	✪✪	2	55.35	13	N.A.	
BEF	86.40	Fixe Belux	B053	31/10/88	LUX	-7.15	13	1.72	13	2.28	39.54	16	✪✪	3	58.92	9	N.A.	
LUF	291.86	G-Bond Fund G-Rentinbel B	G009	31/05/88	LUX	-6.82	5	2.33	5	2.36	40.25	12	✪✪✪	3	59.41	7	N.A.	
LUF	323.40	Generalux Francs B	B064	31/07/91	LUX	-7.33	23	0.59	21	2.42	37.66	21	✪	1	56.61	11	N.A.	

▲ **SIB Approved** ● **Insurance Fund** **Values in US Dollars, on an offer to offer price basis with gross income reinvested** Data Source Micropal™

BEF/LUF Fixed Interest

continued

	CCY	Fund Size ($mil)	Fund Name	Manager Code	Fund Start Date	Domicile Code	3 Mths 97 % Chg	3 Mths 97 Rank	1 Year % Chg	1 Year Rank	Micropal Star Rating 3 Years Volatility	3 Years % Chg	3 Years Rank	3 Years Rating	Risk Return Rating	5 Years % Chg	5 Years Rank	10 Years % Chg	10 Years Rank
		115.98	**Mean/Count**				**-6.08**	**3**	**-2.26**	**3**	**2.42**	**31.04**	**3**		**3**	**44.63**	**3**	**0**	**0**
	BEF	23.95	ING Intl-Belgium Bond Cap	I008	30/09/94	LUX	-6.89	6	1.73	12	N.A.	N.A.				N.A.		N.A.	
▲	LUF	69.18	Inter Optimum BEF/LUF	B069	29/09/89	LUX	-7.47	31	0.24	25	2.37	38.98	18	✪✪	2	57.90	10	N.A.	
	LUF	87.25	Ippa Portf Belgian Bond B	B035	31/05/88	LUX	-7.23	18	1.49	16	2.42	41.46	9	✪✪✪	3	59.10	8	N.A.	
	BEF	N.S.	Isis Belgian Bonds	B026	31/05/95	LUX	-7.29	21	2.36	4	N.A.	N.A.				N.A.		N.A.	
	LUF	N.S.	Isis Bonds Cap	B026	31/01/89	LUX	-7.62	34	-0.52	27	2.39	41.77	8	✪✪✪✪	4	54.74	16	N.A.	
	BEF	117.92	KB Lux Bond BEF B	K011	29/04/88	LUX	-6.99	8	2.02	8	2.30	41.77	7	✪✪✪✪	4	54.87	14	N.A.	
	LUF	318.50	KB Renta Oblirenta Cap	K010	31/10/88	LUX	-7.48	32	1.30	18	2.43	39.30	17	✪✪	2	59.76	5	N.A.	
	BEF	24.73	Lion Belgium Instit Belbonds	C060	08/12/95	LUX	-6.93	7	2.53	3	N.A.	N.A.				N.A.		N.A.	
	LUF	9.08	Lion Interoblig LUF	C062	28/06/85	LUX	-7.50	33	0.08	26	2.31	24.75	25	✪	1	42.63	23	108.87	2
	BEF	2.72	LO Obliflex P Belgian Franc	L019	28/02/91	JER	-7.17	15	2.24	6	2.41	40.15	13	✪✪✪	2	62.04	3	N.A.	
	LUF	290.68	Luxbond Francs A Cap	C002	30/06/95	LUX	-7.37	25	1.55	15	N.A.	N.A.				N.A.		N.A.	
	LUF	47.53	Luxicav Oblilux B	S036	31/07/92	LUX	-7.86	38	-1.19	30	2.39	37.58	22	✪	1	N.A.		N.A.	
	LUF	92.55	Maestro B	S034	30/11/87	LUX	-7.28	20	1.20	19	2.35	40.81	10	✪✪✪	3	54.68	17	N.A.	
▲	BEF	36.35	Mercury ST BEF Global Bond	M021	31/05/93	LUX	-7.38	26	-3.08	32	2.49	24.60	26	✪	1	N.A.		N.A.	
	LUF	31.85	Panelfund Bonds EMU LUF Cap	A037	05/07/96	LUX	-7.20	17	N.A.		N.A.	N.A.				N.A.		N.A.	
	LUF	241.80	Parvest Obli Belux B	B037	30/11/87	LUX	-7.44	30	0.78	20	2.36	42.14	5	✪✪✪✪	4	59.85	4	N.A.	
	BEF	9.85	Portefeuille BG Oblig Belgolux	B063	17/05/96	LUX	-6.71	4	N.A.		N.A.	N.A.				N.A.		N.A.	
	BEF	N.S.	Privalux Bond Invest	C003	31/10/89	LUX	-7.80	36	0.33	23	2.38	39.83	14	✪✪	2	52.21	19	N.A.	
	BEF	64.36	Proventus Belgian Bonds C	P013	29/02/88	LUX	-7.42	27	2.91	1	2.34	42.71	4	✪✪✪✪	4	65.63	1	N.A.	
	LUF	1.56	Sogelux Fd Bonds Belgium	S037	30/11/87	LUX	-7.44	29	0.48	22	2.28	35.93	24	✪	1	50.54	20	N.A.	
	BEF	0.08	Sogenalux Bond A	S037	31/12/91	LUX	-7.12	11	-0.57	28	2.62	38.41	20	✪✪	2	44.93	22	N.A.	

Brazilian Reals Fixed Interest

Funds investing in excess of 70% in Brazilian Real denominated fixed interest securities (corporate, government, index-linked etc) with a maturity of three years or greater.

	CCY	Fund Size ($mil)	Fund Name	Manager Code	Fund Start Date	Domicile Code	3 Mths 97 % Chg	3 Mths 97 Rank	1 Year % Chg	1 Year Rank	Micropal Star Rating 3 Years Volatility	3 Years % Chg	3 Years Rank	3 Years Rating	Risk Return Rating	5 Years % Chg	5 Years Rank	10 Years % Chg	10 Years Rank
		52.50	**Mean/Count**				**2.81**	**20**	**15.48**	**18**	**1.54**	**85.34**	**4**			**0**	**0**	**0**	**0**
●	USD	15.61	Fonte Cindam Strategic	F025	31/08/93	CA	3.30	8	13.46	9	1.10	59.62	4	✪	3	N.A.		N.A.	
	USD	9.28	IB Brazil Income A	I001	16/06/95	CA	7.56	1	15.22	6	N.A.	N.A.				N.A.		N.A.	
	USD	22.27	IB Brazil Income B	I001	30/06/95	CA	7.22	2	15.99	5	N.A.	N.A.				N.A.		N.A.	
	USD	3.60	Liberal F.I.L.M. I	L010	17/11/95	BAH	1.31	17	10.23	17	N.A.	N.A.				N.A.		N.A.	
	USD	24.41	Liberal F.I.L.M. II	L010	17/11/95	BAH	-1.53	20	11.56	13	N.A.	N.A.				N.A.		N.A.	
	USD	1.04	Liberal F.I.L.M. III	L010	17/11/95	BAH	1.64	16	10.92	15	N.A.	N.A.				N.A.		N.A.	
	USD	1.03	Liberal F.I.S.T. I	L010	17/11/95	BAH	4.27	3	35.08	2	N.A.	N.A.				N.A.		N.A.	
	USD	1	Liberal F.I.S.T. II	L010	17/11/95	BAH	1.14	19	12.06	12	N.A.	N.A.				N.A.		N.A.	
	USD	17.71	Opportunity Fixed Exempt	O010	28/02/94	CA	1.73	15	10.99	14	N.A.	N.A.				N.A.		N.A.	
	USD	81.87	Opportunity Fixed Income	O010	31/12/92	CA	1.91	12	13.49	8	1.99	106.22	1	✪✪✪✪	2	N.A.		N.A.	
	USD	2.13	Prosperity Stock Fixed Inc	B012	22/09/95	BAH	1.74	14	10.61	16	N.A.	N.A.				N.A.		N.A.	
	USD	421.45	Star High Yield	B014	30/09/92	CA	2.15	11	13.18	10	1.34	85.52	3	✪✪	4	N.A.		N.A.	
	USD	18.41	UAM Columbus Structure	U004	30/09/96	BAH	3.52	7	N.A.		N.A.	N.A.				N.A.		N.A.	
	USD	195.04	Umbrella Debt	U004	30/11/92	BAH	3.84	5	17.44	3	1.71	89.98	2	✪✪✪	1	N.A.		N.A.	
	USD	140.57	Unifund B	U004	31/03/94	CA	2.75	10	12.84	11	N.A.	N.A.				N.A.		N.A.	
	USD	3.80	Vista Fixed Balanced	B010	03/02/95	CA	4.25	4	36.32	1	N.A.	N.A.				N.A.		N.A.	
	USD	6.20	Vista Fixed Income	B010	24/03/95	CA	1.88	13	8.34	18	N.A.	N.A.				N.A.		N.A.	
	USD	21.80	Vista High Yield	B010	24/03/95	CA	1.28	18	14.48	7	N.A.	N.A.				N.A.		N.A.	
	USD	10.30	Vista Portfolio	B010	15/12/95	CA	3.52	6	16.40	4	N.A.	N.A.				N.A.		N.A.	

▲ SIB Approved **● Insurance Fund** **Values in US Dollars, on an offer to offer price basis with gross income reinvested** Data Source Micropal™

Canadian Dollar Fixed Interest

Funds investing in excess of 70% in Canadian Dollar denominated fixed interest securities (corporate, government, index-linked etc) with a maturity of three years or greater.

	CCY	Fund Size ($mil)	Fund Name	Manager Code	Fund Start Date	Domicile Code	3 Mths 97 % Chg	3 Mths 97 Rank	1 Year % Chg	1 Year Rank	Micropal Star Rating 3 Years Volatility	3 Years % Chg	3 Years Rank	Rating	Risk Return Rating	5 Years % Chg	5 Years Rank	10 Years % Chg	10 Years Rank
		45.24	**Mean/Count**				**-1.18**	**15**	**10.30**	**14**	**2.62**	**19.37**	**12**		**1**	**28.91**	**7**	**128.20**	**1**
▲	CAD	3.95	Aetna IUF Canadian Dllr Bd A	A011	29/04/88	LUX	-1.51	12	9.31	11	2.51	16.62	11	✪		28.66	5	N.A.	
	CAD	10.19	BBL Renta Fd Canadian Dlr C	B052	30/11/93	LUX	-0.93	6	9.82	10	2.51	18.51	9	✪✪	2	N.A.		N.A.	
	CAD	0.85	BBL Renta Fund Obli Cash CAD C	B052	23/08/96	LUX	N.A.	—	N.A.		N.A.	N.A.				N.A.		N.A.	
	CAD	5.77	CIBC PCF Canadian Dollar Bond	C021	30/04/93	GU	-0.93	5	12.14	2	2.55	19.09	7	✪✪	2	N.A.		N.A.	
●	CAD	36.32	Credis Bond CAD A	C054	28/02/92	LUX	-0.92	4	12.41	1	3.29	22.42	2	✪✪✪✪	4	N.A.		N.A.	
●	CAD	75.27	Dit Lux Bondselect CAN $ A	D017	31/12/93	LUX	-0.90	3	10.69	6	2.96	18.58	8	✪	2	N.A.		N.A.	
▲	CAD	16.57	Jupiter Tyndall WUF Mortgage	J008	31/01/84	BER	-0.70	1	7.58	14	1.70	13.18	12	✪		18.25	7	128.20	1
	CAD	26.49	KB Lux Bond CAD B	K011	28/04/89	LUX	-1.71	14	11.62	3	2.38	21.19	4	✪✪✪	5	29.76	4	N.A.	
	CAD	14.94	KB Renta Canarenta B	K010	08/03/96	LUX	-1.40	11	N.A.		N.A.	N.A.				N.A.		N.A.	
▲	CAD	12.23	Lloyds IP CAD Bond	L016	30/11/90	LUX	-1.32	10	8.95	12	2.74	17.36	10	✪✪	1	26.85	6	N.A.	
	CAD	6.43	LO Obliflex X Canadian Dollar	L019	29/03/91	JER	-1.67	13	10.27	7	2.69	22.45	1	✪✪✪✪	3	36.22	1	N.A.	
	CAD	7.59	M.Lynch Global Curr CAD A	M023	31/07/89	LUX	-1.87	15	10.21	8	2.71	21.07	5	✪✪✪	3	29.81	3	N.A.	
	CAD	12.22	Parvest Obli Canada B	B037	28/02/94	LUX	-0.74	2	8.66	13	N.A.	N.A.				N.A.		N.A.	
▲	CAD	399.66	SBC Bond Portfolio CanD /B	S007	30/08/91	LUX	-1.09	8	11.32	4	2.64	22.31	3	✪✪✪✪✪	4	32.79	2	N.A.	
	CAD	37.90	Swissca Bond Invest CAD	S057	31/03/94	LUX	-0.95	7	10.11	9	N.A.	N.A.				N.A.		N.A.	
	CAD	57.53	UBS (Lux) Bond Invest CAD	U001	26/02/93	LUX	-1.11	9	11.06	5	2.71	19.64	6	✪✪✪	1	N.A.		N.A.	

Danish Krone Fixed Interest

Funds investing in excess of 70% in Danish Krone denominated fixed interest securities (corporate, government, index-linked etc) with a maturity of three years or greater.

	CCY	Fund Size ($mil)	Fund Name	Manager Code	Fund Start Date	Domicile Code	3 Mths 97 % Chg	3 Mths 97 Rank	1 Year % Chg	1 Year Rank	Micropal Star Rating 3 Years Volatility	3 Years % Chg	3 Years Rank	Rating	Risk Return Rating	5 Years % Chg	5 Years Rank	10 Years % Chg	10 Years Rank
		56.50	**Mean/Count**				**-7**	**7**	**2.39**	**6**	**2.25**	**40.50**	**4**		**1**	**55.21**	**3**	**217.63**	**1**
	DKK	36.32	BBL Renta Fd Danish Krone C	B052	30/06/95	LUX	-6.59	2	2.28	5	N.A.	N.A.				N.A.		N.A.	
	DKK	104.77	Danske Danish Bd Acc	D003	31/07/89	LUX	-6.75	4	3.39	1	2.15	42.61	1	✪✪✪✪	4	57.35	1	N.A.	
●	DKK	61.39	Frontrunner Danish Bonds	F032	29/06/90	LUX	-8.54	7	2.39	4	2.25	41.62	2	✪✪✪	3	52.40	3	N.A.	
	DKK	20.53	G-Bond Fund G-DKK Bond B	G009	19/01/96	LUX	-6.79	5	N.A.		N.A.	N.A.				N.A.		N.A.	
	DKK	26.29	KB Lux Bond DKK B	K011	30/06/93	LUX	-6.47	1	3.31	2	2.19	40.09	3	✪✪	2	N.A.		N.A.	
	DKK	128.11	KB Renta Decarenta B	K010	31/01/86	LUX	-6.75	3	2.64	3	2.39	37.69	4	✪	1	55.88	2	217.63	1
	DKK	18.07	Parvest Obli DKK B	B037	28/02/94	LUX	-7.08	6	0.31	6	N.A.	N.A.		✪		N.A.		N.A.	

▲ SIB Approved ● Insurance Fund Values in US Dollars, on an offer to offer price basis with gross income reinvested Data Source Micropal™

East Europe Fixed Interest

Funds investing in excess of 70% in Eastern European (Czech Republic, Slovakia, Poland, Hungary, Baltics, Romania, Bulgaria, Slovenia and former Soviet Union (including Central Asia)) denominated fixed interest securities (corporate, government, index-linked etc) with a maturity of three years or greater.

	CCY	Fund Size ($mil)	Fund Name	Manager Code	Fund Start Date	Domicile Code	3 Mths 97 % Chg	3 Mths 97 Rank	1 Year % Chg	1 Year Rank	Micropal Star Rating 3 Years Volatility	3 Years % Chg	3 Years Rank	3 Years Rating	Risk Return Rating	5 Years % Chg	5 Years Rank	10 Years % Chg	10 Years Rank
		22.57	**Mean/Count**				**-3.18**	**1**	**-2.16**	**1**	**0**	**0**	**0**			**0**	**0**	**0**	**0**
	DEM	22.57	IA Central European Fixed Int	E002	29/09/95	LUX	-3.18	1	-2.16	1	N.A.	N.A.				N.A.		N.A.	

Europe Fixed Interest

Funds investing in excess of 70% in European fixed interest securities (corporate, government, index-linked etc) with a maturity of three years or greater.

	CCY	Fund Size ($mil)	Fund Name	Manager Code	Fund Start Date	Domicile Code	3 Mths 97 % Chg	3 Mths 97 Rank	1 Year % Chg	1 Year Rank	Micropal Star Rating 3 Years Volatility	3 Years % Chg	3 Years Rank	3 Years Rating	Risk Return Rating	5 Years % Chg	5 Years Rank	10 Years % Chg	10 Years Rank
		108.46	**Mean/Count**				**-6.69**	**67**	**5.97**	**60**	**2.16**	**29.95**	**50**		**1**	**43.43**	**35**	**133.99**	**5**
▲	USD	20.01	AAF Europe Bond Fund	A001	30/06/94	LUX	0	1	8.80	10	N.A.	N.A.				N.A.		N.A.	
▲	USD	31.04	AEB Worldfolio 4 Non USD Bond	A009	29/11/85	LUX	-5.40	5	3.48	47	2.11	23.15	44	✪	1	42.73	20	139.82	2
	USD	6.49	Aetna IUF Mgd European Bd A	A011	29/04/88	LUX	-6.22	16	5.39	38	1.85	33.15	17	✪✪✪	3	48.08	11	N.A.	
	LUF	N.S.	Bacob Euro Convergence C	B002	08/11/96	LUX	-7.68	57	N.A.		N.A.	N.A.				N.A.		N.A.	
	DEM	N.S.	Bacob Euro Core C	B002	08/11/96	LUX	-7.30	54	N.A.		N.A.	N.A.				N.A.		N.A.	
	ATS	64.65	Baer Multibond Erste EC Bd A	J007	30/06/92	LUX	-6.60	30	2.91	51	2.17	33.41	15	✪✪✪	3	N.A.		N.A.	
	ECU	429.16	Baer Multibond Euro Bond A	J007	29/06/90	LUX	-6.83	40	8.87	8	1.92	33.20	16	✪✪✪✪	3	53.18	6	N.A.	
	ITL	18.43	BIL Euro Rent High Yld Curr C	B067	04/08/95	LUX	-8.45	65	18.17	1	N.A.	N.A.				N.A.		N.A.	
	LUF	54.45	BIL Euro Rent Multi-Curr C	B067	31/01/90	LUX	-7.26	52	5.54	35	1.88	38.15	5	✪✪✪✪✪	4	46.40	15	N.A.	
●	ECU	17.79	BL Multi Tst Bd Zone Eur B	B025	31/01/89	LUX	-6.64	33	7.69	19	1.76	24.39	42	✪	2	31.46	31	N.A.	
	ECU	12.13	Caixa Funds European Bonds	C004	29/11/91	LUX	-6.50	23	0.26	56	2.01	25.25	41	✪✪	1	18.59	35	N.A.	
	CHF	2.45	CIBC PCF EuroBond	C021	30/04/93	GU	-6.50	25	8.46	12	1.91	33.80	13	✪✪✪✪	3	N.A.		N.A.	
▲	ECU	205.71	Citi PF Euro Currencies Bd	C036	31/10/88	LUX	-6.86	41	6.86	23	1.93	27.77	34	✪✪	2	40.98	24	N.A.	
	LUF	11.32	Citibond Sicav A	C036	28/02/90	LUX	-6.98	45	4.66	45	2.80	36.06	8	✪✪✪✪	4	46.64	14	N.A.	
●	ECU	29.86	Clariden European Bond	C039	31/08/90	CA	-6.58	29	5.09	40	1.79	32.12	24	✪✪✪✪	4	42.51	21	N.A.	
	ESP	38.67	Concept Fd Fibanc Euro Rent	B067	05/01/96	LUX	-6.72	36	N.A.		N.A.	N.A.				N.A.		N.A.	
▲	ECU	14.87	Coutts GF Euro Currency Income	C052	31/05/93	IRL	-6.36	20	8.25	13	2.98	27.18	35	✪✪	1	N.A.		N.A.	
●	DEM	258.08	Credis Bond Europe A	C054	28/04/89	LUX	-8.23	64	7.83	16	2.62	37.97	6	✪✪✪✪✪	4	43.31	18	N.A.	
▲●	DEM	2701.11	DBIM Eurorenta	D006	30/11/87	LUX	-6.11	13	10.02	6	2.37	41.63	1	✪✪✪✪✪	5	52.13	7	N.A.	
	DEM	672.25	DekaLux Kapital 3-5	D009	30/11/92	LUX	-6.90	42	-1.44	59	2.44	34.16	11	✪✪✪	2	N.A.		N.A.	
	LUF	N.S.	Demeter Patrimoine Cap	B026	31/01/89	LUX	-6.78	37	6.60	27	2.05	19.44	46	✪	1	40.37	25	N.A.	
●	DEM	325.16	Dit Lux Euro Rentenfonds T	D017	31/12/92	LUX	-7	46	5.43	37	1.95	27.88	33	✪✪	2	N.A.		N.A.	
●	CHF	2.41	Eagle Star European Bd	E001	29/09/95	IOM	-5.68	7	6.97	22	N.A.	N.A.				N.A.		N.A.	
	ECU	65.46	Eufi-Rent Cap	E012	30/04/90	LUX	-6.26	17	8.81	9	1.83	28.02	32	✪✪	3	41.25	23	N.A.	
	NLG	44.47	Euromix Fund-Dutch Gldrs Cap	I008	29/10/93	LUX	-5.81	9	2.96	50	1.63	25.68	40	✪	3	N.A.		N.A.	
	LUF	72.22	Euromix Fund-Income Grwth Cap	I008	31/01/90	LUX	-5.86	10	3.10	48	1.76	25.81	39	✪	2	36.90	27	N.A.	
	ECU	1.60	F&C RAF European Bond	F003	29/11/85	JER	-6.80	38	6.26	30	1.75	32.33	22	✪✪✪	4	44.26	17	151.93	1
▲	ECU	75.21	Fidelity Fds European Bond	F011	28/09/90	LUX	-6.57	27	7.48	20	3.07	26.59	37	✪	1	45.06	16	N.A.	
	USD	0.33	Five Arrows IP European FI	R016	15/03/96	GU	-7.91	60	N.A.		N.A.	N.A.				N.A.		N.A.	
▲	ECU	22.88	Gartmore CSF European Bond	G007	29/11/85	JER	-6.91	43	5.69	34	2.62	32.22	23	✪✪✪	3	42.97	19	128.50	3
	ECU	34.79	Generalux Europe B	B064	31/07/91	LUX	-6.42	21	6.74	25	1.60	29.39	31	✪✪	4	41.50	22	N.A.	
▲●	ECU	26.49	Groupe Indosuez European Bd	G017	31/01/91	LUX	-5.26	4	7.78	17	1.82	41.10	2	✪✪✪✪✪	5	46.77	13	N.A.	
▲●	USD	5.64	Guinness FI IF Euro High Yld	G020	31/12/91	GU	-6.17	14	11.07	5	2.10	18.77	48	✪	1	26.27	34	N.A.	
▲	GBP	26.31	Guinness Flight Euro Hi Bd	G019	30/11/90	GU	-6.34	19	11.68	4	2.01	18.78	47	✪	1	28.15	32	N.A.	
▲	USD	16.45	Guinness Flight European Bd	G019	31/12/85	GU	-6.71	35	9.82	7	2.24	20.24	45	✪	1	33.70	29	122.41	5
▲	DEM	15.71	Hambros EMMA Contl Euro Bond	H002	29/04/88	GU	-7.87	59	1.41	53	2.40	31.20	27	✪✪	2	47.02	12	N.A.	
●	ECU	0.94	Hansard\Fidelity European Bd	H014	31/07/92	IOM	-7.24	51	5.77	33	3.05	27.18	36	✪✪	1	N.A.		N.A.	
●	ECU	0.59	Hansard\Gartmore CSF Euro Bd	H015	31/07/92	IOM	-7.53	55	4.80	42	2.61	31.79	26	✪✪	1	N.A.		N.A.	
●	GBP	2.55	Hansard\GF GSF Euro HI Bd	H017	31/07/92	IOM	-3.23	3	8.67	11	2.63	17.60	49	✪✪	1	N.A.		N.A.	
	FRF	14.58	Hottinger IF-Euro Bds FRF C	H032	30/12/94	LUX	-6.29	18	-0.03	58	N.A.	N.A.				N.A.		N.A.	
	ECU	42.82	HYPO Euro Bond	H024	29/11/91	LUX	-11.02	66	6.70	26	2.22	33.95	12	✪✪✪✪	5	48.59	10	N.A.	

▲ SIB Approved ● Insurance Fund **Values in US Dollars, on an offer to offer price basis with gross income reinvested** Data Source Micropal™

Europe Fixed Interest

continued

	CCY	Fund Size ($mil)	Fund Name	Manager Code	Fund Start Date	Domicile Code	3 Mths 97 % Chg	3 Mths 97 Rank	1 Year % Chg	1 Year Rank	Micropal Star Rating 3 Years Volatility	3 Years % Chg	3 Years Rank	Rating	Risk Return Rating	5 Years % Chg	5 Years Rank	10 Years % Chg	10 Years Rank
		108.46	**Mean/Count**				**-6.69**	**67**	**5.97**	**60**	**2.16**	**29.95**	**50**		**1**	**43.43**	**35**	**133.99**	**5**
	DEM	23.66	INVESCO PS European Bond	I014	29/03/96	LUX	-6.63	32	N.A.		N.A.	N.A.				N.A.		N.A.	
	ECU	15.22	KB European Bond	K007	31/12/90	LUX	-6.21	15	1.74	52	2.39	39.48	3	✪✪✪✪	4	67.35	1	N.A.	
	GRD	13.42	KB Lux Bond Greek Drachma B	K011	13/12/96	LUX	-2.68	2	N.A.		N.A.	N.A.				N.A.		N.A.	
	ECU	10.16	LO Obliflex H Hi Yld Eur Curr	L019	31/10/89	JER	-8.05	62	12.01	2	1.75	34.78	10	✪✪✪✪	4	58.73	3	N.A.	
	ECU	19.58	LO Obliflex L Hi Yld Eur Curr	L019	31/10/89	JER	-7.92	61	11.89	3	1.84	33.74	14	✪✪✪	4	56.05	4	N.A.	
	DEM	1.64	M.Lynch Euro Bond Ptf DM A2	M023	29/01/93	LUX	-7.54	56	6.46	28	1.92	30.37	29	✪✪	3	N.A.		N.A.	
	USD	3.84	M.Lynch Euro Bond Ptf USD A2	M023	29/01/93	LUX	-5.43	6	6.34	29	2.20	4.87	50	✪		N.A.		N.A.	
	DEM	11.41	Merck Finck Invest Lux Rent A	M014	31/12/92	LUX	-6.80	39	-0.03	57	2.04	32.91	18	✪✪✪	2	N.A.		N.A.	
▲	DEM	45.52	Mercury ST European Bond	M021	31/03/94	LUX	-6.63	31	4.90	41	N.A.	N.A.				N.A.		N.A.	
	DEM	45.15	MK Lux Eurorent A	M041	30/06/93	LUX	-7.15	50	5.51	36	2.20	31.05	28	✪✪	2	N.A.		N.A.	
	ECU	8.09	Monceau Europe Obligataire	B028	31/10/84	LUX	-7.11	48	4.27	46	1.79	26.45	38	✪	2	32.10	30	127.31	4
	ECU	21.76	Morgan Stanley Euro Bond	M039	28/02/91	LUX	-6.70	34	8.10	14	2.16	32.73	19	✪✪✪	2	59.26	2	N.A.	
	DEM	8.94	Paneurolife Europe Bond	P003	28/04/95	LUX	-6.57	28	5.93	32	N.A.	N.A.				N.A.		N.A.	
	CHF	520.34	Raiffeisen Euro Obli A	F024	31/03/94	LUX	-6.50	24	6.77	24	N.A.	N.A.				N.A.		N.A.	
▲	DEM	12.73	RBC Gl European Bond	R003	30/11/95	GU	-7.85	58	4.73	43	N.A.	N.A.				N.A.		N.A.	
▲	USD	42.99	Schroder European Bond	S008	29/06/90	GU	-8.10	63	6.15	31	2.09	38.71	4	✪✪✪✪	5	53.89	5	N.A.	
▲	ECU	15.95	Schroder Intl Sel Euro Bond	S010	30/09/94	LUX	-7.11	49	7.78	18	N.A.	N.A.				N.A.		N.A.	
	ECU	2.73	Scot Prov GP European Bond	S014	30/09/91	IOM	-6.44	22	0.31	55	2.34	32.62	21	✪✪✪	2	50.31	9	N.A.	
▲	USD	18.01	Skandifond Europe Bond	S030	30/06/88	LUX	-5.73	8	5.12	39	2.67	34.92	9	✪✪✪✪	3	38.90	26	N.A.	
▲	DEM	8.60	TGA European Bd	T009	30/04/92	LUX	-6.09	12	7.45	21	1.99	32.66	20	✪✪✪✪	4	N.A.		N.A.	
	DEM	398.66	Uni Optima	U012	28/02/94	LUX	-6.95	44	-2.27	60	N.A.	N.A.				N.A.		N.A.	
▲	DEM	1.59	Von Ernst GP Euro Fixed Int	B021	30/11/89	LUX	-7.27	53	4.67	44	1.62	23.68	43	✪	2	26.96	33	N.A.	
	ECU	110.43	Vontobel Fund EC Curr Bond A	B017	31/10/91	LUX	-6.53	26	7.96	15	2.15	37.33	7	✪✪✪✪✪	5	51.25	8	N.A.	
	ECU	44.02	Willer Euro Currencies	W004	31/07/92	LUX	-6.03	11	2.98	49	1.95	32.09	25	✪✪✪	3	N.A.		N.A.	
	DEM	43.40	Wuestenrot Europarent	W008	28/02/89	LUX	-11.55	67	0.56	54	3.19	29.68	30	✪✪	1	36.31	28	N.A.	

Europe (Hard Currency) Fixed Interest

Funds investing in excess of 70% in European Hard Currency (Deutschmark, Guilder, Belgian/Luxembourg Franc) fixed interest securities (corporate, government, index-linked etc) with a maturity of three years or greater.

	CCY	Fund Size ($mil)	Fund Name	Manager Code	Fund Start Date	Domicile Code	3 Mths 97 % Chg	3 Mths 97 Rank	1 Year % Chg	1 Year Rank	Micropal Star Rating 3 Years Volatility	3 Years % Chg	3 Years Rank	Rating	Risk Return Rating	5 Years % Chg	5 Years Rank	10 Years % Chg	10 Years Rank
		60.24	**Mean/Count**				**-5.45**	**9**	**-0.62**	**7**	**2.44**	**35.44**	**4**		**1**	**47.81**	**1**	**0**	**0**
	DEM	N.S.	Astrobal Hard Currency Bonds B	B036	28/06/96	LUX	-6.91	7	N.A.		N.A.	N.A.				N.A.		N.A.	
	DEM	76.01	BIL Euro Rent Strong Curr C	B067	31/01/90	LUX	-6.80	5	-0.30	2	2.41	34.22	4	✪	1	47.81	1	N.A.	
	DEM	85.67	Panelfund Hard Curr Bd DEM C	A037	31/12/92	LUX	-6.63	3	-0.71	5	2.44	35.88	2	✪✪✪✪	4	N.A.		N.A.	
	LUF	85.62	Panelfund Hard Curr Bd LUF C	A037	31/12/92	LUX	-6.75	4	-0.62	3	2.46	35.99	1	✪✪✪	3	N.A.		N.A.	
	NLG	85.64	Panelfund Hard Curr Bd NLG C	A037	31/12/92	LUX	-6.54	2	-0.71	4	2.44	35.67	3	✪✪	2	N.A.		N.A.	
	NLG	65.32	RG Bond Plus	R009	28/04/95	LUX	-7.39	9	-3.62	7	N.A.	N.A.				N.A.		N.A.	
	DEM	3.59	Swiss Life Proteus HC Bd DM	S056	10/11/95	IRL	-6.87	6	-0.76	6	N.A.	N.A.				N.A.		N.A.	
	DEM	19.84	Trinkaus LUXRENT Europa	T011	31/01/94	LUX	-6.95	8	2.41	1	N.A.	N.A.				N.A.		N.A.	

▲ SIB Approved ● Insurance Fund **Values in US Dollars, on an offer to offer price basis with gross income reinvested** Data Source Micropal™

Europe (Mediterranean) Fixed Interest

Funds investing in excess of 70% in Southern European (Mediterranean) fixed interest securities (corporate, government, index-linked etc) with a maturity of three years or greater.

	CCY	Fund Size ($mil)	Fund Name	Manager Code	Fund Start Date	Domicile Code	3 Mths 97 % Chg	3 Mths 97 Rank	1 Year % Chg	1 Year Rank	Micropal Star Rating 3 Years Volatility	3 Years % Chg	3 Years Rank	Rating	Risk Return Rating	5 Years % Chg	5 Years Rank	10 Years % Chg	10 Years Rank
		20.98	**Mean/Count**				**-8.76**	**1**	**2.19**	**1**	**2.60**	**33.60**	**1**		**3**	**0**	**0**	**0**	**0**
	CHF	20.98	LO Obliflex 28 Med Curr	L019	31/05/93	JER	-8.76	1	2.19	1	2.60	33.60	1	✪✪✪	3	N.A.		N.A.	

Eurobonds Fixed Interest

Funds investing in excess of 70% in Eurobonds with a maturity of three years or greater.

	CCY	Fund Size ($mil)	Fund Name	Manager Code	Fund Start Date	Domicile Code	3 Mths 97 % Chg	3 Mths 97 Rank	1 Year % Chg	1 Year Rank	Micropal Star Rating 3 Years Volatility	3 Years % Chg	3 Years Rank	Rating	Risk Return Rating	5 Years % Chg	5 Years Rank	10 Years % Chg	10 Years Rank
		6.25	**Mean/Count**				**-4.86**	**4**	**6.63**	**4**	**1.89**	**23.46**	**4**		**2**	**26.39**	**3**	**108.47**	**2**
	ECU	5.58	BanesFondo Intern. Eurobonos	B030	28/06/91	LUX	-7.96	4	6.24	3	1.74	17.15	3	✪✪	2	15.70	3	N.A.	
	DEM	10.55	EBC IIF Eurobond LT DEM	E004	31/03/93	JER	-7.83	3	8.87	1	2.37	44.57	1	✪✪✪✪	4	N.A.		N.A.	
	USD	4.10	EBC IIF Eurobond LT USD	E004	31/01/84	JER	-0.56	1	8.06	2	2.08	19.37	2	✪✪✪	3	29.51	2	102.48	2
▲	USD	4.78	Jupiter Tyndall WUF Eurobond	J008	31/01/84	BER	-3.07	2	3.36	4	1.38	12.75	4	✪		33.95	1	114.46	1

European Currency Unit Fixed Interest

Funds investing in excess of 70% in fixed interest securities denominated in ECU (corporate, government, index-linked etc) with a maturity of three years or greater.

	CCY	Fund Size ($mil)	Fund Name	Manager Code	Fund Start Date	Domicile Code	3 Mths 97 % Chg	3 Mths 97 Rank	1 Year % Chg	1 Year Rank	Micropal Star Rating 3 Years Volatility	3 Years % Chg	3 Years Rank	Rating	Risk Return Rating	5 Years % Chg	5 Years Rank	10 Years % Chg	10 Years Rank
		95.78	**Mean/Count**				**-6.80**	**36**	**6.77**	**33**	**1.84**	**32.93**	**29**		**2**	**43.04**	**20**	**160.76**	**5**
	ECU	23.95	BBL Renta Fund Ecu C	B052	30/05/86	LUX	-6.43	8	7.42	18	1.61	32.37	19	✪✪	3	46.22	11	158.77	3
	ECU	54.33	BIL Bonds ECU C	B067	31/12/92	LUX	-7.11	29	6.31	25	1.73	32.61	18	✪✪	2	N.A.		N.A.	
	ECU	48.32	Cera Invest EURO Fund Cap	C018	07/06/96	LUX	-6.48	14	N.A.		N.A.	N.A.				N.A.		N.A.	
●	ECU	427.48	Credis Bond ECU A	C054	31/03/87	LUX	-6.61	21	8.23	11	2.54	34.46	12	✪✪✪✪	4	48.97	4	N.A.	
●	ECU	5.50	ECU Capitalisation	C062	30/05/86	LUX	-6.79	25	8.72	4	1.64	33.96	14	✪✪✪	4	42.77	15	144.26	5
	ECU	219.18	Ecupar B	B037	29/11/91	LUX	-6.58	18	6.32	24	1.97	37.78	2	✪✪✪✪	3	48.24	5	N.A.	
	ECU	83.89	Europe Obligations Long Terme	S035	31/10/91	LUX	-6.45	11	7.10	21	1.70	36.03	7	✪✪✪✪	4	42.23	16	N.A.	
	ECU	4.47	Fixe Ecu	B053	28/04/89	LUX	-6.45	12	8.60	5	1.71	32.64	17	✪✪	3	46.48	10	N.A.	
	ECU	22.65	Fructilux Oblig Europeennes	B043	31/10/91	LUX	-7.27	32	1.81	31	2.24	29.46	26	✪	1	35.07	18	N.A.	
	LUF	39.09	G-Bond Fund G-Ecu Bond B	G009	31/01/92	LUX	-6.49	15	7.93	15	1.76	36.16	6	✪✪✪✪✪	3	N.A.		N.A.	
●	ECU	2.04	Hansard Ecu Bond	H011	31/07/92	IOM	-7.13	30	9.67	2	1.93	32.13	21	✪✪	2	N.A.		N.A.	
●	ECU	N.S.	Hansard EU ECU Bond	H010	17/02/95	IRL	-7.37	33	10.08	1	N.A.	N.A.				N.A.		N.A.	
	ECU	14.57	Hottinger IF-Euro Bds Ecu C	H032	31/05/95	LUX	-6.17	3	0.45	32	N.A.	N.A.				N.A.		N.A.	
▲	ECU	49.68	Inter Optimum ECU	B069	30/04/92	LUX	-6.43	7	7.49	17	1.77	36.49	5	✪✪✪✪	4	N.A.		N.A.	
	ECU	0.28	ItalFortune Intl Ecu Bond	F015	31/07/90	LUX	-7.94	35	-2.05	33	1.69	17.59	29	✪	1	3.26	20	N.A.	
	ECU	212.44	KB Renta Ecurenta B	K010	31/01/86	LUX	-6.47	13	7.15	20	1.77	31.96	22	✪✪	2	47.66	7	162.39	2
	ECU	2.13	Lion Interinvest Bds ECU	C062	30/11/87	LUX	-6.90	27	8.55	6	1.71	36.53	4	✪✪✪✪✪	4	39.92	17	N.A.	
	ECU	28.62	Lion Interoblig Ecu	C062	31/03/93	LUX	-7.14	31	7.99	13	1.75	30.71	23	✪	2	N.A.		N.A.	
▲	ECU	9.42	Lloyds IP ECU Bond	L016	30/11/90	LUX	-6.50	16	8.52	8	1.78	34.48	11	✪✪✪	3	46.02	12	N.A.	
	ECU	13.88	LO Obliflex N Euro Curr Unit	L019	31/03/86	JER	-6.05	2	8.74	3	1.79	33.19	16	✪✪	2	52.18	2	182.86	1
	ECU	7.68	MLBS (B) Ecu Fixed Income	M024	30/09/94	LUX	-6.45	10	7.01	23	N.A.	N.A.				N.A.		N.A.	
	ECU	53.60	Multibond Actibond ECU B	C015	28/02/89	LUX	-6.61	20	7.98	14	1.59	34.80	9	✪✪✪	5	47.41	8	N.A.	

▲ SIB Approved ● Insurance Fund Values in US Dollars, on an offer to offer price basis with gross income reinvested Data Source Micropal™

European Currency Unit Fixed Interest

continued

	CCY	Fund Size ($mil)	Fund Name	Manager Code	Fund Start Date	Domicile Code	3 Mths 97 % Chg	3 Mths 97 Rank	1 Year % Chg	1 Year Rank	Micropal Star Rating 3 Years Volatility	3 Years % Chg	3 Years Rank	Rating	Risk Return Rating	5 Years % Chg	5 Years Rank	10 Years % Chg	10 Years Rank
		95.78	**Mean/Count**				**-6.80**	**36**	**6.77**	**33**	**1.84**	**32.93**	**29**		**2**	**43.04**	**20**	**160.76**	**5**
	ECU	32.20	Panelfund Bonds EMU Ecu Cap	A037	05/07/96	LUX	-7.08	28	N.A.		N.A.	N.A.				N.A.		N.A.	
	ECU	133.11	Parvest Obli Ecu B	B037	30/04/91	LUX	-6.32	5	7.05	22	1.84	29.50	25	✪	1	46.53	9	N.A.	
	ECU	69.04	Pictet F.I.F. – Valbond ECU	P016	28/02/92	LUX	-6.58	19	7.20	19	1.85	30.71	24	✪	1	N.A.		N.A.	
	ECU	26.77	Pleiade ECU Bonds	B039	26/02/93	LUX	-5.71	1	6.21	26	1.85	35.28	8	✪✪✪✪	2	N.A.		N.A.	
	ECU	12.34	Proton Fund Intl Bond ECU	P025	29/09/95	LUX	-6.65	23	5.27	28	N.A.	N.A.				N.A.		N.A.	
▲	ECU	0.22	SanPaolo Ecu Obligations	S004	30/11/88	LUX	-6.78	24	5.74	27	1.68	26.74	28	✪	1	27.61	19	N.A.	
▲	ECU	719.17	SBC Bond Portfolio Ecu /B	S007	30/08/91	LUX	-6.45	9	8.45	9	1.68	37.11	3	✪✪✪✪✪	5	50.87	3	N.A.	
	ECU	39.70	Sogelux Fd Bonds Europe	S037	31/07/87	LUX	-6.65	22	8.11	12	1.74	38.15	1	✪✪✪✪	5	48.02	6	N.A.	
	ECU	337.69	Swissca Bond Invest ECU	S057	29/05/92	LUX	-6.50	17	7.61	16	2.53	34.14	13	✪✪✪	3	N.A.		N.A.	
	ECU	2.27	Transoblig Ecu	B041	28/02/86	LUX	-6.88	26	8.32	10	1.68	34.78	10	✪✪✪	4	44.63	13	155.54	4
	ECU	590.55	UBS (Lux) Bond Invest XEU	U001	31/10/89	LUX	-6.39	6	8.55	7	1.80	33.76	15	✪✪✪	2	52.34	1	N.A.	
	ECU	60.98	UBS (Lux) Ptf Inv Fix Inc XEU	U001	30/06/93	LUX	-6.26	4	3.41	29	1.80	29.26	27	✪	1	N.A.		N.A.	
	CHF	4.78	UBZ Euro Income	U002	30/12/88	LUX	-11.07	36	3.30	30	2.27	32.13	20	✪✪	1	44.32	14	N.A.	
	BEF	0.10	World Invest Fixed Income	B022	08/11/96	LUX	-7.80	34	N.A.		N.A.	N.A.				N.A.		N.A.	

Far East & Pacific Fixed Interest

Funds investing in excess of 70% in Far Eastern currency denominated fixed interest securities (corporate, government, index-linked etc) with a maturity of three years or greater.

CCY	Fund Size ($mil)	Fund Name	Manager Code	Fund Start Date	Domicile Code	3 Mths 97 % Chg	3 Mths 97 Rank	1 Year % Chg	1 Year Rank	Micropal Star Rating 3 Years Volatility	3 Years % Chg	3 Years Rank	Rating	Risk Return Rating	5 Years % Chg	5 Years Rank	10 Years % Chg	10 Years Rank
	17.57	**Mean/Count**				**0.26**	**7**	**1.89**	**2**	**2.84**	**8.84**	**2**			**58.57**	**2**	**0**	**0**
BEF	19.48	BBL (L) Invest Equi-Fix Asia1	B052	28/06/96	LUX			N.A.		N.A.	N.A.				N.A.		N.A.	
USD	12.10	HSBC Asian Bond	H034	28/06/96	HK	2.20	1	N.A.		N.A.	N.A.				N.A.		N.A.	
USD	13.96	Indosuez Asian Income	I007	31/03/87	HK	0.65	5	10.11	1	2.26	11.25	1	✪✪✪		64.94	1	N.A.	
USD	64.33	M.Lynch Asia Tiger Bond A1	M023	02/02/96	LUX	1.15	3	N.A.		N.A.	N.A.				N.A.		N.A.	
USD	11.99	Peregrine Asian Bond	P008	30/04/96	CA	1.82	2	N.A.		N.A.	N.A.				N.A.		N.A.	
USD	0.06	RLI/GF Asia Currency & Bond	R026	12/04/96	IOM	-0.47	6	N.A.		N.A.	N.A.				N.A.		N.A.	
USD	1.10	Scot Prov GP Far East Bond	S014	30/09/91	IOM	-4.52	7	-6.32	2	3.42	6.43	2	✪✪		52.20	2	N.A.	

Finnish Markka Fixed Interest

Funds investing in excess of 70% in Finnish Markka denominated fixed interest securities (corporate, government, index-linked etc) with a maturity of three years or greater.

CCY	Fund Size ($mil)	Fund Name	Manager Code	Fund Start Date	Domicile Code	3 Mths 97 % Chg	3 Mths 97 Rank	1 Year % Chg	1 Year Rank	Micropal Star Rating 3 Years Volatility	3 Years % Chg	3 Years Rank	Rating	Risk Return Rating	5 Years % Chg	5 Years Rank	10 Years % Chg	10 Years Rank
	1.97	**Mean/Count**				**-6.76**	**1**	**1.38**	**1**	**3.07**	**56.18**	**1**		**3**	**0**	**0**	**0**	**0**
FIM	1.97	MultiLink Finnish Bonds	I011	29/10/93	LUX	-6.76	1	1.38	1	3.07	56.18	1	✪✪✪	3	N.A.		N.A.	

▲ **SIB Approved** ● **Insurance Fund** **Values in US Dollars, on an offer to offer price basis with gross income reinvested** Data Source Micropal™

French Franc Fixed Interest

Funds investing in excess of 70% in French Franc denominated fixed interest securities (corporate, government, index-linked etc) with a maturity of three years or greater.

	CCY	Fund Size ($mil)	Fund Name	Manager Code	Fund Start Date	Domicile Code	3 Mths 97 % Chg	3 Mths 97 Rank	1 Year % Chg	1 Year Rank	Micropal Star Rating 3 Years Volatility	Micropal Star Rating 3 Years % Chg	Micropal Star Rating 3 Years Rank	Micropal Star Rating Rating	Risk Return Rating	5 Years % Chg	5 Years Rank	10 Years % Chg	10 Years Rank
		50.32	**Mean/Count**				**-6.78**	**38**	**2.24**	**36**	**2.29**	**32.41**	**30**		**2**	**49.52**	**22**	**157.91**	**2**
	FRF	116.99	BIL Bonds Francs Francais C	B067	30/04/93	LUX	-7.23	34	2.87	21	2.32	34.39	7	✪✪✪✪	3	N.A.		N.A.	
	FRF	12.64	Bolux Obligations	C003	31/07/92	LUX	-4.35	2	-1.28	29	2.31	25.44	29	✪	1	N.A.		N.A.	
	FRF	6.26	Capital Gestion Oblig LT	C009	29/04/94	LUX	-7.14	31	5.53	3	N.A.	N.A.				N.A.		N.A.	
	FRF	54.97	Capital Gestion Valeurs	C009	30/12/94	LUX	-2.01	1	5.94	2	N.A.	N.A.				N.A.		N.A.	
●	FRF	58.60	Credis Bond FRF A	C054	31/12/90	LUX	-6.74	15	6.57	1	2.89	38.58	2	✪✪✪✪✪	5	65.64	1	N.A.	
	FRF	14	Eurobc Obligations	O001	31/05/96	LUX	-9.76	38	N.A.		N.A.	N.A.				N.A.		N.A.	
	ECU	23.01	Eurocode	C058	29/04/88	LUX	-7.05	28	2.01	24	2.18	32.86	15	✪✪✪	4	49.17	12	N.A.	
	FRF	21.92	Fixe Franc Francais	B053	31/10/88	LUX	-6.84	21	4.55	9	2.18	34.32	8	✪✪✪✪	4	62.23	3	N.A.	
	FRF	37.53	Fructilux Oblig Francaises	B043	31/10/91	LUX	-6.61	8	0.93	25	2.21	33.03	14	✪✪✪	3	45.52	14	N.A.	
	FRF	1.08	G-Bond Fund G-FRF Bond B	G009	19/01/96	LUX	-6.60	7	N.A.		N.A.	N.A.				N.A.		N.A.	
	FRF	37.44	Generalux FRF B	B064	31/07/91	LUX	-7.05	29	3.48	17	2.07	28.15	27	✪	2	47.44	13	N.A.	
▲●	FRF	21.77	Groupe Indosuez FRF Bond	G017	31/05/91	LUX	-6.54	6	3.79	15	2.23	32.42	17	✪✪	2	54.67	10	N.A.	
	FRF	N.S.	Hansard EU French FI	H010	17/02/95	IRL	-6.63	9	-0.79	28	N.A.	N.A.				N.A.		N.A.	
●	FRF	0.19	Hansard French Fixed Interest	H011	01/07/94	IOM	-7.64	36	2.49	22	N.A.	N.A.				N.A.		N.A.	
▲	FRF	90.88	Inter Optimum FRF	B069	29/09/89	LUX	-6.65	10	4.36	12	2.24	35.18	6	✪✪✪✪	4	56.55	7	N.A.	
	FRF	12.40	KB Lux Bond FRF B	K011	30/10/92	LUX	-6.96	27	5.21	6	2.20	35.82	5	✪✪✪✪	4	N.A.		N.A.	
▲	FRF	14.07	Lloyds IP FRF Bond	L016	30/11/90	LUX	-7.10	30	4.18	13	2.35	36.03	4	✪✪✪✪	4	59.92	5	N.A.	
	FRF	15.48	LO Obliflex S French Franc	L019	30/06/89	JER	-6.74	16	4.51	10	2.30	32.81	16	✪✪	2	61.49	4	N.A.	
	FRF	6.48	MOSAIS Oblig Francaises	C058	30/03/90	LUX	-6.70	12	5.39	4	2.31	33.81	9	✪✪✪	3	57.37	6	N.A.	
	FRF	6.08	Multibond Actibond FRF B	C015	31/03/89	LUX	-6.79	18	3.23	20	2.19	31.84	21	✪✪	2	54.66	11	N.A.	
	FRF	158.70	Parvest Obli Franc B	B037	30/09/86	LUX	-6.93	26	2.30	23	2.34	28.99	25	✪	1	56.30	8	204.51	1
	FRF	18.76	Pictet F.I.F. – Valbond FRF	P016	29/10/93	LUX	-6.73	14	3.57	16	2.24	32.23	20	✪✪	2	N.A.		N.A.	
	FRF	3.98	Pleiade French Franc Bonds	B039	30/06/93	LUX	-7.20	33	3.30	19	2.14	33.08	13	✪✪✪	4	N.A.		N.A.	
	FRF	6.42	Proton IF FRF Fixed Income	P024	29/09/95	BVI	-7.38	35	0.80	26	N.A.	N.A.				N.A.		N.A.	
▲	ECU	1.39	SanPaolo Ecu Obligatns France	S004	28/02/90	LUX	-7.14	32	5.23	5	1.82	27.35	28	✪	3	29.11	22	N.A.	
▲	FRF	348.91	SBC Bond Portfolio FF /B	S007	30/08/91	LUX	-6.68	11	4.77	7	2.20	37.93	3	✪✪✪✪✪	5	65.43	2	N.A.	
	FRF	87.34	Sogelux Fd Bonds France	S037	31/07/87	LUX	-6.89	23	4.59	8	2.25	33.25	12	✪✪✪	3	55.57	9	N.A.	
	FRF	58.14	Swissca Bond Invest FRF	S057	31/05/93	LUX	-6.81	20	3.42	18	2.58	33.61	10	✪✪✪✪	3	N.A.		N.A.	
	FRF	0.40	Transoblig FRF Placement	B041	30/09/86	LUX	-8.50	37	-2.03	31	2.21	22.63	30	✪	1	33.89	21	111.31	2
	FRF	64.26	UBAM FRF Bond	U010	31/03/93	LUX	-6.90	24	3.87	14	2.34	40.15	1	✪✪✪✪✪	5	N.A.		N.A.	
	FRF	106.23	UBS (Lux) Bond Invest FRF	U001	26/02/93	LUX	-6.48	4	4.49	11	2.30	33.33	11	✪✪✪	2	N.A.		N.A.	
	FRF	11.75	UBS (Lux) Ptf Inv Fix Inc FRF	U001	29/07/94	LUX	-6.92	25	0.11	27	N.A.	N.A.				N.A.		N.A.	
	ECU	96.64	Winchester HL Intl Secs D	O008	31/10/88	BER	-6.49	5	-3.82	36	2.34	28.47	26	✪	1	37.94	20	N.A.	
	ECU	42.99	Winchester HL Intl Secs F	O008	30/12/88	BER	-6.88	22	-2.26	32	2.36	31.15	23	✪✪	1	38.16	18	N.A.	
	ECU	44.98	Winchester HL IS Madison	O008	31/07/90	BER	-6.77	17	-2.64	34	2.42	31.32	22	✪✪	1	37.96	19	N.A.	
	ECU	96.64	Winchester RL Intl Secs D	O008	31/10/88	BAH	-6.42	3	-3.54	35	2.34	29.55	24	✪	1	40.15	16	N.A.	
	ECU	117.46	Winchester RL Intl Secs F	O008	30/12/88	BAH	-6.81	19	-1.96	30	2.37	32.34	18	✪✪	2	40.40	15	N.A.	
	ECU	44.98	Winchester RL IS Madison	O008	31/07/90	BAH	-6.71	13	-2.39	33	2.42	32.31	19	✪✪	2	39.78	17	N.A.	

▲ SIB Approved ● Insurance Fund

Values in US Dollars, on an offer to offer price basis with gross income reinvested

Data Source Micropal™

German DMark Fixed Interest

Funds investing in excess of 70% in German Deutschemark denominated fixed interest securities (corporate, government, index-linked etc) with a maturity of three years or greater.

	CCY	Fund Size ($mil)	Fund Name	Manager Code	Fund Start Date	Domicile Code	3 Mths 97 % Chg	3 Mths 97 Rank	1 Year % Chg	1 Year Rank	Micropal Star Rating 3 Years Volatility	3 Years % Chg	3 Years Rank	Rating	Risk Return Rating	5 Years % Chg	5 Years Rank	10 Years % Chg	10 Years Rank
		144.62	**Mean/Count**				**-6.62**	**95**	**-1.33**	**88**	**2.52**	**30.74**	**68**		**1**	**45.46**	**24**	**116.65**	**2**
	DEM	110.86	A.L.S.A. BVB DM Renten 1	A007	31/03/95	LUX	-7.39	90	-2.68	79	N.A.	N.A.				N.A.		N.A.	
	DEM	262.39	A.L.S.A. BVB DM Renten 2	A007	31/03/95	LUX	-6.61	23	-0.66	21	N.A.	N.A.				N.A.		N.A.	
	DEM	25.80	A.L.S.A. BVB DM Renten 3	A007	31/03/95	LUX	-6.50	14	-0.20	13	N.A.	N.A.				N.A.		N.A.	
	DEM	367.31	A.L.S.A. DM Medium Renten	A007	31/03/95	LUX	-7.12	78	-1.19	37	N.A.	N.A.				N.A.		N.A.	
	DEM	96.66	A.L.S.A. DM Renten	A007	30/11/93	LUX	-6.52	15	0.10	10	3.21	34.55	9	✪✪✪✪	3	N.A.		N.A.	
	DEM	857.85	A.L.S.A. Rent	A007	30/10/92	LUX	-6.60	22	-1.85	62	2.46	31.51	34	✪✪✪	3	N.A.		N.A.	
▲	DEM	17.37	AAF Germany Bond Fund	A001	30/06/94	LUX	-6.82	49	-1.53	55	N.A.	N.A.				N.A.		N.A.	
▲	DEM	1.05	Aetna IUF Deutschmark Bd A	A011	29/04/88	LUX	-7.01	74	-3.17	82	2.41	25.84	61	✪	1	39.32	22	N.A.	
	DEM	173.49	Baer Multibond DM Bond A	J007	31/03/92	LUX	-6.77	40	-1.91	66	2.44	29.34	47	✪✪	2	N.A.		N.A.	
	DEM	N.S.	Bank Hofmann Germanrent	B016	31/03/93	GU	-6.67	29	-0.66	20	2.84	35.63	4	✪✪✪✪✪	4	N.A.		N.A.	
	DEM	52.12	BBL Renta Fd Deutsche Mark C	B052	30/10/92	LUX	-6.77	41	-1.56	56	2.51	28.36	54	✪	1	N.A.		N.A.	
	DEM	474.06	BIL Bonds Deutschemark C	B067	31/12/92	LUX	-7.17	81	-1.69	57	2.45	32.44	24	✪✪✪✪	3	N.A.		N.A.	
●	DEM	72.43	BL Multi Tst Bd DM B	B025	31/01/89	LUX	-6.46	13	-1.48	54	2.44	32.94	20	✪✪✪✪	4	43.89	17	N.A.	
	DEM	71.54	CAMCO Fonds DM-Renten	C006	15/12/95	LUX	-6.93	62	-1.14	36	N.A.	N.A.				N.A.		N.A.	
	DEM	23.30	Capital Gestion Oblig Allem	C009	05/07/96	LUX	-7.33	89	N.A.		N.A.	N.A.				N.A.		N.A.	
	DEM	60.37	CB Lux Portfolio DM Media Rnt	A007	31/03/94	LUX	-7.14	79	-1.36	46	N.A.	N.A.				N.A.		N.A.	
	DEM	5.08	CB Lux Portfolio DM Renten	A007	31/03/93	LUX	-6.64	27	-0.93	28	2.58	31.21	36	✪✪	2	N.A.		N.A.	
▲	DEM	20.72	CMI GNF German Bond	C042	30/04/90	LUX	-5.70	10	-1.26	41	2.89	29.99	46	✪✪	1	45.08	16	N.A.	
●	GBP	2.71	CMI Ins Co German Bond	C043	31/01/91	IOM	-7.83	93	-1.89	64	2.88	29.32	48	✪✪	1	38.55	23	N.A.	
●	DEM	0.13	CMI Passport German Bond	C044	20/01/95	IOM	-6.97	68	-2.28	74	N.A.	N.A.				N.A.		N.A.	
▲	DEM	51.72	Coutts GF Deutschmark Income	C052	31/05/93	IRL	-6.62	25	-1.30	45	3.13	30.57	41	✪✪	2	N.A.		N.A.	
●	DEM	220.18	Credis Bond DEM A	C054	31/12/90	LUX	-6.73	34	0.80	7	3.08	36.81	2	✪✪✪✪✪	5	54.50	1	N.A.	
	DEM	63.03	CS Portfolio Income DEM A	C068	31/05/93	LUX	-4.51	7	0.75	9	2.22	26.16	60	✪	3	N.A.		N.A.	
▲	DEM	17.56	CU PP DM Bond	C070	30/11/92	LUX	-7	73	-1.28	44	2.58	27.35	58	✪	1	N.A.		N.A.	
●	DEM	450.68	DBIM Alpha Fonds	D006	30/11/93	LUX	-6.61	24	-1.90	65	2.30	29.11	49	✪✪	2	N.A.		N.A.	
●	DEM	738.10	DBIM DM Renta	D006	30/11/92	LUX	-6.64	26	-0.18	12	2.43	32.64	21	✪✪✪✪	4	N.A.		N.A.	
●	DEM	25.46	DBIM Gerling Luxrent	D006	31/03/93	LUX	-5.61	9	0.86	5	2.15	33.06	17	✪✪✪	5	N.A.		N.A.	
	DEM	42.99	Deuro Rent JPM	J001	30/04/93	LUX	-6.55	18	-0.81	25	2.65	31.18	37	✪✪✪	3	N.A.		N.A.	
	DEM	919.36	Dit Lux Deutsche Renten SK	D017	30/06/94	LUX	-7.20	83	-3	81	N.A.	N.A.				N.A.		N.A.	
●	DEM	449.97	Dit Lux DM Rentenfonds	D017	26/02/93	LUX	-6.82	51	-1.37	47	2.99	24.82	66	✪	1	N.A.		N.A.	
●	DEM	14.46	DM Bond	H009	26/02/93	LUX	-6.96	65	-2.17	72	2.44	33.02	19	✪✪✪✪	4	N.A.		N.A.	
●	DEM	0.83	Eagle Star DEM Bd	E001	29/09/95	IOM	-7.26	87	-0.52	15	N.A.	N.A.				N.A.		N.A.	
	DEM	27.55	Europa Lux DM Rent Invest A	E014	31/12/92	LUX	-6.82	50	-1.38	49	2.43	32.52	23	✪✪✪✪	3	N.A.		N.A.	
	DEM	41.60	Fixe DM	B053	28/02/90	LUX	-6.77	42	-1.26	42	2.44	31.62	32	✪✪✪	3	49.41	3	N.A.	
▲	DEM	49.54	Fleming FF DM Bond	F020	19/05/95	LUX	-7.23	85	-1.06	34	N.A.	N.A.				N.A.		N.A.	
	DEM	27.35	G-Bond Fund G-DEM Bond B	G009	19/01/96	LUX	-6.68	31	N.A.		N.A.	N.A.				N.A.		N.A.	
	DEM	21.41	GAM Bond Deutschmark	G002	29/11/85	IOM	-6.74	37	-1.37	48	2.45	28.70	53	✪	1	42.66	18	102.12	2
	DEM	188.62	Generalux DEM B	B064	31/07/91	LUX	-6.53	16	-1.08	35	2.50	30.47	42	✪✪	2	46.36	12	N.A.	
	USD	0.20	Glbl Mgr German Bond Bear	B066	30/09/94	BER	-8.01	94	-12.40	88	N.A.	N.A.				N.A.		N.A.	
	USD	0.20	Glbl Mgr German Bond Index	B066	30/09/94	BER	-6.97	67	-2.12	70	N.A.	N.A.				N.A.		N.A.	
▲●	DEM	23.75	Groupe Indosuez DM Bond	G017	31/12/90	LUX	-6.81	47	-1	32	2.53	33.80	12	✪✪✪✪	3	46.41	11	N.A.	
	DEM	542.98	HYPO DM Rent	H024	29/12/89	LUX	-11.48	95	-0.99	31	2.38	33.83	10	✪✪✪✪✪	4	49.16	6	N.A.	
	DEM	64.45	HYPO DM Thesaurent	H024	26/02/93	LUX	-6.74	36	-0.95	30	2.40	33.80	11	✪✪✪✪✪	4	N.A.		N.A.	
	DEM	626.92	IHS Fonds 2	U012	30/11/92	LUX	-7	71	-3.60	85	2.58	30.18	44	✪✪	1	N.A.		N.A.	
	DEM	953.57	IHS Fonds 3	U012	26/02/93	LUX	-7	72	-3.23	83	2.58	31.34	35	✪✪✪	2	N.A.		N.A.	
	DEM	303.50	IHS Fonds 5	U012	30/06/93	LUX	-6.83	52	-0.95	29	2.53	35.05	7	✪✪✪	4	N.A.		N.A.	
▲	DEM	14.07	Inter Optimum DEM	B069	31/05/95	LUX	-6.76	38	-2.53	77	N.A.	N.A.				N.A.		N.A.	
	DEM	282.63	Interbond	H009	28/04/89	LUX	-3.71	4	2.71	3	1.59	30.77	40	✪✪	5	41.21	21	N.A.	
●	DEM	0.19	JRIA Deutschmark Bond	J002	29/01/93	IRL	-1.49	1	4.80	1	2.10	26.19	59	✪✪	2	N.A.		N.A.	
	DEM	92.99	KB Lux Bond DEM B	K011	29/04/88	LUX	-6.60	21	-0.48	14	2.43	32.53	22	✪✪✪✪	4	46.94	9	N.A.	
	DEM	76.14	KB Renta Demrenta B	K010	30/11/92	LUX	-6.77	39	-1.03	33	2.55	31.54	33	✪✪✪	2	N.A.		N.A.	
	DEM	101.61	Lion Interoblig DM	C062	31/05/90	LUX	-6.73	35	-0.87	27	2.51	33.53	15	✪✪✪✪	3	47.61	8	N.A.	
▲	DEM	52.07	Lloyds IP DEM Bond	L016	30/11/90	LUX	-6.80	46	-1.40	50	2.52	33.27	16	✪✪✪✪	3	46.21	14	N.A.	
	DEM	110.92	LO Obliflex F Deutschmark	L019	29/03/85	JER	-6.57	20	-0.75	23	2.48	32.29	25	✪✪✪	3	49.30	4	131.17	1
	DEM	62.11	Lux Select	M034	29/12/89	LUX	-6.93	63	-2.34	76	2.44	33.03	18	✪✪✪	4	34.82	24	N.A.	
	DEM	188.95	Luxbond D Mark A Cap	C002	30/06/95	LUX	-6.90	58	-0.58	17	N.A.	N.A.				N.A.		N.A.	
	DEM	22.90	Luxinvest Rentenfonds /A	B061	30/11/92	LUX	-7.47	91	-2.24	73	2.44	24.93	65	✪	1	N.A.		N.A.	

▲ SIB Approved ● Insurance Fund **Values in US Dollars, on an offer to offer price basis with gross income reinvested**

Data Source Micropal™

German DMark Fixed Interest

continued

	CCY	Fund Size ($mil)	Fund Name	Manager Code	Fund Start Date	Domicile Code	3 Mths 97 % Chg	3 Mths 97 Rank	1 Year % Chg	1 Year Rank	Micropal Star Rating 3 Years Volatility	3 Years % Chg	3 Years Rank	Rating	Risk Return Rating	5 Years % Chg	5 Years Rank	10 Years % Chg	10 Years Rank
		144.62	**Mean/Count**				**-6.62**	**95**	**-1.33**	**88**	**2.52**	**30.74**	**68**		**1**	**45.46**	**24**	**116.65**	**2**
	DEM	12.04	Luxinvest Wertgarant	B061	30/11/93	LUX	-7.23	86	-4.93	86	3.14	25.07	63	✪✪	1	N.A.		N.A.	
	DEM	3.29	M.Lynch Global Curr DEM A	M023	28/04/89	LUX	-7.10	77	-1.84	61	2.37	32.14	27	✪✪✪	3	46.32	13	N.A.	
	DEM	N.S.	MeesPierson UF DEM Bond A	M012	01/03/96	LUX	-7.17	80	N.A.		N.A.	N.A.				N.A.		N.A.	
▲	DEM	83.84	Mercury ST DEM Global Bond	M021	30/06/89	LUX	-7.20	82	-2.81	80	2.94	28.21	55	✪	1	48.25	7	N.A.	
	DEM	19.48	MLBS (B) DM Fixed Income	M024	30/09/94	LUX	-6.53	17	0.83	6	N.A.	N.A.				N.A.		N.A.	
	DEM	10.58	Morgan Stanley DM Bond	M039	30/09/92	LUX	-6.84	53	-1.28	43	2.54	30.18	45	✪✪	2	N.A.		N.A.	
	DEM	7.23	MOSAIS Oblig Allemandes	C058	30/11/90	LUX	-6.78	45	-2.10	69	2.49	31.63	31	✪✪✪	2	41.76	20	N.A.	
	DEM	90.98	Multibond Actibond DEM B	C015	28/02/89	LUX	-6.88	57	-0.66	19	2.50	34.70	8	✪✪✪✪	4	49.17	5	N.A.	
	DEM	1.63	OMI (Ire) Dmark Intl FI	O006	29/10/93	IRL	-4.08	6	4.76	2	2.08	24.97	64	✪✪	1	N.A.		N.A.	
	DEM	22.18	Oppenheim Dispo Bond	O009	31/08/92	LUX	-6.96	66	0.77	8	2.33	35.95	3	✪✪✪✪✪	5	N.A.		N.A.	
	DEM	7.22	Panelfund Bonds DEM Cap	A037	30/07/93	LUX	-6.84	54	-0.83	26	2.45	35.39	6	✪✪✪✪✪	4	N.A.		N.A.	
	DEM	14.19	Parvest Obli DM B	B037	29/11/91	LUX	-7.06	76	-1.76	59	2.47	30.21	43	✪✪	2	50.21	2	N.A.	
	DEM	27.55	Pictet F.I.F. – Valbond DEM	P016	29/10/93	LUX	-6.87	56	-1.25	40	2.42	27.61	57	✪	1	N.A.		N.A.	
	DEM	16.61	Proventus DEM Bonds C	P013	22/09/95	LUX	-6.85	55	-1.70	58	N.A.	N.A.				N.A.		N.A.	
	DEM	51.72	Quelle Rent	Q002	30/06/94	LUX	-6.44	12	-2.13	71	N.A.	N.A.				N.A.		N.A.	
	NLG	5.79	Rabobank Select Fixed Income	R001	19/04/96	LUX	-7.20	84	N.A.		N.A.	N.A.				N.A.		N.A.	
▲	DEM	1337.40	SBC Bond Portfolio DM /B	S007	30/04/92	LUX	-6.65	28	-0.77	24	2.47	33.71	14	✪✪✪✪	4	N.A.		N.A.	
▲	DEM	4.10	Skandifond DM Bond	S030	31/10/89	LUX	-7.65	92	-2.07	68	2.96	32.23	26	✪✪	3	45.15	15	N.A.	
	DEM	46.63	SMH OptiPlus	S033	31/12/93	LUX	-1.91	2	0.03	11	2.38	25.12	62	✪	1	N.A.		N.A.	
	DEM	63.43	SMH Optirent	S033	30/11/92	LUX	-6.98	70	-2.55	78	2.68	16.63	68	✪		N.A.		N.A.	
	DEM	95.16	Sogelux Fd Bonds Germany	S037	31/07/87	LUX	-6.78	44	-1.46	52	2.44	31.15	38	✪✪✪	2	46.58	10	N.A.	
▲	DEM	1.69	Sun Life GP DM Bond	S052	31/12/92	LUX	-7.31	88	-5.28	87	2.80	18.50	67	✪	1	N.A.		N.A.	
	DEM	50.93	SVB Portfolio Income DEM	K001	31/12/93	LUX	-3.10	3	1.66	4	2.07	31.77	29	✪✪	5	N.A.		N.A.	
	DEM	286.49	Swissca Bond Invest DEM	S057	31/05/93	LUX	-6.82	48	-1.78	60	2.61	31.88	28	✪✪✪	4	N.A.		N.A.	
▲	DEM	3.83	TGA DEM Bond	T009	28/02/89	LUX	-6.92	61	-1.22	39	2.52	27.85	56	✪	2	42.24	19	N.A.	
	DEM	41.66	Trinkaus DM high-yield	T011	28/02/95	LUX	-5.75	11	-3.29	84	N.A.	N.A.				N.A.		N.A.	
	DEM	137.51	UBAM DEM Bond	U010	30/11/92	LUX	-6.67	30	-1.20	38	2.49	35.56	5	✪✪✪✪	4	N.A.		N.A.	
	DEM	290.94	UBS (Lux) Bond Invest DEM T	U001	26/02/93	LUX	-6.78	43	-0.59	18	2.53	30.79	39	✪✪	2	N.A.		N.A.	
	DEM	103.01	UBS (Lux) Ptf Inv Fix Inc DEM	U001	30/06/93	LUX	-6.68	32	-1.86	63	2.28	28.80	52	✪	2	N.A.		N.A.	
	DEM	133.40	Unico UF DEM Renten	U006	30/11/92	LUX	-5.43	8	-1.48	53	2.70	42.25	1	✪✪✪✪	5	N.A.		N.A.	
	DEM	164.61	UniPlusZins	U012	30/04/93	LUX	-6.56	19	-0.53	16	2.50	33.71	13	✪✪✪✪	4	N.A.		N.A.	
	DEM	90.07	Vereins Lux Portf DM Media Rt	A007	31/03/94	LUX	-7.05	75	-1.43	51	N.A.	N.A.				N.A.		N.A.	
	DEM	32.54	Vereins Lux Portf DM Renten	A007	31/03/93	LUX	-6.68	33	-0.70	22	2.60	31.64	30	✪✪✪	2	N.A.		N.A.	
▲	DEM	23.48	Von Ernst GP DM Bond	B021	31/08/93	LUX	-6.95	64	-2.30	75	2.47	28.81	51	✪	1	N.A.		N.A.	
	DEM	168.65	Vontobel DM Bond A	B017	30/06/93	LUX	-6.91	60	-2	67	2.35	28.84	50	✪	2	N.A.		N.A.	

Global Fixed Interest

Funds investing in excess of 70% in Global fixed interest securities (corporate, government, index-linked etc) with a maturity of three years or greater.

	CCY	Fund Size ($mil)	Fund Name	Manager Code	Fund Start Date	Domicile Code	3 Mths 97 % Chg	3 Mths 97 Rank	1 Year % Chg	1 Year Rank	Micropal Star Rating 3 Years Volatility	3 Years % Chg	3 Years Rank	Rating	Risk Return Rating	5 Years % Chg	5 Years Rank	10 Years % Chg	10 Years Rank
		113.87	**Mean/Count**				**-3.83**	**316**	**4.86**	**305**	**1.96**	**22.38**	**226**		**1**	**40.10**	**161**	**147.07**	**45**
▲	USD	21.58	AAF Global Bond Fund	A001	25/11/94	LUX	-0.68	40	7.40	88	N.A.	N.A.				N.A.		N.A.	
	USD	14.20	AB International Bond	A027	30/11/89	GU	0.43	20	6.52	101	1.07	14.24	174	✪		31.77	122	N.A.	
	USD	2.04	Abtrust Intl Fixed Interest	A003	30/07/82	GU	0.56	16	3.69	172	0.95	8.57	215	✪		19.56	154	66.63	45
	USD	11.02	ACMGI Global Bond Portf AX	A005	31/12/90	LUX	0.29	22	10.47	50	1.76	10.27	206	✪✪		16.03	158	N.A.	
●	GBP	4.38	Adams & Nevile Intrntl Bnd Inc	A006	31/07/85	GU	-2.37	80	16.14	16	2.92	27.87	63	✪✪✪	2	49.10	32	196.69	3
	DEM	1271.49	Adilux	A007	30/09/88	LUX	-5.08	218	4.68	146	2.03	23.97	91	✪✪✪	2	31.26	127	N.A.	
▲	USD	26.60	AEB Worldfolio 5 Global Bonds	A009	30/04/86	LUX	-4.02	157	3.72	171	1.60	20.62	125	✪✪	2	42.13	73	138.14	25

▲ SIB Approved ● Insurance Fund **Values in US Dollars, on an offer to offer price basis with gross income reinvested** Data Source Micropal™

Global Fixed Interest

continued

	CCY	Fund Size ($mil)	Fund Name	Manager Code	Fund Start Date	Domicile Code	3 Mths 97 % Chg	3 Mths 97 Rank	1 Year % Chg	1 Year Rank	Micropal Star Rating 3 Years Volatility	3 Years % Chg	3 Years Rank	3 Years Rating	Risk Return Rating	5 Years % Chg	5 Years Rank	10 Years % Chg	10 Years Rank
		113.87	**Mean/Count**				**-3.83**	**316**	**4.86**	**305**	**1.96**	**22.38**	**226**		**1**	**40.10**	**161**	**147.07**	**45**
	BEF	159.84	AGAM Invest Lux Internat Bds C	A013	31/01/95	LUX	-4	156	3.17	184	N.A.	N.A.				N.A.		N.A.	
	USD	22.39	AIG Multicurrency Bond	A017	29/01/93	IRL	-3.87	148	6.76	98	1.75	25.50	77	✪✪✪✪	3	N.A.		N.A.	
	USD	24	Al Kharejiyah GSF Global Bd	K005	31/05/89	GU	-0.66	39	6.33	103	1.67	3.62	220	✪		19	156	N.A.	
●	DEM	0	Albany Intl Global Bond DEM	A018	29/03/91	IOM	-6.60	271	-2.55	276	2.44	29.21	55	✪✪✪✪	2	50.45	29	N.A.	
●	USD	0	Albany Intl Global Bond Dllr	A018	30/04/91	IOM	-4.08	160	2.92	194	1.56	22.22	105	✪✪✪	3	47.21	39	N.A.	
●	GBP	0	Albany Intl Global Bond Stlg	A018	30/04/91	IOM	-4.60	191	12.98	35	2.13	25.07	81	✪✪✪	2	50.08	31	N.A.	
●	USD	4.94	Allied Dunbar IB Wwide Bond	A021	30/09/93	IOM	-3.97	154	4.23	160	1.51	11.13	198	✪		N.A.		N.A.	
	DEM	74.59	APO 1st Bond	U012	30/11/92	LUX	-6.73	276	-1.99	272	2.40	29.32	54	✪✪✪✪	2	N.A.		N.A.	
●	CHF	39.13	Argus Fund Bond Portfolio	S022	29/01/93	LUX	-2.34	79	7.02	93	1.79	22.64	100	✪✪✪	2	N.A.		N.A.	
▲	GBP	7.10	Ashburton FI Mgmt Fd	A034	06/01/95	IOM	-3.56	129	13.63	28	N.A.	N.A.				N.A.		N.A.	
	USD	3.10	Ashburton Replica Dlr Cash&FI	A035	31/10/94	JER	-0.81	43	5.63	117	N.A.	N.A.				N.A.		N.A.	
	GBP	10.42	Ashburton Replica Stg Cash&FI	A035	31/10/94	JER	-3.81	145	14.87	20	N.A.	N.A.				N.A.		N.A.	
	LUF	N.S.	Astrobal International B	B036	31/08/89	LUX	-4.63	194	5.17	133	1.45	33.61	28	✪✪✪✪✪	5	56.23	11	N.A.	
●	USD	1.16	AXA Eqty&Law ILA Global Acc	A040	12/07/93	IOM	0.49	19	10.97	46	1.85	8.77	211	✪✪		N.A.		N.A.	
	USD	4.99	Bachmann GIF Intl Bond	B001	31/03/89	GU	-2.08	74	2.96	190	0.91	8.67	213	✪		21.35	151	N.A.	
	GBP	2.47	Bachmann GIF Stlg Intl Bond	B001	31/08/93	GU	-4.17	165	8.74	64	1.73	19.02	139	✪✪	1	N.A.		N.A.	
	DEM	20.15	Baer Multibond Global Bond A	J007	29/10/93	LUX	-4.68	199	5.20	132	2	17.26	155	✪✪	1	N.A.		N.A.	
	CHF	15.95	Baer Multicoop Baloise-active	J007	05/04/96	LUX	-2.03	73	N.A.		N.A.	N.A.				N.A.		N.A.	
	CHF	16.83	Baer Multicoop Gerfds Bds A	J007	29/04/94	LUX	-7.88	303	-3.41	282	N.A.	N.A.				N.A.		N.A.	
	USD	12.32	BAII Interportf Intl Bond	B003	29/10/93	LUX	1.03	13	4.98	139	1.17	13.61	178	✪✪		N.A.		N.A.	
●	ECU	17.31	Bank Franck Global Bond ECU	B009	31/05/94	LUX	-5.04	215	0.24	246	N.A.	N.A.				N.A.		N.A.	
●	USD	2.68	Bank Franck Global Bond USD	B009	31/05/94	LUX	0.29	21	4.40	155	N.A.	N.A.				N.A.		N.A.	
▲	USD	55.40	Barclays (Lux) Intl Bond	B047	28/04/78	LUX	-0.41	32	6.91	96	2.16	15.51	167	✪		36.07	98	124.64	33
▲	FRF	20.93	Baring CF World Bond	B049	30/04/92	IRL	-4.90	210	13.83	26	1.65	39.72	13	✪✪✪✪✪	5	N.A.		N.A.	
▲	USD	106.70	Baring GUF High Yield Bond	B049	12/07/93	IRL	2.39	9	26.99	1	2.81	43.99	7	✪✪✪✪	4	N.A.		N.A.	
	USD	261.35	Baring IUF Intl Bond	B049	30/11/78	IRL	-3	100	11.89	40	1.93	24.86	83	✪✪✪	3	53.11	20	177.95	6
	DEM	53.63	Bayernlux International Bond	B051	31/10/91	LUX	-6.41	263	-0.48	254	2.28	29.88	50	✪✪✪✪	2	37.56	90	N.A.	
	DEM	132.59	BBL Renta Fund Hard Curr C	B052	28/02/89	LUX	-6.84	279	0.15	247	2.42	31.56	40	✪✪✪✪	2	50.42	30	N.A.	
	LUF	89.42	BBL Renta Fund High Yield C	B052	28/02/89	LUX	-5.72	243	13.33	33	1.64	33.17	31	✪✪✪✪✪	4	53.35	17	N.A.	
	LUF	327.43	BBL Renta Fund Intl C	B052	30/03/90	LUX	-5.26	225	4.63	147	1.74	21.34	116	✪✪	2	37.25	93	N.A.	
●	AUD	4.23	Bentley/Royal Skandia SAM 1	B057	31/08/88	IOM	N.A.	—	14.16	23	2.23	35.80	20	✪✪✪✪	3	57.74	9	N.A.	
●	GBP	10.40	Bentley/Royal Skandia SAM 3	B057	30/09/88	IOM	N.A.	—	14.52	21	2.18	29.21	56	✪✪✪✪	2	38.50	86	N.A.	
	ECU	10.16	Bermuda Intl Bond ECU Cap	B066	12/07/91	BER	-3.20	109	9.27	59	1.43	40.29	10	✪✪✪✪✪	5	66.73	4	N.A.	
	GBP	28.08	Bermuda Intl Bond GBP Cap	B066	12/07/91	BER	-3.10	105	14.91	19	1.66	40.17	11	✪✪✪✪✪	5	63.09	6	N.A.	
	USD	445	Bermuda Intl Bond USD Cap	B066	30/04/80	BER	-2.22	77	7.06	90	1.24	21.21	117	✪✪	4	44.91	58	119.08	36
	USD	100.38	BIL Bonds USD C	B067	31/12/90	LUX	-0.99	47	3.72	170	1.15	15.51	168	✪✪		26.92	139	N.A.	
	BEF	54.24	BIL Delta Fund Rendement C	B067	28/02/94	LUX	-6.52	268	-0.34	252	N.A.	N.A.				N.A.		N.A.	
	GBP	80.33	Bk of Ire Glbl Intl Bond	B018	30/04/87	IOM	-3.09	104	8.37	71	2.06	28.91	58	✪✪✪✪	3	53.23	19	N.A.	
●	BEF	60.43	BL Multi Tst Bd Global B	B025	28/06/96	LUX	-4.23	170	N.A.		N.A.	N.A.				N.A.		N.A.	
●	ECU	49.16	BL Rentrust F.C.P	B025	28/06/85	LUX	-9.74	312	4.15	163	2.33	27.87	64	✪✪✪✪	3	48.65	33	152.81	17
	GBP	42.29	Blackstone Franks Intl Bond	B068	31/12/91	IOM	-3.95	150	8.36	72	1.98	14.18	175	✪✪		34.70	107	N.A.	
	USD	46.22	Bond Trust Of The World B	S037	31/12/81	LUX	-4.79	206	0.35	244	1.41	15.35	169	✪✪		43.73	65	131.43	29
	BEF	240.59	Bonds Universalis B	P013	31/01/85	LUX	-4.67	197	9.97	54	1.74	38.36	16	✪✪✪✪✪	5	54.36	14	173.03	7
	LUF	N.S.	BR & A Rente Duree Variable B	B019	24/11/95	LUX	-5.98	254	-0.75	259	N.A.	N.A.				N.A.		N.A.	
	FRF	N.S.	BSS Universal Global Bds FRF	B029	06/01/95	LUX	-3.44	120	7.49	87	N.A.	N.A.				N.A.		N.A.	
	USD	N.S.	BSS Universal Global Bds USD	B029	06/01/95	LUX	-1.68	64	6.71	100	N.A.	N.A.				N.A.		N.A.	
▲	USD	50.97	BT GAF Global Bond	B076	29/10/93	IRL	-3.89	149	1.63	223	1.33	17.36	153	✪	2	N.A.		N.A.	
▲	USD	86.92	BT GAF Global High Yield	B076	30/09/93	IRL	3.61	5	23.57	4	5.49	22.15	108	✪✪✪	1	N.A.		N.A.	
	USD	81.83	BT Global Credit	B078	07/10/94	CA	11.33	1	26.65	2	N.A.	N.A.				N.A.		N.A.	
	USD	50.70	Buttress Capital App Bond	B080	28/02/89	BER	-0.58	38	2.66	201	0.88	11.99	191	✪		30.01	131	N.A.	
	USD	22.30	Buttress Intl Income	B080	28/02/89	BER	-1.43	59	8.29	74	1.17	19.39	132	✪✪	4	35.42	101	N.A.	
	CHF	59.40	Cantrade Invest Income	C007	28/02/92	LUX	-4.90	209	0.94	236	2.45	20.06	127	✪✪	1	N.A.		N.A.	
●	USD	9.28	Carlson International Bond A	C011	31/01/91	LUX	-4.32	178	-1.91	269	1.79	10.74	202	✪		20.50	153	N.A.	
	LUF	40.29	Castor & Pollux B	B034	29/07/94	LUX	-7.22	286	2.24	211	N.A.	N.A.				N.A.		N.A.	
▲●	USD	84.53	Chase Vista Global Bond	C019	30/09/87	LUX	-2.46	84	5.25	131	1.03	17.77	151	✪	4	31.03	129	N.A.	
▲●	USD	3.01	Chase Vista Intl Yield	C019	13/10/95	LUX	-1.17	52	14.03	25	N.A.	N.A.				N.A.		N.A.	
	GBP	219.40	CIAM International Bond	C014	05/08/94	JER	-3.25	113	2.94	191	N.A.	N.A.				N.A.		N.A.	

▲ SIB Approved **● Insurance Fund** **Values in US Dollars, on an offer to offer price basis with gross income reinvested** Data Source Micropal™

Global Fixed Interest

continued

	CCY	Fund Size ($mil)	Fund Name	Manager Code	Fund Start Date	Domicile Code	3 Mths 97 % Chg	3 Mths 97 Rank	1 Year % Chg	1 Year Rank	Micropal Star Rating 3 Years Volatility	3 Years % Chg	3 Years Rank	3 Years Rating	Risk Return Rating	5 Years % Chg	5 Years Rank	10 Years % Chg	10 Years Rank
		113.87	**Mean/Count**				**-3.83**	**316**	**4.86**	**305**	**1.96**	**22.38**	**226**		**1**	**40.10**	**161**	**147.07**	**45**
	USD	1.20	CIBC-CEF International Bond	C017	30/12/88	BER	-11.44	315	-5.71	293	2.43	-6.13	225	✪		-3.88	161	N.A.	
	USD	13.48	Citimarkets Global Bond A	C034	29/09/95	LUX	-3.53	128	3.51	179	N.A.	N.A.				N.A.		N.A.	
●	USD	22.85	Citimarkets Global Bond B	C034	27/02/87	LUX	-3.36	117	4.27	159	1.38	22.16	107	✪✪✪	4	45.59	53	N.A.	
▲●	USD	207.68	Citinvest Global Bond Account	C035	31/05/93	LUX	-1.33	57	7.01	94	1.06	14.33	173	✪		N.A.		N.A.	
●	GBP	56.84	CMI Ins Co GBP Security	C043	29/01/88	IOM	-7.24	288	1.69	221	2.29	13.98	177	✪✪		17.81	157	N.A.	
●	USD	4.10	CMI Ins Co USD Security	C043	29/01/88	IOM	-4.21	167	0.26	245	1.57	11.27	195	✪		21.60	150	N.A.	
▲	GBP	62.05	CMI Mgd Intl Bond	C041	29/05/87	LUX	-4.90	211	2.62	202	2.15	15.81	165	✪✪		34.51	108	N.A.	
●	GBP	0.34	CMI Passport Global Bond	C044	20/01/95	IOM	-7.29	291	2.76	199	N.A.	N.A.				N.A.		N.A.	
	DEM	9.44	Concorde Bond Unit Tst DM	C049	30/11/95	BAH	-1.79	67	-6.57	295	N.A.	N.A.				N.A.		N.A.	
	USD	3.96	Concorde Bond Unit Tst USD	C049	30/06/89	BAH	2.25	11	-1.27	262	2.67	21.51	114	✪✪✪	1	56.29	10	N.A.	
	DEM	33.88	Contivest Obli World A	B023	30/06/93	LUX	-5.69	242	2.10	212	2.05	18.70	141	✪✪	2	N.A.		N.A.	
▲	CHF	112.40	Coutts GF Global Income CHF	C052	31/01/80	IRL	-4.61	192	-0.93	260	2.57	19.21	134	✪✪	1	38.23	87	127.15	32
▲	GBP	13.55	Coutts GF Global Income GBP	C052	31/03/80	IRL	-3.68	136	17.43	12	2.37	34.23	25	✪✪✪✪	4	56.15	12	179.69	5
●	CHF	66.19	Credis Bd Prime Currencies A	C054	31/12/87	LUX	-5.66	240	-5.02	288	2.63	28.06	62	✪✪✪	1	54.03	15	N.A.	
	BEF	242.72	Cregem Bonds High Yield Cap	C059	30/06/89	LUX	-6.03	255	12.74	36	1.52	39.83	12	✪✪✪✪✪	5	54.72	13	N.A.	
	BEF	800.96	Cregem Bonds International Cap	C059	31/07/89	LUX	-6.22	260	4.99	137	1.61	30.29	48	✪✪✪✪✪	4	46.14	46	N.A.	
	BEF	N.S.	Cregem Leveraged Investment	C065	31/01/94	LUX	-6.50	267	13.38	32	N.A.	N.A.				N.A.		N.A.	
▲	CHF	17.79	CU PP Worldwide Bond	C070	31/10/88	LUX	-3.09	103	2.46	207	1.56	17.03	158	✪	1	41.01	76	N.A.	
	ECU	10.27	Danske International Bond Acc	D003	29/01/93	LUX	-6.26	261	8.46	69	1.71	36.42	19	✪✪✪✪✪	4	N.A.		N.A.	
	USD	3.40	Dao Heng Fixed Income	D005	11/10/96	HK	-1.73	65	N.A.		N.A.	N.A.				N.A.		N.A.	
●	DEM	137.99	DBIM Rendite Extra	D006	26/02/93	LUX	-4.85	207	5.55	119	1.63	26.24	71	✪✪✪	4	N.A.		N.A.	
●	DEM	45.65	DBIM Zurich Luxrent	D006	30/09/93	LUX	-6.52	269	-0.59	256	2.09	26.08	72	✪✪✪	2	N.A.		N.A.	
	DEM	1920.51	DekaLux Bond	D009	31/10/88	LUX	-6.92	281	3.47	180	2.77	32.68	33	✪✪✪✪	3	48.11	36	N.A.	
	USD	26.08	Deltec Special Situations	D010	31/01/91	BVI	5.89	2	20.12	9	2.31	15.16	171	✪✪		85.25	2	N.A.	
	USD	40.52	Deltec Worldwide Income	D010	31/12/90	BVI	3.79	4	18.56	10	1.84	33.37	29	✪✪✪✪	4	135.96	1	N.A.	
	LUF	N.S.	Demeter Intl Bonds Cap	B026	30/04/90	LUX	-4.41	184	7.75	82	1.85	19.28	133	✪✪	1	39.20	83	N.A.	
●	LUF	0.13	Demeter Patrimoine	D012	31/01/85	LUX	-7.98	304	7.05	92	2.28	19.95	129	✪✪	1	40.26	79	143.62	23
	LUF	196.98	Dewaplus	B027	31/05/85	LUX	-5.16	221	2.62	204	1.75	29.44	52	✪✪✪✪	4	42.59	70	156.43	16
	LUF	1.05	Dewinvest	B027	28/06/85	LUX	-7.84	302	-2.20	273	2.35	34.56	24	✪✪✪✪	3	46.28	45	172.38	8
●	DEM	1762.91	Dit Lux Bondspezial A	D017	30/06/88	LUX	-3.02	101	12.69	37	2.79	32.04	36	✪✪✪✪✪	5	45.67	51	N.A.	
●	DEM	155.03	Dit Lux Uberseeische Renten K	D017	30/06/94	LUX	-1.16	50	2.92	193	N.A.	N.A.				N.A.		N.A.	
▲	USD	2.58	Dolphin IIS Intl Bond	D014	31/05/89	LUX	-0.94	45	1.83	218	1.57	13.61	180	✪		26.91	140	N.A.	
	USD	N.S.	Eagle Star International Bond	E001	27/09/96	IOM	-5.22	224	N.A.		N.A.	N.A.				N.A.		N.A.	
	ECU	5.90	EDM International Cumulative	E009	30/11/90	LUX	-7.67	300	-0.01	250	1.97	14.34	172	✪✪		21.60	149	N.A.	
	DEM	N.S.	EPIC MF International Bonds	A024	20/10/95	LUX	-4.76	204	1.69	222	N.A.	N.A.				N.A.		N.A.	
	USD	N.S.	EPIC MF US World Bonds	A024	20/10/95	LUX	-3.76	141	2.29	210	N.A.	N.A.				N.A.		N.A.	
▲	USD	21.24	Ermitage International Bond	E011	31/05/83	JER	-1.49	60	1.05	233	1.75	10.66	203	✪		45.29	56	118.77	37
	USD	7.53	F&C RAF Multicurr Bonds	F003	31/10/84	JER	-3.30	114	3.54	177	1.30	15.19	170	✪		31.63	124	133.16	27
▲	USD	162.90	Fidelity Fds Intl Bond	F011	28/09/90	LUX	-4.23	169	3.39	181	2.39	10.52	204	✪		33.24	112	N.A.	
	CHF	43.94	Fiduciary Tst Swiss Fr Gl Bd	F014	28/02/95	CA	-5.60	237	4.17	161	N.A.	N.A.				N.A.		N.A.	
	USD	42.11	Five Arrows GOF Worldwide FI	R012	29/01/93	GU	1.30	12	7.97	77	1.36	14.13	176	✪✪		N.A.		N.A.	
▲	GBP	14.56	Five Arrows IBF Global Bd GBP	R013	29/01/93	GU	-3.50	123	5.57	118	1.47	21	120	✪✪	3	N.A.		N.A.	
▲	USD	5.36	Five Arrows IBF Global Bd USD	R013	29/01/93	GU	-4.24	172	4.98	138	1.31	19.16	135	✪✪	3	N.A.		N.A.	
	USD	5.05	Five Arrows IP Gl Fixed Int	R016	30/12/94	GU	-3.79	144	7.06	91	N.A.	N.A.				N.A.		N.A.	
	FRF	13.68	Fixed Income Transworld Bd	S038	30/04/85	LUX	-7.16	284	0.70	238	2.40	17.80	149	✪✪	1	25.93	142	104.79	42
▲	USD	74.90	Fleming FF International Bond	F020	30/11/88	LUX	-4.44	187	6.10	107	1.77	20.98	121	✪✪	2	42.32	72	N.A.	
	DEM	224.48	Fondilux	A007	30/09/88	LUX	-6.69	274	-1.94	270	2.42	31.51	41	✪✪✪✪	2	46	47	N.A.	
	USD	17.66	Franklin Templeton High Yield	T001	29/02/96	LUX	-0.07	26	N.A.		N.A.	N.A.				N.A.		N.A.	
	USD	6.70	Franklin Templeton Intl Bond	T001	29/02/96	LUX	-4.28	176	N.A.		N.A.	N.A.				N.A.		N.A.	
●	DEM	42.96	Frontrunner Global Bonds DEM	F032	31/10/89	LUX	-8.83	308	-1.62	265	2.39	28.19	60	✪✪✪	1	32.53	118	N.A.	
●	DKK	16.13	Frontrunner Global Bonds DKK	F032	31/10/89	LUX	-8.44	307	-0.46	253	2.24	34.66	23	✪✪✪✪	3	46.42	44	N.A.	
▲	DEM	110.66	GAM Total Bond	G002	31/12/92	IOM	-4.64	195	1.89	217	2.28	26.02	74	✪✪✪	2	N.A.		N.A.	
	DEM	30.32	Gamax Funds-Maxi Bond A	G004	29/07/94	LUX	-5.87	249	-4.74	286	N.A.	N.A.				N.A.		N.A.	
▲	USD	44.65	Gartmore CSF Global Bond	G007	31/05/84	JER	-3.63	132	2.77	198	1.98	17.69	152	✪	3	36.86	94	117.47	38
	DEM	18.06	Generalinvest Rendement B	B064	31/01/95	LUX	-6.16	259	-0.58	255	N.A.	N.A.				N.A.		N.A.	
	DEM	101.37	Generalux Multi Currency B	B064	31/07/91	LUX	-5.14	219	5.50	121	1.61	23.16	95	✪✪✪	3	37.56	91	N.A.	
	USD	53	Goldman Sachs World Bond	G013	26/02/93	LUX	-0.31	30	8.54	67	2.63	19.10	137	✪✪	1	N.A.		N.A.	

▲ **SIB Approved** ● **Insurance Fund** **Values in US Dollars, on an offer to offer price basis with gross income reinvested** Data Source Micropal™

Global Fixed Interest

continued

	CCY	Fund Size ($mil)	Fund Name	Manager Code	Fund Start Date	Domicile Code	3 Mths 97 % Chg	Rank	1 Year % Chg	Rank	Micropal Star Rating 3 Years Volatility	% Chg	Rank	Rating	Risk Return Rating	5 Years % Chg	Rank	10 Years % Chg	Rank
		113.87	**Mean/Count**				-3.83	316	4.86	305	1.96	22.38	226		1	40.10	161	147.07	45
	USD	4.43	Govett GSIL Global High Inc	G015	31/01/89	JER	-2.55	86	0.38	243	1.77	5.28	218	✪		29.86	132	N.A.	
▲●	USD	10.55	Groupe Indosuez Global Bond	G017	31/12/90	LUX	-1.29	56	5.80	114	1.40	23.02	97	✪✪✪	4	34.78	106	N.A.	
▲	USD	369	GT Bond A Share	G018	31/01/77	IRL	-2.91	95	10.30	52	2.28	23.83	92	✪✪✪	4	67.05	3	192.12	4
▲	USD	91	GT Strategic Bond A	G018	31/01/94	IRL	-0.52	34	23	5	N.A.	N.A.				N.A.		N.A.	
▲	USD	12.07	Guinness FI IF Intl High Yld	G020	30/06/88	GU	-3.52	127	8.99	62	1.42	9.57	209	✪		35.82	100	N.A.	
▲	USD	36.19	Guinness FI IF Intl Prime Bd	G020	30/06/88	GU	-4.29	177	5.95	110	1.48	10.51	205	✪		43.50	66	N.A.	
▲●	USD	70.43	Guinness Flight Asian Curr&Bd	G019	31/12/93	GU	-0.35	31	11.68	41	1.50	30.81	45	✪✪✪✪	5	N.A.		N.A.	
▲	USD	191.27	Guinness Flight Glbl Bond	G019	31/12/85	GU	-4.21	166	5.82	113	1.66	9.15	210	✪		42.61	69	166.98	12
▲	USD	124.50	Guinness Flight Glbl HI Bd	G019	30/06/87	GU	-3.52	126	8.62	66	1.35	8.71	212	✪		34.82	105	N.A.	
●	USD	N.S.	Hansard EU Intl Bond	H010	17/02/95	IRL	-4.91	212	1.36	226	N.A.	N.A.				N.A.		N.A.	
●	USD	4.12	Hansard International Bond	H011	30/04/90	IOM	-2	72	3.68	173	1.96	12.65	186	✪		40.81	77	N.A.	
●	USD	0.98	Hansard\GF GSF Asian Curr&Bd	H017	08/07/94	IOM	-1.52	61	12.48	39	N.A.	N.A.				N.A.		N.A.	
●	USD	5.30	Hansard\GF GSF Glbl HI Bd	H017	31/08/92	IOM	-2.78	92	6.77	97	1.95	6.62	217	✪		N.A.		N.A.	
●	USD	3.26	Hansard\GT Bond	H016	31/07/92	IOM	-2.76	91	9.69	56	2.11	20.74	123	✪✪	1	N.A.		N.A.	
▲	USD	5.75	Henderson HF Global Bond	H025	30/11/88	LUX	-2.89	93	6.16	106	1.49	16.79	159	✪✪		39.54	82	N.A.	
	ECU	6.77	Hermes Bond	H028	30/04/92	BER	-4.24	171	2.84	196	1.63	25.25	79	✪✪✪	3	N.A.		N.A.	
▲	GBP	4.82	Hill Samuel IBF Sterling Mgd	H030	29/11/85	JER	-3.44	121	4.86	142	1.69	22.48	102	✪✪✪	3	32.03	121	148.40	20
▲	USD	15.48	HSBC GIF Intl Managed Bond	H033	29/09/89	LUX	-3.72	140	5.02	136	2.31	13.25	185	✪		32.44	119	N.A.	
	DEM	30.81	Hypo Classic	H024	29/10/93	LUX	-5.67	241	1.57	225	2.05	26.06	73	✪✪✪	1	N.A.		N.A.	
	DEM	39.83	HYPO Expert Rent	H024	30/12/94	LUX	-7.01	282	-1.62	264	N.A.	N.A.				N.A.		N.A.	
	DEM	310.84	HYPO Lux Interbond	H024	30/06/89	LUX	-8.91	309	6.92	95	1.96	29.99	49	✪✪✪✪✪	5	46.52	43	N.A.	
	DEM	70.66	HYPO Techno Rent	H024	30/12/94	LUX	-7.03	283	-4.07	283	N.A.	N.A.				N.A.		N.A.	
	USD	308	Inc Ptnrs GSF Asian FI	I006	31/12/93	CA	2.29	10	13	34	0.70	37.99	17	✪✪✪✪✪	5	N.A.		N.A.	
▲	USD	30.54	Inter Optimum Interbond	B069	30/03/90	LUX	-2.42	81	1.61	224	0.92	11.07	199	✪		30.09	130	N.A.	
▲	DEM	96.13	Inter Optimum Multi-Devises	B069	29/09/89	LUX	-5.17	222	0	249	1.88	27.45	66	✪✪✪✪	3	46.57	41	N.A.	
	USD	18.30	INVESCO Income Plus	I013	30/04/90	LUX	-4.88	208	1.14	232	2.37	11.17	196	✪		32.91	116	N.A.	
▲	GBP	192	INVESCO Maximum Income	I013	29/06/90	LUX	-3.18	108	16.24	15	2.64	24.05	89	✪✪✪	1	37.33	92	N.A.	
▲	USD	6.40	INVESCO PS Global Bond	I014	30/06/94	LUX	-4.27	175	1.21	230	N.A.	N.A.				N.A.		N.A.	
	LUF	104.83	Ippa Portf Internat Bond B	B035	31/03/88	LUX	-5.18	223	7.60	84	1.62	33.92	27	✪✪✪✪✪	4	51.93	24	N.A.	
	USD	5.56	Irish Life Intl Intl Bonds	I017	30/09/94	IRL	-4.49	189	2.39	208	N.A.	N.A.				N.A.		N.A.	
	USD	1.43	ItalFortune Intl Global Bond	F015	31/07/90	LUX	-6.43	265	3.11	187	0.84	15.70	166	✪✪		4.05	160	N.A.	
	USD	25.09	JF Global Bond and Currency	J004	30/04/79	HK	-1.17	51	5.50	120	2.41	-5.10	224	✪		38.63	85	81.63	44
	USD	7.83	JF International Bond	J004	28/07/95	CA	-4.69	200	5.96	109	N.A.	N.A.				N.A.		N.A.	
	USD	13.10	JRIA/GAM Intl Bond	J002	30/12/94	IRL	-1.23	54	8.35	73	N.A.	N.A.				N.A.		N.A.	
	ECU	7.16	Kaupthing Global Bond Class	K002	18/10/96	LUX	-2.94	98	N.A.		N.A.	N.A.				N.A.		N.A.	
	BEF	609.65	KB Bonds Capital Fund	K010	31/07/73	LUX	-5.81	245	3.88	167	2.67	20.58	126	✪✪	1	31.39	125	131.20	30
	BEF	112.21	KB Bonds High Interest Cap	K010	28/04/89	LUX	-6.08	256	9.20	61	1.85	24.24	88	✪✪✪	2	26.87	141	N.A.	
	BEF	2212.85	KB Bonds Income Fund	K010	31/10/66	LUX	-5.82	246	4.51	152	2.45	20.77	122	✪✪	2	31.08	128	133.78	26
	BEF	132.65	KB Bonds Strong Currency Cap	K010	28/09/90	LUX	-7.30	292	-0.74	258	2.52	31.78	39	✪✪✪✪	2	53.30	18	N.A.	
	GBP	23.07	KB Interntl Accumulation Bond	K007	28/02/83	GU	-3.98	155	5.27	130	1.51	26.55	68	✪✪✪✪	4	53.57	16	171.82	9
▲	GBP	65.82	KB Interntl Income Bond	K007	28/09/79	GU	-4.12	161	4.88	141	1.70	25.46	78	✪✪✪✪	4	52.15	23	166.14	13
	DEM	14.74	KB Lux Bond Interbond B	K011	31/01/94	LUX	-4.17	164	3.28	182	N.A.	N.A.				N.A.		N.A.	
▲	ECU	1.61	KB SEL International Bond	K008	30/04/91	LUX	-5.73	244	3.25	183	2.15	24.03	90	✪✪✪	3	41.39	74	N.A.	
	CHF	24.03	Lake Intertrust Bond C	C062	31/07/89	LUX	-5.63	239	-7.41	298	2.92	18.09	148	✪✪	1	40.13	80	N.A.	
	USD	N.S.	Lazard Diversified Bond A ACC	L001	29/07/83	GU	-5.56	234	5.27	129	1.44	24.44	87	✪✪✪	4	50.68	28	142.27	24
	USD	N.S.	Lazard Diversified Bond A INC	L001	29/07/83	IRL	-3.50	124	5.31	128	1.60	24.70	85	✪✪✪	3	51.49	25	144.14	22
▲	DEM	N.S.	Lazard Diversified Bond DEM	L002	29/07/83	IRL	-4.65	196	6.71	99	1.56	20.73	124	✪✪	2	44.35	61	132.47	28
	USD	N.S.	Lazard Diversified Bond USD	L002	29/07/83	GU	-4.52	190	5.31	127	1.60	24.69	86	✪✪✪	3	51.49	26	144.18	21
	USD	6.99	Lazard Freres Fixed Income	L003	29/01/93	GU	N.A.	—	4.17	162	1.33	0	223	✪		N.A.		N.A.	
	USD	23.37	Lazard Freres Strategic Yield	L003	28/02/94	GU	2.98	7	10.20	53	N.A.	N.A.				N.A.		N.A.	
▲	GBP	N.S.	Lazard International Bond	L002	29/04/94	GU	-5.56	235	20.85	8	N.A.	N.A.				N.A.		N.A.	
	DEM	96.39	Leo Fonds	D017	31/01/90	LUX	-5.83	247	2.59	205	1.79	29.16	57	✪✪✪✪	4	43.48	67	N.A.	
	BEF	67	Lion Belgium Fix	C060	30/06/93	LUX	-7.36	293	-4.41	284	2.46	33.19	30	✪✪✪✪	2	N.A.		N.A.	
	BEF	124.23	Lion Belgium Fix 97	C060	29/07/94	LUX	-7.57	298	-2.62	277	N.A.	N.A.				N.A.		N.A.	
	BEF	76.59	Lion Belgium Fix 98	C060	31/05/93	LUX	-7.56	297	-1.72	267	2.36	38.42	15	✪✪✪✪	4	N.A.		N.A.	
	USD	18.84	Lion Fortune CL Global Bd C	C062	30/04/93	LUX	-2.20	75	7.54	86	1.26	21.66	113	✪✪	4	N.A.		N.A.	
▲	CHF	39.98	Lloyds IP CHF Multicurr Bond	L016	09/09/94	LUX	-3.77	142	-1.26	261	N.A.	N.A.				N.A.		N.A.	

▲ SIB Approved ● Insurance Fund

Values in US Dollars, on an offer to offer price basis with gross income reinvested

Data Source Micropal™

Global Fixed Interest

continued

	CCY	Fund Size ($mil)	Fund Name	Manager Code	Fund Start Date	Domicile Code	3 Mths 97 % Chg	3 Mths 97 Rank	1 Year % Chg	1 Year Rank	Micropal Star Rating Volatility	3 Years % Chg	3 Years Rank	3 Years Rating	Risk Return Rating	5 Years % Chg	5 Years Rank	10 Years % Chg	10 Years Rank
		113.87	**Mean/Count**				**-3.83**	**316**	**4.86**	**305**	**1.96**	**22.38**	**226**		**1**	**40.10**	**161**	**147.07**	**45**
▲	USD	73.60	Lloyds IP Multicurrency Bond	L016	31/03/92	LUX	-3.13	106	4.75	144	1.53	23.67	93	✪✪✪	3	N.A.		N.A.	
	USD	10.68	LM Glbl Global Strategic Yld	L006	08/11/96	NL	0.06	24	N.A.		N.A.	N.A.				N.A.		N.A.	
	USD	132.33	LM Glbl Offs Div Strat Inc B	L006	31/03/92	NL	-2.56	87	9.69	57	1.17	22.73	98	✪✪✪	4	N.A.		N.A.	
	USD	25.70	LO Obliflex A USD Multi Curr	L019	29/03/85	JER	-5.53	231	6.35	102	1.53	17.79	150	✪✪	2	47.39	38	149.27	19
	CHF	177.33	LO Obliflex M Swiss Fr Multi	L019	31/12/85	JER	-8.01	305	-7.29	297	2.90	21.90	111	✪✪✪	1	45.39	55	127.48	31
	CHF	101.27	LO Obliflex T Swiss Fr Multi	L019	30/06/88	JER	-8.23	306	-7.16	296	2.81	21.48	115	✪✪✪	1	45.81	49	N.A.	
	NLG	49.73	LO Obliflex Y Dutch Fl Multi	L019	31/08/88	JER	-5.07	217	1.95	216	1.74	26.26	70	✪✪✪✪	3	48.11	37	N.A.	
	DEM	30.70	Luxinvest GlobalRent /A	B061	26/02/93	LUX	-4.25	173	1.77	219	2.40	19.66	130	✪✪	1	N.A.		N.A.	
	DEM	27.17	Luxinvest SecuraRent	B061	29/12/89	LUX	-4.97	214	-0.04	251	2.72	15.83	164	✪✪		25.89	143	N.A.	
	DEM	16.25	M-Fund DEM Yield	B013	30/11/94	LUX	-6.74	278	11.60	42	N.A.	N.A.				N.A.		N.A.	
	USD	25.27	M-Fund Dollar Income	B013	30/11/94	LUX	-0.93	44	2.59	206	N.A.	N.A.				N.A.		N.A.	
	USD	50.43	M.Lynch Gbl Cur Mlt Cur Bd A2	M023	28/11/86	LUX	-4.70	201	6	108	1.39	12.32	188	✪		35.33	102	150.10	18
	LUF	N.S.	Maxicav	A026	30/11/87	LUX	-7.38	294	-2.77	279	2.47	35.72	21	✪✪✪✪	3	40.31	78	N.A.	
	DEM	2.96	Mega Rent	M034	31/03/93	LUX	N.A.	—	-0.72	257	2.48	28.89	59	✪✪✪✪	2	N.A.		N.A.	
	USD	22.10	Mercury Bond Fd	M017	31/01/78	JER	-1.23	55	2.33	209	1.82	11.70	193	✪		32.43	120	121.36	34
▲	GBP	84.80	Mercury International Bond	M016	30/09/82	IOM	-3.70	137	11.60	43	2.20	27.50	65	✪✪✪✪	3	45.58	54	167.47	11
▲	USD	115.43	Mercury World Bond	M015	30/09/85	LUX	-4.43	185	3.12	186	1.60	22.56	101	✪✪✪	2	48.58	34	167.91	10
	FIM	36.25	Merita Intl Bond	M022	31/10/91	LUX	-3.38	119	3.87	169	1.79	31.96	38	✪✪✪✪	4	34.89	104	N.A.	
	USD	16.35	MFS Intl Fds Charter Inc B1	M026	30/06/94	LUX	-0.77	42	3.54	178	N.A.	N.A.				N.A.		N.A.	
	USD	0.51	MFS Intl Fds Global Govt B1	M026	27/08/93	LUX	-0.26	28	3.59	175	3.06	32.22	35	✪✪✪	1	N.A.		N.A.	
	USD	587.30	MFS Meridian Charter Income	M026	28/06/91	CA	-0.54	37	4.34	156	1.24	16.69	161	✪		39.59	81	N.A.	
	USD	307.50	MFS Meridian Global Govt	M026	31/01/89	CA	-3.45	122	4.40	154	1.74	13.39	182	✪		35.02	103	N.A.	
	USD	35.60	MFS Meridian Ltd Maturity	M026	31/08/94	CA	0.55	17	2.80	197	N.A.	N.A.				N.A.		N.A.	
▲	GBP	26.96	Midland ICF Multicurr Bond	M028	28/02/90	LUX	-3.97	153	5.13	134	1.63	11.17	197	✪		31.69	123	N.A.	
	DEM	9.39	MM Warburg Luxbond	M034	31/07/89	LUX	-5.46	229	2.62	203	2.70	25.89	76	✪✪✪	2	31.37	126	N.A.	
	LUF	3.87	Mobilinvest A+B	D007	28/04/89	LUX	-3.59	130	0.07	248	1.80	18.69	142	✪✪	1	12.64	159	N.A.	
▲	USD	24.40	Morgan Grenfell Global FI	M038	28/02/94	IRL	-5.30	226	4.12	164	N.A.	N.A.				N.A.		N.A.	
▲	USD	7.10	Morgan Grenfell Offshore FI	M038	30/09/94	IRL	-1.62	63	4.94	140	N.A.	N.A.				N.A.		N.A.	
▲	GBP	51.26	Morgan Grenfell Res Assets Bd	M038	29/05/92	IRL	-3.67	135	18.39	11	2.43	29.45	51	✪✪✪✪	2	N.A.		N.A.	
	USD	130.70	Morgan Stanley Global Bond	M039	31/10/89	LUX	-4.37	181	5.87	111	1.43	17.19	156	✪	2	42.34	71	N.A.	
	USD	16.55	Morgan Stanley Real Yield	M039	29/10/93	LUX	-5.88	250	16.32	14	2.16	41.68	9	✪✪✪✪✪	4	N.A.		N.A.	
	FRF	41.88	MOSAIS Oblig Intl Divers	C058	30/03/90	LUX	-4.95	213	1.01	234	1.78	22	110	✪✪✪	2	28.13	137	N.A.	
	DEM	18.34	MultiLink International Bonds	I011	20/09/96	LUX	-12.13	316	N.A.		N.A.	N.A.				N.A.		N.A.	
	USD	24.40	National Mutual Curr & Bond	N001	28/04/89	HK	-4.36	180	1.26	228	1.60	13.36	183	✪		28.64	136	N.A.	
▲	USD	15.40	Newton UGF Intl Bond	N006	29/05/87	JER	-2.43	82	5.78	115	1.53	12.31	189	✪		28.97	133	N.A.	
●	DKK	13.01	North Star Bd & Mortgage Gth	N012	31/12/93	CA	-2.28	78	12.60	38	2.29	73.95	2	✪✪✪✪✪	5	N.A.		N.A.	
	DKK	4.13	North Star Bd & Mortgage Inc	N012	28/02/94	CA	-2.91	96	23.81	3	N.A.	N.A.				N.A.		N.A.	
	DKK	2.76	North Star Concord	N012	31/05/88	CA	-0.28	29	16.87	13	3.63	54.61	3	✪✪✪✪	3	52.28	22	N.A.	
	USD	2.10	North Star Dollar Growth	N012	30/04/90	CA	3.08	6	14.04	24	2.27	25	82	✪✪✪	1	36.36	96	N.A.	
	USD	0.43	North Star Dollar Income	N012	30/04/90	CA	2.70	8	13.54	30	3.16	32	37	✪✪✪✪	2	45.19	57	N.A.	
	GBP	0.47	North Star High Inc (Cayman)	N012	31/05/88	CA	-0.95	46	21.60	7	2.94	47.46	4	✪✪✪✪✪	4	43.74	64	N.A.	
	DKK	11.41	North Star High Performance	N012	29/03/85	CA	-1.20	53	13.40	31	3.12	45.70	5	✪✪✪✪	3	43.91	63	320.51	1
	DKK	10.37	North Star Investment	N012	31/10/84	CA	-2.61	88	9.73	55	2.60	45.48	6	✪✪✪✪✪	4	45.64	52	245.50	2
	SEK	1.31	North Star Swedish High Perf	N012	30/11/93	CA	-3.78	143	14.28	22	2.52	76.48	1	✪✪✪✪✪	5	N.A.		N.A.	
▲	GBP	13.87	Norwich Un JIP Int'l Bond	N013	28/02/90	JER	-4.17	163	-3.09	281	1.61	12.45	187	✪		33.60	111	N.A.	
	CHF	4.26	Obli-Valor	C024	31/03/94	LUX	-5.54	232	-10.15	300	N.A.	N.A.				N.A.		N.A.	
	USD	1.88	Old Mutual HK Intl Fixed Int	O004	28/04/95	HK	-0.51	33	7.85	80	N.A.	N.A.				N.A.		N.A.	
	USD	58.19	OMI (Gnsy) Intl Fixed Int	O005	31/05/82	GU	-1.84	68	7.58	85	1.83	18.64	143	✪✪	1	34.46	109	111.07	39
▲	USD	10.39	OMI Galileo Global Fixed Int	O007	19/07/93	IRL	-0.53	36	8.95	63	2.29	24.73	84	✪✪✪	3	N.A.		N.A.	
	DEM	1.16	Oppenheim Interlux	O009	31/03/89	LUX	-9.35	311	2.72	200	2.15	22.19	106	✪✪✪	3	32.91	115	N.A.	
	DEM	76.44	Optigest Fixed Income Fd	O011	30/01/87	LUX	-1.57	62	-4.52	285	2.69	30.37	47	✪✪✪	1	65.82	5	N.A.	
	USD	6.71	OYSTER World Bonds	B067	31/01/94	LUX	-4.67	198	5.35	126	N.A.	N.A.				N.A.		N.A.	
	LUF	11.39	Panelfund High Yield Bond C	A037	31/05/90	LUX	-5.59	236	15.89	18	1.44	43.73	8	✪✪✪✪✪	5	36.51	95	N.A.	
	ECU	256.41	Panelfund Intl Bonds ECU Cap	A037	30/04/87	LUX	-4.22	168	4.57	149	1.38	30.93	44	✪✪✪✪✪	5	42.74	68	N.A.	
	LUF	253.62	Panelfund Intl Bonds LUF Cap	A037	07/01/94	LUX	-4.34	179	4.55	151	N.A.	N.A.				N.A.		N.A.	
	LUF	120.93	Paribas Rente B	B037	30/12/88	LUX	-5.84	248	3.10	188	2.03	30.79	46	✪✪✪✪	3	45.80	50	N.A.	
	USD	14.58	Parvest International Bond B	B037	31/07/92	LUX	-5.44	228	0.77	237	1.33	12.25	190	✪		N.A.		N.A.	

▲ SIB Approved ● Insurance Fund **Values in US Dollars, on an offer to offer price basis with gross income reinvested** Data Source Micropal™

Global Fixed Interest

continued

	CCY	Fund Size ($mil)	Fund Name	Manager Code	Fund Start Date	Domicile Code	3 Mths 97 % Chg	3 Mths 97 Rank	1 Year % Chg	1 Year Rank	Micropal Star Rating 3 Years Volatility	3 Years % Chg	3 Years Rank	3 Years Rating	Risk Return Rating	5 Years % Chg	5 Years Rank	10 Years % Chg	10 Years Rank
		113.87	**Mean/Count**				**-3.83**	**316**	**4.86**	**305**	**1.96**	**22.38**	**226**		**1**	**40.10**	**161**	**147.07**	**45**
	USD	N.S.	PCP Bond & Currency	P007	31/05/96	CA	-2.91	97	N.A.		N.A.	N.A.				N.A.		N.A.	
	USD	2.34	Peregrine Global Bond	P008	31/05/96	CA	-0.72	41	N.A.		N.A.	N.A.				N.A.		N.A.	
	USD	8.50	Perpetual Offshr Global Bond	P011	31/12/92	JER	N.A.		8.24	75	1.75	8.36	216	✪		N.A.		N.A.	
	USD	N.S.	Perpetual OIA Intl Bond	P012	24/01/97	JER	N.A.		N.A.		N.A.	N.A.				N.A.		N.A.	
	USD	1.48	PFC International Bond Ptfl	P014	31/05/93	CA	0.50	18	5.46	124	2.39	8.66	214	✪		N.A.		N.A.	
	CHF	138.82	Pictet F.I.F. – GFI CHF A Cap	P016	21/07/95	LUX	-5.46	230	-7.84	299	N.A.	N.A.				N.A.		N.A.	
	USD	15.31	Pictet F.I.F. – GFI USD A Cap	P016	21/07/95	LUX	0.88	14	3.12	185	N.A.	N.A.				N.A.		N.A.	
	CHF	168.67	Pictet F.I.F. – Rentoval CHF	P016	30/12/94	LUX	-5.97	253	-14.11	305	N.A.	N.A.				N.A.		N.A.	
	USD	20.42	Pictet F.I.F. – Rentoval USD	P016	21/07/95	LUX	0.66	15	0.46	241	N.A.	N.A.				N.A.		N.A.	
	DEM	N.S.	Pioneer Global Bond	P017	18/08/95	IRL	-5.55	233	7.95	79	N.A.	N.A.				N.A.		N.A.	
	DEM	45.69	Postbank Rendite Global	P019	31/05/95	LUX	-5.04	216	0.95	235	N.A.	N.A.				N.A.		N.A.	
	USD	7.84	Power Capital Maxim High Yld	P020	30/11/95	BVI	0.17	23	10.46	51	N.A.	N.A.				N.A.		N.A.	
	USD	11.49	PRICOA WWIP Global Bond	P022	31/08/95	LUX	-1.03	48	11.11	45	N.A.	N.A.				N.A.		N.A.	
	CHF	21.56	Pro Fonds Lux Interbond (B)	U006	31/01/94	LUX	-3.33	116	7.70	83	N.A.	N.A.				N.A.		N.A.	
	DEM	155.65	Profirent SA	U007	31/10/89	LUX	-7.82	301	5.68	116	1.94	23.06	96	✪✪✪	2	38	88	N.A.	
▲	GBP	54.72	Prolific IF World Bond	P027	28/06/91	IRL	-3.31	115	7.08	89	1.78	25.13	80	✪✪✪✪	3	52.68	21	N.A.	
	USD	9.55	Putnam Embassy Global Govt A	P033	12/07/93	CA	-2.54	85	8.72	65	1.67	19.44	131	✪✪	2	N.A.		N.A.	
	USD	5.19	Putnam Embassy Global Govt B	P033	12/07/93	CA	-2.66	89	8.07	76	1.67	17.17	157	✪✪	1	N.A.		N.A.	
	DEM	34.84	Q High Yield	Q004	30/06/94	LUX	-1.90	69	1.17	231	N.A.	N.A.				N.A.		N.A.	
	GBP	7.65	Quilter Quad Intl Bond	Q003	13/01/95	IOM	-3.17	107	10.75	49	N.A.	N.A.				N.A.		N.A.	
▲	USD	9.50	RBC Gl Intl Bond	R003	24/11/95	GU	-4.13	162	1.98	215	N.A.	N.A.				N.A.		N.A.	
	USD	0.89	RDS Global Intl Bond B	R004	29/10/93	LUX	-1.09	49	-2.54	275	1.13	-6.50	226	✪		N.A.		N.A.	
	LUF	N.S.	Rente Plus B	M025	31/07/86	LUX	-4.77	205	3.58	176	1.59	21.19	118	✪✪	2	25.74	144	108.34	40
▲	NLG	2311.88	RG Divirente Fund	R009	28/04/89	EN	-6.53	270	-5.18	289	3.03	21.83	112	✪✪✪	1	36.24	97	N.A.	
▲	NLG	2169.79	RG Florente Fund	R009	30/04/90	EN	-6.65	272	-5.76	294	2.39	17.30	154	✪✪	1	21.85	148	N.A.	
	USD	1.50	RLI/Baring High Yield Bond	R022	31/08/95	IOM	4.20	3	22.19	6	N.A.	N.A.				N.A.		N.A.	
●	USD	9.70	RLI/GT Bond	R025	28/09/90	IOM	-2.22	76	9.22	60	2.11	18.29	146	✪✪	1	60.87	8	N.A.	
▲	NLG	3878.92	Rorento N.V	R009	31/12/76	EN	-6.14	258	4.02	165	2.21	21.06	119	✪✪	1	51.12	27	166.01	14
●	USD	4.90	Royal Life/Baring Intl Bond	R022	30/10/87	IOM	-4.49	188	13.71	27	2	22.08	109	✪✪✪	1	48.34	35	N.A.	
	USD	27.71	Samba Lux Global Bond	S006	31/01/95	LUX	-3.51	125	4.55	150	N.A.	N.A.				N.A.		N.A.	
	DEM	8.73	Santander Invest Global Bond	B011	30/11/93	LUX	-4.07	158	7.95	78	1.81	39.36	14	✪✪✪✪✪	5	N.A.		N.A.	
▲	CHF	29.45	Sarasin BondSar SICAV	B038	31/08/92	LUX	-4.62	193	-2.74	278	2.52	26.79	67	✪✪✪	1	N.A.		N.A.	
	USD	39.46	Schroder Curr & Bond Acc	S011	30/01/76	HK	-4.07	159	2.93	192	1.43	10.83	201	✪		28.85	134	121.32	35
▲	USD	63.35	Schroder Intl Sel Global Bond	S010	30/06/93	LUX	-4.41	183	2.03	214	1.59	13.25	184	✪		N.A.		N.A.	
	DEM	43.47	Scontinvest Multicurr Bond DM	S012	31/01/94	LUX	-7.26	289	-3.05	280	N.A.	N.A.				N.A.		N.A.	
	FRF	52.09	Scontinvest Multicurr Bond FF	S012	31/01/94	LUX	-7.26	290	-1.97	271	N.A.	N.A.				N.A.		N.A.	
	CHF	13.07	Scontinvest Multicurr Bond SF	S012	30/11/90	LUX	-6.74	277	-12.13	304	3.17	11.58	194	✪✪		25.19	145	N.A.	
▲	ECU	9.79	Scot Equitable IF Intl Bond	S017	31/07/92	LUX	-3.71	139	1.72	220	1.76	18.33	144	✪✪	1	N.A.		N.A.	
	USD	8	Scot Prov GP World Bond	S014	30/09/91	IOM	-2.44	83	4.48	153	1.89	18.30	145	✪✪	1	38.65	84	N.A.	
	USD	76.48	Scudder GOF Global Bond A-2	S019	30/04/93	LUX	-3.86	147	2.87	195	1.38	4.40	219	✪		N.A.		N.A.	
▲	GBP	78.32	Singer & Fried Global Bond	S027	30/04/93	IRL	-2.66	90	5.48	123	2.24	16.49	162	✪✪		N.A.		N.A.	
▲	USD	56.98	Skandifond Intl Bond	S030	31/01/86	LUX	-2.94	99	0.38	242	1.97	16.73	160	✪		32.92	114	104.73	43
	USD	42.51	Sogelux Fd Bonds World	S037	31/07/87	LUX	-3.95	151	3.07	189	1.20	20.05	128	✪✪	4	46.55	42	N.A.	
	USD	49.44	Southern Intl Global Bonds	S041	31/07/96	LUX	-4.72	202	N.A.		N.A.	N.A.				N.A.		N.A.	
	USD	4.40	Strategic GL FI Series	O008	14/07/95	BVI	-4.40	182	0.49	240	N.A.	N.A.				N.A.		N.A.	
	USD	7.10	Strategic Global FI Class A	O008	14/07/95	BVI	-2.90	94	1.27	227	N.A.	N.A.				N.A.		N.A.	
▲	USD	4.37	Sun Life GP Global Bond	S052	31/03/88	LUX	-3.97	152	5.84	112	1.88	16.34	163	✪✪		32.77	117	N.A.	
	USD	0.49	Sun Life Income Dllr	S053	29/01/93	IOM	-1.75	66	3.87	168	0.95	9.76	208	✪		N.A.		N.A.	
	GBP	0.95	Sun Life Intl Bond	S053	31/08/95	IOM	-3.08	102	16.09	17	N.A.	N.A.				N.A.		N.A.	
▲	USD	14.68	Swiss Life Proteus Intl Bond	S056	29/11/91	IRL	-3.22	111	4.31	158	1.71	22.22	104	✪✪✪	2	44.50	60	N.A.	
	CHF	249.25	Swissca Portfolio Income	S059	31/03/95	LUX	-5.34	227	-5.33	291	N.A.	N.A.				N.A.		N.A.	
	CHF	210.26	Swissca Portfolio Yield	S059	31/03/95	LUX	-3.63	131	-1.88	268	N.A.	N.A.				N.A.		N.A.	
	USD	6.30	Syfrets Gl International Bond	S060	30/11/93	CA	-1.35	58	9.52	58	1.46	11.71	192	✪		N.A.		N.A.	
	FRF	5.71	SynalFund Selfi	S061	31/07/90	LUX	-3.23	112	-2.43	274	2.30	28.18	61	✪✪✪	2	28.65	135	N.A.	
▲	DEM	8.34	Templeton GS DM Global Bond	T001	28/02/91	LUX	-5.89	251	6.26	104	2.20	31.13	43	✪✪✪✪	3	44.82	59	N.A.	
▲	USD	33.06	Templeton GS Global Income	T001	28/02/91	LUX	-3.22	110	7.78	81	1.26	19.02	138	✪✪	4	37.84	89	N.A.	
▲	CHF	2.26	Templeton GS Haven	T001	31/07/91	LUX	N.A.	—	-5.58	292	2.72	23.55	94	✪✪✪	1	22.76	147	N.A.	

▲ SIB Approved ● Insurance Fund **Values in US Dollars, on an offer to offer price basis with gross income reinvested** Data Source Micropal™

Global Fixed Interest

continued

	CCY	Fund Size ($mil)	Fund Name	Manager Code	Fund Start Date	Domicile Code	3 Mths 97 % Chg	3 Mths 97 Rank	1 Year % Chg	1 Year Rank	Micropal Star Rating 3 Years Volatility	3 Years % Chg	3 Years Rank	3 Years Rating	Risk Return Rating	5 Years % Chg	5 Years Rank	10 Years % Chg	10 Years Rank
		113.87	**Mean/Count**				**-3.83**	**316**	**4.86**	**305**	**1.96**	**22.38**	**226**		**1**	**40.10**	**161**	**147.07**	**45**
▲	USD	45.36	TGA Intl Bond	T009	30/11/95	LUX	-4.72	203	4.34	157	N.A.	N.A.				N.A.		N.A.	
	USD	1.55	The Sailor's-C & C Bond	B005	28/02/94	LUX	-0.04	25	3.98	166	N.A.	N.A.				N.A.		N.A.	
	ECU	36.29	The Sailor's-Intern Fixed Inc	B005	31/05/91	LUX	-4.44	186	5.49	122	1.92	22.36	103	✪✪✪	2	33.23	113	N.A.	
	ESP	11.71	Top Fund World Fixed Income	F008	30/09/94	IRL	-10.48	313	-1.64	266	N.A.	N.A.				N.A.		N.A.	
▲	GBP	10.83	TSB OIF International Bond	T013	30/04/90	JER	-3.63	133	3.68	174	1.64	18.88	140	✪✪	2	36.04	99	N.A.	
	ECU	0.46	UAP Global Bond	U009	31/03/88	LUX	-5.15	220	4.81	143	1.73	29.38	53	✪✪✪✪	4	46.83	40	N.A.	
	CHF	23.29	UBAM World Bonds CHF	U010	08/12/95	LUX	-6.86	280	-10.59	302	N.A.	N.A.				N.A.		N.A.	
▲	GBP	1.52	Ulster Bank Gl Fixed Int	U003	17/03/95	IOM	-8.98	310	13.56	29	N.A.	N.A.				N.A.		N.A.	
	DEM	16.42	Uni-Global (DM)	U008	28/02/92	LUX	-7.63	299	-1.37	263	2.39	31.30	42	✪✪✪✪	2	N.A.		N.A.	
	ECU	15.60	Uni-Global (ECU)	U008	28/02/92	LUX	-6.40	262	4.58	148	1.79	32.88	32	✪✪✪✪	4	N.A.		N.A.	
	FRF	38.76	Uni-Global (FF)	U008	28/02/92	LUX	-7.38	295	1.24	229	2.25	36.86	18	✪✪✪✪	4	N.A.		N.A.	
	CHF	38.73	Uni-Global (FS)	U008	28/02/92	LUX	-6.70	275	-10.36	301	3.14	22.68	99	✪✪✪	1	N.A.		N.A.	
	USD	5.43	Uni-Global (US$)	U008	28/02/92	LUX	-0.52	35	6.17	105	1.08	13.58	181	✪		N.A.		N.A.	
	CHF	9.19	Uni-Global Systematique (FS)	U008	31/08/94	LUX	-6.13	257	-10.78	303	N.A.	N.A.				N.A.		N.A.	
	DEM	608.76	Unico Investment	U006	29/05/81	LUX	-7.16	285	0.69	239	2.67	9.94	207	✪		19.11	155	107.70	41
	DEM	1316.22	UniLux	U012	31/01/90	LUX	-6.41	264	5.42	125	2.97	32.37	34	✪✪✪✪	4	45.98	48	N.A.	
	DEM	610.85	UniPlusRenta	U012	30/09/92	LUX	-4.25	174	4.73	145	1.70	25.90	75	✪✪✪✪	3	N.A.		N.A.	
	FRF	16.41	Valorive	M040	22/03/96	LUX	-3.71	138	N.A.		N.A.	N.A.				N.A.		N.A.	
▲	USD	7.99	Von Ernst GP Global Bond	B021	30/11/89	LUX	-3.65	134	2.09	213	1.46	13.61	179	✪		21.04	152	N.A.	
	GBP	3.21	W'Invest Excelle Gl Fxd Stlg	W006	30/09/92	JER	-3.36	118	8.48	68	2.11	19.13	136	✪✪	1	N.A.		N.A.	
	USD	47.20	W'Invest Income USD	W006	28/02/77	JER	-3.82	146	5.11	135	1.91	11.07	200	✪		41.17	75	160.38	15
	DEM	155.93	Westrendit	W002	31/01/89	LUX	-10.68	314	-4.87	287	2.55	26.45	69	✪✪✪	1	34.26	110	N.A.	
▲	ECU	35.47	Win GF Intl Bond	W005	31/01/91	LUX	-5.93	252	11.51	44	1.87	34.22	26	✪✪✪✪✪	4	61.57	7	N.A.	
	USD	23.40	Winchester RL Mcurr Govt Bd	O008	31/12/87	BAH	-2	70	10.77	48	2.64	1.61	222	✪		27.61	138	N.A.	
●	USD	1	Winchester RL Mcurr Govt Bd A	O008	31/08/92	BAH	-2	71	10.81	47	2.64	1.71	221	✪		N.A.		N.A.	
▲	CHF	8.99	World Invest Bond	B022	31/12/90	LUX	-5.63	238	-5.18	290	2.41	18.28	147	✪✪	1	24.46	146	N.A.	
	DEM	11.06	World Invest G7 Bond	B022	08/11/96	LUX	-6.50	266	N.A.		N.A.	N.A.				N.A.		N.A.	
	DEM	13.63	Wuestenrot Globalrent	W008	28/02/89	LUX	-7.48	296	8.43	70	2.59	35.11	22	✪✪✪✪	3	44	62	N.A.	

Global Emerging Markets Fixed Interest

Funds investing in excess of 70% in Global Emerging Markets fixed interest securities (corporate, government, index-linked etc) with a maturity of three years or greater.

	CCY	Fund Size ($mil)	Fund Name	Manager Code	Fund Start Date	Domicile Code	3 Mths 97 % Chg	3 Mths 97 Rank	1 Year % Chg	1 Year Rank	Micropal Star Rating 3 Years Volatility	3 Years % Chg	3 Years Rank	3 Years Rating	Risk Return Rating	5 Years % Chg	5 Years Rank	10 Years % Chg	10 Years Rank
		35.32	**Mean/Count**				**2.79**	**30**	**27.31**	**28**	**3.25**	**57.18**	**10**			**110.04**	**4**	**0**	**0**
▲	USD	41.39	AEB Worldfolio 14 Em Mkt Debt	A009	30/09/94	LUX	0.34	28	37.30	6	N.A.	N.A.				N.A.		N.A.	
	USD	N.S.	Credis Bond Fund Emerg Mkt	C054	31/05/94	LUX	2.10	20	29.98	12	N.A.	N.A.				N.A.		N.A.	
	USD	27.18	Deltec Wwide Income Partners	D010	31/08/94	BVI	1.82	23	9.97	28	N.A.	N.A.				N.A.		N.A.	
	USD	N.S.	EPIC MF Emerging Market Debt	A024	20/10/95	LUX	0.92	26	38.21	5	N.A.	N.A.				N.A.		N.A.	
	USD	21	Fleming Frontier Em Mkts Debt	F021	25/08/95	LUX	5.20	4	30.46	10	N.A.	N.A.				N.A.		N.A.	
	USD	83.34	FP Umbrella Debt Class	F029	31/03/95	GU	0.67	27	17.83	21	N.A.	N.A.				N.A.		N.A.	
	USD	23.57	FP Umbrella Global Class	F029	28/02/90	GU	4	11	16.66	24	2.01	32.62	9	✪	2	135.88	2	N.A.	
	USD	N.S.	Garantia Debt	G005	31/12/91	BAH	2.12	18	12.28	26	2.16	76.92	4	✪✪✪	4	143.51	1	N.A.	
	USD	26.70	Global Emerging Markets	G011	31/01/95	GU	4.47	5	47.69	3	N.A.	N.A.				N.A.		N.A.	
	USD	4	Govett Emerging Mkts Inc	G014	24/06/94	JER	1.73	24	18.63	20	N.A.	N.A.				N.A.		N.A.	
	USD	127	GT Emerging Markets Bond	G018	29/01/93	IRL	2.04	21	40.58	4	4.61	47.02	6	✪✪	2	N.A.		N.A.	
	USD	22.81	HYPO Emerging Rent	H024	31/10/94	LUX	-2.71	30	25.65	15	N.A.	N.A.				N.A.		N.A.	
	USD	86.97	IB Emerging Mkts Ptfl	I001	16/09/94	CA	2.47	16	17.35	23	N.A.	N.A.				N.A.		N.A.	
	DEM	57.16	LFM Emerg Mkt Cap Fd DEM Cap	I008	26/02/93	LUX	-1.53	29	35.72	7	3.23	89.49	2	✪✪✪✪	4	N.A.		N.A.	

▲ SIB Approved ● Insurance Fund **Values in US Dollars, on an offer to offer price basis with gross income reinvested** Data Source Micropal™

Global Emerging Markets Fixed Interest

continued

	CCY	Fund Size ($mil)	Fund Name	Manager Code	Fund Start Date	Domicile Code	3 Mths 97 % Chg	3 Mths 97 Rank	1 Year % Chg	1 Year Rank	Micropal Star Rating 3 Years Volatility	3 Years % Chg	3 Years Rank	3 Years Rating	Risk Return Rating	5 Years % Chg	5 Years Rank	10 Years % Chg	10 Years Rank
		35.32	**Mean/Count**				**2.79**	**30**	**27.31**	**28**	**3.25**	**57.18**	**10**			**110.04**	**4**	**0**	**0**
	USD	36.72	LFM Emerg Mkt Cap Fd USD Cap	I008	26/02/93	LUX	5.70	2	54.03	1	4.07	82.99	3	✪✪✪✪✪	3	N.A.		N.A.	
	USD	21.15	LM Glbl Emerging Mkts Bond B	L006	29/11/91	NL	2.19	17	28.79	13	3.94	37.11	8	✪✪	1	87.29	3	N.A.	
▲	USD	20.80	Morgan Grenfell Emerg Mkts FI	M038	28/02/94	IRL	3.59	13	35.48	8	N.A.	N.A.				N.A.		N.A.	
	USD	17.30	Morgan Stanley Emg Mkt Debt	M039	28/04/95	LUX	5.64	3	51.92	2	N.A.	N.A.				N.A.		N.A.	
	USD	0.46	Old Mutual Gnsy Emer Mkt Bd	O003	29/12/95	GU	4.43	6	17.50	22	N.A.	N.A.				N.A.		N.A.	
	USD	13.87	OMI (Gnsy) Emerging Mkt Bd	O005	08/07/94	GU	4.15	9	19.05	19	N.A.	N.A.				N.A.		N.A.	
	USD	0.42	OMI (Ire) Emerging Mkt Bd	O006	15/07/94	IRL	4.19	8	20.52	17	N.A.	N.A.				N.A.		N.A.	
▲	USD	25.95	OMI Galileo Emer Mkt Bond	O007	31/05/94	IRL	2.97	14	12.44	25	N.A.	N.A.				N.A.		N.A.	
	USD	106.54	Recovery Inv Ptfl Co	F029	31/03/92	GU	4.14	10	19.37	18	4.66	40.97	7	✪✪	3	N.A.		N.A.	
	USD	20.48	Schroder Emerging Mkt Debt	S008	29/12/95	GU	1.91	22	11.02	27	N.A.	N.A.				N.A.		N.A.	
	USD	15.30	Scudder GOF Emerg Mkt Inc A-2	S019	30/04/93	LUX	3.65	12	34.02	9	4.14	47.51	5	✪✪✪	2	N.A.		N.A.	
▲	USD	43.42	Templeton GS Emer Mkt FI	T001	31/07/91	LUX	1.31	25	23.48	16	2.81	21.41	10	✪	1	73.48	4	N.A.	
	USD	N.S.	Thornhill Global Deposit	T005	29/10/93	BVI	6.83	1	28.58	14	0.86	95.79	1	✪✪✪✪	5	N.A.		N.A.	
	USD	4.16	VKAC Navigator Emg Mkts FI A	V002	30/06/95	LUX	2.94	15	30.08	11	N.A.	N.A.				N.A.		N.A.	

Iberia Fixed Interest

Funds investing in excess of 70% in Iberian (Spain and Portugal) fixed interest securities (corporate, government, index-linked etc) with a maturity of three years or greater.

	CCY	Fund Size ($mil)	Fund Name	Manager Code	Fund Start Date	Domicile Code	3 Mths 97 % Chg	3 Mths 97 Rank	1 Year % Chg	1 Year Rank	Micropal Star Rating 3 Years Volatility	3 Years % Chg	3 Years Rank	3 Years Rating	Risk Return Rating	5 Years % Chg	5 Years Rank	10 Years % Chg	10 Years Rank
		1.33	**Mean/Count**				**-7.97**	**2**	**8.65**	**2**	**1.96**	**38.53**	**2**		**2**	**17.61**	**1**	**0**	**0**
	ESP	2.56	MOSAIS Oblig Esp & Port	C058	30/11/90	LUX	-8.22	2	12.26	1	1.95	45.14	1	✪✪✪	3	17.61	1	N.A.	
▲	ESP	0.09	SanPaolo Ecu Obligatns Iberie	S004	31/12/93	LUX	-7.72	1	5.04	2	1.97	31.91	2	✪✪	2	N.A.		N.A.	

Italian Lire Fixed Interest

Funds investing in excess of 70% in Italian fixed interest securities (corporate, government, index-linked etc) with a maturity of three years or greater.

	CCY	Fund Size ($mil)	Fund Name	Manager Code	Fund Start Date	Domicile Code	3 Mths 97 % Chg	3 Mths 97 Rank	1 Year % Chg	1 Year Rank	Micropal Star Rating 3 Years Volatility	3 Years % Chg	3 Years Rank	3 Years Rating	Risk Return Rating	5 Years % Chg	5 Years Rank	10 Years % Chg	10 Years Rank
		26.32	**Mean/Count**				**-9.35**	**15**	**24.35**	**12**	**2.54**	**44.75**	**5**			**0**	**0**	**0**	**0**
	ITL	20.98	BBL Renta Fund Lira C	B052	31/03/94	LUX	-9.17	5	27.35	6	N.A.	N.A.				N.A.		N.A.	
	ITL	4.87	Citi PF Italian Lira Bond	C036	25/10/96	LUX	-10.10	13	N.A.		N.A.	N.A.				N.A.		N.A.	
●	ITL	6.03	Credis Bond Lira A	C054	30/09/93	LUX	-9.18	6	25.57	8	3.27	41.15	4	✪✪	1	N.A.		N.A.	
	ITL	0.61	CS Portfolio Income Lira A	C068	29/04/94	LUX	-6.25	1	16.77	11	N.A.	N.A.				N.A.		N.A.	
▲●	ITL	20.46	Groupe Indosuez Ital Lira Bd	G017	22/03/96	LUX	-9.54	7	N.A.		N.A.	N.A.				N.A.		N.A.	
	ITL	12.45	KB Lux Bond ITL B	K011	29/05/92	LUX	-9.66	8	27.96	2	2.33	48.15	2	✪✪✪	3	N.A.		N.A.	
	ITL	6.03	KB Renta Lirarenta B	K010	30/11/94	LUX	-9.92	10	23.50	9	N.A.	N.A.				N.A.		N.A.	
	ITL	21.92	Parvest Obli Lira B	B037	30/07/93	LUX	-10.87	15	27.73	3	2.60	43.59	3	✪✪✪	2	N.A.		N.A.	
▲	ITL	0.09	SanPaolo Ecu Obligatns Italie	S004	26/02/93	LUX	-8.74	4	17.79	10	1.89	39.41	5	✪	4	N.A.		N.A.	
▲	ITL	168.07	SBC Bond Portfolio ITL /B	S007	29/07/94	LUX	-10.09	12	27.41	5	N.A.	N.A.				N.A.		N.A.	
	ITL	5.50	Sogelux Fd Bonds Italy	S037	28/02/94	LUX	-9.91	9	26.01	7	N.A.	N.A.				N.A.		N.A.	

▲ SIB Approved ● Insurance Fund Values in US Dollars, on an offer to offer price basis with gross income reinvested Data Source Micropal™

Italian Lire Fixed Interest

continued

	CCY	Fund Size ($mil)	Fund Name	Manager Code	Fund Start Date	Domicile Code	3 Mths 97 % Chg	3 Mths 97 Rank	1 Year % Chg	1 Year Rank	Micropal Star Rating 3 Years Volatility	3 Years % Chg	3 Years Rank	3 Years Rating	Risk Return Rating	5 Years % Chg	5 Years Rank	10 Years % Chg	10 Years Rank
		26.32	**Mean/Count**				**-9.35**	**15**	**24.35**	**12**	**2.54**	**44.75**	**5**			**0**	**0**	**0**	**0**
	ITL	10.27	Swissca Bond Invest LIT	S057	31/03/94	LUX	-10.28	14	28.96	1	N.A.	N.A.				N.A.		N.A.	
	ITL	28.07	The Sailor's-Lira Fixed Inc	B005	05/01/96	LUX	-8.36	3	N.A.		N.A.	N.A.				N.A.		N.A.	
	ITL	84.20	UBS (Lux) Bond Invest ITL	U001	30/04/93	LUX	-9.93	11	27.67	4	2.59	51.47	1	✪✪✪✪	3	N.A.		N.A.	
	ITL	5.26	UBS (Lux) Ptf Inv Fix Inc LIT	U001	29/07/94	LUX	-8.29	2	15.47	12	N.A.	N.A.				N.A.		N.A.	

Japanese Yen Fixed Interest

Funds investing in excess of 70% in Japanese Yen denominated fixed interest securities (corporate, government, index-linked etc) with a maturity of three years or greater.

	CCY	Fund Size ($mil)	Fund Name	Manager Code	Fund Start Date	Domicile Code	3 Mths 97 % Chg	3 Mths 97 Rank	1 Year % Chg	1 Year Rank	Micropal Star Rating 3 Years Volatility	3 Years % Chg	3 Years Rank	3 Years Rating	Risk Return Rating	5 Years % Chg	5 Years Rank	10 Years % Chg	10 Years Rank
		9.65	**Mean/Count**				**-5.45**	**21**	**-8.14**	**22**	**3.91**	**6.05**	**19**			**43.13**	**16**	**142.21**	**2**
▲	JPY	1.42	Aetna IUF Yen Bond A	A011	29/04/88	LUX	-5.61	15	-9.04	17	4.22	9.36	3	✪✪✪✪		41.65	12	N.A.	
	JPY	3.48	BBL Renta Fund Yen C	B052	28/02/89	LUX	-5.44	11	-7.87	12	3.88	9.74	2	✪✪✪✪		52.46	2	N.A.	
▲	JPY	12.38	CMI GNF Japanese Bond	C042	30/04/90	LUX	-4.26	1	-8.69	13	4.06	4.86	13	✪✪		29.09	15	N.A.	
●	USD	0.60	CMI Ins Co Japan Bond	C043	31/01/91	IOM	-6.16	18	-9.57	19	3.69	0.80	19	✪		16.57	16	N.A.	
●	JPY	0.03	CMI Passport Japan Bond	C044	20/01/95	IOM	-5.51	13	-9.60	20	N.A.	N.A.				N.A.		N.A.	
●	JPY	0.92	Credis Bond YEN A	C054	28/02/92	LUX	-5.70	17	-7.65	7	3.82	6.86	8	✪✪✪		N.A.		N.A.	
	JPY	0.27	Eagle Star Jap Yen Bd	E001	29/09/95	IOM	-5.32	10	-7.87	11	N.A.	N.A.				N.A.		N.A.	
▲	JPY	0.72	Fidelity Fds Yen Bond	F011	28/09/90	LUX	N.A.	—	-6.23	2	4.23	1.55	18	✪		44.46	10	N.A.	
	JPY	0.76	Fixe Yen	B053	31/10/88	LUX	-5.53	14	-8.86	15	3.72	3.82	15	✪		41.52	13	N.A.	
▲	JPY	1.01	Gartmore CSF JPY Bond	G007	31/07/92	JER	-6.40	20	-7.66	8	3.93	8.26	6	✪✪✪✪		N.A.		N.A.	
▲	USD	1.15	Guinness Flight Yen Bond	G019	31/12/85	GU	-6.34	19	-10.06	22	3.90	2.71	16	✪✪		44	11	134.69	2
▲	JPY	0.32	Hambros EMMA Yen Bond	H002	29/04/88	GU	-5.67	16	-9.43	18	3.98	6.48	10	✪✪✪		44.86	8	N.A.	
▲	JPY	8.53	Lloyds IP JPY Bond	L016	30/11/90	LUX	-4.99	5	-7.80	9	3.85	8.24	7	✪✪✪		44.73	9	N.A.	
	JPY	0.92	LO Obliflex D Japanese Yen	L019	28/02/85	JER	-4.87	3	-9.80	21	3.99	3.99	14	✪		49.17	4	149.72	1
	JPY	0.68	M.Lynch Global Curr YEN A	M023	28/04/89	LUX	-5.02	6	-7.83	10	3.83	6.48	11	✪✪✪		47.53	7	N.A.	
▲	USD	81.67	Mercury ST JPY Global Bond	M021	29/05/87	LUX	-7.35	21	-8.79	14	3.44	2.20	17	✪✪		32.90	14	N.A.	
	JPY	0.52	Multibond Actibond Yen B	C015	28/02/89	LUX	-4.97	4	-6.29	3	4.05	9	4	✪✪✪✪		49.34	3	N.A.	
	JPY	12.35	Parvest Obli Yen B	B037	29/11/91	LUX	-5.49	12	-5.79	1	3.70	6.63	9	✪✪		48.83	5	N.A.	
▲	JPY	68.84	SBC Bond Portfolio Yen /B	S007	30/04/92	LUX	-5.18	8	-7.41	5	4.02	9.96	1	✪✪✪✪✪		N.A.		N.A.	
	JPY	7.86	Sogelux Fd Bonds Japan	S037	31/07/87	LUX	-4.43	2	-8.93	16	3.89	5.27	12	✪✪		54.60	1	N.A.	
	JPY	3.92	Swissca Bond Invest YEN	S057	31/03/94	LUX	-5.06	7	-6.51	4	N.A.	N.A.				N.A.		N.A.	
▲	JPY	3.89	TGA Yen Bond	T009	28/02/89	LUX	-5.19	9	-7.42	6	4.08	8.74	5	✪✪✪✪✪		48.31	6	N.A.	

▲ **SIB Approved** ● **Insurance Fund** **Values in US Dollars, on an offer to offer price basis with gross income reinvested** Data Source Micropal™

Latin America Fixed Interest

Funds investing in excess of 70% in Latin American fixed interest securities (corporate, government, index-linked etc) with a maturity of three years or greater.

CCY	Fund Size ($mil)	Fund Name	Manager Code	Fund Start Date	Domicile Code	3 Mths 97 % Chg	3 Mths 97 Rank	1 Year % Chg	1 Year Rank	Micropal Star Rating 3 Years Volatility	3 Years % Chg	3 Years Rank	Rating	Risk Return Rating	5 Years % Chg	5 Years Rank	10 Years % Chg	10 Years Rank
	106.40	**Mean/Count**				**4.90**	**10**	**26.75**	**9**	**3.55**	**48.69**	**8**		**1**	**181.10**	**3**	**0**	**0**
USD	50.46	Deltec Latin American	D010	31/08/90	BVI	7.94	3	35.31	3	8.26	85.88	1	✪✪✪✪	2	341.78	1	N.A.	
USD	12	InverSud Investment	B040	30/11/92	LUX	11.01	1	29.90	5	7.06	11.54	8	✪		N.A.		N.A.	
USD	268.80	JPBT DMA	J003	30/04/93	BAH	2.05	10	12.98	9	0.32	34.10	7	✪	4	N.A.		N.A.	
USD	33.41	JPBT Latin	J003	31/10/91	BAH	2.75	8	36.88	2	3	49.32	4	✪✪✪	2	118.65	2	N.A.	
USD	44.66	JPBT Peso	J003	30/06/93	BAH	2.80	7	16.74	7	0.98	37.50	5	✪✪	3	N.A.		N.A.	
USD	17.40	Lexus Emerging Mkts	S050	31/03/92	BAH	2.73	9	22.14	6	0.69	51	3	✪✪✪	4	N.A.		N.A.	
USD	93.10	Patrimonio Intl Cap Gth	B015	31/03/93	CA	3.86	4	15.29	8	1.95	83.62	2	✪✪✪✪	3	N.A.		N.A.	
USD	218.96	SBC Em Ec Portf Latin Am Bds	S007	28/02/95	LUX	2.93	6	34.08	4	N.A.	N.A.				N.A.		N.A.	
USD	325.18	Sovereign High Yield A	S020	30/11/89	NL	3.68	5	37.41	1	6.13	36.55	6	✪✪	1	82.88	3	N.A.	
BEF	0.02	World Invest Latin America	B022	08/11/96	LUX	9.30	2	N.A.		N.A.	N.A.				N.A.		N.A.	

Mexican Peso Fixed Interest

Funds investing in excess of 70% in Mexican Peso denominated fixed interest securities (corporate, government, index-linked etc) with a maturity of three years or greater.

CCY	Fund Size ($mil)	Fund Name	Manager Code	Fund Start Date	Domicile Code	3 Mths 97 % Chg	3 Mths 97 Rank	1 Year % Chg	1 Year Rank	Micropal Star Rating 3 Years Volatility	3 Years % Chg	3 Years Rank	Rating	Risk Return Rating	5 Years % Chg	5 Years Rank	10 Years % Chg	10 Years Rank
	36.05	**Mean/Count**				**4.40**	**3**	**29.68**	**3**	**6.19**	**0.24**	**3**		**1**	**17.59**	**1**	**0**	**0**
USD	19.39	LM Glbl Mexico Premium Inc B	L006	31/07/90	NL	4.26	2	32.69	2	7.61	-10.61	2	✪✪✪		17.59	1	N.A.	
USD	26.34	M.Lynch Mex Inc Dllr Portf A	M023	31/07/92	CA	2.91	3	17.97	3	2.66	33.14	1	✪✪✪✪	3	N.A.		N.A.	
USD	62.43	M.Lynch Mex Inc Peso Portf A	M023	31/07/92	CA	6.03	1	38.39	1	8.30	-21.81	3	✪✪		N.A.		N.A.	

Netherlands Guilder Fixed Interest

Funds investing in excess of 70% in Netherlands Guilder denominated fixed interest securities (corporate, government, index-linked etc) with a maturity of three years or greater.

CCY	Fund Size ($mil)	Fund Name	Manager Code	Fund Start Date	Domicile Code	3 Mths 97 % Chg	3 Mths 97 Rank	1 Year % Chg	1 Year Rank	Micropal Star Rating 3 Years Volatility	3 Years % Chg	3 Years Rank	Rating	Risk Return Rating	5 Years % Chg	5 Years Rank	10 Years % Chg	10 Years Rank
	90.95	**Mean/Count**				**-6.91**	**16**	**-0.99**	**13**	**2.49**	**31.47**	**9**		**1**	**53.48**	**5**	**150.48**	**1**
NLG	43.55	BBL (L) Invest Equi-Fix Neth.10	B052	28/06/96	LUX	-3.95	1	N.A.		N.A.	N.A.				N.A.		N.A.	
NLG	78.42	BBL Renta Fund Gulden C	B052	30/06/92	LUX	-6.97	9	-0.57	5	2.49	33.38	2	✪✪✪✪	4	N.A.		N.A.	
NLG	175.01	BIL Bonds Florins Neerland C	B067	30/04/93	LUX	-7.46	14	-1.73	12	2.49	30	6	✪✪	2	N.A.		N.A.	
● NLG	148.32	Credis Bond Gulden A	C054	07/04/95	LUX	-6.87	3	-0.31	2	N.A.	N.A.				N.A.		N.A.	
NLG	21.05	Fixe Guilder	B053	30/11/90	LUX	-6.91	7	-1.18	8	2.45	28.39	9	✪	1	51.45	4	N.A.	
NLG	23.31	G-Bond Fund G-NLG Bond B	G009	19/01/96	LUX	-6.88	4	N.A.		N.A.	N.A.				N.A.		N.A.	
NLG	19.90	ING Intl-Dutch Bond Cap	I008	30/06/95	LUX	-7.10	11	-1.68	11	N.A.	N.A.				N.A.		N.A.	
NLG	70.71	KB Lux Bond NLG B	K011	29/04/88	LUX	-6.95	8	-0.43	3	2.45	32.13	5	✪✪✪	3	53.57	3	N.A.	
NLG	99.63	KB Renta Guldenrenta B	K010	30/11/92	LUX	-7.68	16	-1.57	10	2.52	29.94	7	✪	1	N.A.		N.A.	
NLG	4.96	Lion Interoblig Florin	C062	31/01/94	LUX	-6.90	6	0.04	1	N.A.	N.A.				N.A.		N.A.	
▲ NLG	24.92	Lloyds IP NLG Bond	L016	30/11/90	LUX	-6.86	2	-0.87	7	2.59	33.24	3	✪✪✪✪	3	49.11	5	N.A.	
NLG	40.45	LO Obliflex G Dutch Florin	L019	29/03/85	JER	-7.03	10	-0.69	6	2.46	32.28	4	✪✪✪	4	57.56	1	150.48	1
NLG	67.37	Parvest Obli Gulden B	B037	29/11/91	LUX	-7.21	13	-2.06	13	2.48	29.90	8	✪✪	2	55.70	2	N.A.	
NLG	9.12	Rabobank Holland Dutch Bond	R001	19/04/96	LUX	-7.67	15	N.A.		N.A.	N.A.				N.A.		N.A.	

▲ SIB Approved ● Insurance Fund **Values in US Dollars, on an offer to offer price basis with gross income reinvested** Data Source Micropal™

Netherlands Guilder Fixed Interest

continued

	CCY	Fund Size ($mil)	Fund Name	Manager Code	Fund Start Date	Domicile Code	3 Mths 97 % Chg	3 Mths 97 Rank	1 Year % Chg	1 Year Rank	Micropal Star Rating 3 Years Volatility	3 Years % Chg	3 Years Rank	Rating	Risk Return Rating	5 Years % Chg	5 Years Rank	10 Years % Chg	10 Years Rank
		90.95	**Mean/Count**				**-6.91**	**16**	**-0.99**	**13**	**2.49**	**31.47**	**9**		**1**	**53.48**	**5**	**150.48**	**1**
▲	NLG	576.48	SBC Bond Portfolio Hfl /B	S007	30/04/92	LUX	-6.90	5	-0.47	4	2.43	34.01	1	✪✪✪✪✪	5	N.A.		N.A.	
	NLG	52	Swissca Bond Invest NLG	S057	31/03/94	LUX	-7.19	12	-1.38	9	N.A.	N.A.				N.A.		N.A.	

North America Fixed Interest

Funds investing in excess of 70% in North American fixed interest securities (corporate, government, index-linked etc) with a maturity of three years or greater.

	CCY	Fund Size ($mil)	Fund Name	Manager Code	Fund Start Date	Domicile Code	3 Mths 97 % Chg	3 Mths 97 Rank	1 Year % Chg	1 Year Rank	Micropal Star Rating 3 Years Volatility	3 Years % Chg	3 Years Rank	Rating	Risk Return Rating	5 Years % Chg	5 Years Rank	10 Years % Chg	10 Years Rank
		35.14	**Mean/Count**				**-0.59**	**3**	**27.33**	**2**	**1.20**	**16.75**	**1**			**30.44**	**1**	**0**	**0**
	LUF	N.S.	Bacob Dollar Bonds C	B002	08/11/96	LUX	-0.25	1	N.A.		N.A.	N.A.				N.A.		N.A.	
●	USD	40.11	BL Multi Tst Bd Zone Dlr B	B025	31/01/89	LUX	-0.80	3	4.58	2	1.20	16.75	1	✪✪✪		30.44	1	N.A.	
	USD	30.16	M.Lynch Americas Inc Portf A	M023	28/02/94	CA	-0.72	2	50.08	1	N.A.	N.A.				N.A.		N.A.	

Philippine Peso Fixed Interest

Funds investing in excess of 70% in Philippine Peso denominated fixed interest securities (corporate, government, index-linked etc) with a maturity of three years or greater.

	CCY	Fund Size ($mil)	Fund Name	Manager Code	Fund Start Date	Domicile Code	3 Mths 97 % Chg	3 Mths 97 Rank	1 Year % Chg	1 Year Rank	Micropal Star Rating 3 Years Volatility	3 Years % Chg	3 Years Rank	Rating	Risk Return Rating	5 Years % Chg	5 Years Rank	10 Years % Chg	10 Years Rank
		0	**Mean/Count**				**-2.75**	**1**	**14.64**	**1**	**3.12**	**7.97**	**1**			**0**	**0**	**0**	**0**
	USD	0	The Philippine Income Fund	M011	29/01/93	CA	-2.75	1	14.64	1	3.12	7.97	1	✪✪✪		N.A.		N.A.	

Scandinavia Fixed Interest

Funds investing in excess of 70% in Scandinavian fixed interest securities (corporate, government, index-linked etc) with a maturity of three years or greater.

	CCY	Fund Size ($mil)	Fund Name	Manager Code	Fund Start Date	Domicile Code	3 Mths 97 % Chg	3 Mths 97 Rank	1 Year % Chg	1 Year Rank	Micropal Star Rating 3 Years Volatility	3 Years % Chg	3 Years Rank	Rating	Risk Return Rating	5 Years % Chg	5 Years Rank	10 Years % Chg	10 Years Rank
		14.97	**Mean/Count**				**-8.41**	**5**	**9.99**	**4**	**2.44**	**54.42**	**3**		**1**	**40.35**	**2**	**0**	**0**
	SEK	6	Aragon SW High Yield	A028	31/01/90	LUX	-10.17	4	11.80	2	2.59	60.97	2	✪✪✪	4	31.46	2	N.A.	
	ECU	5.15	Danske NSS Nordic Govert Bond	D003	23/06/95	LUX	-6.79	1	6.13	3	N.A.	N.A.				N.A.		N.A.	
▲	NOK	10.12	DNB Investment Nordic Bonds C	D013	29/10/93	LUX	-6.91	2	6.07	4	1.88	36.48	3	✪✪	2	N.A.		N.A.	
	SEK	50.23	MultiLink Scandi Bds	I011	31/12/90	LUX	-10.31	5	15.95	1	2.85	65.80	1	✪✪✪✪	3	49.23	1	N.A.	
	DKK	3.34	Parvest Obli Scandinavia B	B037	04/10/96	LUX	-7.87	3	N.A.		N.A.	N.A.				N.A.		N.A.	

▲ SIB Approved ● Insurance Fund **Values in US Dollars, on an offer to offer price basis with gross income reinvested** Data Source Micropal™

South African Rand Fixed Interest

Funds investing in excess of 70% in South African Rand denominated fixed interest securities (corporate, government, index-linked etc) with a maturity of three years or greater.

	CCY	Fund Size ($mil)	Fund Name	Manager Code	Fund Start Date	Domicile Code	3 Mths 97 % Chg	3 Mths 97 Rank	1 Year % Chg	1 Year Rank	Micropal Star Rating 3 Years Volatility	3 Years % Chg	3 Years Rank	3 Years Rating	Risk Return Rating	5 Years % Chg	5 Years Rank	10 Years % Chg	10 Years Rank
		31.36	**Mean/Count**				**11.89**	**4**	**-16.16**	**1**	**3.06**	**-3.20**	**1**			**20.41**	**1**	**0**	**0**
▲	ZAL	0	Finrand High Yield – Cap	S045	31/08/90	LUX	14.52	1	-16.16	1	3.06	-3.20	1	✪✪✪		20.41	1	N.A.	
	ZAL	N.S.	Five Arrows CFL S African Rd	R010	31/10/96	IRL	9.22	4	N.A.		N.A.	N.A.				N.A.		N.A.	
	ZAL	N.S.	Five Arrows IRL S African Rd	R017	31/10/96	GU	9.38	3	N.A.		N.A.	N.A.				N.A.		N.A.	
	USD	62.72	Southern Intl Sth African Bd	S041	04/10/96	LUX	14.44	2	N.A.		N.A.	N.A.				N.A.		N.A.	

Spanish Peseta Fixed Interest

Funds investing in excess of 70% in Spanish Peseta denominated fixed interest securities (corporate, government, index-linked etc) with a maturity of three years or greater.

	CCY	Fund Size ($mil)	Fund Name	Manager Code	Fund Start Date	Domicile Code	3 Mths 97 % Chg	3 Mths 97 Rank	1 Year % Chg	1 Year Rank	Micropal Star Rating 3 Years Volatility	3 Years % Chg	3 Years Rank	3 Years Rating	Risk Return Rating	5 Years % Chg	5 Years Rank	10 Years % Chg	10 Years Rank
		18.94	**Mean/Count**				**-8.05**	**14**	**9.90**	**12**	**2.06**	**39.10**	**7**		**1**	**22.88**	**2**	**0**	**0**
▲	ESP	23.59	AAF Spain Bond Fund	A001	25/11/94	LUX	-8.34	12	11.14	8	N.A.	N.A.				N.A.		N.A.	
	ESP	7.83	BBL Renta Fund Peseta C	B052	31/03/94	LUX	-8.64	14	11.43	7	N.A.	N.A.				N.A.		N.A.	
	ESP	9.35	Caixa Funds Spanish Bonds	C004	30/10/92	LUX	-7.65	3	-1.41	12	1.96	32.72	6	✪✪	2	N.A.		N.A.	
	ESP	6.73	Cater Allen Paseta Inc Bond	C013	08/03/96	JER	-7.19	1	N.A.		N.A.	N.A.				N.A.		N.A.	
●	ESP	5.99	Credis Bond Peseta A	C054	31/01/94	LUX	-7.58	2	11.50	6	N.A.	N.A.				N.A.		N.A.	
▲	ESP	2.09	CU PP Peseta Bond ACC	C070	31/05/90	LUX	-8.20	8	11.50	5	2.20	43.75	4	✪✪✪	3	27.99	1	N.A.	
	ESP	3.44	Fixe Pesetas	B053	28/02/89	LUX	-8.45	13	9.48	10	2.14	33.93	5	✪✪	2	17.76	2	N.A.	
▲●	ESP	3.86	Groupe Indosuez Spanish Pe Bd	G017	22/03/96	LUX	-7.94	5	N.A.		N.A.	N.A.				N.A.		N.A.	
	ESP	4.32	KB Lux Bond PTAS B	K011	29/05/92	LUX	-8.26	10	13.21	2	1.95	45.09	2	✪✪✪✪	4	N.A.		N.A.	
	ESP	27.48	KB Renta Pesetarenta B	K010	30/11/92	LUX	-8.22	9	12.08	4	2.16	46.40	1	✪✪✪✪	4	N.A.		N.A.	
▲	ESP	26.58	Mercury ST ESP Global Bond	M021	26/02/93	LUX	-7.84	4	2.84	11	1.96	27.89	7	✪	1	N.A.		N.A.	
▲	ESP	114.36	SBC Bond Portfolio ESP /B	S007	31/12/93	LUX	-8.29	11	10.81	9	2.05	43.93	3	✪✪✪	3	N.A.		N.A.	
	ESP	22.75	Sogelux Fd Bonds Spain	S037	30/09/94	LUX	-8.04	6	12.77	3	N.A.	N.A.				N.A.		N.A.	
	ESP	6.76	Swissca Bond Invest ESP	S057	31/03/94	LUX	-8.12	7	13.42	1	N.A.	N.A.				N.A.		N.A.	

Swedish Krona Fixed Interest

Funds investing in excess of 70% in Swedish Krona denominated fixed interest securities (corporate, government, index-linked etc) with a maturity of three years or greater.

	CCY	Fund Size ($mil)	Fund Name	Manager Code	Fund Start Date	Domicile Code	3 Mths 97 % Chg	3 Mths 97 Rank	1 Year % Chg	1 Year Rank	Micropal Star Rating 3 Years Volatility	3 Years % Chg	3 Years Rank	3 Years Rating	Risk Return Rating	5 Years % Chg	5 Years Rank	10 Years % Chg	10 Years Rank
		64.08	**Mean/Count**				**-10.99**	**7**	**11.01**	**7**	**3.18**	**62.81**	**3**		**1**	**47.20**	**2**	**0**	**0**
	SEK	10.67	Alfred Berg Oblig Sverige	A019	13/10/95	LUX	-10.81	5	12.65	3	N.A.	N.A.				N.A.		N.A.	
●	SEK	57.64	Carlson SEK Long Bond A	C011	28/09/90	LUX	-10.13	3	12.05	4	2.91	70.22	1	✪✪✪✪	4	55.42	1	N.A.	
●	SEK	24.39	Frontrunner Swedish Bond SEK	F032	04/08/95	LUX	-12.11	6	12.73	2	N.A.	N.A.				N.A.		N.A.	
●	SEK	N.S.	Hansard EU Swedish FI	H010	17/02/95	IRL	-8.66	1	6.81	7	N.A.	N.A.				N.A.		N.A.	
●	SEK	2.17	Hansard Swedish Fixed Int	H011	22/01/93	IOM	-10.67	4	12.76	1	2.87	59.70	2	✪✪✪	3	N.A.		N.A.	
	SEK	31.47	S-E-Banken Fund Avkastningsfd	S001	10/02/95	LUX	-9.12	2	8.47	6	N.A.	N.A.				N.A.		N.A.	
▲	SEK	258.13	Skandifond Sweden Bond	S030	31/08/89	LUX	-15.40	7	11.60	5	3.75	58.52	3	✪✪	2	38.97	2	N.A.	

▲ SIB Approved ● Insurance Fund **Values in US Dollars, on an offer to offer price basis with gross income reinvested** Data Source Micropal™

Swiss Franc Fixed Interest

Funds investing in excess of 70% in Swiss Franc denominated fixed interest securities (corporate, government, index-linked etc) with a maturity of three years or greater.

	CCY	Fund Size ($mil)	Fund Name	Manager Code	Fund Start Date	Domicile Code	3 Mths 97 % Chg	Rank	1 Year % Chg	Rank	Micropal Star Rating 3 Years Volatility	% Chg	Rank	Rating	Risk Return Rating	5 Years % Chg	Rank	10 Years % Chg	Rank
		216.91	**Mean/Count**				**-5.06**	**34**	**-9.68**	**28**	**3.16**	**24.53**	**22**		**1**	**41.09**	**15**	**83.94**	**3**
	CHF	251.11	Baer Multibond Swiss Bond A	J007	29/11/91	LUX	-5.38	19	-10.41	14	3.25	25.80	8	✪✪✪	3	44.34	4	N.A.	
	CHF	N.S.	Bank Hofmann Swissrent	B016	31/03/93	GU	-5.25	14	-9.91	10	3.63	27.49	4	✪✪✪✪	4	N.A.		N.A.	
●	CHF	1.96	BL Multi Tst Bd CHF B	B025	28/06/96	LUX	-6.79	34	N.A.		N.A.	N.A.				N.A.		N.A.	
▲	CHF	4.53	CMI GNF Swiss Bond	C042	30/04/90	LUX	-4.26	6	-10.61	17	3.31	23.57	14	✪✪	2	37.59	12	N.A.	
●	GBP	1.52	CMI Ins Co Swiss Bond	C043	28/06/91	IOM	-6.16	31	-11.17	22	3.23	21.56	19	✪✪	1	25.34	15	N.A.	
●	CHF	0.30	CMI Passport Swiss Bond	C044	20/01/95	IOM	-4.42	7	-11.61	24	N.A.	N.A.				N.A.		N.A.	
	CHF	N.S.	Credis Bond Fund S-T SFR A	C054	29/12/95	LUX	-5.82	27	-14.24	28	N.A.	N.A.				N.A.		N.A.	
●	CHF	347.05	Credis Bond SFR A	C054	29/11/91	LUX	-5.33	17	-9.93	12	3.49	27.93	3	✪✪✪✪✪	4	46.73	3	N.A.	
	CHF	336.01	CS Portfolio Income SFR A	C068	31/05/93	LUX	-3.65	5	-7.96	5	2.70	22.26	17	✪	4	N.A.		N.A.	
	CHF	38.74	Fixe Francs Suisses	B053	31/12/90	LUX	-5.46	22	-10.84	19	3.22	23.60	13	✪✪	2	40.53	6	N.A.	
	CHF	12.08	GAM Bond Swiss Franc	G002	29/11/85	IOM	-4.99	10	-11.30	23	3.26	22.04	18	✪	1	40.41	7	47.45	3
	CHF	10.01	GAM Swiss Fr Special Bond	G002	30/09/88	IOM	-2.94	4	-0.12	1	2.50	35.81	1	✪✪✪✪	5	57.62	1	N.A.	
▲●	CHF	16.41	Groupe Indosuez Diverbond	G017	31/05/91	LUX	-6.01	30	-9.46	7	3.09	20.07	20	✪	1	35.20	13	N.A.	
	CHF	N.S.	KB Renta Swissrenta B	K010	30/08/96	L	-5.93	28	N.A.		N.A.	N.A.				N.A.		N.A.	
▲	CHF	28.31	Lloyds IP CHF Bond	L016	30/11/90	LUX	-5.20	13	-10.60	16	3.33	26.93	6	✪✪✪	3	40.15	9	N.A.	
	CHF	63.98	LO Obliflex 31 Chf Gl Bal	L019	27/10/95	JER	-2.02	1	-2.64	2	N.A.	N.A.				N.A.		N.A.	
	CHF	16.46	LO Obliflex 33 Chf Conv Dist	L019	16/02/96	JER	-2.29	2	N.A.		N.A.	N.A.				N.A.		N.A.	
	CHF	52.04	LO Obliflex J Swiss Franc	L019	29/03/85	JER	-5	11	-11.73	26	3.26	23.06	16	✪✪	1	40.11	10	73.34	2
	CHF	33.14	LO Obliflex Z Swiss Franc	L019	29/09/89	JER	-4.98	9	-11.73	27	3.19	24.03	11	✪✪✪	2	40.34	8	N.A.	
▲	CHF	9.31	Mercury ST CHF Global Bond	M021	30/11/93	LUX	-6.70	33	-9.92	11	3.31	23.34	15	✪✪	2	N.A.		N.A.	
	CHF	2.24	Multibond Actibond CHF B	C015	31/01/91	LUX	-5.80	26	-10.88	20	3.26	26.95	5	✪✪✪✪	3	39.97	11	N.A.	
	CHF	0.58	Parvest Global 1 CHF B	B037	10/05/96	LUX	-6.44	32	N.A.		N.A.	N.A.				N.A.		N.A.	
	CHF	24.65	Parvest Obli CHF B	B037	02/02/96	LUX	-5.31	16	N.A.		N.A.	N.A.				N.A.		N.A.	
	CHF	251.12	Pictet F.I.F. – Valbond CHF	P016	28/09/84	LUX	-5.68	25	-11.66	25	3.16	17.28	22	✪	1	34.81	14	131.02	1
	CHF	341.69	Raiffeisen Swiss Obli A	F024	31/03/94	LUX	-5.47	24	-9.82	8	N.A.	N.A.				N.A.		N.A.	
▲	CHF	17.94	RBC Gl Swiss Franc Bond	R003	30/11/95	GU	-5.14	12	-10.99	21	N.A.	N.A.				N.A.		N.A.	
▲	CHF	1960.03	SBC Bond Portfolio Sfr /B	S007	30/11/89	LUX	-5.42	20	-10.43	15	3.24	26.43	7	✪✪✪✪	3	44.24	5	N.A.	
▲	CHF	451.59	SBC Dynamic Floor Fd CHF 95%	S007	29/07/94	LUX	-4.42	8	-6.45	3	N.A.	N.A.				N.A.		N.A.	
	CHF	10.56	Sogelux Fd Bonds Switzerland	S037	21/06/96	LUX	-5.47	23	N.A.		N.A.	N.A.				N.A.		N.A.	
	CHF	588.84	SVB Portfolio Income CHF	K001	30/10/92	LUX	-2.29	3	-6.54	4	2.69	24.60	10	✪✪✪	5	N.A.		N.A.	
	CHF	593.89	Swissca Bond Invest CHF	S057	31/05/93	LUX	-5.26	15	-10.68	18	3.31	24.85	9	✪✪✪	3	N.A.		N.A.	
	CHF	523.82	UBS (Lux) Bond Invest CHF T	U001	26/02/93	LUX	-5.33	18	-10.10	13	3.28	23.87	12	✪✪	2	N.A.		N.A.	
	CHF	536.42	UBS (Lux) Ptf Inv Fix Inc CHF	U001	30/06/93	LUX	-5.97	29	-9.44	6	2.73	19.45	21	✪	2	N.A.		N.A.	
	CHF	197.72	Vontobel Swiss Franc Bond A	B017	31/10/91	LUX	-5.43	21	-9.90	9	3.08	28.64	2	✪✪✪✪✪	4	48.99	2	N.A.	

UK Pound Fixed Interest

Funds investing in excess of 70% in British fixed interest securities (corporate, government, index-linked etc) with a maturity of three years or greater.

	CCY	Fund Size ($mil)	Fund Name	Manager Code	Fund Start Date	Domicile Code	3 Mths 97 % Chg	Rank	1 Year % Chg	Rank	Micropal Star Rating 3 Years Volatility	% Chg	Rank	Rating	Risk Return Rating	5 Years % Chg	Rank	10 Years % Chg	Rank
		50.55	**Mean/Count**				**-3.20**	**103**	**16.15**	**101**	**2.43**	**29.06**	**78**		**1**	**40.55**	**66**	**188.83**	**25**
	GBP	8.53	Abtrust Stlg Fixed Interest	A003	29/01/82	GU	-2.61	12	15.85	69	2.03	27.67	52	✪✪	3	25.86	65	161.92	20
▲	GBP	0.47	Aetna IUF Sterling Bd A	A011	29/04/88	LUX	-3.30	65	14.69	89	2.27	27.39	54	✪	2	43.99	21	N.A.	
▲	GBP	46.52	Allied Dunbar Gilt & Income	A020	31/05/84	IOM	-3.72	90	17.74	15	2.73	33.39	15	✪✪✪✪	4	40.04	32	162.85	18
●	GBP	22.90	Allied Dunbar IB Sterling Bond	A021	30/09/93	IOM	-3.73	93	17.64	17	2.22	32.24	18	✪✪✪✪	4	N.A.		N.A.	
	GBP	9.13	AXA Eqty&Law IFM UK Gilt & FI	A039	29/11/85	IOM	-1.95	5	15.60	72	2.49	28.90	39	✪✪✪	2	33.94	54	152.72	24
	GBP	1.93	AXA Eqty&Law ILA Secure Gth	A040	31/01/96	IOM	-3	34	N.A.		N.A.	N.A.				N.A.		N.A.	
	GBP	5.24	AXA Eqty&Law ILA UK Gilt & FI	A040	31/10/85	IOM	-3.43	77	16.30	56	2.19	30.48	30	✪✪✪	4	36.43	46	175.77	16
	GBP	3.54	Bachmann GIF Cash Gilt & Stlg	B001	31/03/89	GU	-2.79	17	16.06	63	1.92	34.24	10	✪✪✪✪	5	34.68	52	N.A.	

▲ SIB Approved ● Insurance Fund **Values in US Dollars, on an offer to offer price basis with gross income reinvested** Data Source Micropal™

UK Pound Fixed Interest

continued

	CCY	Fund Size ($mil)	Fund Name	Manager Code	Fund Start Date	Domicile Code	3 Mths 97 % Chg	Rank	1 Year % Chg	Rank	Micropal Star Rating 3 Years Volatility	% Chg	Rank	Rating	Risk Return Rating	5 Years % Chg	Rank	10 Years % Chg	Rank
		50.55	**Mean/Count**				**-3.20**	**103**	**16.15**	**101**	**2.43**	**29.06**	**78**		**1**	**40.55**	**66**	**188.83**	**25**
▲	GBP	851.30	Barclays Sterling Bond	B046	30/06/72	JER	-3.07	43	18.28	9	2.55	34.73	8	✪✪✪✪✪	4	51.27	5	214.98	6
	GBP	0.25	BBL Renta Fund Obli Cash GBP C	B052	23/08/96	LUX	N.A.	—	N.A.		N.A.	N.A.				N.A.		N.A.	
	GBP	8.88	Bk of Ire Glbl High Inc Gilt	B018	30/04/87	IOM	-2.99	33	17.27	27	2.59	30.60	27	✪✪✪	2	51.31	4	N.A.	
	GBP	7.61	Capel-Cure Myers Stlg Bond	C008	29/05/87	LUX	-3.36	70	15.28	78	2.39	31.78	20	✪✪✪	4	38.37	44	N.A.	
	GBP	8.12	Cater Allen FF High Inc Bond	C013	07/01/00	JER	-3.70	89	17.62	18	N.A.	N.A.				N.A.		N.A.	
●	GBP	16.24	Cater Allen Gilt Income	C013	31/10/95	JER	-2.70	13	16.89	37	N.A.	N.A.				N.A.		N.A.	
●	GBP	12.52	Cater Allen High Yield (2000)	C013	30/10/81	JER	-2.78	15	15.34	77	3.15	27.18	56	✪✪	3	34.74	51	159.65	22
	GBP	33.16	CIAM Sterling Bond	C014	05/08/94	JER	-2.84	21	18.09	12	N.A.	N.A.				N.A.		N.A.	
	GBP	3.21	CIBC PCF Sterling Bond	C021	30/04/93	GU	-3.32	68	19.50	4	2.12	36.93	2	✪✪✪✪	5	N.A.		N.A.	
▲	GBP	37.59	CMI GNF UK Bond	C042	30/04/90	LUX	-1.90	3	16.92	35	2.55	24.88	64	✪	1	41.39	31	N.A.	
▲	GBP	252.89	CMI High Income	C040	31/05/89	IOM	-2.80	18	17.12	31	2.17	34.94	7	✪✪✪✪✪	5	39.69	35	N.A.	
●	GBP	144.46	CMI Ins Co GBP Income	C043	29/01/88	IOM	-3.68	88	17.19	28	2.20	30.42	31	✪✪✪	4	32.78	58	N.A.	
●	GBP	16.07	CMI Ins Co UK Bond	C043	31/01/91	IOM	-3.93	97	16.25	58	3.08	21.18	77	✪	1	34.76	50	N.A.	
●	GBP	0.51	CMI Passport Sterling Income	C044	20/01/95	IOM	-2.56	10	17.11	32	N.A.	N.A.				N.A.		N.A.	
●	GBP	0.34	CMI Passport UK Bond	C044	20/01/95	IOM	-3.14	51	15.88	68	N.A.	N.A.				N.A.		N.A.	
▲	GBP	93.78	CMI Sterling Roll-Up	C040	30/04/93	IOM	-2.85	23	17.87	14	2.30	36.48	3	✪✪✪✪✪	4	N.A.		N.A.	
▲	GBP	45.96	Coutts GF Sterling Income	C052	31/01/79	IRL	-3.29	62	18.12	11	2.55	34.14	11	✪✪✪✪✪	4	41.68	28	190.19	13
●	GBP	26.73	Credis Bond GBP A	C054	31/12/90	LUX	-3.42	76	19.69	3	2.82	38.04	1	✪✪✪✪✪	5	46.20	15	N.A.	
▲	GBP	5.77	CU PP Sterling Bond	C070	31/10/88	LUX	-3.12	49	16.53	47	2.60	25.51	61	✪	1	38.53	41	N.A.	
	GBP	0.25	Eagle Star Sterling Bd	E001	29/09/95	IOM	-3.73	92	16.37	52	N.A.	N.A.				N.A.		N.A.	
	GBP	3.55	F&C RAF Pound Stlg Bonds	F003	31/10/84	JER	-3.06	39	16.57	42	2.46	27.88	49	✪✪	2	45.37	18	210.78	7
▲	GBP	46.01	Fidelity Fds Sterling Bond	F011	30/11/90	LUX	-2.84	22	17.46	23	2.89	22.78	74	✪	1	33.46	57	N.A.	
	GBP	0.66	Finistere Stlg Fixed Int Life	F016	31/12/81	GU	-3.37	73	14.44	90	2.51	21.36	76	✪	1	38.45	42	162.11	19
▲	GBP	28.44	Five Arrows IBF Sterling Bond	R013	31/12/91	GU	-3.11	47	15.83	70	1.99	31.28	24	✪✪✪✪	4	32.63	59	N.A.	
	USD	6.46	Five Arrows IP UK Fixed Int	R016	30/12/94	GU	-3.98	99	11.12	95	N.A.	N.A.				N.A.		N.A.	
▲	GBP	30.26	Fleming FF Sterling Bond	F020	31/03/92	LUX	-3.27	59	17.44	24	2.81	29.39	37	✪✪✪	2	N.A.		N.A.	
	GBP	3.11	Friends Provdnt Fixed Int	F031	31/05/94	GU	-3.37	72	4.31	101	N.A.	N.A.				N.A.		N.A.	
●	GBP	4.94	Frontrunner Sterling Fund	F032	31/10/89	LUX	-2.94	31	16.37	53	1.94	35.51	6	✪✪✪✪	5	31.88	60	N.A.	
	GBP	3.04	GAM Bond Sterling	G002	29/11/85	IOM	-3.09	45	15.22	81	2.26	28.44	45	✪✪	3	40.01	33	161.29	21
	GBP	37.38	GAM Sterling Special Bond	G002	30/11/90	IOM	-1.74	2	21.19	2	2.61	36.38	4	✪✪✪✪	4	59.32	2	N.A.	
▲	GBP	62.13	Gartmore CSF Stlg Bond	G007	31/05/84	JER	-3.24	54	16.31	55	2.52	28.71	41	✪✪	3	44.79	20	180.48	15
	USD	0.09	Glbl Mgr UK Gilt Bear	B066	30/09/94	BER	-3.58	85	10.54	99	N.A.	N.A.				N.A.		N.A.	
	USD	0.10	Glbl Mgr UK Gilt Index	B066	30/09/94	BER	-3.43	78	14.17	93	N.A.	N.A.				N.A.		N.A.	
	GBP	19.88	Govett GSIL UK High Income	G015	31/03/89	JER	-2.93	29	14.92	86	2.50	28.53	44	✪✪	2	42.04	26	N.A.	
▲	GBP	35.52	GT Gilt A	G018	30/07/76	IRL	-3.07	42	16.37	54	2.50	33.59	13	✪✪	2	59.87	1	236.23	1
	GBP	18.51	Guinness Fl IF Stlg High Yld	G020	30/06/88	GU	-3.93	98	16.01	64	2.55	27.72	51	✪✪	2	52.34	3	N.A.	
▲	GBP	115.34	Guinness Flight Gilt&Stlg Bd	G019	31/01/85	GU	-3.99	100	15.63	71	2.47	24.04	70	✪	1	41.85	27	172.84	17
▲	GBP	15.50	Hambros EMMA Sterling Bond	H002	29/04/88	GU	-3.25	58	16.53	48	2.63	31.35	23	✪✪✪✪	4	41.54	29	N.A.	
●	GBP	N.S.	Hansard EU UK Stlg FI	H010	17/02/95	IRL	-2.08	7	10.98	98	N.A.	N.A.				N.A.		N.A.	
●	GBP	6.77	Hansard UK Fixed Interest	H011	28/02/90	IOM	-3.24	56	16.29	57	2.16	33.52	14	✪✪✪✪	4	35.38	47	N.A.	
●	GBP	0.25	Hansard\Gartmore CSF Stlg Bd	H015	27/09/91	IOM	-2.93	30	15.52	74	2.71	28.90	38	✪✪✪	1	36.52	45	N.A.	
	GBP	3.10	Havelet Throg Stlg High Inc	H023	31/08/89	GU	-3.39	74	14.72	88	2.43	30.12	34	✪✪✪	3	33.53	55	N.A.	
▲	USD	13.94	Henderson HF Sterling Bond	H025	31/07/89	LUX	-2.61	11	15.96	67	2.26	28.70	42	✪✪	2	49.23	9	N.A.	
▲	GBP	140.56	Hill Samuel Offshore Hi Yield	H030	31/08/90	JER	-3.33	69	16.89	38	2.30	30.50	29	✪✪✪✪	3	45.67	17	N.A.	
▲	GBP	55.32	Hill Samuel Stlg Fixed Int	H030	31/05/79	JER	-2.85	25	17.30	26	2.72	28.29	46	✪✪✪	2	47.02	13	196.12	12
▲	GBP	3.84	HSBC GIF Sterling Bond	H033	30/01/87	LUX	-2.98	32	15.17	82	2.60	25.18	63	✪	1	39.13	39	N.A.	
●	GBP	0.46	JRIA Sterling Bond	J002	29/01/93	IRL	-2.85	26	11.04	96	2.44	23.55	72	✪	1	N.A.		N.A.	
	GBP	0.63	JRIA/UK Bond Stlg	J002	30/12/94	IRL	-2.83	20	11.03	97	N.A.	N.A.				N.A.		N.A.	
▲	GBP	12.62	Jupiter Tyndall GF High Yield	J010	30/11/90	LUX	-3.29	63	18.43	7	2.11	28.16	47	✪✪	3	43.26	23	N.A.	
	GBP	10.83	Jupiter Tyndall Gilt Acc	J009	31/03/76	JER	-3.16	52	16.43	50	2.51	25.46	62	✪	1	38.43	43	196.49	11
	GBP	10.83	Jupiter Tyndall Gilt Inc	J009	31/03/76	JER	-3.24	55	15.97	65	2.67	23.85	71	✪	1	34.82	49	181.91	14
▲	GBP	88.01	KB Gilt	K007	31/01/79	GU	-3.24	57	17.19	29	2.40	30.21	32	✪✪✪	3	45.13	19	229.62	2
	GBP	8.17	KB Lux Bond GBP B	K011	29/04/88	LUX	-3.31	66	18.59	5	2.14	36.14	5	✪✪✪✪✪	5	45.94	16	N.A.	
▲	GBP	N.S.	Lazard High Yield Bond	L002	31/03/88	GU	-2.41	9	18.37	8	2.35	29.92	35	✪✪✪	3	41.53	30	N.A.	
▲	GBP	34.54	Lloyds IP GBP Bond	L016	30/11/90	LUX	-3.02	37	16.90	36	2.24	32.17	19	✪✪✪✪	4	39.90	34	N.A.	
▲	GBP	900.10	Lloydstrust Gilt	L018	29/12/78	JER	-3.07	41	17.59	20	2.44	32.24	17	✪✪✪✪	3	50.28	8	228.61	4
	GBP	12.18	LO Obliflex E Pound Sterling	L019	29/03/85	JER	-3.43	79	16.96	34	2.53	27.81	50	✪✪	2	50.47	7	229.30	3

▲ SIB Approved ● Insurance Fund Values in US Dollars, on an offer to offer price basis with gross income reinvested Data Source Micropal™

UK Pound Fixed Interest

continued

	CCY	Fund Size ($mil)	Fund Name	Manager Code	Fund Start Date	Domicile Code	3 Mths 97 % Chg	3 Mths 97 Rank	1 Year % Chg	1 Year Rank	Micropal Star Rating Volatility	3 Years % Chg	3 Years Rank	Rating	Risk Return Rating	5 Years % Chg	5 Years Rank	10 Years % Chg	10 Years Rank
		50.55	**Mean/Count**				**-3.20**	**103**	**16.15**	**101**	**2.43**	**29.06**	**78**		**1**	**40.55**	**66**	**188.83**	**25**
	GBP	2.86	M.Lynch Global Curr STG A	M023	28/04/89	LUX	-3.58	84	15.60	73	2.36	27.62	53	✪✪	2	43.73	22	N.A.	
▲	GBP	26.49	Mercury ST GBP Global Bond	M021	26/02/93	LUX	-4.12	102	16.23	59	2.35	33.79	12	✪✪✪✪	5	N.A.		N.A.	
▲	GBP	684.21	Midland Bank Offshore Gilt	M027	31/10/79	JER	-2.87	27	16.52	49	2.31	27.21	55	✪✪	2	42.36	25	196.65	10
▲	GBP	6.65	Midland ICF UK Fixed Int	M028	28/02/90	LUX	-3.02	36	16.09	61	2.41	25.58	60	✪	2	39.38	37	N.A.	
	GBP	17.44	Multibond Actibond GBP B	C015	28/02/89	LUX	-3.56	83	16.40	51	2.16	29.80	36	✪✪✪	3	28.57	64	N.A.	
	GBP	N.S.	Murray Financials Bond	M042	26/04/96	IRL	-2.88	28	N.A.		N.A.	N.A.				N.A.		N.A.	
▲	GBP	9.81	Newton UGF Stlg Bond	N006	29/05/87	JER	-3.40	75	16.58	41	2.48	24.39	66	✪✪	2	35.23	48	N.A.	
	GBP	5.57	Old Mutual Gnsy Stlg Intl FI	O003	21/04/95	GU	-3.07	40	15.97	66	N.A.	N.A.				N.A.		N.A.	
	GBP	4.79	Old Mutual Gnsy UK FI	O003	29/12/95	GU	-2.85	24	14.74	87	N.A.	N.A.				N.A.		N.A.	
	GBP	0.93	Old Mutual HK UK Fixed Int	O004	28/04/95	HK	-3.21	53	15.05	85	N.A.	N.A.				N.A.		N.A.	
	GBP	43.90	OMI (Gnsy) UK Fixed Int	O005	31/05/82	GU	-3.68	87	15.36	75	2.53	21.62	75	✪	1	30.22	62	198.08	9
	GBP	1.22	OMI (Ire) Stlg Intl FI	O006	29/10/93	IRL	-3.37	71	16.65	39	2.15	30.13	33	✪✪✪	4	N.A.		N.A.	
▲	GBP	8.95	OMI UK Gilt Trust	O007	19/07/93	IRL	-3.32	67	16.55	46	3.05	26.29	59	✪✪	1	N.A.		N.A.	
	GBP	13.09	Parvest Obli Sterling B	B037	31/07/90	LUX	-3.46	81	15.35	76	2.42	26.82	58	✪	2	39.19	38	N.A.	
	GBP	N.S.	Perpetual OIA Stlg Bond	P012	24/01/97	JER	N.A.		N.A.		N.A.	N.A.				N.A.		N.A.	
	GBP	5.60	Pictet F.I.F. – Valbond GBP	P016	29/10/93	LUX	-3.12	48	17.64	16	2.56	32.61	16	✪✪✪✪	3	N.A.		N.A.	
	GBP	0.51	Premier Sterling Fixed Int	P021	28/11/86	LUX	-10.50	103	15.23	80	2.59	24.53	65	✪✪	1	22.70	66	153.87	23
▲	GBP	8.80	Prolific IF Stlg High Yield	P027	31/03/89	IRL	-1.94	4	23.65	1	2.74	30.77	25	✪✪✪	2	47.22	12	N.A.	
▲	GBP	22.67	RBC GI UK Bond	R003	15/12/95	GU	-3.09	46	15.24	79	N.A.	N.A.				N.A.		N.A.	
●	GBP	1.52	RLI/Henderson Horizon F I	R027	31/01/89	IOM	-0.69	1	13.73	94	2.43	24.07	69	✪	1	39.04	40	N.A.	
●	GBP	15.06	Royal Life Intl Gilt	R020	31/03/86	IOM	-2.07	6	15.07	84	2.40	24.15	68	✪	1	42.71	24	199.62	8
●	GBP	1.01	Royal Life\Gart Sterling Bond	R024	30/10/87	IOM	-2.31	8	14.29	92	2.44	24.27	67	✪	1	34.47	53	N.A.	
▲	GBP	263.97	SBC Bond Portfolio Stg /B	S007	30/04/92	LUX	-3.45	80	17.98	13	2.34	31.70	21	✪✪✪✪	3	N.A.		N.A.	
	GBP	N.S.	Schroder Offshore Stlg Bond	S008	27/10/95	GU	-2.83	19	16.07	62	N.A.	N.A.				N.A.		N.A.	
●	GBP	20.94	Scot Amicable UK Fixed Int	S015	30/06/94	IRL	-3	35	15.14	83	N.A.	N.A.				N.A.		N.A.	
	GBP	7.27	Scot Eq (SEI) UK Fixed Int	S016	23/06/95	LUX	-3.73	91	17.57	21	N.A.	N.A.				N.A.		N.A.	
	GBP	12.18	Scot Prov GP UK Bond	S014	30/09/91	IOM	-3.28	60	17.60	19	2.19	31.49	22	✪✪✪✪	4	46.74	14	N.A.	
▲●	GBP	26.56	Singer & Fried Preferred Inc	S027	31/05/95	IRL	-3.86	96	16.64	40	N.A.	N.A.				N.A.		N.A.	
	GBP	3.62	Sogelux Fd Bonds UK	S037	31/07/87	LUX	-3.85	94	17.09	33	2.44	28.14	48	✪✪	2	33.48	56	N.A.	
▲	GBP	3.04	Standard Bank Stlg Bond	S044	30/06/78	GU	-3.64	86	14.35	91	2.89	26.95	57	✪✪	1	30.95	61	149.72	25
	GBP	6.21	Sun Life Income Stlg	S053	29/01/93	IOM	-3.49	82	8.78	100	1.54	15.19	78	✪		N.A.		N.A.	
▲	GBP	33.54	Sun Life Secure High Income	S053	31/05/89	IOM	-2.79	16	18.57	6	2.33	34.54	9	✪✪✪✪✪	4	51.09	6	N.A.	
	GBP	25.88	Swissca Bond Invest GBP	S057	31/03/94	LUX	-3.28	61	17.51	22	N.A.	N.A.				N.A.		N.A.	
	GBP	6.26	Syfrets GI Sterling Bond	S060	30/11/93	CA	-3.13	50	18.27	10	2.11	28.77	40	✪✪	3	N.A.		N.A.	
▲	GBP	8.68	TGA Stlg Bond	T009	28/02/89	LUX	-3.86	95	17.30	25	2.74	28.59	43	✪✪	2	39.68	36	N.A.	
	GBP	128.39	TSB Monthly Share	T012	31/03/88	JER	-3.29	64	16.55	45	2.34	30.71	26	✪✪✪	3	47.60	10	N.A.	
▲	GBP	11	TSB OIF High Income	T013	23/06/95	JER	-3.06	38	17.17	30	N.A.	N.A.				N.A.		N.A.	
▲	GBP	200.96	TSB Quarterly Share	T012	28/02/79	JER	-2.72	14	16.55	43	2.40	30.53	28	✪✪✪	3	47.36	11	218.98	5
	GBP	14.43	UBAM GBP Bond	U010	28/02/94	LUX	-3.07	44	16.55	44	N.A.	N.A.				N.A.		N.A.	
▲	GBP	4.20	Von Ernst GP Stlg Fixed Int	B021	30/11/89	LUX	-4.05	101	16.18	60	2.35	23.28	73	✪	1	29.17	63	N.A.	

▲ SIB Approved **● Insurance Fund** **Values in US Dollars, on an offer to offer price basis with gross income reinvested**

Data Source Micropal™

US Dollar Fixed Interest

Funds investing in excess of 70% in American fixed interest securities (corporate, government, index-linked etc) with a maturity of three years or greater.

	CCY	Fund Size ($mil)	Fund Name	Manager Code	Fund Start Date	Domicile Code	3 Mths 97 % Chg	3 Mths 97 Rank	1 Year % Chg	1 Year Rank	Micropal Star Rating: Volatility	3 Years % Chg	3 Years Rank	Rating	Risk Return Rating	5 Years % Chg	5 Years Rank	10 Years % Chg	10 Years Rank
		49.34	**Mean/Count**				**-0.49**	**131**	**4.93**	**120**	**1.36**	**14.81**	**96**			**34.81**	**63**	**87.43**	**15**
▲	USD	18.74	AAF US Bond Fund	A001	25/11/94	LUX	-1.06	98	1.97	103	N.A.	N.A.				N.A.		N.A.	
	USD	31.04	ACMGI American Income Ptf A	A005	30/06/93	LUX	0.19	38	13.38	6	2.70	25.82	7	✪✪✪✪	1	N.A.		N.A.	
▲	USD	8.35	AEB Worldfolio 3 USD Bond Inc	A009	29/11/85	LUX	-0.15	45	3.62	61	0.72	13.94	51	✪✪		25.23	54	79.30	9
▲	USD	1.05	Aetna IUF US Dollar Bd A	A011	29/04/88	LUX	-1.23	107	3.19	76	1.29	12.52	63	✪✪		28.81	43	N.A.	
●	USD	1.72	Allied Dunbar IB Dollar Bond	A021	30/09/93	IOM	-0.73	75	1.96	105	1.31	11.08	79	✪✪		N.A.		N.A.	
	USD	162.12	Baer Multibond Dollar Bond A	J007	29/06/90	LUX	-0.76	76	3.99	56	1.12	15.35	32	✪✪✪✪		30.23	35	N.A.	
	USD	N.S.	Bank Hofmann Dollarrent	B016	28/02/94	GU	-0.45	61	4.10	54	N.A.	N.A.				N.A.		N.A.	
	USD	80.71	Baring Dollar	B049	30/06/92	IRL	0.08	40	3.34	73	0.85	14.83	38	✪✪✪		N.A.		N.A.	
	USD	82.94	BBL Renta Fund Dollar C	B052	28/02/89	LUX	-0.35	58	2.84	83	1.22	14.42	44	✪✪✪		27.34	47	N.A.	
	USD	15	Bermuda US Bond Cap	B066	12/07/91	BER	0.89	20	3.59	64	1.13	2.56	95	✪		11.89	61	N.A.	
	USD	15	Bermuda US Bond Inc	B066	12/07/91	BER	0.83	22	3.52	66	1.53	2.29	96	✪		11.34	63	N.A.	
	USD	22.60	Buttress USD Bond	B080	11/07/86	BER	-0.10	44	3.43	68	1.25	16.86	18	✪✪✪✪	1	36.40	16	N.A.	
	USD	14.31	Caixa Funds US Dollar	C004	31/12/93	LUX	0.25	34	5.26	38	0.60	14.60	41	✪✪✪		N.A.		N.A.	
	USD	11.60	Capel-Cure Myers Dllr Bond	C008	29/05/87	LUX	-1.46	112	3.20	75	1.48	18.47	11	✪✪✪✪	2	32.86	24	N.A.	
	USD	11.71	Captive Fixed Income	P001	31/01/91	BVI	0.78	24	6.29	29	0.38	16.41	22	✪✪✪		29.23	39	N.A.	
▲●	USD	89.90	Chase Vista US Govt Secs	C019	31/01/86	LUX	-1.33	109	2.98	80	1.41	15.36	31	✪✪✪		36.23	17	96.41	5
	USD	3.10	CIBC PCF US Dollar Bond	C021	30/04/93	GU	-0.46	62	4.27	50	0.88	14.83	39	✪✪✪		N.A.		N.A.	
▲	USD	107.92	Citi PF N.America Dollar Bd	C036	30/09/88	LUX	-0.89	83	2.20	99	1.26	12.03	66	✪		31.17	31	N.A.	
▲	USD	10.35	Citi PF USD Bond Opportunity	C036	09/02/96	LUX	-2	122	N.A.		N.A.	N.A.				N.A.		N.A.	
●	USD	17.60	Citi US Govt Inc A	C032	30/06/94	CA	-5.61	129	6.35	27	N.A.	N.A.				N.A.		N.A.	
●	USD	139.94	Clariden US Dollar Bond	C039	31/08/90	CA	-0.47	63	4.20	52	1.12	17.06	17	✪✪✪✪✪	2	37.70	12	N.A.	
▲	USD	34.72	CMI GNF US Bond	C042	30/04/90	LUX	0.01	41	3.18	77	1.95	14.28	47	✪✪✪		33.36	21	N.A.	
●	USD	1.80	CMI Ins Co US Bond	C043	31/01/91	IOM	-1.69	116	2.16	101	1.73	10.80	81	✪✪		26.20	51	N.A.	
●	USD	1.60	CMI Ins Co USD Income	C043	29/01/88	IOM	-0.29	52	3.82	60	0.20	9.32	87	✪✪		11.48	62	N.A.	
●	USD	0.20	CMI Passport US Bond	C044	20/01/95	IOM	-0.96	87	1.95	106	N.A.	N.A.				N.A.		N.A.	
▲	USD	38.65	Coutts GF Dollar Income	C052	31/05/93	IRL	-0.25	48	1.90	107	1.46	9.87	84	✪		N.A.		N.A.	
●	USD	76.21	Credis Bond USD A	C054	31/12/90	LUX	-0.67	72	4.62	47	2.13	16.21	27	✪✪✪✪		36.61	15	N.A.	
	USD	7.75	CS Portfolio Income USD A	C068	31/05/93	LUX	0.38	31	5.27	37	1.53	14.26	48	✪✪		N.A.		N.A.	
▲	USD	8.89	CU PP US Dollar Bond	C070	31/10/88	LUX	-0.51	64	1.73	109	1.59	7.77	92	✪		22.27	56	N.A.	
▲●	USD	475.10	DBIM Dollarrenta	D006	29/07/88	LUX	-1.04	95	8.75	17	1.32	23.88	8	✪✪✪✪✪	3	46.72	8	N.A.	
	USD	30.68	Deltec High Yield	D010	31/08/95	BVI	3.09	3	16.56	2	N.A.	N.A.				N.A.		N.A.	
●	USD	103.16	Dit Lux Bondselect USD A	D017	31/12/91	LUX	-0.83	80	2.79	86	1.70	14.55	43	✪✪		34.83	18	N.A.	
	USD	0.77	Eagle Star US Dllr Bd	E001	29/09/95	IOM	-1.13	102	1.80	108	N.A.	N.A.				N.A.		N.A.	
	USD	N.S.	EPIC MF USD Long Term Govt	A024	20/10/95	LUX	-1.69	115	0.32	114	N.A.	N.A.				N.A.		N.A.	
	USD	N.S.	EV Medallion High Yield B	E003	28/02/95	CA	-1.42	110	12.75	7	N.A.	N.A.				N.A.		N.A.	
	USD	67.65	Federated High Inc Advantage	F006	09/06/95	IRL	1.64	13	13.75	4	N.A.	N.A.				N.A.		N.A.	
▲	USD	38.90	Fidelity Fds Dollar Bond	F011	30/11/90	LUX	-0.58	67	3.52	67	1.47	10.60	82	✪		29.62	37	N.A.	
●	USD	48.10	FIL Leveraged US Govt Bond	F017	23/09/94	HK	2.99	4	28.02	1	N.A.	N.A.				N.A.		N.A.	
	GBP	0.12	Finistere Dllr Fixed Int Life	F016	31/12/81	GU	0.33	32	4.92	43	1.66	13.94	52	✪✪✪		33.18	22	78.98	10
	USD	70.20	Finsbury Fund Ltd	O008	31/10/84	BER	1.91	11	11.78	12	1.80	36.82	1	✪✪✪✪✪	5	86.51	2	114.23	2
	USD	24.80	Finsbury Group Ltd	O008	30/03/84	BER	1.62	14	10.56	13	1.17	32.88	4	✪✪✪✪✪	5	76.01	5	91.50	6
▲	USD	258.47	Five Arrows IBF US Dollar Bond	R013	31/12/91	GU	-0.32	57	4.24	51	0.83	15.06	36	✪✪✪		32.30	26	N.A.	
	USD	2.44	Five Arrows IP USD FI	R016	17/11/95	GU	-1.05	96	1.29	112	N.A.	N.A.				N.A.		N.A.	
	USD	9.43	Fixe US Dollar	B053	31/10/88	LUX	-1.02	93	2.67	87	1.20	13.83	53	✪✪		30.35	34	N.A.	
	USD	N.S.	Fonte Cindam Real	F025	24/11/95	CA	2.04	10	12.28	9	N.A.	N.A.				N.A.		N.A.	
▲	USD	6.70	Franklin Templeton US Govt	T001	28/02/91	LUX	0.25	35	5.20	40	0.93	8.88	89	✪		21.37	57	N.A.	
	USD	2.77	G-Bond Fund G-USD Bond B	G009	19/01/96	LUX	-0.83	79	N.A.		N.A.	N.A.				N.A.		N.A.	
	USD	0.90	GAM Bond US Dollar Ord	G002	29/11/85	IOM	-1.20	105	2.32	97	0.84	11.20	76	✪		25.74	52	64.35	15
	USD	55.10	GAM High Yield	G003	31/08/87	IOM	1.57	15	9.59	15	1.10	28.79	5	✪✪✪✪✪	4	77.69	4	N.A.	
▲	USD	15.81	Gartmore CSF USD Bond	G007	31/07/92	JER	-0.30	53	3.40	69	1.77	16.31	25	✪✪✪✪		N.A.		N.A.	
	USD	55.95	Generalux USD B	B064	26/02/93	LUX	0	42	5.75	34	0.65	13.52	57	✪✪		N.A.		N.A.	
	USD	0.20	Glbl Mgr US Bond Bear	B066	30/09/94	BER	4.87	1	5.20	39	N.A.	N.A.				N.A.		N.A.	
	USD	0.20	Glbl Mgr US Bond Index	B066	30/09/94	BER	-4.21	126	-2.90	119	N.A.	N.A.				N.A.		N.A.	
▲●	USD	11.21	Groupe Indosuez Dollar Bond	G017	31/12/90	LUX	-1.05	97	1.06	113	1.25	13.10	60	✪✪		27.23	48	N.A.	
▲	USD	5.39	Guinness FI IF USD High Yld	G020	31/12/91	GU	0.82	23	12.35	8	2.11	16.24	26	✪✪✪		49.93	7	N.A.	
▲	USD	15.38	Guinness Flight US Dllr Bond	G019	31/01/85	GU	-0.78	77	3.02	79	1.48	14.14	49	✪✪		31.36	30	89.90	7
▲	USD	2.41	Hambros EMMA N Amer EuroBond	H002	29/04/88	GU	-0.25	47	3.37	71	1.68	16.01	29	✪✪✪✪		37.13	14	N.A.	

▲ SIB Approved **● Insurance Fund** **Values in US Dollars, on an offer to offer price basis with gross income reinvested**

Data Source Micropal™

US Dollar Fixed Interest

continued

	CCY	Fund Size ($mil)	Fund Name	Manager Code	Fund Start Date	Domicile Code	3 Mths 97 % Chg	Rank	1 Year % Chg	Rank	Micropal Star Rating 3 Years Volatility	% Chg	Rank	Rating	Risk Return Rating	5 Years % Chg	Rank	10 Years % Chg	Rank
		49.34	**Mean/Count**				**-0.49**	**131**	**4.93**	**120**	**1.36**	**14.81**	**96**			**34.81**	**63**	**87.43**	**15**
●	USD	N.S.	Hansard EU US Dllr FI	H010	15/12/95	IRL	-0.98	90	4.99	41	N.A.	N.A.				N.A.		N.A.	
●	USD	1.44	Hansard US Fixed Interest	H011	28/02/90	IOM	-0.65	69	2.55	93	2.10	13.36	59	✪✪✪		38.44	11	N.A.	
▲	USD	17.12	HSBC GIF US Dollar Bond	H033	30/01/87	LUX	-0.84	81	4.79	45	1.57	11.71	69	✪		29.15	41	N.A.	
	USD	17.24	HYPO Dollar Bond	H024	29/11/91	LUX	-5.68	130	2.67	88	2.05	11.61	70	✪		27.83	45	N.A.	
▲	USD	43.45	Inter Optimum USD	B069	29/09/89	LUX	-0.65	70	2.92	81	0.85	11.44	73	✪		29.22	40	N.A.	
●	USD	0.14	JRIA US Dollar Bond	J002	29/01/93	IRL	-1.30	108	7.98	21	0.91	11.98	67	✪✪		N.A.		N.A.	
	USD	46.47	KB Lux Bond US Dollar B	K011	28/04/89	LUX	-0.95	86	3.22	74	1.08	12.06	65	✪		31.91	27	N.A.	
	USD	42.52	KB Renta Dollarenta B	K010	08/03/96	LUX	-0.43	60	N.A.		N.A.	N.A.				N.A.		N.A.	
▲	USD	N.S.	Lazard US Dollar Bond	L002	28/11/80	GU	-0.54	65	2.56	92	1.34	13.73	54	✪✪		29.62	36	68.08	13
	USD	9.60	Lion Interoblig USD	C062	28/11/86	LUX	-1.16	104	2.80	85	1.31	9.83	85	✪		27.03	50	107.46	3
▲	USD	81.20	Lloyds IP USD Bond	L016	30/11/90	LUX	-0.42	59	2.88	82	1.22	14.13	50	✪✪		31.47	29	N.A.	
	USD	33.01	LM Glbl US High Yield Inv B	L007	22/03/96	NL	2.10	9	N.A.		N.A.	N.A.				N.A.		N.A.	
	USD	14.20	LM Glbl US Intermediate Bond	L007	08/11/96	NL	-0.26	50	N.A.		N.A.	N.A.				N.A.		N.A.	
	USD	54.10	LO Obliflex B USD Medium Term	L019	29/03/85	JER	-1.01	91	2.82	84	2.26	13.63	55	✪✪✪		40.06	10	121.38	1
	USD	2.90	LO Obliflex C USD Long Term	L019	29/03/85	JER	-4.91	128	-3.58	120	3.03	13.62	56	✪✪✪		41.73	9	72.34	12
	USD	38.46	Luxbond Dollars A Cap	C002	30/06/95	LUX	-0.05	43	6.55	25	N.A.	N.A.				N.A.		N.A.	
	USD	9.44	M.Lynch Adjust Sec Portf A	M023	30/08/91	LUX	1.44	16	5.96	33	0.58	12.83	62	✪✪		20.54	60	N.A.	
	USD	7.89	M.Lynch Corp High Income A2	M023	29/10/93	LUX	1.12	18	10.18	14	1.35	23.28	9	✪✪✪✪✪	3	N.A.		N.A.	
	USD	56.11	M.Lynch Gbl Cur US Fed Sec A	M023	30/08/85	LUX	-0.81	78	3.90	58	1.10	15.08	35	✪✪✪		30.51	33	98.33	4
	DEM	N.S.	MeesPierson UF Global Bond A	M012	01/03/96	LUX	-4.71	127	N.A.		N.A.	N.A.				N.A.		N.A.	
	USD	N.S.	MeesPierson UF USD Bond A	M012	01/03/96	LUX	-1.08	100	N.A.		N.A.	N.A.				N.A.		N.A.	
▲	USD	93.06	Mercury ST USD Global Bond	M021	29/05/87	LUX	-0.29	51	6.58	24	1.74	16.40	23	✪✪✪✪		37.29	13	N.A.	
	USD	106.90	MFS Meridian US Govt Bond	M026	31/01/89	CA	0.61	27	-0.03	117	1.86	11.59	71	✪✪		25.27	53	N.A.	
	USD	72.70	MLBS (B) USD Fixed Income	M024	30/09/94	LUX	-1.85	118	4.84	44	N.A.	N.A.				N.A.		N.A.	
	USD	33.26	Morgan Stanley N.Amer Bd	M039	31/08/92	LUX	-0.72	74	4.97	42	1.32	17.73	13	✪✪✪✪	1	N.A.		N.A.	
	USD	23.94	Morgan Stanley US High Yld	M039	30/10/92	LUX	1.20	17	13.59	5	1.48	33.64	3	✪✪✪✪✪	4	N.A.		N.A.	
	USD	3.09	Multibond Actibond USD B	C015	28/02/89	LUX	-1.11	101	2.45	95	1.18	11.96	68	✪		27.62	46	N.A.	
▲	USD	1	Newton UGF US Dllr Bond	N006	29/03/91	JER	-1.96	121	1.43	111	1.32	11.14	78	✪✪		21.17	58	N.A.	
	USD	8.53	Old Mutual Gnsy Dllr Intl FI	O003	21/04/95	GU	-0.66	71	8.34	19	N.A.	N.A.				N.A.		N.A.	
	USD	0.64	OMI (Ire) Dllr Intl FI	O006	29/10/93	IRL	-0.88	82	8.04	20	1.67	16.77	20	✪✪✪✪	1	N.A.		N.A.	
▲	USD	2.38	OMI Galileo US Dollar Bond	O007	19/07/93	IRL	-1.20	106	1.70	110	2.01	11.27	75	✪✪		N.A.		N.A.	
	USD	0.92	OYSTER US & Bonds	B067	13/09/96	LUX	-0.31	55	N.A.		N.A.	N.A.				N.A.		N.A.	
	USD	3.95	Parvest Global 1 USD B	B037	29/10/93	LUX	0.73	26	2.46	94	0.44	5.86	94	✪		N.A.		N.A.	
	USD	64.38	Parvest Obli Dollar B	B037	29/11/91	LUX	-0.57	66	4.08	55	1.28	14.35	45	✪✪		32.64	25	N.A.	
	USD	27.56	Performa USD Internatl Income	P009	26/02/93	LUX	-0.24	46	5.56	35	1.19	17.65	15	✪✪✪✪	2	N.A.		N.A.	
	USD	N.S.	Perpetual OIA USD Bond	P012	24/01/97	JER	N.A.		N.A.		N.A.	N.A.				N.A.		N.A.	
	USD	31.52	Pictet F.I.F. – USD Bond Ptfl	P016	30/04/93	LUX	-0.26	49	3.36	72	1.23	15.86	30	✪✪✪✪		N.A.		N.A.	
	USD	20.42	Pictet F.I.F. – Valbond USD	P016	28/02/92	LUX	0.08	39	3.39	70	1.17	13.41	58	✪✪		N.A.		N.A.	
	USD	5.46	Pleiade Dollar Bonds	B039	26/02/93	LUX	-1.57	113	2.57	91	1.23	7.94	91	✪		N.A.		N.A.	
	USD	10.22	Prima Leveraged Bond	L009	31/01/94	BVI	1.69	12	9.33	16	N.A.	N.A.				N.A.		N.A.	
	USD	8.21	Proton Fund Intl Bond USD	P025	29/09/95	LUX	4.18	2	6.10	31	N.A.	N.A.				N.A.		N.A.	
	USD	N.S.	Putnam Embassy Div Income A	P033	30/07/93	CA	-1.92	120	6.71	23	1.24	18.47	12	✪✪✪✪	2	N.A.		N.A.	
	USD	N.S.	Putnam Embassy Div Income B	P033	30/07/93	CA	-2.06	123	6.03	32	1.24	16.21	28	✪✪✪✪		N.A.		N.A.	
	USD	N.S.	Putnam Embassy US Govt A	P033	30/07/93	CA	-2.24	124	0.10	116	1.51	9.09	88	✪		N.A.		N.A.	
	USD	N.S.	Putnam Embassy US Govt B	P033	30/07/93	CA	-2.37	125	-0.52	118	1.51	7.63	93	✪		N.A.		N.A.	
	USD	19.33	Putnam High Income GNMA	P032	30/09/86	LUX	-1.72	117	2.14	102	2.15	9.55	86	✪		20.72	59	76.30	11
▲	USD	15.20	RBC GI N American Bd	R003	30/11/95	GU	-0.90	84	3.59	63	N.A.	N.A.				N.A.		N.A.	
	USD	N.S.	RTL International	O008	30/04/96	BVI	0.58	28	N.A.		N.A.	N.A.				N.A.		N.A.	
▲	USD	858.47	SBC Bond Portfolio USD /B	S007	30/04/92	LUX	-1.03	94	3.89	59	1.17	16.33	24	✪✪✪✪		N.A.		N.A.	
	USD	145.65	SBC Dynamic Floor Fd USD 95%	S007	31/10/94	LUX	0.57	29	8.45	18	N.A.	N.A.				N.A.		N.A.	
	USD	233.93	Scontinvest Multicurr Dolval	S012	28/02/91	LUX	0.90	19	6.51	26	0.94	8.85	90	✪		24.80	55	N.A.	
	USD	0.50	Scot Prov GP N American Bond	S014	30/09/91	IOM	-1.86	119	1.96	104	1.57	11.59	72	✪✪		27.21	49	N.A.	
	USD	18.33	Scudder GOF US Mtg Bckd A-2	S019	30/04/93	LUX	-0.59	68	2.42	96	1.25	10.95	80	✪		N.A.		N.A.	
▲	USD	21.07	Skandifond US Dollar Bond	S030	30/11/89	LUX	-1.13	103	0.32	115	1.91	14.57	42	✪✪		33.10	23	N.A.	
	USD	22.23	Sogelux Fd Bonds USA	S037	31/07/87	LUX	-1.44	111	3.59	62	0.96	11.15	77	✪		29.06	42	N.A.	
	USD	1.50	Star Series Convertible	S046	29/09/95	BER	-0.98	88	12.16	10	N.A.	N.A.				N.A.		N.A.	
	USD	14.18	SVB Portfolio Income USD	K001	31/12/93	LUX	0.51	30	6.17	30	0.84	16.65	21	✪✪✪✪		N.A.		N.A.	

▲ SIB Approved ● Insurance Fund **Values in US Dollars, on an offer to offer price basis with gross income reinvested** Data Source Micropal™

US Dollar Fixed Interest

continued

	CCY	Fund Size ($mil)	Fund Name	Manager Code	Fund Start Date	Domicile Code	3 Mths 97 % Chg	3 Mths 97 Rank	1 Year % Chg	1 Year Rank	Micropal Star Rating 3 Years Volatility	3 Years % Chg	3 Years Rank	Rating	Risk Return Rating	5 Years % Chg	5 Years Rank	10 Years % Chg	10 Years Rank
		49.34	**Mean/Count**				**-0.49**	**131**	**4.93**	**120**	**1.36**	**14.81**	**96**			**34.81**	**63**	**87.43**	**15**
	USD	83.60	Swissca Bond Invest USD	S057	31/05/93	LUX	-0.69	73	2.23	98	1.96	14.80	40	✪✪✪		N.A.		N.A.	
▲	USD	9.78	TGA USD Bond	T009	28/02/89	LUX	-1.07	99	2.60	90	1.37	12.29	64	✪		29.31	38	N.A.	
	USD	1.61	Transoblig US Dollar	B041	28/02/86	LUX	-1.62	114	2.20	100	1.20	14.95	37	✪✪✪		31.12	32	86.98	8
	USD	60.36	UBAM Med Term Dollar Bond	U010	20/10/95	LUX	2.96	5	4.15	53	N.A.	N.A.				N.A.		N.A.	
	USD	91.50	UBK Select High Yield A	U013	28/02/90	GU	-0.32	56	6.98	22	0.95	17.66	14	✪✪✪✪	3	51.89	6	N.A.	
	USD	2.09	UBK Select High Yield B	U013	31/10/91	GU	0.87	21	4.66	46	0.70	10.30	83	✪✪		34.10	20	N.A.	
	USD	244.59	UBS (Lux) Bond Invest USD	U001	26/02/93	LUX	-1.01	92	2.64	89	1.37	11.32	74	✪		N.A.		N.A.	
	USD	20.02	UBS (Lux) Bond Invest USD E Y	U001	30/11/93	LUX	-15.09	131	3.95	57	1.54	16.77	19	✪✪✪✪		N.A.		N.A.	
	USD	70.79	UBS (Lux) Ptf Inv Fix Inc USD	U001	30/06/93	LUX	0.21	37	4.55	48	0.69	15.10	34	✪✪✪		N.A.		N.A.	
	DEM	107.38	UniDollarBond	U012	30/11/92	LUX	-0.93	85	3.53	65	1.09	14.33	46	✪✪✪		N.A.		N.A.	
	USD	185.32	Vontobel Fund US Dollar Bd A	B017	31/10/91	LUX	-0.98	89	3.04	78	2.05	15.19	33	✪✪✪		31.54	28	N.A.	
	USD	16.49	Willerbond Capital US	W004	30/04/86	LUX	0.22	36	4.39	49	0.76	12.91	61	✪✪		27.97	44	65.92	14
	USD	47.90	Winchester Conv Plus Ltd	0008	31/07/89	BVI	2.82	6	14.66	3	2.40	35.93	2	✪✪✪✪✪	4	104.11	1	N.A.	
	USD	75.30	Winchester GSL PIMCO Low Dur	0008	29/11/91	BVI	0.74	25	5.55	36	1.23	17.24	16	✪✪✪✪	4	34.53	19	N.A.	
	USD	42.20	Winchester GSL PIMCO Tot Ret	0008	31/05/93	BVI	-0.30	54	6.33	28	1.75	20.60	10	✪✪✪✪✪	2	N.A.		N.A.	
	USD	3.60	Winchester HL Conv Plus	0008	30/06/89	BER	2.44	8	12.10	11	1.62	27.10	6	✪✪✪✪	3	83.92	3	N.A.	

▲ SIB Approved ● Insurance Fund **Values in US Dollars, on an offer to offer price basis with gross income reinvested** Data Source Micropal™

LAUFZEITFONDS

Laufzeitfonds are fixed interest bond funds sold primarily in Germany, Switzerland, Luxembourg and Belgium and may be in differing base currencies. These funds are established with a defined maturity, or collapse date, usually within 10 years. When the funds are launched, they usually sell their units for a short period (30 to 90 days) and are then closed. Consequently, only a bid price or net asset value (NAV) price is published until maturity. All interest or capital gains is retained within the fund until the end of the period. The manager of the fund purchases a selection of bonds, in the base currency of the specific laufzeitfond, with the term of the bonds to be similar to the collapse date. Although the manager is not restricted to set maturities for the bond portfolio, it will be liquidated at the term date so that the NAV will be paid out to the investor. These funds have been very popular in the Luxembourg offshore market, as they are relatively risk free and attract investors who wish to have funds invested in fixed securities for a set time, with the income generated by the fund being reinvested.

Due to the type of investment instrument a Micropal Star Rating™ is not calculated for these funds.

BEF/LUF 99 Laufzeitfonds

Funds designated as a laufzeitfond whose charter matures in year 1999 and have invested 70% in BEF/LUX denominated fixed interest securities (corporate, government, index-linked etc).

CCY	Fund Size ($mil)	Fund Name	Manager Code	Fund Start Date	Domicile Code	3 Mths 97 % Chg	Rank	1 Year % Chg	Rank	Micropal Star Rating 3 Years Volatility	% Chg	Rank	Rating	Risk Return Rating	5 Years % Chg	Rank	10 Years % Chg	Rank
	131.52	**Mean/Count**				**-7.40**	**1**	**-0.92**	**1**	**2.56**	**40.02**	**1**			**0**	**0**	**0**	**0**
BEF	131.52	BBL Renta Fd Obli-Fix 99	B052	31/03/92	LUX	-7.40	1	-0.92	1	2.56	40.02	1	—	3	N.A.		N.A.	

BEF/LUF 2000 Laufzeitfonds

Funds designated as a laufzeitfond whose charter matures in year 2000 and have invested 70% in BEF/LUX denominated fixed interest securities (corporate, government, index-linked etc).

CCY	Fund Size ($mil)	Fund Name	Manager Code	Fund Start Date	Domicile Code	3 Mths 97 % Chg	Rank	1 Year % Chg	Rank	Micropal Star Rating 3 Years Volatility	% Chg	Rank	Rating	Risk Return Rating	5 Years % Chg	Rank	10 Years % Chg	Rank
	103.31	**Mean/Count**				**-7.10**	**2**	**1.42**	**2**	**0**	**0**	**0**			**0**	**0**	**0**	**0**
BEF	181.59	BBL Renta Fd Obli-Fix 2000	B052	31/03/95	LUX	-7	1	1.38	2	N.A.	N.A.		—		N.A.		N.A.	
BEF	25.03	KB Fixobli BEF 24/12/2000 Cap	K010	31/07/95	LUX	-7.20	2	1.46	1	N.A.	N.A.		—		N.A.		N.A.	

BEF/LUF 2001 Laufzeitfonds

Funds designated as a laufzeitfond whose charter matures in year 2001 and have invested 70% in BEF/LUX denominated fixed interest securities (corporate, government, index-linked etc).

CCY	Fund Size ($mil)	Fund Name	Manager Code	Fund Start Date	Domicile Code	3 Mths 97 % Chg	Rank	1 Year % Chg	Rank	Micropal Star Rating 3 Years Volatility	% Chg	Rank	Rating	Risk Return Rating	5 Years % Chg	Rank	10 Years % Chg	Rank
	116.04	**Mean/Count**				**-6.63**	**1**	**1.51**	**1**	**2.75**	**43.63**	**1**			**0**	**0**	**0**	**0**
BEF	116.04	BBL Renta Fd Obli-Fix 2001	B052	26/02/93	LUX	-6.63	1	1.51	1	2.75	43.63	1	—	3	N.A.		N.A.	

BEF/LUF 2002 Laufzeitfonds

Funds designated as a laufzeitfond whose charter matures in year 2002 and have invested 70% in BEF/LUX denominated fixed interest securities (corporate, government, index-linked etc).

CCY	Fund Size ($mil)	Fund Name	Manager Code	Fund Start Date	Domicile Code	3 Mths 97 % Chg	Rank	1 Year % Chg	Rank	Micropal Star Rating 3 Years Volatility	% Chg	Rank	Rating	Risk Return Rating	5 Years % Chg	Rank	10 Years % Chg	Rank
	129.64	**Mean/Count**				**-6.99**	**1**	**5.76**	**1**	**0**	**0**	**0**			**0**	**0**	**0**	**0**
BEF	62.29	Cregem Bonds Fix 2002	C059	24/02/95	LUX	-6.99	1	5.76	1	N.A.	N.A.		—		N.A.		N.A.	
USD	197	Proventus BEF Bds Revolving	P013	16/02/96	LUX			N.A.		N.A.	N.A.		—		N.A.		N.A.	

▲ SIB Approved ● Insurance Fund Values in US Dollars, on an offer to offer price basis with gross income reinvested Data Source Micropal™

BEF/LUF 2003 Laufzeitfonds

Funds designated as a laufzeitfond whose charter matures in year 2003 and have invested 70% in BEF/LUX denominated fixed interest securities (corporate, government, index-linked etc).

CCY	Fund Size ($mil)	Fund Name	Manager Code	Fund Start Date	Domicile Code	3 Mths 97 % Chg	3 Mths 97 Rank	1 Year % Chg	1 Year Rank	Micropal Star Rating 3 Years Volatility	3 Years % Chg	3 Years Rank	Rating	Risk Return Rating	5 Years % Chg	5 Years Rank	10 Years % Chg	10 Years Rank
	107.77	**Mean/Count**				**-5.49**	**1**	**4.66**	**1**	**0**	**0**	**0**			**0**	**0**	**0**	**0**
BEF	107.77	BBL Renta Fd Obli-Fix 2003	B052	28/02/95	LUX	-5.49	1	4.66	1	N.A.	N.A.		—		N.A.		N.A.	

BEF/LUF 2004 Laufzeitfonds

Funds designated as a laufzeitfond whose charter matures in year 2004 and have invested 70% in BEF/LUX denominated fixed interest securities (corporate, government, index-linked etc).

CCY	Fund Size ($mil)	Fund Name	Manager Code	Fund Start Date	Domicile Code	3 Mths 97 % Chg	3 Mths 97 Rank	1 Year % Chg	1 Year Rank	Micropal Star Rating 3 Years Volatility	3 Years % Chg	3 Years Rank	Rating	Risk Return Rating	5 Years % Chg	5 Years Rank	10 Years % Chg	10 Years Rank
	2551.00	**Mean/Count**						**0**	**0**	**0**	**0**	**0**			**0**	**0**	**0**	**0**
USD	2551.00	BBL (L) Invest E-Fix Euro Core	B052	29/03/96	LUX	N.A.	—	N.A.		N.A.	N.A.		—		N.A.		N.A.	

BEF/LUF 2005 Laufzeitfonds

Funds designated as a laufzeitfond whose charter matures in year 2005 and have invested 70% in BEF/LUX denominated fixed interest securities (corporate, government, index-linked etc).

CCY	Fund Size ($mil)	Fund Name	Manager Code	Fund Start Date	Domicile Code	3 Mths 97 % Chg	3 Mths 97 Rank	1 Year % Chg	1 Year Rank	Micropal Star Rating 3 Years Volatility	3 Years % Chg	3 Years Rank	Rating	Risk Return Rating	5 Years % Chg	5 Years Rank	10 Years % Chg	10 Years Rank
	422.57	**Mean/Count**				**-4.85**	**1**	**7.71**	**1**	**0**	**0**	**0**			**0**	**0**	**0**	**0**
BEF	422.57	BBL Renta Fd Obli-Fix 2005	B052	28/02/95	LUX	-4.85	1	7.71	1	N.A.	N.A.		—		N.A.		N.A.	

BEF/LUF 2006 Laufzeitfonds

Funds designated as a laufzeitfond whose charter matures in year 2006 and have invested 70% in BEF/LUX denominated fixed interest securities (corporate, government, index-linked etc).

CCY	Fund Size ($mil)	Fund Name	Manager Code	Fund Start Date	Domicile Code	3 Mths 97 % Chg	3 Mths 97 Rank	1 Year % Chg	1 Year Rank	Micropal Star Rating 3 Years Volatility	3 Years % Chg	3 Years Rank	Rating	Risk Return Rating	5 Years % Chg	5 Years Rank	10 Years % Chg	10 Years Rank
	91.67	**Mean/Count**						**0**	**0**	**0**	**0**	**0**			**0**	**0**	**0**	**0**
BEF	91.67	BBL Renta Fd Obli-F Distri2006	B052	29/03/96	LUX	N.A.	—	N.A.		N.A.	N.A.		—		N.A.		N.A.	

Europe 97 Laufzeitfonds

Funds designated as a laufzeitfond whose charter matures in year 1997 and have invested 70% in EUROPE fixed interest securities (corporate, government, index-linked etc).

CCY	Fund Size ($mil)	Fund Name	Manager Code	Fund Start Date	Domicile Code	3 Mths 97 % Chg	Rank	1 Year % Chg	Rank	Micropal Star Rating 3 Years Volatility	% Chg	Rank	Rating	Risk Return Rating	5 Years % Chg	Rank	10 Years % Chg	Rank
	115.15	**Mean/Count**				**-6.96**	**4**	**-1.53**	**5**	**2.32**	**28.45**	**5**			**0**	**0**	**0**	**0**
DEM	154.06	DekaLux EuroPlus 1/97	D009	28/02/92	LUX			0.17	1	2.29	29.44	1	—	3	N.A.		N.A.	
DEM	172.13	DekaLux Europlus 10/97	D009	30/10/92	LUX	-6.85	1	-1.12	2	2.28	28.49	3	—	3	N.A.		N.A.	
DEM	55.68	DekaLux EuroPlus 4/97	D009	30/04/92	LUX	-6.93	3	-1.72	4	2.27	28.13	4	—	2	N.A.		N.A.	
DEM	130.27	DekaLux Europlus 7/97	D009	31/07/92	LUX	-6.91	2	-1.23	3	2.28	28.96	2	—	4	N.A.		N.A.	
DEM	63.58	Luxinvest Zielrent 97	B061	31/03/93	LUX	-7.14	4	-3.76	5	2.50	27.24	5	—	1	N.A.		N.A.	

Europe 98 Laufzeitfonds

Funds designated as a laufzeitfond whose charter matures in year 1998 and have invested 70% in EUROPE fixed interest securities (corporate, government, index-linked etc).

CCY	Fund Size ($mil)	Fund Name	Manager Code	Fund Start Date	Domicile Code	3 Mths 97 % Chg	Rank	1 Year % Chg	Rank	Micropal Star Rating 3 Years Volatility	% Chg	Rank	Rating	Risk Return Rating	5 Years % Chg	Rank	10 Years % Chg	Rank
	50.75	**Mean/Count**				**-6.88**	**5**	**0.33**	**5**	**2.28**	**32.48**	**5**			**0**	**0**	**0**	**0**
DEM	76.26	DekaLux EuroPlus 1/98	D009	29/01/93	LUX	-6.73	1	0.05	4	2.21	31.93	4	—	2	N.A.		N.A.	
DEM	21.03	DekaLux Europlus 10/98	D009	30/09/93	LUX	-6.86	4	3.74	1	2.25	37.27	1	—	4	N.A.		N.A.	
DEM	34.34	DekaLux EuroPlus 4/98	D009	30/04/93	LUX	-6.80	2	0.26	3	2.21	32.18	3	—	3	N.A.		N.A.	
DEM	45.91	DekaLux EuroPlus 7/98	D009	30/07/93	LUX	-6.81	3	0.32	2	2.22	33.31	2	—	5	N.A.		N.A.	
DEM	76.22	Luxinvest Zielrent 98	B061	30/07/93	LUX	-7.18	5	-2.72	5	2.50	27.73	5	—	1	N.A.		N.A.	

Europe 99 Laufzeitfonds

Funds designated as a laufzeitfond whose charter matures in year 1999 and have invested 70% in EUROPE fixed interest securities (corporate, government, index-linked etc).

CCY	Fund Size ($mil)	Fund Name	Manager Code	Fund Start Date	Domicile Code	3 Mths 97 % Chg	Rank	1 Year % Chg	Rank	Micropal Star Rating 3 Years Volatility	% Chg	Rank	Rating	Risk Return Rating	5 Years % Chg	Rank	10 Years % Chg	Rank
	7.29	**Mean/Count**				**-6.90**	**5**	**-0.29**	**5**	**0**	**0**	**0**			**0**	**0**	**0**	**0**
DEM	13.89	DekaLux EuroPlus 1/99	D009	31/01/94	LUX	-6.83	3	0.34	3	N.A.	N.A.		—		N.A.		N.A.	
DEM	3.15	DekaLux EuroPlus 10/99 (A)	D009	07/10/94	LUX	-6.81	2	0.68	1	N.A.	N.A.		—		N.A.		N.A.	
DEM	4.57	DekaLux EuroPlus 4/99 (A)	D009	29/04/94	LUX	-6.88	4	-0.03	4	N.A.	N.A.		—		N.A.		N.A.	
DEM	4.24	DekaLux EuroPlus 7/99 (A)	D009	30/06/94	LUX	-6.79	1	0.50	2	N.A.	N.A.		—		N.A.		N.A.	
DEM	10.60	Luxinvest ZielRent 99	B061	31/05/95	LUX	-7.19	5	-2.96	5	N.A.	N.A.		—		N.A.		N.A.	

▲ SIB Approved ● Insurance Fund **Values in US Dollars, on an offer to offer price basis with gross income reinvested** Data Source Micropal™

Europe 2000 Laufzeitfonds

Funds designated as a laufzeitfond whose charter matures in year 2000 and have invested 70% in EUROPE fixed interest securities (corporate, government, index-linked etc).

CCY	Fund Size ($mil)	Fund Name	Manager Code	Fund Start Date	Domicile Code	3 Mths 97 % Chg	3 Mths 97 Rank	1 Year % Chg	1 Year Rank	Micropal Star Rating 3 Years Volatility	3 Years % Chg	3 Years Rank	Rating	Risk Return Rating	5 Years % Chg	5 Years Rank	10 Years % Chg	10 Years Rank
	179.10	**Mean/Count**				**-7.01**	**3**	**-0.48**	**3**	**2.46**	**33.53**	**2**			**0**	**0**	**0**	**0**
DEM	4.69	DekaLux Europlus 1/2000 (A)	D009	06/01/95	LUX	-6.75	1	1	1	N.A.	N.A.		—		N.A.		N.A.	
DEM	442.32	DekaLux Wachstum 1/2000 (A)	D009	30/09/92	LUX	-7.05	2	-1.75	3	2.43	32.84	2	—	2	N.A.		N.A.	
● DEM	90.28	Dit Lux Zerobond 2000	D017	31/07/92	LUX	-7.22	3	-0.70	2	2.48	34.22	1	—	4	N.A.		N.A.	

Europe 2001 Laufzeitfonds

Funds designated as a laufzeitfond whose charter matures in year 2001 and have invested 70% in EUROPE fixed interest securities (corporate, government, index-linked etc).

CCY	Fund Size ($mil)	Fund Name	Manager Code	Fund Start Date	Domicile Code	3 Mths 97 % Chg	3 Mths 97 Rank	1 Year % Chg	1 Year Rank	Micropal Star Rating 3 Years Volatility	3 Years % Chg	3 Years Rank	Rating	Risk Return Rating	5 Years % Chg	5 Years Rank	10 Years % Chg	10 Years Rank
	93.36	**Mean/Count**				**-6.89**	**2**	**-0.41**	**2**	**2.42**	**31.45**	**1**			**0**	**0**	**0**	**0**
DEM	4.76	DekaLux Europlus 4/2001 (A)	D009	07/04/95	LUX	-6.83	1	0.61	1	N.A.	N.A.		—		N.A.		N.A.	
DEM	181.97	DekaLux Wachstum 1/2001 (A)	D009	31/08/93	LUX	-6.96	2	-1.42	2	2.42	31.45	1	—	3	N.A.		N.A.	

European Currency Unit 2000 Laufzeitfonds

Funds designated as a laufzeitfond whose charter matures in year 2000 and have invested 70% in EUROPE (HARD CURRENCY) fixed interest securities (corporate, government, index-linked etc).

CCY	Fund Size ($mil)	Fund Name	Manager Code	Fund Start Date	Domicile Code	3 Mths 97 % Chg	3 Mths 97 Rank	1 Year % Chg	1 Year Rank	Micropal Star Rating 3 Years Volatility	3 Years % Chg	3 Years Rank	Rating	Risk Return Rating	5 Years % Chg	5 Years Rank	10 Years % Chg	10 Years Rank
	28.29	**Mean/Count**				**-6.60**	**1**	**7.88**	**1**	**1.70**	**34.39**	**1**			**0**	**0**	**0**	**0**
● ECU	28.29	Credis Capital ECU 2000	C055	31/03/93	LUX	-6.60	1	7.88	1	1.70	34.39	1	—	3	N.A.		N.A.	

French Franc 2000 Laufzeitfonds

Funds designated as a laufzeitfond whose charter matures in year 2000 and have invested 70% in FRENCH FRANC fixed interest securities (corporate, government, index-linked etc).

CCY	Fund Size ($mil)	Fund Name	Manager Code	Fund Start Date	Domicile Code	3 Mths 97 % Chg	3 Mths 97 Rank	1 Year % Chg	1 Year Rank	Micropal Star Rating 3 Years Volatility	3 Years % Chg	3 Years Rank	Rating	Risk Return Rating	5 Years % Chg	5 Years Rank	10 Years % Chg	10 Years Rank
	8.44	**Mean/Count**				**-6.61**	**1**	**4.22**	**1**	**2.17**	**30.89**	**1**			**0**	**0**	**0**	**0**
● FRF	8.44	Credis Capital FF 2000	C055	31/03/93	LUX	-6.61	1	4.22	1	2.17	30.89	1	—	3	N.A.		N.A.	

▲ SIB Approved ● Insurance Fund Values in US Dollars, on an offer to offer price basis with gross income reinvested Data Source Micropal™

German DMark 95 Laufzeitfonds

Funds designated as a laufzeitfond whose charter matures in year 1995 and have invested 70% in GERMAN DMARK fixed interest securities (corporate, government, index-linked etc).

CCY	Fund Size ($mil)	Fund Name	Manager Code	Fund Start Date	Domicile Code	3 Mths 97 % Chg	3 Mths 97 Rank	1 Year % Chg	1 Year Rank	Micropal Star Rating 3 Years Volatility	3 Years % Chg	3 Years Rank	Rating	Risk Return Rating	5 Years % Chg	5 Years Rank	10 Years % Chg	10 Years Rank
	1418.20	**Mean/Count**				**-7.21**	**1**	**-2.85**	**1**	**2.50**	**29.19**	**1**			**0**	**0**	**0**	**0**
DEM	1418.20	DekaLux 10/95 (A) (3Y R-O)	D009	30/10/92	LUX	-7.21	1	-2.85	1	2.50	29.19	1	—	3	N.A.		N.A.	

German DMark 96 Laufzeitfonds

Funds designated as a laufzeitfond whose charter matures in year 1996 and have invested 70% in GERMAN DMARK fixed interest securities (corporate, government, index-linked etc).

CCY	Fund Size ($mil)	Fund Name	Manager Code	Fund Start Date	Domicile Code	3 Mths 97 % Chg	3 Mths 97 Rank	1 Year % Chg	1 Year Rank	Micropal Star Rating 3 Years Volatility	3 Years % Chg	3 Years Rank	Rating	Risk Return Rating	5 Years % Chg	5 Years Rank	10 Years % Chg	10 Years Rank
	372.98	**Mean/Count**				**-7.13**	**5**	**-3.59**	**5**	**2.54**	**28.11**	**4**			**0**	**0**	**0**	**0**
DEM	848.50	DekaLux 1/96 (A) (3Y R-O)	D009	26/02/93	LUX	-7.18	5	-3.43	3	2.54	27.61	4	—	1	N.A.		N.A.	
DEM	136.25	DekaLux 10/96 (3Y R-O)	D009	30/09/93	LUX	-7.13	4	-3.98	4	2.54	27.63	3	—	2	N.A.		N.A.	
DEM	378.73	DekaLux 4/96 (3Y R-O)	D009	30/04/93	LUX	-7.12	3	-3.09	2	2.54	28.34	2	—	3	N.A.		N.A.	
DEM	386.25	DekaLux 7/96	D009	30/07/93	LUX	-7.09	1	-3.04	1	2.53	28.87	1	—	4	N.A.		N.A.	
DEM	115.17	Postbank Rendite 96	P019	31/01/94	LUX	-7.12	2	-4.42	5	N.A.	N.A.		—		N.A.		N.A.	

German DMark 97 Laufzeitfonds

Funds designated as a laufzeitfond whose charter matures in year 1997 and have invested 70% in GERMAN DMARK fixed interest securities (corporate, government, index-linked etc).

CCY	Fund Size ($mil)	Fund Name	Manager Code	Fund Start Date	Domicile Code	3 Mths 97 % Chg	3 Mths 97 Rank	1 Year % Chg	1 Year Rank	Micropal Star Rating 3 Years Volatility	3 Years % Chg	3 Years Rank	Rating	Risk Return Rating	5 Years % Chg	5 Years Rank	10 Years % Chg	10 Years Rank
	276.55	**Mean/Count**				**-7.27**	**13**	**-2.86**	**12**	**2.58**	**29.41**	**6**			**0**	**0**	**0**	**0**
DEM	733.20	A.L.S.A. Laufzeitfds 30.06.97	A007	31/12/92	LUX	-7.05	4	-3.55	5	2.56	31.25	2	—	4	N.A.		N.A.	
DEM	427.97	A.L.S.A. Laufzeitfds 31.10.97	A007	31/05/94	LUX	-7.08	8	-3.38	4	N.A.	N.A.		—		N.A.		N.A.	
● DEM	16.87	Credis Capital DM 1997	C055	26/02/93	LUX	-6.98	1	-3.83	10	2.48	27.75	5	—	2	N.A.		N.A.	
DEM	44.43	DekaLux 10/97 (A)	D009	29/07/94	LUX	-7.38	12	-3.66	7	N.A.	N.A.		—		N.A.		N.A.	
DEM	18.33	DekaLux 4/97 (B)	D009	29/04/94	LUX	-7.23	10	-3.95	12	N.A.	N.A.		—		N.A.		N.A.	
DEM	29.26	DekaLux 7/97 (A)	D009	01/07/94	LUX	-7.06	5	-3.80	9	N.A.	N.A.		—		N.A.		N.A.	
DEM	1107.05	DekaLux S Rendite 10/97	D009	30/10/92	LUX	-7.06	6	-3.24	3	2.51	32.24	1	—	5	N.A.		N.A.	
DEM	9.47	Europa Lux 12/97 Invest	E014	29/10/93	LUX	-7.01	2	-3.75	8	2.47	28.85	4	—	2	N.A.		N.A.	
USD	442.08	HYPO DM Cash 97	H024	01/09/95	LUX	-7.28	11	3.34	1	N.A.	N.A.		—		N.A.		N.A.	
DEM	265.08	HYPO DM-Pro Cash 97	H024	01/03/96	LUX	-7.10	9	N.A.		N.A.	N.A.		—		N.A.		N.A.	
DEM	63.05	Postbank Rendite 97	P019	30/06/94	LUX	-7.07	7	-3.64	6	N.A.	N.A.		—		N.A.		N.A.	
DEM	392.87	Uni 93/97	U012	31/12/93	LUX	-7.01	3	-3.91	11	2.84	25.29	6	—	1	N.A.		N.A.	
DEM	45.52	Wuestenrot DM Rent 97	W008	31/12/92	LUX	-9.20	13	-0.92	2	2.62	31.08	3	—	3	N.A.		N.A.	

▲ SIB Approved ● Insurance Fund **Values in US Dollars, on an offer to offer price basis with gross income reinvested** Data Source Micropal™

German DMark 98 Laufzeitfonds

Funds designated as a laufzeitfond whose charter matures in year 1998 and have invested 70% in GERMAN DMARK fixed interest securities (corporate, government, index-linked etc).

	Fund			Fund						Micropal Star Rating				Risk				
	Size		Manager	Start	Domicile	3 Mths 97		1 Year		3 Years				Return	5 Years		10 Years	
CCY	($mil)	Fund Name	Code	Date	Code	% Chg	Rank	% Chg	Rank	Volatility	% Chg	Rank	Rating	Rating	% Chg	Rank	% Chg	Rank
	564.70	**Mean/Count**				**-7.04**	**14**	**-2.49**	**13**	**2.48**	**32.62**	**7**			**0**	**0**	**0**	**0**
DEM	909.66	A.L.S.A. Laufzeitfds 31.03.98	A007	31/03/95	LUX	-6.98	3	-2.97	10	N.A.	N.A.		—		N.A.		N.A.	
● DEM	49.32	DBIM Garantie 100 (1998)	D006	30/06/94	LUX	-7.31	13	-2.77	6	N.A.	N.A.		—		N.A.		N.A.	
DEM	146.73	DekaLux 1/98 (A)	D009	06/01/95	LUX	-7.11	10	-3.46	13	N.A.	N.A.		—		N.A.		N.A.	
DEM	94.46	Dekalux 4/98 (A)	D009	07/04/95	LUX	-7.10	9	-3.32	12	N.A.	N.A.		—		N.A.		N.A.	
DEM	279.19	DekaLux 7/98 (A)	D009	07/07/95	LUX	-7.12	11	-2.85	7	N.A.	N.A.		—		N.A.		N.A.	
DEM	3542.47	DekaLux S Rendite 1/98	D009	31/12/92	LUX	-7.03	4	-3.11	11	2.50	32.30	6	—	1	N.A.		N.A.	
DEM	233.60	DekaLux S Rendite 10/98	D009	30/09/93	LUX	-7.09	8	-2.34	2	2.48	33.88	1	—	4	N.A.		N.A.	
DEM	1273.46	DekaLux S Rendite 4/98	D009	26/02/93	LUX	-7.03	5	-2.90	8	2.50	32.90	5	—	3	N.A.		N.A.	
DEM	352.23	DekaLux S Rendite 7/98	D009	31/08/93	LUX	-7.05	6	-2.59	5	2.49	33.57	3	—	3	N.A.		N.A.	
DEM	110.28	HYPO Lux Zerorent 98	H024	26/02/93	LUX	-7.05	7	-2.58	4	2.56	32.95	4	—	2	N.A.		N.A.	
DEM	18.84	OIM Kapital-Garant 9/98 (B)	O009	02/02/96	LUX	-6.77	2	N.A.		N.A.	N.A.		—		N.A.		N.A.	
DEM	41.27	Postbank Rendite 98	P019	31/01/94	LUX	-7.13	12	-2.50	3	N.A.	N.A.		—		N.A.		N.A.	
DEM	828.18	Uni 92/98	U012	30/04/92	LUX	-6.42	1	1.92	1	2.13	33.77	2	—	5	N.A.		N.A.	
DEM	26.04	Wuestenrot DM Rent 98	W008	30/06/93	LUX	-7.40	14	-2.90	9	2.68	28.95	7	—	1	N.A.		N.A.	

German DMark 99 Laufzeitfonds

Funds designated as a laufzeitfond whose charter matures in year 1999 and have invested 70% in GERMAN DMARK fixed interest securities (corporate, government, index-linked etc).

	Fund			Fund						Micropal Star Rating				Risk				
	Size		Manager	Start	Domicile	3 Mths 97		1 Year		3 Years				Return	5 Years		10 Years	
CCY	($mil)	Fund Name	Code	Date	Code	% Chg	Rank	% Chg	Rank	Volatility	% Chg	Rank	Rating	Rating	% Chg	Rank	% Chg	Rank
	495.11	**Mean/Count**				**-6.97**	**8**	**-1.48**	**8**	**2.43**	**34.40**	**3**			**0**	**0**	**0**	**0**
DEM	101.34	DekaLux S Rendite 1/99	D009	31/01/94	LUX	-7.05	7	-2.05	7	N.A.	N.A.		—		N.A.		N.A.	
DEM	35.24	DekaLux S Rendite 10/99 (A)	D009	07/10/94	LUX	-7	5	-1.23	3	N.A.	N.A.		—		N.A.		N.A.	
DEM	28.23	DekaLux S Rendite 7/99 (A)	D009	01/07/94	LUX	-7.01	6	-1.48	5	N.A.	N.A.		—		N.A.		N.A.	
● DEM	1987.19	Dit Lux DM Laufzeitfonds 99	D017	31/01/92	LUX	-6.98	3	-0.67	2	2.36	33.12	3	—	1	N.A.		N.A.	
DEM	409.87	HYPO Lux Cumrent 99	H024	30/09/92	LUX	-6.87	2	-0.41	1	2.48	36.22	1	—	4	N.A.		N.A.	
DEM	90.92	Oppenheim DM Rent 3/99	O009	03/02/95	LUX	-7.10	8	-2.75	8	N.A.	N.A.		—		N.A.		N.A.	
DEM	22.78	Postbank Rendite 99	P019	30/06/94	LUX	-6.98	4	-1.82	6	N.A.	N.A.		—		N.A.		N.A.	
DEM	1285.35	Uni 92/99	U012	30/10/92	LUX	-6.79	1	-1.40	4	2.45	33.86	2	—	3	N.A.		N.A.	

▲ SIB Approved ● Insurance Fund **Values in US Dollars, on an offer to offer price basis with gross income reinvested** Data Source Micropal™

German DMark 2000 Laufzeitfonds

Funds designated as a laufzeitfond whose charter matures in year 2000 and have invested 70% in GERMAN DMARK fixed interest securities (corporate, government, index-linked etc).

	Fund			Fund						Micropal Star Rating				Risk				
	Size		Manager	Start	Domicile	3 Mths 97		1 Year		3 Years				Return	5 Years		10 Years	
CCY	($mil)	Fund Name	Code	Date	Code	% Chg	Rank	% Chg	Rank	Volatility	% Chg	Rank	Rating	Rating	% Chg	Rank	% Chg	Rank
	819.70	**Mean/Count**				**-6.69**	**6**	**0.12**	**6**	**2.33**	**34.80**	**3**			**0**	**0**	**0**	**0**
● DEM	149.07	Credis Capital DM 2000	C055	31/03/93	LUX	-6.66	3	-0.73	3	2.40	32.44	3	—	1	N.A.		N.A.	
● DEM	4255.81	DBIM Rendite 2000	D006	31/01/92	LUX	-6.19	1	5.15	1	2.11	36.95	1	—	4	N.A.		N.A.	
DEM	98.83	DekaLux S Rendite 4/2000 (A)	D009	06/01/95	LUX	-6.90	5	-0.77	4	N.A.	N.A.		—		N.A.		N.A.	
● DEM	302.60	Dit Lux DM Laufzeitfds 2000	D017	30/11/94	LUX	-7.12	6	-1.93	6	N.A.	N.A.		—		N.A.		N.A.	
DEM	23.19	Postbank Rendite 2000	P019	31/01/94	LUX	-6.81	4	-0.91	5	N.A.	N.A.		—		N.A.		N.A.	
DEM	88.73	UniZero 2000	U012	30/04/92	LUX	-6.47	2	-0.06	2	2.49	35	2	—	3	N.A.		N.A.	

German DMark 2001 Laufzeitfonds

Funds designated as a laufzeitfond whose charter matures in year 2001 and have invested 70% in GERMAN DMARK fixed interest securities (corporate, government, index-linked etc).

	Fund			Fund						Micropal Star Rating				Risk				
	Size		Manager	Start	Domicile	3 Mths 97		1 Year		3 Years				Return	5 Years		10 Years	
CCY	($mil)	Fund Name	Code	Date	Code	% Chg	Rank	% Chg	Rank	Volatility	% Chg	Rank	Rating	Rating	% Chg	Rank	% Chg	Rank
	150.68	**Mean/Count**				**-6.52**	**2**	**-0.35**	**2**	**2.44**	**33.97**	**1**			**0**	**0**	**0**	**0**
DEM	12.65	Postbank Rendite 2001	P019	30/06/94	LUX	-6.49	1	-0.67	2	N.A.	N.A.		—		N.A.		N.A.	
DEM	288.71	Uni 93/01	U012	26/02/93	LUX	-6.55	2	-0.04	1	2.44	33.97	1	—	3	N.A.		N.A.	

German DMark 2002 Laufzeitfonds

Funds designated as a laufzeitfond whose charter matures in year 2002 and have invested 70% in GERMAN DMARK fixed interest securities (corporate, government, index-linked etc).

	Fund			Fund						Micropal Star Rating				Risk				
	Size		Manager	Start	Domicile	3 Mths 97		1 Year		3 Years				Return	5 Years		10 Years	
CCY	($mil)	Fund Name	Code	Date	Code	% Chg	Rank	% Chg	Rank	Volatility	% Chg	Rank	Rating	Rating	% Chg	Rank	% Chg	Rank
	532.79	**Mean/Count**				**-6.23**	**2**	**0.37**	**2**	**2.65**	**34.65**	**1**			**0**	**0**	**0**	**0**
● DEM	527.32	DBIM Rendite 2002	D006	29/07/94	LUX	-6.31	2	1.24	1	N.A.	N.A.		—		N.A.		N.A.	
● DEM	538.25	Dit Lux DM Laufzeitfds 2002	D017	30/09/93	LUX	-6.16	1	-0.50	2	2.65	34.65	1	—	3	N.A.		N.A.	

German DMark 2004 Laufzeitfonds

Funds designated as a laufzeitfond whose charter matures in year 2004 and have invested 70% in GERMAN DMARK fixed interest securities (corporate, government, index-linked etc).

	Fund			Fund						Micropal Star Rating				Risk				
	Size		Manager	Start	Domicile	3 Mths 97		1 Year		3 Years				Return	5 Years		10 Years	
CCY	($mil)	Fund Name	Code	Date	Code	% Chg	Rank	% Chg	Rank	Volatility	% Chg	Rank	Rating	Rating	% Chg	Rank	% Chg	Rank
	9.68	**Mean/Count**				**-4.63**	**1**	**0.46**	**1**	**0**	**0**	**0**			**0**	**0**	**0**	**0**
DEM	9.68	BBL Renta Fd Obli-Fix 2004 DEM	B052	31/05/95	LUX	-4.63	1	0.46	1	N.A.	N.A.		—		N.A.		N.A.	

▲ SIB Approved **● Insurance Fund** **Values in US Dollars, on an offer to offer price basis with gross income reinvested** Data Source Micropal™

Global 2000 Laufzeitfonds

Funds designated as a laufzeitfond whose charter matures in year 2000 and have invested 70% in GLOBAL fixed interest securities (corporate, government, index-linked etc).

CCY	Fund Size ($mil)	Fund Name	Manager Code	Fund Start Date	Domicile Code	3 Mths 97 % Chg	3 Mths 97 Rank	1 Year % Chg	1 Year Rank	Micropal Star Rating 3 Years Volatility	3 Years % Chg	3 Years Rank	Rating	Risk Return Rating	5 Years % Chg	5 Years Rank	10 Years % Chg	10 Years Rank
	363.29	**Mean/Count**				**-6.68**	**1**	**3.78**	**1**	**2.05**	**32.19**	**1**			**0**	**0**	**0**	**0**
DEM	363.29	SchmidtBank Rendite + 2000	F030	31/12/92	LUX	-6.68	1	3.78	1	2.05	32.19	1	—	3	N.A.		N.A.	

Netherland Guilder 2000 Laufzeitfonds

Funds designated as a laufzeitfond whose charter matures in year 2000 and have invested 70% in NETHERLANDS GUILDERS fixed interest securities (corporate, government, index-linked etc).

CCY	Fund Size ($mil)	Fund Name	Manager Code	Fund Start Date	Domicile Code	3 Mths 97 % Chg	3 Mths 97 Rank	1 Year % Chg	1 Year Rank	Micropal Star Rating 3 Years Volatility	3 Years % Chg	3 Years Rank	Rating	Risk Return Rating	5 Years % Chg	5 Years Rank	10 Years % Chg	10 Years Rank
	31.70	**Mean/Count**				**-6.87**	**2**	**-0.69**	**2**	**0**	**0**	**0**			**0**	**0**	**0**	**0**
NLG	51.56	BBL Renta Fd Obli-Fix 2000 NLG	B052	31/03/95	LUX	-6.72	1	-0.53	1	N.A.	N.A.		—		N.A.		N.A.	
NLG	11.85	KB Fixobli NLG 17/01/2000	K010	31/07/95	LUX	-7.02	2	-0.85	2	N.A.	N.A.		—		N.A.		N.A.	

Netherland Guilder 2004 Laufzeitfonds

Funds designated as a laufzeitfond whose charter matures in year 2004 and have invested 70% in NETHERLANDS GUILDERS fixed interest securities (corporate, government, index-linked etc).

CCY	Fund Size ($mil)	Fund Name	Manager Code	Fund Start Date	Domicile Code	3 Mths 97 % Chg	3 Mths 97 Rank	1 Year % Chg	1 Year Rank	Micropal Star Rating 3 Years Volatility	3 Years % Chg	3 Years Rank	Rating	Risk Return Rating	5 Years % Chg	5 Years Rank	10 Years % Chg	10 Years Rank
	58.88	**Mean/Count**				**-5.08**	**1**	**0.94**	**1**	**0**	**0**	**0**			**0**	**0**	**0**	**0**
NLG	58.88	BBL Renta Fd Obli-Fix 2004 NLG	B052	30/06/95	LUX	-5.08	1	0.94	1	N.A.	N.A.		—		N.A.		N.A.	

Swiss Franc 2000 Laufzeitfonds

Funds designated as a laufzeitfond whose charter matures in year 2000 and have invested 70% in SWISS FRANC fixed interest securities (corporate, government, index-linked etc).

CCY	Fund Size ($mil)	Fund Name	Manager Code	Fund Start Date	Domicile Code	3 Mths 97 % Chg	3 Mths 97 Rank	1 Year % Chg	1 Year Rank	Micropal Star Rating 3 Years Volatility	3 Years % Chg	3 Years Rank	Rating	Risk Return Rating	5 Years % Chg	5 Years Rank	10 Years % Chg	10 Years Rank
	379.09	**Mean/Count**				**-5.28**	**1**	**-9.86**	**1**	**3.18**	**25.60**	**1**			**0**	**0**	**0**	**0**
● CHF	379.09	Credis Capital SFR 2000	C055	26/02/93	LUX	-5.28	1	-9.86	1	3.18	25.60	1	—	3	N.A.		N.A.	

▲ SIB Approved ● Insurance Fund

Values in US Dollars, on an offer to offer price basis with gross income reinvested

Data Source Micropal™

MIXED FUNDS

Mixed funds are, as their name suggests, invested in a variety of investment types. Micropal defines a mixed fund as being one which is invested less than 70 per cent in any one asset class – this being an equity, fixed interest or money market security.

Being non-specialist, these funds are useful to investors who wish to leave most of the basic "asset allocation" decisions up to a fund manager. The fund manager will attempt to balance the riskier equity holdings with the lower returning fixed interest investments to produce a portfolio which should achieve a reasonable return at a relatively low level of risk.

Most such funds are globally invested but often have very different styles of management. Some will have a mix which is geared more towards the riskier end of the asset spectrum and will have a higher than average proportion of equity holdings. Others will be more conservative and will carry a high level of bonds and money market instruments. What a fund is trying to achieve is often obvious from its name. For example, Sun Life International has mixed funds with titles such as "managed growth", "balanced" and "defensive".

Brazil Mixed

Funds with a portfolio principally invested (70%) in Brazilian equity, fixed interest and money market securities but typically with no more than 70% in any one asset class.

CCY	Fund Size ($mil)	Fund Name	Manager Code	Fund Start Date	Domicile Code	3 Mths 97 % Chg	3 Mths 97 Rank	1 Year % Chg	1 Year Rank	Micropal Star Rating Volatility	Micropal Star Rating 3 Years % Chg	Micropal Star Rating 3 Years Rank	Micropal Star Rating Rating	Risk Return Rating	5 Years % Chg	5 Years Rank	10 Years % Chg	10 Years Rank
	17.70	**Mean/Count**				**7.85**	**2**	**18.52**	**2**	**11.02**	**87.36**	**1**		**1**	**0**	**0**	**0**	**0**
USD	11.86	Opportunity Balanced Ptfl Cls	O010	28/02/94	CA	7	2	18	2	N.A.	N.A.				N.A.		N.A.	
USD	23.54	SAM Brazil	S003	31/03/93	IOM	8.71	1	19.04	1	11.02	87.36	1	✪✪✪	3	N.A.		N.A.	

Europe Mixed

Funds with a portfolio principally invested (70%) in European equity, fixed interest and money market securities but typically with no more than 70% in any one asset class.

CCY	Fund Size ($mil)	Fund Name	Manager Code	Fund Start Date	Domicile Code	3 Mths 97 % Chg	3 Mths 97 Rank	1 Year % Chg	1 Year Rank	Micropal Star Rating Volatility	Micropal Star Rating 3 Years % Chg	Micropal Star Rating 3 Years Rank	Micropal Star Rating Rating	Risk Return Rating	5 Years % Chg	5 Years Rank	10 Years % Chg	10 Years Rank
	39.53	**Mean/Count**				**-0.32**	**16**	**15.56**	**12**	**2.34**	**40.59**	**5**			**43.98**	**3**	**0**	**0**
● SEK	7.67	Allied Dunbar IB SEK Managed	A021	30/09/93	IOM	6.20	2	21.31	4	2.54	48.05	2	✪✪✪	3	N.A.		N.A.	
BEF	39.36	BBL Patrimonial Belgium C	B052	20/10/95	LUX	-1.38	9	7.65	10	N.A.	N.A.				N.A.		N.A.	
DEM	161.16	BBL Patrimonial Euro-Core C	B052	20/10/95	LUX	-0.51	8	8.56	9	N.A.	N.A.				N.A.		N.A.	
▲ DEM	28.29	Fidelity Fds Euro Balanced	F011	21/10/94	LUX	-2.28	11	18.79	5	N.A.	N.A.				N.A.		N.A.	
CHF	N.S.	Five Arrows IMP Eu Bal In&Gth	R015	31/07/96	GU	1.96	5	N.A.		N.A.	N.A.				N.A.		N.A.	
LUF	85.22	Lux Avantage1 A Cap	C002	30/06/95	LUX	-2.09	10	35.68	1	N.A.	N.A.				N.A.		N.A.	
LUF	99.83	Lux Croissance Francs A Cap	C002	30/06/95	LUX	3.10	3	4.61	12	N.A.	N.A.				N.A.		N.A.	
LUF	3.69	Luxicav Mixed B	S036	31/05/89	LUX	-4.41	14	12.19	7	2.33	51.05	1	✪✪✪✪	4	39.84	2	N.A.	
DEM	60.64	Paneurolife Benelux & Germany	P003	28/02/91	LUX	-2.97	12	6.47	11	2.14	36.35	4	✪✪	3	56.63	1	N.A.	
▲ USD	23.76	PRICOA WWIP European Growth	P022	28/10/94	LUX	0.06	7	23.94	2	N.A.	N.A.				N.A.		N.A.	
DEM	13.84	Scala Germany & Benelux B	B006	29/02/96	LUX	2.85	4	N.A.		N.A.	N.A.				N.A.		N.A.	
▲ GBP	45.22	Sun Life GP Distribution	S052	31/03/93	LUX	9.11	1	22.36	3	2.49	40.38	3	✪✪✪	2	N.A.		N.A.	
DEM	1.74	Syfrets Gl European Bal	S060	10/11/95	CA	1.25	6	10.23	8	N.A.	N.A.				N.A.		N.A.	
ITL	1.15	The Sailor's-Balanced Ptfl	B005	05/01/96	LUX	-3.20	13	N.A.		N.A.	N.A.				N.A.		N.A.	
ITL	4.78	The Sailor's-Italian Equity	B005	05/01/96	LUX	-6.92	16	N.A.		N.A.	N.A.				N.A.		N.A.	
ECU	16.55	UBZ Euro Optimizer	U002	31/07/90	LUX	-5.90	15	14.90	6	2.20	27.14	5	✪	1	35.46	3	N.A.	

Far East & Pacific Mixed

Funds with a portfolio principally invested (70%) in Far Eastern and Pacific equity, fixed interest and money market securities but typically with no more than 70% in any one asset class.

CCY	Fund Size ($mil)	Fund Name	Manager Code	Fund Start Date	Domicile Code	3 Mths 97 % Chg	3 Mths 97 Rank	1 Year % Chg	1 Year Rank	Micropal Star Rating Volatility	Micropal Star Rating 3 Years % Chg	Micropal Star Rating 3 Years Rank	Micropal Star Rating Rating	Risk Return Rating	5 Years % Chg	5 Years Rank	10 Years % Chg	10 Years Rank
	8.59	**Mean/Count**				**-3.46**	**7**	**3.92**	**5**	**3.75**	**3.69**	**3**			**54.14**	**3**	**163.83**	**1**
● HKD	0	CMI Passport HKD Divers'd Mgd	C044	20/01/95	IOM	-0.73	1	3.34	3	N.A.	N.A.				N.A.		N.A.	
● HKD	0	CMI Passport HKD Protectd Mgd	C044	20/01/95	IOM	-1.84	2	1.65	4	N.A.	N.A.				N.A.		N.A.	
USD	34.90	Indosuez Managed	I007	31/01/86	HK	-2.49	3	12.59	1	3.94	5.16	2	✪✪✪		120.74	1	163.83	1
USD	2.15	Orient Growth Fund	B067	31/01/90	LUX	-3.20	5	-4.88	5	3.75	-4.50	3	✪✪		37.30	2	N.A.	
USD	8.43	Paribas Soleil Fund	B037	29/11/91	LUX	-4.34	6	6.88	2	3.55	10.41	1	✪✪✪✪		4.37	3	N.A.	
JPY	6.06	Scala Japan B	B006	14/06/96	LUX	-8.69	7	N.A.		N.A.	N.A.				N.A.		N.A.	
USD	N.S.	Scala Pacific Basin B	B006	29/11/96	LUX	-2.93	4	N.A.		N.A.	N.A.				N.A.		N.A.	

▲ SIB Approved ● Insurance Fund **Values in US Dollars, on an offer to offer price basis with gross income reinvested** Data Source Micropal™

France Mixed

Funds with a portfolio principally invested (70%) in French equity, fixed interest and money market securities but typically with no more than 70% in any one asset class.

	CCY	Fund Size ($mil)	Fund Name	Manager Code	Fund Start Date	Domicile Code	3 Mths 97 % Chg	3 Mths 97 Rank	1 Year % Chg	1 Year Rank	Micropal Star Rating 3 Years Volatility	3 Years % Chg	3 Years Rank	3 Years Rating	Risk Return Rating	5 Years % Chg	5 Years Rank	10 Years % Chg	10 Years Rank
		10.08	**Mean/Count**				**-0.68**	**7**	**8.03**	**5**	**2.36**	**22.95**	**2**			**38.32**	**1**	**0**	**0**
	FRF	5.98	Ace Fund Yield FRF	A004	29/01/93	LUX	-5.51	6	1.55	5	2.15	24.70	1	✪✪✪	3	N.A.		N.A.	
	FRF	5.72	Gallic-Invest	B073	31/03/94	LUX	4.01	1	8.64	4	N.A.	N.A.				N.A.		N.A.	
	FRF	N.S.	Hansard EU French Managed	H010	17/02/95	IRL	2.42	3	9.94	3	N.A.	N.A.				N.A.		N.A.	
●	FRF	0.21	Hansard French Managed	H011	01/07/94	IOM	-7.41	7	10.06	1	N.A.	N.A.				N.A.		N.A.	
	FRF	32.25	Paneurolife France	P003	28/02/91	LUX	-0.03	4	9.95	2	2.58	21.20	2	✪✪	2	38.32	1	N.A.	
	FRF	6.23	Scala France B	B006	08/03/96	LUX	3.95	2	N.A.		N.A.	N.A.				N.A.		N.A.	

Germany Mixed

Funds with a portfolio principally invested (70%) in German equity, fixed interest and money market securities but typically with no more than 70% in any one asset class.

	CCY	Fund Size ($mil)	Fund Name	Manager Code	Fund Start Date	Domicile Code	3 Mths 97 % Chg	3 Mths 97 Rank	1 Year % Chg	1 Year Rank	Micropal Star Rating 3 Years Volatility	3 Years % Chg	3 Years Rank	3 Years Rating	Risk Return Rating	5 Years % Chg	5 Years Rank	10 Years % Chg	10 Years Rank
		2.54	**Mean/Count**				**-1.05**	**4**	**6.39**	**3**	**2.40**	**44.27**	**1**		**1**	**82.99**	**1**	**0**	**0**
●	DEM	0.39	CMI Passport DEM Divers'd Mgd	C044	20/01/95	IOM	-1.62	3	4.92	2	N.A.	N.A.				N.A.		N.A.	
●	DEM	0	CMI Passport DEM Protectd Mgd	C044	20/01/95	IOM	-3.90	4	1.90	3	N.A.	N.A.				N.A.		N.A.	
●	DEM	7.23	Hansard Deutschmark Managed	H011	30/04/90	IOM	0.84	1	12.35	1	2.40	44.27	1	✪✪✪	3	82.99	1	N.A.	

Global Mixed

Funds with a portfolio principally invested (70%) in Global equity, fixed interest and money market securities but typically with no more than 70% in any one asset class.

	CCY	Fund Size ($mil)	Fund Name	Manager Code	Fund Start Date	Domicile Code	3 Mths 97 % Chg	3 Mths 97 Rank	1 Year % Chg	1 Year Rank	Micropal Star Rating 3 Years Volatility	3 Years % Chg	3 Years Rank	3 Years Rating	Risk Return Rating	5 Years % Chg	5 Years Rank	10 Years % Chg	10 Years Rank
		56.96	**Mean/Count**				**-0.40**	**296**	**9.46**	**277**	**2.33**	**22.37**	**198**		**1**	**49.67**	**105**	**127.45**	**25**
	USD	0.21	Abtrust Global Managed	A003	31/07/87	GU	3.77	22	8.47	160	5.77	-34.82	198	✪		-10.48	104	N.A.	
	USD	4.40	Abtrust International Managed	A003	30/07/82	GU	4.09	20	17.38	38	2.50	22.84	106	✪✪	1	55.06	37	89.89	20
	GBP	0.52	Abtrust Star 2	A003	31/10/84	GU	3	34	21.01	12	2.81	25.24	85	✪✪✪	1	53.38	43	112.70	13
	GBP	0.46	Abtrust Star 3	A003	31/10/84	GU	1.30	63	18.23	30	2.44	24.69	89	✪✪✪	2	38.45	81	69.69	21
	GBP	2.20	Abtrust Star 4	A003	31/10/84	GU	3.05	33	21.09	10	2.91	23.78	94	✪✪✪	1	43.70	67	69.17	22
	USD	43.70	ACACIA Balanced Global Secs	O008	29/11/91	BVI	1.56	56	13.20	84	1.70	15.50	153	✪		49.17	52	N.A.	
	USD	0.17	ACMGI Privanza Global Bal. A	A005	28/04/95	LUX	-1.27	182	7.99	168	N.A.	N.A.				N.A.		N.A.	
▲	USD	26.31	AEB Worldfolio 6 Global Bal	A009	30/04/86	LUX	-1.37	185	9.18	147	2	24.77	88	✪✪✪	3	43.51	68	111.42	14
●	GBP	0	Albany Intl International Ptfl	A018	31/08/93	IOM	0.65	93	20.65	14	3.09	38.19	13	✪✪✪✪	3	N.A.		N.A.	
▲	USD	94.70	Allied Dunbar Managed	A020	31/05/84	IOM	0.53	96	11.34	108	2.61	31.33	45	✪✪✪✪	2	59.02	27	136.58	10
	USD	N.S.	Aravis Clipper	A029	19/01/96	BVI	4.99	15	N.A.		N.A.	N.A.				N.A.		N.A.	
▲	GBP	22.26	Ashburton Asset Mgmt Fd	A034	31/05/91	IOM	-1.21	177	19.36	21	2.58	29.81	58	✪✪✪✪	2	56.96	34	N.A.	
	GBP	149.47	Ashburton Replica Sterling	A035	31/12/91	JER	-1.55	197	21.06	11	2.16	31.76	40	✪✪✪✪	3	54.63	40	N.A.	
	USD	49.30	Ashburton Replica US Dollar	A035	31/12/91	JER	1.10	69	12.65	92	1.56	21.87	115	✪✪	4	63.80	19	N.A.	
	USD	10.60	ATC International Dllr	A038	31/08/89	CA	0.88	78	6.26	194	1.62	4.16	183	✪		35.86	86	N.A.	
	GBP	18.95	ATC International Stlg	A038	31/08/92	CA	1.68	53	13.77	71	2.01	23.69	98	✪✪✪	2	N.A.		N.A.	
●	GBP	44.32	AXA E&L Amulet Dist Bd Defer	A040	28/02/94	IOM	-0.80	155	19.02	23	N.A.	N.A.				N.A.		N.A.	
●	GBP	10.78	AXA E&L Amulet Dist Bd Half	A040	28/02/94	IOM	-1.52	196	17.99	33	N.A.	N.A.				N.A.		N.A.	

▲ SIB Approved ● Insurance Fund **Values in US Dollars, on an offer to offer price basis with gross income reinvested** Data Source Micropal™

Global Mixed

continued

	CCY	Fund Size ($mil)	Fund Name	Manager Code	Fund Start Date	Domicile Code	3 Mths 97 % Chg	Rank	1 Year % Chg	Rank	Micropal Star Rating 3 Years Volatility	% Chg	Rank	Rating	Risk Return Rating	5 Years % Chg	Rank	10 Years % Chg	Rank
		56.96	**Mean/Count**				**-0.40**	**296**	**9.46**	**277**	**2.33**	**22.37**	**198**		**1**	**49.67**	**105**	**127.45**	**25**
●	GBP	10.64	AXA E&L Amulet Dist Bd Quart	A040	28/02/94	IOM	-1.47	190	17.84	34	N.A.	N.A.				N.A.		N.A.	
	GBP	80.32	AXA Eqty&Law ILA Intl Mgd	A040	31/10/85	IOM	-1.61	202	13.62	78	2.48	31.43	42	✪✪✪✪	3	68.46	12	147.03	7
	CHF	16.15	Baer Multicoop Baloise-progres	J007	05/04/96	LUX	0.51	99	N.A.		N.A.	N.A.				N.A.		N.A.	
	CHF	18.86	Baer Multicoop Gerfonds A	J007	30/11/93	LUX	-2.73	242	-1.17	261	2.13	4.73	182	✪		N.A.		N.A.	
	CHF	79.59	Baer Multicoop MI FONDS 30 A	M029	31/03/95	LUX	-2.72	241	-2.45	267	N.A.	N.A.				N.A.		N.A.	
	CHF	66.81	Baer Multicoop MI FONDS 50 A	M029	31/03/95	LUX	-1.51	195	0.97	246	N.A.	N.A.				N.A.		N.A.	
▲	GBP	9.52	Barclays Global Income	B046	30/09/87	JER	1.24	64	20.10	18	2.92	26.71	76	✪✪✪	1	63.37	21	N.A.	
	LUF	19.69	BBL Patrimonial Aggressive C	B052	29/07/94	LUX	-2.74	243	10.18	131	N.A.	N.A.				N.A.		N.A.	
	LUF	602.31	BBL Patrimonial Balanced C	B052	30/12/77	LUX	-2.57	235	6.23	195	1.55	32.82	36	✪✪✪✪✪	5	50.28	47	142.39	8
	LUF	24.59	BBL Patrimonial Defensive C	B052	29/07/94	LUX	-5.19	279	3.67	223	N.A.	N.A.				N.A.		N.A.	
●	AUD	3.49	Bentley/Royal Skandia SAM 2	B057	30/04/91	IOM	N.A.	—	-1.34	264	3.01	7.37	178	✪		20.05	101	N.A.	
●	GBP	64.09	Bentley/Royal Skandia SAM 4	B057	30/09/88	IOM	N.A.	—	4.34	217	2.71	10.14	174	✪		16.41	102	N.A.	
	USD	39.02	Bermuda Capital Co Ltd	B059	31/12/81	BER	7.48	8	18.39	28	3.10	33.73	29	✪✪✪✪	2	92.79	3	305.79	1
	BEF	126.03	BIL Delta Fund Balance C	B067	28/02/94	LUX	-4.60	274	2.14	241	N.A.	N.A.				N.A.		N.A.	
●	LUF	57.93	BL Global Asset 100 B	B025	29/10/93	LUX	1.94	48	17.79	36	2.07	40.33	7	✪✪✪✪✪	5	N.A.		N.A.	
●	LUF	13.32	BL Global Asset 30 B	B025	29/10/93	LUX	-0.82	157	8.18	165	1.46	24.81	87	✪✪✪	4	N.A.		N.A.	
●	LUF	40.78	BL Global Asset 50 B	B025	29/10/93	LUX	0.15	116	13.52	81	1.53	31.86	38	✪✪✪✪	5	N.A.		N.A.	
	FRF	8.02	Bolux International	C003	29/04/94	LUX	N.A.	—	2.91	228	N.A.	N.A.				N.A.		N.A.	
	LUF	7.17	BR Fund Global	B070	31/12/86	LUX	-1.82	212	6.73	188	1.70	20.16	133	✪✪	2	35.18	88	55.61	24
●	USD	66.20	Carlson International Equity	C011	28/09/90	LUX	-0.87	161	5.31	208	2.05	19.08	138	✪✪	1	41.19	72	N.A.	
	GBP	4.57	Cater Allen FF Bal Inc & Gth	C013	20/12/94	JER	-2.53	233	12.39	96	N.A.	N.A.				N.A.		N.A.	
	GBP	2.71	CIBC PCF International Managed	C021	03/05/96	GU	3.28	28	N.A.		N.A.	N.A.				N.A.		N.A.	
●	USD	1.24	Citi Balanced A	C032	24/06/94	CA	-1.01	168	6.47	192	N.A.	N.A.				N.A.		N.A.	
▲	DEM	73.39	Citifonds 720	C030	31/01/95	LUX	-4.40	272	-1.67	265	N.A.	N.A.				N.A.		N.A.	
▲●	ECU	28.51	Citinvest Flex Gbl ECU PF	C035	31/03/87	LUX	-5.38	281	8.70	153	1.84	18.90	139	✪	2	23.21	98	N.A.	
	ESP	42.98	Citinvest Flex Gbl ESP PF	C035	23/08/96	LUX	-6.12	287	N.A.		N.A.	N.A.				N.A.		N.A.	
●	USD	189.51	Citinvest Flex Gbl USD PF	C035	30/06/86	LUX	-0.69	151	10.48	121	1.76	5.72	180	✪		8.95	103	28.32	25
	USD	178.15	Citiselect Balanced Growth	C028	21/06/96	LUX	1.20	65	N.A.		N.A.	N.A.				N.A.		N.A.	
	USD	178.51	Citiselect Enhanced Growth	C028	21/06/96	LUX	1.49	57	N.A.		N.A.	N.A.				N.A.		N.A.	
	USD	178.15	Citiselect Growth Fund	C028	21/06/96	LUX	3.20	30	N.A.		N.A.	N.A.				N.A.		N.A.	
●	GBP	217.03	CMI Ins Co GBP Balanced	C043	29/01/88	IOM	-3.18	255	12.27	98	2.15	30.31	52	✪✪✪✪	3	50.18	48	N.A.	
●	USD	0.50	CMI Ins Co GMA Diversified	C043	30/11/92	IOM	-2.62	236	2.52	233	1.90	10.92	169	✪		N.A.		N.A.	
●	USD	0.40	CMI Ins Co GMA Enhanced	C043	30/11/92	IOM	-1.50	193	2.52	234	2.60	25.51	84	✪✪✪	1	N.A.		N.A.	
●	USD	0.70	CMI Ins Co GMA Protected	C043	30/11/92	IOM	-3.22	257	1.30	245	1.64	11.67	165	✪		N.A.		N.A.	
●	USD	23	CMI Ins Co USD Balanced	C043	29/01/88	IOM	-2.84	246	6.95	184	2.04	21.60	118	✪✪	2	39.32	78	N.A.	
▲	GBP	224.44	CMI Intl Mixed	C041	29/05/87	LUX	-1.15	174	13.65	77	2.19	33.75	28	✪✪✪✪✪	4	57.14	33	N.A.	
●	GBP	1.35	CMI Passport Global Mixed	C044	20/01/95	IOM	-3.19	256	13.10	85	N.A.	N.A.				N.A.		N.A.	
	ITL	47	Concept Fd Diversified Ptfl	B067	31/03/94	LUX	5.40	14	31.20	2	N.A.	N.A.				N.A.		N.A.	
	ECU	14.41	Concept Fund Juno	B067	02/12/94	LUX	-4.97	276	-1.26	263	N.A.	N.A.				N.A.		N.A.	
	DEM	7.61	Concorde Global Unit Tst DM	C049	30/11/95	BAH	-3	252	-11.11	276	N.A.	N.A.				N.A.		N.A.	
	USD	7.58	Concorde Global Unit Tst USD	C049	30/12/88	BAH	-0.21	129	-10.21	273	2.86	10.75	170	✪		32.36	90	N.A.	
▲	GBP	21.96	Coutts GF Managed Assets	C052	29/11/91	IRL	-2.32	229	14.34	63	2.32	30.38	50	✪✪✪✪	3	40.38	75	N.A.	
	DEM	236.01	CS Portfolio Balance DEM	C068	31/05/93	LUX	-2.88	248	2.87	229	2.01	23.88	93	✪✪	2	N.A.		N.A.	
	CHF	607.69	CS Portfolio Balance SFR	C068	31/05/93	LUX	-1.85	214	-5.29	270	2.48	21.67	117	✪✪	1	N.A.		N.A.	
	USD	93.85	CS Portfolio Balance USD	C068	31/05/93	LUX	0.79	84	5.41	205	1.54	15.02	156	✪		N.A.		N.A.	
▲	USD	30.57	CU PP Global Managed	C070	31/05/90	LUX	0.91	76	9.68	138	2.64	26.92	74	✪✪✪	2	58.95	28	N.A.	
▲	GBP	7.97	CU PP Monthly Income	C070	31/05/90	LUX	-2.06	220	21.58	8	2.64	23.73	96	✪✪✪	1	47.88	53	N.A.	
●	DEM	803.10	DBIM Delta Fonds	D006	31/12/92	LUX	-2.87	247	0.64	247	2.02	36.25	18	✪✪✪✪	4	N.A.		N.A.	
▲	NOK	27.40	DNB Investment Balanced Ptfl C	D013	29/04/94	LUX	1.49	58	10.84	115	N.A.	N.A.				N.A.		N.A.	
▲	GBP	1.91	Dolphin IIS Contl Cap Builder	D014	30/06/92	LUX	0.87	81	-11.10	275	3.08	-7.74	194	✪		N.A.		N.A.	
●	USD	0.49	Eagle Star Balanced	E001	29/09/95	IOM	-2.03	219	3.94	221	N.A.	N.A.				N.A.		N.A.	
	USD	25.81	Eagle Star Dllr Blue Chip	E001	29/02/88	IOM	1.69	52	17.83	35	2.59	44.46	4	✪✪✪✪✪	4	69.50	11	N.A.	
	USD	15.73	Eagle Star Dllr Performance	E001	29/02/88	IOM	1.70	51	16.03	48	2.55	39.98	10	✪✪✪✪✪	4	65.52	17	N.A.	
●	GBP	80.31	Eagle Star Eagle Blue Chip	E001	29/02/88	IOM	0.13	117	11.98	101	2.72	29.91	55	✪✪✪✪	2	47.75	54	N.A.	
●	GBP	55.82	Eagle Star Eagle Performance	E001	29/02/88	IOM	0.52	97	12.49	94	2.81	28.64	63	✪✪✪	1	47.40	58	N.A.	
●	GBP	24.08	Eagle Star Stlg Blue Chip	E001	29/02/88	IOM	-0.63	149	23.61	3	3.27	40.26	9	✪✪✪✪	3	43.86	66	N.A.	
●	GBP	13.54	Eagle Star Stlg Performance	E001	29/02/88	IOM	-0.08	125	21.55	9	3.10	37.50	15	✪✪✪✪	3	45	62	N.A.	

▲ **SIB Approved** ● **Insurance Fund** **Values in US Dollars, on an offer to offer price basis with gross income reinvested** Data Source Micropal™

Global Mixed

continued

	CCY	Fund Size ($mil)	Fund Name	Manager Code	Fund Start Date	Domicile Code	3 Mths 97 % Chg	3 Mths 97 Rank	1 Year % Chg	1 Year Rank	Micropal Star Rating 3 Years Volatility	3 Years % Chg	3 Years Rank	3 Years Rating	Risk Return Rating	5 Years % Chg	5 Years Rank	10 Years % Chg	10 Years Rank
		56.96	**Mean/Count**				**-0.40**	**296**	**9.46**	**277**	**2.33**	**22.37**	**198**		**1**	**49.67**	**105**	**127.45**	**25**
	ECU	29.95	EDM International Strategy	E009	30/11/90	LUX	-5.09	278	32.86	1	2.88	45.18	3	✪✪✪✪✪	4	44.95	64	N.A.	
	USD	N.S.	EPIC MF Global Strategic Bal	A024	20/10/95	LUX	-0.91	164	5.35	207	N.A.	N.A.				N.A.		N.A.	
	GBP	2.23	Finistere Stlg Managed Life	F016	31/01/83	GU	2.69	36	15.94	50	2.63	31.34	44	✪✪✪✪	2	68.37	13	168.22	5
	GBP	4.28	Five Arrows IMP Bal I & G GBP	R015	30/12/94	GU	-2.25	226	16.15	47	N.A.	N.A.				N.A.		N.A.	
	USD	0.68	Five Arrows IMP Bal I & G USD	R015	30/12/94	GU	-1.24	179	8.82	151	N.A.	N.A.				N.A.		N.A.	
▲	DEM	7.18	Fleming FF DM Balanced	F020	31/08/95	LUX	-5.29	280	4.60	214	N.A.	N.A.				N.A.		N.A.	
▲	USD	38.30	Fleming FF Portfolio	F020	31/03/92	LUX	-0.58	148	11.27	109	2.59	25.97	81	✪✪✪	1	N.A.		N.A.	
	GBP	7.71	Friends Provdnt Managed	F031	31/05/94	GU	0.39	102	16.48	44	N.A.	N.A.				N.A.		N.A.	
	USD	10.20	GAM Universal (Spain)	G003	31/01/90	IOM	14.57	2	21.99	5	3.31	-3.46	191	✪		27.04	96	N.A.	
▲	DEM	236.69	GAM Universal DEM	G002	31/08/90	IOM	2.75	35	7.46	174	3.44	34.32	26	✪✪✪	1	98.98	2	N.A.	
▲	USD	103.10	GAM Universal USD	G003	31/08/90	IOM	11.20	4	18.25	29	2.98	20.48	129	✪✪	1	80.15	6	N.A.	
●	GBP	24.14	Gartmore CSP Sterling L-T Bal	G007	30/04/86	JER	-1.43	188	17.27	39	2.85	29.86	56	✪✪✪✪	2	52.49	45	97.36	18
●	GBP	0.69	Gartmore CSP Sterling M-T Bal	G007	30/04/86	JER	-2.14	221	17.21	40	2.50	30.34	51	✪✪✪✪	3	35.69	87	62.85	23
●	USD	1.85	Gartmore CSP US Dllr L-T Bal	G007	28/02/92	JER	-1.24	180	9.52	142	1.90	21.97	114	✪✪	2	N.A.		N.A.	
●	USD	2.20	Gartmore CSP US Dllr M-T Bal	G007	28/02/92	JER	-2	218	7.91	169	1.65	20	135	✪✪	3	N.A.		N.A.	
	DEM	17.73	Generalinvest Global B	B064	19/04/96	LUX	-2.91	249	N.A.		N.A.	N.A.				N.A.		N.A.	
	CHF	1.76	Govett Glbl Bal Hedge CHF	G014	31/12/93	JER	0.57	95	2.43	236	2.21	12.83	161	✪		N.A.		N.A.	
	USD	1.81	Govett Glbl Bal Hedge USD	G014	31/03/93	JER	0.59	94	5.49	202	2.06	12.36	163	✪		N.A.		N.A.	
	USD	775.83	Green Way	C058	29/02/96	BER	2.20	44	N.A.		N.A.	N.A.				N.A.		N.A.	
	CHF	11.86	GSAM CHF Composite	G003	12/07/96	BVI	7.73	6	N.A.		N.A.	N.A.				N.A.		N.A.	
	USD	150.60	GSAM Composite	G003	31/01/86	IOM	9.11	5	15.76	54	2.23	12.67	162	✪		54.58	41	210.21	3
	DEM	47.39	GSAM DM Composite	G003	27/01/95	IOM	20.42	1	-0.74	257	N.A.	N.A.				N.A.		N.A.	
	GBP	1.18	GSAM GBP Composite	G003	13/12/96	BVI	-1.92	217	N.A.		N.A.	N.A.				N.A.		N.A.	
▲	USD	31.10	Guinness FI IF Intl Bal Gth	G020	30/06/88	GU	-0.30	134	7.55	173	1.48	22.54	110	✪✪	4	54.77	39	N.A.	
▲	USD	5.12	Guinness Flight Glbl Bal Gth	G019	03/02/95	GU	-0.22	131	6.91	186	N.A.	N.A.				N.A.		N.A.	
●	BEF	N.S.	Hansard EU Belgian Mgd	H010	30/06/95	IRL	1.32	61	10.48	120	N.A.	N.A.				N.A.		N.A.	
	DEM	N.S.	Hansard EU DEM Mgd	H010	17/02/95	IRL	3.41	26	9.80	135	N.A.	N.A.				N.A.		N.A.	
●	NLG	N.S.	Hansard EU Dutch Mgd	H010	30/06/95	IRL	3.66	23	13.70	74	N.A.	N.A.				N.A.		N.A.	
●	GBP	N.S.	Hansard EU Intl Mgd	H010	17/02/95	IRL	3.38	27	13.71	73	N.A.	N.A.				N.A.		N.A.	
●	GBP	66.38	Hansard International Managed	H011	28/02/90	IOM	0.88	80	16.99	42	2.45	31.85	39	✪✪✪✪	3	58.41	30	N.A.	
●	GBP	13.19	Hansard UK Sterling Managed	H011	28/02/90	IOM	-0.09	126	21.69	7	2.38	36.19	19	✪✪✪✪✪	4	55.59	36	N.A.	
●	USD	14.10	Hansard US Dollar Managed	H011	28/02/90	IOM	0.10	118	13.02	86	2.06	27.89	70	✪✪✪	3	63.36	22	N.A.	
	USD	9.49	Hermes Global	H028	30/06/92	BER	4.27	18	10.57	119	1.92	8.64	176	✪		N.A.		N.A.	
	USD	83.87	Hermes Strategies	H028	30/04/92	BER	5.41	13	12.88	88	2.99	12.26	164	✪		N.A.		N.A.	
	HKD	95.93	HSBC Managed	H034	31/05/90	HK	-2.76	244	14.08	65	2.67	16.75	149	✪✪		76.61	7	N.A.	
	DEM	32.23	Hypo System	H024	29/10/93	LUX	-2.23	223	2.70	230	1.71	20.72	126	✪✪	3	N.A.		N.A.	
	GBP	1.74	Income Portfolio A	C020	15/12/95	IRL	-4.25	271	9.54	140	N.A.	N.A.				N.A.		N.A.	
	DEM	18.07	Inter Global Fund Mixte DEM	B069	29/12/95	LUX	-3.47	259	2.22	240	N.A.	N.A.				N.A.		N.A.	
	USD	10.90	Inter Global Fund Mixte USD	B069	29/12/95	LUX	0.20	113	2.65	231	N.A.	N.A.				N.A.		N.A.	
	DEM	85.11	Interspar	I012	31/01/83	LUX	-1.46	189	-0.32	255	2.04	17.24	146	✪	1	38.64	80	105.33	15
	GBP	7.44	INVESCO Sterling Managed	I013	30/03/84	JER	2.22	42	14.54	62	2.40	30.14	53	✪✪✪✪	3	47.31	59	101.69	16
	DEM	0.20	Investec European Mgd	I016	17/05/96	BVI	-3.84	262	N.A.		N.A.	N.A.				N.A.		N.A.	
	GBP	N.S.	Investec Sterling Mgd	I016	19/04/96	BVI	-2.18	222	N.A.		N.A.	N.A.				N.A.		N.A.	
	USD	2.61	Investec US Dollar Mgd	I016	29/03/96	BVI	0.28	106	N.A.		N.A.	N.A.				N.A.		N.A.	
	LUF	7.86	Ippa Portf Global Assets B	B035	31/05/94	LUX	-3.96	264	5.40	206	N.A.	N.A.				N.A.		N.A.	
	USD	20.20	Irish Life Intl Bal Mgd Dllr	I017	30/09/94	IRL	0.81	83	13.85	68	N.A.	N.A.				N.A.		N.A.	
	GBP	5.35	Irish Life Intl Bal Mgd Stlg	I017	21/04/95	IRL	1.31	62	17.65	37	N.A.	N.A.				N.A.		N.A.	
	USD	1.99	Irish Life Intl Caut Mgd Dllr	I017	30/09/94	IRL	0.16	114	7.75	172	N.A.	N.A.				N.A.		N.A.	
	GBP	0.37	Irish Life Intl Caut Mgd Stlg	I017	21/04/95	IRL	-1.04	170	15.66	55	N.A.	N.A.				N.A.		N.A.	
	LUF	N.S.	Isis Global Assets Eq Low C	B026	31/12/90	LUX	-4.14	269	3.27	227	1.92	21.02	121	✪✪	2	40.07	76	N.A.	
	LUF	N.S.	Isis Global Assets Eq Medium C	B026	31/12/90	LUX	-1.15	173	7.76	171	1.73	26.77	75	✪✪✪	4	49.31	51	N.A.	
●	DEM	1.41	JRIA Aggressive DEM	J002	29/01/93	IRL	6.32	10	13.72	72	2.86	15.11	154	✪✪		N.A.		N.A.	
●	USD	4.40	JRIA Aggressive Dllr	J002	29/01/93	IRL	7.25	9	16.35	45	2.51	10.23	173	✪		N.A.		N.A.	
●	GBP	8.97	JRIA Aggressive Stlg	J002	29/01/93	IRL	6.13	12	15.90	51	2.49	25.94	82	✪✪✪	2	N.A.		N.A.	
●	DEM	3.92	JRIA Balanced DEM	J002	29/01/93	IRL	3.48	24	10.20	130	2.37	20.68	127	✪✪	1	N.A.		N.A.	
●	USD	4.80	JRIA Balanced Dllr	J002	29/01/93	IRL	3.95	21	12.92	87	1.78	11.31	168	✪		N.A.		N.A.	
●	GBP	17.93	JRIA Balanced Stlg	J002	29/01/93	IRL	3.16	31	12.48	95	2.08	20.90	124	✪✪	1	N.A.		N.A.	

▲ SIB Approved ● Insurance Fund **Values in US Dollars, on an offer to offer price basis with gross income reinvested** Data Source Micropal™

Global Mixed

continued

	CCY	Fund Size ($mil)	Fund Name	Manager Code	Fund Start Date	Domicile Code	3 Mths 97 % Chg	Rank	1 Year % Chg	Rank	Micropal Star Rating 3 Years Volatility	% Chg	Rank	Rating	Risk Return Rating	5 Years % Chg	Rank	10 Years % Chg	Rank
		56.96	**Mean/Count**				**-0.40**	**296**	**9.46**	**277**	**2.33**	**22.37**	**198**		**1**	**49.67**	**105**	**127.45**	**25**
●	DEM	0.61	JRIA Cautious DEM	J002	29/01/93	IRL	-0.44	139	5.18	209	2.09	23.14	100	✪✪	2	N.A.		N.A.	
	USD	0.59	JRIA Cautious Dllr	J002	29/01/93	IRL	1.04	70	9	148	0.98	10.43	172	✪		N.A.		N.A.	
●	GBP	1.40	JRIA Cautious Stlg	J002	29/01/93	IRL	-0.27	133	10.43	122	1.91	16.09	150	✪		N.A.		N.A.	
	GBP	0.29	JRIA/Midland Stlg Aggressive	J002	09/08/93	IRL	-0.30	135	10.22	129	2.49	23.04	103	✪✪✪	1	N.A.		N.A.	
	GBP	0.19	JRIA/Midland Stlg Balanced	J002	09/08/93	IRL	-0.01	121	9.98	134	1.96	19.73	136	✪✪	1	N.A.		N.A.	
	GBP	0.05	JRIA/Midland Stlg Cautious	J002	09/08/93	IRL	0.72	88	8.95	149	1.70	16.07	151	✪		N.A.		N.A.	
	USD	16.51	Lazard Freres Opportunities	L003	29/01/93	GU			18.64	27	3.69	61.83	1	✪✪✪✪✪	4	N.A.		N.A.	
	GBP	9.52	Lazard PP STG Capital Growth	L001	30/11/87	GU	2.21	43	16.91	43	2.19	30.97	47	✪✪✪✪✪	4	65.98	16	N.A.	
	USD	2.36	Lazard PP USD Capital Growth	L001	30/11/87	GU	-0.48	142	7.09	181	1.78	20.39	130	✪✪	3	45.57	61	N.A.	
	USD	79.86	M.Lynch Global Allocation O	M023	30/07/93	LUX	1.64	54	15.56	57	1.54	35.56	22	✪✪✪✪	5	N.A.		N.A.	
	USD	15.14	MAN-GFA MAP Guaranteed 2000	M004	31/05/93	BER	-1.21	176	7.28	177	4.44	-21.75	196	✪		N.A.		N.A.	
	USD	9.46	MAN-GFA MAP Guaranteed 2001	M004	30/06/94	BER	-1.67	204	2.51	235	N.A.	N.A.				N.A.		N.A.	
	USD	1.33	MAN-GFA MAP Leveraged Recovery	M004	30/06/92	BER	0.81	82	-3.60	268	3.56	3.97	184	✪		N.A.		N.A.	
	DEM	3.73	Mega Global	M034	31/03/93	LUX	N.A.	—	7.14	180	2.02	31.27	46	✪✪✪	4	N.A.		N.A.	
▲	GBP	127.12	Mercury International Ptfl	M016	31/05/93	IOM	0.71	89	20.54	15	2.81	37.46	16	✪✪✪✪	3	N.A.		N.A.	
▲	USD	23.70	Mercury ST Global Ptfl	M021	26/02/93	LUX	1.45	59	9.58	139	2.25	22.17	113	✪✪✪	2	N.A.		N.A.	
	USD	73.40	MFS Meridian World Total Ret	M026	31/12/93	CA	-0.83	159	13.39	82	1.75	32	37	✪✪✪✪✪	4	N.A.		N.A.	
▲	GBP	91.66	Midland Intl Circuit Ptfl	M027	28/02/90	JER	-1.23	178	10.69	118	2.24	26.27	79	✪✪✪✪	2	44	65	N.A.	
	ECU	9.54	MLBS (B) Ecu Balanced	M024	30/09/94	LUX	-2.71	240	6.75	187	N.A.	N.A.				N.A.		N.A.	
	USD	120	MLBS (B) USD Balanced	M024	30/09/94	LUX	-0.93	165	7.03	183	N.A.	N.A.				N.A.		N.A.	
	DEM	7.78	North Star Mixed Intl	N012	31/03/86	CA	-1.63	203	9.46	143	2.01	33.48	32	✪✪✪✪	4	40.50	74	213	2
	DEM	7.84	OIM Vermoegensaufbau Fonds	O009	14/10/94	LUX	-1.39	187	2.41	237	N.A.	N.A.				N.A.		N.A.	
	DEM	1.63	Old Mutual Gnsy DEM Mgd	O003	29/12/95	GU	-0.43	138	3.65	224	N.A.	N.A.				N.A.		N.A.	
	USD	5.64	Old Mutual Gnsy Dllr Managed	O003	21/04/95	GU	2.17	45	9.52	141	N.A.	N.A.				N.A.		N.A.	
	USD	3.39	Old Mutual Gnsy Dllr Spec Mkt	O003	21/04/95	GU	-4.11	268	1.39	244	N.A.	N.A.				N.A.		N.A.	
	GBP	26.49	Old Mutual Gnsy Stlg Managed	O003	21/04/95	GU	-0.05	122	14.15	64	N.A.	N.A.				N.A.		N.A.	
	GBP	10.56	Old Mutual Gnsy Stlg Spec Mkt	O003	21/04/95	GU	-6.23	289	4.35	216	N.A.	N.A.				N.A.		N.A.	
	USD	0.40	Old Mutual HK Dllr Managed	O004	28/04/95	HK	1.77	49	8.45	161	N.A.	N.A.				N.A.		N.A.	
	USD	0.75	Old Mutual HK Dllr Spec Mkt	O004	28/04/95	HK	-3.16	254	0.37	251	N.A.	N.A.				N.A.		N.A.	
	GBP	1.12	Old Mutual HK Stlg Managed	O004	28/04/95	HK	-0.06	124	13.82	69	N.A.	N.A.				N.A.		N.A.	
	GBP	0.69	Old Mutual HK Stlg Spec Mkt	O004	28/04/95	HK	-4.24	270	4.75	212	N.A.	N.A.				N.A.		N.A.	
	CHF	20.22	OMI (Gnsy) Cornerstone	O005	31/07/92	GU	-3.06	253	0.47	250	2.31	3.32	185	✪		N.A.		N.A.	
	DEM	17.52	OMI (Gnsy) Deutschemark Mgd	O005	30/04/90	GU	-2.78	245	10.40	126	2.41	16.90	148	✪✪	1	68.04	14	N.A.	
	USD	26.17	OMI (Gnsy) Dllr Special Mkt	O005	31/08/93	GU	-6.01	286	0.54	249	2.96	-5.35	193	✪		N.A.		N.A.	
	USD	40.29	OMI (Gnsy) Dollar Managed	O005	31/05/82	GU	-0.06	123	9.19	145	2.13	11.51	166	✪		63.61	20	92.05	19
	GBP	139.86	OMI (Gnsy) Stlg Managed	O005	31/05/82	GU	-2.25	225	14.94	60	2.34	15.76	152	✪		60.10	23	132.44	12
	GBP	87.54	OMI (Gnsy) Stlg Special Mkt	O005	30/04/84	GU	-7.27	295	4.16	219	2.99	1.07	189	✪		57.36	32	202.81	4
	USD	0.33	OMI (Ire) Dllr Managed	O006	29/10/93	IRL	2.12	46	8.87	150	2.11	18.27	143	✪✪	1	N.A.		N.A.	
	USD	0.60	OMI (Ire) Dllr Special Mkt	O006	29/10/93	IRL	-5.62	283	0.63	248	3.29	-4.19	192	✪		N.A.		N.A.	
	DEM	1.31	OMI (Ire) Dmark Managed	O006	29/10/93	IRL	-0.57	147	7.42	176	2.79	35.40	23	✪✪✪✪	3	N.A.		N.A.	
	DEM	1.31	OMI (Ire) Dmark Special Mkt	O006	29/10/93	IRL	-5.57	282	2.30	238	3.77	0.48	190	✪		N.A.		N.A.	
	GBP	2.67	OMI (Ire) Stlg Managed	O006	29/10/93	IRL	-2.24	224	14.78	61	2.35	20.32	132	✪✪	1	N.A.		N.A.	
	GBP	2.69	OMI (Ire) Stlg Special Mkt	O006	31/08/93	IRL	-6.77	294	4.62	213	3.87	3.10	186	✪		N.A.		N.A.	
▲	USD	8.62	OMI Galileo Global Managed	O007	19/07/93	IRL	-0.91	163	11.26	110	2.43	22.87	105	✪✪	1	N.A.		N.A.	
▲	USD	6.76	OMI Galileo Global Spec Mkt	O007	19/07/93	IRL	-2.55	234	5.59	199	3.60	13.39	160	✪✪		N.A.		N.A.	
	DEM	38.79	Optigest General Fund	O011	30/01/87	LUX	-5	277	-10.28	274	2.13	8.04	177	✪		22.79	100	N.A.	
	ECU	17.27	Paneurolife Fund of Funds	P003	28/02/91	LUX	0.16	115	8.51	159	1.97	22.64	108	✪✪	2	25.08	97	N.A.	
	USD	35.42	Paneurolife Global Equities	P003	28/02/91	LUX	N.A.	—	7.42	175	2.49	25.99	80	✪✪✪	2	31.66	91	N.A.	
	USD	16.40	Paragon Cap Appreciation	P005	31/08/95	BVI	4.12	19	13.79	70	N.A.	N.A.				N.A.		N.A.	
	USD	4.70	Parvest Global 2 USD B	B037	31/03/94	LUX	1.18	66	10.40	127	N.A.	N.A.				N.A.		N.A.	
	LUF	174.95	Parvest Global 3 BEF B	B037	31/07/92	LUX	-5.66	285	0.13	252	2.10	20.08	134	✪✪	1	N.A.		N.A.	
	CHF	13.76	Parvest Global 3 CHF B	B037	10/05/96	LUX	-4.05	266	N.A.		N.A.	N.A.				N.A.		N.A.	
	USD	10.38	Parvest Global 3 USD B	B037	30/09/92	LUX	1.56	55	10.98	112	2.49	21.27	120	✪✪	1	N.A.		N.A.	
	LUF	4.84	Parvest Global 4 BEF B	B037	29/11/91	LUX	-6.40	291	0.09	253	2.28	16.99	147	✪✪	1	30.79	93	N.A.	
	USD	N.S.	PCP Glbl Mgd Balanced	P007	31/05/96	CA	-0.76	153	N.A.		N.A.	N.A.				N.A.		N.A.	
	USD	N.S.	PCP Glbl Mgd Cautious	P007	31/05/96	CA	-1.73	206	N.A.		N.A.	N.A.				N.A.		N.A.	
	CHF	6.02	Performa Global Mix	P009	31/05/90	LUX	-1.78	208	-0.91	260	2.05	18.28	142	✪✪	1	28.21	95	N.A.	

▲ SIB Approved ● Insurance Fund **Values in US Dollars, on an offer to offer price basis with gross income reinvested** Data Source Micropal™

Global Mixed

continued

	CCY	Fund Size ($mil)	Fund Name	Manager Code	Fund Start Date	Domicile Code	3 Mths 97 % Chg	3 Mths 97 Rank	1 Year % Chg	1 Year Rank	Micropal Star Rating 3 Years Volatility	3 Years % Chg	3 Years Rank	3 Years Rating	Risk Return Rating	5 Years % Chg	5 Years Rank	10 Years % Chg	10 Years Rank
		56.96	**Mean/Count**				**-0.40**	**296**	**9.46**	**277**	**2.33**	**22.37**	**198**		**1**	**49.67**	**105**	**127.45**	**25**
	USD	19	PFC Balanced Growth	P014	30/04/85	HK	0	120	12.88	89	2.43	15.11	155	✪		75.04	9	132.60	11
	USD	20.26	PFC GAM Global Ptfl	P014	29/12/89	CA	7.71	7	9.18	146	2.17	5.08	181	✪		44.99	63	N.A.	
	ITL	21.95	PICM Global Portfolio	P016	30/09/93	LUX	-2.92	250	-2.06	266	3.91	18.52	140	✪✪	1	N.A.		N.A.	
	CHF	555.24	Pictet B.F. Global Str Intl	P016	14/07/95	LUX	-1.48	192	-1.20	262	N.A.	N.A.				N.A.		N.A.	
	CHF	166.92	Pictet B.F. Global Str Ref CHF	P016	14/07/95	LUX	-2.47	232	-0.60	256	N.A.	N.A.				N.A.		N.A.	
	USD	35.93	Pictet B.F. Global Str Ref USD	P016	14/07/95	LUX	2.33	41	8.77	152	N.A.	N.A.				N.A.		N.A.	
	CHF	32.23	Pictet F.I.F. – Piclife	P016	31/08/93	LUX	-2.30	228	-6.02	271	2.64	27.36	73	✪✪✪	2	N.A.		N.A.	
	GBP	0.34	Premier Sterling Pension	P021	29/07/88	LUX	-0.80	154	12.12	100	2.98	17.66	145	✪✪	1	38.67	79	N.A.	
	USD	0.30	Premier US Dollar Pension	P021	29/07/88	LUX	-1.89	215	10.42	124	2.21	1.92	188	✪		39.47	77	N.A.	
●	GBP	13.53	Royal Life Intl Pension Gth A	R020	30/10/87	IOM	2.51	39	20.34	16	2.48	43.22	5	✪✪✪✪✪	4	66.13	15	N.A.	
●	GBP	12.18	Royal Life Intl UK Managed	R020	31/03/86	IOM	1.77	50	19.66	19	2.72	45.60	2	✪✪✪✪✪	4	55.78	35	157.54	6
●	USD	2.20	Royal Life/PFC Balanced Gth	R035	29/09/89	HK	2.39	40	10.42	125	2.57	10.62	171	✪		59.07	26	N.A.	
●	USD	1.40	Royal Life/PFC Specialist Gth	R035	29/09/89	HK	6.26	11	6.94	185	2.93	6.82	179	✪		58.76	29	N.A.	
●	GBP	0.68	Royal Life/PFC Stlg Income	R035	29/09/89	HK	-3.87	263	15.98	49	3.01	23.11	101	✪✪	1	37.17	82	N.A.	
	USD	2.82	Royal Skandia Baring Dlr Agg	R038	30/12/88	IOM	0.74	87	11.59	104	2.92	21.77	116	✪✪	1	46.47	60	N.A.	
	USD	7.10	Royal Skandia Baring Dlr Bal	R038	30/12/88	IOM	0.39	103	15.88	52	2.46	29.14	60	✪✪✪	2	50.34	46	N.A.	
	USD	2.98	Royal Skandia Baring Dlr Cau	R038	30/12/88	IOM	-1.60	200	13.69	75	1.98	21.40	119	✪✪	2	32.79	89	N.A.	
	GBP	6.77	Royal Skandia Baring Stg Agg	R038	30/12/88	IOM	0.51	98	19.27	22	2.84	22.91	104	✪✪	1	47.56	56	N.A.	
	GBP	16.61	Royal Skandia Baring Stg Bal	R038	30/12/88	IOM	0.35	104	22.91	4	2.43	28.58	64	✪✪✪	2	47.50	57	N.A.	
	GBP	11.16	Royal Skandia Baring Stg Cau	R038	30/12/88	IOM	-1.81	210	18.02	31	2.12	29.46	59	✪✪✪✪	3	40.74	73	N.A.	
	USD	32.05	Royal Skandia Dlr Bal Fid	R038	31/01/91	IOM	-0.21	130	10.42	123	1.91	27.54	72	✪✪✪✪	3	59.67	24	N.A.	
	ECU	3.57	Royal Skandia Ecu Bal Skandia	R038	31/01/91	IOM	-2.37	231	3.36	226	2.38	22.72	107	✪✪	1	36.14	85	N.A.	
	ECU	1.46	Royal Skandia Ecu Caut Guin Fl	R038	30/10/92	IOM	-3.99	265	12.16	99	2.06	20.96	122	✪✪	1	N.A.		N.A.	
	ECU	3.85	Royal Skandia Gartmore ECU Bal	R038	30/10/92	IOM	-0.99	167	11.73	103	2.22	28.68	62	✪✪✪✪	3	N.A.		N.A.	
	GBP	59.75	Royal Skandia Gartmore STG Bal	R038	30/10/92	IOM	-1.80	209	16.19	46	2.13	28.27	68	✪✪✪✪	3	N.A.		N.A.	
	USD	16.83	Royal Skandia Gartmore USD Bal	R038	30/10/92	IOM	0.26	109	10.04	133	1.75	22.31	111	✪✪	3	N.A.		N.A.	
	ECU	0.69	Royal Skandia Invesco ECU Bal	R038	28/02/92	IOM	0.26	108	12.82	90	2.38	26.70	77	✪✪✪	2	N.A.		N.A.	
	GBP	13.60	Royal Skandia Invesco STG Bal	R038	28/02/92	IOM	-0.14	127	15.57	56	2.48	26.37	78	✪✪✪	2	N.A.		N.A.	
	USD	2.69	Royal Skandia Invesco USD Bal	R038	28/02/92	IOM	-1.83	213	7.19	179	2.09	18.16	144	✪✪	1	N.A.		N.A.	
	GBP	108.70	Royal Skandia Stg Bal Fid	R038	31/01/91	IOM	-0.55	146	20.30	17	2.50	38.20	12	✪✪✪✪✪	4	71.34	10	N.A.	
	GBP	2.93	Royal Skandia Stg Bal Skandia	R038	31/01/91	IOM	-0.53	144	17.14	41	2.27	24.27	90	✪✪✪	2	31.43	92	N.A.	
	GBP	64.06	Royal Skandia STG Caut Guin Fl	R038	30/10/92	IOM	-1.57	198	13.61	79	2.26	23.43	99	✪✪✪	2	N.A.		N.A.	
	USD	9.86	Royal Skandia USD Caut Guin Fl	R038	30/10/92	IOM	-0.51	143	6.56	191	1.55	13.77	159	✪		N.A.		N.A.	
	USD	55.41	SAM Diversified	S003	28/02/89	IOM	1.94	47	6.31	193	0.49	11.43	167	✪		28.87	94	N.A.	
	USD	2.49	Samba Lux Global Balanced	N004	28/04/95	LUX	-3.59	260	13.96	66	N.A.	N.A.				N.A.		N.A.	
▲	ECU	0.22	SanPaolo Ecu Mixte	S004	30/11/88	LUX	-3.41	258	12.58	93	1.62	31.41	43	✪✪✪✪	5	36.51	84	N.A.	
▲	DEM	2.09	Sarasin GlobalSar DM SICAV	B038	07/07/95	LUX	-0.94	166	6.57	190	N.A.	N.A.				N.A.		N.A.	
▲	USD	41.80	Sarasin GlobalSar Dollar	S005	29/01/93	GU	3.47	25	10.90	114	1.75	19.11	137	✪✪	2	N.A.		N.A.	
▲	CHF	11.81	Sarasin GlobalSar SFR SICAV	B038	31/08/92	LUX	-0.82	156	3.85	222	2.09	28.18	69	✪✪✪	3	N.A.		N.A.	
▲	GBP	126.87	Sarasin GlobalSar Sterling	S005	31/12/87	GU	1.18	67	18.75	25	2.24	30.04	54	✪✪✪✪	3	57.59	31	N.A.	
▲	CHF	144.18	SBC Global CHF Balanced B	S007	30/06/94	LUX	-1.51	194	-0.06	254	N.A.	N.A.				N.A.		N.A.	
▲	DEM	110.61	SBC Global DEM Balanced B	S007	30/06/94	LUX	-1.61	201	4.49	215	N.A.	N.A.				N.A.		N.A.	
▲	DEM	118.38	SBC Global DM Growth	S007	31/05/93	LUX	1.04	71	7.86	170	1.82	30.91	48	✪✪✪✪	4	N.A.		N.A.	
▲	DEM	330.78	SBC Global DM Income /B	S007	31/05/93	LUX	-6.50	292	-0.89	258	2.21	29.07	61	✪✪✪	3	N.A.		N.A.	
▲	DEM	376.94	SBC Global DM Yield /B	S007	31/05/93	LUX	-4.41	273	2.56	232	1.83	30.72	49	✪✪✪✪	4	N.A.		N.A.	
▲	ECU	13.10	SBC Global ECU Balanced B	S007	30/06/94	LUX	-2.34	230	8.24	163	N.A.	N.A.				N.A.		N.A.	
▲	ECU	46.74	SBC Global Ecu Growth	S007	30/08/91	LUX	-0.64	150	10.74	117	1.79	35.20	25	✪✪✪✪✪	5	53.04	44	N.A.	
▲	ECU	55.33	SBC Global Ecu Income /B	S007	30/10/92	LUX	-6.23	288	3.36	225	1.83	29.82	57	✪✪✪	4	N.A.		N.A.	
▲	ECU	116.43	SBC Global Ecu Yield /B	S007	31/12/90	LUX	-4.69	275	5.43	204	1.72	33.16	33	✪✪✪✪	5	53.51	42	N.A.	
▲	CHF	237.71	SBC Global SFr Growth	S007	30/09/91	LUX	0.70	90	2.07	242	1.97	27.87	71	✪✪✪	3	47.72	55	N.A.	
▲	CHF	857.88	SBC Global SFr Income /B	S007	30/09/92	LUX	-5.62	284	-8.58	272	2.80	23.77	95	✪✪	1	N.A.		N.A.	
▲	CHF	815.66	SBC Global SFr Yield /B	S007	30/08/91	LUX	-4.06	267	-4.18	269	2.17	24.22	92	✪✪✪	2	42.98	69	N.A.	
▲	USD	153.21	SBC Global USD Balanced B	S007	31/12/93	LUX	0.22	112	11.09	111	1.12	28.50	65	✪✪✪✪	5	N.A.		N.A.	
▲	USD	117.32	SBC Global USD Growth	S007	30/08/91	LUX	1.17	68	13.26	83	1.76	28.41	67	✪✪✪✪	4	49.95	49	N.A.	
▲	USD	211.07	SBC Global USD Income /B	S007	30/09/92	LUX	-1.02	169	5.55	201	0.86	18.35	141	✪✪	5	N.A.		N.A.	
▲	USD	415.55	SBC Global USD Yield /B	S007	30/08/91	LUX	-0.84	160	8.63	155	1.05	22.27	112	✪✪	5	41.87	70	N.A.	
	HKD	205.76	Schroder Asia Balanced Inv	S011	31/01/89	HK	-2.65	239	15.82	53	3.21	14.76	157	✪✪		86.90	4	N.A.	

▲ SIB Approved ● Insurance Fund Values in US Dollars, on an offer to offer price basis with gross income reinvested

Data Source Micropal™

Global Mixed

continued

	CCY	Fund Size ($mil)	Fund Name	Manager Code	Fund Start Date	Domicile Code	3 Mths 97 % Chg	3 Mths 97 Rank	1 Year % Chg	1 Year Rank	Micropal Star Rating 3 Years Volatility	3 Years % Chg	3 Years Rank	3 Years Rating	Risk Return Rating	5 Years % Chg	5 Years Rank	10 Years % Chg	10 Years Rank
		56.96	**Mean/Count**				**-0.40**	**296**	**9.46**	**277**	**2.33**	**22.37**	**198**		**1**	**49.67**	**105**	**127.45**	**25**
	HKD	2.41	Schroder Asia Capital	S011	31/05/93	HK	-6.74	293	11.50	105	3.51	2.64	187	✪		N.A.		N.A.	
	HKD	8.64	Schroder Capital Stable	S011	20/10/95	HK	-1.58	199	7.27	178	N.A.	N.A.				N.A.		N.A.	
	HKD	28.30	Schroder Stable Growth	S011	09/06/95	CA	-1.81	211	9.79	136	N.A.	N.A.				N.A.		N.A.	
●	GBP	6.80	Scot Amicable Adventurous Stg	S015	30/06/94	IOM	0.24	111	11.45	106	N.A.	N.A.				N.A.		N.A.	
●	USD	0.26	Scot Amicable Adventurous USD	S015	30/06/94	IRL	1.04	72	10.06	132	N.A.	N.A.				N.A.		N.A.	
●	GBP	79	Scot Amicable Balanced Stg	S015	30/06/94	IRL	-1.15	172	13.90	67	N.A.	N.A.				N.A.		N.A.	
●	USD	1.10	Scot Amicable Balanced USD	S015	30/06/94	IRL	0.40	101	6	198	N.A.	N.A.				N.A.		N.A.	
●	GBP	18.14	Scot Amicable Conservativ Stg	S015	30/06/94	IRL	-2.64	237	13.67	76	N.A.	N.A.				N.A.		N.A.	
●	USD	0.30	Scot Amicable Conservativ USD	S015	30/06/94	IRL	0.88	79	4.22	218	N.A.	N.A.				N.A.		N.A.	
	GBP	9.64	Scot Eq (SEI) Global	S016	23/06/95	LUX	-0.23	132	12.72	91	N.A.	N.A.				N.A.		N.A.	
	GBP	12.01	Scot Eq (SEI) Mixed	S016	23/06/95	LUX	-0.44	140	15.34	59	N.A.	N.A.				N.A.		N.A.	
▲	ECU	51.17	Scot Equitable IF Intl Mixed	S017	31/07/92	LUX	-1.76	207	8.57	158	2.17	23.73	97	✪✪✪	2	N.A.		N.A.	
	GBP	3.38	Scot Prov GP Stlg Adv Mgd II	S014	31/05/96	IOM	0.66	91	N.A.		N.A.	N.A.				N.A.		N.A.	
	GBP	34.68	Scot Prov GP Stlg Adventurous	S014	30/09/91	IOM	0.76	86	18.73	26	2.56	35.77	21	✪✪✪✪✪	3	84.91	5	N.A.	
	GBP	6.26	Scot Prov GP Stlg Bal Mgd II	S014	31/05/96	IOM	-0.47	141	N.A.		N.A.	N.A.				N.A.		N.A.	
	GBP	66.14	Scot Prov GP Stlg Balanced	S014	30/09/91	IOM	-0.42	137	21.82	6	2.48	42.19	6	✪✪✪✪✪	4	76.48	8	N.A.	
	GBP	2.03	Scot Prov GP Stlg Cau Mgd II	S014	31/05/96	IOM	-1.34	184	N.A.		N.A.	N.A.				N.A.		N.A.	
	GBP	21.99	Scot Prov GP Stlg Cautious	S014	30/09/91	IOM	-1.37	186	17.99	32	2.12	33.55	31	✪✪✪✪	4	54.81	38	N.A.	
	USD	0.10	Scot Prov GP USD Adv Mgd II	S014	31/05/96	IOM	2.54	38	N.A.		N.A.	N.A.				N.A.		N.A.	
	USD	5	Scot Prov GP USD Adventurous	S014	30/09/91	IOM	2.55	37	11.44	107	2.58	20.72	125	✪✪	1	64.37	18	N.A.	
●	USD	0.40	Scot Prov GP USD Bal Mgd II	S014	31/05/96	IOM	4.48	17	N.A.		N.A.	N.A.				N.A.		N.A.	
	USD	8.20	Scot Prov GP USD Balanced	S014	30/09/91	IOM	4.53	16	8.02	167	2.77	25.80	83	✪✪✪	1	59.58	25	N.A.	
●	USD	0.10	Scot Prov GP USD Cau Mgd II	S014	31/05/96	IOM	1.03	73	N.A.		N.A.	N.A.				N.A.		N.A.	
	USD	2.40	Scot Prov GP USD Cautious	S014	30/09/91	IOM	0.98	74	9.74	137	1.83	20.95	123	✪✪	2	41.35	71	N.A.	
▲	USD	89.80	Skandifond International	S030	30/08/85	LUX	-0.90	162	8.63	156	2.07	24.26	91	✪✪✪	2	36.66	83	99.73	17
	USD	3.04	Sun Life Balanced Dllr	S053	31/12/92	IOM	-1.13	171	11.90	102	1.85	20.34	131	✪✪	2	N.A.		N.A.	
	GBP	9.03	Sun Life Balanced Stlg	S053	30/10/92	IOM	-3	251	13.59	80	2.14	23.07	102	✪✪✪	2	N.A.		N.A.	
	USD	1.03	Sun Life Defensive Dllr	S053	29/01/93	IOM	-0.82	158	8.61	157	1.29	20.67	128	✪✪	4	N.A.		N.A.	
	GBP	2.77	Sun Life Defensive Stlg	S053	29/01/93	IOM	-1.19	175	18.96	24	1.90	36.44	17	✪✪✪✪✪	5	N.A.		N.A.	
	GBP	5.85	Sun Life Intl Distribution	S053	31/08/95	IOM	0.91	75	20.90	13	N.A.	N.A.				N.A.		N.A.	
	CHF	0.31	Sun Life Mgd Gth CHF	S053	28/02/94	IOM	-2.64	238	4.81	211	N.A.	N.A.				N.A.		N.A.	
	DEM	0.62	Sun Life Mgd Gth DEM	S053	31/01/94	IOM	-1.31	183	4.09	220	N.A.	N.A.				N.A.		N.A.	
	CHF	59.99	SVB Portfolio Growth CHF	K001	30/10/92	LUX	1.35	60	6.04	197	2.84	33.79	27	✪✪✪	2	N.A.		N.A.	
	DEM	23.19	SVB Portfolio Growth DEM	K001	30/10/92	LUX	0.49	100	10.94	113	2.74	35.26	24	✪✪✪✪	3	N.A.		N.A.	
	CHF	459.90	SVB Portfolio Inc/Gro CHF	K001	30/10/92	LUX	-0.54	145	-0.89	259	2.25	28.48	66	✪✪✪	3	N.A.		N.A.	
	DEM	159.12	SVB Portfolio Inc/Gro DEM	K001	30/10/92	LUX	-1.25	181	5.48	203	1.88	32.86	35	✪✪✪✪	4	N.A.		N.A.	
	USD	23.54	SVB Portfolio Inc/Gro USD	K001	31/12/93	LUX	0.90	77	10.29	128	1.33	24.99	86	✪✪✪	4	N.A.		N.A.	
	CHF	245.23	Swissca Portfolio Balance	S059	31/03/95	LUX	-1.90	216	1.62	243	N.A.	N.A.				N.A.		N.A.	
	CHF	50.60	Swissca Portfolio Growth	S059	31/03/95	LUX	-0.16	128	6.71	189	N.A.	N.A.				N.A.		N.A.	
	GBP	7.95	Syfrets Gl Stlg Balanced	S060	30/11/93	CA	-0.36	136	15.43	58	2.11	32.89	34	✪✪✪✪	4	N.A.		N.A.	
	USD	3	Syfrets Gl USD Balanced	S060	30/11/93	CA	0.34	105	9.26	144	1.58	22.63	109	✪✪	3	N.A.		N.A.	
	USD	1.20	SynalFund Diversifie	S061	31/07/90	LUX	-16.83	296	-12.39	277	1.40	-21.66	195	✪		-19.36	105	N.A.	
▲	USD	4.16	Templeton GS Glbl Balanced	T001	31/05/94	LUX	0	119	8.66	154	N.A.	N.A.				N.A.		N.A.	
	USD	30.20	Thornton SSF Mgd Selections	T006	30/11/92	CA	0.66	92	7.04	182	5.17	-23.20	197	✪		N.A.		N.A.	
	LUF	17.24	Top Fund Allegro-Low Risk	A013	30/09/92	LUX	-3.60	261	5.56	200	1.84	37.96	14	✪✪✪✪	5	N.A.		N.A.	
	LUF	35	Top Fund Crescendo-Medium Risk	A013	30/09/92	LUX	-1.70	205	8.19	164	1.83	39.37	11	✪✪✪✪✪	5	N.A.		N.A.	
	LUF	24.67	Top Fund Fortissimo-High Risk	A013	30/09/92	LUX	0.26	107	10.81	116	2.05	40.30	8	✪✪✪✪✪	5	N.A.		N.A.	
	USD	51.90	Trans Global Investments Ltd	M007	30/08/91	IOM	12.51	3	19.51	20	4.28	31.48	41	✪✪✪	1	168.09	1	N.A.	
	USD	17.50	UBZ Diversified Strategies	U002	30/06/94	IRL	3.23	29	12.33	97	N.A.	N.A.				N.A.		N.A.	
	DEM	107.38	UniAlpha	U012	30/04/92	LUX	-0.76	152	5.09	210	2.15	35.92	20	✪✪✪✪	4	N.A.		N.A.	
	ECU	12.59	Variaplus	B073	30/09/93	LUX	-6.30	290	2.26	239	1.46	8.74	175	✪		N.A.		N.A.	
	CHF	156.68	Von Ernst CSF Intl Mgd	B020	28/02/79	CH	N.A.	—	8.33	162	1.99	33.66	30	✪✪✪✪✪	4	49.60	50	141.83	9
▲	DEM	2.93	Von Ernst GP Global Managed	B021	30/11/89	LUX	-1.48	191	6.19	196	1.79	13.97	158	✪		22.95	99	N.A.	
	USD	5.50	Worldwide Investment	L021	29/04/94	JER	3.10	32	8.09	166	N.A.	N.A.				N.A.		N.A.	

▲ SIB Approved ● Insurance Fund **Values in US Dollars, on an offer to offer price basis with gross income reinvested** Data Source Micropal™

Latin America Mixed

Funds with a portfolio principally invested (70%) in Latin American equity, fixed interest and money market securities but typically with no more than 70% in any one asset class.

	CCY	Fund Size ($mil)	Fund Name	Manager Code	Fund Start Date	Domicile Code	3 Mths 97 % Chg	Rank	1 Year % Chg	Rank	Micropal Star Rating 3 Years Volatility	% Chg	Rank	Rating	Risk Return Rating	5 Years % Chg	Rank	10 Years % Chg	Rank
		64.78	**Mean/Count**				**9.12**	**7**	**24.53**	**5**	**4.81**	**26.31**	**4**			**94.90**	**1**	**0**	**0**
▲	USD	8.05	Aetna IUF Latin American A	A011	30/04/93	LUX	17.65	1	17.08	4	5.39	-2.31	4	✪		N.A.		N.A.	
	USD	13.96	Latin America Income & App A	S020	31/12/91	NL	6.92	5	42.99	1	6.79	35.92	2	✪✪✪	2	94.90	1	N.A.	
	USD	324	Latinvest Value	A023b	31/01/94	BAH	4.97	7	40.72	2	N.A.	N.A.				N.A.		N.A.	
	USD	3.64	Opportunity Brazil Balanced	O010	30/06/93	CA	7.11	4	18.71	3	4.71	63.91	1	✪✪✪✪	3	N.A.		N.A.	
	USD	32.85	SAM Opportunity	S003	30/04/92	IOM	6.32	6	3.13	5	2.33	7.74	3	✪✪		N.A.		N.A.	
	USD	6.16	UAM Columbus Active	U004	30/08/96	BAH	10.99	2	N.A.		N.A.	N.A.				N.A.		N.A.	

North America Mixed

Funds with a portfolio principally invested (70%) in North American (USA and Canada) equity, fixed interest and money market securities but typically with no more than 70% in any one asset class.

	CCY	Fund Size ($mil)	Fund Name	Manager Code	Fund Start Date	Domicile Code	3 Mths 97 % Chg	Rank	1 Year % Chg	Rank	Micropal Star Rating 3 Years Volatility	% Chg	Rank	Rating	Risk Return Rating	5 Years % Chg	Rank	10 Years % Chg	Rank
		16.33	**Mean/Count**				**0.86**	**18**	**12.27**	**16**	**2.12**	**30.42**	**6**			**48.96**	**2**	**0**	**0**
	USD	1.56	Ace Fund Gth USD	A004	29/01/88	LUX	2.82	6	8.28	10	2.54	-0.50	6	✪		14.26	2	N.A.	
●	USD	11.54	Allied Dunbar IB USD Managed	A021	30/09/93	IOM	2.01	9	17.58	5	2.40	57.57	1	✪✪✪✪	4	N.A.		N.A.	
	USD	85.28	Bk of Ire Glbl Intl USD Gth	B018	30/11/88	IOM	2.39	7	21.61	3	2.45	48.84	2	✪✪✪✪	3	83.65	1	N.A.	
	USD	24.70	CIBC PCF Balanced	C021	31/03/94	GU	2.18	8	7.13	13	N.A.	N.A.				N.A.		N.A.	
●	USD	4.80	CMI Passport USD Divers'd Mgd	C044	20/01/95	IOM	-1.28	15	3.55	15	N.A.	N.A.				N.A.		N.A.	
●	USD	3	CMI Passport USD Protectd Mgd	C044	20/01/95	IOM	-2.21	16	2.37	16	N.A.	N.A.				N.A.		N.A.	
●	USD	N.S.	Hansard EU US Dllr Cautious	H010	15/12/95	IRL	1.45	11	7.83	11	N.A.	N.A.				N.A.		N.A.	
●	USD	N.S.	Hansard EU US Dllr Mgd	H010	17/02/95	IRL	2.93	4	11.48	8	N.A.	N.A.				N.A.		N.A.	
●	USD	0.66	Hansard US Dollar Cautious	H011	22/01/93	IOM	-0.21	13	7.43	12	1.72	29.01	3	✪✪✪	3	N.A.		N.A.	
●	USD	19.71	Hottinger IF-US Growth Cap	H032	28/04/95	LUX	1.83	10	21.46	4	N.A.	N.A.				N.A.		N.A.	
	USD	14.60	M.Lynch Capital Portfolio A	M023	30/06/95	LUX	-0.66	14	12.34	7	N.A.	N.A.				N.A.		N.A.	
	USD	17.53	M.Lynch Visionary Portf A	M023	10/11/95	LUX	-7.08	18	25.72	1	N.A.	N.A.				N.A.		N.A.	
	USD	15.02	Paneurolife US Securities Grth	P003	30/11/93	LUX	3.82	3	9.26	9	1.80	22.30	5	✪✪	1	N.A.		N.A.	
	USD	0.06	Scala US & Canada B	B006	09/02/96	LUX	3.95	2	N.A.		N.A.	N.A.				N.A.		N.A.	
	LUF	N.S.	Unicorn Fund of Funds	B060	15/09/95	LUX	-4.07	17	3.65	14	N.A.	N.A.				N.A.		N.A.	
	USD	17.84	US Bondplus	B073	31/05/93	LUX	2.93	5	13.66	6	1.81	25.30	4	✪✪	2	N.A.		N.A.	
	USD	12.35	World Invest Mixed	B022	30/06/94	LUX	4.28	1	22.92	2	N.A.	N.A.				N.A.		N.A.	

South Africa Mixed

Funds with a portfolio principally invested (70%) in South African equity, fixed interest and money market securities but typically with no more than 70% in any one asset class.

CCY	Fund Size ($mil)	Fund Name	Manager Code	Fund Start Date	Domicile Code	3 Mths 97 % Chg	Rank	1 Year % Chg	Rank	Micropal Star Rating 3 Years Volatility	% Chg	Rank	Rating	Risk Return Rating	5 Years % Chg	Rank	10 Years % Chg	Rank
	0.90	**Mean/Count**				**17.47**	**1**	**-15.80**	**1**	**0**	**0**	**0**			**0**	**0**	**0**	**0**
USD	0.90	Syfrets GI South Africa Mgd	S060	31/05/94	CA	17.47	1	-15.80	1	N.A.	N.A.				N.A.		N.A.	

▲ SIB Approved ● Insurance Fund Values in US Dollars, on an offer to offer price basis with gross income reinvested Data Source Micropal™

Switzerland Mixed

Funds with a portfolio principally invested (70%) in Swiss equity, fixed interest and money market securities but typically with no more than 70% in any one asset class.

CCY	Fund Size ($mil)	Fund Name	Manager Code	Fund Start Date	Domicile Code	3 Mths 97 % Chg	Rank	1 Year % Chg	Rank	Micropal Star Rating 3 Years Volatility	% Chg	Rank	Rating	Risk Return Rating	5 Years % Chg	Rank	10 Years % Chg	Rank
	9.62	**Mean/Count**				**-0.58**	**4**	**-4.21**	**2**	**2.89**	**5.46**	**2**			**13.81**	**1**	**0**	**0**
CHF	6.50	Ace Fund Gth CHF	A004	30/10/92	LUX	5.31	1	-3.06	1	3.52	4.13	2	✪✪		N.A.		N.A.	
CHF	12.74	Ace Fund Yield CHF	A004	29/01/88	LUX	-3.56	4	-5.36	2	2.27	6.79	1	✪✪✪		13.81	1	N.A.	
CHF	N.S.	CS Portfolio Focus SFR A	C068	31/01/96	LUX	-2.73	3	N.A.		N.A.	N.A.				N.A.		N.A.	
CHF	N.S.	RMF Swiss Value Fund	R008	07/06/96	LUX	-1.36	2	N.A.		N.A.	N.A.				N.A.		N.A.	

United Kingdom Mixed

Funds with a portfolio principally invested (70%) in UK equity, fixed interest and money market securities but typically with no more than 70% in any one asset class.

	CCY	Fund Size ($mil)	Fund Name	Manager Code	Fund Start Date	Domicile Code	3 Mths 97 % Chg	Rank	1 Year % Chg	Rank	Micropal Star Rating 3 Years Volatility	% Chg	Rank	Rating	Risk Return Rating	5 Years % Chg	Rank	10 Years % Chg	Rank
		61.35	**Mean/Count**				**-0.55**	**17**	**19.88**	**15**	**2.46**	**35.34**	**10**		**1**	**50.74**	**5**	**90.68**	**2**
	GBP	1.51	Abtrust UK Managed	A003	31/12/81	GU	0.50	5	21.16	6	2.43	26.28	10	✪	1	31.47	5	94.18	1
●	GBP	115.71	Allied Dunbar IB GBP Managed	A021	30/09/93	IOM	0.99	4	18.24	10	2.49	41.01	3	✪✪✪✪	3	N.A.		N.A.	
	GBP	62.18	Bk of Ire Glbl Intl Stlg Gth	B018	30/11/88	IOM	-0.63	9	25.56	1	2.62	48.23	1	✪✪✪✪✪	4	88.62	1	N.A.	
●	GBP	5.75	CMI Passport GBP Divers'd Mgd	C044	20/01/95	IOM	-0.88	10	13.98	15	N.A.	N.A.				N.A.		N.A.	
●	GBP	1.86	CMI Passport GBP Protectd Mgd	C044	20/01/95	IOM	-2.04	13	17.19	13	N.A.	N.A.				N.A.		N.A.	
▲	GBP	35.52	F&C PF Sterling Dist	F001	12/07/93	LUX	2.53	2	24.51	2	2.55	29.14	7	✪✪	2	N.A.		N.A.	
●	GBP	N.S.	Hansard EU UK Stlg Cautious	H010	17/02/95	IRL	0.35	6	17.13	14	N.A.	N.A.				N.A.		N.A.	
●	GBP	N.S.	Hansard EU UK Stlg Mgd	H010	17/02/95	IRL	2.66	1	20.36	8	N.A.	N.A.				N.A.		N.A.	
●	GBP	2.10	Hansard UK Sterling Cautious	H011	22/01/93	IOM	-1.58	12	21.68	5	2.01	35.50	6	✪✪	4	N.A.		N.A.	
	GBP	3.30	MultiLink Aaron Cautious Mgd	I011	31/07/96	LUX	-2.30	14	N.A.		N.A.	N.A.				N.A.		N.A.	
▲	GBP	322.93	Norwich Un JIP With Profits	N013	28/02/90	JER	-2.40	15	18.53	9	1.95	44.36	2	✪✪✪✪	5	35.91	4	N.A.	
	GBP	160.06	Paneurolife UK Securities Grth	P003	28/02/91	LUX	-0.32	7	20.72	7	2.28	35.86	5	✪✪✪	3	49.14	2	N.A.	
	GBP	6.28	PFC Stlg Inc & Gth Ptfl	P014	30/04/85	HK	-3.58	17	17.74	11	3.23	27.97	9	✪✪	1	48.57	3	87.18	2
	GBP	2.54	RLI/Gartmore Balanced Gth	R024	29/10/93	IOM	-0.93	11	17.47	12	2.55	28.89	8	✪	2	N.A.		N.A.	
	GBP	N.S.	Scala United Kingdom B	B006	29/11/96	LUX	1.35	3	N.A.		N.A.	N.A.				N.A.		N.A.	
	GBP	17.25	Scot Eq (SEI) UK Deferrd Dist	S016	23/06/95	LUX	-2.48	16	22.20	3	N.A.	N.A.				N.A.		N.A.	
	GBP	121.97	Sun Life Deferred Dist	S053	31/03/93	IOM	-0.63	8	21.78	4	2.48	36.18	4	✪✪✪	2	N.A.		N.A.	

▲ SIB Approved ● Insurance Fund

Values in US Dollars, on an offer to offer price basis with gross income reinvested

Data Source Micropal™

MONEY MARKET FUNDS

Offshore money market funds have the shortest-term outlook of all offshore funds. Basically they invest in debt securities with very short maturity dates, 365 days or less.

These debt securities come in various forms, the most common being government debt issues. Other forms of short-term debt are bank certificates of deposit, bankers' acceptances (debt arising from international trade transactions) and commercial paper (unsecured IOUs from corporations).

Money market funds are the least risky of all offshore funds. Those which invest in the securities of stable governments, such as US Treasury Bills, are virtually free of any risk. However, those money market funds which stray away from "safe" country government debt do run some risk to the investor's capital, albeit a relatively small one.

For instance, funds which invest in private debt or commercial paper leave their investors open to the risk of default should the corporation fail. The fund manager may see this small element of risk as worthwhile given the extra returns to be gained. Only the commercial paper of a senior or high creditworthy company is normally considered by most money market investment managers.

Perhaps more risky are those funds that invest in the short-term debt of weaker economies which have a lower credit rating. Here, the risk of default can be higher than with a blue chip company.

The money market funds are divided into 27 separate categories. The many sectors appear because the majority of the money market funds are invested in just one country. Most investors will invest in those money market funds that are denominated in the currency they use themselves. Consequently, such single-country funds cannot be compared with each other in any meaningful way. The manager of a Canadian dollar money market fund cannot outperform a Danish krone money market fund manager if the markets are against him. Not surprisingly, the largest key single-country sectors are those based on the world's main currencies - deutschmarks, sterling, Swiss francs, US dollars and the yen.

However, by far the biggest category is the managed currency money market sector. These funds are suitable for investors, both individuals or institutions, who want to protect the purchasing power of their liquid assets through a managed diversification of currency and interest rate exposure. Typically the funds invest in a spread of currencies, held largely in the form of bank deposits, certificates of deposits, floating rate notes, and other instruments, such as short-term tail-end bonds. The currencies are monitored on a medium to long-term view, and the manager seeks undervalued currencies or situations in the currency markets that are within the risk parameters of the fund. These funds play a very important part in the global market, as they can be major buyers of Treasury Bills.

Money market funds are popular with many investors because they typically pay higher rates of interest than bank savings accounts. Some single-country money market funds have produced outstanding returns in dollar-converted terms. New Zealand dollar money market funds have returned on average over the past five years, 15.28 per cent per annum, and French franc funds have averaged 7.24 per cent.

Australian Dollar Money Market

Funds investing solely in Australian Dollar denominated money market or cash instruments with durations ranging from overnight to twelve months. Investments will normally be held in bank deposits, short-term monetary investments (e.g. T. Bills and certificates of deposit).

	CCY	Fund Size ($mil)	Fund Name	Manager Code	Fund Start Date	Domicile Code	3 Mths 97 % Chg	Rank	1 Year % Chg	Rank	Micropal Star Rating 3 Years Volatility	% Chg	Rank	Rating	Risk Return Rating	5 Years % Chg	Rank	10 Years % Chg	Rank
		38.12	**Mean/Count**				**-0.09**	**9**	**13.63**	**9**	**1.94**	**38.41**	**7**		**2**	**35.44**	**5**	**183.35**	**3**
	AUD	1.43	Bermuda Money AUD	B066	31/03/94	BER	-0.05	4	13.60	4	N.A.	N.A.				N.A.		N.A.	
●	AUD	138.66	DBIM Australian Dllr Reserve	D006	30/07/93	LUX	-0.19	9	13.51	5	1.91	38.36	3	✪✪✪	3	N.A.		N.A.	
	AUD	14.02	Fidelity AUD Currency Acc	F013	29/11/91	BER	-0.17	8	13.20	9	1.90	37.06	7	✪	2	33.75	4	N.A.	
▲	AUD	0.47	Five Arrows CFL AUD	R010	30/04/84	GU	-0.16	7	13.25	8	2.16	37.09	6	✪✪	1	33.43	5	179.93	3
▲	AUD	9.54	Five Arrows IRL AUD	R017	30/03/84	GU	-0.14	6	13.28	7	1.90	37.63	5	✪✪	3	34.52	3	181.93	2
	AUD	10.75	JF Money Fund AUD	J004	30/04/90	HK	0.01	3	14.14	1	1.90	40.58	1	✪✪✪✪	4	39.69	1	N.A.	
▲	AUD	18.65	Lloyds Intl MMF AUD	L017	30/09/85	GU	-0.13	5	13.50	6	1.95	38.13	4	✪✪✪	2	35.79	2	188.20	1
	AUD	131.31	SBC Money Market Fund AUD	S007	31/08/92	LUX	0.05	1	14.03	3	1.89	40.03	2	✪✪✪✪	4	N.A.		N.A.	
	AUD	18.29	Swissca MM Fund AUD	S058	31/10/94	LUX	0.02	2	14.11	2	N.A.	N.A.				N.A.		N.A.	

Austrian Schilling Money Market

Funds investing solely in Austrian Schilling denominated money market or cash instruments with durations ranging from overnight to twelve months. Investments will normally be held in bank deposits, short-term monetary investments (e.g. T. Bills and certificates of deposit).

	CCY	Fund Size ($mil)	Fund Name	Manager Code	Fund Start Date	Domicile Code	3 Mths 97 % Chg	Rank	1 Year % Chg	Rank	Micropal Star Rating 3 Years Volatility	% Chg	Rank	Rating	Risk Return Rating	5 Years % Chg	Rank	10 Years % Chg	Rank
		9.57	**Mean/Count**				**-7.14**	**3**	**-3.97**	**3**	**2.55**	**26.17**	**3**		**3**	**33.20**	**1**	**0**	**0**
●	ATS	1.01	DBIM Schilling Reserve	D006	31/12/90	LUX	-7.09	1	-2.46	1	2.53	29.59	1	✪✪✪✪	4	33.20	1	N.A.	
	ATS	1.55	Fidelity ATS Currency Acc	F013	31/01/92	BER	-7.23	3	-5.18	3	2.56	23.10	3	✪✪	2	N.A.		N.A.	
	ATS	26.14	SBC Money Market Fund ATS	S007	26/02/93	LUX	-7.11	2	-4.26	2	2.57	25.81	2	✪✪✪	3	N.A.		N.A.	

BEF/LUF Money Market

Funds investing solely in Belgian and Luxembourg Franc denominated money market or cash instruments with durations ranging from overnight to twelve months. Investments will normally be held in bank deposits, short-term monetary investments (e.g. T. Bills and certificates of deposit).

	CCY	Fund Size ($mil)	Fund Name	Manager Code	Fund Start Date	Domicile Code	3 Mths 97 % Chg	Rank	1 Year % Chg	Rank	Micropal Star Rating 3 Years Volatility	% Chg	Rank	Rating	Risk Return Rating	5 Years % Chg	Rank	10 Years % Chg	Rank
		256.75	**Mean/Count**				**-7.36**	**44**	**-4.79**	**40**	**2.58**	**28.10**	**36**		**2**	**30.62**	**22**	**134.23**	**2**
▲	BEF	16.09	ABN AMRO Interest Growth BEF	A001	30/04/92	LUX	-7.51	41	-4.84	27	2.59	28.49	13	✪✪	4	N.A.		N.A.	
	LUF	N.S.	Aqua Europe Cap	B026	31/07/87	LUX	-7.33	17	-4.78	21	2.57	28.70	8	✪✪✪✪	3	30.65	10	N.A.	
	BEF	1244.26	BBL Capital Cash C	B052	31/03/88	LUX	-7.35	24	-4.81	23	2.58	28.48	14	✪✪✪	3	30.08	16	N.A.	
	BEF	950.28	BBL Renta Cash Sht-Med BEF C	B052	31/01/92	LUX	-7.33	16	-4.75	18	2.51	23.05	36	✪	1	N.A.		N.A.	
	BEF	458.61	BIL Money Market BEF	B067	31/01/90	LUX	-7.37	29	-4.95	34	2.58	28.07	27	✪✪	1	30.67	9	N.A.	
●	LUF	68.44	BL Money Trust FB/FLUX B	B025	30/03/90	LUX	-7.29	9	-4.63	9	2.54	27.83	30	✪	2	31.51	4	N.A.	
	LUF	23.72	Cash Fund Belgian Franc	S032	31/10/90	LUX	-7.35	26	-4.92	32	2.58	28.12	23	✪✪	2	30.44	14	N.A.	
	LUF	221	Cera Cash BEF/LUF B	C018	31/12/90	LUX	-7.51	42	-4.69	14	2.53	28.65	10	✪✪✪✪	4	30.04	17	N.A.	
●	BEF	15.82	Citiplus 90 Cat A	C037	30/11/93	LUX	-7.39	33	-4.92	33	2.57	28.57	11	✪✪✪✪	3	N.A.		N.A.	
●	BEF	63.96	Credis Money Market Fund BEF	C057	31/07/92	LUX	-7.33	20	-4.67	11	2.57	28.30	18	✪✪✪	2	N.A.		N.A.	
	BEF	219.31	Cregem Cash Beluf Cap	C059	31/01/90	LUX	-7.34	23	-4.81	24	2.58	28.80	6	✪✪✪✪	4	30.48	12	N.A.	
	BEF	98.90	Currency Mgt Fd Belgian Fcs C	I008	30/10/92	LUX	-7.34	21	-4.77	20	2.57	28.71	7	✪✪✪✪	3	N.A.		N.A.	
	BEF	130.19	European Money Mkt B	B036	31/10/90	LUX	-7.41	34	-5.04	36	2.57	28.34	17	✪✪✪	3	31.19	8	N.A.	
	BEF	511.27	Findico Cap	K010	31/05/89	LUX	-7.34	22	-4.91	30	2.58	28.11	24	✪✪	2	29.55	20	N.A.	
▲	BEF	0.10	Five Arrows CFL Belgian Franc	R010	30/04/84	GU	-7.44	39	-5.49	39	2.68	25.65	35	✪	1	27.25	22	133.55	2

▲ SIB Approved ● Insurance Fund Values in US Dollars, on an offer to offer price basis with gross income reinvested Data Source Micropal™

BEF/LUF Money Market

continued

	CCY	Fund Size ($mil)	Fund Name	Manager Code	Fund Start Date	Domicile Code	3 Mths 97 % Chg	3 Mths 97 Rank	1 Year % Chg	1 Year Rank	Micropal Star Rating: Volatility	3 Years % Chg	3 Years Rank	Rating	Risk Return Rating	5 Years % Chg	5 Years Rank	10 Years % Chg	10 Years Rank
		256.75	**Mean/Count**				**-7.36**	**44**	**-4.79**	**40**	**2.58**	**28.10**	**36**		**2**	**30.62**	**22**	**134.23**	**2**
▲	BEF	4.39	Five Arrows IRL Belgian Franc	R017	31/07/80	GU	-7.44	38	-5.38	38	2.57	26.02	33	✪	1	27.34	21	134.90	1
	BEF	8.75	Force Cash Traditionnel BEF	B073	31/03/93	LUX	-7.32	14	-4.71	15	2.57	28.67	9	✪✪✪✪	4	N.A.		N.A.	
	BEF	211.37	G-Short Term BEF 1 Month	G009	28/02/94	LUX	-7.20	3	-4.51	6	N.A.	N.A.				N.A.		N.A.	
	BEF	19.59	G-Short Term BEF 3 Months	G009	29/04/94	LUX	-7.23	4	-4.44	3	N.A.	N.A.				N.A.		N.A.	
	LUF	1161.66	G-Treasury Belgo-Lux B	G009	31/03/88	LUX	-7.19	2	-4.42	2	2.54	28.24	21	✪✪	3	31.36	5	N.A.	
	LUF	1782.92	G-Treasury Intl Belgo-Lux B	G009	31/03/88	LUX	-7.23	5	-4.51	7	2.55	28.43	15	✪✪✪	4	31.29	6	N.A.	
	BEF	15.65	Inter Cash BEF	B069	23/08/96	LUX	-7.41	35	N.A.		N.A.	N.A.				N.A.		N.A.	
●	BEF	129.90	InvestPlus Money B	B035	31/03/88	LUX	-7.32	11	-4.86	28	2.58	28.08	25	✪✪	1	30.27	15	N.A.	
	LUF	10.84	Ippa Portf Belgian Short B	B035	31/03/92	LUX	-7.42	37	-5.21	37	2.58	27.11	32	✪	1	N.A.		N.A.	
	BEF	613.96	KB Cash Fund BEF	K010	28/02/92	LUX	-7.30	10	-4.81	25	2.58	28.23	22	✪✪✪	2	N.A.		N.A.	
	BEF	78.93	KB Cash Fund BEF Plus	K010	30/04/93	LUX	-7.33	18	-4.79	22	2.56	28.06	28	✪	2	N.A.		N.A.	
	BEF	18.35	Lion Belgium Cash C	C060	30/04/93	LUX	-7.55	43	-4.72	16	2.52	29.43	4	✪✪✪✪	5	N.A.		N.A.	
	LUF	76.57	Lion Interinvest Cash LUF	C062	30/06/87	LUX	-7.24	6	-4.50	5	2.58	29.59	3	✪✪✪✪✪	4	33.09	2	N.A.	
	LUF	166.33	Luxcash Francs A Cap	C002	29/06/90	LUX	-7.33	15	-4.68	13	2.56	28.52	12	✪✪✪	3	30.03	18	N.A.	
	BEF	N.S.	MeesPierson UF BEF Reserve	M012	01/03/96	LUX	-7.71	44	N.A.		N.A.	N.A.				N.A.		N.A.	
	BEF	103.86	Money Plus (Bef) Cap	C061	30/06/89	LUX	-7.16	1	-4.01	1	2.57	30.34	1	✪✪✪✪✪	5	33.51	1	N.A.	
	BEF	136.26	Parvest Short Term BEF A	B037	30/06/93	LUX	-7.42	36	-4.67	12	2.52	28.28	19	✪✪	4	N.A.		N.A.	
	BEF	149.15	Petercam Moneta BEF Liquid B	P013	30/04/90	LUX	-7.28	8	-4.45	4	2.57	29.94	2	✪✪✪✪✪	5	32.97	3	N.A.	
	BEF	N.S.	Privalux Treasury Sicav	C003	29/02/88	LUX	-7.36	27	-4.90	29	2.57	28.34	16	✪✪✪	2	30.50	11	N.A.	
	BEF	60.22	Proventus BEF Liquidity C	P013	29/02/88	LUX	-7.33	19	-4.66	10	2.57	28.82	5	✪✪✪✪	4	31.23	7	N.A.	
	BEF	1.65	Rabobank Holland BEF Cash	R001	19/04/96	LUX	-7.32	13	N.A.		N.A.	N.A.				N.A.		N.A.	
	BEF	67.27	SBC Money Market Fund BEF	S007	31/08/92	LUX	-7.37	28	-4.76	19	2.57	28.24	20	✪✪	2	N.A.		N.A.	
	LUF	1190.14	Short Fund LUF-BEF Cap	A037	31/05/89	LUX	-7.37	30	-4.92	31	2.58	28.08	26	✪✪	1	30.46	13	N.A.	
	BEF	5.37	Sicaro Court Terme B	B019	28/02/95	LUX	-7.26	7	-4.60	8	N.A.	N.A.				N.A.		N.A.	
	LUF	405.79	Sicaro FB/Flux B	B019	28/02/95	LUX	-7.35	25	-4.74	17	N.A.	N.A.				N.A.		N.A.	
	BEF	2.11	Sogelux Fd Money Mkt BEF	S037	21/06/96	LUX	-7.50	40	N.A.		N.A.	N.A.				N.A.		N.A.	
	BEF	52.13	Sogenalux Treasury BEF B	S037	31/07/89	LUX	-7.39	32	-5.01	35	2.58	27.68	31	✪	1	29.78	19	N.A.	
	LUF	3.47	TGA BEF Liquid Assets	T009	31/12/93	LUX	-7.32	12	-5.59	40	2.82	25.71	34	✪	1	N.A.		N.A.	
	BEF	28.25	UBS (Lux) Money Mkt Invst BEF	U001	30/04/93	LUX	-7.37	31	-4.83	26	2.57	28.04	29	✪	2	N.A.		N.A.	

Brazilian Reals Money Market

Funds investing solely in Brazilian Real denominated money market or cash instruments with durations ranging from overnight to twelve months. Investments will normally be held in bank deposits, short-term monetary investments (e.g. T. Bills and certificates of deposit).

CCY	Fund Size ($mil)	Fund Name	Manager Code	Fund Start Date	Domicile Code	3 Mths 97 % Chg	3 Mths 97 Rank	1 Year % Chg	1 Year Rank	Micropal Star Rating: Volatility	3 Years % Chg	3 Years Rank	Rating	Risk Return Rating	5 Years % Chg	5 Years Rank	10 Years % Chg	10 Years Rank
	27.37	**Mean/Count**				**1.72**	**1**	**13.31**	**1**	**0**	**0**	**0**			**0**	**0**	**0**	**0**
USD	27.37	Opportunity Brazilian Eur Sec	O010	17/02/95	CA	1.72	1	13.31	1	N.A.	N.A.				N.A.		N.A.	

▲ SIB Approved ● Insurance Fund **Values in US Dollars, on an offer to offer price basis with gross income reinvested** Data Source Micropal™

Canadian Dollar Money Market

Funds investing solely in Canadian Dollar denominated money market or cash instruments with durations ranging from overnight to twelve months. Investments will normally be held in bank deposits, short-term monetary investments (e.g. T. Bills and certificates of deposit).

	CCY	Fund Size ($mil)	Fund Name	Manager Code	Fund Start Date	Domicile Code	3 Mths 97 % Chg	3 Mths 97 Rank	1 Year % Chg	1 Year Rank	Micropal Star Rating 3 Years Volatility	3 Years % Chg	3 Years Rank	Rating	Risk Return Rating	5 Years % Chg	5 Years Rank	10 Years % Chg	10 Years Rank
		83.90	**Mean/Count**				**-0.19**	**19**	**3.54**	**18**	**1.42**	**11.19**	**17**			**7.23**	**11**	**95.49**	**3**
	CAD	N.S.	Aqua Canada Cap	B026	28/02/92	LUX	-0.13	5	3.81	5	1.20	11.89	7	✪✪✪		N.A.		N.A.	
	CAD	43.95	BBL Renta Cash CAD C	B052	31/05/91	LUX	-0.14	7	3.75	7	4.59	11.69	8	✪✪✪		7.83	5	N.A.	
	CAD	15.28	BBL Renta Cash Sht-Med CAD C	B052	30/09/93	LUX	-0.22	13	3.61	11	1.26	8.54	17	✪		N.A.		N.A.	
	CAD	39.75	Bermuda Money CAD	B066	30/11/93	BER	-0.14	6	3.63	9	1.21	12.18	6	✪✪✪		N.A.		N.A.	
	CAD	57.50	Buttress Money Market CAD	B080	30/11/94	BER	-0.16	8	3.79	6	N.A.	N.A.				N.A.		N.A.	
	CAD	10.52	CIBC PCF Canadian Dollar Money	C021	16/02/96	GU	-0.16	9	N.A.		N.A.	N.A.				N.A.		N.A.	
●	CAD	253.73	Credis Money Market Fund CAD	C057	28/09/90	LUX	-0.04	2	4.23	2	1.20	12.66	3	✪✪✪✪		9.81	2	N.A.	
●	CAD	228.99	DBIM Can Dollar Reserve CAD	D006	30/11/92	LUX	-0.21	12	2.77	17	1.28	10.86	11	✪✪		N.A.		N.A.	
	CAD	53.24	Fidelity CAD Currency Acc	F013	29/11/91	BER	-0.33	17	2.95	16	1.21	9.76	15	✪		5	10	N.A.	
▲	CAD	1.41	Five Arrows CFL Canadian Dllr	R010	30/04/84	GU	-0.37	19	2.65	18	1.22	9.30	16	✪✪		4.19	11	96.16	2
▲	CAD	10.01	Five Arrows IRL Canadian Dllr	R017	31/07/80	GU	-0.33	18	3.02	15	1.21	10.04	13	✪		5.45	8	98.23	1
	CAD	5.28	JF Money Fund CAD	J004	30/04/90	HK	-0.18	10	3.59	12	1.23	12.50	4	✪✪✪✪		9.66	3	N.A.	
	CAD	10.89	Lloyds Intl Liquidity CAD	L015	28/06/91	LUX	-0.19	11	3.66	8	1.22	11.09	10	✪✪		7.39	6	N.A.	
▲	CAD	3.38	Lloyds Intl MMF CAD	L017	31/05/90	GU	-0.32	16	3.03	14	1.21	10.27	12	✪✪		5.91	7	N.A.	
▲	CAD	4.09	RBC ICF Canadian Dollar	R003	30/11/82	GU	-0.27	15	3.06	13	1.21	9.92	14	✪		5	9	92.09	3
	CAD	17.02	RBC IMMF CAD Dist	R002	30/06/92	GU	-0.25	14	3.62	10	1.31	11.29	9	✪✪✪		N.A.		N.A.	
	CAD	424.14	SBC Money Market Fund CAD	S007	28/06/91	LUX	-0.12	4	4.15	3	1.22	12.74	2	✪✪✪✪		9.83	1	N.A.	
	CAD	69.98	Swissca MM Fund CAD	S058	31/07/92	LUX	0	1	4.24	1	1.20	13.02	1	✪✪✪✪✪		N.A.		N.A.	
	CAD	261.12	UBS (Lux) Money Mkt Invst CAD	U001	30/09/91	LUX	-0.06	3	4.14	4	1.22	12.43	5	✪✪✪✪		9.50	4	N.A.	

Danish Krone Money Market

Funds investing solely in Danish Krone denominated money market or cash instruments with durations ranging from overnight to twelve months. Investments will normally be held in bank deposits, short-term monetary investments (e.g. T. Bills and certificates of deposits).

	CCY	Fund Size ($mil)	Fund Name	Manager Code	Fund Start Date	Domicile Code	3 Mths 97 % Chg	3 Mths 97 Rank	1 Year % Chg	1 Year Rank	Micropal Star Rating 3 Years Volatility	3 Years % Chg	3 Years Rank	Rating	Risk Return Rating	5 Years % Chg	5 Years Rank	10 Years % Chg	10 Years Rank
		9.19	**Mean/Count**				**-6.67**	**3**	**-3.43**	**3**	**2.50**	**30.05**	**3**		**3**	**38.59**	**2**	**162.01**	**2**
▲	DKK	0.04	Five Arrows CFL Danish Krone	R010	30/04/84	GU	-6.66	2	-3.49	3	2.58	30.14	2	✪✪✪	2	39.31	1	164.02	1
▲	DKK	27.38	Five Arrows IRL Danish Krone	R017	30/04/84	GU	-6.65	1	-3.32	1	2.46	30.79	1	✪✪✪✪	4	37.87	2	160	2
	DKK	0.15	North Star Intl Money DKK	N012	30/11/92	CA	-6.69	3	-3.47	2	2.47	29.22	3	✪✪	3	N.A.		N.A.	

Europe (Hard Currency) Money Market

Funds investing solely in Europe (Hard Currency) money market or cash instruments with durations ranging from overnight to twelve months. Investments will normally be held in bank deposits, short-term monetary investments (e.g. T. Bills and certificates of deposits).

	CCY	Fund Size ($mil)	Fund Name	Manager Code	Fund Start Date	Domicile Code	3 Mths 97 % Chg	3 Mths 97 Rank	1 Year % Chg	1 Year Rank	Micropal Star Rating 3 Years Volatility	3 Years % Chg	3 Years Rank	Rating	Risk Return Rating	5 Years % Chg	5 Years Rank	10 Years % Chg	10 Years Rank
		5.18	**Mean/Count**				**-7.09**	**1**	**-4.31**	**1**	**2.58**	**26.69**	**1**		**3**	**0**	**0**	**0**	**0**
	NLG	5.18	Currency Mgt Fd NLG/DEM	I008	29/10/93	LUX	-7.09	1	-4.31	1	2.58	26.69	1	✪✪✪	3	N.A.		N.A.	

▲ **SIB Approved** ● **Insurance Fund** **Values in US Dollars, on an offer to offer price basis with gross income reinvested** Data Source Micropal™

European Currency Unit Money Market

Funds investing solely in European Currency Unit money market or cash instruments with durations ranging from overnight to twelve months. Investments will normally be held in bank deposits, short-term monetary investments (e.g. T. Bills and certificates of deposits).

	CCY	Fund Size ($mil)	Fund Name	Manager Code	Fund Start Date	Domicile Code	3 Mths 97 % Chg	Rank	1 Year % Chg	Rank	Micropal Star Rating 3 Years Volatility	% Chg	Rank	Rating	Risk Return Rating	5 Years % Chg	Rank	10 Years % Chg	Rank
		125.88	**Mean/Count**				**-6.20**	**32**	**1.40**	**32**	**2.02**	**29.33**	**28**		**2**	**28.70**	**22**	**124.35**	**3**
	ECU	52.07	Baer Multicash ECU Cash	J007	30/04/91	LUX	-6.49	31	1.59	13	1.94	31.87	2	✪✪✪	5	30.63	4	N.A.	
	ECU	20.12	BBL Renta Cash XEU C	B052	30/09/91	LUX	-6.16	16	1.45	18	2.03	29	18	✪✪	2	27.30	16	N.A.	
	ECU	2.11	Bermuda Money ECU	B066	28/02/94	BER	-6.12	9	1.38	20	N.A.	N.A.				N.A.		N.A.	
	ECU	1.48	CB MMF ECU	A007	31/03/95	LUX	-6.10	3	0.80	31	N.A.	N.A.				N.A.		N.A.	
●	ECU	760.33	Credis Money Market Fund ECU	C057	28/09/90	LUX	-5.92	1	1.91	4	2.03	30.63	7	✪✪✪✪	3	29.38	8	N.A.	
	ECU	3.56	Currency Mgt Fd ECU	I008	30/11/92	LUX	-6.14	13	1.54	16	2.04	29.41	16	✪✪	2	N.A.		N.A.	
●	ECU	252.38	DBIM ECU Reserve	D006	29/03/91	LUX	-6.11	7	1.68	9	1.96	31.31	5	✪✪✪	4	35.78	1	N.A.	
	ECU	12.39	DekaLux Cash ECU (A)	D009	29/05/92	LUX	-6.31	28	1.43	19	1.98	30.44	8	✪✪✪	4	N.A.		N.A.	
	ECU	36.86	Eufi-Cash Ecu Cap	E012	30/03/90	LUX	-6.50	32	1.90	5	2.03	32.55	1	✪✪✪✪	4	30.99	3	N.A.	
	ECU	12.96	Europe Obligations Court Terme	S035	31/10/91	LUX	-6.14	12	1.60	11	2.01	30.32	9	✪✪✪✪	4	28.82	11	N.A.	
	ECU	8.24	Fidelity ECU Currency Acc	F013	29/11/91	BER	-6.25	23	0.98	28	2.03	27.63	25	✪	1	25.77	21	N.A.	
▲	ECU	1.36	Five Arrows CFL ECU	R010	31/10/85	GU	-6.25	24	0.86	29	2.18	27.25	27	✪✪	1	25.19	22	126.08	2
▲	ECU	34.28	Five Arrows IRL ECU	R017	31/10/85	GU	-6.21	22	1.08	25	2.02	27.92	24	✪	1	25.94	19	127.16	1
●	ECU	0.57	Hansard Ecu Deposit	H011	31/07/92	IOM	-6.47	30	-0.55	32	2.01	22.04	28	✪	1	N.A.		N.A.	
▲	ECU	66.47	Inter Cash ECU	B069	29/09/89	LUX	-6.29	26	2.04	1	1.96	29.64	13	✪✪✪	4	28.93	9	N.A.	
	ECU	1.31	JF Money Fund ECU	J004	29/03/91	HK	-6.10	4	1.54	15	2.03	30.30	10	✪✪✪✪	3	29.81	6	N.A.	
	ECU	101.15	Lion Interinvest Cash ECU	C062	29/01/88	LUX	-6	2	1.97	2	2.04	31.59	4	✪✪✪✪✪	4	32.06	2	N.A.	
	ECU	11.65	Lloyds Intl Liquidity ECU	L015	28/06/91	LUX	-6.15	14	1.60	12	2.02	29.29	17	✪✪	2	27.23	17	N.A.	
▲	ECU	16.11	Lloyds Intl MMF ECU	L017	31/03/87	GU	-6.19	19	1.23	23	2.03	28.57	19	✪	2	27.77	15	N.A.	
	ECU	7.92	Luxcash Ecu A Cap	C002	30/06/95	LUX	-6.15	15	1.45	17	N.A.	N.A.				N.A.		N.A.	
▲	ECU	1.49	Newton UGF ECU	N006	31/03/86	JER	-6.20	21	1.05	27	2.02	27.98	23	✪	1	25.89	20	119.79	3
	ECU	22.07	Parvest Short Term Europe B	B037	28/02/91	LUX	-6.19	20	1.32	22	2.01	27.99	22	✪	2	28	14	N.A.	
	ECU	3.16	Proton Fund ECU Cash	P025	29/09/95	LUX	-6.42	29	1.91	3	N.A.	N.A.				N.A.		N.A.	
	ECU	702.95	SBC Money Market Fund XEU	S007	31/05/90	LUX	-6.11	6	1.81	7	2.01	30	11	✪✪✪	3	28.85	10	N.A.	
	ECU	0.37	Scot Prov GP ECU Deposit	S014	30/09/91	IOM	-6.27	25	0.80	30	2.04	27.50	26	✪✪	1	27.10	18	N.A.	
	ECU	5.09	Sogelux Fd Money Mkt Europe	S037	31/05/88	LUX	-6.14	11	1.81	8	1.95	31.83	3	✪✪✪✪	5	29.82	5	N.A.	
	ECU	7.82	Sogenalux Treasury ECU B	S037	30/06/92	LUX	-6.16	17	1.38	21	2.01	29.48	14	✪✪✪	2	N.A.		N.A.	
	ECU	0	Sun Life Money Ecu	S053	30/04/93	IOM	-6.12	10	1.05	26	2.05	28.40	20	✪✪	1	N.A.		N.A.	
	ECU	247.95	Swissca MM Fund ECU	S058	30/04/91	LUX	-6.10	5	1.84	6	2.04	30.80	6	✪✪✪✪✪	3	29.39	7	N.A.	
	ECU	11.31	Trans Monetary ECU	N003	31/01/92	LUX	-6.18	18	1.20	24	2.02	28.29	21	✪	2	N.A.		N.A.	
	ECU	1616.78	UBS (Lux) Money Mkt Invst XEU	U001	31/10/89	LUX	-6.12	8	1.66	10	2.02	29.89	12	✪✪✪✪	3	28.48	12	N.A.	
	ECU	5.76	UBZ Liquidity ECU	U002	12/07/91	IRL	-6.30	27	1.57	14	1.98	29.42	15	✪✪	3	28.20	13	N.A.	

Finnish Markka Money Market

Funds investing solely in Finnish Markka denominated money market or cash instruments with durations ranging from overnight to twelve months. Investments will normally be held in bank deposits, short-term monetary investments (e.g. T. Bills and certificates of deposits).

CCY	Fund Size ($mil)	Fund Name	Manager Code	Fund Start Date	Domicile Code	3 Mths 97 % Chg	Rank	1 Year % Chg	Rank	Micropal Star Rating 3 Years Volatility	% Chg	Rank	Rating	Risk Return Rating	5 Years % Chg	Rank	10 Years % Chg	Rank
	0	**Mean/Count**				**-6.55**	**2**	**0**	**0**	**0**	**0**	**0**			**0**	**0**	**0**	**0**
FIM	N.S.	Five Arrows CFL Finnish Mark	R010	31/10/96	GU	-6.53	1	N.A.		N.A.	N.A.				N.A.		N.A.	
FIM	N.S.	Five Arrows IRL Finnish Markka	R017	31/10/96	GU	-6.57	2	N.A.		N.A.	N.A.				N.A.		N.A.	

▲ SIB Approved ● Insurance Fund Values in US Dollars, on an offer to offer price basis with gross income reinvested Data Source Micropal™

French Franc Money Market

Funds investing solely in French Franc denominated money market or cash instruments with durations ranging from overnight to twelve months. Investments will normally be held in bank deposits, short-term monetary investments (e.g. T. Bills and certificates of deposit).

	CCY	Fund Size ($mil)	Fund Name	Manager Code	Fund Start Date	Domicile Code	3 Mths 97 % Chg	3 Mths 97 Rank	1 Year % Chg	1 Year Rank	Micropal Star Rating 3 Years Volatility	3 Years % Chg	3 Years Rank	3 Years Rating	Risk Return Rating	5 Years % Chg	5 Years Rank	10 Years % Chg	10 Years Rank
		109.27	**Mean/Count**				**-7.07**	**41**	**-2.65**	**39**	**2.43**	**30.61**	**36**		**2**	**36.21**	**26**	**142.88**	**3**
	FRF	N.S.	Aqua France	B026	30/09/87	LUX	-7.04	16	-2.83	23	2.43	30.72	20	✪✪	2	36.40	14	N.A.	
	FRF	18.22	Baer Multicash FRF Cash	J007	30/11/92	LUX	-7.05	18	-1.63	3	2.36	32.08	5	✪✪✪	5	N.A.		N.A.	
	FRF	11.98	BBL Renta Cash Sht-Med FRF C	B052	30/07/93	LUX	-6.99	6	-2.56	16	2.40	27.90	33	✪✪	1	N.A.		N.A.	
	FRF	1.45	Bermuda Money FRF	B066	28/02/94	BER	-7.09	26	-3.50	37	N.A.	N.A.				N.A.		N.A.	
	FRF	74.92	BIL Money Market FRF	B067	30/09/91	LUX	-7.05	17	-2.69	20	2.43	30.91	18	✪✪✪	3	37.05	9	N.A.	
●	FRF	17.41	BL Money Trust FRF B	B025	30/03/90	LUX	-7.03	15	-2.30	10	2.42	31.40	13	✪✪✪✪	3	36.88	11	N.A.	
	FRF	70.68	CCF Elysees Monetaire	C015	29/05/87	LUX	-7.02	13	-2.54	15	2.42	31.52	10	✪✪✪✪	4	38.21	5	N.A.	
●	FRF	402.82	Credis Money Market Fund FRF	C057	31/10/91	LUX	-6.98	5	-2.26	7	2.42	31.50	11	✪✪✪	4	37.14	8	N.A.	
	FRF	0.42	Currency Mgt Fd French Francs	I008	30/11/92	LUX	-7.11	28	-2.90	25	2.43	29.46	28	✪✪	1	N.A.		N.A.	
●	FRF	9.25	DBIM FF Reserve	D006	31/07/89	LUX	-6.65	1	-0.70	1	2.37	34.47	2	✪✪✪✪	5	42.55	1	N.A.	
	FRF	19.71	Eurobonds Plus	C001	31/08/92	LUX	-7.11	27	-3.07	29	2.40	27.46	36	✪	1	N.A.		N.A.	
	FRF	2.63	Europe Investssmt Placement	S037	30/11/87	LUX	-7.24	41	-3.86	39	2.43	27.64	35	✪	1	32.24	25	N.A.	
▲	FRF	13.06	Fidelity FRF Currency Acc	F013	29/11/91	BER	-7.18	36	-3.32	36	2.44	28.47	32	✪	1	33.32	23	N.A.	
▲	FRF	1.59	Five Arrows CFL French Franc	R010	30/04/84	GU	-7.19	38	-3.50	38	2.64	28.54	31	✪✪	1	33.31	24	142.03	3
▲	FRF	10.97	Five Arrows IRL French Franc	R017	31/07/80	GU	-7.15	34	-3.16	33	2.43	29.32	29	✪	1	34.27	21	144.18	1
▲	FRF	6.32	Fleming FF Series II FRF	F020	30/09/92	LUX	-7.03	14	-2.60	18	2.43	31.07	16	✪✪✪✪	3	N.A.		N.A.	
	FRF	1.90	Force Cash Traditionnel FRF	B073	18/10/96	LUX	-7.17	35	N.A.		N.A.	N.A.				N.A.		N.A.	
	FRF	303.67	Fructilux Court Terme FRF	B043	31/10/91	LUX	-7.09	23	-3.04	28	2.44	30.14	23	✪✪	2	36.12	15	N.A.	
	FRF	9.76	G-Treasury French Franc B	G009	29/07/94	LUX	-7.06	19	-2.22	5	N.A.	N.A.				N.A.		N.A.	
	FRF	16.22	G-Treasury Intl Fr Franc B	G009	29/07/94	LUX	-7.09	25	-2.35	13	N.A.	N.A.				N.A.		N.A.	
	FRF	133.35	GFI Lux CEP Court Terme	C016	31/07/87	LUX	-7.01	11	-2.25	6	2.43	32.79	3	✪✪✪✪	4	37.33	6	N.A.	
▲●	FRF	12.99	Groupe Indosuez FRF Reserve	G017	31/01/91	LUX	-7.19	39	-3.18	34	2.46	31.44	12	✪✪✪	3	35.17	18	N.A.	
▲	FRF	287.36	Inter Cash Franc (FRF) C	B069	31/10/89	LUX	-7.14	32	-3.11	32	2.42	28.89	30	✪	1	33.99	22	N.A.	
▲	FRF	789.23	Inter Cash France Securite C	B069	29/01/88	LUX	-7	10	-2.49	14	2.43	31.60	9	✪✪✪✪✪	4	38.99	4	N.A.	
	FRF	2.07	Lazard French Franc Liquidity	L002	30/11/84	GU	-7.18	37	-3.11	31	2.43	29.81	25	✪✪	2	34.61	20	142.44	2
	FRF	569.12	Lion Interinvest Cash FRF	C062	30/06/87	LUX	-6.93	2	-2.31	11	2.44	32.67	4	✪✪✪✪✪	4	40.35	2	N.A.	
	FRF	29.21	Lloyds Intl Liquidity FRF	L015	28/06/91	LUX	-7.06	20	-2.57	17	2.43	30.53	21	✪✪	2	35.37	17	N.A.	
▲	FRF	23.37	Lloyds Intl MMF FRF	L017	31/03/87	GU	-7.12	29	-3.09	30	2.44	29.82	24	✪	2	36.49	13	N.A.	
	FRF	23.50	Luxcash Francs Francais A Cap	C002	29/06/90	LUX	-7	8	-2.28	9	2.41	31.12	15	✪✪✪	3	36.09	16	N.A.	
	FRF	21.51	Matrix French Fr Liquidity A	U011	31/01/96	IRL	-7.14	33	N.A.		N.A.	N.A.				N.A.		N.A.	
	FRF	14.05	MOSAIS Court Terme FRF	C058	30/03/90	LUX	-7.09	24	-3.03	26	2.43	29.69	26	✪	2	34.62	19	N.A.	
	FRF	21.72	Multibond Acticash FRF B	C015	31/01/91	LUX	-7.12	30	-0.92	2	2.33	34.76	1	✪✪✪✪	5	30.04	26	N.A.	
	FRF	0.01	North Star Intl Money FRF	N012	31/05/93	CA	-7.22	40	-3.21	35	2.43	27.85	34	✪	1	N.A.		N.A.	
	FRF	16.47	Oblicic Plac Monetaire FF (m)	C022	31/10/89	LUX	-6.98	4	-2.79	22	2.44	31.06	17	✪✪✪	3	36.82	12	N.A.	
	FRF	238.63	Parvest Short Term FRF B	B037	31/05/93	LUX	-7.08	22	-2.75	21	2.39	30.23	22	✪✪	2	N.A.		N.A.	
	FRF	495.10	SBC Money Market Fund FRF	S007	28/06/91	LUX	-7	9	-2.26	8	2.43	31.79	8	✪✪✪✪✪	4	37.30	7	N.A.	
	FRF	91.61	Sogelux Fd Money Mkt FRF	S037	31/03/88	LUX	-7.01	12	-2.61	19	2.37	31.98	6	✪✪✪	4	40	3	N.A.	
	FRF	32.55	Sogenalux Treasury FRF B	S037	30/06/92	LUX	-7.07	21	-2.87	24	2.43	30.74	19	✪✪	2	N.A.		N.A.	
	FRF	80.37	Swissca MM Fund FRF	S058	31/07/92	LUX	-6.99	7	-2.16	4	2.45	31.82	7	✪✪✪✪	4	N.A.		N.A.	
	FRF	13.59	Trans Monetary FRF	N003	03/01/92	LUX	-7.13	31	-3.03	27	2.43	29.68	27	✪	2	N.A.		N.A.	
	FRF	482.20	UBS (Lux) Money Mkt Invst FRF	U001	30/09/91	LUX	-6.98	3	-2.35	12	2.41	31.19	14	✪✪✪✪	3	36.89	10	N.A.	

▲ SIB Approved ● Insurance Fund **Values in US Dollars, on an offer to offer price basis with gross income reinvested** Data Source Micropal™

German DMark Money Market

Funds investing solely in German Deutschmark denominated money market or cash instruments with durations ranging from overnight to twelve months. Investments will normally be held in bank deposits, short-term monetary investments (e.g. T. Bills and certificates of deposits).

	CCY	Fund Size ($mil)	Fund Name	Manager Code	Fund Start Date	Domicile Code	3 Mths 97 % Chg	3 Mths 97 Rank	1 Year % Chg	1 Year Rank	Micropal Star Rating 3 Years Volatility	3 Years % Chg	3 Years Rank	3 Years Rating	Risk Return Rating	5 Years % Chg	5 Years Rank	10 Years % Chg	10 Years Rank
		339.26	**Mean/Count**				**-7.15**	**101**	**-4.60**	**97**	**2.60**	**25.76**	**76**		**2**	**27.90**	**48**	**105.99**	**14**
	DEM	169.31	A.L.S.A. DM Cash	A007	30/11/93	LUX	-7.06	27	-4.14	12	3.35	28.05	4	✪✪✪✪✪	5	N.A.		N.A.	
	DEM	942.75	A.L.S.A. DM Rentplus	A007	28/02/92	LUX	-7.04	15	-3.72	3	2.57	30.29	1	✪✪✪✪✪	5	N.A.		N.A.	
▲	DEM	48.87	ABN AMRO Interest Growth DEM	A001	31/05/93	LUX	-7.15	69	-4.45	40	2.60	26.49	31	✪✪✪	3	N.A.		N.A.	
▲	DEM	14.22	AEB Worldfolio 2 DM Daily Inc	A009	26/02/93	LUX	-5.68	2	-4.35	33	2.55	26.76	24	✪✪✪✪	3	N.A.		N.A.	
▲	DEM	2.32	Aetna IUF Deutschmark Res A	A011	29/04/88	LUX	-7.20	85	-4.81	72	2.65	25.34	52	✪✪	2	25.72	40	N.A.	
	DEM	N.S.	Aqua Allemagne Cap	B026	31/05/91	LUX	-7.07	33	-4.61	55	2.57	25.93	42	✪✪	2	28.12	28	N.A.	
	DEM	259.71	Baer Multicash DM Cash	J007	30/04/91	LUX	-7.12	58	-4.23	18	2.55	27.48	11	✪✪✪✪	4	30.91	5	N.A.	
▲	DEM	3.67	Barclays MCF Deutschemark	B048	31/10/84	JER	-7.18	79	-5.05	81	2.58	24.09	64	✪	1	25.73	39	104.85	10
	DEM	134.77	BBL Renta Cash DEM C	B052	31/03/89	LUX	-7.11	53	-4.69	61	2.58	25.60	49	✪✪	2	27.90	29	N.A.	
	DEM	60.98	BBL Renta Cash Sht-Med DEM C	B052	30/07/93	LUX	-7.05	19	-4.41	35	2.52	23.07	69	✪	1	N.A.		N.A.	
	DEM	6.43	Bermuda Money DEM	B066	28/02/94	BER	-7.08	37	-4.73	66	N.A.	N.A.				N.A.		N.A.	
	DEM	406.97	BIL Money Market DEM	B067	31/07/90	LUX	-7.08	38	-4.66	60	2.58	26.02	40	✪✪	2	28.68	21	N.A.	
●	DEM	29.06	BL Money Trust DM B	B025	30/03/90	LUX	-7.03	12	-4.14	11	2.56	25.88	43	✪✪	2	28.97	20	N.A.	
	DEM	4439.79	CB Geldmarkt Deutschland I	A007	28/02/95	LUX	-7.04	18	-4.43	38	N.A.	N.A.				N.A.		N.A.	
	DEM	345.61	CB Lux Portfolio DM Cash	A007	31/03/93	LUX	-7.15	68	-4.57	50	2.58	26.62	28	✪✪✪✪	3	N.A.		N.A.	
	DEM	1393.46	CB MMF D-MARK	A007	31/03/95	LUX	-6.98	7	-4.20	15	N.A.	N.A.				N.A.		N.A.	
▲●	DEM	305.43	Citicurr DEM Portfolio	C029	31/03/89	LUX	-7.02	11	-4.40	34	2.57	26.24	34	✪✪✪	3	27.83	30	N.A.	
▲	DEM	251.23	Citifonds 360	C030	31/01/95	LUX	-7.11	51	-4.60	53	N.A.	N.A.				N.A.		N.A.	
▲	DEM	165.58	Citifonds 90	C030	31/01/95	LUX	-7.11	54	-4.57	48	N.A.	N.A.				N.A.		N.A.	
▲	DEM	2.87	CMI GNF DEM Curr Reserve	C042	29/04/94	LUX	-7.14	67	-6.04	97	N.A.	N.A.				N.A.		N.A.	
▲	DEM	45.52	Coutts DEM Liquidity	C053	31/05/83	JER	-7.07	30	-4.65	57	2.57	26.31	33	✪✪✪	3	28.56	22	113.58	2
●	DEM	4092.85	Credis Money Market Fund DEM	C057	30/08/85	LUX	-6.93	4	-4.09	9	2.58	27.87	8	✪✪✪✪✪	4	30.13	11	117.97	1
▲	DEM	7.94	CU PP DM Reserve Acc	C070	31/05/90	LUX	-7.12	55	-4.88	75	2.58	24.47	59	✪	1	24.55	44	N.A.	
	DEM	9.34	Currency Mgt Fd German Marks	I008	30/11/92	LUX	-7.07	35	-4.54	46	2.58	26.20	36	✪✪✪	3	N.A.		N.A.	
▲●	DEM	1076.83	DBIM DM Reserve	D006	29/07/88	LUX	-6.84	3	-3.33	1	2.51	26.59	29	✪✪	4	30.91	6	N.A.	
●	DEM	100.56	DBIM R & S Garant	D006	30/06/92	LUX	-7.21	86	-4.31	21	2.59	27.11	14	✪✪✪✪	4	N.A.		N.A.	
●	DEM	1859.74	DBIM Rendite Garant	D006	31/07/91	LUX	-7.06	26	-4.62	56	2.92	26.81	23	✪✪✪✪	3	29.88	13	N.A.	
	DEM	565.20	DekaLux Cash DM (A)	D009	31/07/91	LUX	-7.12	57	-4.19	13	2.55	27.96	5	✪✪✪✪	5	30.76	7	N.A.	
	DEM	860.97	DekaLux Flex	D009	29/12/89	LUX	-7.12	63	-4.10	10	2.55	27.96	6	✪✪✪✪✪	5	31.35	3	N.A.	
	DEM	1384.70	DekaLux Treasury: DM	D009	26/08/94	LUX	-7.07	29	-4.57	49	N.A.	N.A.				N.A.		N.A.	
	DEM	16.72	DekaLux-MoneyMarket: DM	D009	26/08/94	LUX	-7.05	21	-4.35	31	N.A.	N.A.				N.A.		N.A.	
	DEM	9.65	Deuro Cash JPM	J006	30/04/93	LUX	-7.12	60	-4.29	20	2.56	26.23	35	✪✪✪	3	N.A.		N.A.	
●	DEM	33.13	Dit Lux Cash DM A	D017	30/06/94	LUX	-7.12	59	-4.66	59	N.A.	N.A.				N.A.		N.A.	
●	DEM	362.27	Dit Lux DM Garantie	D017	28/06/91	LUX	-7.08	40	-4.32	27	2.55	27.52	10	✪✪✪✪✪	4	31.24	4	N.A.	
●	DEM	6.06	Eagle Star DM Secure Money	E001	29/09/95	IOM	-7.10	47	-4.80	71	N.A.	N.A.				N.A.		N.A.	
	DEM	N.S.	EPIC MF DM Daily Income	A024	20/10/95	LUX	-7.31	94	-5.06	83	N.A.	N.A.				N.A.		N.A.	
	FRF	4.47	Eurobc Multidevises	O001	30/09/93	LUX	-7.34	95	-5.11	87	2.75	24.26	62	✪✪	1	N.A.		N.A.	
▲	DEM	89.06	Fidelity Cash DEM	F010	30/09/93	LUX	-7.07	34	-4.58	51	2.57	25.24	54	✪✪	2	N.A.		N.A.	
	DEM	133.22	Fidelity DMK Currency Acc	F013	29/11/91	BER	-7.20	83	-5.12	89	2.58	23.95	65	✪	1	25.22	41	N.A.	
▲	DEM	4.91	Five Arrows CFL Deutschemark	R010	30/04/84	GU	-7.20	81	-5.18	90	2.66	23.85	67	✪✪	1	26.02	37	106.66	8
▲	DEM	55.09	Five Arrows IRL Deutschemark	R017	31/07/80	GU	-7.17	77	-5.06	82	2.58	24.35	61	✪	1	26.13	36	109.13	7
▲	DEM	96.98	Fleming FF Series II DEM	F020	30/09/92	LUX	-7.06	24	-4.43	39	2.58	26.90	18	✪✪✪✪	4	N.A.		N.A.	
	DEM	17.07	Force Cash Traditionnel DEM	B073	30/06/95	LUX	-7.12	62	-4.79	70	N.A.	N.A.				N.A.		N.A.	
	DEM	22.25	Fructilux Court Terme DEM	B043	26/02/93	LUX	-7.05	22	-4.60	54	2.58	26.16	38	✪✪✪	2	N.A.		N.A.	
	DEM	126.22	G-Treasury Deutschmark B	G009	29/07/94	LUX	-7.09	45	-4.34	30	N.A.	N.A.				N.A.		N.A.	
	DEM	201.48	G-Treasury Intl Deutschmark B	G009	29/07/94	LUX	-7.08	39	-4.28	19	N.A.	N.A.				N.A.		N.A.	
▲	DEM	12.83	Gartmore CSF DEM Money	G007	31/05/84	JER	-7.28	92	-5.33	92	2.59	23.67	68	✪	1	25.06	42	104.16	11
▲●	DEM	20.94	Groupe Indosuez DM Reserve	G017	31/01/91	LUX	-7.17	78	-4.92	79	2.59	26.49	30	✪✪✪	3	27.72	31	N.A.	
	DEM	2.76	GSAM MMF Deutschemark	G003	30/01/87	IOM	-7.16	72	-3.75	4	2.53	25.98	41	✪✪	3	28.30	24	N.A.	
▲	DEM	2.19	Guinness Fl IF Deutschemark	G020	30/09/83	GU	-7.13	64	-4.75	67	2.58	25.51	51	✪✪	2	28.24	26	112.97	3
▲	DEM	2.19	Guinness Flight DMark Money	G019	31/01/85	GU	-7.11	52	-4.72	63	2.72	25.53	50	✪✪	2	28.18	27	112.70	4
●	DEM	0.80	Hansard Deutschmark Deposit	H011	30/04/90	IOM	-7.24	88	-5.80	94	2.55	21.22	74	✪	1	19.59	48	N.A.	
▲	DEM	1.42	Hill Samuel ICF Deutschmark	H030	30/06/82	JER	-7.26	91	-5.45	93	2.58	22.71	72	✪	1	23.40	45	101.41	13
	DEM	179.95	HYPO DM Cash Plus	H024	31/10/90	LUX	-7.08	41	-4.59	52	2.69	26.07	39	✪✪✪	2	28.47	23	N.A.	
	DEM	116.25	HYPO DM Garantie	H024	30/04/92	LUX	-7.23	87	-4.55	47	2.58	26.99	16	✪✪✪	4	N.A.		N.A.	
	DEM	144.96	HYPO DM Kurz	H024	29/12/89	LUX	-9.89	101	-4.21	16	2.49	27.27	13	✪✪✪✪	4	30	12	N.A.	
	DEM	247.48	Hypo GeldMarkt 1	H024	15/12/95	LUX	-8.07	99	-4.72	65	N.A.	N.A.				N.A.		N.A.	

▲ SIB Approved ● Insurance Fund **Values in US Dollars, on an offer to offer price basis with gross income reinvested** Data Source Micropal™

German DMark Money Market

continued

	CCY	Fund Size ($mil)	Fund Name	Manager Code	Fund Start Date	Domicile Code	3 Mths 97 % Chg	3 Mths 97 Rank	1 Year % Chg	1 Year Rank	Micropal Star Rating 3 Years Volatility	3 Years % Chg	3 Years Rank	3 Years Rating	Risk Return Rating	5 Years % Chg	5 Years Rank	10 Years % Chg	10 Years Rank
		339.26	**Mean/Count**				**-7.15**	**101**	**-4.60**	**97**	**2.60**	**25.76**	**76**		**2**	**27.90**	**48**	**105.99**	**14**
▲	DEM	115.91	Inter Cash DEM	B069	29/09/89	LUX	-7.10	48	-4.20	14	2.56	26.65	27	✪✪✪	3	29.12	18	N.A.	
	DEM	4.70	JF Money Fund DEM	J004	29/04/88	HK	-7.07	31	-4.50	41	2.59	26.88	20	✪✪✪✪	3	30.63	8	N.A.	
●	DEM	0.51	JRIA Deutschmark Deposit	J002	29/01/93	IRL	-7.36	96	-5.85	95	2.57	21.18	75	✪	1	N.A.		N.A.	
●	DEM	0.05	JRIA Spec Deposit Deutschmark	J002	31/12/92	IRL	-7.13	66	-4.89	76	2.58	24.91	55	✪	2	N.A.		N.A.	
	DEM	6.74	Lazard Deutschemark Liquidity	L002	30/11/84	GU	-7.19	80	-4.82	73	2.57	25.31	53	✪✪	2	27.46	33	111	6
	DEM	100.88	Lion Interinvest Cash DM	C062	30/06/87	LUX	-6.96	5	-4.23	17	2.58	27.88	7	✪✪✪✪✪	4	31.76	1	N.A.	
	DEM	83.46	Lloyds Intl Liquidity DEM	L015	29/09/89	LUX	-7.12	56	-4.65	58	2.57	25.63	48	✪✪	2	27.49	32	N.A.	
▲	DEM	29.98	Lloyds Intl MMF DEM	L017	31/05/85	GU	-7.15	70	-4.91	78	2.58	24.91	56	✪	2	27.44	34	111.20	5
	DEM	90.98	Lux Awo	M034	31/10/91	LUX	-7.01	8	-4.71	62	2.56	25.86	44	✪✪	2	26.27	35	N.A.	
	DEM	80.61	Luxcash Deutsche Mark A Cap	C002	29/06/90	LUX	-7.06	25	-4.53	45	2.57	26.19	37	✪✪✪	3	28.30	25	N.A.	
	DEM	81.42	Luxinvest LiquiRent DM	B061	30/04/92	LUX	-7.16	75	-4.78	68	2.53	22.74	71	✪	1	N.A.		N.A.	
	DEM	N.S.	MeesPierson UF DEM Reserve	M012	01/03/96	LUX	-8.24	100	N.A.		N.A.	N.A.				N.A.		N.A.	
	DEM	2.31	Mega Liquid	M034	31/03/93	LUX	N.A.	—	-3.35	2	2.44	25.72	46	✪✪✪	5	N.A.		N.A.	
▲	DEM	26.90	Mercury ST DEM Reserve	M021	30/11/93	LUX	-7.11	50	-4.42	37	2.56	26.73	25	✪✪✪	3	N.A.		N.A.	
	DEM	2.55	MOSAIS Court Terme DEM	C058	28/02/95	LUX	-7.26	90	-4.90	77	N.A.	N.A.				N.A.		N.A.	
	DEM	12.21	Multibond Acticash DEM B	C015	31/01/91	LUX	-7.16	74	-3.91	5	2.56	28.56	3	✪✪✪✪	5	20.99	47	N.A.	
▲	DEM	3.15	Newton UGF Deutschmark	N006	31/03/82	JER	-7.20	84	-5.08	85	2.58	24.52	58	✪	2	25.86	38	105.09	9
	DEM	0.03	North Star Intl Money DEM	N012	31/05/93	CA	-7.54	97	-5.33	91	2.59	22.84	70	✪	1	N.A.		N.A.	
	DEM	17.84	Panelfund Kurz DEM Cap	A037	30/07/93	LUX	-7.04	16	-4.35	32	2.57	26.93	17	✪✪✪✪	4	N.A.		N.A.	
	DEM	141.22	Parvest Short Term DEM B	B037	31/12/92	LUX	-7.13	65	-4.78	69	2.58	25.64	47	✪✪	2	N.A.		N.A.	
	DEM	N.S.	Pioneer Dm Cashfonds	P017	22/12/95	IRL	-7.04	14	-4.09	8	N.A.	N.A.				N.A.		N.A.	
	DEM	454.87	Postbank Rendite DM Cash	P019	31/10/94	LUX	-7.10	49	-4.32	25	N.A.	N.A.				N.A.		N.A.	
	DEM	25.84	Proventus DM Liquidity C	P013	28/02/89	LUX	-7.03	13	-4.34	29	3.03	26.81	22	✪✪	1	29.10	19	N.A.	
▲	DEM	1.41	RBC ICF Deutschemark	R003	30/11/82	GU	-7.16	76	-5.12	88	2.57	23.86	66	✪	1	24.86	43	102.31	12
	DEM	3.34	RBC IMMF DEM Dist	R002	30/09/92	GU	-7.20	82	-4.84	74	2.50	24.41	60	✪	2	N.A.		N.A.	
	GBP	0.68	Royal Life/Guin Fl IFMF DEM	R026	31/12/86	IOM	-7.95	98	-5.06	84	2.71	21.92	73	✪✪	1	23.03	46	70.84	14
▲	DEM	126.30	SBC Dynamic Floor Fd DEM 100%	S007	19/07/96	LUX	-5.66	1	N.A.		N.A.	N.A.				N.A.		N.A.	
	DEM	3103.84	SBC Money Market Fund DEM	S007	28/09/90	LUX	-7.07	32	-4.42	36	2.57	26.38	32	✪✪✪	3	30.14	10	N.A.	
	DEM	23.48	Sicaro Zone DEM B	B019	28/02/95	LUX	-7.09	44	-4.51	42	N.A.	N.A.				N.A.		N.A.	
	DEM	16.63	Sogelux Fd Money Mkt DEM	S037	21/06/96	LUX	-7.07	28	N.A.		N.A.	N.A.				N.A.		N.A.	
	DEM	33.94	Sogenalux Treasury DEM B	S037	30/06/92	LUX	-7.12	61	-4.72	64	2.58	25.80	45	✪✪	2	N.A.		N.A.	
	DEM	N.S.	Sun Life Money DEM	S053	30/04/93	IOM	-7.15	71	-5.91	96	2.60	24.62	57	✪	1	N.A.		N.A.	
	DEM	641.98	Swissca MM Fund DEM	S058	30/04/91	LUX	-7.04	17	-4.32	23	2.59	27.10	15	✪✪✪✪	4	29.43	15	N.A.	
	DEM	0.64	Syfrets GI DEM Money Mkt	S060	10/11/95	CA	-7.24	89	-5.08	86	N.A.	N.A.				N.A.		N.A.	
▲	DEM	4.94	TGA DEM Lqd Ass	T009	31/03/89	LUX	-7.05	20	-4.04	7	2.67	26.69	26	✪✪✪	4	29.27	16	N.A.	
	DEM	29.87	Trans Monetary DEM	N003	31/01/92	LUX	-7.09	46	-4.94	80	2.57	24.19	63	✪	1	N.A.		N.A.	
	DEM	3053.90	UBS (Lux) Short Term Invt DEM	U001	31/07/90	LUX	-7.08	36	-4.53	44	2.57	26.85	21	✪✪✪✪	4	29.51	14	N.A.	
	DEM	24.06	UBZ Liquidity DEM	U002	29/03/91	IRL	-7.02	10	-4.33	28	2.56	27.43	12	✪✪✪✪	4	29.12	17	N.A.	
	DEM	1871.77	UI Money Market DEM	U012	30/12/94	LUX	-7.02	9	-4.32	24	N.A.	N.A.				N.A.		N.A.	
	DEM	399.94	Unicash	U012	31/05/90	LUX	-7.31	93	-4.04	6	2.53	28.79	2	✪✪✪✪	5	31.47	2	N.A.	
	DEM	116.06	Unico UF DEM Reserve	U006	29/05/92	LUX	-6.97	6	-4.32	26	2.49	20.52	76	✪	1	N.A.		N.A.	
	DEM	411.52	UniEuroCash	U012	31/10/91	LUX	-7.09	42	-4.31	22	2.57	27.78	9	✪✪✪✪✪	4	30.30	9	N.A.	
	DEM	186.23	Vereins Lux Portf DM Cash	A007	31/03/93	LUX	-7.16	73	-4.52	43	2.57	26.89	19	✪✪✪✪	4	N.A.		N.A.	

▲ SIB Approved ● Insurance Fund **Values in US Dollars, on an offer to offer price basis with gross income reinvested** Data Source Micropal™

Hong Kong Dollar Money Market

Funds investing solely in Hong Kong Dollar denominated money market or cash instruments with durations ranging from overnight to twelve months. Investments will normally be held in bank deposits, short-term monetary investments (e.g. T. Bills and certificates of deposits).

	CCY	Fund Size ($mil)	Fund Name	Manager Code	Fund Start Date	Domicile Code	3 Mths 97 % Chg	Rank	1 Year % Chg	Rank	Micropal Star Rating: Volatility	3 Years % Chg	Rank	Rating	Risk Return Rating	5 Years % Chg	Rank	10 Years % Chg	Rank
		9.25	**Mean/Count**				**0.90**	**7**	**4.62**	**7**	**0.28**	**13.90**	**5**			**21.79**	**5**	**56.37**	**2**
▲	HKD	19.46	Fidelity HKD Currency Acc	F013	29/11/91	BER	0.80	7	4.48	4	0.09	14.43	3	✪✪✪		22.57	3	N.A.	
▲	HKD	0.07	Five Arrows CFL HK Dllr	R010	30/04/84	GU	0.85	4	4.11	6	0.74	12.29	4	✪✪		18.18	5	55.79	2
▲	HKD	1.23	Five Arrows IRL HK Dllr	R017	30/04/84	GU	0.81	5	3.99	7	0.09	11.88	5	✪		18.27	4	56.95	1
	HKD	14.47	HSBC GMF Hong Kong Dllr	H035	29/03/91	CA	1.02	2	5.14	1	0.08	15.47	1	✪✪✪✪		25.85	1	N.A.	
	HKD	17.31	JF Money Fund HKD	J004	31/12/87	HK	1.02	1	5.12	2	0.38	15.42	2	✪✪✪		24.08	2	N.A.	
	HKD	5.02	Schroder HK Dllr Fixed Income	S011	28/07/95	HK	0.80	6	4.47	5	N.A.	N.A.				N.A.		N.A.	
	HKD	7.20	Schroder Hong Kong Money Mkt	S011	29/12/95	HK	1.02	3	5.03	3	N.A.	N.A.				N.A.		N.A.	

Indonesian Rupiah Money Market

Funds investing solely in Indonesian Rupiah denominated money market or cash instruments with durations ranging from overnight to twelve months. Investments will normally be held in bank deposits, short-term monetary investments (e.g. T. Bills and certificates of deposits).

CCY	Fund Size ($mil)	Fund Name	Manager Code	Fund Start Date	Domicile Code	3 Mths 97 % Chg	Rank	1 Year % Chg	Rank	Micropal Star Rating: Volatility	3 Years % Chg	Rank	Rating	Risk Return Rating	5 Years % Chg	Rank	10 Years % Chg	Rank
	5.34	**Mean/Count**				**1.65**	**1**	**11.83**	**1**	**0.55**	**32.79**	**1**		**3**	**63.11**	**1**	**0**	**0**
USD	5.34	Lippo Indonesia Rup Money Mkt	L012	31/12/91	CA	1.65	1	11.83	1	0.55	32.79	1	✪✪✪	3	63.11	1	N.A.	

Irish Punt Money Market

Funds investing solely in Irish Punt denominated money market or cash instruments with durations ranging from overnight to twelve months. Investments will normally be held in bank deposits, short-term monetary investments (e.g. T. Bills and certificates of deposits).

	CCY	Fund Size ($mil)	Fund Name	Manager Code	Fund Start Date	Domicile Code	3 Mths 97 % Chg	Rank	1 Year % Chg	Rank	Micropal Star Rating: Volatility	3 Years % Chg	Rank	Rating	Risk Return Rating	5 Years % Chg	Rank	10 Years % Chg	Rank
		16.14	**Mean/Count**				**-5.29**	**1**	**9.66**	**2**	**1.75**	**38.62**	**1**		**1**	**34.92**	**1**	**0**	**0**
▲	IEP	0.91	AIB Grofund Irish Pnd Curr	A015	31/05/94	IRL			8.96	2	N.A.	N.A.				N.A.		N.A.	
	IEP	31.37	Bk of Ire Glbl Irish Pnd Curr	B018	30/11/88	IOM	-5.29	1	10.36	1	1.75	38.62	1	✪✪✪	3	34.92	1	N.A.	

▲ **SIB Approved** ● **Insurance Fund** **Values in US Dollars, on an offer to offer price basis with gross income reinvested** Data Source Micropal™

Italian Lire Money Market

Funds investing solely in Italian Lire denominated money market or cash instruments with durations ranging from overnight to twelve months. Investments will normally be held in bank deposits, short-term monetary investments (e.g. T. Bills and certificates of deposits).

	CCY	Fund Size ($mil)	Fund Name	Manager Code	Fund Start Date	Domicile Code	3 Mths 97 % Chg	3 Mths 97 Rank	1 Year % Chg	1 Year Rank	Micropal Star Rating 3 Years Volatility	3 Years % Chg	3 Years Rank	3 Years Rating	Risk Return Rating	5 Years % Chg	5 Years Rank	10 Years % Chg	10 Years Rank
		164.71	**Mean/Count**				**-7.42**	**12**	**13.47**	**9**	**1.79**	**44.19**	**7**		**1**	**19.82**	**5**	**127.89**	**2**
	ITL	0.48	Bermuda Money ITL	B066	31/05/94	BER	-7.38	2	12.92	7	N.A.	N.A.				N.A.		N.A.	
●	ITL	0.02	DBIM Lire Reserve	D006	30/06/92	LUX	-7.19	1	15.87	1	1.75	47.29	1	✪✪✪✪	4	N.A.		N.A.	
▲	ITL	13.48	Fidelity ITL Currency Acc	F013	29/11/91	BER	-7.47	11	12.82	9	1.73	42.69	6	✪	2	19.41	4	N.A.	
▲	ITL	1.07	Five Arrows CFL Italian Lire	R010	30/04/84	GU	-7.46	9	12.88	8	2.14	42.62	7	✪✪✪	1	19.55	3	128.41	1
▲	ITL	9.74	Five Arrows IRL Italian Lire	R017	31/07/80	GU	-7.44	7	12.95	6	1.73	42.83	5	✪✪	2	18.96	5	127.37	2
▲	ITL	15.77	Fleming FF Series II ITL	F020	12/01/96	LUX	-7.46	10	N.A.		N.A.	N.A.				N.A.		N.A.	
	ITL	28.03	Parvest Short Term ITL B	B037	31/10/94	LUX	-7.58	12	13.14	5	N.A.	N.A.				N.A.		N.A.	
	ITL	756.71	SBC Money Market Fund ITL	S007	31/07/91	LUX	-7.42	6	13.59	3	1.72	45.02	3	✪✪✪	4	21.59	1	N.A.	
	ITL	4.32	Sogelux Fd Money Mkt ITL	S037	21/06/96	LUX	-7.41	5	N.A.		N.A.	N.A.				N.A.		N.A.	
	ITL	119.69	Swissca MM Fund ITL	S058	31/07/92	LUX	-7.41	4	13.70	2	1.75	45.41	2	✪✪✪✪	3	N.A.		N.A.	
	ITL	862.54	UBS (Lux) Money Mkt Invst ITL	U001	31/01/91	LUX	-7.40	3	13.35	4	1.74	43.44	4	✪✪	3	19.60	2	N.A.	

Japanese Yen Money Market

Funds investing solely in Japanese Yen denominated money market or cash instruments with durations ranging from overnight to twelve months. Investments will normally be held in bank deposits, short-term monetary investments (e.g. T. Bills and certificates of deposit).

	CCY	Fund Size ($mil)	Fund Name	Manager Code	Fund Start Date	Domicile Code	3 Mths 97 % Chg	3 Mths 97 Rank	1 Year % Chg	1 Year Rank	Micropal Star Rating 3 Years Volatility	3 Years % Chg	3 Years Rank	3 Years Rating	Risk Return Rating	5 Years % Chg	5 Years Rank	10 Years % Chg	10 Years Rank
		10.80	**Mean/Count**				**-6.26**	**22**	**-11.13**	**21**	**3.50**	**-2.12**	**18**			**16.50**	**15**	**86.24**	**4**
▲	JPY	0.92	Aetna IUF Yen Reserve A	A011	29/04/88	LUX	-6.25	15	-10.98	7	3.51	-3.28	18	✪✪		16.56	9	N.A.	
	JPY	2.63	BBL Renta Cash JPY C	B052	28/02/89	LUX	-6.20	6	-11.01	8	3.50	-1.76	6	✪✪✪		16.88	6	N.A.	
	JPY	0.40	Bermuda Money JPY	B066	24/06/94	BER	-6.19	5	-10.95	5	N.A.	N.A.				N.A.		N.A.	
●	JPY	18.55	Credis Money Market Fund JPY	C057	28/02/86	LUX	-6.34	18	-11.21	15	3.51	-1.50	3	✪✪✪✪		18.32	2	91.05	1
▲	JPY	2.95	CU PP Yen Reserve ACC	C070	31/05/90	LUX	-6.58	22	-11.49	19	3.48	-2.16	10	✪✪✪		14.20	15	N.A.	
	JPY	9.94	Eagle Star Jap Secure Money	E001	29/09/95	IOM	-6.15	1	-10.64	1	N.A.	N.A.				N.A.		N.A.	
▲	JPY	3.29	Fidelity JPY Currency Acc	F013	29/11/91	BER	-6.22	10	-11.05	10	3.49	-2.50	13	✪		15.16	11	N.A.	
▲●	JPY	0.40	Groupe Indosuez Yen Reserve	G017	31/01/91	LUX	-6.38	19	-11.65	21	3.52	-2.54	14	✪		14.79	13	N.A.	
▲	JPY	0.57	Guinness Fl IF Japanese Yen	G020	30/09/83	GU	-6.24	13	-11.09	12	3.50	-1.95	8	✪✪✪		16.73	7	87.69	2
▲	JPY	0.25	Guinness Flight Yen Money	G019	31/01/85	GU	-6.23	12	-11.08	11	3.51	-1.86	7	✪✪✪		16.69	8	87.35	3
	JPY	8.44	JF Money Fund JPY	J004	29/04/88	HK	-6.25	14	-11.11	13	3.51	-1.12	1	✪✪✪✪		18.92	1	N.A.	
	JPY	2.74	Lloyds Intl Liquidity JPY	L015	29/09/89	LUX	-6.18	4	-10.89	3	3.50	-1.75	5	✪✪✪✪		17.10	5	N.A.	
▲	JPY	1.51	Lloyds Intl MMF JPY	L017	31/03/87	GU	-6.22	9	-11.04	9	3.50	-2.20	11	✪✪		16.19	10	N.A.	
▲	JPY	5.89	Nikko CF Yen Portfolio	N008	28/04/95	LUX	-6.16	2	-10.91	4	N.A.	N.A.				N.A.		N.A.	
▲	JPY	0.50	RBC ICF Japanese Yen	R003	30/11/82	GU	-6.22	8	-11.32	16	3.50	-2.81	16	✪		14.72	14	78.86	4
	JPY	1.62	RBC IMMF Yen Dist	R002	29/01/93	GU	-6.39	20	-11.54	20	3.47	-2.67	15	✪		N.A.		N.A.	
	JPY	125.72	SBC Money Market Fund JPY	S007	31/05/90	LUX	-6.23	11	-10.95	6	3.49	-2.15	9	✪✪		18.09	4	N.A.	
	JPY	3.05	Swissca MM Fund JPY	S058	31/07/92	LUX	-6.17	3	-10.80	2	3.50	-1.15	2	✪✪✪✪✪		N.A.		N.A.	
▲	JPY	3.59	TGA Yen Lqd Ass	T009	28/02/89	LUX	-6.28	17	-11.46	18	3.51	-2.89	17	✪✪		15.01	12	N.A.	
	JPY	1.06	Trans Monetary JPY	N003	31/01/92	LUX	-6.41	21	-11.38	17	3.51	-2.27	12	✪✪		N.A.		N.A.	
	JPY	32.68	UBS (Lux) Money Mkt Invst JPY	U001	31/10/89	LUX	-6.21	7	-11.14	14	3.51	-1.52	4	✪✪✪✪		18.16	3	N.A.	

▲ SIB Approved ● Insurance Fund **Values in US Dollars, on an offer to offer price basis with gross income reinvested** Data Source Micropal™

Managed Currency Money Market

Funds investing solely in money market or cash instruments with durations ranging from overnight to twelve months with an objective of maximising the value of liquid assets via the management of currency exposure. Investments will normally be held in bank deposits, short-term monetary investments and forward currency contracts.

	CCY	Fund Size ($mil)	Fund Name	Manager Code	Fund Start Date	Domicile Code	3 Mths 97 % Chg	3 Mths 97 Rank	1 Year % Chg	1 Year Rank	Micropal Star Rating: Volatility	3 Years % Chg	3 Years Rank	Rating	Risk Return Rating	5 Years % Chg	5 Years Rank	10 Years % Chg	10 Years Rank
		38.94	**Mean/Count**				**-2.34**	**84**	**3.89**	**81**	**1.58**	**18.57**	**65**		**1**	**24.70**	**52**	**107.79**	**24**
	DEM	420.62	A.L.S.A. BIT	A007	30/10/92	LUX	-5.05	69	4.80	36	1.88	23.68	24	✪✪✪	2	N.A.		N.A.	
●	USD	15.50	AB Managed Currency	A027	30/11/89	GU	0.44	18	6.79	27	0.99	17.72	36	✪✪	5	29.50	13	N.A.	
▲	DEM	6.66	AIB Grofund DEM Mgd Curr	A015	13/01/95	JER	-5.81	72	-4.26	75	N.A.	N.A.				N.A.		N.A.	
▲	ECU	4.27	AIB Grofund ECU Mgd Currency	A015	28/02/86	JER	-4.31	65	0.47	61	1.94	26.12	17	✪✪✪✪	2	32.64	10	135.26	7
▲	IEP	38.61	AIB Grofund Irish Pnd Mgd Curr	A015	12/07/93	IRL	N.A.	—	7.15	24	1.68	30.32	9	✪✪✪✪✪	3	N.A.		N.A.	
▲	GBP	142.43	AIB Grofund Sterling Mgd Curr	A015	31/08/84	JER	-3.25	59	12.56	9	1.97	30.24	10	✪✪✪✪	3	25.26	25	178.84	1
▲	USD	33.13	AIB Grofund US Dllr Mgd Curr	A015	31/10/88	JER	1.10	12	2.40	53	0.58	12.79	43	✪		35.75	8	N.A.	
●	USD	2.56	Allied Dunbar IB Mgd Currency	A021	30/09/93	IOM	-0.28	24	-1.28	64	1.73	11.26	54	✪✪		N.A.		N.A.	
▲	USD	6.20	Allied Dunbar Mgd Currency	A020	31/05/84	IOM	-0.03	21	-1.47	68	1.48	11.79	49	✪		8.51	48	95.51	15
	USD	N.S.	Aqua Patrimoine	B026	30/10/87	LUX	-6.18	73	8.58	19	0.79	12.28	46	✪✪		29.57	12	N.A.	
	GBP	2.03	AXA Eqty&Law ILA Mgd Currency	A040	31/10/85	IOM	-6.94	78	15.99	2	1.69	20.61	30	✪✪✪	2	29.16	14	65.68	21
▲	USD	1.54	Barclays MCF Managed Dllr	B048	31/07/87	JER	-0.83	31	4.31	39	0.37	14.84	38	✪✪		19.87	38	N.A.	
▲	GBP	1.47	Barclays MCF Managed Stlg	B048	29/08/86	JER	-2.90	55	9.35	14	1.18	22.01	29	✪✪✪	3	19.88	37	92.51	16
	USD	19.60	Baring CUF Managed	B049	30/11/87	IRL	-2.10	40	4.73	37	0.94	19.17	34	✪✪	4	25.58	24	N.A.	
	GBP	24.83	Bk of Ire Glbl Mgd Curr	B018	30/04/87	IOM	-2.16	42	6.40	28	1.54	23.07	25	✪✪✪	2	16.13	43	N.A.	
	USD	0.06	CIBC-CEF Managed Currency	C017	30/12/88	BER	-7.04	79	-6.58	76	1.32	-4.05	64	✪		4.79	51	N.A.	
	USD	115.22	CitiLandmark Asia Income Fund	C033	30/11/95	LUX	1.34	10	7.11	25	N.A.	N.A.				N.A.		N.A.	
	USD	24.79	CitiLandmark Mgd Currency	C033	28/02/89	LUX	2.75	3	15.08	4	1.40	20.01	32	✪✪	2	26.83	21	N.A.	
●	CHF	55.39	Clariden Money Mkt CHF	C039	30/06/95	GU	-6.54	75	-12.92	80	N.A.	N.A.				N.A.		N.A.	
●	USD	250.21	Clariden Money Mkt USD	C039	31/07/95	GU	1.14	11	5.01	34	N.A.	N.A.				N.A.		N.A.	
	BEF	7.56	Currency Mgt Fd Liquid Mix C	I008	30/10/92	LUX	-6.19	74	-1.53	69	1.90	25.08	18	✪✪✪	2	N.A.		N.A.	
●	USD	177.10	DBIM Dragon Bond	D006	17/05/96	LUX	1.05	13	N.A.		N.A.	N.A.				N.A.		N.A.	
●	GBP	23.94	Eagle Star Eagle Secure	E001	29/02/88	IOM	-4.58	68	-3.16	73	2.17	11.16	55	✪✪		18.43	40	N.A.	
	CHF	6.82	EBC Traded Currency Capital	E004	31/01/84	JER	-0.27	23	-1.29	65	1.23	11.34	52	✪✪		6.62	49	54.93	23
	CHF	6.82	EBC Traded Currency Income	E004	31/01/84	JER	-0.26	22	-1.29	66	1.22	11.30	53	✪✪		6.43	50	56.20	22
●	GBP	0.17	Finistere Mgd Currency Life	F016	31/12/81	GU	-1.78	37	4.25	40	1.41	9.49	57	✪		25.79	23	92.21	17
▲	DEM	55.09	Five Arrows IRL Mgd DMark	R017	31/12/84	GU	-5.61	70	-3.29	74	2.11	19.63	33	✪✪✪	1	19.93	36	97.25	14
▲	USD	11.75	Five Arrows IRL Mgd Intl	R017	31/07/92	GU	-2.82	53	-1.40	67	0.92	12.27	47	✪		N.A.		N.A.	
▲	GBP	52.98	Five Arrows IRL Mgd Sterling	R017	31/12/84	GU	-3.13	58	13.84	7	1.73	27.43	15	✪✪✪✪	3	25.98	22	140.09	6
▲	USD	14.78	Five Arrows IRL Mgd US Dollar	R017	31/12/84	GU	0.36	20	4.04	42	0.34	11.47	51	✪		14.13	45	88.23	19
▲	GBP	2.88	Gartmore CSF Stlg Global Curr	G007	31/07/92	JER	-3.79	64	9.39	13	1.70	24.93	19	✪✪✪✪	3	N.A.		N.A.	
	USD	16.65	GNI Foreign Exchange	G012	30/06/94	BER	-8.33	82	-9.90	79	N.A.	N.A.				N.A.		N.A.	
	USD	109.70	Goldman Sachs Glbl Curr	G013	30/09/91	CA	0.52	17	11.25	12	0.84	24.59	21	✪✪✪✪	5	48.21	3	N.A.	
	CHF	14.16	Goldman Sachs Glbl Curr CHF	G013	30/11/93	CA	-6.72	76	-7.81	77	3.34	28.75	12	✪✪✪	1	N.A.		N.A.	
▲	USD	106.50	Guinness FI IF Mgd Currency	G020	30/05/80	GU	-2.49	45	2.67	52	0.75	9.92	56	✪		29.15	15	129.91	8
▲	USD	111.33	Guinness Flight Mgd Currency	G019	29/02/84	GU	-2.64	48	2.28	54	1.08	9.45	58	✪		28.64	16	121.77	10
▲	DEM	1.98	Hambros CF European Managed	H001	29/06/84	GU	-3.69	62	-2.97	72	2.25	13.45	42	✪✪		14.64	44	99.59	13
▲	GBP	4.31	Hambros CF Sterling Managed	H001	29/06/84	GU	-2.59	46	15.39	3	1.59	31.88	6	✪✪✪✪✪	3	17.27	42	142.28	4
▲	USD	0.78	Hambros CF US Dollar Managed	H001	29/06/84	GU	-0.38	27	4.85	35	0.36	14.66	39	✪✪		20.51	33	86.88	20
▲	DEM	1.64	Hambros EMMA Contl Euro Money	H002	29/04/88	GU	-7.15	80	-8.58	78	2.75	18.95	35	✪✪✪	1	20.48	34	N.A.	
▲	GBP	100.57	Hambros EMMA Managed	H002	29/04/88	GU	-4.44	67	12.17	11	1.91	30.19	11	✪✪✪✪✪	3	41.90	4	N.A.	
▲	USD	13.81	Hambros EMMA US Dollar Managed	H002	30/06/92	GU	-0.41	28	2.79	50	1.07	11.89	48	✪		N.A.		N.A.	
●	USD	7.85	Hansard\GF GSF Mgd Curr	H017	31/07/92	IOM	-3.50	61	-0.63	62	1.26	8.26	59	✪		N.A.		N.A.	
▲	GBP	23.29	Hill Samuel ICF Sterling Mgd	H030	30/06/82	JER	-2.84	54	9.08	16	1.38	28.11	13	✪✪✪✪✪	4	20.59	32	113.63	11
	USD	105	Inc Ptnrs GSF Asian Money Mkt	I006	25/11/94	CA	1.91	6	8.95	17	N.A.	N.A.				N.A.		N.A.	
●	LUF	14.54	InvestPlus Fix 2001	B035	28/02/95	LUX	-11.09	83	8.75	18	N.A.	N.A.				N.A.		N.A.	
●	LUF	24.59	InvestPlus Fix 2001 Bis	B035	28/04/95	LUX	-6.85	77	3.20	49	N.A.	N.A.				N.A.		N.A.	
	LUF	41.08	Ippa Portf Internat Money B	B035	31/03/88	LUX	-5.68	71	3.64	45	1.69	34.55	2	✪✪✪✪✪	4	38.89	5	N.A.	
	USD	31.73	JF Managed Currency	J004	29/03/91	CA	-3.04	56	12.47	10	1.55	35.35	1	✪✪✪✪	4	54.56	1	N.A.	
●	USD	2.60	JRIA Managed Currency	J002	29/01/93	IRL	-2.78	50	1.43	56	0.78	5.71	61	✪		N.A.		N.A.	
	USD	12.95	Lazard Managed Dllr Liquidity	L002	28/11/86	GU	-2.79	51	1.22	58	1.41	14.23	41	✪✪		19.71	39	106.27	12
▲	GBP	11	Lloyds Intl MMF Managed GBP	L017	31/05/88	GU	-3.04	57	14.73	5	1.93	33.31	4	✪✪✪✪✪	3	22.05	31	N.A.	
▲	USD	5.34	Lloyds Intl MMF Managed USD	L017	31/05/88	GU	0.64	15	3.41	46	0.40	12.72	44	✪✪		10.29	47	N.A.	
	USD	9.89	M.Lynch Sht Term World Inc A	M023	29/06/90	CA	0.41	19	4.36	38	0.59	7.27	60	✪		11.83	46	N.A.	
	USD	65.95	Money Manager I	C028	31/05/95	LUX	1.75	7	5.34	31	N.A.	N.A.				N.A.		N.A.	
	USD	28.93	Money Manager II	C028	31/05/95	LUX	2.30	4	5.24	32	N.A.	N.A.				N.A.		N.A.	
▲	USD	8.20	Newton UGF Mgd Currency	N006	29/05/87	JER	-0.33	25	6.29	30	0.58	14.31	40	✪✪		22.95	29	N.A.	

▲ SIB Approved ● Insurance Fund **Values in US Dollars, on an offer to offer price basis with gross income reinvested** Data Source Micropal™

Managed Currency Money Market

continued

	CCY	Fund Size ($mil)	Fund Name	Manager Code	Fund Start Date	Domicile Code	3 Mths 97 % Chg	3 Mths 97 Rank	1 Year % Chg	1 Year Rank	Micropal Star Rating 3 Years Volatility	3 Years % Chg	3 Years Rank	Rating	Risk Return Rating	5 Years % Chg	5 Years Rank	10 Years % Chg	10 Years Rank
		38.94	**Mean/Count**				**-2.34**	**84**	**3.89**	**81**	**1.58**	**18.57**	**65**		**1**	**24.70**	**52**	**107.79**	**24**
	CHF	0.53	North Star Intl Curr CHF	N012	30/04/90	CA	-2.06	39	-1.27	63	2.88	30.47	8	✪✪✪✪	1	23.49	28	N.A.	
	DEM	0.42	North Star Intl Curr DEM	N012	30/04/90	CA	-2.25	43	2.05	55	2.79	31.46	7	✪✪✪✪	2	24.98	27	N.A.	
	DKK	0.34	North Star Intl Curr DKK	N012	30/04/90	CA	-1.89	38	3.30	47	3	26.66	16	✪✪✪	1	36.80	7	N.A.	
	FRF	0.08	North Star Intl Curr FRF	N012	30/04/90	CA	-2.68	49	3.68	44	2.99	27.93	14	✪✪✪	1	35.66	9	N.A.	
	GBP	0.85	North Star Intl Curr GBP	N012	30/04/90	CA	1.67	8	20.75	1	3.23	32.02	5	✪✪✪	1	27.27	18	N.A.	
	JPY	0.16	North Star Intl Curr JPY	N012	30/04/90	CA	-0.36	26	2.77	51	3.17	34.48	3	✪✪✪✪	2	52.51	2	N.A.	
	SEK	0.10	North Star Intl Curr SEK	N012	30/04/91	CA	-0.69	30	3.24	48	3.12	24.32	22	✪✪✪	1	37.10	6	N.A.	
	USD	1.60	North Star Intl Curr USD	N012	30/04/90	CA	3.55	1	14.53	6	3.06	20.12	31	✪✪✪	1	32.21	11	N.A.	
	USD	0.86	Opportunity Real	O010	06/01/95	CA	1.58	9	9.20	15	N.A.	N.A.				N.A.		N.A.	
	FRF	1.80	Plurigestion PluriForex	M040	30/07/93	LUX	-18.74	84	-24.38	81	3.66	-30.61	65	✪		N.A.		N.A.	
	FRF	3.63	Proton IF Multi-Currency Bond	P024	29/09/95	BVI	-7.75	81	0.85	60	N.A.	N.A.				N.A.		N.A.	
▲	GBP	7.58	Prudential CF Growth D	P030	30/03/84	JER	-0.91	34	7.51	21	1.01	23.76	23	✪✪✪✪	4	28.46	17	147.29	2
▲	GBP	10.47	Prudential CF Income A	P030	29/05/81	JER	-0.91	32	7.21	22	1.25	23.01	27	✪✪✪✪	4	26.94	20	144.77	3
▲	GBP	0	Prudential CF Income B	P030	30/03/84	JER	-0.91	33	7.21	23	1.25	23.01	26	✪✪✪✪	4	26.94	19	140.55	5
▲	USD	2.25	Prudential Curr Mgd Dollar	H031	31/07/84	BER	-0.49	29	4.18	41	0.85	17.57	37	✪✪	5	20.42	35	91.99	18
▲	GBP	26.78	Prudential Curr Mgd Sterling	H031	31/07/84	BER	-1.10	35	6.85	26	1.26	22.13	28	✪✪✪✪	4	25.21	26	128.76	9
▲	USD	2.80	RBC ICF Managed	R003	30/11/82	GU	-2.80	52	1.03	59	0.49	5.12	62	✪		3.05	52	36.43	24
	USD	0.60	RLI/JF Managed Currency	R030	26/04/96	IOM	-3.38	60	N.A.		N.A.	N.A.				N.A.		N.A.	
	USD	3.50	Royal Life/Guin Fl IFMCF USD	R026	30/10/87	IOM	-2.37	44	1.35	57	1.34	3.72	63	✪		22.62	30	N.A.	
	USD	692.41	SBC Em Ec Portf Latin Am MM	S007	28/02/95	LUX	1.92	5	8.35	20	N.A.	N.A.				N.A.		N.A.	
	GBP	0.17	Scot Prov ILA Mgd Curr Stlg	S014	29/09/95	IOM	-4.44	66	5.09	33	N.A.	N.A.				N.A.		N.A.	
	USD	0.30	Scot Prov ILA Mgd Curr USD	S014	29/09/95	IOM	-2.63	47	-2.66	71	N.A.	N.A.				N.A.		N.A.	
▲	USD	37.46	Skandifond Dollar Currency	S030	29/01/88	LUX	1	14	-2.16	70	1.41	12.33	45	✪✪		18.23	41	N.A.	
	USD	35.57	Southern Intl Global Money Mkt	S041	31/07/96	LUX	-3.70	63	N.A.		N.A.	N.A.				N.A.		N.A.	
	GBP	0.51	Syfrets Gl Stlg Mgd Currency	S060	30/11/93	CA	-2.11	41	12.96	8	1.94	24.70	20	✪✪✪	2	N.A.		N.A.	
	USD	0.90	Syfrets Gl USD Mgd Currency	S060	30/11/93	CA	-1.18	36	6.39	29	0.56	11.50	50	✪		N.A.		N.A.	
	USD	0.74	Titan Currency Ptfl	T010	24/02/95	CA	3.54	2	3.92	43	N.A.	N.A.				N.A.		N.A.	

Netherlands Guilder Money Market

Funds investing solely in Netherlands Guilder denominated money market or cash instruments with durations ranging from overnight to twelve months. Investments will normally be held in bank deposits, short-term monetary investments (e.g. T. Bills and certificates of deposit).

	CCY	Fund Size ($mil)	Fund Name	Manager Code	Fund Start Date	Domicile Code	3 Mths 97 % Chg	3 Mths 97 Rank	1 Year % Chg	1 Year Rank	Micropal Star Rating 3 Years Volatility	3 Years % Chg	3 Years Rank	Rating	Risk Return Rating	5 Years % Chg	5 Years Rank	10 Years % Chg	10 Years Rank
		110.53	**Mean/Count**				**-7.30**	**22**	**-5.31**	**21**	**2.57**	**24.73**	**16**		**1**	**27.55**	**11**	**111.38**	**2**
▲	NLG	142.72	ABN AMRO Interest Growth NLG	A001	30/04/92	LUX	-7.34	16	-4.97	10	2.58	25.37	7	✪✪✪✪	4	N.A.		N.A.	
	NLG	104.52	BBL Renta Cash NLG C	B052	30/03/90	LUX	-7.32	15	-5.14	15	2.58	24.49	11	✪✪	2	27.27	8	N.A.	
	NLG	76.89	BBL Renta Cash Sht-Med NLG C	B052	30/07/93	LUX	-7.23	3	-4.92	7	2.52	22.22	16	✪	1	N.A.		N.A.	
	NLG	0.29	Bermuda Money NLG	B066	31/05/94	BER	-7.29	13	-11.36	21	N.A.	N.A.				N.A.		N.A.	
	NLG	105.91	BIL Money Market NLG	B067	30/04/91	LUX	-7.28	9	-5.19	16	2.58	24.65	10	✪✪	2	27.78	6	N.A.	
	NLG	26.93	Cera Cash NLG B	C018	29/07/94	LUX	-7.27	7	-5.13	14	N.A.	N.A.				N.A.		N.A.	
●	NLG	456.88	Credis Money Market Fund NLG	C057	31/10/91	LUX	-7.17	1	-4.74	3	2.59	25.51	5	✪✪✪	3	28.30	4	N.A.	
	NLG	69.85	Currency Mgt Fd Dutch Guilders	I008	31/07/92	LUX	-7.24	5	-4.84	5	2.56	25.40	6	✪✪✪	3	N.A.		N.A.	
●	NLG	27.27	DBIM Gulden Reserve	D006	31/12/91	LUX	-7.30	14	-3.50	1	2.55	28.51	1	✪✪✪✪✪	5	32.30	1	N.A.	
▲	NLG	2.41	Fidelity NLG Currency Acc	F013	29/11/91	BER	-7.41	21	-5.65	19	2.58	22.70	14	✪	1	24.81	10	N.A.	
▲	NLG	0.95	Five Arrows CFL Dutch Guilder	R010	30/04/84	GU	-7.40	20	-5.80	20	2.64	22.32	15	✪✪	1	24.28	11	110.24	2
▲	NLG	10.20	Five Arrows IRL Dutch Guilder	R017	31/07/80	GU	-7.38	19	-5.59	18	2.58	22.96	13	✪	1	25.26	9	112.53	1
	NLG	140.03	G-Treasury Florin B	G009	29/07/94	LUX	-7.20	2	-4.73	2	N.A.	N.A.				N.A.		N.A.	
	NLG	202.71	G-Treasury Intl Florin B	G009	29/07/94	LUX	-7.23	4	-4.76	4	N.A.	N.A.				N.A.		N.A.	
▲	NLG	11.36	Lloyds Intl MMF NLG	L017	31/07/92	GU	-7.35	17	-5.49	17	2.58	23.44	12	✪	2	N.A.		N.A.	

▲ SIB Approved ● Insurance Fund **Values in US Dollars, on an offer to offer price basis with gross income reinvested** Data Source Micropal™

Netherlands Guilder Money Market

continued

	CCY	Fund Size ($mil)	Fund Name	Manager Code	Fund Start Date	Domicile Code	3 Mths 97 % Chg	3 Mths 97 Rank	1 Year % Chg	1 Year Rank	Micropal Star Rating 3 Years Volatility	3 Years % Chg	3 Years Rank	3 Years Rating	Risk Return Rating	5 Years % Chg	5 Years Rank	10 Years % Chg	10 Years Rank
		110.53	**Mean/Count**				**-7.30**	**22**	**-5.31**	**21**	**2.57**	**24.73**	**16**		**1**	**27.55**	**11**	**111.38**	**2**
	NLG	11.42	Luxcash Florins Neerland A Cap	C002	29/06/90	LUX	-7.29	12	-4.98	12	2.56	24.72	9	✪✪	2	27.29	7	N.A.	
	NLG	6.81	Panelfund Short NLG Cap	A037	29/04/94	LUX	N.A.	—	-4.92	8	N.A.	N.A.				N.A.		N.A.	
	NLG	24.07	Parvest Short Term NLG B	B037	08/03/96	LUX	-7.36	18	N.A.		N.A.	N.A.				N.A.		N.A.	
	NLG	18.40	Rabobank Holland NLG Cash	R001	19/04/96	LUX	-7.45	22	N.A.		N.A.	N.A.				N.A.		N.A.	
▲	NLG	152.98	RG Money Plus NLG	R009	30/06/92	LUX	-7.28	10	-5	13	2.53	26.97	2	✪✪✪✪	4	N.A.		N.A.	
	NLG	468.51	SBC Money Market Fund NLG	S007	28/06/91	LUX	-7.28	8	-4.95	9	2.57	24.87	8	✪✪✪	3	28.11	5	N.A.	
	NLG	93.19	Swissca MM Fund NLG	S058	30/04/91	LUX	-7.25	6	-4.85	6	2.60	25.95	3	✪✪✪✪	4	29.07	2	N.A.	
	NLG	387.90	UBS (Lux) Money Mkt Invst NLG	U001	30/09/91	LUX	-7.29	11	-4.98	11	2.57	25.66	4	✪✪✪✪	4	28.63	3	N.A.	

New Zealand Dollar Money Market

Funds investing solely in New Zealand Dollar denominated money market or cash instruments with durations ranging from overnight to twelve months. Investments will normally be held in bank deposits, short-term monetary investments (e.g. T. Bills and certificates of deposits).

	CCY	Fund Size ($mil)	Fund Name	Manager Code	Fund Start Date	Domicile Code	3 Mths 97 % Chg	3 Mths 97 Rank	1 Year % Chg	1 Year Rank	Micropal Star Rating 3 Years Volatility	3 Years % Chg	3 Years Rank	3 Years Rating	Risk Return Rating	5 Years % Chg	5 Years Rank	10 Years % Chg	10 Years Rank
▲		**15.63**	**Mean/Count**				**-0.19**	**4**	**17.09**	**4**	**1.52**	**54.25**	**4**		**2**	**76.39**	**4**	**252.47**	**1**
▲	NZD	20.51	Fidelity NZD Currency Acc	F013	29/11/91	BER	-0.19	2	16.89	4	1.47	53.48	4	✪	2	75.24	4	N.A.	
▲	NZD	0.40	Five Arrows CFL NZD	R010	31/10/88	GU	-0.20	3	17.16	2	1.66	54.64	2	✪✪✪	1	76.35	2	N.A.	
▲	NZD	16.85	Five Arrows IRL NZD	R017	31/10/88	GU	-0.22	4	17.07	3	1.47	53.96	3	✪✪	3	75.67	3	N.A.	
▲	NZD	24.76	Lloyds Intl MMF NZD	L017	30/09/85	GU	-0.15	1	17.21	1	1.48	54.94	1	✪✪✪✪	4	78.28	1	252.47	1

Norwegian Krone Money Market

Funds investing solely in Norwegian Krone denominated money market or cash instruments with durations ranging from overnight to twelve months. Investments will normally be held in bank deposits, short-term monetary investments (e.g. T. Bills and certificates of deposit).

	CCY	Fund Size ($mil)	Fund Name	Manager Code	Fund Start Date	Domicile Code	3 Mths 97 % Chg	3 Mths 97 Rank	1 Year % Chg	1 Year Rank	Micropal Star Rating 3 Years Volatility	3 Years % Chg	3 Years Rank	3 Years Rating	Risk Return Rating	5 Years % Chg	5 Years Rank	10 Years % Chg	10 Years Rank
		4.26	**Mean/Count**				**-2.68**	**4**	**2.39**	**2**	**2.07**	**31.63**	**1**			**0**	**0**	**0**	**0**
▲	NOK	8.38	DNB Investment Norweg'n Csh C	D013	29/04/94	LUX	-2.65	2	2.44	1	N.A.	N.A.				N.A.		N.A.	
▲	NOK	0.13	Fidelity NOK Currency Acc	F013	30/09/93	BER	-2.75	4	2.33	2	2.07	31.63	1	✪✪✪	3	N.A.		N.A.	
	NOK	N.S.	Five Arrows CFL Norwegian Kr	R010	31/10/96	GU	-2.59	1	N.A.		N.A.	N.A.				N.A.		N.A.	
	NOK	N.S.	Five Arrows IRL Norwegian Kron	R017	31/10/96	GU	-2.73	3	N.A.		N.A.	N.A.				N.A.		N.A.	

▲ SIB Approved ● Insurance Fund Values in US Dollars, on an offer to offer price basis with gross income reinvested Data Source Micropal™

Portugese Escudo Money Market

Funds investing solely in Portuguese Escudo denominated money market or cash instruments with durations ranging from overnight to twelve months. Investments will normally be held in bank deposits, short-term monetary investments (e.g. T. Bills and certificates of deposit).

	CCY	Fund Size ($mil)	Fund Name	Manager Code	Fund Start Date	Domicile Code	3 Mths 97 % Chg	Rank	1 Year % Chg	Rank	Micropal Star Rating 3 Years Volatility	% Chg	Rank	Rating	Risk Return Rating	5 Years % Chg	Rank	10 Years % Chg	Rank
		22.24	**Mean/Count**				**-6.24**	**3**	**2.72**	**2**	**2.24**	**45.16**	**2**		**1**	**0**	**0**	**0**	**0**
▲	PTE	43.16	Inter Cash Escudo (PTE)	B069	19/01/96	LUX	-6.22	1	N.A.		N.A.	N.A.				N.A.		N.A.	
▲	PTE	4.05	Lloyds Intl MMF PTE	L017	31/07/92	GU	-6.27	3	2.58	2	2.25	45.13	2	✪✪	2	N.A.		N.A.	
	PTE	19.52	SBC Money Market Fund PTE	S007	26/02/93	LUX	-6.25	2	2.87	1	2.23	45.20	1	✪✪✪	3	N.A.		N.A.	

Singapore Dollar Money Market

Funds investing solely in Singapore Dollar denominated money market or cash instruments with durations ranging from overnight to twelve months. Investments will normally be held in bank deposits, short-term monetary investments (e.g. T. Bills and certificates of deposit).

	CCY	Fund Size ($mil)	Fund Name	Manager Code	Fund Start Date	Domicile Code	3 Mths 97 % Chg	Rank	1 Year % Chg	Rank	Micropal Star Rating 3 Years Volatility	% Chg	Rank	Rating	Risk Return Rating	5 Years % Chg	Rank	10 Years % Chg	Rank
▲		**1.98**	**Mean/Count**				**-2.81**	**3**	**2.69**	**3**	**0.71**	**19.82**	**3**		**3**	**23.43**	**2**	**95.70**	**2**
▲	SGD	1.30	Fidelity SGD Currency Acc	F013	30/09/93	BER	-2.80	2	2.72	2	0.71	19.93	2	✪✪✪	3	N.A.		N.A.	
▲	SGD	0.19	Five Arrows CFL Sing Dllr	R010	30/04/84	GU	-2.81	3	2.58	3	0.72	19.57	3	✪✪	2	23.35	2	94.94	2
▲	SGD	4.46	Five Arrows IRL Sing Dllr	R017	31/07/80	GU	-2.80	1	2.77	1	0.70	19.96	1	✪✪✪✪	4	23.51	1	96.46	1

Spanish Peseta Money Market

Funds investing solely in Spanish Peseta denominated money market or cash instruments with durations ranging from overnight to twelve months. Investments will normally be held in bank deposits, short-term monetary investments (e.g. T. Bills and certificates of deposit).

	CCY	Fund Size ($mil)	Fund Name	Manager Code	Fund Start Date	Domicile Code	3 Mths 97 % Chg	Rank	1 Year % Chg	Rank	Micropal Star Rating 3 Years Volatility	% Chg	Rank	Rating	Risk Return Rating	5 Years % Chg	Rank	10 Years % Chg	Rank
		43.47	**Mean/Count**				**-7.06**	**9**	**0**	**9**	**2**	**36.82**	**8**		**2**	**15.30**	**2**	**0**	**0**
●	ESP	142.60	Credis Money Market Fund PTS	C057	31/03/92	LUX	-6.87	1	0.53	2	1.96	38.54	2	✪✪✪✪	4	N.A.		N.A.	
	ESP	8.14	Fidelity ESP Currency Acc	F013	31/01/92	BER	-7.12	8	-0.46	9	1.96	35.73	7	✪	2	N.A.		N.A.	
▲	ESP	1.44	Five Arrows CFL Spanish Psta	R010	31/10/88	GU	-7.15	9	-0.45	7	2.27	35.76	6	✪✪	1	15.20	2	N.A.	
▲	ESP	18.34	Five Arrows IRL Spanish Psta	R017	31/10/88	GU	-7.09	5	-0.30	6	1.95	36.25	5	✪✪	2	15.40	1	N.A.	
▲	ESP	58.64	Inter Cash ESP	B069	12/07/95	LUX	-7.10	7	0.39	3	N.A.	N.A.				N.A.		N.A.	
▲	ESP	22.05	Lloyds Intl MMF ESP	L017	31/07/92	GU	-7.10	6	-0.18	5	1.96	36.87	4	✪✪✪	3	N.A.		N.A.	
	ESP	0.01	North Star Intl Money ESP	N012	31/03/93	CA	-7.07	4	-0.46	8	1.96	34.69	8	✪	1	N.A.		N.A.	
	ESP	118.45	SBC Money Market Fund ESP	S007	31/08/92	LUX	-7.01	3	0.36	4	1.94	37.75	3	✪✪✪	3	N.A.		N.A.	
	ESP	21.58	Swissca MM Fund PTS	S058	31/07/92	LUX	-7	2	0.59	1	1.97	38.99	1	✪✪✪✪	4	N.A.		N.A.	

▲ SIB Approved ● Insurance Fund **Values in US Dollars, on an offer to offer price basis with gross income reinvested** Data Source Micropal™

Swedish Krona Money Market

Funds investing solely in Swedish Krona denominated money market or cash instruments with durations ranging from overnight to twelve months. Investments will normally be held in bank deposits, short-term monetary investments (e.g. T. Bills and certificates of deposit).

	CCY	Fund Size ($mil)	Fund Name	Manager Code	Fund Start Date	Domicile Code	3 Mths 97 % Chg	3 Mths 97 Rank	1 Year % Chg	1 Year Rank	Micropal Star Rating 3 Years Volatility	3 Years % Chg	3 Years Rank	3 Years Rating	Risk Return Rating	5 Years % Chg	5 Years Rank	10 Years % Chg	10 Years Rank
		21.30	**Mean/Count**				**-8.77**	**9**	**2.49**	**8**	**2.62**	**47.11**	**6**		**1**	**19.02**	**2**	**0**	**0**
	SEK	67.84	Alfred Berg Likviditet Sve	A019	13/10/95	LUX	-8.78	5	2.91	2	N.A.	N.A.				N.A.		N.A.	
▲	SEK	1.68	Fidelity SEK Currency Acc	F013	30/09/93	BER	-8.73	4	1.99	7	2.40	46.15	5	✪✪	2	N.A.		N.A.	
▲	SEK	0.17	Five Arrows CFL Swedish Krone	R010	31/10/88	GU	-8.72	3	2.02	5	2.40	46.90	4	✪✪	4	19.38	1	N.A.	
▲	SEK	44.59	Five Arrows IRL Swedish Krone	R017	31/10/88	GU	-8.71	2	2.29	4	2.39	47.11	3	✪✪✪	2	18.65	2	N.A.	
▲	SEK	2.20	Gartmore CSF Skr Money	G007	13/10/95	JER	-8.80	7	1.84	8	N.A.	N.A.				N.A.		N.A.	
	SEK	N.S.	Lazard Swedish Krona Lqdty	L002	08/11/96	IRL	-8.79	6	N.A.		N.A.	N.A.				N.A.		N.A.	
	SEK	0.03	North Star Intl Money SEK	N012	29/01/93	CA	-8.87	9	2.01	6	2.42	45.02	6	✪	1	N.A.		N.A.	
	SEK	50.98	S-E-Banken Fund Sverge Rantfd	S001	30/06/93	LUX	-8.85	8	4.24	1	3.71	49.92	1	✪✪✪✪	4	N.A.		N.A.	
	SEK	2.90	Sun Life Money Skr	S053	30/04/93	IOM	-8.66	1	2.62	3	2.39	47.54	2	✪✪✪✪	3	N.A.		N.A.	

Swiss Franc Money Market

Funds investing solely in Swiss Franc denominated money market or cash instruments with durations ranging from overnight to twelve months. Investments will normally be held in bank deposits, short-term monetary investments (e.g. T. Bills and certificates of deposit).

	CCY	Fund Size ($mil)	Fund Name	Manager Code	Fund Start Date	Domicile Code	3 Mths 97 % Chg	3 Mths 97 Rank	1 Year % Chg	1 Year Rank	Micropal Star Rating 3 Years Volatility	3 Years % Chg	3 Years Rank	3 Years Rating	Risk Return Rating	5 Years % Chg	5 Years Rank	10 Years % Chg	10 Years Rank
		575.50	**Mean/Count**				**-6.50**	**36**	**-13.29**	**33**	**3.26**	**18.44**	**27**		**1**	**21.15**	**19**	**80.30**	**7**
	CHF	404.19	Baer Multicash Swiss Cash	J007	30/04/91	LUX	-6.48	7	-12.61	2	3.27	21.33	2	✪✪✪✪✪	5	25.53	2	N.A.	
	CHF	17.18	BBL Renta Cash CHF C	B052	30/04/92	LUX	-6.51	8	-13.09	9	3.27	18.54	13	✪✪✪	2	N.A.		N.A.	
	CHF	3.93	Bermuda Money CHF	B066	31/12/93	BER	-6.57	18	-13.32	18	3.27	18.78	12	✪✪✪	2	N.A.		N.A.	
▲	CHF	44.44	Coutts Swiss Franc Liquidity	C053	31/12/93	JER	-6.60	24	-13.12	10	3.28	18.84	11	✪✪✪	3	N.A.		N.A.	
●	CHF	6949.82	Credis Money Market Fund SFR	C057	31/10/91	LUX	-6.44	4	-12.68	3	3.27	20.57	4	✪✪✪✪	4	24.26	4	N.A.	
●	CHF	73.99	DBIM SF Reserve	D006	31/12/91	LUX	-6.36	3	-12.42	1	3.27	21.88	1	✪✪✪✪	5	27.84	1	N.A.	
	CHF	17.47	Fidelity CHF Currency Acc	F013	29/11/91	BER	-6.68	32	-13.73	32	3.27	16.49	25	✪		17.95	16	N.A.	
▲	CHF	5.68	Five Arrows CFL Swiss Franc	R010	30/04/84	GU	-6.69	33	-13.72	31	3.30	16.49	26	✪		17.90	17	78.45	5
	CHF	0.50	Five Arrows IP Swiss Fr Cash	R016	22/03/96	GU	N.A.	—	N.A.		N.A.	N.A.				N.A.		N.A.	
▲	CHF	43.78	Five Arrows IRL Swiss Franc	R017	31/07/80	GU	-6.66	31	-13.58	26	3.27	17.06	22	✪	1	18.87	14	81.14	3
	CHF	101.54	Force Cash Traditionnel CHF	B073	31/05/93	LUX	-6.58	20	-13.29	16	3.27	18.10	15	✪✪	2	N.A.		N.A.	
▲	CHF	3.11	Gartmore CSF SFR Money	G007	31/05/84	JER	-6.74	36	-13.65	29	3.22	16.29	27	✪		17.50	19	77.58	6
	CHF	3.78	GSAM MMF Swiss Franc	G003	30/01/87	IOM	-6.58	23	-13.63	28	3.22	17.38	20	✪✪	1	19.21	13	N.A.	
▲	CHF	3.86	Guinness FI IF Swiss Franc	G020	30/09/83	GU	-6.58	21	-13.38	19	3.28	17.79	17	✪✪	2	19.94	11	85.96	1
●	CHF	0.90	Hansard Swiss Franc Deposit	H011	28/02/90	IOM	-6.73	35	-13.71	30	3.22	17.19	21	✪✪✪	1	18.24	15	N.A.	
▲	CHF	21.12	Inter Cash CHF	B069	30/06/94	LUX	-6.52	11	-13.15	13	N.A.	N.A.				N.A.		N.A.	
	CHF	1.74	JF Money Fund CHF	J004	31/10/90	HK	-6.54	12	-13.13	12	3.28	19.27	7	✪✪✪✪	3	22.69	6	N.A.	
	CHF	3.05	Lazard Swiss Franc Liquidity	L002	30/11/84	GU	-6.61	26	-13.38	20	3.27	17.86	16	✪✪	2	19.77	12	79.43	4
	CHF	66.50	Lloyds Intl Liquidity CHF	L015	29/06/90	LUX	-6.58	19	-13.28	15	3.27	18.30	14	✪✪	2	21.21	9	N.A.	
▲	CHF	18.64	Lloyds Intl MMF CHF	L017	31/05/85	GU	-6.61	25	-13.45	23	3.27	17.53	19	✪	1	20.10	10	84	2
	CHF	N.S.	MeesPierson UF CHF Reserve	M012	01/03/96	LUX	-5.43	2	N.A.		N.A.	N.A.				N.A.		N.A.	
▲	CHF	16.50	Mercury ST CHF Reserve	M021	30/11/93	LUX	-6.48	6	-13.04	7	3.25	19.19	9	✪✪✪	3	N.A.		N.A.	
	CHF	95.09	Parvest Short Term CHF B	B037	28/02/94	LUX	-6.58	22	-13.38	21	N.A.	N.A.				N.A.		N.A.	
	CHF	2.40	Proton Fund Swiss Franc Cash	P025	29/09/95	LUX	-6.65	30	-13.52	24	N.A.	N.A.				N.A.		N.A.	
	CHF	168.09	Raiffeisen Swiss Money A	F024	31/03/94	LUX	-6.55	15	-13.01	5	N.A.	N.A.				N.A.		N.A.	
▲	CHF	0.74	RBC ICF Swiss Franc	R003	30/11/82	GU	-6.64	29	-13.58	25	3.27	16.50	24	✪		17.81	18	75.51	7
	CHF	4	RBC IMMF CHF Dist	R002	30/09/92	GU	-6.64	28	-13.62	27	3.23	16.52	23	✪✪		N.A.		N.A.	
▲	CHF	271.20	SBC Dynamic Floor Fd CHF 100%	S007	19/07/96	LUX	-5.02	1	N.A.		N.A.	N.A.				N.A.		N.A.	
	CHF	5157.63	SBC Money Market Fund CHF	S007	28/06/91	LUX	-6.54	14	-13.06	8	3.27	19.47	6	✪✪✪✪✪	4	22.67	7	N.A.	
	CHF	2.34	Sogelux Fd Money Mkt CHF	S037	21/06/96	LUX	-6.69	34	N.A.		N.A.	N.A.				N.A.		N.A.	
	CHF	35.55	Sogenalux Treasury CHF B	S037	30/06/92	LUX	-6.54	13	-13.25	14	3.27	19.11	10	✪✪✪	3	N.A.		N.A.	
	CHF	0.01	Sun Life Money CHF	S053	30/04/93	IOM	-6.63	27	-13.83	33	3.28	17.67	18	✪✪	1	N.A.		N.A.	
	CHF	1695.56	Swissca MM Fund SFR	S058	30/04/91	LUX	-6.51	10	-13	4	3.28	19.72	5	✪✪✪✪	4	22.87	5	N.A.	

▲ SIB Approved ● Insurance Fund Values in US Dollars, on an offer to offer price basis with gross income reinvested Data Source Micropal™

Swiss Franc Money Market

continued

	CCY	Fund Size ($mil)	Fund Name	Manager Code	Fund Start Date	Domicile Code	3 Mths 97 % Chg	Rank	1 Year % Chg	Rank	Micropal Star Rating 3 Years Volatility	% Chg	Rank	Rating	Risk Return Rating	5 Years % Chg	Rank	10 Years % Chg	Rank
		575.50	**Mean/Count**				**-6.50**	**36**	**-13.29**	**33**	**3.26**	**18.44**	**27**		**1**	**21.15**	**19**	**80.30**	**7**
	CHF	3.76	Trans Monetary CHF	N003	29/09/95	LUX	-6.51	9	-13.31	17	N.A.	N.A.				N.A.		N.A.	
	CHF	5452.45	UBS (Lux) Money Mkt Invst CHF	U001	30/09/91	LUX	-6.55	16	-13.13	11	3.27	19.23	8	✪✪✪✪	3	22.42	8	N.A.	
	CHF	24.42	UBZ Liquidity CHF	U002	28/02/91	IRL	-6.46	5	-13.03	6	3.25	20.74	3	✪✪✪✪	4	25.10	3	N.A.	
	CHF	2.97	UI Money Market SFR	U012	27/10/95	LUX	-6.56	17	-13.39	22	N.A.	N.A.				N.A.		N.A.	

UK Pound Money Market

Funds investing solely in British money market or cash instruments with durations ranging from overnight to twelve months. Investments will normally be held in bank deposits, short-term monetary investments (e.g. T. Bills and certificates of deposit).

	CCY	Fund Size ($mil)	Fund Name	Manager Code	Fund Start Date	Domicile Code	3 Mths 97 % Chg	Rank	1 Year % Chg	Rank	Micropal Star Rating 3 Years Volatility	% Chg	Rank	Rating	Risk Return Rating	5 Years % Chg	Rank	10 Years % Chg	Rank
		53.84	**Mean/Count**				**-2.87**	**87**	**15.81**	**83**	**1.97**	**33.77**	**70**		**2**	**21.60**	**57**	**160.41**	**24**
	GBP	2.13	Abtrust Sterling Deposit	A003	30/07/82	GU	-2.88	52	15.34	66	1.96	32.83	53	✪✪	1	20.97	34	152.75	19
▲	GBP	1.17	Aetna IUF Sterling Res A	A011	29/04/88	LUX	-2.97	72	16.06	31	1.98	33.51	43	✪✪	3	21.35	32	N.A.	
▲	GBP	13.06	AIB Grofund Sterling Currency	A015	31/08/84	JER	-2.80	31	15.39	65	1.93	32.47	57	✪	2	19.74	47	160.31	15
▲	GBP	2.44	AIB Offs Sterling Cash	A016	31/10/89	GU	-3.30	86	14.39	82	2.24	30.15	65	✪	1	16.08	56	N.A.	
●	GBP	0	Albany Intl G'teed Money Stlg	A018	31/03/87	IOM	-2.56	3	16.02	35	1.94	34.61	24	✪✪✪✪	3	23.45	14	N.A.	
	GBP	2.05	AXA Eqty&Law ILA Stlg Deposit	A040	31/10/85	IOM	-2.98	73	16.38	16	1.97	33.30	46	✪✪	1	17.79	53	140.22	23
	GBP	29.11	Baer Multicash STG Cash	J007	31/08/92	LUX	-2.83	38	15.80	46	1.87	36.66	4	✪✪✪	5	N.A.		N.A.	
▲	GBP	63.77	Barclays MCF Sterling	B048	31/10/84	JER	-2.95	69	15.83	43	1.93	34.02	35	✪✪✪	3	21.68	28	163.05	10
▲	GBP	30.96	Barclays Stlg Premium Income	B046	30/11/89	JER	-2.86	44	15.96	37	1.86	34.33	29	✪✪✪	3	22.55	22	N.A.	
	GBP	18.42	BBL Renta Cash GBP C	B052	28/02/89	LUX	-2.86	47	15.96	36	1.94	34.46	27	✪✪✪✪	3	22.87	20	N.A.	
	GBP	26.05	Bermuda Money GBP	B066	31/12/93	BER	-2.72	17	16.41	12	1.93	36.12	6	✪✪✪✪✪	5	N.A.		N.A.	
	GBP	45.11	Bk of Ire Glbl Stlg Curr	B018	30/11/88	IOM	-2.91	60	15.62	56	1.92	34.05	34	✪✪	3	22.09	25	N.A.	
	GBP	65.80	Buttress Money Market GBP	B080	30/11/94	BER	-2.73	19	16.62	5	N.A.	N.A.				N.A.		N.A.	
	GBP	9.47	Cater Allen Acc Stlg Money	C013	07/01/00	JER	-2.65	7	N.A.		N.A.	N.A.				N.A.		N.A.	
	GBP	1.52	CB MMF Pfund Sterling	A007	31/03/95	LUX	-2.81	34	15.44	63	N.A.	N.A.				N.A.		N.A.	
	GBP	8.97	CIBC PCF Sterling Money Market	C021	26/01/96	GU	-2.82	35	N.A.		N.A.	N.A.				N.A.		N.A.	
▲●	GBP	87.62	Citicurr STG Portfolio	C029	31/03/89	LUX	-2.58	4	16.33	19	1.92	35.01	17	✪✪✪✪	4	23.75	11	N.A.	
▲	GBP	94.75	CMI GNF Stlg Curr Reserve	C042	30/04/90	LUX	-2.66	10	16.42	10	2.02	36.18	5	✪✪✪✪	5	26.24	4	N.A.	
●	GBP	75.95	CMI Ins Co GBP Curr Reserve	C043	30/11/90	IOM	-2.75	24	15.72	51	1.95	33.83	40	✪✪	2	22.38	23	N.A.	
▲	GBP	131.52	Coutts Sterling Liquidity	C053	31/05/83	JER	-2.69	13	16.08	29	1.93	35.36	14	✪✪✪✪	4	23.38	16	169.77	3
●	GBP	625.54	Credis Money Market Fund GBP	C057	30/08/85	LUX	-2.68	11	16.42	11	1.94	36.01	7	✪✪✪✪✪	5	24.58	8	168.90	4
▲	GBP	21.64	CU PP Sterling Reserve ACC	C070	30/04/90	LUX	-2.74	21	16.32	20	1.93	34.49	26	✪✪✪	3	21.91	26	N.A.	
	GBP	18.45	CUCIM Trust	C046	31/05/95	GU	-2.69	12	17	3	N.A.	N.A.				N.A.		N.A.	
●	GBP	179.31	DBIM Sterling Reserve	D006	30/11/90	LUX	-2.71	16	17.31	2	1.97	37.78	2	✪✪✪✪✪	5	27.22	1	N.A.	
	GBP	21.48	DekaLux Cash GBP (A)	D009	29/05/92	LUX	-2.80	30	15.79	48	1.93	34.26	31	✪✪✪	3	N.A.		N.A.	
●	GBP	17.92	Eagle Star Stlg Secure	E001	29/02/88	IOM	-2.86	49	16.02	34	1.94	33.74	41	✪✪	2	21.17	33	N.A.	
	GBP	6.60	F&C RAF St Term Stlg Ass	F003	31/01/86	JER	-2.70	14	16.55	7	1.95	35.82	10	✪✪✪✪	4	26.29	3	193.84	1
▲	GBP	121.03	Fidelity GBP Currency Acc	F013	29/11/91	BER	-2.93	64	15.61	57	1.94	32.96	51	✪	2	20.26	42	N.A.	
	GBP	0.15	Finistere Stlg Deposit Life	F016	30/03/84	GU	-2.98	74	15.32	67	1.96	32.56	55	✪	1	20.65	40	140.15	24
▲	GBP	33.49	Five Arrows CFL Sterling	R010	30/04/84	GU	-2.93	63	15.59	58	2.02	33.08	50	✪✪	2	20.76	36	161.38	12
	GBP	10.05	Five Arrows IP Stlg Cash	R016	30/12/94	GU	N.A.	—	14.72	78	N.A.	N.A.				N.A.		N.A.	
▲	GBP	530.22	Five Arrows IRL Sterling	R017	31/07/80	GU	-2.89	57	15.73	50	1.94	33.54	42	✪✪	2	21.35	31	163.04	11
▲	GBP	17.29	Fleming FF Series II GBP	F020	31/03/92	LUX	-2.77	25	16.33	18	1.94	35.81	11	✪✪✪✪✪	4	N.A.		N.A.	
	GBP	0.81	Friends Provdnt Cash Deposit	F031	31/05/94	GU	-2.74	20	14.82	74	N.A.	N.A.				N.A.		N.A.	
▲	GBP	43.37	Gartmore CSF Stlg Money	G007	31/05/84	JER	-3	76	15.43	64	1.93	32.53	56	✪	1	19.80	45	156.85	17
	GBP	25.71	GSAM MMF Sterling	G003	30/01/87	IOM	-2.83	37	16.02	33	2.04	33.96	37	✪✪✪	2	21.55	30	N.A.	
▲	GBP	33.92	Guinness FI IF Sterling	G020	30/09/83	GU	-2.83	36	16.15	27	1.94	35.11	16	✪✪✪✪	4	23.71	12	169.96	2
▲	GBP	8.92	Guinness Flight Stlg Money	G019	31/01/85	GU	-2.87	51	16.25	23	2.24	35.30	15	✪✪✪✪	4	23.95	10	166.76	6

▲ SIB Approved ● Insurance Fund Values in US Dollars, on an offer to offer price basis with gross income reinvested Data Source Micropal™

UK Pound Money Market

continued

	CCY	Fund Size ($mil)	Fund Name	Manager Code	Fund Start Date	Domicile Code	3 Mths 97 % Chg	3 Mths 97 Rank	1 Year % Chg	1 Year Rank	Micropal Star Rating 3 Years Volatility	3 Years % Chg	3 Years Rank	3 Years Rating	Risk Return Rating	5 Years % Chg	5 Years Rank	10 Years % Chg	10 Years Rank
		53.84	**Mean/Count**				**-2.87**	**87**	**15.81**	**83**	**1.97**	**33.77**	**70**		**2**	**21.60**	**57**	**160.41**	**24**
▲	GBP	19.42	Hambros CF Sterling Shr	H001	28/02/79	GU	-2.94	66	15.64	54	1.94	33.37	45	✪	2	21.60	29	164.17	8
▲	GBP	7.39	Hambros EMMA Sterling Money	H002	31/05/85	GU	-2.86	50	11.50	83	2.17	28.96	70	✪✪✪	3	17.81	52	161.23	13
●	GBP	N.S.	Hansard Sterling Deposit Bd	H011	31/03/94	IOM	-2.40	2	15.81	44	N.A.	N.A.				N.A.		N.A.	
●	GBP	7.10	Hansard UK Sterling Deposit	H011	28/02/90	IOM	-3.11	85	14.94	72	1.93	31.21	62	✪✪	1	18.39	51	N.A.	
▲	GBP	21.82	Hill Samuel ICF Sterling	H030	30/06/82	JER	-2.89	56	15.64	55	1.95	33.15	49	✪	2	20.73	38	160.76	14
	GBP	2.88	HSBC GMF Sterling	H035	29/03/91	CA	-2.90	59	15.88	40	1.93	34.29	30	✪✪✪✪	3	23.52	13	N.A.	
▲	GBP	17.25	Inter Cash GBP	B069	31/01/90	LUX	-2.71	15	15.75	49	1.93	34.70	22	✪✪✪	4	23.30	17	N.A.	
▲	GBP	8.12	INVESCO PS Sterling Reserve	I014	31/10/79	LUX	-2.74	23	15.53	60	1.93	32.32	58	✪✪	1	18.94	49	147.62	21
	GBP	5.89	Irish Life Intl Sterling Cash	I017	28/04/95	IRL	-3.05	82	14.77	75	N.A.	N.A.				N.A.		N.A.	
	GBP	22.68	JF Money Fund GBP	J004	29/04/88	HK	-2.73	18	16.40	13	1.94	35.99	8	✪✪✪✪	5	25.17	5	N.A.	
	GBP	5.58	JRIA Spec Deposit Sterling	J002	31/12/92	IRL	-2.80	32	16.34	17	1.93	35.41	13	✪✪✪✪✪	4	N.A.		N.A.	
	GBP	9.64	JRIA Sterling Deposit	J002	29/01/93	IRL	-3.04	80	15.16	70	1.93	31.37	60	✪	1	N.A.		N.A.	
▲	GBP	2.66	Lazard SIT UK Liquid Assets	L001	28/02/89	GU	-2.89	54	20.09	1	2.25	38.12	1	✪✪	1	19.77	46	N.A.	
	GBP	17.73	Lazard Sterling Liquidity	L002	30/11/84	GU	-2.90	58	16.06	32	1.93	34.56	25	✪✪✪	3	22.91	19	168.15	5
	GBP	73.08	Lloyds Intl Liquidity GBP	L015	29/09/89	LUX	-2.85	42	16.19	24	1.94	34.88	21	✪✪✪✪	3	23.43	15	N.A.	
▲	GBP	221.95	Lloyds Intl MMF GBP	L017	30/11/83	GU	-2.88	53	15.87	41	1.94	33.96	36	✪✪✪	2	22.58	21	166.70	7
	GBP	10.23	Matrix Sterling Liquidity A	U011	31/01/96	IRL	-2.84	41	N.A.		N.A.	N.A.				N.A.		N.A.	
	GBP	7.73	Mercury MMT Sterling	M019	31/07/87	JER	-2.81	33	15.80	47	1.93	34.07	33	✪✪✪	3	19.94	44	N.A.	
▲	GBP	15.38	Mercury OST Reserve	M020	30/11/87	LUX	-7.48	87	14.65	79	2.19	29.03	69	✪	1	14.71	57	N.A.	
▲	GBP	40.02	Mercury ST GBP Reserve	M021	30/11/93	LUX	-2.66	9	16.08	28	1.90	34.91	20	✪✪✪	4	N.A.		N.A.	
▲	GBP	2.45	Midland ICF Stlg Liquidity	M028	28/02/90	LUX	-2.86	45	15.68	53	2.12	30.88	64	✪	1	18.43	50	N.A.	
▲	GBP	19.79	Newton Corporate Money	N006	28/06/96	JER	-2.65	8	N.A.		N.A.	N.A.				N.A.		N.A.	
▲	GBP	88.47	Newton UGF Sterling	N006	31/03/82	JER	-2.89	55	15.89	39	1.94	33.94	38	✪✪✪	3	21.83	27	163.41	9
	GBP	2.76	Old Mutual Gnsy Sterling MM	O003	29/12/95	GU	-2.85	43	14.85	73	N.A.	N.A.				N.A.		N.A.	
	GBP	0.29	Old Mutual HK Stlg Mnymkt	O004	28/04/95	HK	-2.92	61	14.60	81	N.A.	N.A.				N.A.		N.A.	
	GBP	12.38	OMI (Gnsy) Stlg Moneymarket	O005	31/05/82	GU	-3.01	77	14.75	76	1.95	30.01	66	✪	1	16.23	54	149.31	20
	GBP	N.S.	Perpetual OIA Stlg Money Mkt	P012	24/01/97	JER	N.A.		N.A.		N.A.	N.A.				N.A.		N.A.	
▲	GBP	12.18	RBC ICF Sterling	R003	30/11/82	GU	-2.86	46	15.69	52	1.94	32.89	52	✪	2	20.49	41	155.39	18
	GBP	37.22	RBC IMMF Stlg Dist	R002	30/06/92	GU	-2.94	68	15.80	45	2	34.14	32	✪✪	1	N.A.		N.A.	
●	GBP	3.04	RLI/Deposit Portfolio	R020	30/04/92	IOM	-2.95	70	14.74	77	1.93	29.58	68	✪	1	N.A.		N.A.	
●	GBP	0.68	RLI/Income Portfolio	R020	29/10/93	IOM	-0.34	1	16.84	4	1.86	31.72	59	✪✪	2	N.A.		N.A.	
●	GBP	16.07	Royal Life Intl Stlg MMkt	R020	31/08/90	IOM	-2.64	5	16.15	26	1.93	34.36	28	✪✪✪	3	23.18	18	N.A.	
	GBP	5.24	Royal Life/Guin Fl IFMF Stlg	R026	30/10/87	IOM	-3.07	84	14.61	80	1.94	29.94	67	✪	1	16.13	55	N.A.	
	GBP	66.24	Royal Skandia Stg B Society	R038	30/12/88	IOM	-2.84	40	16.40	14	1.97	37.22	3	✪✪✪✪	5	26.37	2	N.A.	
	GBP	17.93	Royal Skandia Stg Deposit	R038	30/12/88	IOM	-2.96	71	16.07	30	1.97	33.45	44	✪✪	2	20.17	43	N.A.	
	GBP	640.30	SBC Money Market Fund GBP	S007	31/05/90	LUX	-2.78	26	16.39	15	1.94	35.67	12	✪✪✪✪✪	4	24.81	6	N.A.	
●	GBP	20.80	Scot Amicable UK Deposit	S015	30/06/94	IRL	-3.04	79	15.22	69	N.A.	N.A.				N.A.		N.A.	
	GBP	21.99	Scot Eq (SEI) UK Cash	S016	23/06/95	LUX	-2.99	75	15.59	59	N.A.	N.A.				N.A.		N.A.	
	GBP	37.05	Scot Prov GP Building Society	S014	26/05/95	IOM	-2.64	6	16.29	21	N.A.	N.A.				N.A.		N.A.	
	GBP	6.60	Scot Prov GP Stlg Deposit	S014	30/09/91	IOM	-3.05	81	15.52	61	1.94	31.25	61	✪	1	19.34	48	N.A.	
▲●	GBP	5.75	Singer & Fried Stlg Reserve	S027	31/05/95	IRL	-2.93	65	15.95	38	N.A.	N.A.				N.A.		N.A.	
▲	GBP	7.95	Standard Bank Stlg Capital	S044	31/10/79	GU	-2.94	67	15.51	62	1.93	32.64	54	✪	2	20.76	37	159.37	16
▲	GBP	4.08	Sun Life GP Haven	S052	31/03/88	LUX	-3.02	78	14.97	71	1.99	31.20	63	✪	1	20.67	39	N.A.	
	GBP	7.88	Sun Life Money Stlg	S053	30/10/92	IOM	-2.74	22	16.18	25	1.92	34.93	19	✪✪✪✪	4	N.A.		N.A.	
	GBP	48.68	Swissca MM Fund GBP	S058	30/04/91	LUX	-2.78	27	16.51	9	1.95	35.97	9	✪✪✪✪✪	4	24.77	7	N.A.	
	GBP	6.09	Syfrets GI Stlg Money Mkt	S060	30/11/93	CA	-2.86	48	16.57	6	1.92	33.24	47	✪✪	2	N.A.		N.A.	
▲	GBP	4.35	TGA Stlg Lqd Ass	T009	28/02/89	LUX	-2.80	29	16.53	8	2.30	34.68	23	✪✪✪	4	20.84	35	N.A.	
	GBP	16.39	Trans Monetary GBP	N003	31/01/92	LUX	-2.84	39	15.25	68	1.93	33.23	48	✪✪	2	N.A.		N.A.	
▲	GBP	13.19	TSB OIF Sterling Deposit	T013	31/08/83	JER	-3.06	83	15.85	42	2.03	33.86	39	✪✪	2	22.34	24	146.78	22
	GBP	562.14	UBS (Lux) Money Mkt Invst GBP	U001	30/11/88	LUX	-2.79	28	16.25	22	1.96	34.95	18	✪✪✪✪	4	24.27	9	N.A.	

▲ SIB Approved ● Insurance Fund Values in US Dollars, on an offer to offer price basis with gross income reinvested Data Source Micropal™

US Dollar Money Market

Funds investing solely in US money market or cash instruments with durations ranging from overnight to twelve months. Investments will normally be held in bank deposits, short-term monetary investments (e.g. T. Bills and certificates of deposit).

	CCY	Fund Size ($mil)	Fund Name	Manager Code	Fund Start Date	Domicile Code	3 Mths 97 % Chg	Rank	1 Year % Chg	Rank	Micropal Star Rating 3 Years Volatility	% Chg	Rank	Rating	Risk Return Rating	5 Years % Chg	Rank	10 Years % Chg	Rank
		272.22	**Mean/Count**				**1.03**	**142**	**4.63**	**132**	**0.23**	**13.76**	**103**			**19.54**	**70**	**62.88**	**21**
	USD	448.93	A.L.S.A. USD Cash	A007	30/11/93	LUX	-3.92	142	4.98	39	1.19	15.19	16	✪✪✪✪		N.A.		N.A.	
▲	USD	64.60	ABN AMRO Interest Growth USD	A001	30/04/92	LUX	0.95	117	5.01	36	0.31	11.55	91	✪✪		N.A.		N.A.	
	USD	1.13	Abtrust Dollar Deposit	A003	30/07/82	GU	0.98	110	4.32	101	0.21	10.31	97	✪		13.68	64	52.95	21
	USD	5.46	ACMGI Sht Maturity Dllr Ptf A	A005	31/10/94	LUX	1.21	27	4.58	80	N.A.	N.A.				N.A.		N.A.	
▲	USD	75.11	AEB Worldfolio 1 US Daily Inc	A009	26/02/93	LUX	0.78	134	5.04	32	0	14.98	24	✪✪✪✪		N.A.		N.A.	
▲	USD	9.84	Aetna IUF US Dollar Res A	A011	29/04/88	LUX	1.13	60	4.33	100	0.37	11.89	88	✪✪		16.70	59	N.A.	
●	USD	0	Albany Intl G'teed Money Dllr	A018	31/03/87	IOM	1.29	11	5.42	8	0.11	15.84	9	✪✪✪✪		22.83	10	N.A.	
	USD	N.S.	Aqua Amerique Cap	B026	30/10/87	LUX	1.25	17	5.06	29	0.09	15	23	✪✪✪✪		22.72	12	N.A.	
	USD	3.53	AXA Eqty&Law ILA USD Deposit	A040	31/10/85	IOM	0.93	118	4.97	40	0.16	12.39	81	✪✪		16.85	58	55.28	20
	USD	326.78	Baer Multicash USD Cash	J007	30/09/92	LUX	1.03	96	4.93	49	0.11	14.13	48	✪✪✪		N.A.		N.A.	
	USD	6.23	Barclays ASF USD Liquidity	B044	31/10/90	JER	0.83	129	3.81	116	0.93	10.90	94	✪		12.80	66	N.A.	
▲	USD	11.80	Barclays MCF US Dollar	B048	31/10/84	JER	1.02	102	4.31	102	0.09	12.60	78	✪		17.94	50	61.27	13
	USD	45.35	Baring CUF US Dollar	B049	28/06/85	IRL	1.12	72	4.86	55	0.11	12.52	80	✪		17.95	49	65.58	7
	USD	40.02	BBL Renta Cash Sht-Med USD C	B052	30/07/93	LUX	1.12	68	4.84	57	0.29	11.44	92	✪✪		N.A.		N.A.	
	USD	188.24	BBL Renta Cash USD C	B052	31/03/89	LUX	1.13	64	4.70	69	0.07	14.25	44	✪✪✪✪		20.77	27	N.A.	
	USD	469	Bermuda Money USD	B066	30/11/93	BER	1.24	21	5.11	23	0.07	15.77	10	✪✪✪✪✪		N.A.		N.A.	
	USD	224.72	BIL Money Market USD	B067	31/07/90	LUX	1.15	55	4.84	59	0.08	14.44	40	✪✪✪✪		21.02	25	N.A.	
	USD	12.06	Bk of Ire Glbl USD Curr	B018	30/11/88	IOM	0.85	127	4.19	107	0.09	11.93	85	✪		16.95	57	N.A.	
●	USD	27.52	BL Money Trust Zone Dlr B	B025	30/03/90	LUX	1.07	85	5.09	25	0.15	15.10	20	✪✪✪✪		23.92	6	N.A.	
▲	USD	63.06	BT GAF Enhanced Mgd Dllr Adv	B076	31/05/95	IRL	1.25	18	5.33	11	N.A.	N.A.				N.A.		N.A.	
▲	USD	15.82	BT GAF Enhanced Mgd Dllr Inst	B076	31/05/95	IRL	1.21	25	5.20	14	N.A.	N.A.				N.A.		N.A.	
▲	USD	31.14	BT GAF Mgd Dllr Advisory	B076	30/11/92	IRL	1.32	8	5.52	6	0	16.84	4	✪✪✪✪✪	3	N.A.		N.A.	
▲	USD	39.89	BT GAF Mgd Dllr Institutional	B076	30/11/92	IRL	1.29	10	5.68	4	0	16.55	6	✪✪✪✪✪		N.A.		N.A.	
▲	USD	20.73	BT GAF Mgd Dllr Investor	B076	30/11/92	IRL	1.20	29	5.02	35	0	15.18	17	✪✪✪✪✪		N.A.		N.A.	
	USD	710.40	Buttress Money Market USD	B080	29/07/88	BER	1.24	19	5.36	9	0.09	15.72	11	✪✪✪✪✪		22.74	11	N.A.	
	USD	3.60	Cater Allen Acc USD Money	C013	07/01/00	JER	1.23	22	N.A.		N.A.	N.A.				N.A.		N.A.	
	USD	3.50	CB Lux Portfolio USD Cash	A007	31/03/93	LUX	0.86	126	4.51	89	0.13	13.94	54	✪✪		N.A.		N.A.	
	USD	106.04	CB MMF US Dollar	A007	31/03/95	LUX	1.22	24	5.01	37	N.A.	N.A.				N.A.		N.A.	
	USD	104	Cera Cash USD B	C018	31/05/93	LUX	1.16	48	4.89	52	1.01	14.14	47	✪✪✪		N.A.		N.A.	
●	USD	249.81	Chase Mgd Dllr Inst Class	C019	31/08/95	IRL	0.84	128	4.72	68	N.A.	N.A.				N.A.		N.A.	
●	USD	3.38	Chase Mgd Dllr Investor	C019	30/12/88	IRL	0.78	133	4.11	112	0	14.45	37	✪✪✪		22.98	9	N.A.	
▲●	USD	112.81	Chase Vista Dollar Income	C019	13/10/95	LUX	1.17	45	4.80	62	N.A.	N.A.				N.A.		N.A.	
	USD	21.10	CIBC PCF USD Money Market	C021	16/02/96	GU	1.11	73	N.A.		N.A.	N.A.				N.A.		N.A.	
●	USD	1651.75	Citi Institutional Liquid Res	C032	29/04/94	CA	1.33	7	5.49	7	N.A.	N.A.				N.A.		N.A.	
●	USD	22.17	Citi Liquid Reserves A	C032	31/08/94	CA	1.13	65	4.66	73	N.A.	N.A.				N.A.		N.A.	
●	USD	51.50	Citi Premium Liquid Reserves	C032	28/02/94	CA	1.27	14	5.20	15	N.A.	N.A.				N.A.		N.A.	
▲●	USD	541.92	Citicurr USD Portfolio	C029	30/09/88	LUX	1.12	69	5.06	30	0.08	15.18	18	✪✪✪✪		21.91	18	N.A.	
▲	USD	11.82	CMI GNF USD Curr Reserve	C042	30/04/90	LUX	1.28	13	4.87	53	0.52	13.75	56	✪✪		19.15	40	N.A.	
▲	USD	178.93	Coutts Dollar Liquidity	C053	31/05/83	JER	1.11	74	4.96	43	0.11	15.06	22	✪✪✪✪		21.04	24	69.02	3
●	USD	6558.43	Credis Money Market Fund USD	C057	30/08/85	LUX	1.22	23	4.96	42	0.09	14.91	25	✪✪✪✪		22.51	14	71.90	1
▲	USD	16.03	CU PP US Dollar Reserve ACC	C070	31/05/90	LUX	1.15	54	4.53	85	0.10	13.12	69	✪✪		17.50	52	N.A.	
	USD	17.33	Currency Mgt Fd US Dollars	I008	30/11/92	LUX	1.20	30	4.99	38	0.08	14.54	35	✪✪✪		N.A.		N.A.	
	USD	N.S.	Daily Dollar International	R006	31/05/88	BVI	1.13	62	4.68	70	0	14.05	49	✪✪✪		20.55	29	N.A.	
	USD	1.70	Dao Heng Money Market	D005	11/10/96	HK	0.50	138	N.A.		N.A.	N.A.				N.A.		N.A.	
●	USD	644.60	DBIM Cash USD	D006	18/08/95	LUX	1.25	15	4.95	46	N.A.	N.A.				N.A.		N.A.	
●	USD	1818.60	DBIM US Dollar Reserve	D006	30/11/92	LUX	1.19	33	4.53	86	0.10	14.02	52	✪✪✪		N.A.		N.A.	
	USD	336.70	DekaLux Cash USD (A)	D009	29/05/92	LUX	1.01	104	4.80	63	0.16	13.53	60	✪✪		N.A.		N.A.	
●	USD	566.10	Dit Lux Money Market US$	D017	28/04/95	LUX	1.13	61	4.60	77	N.A.	N.A.				N.A.		N.A.	
●	USD	14.89	Eagle Star Dllr Secure	E001	29/02/88	IOM	1.10	76	4.54	84	0.09	12.62	77	✪		17.33	54	N.A.	
	USD	N.S.	EPIC MF US Daily Income	A024	20/10/95	LUX	0.73	135	4.49	92	N.A.	N.A.				N.A.		N.A.	
	FRF	51.64	Eurobc Dollars US	O001	31/01/94	LUX	1.12	71	5.19	17	N.A.	N.A.				N.A.		N.A.	
	USD	N.S.	Evergreen Daily Dollar Int	R006	26/01/96	BVI	1.13	62	N.A.		N.A.	N.A.				N.A.		N.A.	
	USD	1.31	F&C RAF St Term USD Ass	F003	31/10/84	JER	1.09	78	4.60	78	0.10	13.75	57	✪✪		20.41	31	68.41	5
	USD	95.04	Federated S-T US Govt Inst	F006	28/06/91	IRL	1.17	41	4.92	50	0	14.77	27	✪✪✪		21.84	19	N.A.	
	USD	302.27	Federated S-T US Govt Inv	F006	28/06/91	IRL	1.07	84	4.50	90	0	13.37	64	✪✪		19.99	34	N.A.	
	USD	1.60	Federated S-T US Govt Inv Gth	F006	28/02/92	IRL	1.05	88	4.45	94	0.07	13.29	67	✪		N.A.		N.A.	
	USD	74.24	Federated S-T US Prime	F006	10/02/95	IRL	1.24	20	5.18	18	N.A.	N.A.				N.A.		N.A.	

▲ SIB Approved ● Insurance Fund

Values in US Dollars, on an offer to offer price basis with gross income reinvested

Data Source Micropal™

US Dollar Money Market

continued

	CCY	Fund Size ($mil)	Fund Name	Manager Code	Fund Start Date	Domicile Code	3 Mths 97 % Chg	3 Mths 97 Rank	1 Year % Chg	1 Year Rank	Micropal Star Rating: Volatility	3 Years % Chg	3 Years Rank	Rating	Risk Return Rating	5 Years % Chg	5 Years Rank	10 Years % Chg	10 Years Rank
		272.22	**Mean/Count**				**1.03**	**142**	**4.63**	**132**	**0.23**	**13.76**	**103**			**19.54**	**70**	**62.88**	**21**
	USD	134.67	Federated S-T US Treas Secs	F006	31/07/92	IRL	1.15	56	4.86	54	0	14.54	36	✪✪✪		N.A.		N.A.	
▲	USD	81.90	Fidelity Cash USD	F010	30/09/93	LUX	1.16	50	4.96	44	0.09	13.89	55	✪✪		N.A.		N.A.	
▲	USD	673.26	Fidelity USD Currency Acc	F013	29/11/91	BER	1.01	105	4.35	98	0.07	12.74	75	✪		18.13	48	N.A.	
▲	USD	25.55	Five Arrows CFL US Dollar	R010	30/04/84	GU	1.03	97	4.25	103	0.74	12.64	76	✪✪		17.71	51	63.58	10
	USD	N.S.	Five Arrows GOF Dv Cty Hgh Yl	R012	30/04/96	GU	2.12	2	N.A.		N.A.	N.A.				N.A.		N.A.	
	USD	4.72	Five Arrows IP US Dllr Cash	R016	30/12/94	GU	N.A.	—	3.45	125	N.A.	N.A.				N.A.		N.A.	
▲	USD	193.17	Five Arrows IRL US Dollar	R017	31/07/80	GU	1.05	87	4.38	97	0.07	13.11	70	✪		18.60	43	65.54	8
▲	USD	92.17	Fleming FF Series II USD	F020	30/09/92	LUX	1.21	26	5.25	12	0.08	15.39	14	✪✪✪✪✪		N.A.		N.A.	
	USD	133.26	Force Cash Traditionnel USD	B073	21/10/94	LUX	1.08	80	4.64	75	N.A.	N.A.				N.A.		N.A.	
	USD	124.28	Fructilux Court Terme USD	B043	20/10/95	LUX	1.15	53	4.82	61	N.A.	N.A.				N.A.		N.A.	
	USD	138.46	G-Treasury Dollar US B	G009	29/07/94	LUX	1.15	51	5.22	13	N.A.	N.A.				N.A.		N.A.	
	USD	203.01	G-Treasury Intl Dollar US B	G009	29/07/94	LUX	1.16	47	5.20	16	N.A.	N.A.				N.A.		N.A.	
▲	USD	33.79	Gartmore CSF USD Money	G007	31/05/84	JER	0.88	123	4.20	105	0.97	12.56	79	✪		17.45	53	60.28	15
	USD	0.10	Glbl Mgr US Dollar Cash	B066	16/12/94	BER	0.91	120	3.01	128	N.A.	N.A.				N.A.		N.A.	
	USD	0.90	Govett GSIL Dollar Cash	G015	31/01/89	JER	0.55	137	3.96	113	0.66	12.10	83	✪✪		19.39	38	N.A.	
▲●	USD	51.09	Groupe Indosuez Dollar Res	G017	31/01/91	LUX	1.02	101	4.52	87	0.13	14.44	39	✪✪✪		18.31	45	N.A.	
	USD	101.40	GSAM MMF US Dollar	G003	30/01/87	IOM	1.16	49	7.79	2	0.84	17.70	3	✪✪✪	1	24.01	5	N.A.	
▲	USD	18.28	Guinness FI IF US Dollar	G020	30/09/83	GU	1.14	58	4.77	65	0.08	14.32	41	✪✪✪✪		20.59	28	69.34	2
	USD	13.22	Guinness Flight US Dllr Mny	G019	31/01/85	GU	1.04	90	4.79	64	0.78	14.31	42	✪✪✪✪		20.43	30	68.64	4
▲	USD	0.96	Hambros CF US Dollar Shr	H001	29/06/84	GU	0.99	109	4.15	109	0.07	12.11	82	✪		17.30	55	61.41	11
▲	USD	1.15	Hambros EMMA US Dollar Money	H002	31/05/85	GU	1.03	94	0.40	132	0.90	8.24	103	✪		12.80	67	59.18	16
●	USD	5.75	Hansard US Dollar Deposit	H011	28/02/90	IOM	0.80	131	3.74	121	0.38	11.87	89	✪✪		17.11	56	N.A.	
●	USD	N.S.	Hansard US Dollar Deposit Bd	H011	31/03/94	IOM	1.30	9	4.57	82	N.A.	N.A.				N.A.		N.A.	
▲	USD	1.37	Hill Samuel ICF Dollar	H030	30/06/82	JER	0.95	116	4.12	111	0.07	11.91	86	✪		16.58	60	57.66	18
	USD	12.70	HSBC GMF US Dollar	H035	29/03/91	CA	1.16	46	4.97	41	0.07	15.34	15	✪✪✪✪		24.27	2	N.A.	
	USD	160.65	HYPO Dollar Cash	H024	28/06/91	LUX	-3.62	141	4.96	45	1.17	14.90	26	✪✪✪✪		21.47	22	N.A.	
▲	USD	245.83	Inter Cash USD	B069	29/09/89	LUX	1.03	95	5.02	34	0.19	13.32	65	✪✪		19.95	35	N.A.	
▲	USD	6.90	INVESCO PS Dollar Reserve	I014	31/12/90	LUX	1.02	100	3.90	115	0.14	11.83	90	✪		14.45	62	N.A.	
	USD	2.20	Irish Life Intl Dollar Cash	I017	28/04/95	IRL	0.92	119	3.81	117	N.A.	N.A.				N.A.		N.A.	
	USD	211.50	JF Money Fund USD	J004	29/04/88	HK	1.25	16	5.15	20	0.09	15.67	12	✪✪✪✪		23.43	8	N.A.	
●	USD	1.20	JRIA US Dollar Deposit	J002	29/01/93	IRL	0.83	130	3.61	123	0.06	10.46	96	✪		N.A.		N.A.	
▲	USD	4.63	Jupiter Tyndall WUF Money	J008	31/01/84	BER	0.33	139	3.02	127	0.14	8.76	101	✪		13.39	65	57.38	19
	USD	N.S.	Lazard Dollar Liquidity	L002	30/11/84	GU	1.13	59	4.39	96	0.09	13.41	63	✪✪		18.95	42	63.84	9
	USD	262.68	Lion Interinvest Cash USD	C062	30/06/87	LUX	1.29	12	5.34	10	0.08	16.15	7	✪✪✪✪✪		24.05	4	N.A.	
	USD	308.70	Lloyds Intl Liquidity USD	L015	29/09/89	LUX	1.13	66	4.67	72	0.08	14.04	50	✪✪✪		20.92	26	N.A.	
▲	USD	118.38	Lloyds Intl MMF USD	L017	30/11/83	GU	1.08	83	4.57	81	0.07	13.51	61	✪✪		19.53	37	67.64	6
	USD	216.43	LM Glbl US Money Market (II)	L006	31/03/88	NL	0.97	112	4.73	67	0	14.45	38	✪✪✪		21.15	23	N.A.	
	USD	15.37	LM Glbl US Money Mkt Inv B	L006	29/04/88	NL	0.99	108	4.25	104	0	12.97	72	✪✪		19.13	41	N.A.	
	USD	36.50	Luxcash US Dollars A Cap	C002	29/06/90	LUX	1.19	34	4.90	51	0.09	14.55	34	✪✪✪✪		21.77	20	N.A.	
	USD	30.10	Luxinvest LiquiRent USD	B061	30/11/92	LUX	0.79	132	4.65	74	0.56	10.82	95	✪✪		N.A.		N.A.	
	USD	1063.27	M.Lynch Dollar Asset Portf	M023	29/01/88	CA	1.15	52	5.08	27	0	15.07	21	✪✪✪✪✪		22.68	13	N.A.	
	USD	152.12	M.Lynch Senior Float Rate Cmn	M023	29/12/89	CA	1.76	4	6.37	3	0.10	21.53	2	✪✪✪✪✪	2	35.11	1	N.A.	
	USD	0.24	M.Lynch Super Money Mkt Fd A	M023	31/07/90	LUX	1.08	82	4.83	60	0	14.67	30	✪✪✪✪		22.28	16	N.A.	
	USD	48.24	Matrix US Dlr Liquidity A	U011	31/01/96	IRL	1.12	70	N.A.		N.A.	N.A.				N.A.		N.A.	
	USD	N.S.	MeesPierson UF USD Reserve	M012	01/03/96	LUX	0.17	140	N.A.		N.A.	N.A.				N.A.		N.A.	
▲	USD	44.95	Mercury ST USD Reserve	M021	30/11/93	LUX	0.97	114	4.62	76	0.14	13.65	59	✪✪		N.A.		N.A.	
	USD	48.40	MFS Meridian Money Market	M026	31/01/89	CA	1.09	79	4.48	93	0	13.48	62	✪✪		19.23	39	N.A.	
▲	USD	0.57	Midland ICF USD Liquidity	M028	28/02/90	LUX	2.33	1	3.66	122	0.78	8.32	102	✪		12.19	69	N.A.	
	USD	1.65	Money Plus (USD) Cap	C061	30/06/89	LUX	1.20	31	5.04	33	0.09	14.75	28	✪✪✪✪		20.31	32	N.A.	
	USD	14.52	MOSAIS Court Terme USD	C058	30/03/90	LUX	1.03	98	4.67	71	0.09	13.31	66	✪✪		18.48	44	N.A.	
	USD	108.78	Multibond Acticash USD B	C015	29/03/91	LUX	0.87	125	4.16	108	0.21	14.25	43	✪✪✪		20.18	33	N.A.	
▲	USD	6.80	Newton UGF US Dollar	N006	31/03/82	JER	1.02	103	4.33	99	0.07	12.92	73	✪		18.30	46	61.02	14
	USD	0.04	North Star Intl Money USD	N012	31/05/93	CA	0.88	124	1.97	131	0.66	13.02	71	✪✪		N.A.		N.A.	
	USD	2.13	Old Mutual Gnsy US Dllr MM	0003	29/12/95	GU	0.96	115	3.80	118	N.A.	N.A.				N.A.		N.A.	
	USD	0.33	Old Mutual HK Dllr Mnymkt	0004	28/04/95	HK	1.04	93	3.01	129	N.A.	N.A.				N.A.		N.A.	
	USD	10.73	OMI (Gnsy) Dollar Mnymkt	0005	31/05/82	GU	0.98	111	3.42	126	0.10	9.51	99	✪		12.74	68	59.12	17
	USD	73.50	Oracle Ltd	A008	31/03/93	BAH	1.88	3	8.05	1	0.04	25.45	1	✪✪✪✪✪	4	N.A.		N.A.	

▲ SIB Approved ● Insurance Fund Values in US Dollars, on an offer to offer price basis with gross income reinvested Data Source Micropal™

US Dollar Money Market

continued

	CCY	Fund Size ($mil)	Fund Name	Manager Code	Fund Start Date	Domicile Code	3 Mths 97 % Chg	3 Mths 97 Rank	1 Year % Chg	1 Year Rank	Micropal Star Rating Volatility	Micropal Star Rating 3 Years % Chg	Micropal Star Rating 3 Years Rank	Micropal Star Rating Rating	Risk Return Rating	5 Years % Chg	5 Years Rank	10 Years % Chg	10 Years Rank
		272.22	**Mean/Count**				**1.03**	**142**	**4.63**	**132**	**0.23**	**13.76**	**103**			**19.54**	**70**	**62.88**	**21**
	USD	455.35	Parvest Short Term Dollar B	B037	31/07/90	LUX	1.17	42	5.10	24	0.08	14.57	33	✪✪✪		24.06	3	N.A.	
	USD	5.38	Peregrine USD Money Market	P008	31/05/96	CA	1.17	44	N.A.		N.A.	N.A.				N.A.		N.A.	
	USD	N.S.	Perpetual OIA USD Money Mkt	P012	24/01/97	JER	N.A.		N.A.		N.A.	N.A.				N.A.		N.A.	
	USD	9.21	Proton Fund USD Cash	P025	29/09/95	LUX	1.04	89	4.12	110	N.A.	N.A.				N.A.		N.A.	
	USD	45.14	Proventus Dollar Liquidity C	P013	31/08/92	LUX	1.17	43	5.60	5	0.21	16.09	8	✪✪✪✪		N.A.		N.A.	
▲	USD	0.33	Prudential Money Dllr Dep	H031	31/08/92	JER	0.89	121	3.60	124	0.63	12.08	84	✪✪		N.A.		N.A.	
▲	USD	8.60	RBC ICF US Dollar	R003	30/11/82	GU	1.04	92	4.39	95	0.07	12.81	74	✪		18.18	47	61.37	12
	USD	21	RBC IMMF USD Dist	R002	30/06/92	GU	1.04	91	4.51	88	0.50	14.18	46	✪✪✪		N.A.		N.A.	
	USD	0.20	RLI/JF Dollar	R030	10/05/96	IOM	0.59	136	N.A.		N.A.	N.A.				N.A.		N.A.	
	USD	1.80	Royal Life/Guin Fl IFMF USD	R026	30/10/87	IOM	1.44	5	2.71	130	0.14	9.03	100	✪		11.73	70	N.A.	
	USD	6.46	Royal Skandia Dlr Deposit	R038	30/12/88	IOM	1.02	99	3.80	119	0.09	11.24	93	✪		15.37	61	N.A.	
▲	USD	189.53	SBC Dynamic Floor Fd USD 100%	S007	19/07/96	LUX	1.10	77	N.A.		N.A.	N.A.				N.A.		N.A.	
	USD	2586	SBC Money Market Fund USD I	S007	30/11/87	LUX	1.18	36	5.07	28	0.12	14.65	31	✪✪✪		22.19	17	N.A.	
	USD	3887.64	SBC Money Market Fund USD II	S007	31/08/92	LUX	1.18	38	5.06	31	0.12	14.65	32	✪✪✪		N.A.		N.A.	
	USD	7.58	Schroder US Dollar Money	S011	29/12/95	HK	1.18	37	5.13	22	N.A.	N.A.				N.A.		N.A.	
	USD	0.80	Scot Prov GP USD Deposit	S014	30/09/91	IOM	0.97	113	3.78	120	0.10	9.96	98	✪		14.11	63	N.A.	
	USD	31.56	Sicaro Zone US Dollar B	B019	28/02/95	LUX	1.11	75	4.93	48	N.A.	N.A.				N.A.		N.A.	
	USD	31.36	Sogelux Fd Money Mkt USD	S037	21/06/96	LUX	1.19	32	N.A.		N.A.	N.A.				N.A.		N.A.	
	USD	59.71	Sogenalux Treasury US Dollar B	S037	30/06/92	LUX	1.19	35	5.17	19	0.10	15.55	13	✪✪✪✪		N.A.		N.A.	
	USD	2.64	Sun Life Money Dllr	S053	29/01/93	IOM	1.20	28	4.77	66	0.09	13.69	58	✪✪		N.A.		N.A.	
	USD	588.15	Swissca MM Fund USD	S058	30/04/91	LUX	1.18	39	5.09	26	0.08	15.13	19	✪✪✪✪		22.39	15	N.A.	
	USD	3.80	Syfrets Gl USD Money Mkt	S060	30/11/93	CA	1.12	67	5.13	21	0.51	16.77	5	✪✪✪		N.A.		N.A.	
▲	USD	20.44	Templeton GS USD Liquid Res	T001	31/05/94	LUX	1.08	81	3.90	114	N.A.	N.A.				N.A.		N.A.	
▲	USD	9.94	TGA USD Lqd Ass	T009	28/02/89	LUX	1.40	6	4.49	91	0.86	14.03	51	✪✪		19.75	36	N.A.	
	USD	8.59	Thornton New Tiger USD Liquid	T007	31/07/92	BER	1.01	106	4.19	106	1.43	11.90	87	✪		N.A.		N.A.	
	USD	120.19	Trans Monetary USD	N003	31/01/92	LUX	1.07	86	4.58	79	0.09	13.17	68	✪		N.A.		N.A.	
	USD	6710.09	UBS (Lux) Money Mkt Invst USD	U001	30/11/88	LUX	1.17	40	4.94	47	0.22	14.20	45	✪✪✪		21.51	21	N.A.	
	USD	56.70	UBZ Liquidity USD	U002	28/02/91	IRL	1	107	4.85	56	0.16	14.70	29	✪✪✪		23.83	7	N.A.	
	USD	177	UI Money Market USD	U012	11/08/95	LUX	1.15	57	4.84	58	N.A.	N.A.				N.A.		N.A.	
	USD	57.25	Vereins Lux Portf USD Cash	A007	31/03/93	LUX	0.89	122	4.56	83	0.13	14.01	53	✪✪✪		N.A.		N.A.	

▲ SIB Approved ● Insurance Fund **Values in US Dollars, on an offer to offer price basis with gross income reinvested** Data Source Micropal™

SHORT-TERM BOND FUNDS

Short-term bond offshore funds can be seen as a half-way house between money market funds and fixed interest stock funds. In terms of timescale, they most certainly are. While money market funds hold investment instruments with maturities of less than twelve months and fixed interest stock (bond) funds hold mostly investment instruments which mature in more than three years' time, short-term bond offshore funds, on the other hand, cover the up to the three-year time spectrum.

While money market funds are often seen as an alternative to bank deposits and fixed interest stocks are seen as rather more long-term investments, short-term bond funds fulfil a need somewhere in between. These are essentially very safe investments, but ones which should produce marginally better returns than money market funds.

There is not a large number of offshore funds investing primarily in short-term bonds. Most funds are invested in European fixed interest stocks (bonds) - German bonds are the most popular - although there are some Canadian and US funds. Short-term bond funds are usually dominated by the currency in which the investments are held.

Austrian Schilling Short-Term Bond

Funds investing in excess of 70% in Austrian Schilling denominated fixed interest stock (eg treasury bonds, floating rate notes) with maturities up to three years.

										Micropal Star Rating				Risk				
	Fund			Fund						3 Years				Return	5 Years		10 Years	
CCY	Size ($mil)	Fund Name	Manager Code	Start Date	Domicile Code	3 Mths 97 % Chg	Rank	1 Year % Chg	Rank	Volatility	% Chg	Rank	Rating	Rating	% Chg	Rank	% Chg	Rank
	3.93	**Mean/Count**				**-7.07**	**1**	**-3.34**	**1**	**2.57**	**29.64**	**1**		**3**	**0**	**0**	**0**	**0**
● ATS	3.93	DBIM Schilling Garant	D006	31/08/92	LUX	-7.07	1	-3.34	1	2.57	29.64	1	✪✪✪	3	N.A.		N.A.	

BEF/LUF Short-Term Bond

Funds investing in excess of 70% in Belgian and Luxembourg Franc denominated fixed interest stock (eg treasury bonds, floating rate notes) with maturities up to three years.

										Micropal Star Rating				Risk				
	Fund			Fund						3 Years				Return	5 Years		10 Years	
CCY	Size ($mil)	Fund Name	Manager Code	Start Date	Domicile Code	3 Mths 97 % Chg	Rank	1 Year % Chg	Rank	Volatility	% Chg	Rank	Rating	Rating	% Chg	Rank	% Chg	Rank
	77.30	**Mean/Count**				**-7.41**	**13**	**-3.17**	**9**	**2.45**	**33.98**	**5**		**1**	**37.40**	**1**	**0**	**0**
BEF	230.96	BBL Renta Fund Obli Cash BEF C	B052	01/09/95	LUX	-7.32	3	-2.85	4	N.A.	N.A.				N.A.		N.A.	
BEF	90.07	BBL Renta Fund Obli-C MR BEF C	B052	01/09/95	LUX	-7.17	2	-3.63	8	N.A.	N.A.				N.A.		N.A.	
BEF	2.68	BBL Technix Inv Dur.+ MR BEF C	B052	28/06/96	LUX	-7.38	5	N.A.		N.A.	N.A.				N.A.		N.A.	
BEF	12.58	BBL Technix Inv Durat MR BEF C	B052	01/03/96	LUX	-6.63	1	N.A.		N.A.	N.A.				N.A.		N.A.	
BEF	27.68	Contivest Obli Belux Court-T A	B023	30/06/93	LUX	-7.76	13	-5.08	9	2.44	27.74	5	✪	1	N.A.		N.A.	
BEF	19.77	Findico Short Medium Cap	K010	15/03/96	LUX	-7.53	10	N.A.		N.A.	N.A.				N.A.		N.A.	
LUF	183.29	G-Treasury Intl M-T Bel-Lux B	G009	30/11/93	LUX	-7.38	6	-2.10	2	2.42	35.75	1	✪✪✪	4	N.A.		N.A.	
LUF	234.63	G-Treasury Med Term Bel-Lux B	G009	30/11/93	LUX	-7.35	4	-2.09	1	2.42	35.56	2	✪✪	3	N.A.		N.A.	
LUF	28.19	Ippa Portf Belgian Money B	B035	31/03/92	LUX	-7.55	11	-3.47	7	2.48	35.42	4	✪✪✪	2	N.A.		N.A.	
BEF	57.05	KB Cash Short-Medium BEF	K010	30/11/94	LUX	-7.51	9	-3.25	5	N.A.	N.A.				N.A.		N.A.	
BEF	40.28	KB Lux Bond Short Invest BEF B	K011	08/12/95	LUX	-7.50	8	-3.34	6	N.A.	N.A.				N.A.		N.A.	
LUF	34.15	Panelfund Short BEF-LUF Cap	A037	30/04/90	LUX	-7.46	7	-2.67	3	2.45	35.42	3	✪✪✪✪	3	37.40	1	N.A.	
BEF	43.51	Parvest Medium Term BEF B	B037	11/10/96	LUX	-7.73	12	N.A.		N.A.	N.A.				N.A.		N.A.	

Canadian Dollar Short-Term Bond

Funds investing in excess of 70% in Canadian Dollar denominated fixed interest stock (eg treasury bonds, floating rate notes) with maturities up to three years.

										Micropal Star Rating				Risk				
	Fund			Fund						3 Years				Return	5 Years		10 Years	
CCY	Size ($mil)	Fund Name	Manager Code	Start Date	Domicile Code	3 Mths 97 % Chg	Rank	1 Year % Chg	Rank	Volatility	% Chg	Rank	Rating	Rating	% Chg	Rank	% Chg	Rank
	43.99	**Mean/Count**				**-0.07**	**2**	**5.59**	**1**	**0.47**	**14.07**	**1**			**0**	**0**	**0**	**0**
CAD	43.99	Panelfund Short CAD Cap	A037	29/10/93	LUX	0.57	1	5.59	1	0.47	14.07	1	✪✪✪		N.A.		N.A.	

▲ SIB Approved ● Insurance Fund **Values in US Dollars, on an offer to offer price basis with gross income reinvested** Data Source Micropal™

Danish Krone Short-Term Bond

Funds investing in excess of 70% in Danish Krone denominated fixed interest stock (eg treasury bonds, floating rate notes) withmaturities up to three years.

CCY	Fund Size ($mil)	Fund Name	Manager Code	Fund Start Date	Domicile Code	3 Mths 97 % Chg	Rank	1 Year % Chg	Rank	Micropal Star Rating 3 Years Volatility	% Chg	Rank	Rating	Risk Return Rating	5 Years % Chg	Rank	10 Years % Chg	Rank
	19.24	**Mean/Count**				**-6.84**	**2**	**-2.43**	**1**	**0**	**0**	**0**			**0**	**0**	**0**	**0**
● DKK	9.48	Frontrunner DKK Reserve	F032	31/01/95	LUX	-6.68	1	-2.43	1	N.A.	N.A.				N.A.		N.A.	
DKK	28.99	KB Lux Bond Short Invest DKK B	K011	13/12/96	LUX	-6.99	2	N.A.		N.A.	N.A.				N.A.		N.A.	

Europe Short-Term Bond

Funds investing in excess of 70% in European denominated fixed interest stock (eg treasury bonds, floating rate notes) with maturities up to three years.

CCY	Fund Size ($mil)	Fund Name	Manager Code	Fund Start Date	Domicile Code	3 Mths 97 % Chg	Rank	1 Year % Chg	Rank	Micropal Star Rating 3 Years Volatility	% Chg	Rank	Rating	Risk Return Rating	5 Years % Chg	Rank	10 Years % Chg	Rank
	146.13	**Mean/Count**				**-6.91**	**6**	**0.94**	**5**	**2.35**	**31.91**	**3**		**1**	**38.11**	**1**	**0**	**0**
DEM	75.03	Bayernlux Short Term	B051	31/10/91	LUX	-7.13	4	-0.68	4	2.32	34.08	1	✪✪✪✪	4	38.11	1	N.A.	
ECU	8.41	Danske Short Term Acc	D003	31/10/94	LUX	-6.26	1	2.47	2	N.A.	N.A.				N.A.		N.A.	
DEM	695.92	DekaLux Kapital 1-3	D009	31/03/93	LUX	-7.20	5	-2.90	5	2.52	33.07	2	✪✪✪	3	N.A.		N.A.	
ESP	1.19	KB Lux Bond Short Invest ESP B	K011	13/12/96	LUX	-7.63	6	N.A.		N.A.	N.A.				N.A.		N.A.	
DEM	35.04	Luxinvest EuroFlex	B061	30/11/92	LUX	-6.49	2	-0.19	3	2.21	28.57	3	✪✪	2	N.A.		N.A.	
ECU	61.19	Morgan Stanley SM Euro Bond	M039	31/08/94	LUX	-6.73	3	6.02	1	N.A.	N.A.				N.A.		N.A.	

European Currency Unit Short-Term Bond

Funds investing in excess of 70% in European Currency Unit denominated fixed interest stock (eg treasury bonds, floating rate notes) with maturities up to three years.

CCY	Fund Size ($mil)	Fund Name	Manager Code	Fund Start Date	Domicile Code	3 Mths 97 % Chg	Rank	1 Year % Chg	Rank	Micropal Star Rating 3 Years Volatility	% Chg	Rank	Rating	Risk Return Rating	5 Years % Chg	Rank	10 Years % Chg	Rank
	79.86	**Mean/Count**				**-6.37**	**7**	**2.10**	**6**	**2.04**	**30.41**	**4**		**1**	**36.11**	**2**	**0**	**0**
● ECU	51.17	Dit Lux ECU Garantie	D017	31/03/92	LUX	-6.17	2	1.60	4	1.97	30.39	3	✪✪	3	N.A.		N.A.	
● ECU	8.20	Frontrunner ECU Reserve	F032	31/01/95	LUX	-6.52	6	1.62	3	N.A.	N.A.				N.A.		N.A.	
ECU	5.47	KB Lux Bond Short Invest Ecu B	K011	13/12/96	LUX	-6.33	4	N.A.		N.A.	N.A.				N.A.		N.A.	
ECU	7.94	MOSAIS Court Terme ECU	C058	30/03/90	LUX	-6.23	3	0.53	5	2.34	31.63	2	✪✪✪	2	31.23	2	N.A.	
ECU	1.03	Pleiade ECU Reserve	B039	31/05/93	LUX	-6.91	7	-0.06	6	1.96	26.22	4	✪	1	N.A.		N.A.	
ECU	97.45	UBAM Short Term (ECU)	U010	31/12/90	LUX	-5.92	1	3.58	2	1.88	33.41	1	✪✪✪✪	4	40.99	1	N.A.	
ECU	387.73	UBS (Lux) Med Term Inv ECU	U001	31/07/95	LUX	-6.49	5	5.33	1	N.A.	N.A.				N.A.		N.A.	

▲ SIB Approved ● Insurance Fund

Values in US Dollars, on an offer to offer price basis with gross income reinvested

Data Source Micropal™

French Franc Short-Term Bond

Funds investing in excess of 70% in French Franc denominated fixed interest stock (eg treasury bonds, floating rate notes) with maturities up to three years.

CCY	Fund Size ($mil)	Fund Name	Manager Code	Fund Start Date	Domicile Code	3 Mths 97 % Chg	3 Mths 97 Rank	1 Year % Chg	1 Year Rank	Micropal Star Rating 3 Years Volatility	3 Years % Chg	3 Years Rank	Rating	Risk Return Rating	5 Years % Chg	5 Years Rank	10 Years % Chg	10 Years Rank
	10.65	**Mean/Count**				**-7.08**	**7**	**-1.48**	**6**	**2.33**	**29.64**	**3**		**1**	**47.76**	**1**	**0**	**0**
FRF	2.29	Bolux Court Terme	C003	31/07/92	LUX	-5.87	1	-2.48	3	2.36	23.86	3	✪✪	2	N.A.		N.A.	
FRF	9.39	Capital Gestion Oblig CT	C009	30/12/94	LUX	-7.23	4	-2.61	4	N.A.	N.A.				N.A.		N.A.	
FRF	39.65	Eufi-Cash FRF Cap	E012	28/02/94	LUX	-7.80	7	3.45	1	N.A.	N.A.				N.A.		N.A.	
FRF	9.72	Oblicic Plac Crt Terme FF (m)	C022	31/10/89	LUX	-6.79	2	0.59	2	2.26	35.11	1	✪✪✪✪	4	47.76	1	N.A.	
FRF	1.59	Pleiade French Franc Reserve	B039	30/11/93	LUX	-7.32	5	-3.54	5	2.38	29.94	2	✪✪✪	3	N.A.		N.A.	
FRF	1.28	Transoblig FRF Court Terme	B041	30/12/94	LUX	-7.40	6	-4.31	6	N.A.	N.A.				N.A.		N.A.	
FRF	N.S.	UBS (Lux) Med Term Inv FRF	U001	06/09/96	LUX	-7.15	3	N.A.		N.A.	N.A.				N.A.		N.A.	

German DMark Short-Term Bond

Funds investing in excess of 70% in German Deutschmark denominated fixed interest stock (eg treasury bonds, floating rate notes) with maturities up to three years.

	CCY	Fund Size ($mil)	Fund Name	Manager Code	Fund Start Date	Domicile Code	3 Mths 97 % Chg	3 Mths 97 Rank	1 Year % Chg	1 Year Rank	Micropal Star Rating 3 Years Volatility	3 Years % Chg	3 Years Rank	Rating	Risk Return Rating	5 Years % Chg	5 Years Rank	10 Years % Chg	10 Years Rank
		110.45	**Mean/Count**				**-7.54**	**21**	**-3.79**	**19**	**2.52**	**28.06**	**8**			**41.92**	**1**	**0**	**0**
	DEM	95.81	Apocash DEM	U012	07/07/95	LUX	-7.37	16	-4.41	15	N.A.	N.A.				N.A.		N.A.	
	DEM	30.22	BBL Renta Fund Obli Cash DEM C	B052	19/01/96	LUX	-6.81	1	N.A.		N.A.	N.A.				N.A.		N.A.	
	DEM	0.16	Bcilux DEM Conservation	B007	26/07/96	LUX	-10.43	20	N.A.		N.A.	N.A.				N.A.		N.A.	
●	DEM	0.19	CMI Passport German Curr Res	C044	20/01/95	IOM	-7.38	17	-6.46	18	N.A.	N.A.				N.A.		N.A.	
●	DEM	85.28	Credis Bond Short Term DM A	C054	31/03/87	LUX	-7.05	6	-2.30	3	2.78	31.82	2	✪✪✪✪	4	41.92	1	N.A.	
	DEM	N.S.	CS Portfolio Fixed Inc DM A	C068	28/04/95	LUX	-6.98	2	-6.41	17	N.A.	N.A.				N.A.		N.A.	
	DEM	4.10	Danske Short Term Acc DEM	D003	30/06/95	LUX	-7.27	13	-3.62	9	N.A.	N.A.				N.A.		N.A.	
	DEM	18	Europa Lux DM Cash Invest	E014	30/10/92	LUX	-7.23	11	-4.21	13	2.52	25.73	6	✪✪	2	N.A.		N.A.	
▲	DEM	9.26	Fidelity BF DM Short Term	F009	30/11/93	LUX	N.A.	—	-1.56	1	2.48	28.84	5	✪✪	2	N.A.		N.A.	
●	DEM	9.27	Frontrunner DEM Reserve	F032	31/01/95	LUX	-7.40	18	-3.63	10	N.A.	N.A.				N.A.		N.A.	
	DEM	31.12	G-Treasury Intl M-T D-Mark B	G009	31/08/94	LUX	-7.32	15	-2.63	6	N.A.	N.A.				N.A.		N.A.	
	DEM	32.65	G-Treasury Med Term D-Mark B	G009	31/08/94	LUX	-7.31	14	-2.60	5	N.A.	N.A.				N.A.		N.A.	
	DEM	44.01	KB Lux Bond Short Invest DEM B	K011	08/12/95	LUX	-7.05	5	-3.68	11	N.A.	N.A.				N.A.		N.A.	
	DEM	43.21	LO Obliflex 30 DEM Short Term	L019	31/08/94	JER	-7.15	8	-4.23	14	N.A.	N.A.				N.A.		N.A.	
	DEM	45.07	MK Lux Variogeld	M041	30/06/93	LUX	-7.22	10	-2.96	8	2.43	29.84	4	✪✪✪	3	N.A.		N.A.	
	DEM	16.91	Oppenheim Dispo Cash	O009	31/08/92	LUX	-7.23	12	-3.79	12	2.47	23.99	7	✪	1	N.A.		N.A.	
	DEM	43.47	Scontinvest Short Term DEM	S012	29/02/96	LUX	-7.12	7	N.A.		N.A.	N.A.				N.A.		N.A.	
	DEM	47.53	Swiss Life Proteus DEM Res	S056	30/04/93	IRL	-7.02	3	-2.38	4	2.49	33.59	1	✪✪✪✪	4	N.A.		N.A.	
▲	DEM	8.21	Templeton GS DEM Liq Reserve	T001	31/05/94	LUX	-7.19	9	-5.59	16	N.A.	N.A.				N.A.		N.A.	
	DEM	177.90	UBS (Lux) Med Term Inv DM A	U001	31/07/95	LUX	-11.29	21	-2.10	2	N.A.	N.A.				N.A.		N.A.	
	DEM	1566.34	UniplusKapital	U012	30/04/93	LUX	-7.03	4	-2.91	7	2.49	30.21	3	✪✪✪	3	N.A.		N.A.	
▲	DEM	10.80	Von Ernst GP DM Short Term	B021	31/08/93	LUX	-7.45	19	-6.57	19	2.51	20.43	8	✪	1	N.A.		N.A.	

▲ SIB Approved ● Insurance Fund **Values in US Dollars, on an offer to offer price basis with gross income reinvested** Data Source Micropal™

Global Emerging Markets Short-Term Bond

Funds investing in excess of 70% in Global Emerging Markets fixed interest stock (eg treasury bonds, floating rate notes) with maturities up to three years.

CCY	Fund Size ($mil)	Fund Name	Manager Code	Fund Start Date	Domicile Code	3 Mths 97 % Chg	Rank	1 Year % Chg	Rank	Micropal Star Rating 3 Years Volatility	% Chg	Rank	Rating	Risk Return Rating	5 Years % Chg	Rank	10 Years % Chg	Rank
	157.60	**Mean/Count**				**-4.58**	**1**	**0**	**0**	**0**	**0**	**0**			**0**	**0**	**0**	**0**
● DEM	157.60	DBIM Emerging Markets Bond	D006	19/04/96	LUX	-4.58	1	N.A.		N.A.	N.A.				N.A.		N.A.	

Global Short-Term Bond

Funds investing in excess of 70% in Global denominated fixed interest stock (eg treasury bonds, floating rate notes) with maturities up to three years.

CCY	Fund Size ($mil)	Fund Name	Manager Code	Fund Start Date	Domicile Code	3 Mths 97 % Chg	Rank	1 Year % Chg	Rank	Micropal Star Rating 3 Years Volatility	% Chg	Rank	Rating	Risk Return Rating	5 Years % Chg	Rank	10 Years % Chg	Rank
	73.47	**Mean/Count**				**-4.77**	**7**	**-1.68**	**8**	**1.10**	**9.52**	**2**			**0**	**0**	**0**	**0**
LUF	N.S.	BR & A Rente 3 ans B	B019	24/11/95	LUX	-7.33	6	-1.92	4	N.A.	N.A.				N.A.		N.A.	
USD	1.30	Lazard Freres Liquidity	L003	30/11/92	GU	N.A.	—	0.66	3	0.49	4.19	2	✪✪		N.A.		N.A.	
DEM	5.53	Santander Invest Mgd Short-T	B011	30/11/93	LUX	-6.71	4	-3.32	6	1.71	14.85	1	✪✪✪		N.A.		N.A.	
FRF	14.78	Scontinvest Short Term FRF	S012	31/01/95	LUX	-7.02	5	-2.98	5	N.A.	N.A.				N.A.		N.A.	
USD	67.84	Scontinvest Short Term USD	S012	31/01/95	LUX	1.16	1	4.71	2	N.A.	N.A.				N.A.		N.A.	
CHF	97.49	Uni-Global Max 3 ans (FS)	U008	31/08/94	LUX	-6.70	3	-11.99	8	N.A.	N.A.				N.A.		N.A.	
USD	39.93	Uni-Global Max 3 ans (US$)	U008	28/02/95	LUX	0.56	2	5.50	1	N.A.	N.A.				N.A.		N.A.	
DEM	287.42	Unioptimus	U012	29/09/95	LUX	-7.34	7	-4.11	7	N.A.	N.A.				N.A.		N.A.	

Italian Lire Short-Term Bond

Funds investing in excess of 70% in Italian Lire denominated fixed interest stock (eg treasury bonds, floating rate notes) with maturities up to three years.

CCY	Fund Size ($mil)	Fund Name	Manager Code	Fund Start Date	Domicile Code	3 Mths 97 % Chg	Rank	1 Year % Chg	Rank	Micropal Star Rating 3 Years Volatility	% Chg	Rank	Rating	Risk Return Rating	5 Years % Chg	Rank	10 Years % Chg	Rank
	8.07	**Mean/Count**				**-8.77**	**8**	**4.05**	**1**	**1.37**	**24.56**	**1**			**0**	**0**	**0**	**0**
ITL	2.46	BBL Renta Fund Obli Cash ITL C	B052	19/01/96	LUX	-8.60	5	N.A.		N.A.	N.A.				N.A.		N.A.	
ITL	0.16	Bcilux ITL Conservation	B007	26/07/96	LUX	-10.13	8	N.A.		N.A.	N.A.				N.A.		N.A.	
ITL	4.35	Citi PF ITL Short Term Bond	C036	18/10/96	LUX	-9.52	6	N.A.		N.A.	N.A.				N.A.		N.A.	
ITL	0.77	ItalFortune Intl Short-T & Bds	F015	30/07/93	LUX	-8.23	2	4.05	1	1.37	24.56	1	✪✪✪	3	N.A.		N.A.	
ITL	2.02	KB Lux Bond Short Invest ITL B	K011	13/12/96	LUX	-8.55	4	N.A.		N.A.	N.A.				N.A.		N.A.	
ITL	1.89	ProntoFund Italian Sht Term B	B006	09/02/96	LUX	-8.38	3	N.A.		N.A.	N.A.				N.A.		N.A.	
ITL	44.85	The Sailor's-Short Term	B005	05/01/96	LUX	-7.14	1	N.A.		N.A.	N.A.				N.A.		N.A.	
ITL	N.S.	UBS (Lux) Med Term Inv ITL	U001	06/09/96	LUX	-9.64	7	N.A.		N.A.	N.A.				N.A.		N.A.	

▲ SIB Approved ● Insurance Fund **Values in US Dollars, on an offer to offer price basis with gross income reinvested** Data Source Micropal™

Japanese Yen Short-Term Bond

Funds investing in excess of 70% in Japanese Yen denominated fixed interest stock (eg treasury bonds, floating rate notes)with maturities up to three years.

CCY	Fund Size ($mil)	Fund Name	Manager Code	Fund Start Date	Domicile Code	3 Mths 97 % Chg	Rank	1 Year % Chg	Rank	Micropal Star Rating 3 Years Volatility	% Chg	Rank	Rating	Risk Return Rating	5 Years % Chg	Rank	10 Years % Chg	Rank
	24.14	**Mean/Count**						**6.94**	**1**	**0**	**0**	**0**			**0**	**0**	**0**	**0**
USD	24.14	Parworld Asian Bond	B037	03/11/95	LUX	N.A.	—	6.94	1	N.A.	N.A.				N.A.		N.A.	

Netherlands Guilder Short-Term Bond

Funds investing in excess of 70% in Netherland Guilder denominated fixed interest stock (eg treasury bonds, floating rate notes)with maturities up to three years.

CCY	Fund Size ($mil)	Fund Name	Manager Code	Fund Start Date	Domicile Code	3 Mths 97 % Chg	Rank	1 Year % Chg	Rank	Micropal Star Rating 3 Years Volatility	% Chg	Rank	Rating	Risk Return Rating	5 Years % Chg	Rank	10 Years % Chg	Rank
	25.49	**Mean/Count**				**-7.39**	**6**	**-2.93**	**2**	**0**	**0**	**0**			**0**	**0**	**0**	**0**
NLG	22.23	BBL Renta Fund Obli Cash NLG C	B052	19/01/96	LUX	-7.21	1	N.A.		N.A.	N.A.				N.A.		N.A.	
NLG	18.47	G-Treasury Intl M-T Florin B	G009	31/08/94	LUX	-7.63	6	-2.89	1	N.A.	N.A.				N.A.		N.A.	
NLG	30.29	G-Treasury Med Term Florin B	G009	31/08/94	LUX	-7.63	5	-2.96	2	N.A.	N.A.				N.A.		N.A.	
NLG	30.97	KB Lux Bond Short Invest NLG B	K011	08/03/96	LUX	-7.31	3	N.A.		N.A.	N.A.				N.A.		N.A.	
NLG	N.S.	UBS (Lux) Med Term Inv NLG	U001	06/09/96	LUX	-7.37	4	N.A.		N.A.	N.A.				N.A.		N.A.	

Scandinavia Short-Term Bond

Funds investing in excess of 70% in Scandinavian denominated fixed interest stock (eg treasury bonds, floating rate notes) with maturities up to three years.

CCY	Fund Size ($mil)	Fund Name	Manager Code	Fund Start Date	Domicile Code	3 Mths 97 % Chg	Rank	1 Year % Chg	Rank	Micropal Star Rating 3 Years Volatility	% Chg	Rank	Rating	Risk Return Rating	5 Years % Chg	Rank	10 Years % Chg	Rank
	3.03	**Mean/Count**				**-6.55**	**1**	**-3.10**	**1**	**2.83**	**44.79**	**1**		**3**	**0**	**0**	**0**	**0**
FIM	3.03	MultiLink FIM Short Term	I011	29/10/93	LUX	-6.55	1	-3.10	1	2.83	44.79	1	✪✪✪	3	N.A.		N.A.	

Swedish Krona Short-Term Bond

Funds investing in excess of 70% in Swedish Krona denominated fixed interest stock (eg treasury bonds, floating rate notes) with maturities up to three years.

CCY	Fund Size ($mil)	Fund Name	Manager Code	Fund Start Date	Domicile Code	3 Mths 97 % Chg	Rank	1 Year % Chg	Rank	Micropal Star Rating 3 Years Volatility	% Chg	Rank	Rating	Risk Return Rating	5 Years % Chg	Rank	10 Years % Chg	Rank
	13.09	**Mean/Count**				**-8.91**	**4**	**4.45**	**4**	**2.53**	**49.87**	**3**		**2**	**26.80**	**2**	**0**	**0**
● SEK	10.88	Carlson SEK Short Bond A	C011	28/09/90	LUX	-8.89	3	4.76	2	2.36	52.06	1	✪✪✪✪	4	23.20	2	N.A.	
● SEK	6.70	Frontrunner SEK Reserve	F032	31/01/95	LUX	-8.80	2	3.57	3	N.A.	N.A.				N.A.		N.A.	
SEK	21.73	MultiLink SEK Short Term	I011	31/05/93	LUX	-8.65	1	2.60	4	2.38	46.25	3	✪✪	3	N.A.		N.A.	
SEK	13.04	SSF Swedish Bonds	S055	28/02/91	LUX	-9.31	4	6.86	1	2.87	51.32	2	✪✪✪	2	30.40	1	N.A.	

▲ SIB Approved ● Insurance Fund **Values in US Dollars, on an offer to offer price basis with gross income reinvested** Data Source Micropal™

Swiss Franc Short-Term Bond

Funds investing in excess of 70% in Swiss Franc denominated fixed interest stock (eg treasury bonds, floating rate notes) with maturities up to three years.

	CCY	Fund Size ($mil)	Fund Name	Manager Code	Fund Start Date	Domicile Code	3 Mths 97 % Chg	3 Mths 97 Rank	1 Year % Chg	1 Year Rank	Micropal Star Rating 3 Years Volatility	3 Years % Chg	3 Years Rank	Rating	Risk Return Rating	5 Years % Chg	5 Years Rank	10 Years % Chg	10 Years Rank
		145.55	**Mean/Count**				**-7.31**	**6**	**-13.04**	**4**	**3.27**	**18.90**	**2**			**0**	**0**	**0**	**0**
	CHF	5.29	BBL Renta Fund Obli Cash CHF C	B052	19/01/96	LUX	-6.29	2	N.A.		N.A.	N.A.				N.A.		N.A.	
	CHF	0.19	Bcilux SFR Conservation	B007	26/07/96	LUX	-9.75	6	N.A.		N.A.	N.A.				N.A.		N.A.	
	CHF	N.S.	CS Portfolio Fixed Inc SFR A	C068	28/04/95	LUX	-5.92	1	-14.55	4	N.A.	N.A.				N.A.		N.A.	
	CHF	188.08	LO Obliflex V CHF Short Term	L019	30/11/92	JER	-6.46	3	-13.01	2	3.26	19.11	1	✪✪✪	3	N.A.		N.A.	
	CHF	8.64	Pleiade Swiss Franc Reserve	B039	30/11/93	LUX	-6.53	4	-13.28	3	3.28	18.68	2	✪✪	2	N.A.		N.A.	
	CHF	525.57	UBS (Lux) Med Term Inv SFR A	U001	31/07/95	LUX	-8.91	5	-11.33	1	N.A.	N.A.				N.A.		N.A.	

UK Pound Short-Term Bond

Funds investing in excess of 70% in UK Pound denominated fixed interest stock (eg treasury bonds, floating rate notes) with maturities up to three years.

	CCY	Fund Size ($mil)	Fund Name	Manager Code	Fund Start Date	Domicile Code	3 Mths 97 % Chg	3 Mths 97 Rank	1 Year % Chg	1 Year Rank	Micropal Star Rating 3 Years Volatility	3 Years % Chg	3 Years Rank	Rating	Risk Return Rating	5 Years % Chg	5 Years Rank	10 Years % Chg	10 Years Rank
		21.04	**Mean/Count**				**-3.02**	**10**	**15.97**	**7**	**2.08**	**32.68**	**6**		**1**	**23.79**	**4**	**0**	**0**
▲	GBP	13.48	Abtrust Atlas Sterling	A002	31/03/88	LUX	-2.79	5	16.44	3	1.98	29.65	5	✪✪	2	27.55	1	N.A.	
	GBP	37.64	AXA Eqty&Law IFM Total Income	A039	31/01/90	IOM	-2.72	1	17.32	1	1.89	36.80	1	✪✪✪✪	4	26.67	2	N.A.	
	GBP	10.52	Beckman Reserve Assets	C038	31/08/90	IOM	-2.74	2	15.93	4	2.28	33.63	3	✪✪✪	4	22.38	3	N.A.	
●	GBP	0.34	CMI Passport UK Curr Reserve	C044	20/01/95	IOM	-2.76	3	15.65	5	N.A.	N.A.				N.A.		N.A.	
	GBP	0.83	KB Lux Bond Short Invest GBP B	K011	13/12/96	LUX	-3.10	7	N.A.		N.A.	N.A.				N.A.		N.A.	
	GBP	18.12	Lazard Sterling Reserve	L002	31/05/93	GU	-2.96	6	16.60	2	2.15	34.97	2	✪✪✪✪	3	N.A.		N.A.	
	GBP	85.93	Mercury IIT Reserve	M018	28/02/90	JER	-3.28	8	14.61	7	2.23	29.64	6	✪	1	18.59	4	N.A.	
	GBP	N.S.	Singer & Fried Reserve Roll Up	S027	20/09/96	IRL	-3.58	10	N.A.		N.A.	N.A.				N.A.		N.A.	
▲	GBP	1.47	Swiss Life Proteus Reserve	S056	30/09/92	IRL	-2.77	4	15.24	6	1.95	31.42	4	✪✪	2	N.A.		N.A.	

US Dollar Short-Term Bond

Funds investing in excess of 70% in US Dollar denominated fixed interest stock (eg treasury bonds, floating rate notes) with maturities up to three years.

	CCY	Fund Size ($mil)	Fund Name	Manager Code	Fund Start Date	Domicile Code	3 Mths 97 % Chg	3 Mths 97 Rank	1 Year % Chg	1 Year Rank	Micropal Star Rating 3 Years Volatility	3 Years % Chg	3 Years Rank	Rating	Risk Return Rating	5 Years % Chg	5 Years Rank	10 Years % Chg	10 Years Rank
		126.05	**Mean/Count**				**0.81**	**27**	**4.70**	**19**	**0.67**	**12**	**10**			**20.01**	**6**	**0**	**0**
▲	USD	3.10	Abtrust Atlas Dollar	A002	31/03/88	LUX	0.48	22	4.09	14	1.30	10.85	7	✪✪		20.50	4	N.A.	
	USD	9.93	BBL Renta Fund Obli Cash USD C	B052	19/01/96	LUX	0.37	23	N.A.		N.A.	N.A.				N.A.		N.A.	
	USD	0.31	Bcilux USD Conservation	B007	26/07/96	LUX	-1.16	27	N.A.		N.A.	N.A.				N.A.		N.A.	
	USD	203.20	Buttress Liquid Reserve	B080	28/04/95	BER	1.11	7	1.88	18	N.A.	N.A.				N.A.		N.A.	
●	USD	4.90	CMI Ins Co USD Curr Reserve	C043	29/12/89	IOM	1.01	11	4.39	11	0.24	11.63	6	✪✪		15.53	5	N.A.	
●	USD	0.10	CMI Passport US Curr Reserve	C044	20/01/95	IOM	1.03	10	4.40	10	N.A.	N.A.				N.A.		N.A.	
●	USD	61.49	Credis Bond Short Term USD A	C054	31/03/87	LUX	0.66	16	4.35	12	1.48	14.59	3	✪✪✪✪		28.09	1	N.A.	
	USD	N.S.	CS Portfolio Fixed Inc USD A	C068	28/04/95	LUX	1.14	6	-0.43	19	N.A.	N.A.				N.A.		N.A.	
	USD	39.26	Deltec Dollar Income	D010	28/02/94	BVI	1.71	3	10.43	1	N.A.	N.A.				N.A.		N.A.	
	USD	N.S.	EPIC MF USD Short Term Govt	A024	20/10/95	LUX	-0.48	26	2.46	17	N.A.	N.A.				N.A.		N.A.	
	USD	N.S.	EV Medallion Snr Floating B	E003	28/04/95	CA	1.01	12	5.84	3	N.A.	N.A.				N.A.		N.A.	
	USD	N.S.	EV Medallion Snr Floating C	E003	28/04/95	CA	1.01	13	5.83	4	N.A.	N.A.				N.A.		N.A.	

▲ SIB Approved ● Insurance Fund **Values in US Dollars, on an offer to offer price basis with gross income reinvested** Data Source Micropal™

US Dollar Short-Term Bond

continued

	CCY	Fund Size ($mil)	Fund Name	Manager Code	Fund Start Date	Domicile Code	3 Mths 97 % Chg	3 Mths 97 Rank	1 Year % Chg	1 Year Rank	Micropal Star Rating 3 Years Volatility	Micropal Star Rating 3 Years % Chg	Micropal Star Rating 3 Years Rank	Micropal Star Rating 3 Years Rating	Risk Return Rating	5 Years % Chg	5 Years Rank	10 Years % Chg	10 Years Rank
		126.05	**Mean/Count**				**0.81**	**27**	**4.70**	**19**	**0.67**	**12**	**10**			**20.01**	**6**	**0**	**0**
	USD	2.80	G-Treasury Intl M-T USD B	G009	27/09/96	LUX	0.56	21	N.A.		N.A.	N.A.				N.A.		N.A.	
	USD	9.54	G-Treasury Med Term USD B	G009	27/09/96	LUX	0.64	17	N.A.		N.A.	N.A.				N.A.		N.A.	
▲	USD	2.30	HSBC GIF US Dollar Reserve	H033	30/01/87	LUX	1.36	5	3.12	16	1.19	5.13	10	✪		9.16	6	N.A.	
	USD	0.10	ImPac AP USD Liquidity	I005	31/05/96	CA	2.20	1	N.A.		N.A.	N.A.				N.A.		N.A.	
	USD	53.53	KB Lux Bond Short Invest USD B	K011	08/03/96	LUX	0.60	20	N.A.		N.A.	N.A.				N.A.		N.A.	
	USD	N.S.	Lazard Dollar Reserve	L002	08/11/96	IRL	0.33	24	N.A.		N.A.	N.A.				N.A.		N.A.	
	USD	84.90	LO Obliflex K USD Short Term	L019	28/02/90	JER	0.62	18	5.76	5	0.23	14.24	4	✪✪✪		25.36	2	N.A.	
	USD	35.15	Panelfund Short USD Cap	A037	30/09/93	LUX	1.10	8	5.24	6	0.17	14.94	2	✪✪✪✪		N.A.		N.A.	
	USD	5.52	Pleiade Dollar Reserve	B039	30/06/93	LUX	1.05	9	5.02	7	0.26	13.54	5	✪✪✪		N.A.		N.A.	
▲	USD	830.55	SBC Government Bond 1-3 B	S007	29/10/93	LUX	0.73	15	4.85	9	0.32	15.39	1	✪✪✪✪✪		N.A.		N.A.	
	USD	33.29	Scudder GOF US Sht Term A-2	S019	09/08/93	LUX	0.60	19	3.24	15	0.74	8.95	9	✪		N.A.		N.A.	
	USD	161.62	UBAM Short Term Dollar	U010	31/12/90	LUX	0.98	14	4.92	8	0.80	10.75	8	✪✪		21.43	3	N.A.	
	USD	1207.55	UBS (Lux) Med Term Inv USD	U001	31/07/95	LUX	0.01	25	4.24	13	N.A.	N.A.				N.A.		N.A.	
	USD	2.59	USD Floating Rate B	R006	17/05/96	BVI	1.36	4	N.A.		N.A.	N.A.				N.A.		N.A.	
	USD	21.39	USD Floating Rate C	R006	31/08/94	BVI	1.97	2	9.68	2	N.A.	N.A.				N.A.		N.A.	

▲ SIB Approved ● Insurance Fund

Values in US Dollars, on an offer to offer price basis with gross income reinvested

Data Source Micropal™

SPECIALIST FUNDS

Specialist funds tend to be quite risky, being invested in a narrow range of assets such as precious metals or property. Micropal splits specialist funds into four categories: commodity and natural resources funds, real estate funds, derivative investment funds and actively hedged funds.

The commodity and natural resources sector includes funds invested in the shares of companies operating in commodity related industries, most commonly mining, and/or hold physical assets such as gold bullion and other precious metals.

Real estate funds invest in the shares of companies in property related industries and/or hold physical real estate, quite often development sites.

Derivative investment funds concentrate on investments such as futures and options with the aim of achieving high returns. Futures are shares or commodities (assets) bought or sold for future delivery. A commodity has a price today but also has a price for delivery on a future date. The two prices are likely to be different depending on market expectations of what the price will be in, say, three months' time. A fund may buy a future without the intention of taking up the related asset but instead will rely on price changes in order to sell at a profit ahead of delivery. A profit – or loss – can be made without ever holding the underlying asset. Options are rather similar. An option is the right, but not the obligation, to buy (call) or sell (put) an asset at a fixed strike price within a specified period.

Actively hedged funds tend to behave rather like those in the derivative investment sector but have a somewhat broader scope. Such funds will invest in many areas such as equities, fixed interest stock or money market instruments, but specialist funds will also actively speculate in the derivatives market and/or use hedging techniques involving future and option contracts.

Actively Hedged Specialist

Funds that can invest in equities, fixed interest and money market instruments, whilst having the ability to speculate in the derivatives market and/or to employ hedging techniques utilising various option contracts.

		Fund			Fund						Micropal Star Rating				Risk				
		Size		Manager	Start	Domicile	3 Mths 97		1 Year			3 Years			Return	5 Years		10 Years	
	CCY	($mil)	Fund Name	Code	Date	Code	% Chg	Rank	% Chg	Rank	Volatility	% Chg	Rank	Rating	Rating	% Chg	Rank	% Chg	Rank
		114.74	**Mean/Count**				**4.72**	**78**	**13.30**	**68**	**2.83**	**21.88**	**34**			**78.79**	**18**	**332.79**	**4**
	USD	108.88	Aetos	A033	31/01/86	NL	2.90	50	9.96	45	2.86	53.03	2	✪✪✪✪✪	4	108.44	4	298.20	4
	USD	39.23	Alliance US Grth Strategies A	A005	29/09/95	LUX	5.82	26	20.75	14	N.A.	N.A.				N.A.		N.A.	
	USD	46.29	Alpha Hedge	A023	30/09/88	BVI	4.13	40	16.22	25	2.45	16.07	20	✪✪		61.86	11	N.A.	
	USD	0.47	BCL Currency Fd Dollar US	B023	31/08/94	LUX	-0.57	68	4.73	54	N.A.	N.A.				N.A.		N.A.	
	BEF	1.53	BCL Currency Fd Franc Belge	B023	31/08/94	LUX	-8.04	77	-5	60	N.A.	N.A.				N.A.		N.A.	
	USD	N.S.	BDS Special Situations	M002	29/02/96	BVI	7.55	20	N.A.		N.A.	N.A.				N.A.		N.A.	
	ECU	10.99	Buchanan ECU Euro Hedge	A023	31/12/91	BVI	0.17	65	17.98	22	2.69	52.08	3	✪✪✪✪	4	86.48	8	N.A.	
	CHF	14.38	Contravest	0008	29/12/95	BVI	32.02	1	7.18	52	N.A.	N.A.				N.A.		N.A.	
	CHF	13.94	Conzett Europa Invest	0008	29/12/95	BVI	26.94	2	21.64	11	N.A.	N.A.				N.A.		N.A.	
	USD	80	Cypress Intl	C072	30/09/94	CA	-2.99	74	20.56	15	N.A.	N.A.				N.A.		N.A.	
●	DEM	3.09	DBIM US Protektion Juni '97	D006	30/06/95	LUX	-7.63	76	-11.55	64	N.A.	N.A.				N.A.		N.A.	
	USD	5	Enigma Diversified	K009	29/11/91	CA	2.70	52	19.88	19	3.13	25.04	16	✪✪✪	1	46.05	16	N.A.	
	DEM	15.36	Ermitage Odey Existing Shs	E011	30/11/92	BVI	2.02	60	9.67	46	5	-5.93	32	✪✪		N.A.		N.A.	
	USD	301.57	Ermitage Selz	E011	30/04/84	BVI	2.92	49	18.50	21	3	28.80	12	✪✪✪	2	101.65	6	366.98	2
	USD	165	Everest Capital Frontier	E017	30/12/94	BVI	-2.37	72	69.92	2	N.A.	N.A.				N.A.		N.A.	
	USD	645	Everest Capital Intl	E017	31/01/91	BVI	10.80	11	59.07	3	3.45	76.20	1	✪✪✪✪✪	4	133.11	2	N.A.	
	USD	13	Fortuna International	B004	28/02/94	CA	7.17	22	-23.56	68	N.A.	N.A.				N.A.		N.A.	
	DEM	117.35	Giano Capital	P006	30/11/94	BER	-0.54	67	25.45	8	N.A.	N.A.				N.A.		N.A.	
	USD	2700	Haussmann Holdings	H022	31/12/73	NL	4.79	36	16.89	24	2.60	31.68	11	✪✪✪✪	3	109.16	3	367.46	1
	GBP	6.09	IKOS Hedge Stlg	I004	30/11/92	LUX	-0.87	71	-21.51	66	4.70	-6.70	33	✪✪		N.A.		N.A.	
▲	USD	89.89	Intermarket Fund	B003	31/12/87	LUX	0.41	64	10.33	43	1.23	8.37	25	✪		24.41	18	N.A.	
	USD	7	Key Asia Holdings	K004	31/05/94	CA	7.40	21	4.76	53	N.A.	N.A.				N.A.		N.A.	
	USD	12	Key Global Hedge	K004	29/05/92	CA	7.66	18	26.36	7	2.44	5.70	26	✪		N.A.		N.A.	
	USD	22	Key Hedge Fund	K004	30/03/90	CA	2.21	57	14.44	31	1.59	37.28	8	✪✪✪✪	5	75.32	9	N.A.	
	USD	25	Key Longwood Inc.	K004	03/11/95	CA	-2.72	73	20.42	16	N.A.	N.A.				N.A.		N.A.	
	USD	N.S.	KI Asia Pacific	K006	29/10/93	BER	5.08	33	10.67	41	3.08	2.69	28	✪		N.A.		N.A.	
	USD	22.37	Leu Performance	L009	30/09/93	BVI	3.13	46	8.55	50	1.44	-3.30	30	✪		N.A.		N.A.	
	USD	620.20	Leveraged Capital Holdings	M011	30/12/77	NL	5.34	30	20.04	18	2.74	38.03	7	✪✪✪✪	3	98.92	7	298.51	3
	USD	25.80	Magnum	M002	31/03/94	BVI	15.86	4	11.56	39	N.A.	N.A.				N.A.		N.A.	
	USD	19.60	Magnum Aggressive	M002	31/03/94	BVI	16.26	3	12.98	35	N.A.	N.A.				N.A.		N.A.	
	USD	N.S.	Magnum Capital Growth	M002	29/02/96	BVI	8.03	15	N.A.		N.A.	N.A.				N.A.		N.A.	
	USD	9.20	Magnum Multi	M002	31/03/94	BVI	11.26	9	8.78	49	N.A.	N.A.				N.A.		N.A.	
	USD	N.S.	Magnum Special Situations	M002	29/02/96	BVI	3.73	43	N.A.		N.A.	N.A.				N.A.		N.A.	
	USD	10.50	Magnum US Equity	M002	31/08/95	BVI	5.50	29	42.35	4	N.A.	N.A.				N.A.		N.A.	
	USD	14	Momentum Rainbow	M035	31/12/92	BER	4.83	35	20.09	17	2.72	15.92	22	✪✪		N.A.		N.A.	
	USD	10	Momentum Sandalwood	M035	31/03/95	BER	2.10	59	12.89	36	N.A.	N.A.				N.A.		N.A.	
	USD	24.35	Momentum Stock Master	M035	31/03/92	BER	3.22	45	33.35	5	3.87	33.60	10	✪✪✪	1	N.A.		N.A.	
	USD	9	Momentum Universal Hedge	M035	28/04/95	BER	6.98	23	23.23	9	N.A.	N.A.				N.A.		N.A.	
	USD	10	Momentum USMaster	M035	28/04/95	BER	3.02	47	14.53	30	N.A.	N.A.				N.A.		N.A.	
	USD	6	Myrus Intl	K009	31/10/94	CA	N.A.	—	28.40	6	N.A.	N.A.				N.A.		N.A.	
	USD	N.S.	Needham Omni Fund A	M002	29/02/96	BVI	5.82	25	N.A.		N.A.	N.A.				N.A.		N.A.	
	USD	N.S.	Needham Omni Fund B	M002	29/02/96	BVI	4.27	39	N.A.		N.A.	N.A.				N.A.		N.A.	
	USD	N.S.	Nicholas-Applegate Hedge	A023	31/01/90	BVI	-5.20	75	1.77	57	4.45	26.96	14	✪✪✪	1	40.88	17	N.A.	
	USD	18.80	Olympia Intl Arbitrage	0008	29/12/95	CA	2.86	51	12.12	38	N.A.	N.A.				N.A.		N.A.	
	USD	60.40	Optima	0012	30/12/88	BER	1.74	61	14	33	2.34	27.78	13	✪✪✪	2	64.73	10	N.A.	
	USD	N.S.	Optima Alternative Strategies	0012	30/12/94	BER	1.68	62	12.59	37	N.A.	N.A.				N.A.		N.A.	
	USD	16.81	Optima Emerald	0012	31/12/93	BER	2.37	55	16.10	26	1.17	39.20	6	✪✪✪✪✪	5	N.A.		N.A.	
	USD	14.63	Optima Global	0012	31/12/92	BER	11.89	7	21.79	10	2.93	12.47	23	✪✪		N.A.		N.A.	
	USD	187.26	Optima Platinum	0012	31/05/94	BER	4.92	34	4.07	55	N.A.	N.A.				N.A.		N.A.	
	USD	461.22	Orbis Leveraged Equity	0013	29/12/89	BER	5.22	32	10.15	44	4.49	24.18	18	✪✪	1	103.54	5	N.A.	
	USD	N.S.	Orbitex Dynamic	0014	31/07/95	BAH	-20.92	78	73.80	1	N.A.	N.A.				N.A.		N.A.	
	USD	33.16	Pan International Ltd	P002	28/06/91	BVI	4	42	13.16	34	2.06	-1.73	29	✪		52.05	14	N.A.	
	USD	38.10	Park Place International B	P006	28/02/95	BER	6	24	21.42	12	N.A.	N.A.				N.A.		N.A.	
	USD	N.S.	Permal Asian Holdings	P010	30/12/94	NL	7.56	19	3.65	56	N.A.	N.A.				N.A.		N.A.	
	USD	N.S.	Permal Emerging Mkts Holdings	P010	31/12/93	BVI	14.26	5	19.87	20	3.36	15.95	21	✪✪		N.A.		N.A.	
	USD	N.S.	Permal Investment Holdings	P010	31/03/92	NL	5.26	31	8.79	48	2.25	23.22	19	✪✪	2	N.A.		N.A.	
	USD	N.S.	Permal Noscal	P010	31/12/87	BVI	2.18	58	10.65	42	2.68	41.22	5	✪✪✪✪	4	51.62	15	N.A.	

▲ SIB Approved ● Insurance Fund **Values in US Dollars, on an offer to offer price basis with gross income reinvested** Data Source Micropal™

Actively Hedged Specialist

continued

	CCY	Fund Size ($mil)	Fund Name	Manager Code	Fund Start Date	Domicile Code	3 Mths 97 % Chg	3 Mths 97 Rank	1 Year % Chg	1 Year Rank	Micropal Star Rating 3 Years Volatility	3 Years % Chg	3 Years Rank	Rating	Risk Return Rating	5 Years % Chg	5 Years Rank	10 Years % Chg	10 Years Rank
		114.74	**Mean/Count**				**4.72**	**78**	**13.30**	**68**	**2.83**	**21.88**	**34**			**78.79**	**18**	**332.79**	**4**
	USD	173.21	Prima Capital	L009	31/03/93	BVI	2.99	48	17.85	23	2.10	26.64	15	✪✪✪	3	N.A.		N.A.	
	USD	60.68	Regent Pacific Arbitrage	R005	30/10/92	CA	2.67	53	-2.88	59	2.63	8.54	24	✪✪		N.A.		N.A.	
	USD	29.65	Regent Pacific CB Hedge	R005	24/02/95	CA	11.07	10	-21.37	65	N.A.	N.A.				N.A.		N.A.	
	USD	113.30	Regent Pacific Hedge	R005	29/10/93	CA	7.74	17	-6.62	62	3.63	-5.79	31	✪		N.A.		N.A.	
	USD	N.S.	Rosebud Capital Growth	M002	29/02/96	BVI	2.31	56	N.A.		N.A.	N.A.				N.A.		N.A.	
	USD	25.95	SAM McGarr Hedge	S003	30/11/92	IOM	-0.71	69	14.23	32	3.89	41.92	4	✪✪✪✪	2	N.A.		N.A.	
	USD	37.04	SAM Strategy	S003	31/12/90	IOM	3.71	44	15.15	29	2	24.48	17	✪✪✪	3	53.05	13	N.A.	
▲	USD	32.07	Schroder Intl Sel Hed Gl Bond	S010	30/09/94	LUX	-0.76	70	7.46	51	N.A.	N.A.				N.A.		N.A.	
	USD	203	SCI Global Hedge Net Prf Ind	S039	30/06/87	BVI	9.90	12	20.92	13	3.22	34.53	9	✪✪✪✪	2	146.25	1	N.A.	
	USD	18.20	Spinnaker 100 Series	O008	31/05/96	BVI	11.51	8	N.A.		N.A.	N.A.				N.A.		N.A.	
	USD	N.S.	Spirit Hedge Holdings	S043	29/03/91	BVI	5.63	28	10.88	40	1.86	3.52	27	✪		60.67	12	N.A.	
	USD	N.S.	The Merger	O008	29/12/95	CA	4.63	37	15.90	28	N.A.	N.A.				N.A.		N.A.	
	USD	0.61	Titan Eq Hedge Ptfl	T010	31/03/95	CA	2.50	54	-7.95	63	N.A.	N.A.				N.A.		N.A.	
	USD	0.45	Titan Fixed Income Ptfl	T010	31/03/95	CA	4.03	41	9.55	47	N.A.	N.A.				N.A.		N.A.	
	USD	2.98	Titan Global Hedge	T010	24/02/95	CA	0.72	63	-5.89	61	N.A.	N.A.				N.A.		N.A.	
	USD	0.63	Titan Resource Ptfl	T010	31/03/95	CA	5.67	27	-22.14	67	N.A.	N.A.				N.A.		N.A.	
	USD	0.64	Titan Systematic Ptfl	T010	31/03/95	CA	8.96	14	-1.08	58	N.A.	N.A.				N.A.		N.A.	
	USD	N.S.	VIP Select	M002	31/07/96	BVI	-0.09	66	N.A.		N.A.	N.A.				N.A.		N.A.	
	USD	16.50	Winchester HL Olym Star Gl He	O008	29/01/93	BER	4.28	38	16.07	27	2.24	-7.62	34	✪		N.A.		N.A.	

Commodity & Natural Resources Specialist

Funds investing in shares of companies operating in commodity related industries and/or the holding of physical commodities such as bullion.

	CCY	Fund Size ($mil)	Fund Name	Manager Code	Fund Start Date	Domicile Code	3 Mths 97 % Chg	3 Mths 97 Rank	1 Year % Chg	1 Year Rank	Micropal Star Rating 3 Years Volatility	3 Years % Chg	3 Years Rank	Rating	Risk Return Rating	5 Years % Chg	5 Years Rank	10 Years % Chg	10 Years Rank
		25.32	**Mean/Count**				**-1.99**	**43**	**14.78**	**41**	**5.34**	**34.30**	**29**			**68.09**	**24**	**129.91**	**8**
▲	USD	4.33	Abtrust Atlas Gold	A002	31/03/88	LUX	0.34	14	19.88	11	7.49	4.98	15	✪✪✪		192.97	2	N.A.	
	USD	0.06	Abtrust Gold	A003	31/08/82	GU	-4.18	31	-2.05	35	1.71	-7.63	23	✪		-5.35	23	-20.99	8
▲	USD	7.04	AEB Worldfolio 12 Natural Res	A009	31/08/87	LUX	-0.23	16	8.69	19	4.45	8.42	13	✪✪		65.64	10	N.A.	
▲	GBP	3.65	Barclays Global Resources	B046	31/12/71	JER	0.41	13	0.18	31	4.31	15.69	11	✪✪✪		50.72	15	3.20	7
▲	USD	56.70	Baring GUF Global Resources	B049	02/12/94	IRL	-1.95	23	25.33	10	N.A.	N.A.				N.A.		N.A.	
	USD	16.83	BBL (L) Invest Base Metals C	B052	28/02/94	LUX	0.16	15	7.05	21	N.A.	N.A.				N.A.		N.A.	
	USD	35.24	BBL (L) Invest Goldmines C	B052	30/11/89	LUX	-11.23	41	2.89	25	6.71	-9.02	25	✪✪		58.12	13	N.A.	
	ATS	3.62	Blue Danube Futures Select	B055	30/11/95	LUX	-4.26	32	13.16	18	N.A.	N.A.				N.A.		N.A.	
●	USD	10.87	Credis Equity Gold Mines A	C056	29/12/89	LUX	-4.17	30	15.45	15	7.27	-1.84	19	✪✪✪		49.97	16	N.A.	
▲	USD	3.11	CU PP Gold Share	C070	31/10/88	LUX	-3.80	27	0.75	30	6.10	-14.58	28	✪		32.35	18	N.A.	
●	DEM	49.51	DBIM Gold Plus	D006	31/03/94	LUX	-4.65	33	-6.52	39	N.A.	N.A.				N.A.		N.A.	
	USD	N.S.	EPIC MF Nat Resources Wld Eqs	A024	20/10/95	LUX	-0.29	18	8.39	20	N.A.	N.A.				N.A.		N.A.	
	USD	45.40	Ermitage Global Mining	E011	10/11/95	BER	4.49	3	32.28	6	N.A.	N.A.				N.A.		N.A.	
	USD	8.35	F&C RAF Gold	F003	29/01/93	JER	-5.19	36	-1.10	32	2.82	-3.32	20	✪✪		N.A.		N.A.	
▲	USD	3.08	Gartmore CSF Global Resources	G007	29/05/87	JER	2.33	8	6.33	22	5.22	1.43	16	✪✪		61.94	12	N.A.	
	USD	0.60	Glbl Mgr Gold	B066	30/09/94	BER	-6.67	37	-7.09	40	N.A.	N.A.				N.A.		N.A.	
▲	USD	2.31	Guinness Flight Glbl Energy	G019	31/01/85	GU	2.93	5	25.35	9	2.94	57.32	4	✪✪✪✪	4	90.87	6	157.63	3
▲	USD	5.14	Guinness Flight Glbl Gold	G019	30/11/90	GU	-2.36	25	-4.62	38	6.12	-11.26	27	✪		56.37	14	N.A.	
●	USD	0.50	Hansard\GF GSF Glbl Gold	H017	08/07/94	IOM	-1.95	24	-4.26	37	N.A.	N.A.				N.A.		N.A.	
	USD	12.85	Hermes Gold	H028	30/07/93	BER	11.99	2	2.75	26	5.66	-8.90	24	✪		N.A.		N.A.	
	USD	10.50	Indosuez Pacific Gold	I007	31/10/86	HK	-7.35	39	-1.67	34	6.23	-4.61	21	✪✪		65.57	11	99.72	6
▲	USD	22.59	Lloyds IP Gold	L016	30/11/90	LUX	-2.81	26	2.37	27	6.32	-1.31	18	✪✪✪		37.91	17	N.A.	
	USD	10.02	Luxor	B037	29/11/91	LUX	-4.90	34	-4.23	36	1.67	-5.01	22	✪		3.16	22	N.A.	

▲ SIB Approved ● Insurance Fund **Values in US Dollars, on an offer to offer price basis with gross income reinvested** Data Source Micropal™

Commodity & Natural Resources Specialist

continued

	CCY	Fund Size ($mil)	Fund Name	Manager Code	Fund Start Date	Domicile Code	3 Mths 97 % Chg	3 Mths 97 Rank	1 Year % Chg	1 Year Rank	Micropal Star Rating 3 Years Volatility	3 Years % Chg	3 Years Rank	3 Years Rating	Risk Return Rating	5 Years % Chg	5 Years Rank	10 Years % Chg	10 Years Rank
		25.32	**Mean/Count**				**-1.99**	**43**	**14.78**	**41**	**5.34**	**34.30**	**29**			**68.09**	**24**	**129.91**	**8**
▲	GBP	18.40	M&G Island Gold	M001	30/09/80	GU	-4.94	35	41.05	4	7.35	26.64	7	✪✪✪✪	1	135.29	4	100.46	5
	USD	4.91	M.Lynch World Natural Res O	M023	29/04/88	LUX	-0.28	17	13.30	17	3.17	23.87	8	✪✪✪✪	2	29.21	19	N.A.	
▲	USD	22	Manulife Regent GF Gl Resourc	M006	30/11/93	LUX	-0.64	20	59.54	2	6.37	122.19	2	✪✪✪✪✪	3	N.A.		N.A.	
	USD	87.70	Mercury Energy International	M017	31/12/71	JER	2.22	9	29.05	7	3.22	70.15	3	✪✪✪✪✪	4	89.74	7	261.08	2
	USD	234.50	Mercury Intl Gold & General	M017	31/05/93	JER	-0.54	19	1.82	29	7.10	15.06	12	✪✪✪		N.A.		N.A.	
▲	USD	45.08	Mercury ST Gold & Mining	M021	30/12/94	LUX	-0.96	21	2.15	28	N.A.	N.A.				N.A.		N.A.	
	USD	N.S.	Metal Omni	M002	28/06/96	BVI	14.31	1	N.A.		N.A.	N.A.				N.A.		N.A.	
	USD	8.70	MORES	M032	30/10/81	JER	2.90	6	17.34	14	3.08	29.94	6	✪✪✪✪	2	68.93	9	146.13	4
	USD	23.23	Morgan Stanley Gold	M039	28/04/95	LUX	-11.04	40	18.53	13	N.A.	N.A.				N.A.		N.A.	
	USD	39.67	Multigold	B008	31/01/89	LUX	-7.09	38	-1.21	33	5.37	-10.37	26	✪		15.10	21	N.A.	
	USD	1.80	Olympia Stars Natural Resource	O008	30/12/94	BVI	2.81	7	19.20	12	N.A.	N.A.				N.A.		N.A.	
	USD	35.70	Olympia Stars Natural Trust	O008	29/11/96	BVI	3.26	4	N.A.		N.A.	N.A.				N.A.		N.A.	
●	CAD	109.74	Orbitex Natural Resources	O014	31/12/86	BAH	-3.85	28	38.46	5	5.21	16.11	10	✪✪✪		139.59	3	292.08	1
	USD	28.70	Samba Lux Islamic Trade Fin.	S006	21/04/95	LUX	1.13	12	5.04	24	N.A.	N.A.				N.A.		N.A.	
	USD	7.59	Schroder Asia Energy	S011	30/09/87	HK	-1.87	22	47.14	3	4.53	44.38	5	✪✪✪✪	3	80.73	8	N.A.	
	USD	3.71	Schroder Asia Gold	S011	30/10/87	HK	-4.08	29	5.14	23	5.43	0.55	17	✪✪		26.03	20	N.A.	
▲	USD	11.70	Skandifond Natural Resources	S030	29/04/88	LUX	1.34	11	13.74	16	4.34	7.33	14	✪✪		96.65	5	N.A.	
	USD	33.12	Sogelux Fd Equities Gold Mines	S037	31/05/88	LUX	-16.12	42	27.55	8	6.52	20.53	9	✪✪✪✪	1	222.86	1	N.A.	
	FRF	1.07	SynalFund Or Metal	S061	31/10/90	LUX	-20.22	43	-19.09	41	2.50	-26.60	29	✪		-30.18	24	N.A.	
	USD	8.46	US GSF Prec Met & Nat Res	U014	30/09/93	GU	1.61	10	147.86	1	15.59	634.62	1	✪✪✪✪✪	5	N.A.		N.A.	

Derivative Investments Specialist

Funds that invest substantially in derivative instruments such as futures, forward contracts and options, in order to achieve capital appreciation.

	CCY	Fund Size ($mil)	Fund Name	Manager Code	Fund Start Date	Domicile Code	3 Mths 97 % Chg	3 Mths 97 Rank	1 Year % Chg	1 Year Rank	Micropal Star Rating 3 Years Volatility	3 Years % Chg	3 Years Rank	3 Years Rating	Risk Return Rating	5 Years % Chg	5 Years Rank	10 Years % Chg	10 Years Rank
		116.91	**Mean/Count**				**2.44**	**138**	**8.95**	**141**	**4.87**	**22.57**	**101**			**81.51**	**41**	**272.48**	**12**
●	FRF	23.73	Adelaide FRF	E005	30/04/93	LUX	-9.65	131	-3.63	113	2.44	25.66	43	✪✪✪	3	N.A.		N.A.	
●	USD	28.01	Adelaide USD	E005	31/08/94	LUX	-9.66	132	-4.36	115	N.A.	N.A.				N.A.		N.A.	
	USD	5.72	AHL Athena Gtd Financials Cap	E007	31/03/92	BER	9.98	17	27.67	16	6.28	59.49	13	✪✪✪✪	2	N.A.		N.A.	
	USD	3.73	AHL Athena Gtd Financials Inc	E007	31/03/92	BER	8.12	31	20.91	29	4.94	45.32	25	✪✪✪✪	2	N.A.		N.A.	
	USD	15.53	AHL Athena Guaranteed 1997	E007	31/12/90	BER	8.63	27	26.64	18	4.70	60.66	11	✪✪✪✪✪	3	96.52	12	N.A.	
	USD	1.27	AHL Capital Markets	E007	30/07/93	BER	9.21	23	16	43	7.85	46.20	24	✪✪✪	1	N.A.		N.A.	
	USD	6.40	AHL Commodity	E007	30/07/93	BER	8.27	29	35.44	8	9.19	42.01	29	✪✪✪	1	N.A.		N.A.	
	USD	1.48	AHL Currency	E007	30/07/93	BER	7.26	37	41.72	6	6.90	75.69	6	✪✪✪✪	3	N.A.		N.A.	
	USD	17.21	AHL Diversified Gtd	E007	29/12/95	BER	8.74	26	32.90	11	N.A.	N.A.				N.A.		N.A.	
	USD	6.27	AHL Gtd Capital Markets	E007	28/02/94	BER	9.56	20	19.46	34	N.A.	N.A.				N.A.		N.A.	
	USD	7.65	AHL Gtd Real Time Trading	E007	29/10/93	BER	11.17	14	10.29	64	5.62	5.56	70	✪✪		N.A.		N.A.	
	USD	9	AHL Guaranteed Commodities	E007	30/06/94	BER	6.56	41	23.91	22	N.A.	N.A.				N.A.		N.A.	
	USD	2.64	AHL Real Time Trading	E007	30/07/93	BER	N.A.	—	14.31	51	6.82	14.65	57	✪✪✪		N.A.		N.A.	
	USD	17.67	Albatros Performance II	B042	31/03/93	LUX	-5.71	121	-16.04	129	4.85	7.62	67	✪✪		N.A.		N.A.	
	USD	23.80	Alpha Atlas	A023	31/01/94	BVI	2.10	77	7.09	74	N.A.	N.A.				N.A.		N.A.	
	USD	27.07	Alpha Futures	A023	30/09/88	BVI	4.03	54	13.31	53	2.39	11.71	61	✪✪		53.40	22	N.A.	
	USD	89.72	Aquila Intl	A033	31/12/84	BVI	9.86	18	19.02	36	3.11	15.64	55	✪✪		126.56	8	124.68	6

▲ SIB Approved ● Insurance Fund Values in US Dollars, on an offer to offer price basis with gross income reinvested Data Source Micropal™

Derivative Investments Specialist

continued

CCY	Fund Size ($mil)	Fund Name	Manager Code	Fund Start Date	Domicile Code	3 Mths 97 % Chg	3 Mths 97 Rank	1 Year % Chg	1 Year Rank	Micropal Star Rating 3 Years Volatility	3 Years % Chg	3 Years Rank	3 Years Rating	Risk Return Rating	5 Years % Chg	5 Years Rank	10 Years % Chg	10 Years Rank
	116.91	**Mean/Count**				**2.44**	**138**	**8.95**	**141**	**4.87**	**22.57**	**101**			**81.51**	**41**	**272.48**	**12**
ATS	7.93	Blue Danube Diversified	B055	31/03/93	LUX	-7.69	128	3.83	87	3.64	46.79	22	✪✪✪✪	3	N.A.		N.A.	
ATS	7.71	Blue Danube Garant	B055	31/10/94	LUX	-4.41	116	-2.37	109	N.A.	N.A.				N.A.		N.A.	
USD	39.20	Buchanan European & Atlantic	B079	29/05/92	BER	6.79	40	30.36	13	2.37	18.41	48	✪✪	1	N.A.		N.A.	
CHF	0.30	Buchanan Global - CHF	B079	29/04/94	BER	-6.60	125	-10.46	127	N.A.	N.A.				N.A.		N.A.	
GBP	4.68	Buchanan Global - GBP	B079	29/05/92	BER	-1.25	102	18.31	39	2.40	21.14	45	✪✪✪	2	N.A.		N.A.	
USD	82.33	Buchanan Global - USD	B079	29/05/92	BER	1.04	88	9.77	67	1.55	4.20	73	✪		N.A.		N.A.	
USD	46.51	Buchanan Pacific	B079	29/05/92	BER	-6.04	123	-7.52	119	2.59	-11.03	84	✪		N.A.		N.A.	
USD	288.97	CCIL	C047	31/03/87	CA	10.64	15	18.96	37	3.55	40.45	31	✪✪✪✪	3	107.43	9	N.A.	
● AUD	1.81	CLR Select Div AUD G'teed	C064	30/10/92	LUX	-3.02	111	15.73	46	2.80	28.19	38	✪✪✪	2	N.A.		N.A.	
● AUD	0.19	CLR Select Div AUD Trading	C064	30/10/92	LUX	-6.87	127	10.33	63	5.54	12.59	59	✪✪✪		N.A.		N.A.	
● DEM	0.77	CLR Select Div DEM Trading	C064	30/06/92	LUX	-13.60	136	-3.08	110	5.04	10.16	63	✪✪		N.A.		N.A.	
● FRF	1.26	CLR Select Div FRF Trading	C064	30/06/92	LUX	-13.34	135	-1.29	107	5.11	14.78	56	✪✪✪		N.A.		N.A.	
● USD	1.72	CLR Select Div USD G'teed	C064	30/06/92	LUX	-0.95	100	2.40	93	1.58	3.32	74	✪		N.A.		N.A.	
● USD	8.54	CLR Select Div USD Trading	C064	30/06/92	LUX	-4.41	115	5.88	80	5.09	-0.44	78	✪✪		N.A.		N.A.	
● DEM	0.21	CLR Select Fin DEM Trading	C064	30/06/92	LUX	N.A.	—	-31.03	138	3.88	-31.21	95	✪		N.A.		N.A.	
● USD	0.71	CLR Select Fin USD Trading	C064	30/06/92	LUX	N.A.	—	-21.77	135	2.94	-33.93	97	✪		N.A.		N.A.	
ECU	5.08	Dantrust	D004	30/09/85	GU	-8.21	129	4.02	86	2.47	11.17	62	✪✪		36.75	24	155.79	4
● DEM	12.73	DBIM Forex	D006	31/05/93	LUX	-1.74	106	-5.53	117	2.65	14.45	58	✪✪		N.A.		N.A.	
● DEM	64.34	Dit Lux Staatensanleihen /A	D017	28/02/92	LUX	-4.68	118	6.30	77	2.42	21.26	44	✪✪✪	4	N.A.		N.A.	
DEM	4.60	Ermitage Int Rate Strategy	E011	31/03/94	BER	-6.75	126	-6.15	118	N.A.	N.A.				N.A.		N.A.	
USD	3.90	Europa American Option	E013	31/12/90	CA	-24.53	138	97.56	1	9.13	121.13	2	✪✪✪✪	4	165.48	6	N.A.	
USD	27.59	Fenchurch Gamma	F007	29/05/87	IRL	3.99	55	2.44	92	5.87	-21.96	87	✪		27.86	27	N.A.	
USD	2.16	Floortrader	F023	23/02/96	BVI	6.88	38	N.A.		N.A.	N.A.				N.A.		N.A.	
USD	14.17	Fortitude Group	F027	31/08/93	BVI	-3.34	113	0.12	101	4.58	39.76	32	✪✪✪	2	N.A.		N.A.	
USD	12.29	Fortitude High Risk	F027	28/04/95	BVI	-8.21	130	-8.54	123	N.A.	N.A.				N.A.		N.A.	
USD	1.01	Fountain Futures	F028	31/01/94	BVI	N.A.	—	-32.60	140	N.A.	N.A.				N.A.		N.A.	
USD	1.92	Gaia FX Ltd	G001	30/06/93	CA	8.21	30	4.36	85	7.16	58.08	16	✪✪✪✪	1	N.A.		N.A.	
USD	3.96	Gaia Guaranteed Currency I	G001	29/06/90	CA	1.58	80	6.12	78	1.26	9.54	64	✪✪		19.19	28	N.A.	
USD	2.18	Gaia Guaranteed Currency II	G001	30/11/90	CA	1.34	82	4.62	83	1.34	7.24	68	✪		8.30	32	N.A.	
USD	1.37	Gain B	L022	29/11/91	BER	0.57	92	75.50	3	9.59	70.14	8	✪✪✪✪	1	168.24	5	N.A.	
USD	108.60	GAM Cross Market	G002	31/05/93	IOM	9.22	22	10.42	60	2.02	32.38	35	✪✪✪✪	4	N.A.		N.A.	
USD	59.40	GAM Teleos	G003	29/12/95	BVI	4.15	53	18.77	38	N.A.	N.A.				N.A.		N.A.	
DEM	61.79	GAM Trading DEM	G003	30/10/92	IOM	7.74	33	11.36	57	1.99	15.71	54	✪✪		N.A.		N.A.	
USD	159.20	GAM Trading USD	G003	29/06/90	IOM	7.61	35	16.57	42	1.70	17.94	49	✪✪	3	80.94	13	N.A.	
USD	281.60	GAMut Investments	G003	11/07/86	IOM	17.17	6	21.32	28	4.07	33.13	34	✪✪✪	1	127.58	7	1055.90	2
● USD	25.95	Gems Progressive D	G008	28/02/90	BVI	6.19	43	12.55	55	2.76	7.81	66	✪		68.80	15	N.A.	
● USD	7.64	Gems Progressive J	G008	30/04/92	BVI	3.48	59	28.91	15	3.79	26.67	41	✪✪✪	1	N.A.		N.A.	
● USD	21.18	Gems Progressive T	G008	30/04/92	BVI	2.16	75	15.08	48	2.59	19.40	47	✪✪✪	1	N.A.		N.A.	
CHF	3.83	Global Arbitrage Ltd	E016	31/12/91	BVI	-5.07	119	-8.88	124	2.76	4.75	72	✪✪		16.30	31	N.A.	
NLG	1.86	Global Commodities&Futures	E007	30/11/94	BER	1.10	85	8.54	71	N.A.	N.A.				N.A.		N.A.	
CHF	1.64	Global Fut. & Opt. SICAV CHF	U002	28/02/94	LUX	-12.33	133	-18.60	132	N.A.	N.A.				N.A.		N.A.	
DEM	10.96	Global Futures I	E007	28/02/94	BER	1.05	87	17.08	41	N.A.	N.A.				N.A.		N.A.	
DEM	17.64	Global Futures II	E007	31/08/94	BER	2.19	74	23.53	23	N.A.	N.A.				N.A.		N.A.	
DEM	13.77	Global Futures III	E007	28/04/95	BER	2.34	72	22.44	25	N.A.	N.A.				N.A.		N.A.	
DEM	29.84	Global Futures IV	E007	10/11/95	BER	2.38	70	23.34	24	N.A.	N.A.				N.A.		N.A.	
USD	1.22	GNI Composite	G012	31/12/85	BER	1.49	81	1.32	98	2.15	5.30	71	✪		18.37	30	161.37	3
USD	137.50	GNI Directional	G012	31/07/92	BER	-2.85	110	6.55	76	3.26	54.95	19	✪✪✪✪	4	N.A.		N.A.	
USD	50.16	GNI Diversified	G012	30/06/93	BER	-2.37	109	5.29	81	2.47	28.98	37	✪✪✪	3	N.A.		N.A.	
USD	11.65	GNI Global Financial	G012	31/03/94	BER	-1.57	105	1.79	95	N.A.	N.A.				N.A.		N.A.	
USD	26.70	GNI Technical	G012	31/05/94	BER	3.10	62	7.79	73	N.A.	N.A.				N.A.		N.A.	
USD	N.S.	Graham Financial Futures	O012	29/12/95	BER	1.77	79	12.80	54	N.A.	N.A.				N.A.		N.A.	
USD	86	Hasenbichler Commodities	H021	31/07/90	AUT	6.83	39	20.08	30	7.76	67.56	9	✪✪✪✪	2	282.78	4	N.A.	
USD	79.85	Hermes Neutral	H028	30/04/92	BER	2.95	64	14.38	50	1.38	16.09	53	✪✪		N.A.		N.A.	
GBP	4.03	Hermes Sterling	H028	26/02/93	BER	-0.53	96	25.35	21	2.40	34.14	33	✪✪✪	4	N.A.		N.A.	
DEM	9.30	HYPO Futures Vision	H024	31/12/93	LUX	-6.16	124	2.80	91	3.53	16.77	51	✪✪		N.A.		N.A.	
USD	8.58	Inter Futures Diversified 1	B069	29/09/95	LUX	9.15	24	4.56	84	N.A.	N.A.				N.A.		N.A.	
JPY	13.65	JF Japan Ninja Leveraged	J004	31/01/91	HK	-3.39	114	-21.21	133	12.49	-46.82	99	✪✪		-40.80	39	N.A.	

▲ SIB Approved ● Insurance Fund **Values in US Dollars, on an offer to offer price basis with gross income reinvested** Data Source Micropal™

continued

CCY	Fund Size ($mil)	Fund Name	Manager Code	Fund Start Date	Domicile Code	3 Mths 97 % Chg	3 Mths 97 Rank	1 Year % Chg	1 Year Rank	Micropal Star Rating 3 Years Volatility	3 Years % Chg	3 Years Rank	Rating	Risk Return Rating	5 Years % Chg	5 Years Rank	10 Years % Chg	10 Years Rank
	116.91	**Mean/Count**				**2.44**	**138**	**8.95**	**141**	**4.87**	**22.57**	**101**			**81.51**	**41**	**272.48**	**12**
JPY	9.09	JF Ninja	J004	31/08/90	HK	7.87	32	-58.91	141	20.20	-49.36	100	✪✪		34.06	25	N.A.	
USD	64.01	John Henry Gl Strategies C	J005	31/12/92	BER	2.15	76	30.83	12	5.31	75.10	7	✪✪✪✪✪	4	N.A.		N.A.	
USD	6.65	John Henry Gl Strategies D	J005	31/01/94	BER	1.31	83	33.45	9	N.A.	N.A.				N.A.		N.A.	
USD	0.82	John Henry Gl Strategies F	J005	31/12/92	BER	6.36	42	9.97	65	4.91	27.60	40	✪✪✪	1	N.A.		N.A.	
USD	1.07	John Henry Gl Strategies H	J005	31/12/92	BER	N.A.	—	-9.16	125	5.16	0.73	76	✪✪		N.A.		N.A.	
USD	2.46	John Henry Gl Strategies K	J005	31/05/93	BER	3.62	58	19.87	31	4.60	58.03	17	✪✪✪✪	3	N.A.		N.A.	
USD	90	Kodiak International	M030	30/11/93	CA	-0.75	99	2.85	89	2.34	8.97	65	✪✪		N.A.		N.A.	
USD	91.17	Lehman Currency Adv Ptfl	L008	02/08/93	NL	4.38	50	2.97	88	4.30	-4.41	80	✪		N.A.		N.A.	
AUD	0.36	LPS Intl Australian Issue	L022	30/09/93	BER	0.19	93	45.14	5	9.95	7.05	69	✪✪✪		N.A.		N.A.	
USD	1.40	LPS Intl High Performance B	L022	29/11/91	BER	0.05	95	49.16	4	8.59	27.78	39	✪✪✪	1	59.86	20	N.A.	
USD	0.11	LPS Intl Ordinary A	L022	29/03/91	BER	-1.16	101	14.24	52	4.20	11.77	60	✪✪		31.41	26	N.A.	
USD	N.S.	Magnum Turbo Growth	M002	31/07/96	BVI	5.91	45	N.A.		N.A.	N.A.				N.A.		N.A.	
USD	1.50	McD Financial Arbitrage	A032	31/01/84	BER	2.50	69	2.84	90	5.83	-22.59	88	✪		18.43	29	139.68	5
USD	0.85	MIMC MINT Gtd Nov 2002	M033	31/10/86	BER	N.A.	—	-7.92	121	3.78	-27.58	92	✪		-19.21	36	94.01	8
USD	1.82	MIMC MINT Gtd Spcal Issue	M033	30/05/86	BER	7.72	34	-3.75	114	3.27	-25.42	91	✪		-12.06	34	117.80	7
USD	23	MIMC MINT Ltd Income	M033	31/10/86	BER	17.45	5	1.46	97	6.16	-31.78	96	✪		-29.32	38	52.50	11
USD	4.90	MIMC MINT Ltd Ordinary	M033	31/12/82	BER	17.64	2	1.48	96	6.16	-30.66	93	✪		-24.02	37	64.77	10
USD	7.85	MIMC MINT Plus Guaranteed Bond	M033	31/01/95	BER	7.39	36	-3.56	112	N.A.	N.A.				N.A.		N.A.	
USD	30	Momentum AssetMaster	M035	31/07/91	BER	0.95	89	15.94	45	1.36	47.99	20	✪✪✪✪✪	5	106.28	10	N.A.	
FRF	1.65	MultiFutures	M040	31/03/92	LUX	-22.68	137	-22.64	136	6.42	-42.58	98	✪		N.A.		N.A.	
DEM	6.61	Omega	K003	31/08/94	LUX	3.94	56	11.54	56	N.A.	N.A.				N.A.		N.A.	
USD	3.26	OMI (Gnsy) Gtd Futures Bd 105	O005	31/12/93	GU	-0.60	98	1.84	94	3.69	16.20	52	✪✪		N.A.		N.A.	
USD	5.05	OMI (Gnsy) Gtd Futures Bd I	O005	31/05/91	GU	12.87	8	30.32	14	4.68	46.85	21	✪✪✪✪	2	68.65	16	N.A.	
USD	3.66	OMI (Gnsy) Gtd Futures Bd II	O005	31/12/91	GU	11.22	13	26.26	20	4.08	41.69	30	✪✪✪✪	2	53.85	21	N.A.	
USD	4.36	OMI (Gnsy) Gtd Futures Bd III	O005	30/06/92	GU	11.81	12	26.28	19	4.45	43.27	27	✪✪✪✪	2	N.A.		N.A.	
USD	4.40	OMI (Gnsy) Gtd Futures Bd IV	O005	29/01/93	GU	12.17	10	27.20	17	4.66	44.33	26	✪✪✪✪	2	N.A.		N.A.	
USD	0.70	OMI (Gnsy) Gtd Futures Bd V	O005	31/05/93	GU	-1.27	103	-5.05	116	3.13	-17.45	85	✪		N.A.		N.A.	
USD	0.01	OMI (Gnsy) Mgd Futures Fund	O005	30/11/92	GU	0.93	90	-11.06	128	3.56	-10.73	83	✪		N.A.		N.A.	
USD	54.52	Optima Futures	O012	28/06/91	BER	5.94	44	19.53	33	2.79	21.11	46	✪✪✪	1	100.26	11	N.A.	
USD	4.14	Optima Short	O012	31/05/90	BER	4.19	51	-17.94	131	7.48	-30.87	94	✪		-52.59	40	N.A.	
USD	15.05	Pacific Rim Opportunity	A023	30/07/93	BVI	5.35	47	-0.68	105	2.57	-22.88	89	✪		N.A.		N.A.	
USD	2.03	Paribas Deriv Bond & Curr	B037	27/10/95	LUX	-12.60	134	-21.68	134	N.A.	N.A.				N.A.		N.A.	
USD	4.54	Paribas Deriv Global Futures	B037	30/07/93	LUX	0.87	91	-31.20	139	10.05	-74.99	101	✪		N.A.		N.A.	
USD	N.S.	PCP Futures	P007	31/05/96	CA	2.75	66	N.A.		N.A.	N.A.				N.A.		N.A.	
USD	N.S.	Permal FX Financial & Futures	P010	29/05/92	BVI	5.53	46	17.21	40	2.06	26.67	42	✪✪✪	3	N.A.		N.A.	
USD	16.66	PFC Lev Cross Ccy & Bd Dllr	P014	30/03/90	BER	2.84	65	8.06	72	3.29	-20.54	86	✪		-9.66	33	N.A.	
GBP	1.15	PFC Lev Cross Ccy & Bd Stlg	P014	30/10/92	BER	-1.97	107	15.71	47	2.90	-5.80	81	✪		N.A.		N.A.	
USD	N.S.	Premier Futures Adv Ptfl	L008	31/01/94	BAH	9.34	21	9.53	68	N.A.	N.A.				N.A.		N.A.	
USD	0.71	Privestor Global Diversified	P026	31/03/93	BER	1.99	78	6.07	79	2.92	17.52	50	✪✪	1	N.A.		N.A.	
USD	4611	Quantum	S040	31/12/86	NL	3.16	61	-1.64	108	7.88	42.74	28	✪✪		292.32	2	1172.77	1
USD	1876	Quantum Emerging Gth	S040	31/01/92	NL	17.57	3	38.02	7	8.68	46.57	23	✪✪✪✪	2	N.A.		N.A.	
USD	2489.30	Quantum Industrial Holdings	S040	29/04/94	NL	-5.88	122	19.11	35	N.A.	N.A.				N.A.		N.A.	
USD	1757.80	Quasar International	S040	29/03/91	NL	11.94	11	9.31	69	8.10	63.38	10	✪✪✪✪	3	291.47	3	N.A.	
USD	2250.80	Quota	S040	31/12/91	NL	21.52	1	78.80	2	13.92	327.15	1	✪✪✪✪✪	5	851.64	1	N.A.	
USD	2.54	Sabre Commodity Recovery	S002	15/07/94	BER	13.55	7	-3.39	111	N.A.	N.A.				N.A.		N.A.	
● USD	0.57	Sabre Futures A	S002	28/02/83	BVI	8.97	25	0.98	99	3.73	-0.85	79	✪		37.88	23	84.27	9
USD	N.S.	Signet Offshore	S026	28/02/92	CA	2.36	71	-7.69	120	3.49	2.17	75	✪✪		N.A.		N.A.	
USD	9	SJO Global Fund B	S029	30/09/92	BER	-5.42	120	10.36	61	6.85	60.36	12	✪✪✪✪	2	N.A.		N.A.	
USD	N.S.	Strome Offshore	S049	30/04/92	CA	2.53	68	-16.97	130	9.50	-6.62	82	✪✪		N.A.		N.A.	
USD	5.75	SUN SUN Fund	S025	31/05/91	HK	1.12	84	33.17	10	17.10	0.37	77	✪✪✪		-73.86	41	N.A.	
CHF	N.S.	Swiss Franc Gl Currency	M031	31/05/95	IRL	-3.09	112	-9.22	126	N.A.	N.A.				N.A.		N.A.	

▲ SIB Approved ● Insurance Fund

Values in US Dollars, on an offer to offer price basis with gross income reinvested

Data Source Micropal™

Derivative Investments Specialist

continued

CCY	Fund Size ($mil)	Fund Name	Manager Code	Fund Start Date	Domicile Code	3 Mths 97 % Chg	3 Mths 97 Rank	1 Year % Chg	1 Year Rank	Micropal Star Rating 3 Years Volatility	3 Years % Chg	3 Years Rank	3 Years Rating	Risk Return Rating	5 Years % Chg	5 Years Rank	10 Years % Chg	10 Years Rank
	116.91	**Mean/Count**				**2.44**	**138**	**8.95**	**141**	**4.87**	**22.57**	**101**			**81.51**	**41**	**272.48**	**12**
USD	2.39	Systemtrend Ltd	C064	31/08/84	BER	-0.55	97	-8.02	122	5.49	-23.81	90	✪		-19.08	35	46.19	12
USD	1.75	The Interallianz Warr & Option	I010	28/02/95	LUX	0.11	94	-1.10	106	N.A.	N.A.				N.A.		N.A.	
USD	0.21	Titan Euro Equity	T010	30/09/94	CA	2.65	67	-0.49	103	N.A.	N.A.				N.A.		N.A.	
USD	0.25	Titan Euro Financial	T010	28/10/94	CA	1.06	86	21.68	26	N.A.	N.A.				N.A.		N.A.	
USD	0.28	Titan Forex	T010	30/12/94	CA	-2.03	108	0.03	102	N.A.	N.A.				N.A.		N.A.	
USD	0.40	Titan FX Delta	T010	28/04/95	CA	5.33	48	9.20	70	N.A.	N.A.				N.A.		N.A.	
USD	0.51	Titan Metals	T010	31/08/94	CA	17.49	4	-26.78	137	N.A.	N.A.				N.A.		N.A.	
USD	0.21	Titan US Equity	T010	31/08/95	CA	-1.54	104	6.59	75	N.A.	N.A.				N.A.		N.A.	
USD	0.20	Titan US Financial	T010	31/08/95	CA	N.A.	N.A.	0.15	100	N.A.	N.A.				N.A.		N.A.	
CHF	14.38	TSG General CHF Units	T014	31/07/90	BER	3.27	60	10.35	62	2.86	57.75	18	✪✪✪✪✪	5	64.42	19	N.A.	
GBP	8.27	TSG General GBP Units	T014	31/07/90	BER	3.02	63	10.96	58	2.80	58.17	15	✪✪✪✪✪	5	65.50	17	N.A.	
USD	15.70	TSG General USD Units	T014	31/07/90	BER	2.32	73	10.94	59	2.83	58.45	14	✪✪✪✪✪	5	65.47	18	N.A.	
CHF	1.71	TSG Leveraged CHF Units	T014	31/03/92	BER	8.45	28	15.97	44	4.73	85.99	4	✪✪✪✪✪	4	N.A.		N.A.	
GBP	0.56	TSG Leveraged GBP Units	T014	31/03/92	BER	9.63	19	21.55	27	4.96	89.41	3	✪✪✪✪✪	4	N.A.		N.A.	
USD	0.90	TSG Leveraged USD Units	T014	31/03/92	BER	10.62	16	19.82	32	4.82	84.30	5	✪✪✪✪✪	4	N.A.		N.A.	
USD	N.S.	USD Global Currency	M031	30/12/94	IRL	4.45	49	9.84	66	N.A.	N.A.				N.A.		N.A.	
USD	90	Winchester Futures Olym Star	O008	31/12/90	BVI	4.16	52	15	49	2.08	30.36	36	✪✪✪✪	4	76.67	14	N.A.	
FRF	0.95	Winchester Olm Star FF Hgd	O008	31/07/95	BVI	-4.52	117	-0.67	104	N.A.	N.A.				N.A.		N.A.	
FRF	5.40	Winchester Olm Star FF Mgd	O008	31/07/95	BVI	3.92	57	5.09	82	N.A.	N.A.				N.A.		N.A.	

Real Estate Specialist

Funds investing in shares of companies in property related industries and/or the holding of physical real estate such as development sites.

	CCY	Fund Size ($mil)	Fund Name	Manager Code	Fund Start Date	Domicile Code	3 Mths 97 % Chg	3 Mths 97 Rank	1 Year % Chg	1 Year Rank	Micropal Star Rating 3 Years Volatility	3 Years % Chg	3 Years Rank	3 Years Rating	Risk Return Rating	5 Years % Chg	5 Years Rank	10 Years % Chg	10 Years Rank
		431.77	**Mean/Count**				**-1.65**	**13**	**11.95**	**13**	**3.78**	**7.12**	**8**			**32.36**	**8**	**65.20**	**1**
▲	USD	8.11	American Phoenix US Real Est	A025	28/04/95	LUX	5.44	2	27.77	4	N.A.	N.A.				N.A.		N.A.	
	LUF	6.65	BBL (L) Invest Euro-Immo C	B052	31/05/91	LUX	2.68	5	13.28	7	2.95	1.56	7	✪		14.64	5	N.A.	
	USD	0.40	CIBC-CEF Pacific Prop Shares	C017	30/09/88	BER	-12.20	13	16.73	6	7.37	-19.41	8	✪		110.26	1	N.A.	
	LUF	94.06	Cregem Immo Cap	C065	28/02/94	LUX	-7.12	11	-4.52	10	N.A.	N.A.				N.A.		N.A.	
	LUF	80.74	Immo Royal Immobiliere A	B025	31/05/89	LUX	-7.35	12	-6.10	12	3.06	23.23	1	✪✪✪✪	3	14.55	6	N.A.	
	DEM	194.98	Immocorp SICAV (m)	C048	31/12/87	LUX	-7.06	10	-11.82	13	3.02	4.93	6	✪✪		-7.52	8	N.A.	
	BEF	124.56	International Property Fund C	K010	30/11/88	LUX	-6.66	9	3.93	9	2.22	12.51	3	✪✪✪		5.74	7	N.A.	
	LUF	4.21	Ippa Portf Belgian Immo B	B035	31/05/94	LUX	-4.69	8	-5.21	11	N.A.	N.A.				N.A.		N.A.	
	ECU	6.27	Paneurolife Intl Real Estate	P003	28/02/91	LUX	-3.61	7	29.72	3	3.72	9.60	4	✪✪✪		57.61	2	N.A.	
	USD	63.78	Performa Real Estate Secs	P009	29/07/94	LUX	3.69	3	30.39	2	N.A.	N.A.				N.A.		N.A.	
	USD	53.19	Regent Undervalue Assets Prop	R005	29/04/94	CA	1.27	6	19.32	5	N.A.	N.A.				N.A.		N.A.	
	NLG	4974.42	Rodamco N.V	R009	30/03/79	EN	11.21	1	11.12	8	3.39	5.47	5	✪✪		18.89	4	65.20	1
●	GBP	1.61	Royal Life Intl Property	R020	30/01/87	IOM	2.94	4	30.77	1	4.54	19.07	2	✪✪✪✪	2	44.70	3	N.A.	

▲ SIB Approved ● Insurance Fund **Values in US Dollars, on an offer to offer price basis with gross income reinvested** Data Source Micropal™

WARRANT FUNDS

Warrants are a type of investment instrument which gives the holder the right to subscribe for shares at some time in the future and at prices fixed when the warrants are issued. For a relatively small initial investment, warrants offer the buyer the option of a future stake in a company's equity. Some warrants expire in one or two years' time, while many are for five to 10 years, and others are perpetual. Warrants are basically very speculative. Large sums can be made by investing in warrants and conversely great sums can be lost.

The theoretical value of a warrant can be calculated by subtracting the exercise price of the warrant from the current share price of the underlying share and multiplying this by the number of shares which may be purchased with each warrant. So, for example, if the share price is $10, the exercise price is $3 and each warrant allows the purchase of five shares, then the value of the warrant is ($10 - $3) x 5 = $35.

Warrants are most appealing when the price of the underlying shares is rising because any movement in the share price tends to be exaggerated in the price of the warrant. Of course, this makes them very unappealing when the underlying share price is going downwards. With the above example, if the share price rose by 10 per cent to $11, the value of the warrant would rise by nearly 15 per cent to $40. Likewise, a 20 per cent fall in the share price to $8 would result in a warrant value of just $25 - a price fall of nearly 30 per cent.

Because of this exaggerated or leveraged effect, offshore warrant funds tend to be more volatile than ordinary equity funds. The majority of offshore warrant funds specialise in the markets of Asia Pacific. Just how volatile such funds are can be seen by looking at their performance returns. For example, some funds in the Japan warrant sector have less than 20 per cent of their original assets left after five years of investment. Meanwhile, some warrants funds have made nearly 400 per cent profit.

Consequently, warrant funds are not advisable for most investors. Even for investors happy to take on a bit of speculation, warrant funds should not make up a large portion of a portfolio.

Europe Warrants

Funds investing in excess of 70% in European warrants or related instruments. Funds in this category may leverage or be highly geared.

	CCY	Fund Size ($mil)	Fund Name	Manager Code	Fund Start Date	Domicile Code	3 Mths 97 % Chg	3 Mths 97 Rank	1 Year % Chg	1 Year Rank	Micropal Star Rating 3 Years Volatility	3 Years % Chg	3 Years Rank	Rating	Risk Return Rating	5 Years % Chg	5 Years Rank	10 Years % Chg	10 Years Rank
		14.27	**Mean/Count**				**39.77**	**2**	**97.05**	**2**	**9.76**	**38.03**	**2**		**2**	**194.28**	**2**	**0**	**0**
●	USD	1.15	Hansard\INVESCO European Warr	H018	27/09/91	IOM	38.88	2	94.10	2	10.10	30.46	2	✪✪	2	169.26	2	N.A.	
▲	USD	27.40	INVESCO European Warrant	I013	28/02/90	LUX	40.66	1	100	1	9.43	45.60	1	✪✪✪	3	219.30	1	N.A.	

Far East & Pacific Ex Japan Warrants

Funds investing in excess of 70% in Far Eastern warrants or related instruments excluding Japan. Funds in this category may leverage or be highly geared

	CCY	Fund Size ($mil)	Fund Name	Manager Code	Fund Start Date	Domicile Code	3 Mths 97 % Chg	3 Mths 97 Rank	1 Year % Chg	1 Year Rank	Micropal Star Rating 3 Years Volatility	3 Years % Chg	3 Years Rank	Rating	Risk Return Rating	5 Years % Chg	5 Years Rank	10 Years % Chg	10 Years Rank
		13.64	**Mean/Count**				**-4.68**	**3**	**26.90**	**3**	**11.75**	**-26.76**	**3**			**143.25**	**3**	**0**	**0**
	USD	4.50	CIBC-CEF Malay Thai Sing Warr	C017	30/03/90	BER	-9.20	3	-20.91	3	13.52	-51.93	3	✪✪		20.83	3	N.A.	
●	USD	3.92	Hansard\INVESCO Asia Tgr Warr	H018	27/09/91	IOM	-0.10	1	52.62	1	10.92	-8.76	1	✪✪✪✪		197.68	2	N.A.	
	USD	32.50	INVESCO Asia Tiger Warrant	I013	31/01/90	LUX	-4.75	2	49.01	2	10.80	-19.57	2	✪✪✪		211.24	1	N.A.	

Far East & Pacific Warrants

Funds investing in excess of 70% in Far Eastern and Pacific warrants or related instruments. Funds in this category may leverage or be highly geared.

	CCY	Fund Size ($mil)	Fund Name	Manager Code	Fund Start Date	Domicile Code	3 Mths 97 % Chg	3 Mths 97 Rank	1 Year % Chg	1 Year Rank	Micropal Star Rating 3 Years Volatility	3 Years % Chg	3 Years Rank	Rating	Risk Return Rating	5 Years % Chg	5 Years Rank	10 Years % Chg	10 Years Rank
		6.41	**Mean/Count**				**-10.25**	**5**	**31.57**	**4**	**12.16**	**-35.17**	**4**			**110.16**	**4**	**0**	**0**
	USD	15.24	Baring WUF Tristar Warrant	B049	31/07/89	IRL	-22.57	5	78.85	2	13.78	-33.14	3	✪✪✪		223.67	1	N.A.	
	USD	1.98	ImPac AP Warrant	I005	31/05/96	CA	-17.50	4	N.A.		N.A.	N.A.				N.A.		N.A.	
	USD	12.11	JF Far Eastern Warrants	J004	29/09/89	HK	1.16	1	-40.44	4	13.33	-78.69	4	✪		-10.04	4	N.A.	
	USD	0.58	MBf Pacific Warrants	M010	29/12/89	HK	-1.44	2	81.28	1	11.97	-10.81	1	✪✪✪✪		150.19	2	N.A.	
	USD	2.15	Schroder Asia FE Warrant	S011	31/01/90	HK	-10.88	3	6.60	3	9.55	-18.06	2	✪✪		76.84	3	N.A.	

▲ SIB Approved ● Insurance Fund Values in US Dollars, on an offer to offer price basis with gross income reinvested Data Source Micropal™

Germany Warrants

Funds investing in excess of 70% in German warrants or related instruments. Funds in this category may leverage or be highly geared.

CCY	Fund Size ($mil)	Fund Name	Manager Code	Fund Start Date	Domicile Code	3 Mths 97 % Chg	3 Mths 97 Rank	1 Year % Chg	1 Year Rank	Micropal Star Rating 3 Years Volatility	3 Years % Chg	3 Years Rank	Rating	Risk Return Rating	5 Years % Chg	5 Years Rank	10 Years % Chg	10 Years Rank
	3.38	**Mean/Count**				**7.82**	**2**	**2.72**	**2**	**4.73**	**23.80**	**1**		**1**	**56.18**	**1**	**0**	**0**
DEM	1.22	Aragon Sv German Warrant	A028	30/11/90	LUX	23.38	1	25.43	1	4.73	23.80	1	✪✪✪	3	56.18	1	N.A.	
● DEM	5.53	DBIM DAX Protektion Juni '97	D006	30/06/95	LUX	-7.74	2	-19.99	2	N.A.	N.A.				N.A.		N.A.	

Global Warrants

Funds investing in excess of 70% in Global warrants or related instruments. Funds in this category may leverage or be highly geared.

CCY	Fund Size ($mil)	Fund Name	Manager Code	Fund Start Date	Domicile Code	3 Mths 97 % Chg	3 Mths 97 Rank	1 Year % Chg	1 Year Rank	Micropal Star Rating 3 Years Volatility	3 Years % Chg	3 Years Rank	Rating	Risk Return Rating	5 Years % Chg	5 Years Rank	10 Years % Chg	10 Years Rank
	2.72	**Mean/Count**				**9.86**	**2**	**-20.77**	**2**	**7.29**	**-53.81**	**2**			**-39.67**	**1**	**0**	**0**
▲ USD	2.75	Lloyds IP Warrant	L016	30/11/90	LUX	15.99	1	-20.84	2	9.10	-46.93	1	✪✪✪		-39.67	1	N.A.	
USD	2.68	Regent Lifford Country Warr	R005	31/12/92	CA	3.73	2	-20.69	1	5.48	-60.70	2	✪✪		N.A.		N.A.	

Hong Kong Warrants

Funds investing in excess of 70% in Hong Kong warrants or related instruments. Funds in this category may leverage or be highly geared.

CCY	Fund Size ($mil)	Fund Name	Manager Code	Fund Start Date	Domicile Code	3 Mths 97 % Chg	3 Mths 97 Rank	1 Year % Chg	1 Year Rank	Micropal Star Rating 3 Years Volatility	3 Years % Chg	3 Years Rank	Rating	Risk Return Rating	5 Years % Chg	5 Years Rank	10 Years % Chg	10 Years Rank
	5	**Mean/Count**				**4.07**	**1**	**195.29**	**1**	**17.56**	**53.50**	**1**		**3**	**766.19**	**1**	**0**	**0**
USD	5	CIBC-CEF Hong Kong Warrant	C017	31/08/88	BER	4.07	1	195.29	1	17.56	53.50	1	✪✪✪	3	766.19	1	N.A.	

▲ SIB Approved ● Insurance Fund **Values in US Dollars, on an offer to offer price basis with gross income reinvested** Data Source Micropal™

Japan Warrants

Funds investing in excess of 70% in Japanese warrants or related instruments. Funds in this category may leverage or be highly geared.

	CCY	Fund Size ($mil)	Fund Name	Manager Code	Fund Start Date	Domicile Code	3 Mths 97 % Chg	3 Mths 97 Rank	1 Year % Chg	1 Year Rank	Micropal Star Rating 3 Years Volatility	3 Years % Chg	3 Years Rank	Rating	Risk Return Rating	5 Years % Chg	5 Years Rank	10 Years % Chg	10 Years Rank
		12.97	**Mean/Count**				**-5.34**	**11**	**-44.45**	**11**	**15.11**	**-43.60**	**10**			**-52.26**	**9**	**-84.52**	**2**
	USD	7	Fleming Japanese Warrant	F019	30/04/90	LUX	8.51	2	-59.48	11	17.17	-66.43	7	✪✪✪		-87.73	6	N.A.	
▲	USD	1.80	Gartmore Japan Warrant	G006	31/01/86	LUX	N.A.	—	-54.76	8	18.44	-66.67	8	✪✪✪✪		-87.16	5	-87.52	2
	USD	24	GT Asian Warr & Derivatives A	G018	31/10/91	IRL	14.78	1	27.60	1	10.04	153.05	1	✪✪✪✪✪	3	200.85	1	N.A.	
●	USD	2.08	Hansard\INVESCO Nippon Warr	H018	30/08/91	IOM	-7.95	6	-48.24	5	13.05	-64.80	6	✪		-89.40	9	N.A.	
▲	USD	49.60	INVESCO Nippon Warrant	I013	29/08/86	LUX	-9.62	7	-55.93	9	16.57	-67.09	9	✪✪		-89.03	8	-81.53	1
	USD	41.04	JF Japan Warrants	J004	30/04/91	HK	-0.72	5	-58.42	10	16.85	-62.85	4	✪✪✪		-72.10	3	N.A.	
▲	USD	6.56	KB Japanese Warrant	K007	12/07/91	LUX	-18.68	10	-54.17	7	17.30	-56.38	2	✪✪✪✪		-71.84	2	N.A.	
▲	CHF	4.83	Nippon Growth Warrant	U002	30/11/94	LUX	4.25	3	-48.32	6	N.A.	N.A.				N.A.		N.A.	
●	USD	1.50	RLI/MIM Brit Nippon Warrant	R029	31/08/90	IOM	-25	11	-46.34	3	14.21	-61.74	3	✪✪		-86.21	4	N.A.	
	CHF	N.S.	RMF Warrants Japan	R008	22/03/96	LUX	1.18	4	N.A.		N.A.	N.A.				N.A.		N.A.	
	USD	2.97	Schroder Japan Warrant	S008	30/03/90	GU	-15.79	9	-46.48	4	15.62	-64.15	5	✪✪		-87.74	7	N.A.	
	USD	1.26	Thornton Japan Warrants	T006	28/02/92	BER	-9.73	8	-44.37	2	11.90	-78.90	10	✪		N.A.		N.A.	

▲ SIB Approved ● Insurance Fund **Values in US Dollars, on an offer to offer price basis with gross income reinvested** Data Source Micropal™

SECOND UNITS

Individual funds may have more than one share/unit class issued and these classes may be identified as an A,B,C,D, capitalisation or distributing unit. To avoid distortions in the rankings and mean counts (average) statistics, Micropal lists only one class of each fund in its sectorial sections. The second units, if they exist, are all grouped together in an unsectorised fashion in the following section. The choice of the unit to be displayed in the sectorial rankings usually is the more popular unit as recommended by the investment advisors of the fund.

No Micropal Star Rating™ or risk return ratio is calculated for the non-sectored funds.

Second Units Non-sector

	CCY	Fund Size ($mil)	Fund Name	Manager Code	Fund Start Date	Domicile Code	3 Mths 97 % Chg	Rank	1 Year % Chg	Rank	Micropal Star Rating 3 Years Volatility	% Chg	Rank	Rating	Risk Return Rating	5 Years % Chg	Rank	10 Years % Chg	Rank
		61.14	**Mean/Count**				-2.65	688	7	601	7.41	28.18	366			48.49	206	166.15	29
	USD	27.05	ACMGI American Growth Ptf B	A005	30/06/92	LUX	2.54	100	18.24	96	3.89	50.90	33	N.A.	N.A.	N.A.		N.A.	
	USD	3.92	ACMGI American Growth Ptf C2	A005	30/12/94	LUX	2.54	100	18.24	96	N.A.	N.A.		N.A.	N.A.	N.A.		N.A.	
	USD	106.12	ACMGI American Income Ptf B	A005	30/06/93	LUX	3.97	72	12.65	167	2.70	23.47	235	N.A.	N.A.	N.A.		N.A.	
	USD	27.06	ACMGI American Income Ptf C	A005	30/06/93	LUX	0.02	193	12.65	167	2.70	23.47	234	N.A.	N.A.	N.A.		N.A.	
	USD	4.58	ACMGI American Income Ptf C2	A005	30/11/94	LUX	0.53	173	12.44	169	N.A.	N.A.		N.A.	N.A.	N.A.		N.A.	
	USD	79.89	ACMGI Dev. Regional Mkts B	A005	30/10/92	LUX	9.02	27	18.86	88	5.15	-10.44	351	N.A.	N.A.	N.A.		N.A.	
	USD	2.56	ACMGI Dev. Regional Mkts C2	A005	30/11/94	LUX	8.95	28	18.86	87	N.A.	N.A.		N.A.	N.A.	N.A.		N.A.	
	USD	1.80	ACMGI Global Bond Portf BX	A005	31/07/91	LUX	0.10	191	9.63	203	1.87	7.80	320	N.A.	N.A.	11.84	194	N.A.	
	USD	51.05	ACMGI Global Growth Trends A	A005	28/04/95	LUX	-3.05	319	13.86	154	N.A.	N.A.		N.A.	N.A.	N.A.		N.A.	
	USD	89.64	ACMGI Global Growth Trends B	A005	28/04/95	LUX	-3.30	326	12.70	166	N.A.	N.A.		N.A.	N.A.	N.A.		N.A.	
	USD	49.97	ACMGI Global Growth Trends BX	A005	31/10/91	LUX	-3.19	324	13.32	160	4.02	67.20	15	N.A.	N.A.	114.13	9	N.A.	
	USD	13.36	ACMGI Intl Health Care Ptf A	A005	07/07/95	LUX	3.61	80	1.68	380	N.A.	N.A.		N.A.	N.A.	N.A.		N.A.	
	USD	25.54	ACMGI Intl Health Care Ptf B	A005	07/07/95	LUX	3.37	86	0.66	405	N.A.	N.A.		N.A.	N.A.	N.A.		N.A.	
	USD	5.21	ACMGI Intl Health Care Ptf BX	A005	31/03/92	LUX	3.50	82	1.16	394	4.15	65.62	18	N.A.	N.A.	N.A.		N.A.	
	USD	36.22	ACMGI Intl Privatn Portf B	A005	30/06/94	LUX	6.02	49	16.34	123	N.A.	N.A.		N.A.	N.A.	N.A.		N.A.	
	USD	0.50	ACMGI Privanza Global Bal. B	A005	31/01/95	LUX	-1.51	270	7.32	235	N.A.	N.A.		N.A.	N.A.	N.A.		N.A.	
	USD	31.76	ACMGI Privanza Global Bal. C2	A005	30/12/94	LUX	-1.51	272	7.12	237	N.A.	N.A.		N.A.	N.A.	N.A.		N.A.	
	USD	27.61	ACMGI Sht Maturity Dllr Ptf B	A005	31/10/94	LUX	1.09	144	4.1	320	N.A.	N.A.		N.A.	N.A.	N.A.		N.A.	
	USD	2.98	ACMGI Sht Maturity Dllr Ptf C	A005	31/10/94	LUX	1.09	144	4.1	320	N.A.	N.A.		N.A.	N.A.	N.A.		N.A.	
▲	USD	0.29	Aetna IUF Am Sm Cos B	A011	29/12/95	LUX	-9.03	661	6.06	260	N.A.	N.A.		N.A.	N.A.	N.A.		N.A.	
▲	USD	2.17	Aetna IUF American Equity B	A011	31/05/93	LUX	1.82	114	28.14	31	3.26	67.02	16	N.A.	N.A.	N.A.		N.A.	
▲	USD	78.89	Aetna IUF Asian Equity B	A011	30/04/93	LUX	-0.52	219	19.91	80	6.04	-1.02	338	N.A.	N.A.	N.A.		N.A.	
▲	AUD	0.61	Aetna IUF Aus Dllr Bond B	A011	28/02/94	LUX	-1.61	274	13.82	155	N.A.	N.A.		N.A.	N.A.	N.A.		N.A.	
▲	AUD	1.26	Aetna IUF Australian Eqty B	A011	30/04/93	LUX	-1.92	281	16.22	126	5.05	31.25	148	N.A.	N.A.	N.A.		N.A.	
▲	CAD	1.04	Aetna IUF Canadian Dllr Bd B	A011	31/05/93	LUX	-1.79	279	8.08	220	2.49	13.16	301	N.A.	N.A.	N.A.		N.A.	
▲	DEM	5.32	Aetna IUF Deutschmark Bd B	A011	31/05/93	LUX	-7.29	579	-4.43	519	2.41	21.72	250	N.A.	N.A.	N.A.		N.A.	
▲	DEM	1.05	Aetna IUF Deutschmark Res B	A011	31/05/94	LUX	-7.42	611	-3	494	N.A.	N.A.		N.A.	N.A.	N.A.		N.A.	
▲	USD	5.82	Aetna IUF Emerging Asia B	A011	29/12/95	LUX	8.68	32	0.91	399	N.A.	N.A.		N.A.	N.A.	N.A.		N.A.	
▲	USD	4.13	Aetna IUF Emerging Europe B	A011	29/12/95	LUX	18.67	3	18.08	99	N.A.	N.A.		N.A.	N.A.	N.A.		N.A.	
▲	USD	13.07	Aetna IUF European Eqty B	A011	30/09/93	LUX	4.69	64	18.61	91	2.95	42.98	52	N.A.	N.A.	N.A.		N.A.	
▲	JPY	28.65	Aetna IUF Japanese Eqty B	A011	30/04/93	LUX	-10.23	676	-20.80	599	5.13	-12.11	354	N.A.	N.A.	N.A.		N.A.	
▲	USD	0.73	Aetna IUF Latin American B	A011	30/04/93	LUX	17.43	7	15.96	131	5.28	-5.88	345	N.A.	N.A.	N.A.		N.A.	
▲	USD	2.94	Aetna IUF Mgd European Bd B	A011	31/05/93	LUX	-6.52	446	4.40	317	1.86	29.04	170	N.A.	N.A.	N.A.		N.A.	
▲	GBP	2.11	Aetna IUF Sterling Bd B	A011	19/07/93	LUX	-3.40	328	13.54	157	2.26	23.90	231	N.A.	N.A.	N.A.		N.A.	
▲	GBP	5.80	Aetna IUF UK Equity B	A011	31/05/93	LUX	0.82	160	29.56	26	3.68	48.51	35	N.A.	N.A.	N.A.		N.A.	
▲	GBP	2.88	Aetna IUF UK Sm Cos B	A011	29/12/95	LUX	7.31	41	38.19	11	N.A.	N.A.		N.A.	N.A.	N.A.		N.A.	
▲	USD	1.89	Aetna IUF US Dollar Bd B	A011	31/05/93	LUX	-1.31	261	2.05	372	1.26	9.37	316	N.A.	N.A.	N.A.		N.A.	
▲	USD	1.91	Aetna IUF US Dollar Res B	A011	29/10/93	LUX	0.78	161	5.99	263	0.28	10.85	314	N.A.	N.A.	N.A.		N.A.	
▲	JPY	1.15	Aetna IUF Yen Bond B	A011	31/05/93	LUX	-5.80	404	-9.67	575	4.07	5.78	327	N.A.	N.A.	N.A.		N.A.	
	BEF	N.S.	AGAM Invest Lux Internat Bds D	A013	31/01/95	LUX	-3.99	340	3.17	345	N.A.	N.A.		N.A.	N.A.	N.A.		N.A.	
	BEF	N.S.	AGAM Strategy Bonds BEF Dist	A013	31/12/93	LUX	-7.34	596	2.81	359	2.32	43.53	48	N.A.	N.A.	N.A.		N.A.	
	BEF	N.S.	AGAM Strategy Inter Equities D	A013	28/04/95	LUX	0.02	194	13.42	159	N.A.	N.A.		N.A.	N.A.	N.A.		N.A.	
	USD	9.84	Alliance Intl Technology A	A005	29/09/95	LUX	-9.58	665	16.99	117	N.A.	N.A.		N.A.	N.A.	N.A.		N.A.	
	USD	28.84	Alliance Intl Technology B	A005	29/09/95	LUX	-9.81	668	15.84	135	N.A.	N.A.		N.A.	N.A.	N.A.		N.A.	
	USD	3.90	Alliance Middle East Opps B	A005	31/01/95	LUX	17.95	4	40	8	N.A.	N.A.		N.A.	N.A.	N.A.		N.A.	
	USD	65.61	Alliance US Grth Strategies B	A005	29/09/95	LUX	5.70	52	19.87	81	N.A.	N.A.		N.A.	N.A.	N.A.		N.A.	
	USD	0.10	America Index Plus Fund A	C015	30/06/94	LUX	2.60	98	25.49	46	N.A.	N.A.		N.A.	N.A.	N.A.		N.A.	
	DEM	N.S.	Aqua Allemagne Dis	B026	31/01/94	LUX	-7.07	528	-4.65	525	N.A.	N.A.		N.A.	N.A.	N.A.		N.A.	
	USD	N.S.	Aqua Amerique Dis	B026	31/01/94	LUX	1.25	131	5.01	292	N.A.	N.A.		N.A.	N.A.	N.A.		N.A.	
	CAD	N.S.	Aqua Canada Dis	B026	31/01/94	LUX	-0.13	201	3.76	326	N.A.	N.A.		N.A.	N.A.	N.A.		N.A.	
	LUF	N.S.	Aqua Europe Dis	B026	31/01/94	LUX	-7.32	591	-4.84	541	N.A.	N.A.		N.A.	N.A.	N.A.		N.A.	
	USD	31.34	Asian Technology Portfolio B	A005	31/07/96	LUX	-1.89	280	N.A.		N.A.	N.A.		N.A.	N.A.	N.A.		N.A.	
	USD	9.35	Asian Technology Portfolio H	A005	31/07/96	LUX	-1.67	276	N.A.		N.A.	N.A.		N.A.	N.A.	N.A.		N.A.	
	USD	6.99	Asian Technology Portfolio I	A005	31/07/96	LUX	-1.46	268	N.A.		N.A.	N.A.		N.A.	N.A.	N.A.		N.A.	
	BEF	1.61	Astrobal Belgian Bonds A	B036	28/06/96	LUX	-7.16	555	N.A.		N.A.	N.A.		N.A.	N.A.	N.A.		N.A.	
	DEM	4.57	Astrobal Hard Currency Bonds A	B036	28/06/96	LUX	-6.91	503	N.A.		N.A.	N.A.		N.A.	N.A.	N.A.		N.A.	
	LUF	27.45	Astrobal International A	B036	28/11/86	LUX	-4.63	358	5.13	287	3.04	33.58	128	N.A.	N.A.	56.15	56	183.53	11

▲ SIB Approved ● Insurance Fund **Values in US Dollars, on an offer to offer price basis with gross income reinvested** Data Source Micropal™

Second Units Non-sector

continued

CCY	Fund Size ($mil)	Fund Name	Manager Code	Fund Start Date	Domicile Code	3 Mths 97 % Chg	3 Mths 97 Rank	1 Year % Chg	1 Year Rank	Micropal Star Rating 3 Years Volatility	3 Years % Chg	3 Years Rank	Rating	Risk Return Rating	5 Years % Chg	5 Years Rank	10 Years % Chg	10 Years Rank
	61.14	**Mean/Count**				**-2.65**	**688**	**7**	**601**	**7.41**	**28.18**	**366**			**48.49**	**206**	**166.15**	**29**
LUF	N.S.	Bacob Dollar Bonds D	B002	08/11/96	LUX	-0.25	206	N.A.		N.A.	N.A.		N.A.	N.A.	N.A.		N.A.	
LUF	N.S.	Bacob Euro Convergence D	B002	08/11/96	LUX	-7.68	632	N.A.		N.A.	N.A.		N.A.	N.A.	N.A.		N.A.	
DEM	N.S.	Bacob Euro Core D	B002	08/11/96	LUX	-7.30	582	N.A.		N.A.	N.A.		N.A.	N.A.	N.A.		N.A.	
BEF	N.S.	Bacob Luxinvest Short Term Dis	B002	08/12/95	LUX	-7.32	588	-4.71	530	N.A.	N.A.		N.A.	N.A.	N.A.		N.A.	
ATS	13.59	Baer Multibond Austro Bond D	J007	29/11/91	LUX	-6.58	456	0.10	416	3.02	36.39	102	N.A.	N.A.	51.67	79	N.A.	
CHF	5.86	Baer Multibond Convert Bond D	J007	29/10/93	LUX	0.94	155	5.30	279	2.45	13.01	302	N.A.	N.A.	N.A.		N.A.	
DEM	40.77	Baer Multibond DM Bond D	J007	31/03/92	LUX	-6.77	475	-1.92	465	3	29.30	168	N.A.	N.A.	N.A.		N.A.	
USD	22.90	Baer Multibond Dollar Bond D	J007	29/06/90	LUX	-0.77	228	3.98	323	1.85	15.28	282	N.A.	N.A.	30.13	155	N.A.	
ATS	1.41	Baer Multibond Erste EC Bd D	J007	30/06/92	LUX	-6.60	459	2.89	354	2.96	33.36	129	N.A.	N.A.	N.A.		N.A.	
ECU	108.16	Baer Multibond Euro Bond D	J007	29/06/90	LUX	-6.84	490	8.87	209	2.84	33.12	130	N.A.	N.A.	53.08	73	N.A.	
DEM	17.69	Baer Multibond Global Bond D	J007	29/10/93	LUX	-4.69	362	5.17	284	2.31	17.18	269	N.A.	N.A.	N.A.		N.A.	
CHF	71.02	Baer Multibond Swiss Bond D	J007	29/11/91	LUX	-5.38	383	-10.41	580	3.63	25.79	216	N.A.	N.A.	44.32	108	N.A.	
ATS	2.06	Baer Multicoop Central Eur D	J007	31/10/94	LUX	15.31	11	63.80	1	N.A.	N.A.		N.A.	N.A.	N.A.		N.A.	
CHF	9.98	Baer Multicoop Gerfds Bds D	J007	29/04/94	LUX	-7.88	645	-3.42	500	N.A.	N.A.		N.A.	N.A.	N.A.		N.A.	
CHF	63.01	Baer Multicoop MI FONDS 30 D	M029	31/03/95	LUX	-2.72	302	-2.46	477	N.A.	N.A.		N.A.	N.A.	N.A.		N.A.	
CHF	34.69	Baer Multicoop MI FONDS 50 D	M029	31/03/95	LUX	-1.51	271	0.96	397	N.A.	N.A.		N.A.	N.A.	N.A.		N.A.	
ECU	31.43	Baer Multistock Eur Stk D	J007	29/06/90	LUX	3.53	81	24.91	51	3.02	51.08	31	N.A.	N.A.	69.70	27	N.A.	
DEM	10.28	Baer Multistock German Stk D	J007	31/12/93	LUX	8.84	29	24.23	55	3.04	65.44	19	N.A.	N.A.	N.A.		N.A.	
JPY	17.34	Baer Multistock Japan Stock D	J007	31/05/93	LUX	-4.45	354	-14.46	597	4.88	-5.92	346	N.A.	N.A.	N.A.		N.A.	
USD	1.86	Baer Multistock Korea Stock D	J007	31/12/93	LUX	-5.51	391	-34.88	601	5.55	-51.73	366	N.A.	N.A.	N.A.		N.A.	
USD	35.89	Baer Multistock Pacific Stk D	J007	30/09/91	LUX	-1.30	260	31.89	20	5.08	11.07	311	N.A.	N.A.	88.16	15	N.A.	
DEM	2.43	Baer Multistock Sp Ger Stk D	J007	30/04/96	LUX	9.78	23	N.A.		N.A.	N.A.		N.A.	N.A.	N.A.		N.A.	
CHF	12.74	Baer Multistock Sp Swiss Sk D	J007	30/04/92	LUX	7.03	45	-3.07	495	2.94	12.16	304	N.A.	N.A.	N.A.		N.A.	
CHF	25.75	Baer Multistock Swiss Stock D	J007	29/11/91	LUX	6.88	47	-0.40	426	3.68	36.98	97	N.A.	N.A.	118.33	8	N.A.	
USD	14.53	Baer Multistock US Stk D	J007	29/06/90	LUX	4.54	65	26.78	38	2.91	54.79	25	N.A.	N.A.	74.38	24	N.A.	
USD	N.S.	BAII Interportf Comfort	B003	31/10/95	LUX	N.A.		4.57	310	N.A.	N.A.		N.A.	N.A.	N.A.		N.A.	
USD	5.69	BBL (L) Invest Base Metals D	B052	28/02/94	LUX	0.16	187	7.05	240	N.A.	N.A.		N.A.	N.A.	N.A.		N.A.	
LUF	1.75	BBL (L) Invest Euro-Immo D	B052	28/06/91	LUX	2.68	96	13.28	161	2.94	1.55	334	N.A.	N.A.	14.61	192	N.A.	
LUF	6.27	BBL (L) Invest Europe D	B052	29/01/88	LUX	2.36	105	17.83	104	2.88	35.58	107	N.A.	N.A.	60.47	42	N.A.	
USD	4.83	BBL (L) Invest Food&Bev'rage D	B052	30/08/96	LUX	3.40	85	N.A.		N.A.	N.A.		N.A.	N.A.	N.A.		N.A.	
USD	9.84	BBL (L) Invest Goldmines D	B052	31/10/89	LUX	-11.23	681	2.89	355	1641.03	-10.62	352	N.A.	N.A.	55.22	60	N.A.	
USD	13.98	BBL (L) Invest HealthCare D	B052	14/06/96	LUX	4.32	69	N.A.		N.A.	N.A.		N.A.	N.A.	N.A.		N.A.	
USD	9.69	BBL (L) Invest Tlcom & Media D	B052	17/11/95	LUX	-0.38	213	7.12	236	N.A.	N.A.		N.A.	N.A.	N.A.		N.A.	
LUF	4.90	BBL (L) Invest World D	B052	28/04/78	LUX	-0.24	205	8.81	210	2.72	25.28	221	N.A.	N.A.	40.06	120	67.97	26
BEF	211.95	BBL Capital Cash D	B052	31/03/88	LUX	-7.35	599	-4.81	538	2.80	28.48	182	N.A.	N.A.	30.08	156	N.A.	
LUF	8.30	BBL Patrimonial Aggressive D	B052	29/07/94	LUX	-2.74	305	10.18	193	N.A.	N.A.		N.A.	N.A.	N.A.		N.A.	
LUF	201.44	BBL Patrimonial Balanced D	B052	30/12/77	LUX	-2.57	299	6.23	255	1.90	32.81	134	N.A.	N.A.	49.95	85	141.93	16
BEF	23.78	BBL Patrimonial Belgium D	B052	20/10/95	LUX	-1.37	263	7.65	231	N.A.	N.A.		N.A.	N.A.	N.A.		N.A.	
LUF	12.42	BBL Patrimonial Defensive D	B052	29/07/94	LUX	-5.19	375	3.68	330	N.A.	N.A.		N.A.	N.A.	N.A.		N.A.	
DEM	95.73	BBL Patrimonial Euro-Core D	B052	20/10/95	LUX	-0.51	218	8.56	214	N.A.	N.A.		N.A.	N.A.	N.A.		N.A.	
USD	N.S.	BBL Patrimonial France C	B052	20/12/96	LUX	N.A.	—	N.A.		N.A.	N.A.		N.A.	N.A.	N.A.		N.A.	
USD	N.S.	BBL Patrimonial France D	B052	20/12/96	LUX	-2.18	290	N.A.		N.A.	N.A.		N.A.	N.A.	N.A.		N.A.	
USD	N.S.	BBL Patrimonial Germany C	B052	20/12/96	LUX	N.A.	—	N.A.		N.A.	N.A.		N.A.	N.A.	N.A.		N.A.	
USD	N.S.	BBL Patrimonial Germany D	B052	20/12/96	LUX	0.47	176	N.A.		N.A.	N.A.		N.A.	N.A.	N.A.		N.A.	
USD	N.S.	BBL Patrimonial Netherlands C	B052	06/12/96	LUX	N.A.	—	N.A.		N.A.	N.A.		N.A.	N.A.	N.A.		N.A.	
USD	N.S.	BBL Patrimonial Netherlands D	B052	06/12/96	LUX	-2.28	293	N.A.		N.A.	N.A.		N.A.	N.A.	N.A.		N.A.	
CAD	9.02	BBL Renta Cash CAD D	B052	31/05/91	LUX	-0.14	202	3.75	327	2.04	11.69	309	N.A.	N.A.	7.83	197	N.A.	
CHF	2.16	BBL Renta Cash CHF D	B052	31/01/94	LUX	-6.50	445	-13.09	592	N.A.	N.A.		N.A.	N.A.	N.A.		N.A.	
DEM	25.62	BBL Renta Cash DEM D	B052	31/03/89	LUX	-7.11	543	-4.69	528	2.75	25.60	219	N.A.	N.A.	27.90	169	N.A.	
GBP	4.53	BBL Renta Cash GBP D	B052	28/02/89	LUX	-2.86	311	15.96	132	2.24	34.46	119	N.A.	N.A.	22.87	182	N.A.	
JPY	0.51	BBL Renta Cash JPY D	B052	28/02/89	LUX	-6.20	423	-11.01	584	3.53	-1.76	339	N.A.	N.A.	16.88	191	N.A.	
NLG	26.84	BBL Renta Cash NLG D	B052	30/03/90	LUX	-7.32	590	-5.14	553	2.73	24.49	226	N.A.	N.A.	27.27	173	N.A.	
BEF	83.24	BBL Renta Cash Sht-Med BEF D	B052	31/01/92	LUX	-7.33	593	-4.75	535	2.65	23.05	239	N.A.	N.A.	N.A.		N.A.	
CAD	3.09	BBL Renta Cash Sht-Med CAD D	B052	31/01/94	LUX	-0.21	204	3.61	335	N.A.	N.A.		N.A.	N.A.	N.A.		N.A.	
DEM	7.59	BBL Renta Cash Sht-Med DEM D	B052	30/07/93	LUX	-7.05	521	-4.41	517	2.64	23.09	238	N.A.	N.A.	N.A.		N.A.	
FRF	1.94	BBL Renta Cash Sht-Med FRF D	B052	30/07/93	LUX	-6.99	509	-2.56	480	2.57	27.90	194	N.A.	N.A.	N.A.		N.A.	
NLG	7.10	BBL Renta Cash Sht-Med NLG D	B052	30/07/93	LUX	-7.23	568	-4.92	544	2.63	22.22	246	N.A.	N.A.	N.A.		N.A.	

▲ SIB Approved ● Insurance Fund **Values in US Dollars, on an offer to offer price basis with gross income reinvested** Data Source Micropal™

Second Units Non-sector

continued

CCY	Fund Size ($mil)	Fund Name	Manager Code	Fund Start Date	Domicile Code	3 Mths 97 % Chg	3 Mths 97 Rank	1 Year % Chg	1 Year Rank	Micropal Star Rating Volatility	Micropal Star Rating 3 Years % Chg	Micropal Star Rating 3 Years Rank	Micropal Star Rating Rating	Risk Return Rating	5 Years % Chg	5 Years Rank	10 Years % Chg	10 Years Rank
	61.14	**Mean/Count**				**-2.65**	**688**	**7**	**601**	**7.41**	**28.18**	**366**			**48.49**	**206**	**166.15**	**29**
USD	4.92	BBL Renta Cash Sht-Med USD D	B052	31/01/94	LUX	1.12	142	4.84	301	N.A.	N.A.		N.A.	N.A.	N.A.		N.A.	
USD	40.61	BBL Renta Cash USD D	B052	31/03/89	LUX	1.13	140	4.70	307	1.17	14.25	295	N.A.	N.A.	20.77	186	N.A.	
ECU	8.77	BBL Renta Cash XEU D	B052	30/09/91	LUX	-6.16	421	1.45	386	2.43	29.01	171	N.A.	N.A.	27.30	172	N.A.	
AUD	3.72	BBL Renta Fd Australian Dlr D	B052	30/06/95	LUX	-2.18	291	24.96	50	N.A.	N.A.		N.A.	N.A.	N.A.		N.A.	
CAD	23.54	BBL Renta Fd Canadian Dlr D	B052	30/11/93	LUX	-0.93	240	18.31	94	2.77	27.66	199	N.A.	N.A.	N.A.		N.A.	
DKK	49.87	BBL Renta Fd Danish Krone D	B052	30/06/95	LUX	-6.59	457	7.71	228	N.A.	N.A.		N.A.	N.A.	N.A.		N.A.	
DEM	46.60	BBL Renta Fd Deutsche Mark D	B052	31/12/92	LUX	-6.77	474	5.01	293	3.32	36.84	98	N.A.	N.A.	N.A.		N.A.	
USD	0.78	BBL Renta Fund Asian Curr C	B052	29/11/96	LUX	0.63	168	N.A.		N.A.	N.A.		N.A.	N.A.	N.A.		N.A.	
USD	25.64	BBL Renta Fund Asian Curr D	B052	29/11/96	LUX	0.63	169	N.A.		N.A.	N.A.		N.A.	N.A.	N.A.		N.A.	
USD	44.17	BBL Renta Fund Dollar D	B052	28/02/89	LUX	-0.35	212	10.05	196	2.26	22.41	243	N.A.	N.A.	36.23	139	N.A.	
ECU	48.74	BBL Renta Fund Ecu D	B052	30/04/90	LUX	-6.43	437	15.43	141	2.70	42.15	56	N.A.	N.A.	57.14	54	N.A.	
NLG	76.78	BBL Renta Fund Gulden D	B052	30/09/92	LUX	-6.97	506	6.12	257	3.33	42.27	55	N.A.	N.A.	N.A.		N.A.	
DEM	103.45	BBL Renta Fund Hard Curr D	B052	28/04/89	LUX	-6.84	491	6.87	243	3.28	40.28	70	N.A.	N.A.	60.46	43	N.A.	
LUF	301.69	BBL Renta Fund High Yield D	B052	28/04/89	LUX	-5.72	400	21.83	70	2.96	42.99	51	N.A.	N.A.	64.98	36	N.A.	
LUF	1412.05	BBL Renta Fund Intl D	B052	31/08/66	LUX	-5.26	378	12.44	170	2.97	30.30	155	N.A.	N.A.	47.64	94	156.71	14
ITL	16.44	BBL Renta Fund Lira D	B052	31/03/94	LUX	-9.17	662	39.07	9	N.A.	N.A.		N.A.	N.A.	N.A.		N.A.	
BEF	575.50	BBL Renta Fund Lux D	B052	28/04/89	LUX	-7.03	517	8.75	211	3.39	55.09	23	N.A.	N.A.	74.81	23	N.A.	
BEF	151.15	BBL Renta Fund Obli Cash BEF D	B052	01/09/95	LUX	-7.17	556	-2.85	487	N.A.	N.A.		N.A.	N.A.	N.A.		N.A.	
CAD	0.28	BBL Renta Fund Obli Cash CAD D	B052	23/08/96	LUX	-0.70	225	N.A.		N.A.	N.A.		N.A.	N.A.	N.A.		N.A.	
CHF	2.47	BBL Renta Fund Obli Cash CHF D	B052	19/01/96	LUX	-6.29	430	N.A.		N.A.	N.A.		N.A.	N.A.	N.A.		N.A.	
DEM	15.82	BBL Renta Fund Obli Cash DEM D	B052	19/01/96	LUX	-6.81	485	N.A.		N.A.	N.A.		N.A.	N.A.	N.A.		N.A.	
GBP	0.46	BBL Renta Fund Obli Cash GBP D	B052	23/08/96	LUX	-3.51	333	N.A.		N.A.	N.A.		N.A.	N.A.	N.A.		N.A.	
ITL	2.52	BBL Renta Fund Obli Cash ITL D	B052	19/01/96	LUX	-8.60	658	N.A.		N.A.	N.A.		N.A.	N.A.	N.A.		N.A.	
NLG	17.23	BBL Renta Fund Obli Cash NLG D	B052	19/01/96	LUX	-7.21	564	N.A.		N.A.	N.A.		N.A.	N.A.	N.A.		N.A.	
USD	9.43	BBL Renta Fund Obli Cash USD D	B052	19/01/96	LUX	0.37	179	N.A.		N.A.	N.A.		N.A.	N.A.	N.A.		N.A.	
BEF	60.96	BBL Renta Fund Obli-C MR BEF D	B052	01/09/95	LUX	-7.37	604	-3.63	504	N.A.	N.A.		N.A.	N.A.	N.A.		N.A.	
ESP	6.58	BBL Renta Fund Peseta D	B052	31/03/94	LUX	-8.64	659	21.60	73	N.A.	N.A.		N.A.	N.A.	N.A.		N.A.	
JPY	1.77	BBL Renta Fund Yen D	B052	31/03/89	LUX	-5.44	386	-3.44	501	3.94	15.02	284	N.A.	N.A.	59.81	44	N.A.	
BEF	1.53	BBL Technix Inv Dur.+ MR BEF D	B052	28/06/96	LUX	-5.99	414	N.A.		N.A.	N.A.		N.A.	N.A.	N.A.		N.A.	
BEF	8.21	BBL Technix Inv Durat MR BEF D	B052	01/03/96	LUX	-6.62	462	N.A.		N.A.	N.A.		N.A.	N.A.	N.A.		N.A.	
LUF	581.59	Belicav A	C018	31/01/89	LUX	-7.08	533	2.16	370	2.38	42.11	57	N.A.	N.A.	59.67	45	N.A.	
LUF	126	Belubond Fund LUF Dist	A037	29/01/88	LUX	-7.23	567	1.90	375	2.41	43.63	46	N.A.	N.A.	55.57	58	N.A.	
ECU	10.16	Bermuda Intl Bond ECU Inc	B066	12/07/91	BER	-3.20	325	9.14	207	1.44	39.92	72	N.A.	N.A.	66.11	32	N.A.	
GBP	28.08	Bermuda Intl Bond GBP Inc	B066	12/07/91	BER	-3.08	321	14.30	151	1.90	39.26	76	N.A.	N.A.	61.72	40	N.A.	
USD	445	Bermuda Intl Bond USD Inc	B066	30/04/80	BER	-2.18	289	6.94	242	1.77	20.91	254	N.A.	N.A.	44.55	107	111.64	22
USD	0	Bermuda Money NLG	S011	31/01/86	HK	-3.65	335	2.76	361	1.45	10.91	313	N.A.	N.A.	28.33	167	117.85	20
DEM	N.S.	BIL Bonds Deutschemark D	B067	31/12/92	LUX	-7.17	558	-1.69	460	2.77	32.45	137	N.A.	N.A.	N.A.		N.A.	
ECU	N.S.	BIL Bonds ECU D	B067	31/12/92	LUX	-7.11	542	6.31	252	2.26	32.66	135	N.A.	N.A.	N.A.		N.A.	
NLG	N.S.	BIL Bonds Florins Neerland D	B067	30/04/93	LUX	-7.45	615	-1.73	462	2.77	30.04	158	N.A.	N.A.	N.A.		N.A.	
LUF	N.S.	BIL Bonds Francs D	B067	31/12/93	LUX	-7.27	577	-1.02	448	2.93	36.44	101	N.A.	N.A.	N.A.		N.A.	
FRF	N.S.	BIL Bonds Francs Francais D	B067	30/04/93	LUX	-7.23	569	2.87	357	2.54	34.38	120	N.A.	N.A.	N.A.		N.A.	
USD	N.S.	BIL Bonds USD D	B067	31/12/90	LUX	-0.99	241	3.72	329	2.16	15.59	279	N.A.	N.A.	26.99	174	N.A.	
BEF	N.S.	BIL Delta Fund Balance D	B067	28/02/94	LUX	-4.60	357	2.14	371	N.A.	N.A.		N.A.	N.A.	N.A.		N.A.	
BEF	N.S.	BIL Delta Fund Croissance D	B067	28/02/94	LUX	-1.12	253	5.21	281	N.A.	N.A.		N.A.	N.A.	N.A.		N.A.	
BEF	N.S.	BIL Delta Fund Rendement D	B067	28/02/94	LUX	-6.52	448	-0.34	425	N.A.	N.A.		N.A.	N.A.	N.A.		N.A.	
DEM	N.S.	BIL Equities Allemagne D	B067	30/06/94	LUX	9.69	24	14.06	152	N.A.	N.A.		N.A.	N.A.	N.A.		N.A.	
FRF	N.S.	BIL Equities France D	B067	30/06/94	LUX	5.07	59	18.29	95	N.A.	N.A.		N.A.	N.A.	N.A.		N.A.	
GBP	N.S.	BIL Equities Grand-Bretagne D	B067	30/06/94	LUX	2.64	97	23.70	59	N.A.	N.A.		N.A.	N.A.	N.A.		N.A.	
JPY	N.S.	BIL Equities Japon D	B067	31/01/90	LUX	-5.96	412	-14.73	598	3.89	-12.89	357	N.A.	N.A.	-15.58	205	N.A.	
NLG	N.S.	BIL Equities Pays-Bas D	B067	30/06/94	LUX	4.16	71	21.74	71	N.A.	N.A.		N.A.	N.A.	N.A.		N.A.	
USD	N.S.	BIL Equities USA D	B067	31/01/90	LUX	4.71	63	16.17	127	2.84	41.88	59	N.A.	N.A.	43.89	110	N.A.	
ITL	N.S.	BIL Euro Rent High Yld Curr D	B067	04/08/95	LUX	-8.45	656	18.12	98	N.A.	N.A.		N.A.	N.A.	N.A.		N.A.	
LUF	N.S.	BIL Euro Rent Multi-Curr D	B067	31/01/90	LUX	-7.27	575	5.57	272	2.41	38.16	84	N.A.	N.A.	46.39	98	N.A.	
DEM	N.S.	BIL Euro Rent Strong Curr D	B067	31/01/90	LUX	-6.80	482	-0.29	424	2.79	34.28	123	N.A.	N.A.	47.89	93	N.A.	
LUF	N.S.	BIL Europe Growth All Mkts D	B067	31/01/90	LUX	-0.60	221	17.65	108	2.73	31.13	149	N.A.	N.A.	45.62	104	N.A.	
LUF	N.S.	BIL Luxpart D	B067	29/12/95	LUX	-0.42	215	23.59	61	N.A.	N.A.		N.A.	N.A.	N.A.		N.A.	
● USD	14.24	BL Equities Amer Du Nord A	B025	31/01/92	LUX	0.13	190	15.82	137	3.51	44.43	43	N.A.	N.A.	N.A.		N.A.	

▲ SIB Approved ● Insurance Fund Values in US Dollars, on an offer to offer price basis with gross income reinvested Data Source Micropal™

Second Units Non-sector

continued

CCY	Fund Size ($mil)	Fund Name	Manager Code	Fund Start Date	Domicile Code	3 Mths 97 % Chg	3 Mths 97 Rank	1 Year % Chg	1 Year Rank	Micropal Star Rating 3 Years Volatility	3 Years % Chg	3 Years Rank	Rating	Risk Return Rating	5 Years % Chg	5 Years Rank	10 Years % Chg	10 Years Rank
	61.14	**Mean/Count**				**-2.65**	**688**	**7**	**601**	**7.41**	**28.18**	**366**			**48.49**	**206**	**166.15**	**29**
● ECU	82.31	BL Equities Europe A	B025	28/09/90	LUX	4.33	68	25.81	40	2.41	55.01	24	N.A.	N.A.	76.64	20	N.A.	
● LUF	48.17	BL Global Asset 100 A	B025	29/10/93	LUX	1.94	110	17.79	106	2.05	40.33	69	N.A.	N.A.	N.A.		N.A.	
● LUF	13.28	BL Global Asset 30 A	B025	29/10/93	LUX	-0.82	231	8.16	219	1.55	24.78	225	N.A.	N.A.	N.A.		N.A.	
● LUF	35.55	BL Global Asset 50 A	B025	29/10/93	LUX	0.15	188	13.52	158	1.58	31.83	143	N.A.	N.A.	N.A.		N.A.	
● DEM	29.86	BL Money Trust DM A	B025	30/03/90	LUX	-7.03	515	-4.16	510	2.71	25.82	215	N.A.	N.A.	28.69	164	N.A.	
● LUF	106.88	BL Money Trust FB/FLUX A	B025	30/03/90	LUX	-7.29	580	-4.65	526	2.79	27.76	197	N.A.	N.A.	31.40	146	N.A.	
● FRF	16.22	BL Money Trust FRF A	B025	30/03/90	LUX	-7.03	518	-2.32	474	2.67	31.96	141	N.A.	N.A.	37.43	132	N.A.	
● USD	25.84	BL Money Trust Zone Dlr A	B025	30/03/90	LUX	1.07	146	5.07	289	1.18	15.05	283	N.A.	N.A.	23.85	179	N.A.	
● CHF	N.S.	BL Multi Tst Bd CHF A	B025	28/06/96	LUX	-6.79	478	N.A.		N.A.	N.A.		N.A.	N.A.	N.A.		N.A.	
● DEM	77.19	BL Multi Tst Bd DM A	B025	31/01/89	LUX	-6.46	439	-1.50	456	3.53	32.90	133	N.A.	N.A.	43.85	111	N.A.	
● LUF	115.53	BL Multi Tst Bd FB FLUX A	B025	31/01/89	LUX	-7.42	612	1.63	381	4.07	39.56	75	N.A.	N.A.	53	74	N.A.	
● BEF	N.S.	BL Multi Tst Bd Global A	B025	28/06/96	LUX	-4.23	346	N.A.		N.A.	N.A.		N.A.	N.A.	N.A.		N.A.	
● USD	36.78	BL Multi Tst Bd Zone Dlr A	B025	31/01/89	LUX	-0.80	229	4.97	296	2.54	17.17	270	N.A.	N.A.	30.98	150	N.A.	
● ECU	17.30	BL Multi Tst Bd Zone Eur A	B025	31/01/89	LUX	-6.64	464	7.67	230	3.73	24.33	228	N.A.	N.A.	31.40	147	N.A.	
USD	57.20	Bond Trust Of The World A	S037	31/12/81	LUX	-4.79	368	-6.45	560	2.60	7.39	322	N.A.	N.A.	33.33	142	110.83	23
BEF	23.25	Bonds Universalis A	P013	30/09/86	LUX	-4.67	360	9.96	198	2.41	38.39	83	N.A.	N.A.	54.37	66	171.07	12
LUF	N.S.	BR & A Rente 3 ans A	B019	24/11/95	LUX	-7.33	592	-1.92	466	N.A.	N.A.		N.A.	N.A.	N.A.		N.A.	
LUF	N.S.	BR & A Rente Duree Variable A	B019	24/11/95	LUX	-5.98	413	-0.75	439	N.A.	N.A.		N.A.	N.A.	N.A.		N.A.	
LUF	8.96	Castor & Pollux A	B034	29/07/94	LUX	-7.23	572	2.21	369	N.A.	N.A.		N.A.	N.A.	N.A.		N.A.	
USD	0.01	CCF Sam EMF Asia Indx Track D	C015	30/06/95	LUX	-0.35	211	1.25	392	N.A.	N.A.		N.A.	N.A.	N.A.		N.A.	
USD	0.86	CCF Sam EMF Lat Am Indx Tr D	C015	30/06/95	LUX	16.30	8	16.62	119	N.A.	N.A.		N.A.	N.A.	N.A.		N.A.	
USD	14.01	CCF Sam EMF World Emer Eq D	C015	30/09/93	LUX	10.01	22	6.37	250	5.25	-11.45	353	N.A.	N.A.	N.A.		N.A.	
LUF	221	Cera Cash BEF/LUF A	C018	31/12/90	LUX	-7.35	600	-4.69	529	2.57	28.65	177	N.A.	N.A.	30.04	159	N.A.	
NLG	26.93	Cera Cash NLG A	C018	29/07/94	LUX	-7.27	576	-5.13	552	N.A.	N.A.		N.A.	N.A.	N.A.		N.A.	
USD	104	Cera Cash USD A	C018	31/05/93	LUX	1.16	137	4.89	299	0.08	14.15	297	N.A.	N.A.	N.A.		N.A.	
LUF	N.S.	Cera Invest Emerging Markets D	C018	30/06/94	LUX	0.17	186	17.29	112	N.A.	N.A.		N.A.	N.A.	N.A.		N.A.	
ECU	N.S.	Cera Invest EURO Fund Dis	C018	07/06/96	LUX	-5.83	407	N.A.		N.A.	N.A.		N.A.	N.A.	N.A.		N.A.	
● USD	15.56	Citi Balanced B	C032	24/06/94	CA	-1.11	251	5.73	267	N.A.	N.A.		N.A.	N.A.	N.A.		N.A.	
● USD	14.02	Citi Intl Equity B	C032	24/06/94	CA	-2.09	286	1.41	387	N.A.	N.A.		N.A.	N.A.	N.A.		N.A.	
● USD	0.07	Citi Liquid Reserves B	C032	31/10/94	CA	1.13	141	4.66	308	N.A.	N.A.		N.A.	N.A.	N.A.		N.A.	
● USD	23.03	Citi US Equity B	C032	24/06/94	CA	-0.81	230	11.53	180	N.A.	N.A.		N.A.	N.A.	N.A.		N.A.	
● USD	8.92	Citi US Govt Inc B	C032	24/06/94	CA	0.23	183	6.43	249	N.A.	N.A.		N.A.	N.A.	N.A.		N.A.	
▲● ECU	0.32	CL Earth Fund D	C062	31/12/90	LUX	-16.91	687	11.44	182	4.53	6.87	324	N.A.	N.A.	11.44	195	N.A.	
USD	349.12	Contivest Actions Internat B	B023	30/06/93	LUX	8.69	31	0.13	415	3.18	-16.86	361	N.A.	N.A.	N.A.		N.A.	
BEF	22.38	Contivest Obli Belux Court-T B	B023	30/06/93	LUX	-7.76	638	-5.08	551	2.44	27.74	198	N.A.	N.A.	N.A.		N.A.	
BEF	34.07	Contivest Obli Belux Long-T B	B023	30/11/94	LUX	-7.85	643	-1.36	453	N.A.	N.A.		N.A.	N.A.	N.A.		N.A.	
DEM	0.20	Contivest Obli World B	B023	30/06/93	LUX	-5.80	402	1.70	379	1.61	18.23	266	N.A.	N.A.	N.A.		N.A.	
● CHF	91.74	Credis Bd Prime Currencies B	C054	31/12/87	LUX	-5.66	395	-5.01	548	2.79	28.08	188	N.A.	N.A.	54.66	64	N.A.	
● AUD	37.89	Credis Bond AUD B	C054	28/02/92	LUX	-2.06	285	20.04	79	2.52	45.16	42	N.A.	N.A.	N.A.		N.A.	
● CAD	43.12	Credis Bond CAD B	C054	28/02/92	LUX	-0.92	239	12.42	171	2.58	22.45	242	N.A.	N.A.	N.A.		N.A.	
● DEM	318.84	Credis Bond DEM B	C054	31/12/90	LUX	-6.73	470	0.80	400	2.33	36.84	99	N.A.	N.A.	54.53	65	N.A.	
● ECU	476.02	Credis Bond ECU B	C054	31/03/87	LUX	-6.61	460	8.23	217	1.66	34.53	118	N.A.	N.A.	49.10	89	N.A.	
● DEM	291.01	Credis Bond Europe B	C054	28/04/89	LUX	-8.23	651	7.51	234	1.87	37.59	89	N.A.	N.A.	42.71	114	N.A.	
● FRF	85.16	Credis Bond FRF B	C054	31/12/90	LUX	-6.89	499	6.75	245	2.10	38.85	79	N.A.	N.A.	66.02	33	N.A.	
CHF	N.S.	Credis Bond Fund S-T SFR B	C054	29/12/95	LUX	-5.82	406	-12.09	588	N.A.	N.A.		N.A.	N.A.	N.A.		N.A.	
● GBP	43.44	Credis Bond GBP B	C054	31/12/90	LUX	-3.42	329	19.70	82	2.23	38.08	86	N.A.	N.A.	46.21	101	N.A.	
● NLG	196.71	Credis Bond Gulden B	C054	07/04/95	LUX	-6.86	493	-0.25	423	N.A.	N.A.		N.A.	N.A.	N.A.		N.A.	
● ITL	51.65	Credis Bond Lira B	C054	30/09/93	LUX	-9.18	663	25.61	43	2.65	41.87	60	N.A.	N.A.	N.A.		N.A.	
● ESP	17.64	Credis Bond Peseta B	C054	31/01/94	LUX	-7.82	641	11.50	181	N.A.	N.A.		N.A.	N.A.	N.A.		N.A.	
● CHF	526.05	Credis Bond SFR B	C054	29/11/91	LUX	-5.33	380	-9.93	577	3.24	27.95	192	N.A.	N.A.	46.80	97	N.A.	
● DEM	393.51	Credis Bond Short Term DM B	C054	31/03/87	LUX	-7.06	526	-2.30	473	2.41	31.83	144	N.A.	N.A.	42.01	115	N.A.	
● USD	254.22	Credis Bond Short Term USD B	C054	31/03/87	LUX	0.65	166	4.36	318	0.43	14.58	289	N.A.	N.A.	28.17	168	N.A.	
● USD	143.97	Credis Bond USD B	C054	31/12/90	LUX	-0.67	223	4.63	309	1.22	16.23	276	N.A.	N.A.	36.62	136	N.A.	
● JPY	3.01	Credis Bond YEN B	C054	28/02/92	LUX	-5.70	399	-7.65	568	3.56	6.97	323	N.A.	N.A.	N.A.		N.A.	
● DEM	143.70	Credis Eq Euro Blue Chips B	C056	31/10/89	LUX	2.09	108	27.28	36	2.98	46.36	38	N.A.	N.A.	68.33	29	N.A.	
● ESP	51.23	Credis Eqty Hispano Iberia B	C056	30/03/90	LUX	-4.07	342	43.16	6	4.85	69.60	13	N.A.	N.A.	60.54	41	N.A.	
● FRF	113.02	Credis Equity France B	C056	28/06/91	LUX	0.89	156	25.55	44	3.81	27.46	201	N.A.	N.A.	37.48	131	N.A.	

▲ SIB Approved ● Insurance Fund **Values in US Dollars, on an offer to offer price basis with gross income reinvested** Data Source Micropal™

Second Units Non-sector

continued

	CCY	Fund Size ($mil)	Fund Name	Manager Code	Fund Start Date	Domicile Code	3 Mths 97 % Chg	3 Mths 97 Rank	1 Year % Chg	1 Year Rank	Micropal Star Rating 3 Years Volatility	3 Years % Chg	3 Years Rank	3 Years Rating	Risk Return Rating	5 Years % Chg	5 Years Rank	10 Years % Chg	10 Years Rank
		61.14	**Mean/Count**				**-2.65**	**688**	**7**	**601**	**7.41**	**28.18**	**366**			**48.49**	**206**	**166.15**	**29**
●	DEM	201.58	Credis Equity Germany B	C056	28/02/91	LUX	12.35	15	17.22	114	3.40	29	172	N.A.	N.A.	45.01	106	N.A.	
●	USD	37.97	Credis Equity Gold Mines B	C056	29/12/89	LUX	-4.17	345	15.47	140	7.20	-1.80	340	N.A.	N.A.	50.04	82	N.A.	
●	ITL	49.37	Credis Equity Italy B	C056	30/10/92	LUX	2.38	104	28.04	32	6.24	28.48	181	N.A.	N.A.	N.A.		N.A.	
●	NLG	132.03	Credis Equity Netherlands B	C056	30/09/92	LUX	7.10	43	38.67	10	3.08	104.17	5	N.A.	N.A.	N.A.		N.A.	
●	USD	208.81	Credis Equity North America B	C056	28/06/91	LUX	3.90	75	18.77	89	3.02	45.48	41	N.A.	N.A.	76.42	21	N.A.	
●	DEM	10.58	Credis Equity Oeko Protec B	C056	31/10/90	LUX	1.77	115	4.91	298	2.33	8.18	319	N.A.	N.A.	1.95	199	N.A.	
●	GBP	66.84	Credis Equity UK B	C056	28/06/91	LUX	-1.04	245	22.91	63	3.57	40.65	65	N.A.	N.A.	48.04	92	N.A.	
	BEF	477.21	Cregem Bonds Beluf Dis	C059	31/01/89	LUX	-7.14	551	0.29	412	3.45	40.46	68	N.A.	N.A.	54.89	61	N.A.	
	BEF	142.05	Cregem Bonds High Yield Dis	C059	30/06/89	LUX	-6.03	417	12.73	165	2.80	39.81	74	N.A.	N.A.	54.74	62	N.A.	
	BEF	349.32	Cregem Bonds International Dis	C059	31/07/89	LUX	-6.22	426	4.99	294	2.82	30.28	156	N.A.	N.A.	46.17	102	N.A.	
	BEF	15.92	Cregem Cash Beluf Dis	C059	31/03/94	LUX	-7.34	598	-4.81	539	N.A.	N.A.		N.A.	N.A.	N.A.		N.A.	
	BEF	3.43	Cregem Equities L Emerg Mkts D	C059	24/06/94	LUX	3.89	76	3.05	350	N.A.	N.A.		N.A.	N.A.	N.A.		N.A.	
	BEF	43.82	Cregem Equities L Europe Dis	C059	31/01/90	LUX	4.41	67	29.67	25	2.84	53.35	28	N.A.	N.A.	80.59	19	N.A.	
	LUF	22.02	Cregem Immo Dis	C065	30/11/94	LUX	-7.12	546	-4.52	522	N.A.	N.A.		N.A.	N.A.	N.A.		N.A.	
	DEM	N.S.	CS Portfolio Fixed Inc DM B	C068	28/04/95	LUX	-6.98	508	-3.29	497	N.A.	N.A.		N.A.	N.A.	N.A.		N.A.	
	CHF	N.S.	CS Portfolio Fixed Inc SFR B	C068	28/04/95	LUX	-5.92	410	-12.42	589	N.A.	N.A.		N.A.	N.A.	N.A.		N.A.	
	USD	N.S.	CS Portfolio Fixed Inc USD B	C068	28/04/95	LUX	0.36	181	3.87	324	N.A.	N.A.		N.A.	N.A.	N.A.		N.A.	
	CHF	N.S.	CS Portfolio Focus SFR B	C068	31/01/96	LUX	-2.73	304	N.A.		N.A.	N.A.		N.A.	N.A.	N.A.		N.A.	
	DEM	175.22	CS Portfolio Income DEM B	C068	31/05/93	LUX	-4.51	355	0.95	398	2.03	26.42	211	N.A.	N.A.	N.A.		N.A.	
	ITL	1.27	CS Portfolio Income Lira B	C068	29/04/94	LUX	-6.25	428	17	116	N.A.	N.A.		N.A.	N.A.	N.A.		N.A.	
	CHF	622.54	CS Portfolio Income SFR B	C068	31/05/93	LUX	-3.65	336	-7.89	570	2.67	22.37	244	N.A.	N.A.	N.A.		N.A.	
	USD	73.13	CS Portfolio Income USD B	C068	31/05/93	LUX	0.38	178	5.46	275	1.05	14.50	290	N.A.	N.A.	N.A.		N.A.	
	CHF	0.64	CS Sfr Convert Bd Fd (B)	S023	29/11/91	LUX	-6.81	487	-12.76	590	3.65	11.75	307	N.A.	N.A.	11.28	196	N.A.	
	BEF	30.88	Currency Mgt Fd Belgian Fcs D	I008	30/10/92	LUX	-10.19	675	-4.77	537	3.07	28.71	175	N.A.	N.A.	N.A.		N.A.	
	BEF	1.73	Currency Mgt Fd Liquid Mix D	I008	30/10/92	LUX	-9.28	664	-1.53	457	2.39	25.08	224	N.A.	N.A.	N.A.		N.A.	
	DEM	51.44	DekaLux 1/98 (B)	D009	06/01/95	LUX	-9.70	666	-3.46	502	N.A.	N.A.		N.A.	N.A.	N.A.		N.A.	
	DEM	68.74	DekaLux 10/95 (B) (3Y R-O)	D009	03/11/95	LUX	-7.21	565	-2.85	486	N.A.	N.A.		N.A.	N.A.	N.A.		N.A.	
	DEM	23.73	DekaLux 4/98 (B)	D009	07/04/95	LUX	-7.10	541	-3.32	498	N.A.	N.A.		N.A.	N.A.	N.A.		N.A.	
	DEM	17.94	DekaLux 7/97 (B)	D009	01/07/94	LUX	-7.06	524	-3.80	507	N.A.	N.A.		N.A.	N.A.	N.A.		N.A.	
	DEM	43.34	DekaLux 7/98 (B)	D009	07/07/95	LUX	-7.12	544	-2.85	488	N.A.	N.A.		N.A.	N.A.	N.A.		N.A.	
	DEM	81.53	DekaLux Cash DM (B)	D009	01/07/94	LUX	-7.12	545	-4.19	511	N.A.	N.A.		N.A.	N.A.	N.A.		N.A.	
	ECU	1.86	DekaLux Cash ECU (B)	D009	08/07/94	LUX	-6.34	434	1.45	385	N.A.	N.A.		N.A.	N.A.	N.A.		N.A.	
	GBP	15.22	DekaLux Cash GBP (B)	D009	08/07/94	LUX	-2.80	307	15.79	139	N.A.	N.A.		N.A.	N.A.	N.A.		N.A.	
	USD	94.30	DekaLux Cash USD (B)	D009	08/07/94	LUX	1.01	152	4.80	304	N.A.	N.A.		N.A.	N.A.	N.A.		N.A.	
	DEM	3.41	DekaLux Europlus 1/2000 (B)	D009	06/01/95	LUX	-10.38	677	1	396	N.A.	N.A.		N.A.	N.A.	N.A.		N.A.	
	DEM	12.47	DekaLux EuroPlus 1/99 (B)	D009	31/01/94	LUX	-10.03	672	0.58	409	N.A.	N.A.		N.A.	N.A.	N.A.		N.A.	
	DEM	2.57	DekaLux EuroPlus 10/99 (B)	D009	07/10/94	LUX	-6.81	488	0.68	403	N.A.	N.A.		N.A.	N.A.	N.A.		N.A.	
	DEM	6.62	DekaLux Europlus 4/2000 (B)	D009	07/04/95	LUX	-6.83	489	0.61	406	N.A.	N.A.		N.A.	N.A.	N.A.		N.A.	
	DEM	2.89	DekaLux EuroPlus 4/99 (B)	D009	31/03/94	LUX	-6.88	495	-0.03	420	N.A.	N.A.		N.A.	N.A.	N.A.		N.A.	
	DEM	2.25	DekaLux EuroPlus 7/99 (B)	D009	08/07/94	LUX	-6.79	480	0.58	408	N.A.	N.A.		N.A.	N.A.	N.A.		N.A.	
	DEM	54.14	DekaLux S Rendite 10/99 (B)	D009	07/10/94	LUX	-7	511	-1.23	451	N.A.	N.A.		N.A.	N.A.	N.A.		N.A.	
	DEM	57.16	DekaLux S Rendite 4/2000 (B)	D009	06/01/95	LUX	-6.90	501	-0.77	442	N.A.	N.A.		N.A.	N.A.	N.A.		N.A.	
	DEM	25.53	DekaLux S Rendite 7/99 (B)	D009	01/07/94	LUX	-7.01	514	-1.49	455	N.A.	N.A.		N.A.	N.A.	N.A.		N.A.	
	DEM	20.32	DekaLux Wachstum 1/2000 (B)	D009	09/12/94	LUX	-9.97	671	-1.75	463	N.A.	N.A.		N.A.	N.A.	N.A.		N.A.	
	DEM	32.73	DekaLux Wachstum 1/2001 (B)	D009	02/12/94	LUX	-10.06	673	-1.42	454	N.A.	N.A.		N.A.	N.A.	N.A.		N.A.	
	LUF	N.S.	Demeter Francs Belges Dis	B026	31/01/92	LUX	-7.31	583	1.74	378	2.94	38.50	82	N.A.	N.A.	N.A.		N.A.	
	LUF	N.S.	Demeter Intl Bonds Dis	B026	31/01/94	LUX	-4.41	352	7.68	229	N.A.	N.A.		N.A.	N.A.	N.A.		N.A.	
	LUF	N.S.	Demeter Patrimoine Dis	B026	31/01/92	LUX	-6.78	477	6.53	247	2.91	19.40	261	N.A.	N.A.	N.A.		N.A.	
●	CAD	90.25	Dit Lux Bondselect CAN $ B	D017	31/08/93	LUX	-0.91	237	10.72	191	2.53	18.71	263	N.A.	N.A.	N.A.		N.A.	
●	USD	131.56	Dit Lux Bondselect USD B	D017	31/12/91	LUX	-0.84	233	2.81	358	1.02	14.63	288	N.A.	N.A.	34.96	140	N.A.	
●	DEM	71.49	Dit Lux Bondspezial B	D017	31/03/92	LUX	-3.02	318	12.76	164	1.48	32.18	138	N.A.	N.A.	N.A.		N.A.	
●	DEM	35.13	Dit Lux Cash DM B	D017	30/06/94	LUX	-7.12	548	-4.65	524	N.A.	N.A.		N.A.	N.A.	N.A.		N.A.	
●	DEM	83.11	Dit Lux Staatensanleihen /B	D017	30/04/92	LUX	-4.68	361	6.34	251	1.64	21.36	252	N.A.	N.A.	N.A.		N.A.	
▲	NOK	N.S.	DNB Investment Balanced Ptfl D	D013	29/04/94	LUX	1.49	122	10.84	189	N.A.	N.A.		N.A.	N.A.	N.A.		N.A.	
▲	NOK	13.18	DNB Investment Euro Equities B	D013	31/10/94	LUX	5.41	54	20.08	78	N.A.	N.A.		N.A.	N.A.	N.A.		N.A.	
▲	NOK	N.S.	DNB Investment Nordic Bonds D	D013	29/10/93	LUX	-6.91	504	6.07	259	1.88	36.48	100	N.A.	N.A.	N.A.		N.A.	
▲	NOK	N.S.	DNB Investment Nordic Eq D	D013	29/10/93	LUX	4.48	66	30.49	23	4.35	67.29	14	N.A.	N.A.	N.A.		N.A.	

▲ **SIB Approved** ● **Insurance Fund** **Values in US Dollars, on an offer to offer price basis with gross income reinvested** Data Source Micropal™

Second Units Non-sector

continued

	CCY	Fund Size ($mil)	Fund Name	Manager Code	Fund Start Date	Domicile Code	3 Mths 97 % Chg	3 Mths 97 Rank	1 Year % Chg	1 Year Rank	Micropal Star Rating 3 Years Volatility	3 Years % Chg	3 Years Rank	Rating	Risk Return Rating	5 Years % Chg	5 Years Rank	10 Years % Chg	10 Years Rank
		61.14	**Mean/Count**				**-2.65**	**688**	**7**	**601**	**7.41**	**28.18**	**366**			**48.49**	**206**	**166.15**	**29**
▲	NOK	N.S.	DNB Investment Norweg'n Csh D	D013	29/04/94	LUX	-2.65	300	2.44	365	N.A.	N.A.		N.A.	N.A.	N.A.		N.A.	
▲	USD	N.S.	DNB Investment Worldwide B	D013	31/10/94	LUX	-0.90	236	8.04	221	N.A.	N.A.		N.A.	N.A.	N.A.		N.A.	
	ECU	5.66	Ecupar A	B037	31/07/85	LUX	-6.58	455	6.27	254	2.20	37.72	88	N.A.	N.A.	48.18	91	162.30	13
	BEF	25.44	EMIF Belgium Index Plus A	C015	31/05/90	LUX	2.26	107	16.03	129	2.88	56.63	22	N.A.	N.A.	89.47	14	N.A.	
	FRF	235.99	EMIF France Index Plus A	C015	31/05/90	LUX	7.16	42	22.38	67	4.78	11.44	310	N.A.	N.A.	28.95	162	N.A.	
	DEM	1033.97	EMIF Germany Index Plus A	C015	31/05/90	LUX	7.62	39	15	146	3.53	32.01	140	N.A.	N.A.	57.55	51	N.A.	
	ITL	0.15	EMIF Italy Index Plus A	C015	31/01/94	LUX	2.43	103	17.25	113	N.A.	N.A.		N.A.	N.A.	N.A.		N.A.	
	NLG	945.45	EMIF Netherlands Index Plus A	C015	30/11/92	LUX	4.18	70	26.49	39	3.10	84.03	9	N.A.	N.A.	N.A.		N.A.	
	ESP	0.78	EMIF Spain Index Plus A	C015	31/07/91	LUX	-5.86	409	29.04	28	4.60	66.31	17	N.A.	N.A.	52.64	76	N.A.	
	CHF	131.39	EMIF Switzerland Index Plus A	C015	31/01/94	LUX	10.43	20	-0.67	437	N.A.	N.A.		N.A.	N.A.	N.A.		N.A.	
	GBP	1448.23	EMIF UK Index Plus A	C015	31/05/90	LUX	-1.05	246	23.63	60	3.54	46.26	39	N.A.	N.A.	64.16	38	N.A.	
	ECU	12.05	Eufi-Cash Ecu Dist	E012	30/04/90	LUX	-6.50	444	10.09	195	2.99	52.06	30	N.A.	N.A.	50.01	83	N.A.	
	FRF	0.88	Eufi-Cash FRF Dist	E012	28/02/94	LUX	-7.80	639	9.40	204	N.A.	N.A.		N.A.	N.A.	N.A.		N.A.	
	ECU	73.05	Eufi-Rent Dist	E012	30/04/90	LUX	-6.25	429	15.34	142	2.55	42.83	53	N.A.	N.A.	57.40	52	N.A.	
▲	ECU	25.54	Eufinvest Dist	E012	30/04/90	LUX	5.38	55	22.02	69	2.76	43.86	44	N.A.	N.A.	63.45	39	N.A.	
	NLG	21.61	Euromix Fund-Dutch Gldrs Dis	I008	29/10/93	LUX	-5.80	403	2.93	353	2.24	25.64	218	N.A.	N.A.	N.A.		N.A.	
	LUF	97.83	Euromix Fund-Income Grwth Dis	I008	31/01/90	LUX	-5.86	408	3.03	351	2.99	25.85	214	N.A.	N.A.	36.35	137	N.A.	
	BEF	4.08	European Money Mkt A	B036	31/10/90	LUX	-7.41	609	-5.04	549	2.81	28.25	184	N.A.	N.A.	31.14	149	N.A.	
	ECU	68.26	Europhenix A	B037	29/11/91	LUX	8.21	36	18.62	90	2.91	37.07	95	N.A.	N.A.	67.18	31	N.A.	
	USD	N.S.	EV Medallion Emerging Mkts A	E003	31/10/96	CA	9.69	25	N.A.		N.A.	N.A.		N.A.	N.A.	N.A.		N.A.	
	USD	N.S.	EV Medallion Gr China Gth A	E003	27/09/96	CA	-2.45	297	N.A.		N.A.	N.A.		N.A.	N.A.	N.A.		N.A.	
	USD	N.S.	EV Medallion Greater India A	E003	16/08/96	CA	5.27	57	N.A.		N.A.	N.A.		N.A.	N.A.	N.A.		N.A.	
	USD	N.S.	EV Medallion High Yield A	E003	16/08/96	CA	-1.23	258	N.A.		N.A.	N.A.		N.A.	N.A.	N.A.		N.A.	
	USD	N.S.	EV Medallion Info Age A	E003	31/07/96	CA	-1.74	277	N.A.		N.A.	N.A.		N.A.	N.A.	N.A.		N.A.	
	BEF	0.07	Findico Div	K010	31/05/89	LUX	-7.34	597	-4.98	547	2.80	27.78	196	N.A.	N.A.	28.83	163	N.A.	
	BEF	5.79	Findico Short Medium Div	K010	15/03/96	LUX	-7.53	622	N.A.		N.A.	N.A.		N.A.	N.A.	N.A.		N.A.	
	DEM	14.56	G-Bond Fund G-DEM Bond A	G009	19/01/96	LUX	-11	680	N.A.		N.A.	N.A.		N.A.	N.A.	N.A.		N.A.	
	DKK	6.82	G-Bond Fund G-DKK Bond A	G009	19/01/96	LUX	-11.85	685	N.A.		N.A.	N.A.		N.A.	N.A.	N.A.		N.A.	
	LUF	51.17	G-Bond Fund G-Ecu Bond A	G009	28/02/92	LUX	-11.45	683	7.94	224	2.70	36.15	103	N.A.	N.A.	N.A.		N.A.	
	FRF	0.40	G-Bond Fund G-FRF Bond A	G009	19/01/96	LUX	-11.25	682	N.A.		N.A.	N.A.		N.A.	N.A.	N.A.		N.A.	
	NLG	7.80	G-Bond Fund G-NLG Bond A	G009	19/01/96	LUX	-11.56	684	N.A.		N.A.	N.A.		N.A.	N.A.	N.A.		N.A.	
	LUF	164.92	G-Bond Fund G-Rentinbel A	G009	31/05/88	LUX	-6.81	486	2.31	367	3.06	40.21	71	N.A.	N.A.	59.32	47	N.A.	
	USD	3.02	G-Bond Fund G-USD Bond A	G009	19/01/96	LUX	-5.67	397	N.A.		N.A.	N.A.		N.A.	N.A.	N.A.		N.A.	
	GBP	3.38	G-Equity Fund G-British Eq A	G009	31/03/94	LUX	-0.90	235	24.03	57	N.A.	N.A.		N.A.	N.A.	N.A.		N.A.	
	NLG	5.79	G-Equity Fund G-Dutch Eq A	G009	31/03/94	LUX	3.34	87	25.76	41	N.A.	N.A.		N.A.	N.A.	N.A.		N.A.	
	FRF	6.17	G-Equity Fund G-French Eq A	G009	31/03/94	LUX	4.91	61	17.89	103	N.A.	N.A.		N.A.	N.A.	N.A.		N.A.	
	DEM	4.91	G-Equity Fund G-German Eq A	G009	31/03/94	LUX	7.57	40	17.16	115	N.A.	N.A.		N.A.	N.A.	N.A.		N.A.	
	ITL	9.50	G-Equity Fund G-Italian Eq A	G009	31/03/94	LUX	-1.39	265	20.08	77	N.A.	N.A.		N.A.	N.A.	N.A.		N.A.	
	ESP	0.91	G-Equity Fund G-Spanish Eq A	G009	31/03/94	LUX	-4.56	356	33.53	19	N.A.	N.A.		N.A.	N.A.	N.A.		N.A.	
	LUF	102.77	G-Treasury Belgo-Lux A	G009	30/04/91	LUX	-7.82	640	-4.42	518	2.38	28.23	186	N.A.	N.A.	31.34	148	N.A.	
	DEM	18.45	G-Treasury Deutschmark A	G009	29/07/94	LUX	-7.09	537	-4.34	514	N.A.	N.A.		N.A.	N.A.	N.A.		N.A.	
	USD	27.88	G-Treasury Dollar US A	G009	29/07/94	LUX	1.15	138	5.22	280	N.A.	N.A.		N.A.	N.A.	N.A.		N.A.	
	NLG	12.61	G-Treasury Florin A	G009	29/07/94	LUX	-7.20	563	-4.73	532	N.A.	N.A.		N.A.	N.A.	N.A.		N.A.	
	FRF	2.43	G-Treasury French Franc A	G009	29/07/94	LUX	-7.06	525	-2.22	472	N.A.	N.A.		N.A.	N.A.	N.A.		N.A.	
	LUF	37.06	G-Treasury Intl Belgo-Lux A	G009	31/03/88	LUX	-7.84	642	-4.51	521	2.38	28.43	183	N.A.	N.A.	13.15	193	N.A.	
	DEM	5.51	G-Treasury Intl Deutschmark A	G009	29/07/94	LUX	-7.08	532	-4.29	513	N.A.	N.A.		N.A.	N.A.	N.A.		N.A.	
	USD	5.05	G-Treasury Intl Dollar US A	G009	29/07/94	LUX	1.16	136	5.19	282	N.A.	N.A.		N.A.	N.A.	N.A.		N.A.	
	NLG	3.70	G-Treasury Intl Florin A	G009	29/07/94	LUX	-7.23	570	-4.76	536	N.A.	N.A.		N.A.	N.A.	N.A.		N.A.	
	FRF	0.37	G-Treasury Intl Fr Franc A	G009	29/07/94	LUX	-7.09	538	-2.35	475	N.A.	N.A.		N.A.	N.A.	N.A.		N.A.	
	LUF	12.69	G-Treasury Intl M-T Bel-Lux A	G009	30/11/93	LUX	-7.98	649	-2.10	469	2.27	35.74	105	N.A.	N.A.	N.A.		N.A.	
	DEM	1.10	G-Treasury Intl M-T D-Mark A	G009	31/08/94	LUX	-7.32	589	-2.63	482	N.A.	N.A.		N.A.	N.A.	N.A.		N.A.	
	NLG	0.63	G-Treasury Intl M-T Florin A	G009	31/08/94	LUX	-7.63	631	-2.90	490	N.A.	N.A.		N.A.	N.A.	N.A.		N.A.	
	USD	0.13	G-Treasury Intl M-T USD A	G009	27/09/96	LUX	0.56	170	N.A.		N.A.	N.A.		N.A.	N.A.	N.A.		N.A.	
	LUF	56.29	G-Treasury Med Term Bel-Lux A	G009	30/11/93	LUX	-7.95	647	-2.09	467	2.27	35.55	108	N.A.	N.A.	N.A.		N.A.	
	DEM	4.44	G-Treasury Med Term D-Mark A	G009	31/08/94	LUX	-7.31	585	-2.61	481	N.A.	N.A.		N.A.	N.A.	N.A.		N.A.	
	NLG	3.97	G-Treasury Med Term Florin A	G009	31/08/94	LUX	-7.63	628	-2.96	493	N.A.	N.A.		N.A.	N.A.	N.A.		N.A.	
	USD	1.81	G-Treasury Med Term USD A	G009	27/09/96	LUX	0.64	167	N.A.		N.A.	N.A.		N.A.	N.A.	N.A.		N.A.	

▲ **SIB Approved** ● **Insurance Fund** **Values in US Dollars, on an offer to offer price basis with gross income reinvested** Data Source Micropal™

Second Units Non-sector

continued

	CCY	Fund Size ($mil)	Fund Name	Manager Code	Fund Start Date	Domicile Code	3 Mths 97 % Chg	3 Mths 97 Rank	1 Year % Chg	1 Year Rank	Micropal Star Rating 3 Years Volatility	3 Years % Chg	3 Years Rank	3 Years Rating	Risk Return Rating	5 Years % Chg	5 Years Rank	10 Years % Chg	10 Years Rank
		61.14	**Mean/Count**				**-2.65**	**688**	**7**	**601**	**7.41**	**28.18**	**366**			**48.49**	**206**	**166.15**	**29**
▲	DEM	34.27	GAM Asia Fonds Acc	G002	07/10/94	IOM	-2.53	298	0.73	401	N.A.	N.A.		N.A.	N.A.	N.A.		N.A.	
▲	DEM	25.40	GAM Europa Fonds Acc	G002	30/10/92	IOM	1.03	150	19	86	2.67	40.48	67	N.A.	N.A.	N.A.		N.A.	
▲	DEM	57.48	GAM Orient Fonds Acc	G002	30/09/91	IOM	-1.92	282	-0.14	422	3.44	14.40	292	N.A.	N.A.	70.57	26	N.A.	
▲	DEM	180.04	GAM Tokyo Fonds Acc	G002	31/03/92	IOM	-6.79	479	-7.01	565	3.85	35.61	106	N.A.	N.A.	N.A.		N.A.	
▲	DEM	8.42	GAM Total Bond Acc	G002	31/12/92	IOM	-4.64	359	1.91	374	2.01	25.98	213	N.A.	N.A.	N.A.		N.A.	
▲	DEM	246.85	GAM Universal DEM Acc	G002	31/08/90	LUX	2.75	95	7.88	225	3.37	34.80	113	N.A.	N.A.	99.77	13	N.A.	
	DEM	2.01	Generalinvest Croissance A	B064	31/01/95	LUX	1.76	116	8.49	215	N.A.	N.A.		N.A.	N.A.	N.A.		N.A.	
	USD	0.43	Generalinvest Emerg Mkt A	B064	19/04/96	LUX	8.05	38	N.A.		N.A.	N.A.		N.A.	N.A.	N.A.		N.A.	
	DEM	2.54	Generalinvest Global A	B064	19/04/96	LUX	-2.95	316	N.A.		N.A.	N.A.		N.A.	N.A.	N.A.		N.A.	
	DEM	1.27	Generalinvest Rendement A	B064	31/01/95	LUX	-6.15	420	-0.60	433	N.A.	N.A.		N.A.	N.A.	N.A.		N.A.	
	LUF	23.09	Generalpart A	B064	31/01/91	LUX	2.36	106	33.78	18	3.10	88.85	7	N.A.	N.A.	179.04	4	N.A.	
	DEM	117.21	Generalux DEM A	B064	31/07/91	LUX	-6.50	443	-1	447	3.05	30.39	153	N.A.	N.A.	46.23	100	N.A.	
	ECU	15.78	Generalux Europe A	B064	31/07/91	LUX	-6.48	441	6.66	246	2.47	29.39	166	N.A.	N.A.	41.47	117	N.A.	
	LUF	155.92	Generalux Francs A	B064	31/07/91	LUX	-7.33	594	0.59	407	3.08	37.56	90	N.A.	N.A.	56.53	55	N.A.	
	FRF	8.68	Generalux FRF A	B064	31/07/91	LUX	-7.06	523	3.47	339	2.75	28.06	189	N.A.	N.A.	47.37	96	N.A.	
	DEM	88.97	Generalux Multi Currency A	B064	31/07/91	LUX	-5.15	372	5.62	269	2.26	23.26	236	N.A.	N.A.	37.58	130	N.A.	
	USD	9.98	Generalux USD A	B064	26/02/93	LUX	0	195	5.77	266	1.35	13.53	300	N.A.	N.A.	N.A.		N.A.	
	USD	20.30	GT Africa B Share	G018	24/11/95	BER	7.05	44	21.29	75	N.A.	N.A.		N.A.	N.A.	N.A.		N.A.	
▲	USD	193	GT ASEAN B Share	G018	31/01/79	IRL	3.46	83	17.69	107	6.47	-7.88	349	N.A.	N.A.	107.26	10	357.16	3
	USD	71	GT Asia B Share	G018	28/11/75	IRL	-2.36	295	9.28	206	4.17	5.82	326	N.A.	N.A.	38.41	128	231.13	5
▲	USD	140	GT Asian Small Cos B Share	G018	31/07/92	IRL	-2.85	308	16.23	125	4.44	-13.60	359	N.A.	N.A.	N.A.		N.A.	
	USD	24	GT Asian Warr & Derivatives B	G018	31/10/91	IRL	14.90	12	28.27	30	10.06	154.28	1	N.A.	N.A.	202.70	2	N.A.	
▲	USD	5	GT Australia B Share	G018	30/03/79	IRL	-0.42	214	19.52	83	4.19	26.57	209	N.A.	N.A.	54.23	69	58.99	28
	USD	35	GT Australian Sml Cos B Share	G018	29/03/91	IRL	1.38	126	38.01	13	4.37	18.55	264	N.A.	N.A.	129.02	6	N.A.	
▲	USD	36	GT Berry Japan B	G018	30/09/75	IRL	-4.25	349	-6.71	563	3.40	1.47	335	N.A.	N.A.	-15.19	204	11.34	29
▲	USD	369	GT Bond B Share	G018	31/01/77	IRL	-2.72	303	10.88	188	2.25	23.97	230	N.A.	N.A.	67.71	30	193.27	10
▲	USD	329	GT Emerging Markets B Share	G018	29/06/90	IRL	11.62	17	3.18	344	4.52	-13.91	360	N.A.	N.A.	43.48	112	N.A.	
▲	USD	54	GT Emerging Mkts Small Cos B	G018	30/11/93	IRL	3.20	88	4.98	295	3.96	-12.54	356	N.A.	N.A.	N.A.		N.A.	
▲	USD	158	GT European Smllr Cos B Share	G018	31/10/84	IRL	8.32	35	34.11	16	3.07	48.08	36	N.A.	N.A.	84.85	17	115.73	21
▲	GBP	35.52	GT Gilt B	G018	30/07/76	IRL	-2.92	313	16.92	118	2.58	28.60	178	N.A.	N.A.	53.77	71	223.67	6
	USD	130	GT Healthcare B	G018	31/01/90	IRL	-2.99	317	33.83	17	5.63	127.26	2	N.A.	N.A.	203.02	1	N.A.	
▲	USD	48	GT Hong Kong B Share	G018	30/03/84	IRL	-1.38	264	42.10	7	6.56	8.51	318	N.A.	N.A.	189.68	3	422.42	1
▲	USD	80	GT Honshu Pathfinder B Share	G018	30/11/82	IRL	-9.91	669	-11.51	586	5.69	-13.48	358	N.A.	N.A.	-8.84	203	66.75	27
▲	USD	19	GT Indian Small Cos B	G018	02/12/94	IRL	14.45	13	-2.41	476	N.A.	N.A.		N.A.	N.A.	N.A.		N.A.	
▲	USD	32	GT Japan OTC Stock B	G018	29/12/89	IRL	-7.63	629	-13.71	596	6.15	-12.35	355	N.A.	N.A.	-6.16	202	N.A.	
▲	USD	110	GT Japan Small Companies B	G018	30/04/80	IRL	-8.41	655	-8.36	571	5.65	-7.62	348	N.A.	N.A.	-5.53	201	83.53	24
▲	USD	92	GT Latin America B	G018	30/04/91	IRL	10.22	21	25.53	45	8.01	-5.54	344	N.A.	N.A.	30.74	151	N.A.	
▲	USD	42	GT North America B	G018	30/09/75	IRL	3.10	90	16.26	124	2.91	53.34	29	N.A.	N.A.	106.32	11	213.99	7
▲	USD	60	GT PRC B	G018	31/03/92	IRL	17.82	5	55.62	2	7.06	-18.68	362	N.A.	N.A.	N.A.		N.A.	
▲	USD	91	GT Strategic Bond B	G018	31/01/94	IRL	-0.34	210	23.75	58	N.A.	N.A.		N.A.	N.A.	N.A.		N.A.	
▲	USD	81	GT Technology B Share	G018	28/09/79	IRL	-3.07	320	24.98	49	5.69	122.61	3	N.A.	N.A.	120.66	7	358.85	2
▲	USD	101	GT Telecommunications B	G018	30/06/92	IRL	-2.39	296	9.80	201	4.58	14	298	N.A.	N.A.	N.A.		N.A.	
●	ECU	N.S.	Hottinger IF-Euro Bds Ecu D	H032	31/05/95	LUX	-6.17	422	0.45	410	N.A.	N.A.		N.A.	N.A.	N.A.		N.A.	
	FRF	N.S.	Hottinger IF-Euro Bds FRF D	H032	30/12/94	LUX	-6.29	431	-0.03	419	N.A.	N.A.		N.A.	N.A.	N.A.		N.A.	
●	USD	N.S.	Hottinger IF-US Growth Dis	H032	28/04/95	LUX	1.83	113	21.46	74	N.A.	N.A.		N.A.	N.A.	N.A.		N.A.	
	USD	30.53	India Liberalisation B	A005	31/12/93	LUX	15.36	10	-11	583	6.08	-40.58	365	N.A.	N.A.	N.A.		N.A.	
	USD	0.98	Indosuez Latin America D	B033	29/04/94	LUX	15.96	9	16.41	121	N.A.	N.A.		N.A.	N.A.	N.A.		N.A.	
	BEF	0.86	ING Intl-Belgium Bond Dis	I008	30/09/94	LUX	-6.89	497	1.76	377	N.A.	N.A.		N.A.	N.A.	N.A.		N.A.	
	NLG	5.75	ING Intl-Dutch Bond Dis	I008	30/06/95	LUX	-7.10	540	-1.65	459	N.A.	N.A.		N.A.	N.A.	N.A.		N.A.	
	USD	0.76	ING Intl-Latin Am Equity Dis	I008	30/06/94	LUX	14.43	14	28.27	29	N.A.	N.A.		N.A.	N.A.	N.A.		N.A.	
	USD	0.78	ING Intl-New Asia Equity Dist	I008	30/06/94	LUX	-6.05	418	6.01	261	N.A.	N.A.		N.A.	N.A.	N.A.		N.A.	
▲	FRF	251.74	Inter Cash Franc (FRF) D	B069	29/12/95	LUX	-7.14	550	-3.11	496	N.A.	N.A.		N.A.	N.A.	N.A.		N.A.	
▲	FRF	286.63	Inter Cash France Securite D	B069	29/12/95	LUX	-7	513	-2.49	478	N.A.	N.A.		N.A.	N.A.	N.A.		N.A.	
	BEF	55.59	International Property Fund D	K010	30/11/88	LUX	-6.66	467	-0.58	431	2.48	7.51	321	N.A.	N.A.	1.03	200	N.A.	
	LUF	20.11	Interselex Europa A	G009	31/08/94	LUX	2.79	93	18.47	93	N.A.	N.A.		N.A.	N.A.	N.A.		N.A.	
	LUF	73.51	Interselex World A	G009	31/01/91	LUX	-1.12	255	11.16	184	2.79	39.23	77	N.A.	N.A.	57.32	53	N.A.	
●	BEF	3.90	InvestPlus Money A	B035	31/03/88	LUX	-7.32	586	-4.86	543	2.71	20.24	258	N.A.	N.A.	22.30	184	N.A.	

▲ SIB Approved ● Insurance Fund **Values in US Dollars, on an offer to offer price basis with gross income reinvested** Data Source Micropal™

Second Units Non-sector

continued

CCY	Fund Size ($mil)	Fund Name	Manager Code	Fund Start Date	Domicile Code	3 Mths 97 % Chg	3 Mths 97 Rank	1 Year % Chg	1 Year Rank	Micropal Star Rating: Volatility	Micropal Star Rating: 3 Years % Chg	Micropal Star Rating: 3 Years Rank	Micropal Star Rating: Rating	Risk Return Rating	5 Years % Chg	5 Years Rank	10 Years % Chg	10 Years Rank
	61.14	**Mean/Count**				**-2.65**	**688**	**7**	**601**	**7.41**	**28.18**	**366**			**48.49**	**206**	**166.15**	**29**
LUF	4.46	Ippa Portf Belgian Bond A	B035	31/05/88	LUX	-7.23	571	1.46	384	2.99	41.43	62	N.A.	N.A.	59.08	49	N.A.	
LUF	0.57	Ippa Portf Belgian Immo A	B035	31/05/94	LUX	-4.69	364	-5.21	556	N.A.	N.A.		N.A.	N.A.	N.A.		N.A.	
LUF	0.88	Ippa Portf Belgian Money A	B035	31/03/92	LUX	-7.55	624	-3.48	503	2.84	35.42	110	N.A.	N.A.	N.A.		N.A.	
LUF	0.80	Ippa Portf Belgian Short A	B035	31/03/92	LUX	-7.42	613	-5.21	555	2.80	27.10	203	N.A.	N.A.	N.A.		N.A.	
LUF	1.62	Ippa Portf Global Assets A	B035	31/05/94	LUX	-3.96	338	5.36	278	N.A.	N.A.		N.A.	N.A.	N.A.		N.A.	
LUF	7.79	Ippa Portf Internat Bond A	B035	31/03/88	LUX	-5.18	374	7.59	232	2.46	33.99	125	N.A.	N.A.	52	77	N.A.	
LUF	2.01	Ippa Portf Internat Money A	B035	31/03/88	LUX	-5.68	398	3.63	333	2.25	34.57	117	N.A.	N.A.	38.91	126	N.A.	
LUF	0.48	Ippa Portf Stock Market A	B035	31/05/94	LUX	-1.36	262	9.86	200	N.A.	N.A.		N.A.	N.A.	N.A.		N.A.	
LUF	1.91	Ippa Portf Stock Yield A	B035	31/03/92	LUX	5.07	60	18.06	101	2.91	37.17	94	N.A.	N.A.	N.A.		N.A.	
LUF	N.S.	Isis Bonds Dis	B026	31/01/89	LUX	-7.51	619	-0.69	438	2.98	41.41	63	N.A.	N.A.	54.30	67	N.A.	
LUF	N.S.	Isis Global Assets Eq High D	B026	30/09/93	LUX	0.52	175	9.37	205	2.15	26.62	208	N.A.	N.A.	N.A.		N.A.	
LUF	N.S.	Isis Global Assets Eq Low D	B026	31/12/90	LUX	-4.12	344	3.16	347	2.25	20.88	255	N.A.	N.A.	39.87	122	N.A.	
LUF	N.S.	Isis Global Assets Eq Medium D	B026	31/12/90	LUX	-1.17	256	7.72	226	2.07	26.69	207	N.A.	N.A.	49.15	88	N.A.	
BEF	81.16	KB Bonds High Interest Div	K010	28/04/89	LUX	-6.08	419	7.94	223	2.69	22.58	241	N.A.	N.A.	24.80	177	N.A.	
BEF	47.68	KB Bonds Strong Currency Div	K010	28/09/90	LUX	-7.29	581	0.30	411	2.88	32.94	132	N.A.	N.A.	54.26	68	N.A.	
BEF	10.69	KB Fixobli BEF 24/12/2000 Dis	K010	31/07/95	LUX	-7.19	559	-3.77	506	N.A.	N.A.		N.A.	N.A.	N.A.		N.A.	
ATS	6.58	KB Lux Bond ATS A	K011	31/01/95	LUX	-6.52	447	0.21	414	N.A.	N.A.		N.A.	N.A.	N.A.		N.A.	
AUD	0.44	KB Lux Bond AUD A	K011	31/01/95	LUX	-2.10	287	15.89	134	N.A.	N.A.		N.A.	N.A.	N.A.		N.A.	
BEF	45.53	KB Lux Bond BEF A	K011	31/01/95	LUX	-7.04	520	1.96	373	N.A.	N.A.		N.A.	N.A.	N.A.		N.A.	
CAD	11.24	KB Lux Bond CAD A	K011	31/01/95	LUX	-1.79	278	11.55	177	N.A.	N.A.		N.A.	N.A.	N.A.		N.A.	
DEM	18.46	KB Lux Bond DEM A	K011	30/12/94	LUX	-6.65	465	-0.53	430	N.A.	N.A.		N.A.	N.A.	N.A.		N.A.	
DKK	3.34	KB Lux Bond DKK A	K011	30/06/93	LUX	-6.54	449	3.24	341	2.50	39.91	73	N.A.	N.A.	N.A.		N.A.	
FRF	1.92	KB Lux Bond FRF A	K011	31/01/95	LUX	-7.03	516	5.15	286	N.A.	N.A.		N.A.	N.A.	N.A.		N.A.	
GBP	4.21	KB Lux Bond GBP A	K011	31/01/95	LUX	-3.38	327	18.51	92	N.A.	N.A.		N.A.	N.A.	N.A.		N.A.	
GRD	0.01	KB Lux Bond Greek Drachma A	K011	13/12/96	LUX	-2.68	301	N.A.		N.A.	N.A.		N.A.	N.A.	N.A.		N.A.	
DEM	1.14	KB Lux Bond Interbond A	K011	31/01/95	LUX	-4.23	347	3.22	343	N.A.	N.A.		N.A.	N.A.	N.A.		N.A.	
ITL	1.30	KB Lux Bond ITL A	K011	31/01/95	LUX	-9.73	667	27.85	33	N.A.	N.A.		N.A.	N.A.	N.A.		N.A.	
NLG	14.87	KB Lux Bond NLG A	K011	31/01/95	LUX	-7	512	-0.48	427	N.A.	N.A.		N.A.	N.A.	N.A.		N.A.	
ESP	1.22	KB Lux Bond PTAS A	K011	31/01/95	LUX	-8.35	653	13.11	162	N.A.	N.A.		N.A.	N.A.	N.A.		N.A.	
BEF	4.67	KB Lux Bond Short Invest BEF A	K011	08/12/95	LUX	-7.53	621	-3.34	499	N.A.	N.A.		N.A.	N.A.	N.A.		N.A.	
DEM	12.68	KB Lux Bond Short Invest DEM A	K011	08/12/95	LUX	-7.07	529	-3.68	505	N.A.	N.A.		N.A.	N.A.	N.A.		N.A.	
DKK	0.13	KB Lux Bond Short Invest DKK A	K011	13/12/96	LUX	-6.99	510	N.A.		N.A.	N.A.		N.A.	N.A.	N.A.		N.A.	
ECU	0.08	KB Lux Bond Short Invest Ecu A	K011	13/12/96	LUX	-6.33	433	N.A.		N.A.	N.A.		N.A.	N.A.	N.A.		N.A.	
ESP	N.S.	KB Lux Bond Short Invest ESP A	K011	13/12/96	LUX	-7.63	627	N.A.		N.A.	N.A.		N.A.	N.A.	N.A.		N.A.	
GBP	0.05	KB Lux Bond Short Invest GBP A	K011	13/12/96	LUX	-3.10	322	N.A.		N.A.	N.A.		N.A.	N.A.	N.A.		N.A.	
ITL	0	KB Lux Bond Short Invest ITL A	K011	13/12/96	LUX	-8.55	657	N.A.		N.A.	N.A.		N.A.	N.A.	N.A.		N.A.	
NLG	4.22	KB Lux Bond Short Invest NLG A	K011	08/03/96	LUX	-7.34	595	N.A.		N.A.	N.A.		N.A.	N.A.	N.A.		N.A.	
USD	2.13	KB Lux Bond Short Invest USD A	K011	08/03/96	LUX	0.56	171	N.A.		N.A.	N.A.		N.A.	N.A.	N.A.		N.A.	
USD	12	KB Lux Bond US Dollar A	K011	31/01/95	LUX	-1.01	242	3.16	346	N.A.	N.A.		N.A.	N.A.	N.A.		N.A.	
BEF	0.62	KB Lux Luxinvest D	K011	04/10/96	LUX	0.06	192	N.A.		N.A.	N.A.		N.A.	N.A.	N.A.		N.A.	
CAD	15.02	KB Renta Canarenta A	K010	08/03/96	LUX	-1.40	266	N.A.		N.A.	N.A.		N.A.	N.A.	N.A.		N.A.	
DKK	70.45	KB Renta Decarenta A	K010	31/01/86	LUX	-6.75	471	2.59	362	3.12	37.44	92	N.A.	N.A.	68.95	28	242.49	4
DEM	24.07	KB Renta Demrenta A	K010	30/11/92	LUX	-6.77	473	-1.08	449	2.97	31.35	147	N.A.	N.A.	N.A.		N.A.	
USD	11.20	KB Renta Dollarenta A	K010	08/03/96	LUX	-0.43	216	N.A.		N.A.	N.A.		N.A.	N.A.	N.A.		N.A.	
ECU	128.55	KB Renta Ecurenta A	K010	31/01/86	LUX	-6.47	440	7.09	239	2.60	31.72	145	N.A.	N.A.	59.30	48	207.76	8
NLG	47.11	KB Renta Guldenrenta A	K010	30/11/92	LUX	-7.68	633	-1.61	458	2.99	29.74	163	N.A.	N.A.	N.A.		N.A.	
ITL	1.11	KB Renta Lirarenta A	K010	30/11/94	LUX	-9.92	670	23.42	62	N.A.	N.A.		N.A.	N.A.	N.A.		N.A.	
LUF	81.52	KB Renta Oblirenta Div	K010	31/10/88	LUX	-7.48	618	1.25	393	2.99	39.04	78	N.A.	N.A.	58.91	50	N.A.	
ESP	16.88	KB Renta Pesetarenta A	K010	30/11/92	LUX	-8.22	650	12	174	3.08	46.08	40	N.A.	N.A.	N.A.		N.A.	
CHF	252.05	KB Renta Swissrenta A	K010	30/08/96	LUX	-5.93	411	N.A.		N.A.	N.A.		N.A.	N.A.	N.A.		N.A.	
CHF	7.79	Lake Intertrust Bond D	C062	31/07/89	LUX	-5.63	393	-7.41	566	3.02	18.10	267	N.A.	N.A.	40.14	119	N.A.	
DEM	14.27	LFM Emerg Mkt Cap Fd DEM Dist	I008	26/02/93	LUX	-1.53	273	35.72	14	4.25	89.30	6	N.A.	N.A.	N.A.		N.A.	
USD	21.50	LFM Emerg Mkt Cap Fd USD Dist	I008	26/02/93	LUX	5.70	53	54.03	3	5.17	82.78	10	N.A.	N.A.	N.A.		N.A.	
BEF	1.16	Lion Belgium Cash D	C060	30/04/93	LUX	-7.55	623	-9.13	574	2.67	20.67	256	N.A.	N.A.	N.A.		N.A.	
USD	4.29	Lion Fortune CL Asian Growth D	C062	23/08/96	LUX	1.76	117	N.A.		N.A.	N.A.		N.A.	N.A.	N.A.		N.A.	
USD	0.02	Lion Fortune CL Global Bd D	C062	30/04/93	LUX	-2.20	292	7.54	233	2.35	21.66	251	N.A.	N.A.	N.A.		N.A.	
USD	12	Lion Fortune CL Global Gth D	C062	31/07/91	LUX	-4.11	343	10.17	194	4.47	30.62	151	N.A.	N.A.	87.14	16	N.A.	

▲ SIB Approved ● Insurance Fund Values in US Dollars, on an offer to offer price basis with gross income reinvested Data Source Micropal™

Second Units Non-sector

continued

CCY	Fund Size ($mil)	Fund Name	Manager Code	Fund Start Date	Domicile Code	3 Mths 97 % Chg	3 Mths 97 Rank	1 Year % Chg	1 Year Rank	Micropal Star Rating 3 Years Volatility	3 Years % Chg	3 Years Rank	3 Years Rating	Risk Return Rating	5 Years % Chg	5 Years Rank	10 Years % Chg	10 Years Rank
	61.14	**Mean/Count**				**-2.65**	**688**	**7**	**601**	**7.41**	**28.18**	**366**			**48.49**	**206**	**166.15**	**29**
USD	1.44	Lion Fortune CL Lat Am Eq B	C062	28/02/94	LUX	20.19	2	31.79	21	N.A.	N.A.		N.A.	N.A.	N.A.		N.A.	
LUF	4.56	Lux Avantage1 B Dis	C002	31/07/95	LUX	1.27	129	35.62	15	N.A.	N.A.		N.A.	N.A.	N.A.		N.A.	
LUF	8.85	Lux Croissance Francs B Dis	C002	31/07/95	LUX	-4.40	351	4.56	311	N.A.	N.A.		N.A.	N.A.	N.A.		N.A.	
DEM	37.88	Luxbond D Mark B Dis	C002	30/06/89	LUX	-6.90	502	-0.63	434	3.13	34.31	122	N.A.	N.A.	45.79	103	N.A.	
USD	6.82	Luxbond Dollars B Dis	C002	30/06/89	LUX	-0.05	198	6.50	248	1.72	16.80	272	N.A.	N.A.	28.67	165	N.A.	
LUF	40.25	Luxbond Francs B Dis	C002	30/06/89	LUX	-7.37	603	1.48	383	3.16	41.77	61	N.A.	N.A.	54.13	70	N.A.	
DEM	17.53	Luxcash Deutsche Mark B Dis	C002	31/07/95	LUX	-7.71	634	-6.46	561	N.A.	N.A.		N.A.	N.A.	N.A.		N.A.	
ECU	2.51	Luxcash Ecu B Dis	C002	31/07/95	LUX	-6.97	507	-1.32	452	N.A.	N.A.		N.A.	N.A.	N.A.		N.A.	
NLG	2.04	Luxcash Florins Neerland B Dis	C002	31/07/95	LUX	-7.92	646	-6.84	564	N.A.	N.A.		N.A.	N.A.	N.A.		N.A.	
LUF	4.72	Luxcash Francs B Dis	C002	31/07/95	LUX	-7.95	648	-6.69	562	N.A.	N.A.		N.A.	N.A.	N.A.		N.A.	
FRF	5.60	Luxcash Francs Francais B Dis	C002	31/07/95	LUX	-7.74	637	-5.16	554	N.A.	N.A.		N.A.	N.A.	N.A.		N.A.	
USD	12.18	Luxcash US Dollars B Dis	C002	31/07/95	LUX	-0.04	197	1.37	388	N.A.	N.A.		N.A.	N.A.	N.A.		N.A.	
LUF	0.27	Luxicav Mixed A	S036	31/05/89	LUX	-10.71	678	12.18	173	2.52	50.99	32	N.A.	N.A.	39.80	123	N.A.	
LUF	2.50	Luxicav Oblilux A	S036	31/07/92	LUX	-13.41	686	-1.19	450	2.72	37.55	91	N.A.	N.A.	N.A.		N.A.	
DEM	53.20	Luxinvest GlobalRent /B	B061	30/12/88	LUX	-4.24	348	1.80	376	2.40	19.81	260	N.A.	N.A.	32.45	144	N.A.	
DEM	36.39	Luxinvest Rentenfonds /B	B061	30/11/92	LUX	-7.46	616	-2.18	471	2.83	25.13	223	N.A.	N.A.	N.A.		N.A.	
LUF	19.79	LuxiPrivilege A	S036	31/01/94	LUX	-1.22	257	29.49	27	N.A.	N.A.		N.A.	N.A.	N.A.		N.A.	
USD	6.91	M.Lynch Adjust Sec Portf B	M023	30/08/91	LUX	1.42	124	5.44	276	0.56	11.04	312	N.A.	N.A.	17.55	190	N.A.	
USD	128.93	M.Lynch Americas Inc Portf B	M023	28/02/94	CA	-0.82	232	50.51	4	N.A.	N.A.		N.A.	N.A.	N.A.		N.A.	
USD	22.81	M.Lynch Americas Inc Portf C	M023	28/02/94	CA	-0.91	238	50.51	5	N.A.	N.A.		N.A.	N.A.	N.A.		N.A.	
USD	41.01	M.Lynch Asia Tiger Bond A2	M023	02/02/96	LUX	0.95	154	N.A.		N.A.	N.A.		N.A.	N.A.	N.A.		N.A.	
USD	250.57	M.Lynch Asia Tiger Bond B1	M023	02/02/96	LUX	1.02	151	N.A.		N.A.	N.A.		N.A.	N.A.	N.A.		N.A.	
USD	91.59	M.Lynch Asia Tiger Bond B2	M023	02/02/96	LUX	0.87	159	N.A.		N.A.	N.A.		N.A.	N.A.	N.A.		N.A.	
USD	150.22	M.Lynch Basic Value Portf B	M023	30/03/90	LUX	3.79	77	17.37	110	2.60	54.45	26	N.A.	N.A.	99.91	12	N.A.	
USD	80.82	M.Lynch Capital Portfolio B	M023	30/06/95	LUX	-0.75	227	11.75	176	N.A.	N.A.		N.A.	N.A.	N.A.		N.A.	
USD	10.36	M.Lynch Convert Securities B	M023	30/03/90	LUX	-0.69	224	7.09	238	1.57	16.21	277	N.A.	N.A.	38.07	129	N.A.	
USD	47.70	M.Lynch Corp High Income A1	M023	29/10/93	LUX	1.32	128	10.02	197	1.35	22.92	240	N.A.	N.A.	N.A.		N.A.	
USD	394.48	M.Lynch Corp High Income B1	M023	29/10/93	LUX	1.26	130	9.76	202	1.35	21.99	249	N.A.	N.A.	N.A.		N.A.	
USD	62.84	M.Lynch Corp High Income B2	M023	29/10/93	LUX	1.05	148	9.90	199	1.35	22.22	245	N.A.	N.A.	N.A.		N.A.	
USD	300.05	M.Lynch Dragon Portfolio B	M023	29/05/92	LUX	-3.98	339	15.29	143	5.24	-0.38	336	N.A.	N.A.	N.A.		N.A.	
USD	27.54	M.Lynch Emerg Mkts Portf B	M023	31/05/94	CA	8.69	30	6.15	256	N.A.	N.A.		N.A.	N.A.	N.A.		N.A.	
DEM	3.59	M.Lynch Euro Bond Ptf DM A1	M023	29/01/93	LUX	-7.46	617	6.31	253	1.89	29.95	161	N.A.	N.A.	N.A.		N.A.	
DEM	4.40	M.Lynch Euro Bond Ptf DM B1	M023	29/01/93	LUX	-7.58	625	5.79	265	1.90	28.03	190	N.A.	N.A.	N.A.		N.A.	
DEM	17.67	M.Lynch Euro Bond Ptf DM B2	M023	29/01/93	LUX	-7.63	630	5.87	264	1.92	28.14	187	N.A.	N.A.	N.A.		N.A.	
USD	7.18	M.Lynch Euro Bond Ptf USD A1	M023	29/01/93	LUX	-5.25	377	6.11	258	2.19	4.45	330	N.A.	N.A.	N.A.		N.A.	
USD	9.57	M.Lynch Euro Bond Ptf USD B1	M023	29/01/93	LUX	-5.37	382	5.59	270	2.20	2.90	333	N.A.	N.A.	N.A.		N.A.	
USD	8.80	M.Lynch Euro Bond Ptf USD B2	M023	29/01/93	LUX	-5.46	388	5.68	268	2.20	3.14	332	N.A.	N.A.	N.A.		N.A.	
USD	116.16	M.Lynch Euro Equity Portf B	M023	31/08/90	LUX	7.01	46	22.11	68	3.16	40.82	64	N.A.	N.A.	75.81	22	N.A.	
USD	68.31	M.Lynch Gbl Cur Mlt Cur Bd B2	M023	28/02/91	LUX	-4.87	369	5.17	285	1.39	9.82	315	N.A.	N.A.	30.28	154	N.A.	
USD	58.82	M.Lynch Gbl Cur US Fed Sec B	M023	28/02/91	LUX	-1.08	248	3.13	348	1.09	12.55	303	N.A.	N.A.	25.82	176	N.A.	
USD	421.04	M.Lynch Global Allocation B	M023	30/07/93	LUX	1.46	123	14.68	148	1.52	32.50	136	N.A.	N.A.	N.A.		N.A.	
AUD	4.06	M.Lynch Global Curr AUS B	M023	28/02/91	LUX	-2.90	312	15.93	133	2.51	37.19	93	N.A.	N.A.	51.90	78	N.A.	
CAD	28.03	M.Lynch Global Curr CAD B	M023	31/12/90	LUX	-2.14	288	9.11	208	2.69	17.54	268	N.A.	N.A.	23.44	180	N.A.	
DEM	20.92	M.Lynch Global Curr DEM B	M023	30/11/90	LUX	-7.32	587	-2.82	485	2.38	28.24	185	N.A.	N.A.	39.19	124	N.A.	
GBP	11.64	M.Lynch Global Curr STG B	M023	30/11/90	LUX	-3.83	337	14.52	150	2.31	23.82	232	N.A.	N.A.	36.83	135	N.A.	
JPY	3.84	M.Lynch Global Curr YEN B	M023	30/11/90	LUX	-5.25	376	-8.74	573	3.89	3.41	331	N.A.	N.A.	40.15	118	N.A.	
USD	9.10	M.Lynch Global Equity Portf B	M023	28/02/89	LUX	2.01	109	3.67	331	2.89	16.78	273	N.A.	N.A.	17.57	189	N.A.	
USD	27.64	M.Lynch Global SmallCap B	M023	30/11/94	LUX	-0.09	200	11.96	175	N.A.	N.A.		N.A.	N.A.	N.A.		N.A.	
USD	71.43	M.Lynch Latin Amer Portf B	M023	29/11/91	LUX	17.82	6	18.07	100	6.40	-19.26	363	N.A.	N.A.	25.93	175	N.A.	
USD	37.56	M.Lynch Mex Inc Dllr Portf B	M023	31/07/92	CA	2.75	94	17.81	105	2.77	32.14	139	N.A.	N.A.	N.A.		N.A.	
USD	123.96	M.Lynch Mex Inc Peso Portf B	M023	31/07/92	CA	5.97	50	38.08	12	8.33	-22.39	364	N.A.	N.A.	N.A.		N.A.	
USD	145.62	M.Lynch Pacific EQ Portf B	M023	31/08/94	LUX	3.03	91	6	262	N.A.	N.A.		N.A.	N.A.	N.A.		N.A.	
USD	16.93	M.Lynch Sht Term World Inc B	M023	29/06/90	CA	0.21	185	3.59	336	0.59	4.91	329	N.A.	N.A.	7.72	198	N.A.	
USD	75.14	M.Lynch Super Money Mkt Fd B	M023	31/07/90	LUX	0.75	163	4.83	302	0	14.67	287	N.A.	N.A.	22.40	183	N.A.	
USD	61.66	M.Lynch Technology Portf B	M023	31/03/95	LUX	2.47	102	3.51	337	N.A.	N.A.		N.A.	N.A.	N.A.		N.A.	
USD	39.42	M.Lynch Visionary Portf B	M023	10/11/95	LUX	-7.20	562	25.03	48	N.A.	N.A.		N.A.	N.A.	N.A.		N.A.	
USD	12.13	M.Lynch World Natural Res B	M023	29/04/88	LUX	-0.61	222	12.18	172	3.16	20.29	257	N.A.	N.A.	22.96	181	N.A.	

▲ SIB Approved ● Insurance Fund **Values in US Dollars, on an offer to offer price basis with gross income reinvested** Data Source Micropal™

Second Units Non-sector

continued

CCY	Fund Size ($mil)	Fund Name	Manager Code	Fund Start Date	Domicile Code	3 Mths 97 % Chg	Rank	1 Year % Chg	Rank	Micropal Star Rating: Volatility	3 Years % Chg	Rank	Rating	Risk Return Rating	5 Years % Chg	Rank	10 Years % Chg	Rank
	61.14	**Mean/Count**				**-2.65**	**688**	**7**	**601**	**7.41**	**28.18**	**366**			**48.49**	**206**	**166.15**	**29**
LUF	N.S.	Maestro A	S034	30/11/87	LUX	-7.28	578	1.14	395	2.84	40.53	66	N.A.	N.A.	52.85	75	N.A.	
DEM	N.S.	MeesPierson UF DEM Bond B	M012	01/03/96	LUX	-7.17	557	N.A.		N.A.	N.A.		N.A.	N.A.	N.A.		N.A.	
DEM	N.S.	MeesPierson UF Global Bond B	M012	01/03/96	LUX	-4.71	365	N.A.		N.A.	N.A.		N.A.	N.A.	N.A.		N.A.	
USD	N.S.	MeesPierson UF USD Bond B	M012	01/03/96	LUX	-1.08	247	N.A.		N.A.	N.A.		N.A.	N.A.	N.A.		N.A.	
DEM	4.48	Merck Finck Invest EuroLux B	M014	29/10/93	LUX	-2.75	306	17.35	111	2.60	38.14	85	N.A.	N.A.	N.A.		N.A.	
DEM	1.76	Merck Finck Invest Lux Rent B	M014	31/12/92	LUX	-6.80	483	-5.26	557	3.06	25.17	222	N.A.	N.A.	N.A.		N.A.	
USD	0	MFS Intl Fds Charter Inc A1	M026	30/06/94	LUX	-0.17	203	4.86	300	N.A.	N.A.		N.A.	N.A.	N.A.		N.A.	
USD	0.22	MFS Intl Fds Charter Inc A2	M026	30/06/94	LUX	-1.41	267	1.29	390	N.A.	N.A.		N.A.	N.A.	N.A.		N.A.	
USD	0.87	MFS Intl Fds Charter Inc B2	M026	30/06/94	LUX	-1.12	254	1.53	382	N.A.	N.A.		N.A.	N.A.	N.A.		N.A.	
USD	0	MFS Intl Fds Global Govt A1	M026	30/06/92	LUX	-0.26	208	4.76	305	3.57	28.56	179	N.A.	N.A.	N.A.		N.A.	
USD	0.67	MFS Intl Fds Global Govt A2	M026	30/06/92	LUX	0	195	3.75	328	2.89	27.10	202	N.A.	N.A.	N.A.		N.A.	
USD	1.12	MFS Intl Fds Global Govt B2	M026	30/06/94	LUX	-0.30	209	3.65	332	N.A.	N.A.		N.A.	N.A.	N.A.		N.A.	
USD	1.12	MFS Intl Fds US Emerg Gth A1	M026	30/06/92	LUX	-2.85	310	17.49	109	4.73	71.93	11	N.A.	N.A.	N.A.		N.A.	
USD	7.54	MFS Intl Fds US Emerg Gth A2	M026	30/06/92	LUX	-2.85	309	16.57	120	7.43	70.18	12	N.A.	N.A.	N.A.		N.A.	
USD	6.42	MFS Intl Fds US Emerg Gth B2	M026	30/06/94	LUX	-3.15	323	15.27	144	N.A.	N.A.		N.A.	N.A.	N.A.		N.A.	
USD	1.53	MFS Intl Fds US Equity A1	M026	30/06/92	LUX	1.88	112	25.07	47	2.63	63.16	20	N.A.	N.A.	N.A.		N.A.	
USD	109.55	MFS Intl Fds US Equity A2	M026	30/06/92	LUX	1.93	111	24.85	52	2.95	63.01	21	N.A.	N.A.	N.A.		N.A.	
USD	0.83	MFS Intl Fds US Equity B2	M026	30/06/94	LUX	1.70	118	24.77	53	N.A.	N.A.		N.A.	N.A.	N.A.		N.A.	
BEF	N.S.	Money Plus (Bef) Dist	C061	30/06/89	LUX	-7.16	553	-4.01	509	2.57	30.34	154	N.A.	N.A.	33.51	141	N.A.	
USD	N.S.	Money Plus (USD) Dist	C061	30/06/89	LUX	1.20	132	5.04	291	0.09	14.75	286	N.A.	N.A.	20.31	187	N.A.	
CHF	0.28	Multibond Actibond CHF A	C015	31/01/91	LUX	-5.80	401	-10.88	582	3.48	26.95	204	N.A.	N.A.	39.97	121	N.A.	
DEM	13.43	Multibond Actibond DEM A	C015	28/02/89	LUX	-6.88	494	-0.66	435	2.88	34.70	116	N.A.	N.A.	49.17	87	N.A.	
ECU	0.16	Multibond Actibond ECU A	C015	28/02/89	LUX	-6.61	461	7.98	222	2.40	34.80	114	N.A.	N.A.	47.41	95	N.A.	
FRF	0.37	Multibond Actibond FRF A	C015	28/04/89	LUX	-6.79	481	3.23	342	2.82	31.84	142	N.A.	N.A.	54.66	63	N.A.	
GBP	1.62	Multibond Actibond GBP A	C015	31/01/91	LUX	-3.56	334	16.40	122	3.04	29.80	162	N.A.	N.A.	28.57	166	N.A.	
USD	1.26	Multibond Actibond USD A	C015	28/02/89	LUX	-1.11	252	2.45	364	1.74	11.96	306	N.A.	N.A.	27.62	171	N.A.	
JPY	5.74	Multibond Actibond Yen A	C015	28/02/89	LUX	-4.97	371	-6.29	559	4.10	9	317	N.A.	N.A.	49.34	86	N.A.	
DEM	0.06	Multibond Acticash DEM A	C015	31/01/91	LUX	-7.16	554	-3.92	508	3.10	28.56	180	N.A.	N.A.	20.99	185	N.A.	
FRF	0.35	Multibond Acticash FRF A	C015	31/01/91	LUX	-7.12	547	-0.92	446	2.94	34.76	115	N.A.	N.A.	30.04	158	N.A.	
USD	2.46	Multibond Acticash USD A	C015	29/03/91	LUX	0.87	157	4.16	319	0.98	14.25	294	N.A.	N.A.	20.17	188	N.A.	
DEM	27.46	OIM Kapital-Garant 9/98 (A)	O009	02/02/96	LUX	-6.01	416	N.A.		N.A.	N.A.		N.A.	N.A.	N.A.		N.A.	
DEM	1.74	Panelfund Bonds DEM Dist	A037	30/07/93	LUX	-6.89	498	-0.89	444	2.28	35.17	111	N.A.	N.A.	N.A.		N.A.	
ECU	21.10	Panelfund Bonds EMU Ecu Div	A037	05/07/96	LUX	-7.08	530	N.A.		N.A.	N.A.		N.A.	N.A.	N.A.		N.A.	
LUF	20.87	Panelfund Bonds EMU LUF Div	A037	05/07/96	LUX	-7.20	560	N.A.		N.A.	N.A.		N.A.	N.A.	N.A.		N.A.	
LUF	7.40	Panelfund Emerg Mkts LUF Div	A037	11/11/94	LUX	0.45	177	16.06	128	N.A.	N.A.		N.A.	N.A.	N.A.		N.A.	
USD	7.54	Panelfund Emerg Mkts USD Div	A037	11/11/94	LUX	0.14	189	16.02	130	N.A.	N.A.		N.A.	N.A.	N.A.		N.A.	
DEM	18.96	Panelfund Hard Curr Bd DEM D	A037	28/02/94	LUX	-6.67	468	-0.75	441	N.A.	N.A.		N.A.	N.A.	N.A.		N.A.	
LUF	18.95	Panelfund Hard Curr Bd LUF D	A037	31/03/93	LUX	-6.81	484	-0.67	436	2.20	35.81	104	N.A.	N.A.	N.A.		N.A.	
NLG	18.95	Panelfund Hard Curr Bd NLG D	A037	31/03/93	LUX	-6.59	458	-0.75	440	2.19	35.48	109	N.A.	N.A.	N.A.		N.A.	
LUF	12.20	Panelfund High Yield Bond D	A037	31/05/90	LUX	-5.65	394	15.83	136	2.42	43.57	47	N.A.	N.A.	36.24	138	N.A.	
LUF	150.63	Panelfund Intl Bonds LUF Dist	A037	07/01/94	LUX	-4.40	350	4.48	314	N.A.	N.A.		N.A.	N.A.	N.A.		N.A.	
DEM	32.60	Panelfund Kurz DEM Dist	A037	30/07/93	LUX	-7.09	536	-4.40	516	2.45	26.75	206	N.A.	N.A.	N.A.		N.A.	
LUF	11.90	Panelfund Short BEF-LUF Dist	A037	30/04/90	LUX	-7.51	620	-2.72	483	2.60	35.15	112	N.A.	N.A.	36.90	133	N.A.	
CAD	20.74	Panelfund Short CAD Dist	A037	29/10/93	LUX	0.55	172	5.53	273	1.33	13.94	299	N.A.	N.A.	N.A.		N.A.	
NLG	10.68	Panelfund Short NLG Dist	A037	29/04/94	LUX	-7.25	573	-4.97	546	N.A.	N.A.		N.A.	N.A.	N.A.		N.A.	
USD	16.57	Panelfund Short USD Dist	A037	29/10/93	LUX	1.05	147	5.17	283	1.19	14.81	285	N.A.	N.A.	N.A.		N.A.	
LUF	59.46	Panelfund World LUF Dist	A037	31/05/90	LUX	0.36	180	11.54	179	2.31	30.10	157	N.A.	N.A.	39.05	125	N.A.	
NLG	63.04	Panelfund World NLG Dist	A037	29/04/94	LUX	0.52	174	11.54	178	N.A.	N.A.		N.A.	N.A.	N.A.		N.A.	
LUF	32.51	Paribas Rente A	B037	29/11/91	LUX	-5.81	405	-2.96	492	2.85	23.23	237	N.A.	N.A.	36.85	134	N.A.	
USD	36.26	Parvest ASEAN A	B037	18/11/94	LUX	-4.92	370	4.46	316	N.A.	N.A.		N.A.	N.A.	N.A.		N.A.	
USD	54.17	Parvest Asian Growth A	B037	30/03/90	LUX	-4.76	367	13.68	156	5.65	-5.05	343	N.A.	N.A.	50.24	81	N.A.	
BEF	3.66	Parvest Belgium A	B037	29/09/95	LUX	3.76	78	14.55	149	N.A.	N.A.		N.A.	N.A.	N.A.		N.A.	
ECU	11.47	Parvest Europe A	B037	30/09/85	LUX	2.95	92	22.46	65	2.78	46.71	37	N.A.	N.A.	81.48	18	145.07	15
ECU	40.45	Parvest Europe Mid Cap A	B037	14/06/96	LUX	3.18	89	N.A.		N.A.	N.A.		N.A.	N.A.	N.A.		N.A.	
FRF	8.46	Parvest France A	B037	31/10/91	LUX	-0.47	217	24.73	54	3.89	34.36	121	N.A.	N.A.	71.61	25	N.A.	
DEM	8.09	Parvest Germany A	B037	30/06/93	LUX	8.66	33	24.10	56	3.66	48.84	34	N.A.	N.A.	N.A.		N.A.	
USD	0.21	Parvest Global 1 USD A	B037	29/10/93	LUX	0.73	164	2.40	366	1.59	5.73	328	N.A.	N.A.	N.A.		N.A.	

▲ SIB Approved ● Insurance Fund Values in US Dollars, on an offer to offer price basis with gross income reinvested Data Source Micropal™

Second Units Non-sector

continued

CCY	Fund Size ($mil)	Fund Name	Manager Code	Fund Start Date	Domicile Code	3 Mths 97 % Chg	3 Mths 97 Rank	1 Year % Chg	1 Year Rank	Micropal Star Rating: Volatility	3 Years % Chg	3 Years Rank	Rating	Risk Return Rating	5 Years % Chg	5 Years Rank	10 Years % Chg	10 Years Rank
	61.14	**Mean/Count**				**-2.65**	**688**	**7**	**601**	**7.41**	**28.18**	**366**			**48.49**	**206**	**166.15**	**29**
USD	0.29	Parvest Global 2 USD A	B037	31/03/94	LUX	1.18	133	10.34	192	N.A.	N.A.		N.A.	N.A.	N.A.		N.A.	
LUF	10.75	Parvest Global 3 BEF A	B037	31/07/92	LUX	-5.67	396	0.09	417	2.25	19.97	259	N.A.	N.A.	N.A.		N.A.	
USD	0.57	Parvest Global 3 USD A	B037	30/09/92	LUX	1.56	121	10.96	187	2.54	21.24	253	N.A.	N.A.	N.A.		N.A.	
LUF	0.31	Parvest Global 4 BEF A	B037	29/11/91	LUX	-6.41	436	0.05	418	2.70	16.93	271	N.A.	N.A.	30.71	152	N.A.	
USD	0.15	Parvest Greater China A	B037	15/11/96	LUX	1.63	119	N.A.		N.A.	N.A.		N.A.	N.A.	N.A.		N.A.	
NLG	2.26	Parvest Holland A	B037	29/06/90	LUX	6.04	48	30.69	22	3.44	87.51	8	N.A.	N.A.	140.61	5	N.A.	
USD	0.48	Parvest International Bond A	B037	31/07/92	LUX	-5.41	384	0.67	404	2.03	12.08	305	N.A.	N.A.	N.A.		N.A.	
ITL	0.43	Parvest Italy A	B037	30/09/94	LUX	1.39	125	22.84	64	N.A.	N.A.		N.A.	N.A.	N.A.		N.A.	
JPY	3.70	Parvest Japan A	B037	30/03/90	LUX	-7.73	636	-20.96	600	5.71	-9.54	350	N.A.	N.A.	-20.58	206	N.A.	
BEF	8.88	Parvest Medium Term BEF A	B037	11/10/96	LUX	-7.73	635	N.A.		N.A.	N.A.		N.A.	N.A.	N.A.		N.A.	
LUF	20.34	Parvest Obli Belux A	B037	30/11/87	LUX	-7.43	614	0.72	402	3.03	42.02	58	N.A.	N.A.	59.37	46	N.A.	
CAD	3.30	Parvest Obli Canada A	B037	28/02/94	LUX	-0.74	226	8.59	213	N.A.	N.A.		N.A.	N.A.	N.A.		N.A.	
CHF	0.16	Parvest Obli CHF A	B037	02/02/96	LUX	-5.31	379	N.A.		N.A.	N.A.		N.A.	N.A.	N.A.		N.A.	
DKK	3.71	Parvest Obli DKK A	B037	28/02/94	LUX	-7.08	531	0.24	413	N.A.	N.A.		N.A.	N.A.	N.A.		N.A.	
DEM	7.78	Parvest Obli DM A	B037	31/12/82	LUX	-7.05	522	-1.82	464	3.05	30.03	160	N.A.	N.A.	49.97	84	122.66	19
USD	1.62	Parvest Obli Dollar A	B037	31/01/83	LUX	-0.58	220	4.02	322	1.97	14.20	296	N.A.	N.A.	32.37	145	74.35	25
ECU	30.37	Parvest Obli Ecu A	B037	30/04/91	LUX	-6.32	432	7.72	227	2.49	29.37	167	N.A.	N.A.	46.27	99	N.A.	
FRF	2.77	Parvest Obli Franc A	B037	30/09/86	LUX	-6.93	505	2.24	368	2.96	28.82	174	N.A.	N.A.	56.05	57	203.78	9
NLG	3.28	Parvest Obli Gulden A	B037	29/02/84	LUX	-7.21	566	-2.12	470	3.01	29.72	165	N.A.	N.A.	55.50	59	129.75	18
ITL	0.96	Parvest Obli Lira A	B037	30/07/93	LUX	-10.87	679	27.65	34	3.47	43.33	49	N.A.	N.A.	N.A.		N.A.	
DKK	0.53	Parvest Obli Scandinavia A	B037	04/10/96	LUX	-7.87	644	N.A.		N.A.	N.A.		N.A.	N.A.	N.A.		N.A.	
GBP	0.61	Parvest Obli Sterling A	B037	31/07/90	LUX	-3.46	331	15.26	145	3.22	26.48	210	N.A.	N.A.	38.79	127	N.A.	
JPY	0.11	Parvest Obli Yen A	B037	29/02/84	LUX	-5.50	390	-5.81	558	3.76	6.56	325	N.A.	N.A.	48.79	90	131.82	17
SEK	0.29	Parvest Scandinavia A	B037	04/10/96	LUX	4.82	62	N.A.		N.A.	N.A.		N.A.	N.A.	N.A.		N.A.	
BEF	19.59	Parvest Short Term BEF A	B037	30/06/93	LUX	-7.39	606	-4.73	531	2.84	27.95	191	N.A.	N.A.	N.A.		N.A.	
CHF	1.31	Parvest Short Term CHF A	B037	28/02/94	LUX	-6.58	454	-13.41	594	N.A.	N.A.		N.A.	N.A.	N.A.		N.A.	
DEM	1.81	Parvest Short Term DEM A	B037	31/12/92	LUX	-7.13	549	-4.82	540	2.95	25.45	220	N.A.	N.A.	N.A.		N.A.	
USD	8.67	Parvest Short Term Dollar A	B037	31/07/90	LUX	1.18	134	5.06	290	1.24	14.45	291	N.A.	N.A.	23.86	178	N.A.	
ECU	0.63	Parvest Short Term Europe A	B037	28/02/91	LUX	-6.20	424	1.28	391	2.46	27.80	195	N.A.	N.A.	27.70	170	N.A.	
FRF	1.93	Parvest Short Term FRF A	B037	31/05/93	LUX	-7.08	534	-2.81	484	2.82	30.03	159	N.A.	N.A.	N.A.		N.A.	
ITL	0.87	Parvest Short Term ITL A	B037	31/10/94	LUX	-7.58	626	13.07	163	N.A.	N.A.		N.A.	N.A.	N.A.		N.A.	
NLG	0.37	Parvest Short Term NLG A	B037	08/03/96	LUX	-7.36	602	N.A.		N.A.	N.A.		N.A.	N.A.	N.A.		N.A.	
CHF	0.79	Parvest Switzerland A	B037	31/01/95	LUX	10.90	19	4.55	312	N.A.	N.A.		N.A.	N.A.	N.A.		N.A.	
GBP	0.45	Parvest UK A	B037	31/01/94	LUX	0.28	182	30.26	24	N.A.	N.A.		N.A.	N.A.	N.A.		N.A.	
USD	5.66	Parvest USA A	B037	30/03/90	LUX	2.59	99	25.75	42	3.42	53.86	27	N.A.	N.A.	64.93	37	N.A.	
USD	33.47	Parworld Asian Convertible A	B037	13/01/95	LUX	-6.58	453	11.14	185	N.A.	N.A.		N.A.	N.A.	N.A.		N.A.	
CHF	138.82	Pictet F.I.F. - GFI CHF B Dis	P016	21/07/95	LUX	-5.46	387	-7.85	569	N.A.	N.A.		N.A.	N.A.	N.A.		N.A.	
USD	15.31	Pictet F.I.F. - GFI USD B Dis	P016	21/07/95	LUX	0.87	158	3.12	349	N.A.	N.A.		N.A.	N.A.	N.A.		N.A.	
ITL	N.S.	ProntoFund Italian Sht Term A	B006	09/02/96	LUX	-8.38	654	N.A.		N.A.	N.A.		N.A.	N.A.	N.A.		N.A.	
USD	N.S.	ProntoFund US & CAD Eq A	B006	09/02/96	LUX	-2.04	283	N.A.		N.A.	N.A.		N.A.	N.A.	N.A.		N.A.	
BEF	2.34	Proventus BEF Liquidity D	P013	29/02/88	LUX	-7.31	584	-4.68	527	2.74	28.69	176	N.A.	N.A.	30.53	153	N.A.	
BEF	2.59	Proventus Belgian Bonds D	P013	29/02/88	LUX	-7.41	608	2.87	356	2.89	42.55	54	N.A.	N.A.	65.25	35	N.A.	
DEM	0.64	Proventus DEM Bonds D	P013	22/09/95	LUX	-6.85	492	-1.72	461	N.A.	N.A.		N.A.	N.A.	N.A.		N.A.	
DEM	N.S.	Proventus DM Liquidity D	P013	28/02/89	LUX	-7.03	519	-4.35	515	3.08	26.80	205	N.A.	N.A.	29.09	161	N.A.	
USD	N.S.	Proventus Dollar Liquidity D	P013	31/08/92	LUX	1.17	135	5.58	271	0.45	16.08	278	N.A.	N.A.	N.A.		N.A.	
CHF	43.50	Raiffeisen Euro Actions B	F024	31/03/94	LUX	1.59	120	21.64	72	N.A.	N.A.		N.A.	N.A.	N.A.		N.A.	
CHF	417.28	Raiffeisen Euro Obli B	F024	31/03/94	LUX	-6.57	452	6.83	244	N.A.	N.A.		N.A.	N.A.	N.A.		N.A.	
CHF	40.55	Raiffeisen Swiss Actions B	F024	31/03/94	LUX	5.87	51	-2.89	489	N.A.	N.A.		N.A.	N.A.	N.A.		N.A.	
CHF	119.41	Raiffeisen Swiss Money B	F024	31/03/94	LUX	-6.55	450	-13.01	591	N.A.	N.A.		N.A.	N.A.	N.A.		N.A.	
▲ CHF	320.84	Raiffeisen Swiss Obli B	F024	31/03/94	LUX	-5.47	389	-9.81	576	N.A.	N.A.		N.A.	N.A.	N.A.		N.A.	
CAD	19	RBC IMMF CAD Acc	R002	30/06/92	GU	-0.25	207	3.62	334	1.26	11.69	308	N.A.	N.A.	N.A.		N.A.	
CHF	4.08	RBC IMMF CHF Acc	R002	30/09/92	GU	-6.64	463	-13.62	595	3.27	16.70	274	N.A.	N.A.	N.A.		N.A.	
DEM	2.89	RBC IMMF DEM Acc	R002	30/09/92	GU	-7.20	561	-4.84	542	2.57	24.48	227	N.A.	N.A.	N.A.		N.A.	
GBP	35.69	RBC IMMF Stlg Acc	R002	30/06/92	GU	-2.93	314	15.80	138	1.96	34.10	124	N.A.	N.A.	N.A.		N.A.	
USD	26.40	RBC IMMF USD Acc	R002	30/06/92	GU	1.05	149	4.52	313	0.12	14.25	293	N.A.	N.A.	N.A.		N.A.	
JPY	1.61	RBC IMMF Yen Acc	R002	29/01/93	GU	-6.39	435	-11.53	587	3.52	-2.63	341	N.A.	N.A.	N.A.		N.A.	
USD	N.S.	RDS Global Intl Bond A	R004	29/10/93	LUX	-1.09	249	-2.54	479	1.13	-6.50	347	N.A.	N.A.	N.A.		N.A.	

▲ SIB Approved ● Insurance Fund Values in US Dollars, on an offer to offer price basis with gross income reinvested Data Source Micropal™

Second Units Non-sector

continued

	CCY	Fund Size ($mil)	Fund Name	Manager Code	Fund Start Date	Domicile Code	3 Mths 97 % Chg	3 Mths 97 Rank	1 Year % Chg	1 Year Rank	Micropal Star Rating 3 Years Volatility	3 Years % Chg	3 Years Rank	Rating	Risk Return Rating	5 Years % Chg	5 Years Rank	10 Years % Chg	10 Years Rank
		61.14	**Mean/Count**				**-2.65**	**688**	**7**	**601**	**7.41**	**28.18**	**366**			**48.49**	**206**	**166.15**	**29**
	USD	N.S.	RDS Global Intl Equity A	R004	31/12/93	LUX	3.63	79	2.77	360	3.61	-3.98	342	N.A.	N.A.	N.A.		N.A.	
	JPY	0	RDS Global Pacific Basin A	R004	31/10/94	LUX	-6.76	472	-9.98	578	N.A.	N.A.		N.A.	N.A.	N.A.		N.A.	
	LUF	N.S.	Rente Plus A	M025	26/02/93	LUX	-4.76	366	3.48	338	3.20	-0.84	337	N.A.	N.A.	N.A.		N.A.	
▲	AUD	71.06	SBC Bond Portfolio AusD /A	S007	30/04/92	LUX	-1.27	259	19.20	85	3.64	43.30	50	N.A.	N.A.	N.A.		N.A.	
▲	CAD	110.29	SBC Bond Portfolio CanD /A	S007	30/08/91	LUX	-1.09	250	11.28	183	3.37	22.22	247	N.A.	N.A.	32.65	143	N.A.	
▲	DEM	379.18	SBC Bond Portfolio DM /A	S007	30/04/92	LUX	-5.42	385	-0.79	443	3	33.61	127	N.A.	N.A.	N.A.		N.A.	
▲	ECU	237.29	SBC Bond Portfolio Ecu /A	S007	30/08/91	LUX	-6.65	466	8.41	216	2.46	37	96	N.A.	N.A.	50.33	80	N.A.	
▲	ESP	16.49	SBC Bond Portfolio ESP /A	S007	31/12/93	LUX	-6.45	438	10.75	190	2.82	43.79	45	N.A.	N.A.	N.A.		N.A.	
▲	FRF	121.73	SBC Bond Portfolio FF /A	S007	30/08/91	LUX	-8.30	652	4.73	306	2.84	37.82	87	N.A.	N.A.	65.25	34	N.A.	
▲	NLG	146.38	SBC Bond Portfolio Hfl /A	S007	30/04/92	LUX	-6.68	469	-0.50	428	2.87	33.92	126	N.A.	N.A.	N.A.		N.A.	
▲	ITL	168.07	SBC Bond Portfolio ITL /A	S007	29/07/94	LUX	-3.45	330	27.35	35	N.A.	N.A.		N.A.	N.A.	N.A.		N.A.	
▲	CHF	818.66	SBC Bond Portfolio Sfr /A	S007	30/11/89	LUX	-10.09	674	-10.45	581	3.47	26.37	212	N.A.	N.A.	44.13	109	N.A.	
▲	GBP	45.24	SBC Bond Portfolio Stg /A	S007	30/04/92	LUX	-5.17	373	17.92	102	2.94	31.59	146	N.A.	N.A.	N.A.		N.A.	
▲	USD	126.72	SBC Bond Portfolio USD /A	S007	30/04/92	LUX	-6.90	500	3.84	325	1.77	16.24	275	N.A.	N.A.	N.A.		N.A.	
▲	JPY	3.35	SBC Bond Portfolio Yen /A	S007	30/04/92	LUX	-1.02	244	-7.42	567	4.02	108.46	4	N.A.	N.A.	N.A.		N.A.	
▲	CHF	55.83	SBC Global CHF Balanced A	S007	31/12/93	LUX	-1.51	269	-0.07	421	2.13	38.80	80	N.A.	N.A.	N.A.		N.A.	
▲	DEM	14.64	SBC Global DEM Balanced A	S007	30/06/94	LUX	-1.61	275	4.47	315	N.A.	N.A.		N.A.	N.A.	N.A.		N.A.	
▲	DEM	123.55	SBC Global DM Income /A	S007	31/05/93	LUX	-6.50	442	-0.92	445	2.63	28.99	173	N.A.	N.A.	N.A.		N.A.	
▲	DEM	91.74	SBC Global DM Yield /A	S007	31/05/93	LUX	-4.41	353	2.54	363	2.17	30.66	150	N.A.	N.A.	N.A.		N.A.	
▲	ECU	2.19	SBC Global ECU Balanced A	S007	30/06/94	LUX	-2.34	294	8.22	218	N.A.	N.A.		N.A.	N.A.	N.A.		N.A.	
▲	ECU	24.65	SBC Global ECU Income /A	S007	30/10/92	LUX	-6.23	427	3.33	340	2.38	29.73	164	N.A.	N.A.	N.A.		N.A.	
▲	ECU	25.38	SBC Global Ecu Yield /A	S007	30/09/91	LUX	-4.69	363	5.41	277	2.16	33.09	131	N.A.	N.A.	53.35	72	N.A.	
▲	CHF	606.43	SBC Global SFr Income /A	S007	30/10/92	LUX	-5.62	392	-8.60	572	3.01	23.72	233	N.A.	N.A.	N.A.		N.A.	
▲	CHF	353.02	SBC Global SFr Yield /A	S007	30/09/91	LUX	-4.06	341	-4.20	512	2.38	24.16	229	N.A.	N.A.	42.86	113	N.A.	
▲	USD	8.39	SBC Global USD Balanced A	S007	30/06/94	LUX	0.22	184	11.07	186	N.A.	N.A.		N.A.	N.A.	N.A.		N.A.	
▲	USD	46.27	SBC Global USD Income /A	S007	30/10/92	LUX	-1.02	243	5.52	274	1.67	18.27	265	N.A.	N.A.	N.A.		N.A.	
▲	USD	38.17	SBC Global USD Yield /A	S007	30/09/91	LUX	-0.84	234	8.61	212	1.71	22.20	248	N.A.	N.A.	41.70	116	N.A.	
▲	USD	98.92	SBC Government Bond 1-3 A	S007	29/10/93	LUX	0.73	165	4.83	303	1.09	15.32	281	N.A.	N.A.	N.A.		N.A.	
	FRF	N.S.	Scala France A	B006	08/03/96	LUX	3.95	74	N.A.		N.A.	N.A.		N.A.	N.A.	N.A.		N.A.	
	DEM	N.S.	Scala Germany & Benelux A	B006	29/02/96	LUX	9.11	26	N.A.		N.A.	N.A.		N.A.	N.A.	N.A.		N.A.	
	USD	N.S.	Scala Intl Blue Chips A	B006	09/02/96	LUX	0.77	162	N.A.		N.A.	N.A.		N.A.	N.A.	N.A.		N.A.	
	JPY	N.S.	Scala Japan A	B006	14/06/96	LUX	-8.69	660	N.A.		N.A.	N.A.		N.A.	N.A.	N.A.		N.A.	
	USD	N.S.	Scala Pacific Basin A	B006	29/11/96	LUX	-2.93	315	N.A.		N.A.	N.A.		N.A.	N.A.	N.A.		N.A.	
	GBP	N.S.	Scala United Kingdom A	B006	29/11/96	LUX	1.35	127	N.A.		N.A.	N.A.		N.A.	N.A.	N.A.		N.A.	
	USD	N.S.	Scala US & Canada A	B006	09/02/96	LUX	3.95	73	N.A.		N.A.	N.A.		N.A.	N.A.	N.A.		N.A.	
	LUF	98.08	Short Fund LUF-BEF Dist	A037	31/10/90	LUX	-7.40	607	-4.96	545	2.42	27.91	193	N.A.	N.A.	30.07	157	N.A.	
	BEF	0	Sicaro Court Terme A	B019	28/02/95	LUX	-7.26	574	-4.60	523	N.A.	N.A.		N.A.	N.A.	N.A.		N.A.	
	LUF	18.64	Sicaro FB/Flux A	B019	28/02/95	LUX	-7.35	601	-4.73	533	N.A.	N.A.		N.A.	N.A.	N.A.		N.A.	
	DEM	3.54	Sicaro Zone DEM A	B019	28/02/95	LUX	-7.09	535	-4.51	520	N.A.	N.A.		N.A.	N.A.	N.A.		N.A.	
	USD	7.30	Sicaro Zone US Dollar A	B019	28/02/95	LUX	1.11	143	4.93	297	N.A.	N.A.		N.A.	N.A.	N.A.		N.A.	
	BEF	N.S.	Small Cap European Dis	B026	31/01/94	LUX	8.59	34	26.94	37	N.A.	N.A.		N.A.	N.A.	N.A.		N.A.	
	BEF	39.97	Sogenalux Bond B	S037	31/12/91	LUX	-7.06	527	-0.52	429	2.34	38.66	81	N.A.	N.A.	45.28	105	N.A.	
	BEF	0.05	Sogenalux Treasury BEF A	S037	31/07/89	LUX	-7.41	610	-5.05	550	2.56	27.56	200	N.A.	N.A.	29.49	160	N.A.	
	CHF	6.18	Sogenalux Treasury CHF A	S037	30/06/92	LUX	-6.57	451	-13.26	593	3.23	19.02	262	N.A.	N.A.	N.A.		N.A.	
	DEM	3.31	Sogenalux Treasury DEM A	S037	30/06/92	LUX	-7.15	552	-4.75	534	2.58	25.65	217	N.A.	N.A.	N.A.		N.A.	
	ECU	0.27	Sogenalux Treasury ECU A	S037	30/06/92	LUX	-6.20	425	1.35	389	2.33	29.26	169	N.A.	N.A.	N.A.		N.A.	
	FRF	5.24	Sogenalux Treasury FRF A	S037	30/06/92	LUX	-7.09	539	-2.92	491	2.64	30.53	152	N.A.	N.A.	N.A.		N.A.	
	USD	1.76	Sogenalux Treasury US Dollar A	S037	30/06/92	LUX	1.15	139	5.13	288	0.93	15.44	280	N.A.	N.A.	N.A.		N.A.	
▲	USD	2.31	Templeton GS Emer Mkt FI B	T001	29/07/94	LUX	0.98	153	22.40	66	N.A.	N.A.		N.A.	N.A.	N.A.		N.A.	
▲	USD	10.72	Templeton GS Emerging Mkts B	T001	29/07/94	LUX	8.15	37	19.41	84	N.A.	N.A.		N.A.	N.A.	N.A.		N.A.	
▲	USD	15.02	Templeton GS Global Growth B	T001	29/07/94	LUX	-0.08	199	14.71	147	N.A.	N.A.		N.A.	N.A.	N.A.		N.A.	
▲	USD	4.34	Templeton GS Global Income B	T001	29/07/94	LUX	-3.49	332	6.95	241	N.A.	N.A.		N.A.	N.A.	N.A.		N.A.	
▲	USD	0.28	Templeton GS Latin American B	T001	29/07/94	LUX	11.27	18	13.99	153	N.A.	N.A.		N.A.	N.A.	N.A.		N.A.	
▲	USD	4.79	Templeton GS Smaller Cos B	T001	29/07/94	LUX	5.29	56	21.27	76	N.A.	N.A.		N.A.	N.A.	N.A.		N.A.	
	USD	N.S.	The Emerging Mkts Strategic D	B065	28/02/94	LUX	11.92	16	3.02	352	N.A.	N.A.		N.A.	N.A.	N.A.		N.A.	
	CHF	132.21	UBS (Lux) Bond Invest CHF A	U001	29/09/95	LUX	-5.33	381	-10.10	579	N.A.	N.A.		N.A.	N.A.	N.A.		N.A.	
	DEM	42.05	UBS (Lux) Bond Invest DEM A	U001	29/09/95	LUX	-6.77	476	-0.60	432	N.A.	N.A.		N.A.	N.A.	N.A.		N.A.	

▲ **SIB Approved** ● **Insurance Fund** **Values in US Dollars, on an offer to offer price basis with gross income reinvested** Data Source Micropal™

Second Units Non-sector

continued

CCY	Fund Size ($mil)	Fund Name	Manager Code	Fund Start Date	Domicile Code	3 Mths 97 % Chg	3 Mths 97 Rank	1 Year % Chg	1 Year Rank	Micropal Star Rating 3 Years Volatility	3 Years % Chg	3 Years Rank	Rating	Risk Return Rating	5 Years % Chg	5 Years Rank	10 Years % Chg	10 Years Rank
	61.14	**Mean/Count**				**-2.65**	**688**	**7**	**601**	**7.41**	**28.18**	**366**			**48.49**	**206**	**166.15**	**29**
DEM	817.14	UBS (Lux) Med Term Inv DM T	U001	31/07/95	LUX	-6.89	496	-2.10	468	N.A.	N.A.		N.A.	N.A.	N.A.		N.A.	
CHF	1001.67	UBS (Lux) Med Term Inv SFR T	U001	31/07/95	LUX	-6	415	-11.34	585	N.A.	N.A.		N.A.	N.A.	N.A.		N.A.	

▲ SIB Approved ● Insurance Fund Values in US Dollars, on an offer to offer price basis with gross income reinvested Data Source Micropal™

PART 5
OFFSHORE FUNDS MANAGEMENT DIRECTORY

A001 **ABN AMRO Investment Mgt**
4 Rue Jean Monnet
Kirchberg
L-2180 Luxembourg
Tel 352-4249-49-1
Fax 352-4249-49-399

A002 **Abtrust Atlas Fund (Luxembourg)**
4 Boulevard Royal
L-2449 Luxembourg
Tel 352-22-70-01
Fax 352-22-72-23

A003 **Abtrust International Ltd**
Havelet House PO Box 237
St Peter Port
Guernsey GY1 2PE
Tel 44-1481-727-066
Fax 44-1481-724-468

A004 **Ace Fund Consultants SA**
17 Cote d'Eich BP 687
L-1450 Luxembourg
Tel 352-46-71-71-1
Fax 352-22-48-68

A005 **Alliance Capital Management LP**
1345 Avenue of the Americas
New York NY 10105
U.S.A.
Tel 1-212-969-1000
Fax 1-212-969-1517

A006 **Adams & Nevile Fund Management**
Barfield House PO Box 255
St Julians Avenue
St Peter Port
Guernsey GY1 3QL
Tel 44-1481-710-651
Fax 44-1481-710-284

A007 **ADIG Investment Luxembourg SA (ALSA)**
1a-1b rue Thomas Edison
L-1445 Luxembourg
Tel 352-2511-273
Fax 352-2511-473

A008 **Adyield Inc**
Windermere House
404 E Bay Street
Nassau
Bahamas
Tel 1-242-393-87-77
Fax 1-242-394-32-84

A009 **AEB Worldfolio Management Company**
200 Vesey 23rd Floor
New York NY 10285
U.S.A.
Tel 1-212-640-4931
Fax 1-212-619-9575

A010 **Aetna (Far East) - INVESCO**
Suite 2016 Two Pacific Place
88 Queensway
Hong Kong
Tel 852-2868-3228
Fax 852-2868-5445

A011 **Aetna Investment Management**
21 Avenue Du La Liberté
L-1931 Luxembourg
Tel 352-29-54-94-355
Fax 352-29-54-94-20

A012 **Aetna Capital Management – Wright Investors' Service**
1000 Lafayette Boulevard
Bridgeport
Connecticut 06604
U.S.A.
Tel 1-203-330-5000
Fax 1-203-330-5001

A013 **AGAM-AG Asset Management**
4 Rue de la Reine
L-2418 Luxembourg
Tel 352-47-71-38-605
Fax 352-47-71-38-323

A014 **AGF Management**
87 Rue de Richelieu
Paris 75002
France
Tel 33-1-44-86-2000
Fax 33-1-49-95-08-17

A015 A016
AIB Fund Managers (CI) Ltd
PO Box 468 AIB House
Grenville Street
St Helier
Jersey JE4 8WT
Tel 44-1534-883-000
Fax 44-1534-874-362

A017 **AIG Asset Management Ltd**
Nutley Building Merrion Road
Dublin 4
Ireland
Tel 353-1-283-77-66
Fax 353-1-283-78-23

A018 **Albany International Assurance Ltd**
St Mary's, The Parade
Castletown IM9 1RJ
Isle of Man
Tel 44-1624-823-262
Fax 44-1624-822560

A019 **Alfred Berg Asset Management**
PO Box 2
L-2010 Luxembourg
Tel 352-45-20-30-513
Fax 352-45-20-30-405

A020–A022
Allied Dunbar International Fund Managers
Allied Dunbar International Fund Centre
Lord Street
Douglas IM99 1ET
Isle of Man
Tel 44-1624-661-551
Fax 44-1624-621-513

A023a **Alpha Global International Fund Administration Ltd**
48 Par la Ville Road, Suite 464
Hamilton
Bermuda
Tel 1-441-295-4718
Fax 1-441-295-9637

A023b **Globalvest Management Co**
4 The Cherries, Grange Wood
Rathfarnham, Dublin 16
Ireland
Tel 353-1-493-6282
Fax 353-1-493-6301

GLOBALVEST MANAGEMENT COMPANY, L. P.
Argentina • Brazil • U.S. Virgin Islands

A024 **American Express Bank**
69 route D'Esch
L-1470 Luxembourg
Tel 352-45-90-1
Fax 352-45-90-2010

A025 **American Phoenix Investment Portfolios**
13 Rue Goethe
L-1637 Luxembourg
Tel 352-40-46-46-211
Fax 352-40-46-76

A026 **Anhyp Bank S.A.**
Grotesteenweg 214
Berchem, Antwerpen B-2600
Belgium
Tel 32-3-286-2612
Fax 32-3-286-2545

A027 **Arab Bank Managers**
15 Moorgate
London EC2R 6LP
United Kingdom
Tel 44-171-315-8553
Fax 44-171-600-2617

A028 **Aragon Fondkommission AB**
PO Box 7794
Stockholm S-10396
Sweden
Tel 46-8791-3500
Fax 46-8611-8861

A029 **Aravis Capital Advisors**
300 Park Avenue
New York NY 10022
U.S.A.
Tel 1-212-572-6332
Fax 1-212-572-6432

A030 **Arbitral Finance**
404 East Bay Street
New Providence
Nassau
Bahamas
Tel 1-345-393-8777
Fax 1-345-394-3284

A031 **Archdale Securities Ltd**
9 Kingston Buildings, Abbey Churchyard
Bath BA1 1LT
United Kingdom
Tel 44-1225-460-010
Fax 44-1225-446-434

A032 **Ardent Investment Management Ltd**
48 Par-la-Ville Road
Hamilton
Bermuda HM11
British Virgin Islands
Tel 1-809-293-2765
Fax 1-809-393-4089

A033 **Arnhold & S Bleichroeder Inc**
1345 Avenue of the Americas
New York NY 10105
U.S.A.
Tel 1-212-698-3000
Fax 1-212-299-4475

A034 **Ashburton (IOM) Ltd**
4th Floor Victory House, Prospect Hill
Douglas IM1 1EQ
Isle of Man
Tel 44-1624-620-097
Fax 44-1624-672-338

A035 **Ashburton Replica**
PO Box 239, 35 Don Street
St Helier JE4 8SG
Jersey
Tel 44-1534-222-70
Fax 44-1534-200-65

A036 **AsiaInvest - Impac Asia Funds Ltd**
1205 Universal Trade Centre, 3 Arbuthnot Rd
Hong Kong
Tel 852-2810-1608
Fax 852-2521-5117

A037 **ASLK-CGER Bank**
Rue du Fosse-aux-Loups 48
Bruxelles 1000
Belgium
Tel 32-2-228-61-11
Fax 32-2-228-7199

A038 **ATC - Syfrets International**
20 Abchurch Lane
London EC4 NAD
United Kingdom
Tel 44-171-203-4266
Fax 44-171-220-7141

A039 A040
AXA Equity & Law – Old Mutual Intl Fund Managers
Victory House, Prospect Hill
Douglas IM1 1QP
Isle of Man
Tel 44-1624-683-683
Fax 44-1624-683-684

B001 **Bachmann Asset Management**
Frances House PO Box 175
Sir William Place
St Peter Port GY1 4HQ
Guernsey
Tel 44-1481-723-573
Fax 44-1481-711-353

B002 **Bacob Banque**
25 Rue de Treffle
Bruxelles 1040
Belgium
Tel 32-2-285-12-56
Fax 32-2-230-71-76

B003 **BAII-Banque Arabe et Internationale**
12 Place Vendome
Paris 75001
France
Tel 33-1-47-03-23-45
Fax 33-1-47-03-28-00

B004 **Folkes Asset Management**
Chelsea Wharf, 15 Lots Road
London SW10 OQJ
United Kingdom
Tel 44-171-376-5437
Fax 44-171-351-1454

B005–B007
Banca Commerciale Italiana
19-21 Boulevard Prince Henri
L-1724
Luxembourg
Tel 352-46-14-11-1
Fax 352-22-15-91

B008 **BSI - Banca Della Svizzera Italiana**
Via Magatti 2
Lugano 6901
Switzerland
Tel 41-91-809-3111
Fax 41-91-809-3678

B009 **Bank Franck S.A.**
PO Box 307, 1 Rue Toepffer
Geneva 1211
Switzerland
Tel 41-22-839-4646
Fax 41-22-839-4650

B010 **Banco Boavista**
Praca Pio X- 10 Floor
Rio de Janeiro RJ-20091-040
Brazil
Tel 55-21-211-1437
Fax 55-21-233-9131

B011 **Banco de Santander**
Planta 6,
Paseo de la Castellana 32
Madrid 28046
Spain
Tel 34-1-520-9033
Fax 34-1-575-7881

B012 **Banco Graphus SA**
Av Presidente Vargos 409
17 andar
Rio de Janeiro RJ CEP 20071-003
Brazil
Tel 5521-292-1177
Fax 5521-507-19-14

B013 **Banco Mello SA**
20 Boulevard Emmanuel Servais
L-2535
Luxembourg
Tel 352-47-93-46-1
Fax 352-47-93-46-222

B014
Banco Pactual
Avenue Republica de Chile 230
29 Andar
Rio de Janeiro RJ 20031-170
Brazil
Tel 55-21-272-1229
Fax 55-21-533-1661

B015 **Banco Patrimonio S.A.**
Avenue Brig Faria Liuna 2000
5 Andar
Sào Paulo 01 480-900
Brazil
Tel 55-11-3039-1800
Fax 55-11-3039-1900

B016 **Bank Hofmann Fund Management Ltd**
PO Box 368, Helvetia Court South Esplanade
St Peter Port GY1 3YG
Guernsey
Tel 44-1481-719-000
Fax 44-1481-724-676

B017 **Bank J. Vontobel & Co Ltd**
Bahnhofstasse 3
Zurich CH 8022
Switzerland
Tel 41-1-283-52-69
Fax 41-1-283-53-05

B018 **Bank of Ireland Glbl Funds Ltd – IBI Managers (IOM) Ltd**
4 Christian Road
Douglas
Isle of Man
Tel 44-1624-622-676
Fax 44-1624-662-776

B019 **Bank Van Roeselare NV**
Noordstraat 38
Roeselare 8800
Belgium
Tel 32-51-23-52-11
Fax 32-51-20-63-01

B020 B021
Bank von Ernst & Cie AG
Postfach 5325
Marktgasse 63-65
Bern
CH 3001
Switzerland
Tel 41-31-329-11-11
Fax 41-31-311-63-91

B022 **Banque Arner SA**
19-21 Boulevard Prince Henri
L-1724
Luxembourg
Tel 352-46-14-11
Fax 352-22-15-91

B023 **Banque Continentale du Luxembourg**
2 Boulevard Emmanuel Servais
L-2535
Luxembourg
Tel 352-47-76-881
Fax 352-47-76-88-208

B024 **Banque de Gestion Privee**
26 rue de la Baume
Paris 75008
France
Tel 33-1-40-75-62-62
Fax 33-1-45-63-85-20

B025 **Banque de Luxembourg**
14 Boulevard Royal
L-2449
Luxembourg
Tel 352-49-92-41
Fax 352-47-26-65

B026 **Banque Degroof Luxembourg**
7 Boulevard Joseph 2
L-1840
Luxembourg
Tel 352-45-35-45
Fax 352-25-07-51

B027 **Banque Dewaay**
Boite 39, Boulevard Anspach 1
Bruxelles 1000
Belgium
Tel 32-2-227-8811
Fax 32-2-217-75-40

B028 **Banque du Phenix**
6 Avenue Kleber
Paris 75016
France
Tel 33-1-44-17-21-00
Fax 33-1-45-01-66-88

B029 **Banque Scandinave en Suisse Asset Management**
Case Postale 3754, 11 Cours de Rive
Geneva CH 1211
Switzerland
Tel 41-22-787-31-11
Fax 41-22-735-3370

B030 **Banque Espanol de Credito**
2 Boulevard Royal
L-2535
Luxembourg
Tel 352-46-46-449
Fax 352-46-46-41-41

B031 **Banque Ferrier Lullin**
26 Avenue Monterey, PO Box 547
L-2163
Luxembourg
Tel 352-228-761
Fax 352-449-567

B032 **Banque Harwanne**
103 Boulevard Haussmann
Paris 75008
Tel 33-1-44-94-22-00
Fax 33-1-42-66-26-40

B033 **Banque Indosuez**
39 Allee Scheffer
L-2520
Luxembourg
Tel 352-47-67-1
Fax 352-46-24-42

B034 **Banque Indosuez Belgique SA**
Place Sainte Gudule 14
Bruxelles 1000
Belgium
Tel 32-2-205-92-92
Fax 32-2-512-18-96

B035 **Banque Ippa SA**
Boulevard du Souverain 23
Bruxelles 1170
Belgium
Tel 32-2-676-12-11
Fax 32-2-676-12-13

B036 **Banque Nagelmackers**
12 Place du Louvain
Bruxelles 1000
Belgium
Tel 32-2-211-57-11
Fax 32-2-211-57-63

B037 **Banque Paribas France**
Boite postale 141, 3 Rue d'Antin
Paris 75078
France
Tel 33-1-42-98-12-34
Fax 33-1-42-98-06-82

B038 **Bank Sarasin & Cie**
Elisabethenstraase 62
Basel 4002
Switzerland
Tel 41-61-277-77-77
Fax 41-61-277-75-75

B039 **Banque SCS Alliance SA**
Case Postale 3733, 11 Route de Florissant
Geneva CH 1211
Switzerland
Tel 41-22-346-12-81
Fax 41-22-346-15-30

B040 **Banque Sudamaris**
4 Rue Meyerbeer
Paris 75009
France
Tel 33-1-4801-7777
Fax 33-1-42-46-3213

B041 **Banque Transatlantique Paris**
17 Boulevard Haussmann
Paris 75009
France
Tel 33-1-40-22-80-00
Fax 33-1-4824-0175

B042 **Banque Vernes**
15 Rue des Pyramides
Paris 75001
France
Tel 33-1-44-86-80-00
Fax 33-1-44-86-273

B043 **Banques Populaires Caisse Centrale**
12 Avenue Winston Churchill
Paris 75002
France
Tel 33-1-40-39-30-00
Fax 33-1-40-39-40-01

B044–B046 B048
Barclays Fund Managers Limited
PO Box 152 Sutton House
28-30 The Parade
St Helier
JE4 8RA
Jersey
Tel 44-1534-812-700
Fax 44-1534-608-910

B047 **Barclays Investment Funds (Luxembourg)**
4th Floor Place de la Gare, PO Box 1375
L-1013
Luxembourg
Tel 352-40-43-44
Fax 352-49-23-69

B048 see B044

B049 **Baring International Fund Managers**
2nd Floor IFSC House
Dublin 2
Ireland
Tel 353-1-670-0660
Fax 353-1-670-1181

B050 **Baring International Investment Management**
155 Bishopsgate
London EC2 M5TQ
United Kingdom
Tel 44-171-628-6000
Fax 44-171-214-1659

B051 **BayernLux Management Company**
3 Rue Jean Monnet
L-2180
Luxembourg
Tel 352-42-43-41
Fax 352-42-43-45-099

B052 **Banque Brussels Lambert**
24 Avenue Marnix
Bruxelles 1050
Belgium
Tel 32-2-547-2111
Fax 32-2-738-3886

B053 **Bearbull Investment Products**
18 Avenue Louis Casai
Geneva CH-1209
Switzerland
Tel 41-22-799-9555
Fax 41-22-791-0777

B054 **BEM Management**
65 Front Street
Hamilton HM AX
Bermuda
Tel 1-441-295-1111
Fax 1-441-295-6759

B055 **Benchmark Capital Management**
Lazaristengrasse 12
Vienna 1180
Austria
Tel 43-1-479-1052
Fax 43-1-470-6648

B056 **Bennett Capital Management – Key Asset Mangement**
35-38 Portman Square
London W1H 0EU
United Kingdom
Tel 44-171-465-0315
Fax 44-171-465-0317

B057 **Bentley Capital/Royal Skandia**
Skandia House, Finch Road
Douglas IM99 1NU
Isle of Man
Tel 44-1624-611-611
Fax 44-1624-611-716

B058 **Berkshire Capital Management Ltd**
Seestrasse 17, P.O. Box 53
Zolikon 2
CH-8702
Switzerland
Tel 41-1-396-2720
Fax 41-1-396-2725

B059 **Bermuda Capital Company Ltd**
65 Front Street
Hamiltom HM 12
Bermuda
Tel 1-441-295-1111
Fax 1-441-292-1800

B060 **Beta Capital**
10 Rue Antoine Ans
L-1829
Luxembourg
Tel 352-222-874
Fax 352-222-878

B061 **BfG Luxinvest Management SA**
68 Route de Treves
L-2633
Luxembourg
Tel 352-34-69-411
Fax 352-34-69-40

B062 **BFSC-CDC - Partner Emerg Mkts Global**
2 Boulevard Royal
L-2449
Luxembourg
Tel 352-45-90-1
Fax 352-45-90-2010

B063 **Banque Gestion Edmond de Rothschild (Luxembourg)**
20 Boulevard Emmanuel Servais
L-2535
Luxembourg
Tel 352-47-93-46-1
Fax 352-22-24-94

B064 **Banque Generale du Luxembourg SA**
50 Avenue John F Kennedy
L-2955
Luxembourg
Tel 352-47-99-1
Fax 352-42-42-43-88

B065 **Banque de Gestion Privee**
26 Rue de la Baume
Paris 75008
France
Tel 33-1-40-75-62-62
Fax 33-1-45-63-85-20

B066 **Bermuda International Investment Management Ltd**
Compass Point,
9 Bermudiana Road
Hamilton HM11
Bermuda
Tel 1-441-299-5600
Fax 1-441-299-6518

B067 **BIL-Banque Internationale a Luxembourg**
69 Route d'Esch
L-2953
Luxembourg
Tel 352-45-90-1
Fax 352-45-90-2010

B068 **Blackstone Franks Investment Management**
Frederick House, 19 South Frederik Street
Dublin 2
Ireland
Tel 353-1-605-6193
Fax 353-1-679-0388

B069 **Banque Nartionale de Paris**
16 Boulevard des Italiens
Paris 75008
France
Tel 33-1-40-14-45-46
Fax 33-1-40-14-69-40

B070 **Bonnewijn Renwart & Cie SA**
Rue de la Loi 78
Bruxelles 1040
Belgium
Tel 32-2-287-17-11
Fax 32-2-287-17-10

B071 **Bordier International Bank & Trust Ltd**
80 Harcourt Street
Dublin 2
Ireland
Tel 353-1-790-2400
Fax 353-1-790-2410

B072 **Bowen Capital Management Ltd**
1008A Shui On Centre, 6-8 Harbour Road
Hong Kong
Tel 852-2845-0956
Fax 852-2845-0931

B073 **Banque Privee Edmond de Rothschild SA**
20 Boulevard Emmanuel Servais
L-2535
Luxembourg
Tel 352-47-93-46-1
Fax 352-22-24-94

B074 **Banque Continentale du Luxembourg**
2 Boulevard Emmanuel Servais
L-2535
Luxembourg
Tel 352-47-76-88-1
Fax 352-47-76-88-427

B075 **Brunswick Capital Management (Cayman) Ltd**
Harbour Centre 3rd Floor
George Town
Grand Cayman
Cayman Islands
Tel 1-345-945-9166
Fax 1-345-945-9165

B076 B077
BT Fund Managers Ireland Ltd
80 Harcourt Street
Dublin 2
Ireland
Tel 353-1-790-2400
Fax 353-1-790-2410

B078 **Bankers Trust Luxembourg SA**
PO Box 807, 14 Boulevard FD Roosevelt
Luxembourg
Tel 352-46-0241
Fax 352-47-3136

B079 **Buchanan Capital Management Ltd**
Buchanan House, 3 St James Square
London SW1Y 4JU
United Kingdom
Tel 44-171-973-8070
Fax 44-171-973-8072

B080 **Butterfield Fund Managers (Guernsey) Ltd**
P.O Box 21 Roseneath
The Grange
St Peter Port GY 38P
Guernsey
Tel 44-1481-720-321
Fax 44-1481-714-533

B081 **BZW Asset Management (Guernsey) Ltd – WFNIA**
PO Box 105 Commerce House
Les Banques
St Peter Port GY1 3EZ
Guernsey
Tel 44-1481-729-371
Fax 44-1481-710-001

C001 **Caisse Centrale de Reescompte**
19-21 Boulevard du Prince Henri
L-1724
Luxembourg
Tel 352-46-14-11-1
Fax 352-22-15-91-1

C002 **Caisse D'Epargne de l'Etat**
1 Place de Metz
L-2954
Luxembourg
Tel 352-40-15-5003
Fax 352-48-08-82

C003 **Caisse Privee Banque**
Place du Champ de Mars 2
Bruxelles 1050
Belguim
Tel 32-2-518-92-11
Fax 32-2-518-94-63

C004 **Caixa Management Luxembourg SA**
9 Boulevard d'Italie
Montecarlo 9830
Monaco
Tel 37-79-315-2388
Fax 37-79-315-01430

C005 **Callander Management Company SA**
103 Grand Rue
L-1661
Luxembourg
Tel 352-49-924-2246
Fax 352-22-57-32

C006 **CAMCO Investment Management**
2 Place d'Argent
L-1413
Luxembourg
Tel 352-43-10-90
Fax 352-43-11-80

C007 **Cantrade - UBS Intrag (Services) SA**
36-38 Grande Rue
L-2011
Luxembourg
Tel 352-45-12-11
Fax 352-45-12-12-710

C008 **Capel-Cure Myers Capital Management Ltd**
The Registry, Royal Mint Court
London EC3N 4EY
United Kingdom
Tel 44-171-488-4000
Fax 44-171-480-5681

C009 **Capital Gestion S.A**
55 rue de Luxembourg
Howald
L-2529
Luxembourg
Tel 352-49-92-41
Fax 352-22-57-32

C010 **Capital International SA**
3 places des Bergues
Geneve CH 1205
Switzerland
Tel 41-22-715-15-15
Fax 41-22-731-31-79

C011 **Carlson Investment Management**
Box 70379
Stockholm 10724
Sweden
Tel 46-8-700-63-60
Fax 46-8-700-00-19

C012 **Carnegie Fund Management Company S.A.**
5 Place de la Gare
Centre Europe
L-1616
Luxembourg
Tel 352-40-40-301
Fax 352-49-28-77

C013 **Cater Allen Investment Management (CI) Ltd**
Cater Allen House, Commercial Street
St Helier JE4 8UP
Jersey
Tel 44-1534-828-000
Fax 44-1534-828-201

C014 **Cazenove International Asset Management (CIAM)**
3 Copthall Avenue
London EC2R 7BH
United Kingdom
Tel 44-171-606-0708
Fax 44-171-606-9205

C015 **CCF Structured Asset Management**
115-117 Avenue des Champs-Elysees
Paris 75008
France
Tel 33-1-40-70-74-00
Fax 33-1-40-70-75-23

C016 **CDC Gestion**
7 place des 5 Martyrs du Lycee Buffon
Paris 75507
France
Tel 33-1-42-79-55-00
Fax 33-1-42-79-53-25

C017 **CEF Capital Ltd**
1st–2nd Floor China Building, 29 Queens Road
Central
Hong Kong
Tel 852-2846-3686
Fax 852-2840-0559

C018 **Cera Bank**
Brusselsesteenweg 100
Leuven B-3000
Belgium
Tel 32-16-30-44-84
Fax 32-16-30-33-15

C019 **Chase Asset Management**
5 Rue Plaetis
L-2338
Luxembourg
Tel 352-46-26-85-1
Fax 352-22-45-90

C020 **Christows Investment (Dublin)**
Clifton, St Peter's Road
Bournemouth BH1 2LT
United Kingdom
Tel 44-1202-299344
Fax 44-1202-2931

C021 **CIBC Fund Mngrs (Guernsey) Ltd**
PO Box 447 CIBC House, Rue De Pre
St Peter Port GY1 32X
Guernsey
Tel 44-1481-725-771
Fax 44-1481-726-124

C022 **CIC Paris**
6 Avenue de Provence
Paris 75452
France
Tel 33-1-45-96-96-96
Fax 33-1-45-96-96-66

C023 **Cie Financiere Edmond de Rothschild Banque**
20 Boulevard Emmanuel Servais
L-2535
Luxembourg
Tel 352-47-93-46-1
Fax 352-22-24-94

C024 **Cie Tresorerie Benjamin de Rothschild**
20 Boulevard Emmanuel Servais
L-2535
Luxembourg
Tel 352-47-93-46-281
Fax 352-47-22-39-98

C025 **CITCO Fund Services**
6th Floor World Trade Centre
Tower B
Strawinskylaan 1629
Amsterdam 1077XX
The Netherlands
Tel 31-20-662-8167
Fax 31-20-675-2181

C026 **Citi Investment Fund**
IFSC House, Custom House Quay
Dublin 1
Ireland
Tel 353-1-702-3500
Fax 353-1-702-3550

C027 C029 C030 C033
Citibank Luxembourg SA
58 Boulevard Grande-Duchesse Charlotte
L-1330
Luxembourg
Tel 352-45-14-14-1
Fax 352-45-14-14-75

C028 **Citicorp Investment Services Ltd**
Citibank Plaza 3 Garden Road
45th Floor Citibank Tower
Central
Hong Kong
Tel 852-868-6666
Fax 852-810-0178

C029 C030 see C027

C031 **Citibank (Channel Islands) Ltd**
PO Box 104 , 38 Esplanade
St Helier JE4 8QB
Jersey
Tel 44-1534-608-000
Fax 44-1534-608-291

C032 **Citibank Global Asset Management**
153 East 53rd Steet
New York NY 10043
U.S.A.
Tel 1-212-559-6100
Fax 1-212-793-1812

C033 – C037 see C027

C038 **City Financial (Beckman)**
19-21 Circular Road
Douglas IM99 1IZ
Isle of Man
Tel 44-1624-629-420
Fax 44-1624-627-515

C039 **Clariden Investment Management (Guernsey) Ltd**
PO Box 122, Helvetia Court
St Peter Port GY1 4EE
Guernsey
Tel 44-1481-726-641
Fax 44-1481-724-218

C040 C041 C043 C044
CMI Fund Managers (IOM) Ltd
Clerical Medical House, Victoria Road
Douglas IM99 1LY
Isle of Man
Tel 44-1624-638-888
Fax 44-1624-625-900

C042 **Clerical Medical International**
166 Route d'Arlon, PO Box 71
L-8001
Luxembourg
Tel 352-31-78-311
Fax 352-31-78-31-500

C043 C044 see C040

C045 **Comgest SA**
56 Rue de Londres
Paris 75008
France
Tel 33-1-44-70-75-10
Fax 33-1-42-93-24-14

C046 **Commercial Union Captive Inv**
Galerie Kons 4th Floor,
26 Place De La Gare
L-1018
Luxembourg
Tel 352-402-82-02-40
Fax 352-402-82-02-21

C047 **Commodities Corporation Investment Services SA**
6 Avenue Jules - Crosnier
Geneva CH 1206
Switzerland
Tel 41-22-346-1400
Fax 41-22-346-1733

C048 **Compagnie Financiere de Benelux – Immocorp SICAV**
103 Grande Rue
L-1661
Luxembourg
Tel 352-49-92-42-246
Fax 352-49-92-42-550

C049 **Concorde Asset Management Inc**
PO Box 438 Tropic Isle Building, Road Town
Tortola
British Virgin Islands
Tel 1-809-494-2616
Fax 1-809-994-2116

C050 **Connor Asset Management Ltd**
14 Rue du Rhone, PO Box 3771
Geneva-3 1211
Switzerland
Tel 41-22-31-82-190
Fax 41-22-31-83-190

C051 **Consulta International Ltd**
PO Box 208 Bermuda House,
St Julian's Avenue
St Peter Port GY1 3NF
Guernsey
Tel 44-1481-707-000
Fax 44-1481-726-275

C052 **Coutts & Co Fund Managers Ltd**
Park Avenue Tower, 65 East 55th Street
New York NY 10022
U.S.A.
Tel 1-212-303-2900
Fax 1-212-303-2929

C053 **Coutts & Co (Jersey) Fund Managers Ltd**
PO Box 192, 23-25 Broad Street
St Helier JE4 8ND
Jersey
Tel 44-1534-282-345
Fax 44-1534-282-400

C054–C057
Credis Fund Holding (Luxembourg) SA
5 Rue Jean Monnet, BP 369
L-2013
Luxembourg
Tel 352-43-6161-1
Fax 352-6161-555

C058 **Credit Agricloe Luxembourg SA**
13 Avenue de la Porte Neuve
L-2013
Luxembourg
Tel 352-46-80-81
Fax 352-46-40-62

C059 **Credit Communal de Belgique**
Boulevard Pacheco 44
Bruxelles B-1000
Belgium
Tel 32-2-222-39-74
Fax 32-2-222-52-26

C060 C061
Credit Lyonnais Belgique
Avenue Marnix 17
Bruxelles 1050
Belgium
Tel 32-2-516-05-11
Fax 32-2-511-24-58

C062 **Credit Lyonnais Luxembourg SA**
26a Boulevard Royal
L-2449
Luxembourg
Tel 352-47-68-31-241
Fax 352-47-68-31-382

C063 **Credit Lyonnais Int Asset Management (Singapore) Ltd**
6th Floor Three Exchange Square
8 Connaught Place
Hong Kong
Tel 852-2846-7555
Fax 852-2868-4742

C064 **Credit Lyonnais Rouse Ltd**
Broadwalk House, 5 Appold Street
London EC2A 2DA
United Kingdom
Tel 44-171-374-6100
Fax 44-171-638-0327

C065 **Credit Communal de Belgique**
69 Route D'Esch
L-1470
Luxembourg
Tel 352-45-90-1
Fax 352-45-90-2010

C066 **Cresvale International Asset Management (UK) Ltd**
Shackleton House, 4 Battlebridge Lane
London SE1 2JB
United Kingdom
Tel 44-171-357-6400
Fax 44-171-378-6436

C067 **CRM Asset Management GMBH**
Lichtentaler Strasse 16
Baden-Baden 76530
Germany
Tel 49-72-21-21-59-0
Fax 49-72-21-21-59-21

C068 **Credis Fund Holding (Luxembourg) SA**
5 Rue Jean Monnet, BP 369
L-2180
Luxembourg
Tel 352-43-61-61-1
Fax 352-43-61-61-555

C069 **CS First Boston Investment Management Ltd**
One Cabot Square
London E14 4QJ
United Kingdom
Tel 44-171-516-1616
Fax 44-171-516-3475

C070 **Commercial Union Luxembourg SA**
PO Box 1375
L-1013
Luxembourg
Tel 352-48-90-61
Fax 352-49-23-69

C071 **Custom House Asset Management**
31 Kildare St
Dublin 2
Ireland
Tel 353-1-661-3400
Fax 353-1-661-3601

C072 **Cypress International – Folkes Asset Management**
Chelsea Wharf, 15 Lots Road
London SW10 OQJ
United Kingdom
Tel 44-171-376-5437
Fax 44-171-351-1454

D001 **Daiwa International Capital Management**
The Gateway East, 152 Beach Road
189721
Singapore
Tel 65-297-6811
Fax 65-297-6822

D002 **Daiwa/BNP/Dresdner/Hill Samuel**
69 Route d'Esch
L-1470
Luxembourg
Tel 352-45-90-1
Fax 352-45-90-20-10

D003 **Danske Fund Management Company SA**
2 Rue du Fosse, PO Box 173
L-1536
Luxembourg
Tel 352-46-12-75
Fax 352-4612-75-024

D004 **Dantrust Management Guernsey Ltd**
PO Box 105 Le Tonelle House
Les Banques
St Sampson GY1 3EP
Guernsey
Tel 44-1481-711-818
Fax 44-1481-710-001

D005 **Dao Heng Fund Management Ltd**
33rd Floor - Wu Chung House
213 Queens Rd East
Wanchai
Hong Kong
Tel 852-2831-7853
Fax 852-2891-3370

D006 **DB Investment Management SA**
2 Boulevard Konrad Adenauer
L-1115
Luxembourg
Tel 352-42-101-1
Fax 352-42-101-889

D007 **De Posson & Cie**
103 Grand Rue
L-1661
Luxembourg
Tel 352-40-32-22
Fax 352-49-924-23-90

D008 **Dicam World Wide Investment Fund**
14 rue Aldringen
L-1118
Luxembourg
Tel 352-42-42-3646
Fax 352-42-42-65-00

D009 **Deka International SA**
Deka Fonsmanagement
Mainzerlandstrasse 37
Frankfurt-au-Maine 603029
Germany
Tel 49-69-25-46-01
Fax 49-69-254-63-76

D010 **Deltec Securities**
Deltec House, Lyford Cay
Nassau N-3229
Bahamas
Tel 1-242-362-4549
Fax 1-242-362-4623

D011 **Demachy Worms & CIE**
7 Boulevard Joseph II
L-1840
Luxembourg
Tel 352-45-35-45-1
Fax 352-25-07-21

D012 **Demeter Conseil**
7 Boulevard Joseph II
L-1804
Luxembourg
Tel 352-45-35-45-2048
Fax 352-25-07-21

D013 **Den Norske Bank**
PO Box 1614 VIKA
Stranden 21
Oslo 1 0119
Norway
Tel 47-22-48-10-50
Fax 47-22-94-94-77

D014 **Dolphin - Brewin Dolphin & Co Ltd**
5 Giltspur Street
London EC1A 9BD
United Kingdom
Tel 44-171-236-6441
Fax 44-171-236-0121

D015 D016 D018
Dresdner International Mangement Services Ltd
International Financial Services Centre
La Touche House
Dublin 1
Ireland
Tel 353-1-670-1444
Fax 353-1-670-1414 975

D017 **Dresdnerbank Asset Management SA**
6a Route de Treves
Sennaigerbeirg
L-2633
Luxembourg
Tel 352-46-34-63-1
Fax 352-46-34-63-620

D018 see D015

D019 **Duncan Lawrie**
14/45 Mount Havelock
Douglas IM1 2Q4
Isle of Man
Tel 44-1624-662-200
Fax 44-1624-662-878

E001 **Eagle Star International Services (Luxembourg) SA**
6 Avenue Emile Reuter
L-2420
Luxembourg
Tel 352-47-17-64
Fax 352-47-13-41

E002 **East Fund Management**
Nibelungang 15
Wien 1010
Austria
Tel 43-1-588-84-504
Fax 43-1-588-84-568

E003 **Eaton Vance Management**
24 Federal Street
Boston 2110
U.S.A.
Tel 1-617-482-8260
Fax 1-617-482-2396

E004 **EBC Fund Management (Jersey) Ltd**
PO Box 556, 1-3 Seale Street
St Helier JE4 8XL
Jersey
Tel 44-1534-363-31
Fax 44-1534-394-95

E005 **Etude Bilan Patrimonio Financiere**
17 Avenue George V
Paris 75008
France
Tel 33-1-4723-9090
Fax 33-1-4723-0241

E006 **Ecofin Fund Management Ltd**
19 Buckingham Street
London WC2N 6EF
United Kingdom
Tel 44-171-839-5944
Fax 44-171-930-9714

E007 **ED&F Man Investment Products**
Bahnhofstrasse 15
Pfaffikon 8808
Switzerland
Tel 41-55-415-3636
Fax 41-55-415-3637

E008 **EBC Fund Management (Jersey) Ltd**
1-3 Seale Street, P.O Box 556
St Helier JE4 8XI
Jersey
Tel 44-1534-363-31
Fax 44-1534-394-95

E009 **EDM Servicios Finanieros**
69 Route d'Esch
L-1470
Luxembourg
Tel 352-45-90-1
Fax 352-45-90-20-10

E010 **Eldon Financial Capital Management**
33 Wilson Street
London EC2M 2SJ
United Kingdom
Tel 44-171-696-0082
Fax 44-171-628-0832

E011 **Ermitage Luxembourg SA**
68-70 Boulevard de la Petrusse
BP 1576
L-1015
Luxembourg
Tel 352-40-73-30
Fax 352-40-73-27

E012 **Eufigest Management**
2 place de Metz
L-1930
Luxembourg
Tel 352-40-15-54-55
Fax 352-40-15-54-60

E013 **Europa Funds Limited**
527 Madison Avenue
New York NY 10022
U.S.A.
Tel 1-212-838-6072
Fax 1-212-838-7824

E014 **Europa Luxembourg Invest SA**
14 Rue Aldringen
L-1118
Luxembourg
Tel 352-47-99-23-56
Fax 352-47-99-28-60

E015 **Europacific Advisors**
30 Harbour Road
Wanchai
Hong-Kong
Tel 852-25-21-42-02
Fax 852-28-45-90-86

E016 **European Investement Management**
Route Lavaux
Lutry CH 1095
Switzerland
Tel 41-21-792-1212
Fax 41-21-792-1246

E017 **Everest Capital**
Corner House
20 Parliament Street
Hamilton HM12
Bermuda
Tel 1-441-292-2200
Fax 1-441-292-2285

F001–F003
Foreign & Colonial
Exchange House, Primrose Street
London EC2A 2NY
United Kingdom
Tel 44-171-628-1234
Fax 44-171-628-2281

F004 **F & V Management Company**
F & V Management Co SA
2 Place D'Argent
L-1413
Luxembourg
Tel 352-423-077
Fax 352-423-076

F005 **Falcon Partners**
British American Centre Phase 3
DR.Ray's Drive
George Town
Cayman Islands
Tel 1-345-949-7942
Fax 1-345-949-8340

F006 **Federated International Management Ltd**
14 Hume Street
Dublin 2
Ireland
Tel 353-1-662-4244
Fax 353-1-676-8592

F007 **Fenchurch Capital Management**
311 South Wacker Drive
Suite 4825
Chicago 60606
U.S.A.
Tel 1-312-922-1717
Fax 1-312-554-7761

F008 **FG Asset Management**
Jose Ortega y Gasset 29-5
Madrid 28006
Spain
Tel 34-1-578-26-45
Fax 34-1-577-50-62

F009 F010 F012
Fidelity International Ltd
Pembroke Hall, 42 Crow Lane
Pembroke HM19
Bermuda
Tel 1-441-295-0665
Fax 1-441-236-0319

F011 **Fidelity Funds (Lux)**
Kansallis House
Place de L'Etoile BP 2143
L-1021
Luxembourg
Tel 1-352-250-4041
Fax 1-352-250-340

F012 F013 see F009

F014 **Fiduciary Trust**
Ormonde House
Earlscourt Centre
12 Lower Lesson Street
Dublin-2
Ireland
Tel 353-1-661-3433
Fax 353-1-661-3406

F015 **FIMEDIT**
20 Boulevard Emmanuel Servais
L-2535
Luxembourg
Tel 352-45-90-32-10
Fax 352-45-90-32-43

F016 **Finistere Life Assurance Company Ltd**
Guinness Flight House
PO Box 250
La Plaiderie
St Peter Port GY1 3HQ
Guernsey
Tel 44-1481-710-404
Fax 44-1481-712-065

F017 **First Investments Ltd**
2 Pacific Place, Room 1218
88 Queensway
Hong Kong
Tel 852-2868-1837
Fax 852-2877-6475

F018 **Fisch Asset Management AG**
69 Route d'Esch
L-1470
Luxembourg
Tel 352-45-90-1
Fax 352-45-90-2010

F019–F022
Fleming Fund Management (Luxembourg) SA
6H Route de Treves
European Bank & Business Centre
L-2633
Luxembourg
Tel 352-40-50-40
Fax 352-48-34-49

F023 **Floortrader Capital Management**
World Trade Centre Amsterdam (Tower B - 16th Floor)
Strawinskylaan 1637
Amsterdam 1077XX
The Netherlands
Tel 31-20-67-69-611
Fax 31-20-67-50-881

F024 **Fonds Raiffeisen Suisse (Lux)**
Todestrasse 27
Zurich CH 8022
Switzerland
Tel 41-1-283-52-68
Fax 41-1-283-53-05

F025 **Fonte Cindam**
Avenue Presidente Wilson 231/17
Rio de Janeiro 20030-021
Brazil
Tel 5521-212-1800
Fax 5521-240-3600

F026 **Formosa - Kwang Hua Securities Inv & Trust Co**
1680 Jardine House
One Conaught Place
Central
Hong Kong
Tel 852-2537-9823
Fax 852-2537-9212

F027 **Fortitude Services Ltd**
904-6 Asia Pacific Finance Tower
3 Garden Road
Central
Hong Kong
Tel 852-2509-4490
Fax 852-2509-0827

F028 **Fountain Futures - Citco Fund Services**
World Trade Centre Amsterdam (Tower B - 16th Floor)
PO Box 7241
Amsterdam 1007 JE
The Netherlands
Tel 31-20-6769611
Fax 31-20-6750881

F029 **Financial Portfolio Consulting**
90 Avenue des Champs-Elysees
Paris 75008
France
Tel 33-1-4435-5200
Fax 33-1-4289-3463

F030 **Franken Invest-Schmidtbank**
Johannesgasse 20
Nurenburg 90402
Germany
Tel 49-911-24-70-100
Fax 49-911-24-70-159

F031 **Friends Provident Venturer**
United Kingdom House
Castle Street
Salisbury SP1 3SH
United Kingdom
Tel 44-1722-413366
Fax 44-1722-330298

F032 **Frontrunner Managment Company**
672 Rue de Neudorf, PO Box 782
L-2220
Luxembourg
Tel 352-43-88-73-50
Fax 352-43-39-40

G001 **Gaia Corp Currency Managers**
10 Lower Mount Street
Dublin 2
Ireland
Tel 353-1676-0570
Fax 353-1676-0570

G002 **GAM Fund Management Ltd**
4th Floor
65-66 Lower Mount Street
Dublin 2
Ireland
Tel 353-1-6760-630
Fax 353-1-6613-459

G003 **GAM Fund Managers (IOM) Ltd**
11 Athol Street
Douglas IM99 1HH
Isle of Man
Tel 44-1624-632-777
Fax 44-1624-632-813

G004 **Gamax Managment**
PO Box 220152
Muhlheimestrasse 49
Leverkusen D-51375
Germany
Tel 49-214-8516-0
Fax 49-214-851649

G005 **Garantia Banking Ltd**
Av Brigadero Faria Lima 13704
13 Andar
Sao Paulo 701451000
Brazil
Tel 55-11-821-6000
Fax 55-11-821-6917

G006 **Gartmore Investment Ltd**
Gartmore House
16-18 Monument Street
London EC3R HQQ
United Kingdom
Tel 44-171-782-2000
Fax 44-171-782-2466

G007 **Gartmore Fund Managers International Ltd**
45 La Motte Street
St Helier JE4 8TF
Jersey
Tel 44-1534-886-688
Fax 44-1534-886-689

G008 **Gems Managment Ltd**
404 East Bay Street
PO Box SS-6238
Nassau
Bahamas
Tel 242-393-8777
Fax 242-394-3284

G009 **Generale de Banque**
Rue Montagne du Parc 3
Bruxelles 1000
Belgium
Tel 32-2-565-35-02
Fax 32-2-565-30-44

G010 **Genesis Investment Management Ltd**
21 Knightsbridge
London SW1X 7LY
United Kingdom
Tel 44-171-235-5040
Fax 44-171-235-8065

G011 **Global Portfolio Management**
10 Bridge Street
Castletown IM99 50B
Isles of Man
Tel 44-1624-824-131
Fax 44-1624-823-939

A023b **Globalvest Management Co**

G012 **GNI Fund Managment**
25 Dowgate Hill, Cannon Bridge
London EC4R 2EN
United Kingdom
Tel 44-171-378-3500
Fax 44-171-337-3508

G013 **Goldman Sachs Asset Management International**
140 Fleet Street
London EC4A 2BJ
United Kingdom
Tel 44-171-774-14-74
Fax 44-171-774-51-93

G014 **J. Govett & Co Ltd**
Shackleton House
4 Battle Bridge Lane
London SE1 2HR
United Kingdom
Tel 44-171-378-7979
Fax 44-171-638-3468

G015 G016
Govett (CI) Ltd
AIB House PO Box 335
Grenville Street
St Helier JE4 8NT
Jersey
Tel 44-1534-873-220
Fax 44-1534-888-422

G017 **Groupe Indosuez Fund Management Co**
39 Allee Scheffer
L-2520
Luxembourg
Tel 352-4767-1
Fax 352-462-442

G018 **GT Global**
Alban Gate 14th Floor
125 London Wall
London EC2Y 5AS
United Kingdom
Tel 44-171-710-4567
Fax 44-171-696-0966

G019–G022
Guinness Flight Fund Managers (Guernsey) Ltd
Guinness Flight House
PO Box 250
La Plaiderie
St Peter Port GY1 3QH
Guernsey
Tel 44-1481-710-404
Fax 44-1481-712-065

H001–H006
Hambros Fund Managers
Barfield House
St Julian's Avenue
St Peter Port GY1 3QL
Guernsey
Tel 44-1481-715-454
Fax 44-1481-710-285

H007 **Hamon**
2903-5 Alexandra House
16-20 Chater Road
Hong Kong
Tel 852-2-526-4268
Fax 852-2-526-7277

H008 **Hang Seng Investment Management**
16-th Floor Hang-Seng Building
77 Des Voeux Road
Central
Hong Kong
Tel 852-2825-3916
Fax 852-2868-4241

H009 **HANSA-NORD-LUX Managementgesellschaft**
38-40 Avenue Monterey
L-2163
Luxembourg
Tel 352-45-101-346
Fax 352-45-101-423

H010 **Hansard Europe**
PO Box 43 Enterprise House
Fraskati Road Blackrock
Dublin
Ireland
Tel 353-1-278-1488
Fax 353-1-278-1498

H011–H019
Hansard International
Anglo International House
Bark Hill - North Quay
Douglas IM99 1QL
Isle of Man
Tel 44-1624-688-000
Fax 44-1624-688-218

H020 **Hansberger – Global Fund Services Ltd**
ITI House, Earlsford Terrace
Dublin 2
Ireland
Tel 353-1-478-2411
Fax 353-1-478-2642

H021 **Hasenbichler Asset Management**
Eschenbachgasse 11
Wien 1010
Austria
Tel 43-1-587-3249
Fax 43-1-587-3344

H022 **Haussmann Holdings**
PO Box N-3918
27 Cumberland Street
Nassau
Bahamas
Tel 01-441-326-0282
Fax 01-441-326-5213

H023 **Havelet Throgmorton**
Havelet House, South Esplanade
St Peter Port GY1 3PE
Guernsey
Tel 44-1481-710-491
Fax 44-1481-714-596

H024 **H.C.M. HYPO Capital Management Luxembourg SA**
4 Rue Alphonse Weicker
L-2721
Luxembourg
Tel 352-42-74-44-1
Fax 352-42-19-81

H025 **Henderson**
European Bank and Business Centre
6D Route de Treves
L-2633
Luxembourg
Tel 352-34-66-22-1
Fax 352-34-65-55

H026 **Henderson Crotheswaite International Company**
32 St Mary at Hill
London EC3P 3AJ
United Kingdom
Tel 44-171-623-9992
Fax 44-171-528-0884

H027 **Henderson Touche Remnant**
3 Finsbury Avenue
London EC2M 2PA
United Kingdom
Tel 44-171-638-5757
Fax 44-171-377-5742

H028 **Hermes International Fund Ltd (Bermuda)**
13 Rue Goethe
L-2014
Luxembourg
Tel 352-40-46-46-1
Fax 352-40-46-74

H029 **Hermitage Capital Management**
Rue du Pre
St Peter Port GY1 1OU
Guernsey
Tel 44- 1481-710-901
Fax 44- 1481-711-824

H030 **Hill Samuel Fund Managers (Jersey) Ltd**
PO Box 63, 7 Bond Street
St Helier JE4 4PH
Jersey
Tel 44-1534-604-604
Fax 44-1534-604-606

H031 **Holborn Currency - Prudential Fund Managers (Guersey) Ltd**
PO Box 208, St. Julian's Avenue
St Peter Port GY1 3XS
Guernsey
Tel 44-1481-726-268
Fax 44-1481-726-987

H032 **Hottinger**
69 Route d'Esch
L-2953
Luxembourg
Tel 352-45-90-1
Fax 352-45-90-20-10

H033 **HSBC Investment Funds Luxembourg SA**
7 Rue du Marche-aux-Herbes
L-1728
Luxembourg
Tel 352-47-68-121
Fax 352-47-55-69

H034 H035 **HSBC Asset Management HK Ltd**
15 Floor Peregrine Tower
89 Queensway
Central
Hong Kong
Tel 852-2903-6888
Fax 852-2566-2340

I001 **Icatu Bank**
Avenue President Wilson 231
Rio de Janeiro RJ 20030-021
Brazil
Tel 55-21-217-1300
Fax 55-21-240-4133

I002 **IBJ Asia**
17th Floor Two Pacific Place
88 Queensway
Central
Hong Kong
Tel 852-2103-3000
Fax 852-2845-9187

I003 **IFDC Ltd - Daewoo Securities (Europe) Ltd**
902-904 Two Exchange Square
8 Connaught Place
Central
Hong Kong
Tel 852-284-56-332
Fax 852-285-5374

I004 **IKOS Partners**
7 New Concordia Wharf, Mill St
London SE1 2BB
United Kingdom
Tel 44-171-232-0400
Fax 44-171-231-7590

I005 **ImPac Asset Management Ltd**
1205 Universal Trade Centre
3 Arbuthnot Road
Central
Hong Kong
Tel 852-2810-1608
Fax 852-2521-5117

I006 **Income Partners Asset Management (HK) Ltd**
19th Floor, Cheklang First Bank Centre
1 Duddel Street
Central
Hong Kong
Tel 852-2-869-0186
Fax 852-2-869-6991

I007 **Indosuez Asset Mgmt Asia Ltd**
27th Floor, One Exchange Square
8 Connaught Place
Central
Hong Kong
Tel 852-2521-4231
Fax 852-2868-1450

I008 **ING Bank (Luxembourg) SA**
224 Route d'Arlon
Strassen L-8010
Luxembourg
Tel 352-31-66-11-1
Fax 352-31-68-68

I010 **Interallianz Bank AG**
Ramistrasse 31
Zurich CH 8001
Switzerland
Tel 41-1-262-54-54
Fax 41-1-262-16-43

I011 **International Skandia**
29 Rue Jean Pierre Brassuer
L-1258
Luxembourg
Tel 352-4590-3282
Fax 352-4590-4243

I012 **Interspar Verwaltungsgesellschaft SA**
6c Route de Treves
Senningberg L-2633
Luxembourg
Tel 352-34091
Fax 352-3409-2359

I013 I014
INVESCO International Ltd
PO Box 271 Invesco House
Grenville Street
St Helier JE4 8TD
Jersey
Tel 44-1534-814-000
Fax 44-1534-841-400

I015 **Invest Atlantiques – Casenove Fund Management**
12 Townhouse Yard
London EC2R 7AN
United Kingdom
Tel 44-171-606-0708
Fax 44-171-606-9205

I016 **Investec**
ISFC House
Dublin 1
Ireland
Tel 352-1-670-0660
Fax 352-1-670-1181

I017 **Irish Life International**
Irish Life Centre,
Lower Abbey St
Dublin 1
Ireland
Tel 353-1-704-1500
Fax 353-1-704-1922

Irish Life INTERNATIONAL

J001 **JP Morgan**
Mainzer Landstrasse 46
Boersenstrasse 204
Frankfurt-au-Maine 60325
Germany
Tel 49-69-71-24-0
Fax 49-69-71-24-13-2

J002 **J Rothschild Intl Assurance**
9-13 Grovesnor Street
London W1X 9FB
United Kingdom
Tel 44-171-915-0202
Fax 44-171-915-0203

J003 **Jersey Private Bank & Trust**
Harbour Front Building 2nd Floor
East Bay Street
The Providence
Bahamas
Tel 1-242-394-6231
Fax 1-242-394-5654

J004 **Jardine Fleming Investment Management**
42nd Floor Jardine House, PO Box 70
Central
Hong Kong
Tel 852-2-843-8888
Fax 852-2-845-0808

J005 **John W Henry**
Rosebank Centre, 14 Bermudian Road
Pembroke
Bermuda
Tel 1-441-299-3882
Fax 1-441-295-6759

J006 **JP Morgan**
Mainzer Landstrasse 46
Boersenstrasse 204
Frankfurt-au-Maine 60325
Germany
Tel 49-69-71-24-0
Fax 49-69-71-24-13-2

J007 **Julius Baer Asset Management**
Fraegutstrasse 40
Zurich 8010
Switzerland
Tel 41-1-287-6600
Fax 41-1-202-4161

J008 J010 J011
Jupiter Tyndall Group Plc
11th Floor Knightsbridge House
Knightsbridge
London SW7 1RB
United Kingdom
Tel 44-171-412-0703
Fax 44-171-416-7719

J009 **Jupiter Tyndall (Jersey) Ltd**
7-11 Bath Street
St Helier
JE4 8US
Jersey
Tel 44-1534-879-500
Fax 44-1534-504599

J010 J011 see J008

K001 **Kafag/SFR Convertible Fund Management**
Uraniastrasse 9
Zurich CH 8070
Switzerland
Tel 41-1-333-25-04
Fax 41-1-333-23-19

K002 **Kaupthing Management Company**
20 Boulevard Emmanuelle Servais L-2535
Luxembourg
Tel 352-2-47-93-461
Fax 352-2-47-96-432

K003 **Keppler Asset Management**
47 Boulevard Royal
L-2449
Luxembourg
Tel 352-46-40-10
Fax 352-46-47-0204

K004 **Key Asset Management**
35-38 Portman Square
London W1H 0EU
United Kingdom
Tel 44-171-465-0315
Fax 44-171-465-0317

K005 **KFTCIC Fund Managers Ltd**
PO Box 156, 22 Smith Street
St Peter Port GY1 4EU
Guernsey
Tel 44-1481-717-863
Fax 44-1481-717-860

K006 **KI Pacific Asset Management**
6 Front Street
Hamilton
Bermuda
Tel N/A
Fax N/A

K007 K008
Kleinwort Benson Investment Management
10 Fenchurch Street
London EC3M 3LB
United Kingdom
Tel 44-171-956-6600
Fax 44-171-956-7696

K009 **Kornco - Folkes Asset Management**
Chelsea Wharf, 15 Lots Road
London SW10 0QJ
United Kingdom
Tel 44-171-376-5437
Fax 44-171-351-1454

K010 **Kredietbank Belgique**
Avenue Du Port
Bruxelles B-1080
Belgium
Tel 32-2-422-6944
Fax 32-2-422-8135

K011 **Kredietbank Luxembourg**
11 Rue Aldringen
L-2960
Luxembourg
Tel 352-46-819-3985
Fax 352-48-08-82

L001 L002
Lazard Fund Administration
P.O Box 108 Lazard House
2-6 Church Street
St Helier JE4 8QD
Jersey
Tel 44-1534-620-694
Fax 44-1534-620-629

L003 **Lazard Freres & Co**
20/22 Lower Hatch Street
Dublin 2
Ireland
Tel 353-1-790-50-68
Fax 353-1-790-50-10

L004 **La Cie Financiere Edmond de Rothschild**
20 Boulevard Emmanuel Servais
L-2535
Luxembourg
Tel 352-47-93-46-1
Fax 352-22-24-94

L005 L006 L007
Legg Mason
1 Founders Court
London EC2R 7DB
United Kingdom
Tel 44-171-600-7555
Fax 44-171-600-6788

L008 **Lehman Brothers**
3 World Financial Centre
7th Floor
New York NY 10285
U.S.A.
Tel 1-212-526-0691
Fax 1-212-528-7928

L009 **Leu Capital**
PO Box 8022
Zurich
Switzerland
Tel 41-1-219-11-11
Fax 41-1-219-31-97

L010 **Liberal**
Rua do Carmo 7, 8th Floor
Rio de Janeiro RJ20011
Brazil
Tel 55-21-212-4000
Fax 55-21-333-6104

L011 **Liberty Newport World**
23 Beaufort Court, Admiral Way
London E14 9XL
United Kingdon
Tel 44-171-536-9766
Fax 44-171-536-9767

L012 **Lippo Investment Management**
43rd Floor Lippo Tower
Lippo Centre
89 Queensway
Hong Kong
Tel 852-2867-6818
Fax 852-2596-0388

L013 L014
Lloyd George Investment Management
IFSC House, IFSC Centre
Dublin 1
Ireland
Tel 353-1-670-0660
Fax 353-1-670-1181

L015 L017
LLoyds Bank Plc
PO Box 260 Sarnia House
Le Truchot
St Peter Port GY1 4LL
Guernsey
Tel 44-1481-724-983
Fax 44-1481-727-344

L016 **Lloyds International Portfolio**
1 Rue Schiller
L-1016
Luxembourg
Tel 352-40-22-12-235
Fax 352-40-16-08

L017 see L015

L018 **Lloydstrust**
Waterloo House, Don Street
St Helier JE4 8ZJ
Jersey
Tel 44-1534-284-200
Fax 44-1534-284-888

L019 **Lombard Odier Investment Management**
11 Rue de la Corraterie
Genève CH 1204
Switzerland
Tel 41-22-709-2111
Fax 41-22-709-2911

L020 **Lombardier Management Ltd**
Kirk House, PO Box 1100
Grand Cayman BW1
Cayman Islands
Tel 1-345-949-7212
Fax 1-345-949-0993

L021 **Lonworld Financial Services**
PO Box 845, 19 Seaton Place
St Helier JE4 0UX
Jersey
Tel 44-1534-888-025
Fax 44-1534-888-026

L022 **LPS International**
832 Europort
Gibraltar
Tel 350-791-20
Fax 350-784-28
LPS
London Portfolio Services

L023 **Luxembourg Europe & American Fund Managers**
69 Route d'Esch
L-1470
Luxembourg
Tel 352-56-14-11-1
Fax 352-46-22-37-55

L024 **Luxlife**
4 Rue du Fort Rheinsheim
BP 723
L-2017
Luxembourg
Tel 352-25-27-71
Fax 352-25-27-79

M001 **M&G Guernsey Limited**
PO Box 44 Westbourne
The Grange
St Peter Port GY1 3BG
Guernsey
Tel 44-1481-722-663
Fax 44-1481-716-762

M002 **Magnum Fund Management Ltd**
Harbour Drive Centre 2nd Floor
George Town
Grand Cayman
Cayman Islands
Tel 1-345-949-6770
Fax 1-345-949-6773

M003 **Malabar**
Sterling House, Wesley Street
Hamilton HM1029
Bermuda
Tel 1-441-295-0653
Fax 1-441-292-3677

M004 **MAN-GFA Ltd**
Bahnhofstrasse 15
Pfaffikon CH 8808
Switzerland
Tel 41-55-415-3636
Fax 41-55-415-3637

M005 **Mansion House**
37A Bank of China Tower, 1 Garden Road
Central
Hong Kong
Tel 852-2843-1431
Fax 852-2845-8158

M006 **Manulife Global Fund Ltd**
Room 1305 13th Floor, 9 Queens Road
Central
Hong Kong
Tel 852-2501-9100
Fax 852-2810-9510

M007 **Mapen Advisors – RHR Fund Managers Limited**
19-21 Circular Road
Douglas IM1 1AF
Isle of Man
Tel 44-1624-629-420
Fax 44-1624-662-249

M008 **Martin Currie Fund Mangement Company (Luxembourg)**
15 Avenue Emile Reuter
L-2420
Luxembourg
Tel 352-22-39-82
Fax 352-47-18-13

M009 **Master Consultants**
Myliusstrasse 7
Frankfurt-am-Maine 60323
Germany
Tel 49-69-1700-170
Fax 49-69-1700-1717

(P014) **Matheson PFC Ltd**
29th Floor Hennessy Center
PO Box 20927
Causeway Bay
Hong Kong
Tel 852-2-890-8448
Fax 852-2-890-2524

M010 **MBF Unit Trust Managers Ltd**
17th Floor One Pacific Place
88 Queensway
Hong Kong
Tel 852-2869-0800
Fax 852-2801-7459

M011 **Mees Pierson Capital Management**
Keizersgracht 683
PO Box 293
Amsterdam 1000 AG
The Netherlands
Tel 31-20-527-4871
Fax 31-20-527-4778

M012 **MeesPierson Trust (Luxembourg)**
10 Rue Antoine Gans
L-1820
Luxembourg
Tel 352-476-86 71
Fax 352-476-86-72-29

M013 **Mega Strategic Investment**
8th Floor Jardine House, 1 Connaught Place
Central
Hong Kong
Tel 852-2-525-1087
Fax 852-2845-2503

M014 **Merck Finck & Co**
Pacellistrasse 16
Privatbankiers
Munchen 80333
Germany
Tel 49-89-21-04-0
Fax 49-89-29-98-14

M015 M020
Mercury Asset Management
33 King Williams Street
London EC4R 9AS
United Kingdom
Tel 44-171-2802800
Fax 44-171-280-2820

M016 **Mercury Asset Management(IOM)**
12/13 Hill Street
Douglas IMI IEF
Isle of Man
Tel 44-1624-662255
Fax 44-1624-662850

M017 M018 M019
Mercury Asset Management(Jersey)
Forum House, Grenville Street
St Helier JE4 8RL
Jersey
Tel 44-1534-600-600
Fax 44-1534-600-687

M020 see M015

M021 **Mercury Asset Management (Luxembourg)**
BP 1058
L-1010
Luxembourg
Tel 352-342010-5252
Fax 352-342010-5900

M022 **Merita Bank Luxembourg SA**
PO Box 569
L-2015
Luxembourg
Tel 352-477-6111
Fax 352-477-611251

M023 **Merrill Lynch Asset Management**
68-70 Boulevard de la Petrusse
L-2320
Luxembourg
Tel 352-49-51-561
Fax 352-48-12-71

M024 **Merrill Lynch Bank (Swiss) SA**
18 Rue de Contamines
Case Postale 3070
Geneva CH 1211
Switzerland
Tel 41-22-703-1717
Fax 41-22-703-1515

M025 **Metropolitan Bank**
Boulevard du Souverain 191-197
Bruxelles
B-1160
Belgium
Tel 32-2-228-2943
Fax 32-2-228-8227

M026 **MFS International**
47 Boulevard Royal
L-2449
Luxembourg
Tel 352-46-40-10-1
Fax 352-46-36-31

M027 M028
Midland Bank
PO Box 26, 28-34 Hill Street
St Helier JE4 8NR
Jersey
Tel 44-1534-606-000
Fax 44-1534-606-356

M029 **MIGROSBANK / Julius Baer**
Brandschennestrasse 40
Zurich 8010
Switzerland
Tel 41-1-287-6600
Fax 41-1-212-2581

M030 **Mikles Miller - Folkes Asset Management**
Chelsea Wharf, 15 Lots Road
London SW10 QDJ
United Kingdom
Tel 44-171-376-5437
Fax 44-171-351-1454

M031 **Millenium**
Chase Manhattan House, Georges Dock 1
IFSC
Dublin-1
Ireland
Tel 353-1-612-3000
Fax 353-1-612-3123

M032 **Minerals Oils & Resources**
PO Box 194, 15-21 Broad Street
St Helier JE4 8RR
Jersey
Tel 44-1534-274-41
Fax 44-1534-325-13

M033 **MINT- EDF & Managment**
Sugar Quay, Lower Thames St
London EC3R 6DU
United Kingdom
Tel 44-171-398-6400
Fax 44-171-398-6800

M034 **MM Warburg Luxinvest SA**
PO Box 16
L-2010
Luxembourg
Tel 352-42-63-64
Fax 352-42-45-69

M035 M036
Momentum
140 Brompton Road
London SW3 1HY
United Kingdom
Tel 44-171-581-5841
Fax 44-171-581-5545

M037 **Monument Asset Management Ltd**
Exchange House
Primrose Street Broadgate
London EC2A 2DD
United Kingdom
Tel 44-171-638-5699
Fax 44-171-628-2711

M038 **Morgan Grenfell**
George's Dock House
IFSC
Dublin 1
Ireland
Tel 353-1-676-8600
Fax 353-1-607-6491

M039 **Morgan Stanley Asset Management**
6c Route de Treves
L-2633
Luxembourg
Tel 352-346-461
Fax 352-344-46220

M040 **Multifinance International**
69 Route d'Esch
L-2953
Luxembourg
Tel 352-45-90-32-10
Fax 352—45-90-32-43

M041 **Munchner Kapitalanlagen**
69 Route d'Esch
L-2953
Luxembourg
Tel 352-45-90-1
Fax 352-45-90-2010

M042 **Murray Johnstone (Dublin) Ltd**
7 West Nile Street
Glasgow G1 2PX
United Kingdom
Tel 44-141-226-31 31
Fax 44-141-248 54 20

N001 **National Mutual Investment Management Ltd**
21 Floor National Mutual Centre
151 Gloucester Road
Wanchai
Hong Kong
Tel 852-2536-6366
Fax 852-2536-9411

N002 **Nestor Investment Management SA**
PO Box 858
L-2018
Luxembourg
Tel 352-427-042
Fax 352-427-454

N003 **Neuflize & Schlumberger & Mallet**
50 Avenue J.F. Kennedy
L-2951
Luxembourg
Tel 352-42-42-1
Fax 352-42-42-6500

N004 **Samba Capital Management International Ltd**
Nightingale House, 65 Curzon Street
London W1Y 7PE
United Kingdom
Tel 44-171-629-3966
Fax 44-171-355-4412

N005 **Newport Management International Guernsey Ltd**
PO Box 208 Bermuda House
St Julians Avenue
St Peter Port
Guernsey
Tel 44-1481-707000
Fax 44-1481-726275

N006 **Newton Capital House International Investment Management Ltd**
Newton House Building, Bath Street
St Helier JE4 8UH
Jersey
Tel 44-1534-285-707
Fax 44-1534-285-751

N007 **Nikko Bank Luxembourg**
16-18 Boulevard Royal
L-2449
Luxembourg
Tel 352-46-23-84
Fax 352-46-23-83

N008 **Nikko Capital Mgt (UK) Ltd**
1st Floor, Nikko House, 17 Godliman Street
London EC4V 5BD
United Kingdom
Tel 44-171-248-0592
Fax 44-171-236-1531

N009 **Nikko International**
PO Box 105 La Tonnelle House
Les Banques
St. Sampson GY1 3EP
Guernsey
Tel 44-1481-721-438
Fax 44-1481-710-001

N010 **Nomura Bank International Plc**
20th-21st Floor
Citibank Plaza 3 Garden Road
Central
Hong Kong
Tel 852-2536-1111
Fax 852-2536-1888

N011 **Northgate**
PO Box 83 Ordinance House
31 Pier Road
St Helier JE4 8PW
Jersey
Tel 44-1534-875-141
Fax 44-1534-328-76

N012 **Northstar Fund Managers Ltd**
68 Avenue Des Alpes
Montreux CH 1820
Switzerland
Tel 41-219-637-871
Fax 41-219-637-875

N013 **Norwich Union Performance Management**
PO Box 150, Sentinel House
37 Surrey Street
Norwich NR1 3UZ
United Kingdom
Tel 44-1603-685-302
Fax 44-1603-872-53

O001 **OBC-Odier Bungener Courvoisier**
11 Rue de la Corraterie
Genève 1204
Switzerland
Tel 41-22- 709 24 53
Fax 41-22- 709 29 33

O002 **Odey Asset Management**
12 Upper Grosvenor Street
London W1X 9PA
United Kingdom
Tel 44-171-208-1400
Fax 44-171-208-1401

O003 O005 **Old Mutual Guernsey**
PO Box 121
Fairbairn House
Rahais
St Peter Port GY1 3HE
Guernsey
Tel 44-1481-726-726
Fax 44-1481-728-953

OLD MUTUAL INTERNATIONAL

O004 **Old Mutual Hong Kong**
16th Floor
Sun Hung Kai Centre
30 Harbour Road
Wanchai
Hong Kong
Tel 852-253-166-88
Fax 852-258-790-27

OLD MUTUAL INTERNATIONAL

O005 see O003

O006 O007 **Old Mutual International Fund**
50 Dawson Street
Dublin 2
Ireland
Tel 353-1-662-1555
Fax 353-1-662-1561

OLD MUTUAL INTERNATIONAL

O008 **Olympia Capital International Inc**
Williams House, 20 Reid street
Hamilton HMDX
Bermuda
Tel 1-441-292-1018
Fax 1-441-295-2305

O009 **Oppenheim**
31 Allee Scheffer
L-2520
Luxembourg
Tel 352-22-15-22-441
Fax 352-22-15-22-400

O010 **Opportunity Asset Management**
Avenue President Wilson 231
28th Floor
Rio de Janeiro 20030-21
Brazil
Tel 55-21-532-1000
Fax 55-21-532-2880

O011 **Optigest Luxembourg**
17 Avenue Hoche
Paris 75008
France
Tel 33-1-4075-8700
Fax 33-1-4075-8701

O012 **Optima Fund Management**
73 Front Street
Hamilton HM CX
Bermuda
Tel 1-441-295-8658
Fax 1-441-292-6274

O013 **Orbis**
PO Box 571
Hamilton HM CX
Bermuda
Tel 1-441-292-6666
Fax 1-441-296-3001

O014 **Orbitex Managment Limited**
Maritime House, Frederick Street
Nassau PO Box N-9932
Bahamas
Tel 1-441-356-6456
Fax 1-441-356-5875

O015 **Orion-Heine Securities Corp**
51 John F Kennedy Parkway
Short Hills
New Jersey 07078
U.S.A.
Tel 1-201-912-2086
Fax 1-201-376-6922

O016 **Oswald & Cie**
PO Box1043
George Town
Grand Cayman BWA
Cayman Islands
Tel 1-345-949-0050
Fax 1-345-949-8062

P001 **P.R.P. Performa Ltd**
Beckagaesse 8
FL9490 in Vaduz
Liechtenstein
Tel 41-75-23-32-778
Fax 41-75-23-23-132

P002 **Pan European Life**
7 Rue de La Chapelle
L-1325
Luxembourg
Tel 352-45-67-30-1
Fax 352-45-67-34

P003 **Paneurolife**
B.P. 2408
L-1024
Luxembourg
Tel 352-456-7301
Fax 352-476-86-72-29

P004 **Panurgy Limited**
1202 Tung Wah Mansion
199-203 Hennessy Rd
Wanchai
Hong Kong
Tel 852-2511-4060
Fax 852-2519-7536

P005 **Paragon Asset Management**
2nd Floor TSB House
la Truchot
St Peter Port
Guernsey
Tel 44-1481-726511
Fax 44-1481-713-460

P006 **Park Place**
25 St James' Street
London SW1A 1HA
United Kingdom
Tel 44-171-976-2000
Fax 44-171-930-0424

P007 **PCP Investment Mgmt Ltd**
Harmony House, PO Box 1197
Limassol
Cyprus
Tel 3575-749-754
Fax 3575-749-755

P008 **Peregrine Asset Management (Hong Kong) Ltd**
1704 New World Tower
16-18 Queens Road
Central
Hong Kong
Tel 852-2978-8378
Fax 852-2845-1108

P009 **Performa Investment Advisor**
Avenue J.F. Kennedy
L-2951
Luxembourg
Tel 352-42-42-43-634
Fax 352-42-42-65-00

P010 **Permal Holdings**
PO Box N3918
27 Cumberland Street
Nassau
Bahamas
Tel 1-242-326-0282
Fax 1-242-326-5213

P011 P012
Perpetual Unit Trust Mgmt (Jersey) Ltd
PO Box 459, d'Hauteville Chambers
Seale Street
St Helier JE4 8WS
Jersey
Tel 44-1534-684-48
Fax 44-1534-389-18

P013 **Peterbroeck Van Campenhout & Cie SCS**
19 Rue Place Sainte Gudule
Bruxelles 1000
Belgium
Tel 32-2-229-66-56
Fax 32-2-229-64-44

P014 (PFC) **Matheson PFC Ltd**
29th Floor Hennessy Center
PO Box 20927
Causeway Bay
Hong Kong
Tel 852-2-890-8448
Fax 852-2-890-2524

P015 **Pheim Asset Management**
14th Floor
UBN Tower 10 Jalan P. Ramlee
Kuala Lumpur 50250
Malaysia
Tel 603-201-6407
Fax 603-201-6408

P016 **Pictet and Cie**
29 Boulevard George Favon
Geneva CH1204
Switzerland
Tel 41-22-705-22-11
Fax 41-22-781-3131

P017 **Pioneer Management (Ire) Ltd**
2/4 Ely Place
Dublin-2
Ireland
Tel 353-1-662-3600
Fax 353-1-662-3711

P018 **PMG Fonds Management AG**
14 Hume Street
Dublin 2
Ireland
Tel 353-1-662-4244
Fax 353-1-676-8592

P019 **Postbank International SA Fondsadministration**
2 Route de Treves
L-2633
Luxembourg
Tel 352-349531-283
Fax 352-346206

P020 **Power Capital**
31 Kildare Street
Dublin 2
Ireland
Tel 353-1-661-3400
Fax 353-1-661-3601

P021 **Premier Life – Target International Group**
1 Rue Emilie Bian
L-2016
Luxembourg
Tel 352-405-0751
Fax 352-405-022

P022 **Pricoa**
33 Boulevard Prince Henri
L-1724
Luxembourg
Tel 352-22-66-21-699
Fax 352-47-02-11

P023 **Prime Lipper**
69 Route d'Esch
L-2953
Luxembourg
Tel 352-45-90-32-10
Fax 352-45-90-32-43

P024 P025
Proton
Place Winston Churchill 1
PO Box 897
L-2018
Luxembourg
Tel 352-45-37-81
Fax 352-45-36-97

P026 **Privestor – GNI Fund Management**
25 Dowgate Hill, Cannon Bridge
London EC4R 2EN
United Kingdom
Tel 44-171-337-3743
Fax 44-171-626-5204

P027 **Prolific International Fund Plc**
53 Fiztwilliam Square
Dublin 2
Ireland
Tel 353-1-676-8836
Fax 353-1-676-2136

P028 **Prospect Asset Management**
PO Box 255 Barfield House
St Julians Avenue
St Peter Port
Guernsey
Tel 44-1481-710651
Fax 44-1481-710285

P029 **Prudential Bache Cap Fund**
7th Floor 6 Min Chuan
East Road, Taipei
Taiwan , ROC
Tel 886-2504-2000
Fax 886-2509-293

P030 **Prudential Fund Managers (Jersey) Ltd**
PO Box 26, 28/34 Hill Street
St Helier JE4 8NR
Jersey
Tel 44-1534-606-540
Fax 44-1534-606-356

P031 **Puilaetco**
Ave Herrmann Debrouxlaan 46
Bruxelles B-1160
Belgium
Tel 32-2-679-45-11
Fax 32-2-679-46-22

P032 **Putnam Investments**
47 Boulevard Royal
L-2449
Luxembourg
Tel 352-46-40-10-1
Fax 352-46-36-31

P033 **Putnam Embassy**
Caledonian House 1st Floor
Mary Street
PO Box 1043
George Town
Tel 1-617-292-1000
Fax 1-617-423-9589

Q001 **Quaestor**
River Place House
7-11 Finsbury Circus
London EC2M 7TT
United Kingdom
Tel 44-171-588-8888
Fax 44-171-588-8898

Q003 **Quilter**
PO Box 82, 19/21 Circular Road
Douglas IM99 1EX
Isle of Man
Tel 44-1624-622-699
Fax 44-1624-627-515

Q004 **Quintessenz Sicav**
4 Rue Thomas Edison
L-1445
Luxembourg
Tel 352-44-9031
Fax 352-44-903-2001

R001 **Rabobank**
283 Rue d'Arlon
L-1150
Luxembourg
Tel 352-45-78-801
Fax 352-45-23-96

R002 **Royal Bank of Canada International Fund Management Ltd**
19-21 Broad Street
St Helier
Jersey
Tel 44-1534-274-41
Fax 44-1534-247-60

R003 **RBC Offshore Fund Managers Ltd**
PO Box 246, Canada Court
St Peter Port GY1 3QE
Guernsey
Tel 44-1481-723-021
Fax 44-1481-715-976

R004 **Raggio di Sole Finanziara SA**
19-21 Boulevard Prince Henri
L-2010
Luxembourg
Tel 352-46-22-46-282
Fax 352-22-15-91

R005 **Regent Fund Management**
39 St Jame's Street
London SW1A 1JQ
United Kingdom
Tel 44-171-316-0007
Fax 44-171-316-0008

R006 **Reich & Tang Asset Management**
West Suite 36100
100 King Street
Toronto M5X1A9
Canada
Tel 1-416-956-2980
Fax 1-416-681-3722

R007 **River & Mercantile**
7 Lincoln's Inn Fields
London WC2A 3BP
United Kingdom
Tel 44-171-405-7722
Fax 44-171-405-2955

R008 **RMF Asset Management A.G.**
Poststrasse 4
Pfaffikon CH-8808
Switzerland
Tel 41-55-415-8710
Fax 41-55-415-8799

R009 **Robeco Groep**
Postbus 973, Coolsingel
Rotterdam 3000 AZ
The Netherlands
Tel 31-10-224-12-24
Fax 31-10-224-2114

R010 R012–R017
Rothschild Asset Management (CI) Ltd
PO Box 242, Sausmerez Street
St Peter Port GY1 3HP
Guernsey
Tel 44-1481-719700
Fax 44-1481-723965

R011 **Rothschild Asset Management HK**
16 th Floor, Alexander House
Central
Hong Kong
Tel 852-2522-2432
Fax 852-2537-4989

R012–R017see R010

R018 **Rothschild Asset Management Ltd**
Five Arrows House
St. Swithin's Lane
London EC4N 8NR
United Kingdom
Tel 44-171-280-5000
Fax 44-171-929-1643

R019 **Royal Bank of Scotland Fund Managers (Jersey) Ltd**
PO Box 83 Ordnace House
31 Pier Road
St Helier JE4 8PW
Jersey
Tel 44-1534-875-141
Fax 44-1534-328-76

R020–R037
Royal Life International
Royal Court
Castletown
IM9 IRA
Isle of Man
Tel 44-1624-821-212
Fax 44-1624-824-405

R038 **Royal Skandia Life Assurance**
Skandia House, Finch Road
Douglas IM99 1NU
Isle of Man
Tel 44-1624-611611
Fax 44-1624-611715

S001 **Skandinaviska Enskilda Banken**
Regeringsgatan 45
ST-R2
Stockholm 10640
Sweden
Tel 46-8-676-9051
Fax 46-8-676-9129

S002 **Sabre Fund Management**
Windsor House, St James's St
London SW1
Tel 44-171-316-2800
Fax 44-171-316-0180

S003 **Sodific Asset Management**
18-20 Dumaresq Street
St Helier JE2 3RL
Jersey
Tel 44-1534-58-870
Fax 44-1534-25-361

S004 **San Paolo Gestion International SA**
12 Avenue de Libertie
L-1930
Luxembourg
Tel 352-40-67601
Fax 352-495390

S005 **Sarasin Fund Management (Guernsey) Ltd**
Elisabethenstrasse 62
Basel 4002
Switzerland
Tel 41-61-277-77-77
Fax 41-61-277-75-75

S006 **Samba Capital Management International Ltd**
Nightingale House, 65 Curzon Street
London W1Y 7PE
United Kingdom
Tel 44-171-629-3966
Fax 44-171-355-4412

S007 **Swiss Bank Corporation (Luxembourg)**
PO Box 2, 26 Route d'Arlon
L-2010
Luxembourg
Tel 352-45-20-30-1
Fax 352-45-20-30-700

S008 **Schroder Investment Management (Guernsey) Ltd**
PO Box 255 Barfield House
St Julian's Avenue
St Peter's Port GY1 3QI
Guernsey
Tel 44-1481-710651
Fax 44-1481-710-285

S009 **Schroders Unit Trust**
Senator House
85 Queen Victoria Street
London EC4V 4EJ
United Kingdom
Tel 44-171-658-6000
Fax 44-171-658-3950

S010 **Schroder Investment Management Ltd**
5 Rue Hohenhoff
L-1736
Luxembourg
Tel 352-341-342-202
Fax 352-341-342-342

S011 **Schroder Investment Management (HK)**
25th Floor Two Exchange Square
8 Connaught Place
Central
Hong Kong
Tel 852-2521-1633
Fax 852-2868-1023

S012 **Scontinvest - Discount Bond & Trust Co**
18 Boulevard Royal
L-2449
Luxembourg
Tel 352-228-0071
Fax 352-22-37-67

S013 **Scor (Reafin)**
1 Avenue du President Wilson
La Defense
Paris 92074
France
Tel 33-1-46-98-76-76
Fax 33-1-47-67-04-09

S014 **Scot Provident International Life Assurance**
Scottish Provident House
Ballacottieor Business Park
Douglas IM2 2SP
Isle of Man
Tel 44-1624-677446
Fax 44-1624-612475

S015 **Scottish Amicable European**
Ormond House, 12 Lower Leeson St
Dublin 2
Ireland
Tel 353-1-661-3433
Fax 353-1-661-3406

S016 S017
Scottish Equitable Plc
Edinburgh Park
Edinburgh EH12 9SE
Scotland
Tel 44-131-339-9191
Fax 44-131-339-9567

S018 **Scottish Value Management (Ireland) Ltd**
4 Floor Russell House
Stokes Place
St Stephen's Green
Dublin 2
Ireland
Tel 353-1-475-7601
Fax 353-1-475-7608

S019 **Scudder**
345 Park Avenue
New York 10154-0010
U.S.A.
Tel 1-212-326-6200
Fax 1-212-751-3451

S020 **Scudder Stevens & Clark Ltd**
New London House
6 London Street
London EC3R 7BE
United Kingdom
Tel 44-171-265-0077
Fax 44-171-265-0202

S021 **Seahawk Partners**
1450 East Tower
3343 Peachtree Road
Atlanta, Georgia GA 30326
U.S.A.
Tel 1-404-240-0555
Fax 1-404-240-0552

S022 **SEFI SA - Geneva**
29 Boulevard George Favon
Geneva CH1204
Switzerland
Tel 41-22-705-2211
Fax 41-22-781-3131

S023 **SFR Convert Bond Fd Mgt Co/Kafag**
Uraniastrasse 9
Zurich CH 8070
Switzerland
Tel 41-1-333-25-04
Fax 41-1-333-23-19

S024 **SHK**
4th Floor Admirality Centre
18 Harcourt Road
Hong Kong
Tel 852-2822-5785
Fax 852-2822-5468

S025 **Sun Chan Financial Management**
3rd Floor, Admiralty Centre
Hong Kong
Tel 852-2822-5846
Fax 852-2822-5486

S026 **Signet Inc**
1 Liberty Plaza, 46th Floor
New York NY 10006
U.S.A.
Tel 1-212-406-3380
Fax 1-212-978-1013

S027 **Singer & Friedlander Total Asset Management Ltd**
21 New Street
Bishopsgate
London EC2M 4HR
United Kingdom
Tel 44-171-867-8777
Fax 44-171-867-8780

S028 **Siparex**
20 Boulevard Emmanuel Servais
L-2535
Luxembourg
Tel 352-45-90-32-10
Fax 352-45-90-32-43

S029 **SJO Inc**
PO Box 1194
Hamilton HMEX
Bermuda
Tel 1-441-295-0022
Fax 1-441-292-1277

S030 **Skandia**
PO Box 487, 16 Boulevard Royal
L-2449
Luxembourg
Tel 352-46-17171
Fax 352-22-55-50

S031 **Sloane Robinson Investment Management Ltd**
Der Norske Bank Building
20 St Dunstan's Hill
London EC3R 8HY
United Kingdom
Tel 44-171-929-2771
Fax 44-171-929-3057

S032 **Smeets Verbaet & Co SA**
Kipdorp 10-12
Antwerpen 2000
Belgium
Tel 32-3-233-90-00
Fax 32-3-231-51-52

S033 **Schroder Munchmeyer Hengst & Co**
Friedensstrasse 6-10
Frankfurt-am-Maine 60311
Germany
Tel 49-69-21-79-0
Fax 49-69-21-79-511

S034 **Societe Nationale de Credit a Industrie SA**
4 Rue de la Reine
L-1021
Luxembourg
Tel 352-47-71-38-1
Fax 352-47-71-37-410

S035 **Societe de Gestion Europe Obligations**
1 Place de Metz
L-2954
Luxembourg
Tel 352-40-15-54-10
Fax 352-40-15-54-19

S036 **Societe Europeenne de Banque**
19-21 Boulevard du Prince Henri
L-1724
Luxembourg
Tel 352-46-14-11-272
Fax 352-22-15-91

S037 **Sogenal -Societe Generale Alsacienne Banque**
255 Rue de Mitterhausburgen
Strasbourg 67000
France
Tel 33-88-77-66-55
Fax 33-88-77-60-79

S038 **Societe Gestion Int SA Paris**
69 Route d'Esch
L-2953
Luxembourg
Tel 352-45-901
Fax 352-45-90-2010

S039 **Sofaer Capital Inc.**
Entertainment Building
22nd Floor
30 Queens Road
Central
Hong Kong
Tel 852-252-188-82
Fax 852-2530-29-13

S040 **Soros Fund Management**
14 Ryder Street
London SW1Y 6QB
United Kingdom
Tel 44-171-925-2555
Fax 44-171-925-2625

S041 **Southern International Asset Management SA**
20 Boulevard Emmanuel Servais
L-2535
Luxembourg
Tel 352-45-90-32-10
Fax 352-45-90-32-43

S042 **Special Assets Pacific Advisors Ltd**
6th Floor Terrace, 8 Duddell Street
Central
Hong Kong
Tel 852-2-593-0500
Fax 852-845-5517

S043 **Spirit Fund Managers**
Wickhams Cay PO Box 662
Road Town
Tortola
British Virgin Islands
Tel 1-809-494-2217
Fax 1-809-494-3917

S044 **Standard Bank Fund Management (Jersey) Ltd**
PO Box 583
1 Waverley Place
St Helier
Jersey
Tel 44-1534-675-57
Fax 44-1534-881199

S045 **Standard Bank Investment Corporation Ltd**
PO Box 61017
Marshalltown
Johannesburg 2107
South Africa
Tel 27-11-636-5013
Fax 27-11-636-6477

S046 **Star Series Advisors Limited**
11 Bermudiana Road
Pembroke HM 08
Bermuda
Tel 1-441-299-3882
Fax 1-441-295-6759

S047 S048
State Street Bank Luxembourg SA
47 Boulevard Royal
L-2012
Luxembourg
Tel 352-46-40-10-1
Fax 352-46-36-31

S049 **Strome Offshore Ltd**
Corporate Center P.O Box 31106.SMB
West Bay Road
Grand Cayman
Cayman Islands
Tel 1-345-949-3977
Fax 1-345-949-3877

S050 **Sul America International**
3rd Floor Genesis Building
P.O.Box 30869 SMB
Grand Cayman
Cayman Islands
Tel 1-345-949-0855
Fax 1-345-949-0866

S051 **Sun Alliance**
PO Box 77, Les Echelons Court
St Peter Port GY1 4BN
Guernsey
Tel 44-1481-714-108
Fax 44-1481-712-424

S052 **Sun Life Global Portfolio (Lux)**
PO Box 22, 10 Bridge Street
Castletown IM99 5UB
Isle of Man
Tel 44-1624-824-131
Fax 44-1624-823-939

S053 **Sun Life Management (IOM) Ltd**
PO Box 22, 10 Bridge Street
Castletown IM99 5UB
Isle of Man
Tel 44-1624-824-131
Fax 44-1624-823-939

S054 **Svecia Securities AG**
Alfred Escher-Strasse
Zurich CH 8002
Switzerland
Tel 41-1-201-10-66
Fax 41-1-202-7242

S055 **Svenska Handelsbanken SA**
146 Boulevard de la Petrusse
L-2330
Luxembourg
Tel 352-49-98-11-1
Fax 352-49-00-04

S056 **Swiss Life Investment Management Ltd**
Swiss Life House, South Park
Sevenoaks TN13 IBG
United Kingdom
Tel 44-1732-582000
Fax 44-1732-582001

S057 S058 S059
Swissca Fondsleitung AG
1 Place de Metz
L-2954
Luxembourg
Tel 352-40-15-5410
Fax 352-40-15-54-19

S060 **Syfrets Ltd**
20 Abchurch Lane
London EC4N 7AD
United Kingdom
Tel 44-171-203-4266
Fax 44-171-220-7141

S061 **Synalgest SA**
31 Rue de Courcelles
Paris 75008
France
Tel 33-1-44-35-32-50
Fax 33-1-44-35-32-57

T001 T002
Templeton Investment Management Ltd
Saltire Court, 20 Castle Terrace
Edinburgh EH1 2EH
Scotland
Tel 44-131-469-4000
Fax 44-131-228-45-06

T003 **The Establishment Trust**
13 Rue Goethe
L-2014
Luxembourg
Tel 352-404-6461
Fax 352-404-674

T004 **Thieme Asset Management**
2 Place de Metz
L-1930
Luxembourg
Tel 352-40-15-54-59
Fax 352-40-15-50-60

T005 **Thornhill Asset Managment Ltd**
Suite 298 In-Land Messenger
Road Town
Tortola
British Virgin Islands
Tel 1-809-494-6000
Fax 1-809-494-7277

T006 **Thornton Investment Management Ltd**
Swan House, 33 Queen Street
London EC4R 1AX
United Kingdom
Tel 44-171-246-3000
Fax 44-171-246-3003

T007 **Thornton Investment Management HK Ltd**
7th Floor Hutchinson House
10 Harcourt Road
Central
Hong Kong
Tel 852-2826-8888
Fax 852-2877-2533

T008 **Thornton Dresdner**
International Financial Services Centre, La
Touche House
Dublin 1
Ireland
Tel 353-1-670-1444
Fax 353-1-670-1414

T009 **Threadneedle Asset Management**
6 Avenue Emile Reuter
L-2420
Luxembourg
Tel 352-47-17-64
Fax 352-47-13-41

T010 **Titan Capital Management**
10 Adam Street
London WC2N GAA
United Kingdom
Tel 44-171-379-3937
Fax 44-171-379-3033

T011 **Trinkhaus Luxembourg Investment Management SA**
1-7 Rue Nina et Julien Lefevre
BP 579
L-2015
Luxembourg
Tel 352-47-18-47-714
Fax 352-47-18-47-641

T012 **TSB Fund Managers (CI) Ltd**
25 New Street
St Helier JE4 8XE
Jersey
Tel 44-1534-503-002
Fax 44-1534-617-082

T013 **TSB Fund Managers (CI) Ltd**
25 New Street
St Helier JE4 8XE
Jersey
Tel 44-1534-503-002
Fax 44-1534-617-082

T014 **TSG Investment Mgmt Bermuda**
Bank of Bermuda Building
6 Front Street
Hamilton HMDX
Bermuda
Tel 1-441-299-6537
Fax 1-441-299-6537

U001 **UBS Intrag Zurich**
Bahnofstrasse 45
Zurich CH 8021
Switzerland
Tel 41-1-235-36-36
Fax 41-1-234-93-20

U002 **Uberseebank AG**
Limmatqual 2
Zurich CH 8024
Switzerland
Tel 41-1-267-5555
Fax 41-1-252-2002

U003 **Ulster Bank**
Ulster Group Centre, George's Quay
Dublin 2
Ireland
Tel 353-1608-4000
Fax 353-1608-4588

U004 **Unibanco Asset Management**
Avenue das Nacoes Unidas
Sào Paulo 2101 04578-903
Brazil
Tel 55-11-3043-7512
Fax 55-11-3043-7608

U005 **Unibank SA**
19-21 Circular Road
Douglas IM1 1AF
Isle of Man
Tel 44-1624-629-420
Fax 44-1624-627-515

U006 **Unico Financial Services SA**
26 Boulevard Royal
L-2449
Luxembourg
Tel 352-46-56-51
Fax 352-46-65-900

U007 **Unico Profirent SA**
12-14 Boulevard Grand Duchesse Charlotte
L-1330
Luxembourg
Tel 352-45-27-06
Fax 352-45-21-32

U008 **Unigestion Asset Management**
14 Boulevard Royal
L-2449
Luxembourg
Tel 352-49-92-41
Fax 352-47-26-65

U009 **Union Assurances Paris**
9 Place Vendome
75001
Paris
Tel 33-1-42-86-71-71
Fax 33-1-42-86-78-17

U010 **Union Bancaire Privee SA**
11 Rue Aldringen
L-2960
Luxembourg
Tel 352-46-819-26-86
Fax 352-46-54-52

U011 **Union Fund Management**
Europa House, Harcourt Centre
Harcourt Street
Dublin 2
Ireland
Tel 353-1-407-2000
Fax 353-1-475-2466

U012 **Union Investment Luxembourg SA**
4 Rue Thomas Edison
L-1445
Luxembourg
Tel 352-45-98-66-1
Fax 352-25-18-36

U013 **UBK Asset Management (Guernsey) Ltd**
Sydney Vane House P.O Box 105
Rue du Commerce
St Peter Port GY1 3ET
Guernsey
Tel 44-1481-712-472
Fax 44-1481-710-001

U014 **US Advisors (Guernsey) Ltd**
Butterfield House
Roseneath The Grange
St Peter Port GY1 3NQ
Guernsey
Tel 44-1481-720-321
Fax 44-1481-714533

V001 **Value Partners Ltd**
5th Floor Deven House
979 Kings Road
Quarry Bay
Hong Kong
Tel 852-2-880-9263
Fax 852-2-564-8487

V002 **Van Kampen American Company**
47 Boulevard Royal
L-2449
Luxembourg
Tel 352-46-40-10-1
Fax 352-46-36-31

V003 **Voyager - Covenant Capital Management**
Penhouse Suite, 129 Front Street
Hamilton HM12
Bermuda
Tel 1-441-296-4545
Fax 1-441-232-0637

W001 **Wellington**
75 State Street
Boston, Massachussets
MA 02109
U.S.A.
Tel 1-617-951-5000
Fax 1-617-951-5250

W002 **WestLB International SA**
32-34 Boulevard Grande Duchesse Charlotte
L-2014
Luxembourg
Tel 352-44-74-11
Fax 352-44-741210

W003 **Westman & Leander-Engstrom Inv**
2 Cannon Street
London EC4M 6XX
United Kingdom
Tel 44-171-246-4000
Fax 44-171-248-0208

W004 **Willerfunds Management Company**
43 Boulevard Royal
L-2955
Luxembourg
Tel 352-4681-91
Fax 352-46-35-52

W005 **Winterthur Fund Management Company (Luxembourg) SA**
10 Boulevard Grand Duchesse Charlotte
L-1330
Luxembourg
Tel 352-44-41-70
Fax 352-456179

W006 **Worldinvest**
55 Russell Square
London WC1B 4HP
United Kingdom
Tel 44-171-436-7360
Fax 44-171-637-3322

W007 **Worldsec Asset Mgmt Ltd**
2602 Bank of America Tower
12 Harcourt Road
Central
Hong Kong
Tel 852-2867-7283
Fax 852-2810-4638

W008 **Wustenrot Bank AG**
Im Tambour 1
Ludwigsburg 71630
Germany
Tel 49-71-41-16-28-21
Fax 49-71-41-90-29-41

Y001 **Yamaichi**
74-78 Finsbury Pavement
London EC2A 1AT
United Kingdom
Tel 44-171-638-7050
Fax 44-171-638-7060

PART 6

Appendices and index to funds

Appendix 1 Abbreviations: Offshore Performance Tables and Top 350 Funds

ACCUM, Acc
Accumulation or Accumulating

Actns
Actions, Equities

Adj, ADJ
Adjustable

ADR
American Depository Receipts

Adv
Advantage

ADV
Advisory

ADVT
Advantaged

Agg
Aggregate, Aggressive

Am, Amer
America, American

Ans
Answer

App
Appreciation

ASEAN
Association of S.E. Asian Nations

Ast, Aust
Australia, Australasia

AUD, AUS, Austral
Australian Dollar

B'chip
Blue Chip

Bal
Balance, Balanced

Bckd
Backed

Bd,Bds
Bond(s)

bn
Billion

BVI
British Virgin Islands

BWI
British West Indies

C, Cap
Capital, Capitalisation

CanD
Canadian Dollar

Cat
Category

CBOE
Chicago Board of Trade Options Exchange

CD
Certificate of Deposit

CDSC
Contingent Deferred Sales Charge

CFA
Chartered Financial Analyst

Chf
Swiss Francs

CHF(m)
Swiss Franc Monthly Pricing

CI
Channel Islands

CIS
Commonwealth of Independent States

Cl
Closed

Cmn
Common

Co, Cos
Company, Companies

Cons
Consolidated

CONT
Continued

Contl, CONTL
Continental

Conv, Convert
Convertible

CORP
Corporation

Cos
Companies

CPI
Consumer Price Index

Csh
Cash

CT
Convertible

Ctrys
Countries

Curr
Currency

Cycl
Cyclical

D'mark
Deutsch Mark

DEALING
Day / Frequency

Defer
Deferred

DEPT
Department

Discov
Discovery

Dispo
Disposable Credit

Dist, Dis
Distribution, Distributing

DIV
Dividend

Divers'd, Divsfd, DIVERS
Diversified

Dllr
Dollar

DSC
Deferred Sales Charge

DUR
Duration

EAFE
Europe, Australia and the Far East; as in MSCI'S EAFE Index

EC
European Community

ECU
European Currency Unit

Em, Emer, Emerg
Emerging, Emerging Markets

EMDB
Emerging Markets Database

EMEA
Europe, Middle-East and Africa

ENDWMT
Endowment

ent
Enterprise

Eq, Eqs, Eqty
Equities, Equity

Esp & Port
Spanish & Portugal

Est
Estimated, Established

EU
European Union

Eur, Euro
Europe

EUROPAC
Europe and Pacific

Exp
Export

FCP
Fund managed by separate Mgmt Company-Lux, Fonds Commun de Placement

Fd, Fds
Fond, Fund, Funds

Fed
Federal

FED
US Federal Reserve Bank

FI
Fixed Income, Fixed Interest

Fix
Fixed Debt Instrument

FNMA
Federal National Mortgage Association (FANNIE MAE)

Forex, FX
Foreign Exchange

FRA
Forward Rate Agreement

FT
Financial Times of London

FT100
Financial Times Index of 100 Stocks

FTEP
FT – Actuaries Europac Index

Fut
Futures

Fxd
Fixed

G
Growth

G & I
Growth and Income

G'teed, Garant
Guaranteed

G7
Group of Seven

GDP
Gross Domestic Product

GDR
Global Depositary Receipts

GI
Global Income

Glbl
Global

GNP
Gross National Product

Gnsy
Guernsey

Govt
Government

Grs Pf Fee
Gross Performance Fee

Grth, Grwth, Gth
Growth

H
High

He, Hed
Hedge

HI
High Income

HY
High Yield

I, Inc
Income

IC
Income and Capital

ID
Intermediate Duration

IFC
International Finance Corporation

IFCG
IFC Global Index

IFCI
IFC Investable Index

IFS
International Financial Statistics

ILP
Insurance Life Product

IMF
International Monetary Fund

Indx
Index

Info
Information

Infra
Infrastructure

Ins, Insur
Insurance

INSTL
Institutional

INT
Intermediate

Int, Intl, Intern
International

Interoblig
Interobligation

Inv, Invest, Invst
Investment

IPO
Initial Public Offering

IT
Intermediate-term

Ita
Italy

Jap
Japan

JPM
J P Morgan

L.P. LP
Limited Partners, Limited Partnership

Lat
Latin

Laufzeitfds, Lf, LZ
Laufzeitfonds

LDC
Less Developed Countries

Lqd Ass
Liquid Assets

L-T, LT
Long-Term

Ltd, LTD
Limited

Lux, LUX
Luxembourg

LV
Limited Volatility

m, mo
Monthly

M-T
Medium-Term

MAT
Maturity

MBf.
Management group name

Mgd
Managed

Mgmt, MGMT
Management

Mgr
Manager

Mid
Middle

mil
Million

Min
Minimum

Mixte
Mixterm

MKT
Market

Mkt(s)
Market(s)

MM, MMF, MMkt
Money Market

MNGD
Managed Money Market

Mny
Money

MOF
Ministry of Finance

MORT
Mortgage

MS
Multi-Sector

MSCI
Morgan Stanley Capital International

MSCI EAFE
See EAFE

MT
Medium-Term

MUT
Mutual

MX
Mixed

Natl, NATL
National

NAV
Net Asset Value

NO
Number

Nth
North

O'seas
Overseas

Obli, Oblig
Obligation- Bond

Obli-Fix
Obligation- Fix

Offshr
Offshore

Op, Opps
Opportunity

Opt
Optimum

Or
Organisation

P
Performance

Pac
Pacific

PERF
Performance

Pnd
Pound

PORT, Portf, Ptfl
Portfolio

Port
Portugal

PRC
People's Republic of China

Prec
Precious

Prev
Previous

Prf Ind
Preferred Index

PRTNERS, Ptnrs
Partners

Prop
Property

Protec
Protection

Ptas, PTS
Pesetas

Q
Fund name

QLTY
Quality

QROES
Quarterly Review of Emerging Stock

Quant
Quantities

Quart
Quarterly, Quartile

Rec
Recovery

Rent, Rnt
Renten

Res
Reserve

Ret
Return

RIYd
Real Income Yield

RSRV
Reserves

S&P 500
Standard & Poor's 500 Composite Index

S.E.
South East

SB
Short Bond

Sci
Science

SD
Short Duration

SEC
Securities and Exchange Commission, Securities

Secs
Securities

SEDOL
Stock Exchange Daily Official List (London Stock Exchange)

Sel
Selection

Shr, Shs
Share

Sht
Short

SICAF
Corporate Structure with Fixed Capital

SICAV
Corporate Structure with Variable Capital-Lux, Société d'Investissement à Capital Variable

Sing
Singapore

Sits
Situations

Sm
Small

Sml
Smaller

Sov
Sovereign

SP, Sp
Specialized

Span
Spanish

Spec
Speculative

ST
Short-Term

St.Ass
Standard Assortment

Stk
Stock

Stkmkt
Stock market

Stlg
Sterling

STRAT
Strategic

Sv
SICAV

T-BILL
Treasury Bill

Tech
Technology, Technical

Terme
Maturity, End

Tgr
Tiger

Thai
Thailand

TR
Total Return

Tr
Trans

Treas
Treasury, Treasuries

Tst,Trust
Type of fund

UCITS
Undertakings for Collective Investments in Transferable Securities

UK
United Kingdom

UK FT100
See FT100

Underval
Undervalued

US
United States of America

US S&P 500
See S&P 500

Val
Value

VAR
Variable

WA, Warr
Warrants

Ww
World Wide

XEU
ECU

Yd, Yld
Yield

YOY
Year on Year

YTD
Year To Date

Abbreviations: Currency Country/Domicile

	Currency		Country/Domicile
ARA	Argentine Peso	**AR**	Argentina
AUD	Australian Dollar	**AUS**	Australia
ATS	Australian Schilling	**AUT**	Austria
BAD	Bahamian Dollar	**BAH**	Bahamas
BEF	Belgian Franc	**BEL**	Belgium
BED	Bermuda Dollar	**BER**	Bermuda
BRC	Brazilian Reals	**BZ**	Brazil
USD	British Virgin Island- US Dollar	**BVI**	British Virgin Islands
CAD	Canadian Dollar	**CAN**	Canada
CD	Cayman Dollar	**CA**	Cayman Islands
CLP	Chilean Peso	**CHI**	Chile
COP	Colombian Peso	**CB**	Colombian
DEM	German Mark	**GER**	Germany
DKK	Danish Kroner	**DEN**	Denmark
ECU	European Community Unit	**EU**	Europe
FIM	Finnish Marks	**FIN**	Finland
FRF	French Franc	**FRA**	France
GPD	Guernsey Pound	**GU**	Guernsey
GRD	Greek Drachma	**GRK**	Greece
HKD	Hong Kong Dollar	**HK**	Hong Kong
INR	Indian Rupee	**IND**	India
IDR	Indonesian Rupiah	**INO**	Indonesia
IEP/IRP	Irish Punt	**IRL**	Ireland
IMP	Isle of Man Pound	**IOM**	Isle of Man
ITL	Italian Lire	**ITL**	Italy
JPY	Japanese Yen	**JAP**	Japan
JP	Jersey Pound	**JER**	Jersey
KWD	Kuwaiti Dinar	**KUW**	Kuwait
LUF	Luxembourg Franc	**LUX**	Luxembourg
MXP	Mexican Peso	**MEX**	Mexico
NLG	Netherlands Guilder	**NL**	Netherlands
NTD	NEW Taiwan Dollar	**TW**	Taiwan
NZD	New Zealand Dollar	**NZ**	New Zealand
NOK	Norwegian Krone	**NOR**	Norway
USD	Panama - US Dollar	**PAN**	Panama
PHP	Philippine Peso	**PH**	Philippines
PTE	Portugese Escudo	**PO**	Portugal
SAR	Saudi Arabian Riyal	**SAU**	Saudi Arabia
SGD	Singapore Dollar	**SIN**	Singapore
ZAR	South Africa Rand	**SA**	South Africa
WON	South Korean Won	**KW**	Korea
ESP	Spanish Peseta	**SPA**	Spain
SEK	Swedish Krone	**SWE**	Sweden
CHF	Swiss Franc	**CH**	Switzerland
THB	Thailand Baht	**TH**	Thailand
USD	US Dollar	**USA**	United States
GBP	UK Sterling Pound	**UK**	United Kingdom
VEB	Venezuelan Bolivar	**VZ**	Venezuela

Abbreviations: Publications

	Currency	Country/Domicile
AS	Austrian Standard	
AW	Asian Wall Street Journal	
BG	Bloomberg	
BL	Bourse De Luxembourg	
BP	Belgian Press	
BPN	Banque Paribas Network	
BZ	Borsenzeitung	
CH	Cash	
CL	Cote Official du Luxembourg	
CS	Corriere della Sera	
DI	Dagens Industri	
DN	Dagens Nyheter	
DP	Die Presse	
DS	Der Standart	
EB	Echo DÕel Bourse	
EJ	Economic Journal	
EX	Extel	
FE	Financial Ekonomische	
FN	Finnish Press	
FP	Financial Press	
FT	Financial Times	
FW	Finanz Wirtschaft	
GE	Guernsey Evening Press	
GN	German Newspaper	
HB	Handlesblatt	
HF	Hedge Fund	
HF	HET Financielle Dagblad	
HKEJ	Hong Kong Economic Journal	
HKET	Hong Kong Economic Times	
HTE	Herald Tribune Europe	
HZ	Hanleszentung	
IG	Il Giornale	
IHT	International Herald Tribune	
IN	Internet	
IR	Investir	
IS	Il Sole 24 Ore	
JE	Jersey Evening Post	
JG	Journal de Geneve	
JO	Journal Officiel du Luxembourg	
LE	Les Echos (French Newpaper)	
LEB	LÕEcho (Belgium)	
LN	Luxembourg Newspaper	
LP	Lipper	
LS	Le Soir	
LUX	Luxemburgian	
LW	Luxembourg Wort	
MF	Milano Finanza	
MM	Money Management	
MP	Micropal	
MT	Minitel	
NZZ	Neu Zuricher Zeitung	
PI	Portfolio Investment	
RA	Resident Abroad, The International	
RG	Royal Gazette (Bermuda)	
RL	Royal Life International	
RT	Reuters	
SC	South China Morning Post	
SD	Svenska Dagbladet	
SN	Swedish Newspapers	
TF	Tribune Des Fosses	
TK	Telekurs	
TS	Telekins	
VW	VWD	
WB	Wiener Borse	
WS	Wall Street Journal Europe	

Appendix 2 The Most Frequently Asked Questions about Offshore Funds*

1. **What is an offshore fund?**
Offshore funds are subject to simplified regulation and generally designed for a more sophisticated investor. They can use leverage to increase the performance of the fund and will often invest in instruments or markets that have a higher risk associated with them. Although they are frequently resident in offshore islands such as the Channel or Caribbean islands, the term "offshore" more generally relates to the degrees of external regulation than their location.

2. **What are the tax advantages of an offshore fund?**
Offshore funds are generally managed within a tax neutral environment and will not be subject to most forms of income or capital gains tax. Dividends will generally be paid without deduction, although investors should be aware that certain income receivable by the fund may be subject to withholding taxes deducted from dividends paid on the underlying investments.

3. **What are the main differences between an open-ended investment company, a UK authorised unit trust and a UCITS?**
Unit trusts have been the traditional investment vehicle used for collective investments in the UK but they have largely been ignored by the rest of Europe since they are generally not understood.
To allow the UK industry to sell its products more effectively in the rest of Europe, open-ended investment companies (OEICS) are now being introduced. These are a new form of UK company, but perform a similar function to unit trusts by allowing investors easy access to an investment which benefits from professional investment management and the spreading of risk. They both have similar investment restrictions and may be sold to the general public in the UK.
Both OEICs and UK authorised unit trusts can be a UCITS. A UCITS is an Undertaking for Collective Investments in Transferable Securities and the term relates to funds which comply with the European Union's directive. This allows for the sale of such funds operated in any one state of the Union into all its states.
The major difference between a unit trust and an OEIC is that whilst a unit trust will buy and sell units at bid and offer prices, OEICs will deal at a single price.

4. **Which funds can or can't I buy?**
Investors from certain world-wide jurisdictions may not be eligible to invest in offshore funds. For example, US residents are unlikely to be acceptable as offshore registered investors. Once again, a fund's prospectus should be closely scrutinised for any prevailing restrictions.
The financial regulations in certain jurisdictions mean that fund managers who are neither registered nor authorised in a particular country may not be able to distribute information directly to potential investors. Under certain circumstances, distribution may be permitted through properly regulated financial intermediaries.

5. **I am UK resident, a "sophisticated" investor and don't want to use an intermediary. Why can information on offshore funds only be sent direct to professional advisors?**
Information on SIB registered offshore funds can be issued, but the Financial Services Act imposes tight constraints on the distribution of information on non-SIB recognised funds to private individuals in the UK.

6. **Are offshore funds "PEP-able"?**
No. There are strict rules which specify the type of fund which can be included in a personal equity plan. These include UK authorised unit trusts and investment trusts.

7. **Do offshore funds provide any investor protection or compensation?**
It depends on where the fund is operated. There may be some degree of compensation arrangements in certain jurisdictions but generally, investors would be wise to assume that compensation is unlikely.
For this reason, investors are recommended only to utilise the funds promoted by major investment groups and where there is evidence of a properly structured custodial and administrative regime.

8. **Why can't a US citizen invest in offshore funds?**
They can, but there are SEC regulations which constrain the availability of offshore funds to most US investors. In many cases, an investment house will offer a range of domestic funds designed specifically to meet the needs of US investors.

9. **What is meant by Distributor Status? Can I buy such a fund?**
Distributor status is relevant to UK investors only. If a fund has not been granted UK distributor status, this means that a UK investor will be subject to income tax on any realised capital gains. So the investor will not be able to take advantage of the

annual CGT (Capital Gains Tax) allowance and indexation on any gains.

An investor should examine closely the fund's investment objective/s. For example, if it is to achieve capital appreciation, income may not be available to distribute as dividends. Funds with distributor status will distribute at least 85 percent of their annual income net of expenses.

In addition to reviewing the relevant fund documentation (specifically the prospectus and financial statements) investors should consult their own advisors on taxation and exchange control implications of their acquiring, holding or disposing of shares under the laws of their respective jurisdiction.

Many of the prospectuses do summarise taxation issues based on the law and practice in force in specific countries. Again, investors should examine the relevant prospectus in detail to ensure that the fund is appropriate for their needs.

10. Should I choose "Certificated" or "Inscribed" shares?

The inscribed (non-certificated) approach is designed to speed up redemption procedures. Generally, investors will be required (on their application form) to include details of where proceeds should be paid, together with their full name and registered address.

Subsequently, investors will generally be permitted to give redemption instructions by telephone, fax or other means; and proceeds would be paid only to the designated account.

In the case of certificated shares, the certificates must be sent to the registrar before the proceeds of the investor's sale can be implemented.

11. Is there a different price for buying or selling?

Typically, offshore funds quote a single net asset value (NAV) price to which an initial charge may be added. On redemption, the investor will receive the then current NAV price – generally without further deduction.

Funds are priced on either a forward or historic basis. Most funds are established on a forward price basis, which means that the price is calculated after all the investments for that day have been received. In other words, the investor will not know the price at which the deal is struck until after the completion of the dealing day.

12. What are the charges associated with my investments?

The charges made by offshore funds generally fall into three principal categories.

Initial Charge: This may be anything between 0% to 6% and may be an identifiable charge or may be incorporated into the subscription price or deducted separately.

Annual Charges: These will typically include management and administration fees, investment management fee, promoters fee, "other" expenses (audit, custodian, trustee and general out of pocket expenses). These will generally be effected as a percentage charge based upon the asset value of the fund except in those cases where items are specifically identifiable.

Performance Fees: These are normally fees paid to the investment advisor and computed on the degree of capital appreciation achieved during any designated period and by reference to pre-selected bench marks.

As a general rule, investors should always examine the relevant prospectus of any fund in which they are contemplating an investment in order to ascertain the level of charges and then examine the latest audited accounts of that fund to see how these charges actually impact.

13. What is the minimum investment?

The minimum investment required will vary from fund to fund and can be anything from $1000 USD (or even less) to $50,000 USD (and more in the case of some "institutional" funds).

14. Can I spread my minimum investment across several funds?

This depends on the management group – check with them.

15. Will I receive a discount on a large investment?

Some companies offer discounts on large orders, but it is usually necessary to ask for a discount at the time the order is placed.

16. How can I pay for my shares?

You could send a cheque – but often this introduces delays and costs to the process, particularly if the cheque is not in the base currency of the fund. Investors frequently underestimate the time taken to collect on cheques drawn against some banks, and most companies will not permit investment until cleared funds are obtained.

Where possible, wire transfers (telegraphic transfers) should be used.

17. How do I implement a transfer (switch) between two funds managed by the same group and how much will this cost?

This will depend on the fund group. Usually a simple instruction to make the switch is adequate, but with some funds, particularly those which invest in illiquid markets, a "Notice of Redemption" period may be imposed. In such cases the switch will be carried out at the end of the notice period. Details will be found in the prospectus.

18. I am looking for a fund which will give me a high income; what do you recommend?

You should seek the advice of a professional advisor who will take every aspect of your personal circumstances into account (e.g. your tax position, willingness to accept risk, specific income needs, etc.). Some equity funds generate a fairly high income, but a better yield can often be achieved from a fund investing in fixed interest securities.

However, fixed interest funds may not offer the long-term potential for capital and income growth provided by a well-managed equity fund.

19. What's the difference between yield and total return?

Yield is the calculation of the projected income of the fund as a percentage of the current price per share.

The term "total return" is a measure of the per-share change in total value from the beginning to the end of a specified period, including distributions paid to shareholders. This measure includes income received from dividends, interest and capital gains.

Total return provides the best measure of overall fund performance.

20. Do I have access to my money invested in an offshore fund?

Yes. Unlike some other investments, you can sell your holding in an offshore fund on any day the fund is open for business (each "Dealing Day"). You should note however that some funds, particularly those which invest in illiquid markets, may impose a "Notice of redemption" period. In such cases, the redemption will be carried out at the end of the redemption period.

21. Are money market funds a good investment?

Generally the return from these will be slightly higher than that which could be achieved from a domestic bank. They can also be a convenient place to park your money for the short term, awaiting investment during periods of stock market volatility.

22. How do I know what my fund is doing?

Offshore fund's NAV or prices are published in many newspapers and publications such as the *Financial Times*, *Wall Street Journal (Europe or Asia Edition)*, *International Herald Tribune*, *Singapore Business Times* and *The South China Morning Post*. The Internet is also a fast growing medium through which such information can be obtained.

At least annually, you will also usually be sent financial information containing details of the stocks held in the portfolio and a commentary from the fund manager about the performance of the fund and his views on the market.

23. What is a "fund of funds"?

To offer investors a wide spread of investment – without having too complex a portfolio, some groups offer an asset allocation product investing in the group's other funds. The fund manager will therefore buy and sell shares of "funds" in the portfolio rather than individual stocks.

This may result in some duplication of charges.

24. What is a hedge fund?

A hedge fund is any fund that can use hedging techniques within its portfolio. These can include short selling of stocks or index futures or the use of options or other derivatives. However, within this definition there is an enormous range: at one extreme there are simple equity funds that include a few short positions to reduce their exposure to stock market volatility, while at the other there are global "macro" funds which make enormously leveraged bets on the movement of major bond, equity or currency markets.

25. How is investment risk measured?

There is no satisfactory single measure and much depends on the objectives of the investor. For private investors, two commonly used statistics are standard deviation and maximum drawdown. Standard deviation measures the variability of return from period to period. An investment with very variable returns would be measured as having a high standard deviation (risk), even if the returns were all positive. Maximum drawdown measures the worst ever fall that the investment has suffered from peak to subsequent trough and thus gives an indication of the potential loss to which an investor would have been exposed. Taken together, these two measure provide a useful guide to investment risk.

* *Courtesy of Global Asset Management*

Appendix 3 The Micropal Star Rating™

To assist investors evaluate the performance of a fund and the consistency of that performance relative to other funds in the sector, Micropal has developed the Micropal Star Rating(TM) based on a fund's relative performance. The Micropal Star Rating(TM) is calculated using a funds monthly performance relative to its sector average for each of the 36 months over the three years to date. The average and volatility of these 36 numbers is used to calculate a funds star rating.

RELATIVE PERFORMANCE

This is the performance of the fund less the performance of its sector average. Thus if the fund rises 6% in a month and its sector average by 4% in the same month then the funds relative performance is +2%. This number is calculated for each of the last 36 months.

AVERAGE RELATIVE PERFORMANCE

By calculating the average of the fund's latest 36 monthly relative performances we are measuring its ability on average to out or under perform the other funds in its sector. The higher the average the more the fund has outperformed its peers over the 36 months.

VOLATILITY OF RELATIVE PERFORMANCE

Volatility (Standard Deviation) is a statistical method to measure how much a series of values deviates (how much it moves up and down) about its average. By calculating the volatility of the fund's 36 monthly relative performances we are measuring how consistently the fund has out or under performed its peers. The higher the volatility the less consistent the funds performance relative to its peers.

RELATIVE RETURN / VOLATILITY RATIO

By dividing the funds average relative performance by the volatility of its relative performance we are measuring its ability to not only outperform its peers but to also do so consistently. The higher the ratio the greater the funds ability to out perform its peers and on a consistent basis.

$$\frac{\text{Average monthly relative performance over 3 years (Relative return)}}{\text{Volatility of monthly relative performance over 3 years (Volatility ratio)}} = \text{Micropal Star Ratio}$$

ALLOCATION OF THE MICROPAL STAR RATING(TM)

An Illustration:

Suppose a sector contains 100 funds then:

The Micropal Star Rating(TM)

✪✪✪✪✪	top 10%	10 funds
✪✪✪✪	top 11-30%	20 funds
✪✪✪	top 31-50%	20 funds
✪✪	next 25%	25 funds
✪	bottom 25%	25 funds

ILLUSTRATIONS

Example 1

A fund with a ratio in the top 10% of its sector receives 5 stars, whilst a fund with a ratio in the bottom 25% of its sector receives a 1 star.

	Return	Volatility	Ratio	Rank	Star Rating
Fund A	50%	5	10.0	1	✪✪✪✪✪
Fund B	30%	6	5.0	4	✪✪
Fund C	10%	4	2.5	5	✪
Fund D	30%	4	7.5	2	✪✪✪✪
Fund E	40%	6	6.6	3	✪✪✪

Example 2

Funds with identical performance but different volatility will have different ratio – thus whilst the rewards measured by the return of Fund F and Fund G are identical, the consistency as indicated by the volatility of Fund G is less than the consistency of Fund F, so that the ratio of Fund F is higher than for Fund G.

	Return	Volatility	Ratio	Rank
Fund F	50%	5	10.0	1
Fund G	50%	6	8.3	2

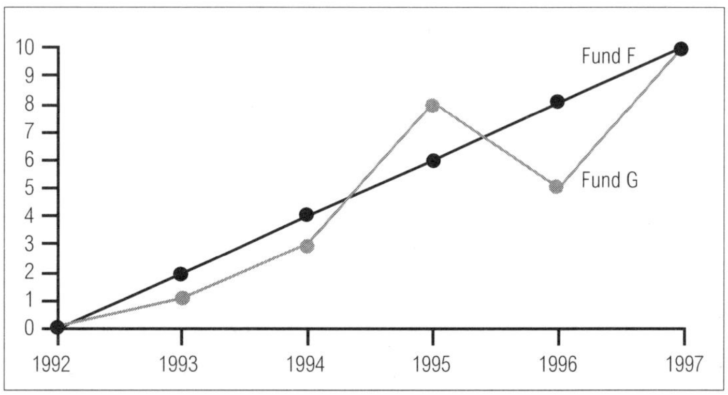

Example 3

However, funds with different performances and different volatilities can have the same Star Rating. Funds H & J have the same ratio. However, Fund H has a higher return than Fund J, while Fund J has the lower volatility.

	Return	Volatility	Ratio
Fund H	50%	5	10.0
Fund J	40%	4	10.0

Under this example both Funds H and J will be awarded the same Star Rating, as although their performance and volatility are different, the relationship of the consistency experienced by each to its performance is identical.

Appendix 4 Publications to Monitor Offshore Investment Funds

PERIODICALS

Expat Investor
Tolley Publishing, 2 Addiscombe Road, Croydon,
Surrey CR9 5AF, UK
Tel 44-171-686-9141 Fax 44-181-760-0588

Global Investing
PO Box 1945, Fort Collins, Colorado 80522-1945, USA
Tel 704-493-3793 Fax 970-221-3964
E-mail 70632,152@compuserve.com

Global Mutual Fund Investor
14 W.Mt. Vernon Pl. Baltimore, MD 21201 USA
Tel 410-783-8440 Fax 410-783-8438

The International
Financial Times Magazines, Greystoke Place,
Fetter Lane, London EC4A 1ND, UK
Tel 44-171-405-6969 Fax 44-171-831-2181

International Fund Investment
63 Long Acre, London WC2E 9JH, UK
Tel 44-171-836-4802 Fax 44-171-240-2254

International Money Marketing
St. Giles House, 50 Poland Street, London W1V 4AX, UK
Tel 44-171-287-5678 Fax 44-171-287-5136

Investment International
4 Tabernacle Street, London EC2A 4LU, UK
Tel 44-171-638-1916 Fax 44-171-638-3128

Offshore Financial Review
Financial Times Magazines, Maple House,
149 Tottenham Court Road, London W1P 9LL, UK
Tel 44-171-896-2508 Fax 44-171-831-9136

Portfolio International
Thames House, 18 Park Street, London SE1 9ER, UK
Tel 44-171-896-2508 Fax 44-171-403-4682

Resident Abroad
Financial Times Magazines, Greystoke Place,
Fetter Lane, London EC4A 1ND, UK
Tel 44-171-405-6969 Fax 44-171-831-2181
Internet http:/www.iii.co.uk/ftmags/international

NEWSPAPERS

The Financial Times
149 Tottenham Court Road, London W1P 9LI, UK
Tel 44-171-873-3000 Fax 44-171-831-9136
USA Tel 1-800-568-7625

The International Herald Tribune
181 Avenue Charles-de-Gaulle,
92521, Neuilly-sur-Seine, France
Tel 41-43-93-00 Fax 41-43-92-10
E-mail iht@iht.com
USA Tel 1-212-752-3890 USA Tel 1-800-882-2884

South China Morning Post
GPO Box 47, Hong Kong
Tel 852-26808661 Fax 852-26808688
UK Tel 44-171-5873683

The Wall Street Journal
Circulation Department, PO Box 2845,
In de Creamer 37, 6401 DH Heerlen, The Netherlands
Tel 31-45-576-1222 Fax 31-45-571-4722
USA Tel 1-800-568-7625
UK Tel 44-181-944-5922 UK Fax 44-181-944-5921
HK Tel 852-5737121 HK Fax 852-8345291

The Wall Street Journal Europe
Rufus Business Centre, Ravensbury Terrace,
London, SW18, UK
Tel 44-181-944-5922 Fax 44-181-944-5921

Website - Micropal
www.micropal.com

Appendix 5 Glossary

Acceptance
A bill of exchange guaranteed by a bank and made eligible to be sold at the maximum rate.

Accumulating Fund
This type of fund re-invests income and capital gains in other investable assets. The investment return from an accumulating fund is included in the appreciation or depreciation of its unit price. At their discretion, fund managers may distribute income to unit holders.

Actively Hedged Funds
These can be invested in equities, fixed interest and money market instruments. The fund managers can speculate in the derivatives market and/or employ hedging techniques, utilizing various option contracts.

Administration Fee
This is the fee paid to the fund administrator and is usually a minimum amount or a percentage of the fund's net asset value.

Advisor
The organization employed by a mutual fund / unit trust to give professional advice on the fund's investments and asset management practices.

Advisory Client
A client who is given investment recommendations by a broker but is responsible for the decisions made. The other types of relationships between broker and client are discretionary, where the broker makes investment decisions, and execution-only, where the client makes decisions but receives no advice from the broker.

Agency Broker
A broker acts as an agent between buyer and seller but is not, in the UK context, a market maker.

Aggressive Growth Funds
These seek maximum capital gains as an investment objective, while income is not a significant factor. Some funds may invest in stocks of businesses that are somewhat out of the mainstream, such as fledgling companies, new industries, companies fallen on hard times, or industries temporarily out of favour. Others may also use specialized investment techniques such as option writing or short-term trading.

American Depository Receipt (ADR)
This is a negotiable certificate representing ownership of shares in a non-US company. ADRs are issued by US banks and are traded in the domestic securities market. The certificates indicate the number of foreign securities held by the US bank in the country of origin. ADRs are also called American Depository Shares.

Amortization
The allocation of portions of an asset's cost to specified periods of time.

Amounts Outstanding
Total balances (including accrued charges) still owed by the debtor at the end of a particular accounting period.

Annualized Mean
Twelve times the annual mean of monthly percent changes.

Annualized Standard Deviation
The standard deviation of the monthly percent changes multiplied by the square root of twelve.

Annual Report
Annual accounts which contain a review of a fund's current financial status and a summary of the changes that have occurred in the past year.

Approved Investment Trust
A trust which satisfies the requirements of Section 842 of the UK's Income and Corporation Taxes Act 1988 as amended by Section 117 of the Finance Act 1988 and is therefore exempt from tax on the capital gains realized from the sale of investments within its portfolio.

Arbitrage
A means of exploiting price differences for similar instruments between different markets. An early example of arbitrage occurred in the dollar/sterling markets in New York and London. Because prices in the two markets sometimes differed, traders could occasionally buy dollars or pounds in one market, and sell them immediately in the other for a profit. As a result of satellite communications, such geographical arbitrage is now rare. Modern arbitrage occurs frequently in the cash and futures markets, or it can involve options. It is a purely professional occupation, since most opportunities are only available for a few seconds.

Asked or Offering Price
The price at which a mutual fund's shares or a unit trust's units can be purchased, or the current net asset value per share plus sales charge, if any.

Asset Protection Trust
A trust established offshore to protect a settlor's assets against those who may attempt to make claims against the settlor-creditors, former spouses and dependents on death.

Asset Swaps
By taking advantage of market imperfections, a fixed-rate asset can, theoretically, be transferred into a floating-rate one, either in the same currency or a different one. Known as synthetic securities, asset swaps can be used to spot pricing anomalies in the bond and swaps markets, which can be exploited accordingly.

Association of Investment Trust Companies (AITC)
The collective voice for UK investment trusts, which acts to protect, promote and advance the common interests of its member trusts and their shareholders.

Back-to-Back Loan
A form of medium- to long-term financing by which a UK company, for example, may borrow foreign currency and at the same time purchase UK government bonds of equal value and maturity, or deposit an equal amount of sterling in a deposit account.

Balanced Funds
These generally have a three-part investment objective: 1) to conserve the investor's initial principal; 2) to pay current income; and 3) to promote long-term growth of both this principal and income. Balanced funds usually have a portfolio mix of bonds, preferred, and common stocks.

Balance Sheet
The statement of the capital position of a company, showing what it owns (assets) and what it owes (liabilities). Normally companies produce an independently audited balance sheet and financial statement once a year in their annual report.

Base Currency
In principle, this is the currency in which a fund maintains its accounts. However, sub-funds within an umbrella structure may be denominated in different currencies. The investments or holdings of a fund may also be denominated in currencies other than the base currency.

Bear
This term describes an investor who thinks that a market will fall. The term also refers to a short position held by a market maker and a market where prices are falling over an extended period.

Bearer Bond
A bond which can be redeemed by whoever presents it at the redemption date, rather than by the person who owns it.

Bearer Security
A bond or share whose ownership is not recorded on a central register and is therefore the equivalent of cash in a capital market. See registered securities.

Beneficial Owner
The person who really owns a security rather than a nominee that may own shares on behalf of others.

Bid or Sell Price
The price at which a mutual fund's shares or a unit trust's units can be redeemed (bought back) by the fund. The bid or redemption price usually means the current net asset value per share.

Bid/Offer Spread
The difference in price between the bid and offer prices at any given time.

Billion (bn)
1,000 million.

Blind Trust
A trust in which the trustees are contractually prevented from providing any information to the beneficiaries about the administration of assets of the trust.

Blue Chip
The term given to shares of well-known, long established companies which often have large market capitalization, a high degree of liquidity within the stock markets and usually pay dividends. The term was named after the highest value chip in poker.

Bonds
An interest-bearing security which charges the issuer to pay to the holder the par value plus interest (coupon value) at some future date or over a period of time. The time schedule of the repayment varies with the type of bond. Be aware that in the UK, bonds are referred to as gilts or stocks.

Bottom-Up
Refers to a type of security analysis. Management that follows this approach is more concerned with the company involved rather than with the economy in general. (See Top-Down.)

Box
An amount of cash reserves required by UK regulations to meet unit holder redemptions at any given time.

Brady Bonds
These are issued to commercial banks by debtor countries to repay defaulted developing country loans. These bonds, named after former US Treasury Secretary Nicholas Brady, are partially collateralized by the US Treasury Department.

Break-up Basis
This is a way of calculating net asset values by which prior charges are deducted at nominal or redemption value. (Commonly used by UK investment trusts.)

Broker/Dealer
A firm that buys and sells mutual fund shares and other securities to the public.

BTANs
(Bons du Tresor a taux annuel) French fixed-rate, two or five year Treasury notes.

BTFs
(Bons du Tresor a taux fixe) French fixed rate, short term discount Treasury bills.

Building Societies
A UK financial institiution that accepts the savings of small depositors and lends them to home buyers in return for the security of a mortgage on the property.

Bull

A term used to describe an investor who thinks the market will rise. It also refers to a long position held by a market maker and to a market where prices are on a rising trend. Investors who think a market will rise are bullish.

Bulldogs

Sterling denominated bonds issued in the United Kingdom by overseas borrowers.

Bunds (Bundesanleihen)

German long term Federal Government bonds.

Call

An option to buy a share or commodity at a set price for a set term.

Capital Gains Distributions

Payments to mutual fund shareholders of profits (long-term gains) realized on the sale of the fund's portfolio securities. These distributions may be paid once a year.

Capital Growth

An increase in the market value of a mutual fund's unit trusts securities, which is reflected in the net asset value of its shares. This is a specific long-term objective of many mutual funds.

Cash Market

The market in the underlying security/ or for immediate delivery.

Cash Ratio

The proportion of a fund's assets which it considers prudent to keep in the form of cash.

Certificate of Deposit (CD)

This is a tradeable bank deposit used by institutional investors who put their money with a bank and get a three-month CD instead of having to deposit that money for three months. If their circumstances change, the institution can sell the bill in the money market. Because they are negotiable, CDs tend to pay a slightly lower rate of interest than conventional deposits.

Certificated Share

A share of stock for which a certificate is issued and registered as being owned by a specific holder or nominee. The majority of shareholders usually find non-certificated (bearer) shares to be more convenient.

Chartered Financial Analyst (CFA)

This is a highly desired title for investment managers who select securities for sale or purchase.

Circulating Capital

A hedged, dollar-denominated subordinated loan bond with current dollar assets.

Closed-Ended Funds

A collective investment scheme, such as a UK investment trust, which has a fixed capital structure. Variations in demand for the shares of the fund are reflected in the movements in their market price which may reflect a premium or a discount in their net asset value.

Commercial Bill

This bill is used as an international payment system that guarantees to pay for exported goods when they are delivered some months hence. For example, to ease his cash flow, an exporter sells a commercial bill to a merchant bank (often an accepting house) at a discount from its total value. The bank guarantees the bill and sells it on at a higher price because of the bank's credit worthiness. The discounted bill is then traded as a money market instrument.

Commodity Funds

These funds invest in shares of companies that operate in commodity related industries or hold physical commodities such as bullion.

Consolidated Accounts

The accounts of a group of companies or subsidiaries which are amalgamated to give an overall financial picture.

Conversion Premium

The difference between the price of a convertible bond or preferred share and the underlying equity conversion value. For example, if the convertible trades at $100 and the underlying shares trade at $80, the conversion premium is $20 (or 25 percent).

Convertibles with high conversion premiums are traded in the same say as straight bonds, while convertibles with low premiums are traded as underlying shares would be.

Convertible

A bond or share which has the option to convert into another bond or share at a fixed date or set of dates and under fixed terms.

Corporate Bond Funds

These funds seek a high level of income by buying corporation bonds as the basis of the portfolio, with the remainder in US Treasury bonds/gilts or bonds issued by a government agency.

Cost of carry

The difference between the cost of borrowing money and the yield which the investment offers.

Country Fund

A mutual fund which may be closed-ended or open-ended and has more than 70 per cent of its assets invested in a specific country.

Coupon

The amount of interest which a bond pays on its nominal value, rather than its yield, which is the rate of interest the bond pays based on the market price of the bond. The coupon refers to the fact that bonds historically have had detachable interest payment coupons attached to them.

Consumer Price Index (CPI)

The commonly used yardstick for measuring the rate of inflation in the US.

Cross-Currency Interest Rate Swaps

A combination currency/interest rate swap, identical to a fixed currency asset except that one or both sets of interest payments are on a floating-rate basis.

Currency Exposure

The net effect in terms of exposure to a currency after taking into account the equity investments, bonds and net cash held in that currency, deducting any prior capital and loans in that currency and adjusting for the effect of any forward exchange or hedging commitments involving that currency.

Currency Forward

see Forward.

Custodian

An organization, usually a bank, that keeps custody of securities and other assets of a mutual fund, and may perform dividend and interest collection services. Custodians normally receive a fee for their services ranging from 0.1% to 0.25% p.a. of the NAV.

Dealings

Day of record when a fund sells or redeems its shares/units.

Debentures

bond or loan which is unsecured by any collateral and ranks as secondary to secured borrowing.

Debt Ratio

The total borrowings divided by the capital employed.

Derivatives

The right or obligation to purchase or sell an equity interest at some future time. Futures, options and warrants, are examples of derivative instruments, which are normally purchased on margin.

Designated Territory

A location recognized by the UK's Securities and Investments Board (SIB) as having investor protection arrangements at least equivalent to those in the UK.

Diluted Net Asset Value

A means of calculating a company's net asset value having factored in outstanding convertible loan stocks, warrants or options and assuming that shareholders have exercised their right to convert or subscribe to the aforementioned, thus increasing the number of shares among which the assets are now divided.

Discount Broker

A broker who provides a "no-frills" service for buying and selling securities. In practice, this means that the commission rates charged are lower, as no investment advice, analysis or research is offered.

The difference between the market price and the net asset value (NAV) of an investment company's ordinary shares. If the market price is less than the NAV per share, the shares are standing at a discount; if the market price is greater than the NAV, the shares are trading at a premium. The discount or premium is expressed as a percentage of the NAV.

For example, if an investment trust's NAV is \$25 per share and the market price of the share is \$20, the discount is \$5 (or 20% of the NAV), that is:

$$\frac{25 - 20}{(25)} \times 100 = 20\%$$

Conversely, if the NAV is \$24 and the market price is \$26.40, the premium is \$2.40 (or 10% of the NAV) – that is:

$$\frac{26.40 - 24}{(24)} \times 100 = 10\%$$

Discretionary

An arrangement made with a stockbroker who has discretion to buy or sell shares best suited to the client's situation. Clients can put limits on discretionary accounts.

Discretionary Trust

The form of trust where the trustees are invested with the powers to decide which of the beneficiaries is to benefit, when and to what extent. Discretionary powers may be excercised under advice of or suggestions from the settlor or protector.

Distributing Fund

A fund which distributes investment income or capital gain to shareholders.

Distributor/Promoter/Marketer

An organization which buys or sells shares of a fund through a custodian and distributes market information about the fund to the investing public. The fund distributor may be the investment manager of the fund as well.

Distributor Status

A fund that pays out dividends equal to at least 85 percent of the fund's income, which are taxed as if they were capital by the Inland Revenue in the UK.

Diversification
The policy of all mutual funds is to spread investments among a number of different securities in order to reduce the risk inherent in investing.

Dividend
That part of a company's annual distributable profits which is paid to the shareholders, usually expressed as an amount per share.

Dividend Yield
Total cash dividends paid as a percent of market capitalization at the end of the period.

Dollar-Cost Averaging
The practice of investing equal amounts of money at regular intervals regardless of whether securities markets are moving up or down. This procedure reduces the average share costs to the investor who acquires more shares during the periods of lower security prices and fewer shares in periods of higher prices.

Domicile
Where funds are registered, i.e. based for tax and regulatory purposes.

Dragon Bonds
Bonds that are priced, launched and syndicated in the Asia-Pacific region outside Japan and may be listed in the Hong Kong, Taiwan or Singapore financial markets.

Earnings Per Share
Total earnings of a company divided by the number of its shares.

Earnings Yield
Earnings per share dividend, divided by the market price per share.

ECU (European Currency Unit)
A basket currency containing fixed percentages of European currencies, except sterling. At present these percentages are renegotiated every five years, with the weighting of each currency in rough proportion to the size of its economy. Because of Germany's economic strength, the ECU is dominated by the mark.

Emerging Markets
Defined by the World Bank as those economies having a GNP per capita of less than $8,626 in 1993.

EMS
The European Monetary System is a package of proposals designed to make the EC's economics move closer together or converge. It includes the European Currency Unit (ECU) and the Exchange Rate Mechanism (the ERM) and the currency bands.

EMTN (Euro medium term note)
Medium term bonds issued as required by governments on the Euromarkets.

Equity
The money value of "shares" and "stock", usually meaning ordinary or preferred shares of a company. These shares represent an ownership interest in a company and may have voting or non-voting privileges.

Eurobond
Corporate or government bonds issued in a currency other than the national currency and floated outside the issuer's home market.

Exchange Rate Per US Dollar
The exchange rate at the end of the period against the US dollar.

Execution Only
Here a broker simply executes his client's orders, without giving any advice. This is the cheapest form of brokerage and is often done by phone. Known in America as discount brokerage.

Federal Reserve
The American central bank.

Feeder Fund
A mutual unit fund which invests only in the shares of other mutual/unit trust funds.

FCP (Fonds common de placement)
A Luxembourg collective investment contractual structure. This type of fund is managed by a separate management company.

FIMBRA
The Financial Intermediaries Managers and Brokers Regulatory Association, which acts as the regulator of independent financial advisors within the UK.

Financial Futures Contracts
An agreement to buy or sell a standard quantity of a specific financial instrument at a future date and at a price agreed between the parties, to take place on the floor of an organized exchange through open outcry (i.e. the method of dealing whereby bids and offers are audible to all other market participants on the floor of the exchange).

Financial Times-Actuaries All-Share Index (The All-Share)
A broadly-based index covering 679 UK industrial, commercial and financial companies.

Financial Times-Actuaries Investment Trust Index
An index covering 66 UK investment trust companies.

Financial Times Industrial Ordinary Share Index (FT Industrial Ordinary or 30-Share Index)
An index covering 30 leading UK industrial and commercial companies, updated automatically every hour. This is the UK index more commonly used in financial comments by the media.

Financial Times Stock Exchange 100 Share Index (FT-SE 100)

The "Footsie" is a computerized Stock Exchange index launched on 13 February 1984 (3 January 1984 = 1000). It is a weighted arithmetic index based on the minute-by-minute share price movements of 100 of the most highly capitalized companies listed on the Stock Exchange.

Fixed Interest Stocks (Bonds)

Funds investing in excess of 70 percent of their assets in fixed interest securities (corporate, government, index-linked, etc.) with a maturity of 3 years or more.

Floating Rate Securities

Interest bearing securities where the interest rate may alter over time.

Forward

In the foreign exchange market, this is a tailor made deal where an investor agrees to buy or sell an amount of currency at a given date. The arrangement is calculated from the current or spot price, with an adjustment for the varying interest rate to cover the period agreed. Forwards are good for investors who need unusual deals which are not negotiable.

Fundamentals

The underlying business or economic conditions of a company or country. The term is used by economists and analysts to assess the investment prospects of a business, a country or a currency, and is usually contrasted with technical analysis.

Fund Manager

A company which manages the day-to-day affairs of a mutual or unit/trust fund. The investment manager and fund manager may be one and the same person.

Fund of Funds

A mutual fund or asset trust which invests only in shares of other mutual funds.

Futures

A contract to buy or sell standardized amounts of a commodity or financial instrument at a specific date in the future. Unlike forwards, futures are negotiable, and because they are standardized they approximate to what many investors want. The aim of this type of instrument is to make futures markets liquid, so that dealing is easy. Futures prices are related to the current price of the commodity, adjusted for the cost of carry.

Gearing (leverage)

The effect that borrowing has on the equity capital of a company. If the assets bought with the funds borrowed appreciate in value, the excess of value over funds borrowed will accrue to the equity shareholder, thus augmenting, or gearing up, the value of his or her capital. Gearing works in the same way – but in the opposite direction – if the asset values fall.

Geographical Spread

The distribution of the investments in a fund's portfolio over different parts of the world, either by country or by larger area.

G7 Nations

The major industrialized nations of the world: USA, Japan, Germany, UK, France, Italy, and Canada.

Gilt-Edged Bonds

Company bonds which have demonstrated over the years the earning capacity to cover interest and principal payments.

Gilts

Bonds issued by the British government and known as gilts or gilt-edged securities. 'Longs' have a redemption date greater than 15 years, 'mediums' between 7 - 15 years and 'shorts' within 7 years.

Global Bond Funds

These invest in the debt securities of companies and countries worldwide, including the US.

Global Equity Funds

Invest in securities traded worldwide, including the US, offering investors an easy avenue to investing abroad. The funds' managers handle the trading and record keeping details and deal with differences in currencies, language, time zones, laws and regulations, business customs and practices. In addition to another layer of diversification, global funds add another layer of exchange-rate risk.

GNMA

The US Government National Mortgage Association (GNMA) invests in US Government backed mortgage securities.

Growth Funds

Invest in the common stock of well-established companies to produce an increase in the value of their investments (capital gains) rather than a flow of dividends. Investors who buy a growth fund are more interested in seeing the fund's share price rise than in receiving income from dividends.

Guaranteed Funds

A type of mutual/unit fund which usually offers the potential of gains plus the guarantee of a return of 90-100 percent of the original investment at some time in the future. Popular in Hong Kong.

Hard Currency

"Hard currency" arises from the days when sound currency was freely convertible into "hard" metal ie: gold. It is used today to describe a currency which is sufficiently sound so that it is generally accepted internationally at face value.

Hard Currency Bond Funds

The objective of this type of fund is to achieve capital growth by investing in a diversified portfolio of high quality bonds and other securitized debt instruments. The fund will usually invest solely in bonds issued in countries which are deemed by the directors to be hard currency countries such as Germany, Switzerland, the Netherlands and Austria.

Hard Currency Growth Companies Fund

The objective of this fund is to produce long-term capital growth by investing in a diversified portfolio of shares of companies whose shares are quoted on a regulated market and which are domiciled in countries which are deemed to have hard currencies such as Germany, Switzerland, the Netherlands, and Austria.

Hedge Fund

A specialist type of mutual fund/unit fund, usually with very few limitations or restrictions on what investments the fund is allowed to make and what investment techniques it may employ. Hedge funds often have high minimum investment requirements and pay performance fees.

Hedging

A strategy for reducing risk by purchasing an investment (or currency) in opposition to another investment (currency) so as to counter any loss made by either. Hedging is used to reduce the risk of loss through adverse movement in interest rates, equity markets, share prices or currency rates.

High Yield Bond Funds

These maintain at least two-thirds of their portfolio in lower-rated corporate bonds (BAA or lower by Moody's rating service and BBB or lower by Standard & Poor's rating service). In return for a generally higher yield, investors must bear a greater degree of risk than for higher-rated bonds.

IMRO

The Investment Management Regulatory Organization; which regulates investment managers, including investment and unit trust managers in the UK.

Income-Bond Funds

These seek a high level of current income for their shareholders by investing at all times in a mix of corporate and government bonds.

Income Equity Funds

Seek a high level of current income for their unit holders by investing primarily in equity securities of companies with good dividend-paying records.

Income-Mixed Funds

Seek a high level of current income for their shareholders by investing in income producing securities, being both equities and/or debt instruments.

Index Funds

A type of mutual fund which attempts to achieve a performance similar to that stated in an index such as the S & P 500 Index, the Nikkei 225 or the FT-SE. The purpose of this fund is to realize an investment return at least equal to the broad market covered by the indices while reducing management costs.

Index Linked

A security such as index linked gilts whose value and/or interest payments are linked to inflation.

Initial Fee

A front-end fee levied by some funds on new clients, which is normally deducted from the initial investment and expressed as a percentage of the invested amount out of which an intermediary is paid if applicable.

Initiation

The conversion of an investment trust company into a unit trust.

Interest Rate Futures

These are contracts on certain three-month interest rates or debt instruments and are available in a variety of currencies and are traded on major futures exchanges throughout the world.

Interim

Formal statement of unaudited results for the first half of the company's financial year.

Investment Advisor

A company which advises and may manage an investment fund's portfolio.

Investment Advisor's Fee

A fee paid to an investment advisor for advisory services by a fund manager.

Investment Objective

The goal, such as long-term capital growth, current income, growth and income, which an investor or a mutual fund/unit trust pursues. Each fund's objective is stated in its prospectus.

Investment Trust

A close-ended, public limited company which invests in the equity of other companies. An investment trust is used by small investors to gain a wide spread of investments easily. Also called an investment fund in the US and normally listed on an exchange.

Large-Cap Stocks
Equities issued by companies with a net worth of at least several billion dollars.

Laufzeitfonds
European Laufzeit funds terminate at the end of the Laufzeit or running period. Initially these were bond funds, so there is little risk involved for the investor because the fund manager buys bonds that terminate around the end of the Laufzeit and yields the amount invested plus interest earned during the period. Usually these funds are closed several weeks or months after launch, so there is only a bid price available once it is closed. Nevertheless, the investor can sell the fund at any time during the running period.

Letter of Wishes
A document prepared by the settlor or grantor of a trust providing guidance on how trustees should exercise their discretionary powers.

LIBOR (London Inter-Bank Offered Rate)
The rate at which banks lend to one another is "fixed" at 11 a.m. on weekdays and is used as the benchmark to determine the interest rate on many large international loans.

Liquid
A market where there are many buyers and sellers (and consequently it is easy to deal) is described as liquid. Investors who hold cash are said to be liquid, and those who have sold their securities for cash have gone liquid.

Listing
For shares (or bonds) to be traded officially on a stock market, they must be listed, which is an endorsement from the market authorities that the securities and their issuer meet certain criteria.

Long
A gilt or other bond with a term of 15 years or more before it can be redeemed.

Long Position
An investor who owns an asset has a "long position" in that asset.

Luxembourg
Funds registered here can be readily marketed in the UK under the UCITS directive which pay income and capital gains gross to investors. Many funds are listed on the Luxembourg Bousse (exchange).

Managed Fund
A posted fund used by insurance companies.

Management Charge
The cost of running a fund, charged annually against its income. The current average level is approximately 0.5 percent to 2 percent of assets under management. The expenses which make up this total usually include the cost of investment management and administration, directors' fees, audit fees and share registration expenses.

Management Company
A company employed by one or more trusts to provide investment management and some or all of the following services: administration, secretarial, registration, accountancy and research.

Market Capitalization
The value of a company on the stock market, calculated by multiplying the number of its issued ordinary shares by its current market price.

Maturity
Another word for redemption or the length of time before a loan or bond will be repaid.

Medium Term Bond
A bond with between five and fifteen years to redemption.

Mixed
(See Balanced Funds).

Money Market Funds
These invest solely in money market or cash instruments with durations ranging from overnight to twelve months. Investments will normally be held in bank deposits, short-term monetary investments and forward currency contracts. Managed currency funds, a type of money market fund, have an objective of maximizing the value of liquid assets via the management of currency exposure.

Mutual Fund
An open-ended investment company (unit trust) that pools money from shareholders and invests in a variety of securities, including, stocks, bonds, and money market instruments. A mutual fund is obligated to buy back (redeem) its shares at their current net asset value; which depends on the market value of the fund's portfolio securities at the time of redemption.

Negotiable
A security which can be bought and sold is said to be negotiable. It is a flexible investment because the holder is not committed to owning it for the full term.

Net Asset Value (NAV)
The market worth of one share of a mutual fund/unit trust, derived by taking a fund's total assets – securities, cash, and accrued earnings – then deducting liabilities and dividing by the number of share units outstanding.

No-load Fund
A mutual fund that does not charge an initial or a redemption fee. The term also refers to a fund selling its shares at unit trust net-asset value without the addition of sales charges.

Nominee
A legal agreement where a person or a firm holds shares on behalf of another person or institution.

OATs (Obligations assimilables du Tresor)
French term for long term Government Treasury Bonds.

"OEICS"
A term used to describe open ended investment companies which are developed as an alternative to open ended unit trusts in the UK and are similar to mutual fund companies in the US.

Offer
The price at which a market maker sells shares; also known as the "ask". Market makers quote two prices: a bid where they buy and an offer where they sell.

Offer Price
The price at which mutual fund/unit shares are sold to shareholders. The offer price may be equal to the bid price, or higher.

Offshore Territories
Generally refers to jurisdictions which have low or no tax regimes for investment schemes, and where investment funds are registered for sale to investors resident in other countries.

Open-ended Funds
A fund or unit trust that can grow or shrink investable capital on demand by issuing new units or shares. Open-ended funds can either be formed as trusts, as with unit trusts, or assume a corporate structure such as open-ended investment companies (so-called OEICs).

Option
This gives the owner the right to buy or sell an asset at a given price within a given period of time. The price at which the option owner can buy or sell is called the striking price.

Option/Income Funds
These seek a higher return by investing primarily in dividend paying common stocks on which call options are traded. Income generally consists of: dividends, premiums from writing options, net short-term gains from the sale of portfolio securities on exercises of options or otherwise, and any profits from closing purchase transactions.

PE Ratio (Price-Earnings ratio)
A relative measure of the price of a company's shares, which also indicates the number of years earnings that are required to equal the current share price.

Performance Fees
Managers of offshore funds are sometimes entitled to a percentage (10-20 percent) of a fund's annual gains as a fee to reflect performance. The fee is supposed to act as an incentive but can have drawbacks.

Portfolio
A collection of securities owned by an individual or an institution, such as a unit trust/mutual fund. A fund's portfolio may include a combination of stocks, bonds, and money market securities.

Portfolio Insurance
A risk-hedging strategy involving the use of stock-index futures.

Precious Metals/Gold Funds
These maintain 70 percent of their portfolios invested in securities associated with gold, silver, and other precious metals.

Preference Share
A type of share in a company, usually with a fixed dividend rate, ranking in priority to ordinary shares for both dividend and return of capital in a liquidation. May have voting rights.

Private Placement
An offering of securities that is made to a select group of investors that may or may not be on preferential terms.

Property
Funds investing in shares of companies involved in property, e.g. construction, letting, etc. and/or owning property within the fund.

Prospectus
A document required by law to be published on the occasion of an issue of shares or fixed-interest securities to the public. A prospectus gives details of the company and the issue. In the case of listed investments, stock exchanges usually require the publication of more information than the minimum legal obligation. A prospectus normally contains: the fund's investment objectives and methods; its policies regarding shareholders; a list of the names and addresses of the fund managers, the trustee/custodian and advisors, and the fees charged. Depending on the jurisdiction, a prospectus may be called "scheme particulars," "product particulars," or "offering memorandum."

Put
An option to sell shares, bonds or a commodity.

Put Option
A right to sell an asset for a specific price (the strike price) within a specified length of time.

Real Rate of Return
The return amount after taking account of inflation – for example, the real rate of interest is the rate with inflation deducted, similarly the real rate of growth after accounting for inflation.

Redemption Date
The date when a bond will be repaid, though some can be redeemed early or "called" by the issuer. If the investor is entitled to redeem the bond early, he has the right to put the bond. Those bonds which are never repaid are known as irredeemables or perpetuals. Some preference shares and convertibles also have redemption or maturity dates.

Redemption Fee
An exit fee charged by a mutual fund/unit trust when a shareholder redeems his shares. This may be different or the same as a switching fee within an umbrella fund.

Regulated
Funds that do not have SIB recognition and cannot therefore be actively promoted to UK private investors.

Reinvestment Privilege
An option available to mutual fund/unit trust shareholders in which fund dividends and capital gains distributions are automatically turned back into the fund to buy new shares, without charge (meaning no sales fee or commission), thereby increasing holdings.

Registered Securities
Shares or bonds whose ownership is recorded on a central register, as opposed to bearer securities.

Repurchase agreement (repo)
An agreement to sell a security or basket of securities and then repurchase them at a particular time and pre-determined price.

Roll-Up Fund
A mutual fund/collective investment scheme which does not make distributions to shareholders. A fund which re-invests rolled-up income on a gross basis can be used by UK residents to defer tax.

RPI (Retail Prices Index)
A measure of consumer inflation within the UK.

Rule 144
The US Securities and Exchange Commission regulation that covers the selling of restricted securities.

Sales Charge
An amount charged to purchase shares in mutual funds/unit trusts sold by brokers or other sales agents. This fee may pay the sales agent and fund the initial set-up fee. The sales charge may occur on initial purchase of the shares (initial fee) or upon redemption of the shares (redemption fee or back-end load). This fee may equate to the bid/offer spread of a unit or be deducted from the gross amount invested. The charge is added to the net asset value per share when determining the offering price.

Saving Scheme
A facility to enable purchases of investment trust company shares to be made easily and cheaply by the investment of regular (usually monthly) sums of money or by occasional lump-sum contributions.

Scheme Particulars
See prospectus.

Secondary Market
A market in which a previously issued security is sold by one investor to another as opposed to the primary market which deals with the original issuance of the security.

Securities and Exchange Commission (SEC)
The primary US federal agency that regulates investment companies and public issuers.

Sedol
Stock Exchange Daily Official List number - London Stock Exchange.

Semi-Annual Report
See interim report.

Sharpe Ratio
A statistical concept used in risk analysis to show the total return of a portfolio in relation to the risk it has undertaken.

Short Term Bonds
Funds investing in fixed interest stock (e.g. treasury bonds, floating rate notes) with maturities up to 3 years.

Short Positions
An investor who has sold securities which he does not own is said to have a "short position". When an investor with a short position buys back the securities, he is said to have "covered" his short position.

SIB (Securities and Investments Board)
The chief regulator under the UK Financial Services Act.

SIB Recognized
An offshore fund which can be actively promoted to UK investors, having been approved by the SIB and offering investors compensation against malpractice equivalent to the UK system.

SICAV (Société d'investissement à capital variable)
The French equivalent of a unit trust and a common structure for offshore funds. Structured as companies rather than trusts, such investment vehicles have a variable share capital.

SICAF (Société d'investissement à capital fixe)
A French corporate structure with fixed capital. A SICAV or SICAF is constituted by articles of incorporation under the legal form of a public limited company.

Single Pricing
Offshore funds may quote one price for buying and selling but may well levy a separate sales charge (often 5–6 percent) when investors buy.

Small-Cap Stocks
These equities are issued by corporations with a stock market capitalization of US$500 million or less.

Specialist-Derivatives Funds
Invest in derivative instruments such as futures, forward contracts and options, in order to achieve capital appreciation.

Split-Capital Trust (Split-Level Trust)
A UK investment trust, usually with a limited or determinable life, whose equity capital is divided into various classes – usually income and capital shares. Holders of income shares receive all or most of the income earned by the company throughout its life, plus a predetermined capital value on liquidation. Holders of capital shares receive little or no income throughout the life of the company but are entitled to all of the assets remaining after repayment of the income shares.

Sponsor
The company which creates a mutual fund/unit trust by underwriting the cash necessary to create the fund and to market the shares to investors. Money from the new shareholders in the fund is used to reimburse the sponsor for the cost of creating the fund and to purchase investment assets. The promoter may be the sponsor.

Spot
Used in a variety of areas to mean good for "immediate" delivery, though the definition of immediate varies between markets. Spot in the foreign exchange market means dealing for settlement two days hence. In the gilt market, it means settlement the next day.

Spread
The difference between a fund's bid and offer (ask) price which may range between 0 and 7 percent.

Stock
In North America a "stock" is generally synonymous with a "share", but in the UK it usually means a bond.

Surrender Charges
A term normally used for life insurance funds (bonds) and pension funds. Instead of making their charges when investors buy, some offshore funds levy charges when holdings are sold or surrendered.

Switching
An option enabling unit fund holders to transfer their investment from one fund to another within the same fund family as their needs or objectives change. Typically, funds allow investors to use the exchange privilege several times a year for a low or no fee per exchange.

Switch or Exchange Privilege
Enables mutual fund shareholders to transfer their investment from one fund to another within the same fund family as shareholder needs or objectives change. Usually funds charge a low or no fee per exchange.

Technical Analysis
Also known as charting, this is a way of predicting future price movements from past movements in prices. Prediction also involves psychology and an understanding of crowd behaviour. Normally technical analysis is seen in contrast to fundamental analysis.

Tokkin Funds
Funds run by Japanese securities firms with the objective of obtaining a higher return than can be achieved through deposit accounts or bonds. Such returns are cash returns, namely dividend income plus net realized capital gains and take no account of any unrealized profits or losses.

Top-Down
Refers to a type of security analysis. Management that follows the top-down approach is concerned with the general level of the economy and any fiscal policy being followed by the government.

Total Return
The return from an investment or portfolio is calculated by combining dividends or interest received with any capital gain or loss. There are two main bases on which total return statistics are computed, and in each case it is assumed that dividends received by the shareholder (but not the tax credit) are reinvested. The first is calculated on the net asset value (NAV) performance of the investment trust, and the dividends are assumed to be reinvested in the assets of the trust at its NAV per share return (NAV total return). The second base is calculated on the share price performance of the investment trust, and the dividends are treated as reinvested in the shares of the trust at the market price, normally at the time when the shares go ex-dividend (share price total return).

Transfer Agent
The organization or custodian employed by a mutual fund/unit trust to prepare and maintain records relating to the accounts of its shareholders. Some funds serve as their own transfer agents.

Treasuries
US Government interest-bearing securities.

Treasury Bills
US Government securities with maturities of one year or less.

Treasury Bonds
US Government bonds with terms from ten to 30 years.

Treasury Notes
US Government bonds with terms of one to ten years.

Turnover Ratio
The total value of shares traded during the period divided by the average market capitalization for the period, calculated in local currency. Average market capitalization is calculated as the average of the end-of-period values for the current and the previous period.

UCITS (Undertakings for Collective Investments in Transferable Securities)
The EC directive adopted in 1985 which allows collective investment schemes authorized in one EC member state to be marketed in another, subject to a two-month notice period. The SIB is responsible for regulating the UK marketing activities of UCITS funds, and investors are protected under the UK Investors Compensation Scheme.

Umbrella Fund
An investment company which has a group of stand-alone sub-funds, (compartments, pools) each having its own investment portfolio, maybe in a different currency from that of the umbrella fund. The purpose of this structure is to provide investment flexibility and widen investor choice.

Underwriter
The organization that acts as the distributor of a mutual fund's shares to broker /dealers and investors.

Unit Investment Trust
A US based investment company that purchases a fixed portfolio of income producing securities. Units in the trust are sold to investors by brokers.

Unit Trust
A common form of collective investment in the UK (similar to a mutual fund) where investors' money is pooled and invested in a variety spread of shares or bonds in order to reduce risks. The fund's basic legal structure is a trust which issues units instead of shares. Its capital structure is open ended as units can be created or redeemed, depending upon demand from investors.

US Person
A resident or citizen of the United States, a partnership or corporation organised under the laws of the US that principally has its residence or place of business in the United States. Such a person as defined is considered to be a "US person" under the security laws of the SEC.

Volatility
The rate of return variability is a measurement of the tendency of a security to rise or fall in value relative to the market. For example if the market was to rise 10 percent and accordingly an equity rose 10 percent, it would be said to have a volatility of 1 or rises equally to the market. Conversely, if the equity rose by 20 percent, it would be said to have a volatility of 2. Volatility ratings are normally calculated after 3 years of market pricing.

Warrant
A financial instrument or type of option given by the company to holders of a particular security giving them the right to subscribe for future issues either of the same kind or some other security

Withholding Tax
Tax deducted from dividends on investments which are paid to investors who are non-residents. Tax can often be reclaimed if there is a double taxation agreement with the investor's country.

Yankee Bonds
US dollar denominated bonds of non-US companies which are issued and approved for the United States.

Yield
The annual grossed-up dividend per share as a percentage of the share price.

Zero Coupon Bonds
Bonds, usually without a coupon rate, which are sold at a discount to their face value, and are redeemed at face or par value. The discounted amount, amortized over the term of the bond, determines the yield to maturity.

Appendix 6 Selected Indices Defined

CLSA CHINA B

There are two official stock markets in China, the Shanghai and Shenzhen where over 70 companies are listed (trading commenced in 1990 and 1991 respectively). Shares which are listed are divided into two categories: A and B shares.

A shares are traded on both stock exchanges in Renminbi, the currency of China and are available only to Chinese citizens.

B shares are traded on both exchanges in US and Hong Kong Dollars.

In the past B shares have only been available to foreign investors, but at the beginning of 1993, local investors were reported to be participating in the B share market.

Shares of one class cannot be exchanged for shares of another class.

CREDIT SUISSE FIRST BOSTON RUSSIAN INDEX

The CSFB ROS 30 Index is a free float weighted index that tracks the 30 largest (by market cap) and most liquid Russian companies (by number of traded days in a year), and is structured so that no single industry sector can dominate. The rules of the CSFB ROS 30 Index dictate that the composition and free-floats of the companies in the index should be reviewed quarterly.

DOMINI SOCIAL INDEX

State Street are the global advisors for this index. 400 stocks make up the index which have passed multiple, broad based social screens to eliminate:

Companies that derive 25% or more of current turnover from weapon-related products, or the manufacture of alcohol, tobacco or gambling products;

Electric companies that own interests in nuclear power plants or companies that derive 4% or more of current turnover from the nuclear power industry;

Companies facing substantial environmental controversies;

Companies experiencing a recent history of notably unstable employee relations.

DOW JONES INDUSTRIAL

This is the longest standing barometer of the US market, having started in 1884 listing 11 shares.

The 30 shares it lists today are blue chip companies. It is a price weighted index and measures the average price movement only. Higher priced stock issues within the index will have a greater impact on the index movement than the lower priced stock issues.

All 30 stocks are listed on the New York Stock Exchange and are components of the S&P 500.

A Utility average is also calculated by Dow Jones and this consists of 20 utility stocks.

EUROTOP 100

The Eurotop 100 index is based on 100 extremely liquid stocks which are traded on security exchanges in nine European countries. The index is a reliable barometer of European economic development. All participating stocks in the index together represent a certain portfolio. The ECU value of this portfolio, divided by 100, is the index quote.

FRANK RUSSELL GROUP OF INDICES

The Russell Indices are US equity indices.

Russell 1000 Index

This index is composed of the 1000 largest companies in the Russell 3000 index. The smallest company in the Russell 1000 index has a market capitalisation of $300 million. This index represents the universe of stocks from which most active money managers typically select.

Russell 2000 Index

This index is composed of the 2000 smallest stocks which make up the Russell 3000. This index represents about 7% of the market capitalisation of the Russell 3000.

Russell 3000 Index

This index is composed of 3000 large US companies by market capitalisation, representing about 98% of the US equity market. The largest company in this index has a market capitalisation of $69 billion, with the smallest company having a market capitalisation of $15 million. The index has been reconstituted annually since 1989.

FINANCIAL TIMES STOCK EXCHANGE INDICES

Financial Times Stock Exchange 100 Share Index

This index is also referred to as the FT-SE 100 or "FOOTSIE". It was the first real time index in the United Kingdom and was created to support a futures contract based upon the UK equity market.

It is a weighted arithmetic index representing the price of 100 securities with a base of 1000 on 3rd January 1984. It is calculated minute-by-minute between the hours of 08:00 and 16:30. The constituents, whose membership by market capitalisation is above £1 billion, are reviewed quarterly. The index covers 72% of the UK equity market-by-market capitalisation.

FT-SE mid 250

This is an index of the next 250 companies after the 100, in market capitalisation. These companies which are substantially nationally based (rather than the UK based international companies in the FTSE 100) are capitalised between £150 million and £1 billion and represent 20% of the UK equity market by market capitalisation.

The index has been calculated since 31st December 1985, using a start value set at the FTSE 100 closing level on that date.

The index is weighted in favour of sectors such as engineering and construction.

FT-SE 350

This index is a combination of the 100 and the 250 indices. It represents approximately 90% of the UK equity market-by- market capitalisation.

It has been calculated since 31st December 1985 with a high correlation to the FT Actuaries All-Share level at that time.

FT/S&P Actuary World Indices

It was to circumvent difficulties with local indexes that the FT-Actuaries World Index series was created in 1987. The publishing rights of these indices were acquired by Standard and Poor's in 1985 and the names of the indices were amended to reflect this, in that the indices are now called FT/S&P Actuary World Indices. The series is designed to represent global equity markets and to reflect the increase in cross-border equity investment, particularly from the United States and Japan.

The series is intended mainly for fund managers, consultants and money managers. Its primary function is global equity performance measurement, hence it is essential that the shares that make up the indices can be purchased and sold. The series is also used for the creation of derivative products such as stock index finds (funds that are used to track the FTA World Indices or one or more of their subseries). Apart from the overall World index, separate figures are published for 24 individual countries and 11 regions such as Europe, the Nordic countries and the Pacific Basin.

The series is based on over 2,200 equity securities from 24 countries and represents at least 70% of the total market capitalisation of the world's main stock market.

FT Industrial Ordinary (FT30)

This index is frequently referred to as the FT Ordinary Share index.

It started its life in 1935 with a base of 100. It is a well established and price sensitive index. The ordinary objective was to track the shares of British industrial companies, but over the years the British economy has switched from an industrial bias to embrace retail and service industries. In 1984 the National Westminster Bank was included in the index when the word industrial was dropped from the title.

The 30 companies currently included are diverse in nature but they are all blue-chip companies.

The index is designed as an indicator of the current market movements rather than for long-term performance comparisons.

FTSE Eurotrack 100

This index was officially launched on the 29th October 1990, with a base of 1000, and gives an overview of the non-UK European markets. The constituents are the top 100 continental European and Irish companies and are based on their stock prices as quoted on SEAQ International.

This index is based on the prices of the constitiuent companies, London dealings only, not those of the home markets. It is intended to reflect the role of the London market as the leading international one in European shares.

It is priced in deutschemarks.

The official index period is 09:45 to 15:30 GMT. It is a real time stock market index. It is designed to be a 'sister' product to the FT-SE 100 share index.

HANG SENG INDEX

This index is compiled by HSI Services Ltd and takes its name from the Hang Seng Bank. It was first published in 1969 and is the most widely quoted index of the Hong Kong Stock Market.

It is a value weighted index of 33 of the largest and most liquid stocks on the Hong Kong Exchange and is calculated daily.

The original base date was 31st July 1964 but this was changed to 13th January 1984, when four subindices were introduced.

This index is made up of four main sectors: commerce and industry, finance, utilities and properties.

IFC GROUP OF INDICES

International Finance Corporation (IFC) produce indices which cover emerging markets, which are defined as 'any stock market located in a developing country, as defined by the World Bank's GNP per capita criterion for a developing country, i.e. a measure of the country's economy – GNP per capita level as:

High income US$ 8,356
Middle income US$ 676–$8,355
Low income US$ 675 or less.

The IFC Indices are broken down into two main groups: IFCG and IFCI.

IFCG (a global indicator)

Represents the performance of the most active stocks in their respective markets, making this the broadest indicator of market movements. These indices include stocks which are only tradable to IFCG local investors as well as stocks which are traded on an international basis.

IFCI (an investable indicator)

Represents more precisely the types of returns foreign portfolio investors might receive from investing in emerging market equity sectors that are legally available to them.

JP MORGAN GROUP OF INDICES

JP Morgan calculate indices from the major government bond markets actively traded by institutional investors. The instruments that are included must be tradable and redeemable for cash, should be fixed coupons and should not appeal exclusively to domestic investors for local tax or regulatory reasons. The eligible instruments are listed below for the various countries included:

Australia
—includes Commonwealth issues
—excludes Index-linked issues
Belgium
—includes State and Road fund issues, including OLO's Canada
—includes Canadian governments
France
—includes OAT's, BTAN's, Emprunts d'Etat
—excludes Index-linked, Perpetuals, FELINS, ORT's, FRN's
Germany
—includes Bund, Bahn, Post (Anleihen), Kassenobligationen, Bundesobligationen

Italy
—includes BTPs, CTOs
—excludes CCTs, CTEs
Japan
—includes 10 and 20 year JGBs, 2, 3 and 4 year medium-term notes
—excludes Private placements, medium term discounts
Netherlands
—includes Dutch State loans
—excludes Perpetuals, private placements
Spain
—includes Bonos and obligaciones
United Kingdom
—includes Gilts, including convertibles
—excludes Index-linked irredeemables
United States
—includes Treasury notes and bonds
—excludes Flower bonds, STRIPS, foreign targeted issues.

The three levels of liquidity per country are tracked:

Benchmark contains:
issues with a high trading volume
recent sizable issues
current coupon issues
latest or most recently opened issues

Active contains Benchmark criteria plus issues:
with significant daily turnover
which may have been benchmarked before actively quoted side issues
so that the universe spans the yield curve

Traded contains Active issues plus:
issues with prices changing regularly
issues for which a two-way market exists
issues that are available for investment.

LOMBARD ODIER & CIE GROUP OF INDICES

Lombard Odier & Cie ('LOC') created a family of bond indices in 1983, having had almost two centuries of experience in global fixed income investment management.

Lombard Odier offers four general types of bond indices:

Domestic Bond Indices

These include solely government issues. The one exception is the Swiss Domestic Bond index which is an aggregate of borrowings by the federal government, cantons and municipalities.

Eurobond Indices

These indices include bonds issued by government and government guaranteed entities; provinces and municipalities; public utilities; banks and financial corporations; private sector companies and international financial institutions.

Composite-Currency Index

The one entry in this area is the ECU Bond, which is made up of borrowings by a group of top-quality issuers, primarily government and sovereign entities. This index has taken on added significance given the decision at the European Community Summit at Maastricht in December 1991, to adopt a single European currency by 1999.

Global and Regional Bond Indices

To track global bond market trends LOC offers the World Bond index, which is expressed in Swiss Franc as well as US Dollar terms. It is an average of all the domestic indices, plus the ECU Bond index, weighted annually by market-capitalisation. Another global index offered is the LOC World Bond index non-Swiss Franc, which does not include the Swiss Franc bond market component, weighted annually by market-capitalisation and expressed in Swiss Franc terms.

The newest benchmark developed by LOC is the LOC Europe Bond index. This is designed to have the performance characteristics of the European domestic bond markets included in the LOC World Bond index using a subset of highly liquid issues. It is a GDP-weighted benchmark of all European domestic bond markets tracked by Lombard Odier and it is expressed in ECU terms. The GDP-weighting is calculated annually.

These indices have been designed to provide investors with a family of benchmarks for use in assessing the performance of investments in the major world bond markets. They can be used for evaluating and implementing investment strategies in different markets. They will be of use to investors interested in creating indexed portfolios, or portfolios designed to track broad market movements.

MAR INDICES

Managed Account Reports (MAR), calculate two indices which track the performance of managed derivatives, trading advisors and investment services:

MAR Trading Advisor Qualified Universe
MAR Fund/Pool Qualified Universe

The indices are equity weighted and track the net performance of the industry since 1980, including both currently active and 'retired' entities.

MAR Trading Advisor Qualified Universe:

This reflects the performance of funds invested with trading advisors world-wide. For inclusion in the 'qualified' universe a trading advisor must have at least $500,000 under management and twelve months of trading clients' assets or act as a trading advisor in a public fund listed in the fund's table of MAR.

As at 31st March 1995, there were 392 advisors in the Universe with a total of $16.10 billion under management.

MAR Fund/Pool Qualified Universe:

This index reflects the performance of investments in managed futures funds and pools world-wide. For inclusion in the 'qualified' universe a fund or pool must appear in MAR's fund table.

As at 31st March 1995, there were 448 advisors with a total of $7.735 billion in equity.

MICROPAL SECTOR INDICES

Micropal has developed a sector indice for each general sector of each database and an overall index for each database, these are calculated as follows:

a) On a month-by-month basis the average change of all funds in a given sector is calculated with income reinvested;

b) The changes are 'chain linked' by multiplying them up successively;

c) The series is scaled such that January 1987 = 100.

The indices contain a spread which is correlated to the spread that is displayed on an overall report of the general sector on an offer-bid basis.

MORGAN STANLEY INTERNATIONAL CAPITAL INDICES

These indices are based on the share price of over 2,000 companies listed on world-wide stock exchanges.

MSCI calculate regional indices as listed below:-

World Index

This is an arithmetical average weighted by market value of the performances of companies listed on the exchanges of USA, Europe, Canada, Australia, New Zealand and the Far East

EAFE

This includes the companies on the exchanges of Europe, Australia, New Zealand and the Far East.

Europe

Consists of the 13 countries of Europe and the companies listed on those exchanges: Austria, Belgium, Denmark, Finland, France, Germany, Italy, Netherlands, Norway, Spain, Sweden, Switzerland and the United Kingdom.

Far East

Includes the companies that are listed on the exchanges of Japan, Hong Kong, Singapore and Malaysia.

Pacific

Contains the above and also Australia and New Zealand.

North America

Includes the companies listed on the exchanges of the US and Canada.

Nordic Countries

Consists of Denmark, Finland, Norway and Sweden.

Individual country indices are also calculated which are expressed in local terms. These regional indices on Micropal's database are denominated in US Dollar terms. All MSCI indices are calculated in local and US Dollar terms.

Not only are the capital indices available but also Net Reinvested and Gross Reinvested series.

Gross Reinvested series take into account actual dividends declared by the companies.

Net Reinvested series take into account those dividends that are net of withholding taxes retained at the source of payment.

Withholding taxes may vary according to the shareholders domicile, and the rates that are used in these calculations are those which are applicable to foreigners not benefiting from double taxation treaties.

A series of 'free' indices are also calculated. These contain only those shares which are readily purchasable by non-local investors. Norway is the only developed market which has significant ownership restrictions. Generally free indices refer to any country defined as being an emerging market.

Emerging Market indices are calculated in US Dollar and local terms and only capital indices are available from Micropal. 'Free' indices are calculated for the countries which have owner restrictions, and 'Global' indices are calculated which contain free shares as well as those shares which are available only to local investors.

NIKKEI 225

This is one of the oldest and most widely followed indices in Japan. It is composed of the stocks of 225 companies which are listed in the Tokyo Stock Exchange First Section. Those stocks are highly liquid and account for approximately 60% of the value of the 1,100+ shares listed on the First Section.

Membership of the index is reviewed annually, when up to six members can be replaced if their shares became illiquid or unrepresentative.

In 1975, Nihon Keizai Shimbun Inc. acquired the right to calculate and publish the old Nikkei – Dow Jones Average, and in 1985 the average was renamed to Nikkei Stock Average.

It is a price weighted average.

When it was first published on May 16th 1949, the average price was ¥176.21 with an original divisor of 225.

SALOMON BROTHERS GROUP OF INDICES

The Salomon Brothers family of international and bond market indices is calculated using similar objective methodologies. Salomons calculate and distribute 17 individual country indices, several composite indices and maturity sector indices. Maturity sectors are defined as being based on the remaining life of the issues in the index, for example, the three- to seven-year index includes those issues with an average remaining life of greater than or equal to three years but less than seven.

Money Market Indices

Salomon Brothers also calculate Money Market Indices, which track the performances of money market instruments in eight global currencies.

They include 20 money market instruments with three-month maturities.

The composite is the World Money Market index, in local and US Dollar terms.

STANDARD & POOR'S 500 COMPOSITE

This index is composed of 500 stocks which are traded on the New York Stock Exchange, American Stock Exchange and the NASDAQ National Market System. These 500 stocks are not the 500 largest companies in terms of market value but are chosen for inclusion because they tend to be leaders in important industries within the US economy.

The origins of the index go back to 1923, when S&P introduced a series of indices which included 233 companies and covered 26 industries. Since then the index has grown to 500 companies, and four major industry sectors have been developed with corresponding indices:

Utilities
Financial
Industrial (400)
Transportation.

Since 1968 the index has been a component of the US Commerce Department's list of leading indicators which track the US economy.

The index is a market value weighted index (shares outstanding times stock price).

A Price return and a Total return index are calculated.

TOKYO PRICE INDEXES – TOPIX

Listed stocks on the Tokyo Stock Exchange (TSE) are classified as being either First Section (ichibu), Second Section (nibu) or Foreign Section. All foreign listed stocks are assigned to the Foreign Section and are not part of TOPIX.

New issue stocks are first assigned to the Second Section.

The top rated and most actively traded First Section listed stocks must have:-

Number of shares – 20+ million shares;

Dividends – ¥5 or more in cash per share for each of the last three years and the ability to maintain dividends of ¥5 or more in cash per share after listing;

Trading volume – must be 200,000+ shares monthly for last six months.

First Section

This is a broad based composite index that includes all domestic stocks listed (1,100+). It is a capitalisation weighted index by Paäsche formula and has a base index level of 100 as at January 4th 1968.

Second Section

This is a composite index of 425+ stocks traded on the Second Section. It is also capitalisation weighted according to Paäsche formula.

TORONTO STOCK EXCHANGE INDICES

This exchange is the main exchange for Canadian shares, and is larger than either the Montreal or Vancouver markets. The main indicators are the Toronto 35 index, the wider TSE 300 Composite index, (the TSE 100 was introduced later than these). These indices are calculated both on a total return basis and on a price return basis.

TSE 300

There are certain criteria that a stock must meet for inclusion in this index:

Shares must be Canadian incorporated and listed on the Toronto Stock Exchange.

All stocks must be listed on the exchange for at least one year before eligibility is considered.

Trading volume of the stock must have been at least 100,00 shares and 100 transactions in the year immediately preceding its consideration.

Stocks are reviewed annually to ensure that they are still eligible by ensuring a qualifying exercise: each stock is ranked according to a one-year average float quoted market value (QMV), this is a one year trade-weighted average price. This is defined as the total value traded for the twelve-month period divided by the total volume of shares traded for the same period. Any stock which falls lower than 325 in QMV is replaced by the stock which has taken its place within the largest 300. Likewise if a stock was not on the TSE 300 but ranked higher than 275 in the eligible pool, then it would replace the displaced stock from the largest 300.

UK RETAIL PRICE INDEX

The Retail Price Index (RPI) is the most generally recognised yardstick used in the UK to measure the rate of inflation, which refers to the general increase in prices and fall in the purchasing power of money.

The index takes into account most items that money is spent on and weights them in such a way that reflects their importance in a consumer's shopping basket.

It is not seasonally adjusted.

US TREASURY BILL INDEX

This index is calculated by Interactive Data Corporation (IDC) and measures the performance of Treasury Bills with a constant maturity of 90 days. Specifically it calculates the change in price of 180 day bills whose maturity is closest to 90 days but not more.

WILSHIRE INDEX

Wilshire 1750 Index

The Wilshire 1750 Index includes the small companies (smallest company has a market capitlisation of $70m) of the Wilshire 2500 Index . These small companies represent 10 percent of the market value of the Wilshire 2500.

The Wilshire 2500 Index

The Wilshire 2500 Index in turn represents the top 2500 companies of the 5000 US companies in the Whilshire 5000 index and makes up 99% of the market capitalisation of the 5000 Whilshire Index.

The Wilshire 5000 Index

The 5000 Index is a market value weighted index of all the public US companies and covers 86 percent of NYSE, 3 percent of AMEX and 11 percent of NASDAQ.

Appendix 7 Examples of Purchase Restrictions

DEFINITION OF 'UNITED STATES PERSON'

For purposes of the applicable prohibitions against ownership and transfer of Fund shares, the term 'United States Person' means:

(1) a resident or citizen of the United States;

(2) a partnership or corporation organized under the laws of the United States;

(3) any entity not organized under the laws of the United States:

(a) that has its principal office or place of business in the United States; or

(b) (i) in which citizens or residents of or entities organized under the laws of or existing in the United States directly or indirectly hold in the aggregate 50 percent or more of the beneficial interests; and

(ii) that will own directly or indirectly, either alone or together with affiliated persons and with any direct or indirect owners of 10 percent of the beneficial interests in the entity, an aggregate of more than 2 percent of the Fund's outstanding shares; or

(c) (i) that is organized principally for passive investment (such as an investment company, a commodity pool or other similar vehicle); and

(ii) (A) in which the amount of units of participation held by United States Persons (other than 'qualified eligible participants' as defined in Rule 4.7 under the United States Commodity Exchange Act) represents in the aggregate 10 percent or more of the beneficial interest in the entity;

(B) that was formed for the purpose of facilitating investment by United States Persons in the Fund, or in any other commodity pool with respect to which the operator is exempt from certain requirements of Part 4 of the regulations promulgated by the United States Commodity Futures Trading Commission by virtue of its participants being non-United States Persons; or

(C) that was formed by United States Persons principally for the purpose of investing in securities not registered under the United States Securities Act of 1933, unless it is formed and owned by 'accredited investors' (as defined in Rule 501(a) under the Securities Act of 1933) who are not natural persons, estates or trusts;

(4) an estate or trust:

(a) of which an executor, administrator or trustee is a United States person, unless:

(i) an executor, administrator or trustee who is not a United Statesperson has sole or shared investment discretion with respect to the assets of the estate or trust; and

(ii) (A) in the case of an estate,, it is governed by non-US law; or

(B) in the case of a trust, no beneficiary (and no settlor if the trust is revocable) is a United States Person; or

(b) the income of which is subject to United States income tax regardless of source;

(5) any agency or branch of a foreign entity located in the United States;

(6) any non-discretionary account or similar account (other than an estate or trust) held for the benefit or account of one or more United States persons; and

(7) any discretionary account or similar account (other than an estate or trust) held by a dealer or other fiduciary organized, incorporated, or (if an individual) resident in the United States, unless it is held by a dealer or other professional fiduciary exclusively for the benefit or account of one or more non-United States Persons.

For purposes of the foregoing, the term 'United States' means the United States of America, its territories and possessions, any state of the United States, and the District of Columbia. Persons requiring details regarding other terms used in the foregoing definition (such as 'qualified eligible participant' and 'accredited investor') should contact the Fund's Managing Director.

FOR RESIDENTS OF ONTARIO AND QUEBEC, CANADA

Contractual Right of Action

Section 32 of the Regulation to the Securities Act (Ontario) provides, in effect, that when in certain circumstances, an offering memorandum is delivered to a subscriber to whom securities are sold, the subscriber must be given a contractual right of action against the issuer of the securities of rescission or damages. This right of action must reasonably correspond to the rights provided in section 130 of the Securities Act (Ontario) applicable to a prospectus and may be summarized as follows.

In the event that this Preliminary Information Memorandum, together with any amendment hereto, contains an untrue statement of a material fact or omits to state a material fact necessary in order to make any statement herein or therein not misleading in light of the circumstances in which it was made (a 'misrepresentation') and it was a misrepresentation on the date of investment, the subscriber will be deemed to have relied on the misrepresentation and shall have, subject as hereinafter provided, a right of action against the Fund, exersisable on written notice given not more than ninety days subsequent to the date of investment, either for damages or alternatively for rescission against the Fund provided that:

(a) the Fund shall not be held liable of the purchaser purchased the shares of the Fund with knowledge of the misrepresentation;

(b) in an action for damages, the Fund will not be liable for all or any portion of such damages that it proves do not represent the depreciation in value of the shares of the Fund as a result of the misrepresentation relied upon;

(c) in no case shall the amount recoverable under this paragraph exceed the price at which the shares of the Fund were sold to the purchaser; and the rights of the action for rescission or damages are in addition to and without derogation from any other right or remedy available at law to the purchaser.

The foregoing rights will be expressly conferred upon each purchaser of shares of the Fund resident in the Province of Ontario in the subscription form to be executed by such purchasers in connection with this offering.

Minimum amount purchased; disclosure of investors' names

Subscriptions for shares of the Fund will not be accepted from any person who is a resident of Ontario, Canada, other than an exempt purchaser, in an amount less than C$150,000. The Fund may be required to disclose the names of purchasers of the shares in this offering to the securities authorities of Ontario, and any person resident in Ontario who subscribes for shares in this offering shall be deemed to have given the Fund such person's consent to follow procedures required by the Ontario securities authorities to make such person's name available.

Minimum amount purchased; disclosure of investors' names

Subscriptions for shares of the Fund will not be accepted from any person who is a resident of Quebec, Canada (other than a sophisticated purchaser within the meaning of Section 43 of the Quebec Securities Act) in an amount less than C$150,000. The Fund may be required to disclose the names of purchasers of the shares of the Fund in this offering in sales reports to be filed with the securities authorities of Quebec, and any person resident in Quebec who subscribes for shares in this offering shall be deemed to have given the Fund such person's consent to include such person's name in any such sales reports.

Restrictions on resale

Shares may not be resold by residents of Quebec except under a resale exemption. Investors should consult their legal advisors before attempting to sell any shares.

Appendix 8 Examples of Investment Restrictions

Example 1

PROSPECTUS EXAMPLE OF THE INVESTMENT RESTRICTIONS FOR A SICAV STRUCTURED FUND FROM LUXEMBOURG WITH UCITS APPROVAL.

INVESTMENT AND BORROWING POWERS AND RESTRICTIONS

The Articles provide that the Board of Directors shall, based upon the principle of spreading of risks, have power to determine the corporate and investment policy and the course of conduct of the management and business affairs of the Company.

The Board of Directors shall also determine any restrictions which shall from time to time be applicable to the investments of the Company.

In exercise of such power the Directors have determined that the following investment and borrowing powers and restrictions shall apply:

(1a) The Company may invest only in:

(i) transferable securities admitted to official listing on a stock exchange in an Eligible State;

and/or

(ii) transferable securities dealt in on other Regulated Market in an member state; and/or

(iii) recently issued transferable securities provided that the terms of issue include an undertaking that application will be made for admission to official listing on an Eligible Market and such admission is achieved within a year of the issue;

(all such securities under (i), (ii) and (iii) above being hereby defined as "Eligible Transferable Securities");

PROVIDED THAT the Company may also invest in transferable securities other than Eligible Transferable Securities or in debt instruments which are treated because of their characteristics as equivalent to transferable securities and which are, inter alia, transferable, liquid and have a value which can be accurately determined on each Valuation Date, PROVIDED FURTHER THAT the total of such debt instruments and of investments other than the Eligible Transferable Securities shall not exceed 10 per cent of the net assets attributable to any fund.

(1b) The Company may hold ancillary liquid assets.

(1c) (i) The Company will invest no more than 10 per cent of the net assets of any or all of the funds (as appropriate) in transferable securities issued by the same issuing body. Moreover where the Company holds on behalf of a fund investments in transferable securities of any issuing body which individually exceeds exceed 5 per cent of the net assets of such fund, the total of all such investments must not account for more than 40 per cent of the total net assets of such fund;

(ii) the limit of 10 per cent laid down in subparagraph (c)(i) above will be increased to a maximum of 35 per cent in respect of transferable securities which are issued or guaranteed by a member state of the European Union ("Member State"), by its local authorities, by another Eligible State or by public international bodies of which one or more Member States are members, and such securities not being included in the calculation of the limit of 40 per cent stated in sub-paragraph (c)(i) above;

(iii) notwithstanding sub-paragraphs (c)(i) and (c)(ii) above, where any fund has invested in accordance with the principle of risk spreading in transferable securities issued or guaranteed by a Member State, by its local authorities, by another OECD Member State or by public international bodies of which one or more Member States are members, the Company is authorized to invest up to 100 per cent of the net assets of such Fund in such securities, provided that fund holds securities from at least six different issues and securities from one issue do not account for more than 30 per cent of the total net assets of such fund.

(1d) The Company will not:

(i) own more than 10 per cent of the outstanding securities of any class of any issuer; or
(ii) acquire shares carrying voting rights which would enable the Company to take legal or management control or to exercise significant influence over the management of the issuing body; or acquire more than 10 per cent of the units of the same collective investment undertaking provided that the limit set out in (i) herein shall not apply to the securities referred to under sub-paragraph (c)(iii) above.

The Company will further not:

(2) make investments in, or enter into transactions involving precious metals, commodities or certificates representing these;

(3) purchase or sell real estate or any option, right or interest therein, provided the Company may invest in securities secured by real estate or interests therein or issued by companies which invest in real estate or interests therein;

(4) invest more than 5 per cent of the net assets attributable to any fund in securities of other collective investment undertakings of the open-ended type. Such investments may be made by the Company, only if:

(i) such collective investment undertaking of the open-ended type is a UCITS within the meaning of the first and second indents of Article 1(2) of the EC directive 85/611 of 20th December 1985;

(ii) in the case of a UCITS linked to the Company by common management or control or by a substantial direct or indirect holding, or managed by a management company linked to the investment manager appointed by the Company (the "Manager"), or any investment advisor appointed by the Company (the "Investment Adviser"), the UCITS must be one that in accordance with its constitutional documents specializes in investment in specific geographical area or economic sector and no fees or costs on account of the transactions relating to the units in the UCITS may be charged by the Company; and

(5) purchase any securities on margin (except that the Company may obtain such short term credit as may be necessary for the clearance of purchases and sales of securities) or make short sales of securities or maintain a short position; deposits or other accounts in connection with option, forward or financial futures contracts, permitted within the limits of clause (10) below, are not considered margins for this purpose;

(6) make loans to, or act as a guarantor for, other persons, or assume, endorse or otherwise become directly or contingently liable for, or in connection with, any obligation or indebtedness of any person in respect of borrowed moneys, provided that for the purpose of this restriction (I) the acquisition of Eligible Transferable Securities in fully or partly paid form and (ii) the lending of portfolio securities subject to all applicable laws and regulations shall not be deemed to constitute the making of a loan or be prohibited by this clause;

(7) borrow for the account of any fund, other than amounts which in the aggregate do not exceed 10 per cent of the total net assets of that fund, taken at market value, and then only from banks as a temporary measure; furthermore borrowings for the account of the Bond Fund or Reserve Funds may only be made to provide moneys to facilitate the redemption of Shares or the payment of expenses; the Company will not purchase securities for any fund while borrowings are outstanding in relation to it, except to fulfill prior commitments and/or exercise subscription rights;

(8) mortgage, pledge, hypothecate or in any manner encumber as security for indebtedness, any securities owned or held by the Company, except as may be necessary in connection with the borrowings, permitted by clause above, and then such mortgaging, pledging, hypothecating or encumbering may not exceed 10 per cent of the relevant fund's total net assets; the deposit of securities or other assets in a separate account in connection with option or financial futures transactions shall not be considered to be a mortgage, pledge or hypothecation or encumbrance for this purpose;

(9) (i) acquire assets which are partly paid or to which a liability is otherwise attached, unless, according to the terms of issue, such asset will or may, at the option of the holder, become free of such liability within one year of such acquisition for the benefit of the relevant fund, or

(ii) underwrite or sub-underwrite securities of other issuers;

(10) purchase or sell commodities or commodity contracts;

(11) make investments in any assets involving assumption of unlimited liability.

If the limitations in clauses (1), (4), (7) and (8) are exceeded for reasons beyond the control of the Company or as a result of the exercise of subscription rights, it must adopt as a priority objective for its sales transactions the remedying of that situation, taking due account of the interests of its shareholders.

The Company may under the conditions and within the limits laid down by law, regulation and administrative practice, employ techniques and instruments:

(i) relating to transferable securities, provided that such techniques and instruments are used for the purpose of an efficient portfolio management; the Company will however not, to the extent of - and as long as required by - any applicable laws and/or regulations, purchase options on securities if the premiums paid therefore would at any time exceed 15 per cent of any fund's net assets. In addition, call options on securities written on behalf of any fund will be to such transactions limited to covered options and the Company will not incur potential net liability with respect in excess of 25 per cent of the value of the portfolio securities of the relevant fund in terms of striking prices, after deducting any options purchased; and/or

(ii) intended to provide protection against exchange risk in the context of the management of Company's assets and liabilities.

In accordance with the above, the Company may, for the above-referred hedging purposes, use options on such futures and forward currency transactions. It will, however, not deal in forward foreign exchange contracts, except to hedge against risks and provided that the value of such contracts does not exceed the value of the net assets denominated in the currency of such contracts and that such contracts do not extend beyond any maturity date of securities forming part of such assets.

The financial instruments referred to here above must be listed on an official stock exchange or dealt in on another regulated market.

The Company in such case, shall further not:

(12) realize at any time an asset of any fund which (i) is carried at the Directors' valuation and (ii) comprises 50 per cent or more of the total net assets of the relevant fund, unless such realization shall be approved by a majority of the votes expressed at a general meeting of the holders of the shares corresponding to the relevant fund;

(13) invest the assets of any fund in any security of a fund in a company or body if Directors and Officers of the Manager or Investment Adviser in relation to such Fund who individually own more than 0.5 per cent of the total nominal amount of all the issued securities of that class collectively own more than 5 per cent of such total nominal amount;

(14) acquire debt securities for the account of any fund with an unexpired period to maturity exceeding 29 years if, upon acquisition, the value of all such debt securities held for the account of the fund would exceed 10 per cent of the net asset value of that fund;

(15) without prejudice to paragraphs (I)(a), (I)(c) and (I)(d) above, hold for the account of any fund any obligations whatsoever of a single person or institution, if more than 25 per cent of the value of the net assets of such fund would consist of such obligations, except that such restriction will not apply to Eligible Transferable Securities as described in sub-paragraph (I)(c)(iii) above;

(16) invest in a mutual fund or unit trust which is managed by any investment manager or advisor appointed by the Directors or any Connected Person of such Investment Manager or Investment Adviser unless (a) that person waives any preliminary or initial charge in relation to the making of such investment and (b) the Investment Manager of the fund for the account of which such

investment is made makes an appropriate reduction in the investment management fee payable to it by the Company for the period during which such investment is held in order to make allowance for any investment management fee received by the Manager of such undertaking.

(17) acquire for the account of any fund any option in respect of securities, if, as a result thereof, the value of all underlying securities in respect of which that fund holds options would exceed 10 percent of the net assets attributable to that fund;

(18) acquire for the account of the Bond Funds and/or Reserve Funds any ordinary shares, redeemable shares or shares convertible into ordinary shares;

(19) without prejudice to the generality of any of the foregoing restrictions, and subject always to paragraph (I)(b), make or acquire any deposit, certificate of deposit, note, bond or other money market instrument for the account of the Bond Funds or Reserve Funds if, as a result:

(i) the aggregate of the values of such deposits, certificates of deposit, bonds, notes and other money market instruments made or held for the account of the relevant fund which constitute or represent obligations of any one bank or other financial institution other than with the Custodian Bank, would exceed 25 per cent of the net assets attributable to such fund; or

(ii) the aggregate of the values of all such deposits, certificates of deposit, bonds, notes and other money market instruments made or held for the account of the relevant fund which constitute or represent obligations of any investment manager or investment advisor appointed by the Directors or any Connected Person of any thereof would exceed 10 per cent of the net assets of such fund;

(20) acquire, for the account of any fund, any investment in or other obligation of any company or other entity, situated in any country or other territory which is at that time a restricted territory if as result thereof the aggregate value of all investments in and other obligations of companies and other entities situated in countries and other territories which then are restricted territories would exceed 20 per cent of the net assets of that fund and, for this purpose, the expression "restricted territory" means a country or other territory from which the repatriation of invested capital is under the law and practice applicable at the relevant time unlikely to be effected within one month after a decision to repatriate such invested capital is made; or

(21) permit any deposit of cash to be made with any company appointed (a) to manage the business of the Company or (b) to manage the portfolio investments of the Company or (c) to act as the distributor of Shares, or (d) to act as investment advisor in relation to the Company's portfolio of investments or with any Connected Person of any such company unless such company or Connected Person allows interest on such deposit at a rate which is not less than the prevailing rate for a deposit of a similar amount and for the same period.

The expression "Connected Persons" means:

(i) in relation to the Manager (as defined in Article 27), to any other manager, any investment advisor appointed by the Manager (an "investment advisor" or any company appointed for the purpose of distributing Shares (a "share distributor") (the relevant such company being referred to below as the "relevant company").

(a) any person, or company beneficially owning directly or indirectly 20 per cent or more of the ordinary share capital of the relevant company, or able to exercise, directly or indirectly, 20 per cent or more of the total votes in the relevant company;

(b) any person or company controlled by a person who falls within (a) above;

(c) any company 20 per cent or more of whose ordinary share capital is beneficially owned, directly or indirectly, by the relevant company and each of the others of the Manager and each investment manager, investment advisor and share distributor taken together and any company 20 per cent or more of the total votes of which can be exercised, directly or indirectly by the relevant company and each of the others of the Manager and each investment Manager, investment advisor and share distributor taken together; and

(d) any director or officer of the relevant company of any Connected Person of the relevant company as defined in (a), (b) and (c) above; and

(ii) in relation to the Custodian:

(a) any person or company beneficially owning directly or indirectly 20 per cent or more of the ordinary share capital of the Custodian or able to exercise, directly or indirectly 20 per cent or more of the total votes in the Custodian;

(b) any person or company controlled by a person who falls within (a) above;

(c) any company 20 per cent or more of whose ordinary share capital is beneficially owned, directly or indirectly by the Custodian and any company 20 per cent or more of the total votes of which can be exercised, directly or indirectly, by the Custodian; and

(d) any director or officer of the Custodian or of any Connected Person of the Custodian, as defined in (a), (b) or (c) above.

For the purposes of these restrictions the following definitions shall apply:

Eligible Market means an official stock exchange or Regulated Market in an Eligible State.

Regulated Market means a regulated market which operates regularly and is recognized and open to the public.

Eligible State means a member state of the Organization for the Economic Co-operation and Development, Hungary, Jamaica and any country in Africa, Asia, Central America and South America.

Example 2

PROSPECTUS EXAMPLE OF THE INVESTING RESTRICTIONS FOR A FUND THAT IS A NETHERLANDS ANTILLES OPEN-ENDED INVESTMENT FUND WHOSE PRINCIPAL OBJECTIVE IS CAPITAL APPRECIATION WORLDWIDE AND MAY TRADE IN COMMODITIES AND CURRENCY MARKETS.

The Fund observes the following restrictions in its investment activities:

(1) The Fund will not effect any purchase that would result in an investment of more than 20 percent of the value of its aggregate net assets in securities of any single issuer, other than securities issued by governments or any instrumentalities thereof.

(2) The Fund will not effect any purchase that would result in an investment of more than 50 percent of the value of its total assets in shares of any single private industry or sector.

(3) The Fund will not purchase securities of any issuer having fewer than three years of continuous operations (including operations of any predecessors) if such purchases would cause the cost of investments in securities of all such issuers to exceed 30 percent of the Fund's aggregate net assets.

(4) The Fund will not purchase non-marketable securities (i.e. securities which are not traded on a recognized securities exchange or in an organized inter-dealer market) if such purchase would cause the cost of all non-marketable securities held by the Fund to exceed 25 percent of the Fund's aggregate net assets or the cost of non-marketable securities of any single issuer to exceed 10 percent of the Fund's aggregate net assets.

(5) The Fund will not commit more than 5 percent of its total assets to initial margin deposits and premiums for futures contracts and options thereon.

(6) The Fund will not purchase or sell real estate or real estate interests, other than securities issued by real estate investment trusts or similar entities.

The foregoing investment policies and restrictions cannot be changed without the consent of the Board of Supervisory Directors of the Fund. Shareholders will be informed of any such change approved by the Board in the next annual or quarterly report following such action. The Fund's investment restrictions should not be construed as providing any protection against the risk of a decline in the Fund's net assets.

Subject to the foregoing limitations, the investments of the Fund are executed in the manner and diversified to the extent deemed desirable by the Fund's portfolio managers. There are no other material restrictions on the particular types of investments or on the particular trading markets in which the Fund may invest.

Appendix 9 Sample application form

1. NAME(S) AND ADDRESS **FULL NAME(S) OF APPLICANT(S)**

1 ....

2 ....

ADDRESS OF FIRST NAMED APPLICANT (to be used for all communications)

....

....

Post Code .... Telephone ....

2. INVESTMENT I/We wish to invest the following amounts:

	CURRENCY OF FUND	LUMP SUM INVESTMENT MIN. INVESTMENT	LUMP SUM INVESTMENT YOUR INVESTMENT	REGULAR INVESTMENT MIN. INVESTMENT	REGULAR INVESTMENT YOUR INVESTMENT
GLOBAL INCOME	$	($1000)	....	($250)	....
GLOBAL EQUITY	$	($1000)	....	($250)	....
US BOND	$	($1000)	....	($250)	....
		TOTAL INVESTMENT		TOTAL INVESTMENT	

3. PAYMENT

FOR LUMP SUM INVESTMENT ONLY
I/We enclose Bank Instruction Letter/cheque(s)/bankers draft(s) for the sum(s) listed in section 2 above, in respect of my/our investment(s).

FOR REGULAR INVESTMENT
I/We enclose a Bank Instruction Letter, which please lodge with my/our Bank.

Payment Notes:
1. Remittance(s) should be made payable to Bank XXY 2. Investment will be made at the subscription price(s) ruling on the appropriate dealing day following receipt of funds.

4. INCOME

INCOME CAN BE REINVESTED TO PURCHASE ADDITIONAL SHARES FOR YOU. IF YOU PREFER TO RECEIVE YOUR INCOME, PLEASE COMPLETE ONE OF THE FOLLOWING:
(This facility is not available for shares acquired under a Regular Investment Plan)

INCOME TO BE PAID TO THE FOLLOWING BANK ACOUNT **or** **INCOME TO BE SENT TO THE FOLLOWING ADDRESS**

BANK .... SORT CODE ....

ADDRESS OF BANK ....

....

ACCOUNT NAME ....

ACCOUNT NUMBER ....

5. CERTIFICATES

ONLY COMPLETE THIS SECTION IF YOU WISH TO RECEIVE A CERTIFICATE.
I/We wish to be issued with registered CERTIFICATED SHARES, please tick box ☐ The certificate should be forwarded to address:

....

NOTE: Non-certificated shares will be more convenient for the majority of shareholders. In particular, investors may receive redemption proceeds direct into a nominated bank account without instructions (see Section 6 below).

6. RAPID REDEMPTION AUTHORITY

DO NOT COMPLETE THIS SECTION IF YOU HAVE COMPLETED SECTION 5 ABOVE
For holders of non-certificated shares, redemption proceeds can be forwarded quickly to a nominated bank account, without the need for written instructions
I/We will wish the redemption proceeds to be paid to:

BANK .... SORT CODE ....

ADDRESS OF BANK ....

....

ACCOUNT NAME ....

ACCOUNT NUMBER ....

These instructions can only be changed by written request, signed by all joint shareholders.

7. NOMINEE SERVICE

☐ (I/We* do not wish to have my/our* investment registered in my/our* names and therefore wish to use the nominee service provided. (Tick box.) Please register the investment (and further shares arising from future reinvestments of dividends) in the name of XXXX Nominees Company. I/We* understand that there is an annual charge of $30 per year for the use of this nominee service.

8. DECLARATIONS ALL APPLICANTS MUST COMPLETE THIS SECTION

I/We acknowledge that my/our investment(s) is/are subject to the terms of the Prospectus dated XXXX, a copy of which was offered to me/us, and to the provisions of the Memorandum and Articles of Association and Fund Rules of the Company.

I/We hereby represent and declare that I am not/none us is a United States Person and I am not/none of us is acquiring shares for the account benefit of any United States Person or with a view to their offer, sale, transfer or delivery, directly or indirectly, in the United states or to or for the benefit of any United States Person
(as such terms are defined in the Prospectus).

I/We declare that I am/we are over 20 years of age. Agency / Intermediary for commission payable

ALL APPLICANTS MUST SIGN HERE 1 .... DATE ....
2 ....

Where a corporation is applying, it must sign under the hand of a properly authorised official, who must state his representative capacity. If the Form is signed under a form of authority, such authority, or a duly certified copy therefore, must be attached to this Form.

Index to Funds

http://www.intl-offshore.com

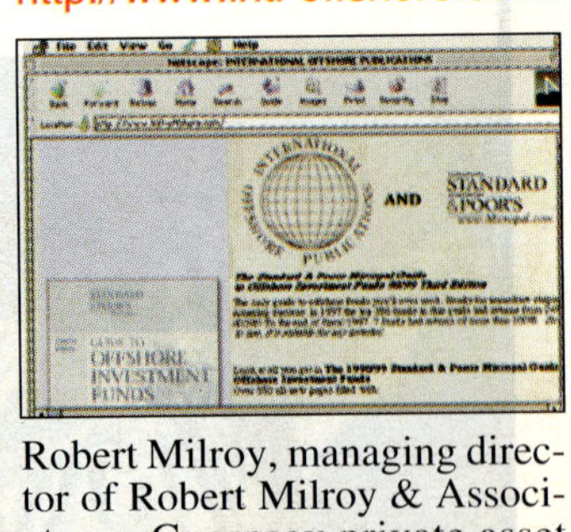

Robert Milroy, managing director of Robert Milroy & Associates, a Guernsey private asset management firm, aligns his offshore investment fund expertise with the data collection people at Standard & Poors and produces publications for International Offshore Publications including the S&P Guide to Offshore Investment Funds.